THE INTERNATIONAL CONFERENCE ON THE FORMER YUGOSLAVIA

VOLUME 1

THE INTERNATIONAL CONFERENCE ON THE FORMER YUGOSLAVIA

OFFICIAL PAPERS

VOLUME 1

Edited by

B.G. RAMCHARAN

KLUWER LAW INTERNATIONAL
THE HAGUE / LONDON / BOSTON

A C.I.P. Catalogue record for this book is available from the Library of Congress.

ISBN 90-411-0429-1 (Vol. 1)
ISBN 90-411-0436-4 (Vol. 2)
ISBN 90-411-0437-2 (Set of 2 volumes)

Published by Kluwer Law International,
P.O. Box 85889, 2508 CN The Hague, The Netherlands.

Sold and distributed in the U.S.A. and Canada
by Kluwer Law International,
675 Massachusetts Avenue, Cambridge, MA 02139, U.S.A.

In all other countries, sold and distributed
by Kluwer Law International, Distribution Centre,
P.O. Box 322, 3300 AH Dordrecht, The Netherlands.

Printed on acid-free paper

Printed in the Netherlands

TABLE OF CONTENTS

PART TWO

Volume II   **PART THREE**

TABLE OF CONTENTS AND DOCUMENTS

PART TWO

LIST OF ABBREVIATIONS

AAA	Anti-Aircraft Artillery
ACVs	Armoured Combat Vehicles
ATC	Air Traffic Control
ATS	*Schillings* (Austrian currency)
AWACS	Airborne Warning And Control System
B & H	Bosnia and Herzegovina
BCP	Border Crossing-Point
BGL	*Lev* (Bulgarian currency)
BiH	Bosnia and Herzegovina
BN	grid reference
BRC	Bulgarian Red Cross
BS	Bosnian Serbs
BSA	Bosnian Serb Army
CARITAS	*Caritas Internationalis*: International Confederation of Catholic Organizations for Charitable and Social Action
CASEVAC	Evacuation of Casualties
CCP	Controlled Crossing-Point
CEDAW	Committee on the Elimination of Discrimination Against Women
CEE	Communauté européenne economique
CERD	Committee on the Elimination of Racial Discrimination
CFE	Treaty on Conventional Armed Forces in Europe
CGRA	General Commission for Refugees and Stateless Persons (Belgium)
CGS JA	Yugoslav Army Command

CICR	*Comité international de la Croix-Rouge*
CN	grid reference
COCOM	Coordination Committee for Multilateral Export Controls
CP	grid reference
CQ	grid reference
CRHC/FC	Follow-up Committee of the Comprehensive Response
CSBMs	Confidence- and Security-Building Measures
CSCE	Conference on Security and Cooperation in Europe
CSFR	Czecho-Slovak Federal Republic
CSO	Committee of Senior Officials (CSCE)
cu m	cubic metres
D Day	Seven days after midnight of the day the Agreement relating to Bosnia and Herzegovina is signed in Geneva
D-Day	Seven days after midnight (New York time) of the day on which the Security Council approves the arrangements implementing the Military Agreement of 11 August 1993, as amended
DHA	Department of Humanitarian Affairs (UN)
DM	*Deutsch Mark* (German currency)
EBRD	European Bank for Reconstruction and Development
EC	European Community/Communities
EC-COY	European Community Conference on Yugoslavia
ECHO	European Community Humanitarian Office
ECMM	European Community Monitor Mission
ECOSOC	Economic and Social Council (UN)
ECTF	European Community Task Force
ECU	European Currency Unit
EEC	European Economic Community
EST	Eastern Standard Time (New York time)
EU	European Union
FAO	Food and Agriculture Organization
FAP	Truck factory
FORPRONU	*Force de protection des Nations unies*
FRY	Federal Republic of Yugoslavia
FSC	Forum on Security Cooperation (OSCE)
FYR	Former Yugoslavia Republic
FYROM	Former Yugoslavia Republic of Macedonia

GDP	Gross Domestic Product
GNP	Gross National Product
HCR/IMFY	International Meeting on Humanitarian Aid for Victims of the Conflict in the Former Yugoslavia (Comprehensive Response to the Humanitarian Crisis in the Former Yugoslavia)
HDZ	*Hrvatska Demokratska Zajednica* (Croatian Democratic Union; party of Bosnian Croats)
HQ	Head Quarters
HVO	*Hrvatska Vojska* (Croatian Defence Council)
I	Implementation
IBRD	International Bank for Reconstruction and Development
ICFY	International Conference on the Former Yugoslavia
ICJ	International Court of Justice
ICR	International Christian Relief (UK)
ICRC	International Committee of the Red Cross
IFOR	Implementation Force
IFRC	International Federation of Red Cross/Crescent Societies
IMCR	Inter-Ministerial Commission for Refugees
IMG	Infrastructure Management Group
IMG-IBH	IMG - Infrastructure for Bosnia and Herzegovina
INA	Immigration and Nationality Act (USA)
INTERPOL	International Police Cooperation
IOM	Intergovernmental Organization for Migration
IPTF	International Police Task Force (UN)
JA	Yugoslav Army *also*: Yugoslav Army's military compounds from where the controlled crossing-points are patrolled
JNA	Yugoslav National Army
kV	kilo Volt
LC	London Conference
LDK	Democratic Alliance of Kosovo
Lt	Lieutenant

MCCC	Monitoring Command Coordination Centre (NATO)
MEDEVAC	Medical Evacuation
MFA	Military Force of Albania
Mi-B	Type of helicopter
MMWG	Mixed Military Working Group
MOU	Memorandum of Understanding
MP	Member of Parliament
MSF	*Médecins sans Frontières*
MT	Mechanical Transport
MUP	Ministry of Internal Affairs Special Police
N	Negotiations (+ decision-making)
NAC	North Atlantic Council
NATO	North Atlantic Treaty Organisation
NBY	National Bank of Yugoslavia
NGOs	Non-Governmental Organizations
ODA	Overseas Development Administration (UK)
OE	Aliens Office (Belgium)
OECD	Organization for Economic Cooperation and Development
OFPRA	Office for the Protection of Refugees and Stateless Persons (France)
OIC	Organization of the Islamic Conference
OICCG	OIC Contact Group
ONU	*l'Organisation des Nations unies*
OSCE	Organization for Security and Cooperation in Europe
PCIJ	Permanent Court of International Justice
PDP	*Partija za Demokratski Prosperitet* (Party of Democratic Prosperity; Albanian party in the former Yugoslav Republic of Macedonia)
PHARE	Poland and Hungary: Aid for the Restructuring of Economies (EU Programme of Assistance for Economic Restructuring in the Countries of Central and Eastern Europe)
PKOs	Peace-Keeping Operations
POW	Prisoner of War
PRA	Principal Applicant

R	Resettlement
RATCR	Regional Arms Transfer Control Regime
RS	*Republika Srpska*
RSK	Republic of Serb Krajina

SAA	Special Area(s) of Attention
SAC	Special Assistance Category (Australian initiative)
SACEUR	Supreme Allied Commander Europe
SAMs	Surface-to-Air Missiles
SAMs	Serbia and Montenegro Assistance Missions
SAMs	Sanctions Assistance Missions
SAMCOMM	Sanctions Assistance Missions Communication Centre
SC	Security Council (UN)
SDA	*Stranka Demokratske Akcij* (Party of Democratic Action; party of Bosnian Muslims)
SDS	*Srpska Demokratska Stranka* (Democratic Party of Bosnian Serbs)
SFRY	Socialist Federal Republic of Yugoslavia
SG	Secretary-General (UN)
SHAPE	Supreme Headquarters of the Allied Powers in Europe
SIB	Swedish Immigration Board
SM, S/M	Serbia and Montenegro
SPO	*Srpski Pokret Obnove* (Serbian Renewal Movement in Serbia/Montenegro)
SRBH	Socialist Republic of Bosnia and Herzegovina
SRSG	Special Representative of (UN) Secretary-General

TDF/TDH	*Terre des femmes/hommes*
TLE	Treaty Limited Equipment
TPS	Temporary Protected Status
TROO	*Tijdelijke Regeling Opvang Ontheemden* (Displaced persons in the Netherlands)

UCP	Uncontrolled Crossing-Point
UHF	Ultra High Frequency
UK	United Kingdom
UN	United Nations
UNCHR	United Nations Commission on Human Rights
UNCITRAL	United Nations Convention on International Trade Law

UNCIVPOL	United Nations Civilian Police
UNCRO/	United Nations Confidence Restoration Operation in UNCROIC Croatia
UNDP	United Nations Development Programme
UNESCO	United Nations Educational, Scientific and Cultural Organization
UNHCR	United Nations High Commissioner for Refugees
UNICEF	United Nations Children's Fund
UNIDO	United Nations Industrial Development Organization
UNIFIL	United Nations Interim Force in Lebanon
UNMOs	United Nations Military Observers
UNPAs	United Nations Protected Areas
UNPF	United Nations Peace Force
UNPF-HQ	United Nations Peace Force Headquarters
UNPREDEP	United Nations Preventive Deployment Force
UNPROFOR	United Nations Protection Force
UNSCR	United Nations Security Council Resolution
UNSG	United Nations Secretary-General
UNV	United Nations Volunteers
US(A)	United States of America
USD	US Dollars
USSR	Union of Soviet Socialist Republics
UTM	grid references
VJ	Yugoslav Army
VMA	Hospital in Belgrade
VMRO	*Vnatresna Makedonska Revolucionerna Organizacija* (Internal Macedonian Revolutionary Organization)
VtV	*Vergunning tot Verblijf* (permission to stay on humanitarian grounds in the Netherlands)
WEU	Western European Union
WFP	World Food Programme
WHO	World Health Organization

THE INTERNATIONAL CONFERENCE ON
THE FORMER YUGOSLAVIA

* Initiated the highly-successful preventive deployment of peacekeeping forces in the Former Yugoslav Republic of Macedonia - the first-ever preventive deployment of United Nations peacekeeping forces.

* Established and operated the International Monitoring Mission along the Drina River for over eighteen months. This key stabilisation regime has had a staffing of over 500 persons.

* Negotiated the withdrawal of the Yugoslav National Army from the Prevlaka Peninsula, and thus avoided further conflict between Croatia and the Former Republic of Yugoslavia in the fall of 1992.

* Negotiated the de-mining of the Peruca Dam which, in the fall of 1992, threatened several communities in the vicinity of the Dam in Croatia.

* Helped raise awareness and funds for dealing with humanitarian problems in the former Yugoslavia through the winters of 1992, 1993, 1994 and 1995. Negotiated, in September 1992 (following the shooting down of an aircraft), an agreement on safe corridors for aircraft engaged in the humanitarian airlift.

* Initiated the excavation of the only mass-grave site dug up to date: that at Ovcara near Vukovar. Worked for an international penal tribunal.

* Negotiated the March 29, 1994 Cease-fire Agreement in Croatia.

* Negotiated the December 2, 1994 Economic Agreement in Croatia that led to the re-opening of the Zagreb-Belgrade Highway.

* Negotiated the settlement of the highly-dangerous problem of Sector East in Croatia.

* Did the groundwork negotiations that laid the basis for the Dayton/Paris accords on Bosnia-Herzegovina. Two earlier agreements negotiated by the International Conference on the Former Yugoslavia in 1993 were first accepted by the parties and subsequently repudiated by one side and then another.

* Drafted in 1993 the treaty that was eventually signed by Greece and the Former Yugoslav Republic of Macedonia to settle their dispute.

* Mediated highly dangerous inter-ethnic problems in the Former Yugoslav Republic of Macedonia, organized, helped raise funds and arranged for international monitoring of the crucial national population census, provided good offices for its national elections, and generated international assistance for a multi-ethnic media to promote inter-ethnic harmony.

* Provided good offices for dealing with problems affecting other ethnic communities, nationalities or minorities in the whole of the former Yugoslavia.

* Drafted a treaty on succession issues which is awaiting finalisation among the successor republics.

* Initiated studies on future confidence-building measures in the former Yugoslavia.

* Initiated studies on future development cooperation in the former Yugoslavia.

* THUS CONTRIBUTING TO CONFLICT PREVENTION, PEACEMAKING, PEACEKEEPING, PEACE-BUILDING, HUMANITARIAN AND HUMAN RIGHTS EFFORTS IN THE FORMER YUGOSLAVIA FOR A PERIOD OF THREE AND A HALF YEARS

* For a year (1993), the UN Co-Chairman of the International Conference on the Former Yugoslavia also, as Special Representative of the UN Secretary-General, led all peacekeeping, humanitarian and other operations of the United Nations in the former Yugoslavia.

*****

PART ONE

INTRODUCTION

The International Conference on the Former Yugoslavia was established at the end of August 1992 to remain in being until a final settlement of the problems of the former Yugoslavia is reached. It builds on the work done by the European Community Conference on Yugoslavia, and is guided by the Statement of Principles agreed at its London sessions, which are discussed below. The Permanent Co-Chairmen are the Head of State/Government of the Presidency of the European Union and the Secretary-General of the United Nations. The Conference can be re-convened in plenary session by the Permanent Co-Chairmen on the recommendation of the Co-Chairmen of the Steering Committee.

1. The Main Decisions of the Conference at its London Session (August 1992)

A. PRINCIPLES

At its London session, the International Conference endorsed a set of principles as the basis for a negotiated settlement of problems in the former Yugoslavia. They provided, *inter alia*, for:

(i)   all parties and others concerned to cease fighting and the use of force;

(ii)   non-recognition of advantages gained by force;

(iii)   the need for all the parties concerned to engage in negotiations;

(iv)   respect for the highest standards of individual rights and fundamental freedoms in a democratic society;

3

(v)   implementation of constitutional guarantees of the human rights and fundamental freedoms of persons belonging to ethnic and national communities and minorities, the promotion of tolerance and the right to self-determination;

(vi)   total condemnation of forcible expulsions, illegal detentions and attempts to change the ethnic composition of populations, and effective promotion of the closure of detention camps, and of the safe return to their homes of all persons displaced by the hostilities who wish this;

(vii)   compliance by all persons with their obligations under international humanitarian law;

(viii)   respect for the independence, sovereignty and territorial integrity of all states in the region and respect for the inviolability of frontiers;

(ix)   a final settlement of all questions of succession to the former Socialist Federal Republic of Yugoslavia to be reached by consensus or by arbitration and the commitment of all parties to recognise each other mutually;

(x)   compliance in full with all UN Security Council Resolutions;

(xi)   the vital need for humanitarian aid with special consideration for the needs of children;

(xii)   cooperation in international monitoring, peace-keeping and arms control operations;

(xiii)   the need to provide international guarantees to ensure the full implementation of all agreements reached within the framework of the International Conference.

B. THE OFFICE OF THE CO-CHAIRMEN

The Co-Chairmen of the Steering Committee work in continuous sessions at the Office of the United Nations in Geneva. There are six Working Groups in continuous session:

(a)   *Bosnia and Herzegovina Working Group* which promotes a cessation of hostilities and a constitutional settlement;

(b)   *Humanitarian Issues Working Group* which promotes humanitarian relief in all its aspects, including refugees;

(c)   *Ethnic and National Communities and Minorities Working Group* which recommends initiatives for resolving ethnic questions;

(d)   *Succession Issues Working Group* which seeks to resolve succession issues;

(e) *Economic Issues Working Group* which addresses economic issues arising from the emergence of new states;

(f) *Confidence and Security-building and Verification Measures Working Group* which seeks to develop confidence-building measures covering military movements, arms control and arms transfers and limitations, and measures for their monitoring and verification.

C. ARBITRATION COMMISSION

The Conference is assisted by an Arbitration Commission.

D. SECRETARIAT

A small Secretariat operates from the Office of the United Nations in Geneva. It is headed by an Executive Director and is staffed by personnel from the United Nations and from the European Community.

E. COSTS

Participants in the Conference agreed to bear the costs related to the administrative implementation of its Work Programme and the provision of the Secretariat, with a scale of contributions approved every six months by the Steering Committee.

F. SPECIFIC DECISIONS ADOPTED BY THE CONFERENCE AT ITS LONDON SESSION

The following specific decisions were adopted by the International Conference meeting in London in August 1992.

Cessation of Violence

The *overall aim* was an effective and durable cessation of hostilities in the whole of the former SFRY and in particular in Bosnia and Herzegovina in order to facilitate the negotiation of a lasting political settlement. This required urgent action including:

- early lifting of the sieges of towns and cities;
- international supervision of heavy weapons;
- bringing all forces, including irregulars, under central control;
- withholding of direct or indirect military assistance to self-proclaimed governments and the internal components of neighbouring states;
- the progressive reduction of weapons in the region under international supervision.

Participants agreed confidence-building measures including:

- the notification of all mortars and heavy weapons to the UN within 96 hours as a prelude to their disengagement from the conflict;
- a ban on military flights;
- early setting up of hot lines between local commanders and Headquarters;
- improved contact through liaison visits;
- the identification of Headquarters and commanders of all armed units, including para-militaries;
- the posting of observers on the Bosnian/Serbian and Bosnian/Montenegrin borders;
- the deployment of observers in Bosnia to monitor heavy weapons.

Further confidence-building measures were to be urgently examined.

Humanitarian Issues

In London, the Co-Chairmen of the Conference agreed a programme of action with the parties to the conflict. This included:

a. Effective delivery of humanitarian aid

    (i)   Full collaboration in delivery of humanitarian relief by road throughout Bosnia and Herzegovina, with the following specific steps:

- progressive development of relief missions and road convoys from Croatia and Serbia and Montenegro into all areas of Bosnia where relief is required;
- priority to repairing the road and railway between Ploce, Mostar and Sarajevo;

- parties to designate local representatives with whom practical arrangements for relief missions and road convoys can be made;
- acceptance of and arrangements for international monitors.

(ii) Parties to exercise authority over undisciplined elements in their areas.

b. Refugees

(iii) Progressive return of refugees to their homes and response to the needs identified by the UN.

c. Dismantling detention camps

(iv) Unconditional and unilateral release under international supervision of all civilians detained, and the closure without delay of the detention camps.

(v) Parties to take responsibility for security and protection of those detained until freed under international supervision.

(vi) International community to be given immediate access in order to monitor the situation of those in detention.

(vii) Pending release and return home of those detained, urgent action by humanitarian organizations to examine temporary options.

d. Safe Areas

(viii) Further examination of options including neutral zones or safe areas.

International Action

In order to promote these objectives all governments and international organizations would:

- collaborate fully with the Secretary-General of the United Nations in providing to him information in implementation of UNSCR 771;
- ensure the compliance by all persons with their obligations under international humanitarian law;
- take all possible legal action to bring to account those responsible for committing or ordering grave breaches of the Geneva Conventions;
- draw up a register of verified breaches of international humanitarian law;

- set up the monitoring missions called for by the CSCE in the territories of the former SFRY and in neighbouring countries;
- not consider help for the reconstruction of the Serbian economy before Serbia has complied with the demands of the Conference;
- provide the means for:
  - passage and protection of humanitarian convoys at the request of the United Nations;
  - control and monitoring of heavy weapons in Bosnia and Herzegovina under the auspices of the United Nations.

Sanctions

The relevant governments agreed that they would:

- implement an agreed action plan to ensure the rigorous application of sanctions;
- enforce sanctions on the Danube, consistent with their view that riparian states have the authority and obligation to do so;
- provide practical advice, manpower and equipment to help neighbouring countries to enforce sanctions rigorously;
- contribute experts to advise on the application of sanctions in all neighbouring countries to take part in the monitoring missions which will be established in the neighbouring countries to ensure full implementation of sanctions;
- ask the Security Council to:
  - take necessary measures to tighten up the application of sanctions in the Adriatic;
  - prevent illegal transfers of financial assets to Serbia and Montenegro; and
  - eliminate diversion of goods in transmit.

Conference parties asked the European Community and the CSCE to coordinate all necessary practical assistance to all neighbouring countries.

Violations of International Humanitarian Law

The Co-Chairmen undertook to carry forward a study of the creation of an international criminal court.

2. Activities of the International Conference since its Establishment (September 1992 to June 1995)

Since its establishment the International Conference has carried out the following activities:

A. BOSNIA AND HERZEGOVINA

The Co-Chairmen of the Steering Committee and the Chairman of the Working Group on Bosnia and Herzegovina have worked continuously since the establishment of the Conference to help bring about a settlement of the conflict in Bosnia and Herzegovina. On 2 May 1993, all three parties signed a comprehensive peace plan subject, in the case of the Bosnian Serbs, to ratification by the Bosnian Serb assembly. The Bosnian Serb side repudiated its acceptance shortly thereafter on the grounds that the assembly had not ratified its signature.

Subsequently, two other peace plans were worked out with the parties to the conflict in Bosnia and Herzegovina, one in August 1993 and the other in September 1993. The Bosnian Serb and the Bosnian Croat sides accepted these plans. The Bosnian Muslims also accepted it at one stage - on condition, however, that additional territory be allocated to the Bosnian Muslims in drawing up the map of the boundaries of the three constituent republics: a Croat majority republic, a Muslim majority republic, and a Serb majority republic. In the end they decided against acceptance.

Subsequently, the Co-Chairmen have worked closely with the members of a Contact Group, consisting of France, Germany, the Russian Federation, the United Kingdom, and the United States of America on a further plan, known as the Contact Group plan, which has been widely supported internationally. The Bosnian-Croat Federation, comprising Bosnian Croats and Bosnian Muslims have accepted the Contact Group map. The Bosnian Serbs have so far declined to do so.

B. CROATIA

The Co-Chairmen of the Steering Committee have worked for the resolution of problems in the United Nations Protected Areas (UNPAs). They have organised meetings between the President of the Republic of Croatia and the President of the Federal Republic of Yugoslavia, as well as between the President of the Republic of Croatia and the President of Serbia. The outcome of these meetings included the adoption of joint declarations providing inter alia for the establish-

ment of a joint commission and for the demilitarisation of the Prevlaka Peninsula. Pursuant to the agreements thus reached the Federal Republic of Yugoslavia (Serbia and Montenegro) withdrew its forces from the Prevlaka Peninsula.

Following offensives by Croatian armed forces on 22 January 1993, and in
the light of Security Council resolutions calling for a cessation of hostilities and
for a return to the situation obtaining before 22 January 1993, the Co-Chairmen
and senior officials of the Conference have engaged in continuous efforts to
bring about a cessation of hostilities and to promote a process that would lead to
the resolution of outstanding problems. These led to the signature of an agreement on 29 March, 1994.

C. FYROM

The Co-Chairmen have followed the situation in FYROM closely. Upon their
proposal the Secretary-General recommended, and the Security Council mandated, the first-ever preventive deployment of United Nations peace-keeping
forces in the Former Yugoslavia Republic of Macedonia. It has made a significant contribution to stabilisation of the situation in that part of the former Yugoslavia.

The Co-Chairmen of the Conference also extended their good offices in the
situation between the FYROM and the Republic of Greece and put forward a
draft treaty in future relations between the two countries. The draft convention is
the subject of continuing contacts.

D. COOPERATION WITH UNPROFOR

Relations between the Conference and UNPROFOR have been close from the
outset. From May 1993 to January, 1994 the United Nations Co-Chairman of the
Steering Committee was simultaneously the Secretary-General's Special Representative for the former Yugoslavia, in charge of UNPROFOR and all other UN
activities in the former Yugoslavia.

E. HUMANITARIAN ISSUES

Programmes of humanitarian assistance undertaken under the auspices of the
Conference's Humanitarian Issues Working Group, chaired by the United
Nations High Commissioner for Refugees, helped to avert a humanitarian disas-
ter during the winters of 1992/1993, 1993-94 and 1994/1995. Notwithstanding

severe security risks and problems of access, humanitarian activities are continuing.

F. ETHNIC AND NATIONAL COMMUNITIES AND MINORITIES

Since the establishment of the Conference, contacts have been maintained with the Governments and communities concerned in order to deal with the situation in the UNPAs, in Kosovo, Sandjak and Vojvodina, and in the FYROM. These contacts are continuing.

G. SUCCESSION ISSUES

Meetings have been held among the successor states to discuss succession issues. At the request of the Chairman of the Working Group on Succession Issues, the Arbitration Commission provided its opinions on six legal issues. A draft treaty on succession issues has been submitted to the parties.

H. ECONOMIC ISSUES

Preparatory work has been done, including an in-depth survey, for the convening of a conference on reconstruction and development in the former Yugoslavia. Further work on the convening of the conference has been held in abeyance pending the achievement of progress in settling the prevailing conflicts.

I. CONFIDENCE AND SECURITY-BUILDING MEASURES

The Conference's Working Group on this subject made a special contribution to preventing threats to aircrafts engaging in humanitarian relief operations, especially in the aftermath of the shooting down of an aircraft in September 1992. An important study on confidence-building measures was commissioned and submitted to the States of the region for their consideration.

J. ARBITRATION COMMISSION

The Arbitration Commission has rendered legal opinions on several questions submitted to it by the Co-Chairmen.

K. Cooperation with Special Rapporteur of Commission on Human Rights

The Co-Chairmen and other officials of the Conference have worked closely with the Special Rapporteur and members of his staff.

L. Cooperation with Commission of Experts and International Tribunal

The Co-Chairmen and other officials of the Conference also cooperated closely with members of the Commission and the Tribunal and their secretariats.

1. THE EUROPEAN COMMUNITY CONFERENCE
(1991-1992)

A. DRAFT CONVENTION

Editor's Note: The efforts of the European Community Conference, chaired by Lord Carrington, were focused on a draft Convention containing articles dealing with: general provisions; human rights and rights of national or ethnic groups; cooperation in the areas of economic relations, foreign affairs and security, and legal cooperation; and institutions to deal with human rights, economic relations, political and security cooperation, legal cooperation, parliamentary affairs, arbitration and the location of institutions. The text of the draft Convention, as at November 1991, is reproduced below.

1. TREATY PROVISIONS FOR THE CONVENTION OF 4 NOVEMBER 1991

CHAPTER I: GENERAL

Article 1
1. The new relations between the Republics will be based on the following:
    a) sovereign and independent Republics with an international personality for those that wish it;
    b) a free association of the Republics with an international personality as envisaged in this Convention;
    c) *a common state of equal Republics for those Republics which wish to remain a common state*;
    d) comprehensive arrangements, including supervisory mechanisms for the protection of human rights and special status of certain groups and areas;
    e) European involvement, where appropriate;
    f) in the framework of a general settlement, recognition of the independence, within the existing borders, unless otherwise agreed, of those Republics wishing it.

13

2. The Republics recognize that cooperation between them and the creation of this association is part of the process of building a new Europe envisaged in the Paris Charter of November 1990, and will improve the prospects for cooperation and closer relations with the European Community. They will cooperate in the fields for which these arrangements provide and other agreed fields, without thereby precluding closer forms of cooperation in such areas between Republics that so wish.

CHAPTER II: HUMAN RIGHTS AND RIGHTS OF NATIONAL OR ETHNIC GROUPS

Article 2
a) Human rights
1. The Republics shall guarantee the following human rights:
   a) the right to life
   b) the right not to be subjected to torture or to inhuman or degrading treatment
   c) the right not to be subjected to slavery or compulsory labour
   d) the right to liberty
   e) the right to a fair and public hearing by an impartial tribunal and not to be subject to retrospective criminal proceedings
   f) the right to respect for private and family life, the home and correspondence
   g) the right to freedom of thought, conscience and religion
   h) the right to freedom of expression
   i) the right of freedom of peaceful assembly and freedom of association
   j) the right to marry and form a family
   k) the right to an effective remedy determined by law and available to all persons whose human rights have been violated, and
   l) all the other rights envisaged in the instruments listed below,
subject only to the exceptions and restrictions set out in those instruments, and without discrimination on any ground such as sex, race, colour, language, religion, political or other opinion, national or social origin, association with a national minority, property, birth or other status.

   The instruments referred to above are:
   - the Universal Declaration of Human Rights, the International Covenant on Civil and Political Rights, the International Covenant on Economic, Social and Cultural Rights of the United Nations;
   - the Final Act of the Conference on Security and Co-operation in Europe, the Charter of Paris for the New Europe and the other CSCE documents

relating to the human dimension, in particular the Document of the
Copenhagen Meeting of the Conference in the Human Dimension of the
CSCE and the document of the Moscow meeting of the Conference on the
Human Dimension of the CSCE;
- The Council of Europe Convention for the Protection of Human Rights
  and Fundamental Freedoms and the Protocols to that Convention.

b) Rights of members of national *or* ethnic groups

2. The Republics *shall* guarantee human rights as applied to national or ethnic
groups, in particular, and embodied in:
- the instruments of the United Nations, CSCE and the Council of Europe
  referred to in paragraph 1 of this Article;
- the Convention of the Elimination of Racial Discrimination, the Convention on the Prevention and Punishment of the Crime of Genocide and the
  Convention on the Rights of the Child of the United Nations;
- the report of the CSCE meeting of experts on national minorities held in
  Geneva.

In giving effect to this Convention, they shall also take appropriate account of
- proposals for a United Nations Declarations *on* the Rights of Persons
  belonging to National *or* Ethnic, *Religious* and Linguistic Minorities;
- the proposals for a Convention for the Protection of Minorities of the
  European Commission for Democracy and Law in the framework of the
  Council of Europe.

3. The Republic shall guarantee to persons belonging to a national or ethnic
group the following rights:
- the principle of non-discrimination as set out in the legal instruments
  mentioned in paragraph 2 of this Article;
- *the right to be protected against any activity capable of threatening their
  existence*;
- all cultural rights as set out in the instruments mentioned in paragraph 2 of
  this Article, in particular the right to identity, culture, religion, use of
  language and alphabet, both in public and *in* private, and education;
- protection of equal participation in public affairs, such as the exercise of
  political and economic freedoms, in the social sphere, in access to the
  media and in the field of education and cultural affairs generally;
- the right to decide to which national or ethnic group he or she wishes to
  belong, and to exercise any rights pertaining to this choice as an individual or in association with others. *No disadvantage shall arise from a
  person's choice to belong or not to belong to a national or ethnic group.*

This right shall particularly apply in the case of marriage between persons of different national or ethnic groups.

Those persons of the same national or ethnic group living distant from others of the same origin, for example, in isolated villages, shall be granted self-administration, to the extent that it is practicable.

The above principles shall also apply in areas where members of the main national or ethnic group of a Republic are numerically inferior to one or more other national or ethnic groups in that area.

4. The Republics shall guarantee to persons belonging to a national or ethnic group forming a substantial *percentage* of the population in the *Republic* where they live but not forming a majority, in addition to the rights set out in paragraph 3 of this Article, a general right of participation of members of this group in public affairs, *including participation in the* government *of the Republics* concerning their affairs.

c) Special status

5. In addition, areas in which persons belonging to a national or ethnic group form a majority, shall enjoy a special status of autonomy.

Such a status will provide for:

a. the right to have and show the national emblems of that *area;*
b. (deleted)
c. an educational system which respects the values and needs of that group;
d. i.   a legislative body,
   ii. an administrative structure, including a regional police force, and
   iii. a judiciary,

responsible for matters concerning the area, which reflects the composition of the population of the area;

e. provisions for appropriate international monitoring.

These areas are listed in Annex A.

5A Such areas, unless they are defined in part by an international frontier with a State not party to this Convention, shall be permanently demilitarised and no military forces, exercises or activities on land or in the air shall be permitted in those areas.

5B a   The Republics shall provide for international monitoring of the implementation of the special status of autonomy. To this end, they shall conclude agreements which would provide for a permanent international body to monitor implementation of this paragraph.

b The monitoring missions thus established shall
- report to the Republics in question as well as to the other parties to the agreement, and
- as appropriate formulate recommendations on the implementation of the special status.

c The Republics shall give effect to such recommendations through legislation or otherwise. In case of dispute, the Court of Human Rights shall be requested to give its decision.

6. (deleted)

d) General provisions

7. Persons belonging to a national or ethnic group, in exercising their rights, respect the rights of the majority and of persons belonging to other groups.

8. The Republics should jointly, or individually as the case may be, become parties to international instruments in the field of human rights, including *all* related complaint procedures.

9. The Republics shall provide, by legislation and through national institutions, in respect of the rights referred to in this Article, full implementation of the rights and an effective remedy for breaches of any of those rights.

10. As none of the Republics will have an ethnically homogeneous population, they shall cooperate and consult one another directly or through a mixed commission in respect of matters dealt with in paragraph 3 to 5 of this Article.

CHAPTER III: OTHER AREAS OF COOPERATION

Article 3
a) Economic Relations

1. The Republics recognise their interest in establishing appropriate measures for economic cooperation among themselves.

2. The Republics shall base their economic system and their politics on the principles of market economy, private *and other forms of* property and free enterprise, and openness to world trade.

3. *The Republics agree to start their economic cooperation according to either of the following regimes*:
- The Republics hereby establish between themselves a customs union, in order to maintain a common internal market, within which goods shall move without either tariff barriers or quantitative restrictions. The customs union shall have a common external tariff, a common external trade policy and arrangements for sharing customs receipts. Subject to any

decision by the Council of Ministers for Economic Cooperation, (in this Part a) referred to as "the Council") the common external tariff shall be based on that applied for imports into Yugoslavia at 1 July 1991 subject to the changes set out in Annex…, and the external trade policy shall include the continued implementation of external regimes and external agreements as applied by Yugoslavia at 1 July 1991. Customs receipt shall be shared in accordance with the provisions of Annex..

- *The Republics establish between all or some of them a single internal market with an appropriate monetary arrangement. The single internal market will consist of a customs union and appropriate arrangements for full freedom of movement of factors of production, including the right of establishment of firms, common policies in agriculture, transport, energy and regional development of less developed regions. There will be a necessary degree of harmonisation of macro-economic, including fiscal and social, policies. Common economic and harmonised social policies will be backed by the establishment of appropriate structural funds.*

4. The Republics shall cooperate to limit the adverse effects of other obstacles impeding the free movement of goods *and, for those republics entering into the more extensive arrangements outlined in the second part of the previous paragraph, of services and of factors of production,* such as technical standards, subsidies and regulations affecting trade, by taking measures, such as sharing information, concerting policy objectives and, if necessary, harmonising rules and regulations which distort competition.

5. The Republics shall cooperate and, subject to any decision of the Council shall maintain existing arrangements, in the fields of transport and infrastructure, The Council shall take measures to maintain competition, especially for the protection of the common internal market *or for those republics entering into the more binding arrangements outlined in the second part of paragraph 3, of the single internal market, as well as* the freedom to supply services.

6. Rights of establishment *of firms* and freedom to provide services shall be maintained, in particular for the professions, where they exist at present.

7. The Republics shall cooperate, for the protection of the environment.

8. The Republics shall cooperate in monetary matters with a view to maintaining or achieving monetary stability and the highest possible degree of currency convertibility as the best support for the market economy.

The appropriate monetary mechanism for those Republics entering into the more binding arrangements outlined in the second part of paragraph 3 will be built on the basis of a common currency, or of the experiences of the European Monetary System.

As a minimum, in the absence of a common currency convertibility, they shall consider, for their mutual transactions, the establishment of a common payments system, based upon a clearing mechanism and a reserve fund.

9. This Article shall be reviewed by the Republics at the end of a period of five years from the entry into force of this Convention.

10. The Republics shall examine *during the first five years* the impact of the customs union on each of their economies. On the basis of this examination, and taking into account the trend towards increased economic cooperation throughout Europe, they shall also consider their interest in extending their economic cooperation and, if necessary, the means for doing so, including measures to encourage economic convergence among the republics within the framework of the association.

Article 4
b) Foreign Affairs and Security

1. The Republics shall consult on all matters of common interest in the areas of foreign affairs and security, and shall cooperate where they can agree common positions, including the possibility of common representation in specific areas agreed between them.

2. Relations between the Republics, individually or jointly, shall be based on CSCE commitments. They may decide to apply between themselves the practices and procedures agreed in the CSCE, among others.

3. The Republics shall decide for themselves what armed forces to have or allow on their territory and what cooperative defence arrangements to have among themselves.

Article 5
c) Legal Cooperation

1. The Republics shall consult and cooperate in the field of legal cooperation, such as control of international crime, terrorism and drug trafficking, in accordance with European and international standards, such as those developed in the Council of Europe and the United Nations, and shall seek, individually or jointly, to become parties to international conventions in these matters.

2. In the field of international crime, terrorism and drug trafficking, the law enforcement authorities of the Republics, including the police forces, shall establish and maintain close links and cooperation with a view to the effective prevention and punishment of these crimes.

CHAPTER IV: INSTITUTIONS

Article 6

The Republics establish hereby the institutions for which this Chapter provides, in order to give effect to their cooperation under this Convention. They may establish additional institutions to the extent that they agree to further cooperation in these or other fields. *They agree to adapt these institutions, as appropriate, to take account of higher forms of economic or other integration which may be agreed between them.*

Article 6A

A Council composed of the President *of each of the Republics, or the President of the Presidency*, shall meet together in a Council at least twice a year.

Article 7

a) Human Rights

1. A Court of Human Rights is established by this Convention. It shall have jurisdiction within the Republics to consider appeals from courts in the Republics involving questions dealt with in paragraph 1 to 5 of Article 2. The Court shall consist of members, one to be nominated by each Republic, and an equal number and one additional member, being nationals of European States other than the Republics, to be nominated by the Member States of the European Community. The persons nominated shall be of high moral character and must either possess the qualifications required for appointment to high judicial office or be jurisconsults of recognised competence. No two judges shall be *nationals* of the same *Republic or European State*. The Court shall take its decisions by a majority. The Republics hereby request the Member States of the European Communities to make the nominations for which this paragraph provides. The Statute of the Court is set out in Annex....

2. Mixed Commissions shall be established under this Convention by any Republics which jointly decide to do so, for the purpose of making recommendations or taking decisions on matters entrusted to them, by the Republics concerned where such Mixed Commissions might assist in avoiding or dealing with disputes concerning human rights and the rights of ethnic or national groups and areas having special status. Such mixed Commissions shall include members nominated by the Republics concerned on a basis of parity. If the decision establishing them so provides, a Mixed Commission shall also include appropriately qualified independent persons nominated by the Member States of the European Community, and the Mixed Commission shall then have a power of decision by

majority vote. The Republics hereby request the European Communities to make the nominations for which this paragraph provides. Subject to the decision by which they are established, Annex ... shall apply to the Mixed Commissions.

Article 8
b) Economic relations

1. The Republics hereby establish a Council for Economic Cooperation, which shall meet every month, unless otherwise agreed. The Council shall consist of one Minister from each Republic and shall take decisions by consensus, unless otherwise agreed. It shall normally be composed of Economic Ministers, but may also be composed of Ministers of Transport, Energy, Environment or other Ministries according to the subject matter under discussion. Specialist ministers may attend whenever appropriate.

1A *The Council for Economic Cooperation, composed of one Minister from each of the Republics concerned, shall meet to take decisions on matters arising under Article 3.3 second part, which are additional to those arising under Article 3.3 first part and the subsequent provisions of this Article shall be applied accordingly.*

2. Meetings of the Council shall be prepared by a Committee of Senior Officials from each Republic, meeting weekly. Standing committees shall, in addition, be established to prepare proposals for the Council in the specialised areas mentioned in paragraph 1 above. It may at any time set up additional institutional arrangements to meet specific needs.

3. An Executive Committee, headed by a Secretary-General appointed for four years and assisted by a permanent Secretariat, shall make recommendations, monitor decisions and service meetings.

4. In external relations on matters covered by agreed arrangements or policies in the internal market, customs union or economic and monetary cooperation, the Council shall, where necessary, agree on common positions for the conduct of negotiations with third countries including the making of international agreements with States and international organizations. In such negotiations it shall decide whether to be represented by the Presidency of the Secretary-General of the Executive Committee.

5. The Republics hereby establish a Board for Transport consisting of one member and one alternate from each Republic which shall be responsible for the proper functioning from day to day of railways, roads and other transport operations between the Republics.

The Republics hereby establish a Board for Energy consisting of one member and one alternate from each Republic which shall be responsible, for the proper functioning from day to day of pipelines, electricity grids and other arrangements concerning energy between the Republics.

Article 9
c) Political and Security Cooperation

1. The Republics hereby establish a Council for Political and Security Cooperation composed of Foreign Ministers for the purpose of the cooperation envisaged in Article 4.1 to 3. It shall take decisions by consensus. It shall meet monthly, unless otherwise agreed. *Other Ministers shall attend whenever appropriate.*
2. When agreement on a common approach can be reached by all or some republics, those republics shall be guided by it.
3. When common positions can be reached by consensus, a decision shall be taken whether to invite the President or one of the Republics to speak or act for the association.
4. The Council may discuss any security matters raised by any Republic. The Council may decide by consensus on defence cooperation.
5. Meetings of the Council shall be prepared by senior officials from Foreign Ministries.

Article 10
d) Legal Cooperation

1. The Republics shall establish a Council for Legal Cooperation *composed of Ministers* for the purpose of cooperation as envisaged in Article 5. It shall take decisions by consensus. It will meet every six months, unless otherwise agreed.
2. The Council may discuss any matters raised by any Republic within the specific fields expressly mentioned in Article 5 and it may discuss any other topic to which it decides to extend its discussion.
3. Meetings of the Council shall be prepared by senior officials from appropriate Ministries.

Article 10A

The presidency of the Councils for which Chapter III provides shall be held for a term of six months by each member of the Council in turn, in alphabetical order, the first President being from ... (to be determined by lot).

Article 11

e) Parliamentary body

The Republics shall consider the establishment of a parliamentary body, composed on the basis of parity of delegates from the legislature of each Republic, to discuss matters arising out of these arrangements.

Article 12

f) Arbitration

The Chairman of the Arbitration Commission established in the framework of the Conference of Yugoslavia will submit a text for this article.

Article 13

g) Locations of institutions

The seat of the institutions for which provision is made by this Convention shall be located in different Republics.

B. STATEMENT OF PRINCIPLES

Editor's Note: The following Statement of Principles was agreed upon by the leadership of the three sides to the conflict in Bosnia and Herzegovina in March 1992. However, it was subsequently repudiated by the Bosnian Presidency.

2. STATEMENT OF PRINCIPLES OF 18 MARCH 1992 FOR NEW CONSTITUTIONAL ARRANGEMENTS FOR BOSNIA AND HERZEGOVINA

A. INDEPENDENCE

1. Bosnia and Herzegovina would be a state, composed of three constituent units, based on national principles and taking into account economic, geographic and other criteria.

2. Bosnia and Herzegovina would continue to have its existing borders and neither the government of Bosnia and Herzegovina nor the governments of the constituent units will encourage or support claims to any part of its territory by neighbouring states.

3. Sovereignty resides in the citizens of the Muslim, Serb and Croat nations and other nations and nationalities, who realise it through their civic participation in the constituent units and the central organs of the republic.

B. GENERAL PRINCIPLES

1. Bosnia and Herzegovina and its constituent units would be governed in accordance with the following constitutional principles, as understood and generally practised among the democratic states of Western Europe and as set out in draft convention under discussion in the conference:

    a. Respect for human rights at the highest standards as envisaged in the draft convention, respect for private ownership, the market economy and free enterprise;

    b. The general and equal right to vote, free elections and secret voting;

    c. Freedom for political and trade union activities;

    d. A secular state system with full religious freedom and separation of church and state, separation of powers between the branches of government, the rule of law and a democratic and effective system of control and protection of constitutionality and legality;

e. International control and jurisdiction for the protection of human rights and freedom.

C. THE ASSEMBLY AND GOVERNMENT OF BOSNIA AND HERZEGOVINA

1. The assembly of Bosnia and Herzegovina would be composed of a chamber of citizens, which would be directly elected, and chamber of constituent units in which each of the constituent units would have an equal number of representatives.
2. The assembly, acting through the chamber of citizens and the chamber of constituent units, and the government, would have competence to legislate, to consider and adjust proposals from the constituent units and to administer in the following fields: central bank and monetary policy, foreign relations, defence,[1] general economic policy, economic relations, including, where any of the following affect more than one constituent unit, transport, energy supplies, pipelines and water management, and other items to be decided. Decisions concerning the flag and emblem, higher education, religion, matters concerning defence, macro-economic policy, important or general matters concerning economic policy, decisions concerning relations between Bosnia and Herzegovina and states neighbouring Bosnia and Herzegovina and other items to be decide would be decided in the chamber of constituent units by a majority of four-fifths of the total number of the representatives in it.
3. The composition of the civil service and the judiciary of Bosnia and Herzegovina would reflect proportionally the national composition of Bosnia and Herzegovina.
4. In order to resolve constitutional questions between the authorities of Bosnia and Herzegovina and of the constituent units, a special tribunal would be established, which would, for a period of not less than five years, include impartial elements drawn from outside Bosnia and Herzegovina and its neighbouring states. This tribunal will have one member from each unit and the same number and one more drawn from outside. It takes decisions by simple majority.

---

[1] Matters concerning the future armed forces of Bosnia and Herzegovina will be defined in the course of these negotiations. This does not refer to the present army, the question of which will be solved separately.

D. THE CONSTITUENT UNITS

1. Within Bosnia and Herzegovina, constituent units would be established, which are defined in part E below.
2. The assembly and the government of the constituent units would have power, subject to any legislation of Bosnia and Herzegovina in the limited fields specified above and in accordance with the procedures set out above, to legislate and to administer in matters of concern to the constituent units, namely, the administration of the services and officials of a constituent unit, expropriation of property for public use, land registries, fire prevention, chambers of commerce, supervision of co-operative trading organizations, saving banks and credit institutions, supervision of charitable institutions, social security, sickness insurance, conservation of the historic, artistic and cultural heritage, cultural institutions, such as libraries, institutions and museums, the use of land, environmental controls, housing, markets, roads, emergency services, mining, hunting and fishing, nature reserves, aqueducts, water management, pipelines, transport within the constituent unit, tourism, agriculture and forests, social assistance, education schools, police, trade and other aspects of economic policy, security at public performances, hygiene, sport and recreation and other items to be decided. Each constituent unit would organise its own institutions. A constituent unit may establish and maintain relations and links with the other republics and with organizations in them provided that these relations and links are consistent with the independence and integrity of Bosnia and Herzegovina.
3. All the institutions (civil service, the judiciary, etc.) established by a constituent unit would reflect proportionally the national composition of the constituent unit.
4. Members of the nations who would be in a minority in a particular constituent unit would receive protection similar to that in article 2(3) of the draft convention.

E. DEFINITION OF THE CONSTITUENT UNITS

A working group will be established in order to define the territory of the constituent units based on national principles and taking into account economic, geographical and other criteria. A map based on the national absolute or relative majority in each municipality will be the basis of work in the working group, and will be subject only to amendments, justified by the above-mentioned criteria. A copy is annexed to this statement.

F. TRANSITIONAL STEPS

1. Subject to the definition of the constituent units for the purpose of the future arrangements in accordance with part E of this statement, a constitutional law to modify the constitution in order to give effect to these principles will be prepared and submitted to assembly as soon as possible, and will have to be confirmed by a referendum of the people under international supervision.

This paper is the basis of further negotiations.

Annexes of 2 April 1992

ANNEXE 1

The leaders of the three main parliamentary parties meeting in Brussels under the auspices of the European Community for the sixth round of talks on future constitutional arrangements for Bosnia and Herzegovina:

-   Solemnly undertake to do all in their power to bring down the level of violence in Bosnia and Herzegovina,
-   Urgently appeal to all in Bosnia and Herzegovina, regardless of ethnic origins, religious beliefs and political affiliation, to refrain from violence, provocation of violence and from any other military or political action that might jeopardise the agreements already made by the three parties and cast doubts on a successful outcome of the talks.

They are firmly convinced that a peaceful environment will facilitate understanding, speed up negotiations and allow for the drafting of a new constitution acceptable to all in the shortest possible time.

ANNEXE 2

Additional part to be added after part B of the Statement of Principles of 18 March 1992

Human Rights

1. The Constitution would include provisions providing for the protection of human rights and rights of minorities as envisaged in article 2 a), b) and d) of the

draft convention of the EC Peace Conference on Yugoslavia and full effect would be given to those rights by the authorities of Bosnia and Herzegovina and the authorities of the constituent units.

2. Cases in courts involving allegations of a breach of those rights would be decided, as a final court of appeal by the special tribunal, envisaged in paragraph C4 of the agreed Statement of Principles the jurisdiction of that tribunal would extend to cover such cases.

3. A mixed commission for human rights would be established, composed of one representative of each of the three nations and four representatives including the chairman for the European Community. The mixed commission would consider and make recommendations by majority vote on any question relating to those rights which are brought before it.

4. A monitoring mission including members drawn from the European Community would be established which could, at the request of 2 representatives on the Mixed Commission for human rights, investigate and report on any allegation of infringement of the rights referred to in paragraph 1 above.

ANNEXE 3

The working group on definition of the constituent units in Bosnia and Herzegovina

1. The working group will consist of three persons from each of the three parties represented in the talks on future constitutional arrangements for Bosnia and Herzegovina, together with three persons, including a chairman, nominated by the European Community.

2. It will meet as soon as all its members have been nominated and will make recommendations by 15 May 1992 to the chairman of the constitutional talks.

3. The working group will draw a map of the constituent units. While basing its work on national principles, the criteria which the working group will take into account in addition to economic and geographical criteria, include historical, religious, cultural and educational, transport and communications, and the will of inhabitants, to the extent that the members of the working group consider that the application of these criteria are justified.

4. The working group will endeavour to reach unanimous recommendations reconciling the competing claims and considerations presented to it. But, if it is unable to reach agreement its members may present separate recommendations.

2. INTERNATIONAL CONFERENCE ON THE FORMER YUGOSLAVIA: LONDON SESSION (AUGUST 1992)

Editor's Note: The "London Conference" was held on 26 and 27 August 1992. The outcome of the Conference is reflected in the documents reproduced in Section A below. Other significant papers of the Conference are the Statements of participants, reproduced in Section B below.

A. DOCUMENTS APPROVED AND ENDORSED

3. PROPOSED PROVISIONAL RULES OF PROCEDURE*

GENERAL

1. (1)   The following Rules of Procedure are established for the International Conference on the Former Socialist Federal Republic of Yugoslavia.

(2)   The Conference shall meet in London from 26 to 28 August 1992 inclusive, under the title of the London Conference on the Former Socialist Federal Republic of Yugoslavia.

(3)   The second stage of the Conference will be held at the United Nations Office at Geneva.

(4)   The Conference shall hold subsequent plenary meetings at a date and place to be decided by the Co-Chairmen.

---

*   The London Conference, LC/C1 (Revised), 25 August 1992.

AGENDA

2. The draft agenda for each meeting of the Conference shall be prepared by the Co-Chairmen, and shall be submitted to the meeting for approval.

ATTENDANCE

3. The following shall be invited to attend the Conference:-
   (a) the representatives of States and organizations, as well as other persons, invited by the Co-Chairmen, and
   (b) those persons invited by Lord Carrington, as the Chairman of the EC Conference on Yugoslavia.

CO-CHAIRMEN

4. (1) The Co-Chairmen of the Conference shall be the Secretary General of the United Nations and the Head of Government of the State currently holding the Presidency of the Council of Ministers of the European Community.

(2) If either of the Co-Chairmen finds it necessary to be absent during a meeting or any part thereof, he shall designate another person to take his place; any person so designated shall have the same powers and duties as the absent Co-Chairman.

5. In addition to exercising the powers conferred upon them elsewhere by these rules, the Co-Chairmen shall declare the opening and closing of each meeting, direct the discussions in meetings, ensure observance of these rules, accord the right to speak, put questions and announce decisions. They shall rule on points of order and, subject to these rules, shall have complete control of the proceedings at any meeting and over the maintenance of order thereat. The two Co-Chairmen will decide which of them shall speak on behalf of the Co-Chairmen during a particular meeting.

SECRETARIAT

6. (1) The Secretariat for the London Conference shall be provided by the Government of the United Kingdom; for subsequent meetings of the Conference, the Co-Chairmen shall make arrangements for the provisions of a Secretariat.

(2) The Secretariat shall:

    (a) provide and direct the staff required by the Conference and any committees which it may establish;

    (b) distribute documents of the Conference and its committees;

    (c) interpret speeches made at the Conference;

    (d) generally perform all other work which the Conference may require.

LANGUAGES

7. (1) English, French and Serbo-Croat shall be the languages of the Conference and its committees.

(2) Speeches made in any of the languages of the Conference shall be interpreted into the other languages.

(3) Any participant may make a speech in a language other than the languages of the Conference. In this case, he shall himself provide for interpretation into one of the languages of the Conference. Interpretation into the other languages of the Conference by the interpreters of the Secretariat may be based on the interpretation given in the first such language.

RECORDS

8. The records of the meetings of the Conference and its committees shall be in such form as the Co-Chairmen decide.

MEETINGS

9. The meetings of the Conference and its committees shall be held in private.
10. No participant may address the Conference without having previously obtained the permission of the Co-Chairmen, who shall have discretion as to the order in which they call those who have signified a desire to speak. The Co-Chairmen may call a speaker to order if his remarks are not relevant to the subject under discussion.
11. Either of the Co-Chairmen may at any time make either oral or written statements to the Conference concerning any question under consideration by it.
12. During the discussion of any matter, a participant may raise a point of order, and the point of order shall be immediately decided by the Co-Chairmen.

13. The Co-Chairmen may limit the time to be allowed to each speaker and the number of times each person may speak on any question. When the debate is limited and a speaker exceeds his allotted time, the Co-Chairmen shall call him to order without delay.

14. The Co-Chairman may allow any participant the right of reply, to be made at a time to be decided by the Co-Chairmen.

15. The Co-Chairmen may at any time:-

    (a) close the debate on the item under discussion, whether or not any participant has signified his wish to speak;

    (b) suspend or adjourn the meeting.

16. (1) Any participant invited to attend the Conference may submit proposals for discussion at the Conference to the Co-Chairmen for their consideration. The basic proposals for discussion at the Conference shall be those put forward by the Co-Chairmen.

(2) Where a participant makes a request that a document is circulated to the Conference, the Secretariat will circulate the document to the Conference if either of the Co-Chairmen authorises its circulation. No document will be circulated to the Conference except in accordance with this Rule.

(3) If a person other than a participant in the Conference makes a request that a document be made available to the participants in the Conference, he must likewise obtain the authorisation of either of the Co-Chairmen. The person who wishes the document to be made available shall provide the Secretariat with a sufficient number of copies of the document, and the Secretariat will place those copies at a location which the Secretariat consider suitable in or near the meeting-place of the Conference.

(4) Documents will be circulated under sub-paragraph (2) above or made available under sub-paragraph (3) in the language in which they were submitted to the Secretariat.

TASK GROUPS

17. The Co-Chairmen may establish such Task Groups as they deem necessary for the performance of the functions of the Conference.

18. The Co-Chairmen of the Conference will:

    (a) choose the Chairman of any Task Group;

    (b) designate the membership of the Task Group.

19. The Chairman of a Task Group shall have the same powers and duties, in relation to a Task Group, as the Co-Chairmen have in relation to the Conference under these Rules.

20. A Task Group shall meet at the time and place decided by its Chairman.

21. Each Task Group may set up sub-groups, whose chairmanship and member-ship shall be decided by the Chairman of the Task Group.

4. STATEMENT OF PRINCIPLES*

The London Conference has endorsed the following principles as the basis for a negotiated settlement of the problems of former Yugoslavia:

(i)   the imperative need that all parties and others concerned should cease fighting and the use of force, should respect agreed ceasefires and restrain those who commit or seek to provoke breaches of them;

(ii)   non-recognition of all advantages gained by force or fait accompli or of any legal consequence thereof;

(iii)   the need for all parties concerned to engage actively, directly or through intermediaries, in negotiations on the basis of these principles;

(iv)   respect for the highest standards of individual rights and fundamental freedoms in a democratic society, as embodied in the International Coven-ants of the United Nations on Human Rights, the European Convention of Human Rights and its protocols and other instruments of the United Nations, the Conference on Security and Cooperation in Europe and the Council of Europe;

(v)   implementation of constitutional guarantees of the human rights and fundamental freedoms of persons belonging to ethnic and national com-munities and minorities, the promotion of tolerance and the right to self determination in accordance with the commitments entered into under the CSCE and in the EC Conference on Yugoslavia;

(vi)   total condemnation of forcible expulsions, illegal detentions and attempts to change the ethnic composition of populations, and effective promotion of the closure of detention camps, and of the safe return to their homes of all persons displaced by the hostilities who wish this;

(vii)   compliance by all persons with their obligations under international hu-manitarian law and particular the Geneva Conventions of 12 August 1949, and the personal responsibility of those who commit or order grave breaches of the Conventions;

---

*   The London Conference, LC/C2 (Final), 26 August 1992.

(viii) the fundamental obligation to respect the independence, sovereignty and territorial integrity of all states in the region; and to respect the inviolability of all frontiers in accordance with the UN Charter, the CSCE Final Act and the Charter of Paris. Rejection of all efforts to acquire territory and change borders by force;

(ix) the requirement that a final settlement of all question of succession to the former Socialist Federal Republic of Yugoslavia must be reached by consensus or by arbitration and the commitment of all parties to recognise each other mutually, to respect each others' status and rights under any such settlement and to share the duties and responsibilities of successor states;

(x) the obligations on all states and parties concerned to comply in full with all UN Security Council Resolutions on the crisis in the former Socialist Republic of Yugoslavia and to do their utmost to secure their implementation;

(xi) the vital need for humanitarian aid to be provided and, under appropriate protection and with the full cooperation of the local authorities, to reach the populations in need, with special consideration for the needs of children;

(xii) the obligation on all parties to cooperate wholeheartedly in the international monitoring, peace-keeping and arms control operations in the territory of the former Socialist Federal Republic of Yugoslavia and to contribute constructively to the suppression of violence throughout the area;

(xiii) the need to provide international guarantees to ensure the full implementation of all agreements reached within the framework of the International Conference.

5. WORK PROGRAMME OF THE CONFERENCE[*]

INTERNATIONAL CONFERENCE ON THE FORMER YUGOSLAVIA

1. The International Conference on the former Yugoslavia will remain in being until a final settlement of the problems of the former Yugoslavia has been reached. It will build on the work already done by the EC Conference on Yugoslavia, especially the documents already produced, and will be guided by the provisions of the statement of principles agreed today. The Permanent Co-Chair-

---

[*] The London Conference, LC/C4 (Final), 27 August 1992.

men will be the Head of State/Government of the Presidency of the of the European Union and the Secretary-General of the United Nations. The Conference will be re-convened on plenary session by the Permanent Co-Chairmen on the recommendation of the Co-Chairmen of the Steering Committee.

STEERING COMMITTEE

2. A high-level Steering Committee will be set up. The Co-Chairmen will be a representative of the Secretary-General of the United Nations and a representative of the Presidency of the European Community. It will include representatives of the Troika of the European Community, the Troika of the CSCE, the five permanent members of the UN Security Council, and one representative from the OIC, two representatives from the neighbouring States and Lord Carrington. It will meet at the request of the Co-Chairmen to guide the work of the Conference and to coordinate its work with related work in other organizations. The Office of the Co-Chairmen

3. The Co-Chairmen of the Steering Committee will be assisted by the Chairmen of the Working Groups (on which see below). They will work in continuous session at the Office of the United Nations in Geneva. The Co-Chairmen will direct the Working Groups and prepare the basis for a general settlement and associated measures. They will also meet as necessary with representatives from the former Yugoslavia, who will attend meetings without preconditions.

4. There will be six Working Groups in continuous session at the Office of the United Nations in Geneva:

(a) Bosnia and Herzegovina Working Group. The Group's task is to promote a cessation of hostilities and a constitutional settlement in Bosnia and Herzegovina;

(b) Humanitarian Issues Working Group. The Group's task is to promote humanitarian relief in all its aspects, including refugees;

(c) Ethnic and National Communities and Minorities Working Group. The Group's task is to recommend initiatives for resolving ethnic questions in the former Yugoslavia. A special group on the former autonomous province of Kosovo will be set up;

(d) Succession Issues Working Group. The Group's task is to resolve succession issues arising from the emergence of new states on the territory of the former Yugoslavia;

(e) Economic Issues Working Group. The Group's task is to address economic issues arising from the emergence of new states in the territory of the former Yugoslavia.

(f) Confidence and Security-building and Verification Measures Working Group. The Group's task are to develop confidence-building measures covering military movements, arms control and arms transfers and limitations, and measures for their monitoring and verification.

ARBITRATION COMMISSION

5. The Conference will seek the continued assistance of the Arbitration Commission.

SECRETARIAT

6. A small Secretariat will be established at the Office of the United Nations in Geneva. It will be headed by an Executive Director. It will be staffed by personnel from the United Nations and from the European Community.

COSTS

7. Participants in the Conference agree to bear the costs related to the administrative implementation of this Work Programme and the provision of the Secretariat, with a scale of contributions to be approved by the Steering Committee.

6. WORK PROGRAMME OF THE CONFERENCE (ADDENDUM)*

Memorandum of Albania, Austria, Bulgaria, Hungary, Romania, Greece, and Italy of 26 August 1992 to the Co-Chairmen of the London Conference on the Draft Action Programme

The undersigned Ministers have agreed the following formula for selection of the representative for the "neighbouring States":

1. Given the fact that there will be two seats for "Neighbouring Countries", one will be allocated to the Community Countries, Italy and Greece, the other one to non-Community Countries. Italy and Greece have decided on their own rotation

---

*   The London Conference, LC/C4 (Final), Addendum, 27 August 1992.

system, on a six months basis.

2. The Representatives of the non-Community neighbouring States have agreed to the following representation on the Steering Committee:

a) the system will be based on rotation in alphabetical order (English alphabet) with Romania starting the process;
b) the tenure will be for a period of three months;
c) it has been agreed that the member representing the non-Community neighbouring States in the Steering Committee will keep the representatives of the other neighbouring States informed in a timely fashion so as to ensure complete collaboration and the best possible hand-over of responsibilities to the next appointee.

7. STATEMENT ON BOSNIA[*]

The participants in the London Conference on the former Socialist Republic of Yugoslavia condemn the continuing violence in Bosnia and Herzegovina and the attempts to gain territory by the use of force. They reject as inhuman and illegal the expulsion of civilian communities from their homes in order to alter the ethnic character of any area. They welcome the adoption by the United Nations Security Council of Resolution 771 and other Security Council Resolutions, and the Resolution of the UN Commission on Human Rights on the situation of human rights in the territory of the former Yugoslavia. They undertake to collate substantiated information on violations of international humanitarian law and to make this information available to the United Nations. They reaffirm that persons who commit or order the commission of grave breaches of the Geneva Conventions are individually responsible in respect of such breaches.

A political settlement in Bosnia and Herzegovina must include the following provisions:

a) a full and permanent cessation of hostilities and an end of all violence and repression, including the expulsion of populations;
b) recognition of Bosnia and Herzegovina by all the former Yugoslav Republics;
c) respect for the integrity of present frontiers, unless changed by mutual agreement;

---

[*] The London Conference, LC/C5 (Final), 27 August 1992.

d) implementation of guarantees for the rights of persons belonging to all national communities and minorities in accordance with the UN Charter and CSCE provisions;

e) just and adequate arrangements for people who have been forcibly expelled from their homes including the right to return and compensation for their losses;

f) democratic and legal structures which properly protect the rights of all in Bosnia and Herzegovina, including national communities and minorities;

g) assurances of non-intervention by outside military forces whether formed units or irregulars, except as provided for in relevant UN Security Council Resolutions:

h) respect for all international Treaties and Agreements;

i) restoration of trade and other links with neighbouring countries.

Further urgent steps are now required to achieve a settlement. The participants in the London Conference urge all parties immediately and without preconditions to resume negotiations on future constitutional arrangements within the framework of the Conference. All parties involved must participate in these negotiations with a genuine will to secure peace and a respect for the interest of the other parties.

The negotiations will also need to cover the following arrangements:

a) a genuine and lasting end to the conflict throughout the Republic, and return of territory taken by force;

b) the cessation of all outside interference, in terms of personnel or material support, in the present conflict;

c) the grouping of heavy weaponry under international control;

d) the demilitarisation of major towns and the monitoring of them by international observers:

e) the establishment of refugee and relief centres for those citizens of Bosnia and Herzegovina who have lost or been expelled from their homes, pending their return;

f) the extension of humanitarian relief to all areas of Bosnia-Herzegovina where supplies are needed, with the cooperation of local parties;

g) an international peace-keeping force under UN auspices may be created by the Security Council to maintain the ceasefire, control military movements, and undertake other confidence-building measures.

As and when parties are ready to reach a settlement on the above basis, the International Community will join with them in a major reconstruction programme to cope with humanitarian needs and to restore economic activity.

THE LONDON CONFERENCE

At a meeting with FCO Minister of State Douglas Hogg, Drs Karadzic and Koljevic representing the Bosnian Serbs signified their agreement to the following:

i) That the Bosnian Serb side would notify to the UN within 96 hours the positions of all heavy weaponry to be grouped around the 4 towns of Sarajevo, Bihac, Gorazde and Jajce, this grouping to be completed within a period of 7 days. The weaponry once grouped would be put under the continuous supervision of permanent UN observers. The Bosnian Serb side would expect the Bosnian Government to take reciprocal action, but would not impose this as a precondition for their own action, which would be unilateral. The Bosnian Serb side further undertook with immediate effect not to initiate fire from any of this heavy weaponry.

ii) That the Bosnian Serb side recognised that in negotiations between the three Bosnian parties, they would agree to withdraw from a substantial portion of the territory now under the control of their forces.

8. SPECIFIC DECISIONS BY THE LONDON CONFERENCE*

1. Acting under the principles set out in the relevant Conference documents, all parties at the Conference formally accept and agree to cooperate in a number of actions.

CESSATION OF VIOLENCE

2. The *overall aim* was an effective and durable cessation of hostilities in the whole of the former SFRY and in particular in Bosnia and Herzegovina in order to facilitate the negotiation of a lasting political settlement. This requires urgent action including:

---

*   The London Conference, LC/C7 (Final), 27 August 1992.

- early lifting of the sieges of towns and cities;
- international supervision of heavy weapons;
- bringing all forces, including irregulars, under central control;
- withholding of direct or indirect military assistance to self-proclaimed governments and the internal components of neighbouring states;
- the progressive reduction of weapons in the region under international supervision.

3. Participants agreed confidence-building measures including:

- the notifications of all mortars and heavy weapons to the UN within 96 hours as a prelude to their disengagement from the conflict, which will be the first item in negotiations;
- a ban on military flights;
- early setting up of hot lines between local commanders and Headquarters;
- improved contact through liaison visits;
- the identification of Headquarters and commanders of all armed units, ineluding para-militaries;
- the posting of observers on the Bosnian/Serbian and Bosnian/ Montenegrin borders;
- the deployment of observers in Bosnia to monitor heavy weapons.

4. Further confidence-building measures, covering military movements, arms limitation and verifications will be urgently examined.

HUMANITARIAN ISSUES

5. The Co-Chairmen have agreed a programme of action with the parties to the conflict. This includes:

Effective Delivery of Humanitarian Aid

(i)   Full collaboration in delivery of humanitarian relief by road throughout Bosnia and Herzegovina, with the following specific steps:

- progressive development of relief missions and road convoys from Croatia and Serbia and Montenegro into all areas of Bosnia where relief is required;

- priority to repairing the road and railway between Ploce, Mostar and Sarajevo;
- parties to designate local representatives with whom practical arrangements for relief missions and road convoys can be made;
- acceptance of and arrangements for international monitors.

(ii)   Parties to exercise authority over undisciplined elements in their areas.

Refugees

(iii)   Progressive return of refugees to their homes and response to the needs identified by the UN.

Dismantling Detention Camps

(iv)   Unconditional and unilateral release under international supervision of all civilians detained, and the closure without delay of the detention camps.

(v)   Parties to take responsibility for security and protection of those detained until freed under international supervision.

(vi)   International community to be given immediate access in order to monitor the situation of those in detention.

(vii)   Pending release and return home of those detained, urgent action by humanitarian organizations to examine temporary options.

Safe Areas

(viii)   Further examination of options including neutral zones or safe areas.

INTERNATIONAL ACTION

6. In order to promote these objectives all governments and international organizations will:

- collaborate fully with the Secretary-General of the United Nations in providing to him information in implementation of UNSCR 771;
- ensure the compliance by all persons with their obligations under international humanitarian law;
- take all possible legal action to bring to account those responsible for com-

mitting or ordering grave breaches of the Geneva Conventions;
- draw up a register of verified breaches of international humanitarian law;
- set up the monitoring missions called for by the CSCE in the territories of the former SFRY and in neighbouring countries;
- not consider help for the reconstruction of the Serbian economy before Serbia has complied with the demands of this Conference;
- provide the means for:
  - passage and protection of humanitarian convoys at the request of the United Nations;
  - control and monitoring of heavy weapons in Bosnia and Herzegovina under the auspices of the United Nations.

SANCTIONS

7. The relevant governments agreed that they will:

- implement an agreed action plan to ensure the rigorous application of sanctions;
- enforce sanctions on the Danube, consistent with their view that riparian states have the authority and obligation to do so;
- provide practical advice, manpower and equipment to help neighbouring countries to enforce sanctions rigorously;
- contribute experts to advise on the application of sanctions in all neighbouring countries to take part in the monitoring missions which will be established in the neighbouring countries to ensure full implementation of sanctions;
- ask the Security Council to:
  - take necessary measures to tighten up the application of sanctions in the Adriatic;
  - prevent illegal transfers of financial assets to Serbia and Montenegro; and
  - eliminate diversion of goods in transit.

Conference parties asked the European Community and the CSCE to coordinate all necessary practical assistance to all neighbouring countries.

VIOLATIONS OF INTERNATIONAL HUMANITARIAN LAW

8. The Co-Chairmen have undertaken to carry forward a study of the creation of an international criminal court.

9. Conclusions on Implementation of Existing Sanctions[*]

1. The London Conference welcomes the steps taken by the international community to implement United Nations Security Council Resolutions 713 and 757 imposing mandatory sanctions against Serbia and Montenegro, but regrets that there remain gaps in implementation. The following proposals deal with the gaps identified so far.

COMPLIANCE WITH UNSCR 757: NEED FOR ENFORCEMENT

2. The Conference notes that many countries are cooperating with the UN Sanctions Committee but is concerned that compliance remains incomplete. The Conference calls on all governments forthwith to comply fully with the requirements of UNSCR 757. All governments should respond to the appeal issued by the UN Sanctions Committee for information regarding violations of the sanctions regime.

3. The Conference recommends that the Security Council should consider any request made to it under Article 50 of the UN Charter by any state which considers that it is confronted by special economic problems arising from carrying out the requirements of UNSCR 757.

ENFORCEMENT OF SANCTIONS BY NEIGHBOURING STATES

4. Neighbouring states are encountering practical problems in the enforcement of sanctions. The Conference notes with approval the fact that the Romanian government invited experts to give advice on ways of overcoming difficulties in the application of sanctions and that officials from a number of Conference countries will shortly go to Romania to help the Romanian authorities with enforcement. Further missions are currently visiting Hungary and Bulgaria with the same purpose. The Conference looks forward to similar missions taking place to all other neighbouring countries, and welcomes the offer of assistance by the Conference on Security and Cooperation in Europe to these countries. It also welcomes the intention to establish monitoring missions from representatives of individual Conference countries to assist in the implementation of sanctions in neighbouring countries. The Conference invites the European Commu-

---

[*]   The London Conference, LC/C8, 27 August 1992.

nity and the Conference on Security and Cooperation in Europe to coordinate these activities.

THE DANUBE

5. The Conference notes that Article 103 of the UN Charter obliges the riparian states of the Danube to do whatever is necessary, including the stopping and searching of vessels, to prevent the use of the River Danube for the purposes of circumventing or breaking the sanctions imposed in UNSCR Resolutions 713 and 757, notwithstanding the provisions of the Belgrade Convention.
6. The Conference calls upon the riparian countries to prevent sanctions being broken or circumvented by trade along the Danube. Individual Conference countries will provide expertise, technical assistance and equipment to the governments concerned to help with enforcement.

UNAUTHORISED TRANSFERS OF SERBIAN AND MONTENEGRIN ASSETS

7. The Conference is concerned that financial transfers for the benefit of Serbia and Montenegro in breach of UNSCR 757 are taking place. The Conference countries reaffirm their commitment to prevent such transfers and call on other states to do the same. The Conference invites the UN Sanctions Committee to consider whether its guidelines need to be tightened for this purpose.

TRANSIT TRAFFIC

8. Illegal diversion of goods in transit across Serbia and Montenegro is taking place. The Conference calls on the authorities of bordering countries to do all they can to prevent this diversion and to report violations to the UN Sanctions Committee. The Conference also invites the UN Security Council to ask the Sanctions Committee to define more precisely its guidelines on the subject of transit traffic.

STRENGTHENING THE LEGAL FRAMEWORK

9. The Conference invites the Security Council to take such further measures as may be necessary to ensure the full implementation of UNSCRs 713 and 757. Existing sanctions are possibly being breached by maritime traffic in the Adriatic

Sea. The Security Council is therefore invited to consider further measures to ensure rigorous implementation of sanctions in the Adriatic.

FOLLOW UP TO THE CONFERENCE

10. The Conference agrees that member states of the European Community and of the Conference on Security and Cooperation in Europe will keep the UN Sanctions Committee informed on a regular basis about the action they have committed themselves to take to enforce sanctions rigorously, including any problems that may be encountered. In addition, as part of the follow up to the Conference, the Representatives of the Co-Chairmen of the Steering Committee will take action necessary to remedy defects in enforcement and generally to ensure rigorous application of sanctions in accordance with SCR 757.

10. PROGRAMME OF ACTION ON HUMANITARIAN ISSUES AGREED BETWEEN THE CO-CHAIRMEN TO THE CONFERENCE AND THE PARTIES TO THE CONFLICT*

Programme of Action by Radovan Karadzic

Recognising that an effective humanitarian response with the full collaboration of the parties to the conflict would greatly contribute to efforts to find an overall political solution and bring an end to hostilities, the Co-Chairmen of the Conference, the UN High Commissioner for Refugees and the parties to the conflict in Bosnia have agreed the following Programme of Action:

1. The parties to the conflict commit themselves to full collaboration in ensuring the delivery of humanitarian relief by road throughout Bosnia and Herzegovina.
2. In order to enhance the development of the system of land convoys to deliver humanitarian assistance on the basis of negotiated safe passage. The following specific steps will be undertaken:

   a. Priority will be given to repairing the road and railway between Ploce, Mostar and Sarajevo.
   b. The parties to the conflict will no later than 3 September identify to UNHCR representatives at Sarajevo (or at Belgrade, Split or Zagreb as

---

* The London Conference, LC/C9, 27 August 1992.

appropriate) designated representatives of the local authorities (at a military police and political level) at all relevant locations with whom the practical arrangements for the expansion of the forthcoming relief missions and road convoys for the benefit for all victims in need will be made.

c. UN and UNHCR representatives will meet regularly with designated representatives of the parties to make arrangements for forthcoming relief missions and road convoys from Croatia and from Serbia and from Montenegro to Sarajevo and also to Banja Luka, Bihac, Bileca, Duboj, Foca, Gorazde, Mostar, Tuzla, Vitez, and Vlasenica. This pattern will be extended to all areas within Bosnia and Herzegovina where humanitarian assistance is required.

d. It was recognised that in addressing the acute problem of the unlawful detention of civilians and the deplorable condition in which they were held. The primary objective to secure their release and return to their homes. If not immediate feasible, they identified the following possible options in the light of the wishes of those detained and in keeping with the provisions set out at para 3 below:
   - repatriation to areas under the control of their respective ethnic authorities;
   - choosing to stay temporarily in the area of detention;
   - relocation in areas away from the conflict under international supervision;
   - temporary refuge in third countries.

e. The international humanitarian agencies will explore urgently with the parties all possible ways to secure the safe release of those detained.

f. In the meantime, the parties undertook to ensure that arrangements are made to ensure that those in detention are cared for and protected, until such time as their safe release is feasible, and accepted that the international community will monitor the situation closely to ensure that the security and well-being of those held in detention is assured. To this end, they undertook to give free access to representatives of the international community including the UN, ICRC, EC and CSCE.

g. In the light of the need for the immediate evacuation of critical medical cases under ICRC supervision, the parties agreed to arrange security guarantees to permit the use of Banja Luka airport for this purpose. The evacuation would take place with the shortest delay. The parties undertook to identify the names of local commanders/authorities who would make the arrangements with the ICRC delegate, in close coordination with the UN, and who would be individually responsible for the safe passage and security of those to be evacuated.

3. In carrying out the Programme of Action, the parties to the conflict under-took to abide by the following provisions:

i)   all the parties to the conflict are bound to comply with their obligations under International Humanitarian Law and in particular the Geneva Conventions of 1949 and the Additional Protocols thereto, and that persons who commit or order the commission of grave breaches are individually responsible.

ii)   all the parties to the conflict have the responsibility to exercise full authority over undisciplined elements within their areas so as to avoid anarchy, breaches of international humanitarian law and human rights abuse.

iii) that refugees and displaced persons should be allowed to return volun-tarily and safely to their places of origin.

iv)   all practices involving forcible displacement, all forms of harassment, humiliation or intimidation, confiscation and destruction of property and all acts involved in the practice of ethnic cleansing are abhorrent and should cease forthwith.

v)   there should be unconditional and unilateral release under international supervision of all civilians currently detained;

vi)   that the parties to the conflict are responsible for the provision of secur-ity and protection for those currently detained until they can be freed under international supervision;

vii) that all such action should be in accordance with the agreement with the parties reached in Geneva on 22 May under auspices of the ICRC;

viii) that the provision of humanitarian assistance should be carried out im-partially and on a non-political basis for the benefit of all those affected by the conflict.

The representatives of the Co-Chairmen also noted the following points made by the parties:

a.   that humanitarian assistance should be carried out impartially to the bene-fit of all those in need.

b.   that no party can be expected to give guarantees of security on behalf of the other parties to the conflict.

c. that in granting safe access to the international humanitarian organizations there would be a clear understanding that no party would gain military advantage.

Programme of Action by Alija Izetbegovic, President of the Republic of Bosnia and Herzegovina

Recognising that an effective humanitarian response with the full collaboration of the parties to the conflict would greatly contribute to efforts to find an overall political solution and bring an end to hostilities, the Co-Chairmen of the Conference, the UN High Commissioner for Refugees and the parties to the conflict in Bosnia have agreed the following Programme of Action:

1. The parties to the conflict commit themselves to full collaboration in ensuring the delivery of humanitarian relief by road throughout Bosnia and Herzegovina.
2. In order to enhance the development of the system of land convoys to deliver humanitarian assistance on the basis of negotiated safe passage. The following specific steps will be undertaken:

a. Priority will be given to repairing the road and railway between Ploce, Mostar and Sarajevo.
b. The parties to the conflict will no later than 3 September identify to UNHCR representatives at Sarajevo (or at Belgrade, Split or Zagreb as appropriate) designated representatives of the local authorities (at a military police and political level) at all relevant locations with whom the practical arrangements for the expansion of the forthcoming relief missions and road convoys for the benefit for all victims in need will be made.
c. UN and UNHCR representatives will meet regularly with designated representatives of the parties to make arrangements for forthcoming relief missions and road convoys from Croatia and from Serbia and from Montenegro to Sarajevo and also to Banja Luka, Bihac, Bileca, Duboj, Foca, Gorazde, Mostar, Tuzla, Vitez, and Vlasenica. This pattern will be extended to all areas within Bosnia and Herzegovina where humanitarian assistance is required.
d. It was recognised that in addressing the acute problem of the unlawful detention of civilians and the deplorable condition in which they were held. The primary objective to secure their release and return to their

homes. If not immediate feasible, they identified the following possible options in the light of the wishes of those detained and in keeping with the provisions set out at para 3 below:
- repatriation to areas under the control of their respective ethnic authorities;
- choosing to stay temporarily in the area of detention;
- relocation in areas away from the conflict under international supervision;
- temporary refuge in third countries.

e. The international humanitarian agencies will explore urgently with the parties all possible ways to secure the safe release of those detained.

f. In the meantime, the parties undertook to ensure that arrangements are made to ensure that those in detention are cared for and protected, until such time as their safe release is feasible, and accepted that the international community will monitor the situation closely to ensure that the security and well-being of those held in detention is assured. To this end, they undertook to give free access to representatives of the international community including the UN, ICRC, EC and CSCE.

g. In the light of the need for the immediate evacuation of critical medical cases under ICRC supervision, the parties agreed to arrange security guarantees to permit the use of Banja Luka airport for this purpose. The evacuation would take place with the shortest delay. The parties undertook to identify the names of local commanders/authorities who would make the arrangements with the ICRC delegate, in close coordination with the UN, and who would be individually responsible for the safe passage and security of those to be evacuated.

3. In carrying out the Programme of Action, the parties to the conflict undertook to abide by the following provisions:

i)   all the parties to the conflict are bound to comply with their obligations under International Humanitarian Law and in particular the Geneva Conventions of 1949 and the Additional Protocols thereto, and that persons who commit or order the commission of grave breaches are individually responsible.

ii)   all the parties to the conflict have the responsibility to exercise full authority over undisciplined elements within their areas so as to avoid anarchy, breaches of international humanitarian law and human rights abuse.

iii) that refugees and displaced persons should be allowed to return voluntarily and safely to their places of origin.

iv) all practices involving forcible displacement, all forms of harassment, humiliation or intimidation, confiscation and destruction of property and all acts involved in the practice of ethnic cleansing are abhorrent and should cease forthwith.

v) there should be unconditional and unilateral release under international supervision of all civilians currently detained;

vi) that the parties to the conflict are responsible for the provision of security and protection for those currently detained until they can be freed under international supervision;

vii) that all such action should be in accordance with the agreement with the parties reached in Geneva on 22 May under auspices of the ICRC;

viii) that the provision of humanitarian assistance should be carried out impartially and on a non-political basis for the benefit of all those affected by the conflict.

The representatives of the Co-Chairmen also noted the following points made by the parties:

a. that humanitarian assistance should be carried out impartially to the benefit of all those in need.

b. that no party can be expected to give guarantees of security on behalf of the other parties to the conflict.

c. that in granting safe access to the international humanitarian organizations there would be a clear understanding that no party would gain military advantage.

Programme of Action by Mate Boban

Recognising that an effective humanitarian response with the full collaboration of the parties to the conflict would greatly contribute to efforts to find an overall political solution and bring an end to hostilities, the Co-Chairmen of the Conference, the UN High Commissioner for Refugees and the parties to the conflict in Bosnia have agreed the following Programme of Action:

1. The parties to the conflict commit themselves to full collaboration in ensuring the delivery of humanitarian relief by road throughout Bosnia and Herzegovina.

2. In order to enhance the development of the system of land convoys to deliver humanitarian assistance on the basis of negotiated safe passage. The following specific steps will be undertaken:

    a. Priority will be given to repairing the road and railway between Ploce, Mostar and Sarajevo.

    b. The parties to the conflict will no later than 3 September identify to UNHCR representatives at Sarajevo (or at Belgrade, Split or Zagreb as appropriate) designated representatives of the local authorities (at a military police and political level) at all relevant locations with whom the practical arrangements for the expansion of the forthcoming relief missions and road convoys for the benefit for all victims in need will be made.

    c. UN and UNHCR representatives will meet regularly with designated representatives of the parties to make arrangements for forthcoming relief missions and road convoys from Croatia and from Serbia and from Montenegro to Sarajevo and also to Banja Luka, Bihac, Bileca, Duboj, Foca, Gorazde, Mostar, Tuzla, Vitez, and Vlasenica. This pattern will be extended to all areas within Bosnia and Herzegovina where humanitarian assistance is required.

    d. It was recognised that in addressing the acute problem of the unlawful detention of civilians and the deplorable condition in which they were held. The primary objective to secure their release and return to their homes. If not immediate feasible, they identified the following possible options in the light of the wishes of those detained and in keeping with the provisions set out at para 3 below:
       - repatriation to areas under the control of their respective ethnic authorities;
       - choosing to stay temporarily in the area of detention;
       - relocation in areas away from the conflict under international supervision;
       - temporary refuge in third countries.

    e. The international humanitarian agencies will explore urgently with the parties all possible ways to secure the safe release of those detained.

    f. In the meantime, the parties undertook to ensure that arrangements are made to ensure that those in detention are cared for and protected, until such time as their safe release is feasible, and accepted that the international community will monitor the situation closely to ensure that the security and well-being of those held in detention is assured. To this end, they undertook to give free access to representatives of the international community including the UN, ICRC, EC and CSCE.

g. In the light of the need for the immediate evacuation of critical medical cases under ICRC supervision, the parties agreed to arrange security guarantees to permit the use of Banja Luka airport for this purpose. The evacuation would take place with the shortest delay. The parties undertook to identify the names of local commanders/authorities who would make the arrangements with the ICRC delegate, in close coordination with the UN, and who would be individually responsible for the safe passage and security of those to be evacuated.

3. In carrying out the Programme of Action, the parties to the conflict undertook to abide by the following provisions:

i)   all the parties to the conflict are bound to comply with their obligations under International Humanitarian Law and in particular the Geneva Conventions of 1949 and the Additional Protocols thereto, and that persons who commit or order the commission of grave breaches are individually responsible.

ii) all the parties to the conflict have the responsibility to exercise full authority over undisciplined elements within their areas so as to avoid anarchy, breaches of international humanitarian law and human rights abuse.

iii) that refugees and displaced persons should be allowed to return voluntarily and safely to their places of origin.

iv) all practices involving forcible displacement, all forms of harassment, humiliation or intimidation, confiscation and destruction of property and all acts involved in the practice of ethnic cleansing are abhorrent and should cease forthwith.

v)   there should be unconditional and unilateral release under international supervision of all civilians currently detained;

vi) that the parties to the conflict are responsible for the provision of security and protection for those currently detained until they can be freed under international supervision;

vii) that all such action should be in accordance with the agreement with the parties reached in Geneva on 22 May under auspices of the ICRC;

viii) that the provision of humanitarian assistance should be carried out impartially and on a non-political basis for the benefit of all those affected by the conflict.

The representatives of the Co-Chairmen also noted the following points made by the parties:

a. that humanitarian assistance should be carried out impartially to the benefit of all those in need.
b. that no party can be expected to give guarantees of security on behalf of the other parties to the conflict.
c. that in granting safe access to the international humanitarian organizations there would be a clear understanding that no party would gain military advantage.

11. SERBIA AND MONTENEGRO (PAPER BY THE CO-CHAIRMAN)[*]

We welcome the fact that all participants in the Conference have subscribed to the Statement on Bosnia and Herzegovina. All participants must fulfil the obligations to which they have agreed. In particular, Serbia and Montenegro face a clear choice. They have undertaken to:

- cease intervention across their borders with Bosnia and Croatia;
- to the best of their ability restrain the Bosnian Serbs from taking territory by force and expelling the local populations;
- restore in full the civil and constitutional rights of the inhabitants of the Kosovo and Vojvodina and also to ensure the civil rights of the inhabitants of the Sandjak;
- use their influence with the Bosnian Serbs to obtain the closure of their detention camps, to comply with their obligations under international humanitarian law and in particular the Geneva Conventions, and to permit the return of refugees to their homes. The Bosnian Croats and Muslims have given similar undertakings;
- fully observe the relevant resolutions of the UN Security Council;
- declare that they fully respect the integrity of present frontiers;
- guarantee the rights of ethnic and national communities and minorities within the borders of Serbia and Montenegro in accordance with the UN Charter, the CSCE and the draft convention of the EC Conference on Yugoslavia;

---

[*] The London Conference, LC/C10 (Final).

- work for the normalisation of the situation in Croatia, for implementation of the Vance Plan and for acceptance by the Serbs in the Krajina of special status as foreseen in the draft convention of the EC Conference on Yugoslavia;
- respect all relevant international treaties and agreements.

If, as suggested by Mr. Panic's recent letter to the President of the Security Council of the UN, Serbia and Montenegro do intend to fulfil these obligations in deed as well as word they will resume a respected position in the international community. They will be enabled to trade, to receive assistance and to enjoy the full cooperation of all members of the international community. If they do not comply the Security Council will be invited to apply stringent sanctions leading to their total international isolation.

12. CONFIDENCE, SECURITY-BUILDING AND VERIFICATION*

I PURPOSE

1. There is an urgent need to identify and promote steps in the military sphere in all or part of the former Socialist Republic of Yugoslavia (SFRY) which could underpin a cessation of hostilities and a durable political settlement. To this end, the Conference has taken some immediate decisions and set up a Working Group to develop confidence-building measures, covering military movements and arms transfers and limitations, as well as measures for their monitoring and verification. This work will be under the direction of the Co-Chairmen of the Steering Committee (see Work Programme). The results of this work will be compatible with action authorised by the Security Council in respect of the United Nations peace-keeping operations in the former SFRY.
2. Such military measures need to be seen in the context of measures of a political and humanitarian nature, including, for example, convoys under UNHCR auspices, and exchanges of prisoners of war under ICRC auspices.

---

*   The London Conference, LC/C11 (Final); Conference Document produced by the Co-Chairmen on the basis of extensive consultations with Delegations on 26/27 August 1992.

II IMMEDIATE DECISIONS OF THE CONFERENCE

3. The most immediate task is to alleviate the suffering in Bosnia and Herzegovina through a permanent identifying HQ locations and names of commanders, covering all armed units, including paramilitary units.

4. It will be for the Co-Chairmen of the Steering Committee to recommend how these measures should be implemented, taking account of international peace-keeping and other related activities in progress in the region. Breaches of agreed measures will be reported (with, where possible, an indication of who is responsible) by the Co-Chairmen to the Conference, and, where appropriate, by the Secretary-General of the United Nations to the Security Council.

5. Priority should be given to assuring that there is immediate follow-up to the agreement on international supervision of all mortars and heavy weapons in Bosnia and Herzegovina, proceeding by agreed steps, which could include tagging, monitoring, deactivation, corralling under local supervision and eventually centralisation of such weapons. It will be for the Co-Chairmen of the Steering Committee to decide whether this work would more appropriately be done by the Working Group on confidence, security-building and verification or the one on Bosnia and Herzegovina.

III WORKING GROUP PROGRAMME

6. The Working Group should seek early agreement on measures aimed to enhance transparency between the parties in the former SFRY. The purpose of these provisions would be to build confidence and to ensure that any ceasefire is durable. Such measures may include, inter alia:

- information exchange on numbers and location of certain categories of equipment (to be defined) held by the parties;
- advance notification of movements of personnel, or movements/transfers of equipment;
- information on personnel levels of formations and units above a given strength;
- extension of observer missions both in inter-republican borders and within certain republics;
- short-notice on-site inspection (within 24 hours) in the event of suspect activities.

7. In addition, though perhaps on a different timescale, other measures should be considered in the former SFRY, including:

- restriction on the movement of paramilitary or military forces;
- no acquisition of certain types of equipment;
- measures of demilitarisation, for example declaring that areas around specific locations, such as refugee camps or major cities, should be free from certain categories of equipment;
- other verification measures, for example, assessment visits by parties to evaluate compliance with agreed provisions, or overflights by outside states;
- more systematic liaison provisions, for example, establishment of local standing liaison commissions, cessation of hostilities and safe delivery of humanitarian assistance. Achievement of these aims can be facilitated considerably through agreement of measures aimed at clarifying the military situation in Bosnia and Herzegovina and increasing the possibilities for liaison and verification. As a first step, the Conference has decided to adopt the following measures with regard to Bosnia and Herzegovina:
- improved communications between the parties, including direct and immediate liaison between commanders on forward deployment lines, for example, by local radio and telephone hot lines;
- improvements in contacts between the parties, for example, by liaison visits, and by establishing joint teams to resolve local incidents;
- immediate acceptance of reconnaissance teams to prepare for the deployment of observers around designated locations;
- posting of observers on the Bosnian/Serbian, Bosnia/Montenegrin and Bosnian/Croatian borders;
- immediate acceptance of the principle that all mortars and heavy weapons will be subject to international supervision and, as a first step, should be notified to the UN by type and location within 96 hours, as a prelude to their disengagement from the conflict;
- no military use of aircraft or helicopters;
- information exchange on command structure, involving outside observers such as EC Monitors or UN Military Observers:
- other arms limitation measures.

8. Although the group will focus on new measures, it will also be important to ensure that existing obligations under the terms of the Vienna Document 92 in respect of provision of information are fully implemented. Consideration should

also be given to applying in the former SFRY some of the mechanisms of the Vienna Document which are designed to enhance transparency, for example, the unusual military activity, verification and border tours measures.

IV WORKING GROUP ORGANIZATION

9. It will be for the Co-Chairmen of the Steering Committee to decide how to develop work on these lines as soon as possible.

B. STATEMENTS

13. ADDRESS BY SECRETARY-GENERAL BOUTROS BOUTROS-GHALI TO THE INTERNATIONAL CONFERENCE ON THE FORMER SOCIALIST FEDERAL REPUBLIC OF YUGOSLAVIA
(26 AUGUST 1992)

An international era has just ended. With its passing, a dimension of fear has departed; but a dimension of stability has disappeared as well. No problem of today, however familiar in its form, is exactly like the problems of the era past. There is a new specificity to conflict now.

The closing of the cold war opened a Pandora's box of causes and conflicts that had been kept down by the ideological struggle of that era. Old disputed ambitions and hatred have burst forth. In the years just past, such activities would have been regarded as points of loss or gain in the calculation of the bi-polar powers. Without that cold war structure to deal with them, it is left to us here in this room to provide the approaches and ultimately the answers.

There is one specific feature of the critical situation which is the purpose of this Conference. Territories of the former Yugoslavia now locked in military confrontation have been recently recognized by the international community and have taken their place in the General Assembly of the United Nations as Member States. This is, then, an international conflict. Not only the future shape and security of one or more Member States is at risk, but perhaps their very existence.

The unfolding of this crisis is being closely watched by others who, in similar conditions of instability and new confrontation, could resort to war and destruction rather than choose the road of negotiation and dialogue. They must understand, they must accept that the only route for change is one that is legal, peaceful, and which contributes to a structure of international peace and security.

In response to the crisis that has erupted with the collapse of the former Yugoslavia, the United Nations has undertaken an intensive and extensive array of actions.

It is important to review in some detail the difficult process which has led to the establishment of a United Nations presence in the former Yugoslavia and to its present situation:

On 25 September 1991 the Security Council met and adopted by consensus Resolution 713 expressing deep concern at the fighting, the continuation of which it considered to be a threat to international peace and security, and asking the Secretary-General to offer his assistance in resolving the crisis.

As a consequence of Resolution 713 my predecessor appointed Mr. Cyrus Vance as his personal envoy. Between October 1991 and January 1992 Mr. Vance undertook five missions to the area as part of the international community's collective efforts to stop the fighting and find a peaceful solution. It soon became clear that the most valuable contribution the UN could offer towards the establishment of a peaceful settlement was a peace-keeping operation that could create the necessary conditions for the pursuit of political negotiations.

On 23 November 1991 Mr. Vance convened in Geneva, in the presence of Lord Carrington, a meeting of the Presidents of Croatia and Serbia and the Yugoslav Secretary for Defense to discuss measures to end the conflict. A cease-fire was agreed, but not honoured on the ground.

The Security Council approved Mr. Vance's efforts in Resolution 721 of 27 November 1991, but stressed that a United Nations peace-keeping operation could not be considered in the absence of full compliance by all the parties with the agreement reached at Geneva.

A United Nations peace-keeping plan was broadly agreed to by the parties as the result of Mr. Vance's continuing efforts. The plan was approved by the Security Council in Resolution 724 of 15 December 1991 which stated, however, that conditions did not yet exist for the dispatch of United Nations peace-keepers. The Security Council endorsed the Secretary-General's proposal that a military team be sent to Yugoslavia to carry forward preparations for a possible peace-keeping operation. The first Blue Berets arrived on 8 December 1991.

On 2 February 1992, in Sarajevo, Mr. Vance gained agreement by the warring parties to accept international assistance in maintaining a ceasefire. This was approved by the Security Council in Resolution 727 of 8 January 1992. Fifty military liaison officers from other UN peace-keeping operations were sent to Yugoslavia to promote maintenance of the ceasefire.

On 7 February 1992 the Council's Resolution 740 increased the United Nations military liaison contingent from 50 to 75 and requested me to prepare for a peace-keeping mission.

Following intensive negotiation with the authorities in Belgrade and Zagreb, I recommended that the United Nations Protection Force (UNPROFOR) be established. This was approved by the Council in Resolution 743 of 21 February 1992. After the advance elements of UNPROFOR had done the necessary preparatory work, the Council authorized the full deployment of the force in Resolution 749 of 7 April 1992.

As you know, the European Community Monitoring Mission, comprising both military and diplomatic personnel, had the task at this time of monitoring ceasefire and other military arrangements negotiated with the parties locally. Political decisions by the European Community had an impact on the parties;

perceptions, however, with the result that United Nations personnel were increasingly asked to perform functions that - in the agreed division of labour between the EC and the UN - properly were those of the European Community Monitoring Mission.

This division of labour was eroded on two fronts. First, in Croatia, UNPROFOR's functioning inevitably brought it into discussions with the parties in the political issues that divided them and which had operational implications for UNPROFOR.

Second, as fighting broke out in Bosnia and Herzegovina, the European Community Monitoring Mission and the International Committee of the Red Cross withdrew their personnel from Sarajevo, leaving the United Nations head-quarters of UNPROFOR and UN military observers in Mostar and Bihac as the only international presence in Bosnia and Herzegovina. This meant that UNPROFOR had to lead negotiations with the parties on a ceasefire and in a number of humanitarian issues.

On 5 June 1992 the United Nations Protection Force concluded an agreement which permitted the reopening of Sarajevo airport. The Force has continued since then to arrange safe passage of humanitarian relief in Sarajevo. To date, some 8.000 metric tonnes of supplies have been airlifted by 850 sorties to the city's population. Almost 2 million refugees and displaced persons are in the former Yugoslavia. The lead agency, the Office of the UN High Commissioner for Refugees, estimates that up to a half a million people will require shelter before the onset of winter.

In performing its functions, the United Nations Protection Force was com-pelled to go beyond the original peace-keeping plan which had been approved by the Security Council in December 1991. The Council, in Resolutions 761, 762, and 769, enlarged the role of the Force to cope with its evolving responsibilities.

The expectations of the international community - which has been shocked by the horror of the conflict in Bosnia and Herzegovina - continue to exceed the resources and capacity of the United Nations Protection Force.

It is not widely understood that although the Security Council has called for a number of actions by all sides to the conflict in Bosnia and Herzegovina, the United Nations Force has been explicitly authorized and equipped to implement only the 5 June 1992 Agreement. This it has done in most difficult and danger-ous conditions.

United Nations soldiers in Sarajevo have suffered casualties in a situation of considerable hardship.

Today they remain vulnerable to attack both at the airport and on the hillsides around the city, where its observers are monitoring the employment of heavy weapons of the warring sides.

In this situation: as increasingly is becoming true for other United Nations Mission, the success of the operation depends on the cooperation of irregular forces in the conflicting parties. This presents the United Nations operation with an unprecedented set of problems:

- the lack of a clear chain of command;
- political and legal implications of dealing with various factions and groups;
- the inability of such groups to make an agreement or to keep one, and
- the difficulties which attend dealings with irregular forces: geographical remoteness, clandestine practices, and suspicion and bitter hostility toward external attempts to stop the bloodshed and to restore peace.

I wish to insist that the UN mission with its present mandate cannot, by itself, bring this crisis to an end or to a durable political solution. More, much more, is urgently required. That is why we are here today in London.

The Charter of the United Nations devotes Chapter VIII to regional organizations for dealing with regional actions related to peace and security. The cold war crippled the proper use of Chapter VIII and indeed, in that era, regional arrangements worked on occasion against resolving disputes in the manner foreseen in the Charter.

In the past, regional arrangements were created because of the absence of a universal system for collective security; thus their activities often worked at cross purposes with the sense of solidarity required for the effectiveness of the World Organization. But in the post cold war period regional organizations can play a crucial role, if their activities are undertaken in a manner consistent with the principles of Chapter VIII of the United Nations Charter.

There could be no more critical moment than the present for the advancement of this concept and for the fulfilment of this opportunity.

On 13 August the Security Council in Resolution 770 called upon States to take "all measures necessary" to facilitate in coordination with the United Nations the delivery of humanitarian assistance.

Such action, the resolution stated, may be taken either nationally or through regional agencies and arrangements.

The resources of Europe are vast: they are moral, economic and military. I call upon this Conference to bring about urgent cooperation between the regional arrangements and agencies of Europe, including NATO, and the United Nations Security Council. The purpose should be clear: to turn back the march of misery, devastation and terror.

In this context the following ideas should be considered.

First, the international community cannot step into every instance of violence that erupts around the world. But some disputes compel our attention: those that threaten international peace and security; those that transgress the fundamental moral standards which humanity holds in common, including those human rights whose violation inflicts unacceptable suffering on ordinary people; and those which, unless resolved rightly, would send to undermine the foundations of the international system.

In this last regard falls the recognition that the foundation-stone of the world community's work is and must remain the State. Respect for its basic sovereignty and territorial integrity are crucial to any common international progress.

The former Yugoslavia has been transformed into several Member States of the United Nations. They possess all the rights and duties held by their fellow-States in the international community.

Second, what we observe today in the former Yugoslavia is the challenge of finding a formula through which diversity can be respected yet the government may serve a common purpose and enjoy a common allegiance.

When the ideology that held different peoples together disappears, it is not a surprise that new States emerge. Yet it cannot be denied that if every ethnic, religious or linguistic group claimed statehood, there would be no limit to fragmentation. Peace, security and economic well-being for all would become even more difficult to achieve.

One requirement for solutions to these problems lies in commitment to human rights with a special sensitivity to those of minorities, whether ethnic, religious, social or linguistic.

The General Assembly will soon have before it a declaration on the rights of minorities.

That instrument, together with the increasingly effective machinery of the United Nations dealing with human rights, should enhance the situation of minorities as well as the stability of States. One approach to the solution of this crisis should include a special appeal to the leaders of all religious denominations. In them is enshrined the moral and spiritual responsibility to defend and uphold the dignity and life of each human being regardless of faith.

Third, in this century, is the consequence of too many examples of man's inhumanity to man, a generally shared perception has taken hold, supported by basic international legal instruments. The systematic torture and killing along racial, ethnic, or religious lines can no longer be tolerated. There are some acts of governments that sovereignty cannot shield.

Those positions of leadership who preside over such crimes must know that they personally will be held accountable by the international community: Security Council Resolution 771 of 13 August strongly condemns those who violate international humanitarian law, and warns that they will be held responsible for their actions.

Fourth, the critical humanitarian situation prevailing in the area is deeply linked to a political settlement. History and geopolitics have thrown diverse peoples together. The final aim must be the overall settlement of the dispute in all its aspects. Whether the differences are between States or within States, the answers lie not in segregation or separation, but in patterns of agreement under which diversity and unity both have a place.

Fifth, a negotiating structure needs to be found to assist the contending parties sort the issues between them. It is necessary to begin the work of reconciliation, rehabilitation and reconstruction, in order to reshape the involved economic, political and social relations which are their common destiny. The United Nations stand ready to fulfil its role as peace-keeper, peacemaker and peace-builder, whatever form and format emerges as the most promising avenue towards a settlement.

Sixth, the decisions of nations in this end other forums that address questions of international peace and security cannot expect to succeed as declarations or proclamations alone. Mandates must be carefully measured against the capacity and the resources provided to carry them through.

When United Nations personnel are deployed in conditions of strife, whether for preventive diplomacy, peace-keeping, peace-building or humanitarian purposes, it is essential to guarantee the safety of the people involved. And for the credibility of the Organization, there should be contingency planning in case the purpose of the United Nations operation is systematically frustrated and hostilities resume or intensify.

The world's priorities are no longer set by the bipolar confrontation of the past. For the present and the future, we must not allow our priorities to be set, nor our emotions celebrated, by the extent of media coverage which a given crisis generates.

It now appears certain that the world community will face for the foreseeable future sporadic regional outbreaks of violence and warfare in various areas around the globe.

In the decades just past, the intellectual and policy framework in which responses to such crises were designed was provided by the culture of the cold war.

What is needed now is a new intellectual and practical foundation for approaching such conflicts, and new principles under which they may be stopped by collective effort and their causes resolved. This is the challenge which we

face. Let us hope that in taking up this challenge our conference will make a
lasting contribution to peace and security.

14. OPENING SPEECH GIVEN BY THE PRIME MINISTER THE RT HON JOHN MAJOR PP, AT THE LONDON CONFERENCE ON THE FORMER YUGOSLAVIA TERRITORIES (26 AUGUST 1992)

PEACE WITH JUSTICE

May I first welcome you all to the London Conference, a Conference sponsored
jointly by the United Nations and the European Community. I think no explanation is necessary to the people present today as to why we are here or to the size
of the problem that lies before us. What we are hoping from this Conference is
that it will prove to be a decisive turning point, that it will mark a decisive new
phase in the search for the peace in the former Yugoslavia territories that all of
us wish to see.

What I fear we can see daily as we look around is the tragedy of Yugoslavia
unfolding. Throughout the world our fellow citizens in each of our individual
countries have seen the waste, the despair and the growing danger of the continuing conflict in Yugoslavia.

In this room are the people who can stop this war, end the bloodshed, reach a
lasting settlement. I do not believe that world opinion will easily forgive anyone
who impedes that work over the next couple of days and beyond.

The people that we represent at this Conference have been appalled by the
destruction, the killing, the maiming and the sheer cruelty which has disfigured
the former Yugoslavia. We all seek a just peace and against that background it
seemed to the Secretary General and to me that the United Nations and the European Community should join together in holding this Conference.

Fortunately, we will not be beginning our work from scratch. The European
Community has given monitors and sponsored a Peace Conference. Lord Carrington, to whom I pay a very warm and well deserved tribute, has made substantial progress and we should build on that. The United Nations has passed
Resolutions bringing in an arms embargo on Serbia and Montenegro. Ten days
ago the Security Council agreed that all necessary measures could be used to
deliver humanitarian aid. The UN agencies have supplied and distributed emergency aid and cared for refugees and individual countries, many represented here
today, have contributed too, often by taking in large numbers of refugees.

But I think we have all felt that the time has come to broaden and to intensify our work. And let me suggest to you, as Co-Chairman, how I believe we should tackle that task.

Humanitarian Aid

Firstly, humanitarian help. Even if peace were achieved tomorrow, hundreds of thousands of people would still be involved in hunger, sickness, desperation, and those problems are bound to worsen as winter approaches.

The United Nations High Commissioner for Refugees estimates that some two and a half million people remain in the former Yugoslavia and over one and a quarter million of these will depend on outside help for shelter, food and medicines to see them through the coming winter. Without that help many of that 1.3 million may not survive. And this is not a natural disaster we are dealing with, it is a man-made disaster and it needs a man-made solution and this Conference can make its contribution to that.

We must ensure that humanitarian supplies are distributed to the victims of this conflict, particularly those victims still trapped in the war zones in Bosnia. I believe that the humanitarian agencies have done an outstanding job, they have put their lives on the line to assist in the survival of others. The Security Council Resolution 770 is a guarantee the international community has given that we will not leave the United Nations and its agencies without help and protection in the task they have overtaken.

It cannot be done by force but it must be done in safety. And that is why my country and others are willing to provide armed escorts to help the relief convoys on their missions of mercy. We have no hostile intent to any party in Bosnia, but I have to say to the Conference that we will not be deflected from our determination to deliver aid wherever it is needed.

Human Rights Obligations

And secondly, I believe we must tackle respect for human rights. Violations of international humanitarian law must stop. I welcome unreservedly the Security Council Resolution condemning human rights violations and this conference must call on all parties to respect human rights, regardless of nationality, regardless of religion.

At present let us be frank, that is not happening. Civilians are detained against their will and subjected to ill treatment, especially in Bosnia. Those detention camps must be shut but while they exist humanitarian agencies should have immediate unimpeded and constant access to them and individuals must accept their own responsibility for any war crimes they order or commit.

Some action has already been taken and I welcome the recent rapporteur missions to investigate detention centres throughout the former Yugoslavia and the attacks on civilians in Croatia and Bosnia. And I warmly support, too, the United Nations decision to appoint a Special Rapporteur to investigate allegations of human rights abuses in particular Bosnia Herzegovina. The human rights situation throughout former Yugoslavia must continue to be closely monitored.

But humanitarian help and greater respect for human rights, however desperately needed, do not cure, even though they may ease, the basic problem that we seek to solve.

Peace Process

And thirdly, therefore, we must work for peace with justice with as much energy as we relieve those already suffering from war as a result of injustice. It is clear that we need a peace process and that this should be coupled with the necessary international pressure to bring success.

That peace process is vital but is must be based, I believe, on certain fundamental principles. The first is that frontiers cannot be altered by force; the international community will not accept that Bosnia can be partitioned by conquest. Those who suppose they can secure international acceptance of military advantages gained by force are mistaken in that judgment.

The second principle is that within those fixed frontiers minorities are entitled to full protection and respect to their civil rights, this applies universally whether in Bosnia, Croatia or Serbia. And those two principles go together, neither can be effective without the other.

And so the principles and how we hope to achieve them are set out in the two key documents which I hope the Conference will adopt. The statement of principles sets out the basic international standards which must govern a settlement, I cannot believe after further discussion that any of us here will not be able and prepared to subscribe to it.

But what counts of course is not just the acceptance of those principles but the subsequent application of those principles and they are in reality not being completely fulfilled by any of the main parties to the crisis at present.

International Task Groups

We must therefore help the parties to come closer to doing so and that is the purpose of the work set out un the action programme. This Conference will remain in being and will remain active. Its work will be handled in partnership by the United Nations and the Presidency of the European Community and in addition we urgently need a high level international task group to tackle each main problem that we face. Those task groups will build on the work already done by the European Community Peace Conference and the United Nations. They must then get down to work energetically and unremittingly on the problems they have been set and we must also strive for further practical progress during the Conference on various key questions - humanitarian issues confidence-building measures and the implementation of the UN Security Council Resolutions.

We shall also be looking tomorrow at two further documents. These are the draft statements, one on Serbia, one on Bosnia. I hope that all parties will be able to adopt them. Like the Statement of Principles, they should be uncontentious. We believe, for example, that they are consistent with Mr. Panic's recent letter to the United Nations Security Council which struck a note of realism and of moderation.

It is essential that this is followed up in deeds as well as in words and if all the Yugoslav parties at this Conference, including Serbia, are prepared to subscribe to the draft statements this will be an encouraging sign. And if not, the world will be entitled to doubt the goodwill of those who stand out against it and to draw the appropriate conclusions.

What are those conclusions? These conclusions must mean bringing pressure to bear on governments or factions which do not abide by those principles. That in turn means sanctions. We need to enforce them more effectively and if necessary intensify them and that will be an inevitable issue at this Conference and perhaps beyond it too.

No-one should underestimate the anguish that is felt around the world at the events that unfold daily. The different former Yugoslav delegations, and in particular I think those from Serbia and Montenegro, must ask themselves these questions ;"Do you wish to be considered as part of Europe? Do you wish to belong to the world community?" If so, good, but that does mean accepting the standards of the rest of Europe and of the world community.

Settlement by Negotiations

In this Conference and beyond it we are ready to work with the republics of the former Yugoslavia to settle the final new constitutional arrangements in accordance with the principles I have set out. Our aim is to take into account the legitimate interests of all parties. Parties who choose to ignore settlements by negotiation will find no support from other governments or international organizations. All the countries and organizations who have a role to play are represented here today at this Conference. They will all set out their own view but I believe there is a common determination.

For those who accept negotiation, and that means a willingness to make concessions and a genuine desire to find compromises, we have everything to offer. We will speed up your integration into the international community, we will begin with reconstruction aid, we will offer economic help through trade agreements, through export credits, through a full partnership in Europe. But if we do not get cooperation, the pressure will inexorably increase, condemnation, isolation, parties who stand in the way of agreement can expect even tougher sanctions, even more rigorously policed. No trade, no aid, no international recognition or role. Economic, cultural, political and diplomatic isolation, Those are the choices.

So I see our task at this Conference as ensuring humanitarian help, restoring respect for human rights and setting in hand a process which will lead to a just and enduring peace by agreeing on the necessary principles, on the pressures needed to put those principles into effect, and on the intensive programme of work needed to bring our process to success.

That is what lies ahead of us at this Conference and in the continuing work that may follow it. This I hope will prove to be a decisive break towards peace in the former Yugoslavia and that, I hope, is why everyone who is here has chosen to attend.

15. SUMMARY OF STATEMENT BY LORD CARRINGTON (26 AUGUST 1992)

Lord Carrington rehearsed the historical background to the London Conference and the EC Peace Conference following the disintegration of the former Yugoslavia. The rise of a suppressed nationalism in the Serbian Krajina had produced an over-reaction by the JNA and a continuing cycle of conflict, military over-reaction and abuses of the civil population.

The EC Peace Conference as originally mandated by the CSCE had three guiding principles:

a) Establishment of a genuine ceasefire;
b) No recognition of states without an overall settlement; and
c) No change of borders without mutual agreement.

Of these three principles only the latter remains following the escalation of the conflict and recognition of several of the former Yugoslavia republics. Recognition of the republics had removed international leverage over the parties, and Serbia in particular. The only remaining common interest shared by the republics was a wish to divide the assets of the former Yugoslavia. Most recently negotiations had been about specific bilateral disputes.

Lord Carrington stated that there were six unresolved problems, namely Bosnia, the Serbian Krajina, Vojvodina, Kosovo, Sandjak and Macedonia.

Bosnia and Herzegovina

Lord Carrington reiterated that the 18 March principles had been agreed by all three parties, although since rejected by the Muslim SDA. The principles formed an adequate basis for a solution and recognition of Bosnia and Herzegovina had been right. Nonetheless, this had led to the current conflict and Bosnia's very existence now hangs in the balance. The international community could accept a fait accompli. All three parties had to show flexibility or peace would not be achieved by any amount of diplomacy.

Serbian Krajina

The Serbs continued to demand complete independence but the only valid settlement was one respecting the territorial integrity of Croatia. The Serbs in he Krajina felt safer under UN authority but the Croatians were impatient to regain control. The international community had to persuade the Serbs in Krajina to negotiate and the Croats to show restraint.

Kosovo

Despite the fact that the population of Kosovo had voted for independence this could not be an acceptable solution in view of the recognised borders. The Kosovars have now declared their readiness to negotiate without preconditions, Serbia had not. Both should come to the table.

Vojvodina and Sandjak

Vojvodina and Sandjak also gave rise to concern and must be addressed in the Conference.

Macedonia

Lord Carrington stated that recognition was a matter for governments, not the Peace Conference. The EC arbitration Commission (Badinter) has made clear that Macedonia satisfied the conditions for recognition. The Greek position was clear. A solution had to be found to the recognition issue. He noted that the problems of the Albanian minority in Macedonia seemed close to solution and that this would have a positive impact on the Kosovo problem. He paid tribute to the consistent goodwill shown by the Macedonian side in all their dealings with the Peace Conference.

Conclusion

Lord Carrington concluded that with the exception of Macedonia all the problems facing the London Conference involved Serbia. He stressed that responsibility for finding lasting solutions rested both on those fighting and on the leaders encouraging them to fight. He deplored the practice of ethnic cleansing and human rights abuses in all forms.

16. STATEMENT BY MR. ALFRED SERREQI[*]

Mr. Chairman, We have come to London today in a gathering of European and world significance. London - the venue of conferences of crucial historic importance - stands today at the parting of the ways of raising over old animosities and artificial models. The history of the Europe after World War II provides the groundwork for a new qualitative start.

The process of the disintegration of former Yugoslavia proves to be a painful and tragic development. The continuing fighting and genocide in Bosnia and Herzegovina, the toll in human lives, hundreds and thousands of refugees and displaced persons, this is what is going on in the very heart of Europe. Bosnia and Herzegovina but not only it, are trial cases of the Europe we are trying to build. Unchecked Serbian nationalism is defying democracy. But, democracy, which our peoples had yearned for for years, cannot and will not be marred by such developments. The EC Peace Conference took upon itself the hard but noble task of ensuring a peaceful dismantlement of the former federation of Yugoslavia. It worked out a platform and an action programme to establish new

---

[*] The London Conference, General Debate: 26 August 1992.

states in peace. To the dismay of all of us, there was war and crimes unbeknownst to the younger generations of this century. The process could not be moulded into the peaceful framework of the Peace Conference.

We are today convening under another format in a new Conference, which has nourished many hopes. Enlarged representation is only one feature of this format and a guarantee of success. The mission of this new Conference will be to complete that process of disintegration peacefully. Its mission will be to make sure that the voice of all and everyone is equally heard and heeded. Its mission will be to settle burning issues of considerable complexity. Another approach to issues of historic bearing will contribute to the overall settlement on the Yugoslav crisis. The invitation extended to Albania is an honour and an assessment of the role played and to be played in the future with regard to this crisis at large as well as portions of it in particular. Its attitude concerning the EC Peace Conference has already been voiced in the CSCE and elsewhere.

Mr. Chairman, Yugoslavia has already dismantled. The peoples which once formed the SFRY went into the states created. Yugoslavia, however, was not drawn upon ethnic lines, and Albania does not seek to do so. Nonetheless, the question arises: what became of the Albanians of Kosova, Macedonia and others in the former federation? Where did the third of the peoples of former Yugoslavia go? The deeds of Serbian nationalism must be horrendous remembrances of what connivance on the part of Europe means, of what giving Serbia a free hand may lead to.

Mr. Chairman, Kosova has never been an exclusive part of Serbia. Suffice it to go through the Yugoslav constitutions and pick out the relevant articles which testify that the Socialist Autonomous Province of Kosova was a constituent unit of the former SFRY. It took the presidency upon rotarian as all the other federal units, it had its representatives in the federal parliament and all other federal structures, it had its own constitution and constitutional court, its territory could not be changed but by a decision of its own parliament, its parliament could decree laws, proclaim a referendum, and many more competences on which my experts could delve at length. I leave it up to you, distinguished colleagues, to draw the relevant conclusions.

Today the situation of the Albanians in former Yugoslavia is worsening very quickly, and not only in Kosova, but also elsewhere. In Kosova, large-scale repression continues. Unconstitutional arrangements have led the situation to their complete alienation from all the Serb-led state structures, to an overall paralysis. Peaceful pursuit, which has enjoyed considerable support by the peaceful Albanians, is being questioned. The London Conference could restore the lost confidence by providing the right frame towards the solution of their problem.

The Albanian delegation has come here to precisely contribute to a solution. A solution which would be fair and acceptable. Such a solution has to be sought by all of us, but it has to be sought and accepted by the Albanians of Kosova themselves. Only they can have the final say. Albania does not have any mandate to represent them. Serbia simply cannot either.

Mr. Chairman, Our heads of state and government gathering in Helsinki last month, called on the Belgrade authorities to "refrain from further repression and engage in serious dialogue with representatives of Kosova, in the presence of a third party". It is high time the setting were provided to this end. But, first of all, the whole of Kosova must be put under permanent international observers. Then, this Conference, by including Kosova into the agenda of talks on future arrangements within the territory of the former Yugoslavia can constructively play an irreplaceable role in averting the use of violence. The establishment of a separate task-group on Kosova is the first indispensable step to proceed in the right direction. Chapter II of the Draft Convention of the EC Peace Conference is not the proper frame towards a solution. The Kosovars made it clear that they will not accept a solution under those terms, and Albania, on its part, has also made it clear that it will only accept what is acceptable to them, and will only exercise its margin of discretion on the representatives of Kosova. The institutionalization of dialogue will prove to be the only way to keep an already deteriorating situation under control.

Kosova has mandated its representatives to conduct talks on their future. The will of the people, of which all international documents speak, has materialized peacefully and democratically. A referendum has ben held on September 26-30, 1991, elections on May 24, 1992. The new parliament attempted to convene and constitute a government: it was not allowed to. All has gone in full accordance with the laws. What was against the laws, was the violation of the will of the people by Serbia, through illegal arrangements and open violence. In 1945, under martial law, unification with federal Serbia within Federal Yugoslavia took place. It was proclaimed as an act of the will of the people. In 1989, the will of the people decided to lead a new life. This time the act was nicknamed "illegal". Self-determination seemed to have lost the marvel of its doings, while the Helsinki Final Act does not say so. This delegation finds it difficult to understand double standards.

Mr. Chairman, Everyone around this table must understand that concealing reality will only worsen it. Confining and limiting the scope of the problem will only keep tensions ever present and European security in constant danger. Kosova is not a case of human rights abuses, however gross they be. It is not a minority issue, and solutions along those lines will not be accepted. Albania believes that the London Conference will be able to overcome all that could not stop the war in former Yugoslavia, and the other obstacles towards a peaceful and comprehensive solution. Albania, on its part, will continue to do its best in the service of peace.

Thank you, Mr. Chairman.

17. STATEMENT BY MR. DAVID ANDREWS, MINISTER FOR FOREIGN AFFAIRS OF IRELAND*

Distinguished Co-Chairmen, Secretary of State Hurd will set out comprehensively the approach of the European Community and its member States to the situation on former Yugoslavia and our collective attitude to the work of the Conference. My delegation is fully associated with that intervention.

On behalf of the Irish delegation, I wish to welcome the convening of the Conference. It is a continuation and intensification of the EC Peace Conference which, under Lord Carrington's Chairmanship, has played a pivotal role in the search for a comprehensive political settlement to the crisis in former Yugoslavia.

I welcome the participation in this Conference of the UN, CSCE and States beyond the European Community. Their involvement demonstrates the gravity of the situation in the former Yugoslavia and the urgent need for a settlement.

Co-Chairmen, The Irish people fully share the international community's outrage at the killing, destruction and human rights violations which have taken place over the past twelve months in the former Yugoslavia. Events there have ensured that the Yugoslav crisis will be catalogued in the litany of horrors of twentieth century history.

Also, the European Community Monitor Mission and UNPROFOR have sustained many casualties - an Irish officer was injured in Sarajevo yesterday. I condemn the parties responsible for the attacks on those who are prepared to serve interests of peace.

In Bosnia and Herzegovina, it is self-evident that basic principles of international law are being violated, systematically and comprehensively. Forced expulsions and deportation of Bosnians, wanton destruction of homes and symbols of cultural identity continue; civilians, unable to seek refuge, have been subject to ruthless and relentless bombardment; towns and villages have been denied food and medicine; hospitals have been shelled; non-combatants - men, women and

---

* The London Conference, General Debate: 26 August 1992.

children - have been coldly singled out by snipers' bullets; many are held in appalling detention camps; some have disappeared, and evidence of summary executions is mounting.

These outrageous violations of the basic principles of international humanitarian law must stop now. This has been made clear by the CSCE, the United Nations Commission on Human Rights and by UN Security Council Resolution 771. The perpetrators of these heinous acts must be made to account for their actions.

Detention camps must be closed and we look to this Conference to agree practical and effective measures to this end. Pending their closure, the ICRC and other international agencies must have access to the camps without impediment, as stipulated by Security Council Resolution 771. The important CSCE and UNHCR mission on detention camps and ethnic cleansing must be supported.

It is vital to ensure the unimpeded delivery of humanitarian assistance by the United Nations organisations. Their efforts, and those of the ICRC, in conditions of extreme danger, deserve our fullest praise and support. It is imperative that the parties concerned guarantee the safe passage of the relief convoys. I hope that we can go further at this Conference and agree on a range of practical measures on how best to respond to the critical needs of those who have fled or been forced from their homes.

Co-Chairmen, We do not consider that the responsibility for the tragedy in Bosnia rests exclusively with one party. However, we believe that the leaders of the Serbian Community in Bosnia and also in Serbia bear primary responsibility.

It is essential, therefore, that the Conference should categorically reject the notion that a *de facto* partition of *Bosnia* will be tacitly accepted by the international community.

It is not for us to prescribe the nature of the internal political arrangements for Bosnia. But the Conference should underline that a formula, acceptable to the three ethnic groups within that Republic, must be negotiated. All parties must participate constructively to this end.

A ceasefire, underpinned by firm and binding commitments from all parties, must also be established; if not secured during the Conference, an effective ceasefire should be a priority for follow-up work, which I am glad to know is to begin immediately.

Co-Chairmen, We must make it clear that the international community will not accept military gains in the other Republics of former Yugoslavia. The repressive policies being pursued against these communities are unacceptable and run the risk of precipitating a wider conflict in the region.

Special status must be negotiated for Kosovo and Vojvodina to ensure the protection of human rights of their populations and to enable them to live in peace and security. Observers must be stationed in these and other sensitive areas.

Failure by Serbia to abandon its policies of territorial conquest and its harsh treatment of minorities will lead to continuing political isolation which should be accompanied by a further tightening of the sanctions regime.

Co-Chairmen, The principles I have emphasised in my statement - for example, the non-use of force and respect for minority rights - must, of course, apply throughout the region. They are as valid with regard to Croatian Krajina as to Serbia and Bosnia.

Above all, the fundamental principle which this Conference must establish is that a lasting solution can only be achieved by peaceful means and by negotiation among all the parties concerned. There is simply no alternative to this approach.

We do not underestimate the difficulties which lie ahead. The bitterness and distrust created on all sides by events in the former Yugoslavia will not be easily overcome. The international community must, through both its pressure and assistance, work relentlessly through the new Conference structure to achieve a political settlement. I earnestly hope that it will succeed.

Thank you, Co-Chairmen.

18. STATEMENT BY MR. WILLY CLAES[*]

La communauté internationale est confrontée en Yougoslavie à une situation intolérable: le refus des droits démocratiques les plus élémentaires, le culte aveugle de la supériorité ethnique, et l'exaltation perverse du nationalisme: il faut que cela cesse.

Pour que cette Conférence aie un sens, if faut, aux yeux de la Belgique, qu'un cessez-le-feu effectif et crédible soit immédiatement instauré. Toutes les parties au conflit ont délégué leurs négociateurs à cette conférence: que leurs troupes en Bosnie-Herzégovine respectent le dialogue que nous attendons. C'est une condition première.

La population civile est devenue la cible de pratiques effroyables.

La Belgique condamne et exige qu'il soit mis fin à la politique d'épuration ethnique pratiquée dans diverses régions de l'ancienne Yougoslavie et particul- ièrement en Bosnie-Herzégovine. Non seulement ces pratiques sont criminelles, mais de plus, cette politique est totalement inutile, car la communauté internatio-

---

[*] The London Conference, General Debate: 26 August 1992.

nale n'acceptera pas que des modifications de frontières viennent entériner cette politique de transfers de populations et de déportations, condamnées par les traités internationaux.

La Belgique condamne également et avec la même force la politique délibérée d'emprisonnement dans les camps de civils innocents: elle exige que les organisations internationales puissent à l'instant avoir l'accès le plus complet aux camps en vue de s'assurer que les reponsables de ceux-ci remplissent leurs obligations élémentaires pour ce qui est de l'approvisionnement et des soins médicaux indispensables aux détenus. La Belgique partage l'opinion des organisations humanitaires compétentes selon lesquelles cette politique des camps est une violation flagrante du droit humanitaire et que l'emprisonnement et la détention dans des conditions épouvantables de dizaines de milliers de personnes constitue un nouvel aspect d'une politique de terreur ethnique.

Que ceux en Yougoslavie qui commettent, permettent ou ordonnent ces crimes contraires au Droit international et plus spécifiquement aux Conventions de Genève soient bien conscients de ce que leur reponsibilité individuelle est engagée devant la cammunauté international, qu'aucune protection ne leur évitera d'avoir à répondre de leurs crimes, et que la justice saura avoir la mémoire suffisamment longue pour les retrouver.

Il faut que toutes les parties au conflit en Bosnie-Herzégovine garantissent le libre acheminement de l'aide humanitaire qui sera organisé dans les conditions prévues par la résolution 770 du Conseil de sécurité. La Belgique participera à cette action menée en coordination avec les Nations Unies. Il faut donc que toutes les parties au conflit s'assurent du respect de leurs décisions par tous les irréguliers qu'elles ont armés et que, le cas échéant, elles leur imposent leur volonté.

La Belgique souhaite que les parties au conflit en Bosnie-Herzégovine confirment et mettent enfin en oeuvre leur accord du 17 juillet relatif à la supervision, sous l'égide de Nations Unies, de leur armement lourd. Elle demande l'etablissement prochain d'un inventaire le plus complet possible des arsenaux d'armes sur l'ensemble du territoire de l'ancienne Yougoslavie et considère que l'offre de déploiement d'observateurs internationaux chargés de contrôler les aéroports militaires de la Serbie et Monténégro doit faire l'objet d'un examen approfondi.

En l'absence de coopération des parties avec la Communauté internationale pour atteindre et mettre en pratique l'ensemble des principes établis par la présente Conférence, la Belgique estime qu'une pression plus forte devra alors être exercée par un raffermissement des embargos militaire, économique et aérien établis par les résolutions 713 et 757, et, le cas échéant, par la mise en place d'un blocus effectif tant fluvial que maritime.

La Belgique considère également que d'autres sanctions devront également peser sur la Serbie et le Monténégro; avec ses partenaires des Douze la Belgique s'oppose à la participation de cet Etat aux travaux des organisations internationales. Elle pourrait, si cet Etat persiste dans sa politique, recommander son exclusion complète des organisations en question.

La Conférence sur la Yougoslavie doit permettre la mise au point de méchanismes politiques suspectibles de renforcer toutes tentatives de cessez-le-feu afin de bâtir un espace de paix. Au centre de ces méchanismes, ill est évident que les répresentants des différentes Communautés concernées doivent reprendre un dialogue politique. Ce dialogue doit se fonder sur des principes universellement reconnus que je réaffirme à cette Conférence de Londres: le respect des droits de l'homme et des minorités, le respect de l'intégrité territoriale des Etats dans des frontières qui ne peuvent être modifiées par la force, le retour des réfugiés dans leur lieu d'habitation d'origine et leur dédommagement pour les pertes éprouvées. Je songe ici également à l'acquis identifié et obtenu par les efforts remarquables déployés par Lord Carrington au cours de l'année écoulé. Il n'y aura pas de solution à ce conflit sans que de difficiles concessions politiques ne soient consenties.

Les responsables qui ont voulu toléré ou subi ce conflit sont aujourd'hui présents à cette table. Dans la situation actuelle, c'est vous, les représentants de toutes les parties yougoslaves, qui ferez la paix. Votre sort est entre vos mains. La Communauté internationale vous a amené à la table de négociations et vous a encouragé à établir un dialogue.

En prolongeant le conflit, les belligérants assument une responsabilité historique car ils exposent leur peuple à l'ostracisme le plus complet, à un isolement économique et financier pendant une longue période. Tout au contraire, si les cessez-le-feu se consolident, si un dialogue s'établit, alors ces diverses républiques nées de l'ancienne Yougoslavie prendront leur place légitime dans la société des Nations, au sein des divers organismes européens ou internationaux de coopération économique, sociale et culturelle. Elles auront ainsi l'occasion de consolider leurs institutions démocratiques et pourront espérer jouir d'un épanouissement général dont doivent profiter l'ensemble de leurs citoyens. Cette Conférence sur la Yougoslavie les place devant ce choix historique.

19. Statement by Mr. Stoyan Ganev, Minister for Foreign Affairs of the Republic of Bulgaria[*]

Mr. Chairman, Excellencies, Ladies and Gentlemen, Please, allow me first to welcome the initiative to hold the London Conference on the former Socialist Federal Republic of Yugoslavia and to thank the UK Government for inviting Bulgaria to participate in it and for providing excellent working conditions.

The Yugoslav crisis has set one of the most serious challenges to the democratic world for the last decades. We are all horrified by the barbarities in Bosnia and Herzegovina. At the same time we are disappointed with the so far unsuccessful efforts to have these barbarities stopped.

The potential of the international community, of all basic institutions on which the solution of the crisis in former Yugoslavia depends, is centered here, in London, now. This determines the responsibility of all participants for the success of this unique forum. We see two basic goals before this Conference - to find the solutions, which would prevent the conflict from spilling over to other regions of former Yugoslavia and the neighbouring countries so as to contribute to a just and complete settlement of all problems resulting from the dissolution of the former SFRY.

The Yugoslav crisis cannot be solved solely by stopping the fighting. Its lasting settlement is a question of the Balkans' future. To eliminate the risks of a conflict in this region would be impossible, unless overall regulation of relations is achieved, relations binding together the new post-communist realities with the complicated historic legacy. Such a regulation can be done by adhering to the standards of civilized international communication. Led by this concept, at a number of international meetings, Bulgaria has suggested that a Forum be held, which would promote the practical application of the principles, values and mechanisms of the Helsinki process in the Balkans. That is why we are pleased to find our idea in accord with the logic underlying the convening of The London Conference.

This Conference is in a position to offer concrete action to put an end to the war in Bosnia and Herzegovina and to render humanitarian relief. Serbian authorities bear the main responsibility for what is happening there and at the same time they genuinely have the greatest capability of positively influencing future developments. It is necessary to seek opportunities now, to strengthen international political and economic pressure on Belgrade, with a consistent and resolute position taken by all countries. The role of former Yugoslavia's neighbour-

[*] The London Conference, General Debate: 26 August 1992.

ing countries is of particular importance. Bulgaria is resolved to further strictly comply with the UN Security Council Resolution 757, despite the enormous economic cost the country cannot afford at this juncture. My country is ready to cooperate with all international monitoring mechanisms for the observance of sanctions including the control of traffic of goods with the Bulgarian sector of the Danube.

Should the international community decide as a last resort to use military force to facilitate the delivery of humanitarian assistance, Bulgaria confirms its position, that it will not take part with armed forces or armaments in such operations, and is of the opinion that a similar approach on behalf of the other Balkan countries will help overcome the historically accumulated doubts for a lasting stability in the region.

Bulgaria is ready to provide humanitarian aid and we consider the suggestion of reconstruction of war-torn Bosnia and Herzegovina as most positive.

The cessation of the war in Bosnia and Herzegovina will open the road to the return of the hundreds of thousands refugees to their homes and to the reinstatement of the ethnic composition, forcefully altered by the policy of systematic "ethnic cleansing". The London Conference should clearly declare the principle of non-recognition of the *fait accompli* with regard to the minorities on the territory of the former Yugoslavia. We propose that the acute problems, related to the violations of the rights of representatives of the Bulgarian minority in Serbia, be brought to the attention of the Conference and be invited to participate in its future activities.

The London Conference will fulfil its tasks by speeding up the international recognition of all former Yugoslav republics, which have proclaimed their independence in a constitutional way, and by promoting the recognition of their sovereignty, territorial integrity and political independence. As a first step, the former republics themselves should at this very conference recognize each other, as well as the frontiers, which existed between them before the start of the conflict.

We are worried by the delay on recognizing the former Yugoslav Republic of Macedonia. This brings the threat of its destabilization and possible further complications in the entire region.

The principles of recognition of the borders' inviolability and of the territorial integrity are of real value only when they relate to internationally recognized frontiers and territories.

The London Conference should recognize the existing facts, namely, the existence of an independent state in actual boundaries. At the same time, the open questions, related to the former Yugoslav Republic of Macedonia, should be solved. Bulgaria believes this should be done through negotiations between the parties concerned; Lord Carrington suggests this is a matter for Governments. All Governments concerned are represented here. We suggest creating a special "ad hoc" group to help solve this important question.

The Balkans' future will depend to a great extent on the quick solution of the economic backwardness, which is the cause of a number of the existing controversies and problems. We believe that this Conference is the place where an urgent plan should be proposed to economically assist the Balkan region, to stabilize it and to speed up the process of its integration into Europe.

In conclusion, I would like to emphasize the fact, that had we not found a civilized solution to the ethnic problem in our country, today Bulgaria should have been in a situation similar to that of the former Yugoslavia, and could have further added to Europe's concerns. Given this background Bulgaria is aware of its great responsibility to promote the optimal realization of this unique conference potential, the beginning of which we lay today.

20. STATEMENT BY MR. MA YUZHEN, HEAD OF CHINESE DELEGATION AT THE INTERNATIONAL CONFERENCE ON THE FORMER SOCIALIST FEDERAL REPUBLIC OF YUGOSLAVIA*

Messrs. Co-Chairmen, First of all, please allow me to extend, on behalf of the Chinese Government, our congratulations on the convocation in London of the International Conference of the former Socialist Federal Republic of Yugoslavia and to express our appreciation for the latest peace efforts made by the United Nations and the British Government aimed at solving the crisis in the former Yugoslavia. I would also like to take this opportunity to thank our host for providing this Conference with needed facilities.

The past year or more have witnessed a drastic sharpening of the ethnic, religious and territorial conflicts among the republics of the former Yugoslavia. Continuous ethnic hostilities have turned the former Yugoslav region into the largest war zone with mounting casualties that the post-war Europe has ever seen, inflicting untold sufferings on the people there. The Chinese people are deeply sympathetic with the agony and predicament of the people of all nationalities in the former Yugoslavia and strongly appeal for the earliest possible end to the bloodshed.

Historical experience has proved that war can hardly solve anything, whether

---

* The London Conference, General Debate: 26 August 1992.

it be ethnic conflict or interstate dispute. It is only through dialogue and negotiation that fighting can be brought to an end and it is only by a peaceful settlement of dispute can peace be achieved and maintained. What is most urgent, in our view, is that the various parties to the conflict in the former Yugoslavia, particularly in Bosnia and Herzegovina, reach a ceasefire as soon as possible and reopen their negotiations, for this settlement and also where the fundamental interest of the people of various nationalities in the former Yugoslavia lies. The continued use of force will only aggravate the confrontation and animosity and make the issue all the more difficult to resolve. It is also unrealistic to try to stop a war by waging another war. Such attempt is likely to be counterproductive and invite even greater disasters.

Today, to our delight, the representatives of all the independent states of the former Yugoslavia have once again sat together in a joint effort to seek a political solution. We appeal for their renewed efforts to keep the good momentum going. We are aware of the difficulties involved, but the parties can very well set aside their differences and reach an unconditional ceasefire first so as to create conditions and win time to conduct peaceful negotiations. Their differences will be reconciled so long as they can enter into calm and genuine dialogue and consultation. It is our sincere hope that the people of various nationalities in the former Yugoslavia will forego their past grievances, state anew a life of amity and good-neighbourliness and dedicate themselves to the rebuilding of their homeland.

Messrs. Co-Chairmen, The crisis in the former Yugoslavia has become a hot spot in the present-day world, posing a grave threat to peace and stability in Europe and the world at large. It is only natural that China and the rest of the international community are seriously concerned and anxious about it. Heretofore, the United Nations, the European Communities, the CSCE and other international and regional organizations have carried out a great deal of mediation and made major efforts for resolving the crisis and restoring peace in that region. The Chinese Government appreciates and supports all these efforts and has also done its share to this end within its capabilities. We have all along held that the international mediation should always be fair and reasonable, must follow the norms governing international relations and should aim solely at restoring peace and stability in the former Yugoslavia. Any move that may aggravate the difference and confrontation among the conflicting parties must be avoided, and no direct involvement in the conflict should be carried out.

Messrs. Co-Chairmen, I would like to take this opportunity to reiterate that China has all along been committed to a peaceful settlement of the crisis in the former Yugoslavia. China does not seek, and has never sought, any selfish interest in that region. We respect the choice made by the people of various countries in the former Yugoslavia, endeavour to maintain and develop friendly relations and cooperation with the independent states and the people of various nationalities in the former Yugoslavia on the basis of the Five Principles of Peaceful Coexistence and have never interfered in their internal affairs. As a permanent member of the U.N. Security Council, China will, together with the other participating countries at the conference and the rest of the international community, continue to make its efforts to promote a fair and reasonable settlement of the crisis in the former Yugoslavia and restore peace and stability in the region.

Thank you.

21. STATEMENT BY MR. JOZEF MORAVCIK, CHAIRMAN-IN-OFFICE OF THE CSCE COUNCIL OF MINISTERS*

Dear Prime-Minister Major, Dear Secretary-General Boutros Ghali, Dear Colleagues and Friends, We are here in London to give a new impetus to international search for a political solution to the Yugoslav conflict.

So far, efforts to bring peace and justice to this troubled region have yielded meagre results. This is not, however, to underestimate the work done by the Conference on Yugoslavia chaired by Lord Carrington. Our conference will no doubt profit from the work done in the Hague and in Brussels.

The problem we are facing is not limited strictly to the former Yugoslavia. This is a Euro-Atlantic, indeed a worldwide problem. We are dealing with fundamental human values expressed in basic CSCE documents, including the Charter of Paris and the one called Challenges of Change, adopted recently in Helsinki.

The CSCE is attempting to develop means by which to protect the values it cherishes. It may do it only with the assistance and cooperation of other international institutions: the United Nations, the European Community, NATO, Western European Union and the Council of Europe.

Let me inform you briefly on activities the CSCE has undertaken with respect to this conflict.

Five CSCE Missions have travelled to the area so far. They focused on human rights, fundamental freedoms, minority problems and elections. The sixth mission is about to be dispatched, to inspect detention camps. Preparations are under way to send - for the first time ever - missions of long duration to Kosovo,

---

* The London Conference, General Debate: 26 August 1992.

Vojvodina and Sandjak decided by the 15th Meeting of the CSCE Committee of Senior Officials (CSO) held recently in Prague.

It is important to mention in this context other results of the 15th CSO Meeting including the establishment of a joint CSCE Mission with the authorities in Skopje in order to prevent the spillover of tension to countries neighbouring with Serbia and Montenegro. This decision - together with expansion of the EC monitoring mission activities to Hungary, Bulgaria and Albania - is meant, e.g., to tighten conditions of implementing the sanctions imposed by the UN on Serbia and Montenegro.

Responding to the request of Mr. Boutros Ghali, the UN Secretary-General, the CSCE has decided to help the United Nations in carrying out its peacekeeping activities in Ex-Yugoslavia including its involvement in supervising the heavy weapons in Bosnia and Herzegovina.

In my capacity of the Chairman-in-Office of the CSCE Council I visited last week, in the company of the other partners of the CSCE Troika, Belgrade, Skopje, Ljubljana, Zagreb and Sarajevo to see how the latest CSO decisions can be best implemented and in more general terms what role the CSCE may play in the conflict.

During my talks in Belgrade I transmitted the strong political message contained in the decision document of the last CSO Meeting. I pointed out that evidence continued to mount that Serbian authorities are using the conflict to carry out so called "ethnic cleansing".

The talks we had in Belgrade were not easy. However, I am pleased to announce that there is an agreement, in principle, that all CSCE Missions can be dispatched as foreseen by the CSO. In organising these Missions the CSCE will bear in mind that problems in those three regions of Serbia where the Missions are to be deployed - namely in Vojvodina, Kosovo and Sandjak - should be treated in a differentiated way.

Let me now dwell a bit in one of the essential conclusions I drew from my trip to former Yugoslavia: the problem of coordination.

In Zagreb I met briefly with Mr. Mazowiecki, the UN Special Rapporteur for Human Rights and Detention Camps. We discovered that we knew virtually nothing about each other's schedules and long-term plans. Duplication is most evident in human rights activities.

I am therefore satisfied that the Steering Committee has as one of its duties to facilitate coordination of international activities concerning the conflict. It should also cover coordination of activities relating to human rights, fundamental freedoms, minority problems and election processes where the CSCE can play its role.

I think it is self-evident that any serious coordination effort covering human rights should include the Council of Europe. The CSCE has already profited from high expertise of the Council in this respect and intends to continue to do so. Indeed, I assume we will simply follow the logic of events if this Conference involves the Council of Europe in its activities.

I assume that this Conference and the follow-up do in fact represent in political terms the very first practical effort of creating an ad hoc interlocking system of major international institutions dealing with a particular problem. If I am right then what we need to do is to invite at an appropriate time other international organizations to join this exercise. Some of them have facilities and infrastructure that certainly can be used for implementing any of the options that are or will be discussed here.

My recent visit to former Yugoslavia clearly proves the CSCE has an important role to play in any further efforts to find a political solution to the Yugoslav tragedy. Despite some doubts and hesitations the CSCE's role is required by all parties to the conflict. By dispatching long-duration Missions to Vojvodina, Kosovo and Sandjak the CSCE enters into its first large-scale exercise of preventive diplomacy and I am sure it is able to seriously contribute to prevent spreading of the conflict.

We should all give serious thought to what can be done for the population of Bosnia and Herzegovina before winter time. Humanitarian efforts will have to be redoubled if we are to avoid large and uncontrolled movements of refugees within and beyond the Balkans.

In this context, I also discussed the problems of safe havens. I came to realize that we have to carefully consider that dangers might be entailed on concentrating a lot of refugees on a small area for an indefinite time.

Problems facing this Conference are immense, indeed. But I strongly believe that it will bring success so much needed for the future of Europe.

Thank you for your attention.

22. STATEMENT BY MR. UFFE ELLERMANN-JENSEN, MINISTER FOR FOREIGN AFFAIRS OF DENMARK*

Co-Chairman, My friend and colleague, Mr. Douglas Hurd, has already made a statement on behalf of the Twelve. Needless to say, I fully subscribe to what he has said.

For my own part, I would like to add a few supplementary remarks.

---

* The London Conference, General Debate: 26 August 1992.

The situation in the former Yugoslavia is appalling, and especially tragic in Bosnia and Herzegovina - a fellow member in the UN and the CSCE. The greatest responsibility for this tragedy falls on the Serbian leadership and on the Serbs in Bosnia and Herzegovina.

Daily reports of bombings, murder, torture, depict a desperate situation for millions of people.

We thought we had left all this behind us. But images of emaciated prisoners in camps with barbed wire appear in Europe again. Repulsive methods of breaking down the human spirit are being employed once more.

We are now faced with by far the most massive refugee situation in Europe since the Second World War.

This situation is intolerable, and the international community in its revulsion must do everything possible to turn it around.

The big question, of course, is: what can be done that hasn't been done before?

Ever since the beginning of the break-up of Yugoslavia, the European Community, the CSCE and the United Nations have employed all possible measures short of the use of force: Mediation, sanctions, observer missions, peace-keeping forces.

And what has been the result ? Peace in Slovenia and a comparatively stable situation in Croatia. This we all welcome, even though many issues in Croatia remain to be resolved.

But the war moved south to Bosnia and Herzegovina with unrestrained ferocity, and the risk of its spreading further south looms ever larger.

The failure to establish a durable and just peace cannot be attributed to outside mediators. On the contrary. They have skilfully done all in their power and we pay tribute to their efforts. And a very special tribute to Lord Carrington for his untiring efforts over so many months.

Rather, it is those who employ military force to establish territorial faits accomplis, to bomb cities, to conduct ethnic cleansing, to herd people into camps, it is those people who bear the responsibility for the continued massive hardship and suffering.

An analysis of the overall developments in the former Yugoslavia unfortunately leads to the conclusion that we are faced with a Lebanon-like situation. Let's be frank about it.

But this situation must not lead to despair, cynism and inaction.

We must continue and expand our efforts to bring the parties to their senses and to help them bring about a comprehensive, lasting and just negotiated solution. Only a solution arrived at through negotiations, without the threat or use of force, will be acceptable and have a chance to last.

It is a daunting task, as realistically we must recognize that there are no quick fixes.

This Conference constitutes a major effort by the international community to avert further senseless suffering and destruction. The negotiation process started by the European Community is now broadened and intensified, in particular with the full involvement of the Secretary-General of the United Nations in this Conference.

We offer the parties a framework for settling their disputes through negotiations, permitting fair interaction of the legitimate aspirations of all parties.

In parallel to this offer, we must make it clear that we will not allow alternative methods. We shall not tolerate acquisition of territory by force, human rights violations and the suppression of national minorities. Those who perpetrate such acts must know that they will be considered international outcasts, pariahs. And these individuals who commit, or order others to commit, war crimes must know that they will be held personally accountable for their acts as argued so convincingly by Dr. Boutros Ghali. Not only will they never be allowed to hold what they are grasping. As outlaws, they shall never find peace. And we have to establish, in the UN, the necessary international instruments to deal with this issue. In today's and tomorrow's interdependent Europe they will never be able to develop a viable society. This is the message - loud and clear - contained in the UN-resolution on individual responsibilities and in the sanctions. The sanctions must therefore be more forcefully applied. All circumvention must cease. And those breaking the sanctions should be held responsible as accomplices.

Mr. Chairman, We support the idea of having a set of basic, general principles emanate from this gathering. Principles which must form the foundation for our continued efforts in the negotiating process.

We must ensure an active and effective follow-up to keep the parties at the negotiating table.

We must maintain maximum pressure to bring military operations and human rights violations to a halt and to move genuine negotiations forward.

We must make use of all relevant procedures to prevent the outbreak of hostilities in other explosive areas such as Kosova and Vojvodina.

We must continue to provide humanitarian aid to those millions who need it, if necessary by employing military units on the basis of Security Council Resolution 770.

And our efforts must be closely coordinated with other international bodies, in particular the United Nations, the CSCE, and NATO to ensure maximum impact.

I think we can all agree on this.

But we must also recognize that no success is possible without the necessary political will on the part of those directly concerned to respect the basic principles and to seek a negotiated solution on the basis of international law.

Therefore, this Conference must also send a strong signal to those who substitute military force for genuine negotiations.

During 40 years of Cold War, no large armed clashes took place in Europe. It is a tragic irony, therefore, that now, after the end of the Cold War and the collapse of totalitarianism, Europe is faced with a major conflagration in the Balkans.

This Conference offers us - and especially the parties directly involved - the opportunity to avert further disaster with incalculable consequences. Let us not miss the opportunity. As John Major said: In this room are the people who can stop the fighting. Let the parties realize that their maximum aims are unattainable, and that they must negotiate to achieve peace.

In the continued efforts to bring the tragedy to an end, we have great confidence in the British Presidency of the European Community in co-operation with the Secretary-General of the United Nations to move us forward in a constructive and farsighted manner.

Denmark, in our national capacity as well as future presidency of the EC, will play an active part.

Thank you, Mr. Chairman.

23. STATEMENT BY MR. DOUGLAS HURD, THE FOREIGN SECRETARY OF THE UNITED KINGDOM[*]

War in the former Yugoslavia is a tragedy - thousands have been killed, millions have been driven from their homes. It is not the only such tragedy occurring in the world, but this tragedy of Yugoslavia is a particular reproach to the whole of Europe - the prison and refugee camps, the mortar bombs falling on funerals, the ethnic cleansing, challenge the principles of international law and decent behaviour, and thus challenge us who claim to defend these principles and that behaviour.

The Community and its member states strongly condemn the continuing violence. No party to the conflict is blameless. But the greatest responsibility falls on the Serbian leadership and on the Serbs in Croatia and Bosnia. The

---

[*]   The London Conference, General Debate: 26 August 1992.

immediate step forward is clear. The Serbs and all other parties should immediately respond to the terms of successive mandatory Security Council resolutions and implement and observe the agreement signed by all the Bosnian parties on 17 July at the EC Conference.

Sadly, there might be still greater suffering. The Kosovar Albanians have shown admirable restraint in the face of the consistent denial of their basic human rights. We recognise their legitimate wish that their past autonomy should be restored. Serbia should refrain from further repression and engage in serious dialogue with representatives of this territory. At the same time the Kosovars should understand that they must proceed by negotiation and that the international community cannot accept the alteration of international frontiers by force. We welcome the CSCE's plan to station observers in Kosovo, and also in Vojvodina and the Sandjak, to deter violence and help to restore confidence.

The immediate focus - rightly - has been on ensuring the prompt and effective delivery of humanitarian aid. The international agencies face a formidable task. Thousands are still trapped in the conflict zones. Their suffering is made worse by the widespread disregard for basic humanitarian principles shown by some combatants. Violations of international humanitarian laws must stop. All detention camps should be shut. While they do continue to exist, international humanitarian agencies, notably the Red Cross, should, as UN Security Council Resolution 771 puts it, have "immediate, unimpeded and constant access" to them. We support the parallel initiative for the CSCE in close cooperation with the Red Cross and the UNHCR to ensure that all detention centres are inspected as soon as possible.

All parties to the conflict are bound to comply with international humanitarian law and in particular the Geneva Conventions. SCR 771 reaffirmed that obligation. The Bosnian Serbs' attempt forcibly to expel 25,000 people from Bihac flew in the face of that obligation, the latest in a long line of such expulsions. We shall take careful note of the perpetrators of these criminal acts and shall do all we can to bring them to account.

As part of this effort, the Community and its member states support two separate courses of action. It is right that the UN Human Rights Commission should have appointed a special rapporteur to investigate human rights abuses. We shall give Mr. Mazowiecki all possible support. We also took the initiative in invoking the CSCE mission which will now investigate the treatment of unarmed civilians by all sides.

The UN Humanitarian Agencies and the International Committee of the Red Cross have done an outstanding job, working against the odds in increasingly dangerous circumstances. They will continue to get our support. The Community has so far pledged 48.5 M ECU for emergency humanitarian aid since November 1991, and is now discussing a further 120 M ECU.

We welcome UN Security Council Resolution 770 which reinforces the humanitarian effort by authorising use of all necessary measures in coordination with the UN. Our aim remains to deliver aid where it is needed. Help is getting in by land as well as by air. We now need to increase the scale and scope of these operations so that they get to all places where relief is needed, including the camps.

Until there is progress on all these points the UN sanctions regime should remain in force. We shall work for its strict enforcement and, if necessary, strengthening. We shall also work to extinguish the Yugoslav seat at the UN.

Suffering in the former Yugoslavia is not some act of God. It is a direct result of blatant aggression and the failure of the leaders principally concerned to agree how their peoples should live together. Relieving suffering, however important, is not enough. We must help - and where necessary bring pressure on - those leaders to remove the cause of that suffering.

This is not easy. There are real limits on what any outsider can do. Ancient hatreds are not easily soothed by outsiders. Political leaders are not necessarily in full command of local warlords.

At the same time, we are conscious, as the Community, of the extent to which Yugoslavia is a European problem.

These areas of conflict border with two member states, the fleeing refugees are arriving in several member states. There are risks of the fighting spreading to engulf the wider Balkan region. The Community therefore carries a particular responsibility.

The Community and its member states will not accept that Bosnia can be partitioned by force. Its inhabitants have voted in a referendum for independence: it has been internationally recognised and admitted to the UN. We cannot accept that outside countries should carve it up. We must work for an early ceasefire and for progress on a *political* solution. This must be based in respect for the existing frontiers and on a political arrangement which satisfies all three ethnic communities. The follow-up work to this Conference should address these questions right away. We need not specify what constitutional arrangement they should reach. But that there should be one is clear.

Yugoslavia in general and Serbia in particular face a sombre choice. The Serbs must abandon the policies which have brought the region to disaster. Mr. Panic has given clear promises to do so. I am encouraged to hear it. But *Serbia* must agree that it will be bound by this. It says that the federation is responsible for its foreign relations: in that case Serbia must comply with the federation's policies. Serbia's behaviour will be measured against the undertaking which Mr. Panic has made. If it does not abide by them it will drag Yugoslavia into ever increasing isolation.

Against this background what does the Community and its member states hope to see as the outcome of his Conference?

The aim must be to intensify and broaden international pressure on the parties to work wholeheartedly for political settlement. It will be important to build on the firm foundation already established by the excellent work of Lord Carrington. I pay tribute to his untiring and ingenious efforts over the past year. He has not only laboured unremittingly to bring about successive ceasefires. He has also produced an admirable basis for a draft agreement. He deserves the heartfelt thanks of all of us here today. This will continue within the new Conference framework.

As he found so clearly, broking agreements entails convincing awkward and highly distrustful people that their interests will be best served by compromise. There are no guarantees that our efforts will succeed in establishing a lasting peace in the region. But we must take maximum advantage of every channel available.

The key mechanisms for future work are set out in the draft action programme. Clearly, we need a task group to deal with Bosnia, which poses the most difficult and the most immediate problems. With the help of that group the three communities must resume talks on a new constitution so that they are enabled to live peacefully together. The task group must also negotiate political conditions to allow humanitarian activities to be undertaken safely. It should, finally, work to establish a durable ceasefire. A key part of that ceasefire will be bringing heavy weapons belonging to all sides under international supervision.

Secondly, work on the status of the various minorities must be taken forward rapidly. The minorities in Kosovo, Krajina, Vojvodina, Sandjak and in the former Yugoslav Republic of Macedonia - all need a special status within their respective republics which guarantees their rights and enables them to live in confidence.

A high-level body will be needed to ensure that our efforts are coherent and speedy. It should, we believe, be composed of eminent people who are willing to dedicate considerable time and energy to the task and should bring together the Chairmen of the task groups and representatives of the UN, the EC, the CSCE, and perhaps others with valuable influence to contribute. The body should meet frequently to keep progress in the task groups under close review, to prepare the basis for an overall settlement and coordinate with other international organisations. It should also meet, as necessary, with the republics of the former

Yugoslavia. It will be the focus of all our combined efforts for peace.

Close liaison between those primarily involved in negotiations in capitals, and those active on the ground will be essential. The work of the Conference must not duplicate or undermine the operations of the United Nations or other international bodies, which will remain the proper fora for action in their particular areas of competence.

To work, these arrangements will need the full support of everyone gathered at this Conference. If we cannot present a united approach, we only make ourselves vulnerable to those who seek to achieve their ends by force. We urge the Conference to endorse the draft Statement of Principles as the basis of our approach. This sets out, in simple and forceful terms, the basic principles for a negotiated settlement. The essentials are clear; the fighting and "ethnic cleansing" must stop: human rights must be respected; the rights of minorities must be guaranteed; frontiers cannot be changed by force, only by mutual agreement; sanctions must be maintained; and, perhaps most importantly, all parties must engage actively in negotiations to resolve their differences, rather than resort to force.

24. STATEMENT BY MR. ROLAND DUMAS[*]

Messieurs les Presidents, Messieurs les Ministres, Mesdames et Messieurs, Depuis plus d'un an, au coeur de l'Europe, à deux heures d'ici, sevit un conflit meurtrier et destructeur. Tous les efforts déployés par la communauté internationale ont été jusqu'ici impuissants à l'éteindre.

Il y a un an à peine la Bosnie était le symbole de la coexistence harmonieuse entre plusieurs peuples aux cultures et aux réligions différentes et rêvait de devenir la suisse des Balkans, cela parait si loin.

Aujourd'hui un habitant sur trois a du quitter son foyer, victime des combats et d'une politique systématique de "purification ethnique" aux relents idéologiques que l'on croyait a jamais bannie de notre continent.

Dans ces conditions la nécessité de l'action n'est plus à démontrer, tout est urgent: faire cesser les combats, assurer les besoins les plus élémentaires de tous alors que s'approche l'hiver, libérer les prisonniers, et enfin trouver au conflit une solution politique qui soit équitable et durable. La France y est prête. Elle l'a montré concrétement à toutes les étapes. La France veut poursuivre et accroître cet effort.

---

[*] The London Conference, General Debate: 26 August 1992.

Avant d'évoquer quelques propositions concrètes pour l'avenir, je voudrais m'arrêter un instant pour saluer ceux que se sont engagés au service de la paix. Je veux rendre d'abord pleinement hommage au dévouement de tant de femmes et d'hommes, qui resteront inconnus, qui risquent leur vie et parfois la perdent par pur sens de la solidarité: observateurs, soldats, secouristes, infirmières, médecins et tant d'autres. Gardons leur courage a l'esprit. Leurs geste et, dans le même esprit, celui du Président de la République allant à Sarajevo montrent les chemins que peut ouvrir la volonté de paix.

Si nous voulons agir efficacement face à la complexité du drame Yougoslave, il convient de rappeler quelques principes politiques simples mais fondamentaux: droit à l'autodétermination des peuples, respect du droit des minorités, rejet de la politique de fait accompli... La France, pour sa part, n'a cessé de rappeler ces principes à l'ensemble des parties. Plus que jamais il importe de souligner ces obligations essentielles à tous les protagonistes, et particulièrement à ceux qui portent la plus grande responsabilité dans ces violations.

Mais il faut aussi reconnaître l'évidence: pour que cessent les souffrances, il faut retrouver la paix, ce qui veut dire non seulement la fin des combats mais aussi un climat d'apaisement. Il n'y a pas d'autre voie: l'escalade de la guèrre est sans issue. L'internationalisation du conflit, dans une région aussi instable, serait lourde de tous les risques. C'est pourquoi il faut une relance du processus politique servant de cadre à une véritable négociation.

C'est ce constat qui a conduit la France a proposer l'élargissement de la conférence de paix afin de lui donner une nouvelle impulsion.

A cet régard, la France estimait depuis longtemps nécessaire une implication plus importante de l'ONU. C'est sous ma présidence que le Conseil de Sécurité a adopté le 25 Septembre la Resolution 713, la première consacrée à la Yougoslavie, qui soutenait les efforts de la CEE et invitait le Sécrétaire Général a proposer son assistance sans délai.

Aujourd'hui, la participation de l'ONU dans les efforts de paix, l'autorité particulière qui est la sienne, justifient pleinement sa présence dans cette conférence. Nous avons souhaité aussi la présence des pays voisins de l'ex-Yougoslavie. Ils sons directement concernés par le conflit et peuvent exercer sur les belligérants une influence positives.

Mesdames et Messieurs, L'annonce de notre réunion a soulevé une grande espérance qu'il ne faut pas décevoir. Pour cela nous devons être réalistes. Ce qui compte vraiment ce n'est pas de s'être réunis deux jours. C'est ce que nous allons bâtir. Quels outils allons-nous créer pour faire avancer la paix? Il ne s'agit pas de la promettre pour demain. Il s'agit de se donner les moyens que la paix progresse de manière sure et durable. Voilà le but véritable de notre conférence et du processus qu'elle doit lancer. Je voudrais faire quelques propositions concrètes en ce sens. Quatre objectifs me semblent prioritaires.

Le premier est la relance du dialogue politique. La négociation sur les arrangements institutionnels en Bosnie-Herzegovine, aujourd'hui bloquée, revêt une urgence particulière alors que sur le terrain une solution de force est en train de prévaloir. Les Républiques issues de l'ancienne Yougoslavie doivent donc s'engager a se reconnaître par consentement mutuel comme états souverains. Elles doivent donc souscrire au respect des principes de l'inviolabilité des frontières et de l'intégrité territoriale, conformément à la charte des Nations-Unies, à l'acte final d'Helsinki et à la charte de Paris.

Mais le dialogue politique doit également s'instaurer partout où se posent des problèmes de minorités, au Kosovo, au Sandjak, en Voivodine, en Macédoine et en Krajina. C'est indispensable pour apaiser les crises ouvertes qui existent et désamorcer d'autres conflits potentiels tout aussi explosifs. Nous n'avons pas le droit d'échouer dans la prévention de ces crises-là. Pour contribuer à cela, il me paraitrait souhaitable que des observateurs soient envoyés partout où cela parait utile.

Le deuxième objectif est la diminution de la violence. Elle ne sera pas rapide mais elle doit être certaine. Ces derniers mois ont été riches en promesses non tenues et en cessez-le-feu rompus. Je suggère donc une approche progressive encadrée par un plan précis de désescalade du conflit qui conduira à un véritable cessez-le-feu.

Cependant les armes se tairont d'autant plus facilement qu'elles se feront rares. Il faut donc renforcer l'embargo. Nous en avons les moyens juridiques grâce à la résolution 757, nous en avons aussi les moyens technique. En accord avec les pays frontaliers - et à la demande, d'ailleurs, de certains d'entre eux - je demande que soit mis en place un contrôle véritable aux frontières y compris sur le Danube. Plusieurs pays, l'Allemagne notamment, sont prêts à fournir les hommes et les équipements nécessaires. Il est également important que les organisations humanitaires exercent un strict contrôle sur leurs fournitures. Dans le même esprit, je souhaite que le gouvernement Bosniaque autorise les vols de surveillance et de reconnaissance au-dessus de son territoire. Peut-être faudrait-il même réflechir dès maintenant à un contrôle de l'espace aérien de la Bosnie. Agissons vite. Tout cela est à notre portée.

Le troisième objectif est d'assurer la couverture des besoins minimaux des populations. L'hiver approche. Dans un mois, il fera froid, les routes seront difficiles. Nous devons être organisés avant ou la Bosnie sera un mouroir. Les mèsures à prendre sont claires. L'aide doit pouvoir être acheminée partout sans aucun obstacle et l'action des organisations humanitaires doit être partout et par tous protégée et facilitée. En particulier, l'acces à tous les camps doit être permanent. Progressivement, ils devront soit être fermés soit être placés sous le contrôle des organisations internationales. Dès maintenant, il faut installer dans chaque camp une antenne humanitaire chargée d'évaluer les besoins mais aussi de marquer la vigilance de la communauté internationale.

A cet égard, je souhaiterais que nous chargions une personnalité reconnue, d'une mission de témoignage sur les camps de prisonniers. Je pense pour cela à Elie Wiesel, Prix Nobel de la Paix pour son oeuvre en faveur de la mémoire vivante de l'holocauste. C'est une haute figure d'étique et d'histoire dont la vie a fait un témoin devant notre conscience à tous.

Car tel est le quatrième et dernier objectif. Il s'agit d'obtenir le strict respect du droit humanitaire. Nous constatons en effet de très graves violations des droits les plus élémentaires de la personne: exactions à l'encontre des populations, politique de "purifications ethniques", création de camps de détention ou les conventions internationales ne sont pas appliquées. Il ne s'agit pas seulement de dénoncer ces crimes, leurs auteurs doivent savoir qu'il n'y aura pas d'impunité pour de tels agissements et qu'ils seront poursuivis.

Je voudrais à ce propos faire deux suggestions. La première serait que nous demandions à la commission Badinter de nous donner d'ici un mois un avis sur les droits et garanties des minorités afin que nous disposions d'un cadre juridique. La seconde serait, comme l'a proposé l'Allemagne, de réfléchir à la mise en place d'une cour pénale internationale pour juger de ces crimes.

Voilà nos objectifs, voilà des moyens concrets pour réaliser chacun d'eux. Il en faudra d'autres. Encore une fois, ce que nous lançons aujourd'hui est un processus dans la durée.

Messieurs Les Presidents, Messieurs les Ministres, Mesdames et Messieurs, Ce n'est pas seulement le sort de peuples et d'états qui est en jeu, c'est aussi un certain sens de l'Europe qui se joue dans cette paix. Ce conflit n'est pas seulement une monstruosité sur le plan humain, c'est aussi une aberration historique. Je le dis à tous les belligérants: il n'y a plus de place en Europe pour les ennemis héréditaires vous devez le comprendrez. L'Europe a payé très cher pour apprendre cette leçon elle ne l'oubliera jamais.

25. STATEMENT BY DR. KLAUS KINKEL[*]

Chairmen, For more than twelve months now, a terrible war of destruction and expulsion has been raging in the heart of Europe. Each day on which inno-

---

[*] The London Conference, General Debate: 26 August 1992.

cent civilians continue to be bombarded with heavy artillery and driven out of their native regions, each day on which prisoners of war are caused suffering, undermines the credibility of the new beginning we have embarked upon together in Europe. Clearly, problems that have remained unsolved for centuries cannot be settled overnight, even with the best intention in the world. Nevertheless, all concerned must realize that people who have been disappointed time and time again now desperately pin their hopes on this Conference. Anyone who fails here in London to meet his responsibility to secure peace, to uphold international law and defend human dignity, will exclude himself from the community of European democracies for a long time to come. Not last due to the terrible images that can be seen daily on television screens all over the world, world public opinion shows less and less understanding for the fact that the community of nations is not capable to solve the problems in former Yugoslavia. We must not and cannot allow a situation to continue where, after the end of the East-West conflict, that constituted a threat to all of us such terrible ethnic conflicts arising in multi-national states cause new devastation for the whole world.

Foreign Secretary Hurd has spoken on behalf of the Community. His demands have our full support. From the German point of view I should like to add the following:

This Conference must send a clear message: "Enough of the killings and expulsions!" We cannot and will not allow ourselves to be put off any longer with empty promises while heavy artillery continues to reduce one town after the other in Bosnia and Herzegovina to ruins. There must now be unequivocal commitments, and we expect them to be honoured as innocent people are killed.

I appeal to the Serbian leadership: Realize that you stand at the crossroads. One of the roads leads back into the community of nations, to peace and prosperity. The other leads to absolute isolation and impoverishment. And make no mistake: The community of nations will never countenance acquisitions of territory or drawing of new borders resulting from the use of force and terror. Those responsible for the devastation will be held accountable for what has been senselessly destroyed. They cannot expect any assistance from the community of nations in the reconstruction process if they continue with this senseless war. This, in any case, will be the position advocated with great resolve by the Federal Republic of Germany.

All victims of this conflict have our sympathy and solidarity, regardless of their nationality. Germany is neither anti-Serbian nor pro-Croatian, but it opposes aggression and terror, seizure of territory and expulsion, no matter who is responsible.

Undoubtedly, war crimes and grave violations of human rights are not perpetrated by only one side. But in political terms the crucial question is: Where does the main source of the evil lie?

The answer is obvious: in Belgrade! The response to the disintegration of former Yugoslavia - which was their own fault - was a ruthless war aimed at creating an ethnically cleansed greater Serbia. They are deterred neither by violations of international law, nor by deliberate and systematic acts of terror against the other nations. This is the root of the crimes against humanity which stun us day by day. What is happening here is genocide and this we condemn before the world community. The community of nations will pursue all crimes no matter who has committed them. Let no one believe that these atrocities will be forgotten.

What must be done? What can be done?

First, in Bosnia and Herzegovina there must be a genuine and lasting cease-fire, coupled with international controls on heavy artillery. The cantonalization concept must not turn out to be the disintegration of this republic and the occupation of two thirds of the territory on behalf of one third of the population.

Second, after this Conference all parties must engage in serious negotiations to find a political solution. We fully support the programme of action put forward by the presidency. What Lord Carrington and his aides have worked out must form the basis for substantive negotiations. The draft agreement of 4 November 1991 establishes an optimum balance between preserving territorial integrity and the need to guarantee extensive and equal rights for all national communities and ethnic groups. All decisions of the CSCE and the European Community on Yugoslavia are contained in that draft.

Third, it is crucial for the credibility of peace-making efforts below the military threshold that the Security Council sanctions should prove genuinely effective, whether on the mainland or at sea. Germany will participate in appropriate measures within the limits set by its constitution.

Fourth, and this is a particularly urgent demand, all detention camps must be closed immediately. The detainees must be allowed to return to their home towns to be temporarily accommodated in safe places. Those responsible for all crimes and violations of human rights, both inside and outside the camps, must be brought to account. An international court of criminal justice has to be created.

Fifth, in accordance with Security Council resolution 770, humanitarian supplies must be given military protection if necessary.

Sixth, before winter arrives, the countless numbers of refugees must be found accommodation, and as far as possible near their home regions. The question of creating security zones therefore remains on the agenda. In emergencies we are prepared to take in more refugees. But we appeal to all other countries to help, too, alleviating the suffering of despairing victims of the war - financially, and where necessary by taking them in. The Europeans, acting as partners, must share the burden fairly.

Seventh, the Serbian-Montenegrin state, or whatever it may call itself, has no rightful claim to the place in international organizations once held by highly respected Yugoslavia. The Conference's arbitration commission has said all that needs to be said on the legal aspect of this issue. Let us not be deceived by the pseudo-Yugoslavism of those who want a greater Serbia: their "Yugoslavia" has nothing in common any more, either ethnically, historically or culturally, with the community of southern Slavic and other nations enjoying equal rights envisaged by the state's founders in 1917/1918 and between 1943 and 1945. The claim to continuity serves rather to justify expansion by the use of force. If only for this reason, the community of nations should not recognize it.

Thank you.

26. Statement by Mr. Taizo Nakamura, Representative of the Government of Japan to the International Conference on Yugoslavia*

Mr. Chairmen, Having the honour to represent the Government of Japan, I should like, first, to express my profound thanks for all the British Government has done to convene this very significant International Conference on Yugoslavia.

It gives cause for the very gravest concern that the situation in the former Yugoslavia, especially in Bosnia and Herzegovina, shows no sign of any significant improvement, despite the continuous efforts of the international community. Recourse to the use of force for the purpose of acquiring territory, which has been demonstrated primarily by the Serbs, threatens to jeopardize the newly emerging order in Europe, and ultimately of the world. The international community is deeply shocked to see innocent civilians - forced to flee their homes or, reportedly, detained in camps - being those who must pay the price.

That situation makes it all the more important that we have here an opportunity to reaffirm our shared commitment to finding a peaceful political solution for Yugoslavia and to define a common approach to attaining that objective. We evaluate very highly the cooperation between the two leading organizations in the peace efforts, the European Community and the United Nations, one result of that cooperation being the holding of this Conference.

---

*   The London Conference, General Debate: 26 August 1992.

Let me, here, reaffirm the intention of the Government of Japan to make any constructive contribution it can to the common search for a peaceful solution.

Mr. Chairmen, We are deeply impressed by the role the European Community, through successive Presidencies and the work of Lord Carrington, as Chairman of the Conference on Yugoslavia, has been playing, with the United Nations, in addressing Yugoslav problems. The Government of Japan, which has resolutely supported those efforts, considers what has been achieved to be of great value. Convinced that the European Community will continue to play a central role in the area that was formerly Yugoslavia, we would like to renew, as the Community's partner, our firm support for any constructive initiative the European Community may undertake.

Mr. Chairmen, As the situation in the former Yugoslavia continues to deteriorate, especially in Bosnia and Herzegovina, it is our view that the international community should, anew, address with the utmost urgency the question of what kind of political framework is needed to ensure a lasting peace in the area and what means should be adopted to attain peace. We, therefore, support the draft "Statement of Principles", as a document which provides a solid basis for our future work in that direction.

We strongly urge all the parties to the conflict in the former Yugoslavia to accept those principles and to proceed to the negotiation table immediately. We appeal, especially, to the leaders of the Republic of Serbia and the Federal Republic of Yugoslavia to exert all the influence at their command on all Serbian armed elements in Bosnia to this end.

Concerning the goals of those negotiations, we would like to stress that a legal guarantee of the rights of minorities alone cannot ensure lasting peace and stability in the region. It is necessary to negotiate a constitutional arrangement which will enable all ethnic groups to feel completely safe, even when living as a minority.

Although it is regrettably true that enmity and hatred among the ethnic groups is unlikely to subside soon, it is, nonetheless, feasible to prevent such hostility from crossing the line into violence and bloodshed, if we can attain effective control of weapons. It is with this in mind that we would like to emphasize, as a nation with the most rigorous self-restraint policy on arms export in the world, the imperative need to maintain and strictly enforce the arms embargo for the entire territory of the former Yugoslavia and, at the same time, to find a way to place all weapons under international supervision.

We join other delegates in expressing the view that the Republics of Serbia and Montenegro should take the primary responsibilities for halting hostilities in Bosnia and Herzegovina. We, therefore, attach great importance to the UN

Security Council Resolution on the sanctions against the two Republics, and support measures to enhance effectiveness of those sanctions.

The Government of Japan condemns absolutely the concept and practice of "ethnic cleansing". We can never accept, as a "fait accompli", any change of ethnic composition brought about by the use of force or intimidation.

As for the human rights situation, we need, before anything else, accurate knowledge of what is actually happening. We attach great importance to ensuring unimpeded and continuous access for the ICRC to all places of detention. We also support the appointment of a "Special Rapporteur" by the Commission of Human Rights of the United Nations. We strongly hope that by such measures a clear picture of the situation will soon be available.

Concerning refugees and displaced persons, we support, as a means of solving the problems involved, the "comprehensive approach" the UNHCR put forward in July. Permanent solutions to those problems will call for yet greater involvement by the international community, and we will continue to give the humanitarian activities of the UNHCR and other international organizations the fullest possible support, and intend to make further contributions to the greatest extent possible.

Japan was a party to the G7 Summit Declaration on the former Yugoslavia and voted for UN Security Council Resolution 770, which calls upon States to take all measures necessary to facilitate the delivery of humanitarian assistance to Bosnia and Herzegovina, in view of the urgent need to lessen the sufferings of the Bosnian people and save every life possible.

We believe, however, that such measures should be taken in close coordination with the United Nations and other humanitarian organizations so that the people involved in the humanitarian activities should carry out their tasks in safety.

Mr. Chairmen, We believe that this International Conference is, in many ways, a beginning, intended to give a fresh start for a sustained negotiation process, a task that will undoubtedly require a very great deal of work and great perseverance. With this in mind, we welcome and support the "Action Programme", which proposes the establishment of a Steering Committee and Six Task Groups within the framework of the Conference and define their respective mandates. We believe that this document can serve as a useful guide for future negotiations.

Mr. Chairmen, I would like to conclude my statement by reaffirming our readiness to participate in any activity of the Conference to which it is felt we can make a useful contribution.

Thank you, Mr. Chairmen.

27. STATEMENT BY MR. JACQUES F. POOS[*]

Monsieur le Président, Monsieur le Secrétaire Général, Excellences, Mesdames et Messieurs, La Présidence de la Communauté européenne a dans son intervention clairement situé les enjeux de la Conférence d'aujourd'hui et a indiqué les principes et les lignes d'action qui devront être les nôtres dans les mois à venir. Le Luxembourg fait siennes les conclusions de la Présidence brittanique.

Je souhaite cependant très brièvement ajouter quelques réflexions à l'intention de la Conférence.

Pour le Luxembourg les travaux de la Conférence sur la Yougoslavie présidés par Lord Carrington ont dégagé la base pour un règlement politique du conflit dans l'ex-Yougoslavie et constituent la base pour tout arrangement futur.

Aucune situation de fait créé par la voie de l'expansionisme par une des parties ne saurait de quelque façon que ce soit affecter la validité des solutions proposées. La communauté internationale ne peut accepter une politique basée sur la force.

La modération éventuelle qu'une des parties pourrait montrée une fois sa politique de conquête territoriale achevée, serait bienvenue mais ne saurait nous tromper.

Les images qui nous parviennent de Bosnie-Herzégovine rappellent les pires heures de l'histoire européenne. Aucune justification ne saurait être trouvée aux exactions commises de quelque côté que ce soit. La politique de purification ethnique est l'expression la plus basse d'une politique d'agression essentiellement dirigée contre des populations civiles désarmées et innocentes.

Toutes les parties sont certes responsables de la situation actuelle règnant dans l'ex-Yougoslavie. Il est une partie qui est responsable de l'ampleur et de la nature inhumaine qu'a pris ce conflit.

Il faut certes que tous fassent preuve de raison, notamment pour ce qui concerne un arrangement futur garantissant l'indépendance et l'intégrité territoriale de la Bosnie-Herzégovine tout en assurant l'égalité des communautés qui la constituent. L'on ne saurait nier cependant qu'il revient en priorité à la partie serbe de mettre fin à sa politique de conquête.

De même convient-il pour cette partie de se retirer des territoires saisis indûment en Croatie.

Les revendications légitimes de la Serbie à voir des droits des communautés serbes garantis dans les autres Etats constitutifs de l'ex-Yougoslavie, doivent

---

[*]   The London Conference, General Debate: 26 August 1992.

trouver comme pendant la possibilité pour les communautés non serbes du Kosovo, du Sandjak et du Voivodine de se prévaloir des mêmes droits.

La situation des réfugiés sur les territoires de l'ex-Yougoslavie et sur le reste de l'Europe est dramatique et appelle l'action de la communauté internationale. A côté de contributions importantes au HCR et à sa participation du pont aérien sur Sarajevo, mon pays a déjà accueilli plus de mille réfugiés en provenance de Bosnie-Herzégovine, ce qui constitue 0.25 % de sa population.

Il est particulièrement important également que l'aide humanitaire parvienne dans des conditions de sécurité satisfaisantes aux populations concernées de Bosnie-Herzégovine. Mon pays soutient les efforts en cours en vue de doter d'une protection militaire les convois humanitaires en Bosnie-Herzégovine. Il appuie aussi l'idée de la supervision des armements lourds dans cette république. Mon gouvernement déterminera bientôt la nature de sa contribution à ces deux opérations, sachant que le Luxembourg participe déjà avec un petit contingent à l'opérations FORPRONU en Yougoslavie.

Enfin il me paraît essentiel de renforcer l'embargo porté par la résolution 757 du Conseil de Sécurité. J'escompte qu'un plan d'action cohérent à cet effet pourra être adopté par les Etats participant à la Conférence de Londres.

28. Statement by Dr. Hamid Algabid, Secretary-General of the Organization of the Islamic Conference[*]

Excellency John Major, Prime Minister of the United Kingdom, Excellency Mr. Boutros Boutros Ghali, Secretary-General of the United Nations, Excellencies, Heads of delegations, Ladies and Gentlemen, First of all I would like to express to the Prime Minister of the United Kingdom on behalf of the Organization of the Islamic Conference, our sincere expression of gratefulness for the kind invitation you have kindly extended to us to participate in this important Conference on Yugoslavia. We welcome this auspicious initiative taken by the European Community to convene this Conference which we hope will not fail to make a substantive contribution towards the restoration of peace in former Yugoslavia. I may assure you of our full cooperation and support.

The Organization of the Islamic Conference has been following with great concern the tragic developments which have cast a shadow and destroyed Bosnia and Herzegovina since the declaration of independence of this young Republic following a referendum organized early this year. Against every expectation and

[*]   The London Conference, General Debate: 26 August 1992.

when a powerful wind of liberty is blowing in this part of the world, Serbia has started to stop and subvert by force the peaceful and democratic course chosen by the people of Bosnia and Herzegovina to realise their legitimate aspirations.

The nature and extent of atrocities that the Serbian forces are committing every day against the populations of Bosnia and Herzegovina sadly remind, in their cruelty and perfidious designs motivating them, of not a very distant past. These serious facts are known throughout the world; day-to-day news provides us with its afflicting proof.

These facts have been denounced, reproved and condemned unanimously by the civilized nations of the world. These events question our conscience and underscore the pressing need of checking the destructive and murderous fury of Serbian forces in Bosnia and Herzegovina. This should not continue any further.

The consideration of the present situation in Bosnia and Herzegovina requires that principal aspects of the conflict be dealt with very urgently. It is urgent, prior to everything, to put an end to the Serbian aggression which is aimed at undermining the political independence, unity and territorial integrity of the Republic of Bosnia and Herzegovina, a member state of the United Nations.

It is-well known to all that the ambitions of Serbian leaders are to substitute "a greater Serbia" for former Yugoslavia. In this way, Serbia, by occupying through force two-thirds of the territory of the Republic of Bosnia and Herzegovina through "ethnic cleansing" operations, undertook to alter the situation on the ground and to present the international community with a fait accompli.

It is also necessary to look into the serious violations of international humanitarian law and the humanitarian dimensions of the conflict which has led to a massive exodus of refugees. Lastly, it is imperative to see to it that the conflict may not extend to other regions, particularly, to Sandjak, Kosovo and Macedonia.

The Extraordinary Session of the Islamic Conference of Foreign Ministers held in Istanbul in June 1992 on the situation in Bosnia and Herzegovina had not only strongly condemned the violence and blind use of force by the Yugoslav army and the Serbian irregular forces in Bosnia and Herzegovina but also especially reaffirmed its commitment to the preservation of political independence, unity and territorial integrity of this country.

The Conference demanded the withdrawal of the units of Yugoslav army at present in Bosnia and Herzegovina or their subjection to the legal governmental authorities of Bosnia and Herzegovina. I also called for the disarming and disbanding under international supervision of all the Serbian irregular forces and other armed elements found in Bosnia and Herzegovina.

The Conference condemned the non-compliance by the Serbian leaders of relevant Security Council resolutions and urges the latter to have recourse to Article 42 of Chapter VII of the UN Charter when measures provided under Article 41 proved to be inadequate.

Moreover, the Conference emphasised the irrefutable responsibility of the Serbian leaders vis-à-vis the violations of humanitarian law committed against the Bosnian people. The Conference also committed itself to provide humanitarian relief and assistance to the victims of the conflict in Bosnia and Herzegovina.

Such are the main elements which the Organization of the Islamic Conference has set out in its approach for a political solution to the problem. This is an approach which is based on international legality and on the logic of actions undertaken by the Security Council and the initiatives taken by regional bodies and especially those taken within the framework of European Community and the Conference on Security and Cooperation in Europe in order to put an end to the violence which is raging in Bosnia and Herzegovina.

Faced with these initiatives, the Serbian leadership has remained intransigent in its defiance of international law and has not complied with the relevant Security Council resolutions, as if they are assured in their impunity; as if they have not understood at all that the international community could no more tolerate their conduct in Bosnia and Herzegovina.

We should stress openly and strongly here that any negotiated political settlement must of course be based on law and conform to the UN resolutions. Similarly, the negotiations cannot succeed in a climate of hatred and murderous violence such as is being witnessed in Bosnia and Herzegovina. It is in this spirit and to promote political settlement that the Organization of the Islamic Conference is of the view that it is necessary that the London Conference should first of all obtain from the parties to the conflict in Bosnia and Herzegovina the following commitments:

One: solemn commitment to establish without further delay a verifiable ceasefire and to abide by it;

Two: respect and comply with all the provisions of the relevant U.N. Security Council resolutions:

Three: respect the principles and norms of international humanitarian law;

Four: guarantee the safety and freedom of movement of all international personnel in Bosnia and Herzegovina, engaged in peace-keeping or humanitarian activities;

Five: allow the return of all displaced persons and refugees from Bosnia and Herzegovina to their homes, under international supervision;

Six: undertake the withdrawal of all units of the Yugoslav National Army and the demobilization and disarming of all irregular armed units, operating in the territory of the Republic of Bosnia and Herzegovina under effective international supervision.

The Conference must also make it absolutely clear that if the aforementioned minimum requirements are not met, it would be obliged to recommend to the Security Council, to resort to the provisions of Article 42 of Chapter VII of the Charter of the United Nations for the enforcement of its resolutions pertaining to Bosnia and Herzegovina.

Moreover, the OIC is of the view that the fundamental legal framework for a negotiated settlement of the conflict in Bosnia and Herzegovina must provide for respecting the unity, sovereignty, political independence and territorial integrity of the Republic and upholding democratic values and human rights.

We in the Organization of the Islamic Conference reject the blind and brutal use of force aimed at imposing its sectarian and nihilistic law in the former Yugoslavia.

We are committed to work for establishing a fresh era of understanding and cooperation among the new Republics of former Yugoslavia in the interest of their various peoples. We do not make any distinction between these people; all of them form a part of humanity. Whatever be their nationality, their ethnic leanings or their faith, we entertain an equal dignity for them. We wish to them peace, security and happiness on an equal basis.

We are conscious of the challenge to peace in the former Yugoslavia. At stake is not only the future of this region but also the very values of the civilized behaviour which the international community has to uphold.

It is for this main reason that the organization of the Islamic Conference has wished to be represented at the London Conference at three levels; that of the current Summit Chairman, that of the current Chairman of the Islamic Conference of Foreign Ministers and in the person of the Secretary General.

It is our earnest hope that all parties to the conflict in the former Yugoslavia would seize this valuable opportunity to work for ushering a new era of peace and good neighbourliness in the region. It is incumbent upon them to extinguish the all consuming flames of hatred so that in a spirit of mutual confidence and cooperation that they may build a promising future for their proud peoples.

Men and women are working with faith and conviction to contribute to the realization of this objective. I see at the very first rank of the latter, the United Nations forces which with courage are accomplishing, in a climate characterized by violence and hostility, the noble mission which has been entrusted to them within the framework of the application of United Nations Security Council resolutions. I reaffirm to them through the United Nations Secretary-General, his Excellency Mr. Boutros Boutros Ghali, our appreciation and active support of the member states of the Organization of Islamic Conference which are pre-pared to strengthen with their human and material potentials the credibility of their action in Bosnia and Herzegovina.

I also join in paying this tribute to the numerous humanitarian organisations which have hastened to these places in order to bring their support, assistance and comfort to the millions of victims of this grave tragedy.

We also owe a lot to the efforts of Lord Carrington to be at this place today to speak and espouse together peace in the former Yugoslavia. He has worked in a persevering manner and with great talent, which we have always acknowledged, for paving the way for holding this Conference. I would like to pay to him a very sincere tribute.

I wish this Conference every success.

Thank you.

29. STATEMENT BY DR. JOAO DE DEUS PINHEIRO[*]

I would like, first of all, to thank Lord Carrington for the excellent job he has been doing as Chairman of the EC Conference on Yugoslavia for almost a year now, in circumstances of extreme difficulty. It was my privilege, as President of the Council of Ministers of the European Community, to work closely with him from January through June. During that time the political and military actions of the several Yugoslav parties on one side and the political decisions of the twelve on the other contributed in their different ways to a situation of frustrating com-plexity. In spite of this, Lord Carrington managed to steer the course of the Conference with insight and perseverance for which we must all be grateful.

Here, we build on the foundations that he laid down, reinforced by the wel-come UN participation and with some adjustment of terms of reference, work in progress will continue. The London Conference will give to it a wider political backing and a renewed sense of urgency. Time is indeed of the essence - not only because each day more fighting and unresolved tension prolong human suffering and keep alive the dangers of a wider Balkan conflict, but also because winter will soon be with us. If by mid-October peace will not have been achieved, particularly in Bosnia and Herzegovina, a catastrophe of major pro-portions will engulf the region.

Which then should the aims of this Conference be? Fundamentally, two. First - to find political solutions, along the lines established by the EC Conference, of

---

[*] The London Conference, General Debate: 26 august 1992.

the Bosnian question, of the Kosovo question and of the UN protected areas in Croatia question. On Bosnia the three parties must be made to sit again round the table: Serbs (and Croats) will have to give land back, displaced persons must be allowed to return home if they so wish, the international borders of Bosnia must be recognized by all concerned, and satisfaction must be given to the legitimate aspirations of the three nations of Bosnia and Herzegovina. The war has placed the most numerous of them in a weak and invidious position. This will not do and must be redressed. A fair constitutional agreement must be brokered by the Conference and the international community should then take all measures necessary to make the parties respect that agreement.

The Government in Belgrade and representatives of the Albanians of Kosovo must also sit round the Conference's negotiating table. Kosovans have to understand once and for all that independence is not an option open to them. The Serbian authorities, on the other hand, have to guarantee to the Kosovans, without subterfuges and procrastination, the fullest form of autonomy foreseen in the Draft Convention of the EC Conference. We know that both sides have to come some way from their extreme position - but there is no other peaceful solution to the question.

The Serbs in the Croatian Krajina and the other UN protected areas must start negotiating in the Conference the provisions of their special status. The Croatian constitution has been changed and other legislation passed in Zagreb to accommodate their interest. A speedily and good-faithed process has now to take place. Again, like the Kosovans, they cannot aspire to independence nor can they aspire to join Serbia. International borders have to be kept. Within Croatia, however, they will enjoy a wide measure of self-government.

The other aim of this Conference is to bring back peace to former Yugoslavia, taking, if need be, all necessary measures to do so. The present war in Bosnia and Herzegovina has to be stopped. Military actions in the UN protected areas of Croatia have to be stopped as well. We have to prevent war breaking out in other politically disturbed areas of the region.

Such peacemaking activity will at times have to be robust. All warring parties must know that from now on they have to abide by ceasefires and by confidence-building measures that they have signed or will sign - or else be prepared to confront the might of the international community.

Humanitarian relief must be allowed to proceed unimpeded. Human rights violations, so gross and blatant in many cases, cannot take place anymore. Those responsible for "ethnic cleansing" by murder or expulsion, and for the inhuman treatment of prisoners must be brought to justice. Regrettably, all parties in the Yugoslav conflict have committed atrocities, some however on a bigger scale than others. The senseless pounding of civilian populations in cities by Serbian artillery, whatever the provocation, seems to have been part of a deliberate policy that cannot go unpunished.

This Conference builds on the political foundations established by the Carrington Conference and on the ongoing commitment of the United Nations to bring the mechanisms provided by its Charter to the restoration of peace in former Yugoslavia.

With he support of all of us it cannot fail.

30. STATEMENT BY MR. ADRIAN NASTASE, MINISTER OF FOREIGN AFFAIRS OF ROMANIA*

Distinguished Co-Chairmen, Your Excellencies, Let me begin with a word of thanks and appreciation for the timely initiative of the Presidency of the European Communities, personally of Prime Minister John Major, and of the United Nations Secretary-General, Dr Boutros Boutros Ghali, to convene this Conference on Yugoslavia here in London.

Although rather late in the day, this Conference is more than welcome. It is also positive that the Conference is not building on barren land, but can rely on the strenuous efforts undertaken in different fora during the past few months with growing direction and coherence. In this respect, we must commend the comprehensive, though sometimes frustrating, work carried out so far by Lord Carrington's Group enabling us now to focus attention on the real issues.

We are all aware that there are no simple solutions to complex problems. The Yugoslav crisis is confronting us here, and the international community, with painful decision-making dilemmas due, among other things, to the emotional charge of the situation.

The Conference is now the focal point of public attention and scrutiny. Expectations are uncomfortably high. The world is waiting for practical solutions and concrete ways to stop the fighting. The enormity of the task and of the pressures we are all under should be an additional incentive of this Conference to show real statesmanship and to take the lead in making a sense of balance and reason prevail.

We have examined the main draft documents of the Conference. They provide both the lowest common multiplier and the highest common denominator for the task in hand. Probably, it is the maximum that may realistically offer a

---

* The London Conference, General Debate: 26 August 1992.

basis for consensus considering the complexity of the prevailing circumstances.

The question of establishing an agreed set of basic principles is, in our view, of crucial importance. The draft submitted to us offers a good basis for an agreement here, in London, and we are ready to support it. Equal treatment for all parties concerned might be one of the keys for an early, lasting and successful settlement of the crisis we are dealing with in a new, promising framework.

We regard as a basic task of this Conference to highlight the peaceful settlement as the only acceptable alternative to all the parties to the conflict. As we have already seen, any other option cannot but lead to war. Until now, the fighting has been confined within the frontiers of former Yugoslavia, recognized by international treaties. If it spills over those frontiers or questions them, that is real war in Europe.

The action programme is comprehensive and realistic. We must send a clear signal of our common resolve to start a meaningful process and to establish a structure of negotiations conducive to a viable and lasting solution.

Romania is in a unique position in this area haunted by the storms of history of having never fought a fighting war against any of the peoples of former Yugoslavia. We have also succeeded in having a balanced conduct and good relations with all the Yugoslav republics. This enables us to act as a factor of stability in the region. As one of the neighbours whose perceptions are in no way burdened by territorial and other ambitions, Romania can afford, and can be counted on, to take an unbiased and constructive stand.

That is one more reason why we welcome the initiative to invite the neighbouring countries to this Conference. Despite the vicissitudes of history, we have learnt to know each other, we are familiar with the issues confronting the region as a whole and we have a vital stake in what is happening there. Due representation of the countries of the region in the Conference working bodies is therefore of essence. As for us, we are prepared to make a meaningful contribution to, at least, the Secretariat and the task groups on minorities, and on confidence and security building measures.

Romania is a law-abiding member of the international community. Whatever our own interests and preferences might have been, we have scrupulously complied with the resolutions of the Security Council on Yugoslavia and fully cooperated with other national and international agencies in order to make the sanctions work.

It is most unfortunate when such a commitment could be construed as a liability rather than an asset. I therefore strongly urge the other neighbouring countries of Yugoslavia to accept, as we have already done, international observers in order to monitor implementation of the sanctions.

The specific patchwork of Yugoslavia, composed of many nationalities and different religions, in an odd entanglement all over its territory has always challenged conventional wisdom. Now it also challenges the application of the basic concepts of international law.

There cannot be a separate international law for Yugoslavia. Although conditions are historically and psychologically peculiar, international law is one for all. We may think of arrangements, adapted to the specific situation, acceptable to the parties concerned. Whichever their contents, they will remain what they are, i.e. one-time solutions which do not create international law.

Even if, due to the irrational logic of the war, there is a clear tendency to ignore its economic consequences, such aspects can no longer be overlooked. Irrespective of their ethnic origin, millions of individual human beings all over the former territory of Yugoslavia are tragically affected by them. A valuable infrastructure which has taken decades to put into place is being destroyed in a matter of days. This puts in jeopardy not only the normal life of the population, but also any reasonable prospects for the future recovery. The belligerents themselves, and first of all the civilians, are those who carry the burden of a conflict the costs of which have already exceeded the most pessimistic evaluations. But there are and will be many more others, outside the Yugoslav theatre of war, who, in some form or another, will have to pay the high bill of protracted violence there.

This is one more reason for the international community to reach, at last and at least, the conclusion that early investments in conflict prevention are both cheaper and more effective than those eventually required by reconstruction efforts, and to act accordingly.

Finally, I would like to stress once more that, fortunately, at this stage we are not totally barehanded. A set of principles, an action programme, a promising framework of debate, and rules of procedure have been outlined and agreed upon.

The very fact that such a Conference has become possible at all is probably a sign of the times. We delegate a lot of responsibility to our Co-Chairmen, but we undertake, each of us, a major responsibility as well. Now, we, all of us here, are involved. Our commitment should be total and without reservation. We will all have to do our share. Romania certainly will.

31. STATEMENT BY MR. ANDREI KOZYREV, MINISTER OF FOREIGN AFFAIRS OF THE RUSSIAN FEDERATION*

Mr. Prime Minister, Mr. Secretary-General, Russia welcomes the London Conference as a new stage in combining efforts of all those who are directly interested in settling the Yugoslav conflict and have a real influence in the region. Without it, as we all found out, the issue would not move an inch.

All parties to the conflict bear responsibility for what is happening, though to a different degree.

All sides constantly violated the ceasefire agreements. At the same time people in Yugoslavia today are clearly tired of war and more constructive voices are starting to be heard.

Among other measures we considered necessary:

1. - speediest achievement of specific agreements on a rapid ceasefire in Bosnia and Herzegovina by all sides and their separation under international control;
2. - to negotiate a political settlement of problems in relations between the former Yugoslav republics. We urge their mutual recognition;
3. - to recognise the inviolability of all outer borders and introduce a moratorium on changing internal (inter-republican) borders of former Yugoslavia, not to accept territorial changes achieved by force, stop ethnic cleansing;
4. - to implement the resolutions of the UN Security Council on the Yugoslav crisis and he conditions of settlement approved by the world community;
5. - to establish strict international control over the compliance with the conditions of settlement punishing any violations;
6. - to reject any attempts to turn the crisis on Bosnia into a religious war either internally, or internationally;
7. - to guarantee rights and special status of national minorities either in Kosovo or Krajina within the states they belong to.

We support the proposed principles and the plans of action, and consider it necessary to concentrate on the Statement on Bosnia. Russia proceeds on the understanding that implementation of the UN and CSCE demands would lead to a recognition of the Federal Republic of Yugoslavia as a legitimate member of

---

* The London Conference, General Debate: 26 August 1992.

the international community.

We agree with Prime Minister J. Major that there is a choice - either all parties to the conflict comply with the demands of the UN and CSCE and thus integrate in the international community to make it possible to proceed to gradually lift the sanctions, or there will be movement in the opposite direction.

In our view the task of the London Conference is firmly, but without dictate by anyone, to help in making the right choice.

32. Statement by Dr. Ghazi Algosaibi, Head of Saudi Arabia's Delegation to the London Conference*

Your Excellencies, The Chairmen, Your Excellencies, Heads and Members of Delegations, I have the honour to convey to this August Conference the greetings of the Custodian Of The Two Holy Mosques, King Fahad bin Abdul Aziz, and his warmest wishes for success in your deliberations upon the fate of a very sensitive area that captures the attention of the whole world.

What unfolds now in Bosnia and Herzegovina - families scattered; children orphaned, and innocent bloodshed - is a real tragedy that touches the heart of every human being everywhere, regardless of religion, race or political creed.

The Government of Saudi Arabia, which has done its utmost to alleviate human suffering in Bosnia and Herzegovina, feels that now is the time for the international community to put an end to the tragedy, through a just solution reached through peaceful methods.

The Government of Saudi Arabia is willing to exert all its efforts toward achieving such a just solution that would end the blood-letting and establish peace in that troubled land.

The situation requires all parties concerned to meet their historic responsibilities and to face the bloody scenes of destruction and wanton murder with a combination of compassion, wisdom, and a keen sense of justice. Thus, and only thus, can a happy end crown the unhappy conflict; peace and security replace fear and strife.

I pray to God Almighty to bless you in your peaceful endeavours and to fulfill the hopes attached to this historic meeting.

Thank you very much.

---

* The London Conference, General Debate: 26 August 1992.

33. STATEMENT BY MR. HIKMET CETIN*

Mr. Chairman, The London Conference will mark a turning point in the history of Europe, whether we succeed or not. Succeed we must if we are to bring peace and security to Bosnia and Herzegovina and the rest of former Yugoslavia. If we fail, the consequences could be disastrous for all of us.

Aggression, bloodshed, brutality, fear, ethnic cleansing, forced deportations, mass expulsions, concentration camps, murder, rape, starvation. This today, is the vocabulary of the tragedy in Bosnia and Herzegovina. Is it going to be the vocabulary of Europe?

The answer will, in part, depend on what we accomplish in this Conference. We are gathered here under the expectant, indeed demanding gaze of the entire international community to find a settlement for Bosnia. What is taking place in Bosnia today is tragic and a source of shame for each and every one of us. But worse things may yet be in the offing in Kosovo, Vojvodina and the Sandjak. We thus bear a heavy responsibility and history will surely sit in judgement of what we achieve, or fail to achieve, at The London Conference.

The effectiveness of any solution shall depend on how properly we diagnose the problem and its causes. We can no longer afford to skirt the issues before us by focusing on the symptoms only; we must go directly into the essence and the root of what afflicts former Yugoslavia.

The problem we are facing in Bosnia is no civil war, nor is it a humanitarian crisis. It is one of aggression, the unbridled use of force, the attempt to gain territory through the use of force and ethnic cleansing. It also involves crimes against humanity and a deliberate design to wipe out an entire community through murder or forced displacement. Even children are being killed. While the Serbian aggressor has a free hand, the Bosnian victim continues to be denied the legitimate right of self-defence. Cultural heritage, property and the environment are being wantonly destroyed. The humanitarian crisis is the consequence of aggression.

In short, what is happening in Bosnia and Herzegovina is a flagrant violation of just about every principle enshrined in the United Nations and Paris Charters and other UN and CSCE documents. Our values are being tested, the new world order is being challenged at its very onset. We cannot, and must not, allow this sinister challenge to everything we stand for continue unchecked.

Further failure on our part to respond effectively to the conflict in Bosnia would carry many dangers. The intolerable costs in terms of human lives and

---

* The London Conference, General Debate: 26 August 1992.

material losses will get bigger, which would make wounds and feelings harder to heal. The conflict may spill over to other parties of former Yugoslavia. What is worse, it may lead to its being increasingly viewed as a war between religions. Being the current chairman of the Islamic Conference of Foreign Ministers, I know the depth of concern in the Muslim world. The Islamic Conference has so far taken a very constructive stand in support of UN efforts in Bosnia and will do the same for the London Conference, provided that we deliver some concrete results in favour of justice and legitimacy.

The London Conference must build upon what has already been achieved in the United Nations and the CSCE, but we must go further. A number of decisions have been adopted in those forums. We should also take into account the important support of our public for decisive action against Serbian aggression. The press and media deserve our special thanks here for bringing, at the risks of their lives, the horrors of the crimes and atrocities committed in Bosnia to our knowledge and for thus having galvanized world public opinion.

The Government of Turkey has taken a number of initiatives in pursuit of a peaceful settlement of the conflict in Bosnia. We have been active in stressing the issue in various international organizations such as the UN, the CSCE, the Islamic Conference and NATO. We will persist in our efforts until peace returns to the former Yugoslavia.

We have submitted a comprehensive plan of action for Bosnia and handed it over to the permanent members of the UN Security Council on the 7th of August. I think this makes Turkey the only individual country that has proposed a precise line of action to the subject. I have personally visited Sarajevo. We keep in touch with all the parties, including the Serbs. Turkey is a Balkan Country and has intimate historical and cultural ties with Bosnia, Serbia and the other republics. We look forward to enjoying our traditional ties of friendship with all the peoples of former Yugoslavia, including the Serbian people who we regard close to us. We have recognized the four new republics of Slovenia, Croatia, Bosnia and Herzegovina and Macedonia and we are about to establish diplomatic relations with them as well. There is, in Turkey, a large population of Bosnian origin, probably in the millions. Today more than 15,000 Bosnians have taken temporary refuge in my country. An equal number are staying with family and relatives in Turkey. To date, Turkey has given 1,7 million dollars worth of aid to Bosnia and the other republics. We have contributed cargo aircraft to the UN air shuttle between Zagreb and Sarajevo. We have announced our readiness to contribute military as well, if called upon by the UN.

Accordingly, we have a close and priority interest in what happens in Bosnia and the other republics. We have the accumulated experience, the knowledge and the proximity to make substantial contributions to the peace process, particularly in Bosnia. The Balkans is a region fraught with danger. History is our witness. The Government of Turkey is determined to act as an element for peace, stability and prosperity in this critical region. We will strive to promote cooperation and solidarity in the Balkans, not sub-divisions or axis.

In the light of what we have done and stated regarding the situation and developments in the former Yugoslavia, I submit that we be guided by the following principles and considerations in our approach to the matters on our agenda.

Our general frame of reference will be the UN Charter, the Paris Charter and other CSCE documents as well as the rules of international law and legitimacy. More specifically, we will also keep in mind the various decisions already adopted on Yugoslavia and preserve and implement what is good in them.

We will remember that the Balkans are a sensitive region and the Balkan countries will one day become full partners in the process of European integration politically, economically and otherwise.

We will have confidence in the proven ability of the people of Bosnia and of all the other republics to live together in peace and harmony, despite a number of traumatic confrontations in the course of their shared history. They have lived together before and they can and will live together again.

We will be aware of the fact that the Serbian people are also suffering from this tragedy and that not all of them approve of what some of their leaders are doing. While we punish the aggressor, we will have compassion for the victims, irrespective of their ethnic origin.

We will not allow the London Conference to turn into a platform for dealing with the symptoms rather than the causes of the disease or have it abused by the aggressor. We will press for some immediate results, in particular the ending of bloodshed. We will see to it that the London Conference proceeds in harmony with the other forums, in particular the UN Security Council, in generating appropriate action and decisions to help bring about a settlement. The CSCE, NATO and the Western European Union can and must also be asked to contribute to the UN effort.

We will work for a solution that preserves and respects the independence, sovereignty and territorial integrity of Bosnia and Herzegovina as well as the other republics. We will, under no circumstances, recognise territorial gains obtained by use of force or any changes in borders except through peaceful negotiations.

We will not prescribe any constitutional formulas for anyone. We will leave it to the ethnic groups and minorities themselves to work out their own arrangements, but extend all assistance to them if they so request.

Our first priority will be to stop the bloodshed and effect a lasting ceasefire.

Aggression, sustained by the leadership in Belgrade and carried out by their proxies in Bosnia, must be halted. The guns should fall silent and be removed. In attaining these and other agreed objectives, we will not rule out the use of force. We will make sure that any military intervention is under the full authority of the UN Security Council.

All occupied territory will be evacuated.

Humanitarian assistance will be delivered through coordinated international actions.

We will see to it that all those expelled and displaced return to their homes and properties in safety and be adequately indemnified. International effort for the rehabilitation of those in need and without discrimination, especially the children, will be undertaken without delay.

All concentration camps and prisons shall be made accessible to UN and international inspection and control.

All those found to have committed crimes against humanity, or violated human rights, will be appropriately punished.

An international fund will be established to achieve any of the aims agreed upon at the London Conference where and as appropriate.

There will be no imposed political settlement in Bosnia. The solution agreed upon by the people of that country will be secured and implemented under effective international guarantees.

Mr. Chairman, In the short time available to us, we cannot be exhaustive in explaining our thinking. So my statement reflects only a summary analysis of how we view the situation in the former Yugoslavia and what we want to see come out of this Conference. Turkey is ardently determined to work for peace, stability, security, for respect of human rights and the values we all stand for as civilised members of the international community. We, therefore, look forward to the possibility of continuing our contributions in this direction within the bodies to be created by this Conference. We are ready to accept the responsibility because we know we have the capacity, the assets and the desire to do so. Our participation will significantly enhance the chances of success in the difficult tasks that lie before us.

Thank you, Mr. Chairman.

34. STATEMENT BY LAWRENCE S. EAGLEBURGER, ACTING SECRETARY OF STATE OF THE UNITED STATES OF AMERICA[*]

We have gathered here today because, as members of the family of nations - East and West, Moslem, Christian or Jew - we are compelled to help the peoples of the former Yugoslavia in their hour of suffering and need. But the decisions we make in London on their behalf will have consequences beyond the crisis at hand. For what we accomplish - or fail to accomplish - cannot help but influence the future of Europe and the shape of the post-Cold War international system.

Just three years ago, mankind began anew its long-interrupted march towards freedom, enlightenment and the rule of law. We had every reason then to hope that all nations liberated from communism would join not only the Western circle of democracy, but also the circle of peace created by the reconciliation of historical enemies. We envisaged, in short, an enlarged commonwealth of democracies poised to enter the 21st century having transcended the hatreds and rivalries which had so blighted the century we were about to leave.

Those hopes remain undiminished, but in the meantime events in the former Yugoslavia have confronted us with the specter there of history not transcended, but relived; and of the vision of that land's future as a reenactment of it tragic past.

Indeed, there is a chilling echo today in the former Yugoslavia of some of Europe's darkest moments - of previous examples of racially-inspired repression, aggression and territorial expansion. However, history teaches that the conquests of past ethnic cleansers have tended to be short-lived, and that peoples in whose name their crimes were committed have tended to enjoy an unhappy fate.

True friends of the peoples of the former Yugoslavia must acknowledge that history did not begin there yesterday, and that the tragedy now unfolding has ancient and complicated roots. They are aware, in particular, that the people of Serbia were one of World War II's principal victims; and they sympathize with their suffering which is still fresh in the minds of many.

I represent a government, in fact, which historically has enjoyed a special relationship with the people of Serbia. And I recognize that in the ongoing Yugoslav turmoil, crimes have been committed on all sides. But it is Serbs, alas, who are most guilty today of crimes which mimic those of their former tormentors, and which violate the sacred memory of ancestors who suffered at their hands. And it is the Serbs who face a spectacularly bleak future unless they manage to

---

[*]   The London Conference, General Debate: 26 August 1992.

change the reckless course their leaders chose for the new nation.

I make this prediction without satisfaction, but I make it because we must be absolutely clear: the civilized world simply cannot afford to allow this cancer in the heart of Europe to flourish, much less spread. We must wrest control of the future from those who would drag us back into the past, and demonstrate to the world - especially to the world's one billion Moslems - that the Western democracies will oppose aggression under all circumstances, not oppose it in one region and appease it in another.

To be sure, we will not settle this conflict here today in London. But neither will we acquiesce in the de facto constitution of a Greater Serbia. What we will do, I hope, is to establish a coordinated, integrated and ongoing process of negotiation which will culminate in a reversal of Serb aggression and the integration of the former Yugoslav republics into the wider framework of a democratic Europe. Here at this Conference we should offer leaders throughout the former Yugoslavia the choice of cooperating with the international community or paying what we will ensure is an unacceptable price for aggression. And we should, here at this Conference, place squarely before the people of Serbia the choice they must make between joining a democratic and prosperous Europe or joining their leaders in the opprobrium, isolation and defeat which will be theirs if they continue on their present march of folly.

In brief, the United States expects this Conference to undertake the following specific tasks:

Humanitarian Relief

First, the delivery of humanitarian relief to the victims of this conflict, and the granting of immediate, complete and unimpeded access to all detention camps.

With winter approaching, our immediate priority is to address urgently the task of housing and feeding the hundreds of thousands who have been left homeless in Bosnia, Croatia, Slovenia, Serbia and Macedonia. We must also funnel humanitarian assistance to hundreds of thousands more who are besieged *inside* Bosnia, so that they do not become the next wave of refugees. It will require the opening of safe corridors to accomplish this goal. The international community must have unimpeded access by ground and air to deliver humanitarian relief. And while we seek to cooperate peacefully with all sides, we must be prepared to use all means necessary to ensure that help reaches its destination.

To date, the United Nations and the ICRC have helped deliver some $ 500 million dollars' worth of assistance to the war zone. But the UNHCR has now called concerned governments to meet again on September 4 to implement a concrete plan for expanding convoys into Bosnia and meeting the winter shelter needs of refugees everywhere in the former Yugoslavia. The United States will make an initial contribution of more than $ 40 million, and an additional contribution after October. Beyond direct financial assistance, our support will include food, medicine, shelter materials, transportation and technical assistance.

Let me say, parenthetically, that we are aware of the risk that humanitarian assistance could, if we are not careful, help consolidate the land-grab in Bosnia and the political cantonization which the United States categorically opposes. Therefore, we believe it is not too soon for the international community to begin addressing the issue of how we will assist refugees to return to - and to rebuild - what is left of their homes and villages. This is an issue which will have to be part of any political settlement of the present crisis which obtains the support of the United States, and it will require another substantial infusion of the international assistance.

Finally, we must insist upon an end to the abuses being committed in detention camps throughout Bosnia, and the disbandment of these camps. The international community must receive full access to all such camps at once and on a continuing basis. The ICRC should do all it can to accelerate its ongoing inspections and be joined in its efforts by rapporteurs from the UNHCR and CSCE.

A Negotiating Process

Our *second* task here is to seek a definitive halt to the violence inflicted day after day on the people of Bosnia. As a first step, I call upon the Serbian forces to lift the sieges of Sarajevo, Gorazde, Tuzla, Bihac, Mostar and other Bosnian cities - a step which must be part of a larger diplomatic process. Towards this end, we must create a durable international negotiating mechanism, one that will operate permanently with all the relevant parties present to achieve a just and lasting settlement.

I emphasize the words "just and lasting". The Government of Serbia has stated its willingness in London to negotiate peace. But we must make certain that in agreeing to a negotiating mechanism, all parties agree as well to negotiate on the basis of principles enshrined in the UN Charter and CSCE - namely, a commitment to the peaceful resolution of disputes; respect for the territorial integrity of other states; rejection of efforts to change borders by force; guarantee on fundamental human rights - including the rights of minorities; safe return to their homes of populations victimized by "ethnic cleansing"; and mandatory compliance with efforts to deliver humanitarian assistance, only by agreeing to a peace process based on these principles can we ensure that negotiations do not become a vehicle for consolidating the fruits of aggression.

Punishing and Quarantining Aggression

But successful negotiations will require us, above all, to raise the costs now for those who perpetuate the violence and continue to hold territory acquired by force. Thus we believe the third task of this Conference is to reaffirm the international community's resolve to tighten comprehensive economic sanctions against Serbia/Montenegro, and to maintain its political isolation until all relevant Security Council Resolutions are complied with. At the same time, we should make all other parties to the conflict aware that we will impose sanctions against them, too, if they act with similar viciousness.

We understand that tightening sanctions will impose hardships on the traditional trading partners of Serbia/Montenegro, and we encourage efforts to help compensate those states whose strict compliance with the sanctions is causing them undue pain. But we must resolve no longer to tolerate continuing and flagrant violations of the sanctions regime.

Several steps are necessary. *One*, the UN Sanctions Committee transshipment guidelines must be strengthened to include strict documentation and inspection procedures. *Two*, in agreement with the Government of Romania, we will move quickly to place multinational sanctions monitors in Romania. The United States is ready to contribute experts and equipment to this operation. Similar arrangements should also be established in other areas bordering Serbia/Montenegro, including Hungary, Bulgaria, Albania, and Macedonia. *Three*, we must implement new measures to eliminate violations occurring via the Danube River.

Preventive Diplomacy

The *fourth* task for this Conference must be in the realm of preventive diplomacy - namely, to ensure the conflict does not expand into areas and countries not yet directly affected by the fighting.

The immediate step must be to implement decisions taken two weeks ago by the CSCE to insert continuous human rights monitors into those areas of Serbia - Kosovo, Vojvodina, and the Sandjak - that could become the next targets of aggression. Further, Serbian leaders have expressed their readiness to permit international observers on their territory, including along the Bosnian-Serbian border, and at airbases in Serbia and Montenegro. Now is the time to turn these words into effective actions by deciding, here today, to place observers along that border and at those airbases.

These monitors must be complemented by others in the states and regions bordering Serbia. Their function would be to serve both as a deterrent to an expansion of the fighting and as an "early warning" of its imminent occurrence.

The European Community is actively working with Albania, Hungary, Bulgaria, Romania, and Greece to put into place such monitoring teams. We applaud these efforts, urge that they be completed as a soon as possible, and stand ready to help as we can. At the same time, the United States is making efforts to put monitors on the ground in the former Yugoslav republic of Macedonia, and we will cooperate with the EC to provide the residents of this region with economic help as well.

Conclusion

I began by describing the tragedy of the former Yugoslavia in terms of the seemingly endless cycle of violence and vengeance which has characterized that region for so many centuries. But in truth, there is nothing fatalistic about what is going on in those lands. The fact of the matter is that the conflict was willed by men seeking to perpetuate Europe's last communist regime by manipulating age-old hatreds and fears. The fact of the matter is that the peoples of the former Yugoslavia can still refuse to drink the lethal brew which their leaders have put before them.

If they should so refuse, they will be able to join a democratic Europe in a process of integration which is rendering obsolete traditional notions of sovereignty, and which is enhancing the interests of minorities across the continent. The world's democracies -- most certainly including the United States -- will welcome the Serbs to their midst, and offer them greater security than they could ever hope to enjoy under the law of the jungle now prevailing.

But those peoples who choose the irrational path of hatred and aggression cannot expect membership in the newly enlarged community of democratic nations. We will simply not allow them to make a mockery of the more human and rational future that the collapse of communism and the end of the threat of nuclear holocaust promise.

35. STATEMENT BY DR. CORNELIO SOMMARUGA[*]

The ICRC has rarely been so outspoken while active in a country affected by conflict.

- Following several public appeals launched since the ICRC first began work in the former Yugoslavia on June 1991, I presented our point of view on 29 July 1992 during the UNHCR meeting in Geneva.
- The ICRC issued a solemn appeal to the parties to the conflict on 13 August 1992, urging them to respect civilians and prisoners and to comply with the Geneva Conventions in general.

All these appeals were made necessary by the seriousness of the humanitarian situation in former Yugoslavia, particularly in Bosnia and Herzegovina. They were launched following meetings held under ICRC auspices with representatives of the parties involved in this armed conflict. These meetings were important and we are ready to organize others.

However, when bilateral steps are not sufficient to improve the plight of the victims, showing that traditional means are insufficient to restore respect for international humanitarian law, we have to move on to other measures, such as public statements and appeals to all the States party to the Geneva Conventions of 1949.

Indeed, the 170 States party to the Conventions have undertaken to "respect and to ensure respect for [the Convention] in all circumstances", as specified in Article 1 common to all four Conventions.

Today I appeal to you again. The way in which hostilities are being conducted in Bosnia and Herzegovina leaves no room for humanity.

- The civilian population is systematically harassed; thousands of civilians are arrested in their homes, brutalized or even killed.
- Whole minority groups comprising tens of thousands of civilians are systematically transferred by force or, as is currently the case in Sanski Most, driven without any protection towards and across the front lines.
- Hundreds of thousands of civilians have been besieged for several months in cities such as Bihac, Bosanski Brod, Derventa, Gorazde and Sarajevo.
- Detainees, the majority of whom are civilians, are held in conditions of extreme hardship in places of detention which are totally inadequate for the

---

[*] The London Conference, General Debate: 26 August 1992.

purpose. They are ill-treated and hundreds of them have been executed, either in places to which the ICRC has been denied access or in places it has been allowed to visit only after the executions had stopped.

- Hospitals and other public and private property are not respected, to say the least. The Red Cross emblem is totally disregarded, so humanitarian convoys have in some instances to be accompanied by armed escorts.
- The ICRC has not been allowed to monitor the situation properly in the field. Indeed, it has been denied access to several areas of Bosnia and Herzegovina for lack of the necessary authorizations and/or security guarantees. The ICRC has therefore not been able to bring protection and assistance in time to all civilians affected by the conflict.

This unacceptable situation cannot go on. The humanitarian organizations have done everything within their power to bring about more humanity in this conflict, but I can only say that this is not enough. The time has come for the international community of States to assume its responsibilities.

This is now imperative. Failure to restore compliance with international humanitarian law would mean that the international community is powerless to prevent the worst.

That could also set a dangerous precedent for other countries particularly those recently created, which might encounter similar problems with their own borders and minorities.

That is why we warmly support your efforts to resolve the conflict in Bosnia and Herzegovina. We also appeal to you to decide urgently on practical measures to restore respect for international humanitarian law. My appeal is addressed first and foremost to the parties to the conflict.

Please, behave with more humanity, respect prisoners and civilians, and envisage solutions that will permit a return to normal life.

As leaders of the different parties, you have a tremendous responsibility to deliver a message of peace to the population, to advocate respect for humanitarian principles and human dignity, to instruct and control your troops accordingly and, finally, to fight against the scourge of racism and discrimination.

The international community also has a vital role to play.

As a first step, immediate measures must be taken to guarantee respect for the civilian population throughout Bosnia and Herzegovina. Forced transfers, harassment, arrests and killings must cease at once. The whole civilian population must enjoy all the security guarantees necessary to live in peace and dignity, whether in Bosnia and Herzegovina or elsewhere.

As a second step, a haven must be found for some 10,000 detainees already visited by the ICRC in northern and eastern Bosnia and Herzegovina and for others still to be visited. These people, most of whom are civilians, must be released before mid-September, because of the lack of protection in these places and the inadequate conditions of detention, which will be aggravated by the coming winter season. Today, there is nowhere in Bosnia and Herzegovina for them to go.

If they go back to their places of origin, they might be killed or find that their homes have been destroyed. Is it possible to ensure their safe return and a normal life at home? Should they be transferred in proper conditions of security to other parts of Bosnia and Herzegovina or to other countries for temporary resettlement? Should protected zones be established?

The urgent answers to these question rest with you, because the ICRC cannot assume such a momentous responsibility alone. From the legal standpoint, all civilians must be able to live in safe places, with a decent way of life and reunited with their families. Whatever solution is chosen by the international community, it should be in accordance with those standards.

I hope, that this Conference will be able to work out a peaceful settlement to this conflict, which has already gone on far too long. The most pressing needs are to ensure better protection for the civilian population and to make safe and acceptable arrangements for detainees.

The ICRC of course stands ready to offer its services, in accordance with its traditional role as a neutral intermediary, to help restore a measure of humanity in this terrible war and to promote the implementation of international humanitarian law.

Thank you.

36. STATEMENT BY ALIJA IZETBEGOVIC, PRESIDENT OF THE REPUBLIC OF BOSNIA AND HERZEGOVINA[*]

Ladies and Gentlemen, Dear Friends, I speak to you on behalf of the people of Bosnia and Herzegovina, the youngest member state of the United Nations, the country which is a victim of brutal aggression that has stunned the world.

While I convey the greetings of our citizens and their appreciation for all you have done to provide humanitarian assistance, I must also express our disappointment for all that the world community has failed to do at this crucial time.

Not only has the international community failed to come to the aid of Bosnia

---

[*]   The London Conference, General Debate: 26 August 1992.

and Herzegovina, it has failed to fulfill its commitment to the principles of world peace and democracy.

There is a struggle underway in Bosnia that pits a well-armed military force against men and women who have lived peacefully together in a multi-ethnic and multi-cultural society.

In Bosnia, an eminently European principle of peaceful co-existence between and among people, social and ethnic groups, is being defended with our lives.

That is the principle of diversity and mutual tolerance of which Bosnia and Herzegovina, in spite of all historical challenges, has always been an exceptional example. Today, we cling to this commitment with an idealistic persistence.

According to the Belgrade strongmen, the representatives who are present in this room, Bosnia and Herzegovina should have, after the dissolution of Yugoslavia, remained within a kind of rump Yugoslavia - or a "greater Serbia" as it is usually called - together with Serbia and Montenegro.

In the referendum we held, our people refused to follow that course by a vast majority. The will of the people has been acknowledged by Europe and most of the civilized world who have extended diplomatic recognition. However, the Belgrade regime has not recognized this will.

Our democratic decision was followed by revenge and attempts to impose a "greater Serbia" by naked force. One of the best equipped military forces was used against a newly born state and its unarmed people. More than 2,400 armored vehicles and tanks, some 1,800 artillery weapons of large calibre, aircraft and multiple rocket launchers of the JNA, plus more than 100,000 JNA troops joined by an equal number of paramilitary forces of the SDS launched an aggression on the young, unprotected and defenceless state.

With a few light weapons collected in haste, our people resisted and still resists in the towns of Sarajevo, Gorazde, Srebrenica, Bosanski Brod, Brcko, Jajce, as well as in large regions of Herzegovina and central Bosnia, Cazin-Krajina and relatively large areas in the valleys of the Bosnia and Neretva River.

Dear friends, this is not an ordinary war, nor is the aggression undertaken by Serbia an ordinary invasion. This is a genocidal war against civilian populations and its religions, national and cultural values. The towns have been destroyed, non-desirable citizens have been killed or expelled.

Like black mushrooms, the concentration camps have strung up throughout Bosnia and Herzegovina, in which men, women and children are being massacred or all slowly dying of starvation and torture.

The languages of the civilized world do not have a word ugly enough to express and describe the atrocious crimes that are being perpetrated by the Serb extremists.

All of this is happening in Europe, at the end of the 20th century, in front of your very eyes and in your very presence.

As you are aware, early this year the three largest political parties in the Bosnian parliament began negotiations on the principles of the future constitutional arrangements for Bosnia and Herzegovina, under the auspices of the European Community.

During the negotiations, one of the participants - the SDS - joined the aggressor and initiated was against the legally constituted government of our country. The worst crimes against civilian populations in our country have been ordered or committed by the very leaders and members of this party.

Now we are requested to continue negotiations as if nothing has happened; as if our towns have bot been destroyed; as if our people have not been killed and expelled; as if hatred and mistrust have not been created.

It is possible to negotiate, but first the aggression must be stopped. Then we can talk about the future arrangements of Bosnia and Herzegovina.

Stopping the aggression and removal of its consequences demands:

- An immediate ceasefire;
- Withdrawal of the JNA and of its paramilitary forces from the territory of Bosnia and Herzegovina, in accordance with Security Council Resolution 752;
- Return of the expelled population to their homes and villages;
- Return of the stolen property and compensation for the war damage;
- Establishing a war crimes tribunal to prosecute and punish those who are guilty of these crimes against humanity.

If the aggressor does not accept these conditions he should be forced to do so by the following means:

1. Effective implementation of sanctions against Serbia and Montenegro imposed by Security Council Resolution 757. There are serious breaches in the sanctions which must be stopped.
2. Tightening of the sanctions on all fronts.
3. Elimination of the aggressor's heavy weapons by concentration of the weaponry under control of the legal government of Bosnia and Herzegovina or international organizations, or destruction of the weaponry by air strikes.

The first is requested by Security Council Resolution 752 which has not been implemented. The second would need a new resolution. I ask you to support such a measure, if needed.

4. Making it possible for the legal authorities of Bosnia and Herzegovina to arm their troops. In this connection, we have requested a lifting of the arms embargo or exempting Bosnia and Herzegovina from that embargo. I believe that you all agree that an internationally recognized state, exposed to aggression, has the right of self-defence.
5. Establish a control area along the border with Serbia and Montenegro in order to prevent the flow of new arms and fresh troop reinforcements for further aggression. This would require deployment of 1,500 troops of the international forces at some 30 check-points.

As you can see, we do not request, except in the previous point, any ground troops. We do not ask for 150,000 to 300,000 soldiers, which is an argument used by some of those who oppose helping Bosnia and Herzegovina and who are attempting to frighten European governments and the public. We have enough men ready to fight for liberation of the country, but they need weapons.

We learned from the Conference documents that a working group for Bosnia and Herzegovina will be established. We are prepared to cooperate with it, but we think that it should be much broader than the former one. It should include one CSCE representative and, if possible, one representative of the Congressional Human Rights Foundation, which has offered its help and cooperation in this respect.

In any case, the working group will first have to study very carefully the demographic map of Bosnia and Herzegovina in order to understand that Bosnia and Herzegovina is a mixed nation. Ethnically pure territories are an exception, and no solution can be based on exceptions.

Our Government has prepared a study of future constituencies of Bosnia and Herzegovina. While I will not discuss it in detail now, I want to point out only two main points which will be the foundation of the future constitution of our country.

1. Bosnia and Herzegovina will be a democratic, secular state, based on the sovereignty of its citizens and the equality of nations.
2. It will be a decentralized state with broad regional and local self-administration.

Two main instruments have been envisaged for implementation of these principles:

1. A new Chamber of Nations will be a second chamber of the parliament. Decision making will be on the basis of consensus for the most important issues, which implies the right of veto.
2. A Tribunal for supervision of the implementation of the Constitution and of respect for human and ethnic rights would consist of nine respected lawyers, three from Bosnia and Herzegovina and six designated by international institutions. The mandate of the Tribunal would be five years.

With respect to solving problems relative to the dissolution of Yugoslavia, I would briefly say the following:

We accept all attitudes and criteria adopted by the EC Arbitration Commission (Mr. Badinter's Commission) including those concerning the international recognition of the new states as well as those concerning the succession.

The Federal Republic of Yugoslavia (Serbia and Montenegro) cannot be direct successors to Yugoslavia. The new state can be recognized only after it has been confirmed that human and national rights of its citizens, nations and minorities have been fully guaranteed by law and in practice. No compromises are acceptable.

Reject the plans on partition of Bosnia and Herzegovina and suppress any intentions of that kind. If you do not do that, the aggressor will, instead of punishment, receive a reward, while two million Muslim people of Bosnia and Herzegovina would be deprived of their homeland.

It such a case, its worse part would become criminals and its better part would become avengers. The latter would then seek revenge for the aggressor's atrocities and the world's indifference. It could last for years.

Finally, Bosnia and Herzegovina is a European country, and its people are European people. Even the evil inflicted upon us has not come from Asia, but has a European origin. The aggressor has mixed two poisons in himself: fascism - which is racism and extreme nationalism - and bolshevism - total absence of a feeling for law and human rights. Both are European-made products.

You cannot let Bosnia and Herzegovina die under the boots of these two evils, and then go to meeting to discuss a New World Order and a New Europe.

Today, Europe itself is being defended and built and even may be buried in Bosnia.

It has been said that after Auschwitz any poetry becomes senseless. After Sarajevo is destroyed and Bosnia enslaved, any talks on New Europe will become senseless too.

Thank you for your attention.

37. STATEMENT BY DR. FRANJO TUDJMAN, PRESIDENT OF THE REPUBLIC OF CROATIA*

Mr. Prime Minister, Mr. Secretary-General, Your Excellencies, Ladies and Gentlemen, Let me first of all express my gratitude to the European Community, the Conference on Security and Cooperation in Europe, the United Nations and all other organisations, agencies and associations for their endeavours to solve the state-political and war crisis in the territory of former Yugoslavia, and for the great effort and good will shown in trying to arrive at a peaceful and just solution.

I would also like to thank the conveners of this Conference who have decided, at a time when the efforts exerted so far no longer appear to be efficient, to provide a new, more energetic stimulus to the solution of the crisis which threatens to outgrow into conflicts of a much broader scale which could bring about the expansion of the disaster of war to the entire continent, and possibly to the entire world. As also indicated in the programme of its work, the London Conference should represent the continuation of the Conference chaired by Lord Carrington, and must not depart from its results and from the agreed document. One should in every respect prevent the repetition of extended talks on matters about which decisions have already been made.

While expressing my thankfulness I nevertheless have to observe, noting that is also the view of many other concerned people familiar with the crisis in former Yugoslavia, that the international community has not yet found an efficient mechanism for stopping aggression, and that it has not summoned enough will and ways and means to end the brutal destruction wrought by a war such as Europe has hardly known, associated with the most barbaric form of "ethnic cleansing" in order to create "ethnically pure areas" within the scope of the programme of the conquest of territories of other states.

Therefore, I make a plea for efficient ways to terminate the horrors of war, to stop the loss of human life, civilians in particular, and the vast damage of property, as prerequisites for the gradual re-establishment of peaceful life and good relations among states emerged in the areas of former Yugoslavia, and their integration into civilized Europe. In this connection, I cannot but remind you of some facts related to the occurrence and spreading of the crisis in the area of the former Yugoslav community.

The Republic of Croatia has spared no efforts in order to prevent the escalation of the state and political crises in former Yugoslavia into an armed conflict.

---

* The London Conference, General Debate: 26 August 1992.

Accordingly, Croatia proposed the transformation of the former state into a confederal association of sovereign states. When this proposal was turned down, and when war ensued, Croatia agreed to the peaceful solution by accepting the Vance plan.

Croatia will continue to do everything in its power to see that the UNPROFOR mandate is implemented as quickly as possible and completely. However, it should be noted that the pace of implementation of the task of the peace-keeping force must be substantially accelerated. So far UNPROFOR has fallen behind schedule in disarming the irregular forces still present in the zones under its control, in providing the conditions for the return of displaced persons to their homes, in the re-establishment of communications and control along Croatia's international borders. Croats are still being expelled from areas under the control of the peace-keeping force while, on the other hand, settlement of people who had never inhabited these areas is even being permitted.

Such an incomprehensible slowness and the breach of all set deadlines are becoming intolerable. It should be noted that the Republic of Croatia, in the area from Slavonski Brod to Zupanja, is continuously being attacked from the territory of Bosnia and Herzegovina. Forces of the former Yugoslav Army, that is, Serbo-Montenegrin military formations, still occupy purely Croatian areas south of Dubrovnik, which are not within the UNPA's because there is no Serbian population in those areas, According to the Vance Plan the aggressor army had to withdraw from this region a long time ago.

In its Constitution and subsequent Constitutional Law the Republic of Croatia has guaranteed to the Serbs in Croatia all civil and ethnic rights, in line with strictest international standards, as well as the self-government of the Serbian national minority in areas where Serbs account for the majority of the population. All this has been done in accordance with the proposals and recommendations of the EEC Conference and views of the Arbitration Commission. Croatia has had no problems with the Serbian population in this territory except with that part of the Serbian minority who, armed by the Yugoslav Army and incited from Serbia, associated themselves with the attempt to forcibly restore the communist regime and conquer - for Serbia - Croatian territories that have never in history belonged to the Serbian state.

Croatia has consistently adhered to the principles and legal provisions of its democratic Constitution and constitutional laws, and international commitments which it has accepted. In proof of such a policy let me note that two months ago about 3,500 residents of Serbian nationality in the region of Gorski Kotar, armed by the former Yugoslav Army, voluntarily surrendered their weapons and took part in the elections for members of the Croatian Parliament. Today the Serbs have 13 representatives in the Croatian Parliament, they had and still have their ministers in the Government, and representatives in the Constitutional Court and the Supreme Court of the Republic of Croatia.

In order to reduce the tension, which is still present, and normalize the situation as soon as possible, the government will propose to the Croatian Parliament to consider at this autumn session the abolition and amnesty of those who were misled into joining the armed revolt and who are not guilty of war crimes.

In view of all these considerations, we firmly believe that UNPROFOR will be able to implement its task within the terms specified in its mandate, and that there will be no need to extend the mandate from the standpoint of the stability of the legal system in the Republic of Croatia.

Because of the aggression of the former Yugoslav Army and Serbian territorial and irregular formations, perpetrated in a truly criminal and barbaric fashion, Croatia has suffered appalling losses of life which exceed the figure of 10,000 killed (predominantly civilians) and 30,000 wounded persons, and direct material damage of more than 20 billion US dollars. The names of the destroyed towns and villages such as Vukovar, Pakrac, Lipik, Vinkovci, Nuštar, Slavonski Brod, Dalj, Petrinja etc., are widely known. Unfortunately, this list of suffering also has to include the historical and civilizational jewel of Croatian and world history - Dubrovnik!

Croatia still has more that 270,000 persons displaced from various Croatian regions, while an additional number of more than 80,000 are being provided relief in other countries (Hungary, Austria, Germany, Switzerland), and I take this opportunity to thank them particularly for their help. Moreover, more than 400,000 refugees have fled to Croatia from Bosnia and Herzegovina, together with an additional 35,000 Croatian refugees from Vojvodina and Kosovo. Unless urgent steps are taken, a new wave of hundreds of thousands of refugees may be expected to flee Bosnia and Herzegovina. For Croatia the daily costs of refugee care is three million US dollars. So far, the Republic itself has spent more than 550 million US dollars in addition to assistance from other countries and agencies which has not been nearly adequate to meet requirements. Devastated and exhausted by the war Croatia can no longer bear the burden of providing for the needs of these unfortunate people. The international community will have to do much more than just showing sympathy for their sufferings. Urgent and efficient steps must be taken in order to stop this senseless aggression and to produce the prerequisites for the return of refugees to their homes in Croatia and Bosnia and Herzegovina.

Finally, let me draw our attention to the need for an urgent abrogation of the legitimacy of the former SFR of Yugoslavia, and for its expulsion from all international organizations. That is a country which exists no more! One should accelerate the process of succession, and of the division of assets, liabilities and commitments. The Republic of Croatia is ready to assume its own share of such assets and liabilities as soon as agreement is reached in their divisions.

As far as the future is concerned, the Republic of Croatia wants to be a factor of peace and stability in this part of the world. Croatia is ready to cooperate with all the new independent states in the territory of former Yugoslavia, and with all other countries of Europe and the world.

Thank you for your attention.

38. STATEMENT BY MR. KIRO GLIGOROV*

Honorable Chairmen, Ladies and Gentlemen, I would like to thank Lord Carrington for his efforts to find a just, peaceful, and lasting settlement of the crisis in former Yugoslavia. I would also like to thank Monsieur Badinter for his efforts to demonstrate that the future of Europe is not in *war* but in the *respect of law*.

There are great expectations in the Republic of Macedonia that this Conference will strengthen the peace process in the Balkan region and create preventive conditions for surpassing new potential foci of crisis. In the opposite case, violence and war in that area will be an introduction into a wider and ultimately senseless Balkan and European war.

One of the serious causes stimulating instability which can put peace in the region under question is the manner and essence by which for more than six months, the international recognition of the Republic of Macedonia is continuously being postponed.

The Republic of Macedonia, in a peaceful and legitimate way, gained its independence without war. At the general referendum, it voted yes for a sovereign and independent state. The free, multiparty elections which were carried out and the new civilian Constitution which was adopted are the foundations on which our democratic government is constituted.

Inter-ethnic equality and understanding are the confirmation of the legitimacy of a small nation to self-determination and to its own state.

Since the beginning of the Yugoslav crisis and war, the Republic of Macedonia is a force for peace and political dialogue in the region. We refused to participate in the bloody inter-ethnic war. The Yugoslav Army has left the Republic of Macedonia and without incidents or conflicts.

---

* The London Conference, General Debate: 26 August 1992.

Since the beginning of the crisis, the Republic of Macedonia has based its peaceful policy on a number of basic principles:

1) Inviolability of the frontiers between the Republics of the former SFRY and the other countries in the immediate region as internationally recognized and guaranteed state frontiers;
2) political dialogue and peaceful methods as the only possible way to resolve the relations among these independent states;
3) guarantees for human rights and the rights of national minorities, as the only guarantee for peace and democracy in the ethnically-mixed Balkans.

In the Republic of Macedonia, there is a permanent open dialogue with the national minorities and they participate directly in the administration of the Constitution of the Republic. This is one of the greatest reasons for the preservation of peace in the Republic of Macedonia.

- Free movement of people, goods, and ideas, open frontiers, good neighbourliness, and general cooperation among the Balkan states, as a condition for its adjustment to the European integrative processes and politics.

So, what are the results of such an internationally known and confirmed policy of the Republic of Macedonia? We have acquired our independence and sovereignty and we control our own frontiers, we have preserved peace and internal stability within the Republic. This situation has prevented the escalation of war so that it could not reach the frontiers of the neighbours of the Republic of Macedonia. As a result, the arbitration commission of Dr. Badinter stated in its report of 15 January 1992 that "only the Republic of Slovenia and the Republic of Macedonia fulfil the conditions to be internationally recognized" and that the "name 'Macedonia' does not imply any territorial claims". That is the only possible legal and just conclusion which could have been reached.

After that, a new typically Balkan affair started which, unfortunately, by the power of its dealings, had dragged the European Community with it, and created a precedent unknown in international relations by testing the basic principles of the new European architecture and the elementary and sovereign rights of a small and peaceful nation to self-determination. For the peace and democracy for which the Republic of Macedonia has received high marks by the whole international community, it has also gained silently an unseen punishment: it remained the last to await recognition. And, by the last Lisbon Declaration of the European Community it got an offer: to change the name so that it can be recognized!

A small nation of about 2,100,000 inhabitants is pushed into uncertainty, through strong methods of economic pressure, blockades by certain neighbours and isolation as well: an unrecognized state has no right to membership in the international finance organizations and institutions.

The humanitarian and economic assistance offered is most often symbolic, and it remains as a sole question to the unquiet international consciousness. The request then that it change its name, to deface itself, is not only outside of any principle of international law and practice, but is also a defeating fact, where we were not only isolated in the possibility to present our argument equally for a longer period, but we were facing a new phenomenon -- the whole international mechanism up to the United Nations was stopped to consider the recognition of the Republic of Macedonia. This fact is insulting for our national pride and a defeat as an example of the rights and justice for the small nations.

We are aware of the principle of consensus in the EC and of the logic of protection and solidarity with the internal interests of certain of its member-states. But, is it possible that this is the cover for making it impossible for a nation to have the right to self-determination, for its economic and social suffo-cations, for the creation of a new, potentially military, focus? Unrecognized Macedonia means application of the logics of the Balkan wars, a century old already. Today, it means an adventure with military consequences and wider European involvement.

I am repeating today our persistently expressed good will and readiness to find a solution. We have been cooperative during the whole time, and construc-tive within the activities of the EC. We have initiated, and we are even now ready for equal, friendly, and open discussions. But, we cannot accept solutions which will destabilize Macedonia and would create a new focus of conflict in the Balkans with the danger of expansion of the war.

Immediately after our request to the EC to be internationally recognized, and at the request of the Badinter Commission, we have stated that we have no terri-torial claims towards any of our neighbours, and that we do not want to interfere in the internal affairs of our neighbours. Not only this, not to remain only on declarations, but we have also undertaken concrete changes in the constitution of the Republic of Macedonia, which is the only example in the world, with such provisions, that we have no territorial claims towards any of the neighbors and we shall not interfere in the internal affairs of other countries. In spite of the strongest declaration, the constitutional guarantee, we have adopted in connec-tion to this a special declaration of the Parliament and we have proposed signing a bilateral agreement with the Republic of Greece providing European guaran-tees on the inviolability of the frontiers and for friendship and cooperation which is a practice in the whole world and an acquisition.

The Republic of Macedonia will continue on the path of peace and dialogue. Because of that we support the activities for the establishment of peace in Bosnia and Herzegovina. We support the decision of the CSCE for sending missions in the foci of this crisis and observers in the neighboring countries. We support all the activities of preventive diplomacy, so as to avoid escalation of the war into other areas, especially in Kosovo. In these efforts, we are even now with a full goodwill and readiness for friendship and cooperation with all our neighbors. Such an atmosphere is already prevailing in our relations with some of our neighbors. We are prepared for discussions with the Republic of Greece and for cooperation with the EC.

In this respect, we have started a really constructive dialogue with the President of the EC.

The Republic of Macedonia should receive its international recognition. Not only because of the principle of law and justice, but because of the international political interest, too, for peace in that region of the Balkans. In this framework, the act of its international recognition is an essential element of the preventive diplomacy on the peace process in the Balkans.

39. STATEMENT BY DR. DIMITRIJ RUPEL, MINISTER OF FOREIGN AFFAIRS OF THE REPUBLIC OF SLOVENIA*

Mr. Chairman, We are grateful to the government of the United Kingdom for its hospitality and for the effort invested in the organization of this Conference. We understand this initiative as an expression of the deepest concern shown by the government of the United Kingdom, the UN, CSCE, EC and the entire world, for the war which in all its terror is being waged against Bosnia and Herzegovina (B&H) and which is threatening to spill across the borders of former Yugoslavia.

Let me use this occasion to thank the international communities, agencies and organisations for their efforts so far to help the peace process on former Yugoslavia: the EC-monitors, UNPROFOR, UNHCR, Red Cross and others who have provided assistance.

Let me use this occasion to express appreciation of and thank the introductory speakers: Prime Minister Major, Secretary-General Boutros Ghali and Lord Carrington for their energetic contributions and new ideas.

Let me also use this occasion to regret the rules of procedure which have

---

*   The London Conference, General Debate: 26 August 1992.

inappropriately prescribed the languages of the Conference and which have avoided the identification of the countries present at this Conference.

The London Conference has a solid basis in the work accomplished so far by the EC Conference on Yugoslavia, under the able chairmanship of Lord Carrington.

Lord Carrington conducted the work of the EC conference on Yugoslavia with dignity and honour as a truly great international figure. He spared no effort to address any issue, irrespective of its complexity.

In some respects his Lordship led to important results which are basic for the future:

1. Independence of the republics, now sovereign states;
2. Questions posed to the Arbitration Commission and its opinions;
3. The principle that the Conference on Yugoslavia is a conference of six republics which are equal - and some of them internationally recognised;
4. Last, but not least, that Yugoslavia has dissolved and ceased to exist.

Slovenia participates at the London Conference as a member of the UN and a CSCE participating state. Our presence here is an expression of responsibility which Slovenia feels as a member of the international community. Slovenia is not involved in any of the armed conflicts which are taking place on the territory of former Yugoslavia and participates in the efforts to find solutions for the crisis in the Balkans with good will, objectivity and an interest to stop the war - as any other state - neighbour of the area of conflict.

In the opinion of the Republic of Slovenia, the following four points provide a framework for ending the war and finding a political solution to the problems in Bosnia and Herzegovina:

1. In accordance with Security Council resolution 770 (1992) of 13 August 1992, immediate and effective humanitarian assistance to all those who are endangered should be provided, thus contributing essentially to a gradual cessation of war activities;
2. Safety zones should be established in which the threatened population, especially the Moslems, will find safe haven and to which the refugees could return;
3. Negotiations among the representatives of the three constituent nations of Bosnia and Herzegovina (Muslims, Croats and Serbs) should be promoted in order to establish political and constitutional arrangements for their coexistence in the territories of their own administrative units; the statehood of Bosnia and Herzegovina, the integrity of its territory, its

sovereignty and political independence should be preserved;

4. Two of the nations involved in the conflict enjoy the full support of their respective states, which is however not the case with the Moslems. In our opinion, all three nations should enjoy the equal (legal) support of the international community, especially of the European countries. The international community should assume a more active role in negotiations concerning the future of Bosnia and Herzegovina and provide relevant international guarantees of its political stability, constitutional order safety, and integrity of the territory, based on the equality of these three constituent nations.

The Conference will succeed and gain public credibility only if it succeeds in stopping the hostilities. This is a precondition for the start of a political settlement of issues which are twisted into a justification for the crisis and war with its tragic consequences, including genocide, ethnic cleansing, change of borders through violence, concentration camps, destruction of cities and killing of the civilian population, together with the largest exodus recorded in Europe since World War II.

We are faced with a faithless policy which has hitherto unscrupulously used the indecisiveness and leniency of the international community, and rejected political solutions to the crisis. Through violence, war, extreme cruelty, it has succeeded in the realization of its political aims. This is a policy which speaks only in the cruel language of violence. It is for this reason that it expects to be rewarded in the end, through war-extorted recognition of de facto gains. This kind of policy can only be stopped by a decisive and firm reply, supported by the necessary force. The demand for a ceasefire must be supported by a demand for a withdrawal of foreign armed forces and heavy artillery from B&H. We propose that all mechanisms - economic, military and diplomatic - be used against the Serbian political machine. We consider the latter mechanism to have the greatest effect, that is, breaking of diplomatic relations with Belgrade and the exclusion of Serbia and Montenegro, or their common state, the Federal Republic of Yugoslavia (FRY), from international organizations and forums, for membership in which they neither have any legal basis nor international recognition. In this way we would be excluding from the international community all those who do not wish to recognize or live by the rules which are the guidelines for life in this community.

It is fortunate that the UN, through its eminent presence at the London Conference, serves as a reminder that this world organization is prepared to cooperate in the process of "peace-building". A saying is attributed to Sir Winston

Churchill that "the UN was not created for the purpose of leading nations into heaven but to save them from hell". Today such a condition could exist throughout the Balkans and the entire south-eastern part of Europe. The cooperation and intensive engagement of the UN is vital. It would be fitting if in the heart of the Balkans, an area which is through its historical, cultural, religious, and ethnic differences so specific in nature but is at the same time so similar to some other parts of the world where the type of Balkan trauma and problems could recur tomorrow, the peace-building ability of the UN could come to fruition. A successful settlement of this crisis could greatly contribute to the establishment of a model for treating similar problems in Europe and elsewhere in the world.

The war now raging in Bosnia and Herzegovina is the only war in Europe that goes against the new world order based on recognition of democratic principles, human rights and the principles laid down in the UN Founding Charter and the CSCE documents. The primary responsibility for the war against B&H which is the extension of the former aggression against Croatia and the start of the violent break-up of the former SFRY that began in Slovenia, is in the hands of the Belgrade authorities. We have already paid a price for giving way to the aggression of Serbia and Montenegro and feigning ignorance of the international position of their common state, the FRY, and this has further stimulated their policies of conquest and violation of human rights and humanitarian law. Such appeasement has weakened the UN imposed sanctions and helped to break the political blockade of Belgrade. It has allowed Serbia, by applying a "smoke screen" of a kind of "soft" government in the FRY and the benevolent acquiescence by the international contacts towards its Prime Minister, to continue the war, the ethnic cleansing and violation of human rights and the rights of national minority groups on its territory. Furthermore, the FRY is creating an impression that all of the above in no way affects its acceptance into the international community. Leniency from the international community also enables Serbia to avoid implementing the decisions of the Arbitration Commission which were also confirmed on 20 July 1992 by the Foreign Ministers of the European community, according to which the FRY has equal status to other successors to the former SFRY and could thus not expect to enjoy automatic and monopolistic continuity of the disintegrated state. For this reason Slovenia did not oppose and is not against the participation of the Serbian and Montenegrin representatives at the London Conference. However, it did oppose, and it is against, the participation of the FRY at this Conference.

Refugees from B&H are still flooding into the neighbouring countries and increasingly into the whole of Europe. The majority of the refugees are Muslims, who are, due to cynical plans for the division of B&H, being left without their homeland. Can we allow Europe to create the nucleus of long-term terrorist activities within its bosom? This problem has to be resolved at the roots, ending the war and the ethnic cleansing and enabling the people to return to their homes.

The existence of concentration camps is a disgrace and degrading for humanity. It is cynical to talk about the state of affairs in these camps. The important thing is to issue a demand that the camps be immediately disbanded. It is also important to demand an immediate prosecution of those responsible for war crimes and crimes against humanity in B&H. We support the proposal for establishment of an international tribunal which would judge the perpetrators of these crimes in B&H.

Mr. Chairman! I am firmly convinced that there is a solution to all the problems which I have mentioned. This primarily concerns the perseverance of this eminent Conference with the basic points of the contractual specifications for the resolutions which were proposed by Lord Carrington for an integral solution to the Yugoslav crisis last November. This includes the perseverance with the opinion provided by the Arbitration Commission of the Conference on Yugoslavia, presided over by Mr. Badinter. Last, but not least, it also includes perseverance with the UN Security Council resolution which speaks of the fact that the war waged against B&H also threatens world peace and security. For this reason all means of exerting pressure on the aggressors, and their immediate political isolation, are acceptable.

If I am not mistaken, the worst bombing of Sarajevo so far took place last night. If I am not mistaken those responsible are sitting in this room.

Action must be taken, and Slovenia is prepared to contribute to the international action to end suffering and senseless ambition to get stronger through territorial conquest and destruction. Nowadays Europeans get stronger through more work and constructive imagination.

40. STATEMENT BY MR. DOBRICA COSIC[*]

Gentlemen, The future of Europe will not forgive us if this Conference also fails to put an end to the horrendous sufferings of hundreds of thousands of men, women, and children on the soil of former Yugoslavia, if this Conference does not mark a turning point in the policy of all internal and external factors in the Yugoslav agony, in the cessation of the inter-ethnic, religious and civil war in Bosnia and Herzegovina, the completion of the state-political reorganization of

---

[*]   The London Conference, General Debate: 26 August 1992.

Yugoslavia and in ensuring objective preconditions for stabilization and lasting peace in the Balkans.

For this turnabout to be achieved it is necessary that all the Yugoslav factors renounce every use of force and nationalistic exclusivism in attaining the stated objectives of their national ideologies;

- that they seek, primarily themselves, through dialogue, agreements and compromises, solutions for ending the Yugoslav agony and embark on an integral normalization of mutual relations and the observance of the existential interdependence of all the Yugoslav and Balkan peoples;
- that, in the processes of democratic revolution which has emerged after the collapse of "real socialism" and which has, through the basic principles of human rights, become universal through the fora of the world community as a global process, they accelerate and finalize the democratic transformation of their societies, ensure all human rights and the rights of national minorities according to the highest CSCE standards and thereby make a final break with the totalitarian past and the regime of the communist party and also, through the rule of law, prevent the further stirring up of the residual energies of Nazi, clerical and chauvinist provenance, which have become powerful factors of war on the soil of former Yugoslavia;
- that all the three parties in Bosnia and Herzegovina put an immediate end to their mutual killings, "ethnic cleansing", the setting up of camps for civilians, enable all refugees and exiled persons to return to their homes, abolish all forms of national, religious and civil discrimination and under the wing of the European Community continue and finalize negotiations on the political set-up of Bosnia and Herzegovina;
- that the Federal Republic of Yugoslavia, with its constituent republics of Serbia and Montenegro, be consistent in not extending military aid to the Serbs in Bosnia and Herzegovina, prevent any participation of citizens of the Federal Republic of Yugoslavia in paramilitary formations in Bosnia and Herzegovina, not engage again in any form of political and other participation in the antagonisms of the Yugoslav peoples and embark on bilateral negotiations on the normalization of relations with all the newly-formed states;
- that Croatia immediately withdraw its Army from Bosnia and Herzegovina, abandon its military coalition with the Moslems and initiate political negotiations with the Serbian Republic and with representatives of other Serbs in Croatia;
- that the Moslem leadership abandon its aspirations for political hegemony in Bosnia and Herzegovina, cease to obstruct the negotiation for achieving

a political agreement with the Serbs and the Croats and relinquish the confessional and military internationalization of the civil war in Bosnia and Herzegovina;

- that the Serb leadership in Bosnia and Herzegovina make appropriate territorial concessions to the Moslems in areas which are now being defended by the Serbs as their own, and thereby create a sound basis for the future set-up based on agreement between the three constituent peoples;
- that all the former republics and nations immediately discontinue the media war, renounce chauvinistic exclusivism and political struggle employing all means, which has already caused pathological hatred among people and nations, thwarting any ethnic and democratic communication. If we wish this Conference to mark a turning point in the policy of international factors and change the situation on the Yugoslav soil, which we all wish, in my opinion, it would be reasonable;
- that the international factors of the Yugoslav crisis overcome their role of biased arbitrators and establish the equality of all Yugoslav participants in decisions and rights in completing the state-political reorganization on the space of the former Yugoslavia;
- that they rehabilitate the denied principles and norms of international law, primarily the rights of all peoples to self-determination, as a fundamental principle of the United Nations;
- that they give up double standards in interpreting the rights of the Yugoslav nations, which have caused great damage to the Serbian people, especially through the too ready legalization of secession and change of the external state borders established by the Versailles Treaty and peace treaties after World War II and guaranteed by the Helsinki Accord as well as by the simultaneous proclamation of internal republican borders as inviolable although those borders were imposed by the decisions of the Comintern and the Communist Party of Yugoslavia, which has in fact caused the interethnic wars on the Yugoslav soil;
- that they free the Federal Republic of Yugoslavia of the sanctions of the Security Council based on unfair assessment of the nature of the war in Bosnia and Herzegovina, and on stereotyped arbitrariness and falsehoods of the mass media which have satanized the Serbian people and psychologically prepared the world public for making Serbia and Montenegro the "scapegoats" of the projected new world order and made the Serbs the Jews of the end of the 20th century;
- that the Security Council withdraw Resolution 770 approving military intervention even to individual states or groups of states, which in fact puts

the Federal Republic of Yugoslavia in the position of a hostage of the participants of the civil war in Bosnia and Herzegovina;
- that the mass media of the countries participant in this Conference put an end to the ethnic cleansing of information;
- that the function of pressures, arbitration and the punishing of the participants in the war in which three sides are participating be replaced by the function of good offices and a peace-making mission.

In order to attain the basis objectives of this Conference I deem it rational to reach agreement on the following decisions:

1. The demilitarization of Bosnia and Herzegovina and the placing of all armaments under UNPROFOR control.
2. The demilitarization, in stages, of the entire Balkan region and of states having territorial claims vis-à-vis the Balkans.
3. The recognition of the state continuity and personality of the Federal Republic of Yugoslavia, the lifting of sanctions, and its participation as an equal partner in rights and responsibilities for the peaceful and political resolution of all issues related to state-political reorganization on the Yugoslav soil.
4. The International Conference on Yugoslavia should be turned into a standing conference with its headquarters in Geneva, and with a Yugoslav appropriate United Nations and CSCE commissions alternately meet in cities of the former Yugoslav republics until state agreements are concluded and relations among the newly created states fully normalized.
5. An economic, political and communication association as a region correlative to the European Community and an association aspiring towards the creation of a Balkan confederation should be created of the states established on the principles of the self-determination of peoples.

These are, I am convinced, the roads of constructive and preventive diplomacy towards turning the traditional Balkan instability into a region of peace, integral democracy, the freedom of nations and people.

Gentlemen, I would like to draw your attention to an aspect of the future not only of the Yugoslav and the Balkan peoples. The virus of national-statism and secessionism which has in the post-communist era affected multi-national societies, nations in diaspora, and national minorities in the south-east and east of Europe and in the former Soviet Union, is the heritage of communism and of traditional policies.

"Balkanisation" which is precisely at this moment assuming tragic proportions on our soil, among other things due both to the operation of external factors and political manipulations with human rights, might turn into a source of permanent conflict and trigger a destructive process in the international community at the beginning of the third millennium.

It is not possible to restrict and control "balkanisation" by way of sanctions. The international ghettoization of various regions of the world is incompatible with the proclaimed principles of the new world order. Such a hazardous game in the Balkans will backfire like a boomerang on Europe, Russia and the new world at large.

International sanctions and military intervention would not remove the real causes of the conflict but only multiply the evil consequences of a bad policy and exacerbate the problem of accelerated "balkanisation" of other multi-national and multi-confessional areas.

The peaceful rearrangement of Yugoslavia hence calls for the introduction of new and anticipatory principled solutions on the exercise of national and state rights so as to enable it to carry out and complete the state-political reorganization in the Balkans, and even further afield, by peaceful means and practices.

Hoping that this Conference will lend a fresh impetus to efforts aimed at defining and establishing a new democratic order ushering in a new democratic era in the Balkans, I wish that we eventually abandon arms and become, through reason, the masters of our fate. Finally, I wish to express my thanks to Prime Minister Major and to UN Secretary-General Boutros Ghali and to all those participants who have sought with their political astuteness and benevolence to ensure a successful outcome of this distinguished gathering.

Thank you.

41. STATEMENT BY MR. MICHAEL PAPACONSTANTINOU, MINISTER OF FOREIGN AFFAIRS OF GREECE[*]

The convening of the London Conference on the former Socialist Federal Republic of Yugoslavia demonstrates the wish of the entire international community to actively pursue a solution of the Yugoslav crisis which constitutes a threat to peace and stability. The Foreign Secretary of the United Kingdom, speaking on behalf of the European Community and its member states, has already described the major challenges we are confronted with, as well as the main points of the Twelve's position.

---

[*]   The London Conference, General Debate: 26 August 1992.

Greece as a Balkan country and a direct neighbour to former Yugoslavia welcomes the convening of this important Conference and feels that she has a particular responsibility to actively contribute to the search of a negotiated and comprehensive solution of the Yugoslav crisis. This crisis has already turned into a major tragedy. Even more, it constitutes a potential danger of destabilisation of the whole area. Thousands of innocent people have been killed. Many more have become refugees. Atrocities have been committed from all sides against the civilian population to such an extent that they represent an affront to mankind. It is inconceivable that such a war is waged in Europe in the present day. Greece condemns vigorously the continuing acts of violence and the attempts to impose solutions by force. Nevertheless, there is no time to lose in searching for those who first started in trying to justify the continuing use of violence by invoking the responsibilities of the other side, whichever it is. All parties, including Serbia, must immediately cease fire and comply with all mandatory resolution of the United Nations Security Council before it is too late.

The European Community has been actively involved, from the very beginning of the crisis, in efforts to assist the parties to find, through dialogue, a lasting solution. A proper negotiating framework has been set up, under Lord Carrington's guidance, to help the parties in this effort. Greece has been actively participating in these efforts, advocating moderation, even-handedness, impartiality and negotiated procedures.

I wish to use this opportunity in order to express the Greek Government's deep appreciation for the outstanding work accomplished by Lord Carrington, whose mission my country has fully supported during its very difficult stages.

As regards the former Yugoslav Republic of Macedonia on which Lord Carrington made a remark, I would prefer to refer to the statement made by the Co-Chairman of the Conference and President of the European Community, Mr. Hurd. Indeed, once the prerequisites mentioned in the decision of the European Community taken in Lisbon on 27 June 1992 concerning recognition of that Republic are fulfilled, Greece will be ready to extend its full cooperation and friendship to the new Republic.

Today's Conference will continue the work already done and will try using our collective weight to encourage the Yugoslav parties to reach a viable and lasting solution which will be acceptable to all and which will offer the necessary guarantees for stability and peace.

But no solution can prove viable and lasting unless all parties to the conflict show determination to achieve this goal. Thus, the heaviest responsibility falls upon all the Yugoslav parties themselves.

We expect all the parties to the conflict to cease fighting immediately and to engage without delay, in good faith, in serious negotiations for a comprehensive political settlement.

The international community cannot and should not accept solutions based on situations created by force or faits accomplis and must be determined not to recognise any acquisitions or gains which are the result of aggression.

A major tool in our hands is the strict commitment to the principles of the inviolability of all frontiers and territorial integrity of all former Yugoslav Republics in accordance with the UN Charter, the CSCE Final Act and the Charter of Paris. It should not be forgotten that the Yugoslav Parties have already subscribed to this principle at the beginning of the Hague Conference. It is, nevertheless, of paramount importance that their commitment to this principle be repeated along with the whole set of principles which this Conference will be called to adopt. The importance for the whole Balkans of this principle of the inviolability of frontiers is self-evident. Insistence, however, on practices and targets incompatible with these principles will perpetuate the crisis with unforeseen results.

Another basic principle should be the protection of minorities and the respect for human and civil rights of all the citizens in the new Republics of former Yugoslavia. These rights should be guaranteed, by special arrangement, by the international community throughout.

The situation in Bosnia and Herzegovina has reached alarming dimensions. All three ethnic communities should immediately cease fire and grasp the opportunity offered to them to continue negotiations in good faith with a view to reaching an early comprehensive solution as to the future of their state. Greece vigorously condemns the inhuman policy of ethnic cleansing. The atrocities committed there by various parties have outraged international opinion. Those who commit them will be held accountable. What is of primary importance at this stage is to ensure the unhindered and prompt delivery of humanitarian aid to all who need it. It is unacceptable that thousands of innocent civilians are deprived of urgently needed humanitarian and medical aid by the acts of a small number of people. We must ensure that all refugees will be able to return to their homes and properties in safety, and in accordance with international law and the human rights covenants.

All parties to the conflict have the obligation, under international law, to respect the rights of prisoners and civil populations. It is their obligation to allow the unhindered dispatch of humanitarian aid wherever it is needed, including the camps. Until these camps are dismantled, free access to them by the ICRC should be guaranteed. In this context, we welcome the efforts undertaken by the UN and their agencies to contribute to alleviating human suffering there.

Greece has already taken the initiative on this issue and has introduced the idea of an international investigation into accusations about abuses on any civilians and the punishment of the perpetrators of such acts.

We reaffirm our support of all Security Council Resolutions and mainly 713 and 757. The arms embargo should be reinforced vis-à-vis all sides. Nobody should be allowed to attempt to violate it. The strict implementation of the general trade embargo adopted by Resolution 757 should remind all parties of the determination of the international community to genuinely press for a quick solution of the crisis and to isolate those who do not cooperate in a peaceful way in the settlement of the crisis.

We must act swiftly and stop the war before it is too late. The dangers of the spill-over of the crisis are real. Therefore, our efforts to find solutions to all aspects of the Yugoslav crisis should be decisive and reinforced.

In Kosovo, a serious and open dialogue between the Serbian Government and the Albanian population should start without delay. The rights of this population should be restored as soon as possible.

In Bosnia and Herzegovina, the three main ethnic groups should agree at the earliest on a new constitution based on the 18th March agreement of the three Bosnian ethnic communities. This seems to be the only realistic solution at the time.

There is no time to lose. The acquis of the European Community Conference should be preserved and further built upon. If we fail to settle the crisis soon, the coming generations will not understand why the will of the entire world to achieve peace has been disregarded and how this opportunity has been lost, causing enormous suffering and destruction.

42. STATEMENT BY MR. H. VAN DEN BROEK, MINISTER FOR FOREIGN AFFAIRS OF THE NETHERLANDS*

Mr. Co-Chairman, This meeting is one in a long series dealing with the break-up of Yugoslavia. We can look back on a year marked by broken promises, false expectations deliberately aroused, a drive for territorial expansionism by violent means, violations of the most basic human rights including that most repellent manifestation, the revival of "ethnic cleansing", combined with the setting up of internment camps. By means of aid and political and diplomatic interventions, the EC, the CSCE and the UN - both separately and in concert - have succeeded so far maybe in delaying, but not in preventing, the spread of

---

* The London Conference, General Debate: 26 August 1992.

violence. Violence has spread from Slovenia to Croatia, from Croatia to Bosnia, while there seems to be no doubt that the next victim is most likely to be Kosovo, with all the risks of escalation over the borders that such a development would entail. In the meantime, the Serbs control more than 2/3 of Bosnia and Herzegovina and continue to extend the area under their control by means of ethnic terrorism.

We do not need to repeat here today all the principles to which a political solution should adhere. The Carrington Conference and the Badinter Commission have formulated them in careful and expert terms. At this point I wish to pay tribute to Lord Carrington and the magnificent work he has done. Conditions such as respect for existing borders and the rights of minorities have been discussed in the Carrington Conference, from every angle with all parties concerned, as have the numerous variations on the issue of future cooperation between the new republics. These discussions of course remain of value. However, they lose credibility and become counter-productive when certain parties use them as a cover in order to continue their policy of creeping expansionism. The most important aim of this Conference in London, in our view, is therefore to increase the pressure of the chief culprit, Serbia, with its abhorrent practice of ethnic cleansing, and to prevent the prospect of total political, diplomatic and economic isolation, without even excluding military options as a means of last resort, against the parties who are unwilling to cooperate. The crisis, this inhuman suffering, cannot continue with the international community indefinitely remaining powerless to act.

The Netherlands warmly welcomes the presence here today of the UN Secretary-General and the representatives of the five permanent members of the Security Council. We have, I believe, arrived at a point where intervention and sharpening up of the sanctions can in principle only be legitimised by the Security Council.

In this sense, resolution 770 - which made it possible to provide military protection for aid convoys - was indispensable and opportune. We also feel obliged to help organisations such as the UNHCR and the ICRC to reach the many victims in safety. My country is therefore willing to make a new, substantial military contribution to allow full implementation of SC-resolution 770, in addition to our existing contribution to UNPROFOR in Croatia and Bosnia. Because the Netherlands is participating in UNPROFOR it understands all too well the Secretary-General's concern that the UN peace force might be compromised in the event of a greater military involvement. Obviously, careful thought and planning remain of the utmost importance. The dilemma presented by the fact of those who are being oppressed and expelled from their homes on the one hand, and by the risk of escalation when providing sufficient military protection for our troops and aid workers on the other, leads indeed to painful choices. But the complexity of this dilemma should never turn the international community into the hostage of those who wish to use violence in furthering their reprehensible, ethnically inspired power politics. At this stage this means that Resolution 770 should be out into effect immediately and in full.

A second task which has high priority is to place the heavy weapons in Bosnia and Herzegovina under international supervision. Agreements to this effect have previously been reached between the parties but have not so far been observed. NATO and the WEU should now complete their study of their contribution to such a control mechanism and present the results forthwith to the UN Secretary-General. My country has already offered to make available observers for this task. The Security Council should now consider a resolution which will sanction the use of force where necessary to ensure compliance with agreements on disarmament. Here too, the international community can no longer tolerate broken promises on pain of appearing to be capitulating to aggression.

Furthermore, in order to enable the negotiations on a political solution to progress, the pressure on Serbia should be increased for as long as ethnic cleansing continues, the existing borders remain unrecognised, the problem of the minorities is not satisfactorily settled and the internment camps remain open. Together with other delegations, therefore, we ask that this Conference, in addition to its support for the UN measures I referred to a moment ago, also express support for:

1. the admission of permanent observers to Kosovo, Vojvodina and Sanjak, with the cooperation of the CSCE;
2. a tightening up of the trade embargo and its supervision and enforcement through a supplementary Security Council resolution;
3. expulsion of Serbian representatives from international bodies and recognition of the Yugoslav Federation solely subject to the EC conditions formulated by the EC Conference headed by Lord Carrington;
4. the compiling of a black list - perhaps by the UN Human Rights Commission - of those who are guilty of or responsible for crimes against humanity and in this connection a study - in line with the proposals put forward by Mr. Kinkel, the German Foreign Minister - of the scope for setting up an International Tribunal; this should all be done in consultation with the UN Human Rights Commission and its rapporteur, Mr. Mazowiecki.

There is no certainty whatsoever that the action currently being taken by the international community will be sufficient to call a halt to the totally unacceptable aggression, let alone to reverse it in order to allow the displaced persons to return home. We therefore feel that this Conference must keep the option of more radical measures open in an explicit manner, and in this, the primary role falls to the Secretary-General and the Security Council.

Last but not least, I should like to express on behalf of the Netherlands our appreciation and respect for the tireless efforts of UNHCR and all the other aid organisations in the gigantic task facing them. They can count on our continuing support in their efforts to provide facilities in the region. In cases where that has proved possible, the Netherlands, like many other countries, has said it is prepared to admit a number of displaced persons after thorough consultations. We are fully aware that such an offer may carry the undesirable implication that ethnic cleansing practices have been accepted as a fait accompli. In view of this, we would like to see requests from UNHCR for aid in setting up or equipping facilities in the region which could be "adopted" by countries or groups of countries. This Conference might also express support for such an idea. The arrival of winter will make extra measures necessary.

Mr. Co-Chairman, We are grateful for your initiative in preparing this Conference. We hope most sincerely that it will produce concrete results, particularly for those in Bosnia and Herzegovina who are the victims of violence, who have been uprooted and robbed of so much that is dear to them. If we do not, together, succeed in restoring their confidence in their future as free citizens in a multi-ethnic, democratic society, then the dreadful consequences will be felt most keenly throughout Europe and Europe will run the risk of being left behind by the tide of its own history.

43. STATEMENT BY MRS. BARBARA McDOUGALL, SECRETARY OF STATE FOR EXTERNAL AFFAIRS OF CANADA*

Mr. Chairmen, As you have both underlined, this Conference faces a daunting challenge and we all must be determined to succeed, despite the thread of pessimism that runs through all discussion of this topic. What are our goals? I don't think that anyone expects us to resolve the crisis in two days. We pray for - and work for - a durable ceasefire. That may be unrealistic this week, but what we can achieve, with determination and political will, is the intensification of a peace process with a real chance of success.

Leaders in the former Yugoslavia have not responded to the efforts of

---

*   The London Conference, General Debate: 26 August 1992.

regional organizations to help resolve the crisis. We are here, therefore, in a context which includes the broader international community, and reflects its determination to see this crisis ended.

Canada, among others, has tried to make a meaningful contribution to resolving the crisis in the former Yugoslavia, through peacekeeping, humanitarian assistance and monitoring missions.

But, as with other members of the Conference, Canada has been horrified and frustrated by the failure of the parties, particularly but not exclusively Serbians, to stop the senseless killing.

Our citizens are angry. They are outraged by the acts of barbarism. They are offended by the farce of endless ceasefires; of agreements cynically reached and violated; of promises made and broken. Their hearts go out to the civilians directly affected; their disgust with the leadership that allows this to continue grows daily.

Representatives here, today, are charged with a heavy responsibility. Time has run out. This may be the last chance to avoid disaster of even more tragic dimensions. There is no room in this Conference for those who are not prepared to participate in good faith and who are not motivated by a sincere desire to bring this tragedy to an end.

There can be no possibility of success unless each of us shares sincerely the objectives of this meeting. We all must be prepared to make it work.

We must stop the killing. Already too many lives have been lost, too many homes shattered, too many people put to flight. In human terms, the costs have been unspeakable. The warring parties themselves must agree to lay down their arms. The responsibilities for ensuring that this happens rests directly with the political and military leaders of communities in Bosnia, Serbia/Montenegro and Croatia. There must be a general ceasefire.

We are all painfully aware that previous ceasefires have failed to hold. While leaders meet and reach agreement, the killing continues and the hideous process of "ethnic cleansing" goes on. This is dreadfully wrong.

We have before us an essential and well-thought out set of principles to form the basis of a negotiated settlement. We must adopt this here in London and see that all parties concerned abide by it. Agreement to these principles is essential to making progress; I think it crucial that the principles emphasize the dreadful issues of detention camps, forcible expulsion of civilian populations, and the deliberate interference with the delivery of humanitarian aid.

There can be *no* exceptions to these principles. If armed bands on any side are led by local warlords not answerable to anyone, then surely all delegates to this Conference must brand them as outlaws. I choose this word carefully, and I mean it in its most literal sense. These groups would be declared outside the law. Accordingly, they would not receive support or protection from any of the states or leaders represented at this Conference and they will be answerable before the appropriate judicial tribunals, including, possibly, war crimes tribunals - a proposal we believe should be considered by this Conference.

Genuine, direct negotiations, as opposed to rhetorical battering among all parties, must begin. The existence of extremists on all sides cannot be used as an excuse to prevaricate. The parties must come together, mindful that CSCE principles are fundamental to this process.

There is surely no reason why differences, deep as they may be, cannot be resolved through peaceful negotiations rather than bloody violence. There is nothing mysterious about ending the killing. The only way to stop is to stop. The role of the international community in this Conference, has to be that of the honest broker. The international community must be prepared to accept its responsibility to see that a just and fair-minded peace is achieved. We need imagination, flexibility, and the determination to end the suffering.

This Conference and the negotiations it will launch have another equally important purpose -- to provide a framework within which all the Republics of the former Yugoslavia can settle their differences and work out their long-term future together. Here again, the international community has a vital role. But our presence as an international community, our willingness to assist, does not let the peoples and governments of the former Yugoslavia off the hook. They themselves must find new ways to live together. Think ahead, to when today's children, in the region physically and emotionally scarred by war and hatred, are grown up; they will have to live in the future as neighbours. Geography will see to that. The sooner this reality is faced the better.

We are concerned that tension in Kosovo could lead to another tragic outbreak of fighting. It is not good enough for the Serbian authorities to say this is an internal matter. Human rights and minority rights are *not* internal matters. We must address this issue here this week. If there is any place in Europe that is ripe for preventive diplomacy, *Kosovo* surely is.

The principle of human rights is also still at issue in the Krajina. Tenuous progress is being made. To advance further, the Government in Zagreb must make greater efforts to give the residents of Krajina the sense of security they need. Serbs there must, for their part, accept that Krajina is and will remain part of Croatia.

We in the international community have stressed the need to bring humanitarian relief to the people of Sarajevo and other parts of Bosnia and Herzegovina. We have taken active measures with the help of UNPROFOR, to get supplies in to those who most need them. These efforts have been beset with difficulties.

Two weeks ago the Security Council reaffirmed the determination of the international community to make deliveries possible. Surely compassion in among even the most black-hearted dictates that Resolution 770 must be implemented fully.

Canada believes this can be best be accomplished by enlarging the mandate and size of UNPROFOR. Peacekeeping will have to become more active, more dynamic. The people of Sarajevo are not alone in their needs. There are many others and we must help them too.

The Canadian Government is ready to make further efforts in support of this essential humanitarian work, and has decided to make available to the United Nations 1200 more Canadian troops for this purpose. We welcome the commitment of others to this common effort. We remind the representatives of all parties in Bosnia of their obligation to facilitate, not to impede, deliveries of food and medicine to civilians whatever their ethnic group. It is totally unacceptable and loathsome that aid convoys are fired upon or mined.

If the fighting is not stopped immediately, the Security Council must consider a resolution authorizing enforcement of the sanctions imposed in Resolution 757 and the arms embargo imposed by Resolution 713. This should apply to the Adriatic, the Danube and the land frontiers. This would be another important demonstration of international will and determination.

This Conference must stress that the international missions of the UN Commission on Human Rights and the CSCE must be given immediate and complete access to all camps, wherever they are.

I denounce, in the strongest manner possible, the non-cooperation of Bosnian Serbs at Manjaca in refusing to open the camp to inspection by the Special Rapporteur of the UN Commission on Human Rights, Mr. Mazowiecki. This is flagrant disrespect for the collective will of the international community, to say nothing of inhumane and cruel treatment of inmates, innocent or otherwise. No wonder our public have every reason to believe the worst concerning these camps.

The courage of the International Red Cross is exceptional, but it must be assisted in its vital work of ensuring humane treatment of all prisoners and captives.

Representatives of those engaged in the conflict in Bosnia, present here today, must bear in mind their *personal* duty to ensure that the Geneva Conventions are fully observed, in every village and every camp.

The tragic plight of those driven from their homes by fear, by fighting or by "ethnic cleansing" has touched us all. Neighbouring areas and countries have had to bear particularly heavy burden, and need international help and support.

The international organisations that are central to dealing with the humanitarian situation require generous support. Canada will contribute $ 15 million to the UNHCR's next appeal, and will also contribute $ 5 million to the ICRC to help specifically with its work with prisoners of war and hostages/others in the camps.

With such issues as these at stake, and so many lives at risk, this Conference cannot afford to fail. We cannot accept the implications of such a defeat. We cannot accept that "ethnic cleansing" be legitimized and that those outside the law continue to impose their will with impunity. The parties that are responsible will be liable and the States than condone what is happening will be ostracized. They will find themselves pariahs, cut off from the community of nations in every aspect of normal discourse and relations.

There can, and should be another way ahead. Leadership in the region must abandon their unrealistic dug-in positions that serve no purpose except that of their own ambition. Surely it's not too much to ask for good faith, and *sincere* commitment to the pursuit of peace, we can make real progress here towards reaching a future free of violence and cruelty and discord, one that is in the interest of everyone present and most particularly of the people they lead.

44. Statement by Mr. Géza Jeszenszky, Minister for Foreign Affairs of the Republic of Hungary[*]

Messrs. Co-Chairmen, The Hungarian Government welcomes the initiative to convene the London Conference on Yugoslavia. We see it as probably the last chance to find a solution to the crisis without major military involvement from outside. Should we fail to achieve this task we will have to have the largest military conflict in Europe since World War II, which would put the whole subcontinent in fire and would not leave the other parts of Europe untouched. On the basis of out historical experience and our proximity to the conflict we feel Hungary can contribute in a constructive and, at he same time, resolute manner to the work and hopeful success of the Conference.

I would like to restrict my intervention to a few issues, which we, from the Hungarian point of view, see as decisive for a lasting solution to the crisis. We are convinced that the solution must be comprehensive, i.e. it must offer a solution for all the national and ethnic groups that live in what for the last 75 years

---

[*] The London Conference, General Debate: 26 August 1992.

was known as Yugoslavia.

No effort can bring results unless the fighting on the territory of the former SFRY stops immediately. All means at our disposal must be used to achieve this objective. States as well as international organisations such as the UN, NATO, WEU and the CSCE must do their utmost to achieve this goal. Ceasefires must be respected, armed forces must be brought under political control. The solution of the problem must be based on the recognition of the border of the republics which composed the former SFRY, and the territorial integrity and sovereignty of all the successor states must be respected.

The status and future of national minorities is one of the greatest challenges we have to face and handle in the post-Communist world, and in particular on the successor states of the former SFRY. Many national groups live there whose language and culture are different from that of the majority. All of them have some specific characteristics and their situations and aspirations vary. There is, however, one feature, which is common for all: all of them want to preserve their national, cultural, linguistic and religious identity and all of them want theirs to be fully ensured by law and respected in practice. These people do not want more than all the other people who belong to the majority. But their situation is different - since they are a minority - and this different situation requires different methods to ensure the same result: equality, freedom and the preservation of their national identity.

All those who present the case and aspirations of national minorities as a tendency leading to undermining the integrity of a state or endangering the rights of the majority, either do not understand the real situation or pretend that. All those who wish to present the natural aspiration of a nation to support the legitimate aspirations of all their co-nationals as interference with internal affairs or as an effort of trying to change the borders between their states, either do not understand or do not want to understand the very substance of the problem. All those who vehemently and with full conviction support the strive of national minorities for their rights to be ensured by the state in which they live, prove two things: first, that they are ready to engage themselves for the rights of those others who happen to be unlucky enough to live outside the borders of their nation-state, due to unwise peace settlements in this century. Secondly, that they do not question these borders, they do not want to revise former, in many cases unfair settlements, since the only objective they follow is to ensure that the situation of these minorities *in the state where they now live* be ensured in accordance with internationally recognised norms and commitments.

A lasting solution to the problem of national minorities must ensure both guarantees for the rights of minorities and all conditions necessary to preserve their national identity and, at the same time, offer assurances to the state in which they live that these rights and aspirations do not undermine the territorial integrity and sovereignty of that state. The best way to achieve these goals is to offer and ensure various forms of autonomy to the national minorities.

Autonomy is the most appropriate form of self-government in which these double requirements in which they live would be the best safeguard for stability and security, but also for freedom and democracy for the minority and majority. In this respect I would like to recall Hungary's support for the efforts of the Democratic Community of Hungarians in Vojvodina as a body whose legitimacy and constructive attitude has been confirmed in several elections and as a political organization which is loyal to the Republic of Serbia.

The concept of autonomy they devised is completely in line with the solutions offered for the protection of minorities in the Carrington plan, which we continue to support.

A lasting and satisfactory settlement is inconceivable without managing and solving the refugee problem. In addition to the unimaginable suffering of now millions of women, men and children and the huge burden of the states receiving them, a failure to solve the problem would legalize the violent deportation of them, which has no precedent in modern history other than the deportation of people by the Nazis and by Stalin's henchmen.

Security and stability in this region requires the establishment of a certain balance of forces, at the lowest possible level, both between the successor states of the former SFRY and their neighbours. To this end a legally binding treaty, with the participation of all successor states and neighbouring states is needed. This treaty should limit and, as necessary, reduce both the armament and equipment and manpower of the armed forces and the paramilitary capabilities, activities and intentions of the parties to the treaty through an extensive exchange of information and an intrusive verification regime.

The solution of the crisis must be elaborated with the participation of all parties concerned, including the six successor states, their neighbours and the legitimate representatives of the national minorities. The solution must be internationally guaranteed and controlled.

This Conference must continue its work concentrating on specific issues whose solution is indispensable. Hungary is willing and ready to participate in all task groups which may be set up by the conference.

Mr. Chairman, In this context allow me a few remarks concerning the drafts before us. First we consider the Provisional Rules of Procedure valid only for this ministerial phase of the Conference.

The substantial participation of all interested states in the preparation of, decisions, as well as decision-taking at all stages and in all bodies of the Conference must be ensured.

We support the set of Principles contained in the draft, as we have supported all the UN resolutions and the principles of the Carrington plan. This is, however, not enough: concrete steps and actions are needed.

We also support the very good ideas expressed by many speakers of the Conference as well as by the Badinter Commission and others. All of them deserve our attention and, even more, full implementation.

Mr. Chairman, After Friday the Conference must continue its work concentrating on specific issues whose solution is indispensable.

We are also ready to help in convening and organizing some of the future meetings and naturally implementing their decisions.

The most important task however, is that we all agree and decide that the Conference must, within a short period of time and through intensive and permanent efforts, devise the framework for the solution of the crisis, building also on the results and integrating the efforts of other organizations and institutions. We cannot fail, since our failure would signal a failure of historic effort to make the world really safe for democracy following the end of communism and the victory of freedom.

45. STATEMENT BY THE SPOKESMAN OF THE MINISTRY OF FOREIGN AFFAIRS OF ROMANIA ON COMPLIANCE WITH THE SANCTIONS AGAINST YUGOSLAVIA DECIDED BY THE SECURITY COUNCIL RESOLUTIONS*

In the context of the constant preoccupation of the Romanian Government to contribute toward a political settlement of the conflict in Yugoslavia, Romania has permanently supported the endeavours of the international community aiming at restoring peace in the region.

At the same time, Romania has complied with the decision adopted by the United Nations Security Council, fully observing the provisions of Resolution 713 of 25 September 1991 banning the supply of weapons and military equipment to Yugoslavia, as well as Resolution 757 of 30 May 1992 deciding economic sanctions against the Federal Republic of Yugoslavia (Serbia and Montenegro).

To that effect, the Romania Government established the necessary mechanisms for the purpose of implementing and observing the military embargo and

---

* Press Release, Ministry of Foreign Affairs of Romania, 22 August 1992.

the above-mentioned economic sanctions by all Romanian agencies and organisations.

The Romanian Government's statement of 3 June and 15 July 1992 and the directives issued by the Ministry of Trade and Tourism, Ministry of Agriculture and Food, Ministry of Industry, and Ministry of Transport spelled out specific measures or the implementation of the sanctions provided for by Resolution 757 (1192). Those measures were reported to the Security Council in the Memorandum of the Romanian Government of 20 June 1992 and the addendum to that Memorandum of 16 July 1992.

On 20 August 1992, the Romanian Government issued a special decision containing detailed instructions for the enforcement of sanctions with a view to consolidating the mechanisms designed to ensure strict compliance with the sanctions.

The instructions indicate the precise implementations of measures:

- to ban import into Romania of goods exported by the Federal Republic of Yugoslavia;
- to ban any transactions by Romanian nationals or Romanian flag vessels or aircraft involving any commodities and products originating in the Federal Republic of Yugoslavia, including any transfer of funds;
- to ban the sale or supply by Romanian nationals or from Romanian territory, or using Romanian flag vessels or aircraft of any goods, whatever their origin, to any person or legal entity in the Federal Republic of Yugoslavia;
- to abstain from making available to the authorities of the Federal Republic of Yugoslavia or to any commercial or industrial company or public utility in that country any funds or any financial or economic resources;
- to deny take-off or landing permission in Romania or overflight of Romanian territory to any aircraft intending to land in the territory of the Federal Republic of Yugoslavia or that took off from its territory;
- to specify delivery conditions for supplies strictly intended for medical use, food or goods designed for basic human needs;
- to monitor transport of goods to or from the Federal Republic of Yugoslavia, as well as transmit or transshipment through that country;
- to indicate the regime of exceptions from such interdictions, in case of supplies intended strictly for medical use, foodstuffs or deliveries for other humanitarian purposes, as approved expressly by the Sanctions Committee of the Security Council.

The military embargo and economic sanctions have been observed strictly and in good faith despite the severe consequences that the discontinuance of trade and economic cooperation with the Federal Republic of Yugoslavia have entailed to the Romania economy. Nevertheless, there have been some suspicions about Romania's compliance with the United Nations sanctions.

Starting from the fact that Romania has nothing to hide and from its real willingness and firm determination to comply with the UN Security Council decision, the Romanian Government made public its readiness to cooperate with the states and international organisations that are interested in assisting Romania to implement the sanctions. In that spirit, the Romanian Government conveyed to the partner countries in the North-Atlantic Co-operation Council an invitation to designate their observers at the Romanian border crossing-point, ports and airports that are relevant for the implementation of sanctions. That initiative was welcomed with interest. With the view to establishing such a mission intensive bilateral and multilateral consultations have already taken place in various capitals and in Brussels. The mission implies on-site deployment of multinational teams of experts for monitoring, jointly with the Romanian authorities, the flow of goods at border crossings and customs checkpoints.

Following agreement on organisational details and on the institution framework for action, the mission will state its activity in Romania before long. At the same time, it is envisaged to establish a mechanism designed to report the results of the mission to the Romanian Government and probably also through the CSCE, the European Communities, the North-Atlantic Cooperation Council and the United Nations.

In the same context, between 15-18 August 1992, at the invitation of the Romanian side, an exploratory team of the EEC Presidency (United Kingdom) and of the EEC Commission visited some border crossing-points and ports on the Danube in Romania. The team members appreciated favourably the activity of the Romanian authorities with respect to the implementations of the relevant resolution of the UN Security Council.

Certainly, the transit of foreign vessels along the Danube remains an open issue, since the provisions of the Belgrade Convention on navigation on the river impose limitations on the authority of transit countries to control the vessels which do not call at the ports of the riparian states. This question, however, is beyond the ability of the Romanian authorities to take action. Actually, the question is being considered by the security Council Sanctions Committee with a view to preparing possible further guidelines on that matter.

The Ministry of Foreign Affairs of Romania is confident that the above-mentioned attitude and the actions taken by the Romania Government provide enough evidence to the effect that Romania is a reliable partner in the efforts being made by the international community toward strengthening international legality and ensuring political stability and peace in the region and in Europe.

46. Open Letter of 25 August 1992 by Jacques Attali, President of the European Bank for Reconstruction and Development, to the Participants in the London Conference on the Former Socialist Republic of Yugoslavia*

Your Excellencies, The London Conference provides the countries of the former Yugoslavia with a new opportunity to find a peaceful solution, with the international community, that will bring relief to the suffering of large numbers of people by opening the way to a long-term settlement of the conflict and to future prosperity. I would like to offer my best wishes for a successful conference.

Modern Europe must be based on mutually beneficial cross-cultural relations, in the strengthening of democracy, on the implementation of the fundamental principles of internationally recognised individual human rights and minority rights as well as on economic progress.

The European Bank which was specifically created to finance reconstruction and development in Central and Eastern Europe, stands ready to assist in rebuilding the former Yugoslav republics and is prepared to participate in any relevant international task groups. The Bank will also prepare, if asked, a report on anticipated needs.

Once again, may I wish you every success in your work during the Conference.

---

*   The London Conference, 25 August 1992.

3. INTERNATIONAL CONFERENCE ON THE FORMER YUGOSLAVIA: GENEVA

A. A CHRONOLOGY: SEPTEMBER 1992 - MARCH 1995

Editor's note: The International Conference on the Former Yugoslavia started its activities in Geneva on 3 September 1992. The following is a chronology of significant events.

SUMMARY OF ACTIVITY

1992

3 September
- First meeting of Steering Committee in Geneva.

4 September
- Co-Chairmen attend UNHCR Follow-Up Committee meeting.

4-6 September
- Co-Chairmen's meetings with Working Group Chairmen, ICRC, UNHCR, UN Under-Secretary-General Goulding and UNCHR Rapporteur, Mazowiecki.

4-16 September
- Seven meetings of Working Group on Confidence and Security Building Measures.

7-9 September
- Meeting of Working Group on Succession Issues.

9-12 September
- Visit by Co-Chairmen to Zagreb, Sarajevo and Belgrade.
- Mr. Vance also visits Ljubljana en route to Geneva.

12-13 September
- Lord Owen participates in EC Foreign Ministers informal meeting at Brocket Hall.

14 September
- UNSCR 776 authorises additional UNPROFOR deployment.

14-15 September
- Meetings in Brussels of expert sub-groups of Working Group on Economic Issues on inventory of assets and liabilities of Federal Republic of Yugoslavia (Serbia and Montenegro).

14-17 September
- Meeting of Working Group on Ethnic and National Communities and Minorities. In the margins the Co-Chairmen meet leaders and representatives of other interest groups.

16 September
- Co-Chairmen meet Macedonian Minister for Internal Affairs, Frckovski.
- Meeting with Ibrahim Rugova, leader of Kosovar Albanians.

18 September
- Mr. Vance meets Chairman of Arbitration Commission, Mr. Robert Badinter.

18-19 September
- Meeting of Working Group on Bosnia and Herzegovina.

19 September
- Geneva agreement with Bosnian parties on humanitarian assistance.

21 September
- Mr. Vance meets Director of UNICEF, Mr. James Grant.

22-23 September
- Visit by Co-Chairmen to Athens for talks with Greek Prime Minister Mitsotakis.

22-24 September
- Visit by Chairman of Working Group on Ethnic and National Communities and Minorities to Belgrade for meetings with Kosovar leadership.

23-24 September
- Meeting of Working Group on Confidence and Security Building Measures.

25-26 September
- Visit by Co-Chairmen to Zagreb and Banja Luka to examine humanitarian situation.

28 September
- Visit by Co-Chairmen to Belgrade.

29 September
- Co-Chairmen meet President Izetbegovic in Geneva.
- Mr. Vance meets ICRC President, Mr. Sommaruga.

30 September
- President Tudjman and President Cosic meet in Geneva under the auspices of the Co-Chairmen.

1 October
- Ambassadors Hall and Okun brief Steering Committee Delegations in Geneva.
- Meeting of Working Group on Confidence and Security Building Measures.

2 October
- Co-Chairmen meet Macedonian Foreign Minister Maleski in Geneva.

3 October
- Resumption of Sarajevo airlift.
- Mr. Vance meets with Mrs. Ogata and Mr. Sommaruga.
- Lord Owen briefs Council of Europe.

5 October
- Declaration of EC Foreign Affairs Council in Luxembourg.
- UNSCR 779 on Prevlaka.

6 October
- UNSCR 780 establishes Commission of Experts to investigate alleged war crimes.
- Mr. Vance meets Croatian Deputy Prime Minister and Bosnian Government representatives in Geneva.
- Meeting of Working Group on Confidence and Security Building Measures.

7 October
- Meeting of Mixed Military Working Group chaired by General Morillon in Sarajevo; not attended by Bosnian Government representatives.

8 October
- Co-Chairmen meet UNCHR Rapporteur, Mazowiecki.

9 October
- UNSCR 781 establishes a no-fly zone over Bosnia and Herzegovina.

10 October
- Co-Chairmen visit Moscow for talks with Russian Foreign Minister Kozyrev.

11 October
- Mr. Vance meets Bosnian Serb leader Dr. Karadzic.

12 October
- Second meeting of Mixed Military Working Group meets in Sarajevo; again is not attended by Bosnian Government representatives.

13 October
- Lord Owen negotiates with Dr. Karadzic on withdrawal of Bosnian Serb aircraft.

13-14 October
- Ambassadors Ahrens and Hall hold first round of Conference-brokered talks on education in Pristina.

14 October
- Mr. Vance briefs UN Security Council on ICFY developments.

16 October
- Co-Chairmen meet Macedonian President Gligorov in Geneva.
- Declaration by European Council in Birmingham.
- Special Advisors and Deputies to Co-Chairmen brief Geneva-based delegations of Steering Committee.

17 October
- Co-Chairmen meet Federal Republic of Yugoslavia (Serbia and Montenegro) Prime Minister Panic.

18 October
- Mr. Vance meets Federal Republic of Yugoslavia (Serbia and Montenegro) Prime Minister Panic.
- Mr. Vance meets Bosnian Serb, Mr. Koljevic.

19 October
- President Cosic and President Izetbegovic meet in Geneva under the auspices of the Co-Chairmen.

20 October
- Second meeting of President Tudjman and President Cosic in Geneva under auspices of Co-Chairmen.
- JA withdrawal from Prevlaka completed.

21 October
- Co-Chairmen meet with President Izetbegovic.
- Lord Owen meets Federal Republic of Yugoslavia (Serbia and Montenegro) Prime Minister Panic.

22 October
- Second round of Conference-brokered talks on Kosovo held in Belgrade.

23 October
- First meeting of Mixed Military Working Group with all three parties participating, chaired by General Morillon in Sarajevo.

24 October
- Lord Owen meets Irish Prime Minister in Dublin.

26 October
- Second full meeting of Mixed Military Working Group in Sarajevo.
- Mr. Vance meets ICRC President, Mr. Sommaruga.

27 October
- Second meeting of Conference Steering Committee in Geneva.

28 October
- New constitutional proposals for Bosnia and Herzegovina released.

28-30 October
- Co-Chairmen visit Belgrade, Zagreb, Pristina, Tirana, Skopje and Podgorica.

3 November
- Ambassadors Okun and Hall brief Geneva-based delegations of Steering Committee.

4 November
- Co-Chairmen meet Turkish Prime Minister Demirel in Ankara.
- Meeting of Working Group on Confidence and Security Building Measures.

5 November
- Co-Chairmen meet Bosnian Foreign Minister Silajdzic and Bosnian Serb leaders, Dr. Karadzic and Mr. Koljevic.

6 November
- Lord Owen addresses European Parliament Foreign Affairs Committee in Brussels.
- Lord Owen meets German Foreign Minister Kinkel.
- Mr. Vance meets Bosnian Serb leaders, Dr. Karadzic and Mr. Koljevic.

7 November
- Co-Chairmen meet President Gligorov of Macedonia.

9 November
- Lord Owen briefs EC Foreign Affairs Council in Brussels.

10 November
- UNSCR 786 on humanitarian flights to Bosnia and Herzegovina.
- Cease-fire agreement signed in Sarajevo.

10-12 November
- Working Group on Ethnic and National Communities and Minorities, chaired by Ambassador Ahrens, visits Novi Sad for trilateral meeting.

11-14 November
   Co Chairmen address UN Security Council in New York.

12 November
- Lord Owen meets EC Ambassadors in New York.
- Co-Chairmen meet Ambassadors of the Permanent Members of the UN Security Council in New York.

13 November
- UN Security Council Debate in New York.

14 November
- Mr. Vance meets Ambassador Sacirbey, Permanent Representative of Bosnia and Herzegovina to the UN.

16 November
- UNSCR 787 bars trans-shipment of oil and other products and allows stop and search of vessels in the Adriatic.
- Working Group on Confidence and Security Building Measures meets in Geneva.

18 November
- Working Group on Bosnia and Herzegovina resumes talks.
- Members of the Working Group on Ethnic and National Communities and Minorities meet with representatives of the Muslims from Sandjak.
- Special Group on Kosovo meets with delegation of the Kosovar Albanians.
- Meeting of the Working Group on Confidence and Security Building Measures.

- Ambassadors Okun and Hall brief Geneva-based delegations of Steering Committee.

19-20 November
- Co-Chairmen visit UNPAs in Croatia.

23 November
- Co-Chairmen meet Greek Prime Minister Mitsotakis in Geneva.

23-26 November
- Delegation of Working Group on Ethnic and National Communities and Minorities in Skopje.

24 November
- Meeting of the Working Group on Confidence and Security Building Measures.

24-27 November
- Working Group on Succession Issues meets for the first time in Geneva under its new Chairman, Ambassador Bojer.

25 November
- Lord Owen meets Spanish Prime Minister and Foreign Minister Solana in Madrid.
- Co-Chairmen meet Federal Republic of Yugoslavia (Serbia and Montenegro) Prime Minister Panic.
- Working Group on Bosnia and Herzegovina meets Bosnian Serb and Bosnian Government representatives.

26 November
- Mr. Vance meets Professor Kalshoven, Chairman of the UN Commission of Experts, established by UNSCR 780.

27 November
- Co-Chairmen meet UNPROFOR Deputy Chief of Mission, Mr. Thornberry in Geneva.

28-29 November
- Co-Chairmen have private meeting with President Tudjman at Brioni.

30 November-2 December
- Co-Chairmen attend the Extraordinary Session of the Organization of the Islamic Conference Foreign Ministers in Jedda.

1 December
- Chairman of the Working Group on Bosnia and Herzegovina, Mr. Ahtisaari, meets delegation of Bosnian Serbs headed by Mr. Buha.

1-2 December
- Sub-Group on Macedonia meets in Geneva for trilateral talks between representatives of the Macedonian Government and Macedonian Albanians, under the chairmanship of Ambassador Ahrens.
- Trilateral meeting under chairmanship of Ambassador Rey between representatives of the Macedonian Government and Serbs from Macedonia.

2 December
- Co-Chairmen meet UNPROFOR officials and troops in Split.
- Ambassador Rey meets Albanians from the communities of Preseva, Bujanovac and Medvedja in southern Serbia.

3 December
- Working Group on Confidence and Security Building Measures meets in Geneva.

4 December
- Lord Owen meets NATO Secretary-General and Belgian Foreign Minister in Brussels.
- Mr. Vance addresses high-level stocktaking meeting of the Humanitarian Issues Working Group chaired by Mrs. Ogata.
- Ambassadors Okun and Hall brief Geneva-based delegations of Steering Committee.

7 December
- Mr. Ahtisaari meets delegations of the Bosnian Government and of the Bosnian Serbs.
- Working Group on Confidence and Security Building Measures meets.

7-10 December
- Working Group on Ethnic and National Communities and Minorities visits Skopje and Pristina.

8-9 December
- Co-Chairmen attend separate high-level meetings on constitutional arrangements with the three Bosnian parties, chaired by Mr. Ahtisaari.

9 December
- Co-Chairmen meet Crown Prince Alexander of Yugoslavia and Mrs. Ogata.

10 December
- Mr. Vance meets with Mr. Wourgaft, Secretary-General of the World Veterans Foundation.

11 December
- UNSCR 795 authorises deployment of UNPROFOR contingent to Macedonia.

14 December
- Lord Owen attends meeting of CSCE Council of Ministers in Stockholm.
- Lord Owen meets Swedish Prime Minister.
- Working Group on Confidence and Security Building Measures meets.

15 December
- Delegation of Working Group on Ethnic and National Communities and Minorities travels to Subotica in Vojvodina to meet representatives of the Croat and Hungarian minorities.

16 December
- Expanded Steering Committee Meeting at Ministerial level in Geneva.
- Sub-Group on Kosovo meets group of medical experts.

17 December
- Co-Chairmen meet President Tudjman and President Izetbegovic in Zagreb.
- Lord Owen meets Fikret Abdic, member of Bosnian Presidency in Velika Kladusa, Bihac pocket.

18 December
- Mr. Vance meets UN Secretary-General Boutros-Ghali and members of the Security Council in New York. He also meets President Bush and Secretary of State James Baker in Washington.

18-21 December
- Lord Owen visits Sarajevo, Kiseljak and Pale for talks with senior political and military leaders of the three Bosnian parties.

19 December
- Mr. Vance meets foreign policy team of the incoming Administration in Washington.

23 December
- Ambassadors Okun and Hall brief Geneva-based delegations of Steering Committee.

26 December
- Mr. Vance meets UN Secretary-General Boutros-Ghali.

27 December
- Co-Chairmen meet President Tudjman and President Izetbegovic in Geneva.
- Co-Chairmen meet Russian Foreign Minister, Kozyrev.

28 December
- The UN Secretary-General Boutros-Ghali and the Co-Chairmen meets President Tudjman, President Izetbegovic and President Cosic.

29 December
- Lord Owen meets Croatian Defence Minister Susak, in Zagreb.
- Mr. Vance meets Chairman of the Arbitration Commission, Mr. Badinter.

30 December
- Lord Owen meets President Milosevic and Dr. Karadzic in Belgrade.

31 December
- Mr. Vance and UN Secretary-General Boutros-Ghali visit Sarajevo.

1993

2-4 January
- Co-Chairmen convene first round of Summit Meeting on Bosnia and Herzegovina in Geneva with representatives of the Bosnian Presidency, Bosnian Croats, Bosnian Serbs, Croatia and the Federal Republic of Yugoslavia (Serbia and Montenegro).

5-6 January
- Co-Chairmen visit Belgrade and Zagreb. Meet with President Cosic, President Milosevic and President Tudjman.

7 January
- Co-Chairmen meet President Gligorov of Macedonia in Geneva.

10-12 January
- Second Round of five-party Summit Meeting on peace plan for Bosnia and Herzegovina.

13 January
- Ambassador Okun briefs Geneva-based delegations of Steering Committee.

15 January
- Co-Chairmen meet President Tudjman and President Izetbegovic in Zagreb.
- Ambassadors Hall and Okun meet delegation of Bosnian Serbs led by Mr. Buha in Geneva.

20-21 January
- Co-Chairmen visit Sarajevo and Zagreb for meetings with President Tudjman and Bosnian Croat and Muslim leaders.

23 January
- Third round of Summit Meeting on peace plan for Bosnia and Herzegovina.

24-27 January
- Mrs. Ogata visits former Yugoslavia to review the humanitarian relief operation in Bosnia.

28 January
- Mrs. Ogata meets separately President Izetbegovic, Dr. Karadzic and Bosnian Croat leader, Mr. Boban and calls on them to end abuses of humanitarian rights and of humanitarian law.

30 January
- At a plenary session of the Peace Conference on Bosnia, Mr. Boban signs the entire three part package, Dr. Karadzic signs the Constitutional Principles and the Military package, while President Izetbegovic signs the Constitutional Principles and agrees to hold talks with UNPROFOR.

31 January
- Lord Owen reports to the President of the EC Council of Ministers, Niels Helveg Petersen of Denmark.

1 February
- Co-Chairmen meet UN Secretary-General Boutros-Ghali and US Secretary of State Christopher.

10 February
- In New York, Lord Owen meets the Canadian, New Zealand, Belgian and Venezuelan Ambassadors. Later holds talks with US Secretary of State Christopher and the Head of UN Peace-keeping Operations, Mr. Goulding.
- Ambassador Ahrens meets representatives of the Macedonian Government and of the Macedonian Albanians to discuss language and educational issues.

11 February
- Lord Owen holds talks with Dr. Karadzic and the Greek special Envoy.
- Mr. Vance meets Federal Republic of Yugoslavia (Serbia and Montenegro) Foreign Minister Djukic, while Lord Owen briefs EC Ambassadors. The Co-Chairmen also hold bilateral meetings with Dr. Karadzic and Mr. Papoulias, Under-Secretary of State in the Greek Foreign Ministry.

12 February
- Co-Chairmen meet troop contributors to former Yugoslavia.

15 February
- Co-Chairmen brief President of the EC Council of Ministers on recent developments.

16 February
- Krajina talks to discuss demilitarisation and repatriation of refugees begin in New York.

17 February
- Co-Chairmen meet the Russian Envoy to former Yugoslavia, Mr. Churkin.
- Krajina talks continue in New York.
- Ambassador Rey meets Yugoslav and Kosovar Albanian representatives to discuss educational issues in the Kosovo.

18 February
- Co-Chairmen meet US Envoy to former Yugoslavia, Mr. Bartholomew and Russian Envoy Churkin.
- Co-Chairmen hold separate talks with the Krajina Serbs and the Croatian Defence Minister Susak on the situation in the Krajina.

19 February
- Krajina talks continue.
- Lord Owen meets Croatian Defence Minister Susak.
- Co-Chairmen meet the UN Secretary-General Boutros-Ghali and EC Ambassadors.

22 February
- Talks continue with the Krajina Serbs in New York to secure a ceasefire in the UNPAs and the "pink zones".
- Co-Chairmen subsequently meet UN Secretary-General Boutros-Ghali, Greek Foreign Minister Papaconstantinou, and the EC Foreign Affairs Commissioner Van den Broek.

23 February
- Co-Chairmen meet Macedonian Deputy Prime Minister Crvenkovski.
- Co-Chairmen also brief the Security Council on the latest developments in the negotiations on Bosnia and Herzegovina and on Krajina.

24 February
- Co-Chairmen meet Mr. O'Brien, new President of the Steering Committee and permanent members of the Security Council.
- Co-Chairmen also hold talks with the New Zealand Ambassador to the UN and the Russian Special Envoy Churkin.

25 February
- Co-Chairmen meet Bosnian Croat leader Mr. Boban and Bosnian Prime Minister Mr. Akmadzic to discuss implementation of the peace plan.
- Co-Chairmen attend separate meetings with EC Ambassadors and UN Military leaders.

26 February
- Lord Owen meets the UN Secretary-General Boutros-Ghali.

1 March
- Co-Chairmen hold talks with Mr. Bartholomew and Mr. Churkin.
- They also have bilateral meetings with Dr. Karadzic, President Izetbegovic and Mr. Boban.
- Co-Chairmen also meet the Ambassador of the OIC, the Moroccan Ambassador and the UN Secretary-General Boutros-Ghali.
- Ambassadors Okun and Ahrens open the Krajina talks in New York meeting Krajina Serb and Croatian Government representatives.

2 March
- Lord Owen holds talks with Mr. Bartholomew and Mr. Churkin.
- Co-Chairmen meet President Izetbegovic, Bosnian Prime Minister Akmadzic and Mr. Boban to discuss Muslim/Bosnian Croat relations in the light of recent fighting.
- Lord Owen later meets Dr. Karadzic.

3 March
- President Izetbegovic signs the Military Agreement for peace in Bosnia.
- Lord Owen meets the British Secretary of State, Mr. Hurd.
- The Co-Chairmen hold talks with Dr. Karadzic and Mr. Boban.

4 March
- Lord Owen meets the Foreign Minister of New Zealand, Mr. McKinnon.
- The Co-Chairmen and UN Secretary-General Boutros-Ghali meet Dr. Karadzic, who continues to refuse to sign the complete Peace Plan.
- They later meet President Izetbegovic, Mr. Boban and Mr. Churkin.
- Ambassadors Ahrens and Okun continue talks with the Croatian Government and the Krajina Serbs on a ceasefire agreement, but talks falter over deployment of Serbian police in the area.

5 March
- Lord Owen meets French Permanent Representative to the UN, Ambassador Merimee.

8 March
- Lord Owen briefs the EC Foreign Affairs Council in Brussels, which then reaffirms its 1 February Declaration of support for the Vance/Owen Peace Plan.

8-10 March
- Ambassador Ahrens chairs talks with the Croatian Government and Knin Serb representatives in Zagreb and Belgrade. Talks with Federal Republic of Yugoslavia (Serbia and Montenegro) Foreign Minister Jovanovic focus on Kosovo and Vojvodina.

8-11 March
- Working Group on Succession Issues meets in Geneva without Serbian, Montenegrin and Federal representatives.

11 March
- Co-Chairmen travel to Paris for talks with Chairman of the Arbitration Commission, Mr. Badinter, President Mitterand and Foreign Minister Dumas. They are later joined by President Milosevic.

12 March
- Lord Owen meets the UN Secretary-General Boutros-Ghali and representatives of the Security Council.

16 March
- Co-Chairmen brief representatives of the Permanent Five in New York.
- Lord Owen later holds talks with Mr. Bartholomew and with the Danish Ambassador to the UN.

17 March
- Ambassadors Ahrens and Okun resume talks with Croatian Government representatives in Geneva.
- The Co-Chairmen meet separately Bosnian Prime Minister Akmadzic, Mr. Boban and Dr. Karadzic to discuss maps and interim arrangements for the Bosnian Peace Plan.

18 March
- In response to the Bosnian Serb blockading of a humanitarian aid convoy heading for Srebrenica, the Co-Chairmen meet Federal Republic of Yugoslavia (Serbia and Montenegro) Foreign Minister Jovanovic, calling on him to intervene.
- Co-Chairmen hold talks with President Izetbegovic and Dr. Karadzic.

19 March
- Lord Owen continues to try to lift the blockade on the humanitarian aid convoy, talking with Dr. Karadzic and the Bosnian Serb Army Command.
- Co-Chairmen also meet President Izetbegovic, Mr. Boban and the Spanish Foreign Minister Solana.

20 March
- Co-Chairmen hold talks with Mr. Churkin and with the Norwegian Defence Minister Holst.

21 March
- Lord Owen holds meetings with UN Secretary-General Boutros-Ghali, Mr. Bartholomew, Mr. Churkin and Dr. Karadzic, while Mr. Vance is indisposed through ill health. Discussions focus on the evacuation of the wounded from Srebrenica, the question of detainees and release of POWs.

22 March
- Co-Chairmen hold meetings with the President of the UN Security Council, the Permanent Five and members of the Security Council.

23 March
- Lord Owen hosts talks with President Izetbegovic, Dr. Karadzic and Mr. Boban.
- Co-Chairmen meet Mr. Bartholomew and Security Council representatives.

24 March
- Co-Chairmen hold separate talks with President Izetbegovic, Dr. Karadzic and Mr. Boban. They later meet Mr. Bartholomew and the Macedonian Deputy Prime Minister Crvenkovski.

25 March
- Co-Chairmen chair a plenary of the Bosnian Peace Conference. President Izetbegovic and Mr. Boban sign the interim arrangements and the revised provincial map.

26 March
- UN Secretary-General Boutros-Ghali submits a report to the Security Council recommending further and decisive action on Bosnia.

30-31 March
- Ambassadors Ahrens and Okun resume talks on the Krajina talks in New York.

31 March
- Mr. Vance meets the Norwegian Foreign Minister Stoltenberg.

2 April
- Official announcement of Mr. Stoltenberg as successor to Mr. Vance.

5 April
- In Luxembourg, Lord Owen attends a session of the EC Foreign Affairs Council, which reaffirms support for the Vance/Owen Peace Plan and for strengthening sanctions.

5-7 April
- A session of the Working Group on Succession Issues is attended by all delegations, including new Federal Republic of Yugoslavia (Serbia and Montenegro) representatives.

7 April
- Lord Owen and Ambassadors Okun and Ahrens chair talks with representatives of the Croatian Government in Geneva.

14 April
- Lord Owen meets the non-aligned members of the Security Council in New York.
- UNSCR 819 condemns Serbian activity in Bosnia and Herzegovina, calls for Srebrenica to be made a safe area and demands that the relief effort be allowed to proceed unhindered.

16 April
- Lord Owen discusses the humanitarian relief situation in Srebrenica with President Milosevic but receives no guarantees that Bosnian Serb blockades will be lifted.
- UNSCR 820 calls on the Serbs to sign the Vance/Owen Peace Plan and threatens tightening of sanctions.

21 April
- Lord Owen, accompanied by Ambassadors Ahrens, Hall and Okun, meets Croatian Defence Minister Susak in Zagreb. Meetings are later held in Belgrade with President Cosic, President Milosevic, Dr. Karadzic and General Mladic.

22 April
- Lord Owen meets Macedonian President Gligorov in Skopje and Greek Prime Minister Mitsotakis in Athens to discuss Greek/Macedonian disputes.

23 April
- Lord Owen participates in Bilderberg Conference in Athens. He later holds talks with Macedonian President Gligorov in Skopje, with Montenegrin President Bulatovic in Podgorica and with President Milosevic in Belgrade.

24 April
- Talks continue with the Bosnian Serb leaders Dr. Karadzic, Mr. Krajisnik and General Mladic. In Zagreb, Lord Owen again meets Croatian Defence Minister Susak and Mr. Boban. President Izetbegovic and President Tudjman later join the talks and sign a cease-fire agreement in Central Bosnia.

25 April
- Lord Owen holds talks with UNPROFOR Force Commander General Wahlgren to discuss implementation of the Vance/Owen Peace Plan.

26 April
- Lord Owen goes to Bonn to brief German Foreign Minister Kinkel and to Copenhagen to meet the President of the EC Council of Ministers.

27 April
- Lord Owen meets French Prime Minister Balladur and Foreign Minister Juppé in Paris.

28 April
- UNSCR 821 recommends exclusion of Federal Republic of Yugoslavia (Serbia and Montenegro) from ECOSOC.

28-30 April
- Co-Chairmen hold talks with Greek and Macedonian representatives in New York.

30 April
- Ambassador Ahrens meets Knin Serb representatives led by Mr. Hadzic.
- Mr. Vance resigns as Co-Chairman of the Steering Committee of the International Conference on the Former Yugoslavia.

1 May
- Mr. Stoltenberg assumes responsibilities as Co-Chairman.

1-2 May
- Lord Owen and Mr. Vance co-chair a conference in Athens with representatives from the Federal Republic of Yugoslavia (Serbia and Montenegro), Croatia and all three ethnic groups in Bosnia. The Conference is also attended by Prime Minister Mitsotakis, Mr. Bartholomew and Mr. Churkin. Dr. Karadzic signs the Interim Arrangements and the provisional provincial map.

4 May
- Mr. Vance and Mr. Stoltenberg hold informal consultations in the Security Council and later meet UN Secretary-General Boutros-Ghali.

5 May
- Lord Owen meet NATO Secretary-General Worner and Dutch Foreign Minister Van den Broek in Brussels.
- Mr. Stoltenberg continues meetings with senior UN staff in New York and representatives of the Permanent Five.

6 May
- UNSCR 824 designates towns including Sarajevo as "safe areas".

7 May
- Lord Owen meets Mr. Stoltenberg in London.

9 May
- Lord Owen travels to Brussels where he meets the British Secretary of State Hurd.

10 May
- Lord Owen holds talks with Danish Foreign Minister Petersen and later attends the meeting of the EC Foreign Affairs Council in Brussels.

10-12 May
- Working Group on Succession Issues meets in Geneva under the Chairmanship of Ambassador Bojer.

11 May
- Mr. Stoltenberg, accompanied by his Political Adviser, Mr. Egeland, arrives in Geneva for briefings with Ambassadors Ahrens and Hall, Mr. Thornberry, General Wahlgren and Brigadier Wilson. He later meets Mrs. Ogata and then holds a press briefing.

12 May
- Mr. Stoltenberg and Mr. Egeland meet French Foreign Minister Juppé in Paris before travelling on to New York.
- Ambassador Ahrens meets Ambassador Miomir and Mr. Lerotic of the Croatian Government.

14 May
- Ambassador Ahrens holds talks in the Hague with the CSCE High Commissioner for National Minorities Van Der Stoel.

15 May
- The Co-Chairmen travel to Moscow where they hold talks with the Ambassadors of the EC Troika and of Norway.

16 May
- The Co-Chairmen meet Russian Foreign Minister Kozyrev and Mr. Churkin to discuss implementation of the Vance-Owen Peace Plan.

17 May
- Mr. Stoltenberg and Mr. Egeland meet British Secretary of State Hurd.

18 May
- Co-Chairmen meet President Izetbegovic and President Tudjman in Split and Mostar.

19 May
- Co-Chairmen attend meetings in Naples with Admiral Boorda and SACEUR.

20 May
- Lord Owen visits Minsk and Kiev to obtain Belorus and Ukrainian agreement to deploying additional troops to former Yugoslavia.

24 May
- General Morillon arrives in Geneva for a meeting with Lord Owen.

25 May
- UNSCR 827 establishes war crimes tribunal.
- Lord Owen meets Norwegian Foreign Minister Holst.

26 May
- Lord Owen briefs EC Ambassadors in Geneva on latest developments in the negotiating process.
- British Minister of State, Mr. Hogg, visits Geneva for talks with Lord Owen.

27 May
- Lord Owen meets the Chairman of the Working Group on Confidence Building Measures, Mr. Berasategui. He later holds talks with the Canadian Ambassador in Geneva and the Argentinean Permanent Representative to the UN.

28 May
- Bosnian Foreign Minister Silajdzic attends a meeting with Lord Owen.
- Lord Owen meets the Chairman of the Succession Issues Working Group, Ambassador Bojer.

2 June
- Co-Chairmen travel to Zagreb for talks with President Tudjman and with UNPROFOR.

3 June
- Co-Chairmen meet Dr. Karadzic in Pale.

4 June
- UNSCR 836 enforces protection of "safe areas".
- Co-Chairmen meet President Izetbegovic in Sarajevo and Mr. Boban in Split.

6 June
- Lord Owen briefs the British Secretary of State Hurd on the latest negotiations in former Yugoslavia.

7 June
- In Paris, Lord Owen meets French Foreign Minister Juppé and Co-Chairmen meet the Russian Envoy to former Yugoslavia, Mr. Churkin.

8 June
- Mr. Stoltenberg meets the UN Secretary-General Boutros-Ghali in Paris. In Luxembourg, Lord Owen has talks with Danish Foreign Minister Petersen.
- Lord Owen attends the EC Foreign Affairs Council, which focuses on European support for the Vance/Owen Peace Plan and considers the Washington proposal on safe areas.
- Lord Owen returns to Paris where he meets the French Chief of Defence Staff, Admiral Lanxade.

9 June
- Co-Chairmen meet the UN Secretary-General Boutros-Ghali in Paris.
- Co-Chairmen visit Belgrade for talks with President Milosevic. They also receive a delegation from the opposition Serbian Renewal Movement (SPO) which protests at the arrest and ill-treatment of its leader, Draskovic.

10 June
- In Tirana, the Co-Chairmen meet President Berisha. The Co-Chairmen travel to Podgorica to meet President Bulatovic and return to Belgrade for further talks with President Milosevic.
- UNSCR 838 agrees on need to establish border monitors.

12 June
- Co-Chairmen host a meeting of the Co-ordination Body in Geneva.

13 June
- Meeting of the Co-ordination Body continues.

14 June
- Co-Chairmen travel to Bonn for talks with German Foreign Minister Kinkel and Chancellor Kohl.

15 June
- Co-Chairmen attend Co-ordination Body meeting.

16 June
- Co-Chairmen host talks with President Milosevic, President Tudjman and President Izetbegovic, as well as representatives of the Bosnian Serbs and Croats.

17 June
- Co-Chairmen hold a press briefing on the latest negotiations. They later also brief EC Ambassadors.
- Co-Chairmen meet separately Bosnian Presidency member, Mr. Abdic, and Krajina Serb leader, Mr. Hadzic.

18 June
- Co-Chairmen travel to Copenhagen for talks with Danish Foreign Minister Petersen and Prime Minister Rasmussen.
- UNSCR 842 extends mandate to allow deployment of US troops in Macedonia.
- UNSCR 843 refers requests for sanctions assistance to the sanctions committee.
- UNSCR 844 provides for implementation of "safe areas" resolution and for reinforcement of UNPROFOR.
- UNSCR 845 urges settlement of Greek/Macedonian differences.

20 June
- Lord Owen returns to Copenhagen to meet Danish Foreign Minister Petersen and EC Foreign Ministers.

21 June
- Lord Owen attends European Council in Copenhagen.

22 June
- The European Council adopts a declaration on Bosnia and Herzegovina, in which it expresses its full confidence in the Co-Chairmen, calls for an immediate cease-fire and for the speedy implementation of UN SCRs on safe areas.
- Co-Chairmen attend talks between Croatian Government and Krajina representatives, hosted by Ambassador Ahrens, in Geneva.
- Lord Owen receives Monseigneur Tauran, Secretary of State for the Holy See.

23 June
- Co-Chairmen meet members of the Bosnian Presidency in Geneva. They then hold talks at a Swiss government villa with President Milosevic, President Tudjman, President Bulatovic, Dr. Karadzic and Mr. Boban. After a further separate meeting with the Co-Chairmen, the Presidency joins the Serb, Croat and Montenegrin Presidents for discussions at the villa.

24 June
- Krajina talks continue in Geneva.
- Co-Chairmen hold bilaterals with Dr. Karadzic and Mr. Boban.

28 June
- Co-Chairmen meet members of the Bosnian Presidency in Geneva.
- Mr. Stoltenberg attends a farewell dinner for General Wahlgren in Zagreb.

29 June
- Lord Owen travels to Brussels for a meeting with Belgian Foreign Minister Claes.
- In Geneva, Co-Chairmen host a dinner for the new Force Commander, General Cot and also for Mr. Eide, deputy SRSG.

30 June
- Ambassador Jean-Pierre Masset arrives in Geneva to take up his appointment as Deputy to Lord Owen.
- UNSCR 847 extends UNPROFOR's mandate by three months.

1 July
- Co-Chairmen host a meeting of the Expanded Steering Committee in Geneva.

5 July
- Ambassador Masset travels to Sarajevo to meet President Izetbegovic.

6 July
- Ambassadors Vollebaek and Ahrens hold talks in Geneva with representatives of the Croatian Government and of the Knin authorities.
- Lord Owen travels to Dublin for talks with Irish Foreign Minister Spring.
- Mr. Stoltenberg travels to Zagreb where he meets the Force Commander, General Cot and UNPROFOR staff.

7 July
- Lord Owen and Mr. Ahtisaari join Mr. Stoltenberg's party in Zagreb and have dinner with President Tudjman.

8 July
- Lord Owen and Mr. Stoltenberg travel to Belgrade, where they meet UNPROFOR and UNHCR representatives. Co-Chairmen meet representatives Draskovic's party (SPO) and Dragan Veselinov of the Farmers Party. Lord Owen later meets doctors treating Draskovic.
- Co-Chairmen hold talks with Federal Republic of Yugoslavia (Serbia and Montenegro) President Lilic and Foreign Minister Jovanovic. They later meet President Milosevic and Bosnian Serb leaders Dr. Karadzic and Mr. Krajisnik.

9 July
- Lord Owen returns to Zagreb where he meets Croatian Defence Minister Susak. President Tudjman joins them for lunch.
- Mr. Stoltenberg meets President Milosevic in Belgrade.

10 July
- Co-Chairmen meet President Tudjman in Zagreb.
- Co-Chairmen host a meeting of the Bosnian Presidency in Zagreb.

11 July
- Meeting of Bosnian Presidency continues.

12 July
- Mr. Stoltenberg meets the UN Secretary-General Boutros-Ghali in New York.
- Mr. Stoltenberg briefs the UN Security Council and representatives of the OIC.
- Ambassadors Vollebaek and Ahrens begin two days of talks with the Croatian authorities on the Krajina issue.

13 July
- Mr. Stoltenberg meets the Under Secretary-General for Peacekeeping Operations, Mr. Annan, Non-Aligned Members of the Security Council and the Belgian Permanent Representative to the UN.

14 July
- Mr. Stoltenberg meets Ambassador Nobilo, Croatian Permanent Representative to the UN in New York.
- Ambassadors Vollebaek and Ahrens travel to Belgrade for meetings with the Federal Republic of Yugoslavia (Serbia and Montenegro) authorities.

15 July
- Ambassadors Vollebaek and Ahrens meet local Serb representatives at Erdut in UNPA Sector East.

16 July
- In Geneva, Co-Chairmen attend meeting of the Working Group on Humanitarian Issues Working Group, chaired by Mrs. Ogata.
- Co-Chairmen hold talks with the representative of the Indonesian President.
- Ambassadors Vollebaek and Ahrens return to Zagreb for further talks with Croatian Government representatives.

17 July
- Co-Chairmen host talks between President Milosevic and President Tudjman at the Hotel de Ville in Geneva.

18 July
- Ambassador Vollebaek travels to Knin to meet the Krajina Serbs.

19 July
- Lord Owen attends the Foreign Affairs Council in Brussels.

26 July
- In Geneva, the Co-Chairmen hold talks with Mr. Abdic and have dinner with President Izetbegovic.
- In Zagreb, Ambassador Vollebaek begins two days of talks with Croatian Defence Minister Susak and General Bobetko.

27 July
- New round of negotiations begins in Geneva. Co-Chairmen hold separate talks with President Milosevic and Dr. Karadzic, the Bosnian Presidency, Mr. Bartholomew and Mr. Churkin. The day ends with a meeting attended by President Milosevic, President Tudjman, President Izetbegovic, President Bulatovic, Dr. Karadzic and Mr. Boban.

28 July
- Co-Chairmen host a series of bilateral discussions between the Bosnian Presidency, President Milosevic and Dr. Karadzic and President Tudjman and Mr. Boban. The day ends with a meeting of all heads of delegations.

29 July
- Co-Chairmen hold bilateral meetings with President Milosevic, Dr. Karadzic, President Tudjman and Mr. Boban, followed by a meeting of all heads of delegations.
- Lord Owen meets Mr. Borges, a Portuguese financial expert, to discuss the future economic structure of Bosnia and Herzegovina.

30 July
- Co-Chairmen host further talks with the heads of all delegations, as well as with Bosnian Opposition leaders.

31 July
- Co-Chairmen hold separate bilaterals with President Izetbegovic and Dr. Karadzic and Mr. Boban and Dr. Karadzic. The day ends with a trilateral with President Izetbegovic, Dr. Karadzic and Mr. Boban.

1 August
- Co-Chairmen meet Bosnian Opposition leaders and Mr. Bartholomew. After separate talks with Dr. Karadzic and Mr. Boban, a further trilateral is held with President Izetbegovic and the Bosnian Serb and Croat leaders.

2 August
- Co-Chairmen hold separate talks with members of the Bosnian Opposition and with Dr. Karadzic. A meeting of heads of delegations lasts only 40 minutes.

3 August
- Following the Bosnian Presidency's refusal to continue to attend talks, the Co-Chairmen hold a bilateral with Dr. Karadzic and Mr. Boban. On their return to Geneva, President Milosevic, President Tudjman and President Bulatovic join the Co-Chairmen and President Izetbegovic for dinner at the villa.

4 August
- Co-Chairmen host bilaterals between President Milosevic and Dr. Karadzic, and President Tudjman and Mr. Boban.

5 August
- The Foreign Ministers of Senegal, Pakistan, Tunisia and Turkey, and the OIC Secretary-General call on the Co-Chairmen.
- Bosnian Presidency resumes talks with the Co-Chairmen.

6 August
- Co-Chairmen brief members of the Steering Committee on latest round of negotiations.

9 August
- Mr. Stoltenberg receives Mitsotakis' Chef de Cabinet and the Federal Republic of Yugoslavia (Serbia and Montenegro) Ambassador, Mr. Pavicevic.
- Talks resume, with a meeting attended by President Izetbegovic, Dr. Karadzic and Mr. Boban.

10 August
- Co-Chairmen hold separate meetings with President Izetbegovic, Dr.Karadzic and Mr. Boban.

11 August
- Mr. Bartholomew calls on the Co-Chairmen to introduce his successor as US Special Envoy, Ambassador Charles Redman.
- Co-Chairmen hold separate talks with Dr. Karadzic, President Izetbegovic and Mr. Boban.
- Ambassadors Vollebaek and Ahrens begin a new round of talks in Geneva with Croatian Government and Krajina Serb representatives.

12 August
- Co-Chairmen have separate meetings with Krajina Serb leader, Mr. Hadzic and the head of the Croatian delegation, Mr. Degoricia.
- Co-Chairmen meet the Bosnian Presidency, Dr. Karadzic and Mr. Boban. They also brief Mr. Bartholomew and Ambassador Redman.

16 August
- After a weekend break, the Co-Chairmen resume talks with President Izetbegovic, Mr. Boban and Dr. Karadzic.

17 August
- Co-Chairmen host bilaterals first with President Izetbegovic and Dr. Karadzic, then with President Izetbegovic and Mr. Boban. The day ends with a meeting of the three heads of delegations.
- Ambassadors Vollebaek and Ahrens travel to Zagreb to continue discussions with Croatian Government representatives on the Krajina.

18 August
- Co-Chairmen hold a meeting with President Izetbegovic and Mr. Boban. Dr. Karadzic joins the meeting later. All three parties approve the text of an agreement on Sarajevo.
- Ambassadors Vollebaek and Ahrens are received by President Tudjman on Brioni to further discuss the situation in the Krajina.

19 August
- Ambassador Redman calls on the Co-Chairmen for a briefing on latest developments regarding the map. President Milosevic, President Tudjman and President Bulatovic return to Geneva and attend a meeting of all heads of delegations.
- Ambassadors Vollebaek and Ahrens continue their talks, meeting the Krajina Serbs at Plitvice.

20 August
- Co-Chairmen host a series of talks with all parties and issue a package containing the constitutional papers and maps agreed upon during the negotiations. It is decided that the talks will resume on 30 August. They then brief Ambassador Redman to this effect.

23 August
- Lord Owen briefs EC Ambassadors. The Co-Chairmen then hold a press conference.

30 August
- Co-Chairmen hold a meeting with Ambassador Redman.

31 August
- Co-Chairmen hold a series of talks. First, with President Izetbegovic and Mr. Silajdzic. Second, with President Milosevic, President Tudjman, President Bulatovic, Dr. Karadzic and Mr. Boban. Briefing with Ambassador Redman.

2 September
- Lord Owen briefs EC Ambassadors.

7 September
- Co-Chairmen meet Russian Ambassador.

14 September
- Co-Chairmen meet President Izetbegovic and Foreign Minister Silajdzic

14 September
- Meeting in Geneva of ICFY expanded Steering Committee

16 September
- Co-Chairmen meeting Mr. Krajisnik and Mr. Buha in Podgorica. Mr. Krajisnik accompanies Co-Chairmen to Geneva for meeting with President Izetbegovic and Foreign Minister Silajdzic.

17 September
- Co-Chairmen meet President Izetbegovic, Mr. Filipovic, Mr. Krajisnik and Mr. Buha - Muslim-Serb joint statement issued.

17 September
- Co-Chairmen travel to Istanbul for meeting with Foreign Minister Cetin.
- Co-Chairmen meet President Gligorov and Prime Minister Crvenkovski in Skopje, followed by a visit to UNPROFOR contingent in Skopje and to the troops on the border with Serbia
- Co-Chairmen meet President Milosevic and Dr. Karadzic in Belgrade

18 September
- Co-Chairmen meet President Tudjman, Mr. Boban and Mr. Susak in Split

19 September
- Co-Chairmen visit Neum area and have discussions with Franco-German technical team.

20 September
- Co-Chairmen meet parties and President Milosevic, President Bulatovic and President Tudjman on HMS Invincible.

22 September
- Co-Chairmen attend North Atlantic Council meeting.

28 September
- Meeting of Muslim Sabor in Sarajevo.

29 September
- Bosnian Assembly votes for peace plan but only if territories captured by force are returned.

30 September
- Lord Owen meets Ambassador Redman.
- Co-Chairmen meet Mrs. Ogata.

30 September
- UNSCR 869 is passed extending UNPROFOR mandate to 1 October 1993.

1 October
- UNSCR 870 is passed extending UNPROFOR mandate until 5 October 1993.

4 October
- UNSCR 871 extends UNPROFOR mandate until 31 March 1994.

5 October
- Co-Chairmen brief Foreign Affairs Council in Luxembourg.

6 October
- Lord Owen meets Chairman of Working Group on Economic Issues, Mr. Durieux.

11 October
- Lord Owen meets Foreign Minister Kinkel in Bonn.

12 October
- Ambassador Masset and Ambassador Ahrens brief FCO officials in London, and Quai d'Orsay officials in Paris.
- Lord Owen meets Portuguese Foreign Minister in Lisbon.

15 October
- Lord Owen in Rome for meetings with the Pope and Foreign Minister Andreatta.

17 October
- Co-Chairmen meet President Milosevic and Foreign Minister Jovanovic outside in a government villa near Belgrade.

18 October
- Co-Chairmen arrive in Zagreb.

20 October
- Lord Owen meets Ambassador Redman in London.

21 October
- Lord Owen meets Foreign Minister Kooijmans in The Hague.

25 October
- Lord Owen meets Foreign Minister Papoulias in Athens.

26 October
- Lord Owen meets Irish Foreign Minister Spring in Luxembourg.

26 October
- Lord Owen briefs Foreign Affairs Council meeting in Luxembourg.

28-31 October
- Mr. Stoltenberg in Zagreb and Belgrade.

3 November
- Co-Chairmen meet UNHCR officials.

4 November
- Co-Chairmen give Press Conference.

8-9 November
- Mr. Stoltenberg in Sarajevo and Split.

11 November
- Lord Owen meets Croatian Defence Minister Susak and Ambassador Zuzalj in London.

12 November
- Lord Owen meets President Milosevic and Dr. Karadzic in a government villa near Belgrade.

17 November
- International War Crimes Tribunal (set up by UNSCR 827) holds inaugural meeting in The Hague.

17 November
- Lord Owen meets President Mitterand in Paris.

18 November
- Lord Owen meets Ambassador Redman.
- Lord Owen meets leaders of Bosnian Parties in Geneva for meeting with Mrs. Ogata on humanitarian issues.
- Lord Owen meets Mrs. Ogata.

21 November
- Lord Owen meets British Secretary of State Hurd in Luxembourg.

22 November
- Lord Owen meets Belgian Foreign Minister Claes in Luxembourg.

22 November
- Lord Owen briefs Foreign Affairs Council attended by Generals Cot and Briquemont.

29 November
- Meeting EC Foreign Ministers with parties, President Milosevic, President Bulatovic and President Tudjman in Geneva hosted by Co-Chairmen.
- Co-Chairmen have dinner with President Tudjman and President Milosevic.

30 November -2 December
- Co-Chairmen continue talks with parties.
- Lord Owen briefs EC Ambassadors.

3 December
- Mr. Yasushi Akashi appointed as UN Secretary-General's Special Representative for ex-Yugoslavia: Mr. Stoltenberg to continue as Co-Chairman.

9 December
- Co-Chairmen meet President Milosevic and Dr. Karadzic in a government villa near Belgrade.

10 December
- Lord Owen briefs EC Foreign Ministers in Brussels.

17 December
- Co-Chairmen, Belgian Foreign Minister Claes, and EU Commissioner Van den Broek meet Prime Minister Silajdzic and Foreign Minister Ljubljankic in Vienna.
- Co-Chairmen meet President Milosevic, Dr. Karadzic, Croatian National Security Adviser Sarinic and Mr. Akmadzic in Belgrade.
- Sarinic returns with Co-Chairmen to Vienna to meet Foreign Minister Silajdzic.

21 December
- Co-Chairmen meets parties, President Milosevic, President Bulatovic and President Tudjman in Geneva.

22 December
- Co-Chairmen and EU Ministers meet Parties in Brussels.

23 December
- Co-Chairmen continue talks.

1994

4 January
- Co-Chairman meet Bosnian Prime Minister Silajdzic and Croatian Foreign Minister Granic in Vienna.

5 January
- Co-Chairmen meet President Milosevic and Dr. Karadzic in a government villa near Belgrade.

16-17 January
- Co-Chairmen brief Greek Foreign Minister Papoulias in Athens.

17 January
- Co-Chairmen meet OIC Contact Group in Geneva

18 January
- Next round of peace negotiations begin in Geneva.

19 January
- Negotiations continue in Geneva.

31 January - 1 February
- Co-Chairman meet Russian Foreign Minister Kozyrev in Moscow.

2 February
- Steering Committee meeting in Geneva.

2-4 February
- Co-Chairmen visit neighbouring countries: Romania, Bulgarian and Albania. In Romania they have meetings with Romanian Foreign Minister Melescanu and President Iliescu, in Bulgaria they have meetings with Bulgarian Foreign Minister Daskalov and President Zhelyu Zhelev and in Albania, they have a meeting with President Berisha.
- Co-Chairmen then fly to Rome for meeting with Italian Foreign Minister Andreatta.

6 February
- Co-Chairmen go Belgrade for meetings with Dr. Karadzic etc

7 February
- Lord Owen attends Foreign Affairs Council in Brussels.

9 February
- Co-Chairmen meet Balkan Foreign Ministers in Geneva.

10 February
- Co-Chairmen meet with all parties in next round of peace negotiations

11 February
- Co-Chairmen have breakfast meeting with senior Canadian Officials in Geneva.

12-13 February
- Talks continue.

16 February
- Lord Owen addresses Foreign Affairs Committee in Brussels.

16 February
- Lord Owen meets Foreign Minister Apostolides in Brussels.

23 February
- Co-Chairmen go to Zagreb for a meeting with Mr. Akashi and Mr. Annan.

1 March
- Bosnian Prime Minister Silajdzic, Croatian Foreign Minister Granic and Bosnian Croat leader Mr. Zubak in Washington sign framework federation agreement between Muslims and Bosnian Croats as well as outline agreement on a confederation of the federation with the Republic of Croatia.

2 March
- Lord Owen briefs EU Ambassadors in Geneva

4 March
- UN Security Council adopt Resolution 900 calling for a final lifting of the siege of Sarajevo and for the restoration of public services in the city.

12 March
- General Delic and General Roso, on behalf of the Bosnian Muslims and Croats respectively, sign agreement in Split on the future formation of a federal army.

17 March
- Agreement on opening of 'blue routes' on the Sarajevo-Visoko route and between Muslim and Serb populated areas of Sarajevo from 23 March signed by Dr. Hasan Muratovic, Deputy Prime Minister of the Bosnian government and Momcilo Krajisnik, President of the Bosnian Serb parliament.

17 March
- Co-Chairmen go to Washington for signing of the Federation agreement between the Bosnian Muslim and Bosnian Croats.

18 March
- In Washington cover letter committing parties to establish a federation, to negotiate jointly with the Serbs and to work towards setting up a Confederation with Croatia signed by President Izetbegovic, President Tudjman, Mr. Zubak and Bosnian Prime Minister Silajdzic. Mr. Zubak and Foreign Minister Silajdzic sign a document endorsing the draft constitution of the federation. President Izetbegovic and President Tudjman sign a letter of intent on the confederation.

22 March
- Tuzla airport re-opened for UN flights.
- Ceasefire negotiations in Zagreb between delegations of the Croatian government and of the Krajina Serbs hosted by the Russian Embassy and attended by Russian special envoy Churkin and US Ambassador to Croatia Galbraith.

24 March
- Bosnian Serb parliament rejects joining Muslim/Croat Federation and demands that sanctions against Serbs are lifted.

25-26 March
- Lord Owen attends EU Foreign Ministers meeting in Ioannina, Greece.

27 March
- Bosnian Croat parliament endorses the federation agreement and proposes Mr. Zubak for president of the Federation.

27 March
- Lord Owen meets with President Milosevic in a government villa near Belgrade.

28 March
- Bosnian parliament approves framework agreement for Federation.

29 March
- Ceasefire agreement signed at Russian Embassy in Zagreb by Croatian Government representative Mr. Sarinic and Admiral Rakic for the Krajina Serbs.

30 March - 1 April
- Constituent Assembly of the Federation of Bosnia and Herzegovina established as Bosnian parliament adopts Constitutional Law on amendments to Bosnian Constitution.

31 March
- UN Security Council adopt Resolution 908 extending UNPROFOR mandate until 30 September 1994 authorising increase of UNPROFOR personnel by 3,500 troops with decisions on further troop requirements by 30 April and authorising extension of Close Air Support to Croatia.

11 April
- Lord Owen visits Paris for meeting with Chairman of Bosnian Serbs Krajisnik and Bosnian Vice President Koljevic.

12 April
- Co-Chairmen visit Zagreb for meeting with Akashi.

13 April
- Co-Chairmen travel to Sarajevo for meetings with General Rose, Mr. Churkin, Mr. Redman and President Izetbegovic. They then go on to Pale to meet with Dr. Karadzic and General Mladic.

18 April
- Lord Owen attends Foreign Affairs Council in Luxembourg

20 April
- Co-Chairmen travel to Moscow for meeting with Foreign Minister Kozyrev.

26 April
- First meeting of new Contact Group; Ambassador De Sedouy (France), Mr. Ludlow (UK), Mr. Steiner (Germany), Mr. Manning (UK), Mr. Redman (USA).

28 April
- Contact Group go to Zagreb, Sarajevo and Pale for meetings with parties.

29 April
- Lord Owen goes to Oslo for a meeting with Mr. Stoltenberg and Mr. Churkin.

5-6 May
- Contact Group goes to Zagreb, Sarajevo and Pale for meetings with Dr. Karadzic and President Izetbegovic.

11 May
- Vienna Agreement gives Bosniac-Croat Federation 58% of Bosnian territory; divides federation into 8 cantons; and determines composition of interim federal government.

12 May
- US Senate votes both for a mandatory unilateral lifting of the arms embargo and for a multilateral approach.

12 May
- Co-Chairmen go to Paris for meeting with Secretary-General, Mr. Akashi and General de Lapresle.

13 May
- Foreign Ministers of France, Russia, UK, USA, EU Troika (Greece, Belgium, Germany) plus Vice-president of Commission meet in Geneva: call for 4 month cessation of hostilities and call for negotiations to commence within 2 weeks under aegis of Contact Group on the basis of 51%/49% territorial division.

16-19 May
- Co-Chairmen travel to Belgrade and Zagreb for meetings with President Milosevic, Dr. Karadzic etc.

17-20 May
- Contact Group meet in Washington.

24-25 May
- Vienna conference on reconstruction of Sarajevo.

24 May
- Co-Chairmen meet with Contact Group in Geneva.

25-26 May
- Contact Group talks with Bosnian Federation and Bosnian Serbs in Talloires, France.

31 May

- Bosnian Constituent Assembly unanimously elects Mr. Zubak and Mr. Granic as President and Vice-President of Federation until federal elections, scheduled in 6 months. Assembly also endorses Washington and Vienna Agreements.

2 June

- Parties come to Geneva for cessation of hostilities talks chaired by Mr. Akashi.

4-5 June

- Contact Group meet with the Bosnian Federation and Bosnian Serbs at the French Mission in Geneva.

6 June

- Ceasefire talks, under auspices of Mr. Akashi, begin after delay in Geneva, once Muslim side acknowledge that Bosnian Serb forces have left the Gorazde exclusion zone.

7 June

- Milan Martic, President of the "RSK" meets Co-Chairmen and agrees to meeting with Croatian side in Plitvice on 16 June.

8 June

- Bosnian Federation and Bosnian Serbs agree cessation of offensive operations and provocative action for one month from 10 June. All prisoners of war to be liberated.

9 June

- US Congress votes for unilateral mandatory lifting of arms embargo.

10 June

- Draft Memorandum Of Understanding on the EU administration of Mostar initialled ad referendum by enlarged EU Troika and Bosniac and Bosnian Croat sides.

16 June

- Plitvice talks between Krajina Serbs and Croatian authorities cancelled.

21 June
- EU members of the Contact Group go to Brussels to brief the Ad Hoc Group on Former Yugoslavia.

24-25 June
- Co-Chairmen attend EU Summit in Corfu.

25 June
- Co-Chairmen go to Skopje to see President Gligorov then to Belgrade and Zagreb.

28 June
- Contact Group meet in Paris.

4 July
- Contact Group meet in Geneva at German Mission.

5 July
- Contact Group Foreign Ministers meet at Russian Mission in Geneva to discuss territorial division of Bosnia and Herzegovina.

7 July
- EU members of Contact Group brief the Ad Hoc Group on Former Yugoslavia in Brussels.

10 July
- Co-Chairmen go to Belgrade for a meeting with President Milosevic.

11 July
- Co-Chairmen go to Zagreb for a meeting with Mr. Akashi and President Tudjman.

15 July
- Contact Group meet in Washington.

18 July
- Lord Owen attends Foreign Affairs Council in Brussels.

19 July
- Contact Group meet in Geneva.

20 July
- Contact Group meet with parties in Geneva.

21 July
- Contact Group meet at US Mission in Geneva.

25 July
- Contact Group meet in Moscow.

28-29 July
- Contact Group meet in Geneva.

30 July
- Lord Owen attends ministerial meeting in Geneva with Foreign Ministers of Contact Group.

1 August
- Steering Committee Meeting in Geneva chaired by Mr. Stoltenberg.

12 August
- Mr. Stoltenberg and Brig-General Pellnäs go to Belgrade to meet President Milosevic.

13 August
- Mr. Stoltenberg travels to Pale to meet Dr. Karadzic. Brig-General Pellnäs visits border areas.

14 August
- Mr. Stoltenberg returns to Belgrade.

15 August
- Mr. Stoltenberg travels to New York to brief Secretary-General Boutros-Ghali.

23 August
- Co-Chairmen attend Succession Issues Working Group meeting in Geneva.

29 August
- Lord Owen holds meeting with German Foreign Minister Kinkel and President of the EU Council of Ministers.

31 August
- Co-Chairmen hold talks with Ambassadors Ahrens and Eide on the Krajina.

4 September
- Co-Chairmen, accompanied by Brig-General Pellnäs and Ambassador Ahrens, travel to Belgrade for evening meeting with President Milosevic.

5 September
- Co-Chairmen hold meeting with Mr. Mikelic in Belgrade, then travel via Dubrovnik and Prevlaka to Podgorica for meeting with President Bulatovic.

6 September
- Co-Chairmen travel to Zagreb to hold meeting with President Tudjman. After meeting in Zagreb they travel to Knin.

10 September
- Lord Owen attends informal meeting of EU Foreign Ministers, Usedom, Germany.

13 September
- Lord Owen meets Contact Group in Geneva.
- Establishment of ICFY Monitoring Mission to Federal Republic of Yugoslavia (Serbia and Montenegro). Brig-General Pellnäs to be Mission Coordinator.

20/21 September
- Lord Owen visits Washington during which he meets with US officials dealing with Bosnia and Herzegovina.

26 September
- Co-Chairmen visit Belgrade and meet with Brig-General Pellnäs for update on Border Monitoring Mission. They view border crossing point at Sremska Raca.

27 September
-   After further briefing at Mission Headquarters, Co-Chairmen hold a meeting with President Milosevic.

28 September
-   Co-Chairmen go to Budapest for a meeting with Prime Minister Guyla Horn.

30 September
-   Lord Owen meets Russian Foreign Minister Kozyrev in New York.

4 October
-   Lord Owen attends EU Foreign Affairs Council, Luxembourg.

5 October
-   Co-Chairmen travel to Geneva for Senior Official Level Expanded Steering Committee meeting.

10 October
-   Mr. Stoltenberg travels to New York to brief Security Council.

12 October
-   Co-Chairmen travel to Moscow for meeting with Russian Foreign Minister Kozyrev.

13 October
-   Co-Chairmen travel to Zagreb for meetings with President Tudjman.

14 October
-   Co-Chairmen travel to Belgrade for working lunch with President Milosevic; return to Zagreb.

15 October
-   Mr. Stoltenberg meets Brig-General Pellnäs in Vienna.

25 October
-   Lord Owen addresses lunchtime lecture on "The Break-up of Yugoslavia", Royal Geographical Society, London.

26 October
- Co-Chairmen travel to Belgrade to meet President Milosevic. They then travel to Zagreb to meet President Tudjman.

27 October
- Meeting in Zagreb with representatives from Croatian Government, headed by Mr. Sarinic, and Krajina Serbs headed by Mr. Mikelic.

31 October
- Lord Owen attends EU Foreign Affairs Council, Luxembourg

2 November
- Co-Chairmen travel to Zagreb.

3 November
- Co-Chairmen travel to Knin to meet Mr. Sarinic and Mr. Mikelic.

4 November
- Co-Chairmen in Zagreb to meet Foreign Minister Granic and Foreign Minister Jovanovic.

7 November
- Mr. Stoltenberg meets Secretary-General Boutros-Ghali, Mr. Akashi, Mr. Goulding, General de Lapresle and Major General Baril at the Palais des Nations, Geneva.

9 November
- Co-Chairmen travel to Belgrade to meet President Milosevic.

14 November
- Co-Chairmen travel to Zagreb.

15 November
- Negotiations on economic matters resume with Mr. Sarinic and Mr. Mikelic in Zagreb.

25 November
- Co-Chairmen travel to Zagreb to meet President Tudjman. They then travel to Belgrade to meet President Milosevic and the return to Zagreb to meet President Tudjman.

1 December
- Lord Owen travels to Geneva to finalise wording of Economic Agreement. The Co-Chairmen then travel to Zagreb.

2 December
- Co-Chairmen attend Economic Agreement signing ceremony with Mr. Sarinic and then travel to Knin for signing ceremony with Mr. Mikelic.

2 December
- Co-Chairmen leave Zagreb for Brussels to attend meeting of Foreign Ministers of Contact Group.

3 December
- Mr. Stoltenberg returns to Geneva for meeting with Secretary-General.

5 December
- Lord Owen travels to Poole, Dorset to address NATO senior officers Joint Warfare Seminar.

6 December
- Co-Chairmen travel to Belgrade for talks with President Milosevic and Mr. Mikelic.

23 December
- Lord Owen to Belgrade to meet President Milosevic and Mr. Mikelic.

1995

15 January
- Mr. Nieminen takes over as Coordinator of the ICFY Mission in Belgrade.

17 January
- Lord Owen meets with French officials in Paris.

23 January
- Lord Owen attends EU Foreign Affairs Council in Brussels.

30 January
- Lord Owen meets with French Foreign Minister Juppé in Paris.

31 January
- Co-Chairmen attend ICFY Steering Committee in Geneva.

1 February
- Co-Chairmen meet Mr. Mikelic and Mr. Sarinic in Belgrade.

2 February
- Co-Chairmen meet President Milosevic in Belgrade.
- Co-Chairmen meet President Tudjman in Zagreb.
- Co-Chairmen meet French officials in Paris.

6 February
- Lord Owen attends Foreign Affairs Council in Brussels.

9 February
- Mr. Stoltenberg meets Swedish Foreign Minister and Defence Minister.

14 February
- Co-Chairmen meet with Italian Foreign Minister Agnelli in Rome.

15 February
- Co-Chairmen meet President Milosevic in Belgrade.

16 February
- Co-Chairmen meet Foreign Minister Kozyrev in Moscow.

23 February
- Mr. Stoltenberg meets Secretary-General in New York.

3 March
- Mr. Stoltenberg meets Secretary-General in Vienna.

5 March
- Co-Chairmen meet Mr. Akashi in Zagreb.
- Co-Chairmen meet Mr. Nieminen in Belgrade.

6 March
- Co-Chairmen meet President Milosevic in Belgrade.

7 March
- Co-Chairmen meet Mr. Sarinic in Zagreb.

8 March
- Mr. Stoltenberg meets American Ambassador Galbraith in Zagreb.

10 March
- Co-Chairmen attend Steering Committee in Geneva.

10 March
- Lord Owen lunches with EU Heads of Mission in Geneva.

14 March
- Lord Owen meets with House of Commons Foreign Affairs Committee

16 March
- Lord Owen meets with Spanish Foreign Minister Solana in Madrid.

16 March
- Mr. Stoltenberg meets Finnish Under-Secretary of State .

17 March
- Lord Owen meets with Russian Ambassador Adamishin in London.

19 March
- Mr. Stoltenberg meets Mr. Akashi in Zagreb.

20 March
- Mr. Stoltenberg meets President Milosevic in Belgrade.

21 March
- Mr. Stoltenberg meets Mr. Sarinic in Zagreb.

22 March
- Lord Owen meets with French officials at Quai d'Orsay in Paris.

23 March
- Co-Chairmen meet Mr. Mikelic in Belgrade.
- Mr. Stoltenberg meets President Tudjman in Zagreb.
- Lord Owen meets Robert Fraser, US representative on Contact Group, in Belgrade.

24 March
- Lord Owen meets Prime Minister Major.

27 March
- Lord Owen meets for briefing with Foreign Press Association in London.
- Lord Owen meets British Foreign Secretary Hurd.

B. MINISTERIAL MEETING, 16 DECEMBER 1992

Editor's Note: On 16 December 1992, a Ministerial Level Meeting of the Steering Committee of the International Conference on the Former Yugoslavia was held in Geneva to review the efforts of the Conference since it began working on 3 September 1992. The Statements made at the Ministerial meeting provide an indication of the international community's reaction to continuing conflict in the former Yugoslavia. The texts of Statements distributed at the meeting are reproduced below.

47. OPENING STATEMENT OF MR. CYRUS VANCE*

President Felber, Honourable Ministers, Your Excellencies, Ladies and Gentlemen, Lord Owen and I extend to you our warmest good wishes and welcome you to this Ministerial Meeting of the Steering Committee of the International Conference.

At the outset it is my privilege to read a message from the Secretary-General, Dr. Boutros-Ghali.

Distinguished delegates, your presence here today demonstrates the deep concern of the international community over the grave situation in former Yugoslavia. Conflict persists in Bosnia and Herzegovina. More than 3 million refugees and displaced persons from the three communities continue to depend on international aid for their survival. Over the last three months more than 7,000 troops have joined the command of the United Nations Protective Force in Bosnia and Herzegovina, helping to bring urgently-needed humanitarian assistance to the civilian populace. While much has been done, the conflict endures - with the risk of spreading to other areas of the Balkans.

The Conflict in Bosnia and Herzegovina is but the most recent explosion in the violent break-up of post-Tito Yugoslavia. The roots of the violence lie deep in the region's complex history of mutual grievances, political ambitions, territorial claims, religious differences, and ethnic rivalries.

But to say that the causes of the conflict are complex does not relieve us of the responsibility to seek just and equitable solutions. It is essential that we bend every effort to unify our actions to bring the fighting to an end, to prevent the conflict from spreading, to provide humanitarian assistance to all, and to find a lasting political solution to the problems of Bosnia and Herzegovina and the former Yugoslavia as a whole.

---

* Ministerial Level Meeting of the Steering Committee of the International Conference on the Former Yugoslavia, Geneva, 16 December 1992.

In the 104 days since the International Conference began, we and our many colleagues, civilian and military, and other institutions and organizations, have worked to push forward on a wide range of problems. All are difficult, but all are essential.

They have included:

- Improving relations between Croatia and the Federal Republic of Yugoslavia;
- Initiating serious dialogue among the leaders of Croatia, the Federal Republic of Yugoslavia, and Bosnia and Herzegovina;
- Working to stabilize the situation in the UN Protected Areas in Croatia, including such thorny problems as the return of refugees;
- Demilitarizing the Prevlaka peninsula in the context of an agreed withdrawal of the Yugoslav army from Croatian territory on October 20;
- Deploying a large United Nations peace-keeping operation in Bosnia and Herzegovina to protect humanitarian convoys;
- Establishing a Mixed Military Working Group in Sarajevo to bring about a cessation of hostilities and to address other important military issues:
- Constructing a constitutional framework for Bosnia and Herzegovina;
- Working to strengthen existing sanctions and measures for enforcement;
- Deploying preventive peace-keeping troops in Macedonia, as well as conducting preventive diplomacy in Kosovo, Sandjak, and Vojvodina.
- Actively cooperating with the UN Commission on Human Rights and its Special Rapporteur, as well as with the Commission of Experts on violations of humanitarian law, including war crimes.

Promoting a cessation of hostilities and constitutional settlement in Bosnia and Herzegovina, remain our priority objectives. It has not been easy, and I must tell you that all three sides have at different times created obstacles to the realization of these goals. Nonetheless some progress - although not nearly enough - has been made. After lengthy and strenuous efforts by the United Nations Commanders, a tripartite Mixed Military Working Group has been established in Sarajevo. The results have not been negligible and the overall level of violence has been reduced, although not ended.

From the outset Lord Owen and I have proceeded on the basis that our essential task is to bring about a durable political solution. Practically speaking, there are no serious alternatives to a negotiated political settlement. It is important, therefore, that our actions work consistently to this end. We hope very much that this meeting will send a clear message to all parties concerned that incentives are available to those who cooperate in the peace process, and that costs will be borne by those who do not. Let me briefly share with you our thinking on a range of specific issues which concern us all.

Macedonia is undergoing an acute crisis. To help defuse it, the Security Council has just approved the Secretary-General's recommendation that a United Nations peace-keeping operation - a preventive deployment - be established in Macedonia. An infantry battalion consisting of some 700 armed troops, with logistic support, military observers, and UN civilian police will perform this task. The Co-Chairmen join the Security Council in attaching great urgency to some immediate deployment.

Kosovo is no less pressing a problem. It is doubtful whether at present we could receive the required consent to insert United Nations peace-keeping forces into this province of Serbia, but in any event the CSCE already maintains a presence in Kosovo. We welcome the CSCE decision in Stockholm to enlarge its civilian monitor mission. Given the heightened tension on all sides involved in the Kosovo issue, conflict could break out there as much by misadventure as by design. Therefore the good offices role of the CSCE mission is of critical importance. Over the long run serious improvements must be made in Kosovo. During the last three months the Conference's Special Group on Kosovo has carried out intensive discussions with all sides on a broad range of social, educational, and political issues. We believe that these efforts will help to improve stability and will bear fruit. Restoration of genuine autonomy to Kosovo remains a principal goal.

With respect to the *no-fly zone* over Bosnia and Herzegovina, we believe that breaches of the Security Council's resolution need to be examined. In this connection it is essential to understand the factual situation. The fact is that UNPROFOR thus far has *not* seen any use of fixed-wing fighter aircraft in support of combat operations in Bosnia and Herzegovina sin^Oe the no-fly-zone resolution was passed more that two months ago. UNPROFOR has tracked helicopters on a number of occasions and has been informed of allegations that helicopters have been used in an offensive role. This, however, has *not* been confirmed by UNPROFOR. These facts should be taken into account in any consideration of a Chapter VII determination. The Security Council must also consider the probable consequences of an enforcement action, particularly the endangerment of UNPROFOR personnel, and UNHCR, ECMM and unarmed humanitarian workers in Bosnia and Herzegovina and elsewhere in the former Yugoslavia.

Another important issue is the suggested lifting of the *arms embargo*. Two weeks ago in Jeddah, Lord Owen and I were able to assess the depth of feeling of the Islamic countries in favour of this actions. Yet I must tell you that, in our view, such action would be unwise. It would widen and deepen the war in Bosnia and Herzegovina. It would encourage the delivery of more sophisticated and more destructive weapons to all the warring parties, and could also lead to the spread of the conflict throughout the Balkan region.

Another subject under consideration is that of *security zones* or safe havens for civilians caught up in the fighting. Advocates of this policy offer several variants and it is not always clear what is being proposed, I believe we should examine such proposals carefully, but Lord Owen and I cannot support any policy that would contribute to ethnic cleansing. We continue to believe the best "safe haven" lies in an overall cessation of hostilities.

With respect to the *refugee situation*, Mrs. Ogata will be reporting on her activities and the requirements on the ground. Inside and outside of Bosnia and Herzegovina more than 3 million refugees and displaced persons still need assist ance. Inside the country, thanks to the heroic efforts of UNHCR workers, UNPROFOR and others, food and other supplies are getting through to many places that had not been reached before. But international relief efforts remain dangerous, and still encounter obstruction and intimidation. More must be done by all of us to improve the lot of innocent civilians.

Human rights issues have been at the forefront of or concerns since our first day in Geneva. In a message we sent to the UN Commission on Human Rights on November 30 we again condemned ethnic cleansing and other violations of human rights and invited the Commission to give attention to the important question of protecting the rights of minorities.

We have cooperated with the International Committee of the Red Cross, and we pay tribute to President Sommaruga and his colleagues for their noble and unsung work day in and day out - particularly on prisoners release and evacuation. In view of the urgency of this matter, and deep interest in it, he will report on the latest developments.

We have also taken action on allegations of war crimes and other breaches of international humanitarian law. We have sought to help the Commission of Experts bring about a forensic examination of the mass grave site of Ovcara near Vukovar and this is in train this week. Lord Owen and I believe that atrocities committed in the former Yugoslavia are unacceptable, and persons guilty of war crimes should be brought to justice. We, therefore, recommend the establishment of an international criminal court.

This is the path we have followed since assuming our mission, and we shall continue to press ahead the strategies I have indicated. Finally, in his remarks Lord Owen will address the steps we plan to take in the immediate future to expedite our endeavours. Thank you.

48. Speech by the Rt. Hon. the Lord Owen[*]

As Co-Chairmen we are both convinced that we should press for an overall settlement to be achieved as soon as humanly possible. This will have to include the restoration of full autonomy for Kosovo where the situation is particularly dangerous. Realism tells us that there are many formidable problems ahead.

We never doubted that the parties in Bosnia and Herzegovina cannot negotiate a settlement on their own and that there will have to be considerable pressure brought to bear on all three parties at various times. Many of the countries sitting around this table have a part to play in that process.

One of our concerns is that the Bosnia and Herzegovina Government is sadly increasingly becoming representative only of the Muslim population. We are travelling tomorrow to Zagreb to meet with President Tudjman and President Izetbegovic in an attempt to bring together the Bosnian Muslims and Bosnian Croats into a more representative Presidency. We will try, though we know it will be very difficult, to persuade both sides to come to some measure of agreement on a provincial map for Bosnia and Herzegovina.

So far we have failed to get the Bosnia and Herzegovina Government, at political level, to come around the same table with the Bosnian Serbs and Bosnian Croats. With so much of the territory in which they would normally be in the majority under the control of the Bosnian Serbs they are afraid of negotiating now, as they see it, from a position of weakness. We will, I expect, need the support of countries particularly in the Islamic world to encourage President Izetbegovic to participate constructively in January. But if he is to compromise we will have to be able to demonstrate that we are capable of rolling back the present Bosnian Serb front line and obtaining their agreement to live under a rule of law that allows for ethnic cleansing to be reserved.

The Bosnian Croatian position presents for the moment the least difficulty and indeed could become a helpful factor in negotiations but there are still parts of the Croatian Army in Bosnia and Herzegovina and some unauthorised flights from Zagreb.

The overriding challenge is, however, to roll back the Bosnian Serbs and here General Mladic is becoming even more important. He is a determined officer. While he probably listens to President Cosic and General Panic he is not controlled by them. He answers to President Milosevic.

It is Belgrade, above all, who control the main pressure points on the Bosnian

---

[*] Ministerial Level Meeting of the Steering Committee of the International Conference on the Former Yugoslavia, Geneva, 16 December 1992.

Serbs. Dr. Karadzic ultimately answers to Belgrade and in effect the Bosnian Serb military efforts and economy, apart from food, is critically dependent on decisions taken in Belgrade. We are right therefore in believing that Belgrade has - if it cares to exercise it - the capacity to deliver a settlement.

That is why it is fundamentally important that all existing sanctions against Serbia and Montenegro are maintained and indeed reinforced. We cannot afford to allow sanctions to be evaded as happened a few weeks ago with the oil embargo. We need a person who can string together intelligence information from different countries and report evasion and potential sanctions busting to the Sanctions Committee. Having adopted at last stop and search in the Adriatic we must have stop and search on the Danube. It is prudent too for us all to plan for new and tougher sanctions. They may be needed against an intransigent new Serbian Government, but we as Co-Chairmen do not believe that they should be applied or even threatened until we have given whatever new government emerges in Belgrade the opportunity to contribute positively to the negotiation process. Whatever happens on 20 December, President Cosic will remain the President.

We intend to proceed on a determined and persistent path towards a negotiated settlement.

Between Christmas and New Year Dr. Boutros Boutros-Ghali will be visiting Geneva and during that time he has agreed to meet with us and President Cosic and also separately with President Tudjman. We may or may not seek to bring the Presidents together.

If no candidate in the Serbian Presidential elections obtains more than 50 per cent of the vote there will have to be a run-off, and the most likely time for a second election is thought to be 3 January. The results would not be known before 4 or 5 January and there will be a public holiday because of the Orthodox Christmas on 7 and 8 January. We may find therefore that we have not an authoritative government to deal with in Belgrade until the week beginning 11 January. Yet neither of us believes it is acceptable in terms of the situation on the ground in Bosnia and Herzegovina or indeed in terms of world opinion for us to wait until then.

We are therefore inviting to Geneva on 2 January President Izetbegovic, Dr. Karadzic and Mr. Boban and asking them to bring their senior military commander. We want not only a sustainable cessation of hostilities and the demilitarisation of Sarajevo, but also to try to reach an agreement on a pull back from the military front line in a way which reinforces and goes with the grain of an overall political settlement. We will also be trying to ensure free access of all citizens in and out of cities and towns that have been under siege and the free movement of humanitarian aid. We will be inviting Belgrade and Zagreb to send representation at the level they think appropriate to these talks. We will plan to follow these talks up when the political situation is clearer in Belgrade with further meetings in the middle of January.

We believe that only when this process has been undertaken will we be able to analyse the potential for a genuine negotiated settlement which fulfils the principles laid down for this Conference at the end of August in London. If any party in Bosnia and Herzegovina or any government in Zagreb or Belgrade is obstructing such a settlement we will not hesitate to bring their attitude and action to the attention of this Conference. We cannot fix deadlines or milestones but when a new administration is established in the United States it may well be appropriate to adopt new measures in the Security Council and even meet again at Ministerial level.

At this stage, however, neither Cyrus Vance nor I are faint hearted about the prospect of a negotiated settlement. A great deal of time and effort has been invested in a negotiated settlement since we met together for the first time here on 3 September. We intend to capitalise on that investment. We do believe, however, that four additional new measures should be considered.

Firstly, consideration of the establishment of an international Criminal Court through a Resolution by the Security Council. It would surely be wrong if the practitioners of ethnic cleansing are not brought to justice.

Secondly, consideration of a Chapter VII determination to make it possible to enforce a no-fly ban by the Security Council if and only if infringements continue. This is a two stage process for the implications of any actual enforcement for UN troops, UNHCR and others on the ground in Bosnia and Herzegovina demand the deepest analysis by members of the Security Council. The Secretary General will also need to be fully involved in any decisions in the timing and the type of any enforcement action and his decision to ask NATO for planning assistance will help this process.

Thirdly, consideration to toughening existing sanctions through a mechanism for using delicate intelligence and other information so as to report evasions to the UN Sanctions Committee at the earliest moment.

Fourthly, consideration to a Security Council Resolution on Kosovo making it clear that all parties should show restraint but that any further internal suppression would be considered a threat to the peace and that negotiated autonomy is an essential and urgent priority.

We both remain firmly against making any change in the Security Council arms embargo which was passed in September 1991 and covers the whole territory of the former Yugoslavia. Now is the time to test the parties inside Bosnia and Herzegovina and the countries surrounding Bosnia and Herzegovina at the negotiating table. It must never be forgotten that peace will only come to the former Yugoslavia through negotiations. To bring that about we need a judicious use of moral, political, economic and military pressures.

49. PRESENTATION BY GENERAL NAMBIAR, UNPROFOR*

INTRODUCTION

1. I have been asked by the Co-Chairmen of the International Conference on former Yugoslavia to apprise you of the activities of UNPROFOR in the region. This I shall do by first very briefly recapitulating some of the more important aspects of the various Security Council Resolutions and reports of the Secretary-General that impact on our mandate and the scope of our activities in the UNPAs and in Bosnia and Herzegovina.

2. I shall then briefly apprise you of the activities in the UNPAs since the Mission was set up, the present status, an assessment of the problems we face, and some recommendations. I shall then do the same, in some greater detail, in regard to Bosnia and Herzegovina.

3. My colleagues Mr. Cedric Thornberry, Director of Civil Affairs and Deputy Chief of Mission, and Maj Gen Phillipe Morillon, Commander B & H Command, and I, would then be available to field your questions.

MANDATE

4. Allow me to first display a few extracts from Annex III to the Secretary-General's report of 11 December 1991 (Security Council document S/23280) ("the Vance Plan") which outlined a concept for the peace keeping operation:-

   (a) "United Nations troops and police monitors would be deployed in certain areas in Croatia, designated as United Nations Protected Areas."

   (b) "The UNPAs would be areas in Croatia in which the Secretary General judged that special arrangements were required during an *interim period* to ensure that a lasting ceasefire was maintained. They would be areas in which Serbs constitute the majority or a substantial minority of the population and where inter communal tensions have led to armed conflict in

---

* Ministerial Level Meeting of the Steering Committee of the International Conference on the Former Yugoslavia, Geneva, 16 December 1992.

the recent past. As already stated, the special arrangements in these areas would be of an interim nature and would not prejudge the outcome of the political negotiations for a comprehensive settlement of the Yugoslav crisis."

(c) "The infantry units would be deployed throughout the UNPAs. They would be lightly armed but would use armoured personnel carriers and helicopters. They would control access to the UNPAs by establishing check points on all roads and principal tracks leading into them and at important junctions inside them. At these check points they would stop and, if necessary, search vehicles and individuals to ensure that no military formations or armed groups entered the UNPAs and that no weapons, ammunition, explosives or other military equipment were brought into them."

5. When the decisions were being taken in February 1992, a number of complications remained; however as the Secretary General stated in his report of 15 February 1992 (Security Council document S/23592):

> "... after careful deliberation, I have come to the conclusion that the danger that a United Nations peace-keeping operation will fail because of lack of cooperation from the parties is less grievous than the danger that delay in its despatch will lead to a break down of the ceasefire and to a new conflagration in Yugoslavia." (Prophetic words indeed!)

6. In so far as the period was concerned, Para 3 of SCR 743 (1992) of 21 February 1992 states, "The Force is established .... for an initial period on 12 months unless the Council subsequently decides otherwise."

7. Since the Mission was set up under the provisions of SCR 743, there have been nine extensions of the mandate (- in fact, since June 1992):

(a) Reopening of Sarajevo airport for humanitarian purposes;
(b) Establishment of Joint Commission and functions in "Pink Zones";
(c) Monitoring of heavy weapons;
(d) Immigration and customs functions on UNPA boundaries that run along state borders;
(e) Deployment in Bosnia and Herzegovina for escort of humanitarian aid convoys;
(f) Monitoring of demilitarisation of Prevlaka Peninsula;
(g) Deployment of observers at airfields and monitoring of "No Fly Zone" over Bosnia and Herzegovina;

(h) Control of Peruca Dam;
(i) Preventive deployment in Macedonia.

STRENGTH OF FORCE

8. The strength of force has taken the following shape:

		Military (including observers)	UNCIVPOL	Civil Affairs	Civil Admin.	Total
(a)	Original Mandate	13053	515	104*	435*	14107*
(b)	Sector Sarajevo	1419	10	6*	52*	1487*
(c)	Pink Zones	60 (obsrs)	82	-	3	145
(d)	Monitoring Heavy Weapons	63 (obsrs)	-	-	-	63
(e)	B-H Command	7175	-	57*	55*	7287*
(f)	"No-Fly Zone"	66 (obsrs)	8	-	12	86*
Total		21645	615	167*	557*	22985**

*   Includes local civilian staff
** Includes 361 local civilian staff

UNITED NATIONS PROTECTED AREAS

Induction and Deployment

9.   Deployment of the Force commences with the arrival in theatre on 08 March 1992 of some command elements and advance parties. Other elements of the Force were inducted subsequently and the military component was complete in the Sectors by end of June 1992. Civilian staff both political and administrative are in fact still in the process of arriving to meet the projections for the original mandate. UN severely stretched as regards staff because of so many PKOs.
10. Deployment of the Force into the four Sectors is as indicated on the Map. Peculiarity of each UNPA.

Central Elements of the Plan

11. Agreement by the parties to the conflict and cooperation with UNPROFOR.

12. Withdrawal of the JNA from all of Croatia.

13. Continued functioning, on an interim basis, of existing local authorities and police, under UN supervision, "pending achievement of an overall political solution to the crisis". Note: No specific time limits.

Manner of Implementation

14. Withdrawal of the JNA.

15. Disbandment of TDF and concentration of weapons in storage.

16. Demilitarisation of para military and irregulars.

17. Protection of UNPAs to be assumed by UNPROFOR.

18. Return of displaced persons, recreation of police forces etc.

Pink Zones

19. What they are; Joint Commission - 9 meetings; currently stalled; additional basis of instability.

Complications

20. Disintegration of one of the states that was a signatory to the Plan and its proclaimed lack of authority over the groups in the UNPAs.

21. Fighting in Bosnia and Herzegovina and spill-over effects.

22. "Knin authorities" claim to be an independent republic and say they do not accept Belgrade's authority to negotiate and discuss on their behalf.

23. Creation of militia forces of various types and refusal to demilitarise on grounds of threat from Croatia, including infiltration by terrorist groups, UNPROFOR's inability to provide protection particularly in "Pink Zones" and claim that any state is authorised to have such armed police or militia.

24. Harassment and intimidation of minorities (also in Croat controlled areas of Sector West). Also threats to moderate Serb elements.

25. Resettlement of Serbs displaced from other parts of Croatia and recently from Bosnia and Herzegovina; do not have jobs and hence more prone to lawlessness.

26. Statements by Croatian leaders, talks of military resolution of the problem and threatened marches for mass return of displaced persons; these further fuel

adverse reactions. Anti-UNPROFOR propaganda constantly produced by Croatian media, often coming from some Government quarters.

27. Intense hostility and suspicion towards each other; rigidity of positions.

28. All parties lack credibility in their dealings with UNPROFOR.

29. Severe economic situation made worse by damage and destruction of infrastructure.

29a. Most progress halted since mid-October by forthcoming elections in FRY.

Assessment

30. Serbs will continue attempts to gain recognition and legitimacy; hence we may expect continued intransigence, particularly on demilitarisation and border control.

31. Developing attitudes will however depend very much on the degree of independence or autonomy the Bosnian Serbs manage to achieve.

32. However, economic pressures will take their toll.

33. Croatian rhetoric will continue; particularly on return of displaced persons. Also, pressure will grow for restoration of facilities and infrastructure that affect economy in various areas.

33a. Croats will seek to get international intervention to force reintegration of UNPAs into Croatia. Main achievement so far is that there has been no return to war, despite the pressures; and the desire for peace is probably strengthening overall.

Thrust of Efforts

34. Continue to make it clear to the Serbs that no change of borders is acceptable.

35. Get the Croatian authorities to talk constructively to Serb leadership in Croatia, including UNPAs; and stop issuing threats, including early termination of UNPROFOR mandate, which is construed as threat to go to war again.

36. Work towards a solution granting the Serbs mutually acceptable degree of autonomy.

37. Comprehensive amnesty legislation by Croatia.

38. Exploit carrot of economic assistance to both sides, particularly in restoration of facilities and infrastructure damaged or destroyed by the conflict.

38a. Continue to press toward normalisation of infrastructure relationships.

38b. Concurrently direct efforts towards resettlement/return of displaced persons in an organised manner under the aegis of the Joint Mechanisms set up for the purpose under conditions of some stability.

BOSNIA AND HERZEGOVINA

Initial Presence

39. The Force Headquarters was set up in Sarajevo in mid March 1992 and was to control the activities in the UNPAs from that locations.

40. It became evident soon after our arrival that the then impending recognition of B & H independence and the Bosnian Serbs' reservations about such recognition, could lead to conflict. These fears soon came true and the rest is recent history.

41. A couple of points that may be made pertaining to the initial developments may be of interest. It appeared that, in so far as Sarajevo was concerned, the situation really started getting bad subsequent to the attacks on the JNA, particularly the 03 May 1992 incident. In regard to other areas in B & H, UNPROFOR did not have any presence and hence no authentic comments can be made.

42. The presence of UNPROFOR was, looked upon by the local people and leadership as an insurance against any serious outbreak of trouble in Sarajevo and an expectation raised that we were in a position to intervene. This was unfortunate because neither did we have a mandate for B & H nor the resources. Even so, we did whatever we could in providing limited humanitarian assistance, our good offices in negotiations and discussions and even in providing some presence in accompanying convoys under possible threat.

43. The worsening situation and the fact that the Force Headquarters was getting so totally embroiled in the local situation to the detriment of its main task in the UNPAs, compelled us to move the major component of the Headquarters to Belgrade on 16 and 17 May 1992. A component of about a hundred personnel under the Chief Military Observer remained in Sarajevo to provide good offices for negotiation between the parties and limited humanitarian assistance. The situation, however, continued to deteriorate.

Sarajevo Airport Agreement

44. On 05 June 1992, Cedric Thornberry negotiated an agreement that UNPROFOR take over full operational responsibility for the functioning and security of Sarajevo airport to facilitate induction of humanitarian aid supplies.

45. All parties reaffirmed the ceasefire declared for 01 June 1992.

46. Agreed to withdraw anti-aircraft weapon systems from the vicinity of the airport and air approaches.

47. Agreed to concentrate in agreed areas all artillery, mortars, ground-to-ground missile systems and tanks that were within range of the airport.

Deployment into Sarajevo

48. Brig. Gen. L.W. MacKenzie and an advance element moved to Sarajevo on 10 June 1992; airport management elements from France. Serbs hand over the airport to UNPROFOR.

49. Canadian battalion from Sector West redeployed.

50. SCR 761 of 29 June 1992 authorised additional deployment.

51. Humanitarian aid flights commenced on 29 June 1992.

52. Additional unites arrived end of July 1992.

53. Ceasefire however never held; situation remained unsatisfactory and dangerous. No humanitarian corridors in the city; no full concentration of heavy weaponry.

Use of Airport

54. A total of 1747 humanitarian aid flights to date; airport was closed for about a month in September 1992 following the shooting down of the Italian aircraft.

55. There have also been a number of temporary suspensions; latest suspension was from 02 December 1992.

56. A total of approx. 20,000 metric tonnes of supplies have been flown into Sarajevo.

57. The airlift has also been used for visits of a number of official and non-official delegations.

58. B & H Government officials have been transported in and out.

59. Troops in Sarajevo have been heavily committed in escort of humanitarian aid convoys to the city and to escort various delegations and visitors. This has placed a heavy strain on them.

Mandate for Bosnia and Herzegovina

60. SCR 776 of 14 September 1992 authorised enlargement of UNPROFOR's mandate and strength in Bosnia and Herzegovina to provide protection to UNHCR organised humanitarian aid convoys as well as to convoys of released

detainees if requested by the ICRC. *Not* a traditional peace-keeping mandate because no peace was ever negotiated.

61. Deployment and effort in support of UNHCR Plan; UNHCR the lead agency.

62. Resources for this mandate including troops and equipment to be provided by member states of the European Community, Canada and USA, at no cost to the United Nations.

63. A transport battalion was included for conveyance of supplies by military drivers in more sensitive areas.

Deployment

64. The proposed deployment areas and present locations of troops are as explained on the map.

Achievements

65. Effective deployment was achieved in mid November.

66. Convoy escorting capability is growing as units understand their areas of responsibility.

67. Also, as liaison and cooperation between units and air agencies improve.

68. In November 1992, 56 convoys were escorted.

69. From 01 to 13 December 1992, 72 convoys were escorted.

70. Since 30 October 1992, approx. 11,000 MT escorted.

71. In areas like Velika Kladusa, daily runs from Zagreb stated at 40/50 MT per day, now run at 200 MT per day.

72. Presence of troops on UNHCR priority routes has given greater confidence to civilian drivers and convoy operators, who are now prepared to move unescorted.

73. Sarajevo receives 5 convoys per week.

74. Aid convoys have secured access to places like Gorazde, Srebrenica and Tuzla; regular convoys are now running.

75. UNPROFOR presence and movement on various routes have assisted in calming the situation.

76. Regular meetings and discussions held with political and military leadership to defuse tensions.

77. MMWG meetings between military commanders held at regular intervals.

78. Assistance in restoration of facilities.

Problem Areas

79. Some parts of Bosnia and Herzegovina are uncovered by deployment; hence authentic information is lacking.
80. Banja Luka deployment stalled by Serb leadership.
81. Also deployment into Bosanski Prtrovac area.
82. Inappropriate deployment of Spanish Battalion.
83. Assurances and agreements of parties not credible.
84. Muslim leadership keenness for foreign military intervention. Status quo is not to their advantage.
85. Presence of mercenaries; many armed groups not under control.
86. Croatian Army presence.
87. Winter conditions may affect to some areas.

No Fly Zone

88. SCR 781 adopted on 09 Oct '92.
89. Monitoring Command Coordination Centre established on 20 October 1992 and UNMO/ECMM deployment at airfields commences 02 November 1992.
90. Violations being monitored by MCCC and reported on daily basis; protests lodged locally and at higher levels.
91. Major activity now is of helicopters from Banja Luka (claimed to be in casualty evacuation and training flights) and fixed wing aircraft at Cazin; in latter case some flight confirmed from/to Pleso (Zagreb).
92. No confirmed evidence of use of aircraft in support of ground operations.

Assessment

93. Serbs and Croats have achieved control of areas they are interested in.
94. Muslim leadership cannot accept status quo. Hence will continue to insist on foreign military intervention or lifting of arms embargo. UN presence now seen as obstruction.
95. Attempts will be made at local levels to improve positions; Serbs will continue to respond with heavy weapons.
96. Fighting will continue in North East - Corridor.
97. Unlikely to be any serious obstructions to delivery of humanitarian supplies, except weather and logistics.

Recommendations

98. Work towards political settlement must continue - coordinated strategy. Full bilateral support required to assist UNPROFOR in its tasks in whole area of operations.

99. Must persevere in attempts to obtain cessation of hostilities. Bosnia and Herzegovina Government must be disabused of hopes of foreign military intervention while being reassured that a just constitutional settlement will be achieved and guaranteed by the international community.

100. Persist in effort towards demilitarisation in Sarajevo.

101. Continue with humanitarian aid efforts.

Casualties Suffered

	B-H		UNPAs		Other Areas		Total	
	F	W	F	W	F	W	F	W
101. Operational								
(a) Bullet injuries	3	17	-	9	-	-	3	26
(b) Mines and explosives	1	16	4	39	-	-	5	55
(c) Shelling	1	68	-	12	-	-	1	80
Total	5	101	6	60	-	-	9	161
102. Non-operational	-	9	12	101	-	39	12	158
103. Overall total	5	110	16	160	-	39	21	319

Tribute

104. Dedication and selflessness.

105. Morale.

Violations of SCR 718 - from 08 nov to 12 Dec 92

1. Violations within B & H	Serbs	Croatians
a. *Fixed Wing*		
(i) Tracked by AWACS	21	0
(ii) Observed by UNMOs	29	18
b. *Rotary Wing*		
(i) Tracked by AWACS	36	0
(ii) Observed by UNMOs	164	0

2. *Violations where trucks observed entering or exiting borders of B & H*

	From B & H	To B & H
a. Serbia/Montenegro:	1	1
b. Croatia	5	5

Note: No aircraft were observed carrying weapons.

50. ORAL REPORT BY M. AHTISAARI, CHAIRMAN OF THE BOSNIA AND HERZEGOVINA WORKING GROUP[*]

The terms of reference of the Bosnia and Herzegovina Working Group are: "... to promote a cessation of hostilities and a constitutional settlement in Bosnia and Herzegovina". As General Nambiar has dealt with much of what can be said about the first part of this dual mandate, I shall immediately turn to the constitutional issues.

At our last meeting I outlined the proposals that the Co-Chairmen were then about to present to the parties on a "Possible Constitutional Structure for Bosnia and Herzegovina".

These proposals were the next day also communicated to the Security Council -- which subsequently specifically endorsed them as the basis for the constitutional negotiations.

---

[*] Ministerial Level Meeting of the Steering Committee of the International Conference on the Former Yugoslavia, Geneva, 16 December 1992.

Following are the principal points of these proposals:

(1) Bosnia and Herzegovina is to be a centralized state with 7 to 10 autonomous provinces whose boundaries would take into account ethnic and other considerations. Many governmental functions, especially those relating to normal contacts of public authorities with citizens would be assigned to the provinces.

(2) The Constitution is to recognize three major "ethnic" groups, as well as of a group of "others".

(3) As most important feature is to be insistence on the highest level of internationally proclaimed human rights, whose implementation is to be ensured and monitored by a variety of national and international organs.

(4) Another important feature would be various international supervisory and control mechanisms, to continue for some time.

The *Bosnian Government* accepted the general outline of the Co-Chairmen's proposals, though it considers that they provide for excessive decentralization and that ethnic and other group considerations are overemphasized.

The *Bosnian Croats* declared the constitutional proposals to be a relatively acceptable basis for further talks, subject to three principal reservations: the constitutional arrangements should more adequately reflect that Bosnia and Herzegovina is a state of three constituent nations; that it should not become a protectorate of the international community; and there should be complete demilitarizations.

The *Bosnian Serbs* on 19 November presented a counter-proposal, to be considered together with that of the Co-Chairmen. Under it, Bosnia and Herzegovina is to be divided, on an ethnic basis, into three sovereign states, each with international legal personality and only loosely confederated in a central unit. All the organs of the central government would be constituted by appointees of the three states on an equal basis, and would generally only be able to take decisions by consensus. Human rights would be guaranteed at the highest international level, but there would be no international monitoring of compliance.

Clearly, the positions of the parties remain far apart, and their proposals for altering features of the Co-Chairmen's proposal tend in at least partly divergent directions.

Although the Co-Chairmen's proposal specified criteria for the delimitation of the provinces, no boundaries were suggested as part of the original package. Instead the parties were again requested to provide their own conceptions as to the boundaries to be drawn - as a starting point for the development by the Conference of a set of proposals. It was only at the beginning of last week that the parties presented their ideas concerning boundaries.

The map of the *Bosnian Government* would divide the country into 13 provinces, with populations ranging from 564 thousand to 67 thousand. All of these would have an ethnically varied population, though in each province one of the ethnic groups would predominate - sometimes distinctly, sometimes just barely.

The *Bosnian Croats* submitted a map merely indicating those territories - consisting of one large, one medium-sized and four small ones - within which Croats allegedly constituted a majority of 60% or more. No indication was given as to how provincial boundaries might be drawn in this light, though it was explained that it was expected there would be two provinces and that other concentrations of Croat populations would end up in provinces with other majorities.

The *Bosnian Serbs* submitted a map that defined as Serb territory about 75% of the country, with a population of some 1.6 million Serbs - that is almost all the Bosnian Serbs - plus about 300 thousand Muslims and 100 thousand Croats.

The Government and the Croat delegations informed us that they would try to submit a joint proposal as to the delimitations of the provinces.

We intend to use the maps submitted or to be submitted by the parties to narrow the differences between them.

In my view, the immediate objective of the Conference in respect of Bosnia and Herzegovina will have to be two-folded; First, to induce all three parties to observe the ceasefire scrupulously. Each must refrain from any actions that could be interpreted as a breach of the ceasefire, and not over-react to apparent breaches by others so as not to escalate violence. A procedure must be established to examine swiftly all allegations of ceasefire violations, the reports of which would be immediately submitted to the parties and, through UNPROFOR to the Secretary-General and the Co-Chairmen.

Secondly, all parties must participate immediately and unconditionally in continuous negotiations, in both the Mixed Military Working Group, and in the Bosnia and Herzegovina Working Group on the formulation of the future constitution. In both these settings the three parties must sit together. In this connection it might be recalled that the three-week delay, from 30 September until 21 October, in convening the Mixed Military Working Group was largely due to the refusal of one of the parties to participate in joint meetings -- and that meanwhile many lives were lost and the military situation deteriorated further with respect to that party.

It is my perception that the *Bosnian Serbs* are ready to engage in serious negotiations and recognize the need to make concessions from the initial position that they have presented to the Working Group in respect of the delimitation of the provinces. The *Croats* are also prepared to participate.

Obviously all parties will have to make concessions in respect of positions they have advanced. At the same time, the Conference itself -- as the custodian representing the international community -- must make sure that certain principles are not compromised, such as the need for Bosnia and Herzegovina to become a functionally viable state able to carry out its international obligations and to ensure for all its citizens an assured existence in conformity with internationally recognized human rights.

Finally, the problems of Bosnia and Herzegovina cannot be separated from those of the other successor states to former Yugoslavia, and the fulfilment of the tasks of our Working Group may therefore only be possible in the context of an overall accomplishment of the mandate of this Conference.

51. Statement by Mr. Cornelio Sommaruga, President of the International Committee of the Red Cross[*]

Le souhait le plus cher que je tiens à vous exprimer aujourd'hui est que des solutions politiques soient apportées au conflit de l'ex-Yougoslavie, qui a fait de trop nombreuses victimes.

Il faut éviter que cette guerre s'étende. J'en appelle à travers vous aux dirigeants de la région, mais aussi à vous tous félicitons de l'excellente collaboration avec le HCR et la FORPRONU, ainsi qu'avec les Coprésidents de cette Conférence et leur équipe.

En Bosnie-Herzégovine, la situation humanitaire est terrible. Le CICR a déjà pris des positions très fermes pour dénoncer les violations gravissimes du droit international humanitaire et pour amener les parties au conflit à s'entendre sur le respect des règles humanitaires.

Dans ce but, le CICR a demandé l'appui de la Communauté des Etats. En effet, si les dispositions du droit international humanitaire étaient effectivement respectées, une grande partie des souffrances seraient évitées à la population civile.

Je dois malheureusement constater que ces efforts n'ont pas encore abouti. La population civile n'est toujours pas respectée, à l'arrière des lignes de front, comme dans les villes assiégées. Des milliers de victimes risquent de s'ajouter à

---

[*] Ministerial Level Meeting of the Steering Committee of the International Conference on the Former Yugoslavia, Geneva, 16 December 1992.

une liste déjà trop longue.

A la Conférence de Londres, les parties au conflit ont pris l'engagement de libérer tous les prisonniers. Elles sont signé un accord à cet effet à Genève le 1er octobre. Elles doivent maintenant tenir cet engagement, qui a été confirmé dans mon bureau par les leaders des parties la semaine dernière.

Sur l'ensemble des prisonniers concernés par cet accord, 3.944 ont été libérés à ce jour, dont 1.008 le 14 décembre. J'espère que ce processus permettra de fermer les camps de Manjaca et de Batkovic, ainsi que ceux qui se trouvent dans les villes de Livno, Tomislavgrad, Orasje, Celebici, Konjic, Tarcin, Visoko et Zenica, et ailleurs encore. Cela signifie que 4.345 prisonniers doivent être libérés dans les meilleurs délais, - cette semaine encore - soit: 2.780 par la partie serbe de Bosnie, 1.027 par la partie musulmane de Bosnie et 538 par la partie croate de Bosnie. Le CICR est prêt à continuer de jouer son rôle d'intermédiaire neutre dans cette opération humanitaire.

J'espère également qu'il pourra enfin obtenir l'accès aux milliers de prisonniers que ses délégués n'ont pas encore pu visiter en Bosnie-Herzégovine. Il faut que la pression international soit maintenue sur toutes les parties au conflit.

Je tiens ici aussi à vous remercier du soutien que vous apportez au processus de libération des prisonniers, notamment par l'accueil de réfugiés venant de ces lieux de détention selon les accords que vous avez pris avec le HCR.

L'engagement de respecter la population civile doit maintenant se traduire par des actes sur le terrain. Ce que le CICR fait aujourd'hui en Bosnie-Herzégovine est important. Nous sommes en mesure d'apporter une assistance à 500.000 personnes déplacées sur les 80% du territoire que nous pouvons atteindre.

Mais face au non-respect généralisé du droit international humanitaire, ces actions ne suffisent pas. Il faut trouver d'autres solutions pour protéger la population civile.

Vous vous souvenez que le CICR a envisagé la création de zones protégées en Bosnie-Herzégovine. En effet, des dizaines de milliers de civils proches des zones de combats se trouvent sans protection. Des minorités sont trop souvent à la merci de ceux qui se sont arrogé le pouvoir avec leur fusil. Cela n'est pas acceptable.

Je continue de penser que des formules efficaces de protection à l'intérieur de la Bosnie-Herzégovine, sans favoriser le transfert de population, amis avec une présence extérieure accrue, doivent être mises en oeuvre d'urgence, malgré les difficultés et les risques qui y sont liés. Ces formules doivent contribuer à mettre un terme à l'abominable processus de "purification ethnique". Et puis il s'agit de continuer à sauver des vies humaines à l'intérieur de cette République.

Je vous parle, au nom aussi, des 150 délégués du CICR, qui sont sur le terrain et qui sont donc témoins de ce qui se passe.

Face au sort de milliers de civils en danger de mort, la communauté internationale se doit d'agir immédiatement. Il est de mon devoir de vous le rappeler et de demander votre coopération pour que les engagements pris à Londres et Genève soient enfin mis en oeuvre. Il est de votre devoir - Mesdames et Messieurs les Ministres - de réagir afin de mettre un terme à l'horreur. Il est du devoir de nous tous, et notamment des responsables politiques et militaires sur place, de respecter et faire respecter le droit international humanitaire, en ex-Yougoslavie comme partout dans le monde.

52. STATEMENT BY LAWRENCE S. EAGLEBURGER, SECRETARY OF STATE OF THE UNITED STATES OF AMERICA*

Ladies and Gentlemen, Just under four months ago, an important milestone was reached with the convening of the London International Conference on the Former Yugoslavia. Commitments were made both by the parties to the Yugoslav conflict and by the international community itself - commitments to ensure unimpeded delivery of humanitarian aid; to lift the barbaric siege of cities; to halt all military flights over Bosnia and Herzegovina; to group all heavy weapons under UN monitoring; to open up and shut down all detention camps; to tighten sanctions against the aggressor; and to prevent the conflict's spread to neighboring regions and countries.

Some of those commitments have been kept, particularly in the area of sanctions monitoring and in efforts to prevent a further widening of the war. Most importantly, London established a negotiating mechanism centered here in Geneva, which has brought the international community and the various ex-Yugoslav parties together on an ongoing basis, and which, thanks to the efforts of Cyrus Vance and Lord Owen, remains a viable forum for an eventual settlement of the war.

But let us be clear: we find ourselves today in Geneva because most of the commitments made in London have not been kept, and because the situation inside the former Yugoslavia has become increasingly desperate. Thus we meet to discuss how the international community will respond in order to force compliance with the London agreements, and thereby accelerate an end to the war.

It is clear in reviewing the record since London that the promises broken

---

* Ministerial Level Meeting of the Steering Committee of the International Conference on the Former Yugoslavia, Geneva, 16 December 1992.

have been largely Serbian promises broken. It is the Serbs who continue to besiege the cities of Bosnia; Serb heavy weapons which continue to pound the civilian populations in this cities; the Bosnian Serb air forces which continue to fly in defiance of the London agreements; and Serbs who impede the delivery of humanitarian assistance and continue the odious practice of "ethnic cleansing". It is now clear, in short, that Mr. Milosevic and Mr. Karadzic have systematically flouted agreements to which they had solemnly, and yet cynically, given their assent.

Today we must, at a minimum, commit ourselves anew to the London agreements by:

- redoubling our assistance efforts, and continuing to press for the opening of routes for aid convoys, so that widespread starvation can be avoided this winter;
- strengthening our efforts to prevent the war's spill over particularly in the Kosovo, which we will not tolerate; and
- tightening and better enforcing sanctions, the surest means of forcing an early end to the war.

But we must also do more. It is clear that the international community must begin now to think about moving beyond the London agreements and contemplate more aggressive measures. That, for example, is why my government is now recommending that the United Nations Security Council authorize enforcement of the no-fly zone in Bosnia, and why we are also willing to have the Council reexamine the arms embargo as it applies to the government of Bosnia and Herzegovina.

Finally, my government also believes it is time for the international community to begin identifying individuals who may have to answer for having committed crimes against humanity. We have, on the one hand, a moral and historical obligation not to stand back a second time in this century while a people faces obliteration. But we have also, I believe, a political obligation to the people of Serbia to signal clearly the risk they currently run of sharing the inevitable fate of those who practice ethnic cleansing in their name.

The fact of the matter is that we know that crimes against humanity have occurred, and we know when and where they occurred. We know, moreover, which forces committed those crimes, and under whose command they operated. And we know, finally, who the political leaders are to whom those military commanders were - and still are - responsible.

Let me begin with the crimes themselves, the facts of which are indisputable:

- *the siege of Sarajevo*, ongoing since April, with scores of innocent civilians killed nearly every day by artillery shelling;
- *the continuing blockade of humanitarian assistance*, which is producing thousands upon thousands of unseen innocent victims;
- *the destruction of Vukovar* in the fall of 1991, and the forced expulsion of the majority of its population;
- *the terrorizing of Banja Luka's 30.000 Muslims*, which has included bombings, beatings and killings;
- *the forcible imprisonment, inhumane mistreatment and wilful killing of civilians at detention camps*, including Banja Luka/Manjaca, Brcko/Luka, Krajina/Prnjavor, Omarska, Prijedor/Keraterm, and Trnopolje/Kozarac;
- *the August 21 massacre* of more than 200 Muslim men and boys by Bosnian Serb police in the Vlasica mountains near Varjanta;
- *the May-June murders of between 2,000 and 3,000 Muslim men, women and children* by Serb irregular forces at a brick factory and a pig farm near Brcko;
- *the June mass execution of about 100 Muslim men at Brod*;
- *and the May 18 mass killing of at least 56 Muslim family members* by Serb militiamen in Grbavci, near Zvornik.

We know that Bosnian Serbs have not alone been responsible for the massacres and crimes against humanity which have taken place. For example, in late October Croatian fighters killed or wounded up to 300 Muslims in Proxzor; and between September 24-26 Muslims from Kamenica killed more than 60 Serb civilians and soldiers.

We can do more than enumerate crimes; we can also identify individuals who committed them:

- for example, *Borislav Herak* is a Bosnian Serb who has confessed to killing over 230 civilians; and
- *"Adil" and "Arif"* are two members of a Croatian paramilitary force which in August attacked a convoy of buses carrying more than 100 Serbian women and children killing over half of them.

We also know the names of leaders who directly supervised persons accused of war crimes, and who may have ordered those crimes. These include:

- *Zeljko Raznjatovic*, whose paramilitary forces, the "Tigers", have been linked to brutal ethnic cleansing in Zvornik, Srebrenica, Bratunac and Grabnica; and who were also linked to the mass murders of up to 3,000 civilians near Brcko;
- *Vojislav Seselj*, whose "White Eagles" force has been linked to atrocities in an number of Bosnian cities, including the infamous incident at Brcko;
- *Drago Prcac*, Commander of the Omarska Detention Camp, where mass murder and torture occurred; and
- *Adem Delic*, the camp commander at Celebici where at least 15 Serbs were beaten to death in August.

I want to make it clear that, in naming names, I am presenting the views of my government alone. The information I have cited has been provided to the UN War Crimes Commission, whose decision it will be to prosecute or not. Second, I am not prejudging any trial proceedings that may occur; they must be impartial and conducted in accordance with due process. Third, the above listing of names is tentative and will be expanded as we compile further information.

Finally, there is another category of fact which is beyond dispute -- namely, the fact of political and command responsibility for the crimes against humanity which I have described. Leaders such as Slobodan Milosevic, the President of Serbia, Radovan Karadzic, the self-declared President of the Serbian Bosnian Republic, and General Ratko Mladic, Commander of Bosnian Serb military forces, must eventually explain whether and how they sought to ensure, as they must under international law, that their forces complied with international law. They ought, if charged, to have the opportunity of defending themselves by demonstrating whether and how they took responsible action to prevent and punish the atrocities I have described which were undertaken by their subordinates.

I have taken the step today of identifying individuals suspected of war crimes and crimes against humanity for the same reason that my government has decided to seek UN authorization for enforcing the no-fly zone in Bosnia, and why we are now willing to examine the question of lifting the arms embargo as it applies to Bosnia and Herzegovina. It is because we have concluded that the deliberate flaunting of Security Council resolutions and the London agreements by Serb authorities is not only producing an intolerable and deteriorating situation inside the former Yugoslavia, it is also beginning to threaten the framework of stability in the new Europe.

It is clear that the reckless leaders of Serbia, and of the Serbs inside Bosnia, have somehow convinced themselves that the international community will not stand up to them now, and will be forced eventually to recognize the fruits of their aggression and the results of ethnic cleansing. Tragically, it also appears that they have convinced the people of Serbia to follow them to the front lines of what they proclaim to be an historic struggle against Islam on behalf of the Christian West.

It is time to disabuse them of these most dangerous illusions. The solidarity of the civilized and democratic nations of the West lies with the innocent and brutalized Muslim people of Bosnia. Thus we must make it unmistakably clear that we will settle for nothing less than the restoration of the independent state of Bosnia and Herzegovina with its territory undivided and intact; the return of all refugees to their homes and villages and, indeed, a day of reckoning for those found guilty of crimes against humanity.

It will undoubtedly take some time before all these goals are realized; but then there is time, too, though not much, for the people of Serbia to step back from the edge of the abyss. There is time, still, to release all prisoners; to lift the siege of the cities; to permit humanitarian aid to reach the needy; and to negotiate for peace and for a settlement guaranteeing the rights of all minorities in the independent states of the former Yugoslavia.

But in waiting for the people of Serbia, if not their leaders, to come to their senses, we must make them understand that their country will remain alone, friendless and condemned to economic ruin and exclusion from the family of civilized nations for as long as they pursue the suicidal dream of a Greater Serbia. They need, especially, to understand that a second Nuremberg awaits the practitioners of ethnic cleansing, and that the judgment, and opprobrium, of history awaits the people in whose name their crimes were committed.

53. STATEMENT BY THE MINISTER OF FOREIGN AFFAIRS OF THE REPUBLIC OF ALBANIA*

Mr. Chairman, Since the inception of the International Conference on former Yugoslavia, the delegation of the Republic of Albania has seen it as the forum for a comprehensive solution to the Yugoslav crisis. Let me take this occasion to thank the Co-Chairmen for their onerous efforts in this regard. Today's Meeting, however, reveals the understanding that complex issues of the Yugoslav crisis can better be addressed in the framework of special meetings with a clearly-defined agenda and status. In this context, we welcome this new meeting and hope it comes with concrete results. This delegation, however, considers that the participation of the victim of aggression here today, the Republic of Bosnia and Herzegovina, whose contribution has been invaluable in other occasions, would have been a positive factor.

Mr. Chairman, the Republic of Albania is of the opinion that the Belgrade authorities have not kept their commitments. The situation has continued to worsen. A fact which calls for more resolute response on the part of the international community, which must now set clear cut deadlines to deal with the aggressor. Concerted action to this end must be translated into concrete steps aimed at eliminating the sources of aggression and enforcing the implementation of commitments undertaken. In this respect, Albania endorses the future action presented here by Lord Owen, namely, the establishment of an international court to held account on war crimes., strict implementation of the no-fly zone, and, above all, reinforcement of sanctions against Belgrade. This action has to take life immediately in order to give an end to the tragedy of the Bosnian people.

Mr. Chairman, the Republic of Albania is also deeply concerned at recent open signs of the intention to escalate the conflict to Kosova. People are being openly killed in broad daylight in Kosova, provoking thus the population to resign peaceful opposition and become the targets of a slaughter with unpredictable regional consequences. The leadership of Kosova, while giving concrete proofs of civilized approaches, has hitherto managed to control the rising feelings of its people who, despite the pangs of further division into other states, have not yielded to violence. The response of the Serbian side is now well-known.

These are, in short, the alarming concerns that impel Albania to renew its

---

* Ministerial Level Meeting of the Steering Committee of the International Conference on the Former Yugoslavia, Geneva, 16 December 1992.

strong appeal on the international community to take quick preventive action before the scenario unfolds. Developments in Kosova must be monitored by, inter alia, sending in UN preventive forces, that would maintain peace while negotiations continue. The CSCE support for the UN presence in Kosova paves the way for the adaptation of measures towards its implementation. It is obviously clear that the Belgrade authorities are responsible and guilty for the Yugoslav crisis and human tragedy there. Especially, in the case of Kosova, this conclusions is clear enough. In respect to this, I would like to stress here that the pressure of the international community for a stable and lasting solution must be exerted on Belgrade regime. Concerning the future status of Kosova, Albania states its resolute position. This Conference, with the consent of all its participating states, should be the only forum to discuss and decide about it.

Since the outbreak of the Yugoslav crisis, Albania has maintained that the dialogue should be pursued for a peaceful solution, joining to this end its efforts with those of international community. In spite of the heavy economic burden, the Albanian government has strictly implemented a constructive attitude towards the former Yugoslav republic of Macedonia, promoting friendly relations with this country. We consider the deployment of the UN peace-keepers there as a means to further ensure stability and peace in the area. At the same time, I would like to state that no danger would come to this country from the Albanian territory.

Thank you.

54. STATEMENT BY DR. HAMID ALGABID, SECRETARY-GENERAL OF THE ORGANIZATION OF THE ISLAMIC CONFERENCE[*]

Co-Chairmen, Excellencies the Ministers, Distinguished Delegates, We welcome the initiative to convene this Ministerial level expanded Steering Committee Meeting of the International Conference on former Yugoslavia.

We appreciate the relentless efforts made by the Co-Chairmen of the Steering Committee so as to ensure the implementation of the London Conference decisions with respect to former Yugoslavia.

More than three months have elapsed since the holding of the London Conference. The period may appear short for evaluating the actions taken since the formation of the Steering Committee. However, the seriousness of the situation

---

[*] Ministerial Level Meeting of the Steering Committee of the International Conference on the Former Yugoslavia, Geneva, 16 December, 1992.

on the ground is such that this period appears long to the most of us and especially to Bosnian people subjected to a regime of terror and violence of a rare barbarous nature.

It could be said today that with regard to the hopes raised by the London Conference and the laudable efforts put in by Cyrus Vance and Lord Owen that three months have been a period of challenge and frustration because of Serbian obstinacy.

The Serb aggressor has in fact with cleverness multiplied the obstacles on way to peace; it has redoubled with ardour its cruelties and excesses and tried by all means to put before the international community a fait accompli.

All international efforts notably those made within the framework of the International Conference on former Yugoslavia and the United Nations to find a peaceful solution to the problem have effectively been stone walled by the Serbs.

The repugnant policy of ethnic cleansing continues to be applied with same criminal and murderous ardour. However, the humanitarian operations being undertaken under Security Council resolutions have cruelly been frustrated and thousands of people of Bosnia continue to live in besieged towns for months hoping for humanitarian assistance which is tragically being delayed.

The UN sanctions against Serbia and Montenegro continue to be violated. While strong Serb forces, assured of military supremacy by the arms embargo decreed by the Security Council, are pursuing and increasing their aggression in Bosnia and Herzegovina.

In fact, the Geneva process in former Yugoslavia has had no serious impact on the actual situation in Bosnia and Herzegovina, where the aggression continues.

It is in this context that an Extraordinary Session of the Islamic Conference of Foreign Ministers was held in Jeddah on 1-2 December 1992 to consider the serious situation in Bosnia and Herzegovina.

Besides, expressing the deep distress and grave concern of the Organisation of Islamic Conference over the deteriorating situation in Bosnia and Herzegovina, the Conference expressed the disquiet of the Islamic countries over the lack of effective action by the Security Council to implement its resolutions on Bosnia and Herzegovina.

The Conference was of the view that in the absence of effective action by the Security Council to end the Serbian aggression, the arms embargo imposed against former Yugoslavia by the Security Council Resolution 713 (1991) has in actual fact worked to the detriment of the Government of Bosnia and Herzegovina impairing its ability to exercise its legitimate right of individual or collective self-defence under Article 51 of the Charter of the United Nations.

The OIC member states requested the Security Council to clarify and declare explicitly that the arms embargo imposed by Resolution 713 does not apply to the Republic of Bosnia and Herzegovina and to allow the immediate delivery of defensive arms to the Republic of Bosnia and Herzegovina by member states which were urged to extend their cooperation to the Republic of Bosnia and Herzegovina in the exercise of its inherent right of individual and collective self-defence in accordance with Article 51 of the Charter of the United Nations.

The Conference also requested the Security Council to review by 15 January 1993, the situation in Bosnia and Herzegovina and the implementation of its relevant resolutions including Resolution 752 (1992) as well as relevant commitments reached during the London Conference on former Yugoslavia.

The OIC member states are finding it increasingly difficult to understand the hesitations, which could be likened to eschewing responsibility, which have so far characterized the international reaction to Serb aggression in Bosnia and Herzegovina. These hesitations leave us a bitter taste; they are revolting and favour those who characterize and denounce to policy of double standards practised within the Security Council by those countries, which by virtue of the Charter, have special responsibility for the maintenance of peace.

These hesitations and procrastination have encouraged the Serbs in their criminal undertakings while at the same time the Bosnian people have been denied their legitimate rights to individual and collective self-defence, which is conferred upon them by the United Nations. One cannot refuse them this rights and continue to do nothing to check the Serb aggression.

We are hardly convinced by the arguments of those who speak of the complexity of the situation on the ground and the risk of escalation of the conflict to justify the refusal to resort to Article 42 of the UN Charter against Serbia and to lift partially the embargo so as to enable Bosnia to secure the means to defend itself. These arguments lead to inaction and encourage the Serb aggressor, which is moreover being favoured by the arms embargo unjustly instituted against Bosnia and Herzegovina. We should admit, as I emphasized before the Sixth Extraordinary Session of the Islamic Conference of Foreign Ministers, in response to all those arguments that the responsibility of maintaining peace is not without risks.

It is high time that the Security Council is provided the means necessary for implementing its decisions on Bosnia and Herzegovina. It is urgent that the Security Council established a time-frame for the realization of its actions.

The rapidly deteriorating situation in Kosovo, the Sandjak, Vojvodina and the Republic of Macedonia is also a matter of serious concern to the OIC. It is absolutely necessary for the Security Council to take effective action to prevent the conflict from spreading and enveloping the entire region.

I wish to reiterate here the readiness of the OIC member states to cooperate fully with the Security Council and to contribute financially as well as in terms of personnel to any enforcement action that the Council may deem necessary to undertake under article 42 of the UN Charter to restore peace in Bosnia and Herzegovina.

The member States of OIC are also determined to act in order to extend help to the Government of the Republic of Bosnia and Herzegovina in the exercise of its inherent right of individual and collective self-defence.

We warmly welcomed the recent humanitarian, much publicised drive which led to the sending to Somalia of so many troops to restore state authority undermined by armed factions and gangs of plunderers and bring to an end the terrible suffering of the Somali people.

Now why, yes why is it that the fate of the Muslim people of Bosnia and Herzegovina does not move that much?

I read in the aeroplane while coming to Geneva the evidence of a Bosnian who survived from the Serb concentration camp.

Demir described the torture carried out in the Omarska Camp as follows:

"At seven o'clock in the morning started first session. We were called one by one to be beaten with riding whips, butts of guns, iron bars, knives. The strokes fell everywhere on the body and the head. Each of us had an arm, leg broken. If one of us cried out of pain, he was immediately gunned down or beaten to death.

Special tortures are also carried out like the ones inflicted on a Demir's friend, who was tortured to death by a Muslim emblem made of iron crescent with star inside."

This poignant proof shows the unlimited extent of crimes committed by Serbs in Bosnia and Herzegovina. Excesses of all sorts, gang rapes of Muslim women, villainous murder of children and elderly persons have also become the daily lot of the Bosnian people. Bosnia and Herzegovina, as is evident from this survivor, has become the cemetery for Muslims.

Till when will the civilized world continue to tolerate this?

Thank you.

55. Statement by Teodor Melescanu, Minister of State and Minister of Foreign Affairs of Romania[*]

Distinguished Co-Chairmen, Ladies and Gentlemen, With your permission, before anything else, I would like to discharge myself of an honouring duty, that of hailing the initiative taken by the two Co-Chairmen to convene an expanded meeting of the Steering Committee on an issue of an utmost importance at a sensitive time for the developments in the former Yugoslavia.

I am taking the opportunity to extend to the two Co-Chairmen the appreciation of the Government of Romania on their delicate and laborious undertakings and to wish them strive along the same avenue since that has proven to be the most suitable under the present circumstances.

There are indeed voices that claim that the international community has performed too little and has acted too late to prevent and to stop eventually the escalation of conflicts in former Yugoslavia. Nevertheless, an ever growing number of deeds do challenge such a view.

The whole range of activities that have been taking place, here in Geneva, as of September last provide the best clear evidence that the international community, especially its two most important collective players - UN and EC - are sparring no efforts to restore peace on the territories of former Yugoslavia.

The very structure of the world organization allows for a direct and continuous dialogue with the body that holds the primary responsibility in maintaining and, when necessary, restoring international peace and security, and that is the Security Council. The already established practice of consultations between the Security Council and the two Co-Chairmen of the Conference is in itself a guarantee that all relevant interests and suggestions enjoy due attention.

The most recent confirmation of the positive results of the above-mentioned cooperation is offered by the decision taken by the Security Council in its Resolution 795. The adoption of a UNSC Resolution providing for the establishment of the presence of the United Nations Protection Force in the former Yugoslav Republic of Macedonia, to be closely coordinated with the CSCE mission here indicates that preventive diplomacy is not just words on paper.

Also, there have been new steps taken by EC in respect to the Yugoslav crisis which come to substantiate the same former assessment. We totally support the decisions of the EC Summit in Edinburgh, sharing the view that their rapid and comprehensive implementation will, on the one hand, decisively deter any

---

[*] Ministerial Level Meeting of the Steering Committee of the International Conference on the Former Yugoslavia, Geneva, 16 December 1992.

attempts at an escalation of the current conflicts, and, on the other hand, will prevent their most dangerous extension in other parts of former Yugoslavia.

The London Conference on Yugoslavia had the merit of involving the neighbouring countries in the efforts aimed at a peaceful resolution of the Yugoslav crisis.

In this respect, the Conference in Geneva has provided a valuable framework for a balanced, constructive involvement of each and every of the neighbouring countries. It has favoured and should favour an essential process of learning capable of strengthening a cooperative behavior among us. One based on the firm conviction that an early peaceful settlement of the conflicts in former Yugoslavia would turn beneficial to all our countries. The more so, because, except for the Yugoslav peoples, our peoples are the most affected by the risks and costs of the continuation of those conflicts. In both economic and political terms.

Taking into account the importance of preventing a possible spill-over of the civil war in former Yugoslavia, it might prove useful, perhaps, to think of new ways of ensuring an increased coordination of our individual efforts under the aegis of the Conference in Geneva and its Co-Chairmen.

Needless to say, full compliance with the embargoes established by the UN Security Council is essential for the success of all joint international efforts meant to curb and finally put an end to the tragic confrontations in former Yugoslavia.

Although my country is paying a very high price for the strict application of the embargo which deeply affects our economic situation, the Romanian government is strongly committed to abide firmly by the regime of sanctions. To this end Romania intends to develop cooperation with both the CSCE missions and the neighbouring countries, namely Bulgaria and Hungary, to fully comply with the embargo and ensure a safe traffic on the Danube.

Distinguished Co-Chairmen, there is no secret that a viable and lasting solution to the crisis in ex-Yugoslavia cannot be reached at without the constructive involvement - via the working groups set up in Geneva - of all parties in conflict.

In our view, the main lines of action able to encourage the domestic forces favourable to peace, and to discourage those who, for various reasons, continue to fuel to conflicts respectively should be the following:

a) isolating the crisis, and in particular armed violence, within the already affected areas of former Yugoslavia; and to this effect:
   - take all necessary measures for a strict application of the embargoes established by the UN Security Council, including the existing one on weapons, with the clear support of all the neighbouring countries;

- undertake a decisive international action to stop any flow of arms and military equipments towards the ex-Yugoslav republics. More arms into former Yugoslavia will just stimulate fighting;
- pay due attention to the risks that might stem from a possible unbalanced assessment of the responsibilities of each of the parties in conflict, in order to allow none of the proven perpetrators of the war to elude appropriate sanctions;
- ensure that the much needed humanitarian assistance reaches safely its destination.

b) underlying the particular responsibility of all neighbouring countries to refrain from any action that might lead to the continuation and the aggravation of the conflict and of inter-ethnic tensions, and also their obligation to act in their relations with the new independent republics of former Yugoslavia in keeping with the principles of international law, including respect of existing borders.

c) finding the appropriate ways to encourage and support, everywhere in former Yugoslavia, all political forces that take a responsible, constructive attitude, in accordance with CSCE and UN requirements.

d) Encouraging the adoption of specific and practical measures in order to support the neighbouring countries in applying in practice the embargo, including on the Danube, and assisting them in overcoming the losses they have registered.

e) aligning all diplomatic initiatives, especially those taking place outside this framework, to the efforts for the peaceful settlement in Geneva. Otherwise, they will run the risk of steering unexpected water to the mills of the civil war in former Yugoslavia.

56. STATEMENT BY THE TURKISH REPRESENTATIVE*

I wish to thank the Co-Chairmen of the ICFY for organizing this timely meeting. We are grateful to the Co-Chairmen, UNPROFOR, UNHCR, ICRC and the NGO's for their efforts in Bosnia and Herzegovina.

Turkey has done its utmost to help stop the aggression and bloodshed in Bosnia and Herzegovina and to avert the dangers of the spreading of the conflict over the Balkan peninsula. To this effect, we convened a Balkan Conference in

---

* Ministerial Level Meeting of the Steering Committee of the International Conference on the Former Yugoslavia, Geneva, 16 December 1992.

Istanbul, initiated two meetings of the Islamic Conference of Foreign Ministers and called for the 2nd Special Session of the Human Right Commission.

Decisions adopted in these meetings reflect the views of a sizeable segment of international community. The measures contained in these decisions provide valuable guidelines for the work of our Co-Chairmen in their endeavours.

Nevertheless, the situation on the ground has continuously deteriorated.

It is high time to come to grips with our failures:

1. We could not put under control the Serbian artillery around Sarajevo;
2. We could not establish an effective ceasefire;
3. We could not stop the shipments of weapons from Serbia to its troops and paramilitary forces;
4. We could not strengthen the terms of reference of the UNPROFOR;
5. We could not maintain humanitarian corridors;
6. We could not create safety zones;
7. We could not bring war criminals to justice;
8. We could not enforce a no-fly zone;
9. We could not allow Muslim-Croat joint operations;
10. We could not lift the one-sided embargo on the victim;
11. We could not mount a military intervention, limited or not.

Today we all further agree that:

- the aggressor is the Republic of Serbia, the Yugoslav army and Serbian paramilitary forces;
- the victim is the Muslims of Bosnia and Herzegovina; and
- the crime is genocide committed in the form of ethnic cleansing which aims at "extermination" or "destruction" of the victim population.

Half of the Muslim population have been uprooted and deported, the other half of the remaining population are living in besieged cities and towns and awaiting the winter to take its toll.

I am afraid, we will do, as before, too little too late.

For example:

- An enforcement of no-fly-zone, useful by itself, is not decisive enough to stop the aggression.
- We cannot pin any hope on the elections in Serbia.
- The Serbians cannot be expected to stop their aggression on their own.

-    We cannot envisage meaningful negotiations while Serbia controls an ethnically cleansed Bosnia and Herzegovina.

The measures we have to take should be proportionate to the nature and the scope of the conflict.

1.   All Serbian heavy weapons including artillery should be immediately put under UN control or silenced,
2.   The Serbian side should lift the sieges on Sarajevo and other town,
3.   Effective and viable measures should be taken to stop arms shipments from Serbia to its surrogates in Bosnia and Herzegovina,
4.   A no-fly-zone should be enforced by the UN Security Council,
5.   The embargo on the Government of Bosnia and Herzegovina should be lifted to uphold the right of legitimate self-defence. The CSCE Stockholm decision is a step in this direction,
6.   Safety zones to be protected by UNPROFOR should be established in areas where vulnerable populations live,
7.   The ICFY and UNSC should reaffirm the principles of the London Conference taking into account the worsening situation on the ground.
8.   The constitutional structure proposed by the Co-Chairmen should remain as the basis for negotiations and the other proposals which are not compatible with the enunciated principles should be discarded.

The implementation of these measures is essential for the Co-Chairmen to fulfil the tasks assigned to them by the international community.

Time is of utmost importance. We cannot afford or permit the Republic of Bosnia and Herzegovina to die.

57. STATEMENT BY THE HEAD OF THE SAUDI DELEGATION[*]

The Conference which was held in London last August to discuss the situation in former Yugoslavia has raised hopes of finding a negotiated solution that would satisfy all parties concerned and be compatible with United Nations resolutions and international legitimacy. Unfortunately, however, the developments that followed the conference have dashed those hopes.

---

[*] Ministerial Level Meeting of the Steering Committee of the International Conference on the Former Yugoslavia, Geneva, 16 December 1992.

The situation, as we all know, has become worse: the Serbian forces have extended the scale of their military operations and occupied most of the strategic outlets and most of the Bosnian territory: they now besiege the Bosnian capital at close range and from all sides while shelling and bombarding the city continuously; acts of killing, plunder and rape accompany ethnic cleansing; the Serbs go on defying United Nations resolutions and the international community.

This situation has caused concern all over the world. It was natural that it aroused particular concern in the Islamic World. That is why the Organisation of Islamic Conference held an extraordinary conference recently in Jeddah at Foreign Ministers level. In his opening address the Custodian of the Two Holy Mosques King Fahd referred to resolutions of the UN and the decisions of the London Conference and affirmed Saudi Arabia's support for those resolutions and decision, saying that collective efforts should be exerted in order to imple ment a solution decisively and effectively.

The Kingdom of Saudi Arabia confirms its commitment to support those international resolutions and to act within the bounds of international legitimacy for peace in former Yugoslavia. It expresses sincere hope that this Conference will lead to a just and peaceful end to the tragedy in Bosnia.

We wish the participants in this conference every success.

4. PEACEMAKING IN BOSNIA AND HERZEGOVINA

Editor's Note: To date, there have been at least five Peace Plans to settle the conflict in Bosnia and Herzegovina: the Carrington-Cutileiro Plan, the Vance-Owen Plan, the Stoltenberg-Owen Plan (often referred to as "the Invincible Package"), the European Union Action Plan, and the Contact Group Plan. The Statement of Principles worked out by Lord Carrington and Ambassador Cutileiro with the parties in March 1992 was reproduced earlier. The text of the Vance-Owen Plan and the Invincible Package are reproduced below, as are the European Union Plan and Ministerial Statements of the Contact Group on Bosnia and Herzegovina.

A. THE VANCE-OWEN PLAN

58. AGREEMENT RELATING TO BOSNIA AND HERZEGOVINA[*]

THE UNDERSIGNED,

Guided by the principles of the Charter of the United Nations, the Universal Declaration of Human Rights[a] and the Declaration on the Rights of Persons belonging National or Ethnic, Religious and Linguistic Minorities,[b]

Recalling the Statement of Principles and the Statement on Bosnia adopted by the International Conference on the Former Yugoslavia at its session in London and the Programme of Action on Humanitarian Issues agreed to at that session,

---

[*] Signed in Geneva on 30 January 1993 by A. Izetbegovic, R. Karadzic, and M. Boban; and, as witnesses, by C.R. Vance and D. Owen.

[a] General Assembly resolution 217 A (III).

[b] General Assembly resolution 47/135.

Considering the decisions of the United Nations Security Council relating to the former Yugoslavia,

Reaffirming their commitment to peace and security among the successor States to the former Yugoslavia,

Hereby agree as follows:

I. CONSTITUTIONAL FRAMEWORK FOR BOSNIA AND HERZEGOVINA

Tripartite negotiations shall proceed on a continuous basis in Geneva, under the auspices of the International Conference in the Former Yugoslavia, in order to finalise a Constitution for Bosnia and Herzegovina in accordance with the following principles:

(1)   Bosnia and Herzegovina shall be a decentralized State, the Constitution shall recognize three constituent peoples, as well as a group of others, with most governmental functions carried out by its provinces.

(2)   The provinces shall not have any international legal personality and may not enter into agreements with foreign States or with international organisations.

(3)   Full freedom of movement shall be allowed throughout Bosnia and Herzegovina, to be ensured in part by the maintenance of internationally controlled throughways.

(4)   All matters of vital concern to any of the constituent peoples shall be regulated in the Constitution, which as to these points may be amended only by consensus of these constituent peoples; ordinary governmental business is not to be veto-able by any group.

(5)   The provinces and the central Government shall have democratically elected legislature and democratically chosen chief executives and an independent judiciary. The Presidency shall be composed of three elected representatives of each of the three constituent peoples. The initial elections are to be United Nations/European Community/Conference on Security and Cooperation in Europe supervised.

(6)   A Constitutional Court, with a member from each group and a majority of non-Bosnian members initially appointed by the International Conference on the Former Yugoslavia, shall resolve disputes between the central Government and any province, and among organs of the former.

(7)   Bosnia and Herzegovina is to be progressively demilitarized under United Nations/European Community supervision.

(8)   The highest level of internationally recognized human rights shall be provided for in the Constitution, which shall also provide for the ensurance of implementation through both domestic and international mechanisms.

(9)   A number of international monitoring or control devices shall be provided for in the Constitution, to remain in place at least until the three constituent peoples by consensus agree to dispense with them.

II. COOPERATION IN RESPECT OF HUMANITARIAN EFFORTS

1. Maximum cooperation shall be extended to the High Commission for Refugees, the International Committee of the Red Cross, the United Nations Protection Force, the European Community Monitoring Mission and other humanitarian organisations working to provide assistance to refugees and displaced persons.

2. Full cooperation shall also be extended to the High Commissioner for Refugees in drawing up and implementing programmes for the return of refugees and displaced persons to their homes.

59. Map of Bosnia and Herzegovina

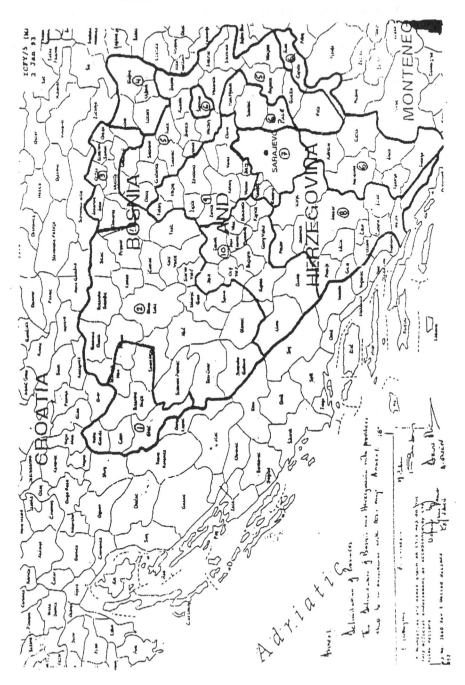

60. AGREEMENT FOR PEACE IN BOSNIA AND HERZEGOVINA*

THE UNDERSIGNED,

Welcoming the invitation of the Co-Chairmen of the Steering Committee of the International Conference on the Former Yugoslavia to participate in talks for the restoration of peace in Bosnia and Herzegovina,

Taking account of the constructive atmosphere of the peace talks held in Geneva from 2 to 5 January and the assistance of the Force Commander of the United Nations Protection Force, Lieutenant-General Satish Nambiar,

Keeping in mind the principles of the International Conference and the Resolutions of the United Nations Security Council, in particular Resolutions 752 (1992) and 787 (1992) pertaining to withdrawal of all outside forces from Bosnia and Herzegovina,

Wishing to bring the conflict in Bosnia and Herzegovina to an end without any further delay and to re-establish peace throughout the country,

Desiring to work out arrangements for bringing about compliance with a cessation of hostilities, and for monitoring it so as to ensure that it is effective and lasting,

Hereby agree on the following:

1. Measures for the achievement of an unconditional cessation of hostilities throughout Bosnia and Herzegovina, as set out in Annex I to the present agreement;
2. Measures for the restoration of infrastructure in Bosnia and Herzegovina, as set out in annex II to the present agreement;
3. Measures on the opening of routes, as set out in annex IV to the present agreement;
4. Arrangements on the separation of forces, as set out in annex IV to the present agreement;
5. Measures for the demilitarization of Sarajevo, as set out in annex V to the present agreement;
6. Measures for the monitoring of the borders of Bosnia and Herzegovina, as set out in annex VI to the present agreement;
7. Return of forces to the designated provinces, as set out in annex VII to the present agreement.

---

* Signed in Geneva on 30 January 1993 by A. Izetbegovic, R. Karadzic, and M. Boban; and, as witnesses, by C.R. Vance and D. Owen.

Annex I
Cessation of Hostilities

Broad Principles

All parties agree to support the broad principles required to support a cessation of hostilities. These broad principles will be translated into concrete action through additional discussion within the Mixed Military Working Group. Several of the principles will be dealt with on a stand-alone basis, although they remain an integral part of the overall framework of the cessation of hostilities.

The broad principles are:

A ceasefire must be put in place and remain effective. This is to be implemented 72 hours from midnight (New York time - EST) of the day on which the Security Council endorses this plan.

Monitoring and control measures are to be put in place to ensure compliance and should include as a minimum:

- Links between Commanders in conflict areas (hot lines);
- Provision of United Nations Protection Force/European Community Monitoring Mission liaison and monitors;
- Establishment of joint crisis management teams;
- Opening of confrontation line crossing-points. For use by the United Nations Protection Force and monitoring agencies.

The separation of forces is to be achieved.

Routes supporting the general freedom of movement of people, commerce and humanitarian aid are to be opened.

The restoration of infrastructure will proceed as a priority. Restoration will not be linked to any negotiations.

Essential Elements

- Security Council endorses the plan - initiates all follow-on action (D-3). The 72 hours permit passage of information;
- Cessation of hostilities effective (D-Day);
- Declaration of forces - this is to take place in D-1 and should include:
  - Numbers and locations of all heavy weapons,
  - Detailed documentation of mine fields,

- Locations of front lines (traces),
- Defensive works and positions;
- Establish demarcation line (joint actively);
- Move in United Nations Protection Force forces to establish security (commencing D+1):
  - Monitor lines of conflict,
  - Monitor heavy weapons,
  - Reporting system (all parties);
- Withdrawal of heavy weapons:
  - Of calibre 12.7 mm and above; 5 days for Sarajevo and 15 days for remaining areas;
  - Locations to be determined based on effective ranges of weapon systems.
  - All such withdrawals will be supervised by the United Nations Protection Force and subsequently monitored at the designated locations by the United Nations Protection Force in order to prevent their use.
- Separation of forces:
  - Abandon defensive works on confrontation line,
  - Area of separation to be agreed,
  - Distance in which no forces, except police, allowed,
  - Distance within which no defensive works will be manned.

The separation of forces and withdrawal of heavy weapons are linked.

Mixed Military Commission is established to deal with any clarifications and breaches of the cessation of hostilities.

Annex II
Restoration of Infrastructure

All parties agree that denial or use of civil utilities as a weapon of war is unacceptable, and all affirm their commitment to the full restoration of the civil infrastructure across Bosnia and Herzegovina, and in particular, Sarajevo.

The provision of humanitarian aid cannot be linked in any way with the military steps of the process of demilitarization or cessation of hostilities. Being humanitarian in nature, its priority is strictly governed by the ability of all three parties to support its implementation.

Restoration will be the first priority. Therefore, immediate efforts must be placed on the restoration of infrastructure. This is equally applicable to the city of Sarajevo as well as the rest of Bosnia and Herzegovina. It includes where applicable:

Power grids;
Power stations;
Bridges;
Gas;
Telecommunications;
Railway lines;
Routes;
Water supply.

Guarantees of security will be requested and must be provided and the restoration of power/water/heat will be fully supported by the warring parties.

A joint committee is already in place in Sarajevo; the work of this committee is to be facilitated with immediate effect to enable early restoration of utilities in Sarajevo.

Assistance will be provided through all the appropriated agencies, including United Nations and civilian expertise. However, within Bosnia and Herzegovina, a joint commission composed of representatives of all sides is to identify the priorities, define the needs and execute the work in conjunction with civil authorities. To this end, vital installations will be identified in conjunction with Bosnia and Herzegovina joint commission:

- Access will be guaranteed after local arrangements are made.
- Forces will be withdrawn from sites consistent with security.
- Warring parties will provide, when necessary, liaison for the repair teams.
- Civil agencies/workers will be assisted.

Parties will work to re-establish infrastructure, including railways/power grids/water supplies, across borders with neighbouring republics.

Respect for infrastructure facilities must be developed and they must remain free from attack or use as defensive positions.

All parties agree to develop a common instruction for passage down chains of command to demonstrate an equal endorsement of support.

Annex III
Opening of Routes

The opening of routes is directly related to the political issue which concerns the freedom of movement of all people in the context of constitutional principles. It is equally applicable to Sarajevo as well as all other areas of Bosnia and Herzegovina.

It is to be achieved through:

- Security guarantees by all parties to ensure non-interference and protection of personnel and material using the routes;
- Non-interference on the route;
- Checkpoints, patrols, and monitoring by United Nations Protection Force/European Community Monitoring Mission, as appropriate;
- Supervised inspection at entry points;
- Freedom of passage of humanitarian aid;
- Absolute freedom of movement of United Nations forces.

The concept of blue routes for Sarajevo is appended hereto. This format is applicable for the establishment of all other similar types of routes within Bosnia and Herzegovina. Additional routes can be negotiated under the aegis of the Mixed Military Working Group.

APPENDIX

SARAJEVO "BLUE ROUTE" CONCEPT

The parties have decided to establish three free passage routes with mutually agreed measures to guarantee and ensure safe passage for freedom of movement of civilians, commercial goods and humanitarian aid to and from Sarajevo.

These routes are:

- Sarajevo-Zenica-Sarajevo;
- Sarajevo-Mostar-Sarajevo;
- Sarajevo-Zvornik-Sarajevo.

Outline Plan for Blue Routes

1.   Execution
1.1   Prerequisites

The following prerequisites are to be required:

1.1.1 Cessation of hostilities.
1.1.2 Complete freedom of movement for United Nations Protection Force on the three blue routes.

1.2   Use of the Blue Routes

1.2.1 Timings
Routes will be open during daylight hours for convoys. United Nations Protection Force will use the route 24 hours a day.

1.2.2 Access for Civilians
All civilians, regardless of sex, age, or ethnic origin, and without weapons or ammunition, will be allowed to use the routes. Private and commercial vehicles will also be permitted on each route subject to inspection outlined on paragraph 1.5.1 below.

1.2.3 Access for Humanitarian Aid
All international and local humanitarian aid agencies will be allowed to use the routes. Humanitarian aid includes, but is not limited to, food, water, medical supplies and fuel.

1.2.4 Access for Commercial Goods
Normal commerce will be progressively restored to and from Sarajevo.

1.3   Establishment of Routes

1.3.1 Sarajevo-Zenica-Sarajevo
This route incorporates Sarajevo-Rajlovac-Ilijas-Visoko-Zenica.

1.3.2 Sarajevo-Mostar-Sarajevo
This route incorporates Sarajevo-Ilidza-Hadzici-Tarcin-Jablanica-Mostar.

1.3.3. Sarajevo-Zvornik-Sarajevo
This route incorporates Sarajevo-Bentbasa-Mokro-Sololac-Vlasenica-Zvornik.

1.4   Checkpoints

Checkpoints will be established and manned by United Nations Protection Force forces at the entrance and exit of each route and when crossing a line of confrontation. Each United Nations Protection Force checkpoint will be located near or with the checkpoint of the force controlling the territory involved consistent with the security requirements of the factions. No side will be permitted to erect a new checkpoint.

1.5 Control Measures

1.5.1 Inspection Procedures

(a) Inspections will be conducted by United Nations Protection Force forces. Each side is permitted to monitor the events in close coordination with the United Nations Protection Force.

(b) War-related material, weapons or ammunition are forbidden. If found, the items will be confiscated and subsequently destroyed under control of the United Nations Protection Force and the parties.

(c) Humanitarian aid convoys may be subjected to inspections.

(d) Checkpoints will be activated only during daylight hours as a safety measure for civilians and convoys.

1.5.2 Escorts

(a) Each convoy will be escorted with the appropriate United Nations Protection Force vehicles.

(b) Convoys and escorts will take priority over military activities.

(c) The army controlling the territory involved may provide civilian police as an additional means of security.

1.5.3 Patrols

(a) United Nations Protection Force forces will patrol the blue routes as necessary.

(b) Patrols will consists of at least two vehicles suitably equipped and will contain an appropriate communications net.

(c) All United Nations Protection Force patrols will be permitted to cross all checkpoints.

1.6 Implementation

1.6.1 Suggested Timeframe

D-3   - Security Council endorses the plan
D+1 - Erecting checkpoints
        - Inspection procedures agreed
        - Routes cleared of all obstacles

- Repairs carried out as required
- Reconnoitre by the United Nations Protection Force
D+5 - Opening of blue routes for civilians and humanitarian aid

Annex IV
Separation of Forces

The parties agree that the separation of forces is an element of the overall cessation of hostilities. An agreement will be based on the steps and control measures and sequence of events outlined below:

Steps

The concrete steps envisaged in the process include:

- An absolute ceasefire.
- Temporary freezing of the military situation, pending agreement in return of forces to designated provinces.
- No forward deployments or offensive action.
- No move of additional forces, explosives and weapons forward will be permitted. Rotation on an individual basis is acceptable.
- Withdrawal of heavy weapons (direct and indirect fire) of all parties from areas of confrontation to areas of range, decided upon by the parties in conjunction with the United Nations Protection Force.
- Physical separation of forces in contact.
- Security and monitoring of the demilitarized zone.

Control Measures

The control measures required include:

- Declaration of forces in being, including location of minefields.
- Monitoring of front lines.
- Declaration of heavy weapons in separation areas.
- Establishing agreed lines in which forces may be located.
- Staged withdrawal of forces culminating in their relocation to designated provinces.

Sequence of Events

- Ceasefire under aegis of the overall cessation of hostilities.
- Establishment and patrol of the demarcation line by United Nations Protection Force personnel.
- Withdrawal of designated weapons systems of all parties.
- Search and clearance of the affected area by joint patrols.
- Conduct of joint and United Nations-only patrols within the area. Composition of the patrols to be negotiated at the Mixed Military Working Group.

UNPROFOR Concept for Heavy Weapons Control

- All heavy weapons 12.7 mm calibre and above are included.
- These weapons will be withdrawn out of effective range to areas decided between the United Nations Protection Force and the parties.
- The withdrawal will be monitored by the United Nations Protection Force.
- Once in location the weapons will be monitored to ensure that they are not used.
- The United Nations Protection Force will not physically take over the weapons.
- Where terrain such as towns preclude moving weapons out of range, they will be gathered in agreed location under United Nations Protection Force control to ensure that they are not used.

Annex V
Demilitarization of Sarajevo

The demilitarization of Sarajevo is based on one requirement: an effective cessation of hostilities.

The other elements are:

- Establishment of control on an designated line;
- Restoration of civil utilities;
- Land routes and freedom of movement;
- Separation of forces along lines of confrontation.

Control measures include:

- Patrol and monitoring of the demarcation line;
- Checkpoints at major crossings until confidence is restored;
- Mixed patrols in the demilitarized zone.

A military/civil joint commission as previously proposed should oversee the implementation of the accord.

Appended hereto is a draft agreement covering first stage of a potential agreement on the demilitarization of Sarajevo. This stage covers the airport area as already discussed at the Mixed Military Working Group.

APPENDIX

PROPOSED AGREEMENT ON THE FIRST STAGE OF DEMILITARIZATION
OF SARAJEVO

The authorized representatives of all three conflicting sides with the presence of the United Nations Protection Force representative agree on the implementation of an area in the western and southern districts of Sarajevo.

Cessation of Hostilities

The cessation of hostilities will be implemented as follows:

(a) The freezing of the military situation on the existing lines.
(b) No offensive action allowed.
(c) No forward redeployments.
(d) All heavy weapons will be withdrawn from positions from which they can engage.
(e) No movement or any additional forces although rotation of personnel on a one-for-one basis shall be permitted.
(f) No movement or resupply of ammunitions, explosives or incendiary devices.

Freedom of Movement for All Civilians

The agreement on blue routes will re-establish the freedom of movement of all civilians in support of this plan.

Restoration of Civil Utilities

A Joint Commission composed of representatives from each side will identify priorities, define needs and execute the implementation of civil utilities. Details can be found in annex II, Restoration of infrastructure.

Removal of Heavy Weapons

(a) *Area.* All heavy weapons will be withdrawn to designated locations from the following: Mojmilo, Dobrinja, Lukavica, Gornji, Kotorac, Vojkovici, Hrasnica, Sokolovici, Butmir, Ilidza, Otes, Stup, Nedarici.
(b) *Joint Commission.* A Joint Commission will be created.

(1) The mission of this Joint Commission will be to execute and implement details of this plan and subsequent phases.
(2) This Joint Commission will be composed of:

(a) A United Nations Protection Force command and support element;
(b) A team of each side commanded by an officer senior enough to make decisions and designated as the authorised commander for the troops in the areas affected;
(c) A joint communications system which includes a command set and the necessary guaranteed communications link to each individual headquarters.

(c) *Time-frame.* From each district the withdrawal of heavy weapons out of the designated area will be carried out in two stages within a period of five days:

(1) Stage 1 - Withdrawal of all direct fire weapons of 12.7 mm calibre and above (tanks, armoured personnel carriers, anti-tank, anti-aircraft and heavy machine guns).
(2) Stage 2 - Withdrawal of all heavy indirect fire weapons (mortars, field artillery).

(d) *Control measures.* The following implementation and control measures will be used:

(1) United Nations Protection Force forces will patrol the area of separation between the conflicting sides.

(2) United Nations Protection Force forces will be deployed on the confrontation lines and in agreed mixed checkpoints proposed by the Joint Commission.

(3) All parties are to identify weapons by type and location and will provide the United Nations Protection Force with detailed maps of areas considered to be under their respective control.

(4) Complete freedom of movement for all United Nations Protection Force personnel and vehicles within the affected areas.

(5) The Joint Commission will establish mixed patrols as appropriate.

Annex VI
Monitoring of Borders

Pursuant to United Nations Security Council resolution 787 (1992), Paragraph 5, to prevent interference from outside the Republic of Bosnia and Herzegovina, the United Nations Protection Force/European Community Monitoring Mission will monitor borders with neighbouring republics.

Principles

United Nations Protection Force/European Monitoring Mission forces will monitor crossings to prevent weapons, munitions, military personnel or irregular forces from entering the country.

Borders with adjoining republics will be monitored.

United Nations Protection Force actions to observe, search and report will be facilitated by the authorities of the Republic of Croatia and the Federal Republic of Yugoslavia.

Annex VII
Return of Forces to Designated Provinces

To enable the process of return to normalcy, and as a direct follow-on from the cessation of hostilities and the separation of forces, a return of forces to designated provinces will be conducted. This can start as part of the withdrawal of heavy weapons but, given the winter weather conditions, it is hard to fix a definite date for the completion of this process. We should however aim to achieve the return of forces within 45 days.

This stage will be coordinated with an agreed demobilization of forces in being.

The United Nations Protection Force/European Community Monitoring Mission will monitor the withdrawal of these forces in conjunction with national and provincial authorities.

The Mixed Military Working Group would be the technical negotiating agency.

61. INTERIM ARRANGEMENTS FOR BOSNIA AND HERZEGOVINA (29 JANUARY 1993)

INTRODUCTION

In 1990, the Bosnian Parliament adopted amendment LXXIII to the Constitution of the Republic of Bosnia and Herzegovina. Following the outbreak of hostilities in 1992, this provision of the Constitution was invoked and the Presidency was expanded from 7 to 10 members with the inclusion of the Prime Minister, The President of the Assembly and the Commander-in-Chief of the Armed Forces. The powers of the Parliament were transferred to the Presidency.

Following the signing of the peace agreement and their endorsement by the United Nations Security Council, it is proposed that each of the three parties represented at the Conference (the "parties") nominate three representatives to serve in an interim central Government. The confirmation of these nine representatives will be subject to the approval of the Co-Chairmen of the Steering Committee of the International Conference on the Former Yugoslavia (the "Co-Chairmen"). Once the composition of the interim central Government has been confirmed, it is proposed that the Presidency, acting in accordance with its powers under amendment LXXIII, will transfer its powers and authority to this interim central Government.

Those aspects of the existing Constitution which relate to the Presidency will then be suspended. To the extent practicable, the other provisions of the existing Constitution of Bosnia and Herzegovina will continue to apply, in particular those provisions relating to the courts and legal system.

During the interim period, which is defined as the period between the transfer of authority to the interim central Government and the holding of free and fair elections, a new Constitution for Bosnia and Herzegovina will be drafted by the parties with the assistance of the Co-Chairmen and will be the basis upon which the elections will take place.

In each province, there will be an interim provincial government composed of a Governor, Vice-Governor and 10 other members.

Throughout the interim period, *opstina* authorities will retain their existing powers. The *opstina* boundaries will remain as at present except where they are crossed by provincial boundaries or where the boundaries have been changed by agreement under the auspices of the International Conference on the Former Yugoslavia.

This document contains proposals for the functioning of an International Access Authority, the national power authority, the National Bank, the Post, Telegraph and Telecommunications Authority of Bosnia and Herzegovina and an independent National Civil Aviation authority.

I. INTERIM CENTRAL GOVERNMENT

A. In the interim period, there will be a nine-member interim central Government.

1. Three representatives will be nominated by each of the parties. These nominations will then be conformed by the Co-Chairmen.
2. The interim central Government will take decisions by consensus. In the event that a decision will be referred to the Co-Chairmen for their urgent consideration.
3. The interim central Government will be located in Sarajevo, within that *opstina* designated as the capital. In addition to its national responsibilities, the interim central Government will administer the capital and have responsibility for its policy.
4. The position of President of the interim central Government will rotate every four months among the representatives of the parties. The President of the interim central Government will perform the role of head of State.

B. The principal responsibilities of the interim central Government will be as follows:

1. Preparations for the holding of free and fair elections, on the basis of the new Constitution, under international supervision;
2. Relations with the Mixed Military Working Group, the United Nations Protection Force (including the United Nations Civilian Police), the European Community Monitoring Mission and the International Conference on the Former Yugoslavia;

3. Coordination with the Office of the United Nations High Commissioner for Refugees, The International Committee of the Red Cross, the World Health Organization and other relevant agencies on the return and rehabilitation of refugees and displaced persons.
4. Foreign Affairs (including membership in international organizations);
5. International commerce (customs duties, quotas);
6. Citizenship;
7. Raising of any taxes required to carry out its functions.

C. The interim central Government will be responsible or appointing ministers and determining the role of such ministries as are deemed appropriate.
D. The Co-Chairmen will be involved with the parties in the preparation of the Constitution for Bosnia and Herzegovina and will also be available to assist the interim central Government in its work.

II. INTERIM PROVINCIAL GOVERNMENTS

A. During the interim period, each province will have an interim provincial government composed of a Governor, a Vice-Governor and 10 other members. The Governor, the Vice-Governor and the 10 other members of the interim provincial government will be nominated by the parties on the basis of the composition of the population of the province* provided that none of the three constituent peoples will be left unrepresented in any province. The interim provincial governments will be composed as in annex A.
B. Decisions will normally be taken by a simple majority, except that the adoption of the provincial constitution and the setting of *opstina* boundaries will be taken by consensus.
C. The principal functions of the interim provincial governments will be:

1. The drafting of provincial constitutions in accordance with the new Constitution of Bosnia and Herzegovina;
2. The preparation of free and fair elections, which should be held as soon as possible, on the basis of proportional representation and under international supervision;

---

* To determine these relative percentages, the 1991 census will be used.

3. Relations with the Mixed Military Working Groups, the United Nations Protection Force (including the United Nations Civilian Police), the European Community Monitoring Mission and the International Conference on the Former Yugoslavia;
4. Coordination with the Office of the United Nations High Commissioner for Refugees, The International Committee of the Red Cross, the World Health Organization and other relevant agencies on the return and rehabilitation of refugees and displaced persons;
5. Supervision of Police Force;
6. Restoration of infrastructure;
7. Raising of any taxes necessary to carry out their functions.

D. There will be attached to the staff of each provincial Governor a United Nations Protection Force Military Liaison, including a United Nations Civilian Police Liaison Officer, to assist in the carrying out of the above tasks.

III. INTERIM ARRANGEMENTS FOR THE PROTECTION OF HUMAN RIGHTS

A. The three parties have accepted principle No. 8 of the Constitutional Framework for Bosnia and Herzegovina which states that the highest level of internationally recognized human rights shall be provided for in the Constitution. The international community has repeatedly condemned ethnic cleansing and has demanded that its results be reversed. In order that the provisions of principle No. 8 be implemented in the interim period, the following measures will be taken, with particular emphasis placed on reversing ethnic cleansing wherever it has occurred.

1. All statements or commitments made under duress, particularly those relating to the relinquishment of rights to land and property, are wholly null and void.
2. Four ombudsmen will be appointed immediately by the Co-Chairmen, as per paragraph VI.B.2 of the *Proposed Constitutional Structure for Bosnia and Herzegovina* (ICFY/6, annex).
3. All citizens, through their representatives, will have the right to request international monitoring in areas where they believe that human rights were being, are being, or are about to be infringed. This may involve the monitoring of the area by the United Nations Civilian Police or other appropriate bodies such as the European Community Monitoring Mission, with or without the assistance of United Nations Protection

Force military personnel. In the same way, they will also be able to make representations to the Mixed Military Working Group to request a redeployment of any armed forces in their area.

IV. Appointment of a Representative of the Co-Chairmen in Bosnia and Herzegovina

The Co-Chairmen shall appoint a representative in Bosnia and Herzegovina, who will be resident in Sarajevo and available as and when necessary to he interim central Government and the interim provincial governments.

V. Establishment of an International Access Authority

A. Principle 3 of the Constitutional Framework for Bosnia and Herzegovina states that "full freedom of movement shall be allowed throughout Bosnia and Herzegovina, to be ensured in part by the maintenance of internationally controlled throughways".

In order to implement this principle, an international access authority will be established with representatives from the interim central Government and the interim provincial governments, which:

1. Will have sole responsibility for all railway lines in Bosnia and Herzegovina and those roads which are declared as internationally controlled throughways.
2. Will regulate the operation of port facilities on the River Sava.

The Authority's essential purpose will be to guarantee full freedom of movement between and within the provinces of Bosnia and Herzegovina and also to and from these provinces to the Republic of Croatia and to the Republic of Serbia (the proposed routes are set forth in annex B).

B. It is intended that the International Access Authority will be in operation as soon as possible during the interim period. Following the endorsement of the Agreement on Peace in Bosnia and Herzegovina by the United Nations Security Council, all designated throughways will come under the overlapping responsibility of the United Nations Protection Force. A period of overlapping responsibility is envisaged for the United Nations Protection Force and that of the International Access Authority. During this period of overlapping responsibility, the United Nations Protection Force's involvement will be phased out and its responsibilities assumed by traffic police employed by the International Access

Authority, This transfer of responsibility will only happen by agreement of all those involved in the International Access authority.

VI. FUNCTIONING OF THE NATIONAL POWER AUTHORITY

A Board of Directors will be appointed by the interim central Government and the interim provincial governments to manage Elektro Priveda, the existing national power authority, which will be responsible for the transmission and distribution of electricity in Bosnia and Herzegovina. The Board will be responsible for ensuring the uninterrupted supply of electricity to the whole of the country and to make appropriated links with neighbouring countries.

1. The interim central Government and each of the interim provincial governments will appoint one representative to the Board of Directors of Elektro Priveda.
2. Elektro Priveda will continue to have its headquarters in Sarajevo.

VII. FUNCTIONING OF THE NATIONAL BANK OF BOSNIA AND HERZEGOVINA

The functions of the Governor and Council of the National Bank (Naroda Banka) of Bosnia and Herzegovina will be taken over by a Board of Governors. The National Bank will continue to have responsibility, *inter alia*, for issuing currency and for exercising a regulatory function over provincial banks, as well as for relations with international financial institutions.

1. The interim central Government and each of the interim provincial governments will appoint one representative to the Board of Governors of the National Bank.
2. The National Bank will remain located in Sarajevo.

VIII. FUNCTIONING OF THE NATIONAL POST, TELEGRAPH AND TELECOMMUNICATIONS AUTHORITY

A Board of Directors will be appointed by the interim central Government and the interim provincial governments to manage to National Post, Telegraph and Telecommunications services throughout Bosnia and Herzegovina, and necessary international links. It will also have responsibility for the allocation of radio and television transmission frequencies in Bosnia and Herzegovina.

1. The interim central Government and each of the interim provincial governments will appoint one representative to the Board of Directors of the National Post, Telegraph and Telecommunications Authority.
2. The National Post, Telegraph and Telecommunications Authority will be located in Sarajevo.

IX. ESTABLISHMENT OF AN INDEPENDENT NATIONAL CIVIL AVIATION AUTHORITY

An independent National Civil Aviation Authority will be established as soon as possible by the interim central Government and the interim provincial governments.

The National Civil Aviation Authority will, when appropriate, assume responsibilities for the control of all civilian traffic in the airspace of Bosnia and Herzegovina, as well as for relations with the International Civil Aviation Organization and other relevant international authorities. Initially, a period of overlapping responsibilities is envisaged for the United Nations Protection Force and the National Civil Aviation Authority.

The United Nations Protection Force will continue operating and controlling Sarajevo airport until other arrangements are agreed with the United Nations Protection Force.

1. The interim central Government and each of he interim provincial governments will appoint one representative to the Board of Directors of the National Civil Aviation Authority.
2. The National Civil Aviation Authority will have its headquarters in Sarajevo.

Annex A
Structure of Interim Provincial Governments

For the purposes of this annex, the parties will be designated "Party A", "Party B" and "Party C", denoting the delegations of Mate Boban, Alija Izetbegovic and Radovan Karadzic respectively.

Province No. 1
Province capital: Bihac
Governor: Nominated by Party B
Vice-Governor: Nominated by Party C
Other members of interim provincial government:
seven members nominated by Party B, two members, nominated by Party C, one member nominated by Party A

Province No. 2
Province capital: Banja Luka
Governor: Nominated by Party C
Vice-Governor: Nominated by Party B
Other members of interim provincial government:
seven members nominated by Party C, two members nominated by Party B, one member nominated by Party A

Province No. 3
Province capital: Bosanski Brod
Governor: Nominated by Party A
Vice-Governor: Nominated by Party C
Other members of interim government:
Five members nominated by Party A, three members nominated by Party C, two members nominated by Party B

Province No. 4
Province capital: Bijeljina
Governor: Nominated by Party C
Vice-Governor: Nominated by Party B
Other members of interim provincial government:
five members nominated by Party C, four members nominated by Party B, one member nominated by Party A

Province No. 5
Province capital: Tuzla
Governor: Nominated by Party B
Vice-Governor: Nominated by Party C
Other members of interim provincial government:
five members nominated by Party B, three members nominated by Party C, two members nominated by Party A

Province No. 6
Province capital: Nevesinje
Governor: Nominated by Party C
Vice-Governor: Nominated by Party B
Other members of interim provincial government
seven members nominated by Party C, two members nominated by Party B, one member nominated by Party A

Province No. 7
Province of Sarajevo
Because of its special position with the capital in its midst, it is proposed that each of the parties will nominate three members in the interim provincial government.

The *opstina* boundaries in Sarajevo will be referred immediately to a committee to which each party will nominate a member. The Committee will meet in Sarajevo under the chairmanship of the Co-Chairmen's representative, and will report to the Co-Chairmen before Sunday, 7 February 1993. The Co-Chairmen will arbitrate in the event of any differences.

It is envisaged that one of the *opstina*s will be called the "Capital *opstina*" and encompass the government buildings, historic buildings, the university, hospital, the railway station and sports facilities and will come under the administration of the interim central Government.

Province No. 8
Province capital: Mostar
Governor Nominated by Party A
Vice-Governor: Nominated by Party B
Other members of interim provincial government:
six members nominated by Party A, three members nominated by Party B, one member nominated by Party C

Province No. 9
Province capital: Zenica
Governor: Nominated by Party B
Vice-Governor: Nominated by Party A
Other members of interim provincial government:
six members nominated by Party B, two members nominated by Party A, two members nominated by Party C

Province No. 10
Province capital: Travnik
Governor: Nominated by Party A
Vice-Governor: Nominated by Party B
Other members of interim provincial government:
five members nominated by Party B, four members nominated by Party A, one
member nominated by Party C

Annex B
Throughways to be Controlled by the International Access Authority

- That part of the road from Bihac to Livno that passes through Banja Luka
  Province;
- That part of the road from Bihac to Jajce that passes through Banja Luka Prov-
  ince;
- That part of the road from Banja Luka to Brcko that passes through Posavina
  Province;
- Those parts of the roads from Tuzla to Orasje and from Tuzla to Brcko that
  pass through Posavina and Bijeljina Provinces;
- Those parts of the roads from Han Pijesak to Sekovici and from Sekovici to
  Zvornik that pass through Tuzla Province;
- That part of the road from Pale to Kalinovik that passes through Sarajevo
  Province;
- That part of the road from Foca to Sarajevo that passes through East Herzeg-
  ovina Province;
- The road from Sarajevo to Mostar and to the Croatian border towards Split;
- That part of the road from Ljubinja to Neum that passes through Mostar Prov-
  ince.

International road border crossings affecting the International Access Authority:

- Bihac Province: Velika Kladusa, towards Karlovac and Zagreb;
- Banja Luka Province: Bosanski Gradisja, towards Zagreb-Belgrade auto-
  route;
- Posavina Province: Orasje, towards Zagreb-Belgrade autoroute;
- Bijeljina Province: Sremska Race, towards Zagreb-Belgrade autoroute;
- Tuzla Province: Zvornik, towards Zagreb-Belgrade autoroute;
- Mostar Province: Osoje, towards Split.

B. THE STOLTENBERG-OWEN PLAN

Editor's Note: This Plan, it being negotiated on board HMS *Invincible*, is often referred to as "the Invincible Package". It consists of the following documents:

62. MAPS

Map of Bosnia and Herzegovina

UNION OF REPUBLICS OF BOSNIA AND HERZEGOVINA

− − − − − EXACT LINE TO BE CONFIRMED

Map of Sarajevo

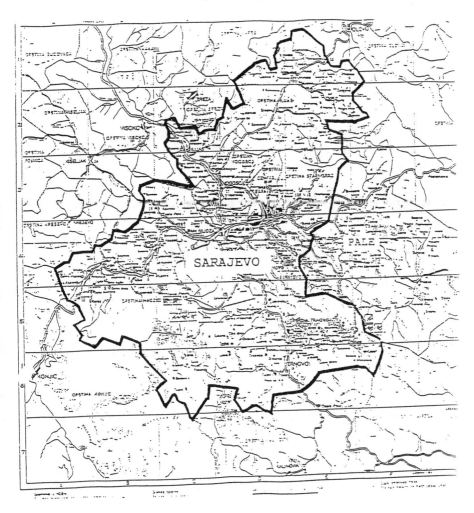

Explanation of Detailed Maps

GORNJI VAKUF

Three constructions to assist in demarcation between Croat and Muslim majority republics:

- *Flyover complex* at existing junction at *Padgrade*;
- *Road* along line of existing mining railway from *Humac* to *Flyover*;
- *Bypass* south of *Gornji Vakuf* from the *Flyover complex* at *Podgrade* to the main *Prozor Road* near *Pidris*.

These works will enable uninterrupted access on home territory for:

- Croat majority republic between *Prozor*, *Jaijce* and *Novo Travnik*;
- Muslim majority republic between *Gornji Vakuf* and *Bugojno*.

BUGOJNO-DONJI VAKUF

Two constructions to assist in demarcation between Croat and Muslim majority republics:

- Upgraded *Road* over the *Vrbas* northwest of *Trnjak*.

These works will enable uninterrupted access on home territory for:

- Croat majority republic between *Kupres*, *Prozor* and *Jaijce* (via *Porice* and *Prusac*);
- Muslim majority republic between *Travnik*, *Bugojno* and *Gornji Vakuf*.

JABLANICA

One construction to assist in demarcation between Croat and Muslim majority republics:

- *Bypass* on east bank of the *Neretva* between *Aleksin Han* and *Jablanica*.

This work will enable uninterrupted access on home territory for:

- Croat majority republic between the western edge of *Jablanica* and *Prozor*;
- Muslim majority republic between *Mostar* and *Sarajevo Districts*.

Before this work is complete the boundary between the Croat and Muslim majority republics shall be (*see map 1*):

- The *Neretva* south of *Aleksin Han*;
- The western edge of the main road north of *Aleksin Han* as far as *Jablanica*.

After this work is complete the boundary between the Croat and Muslim majority republics shall be (*see map 1*):

- The *Neretva* south of *Jablanica*.

Map of Gornji Vakuf

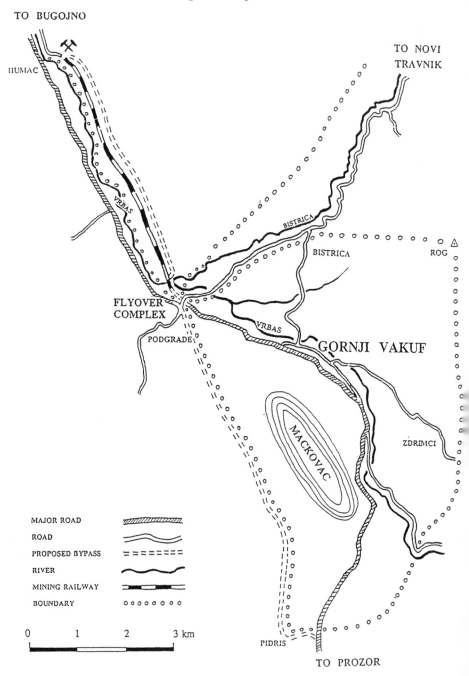

TO BUGOJNO

HUMAC

TO NOVI
TRAVNIK

VRBAS

BISTRICA

BISTRICA

ROG

FLYOVER
COMPLEX

VRBAS

PODGRADE

GORNJI VAKUF

MACKOVAC

ZDRIMCI

PIDRIS

TO PROZOR

MAJOR ROAD

ROAD

PROPOSED BYPASS

RIVER

MINING RAILWAY

BOUNDARY

0   1   2   3 km

Map of Bugojno-Donju Vakuf

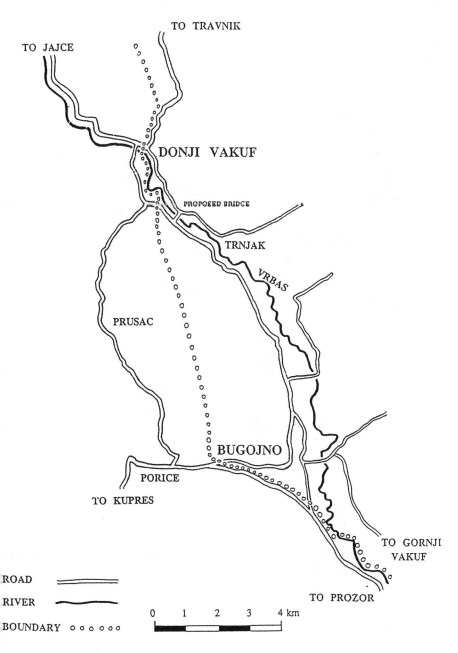

Map of Jablanica

MAP 1

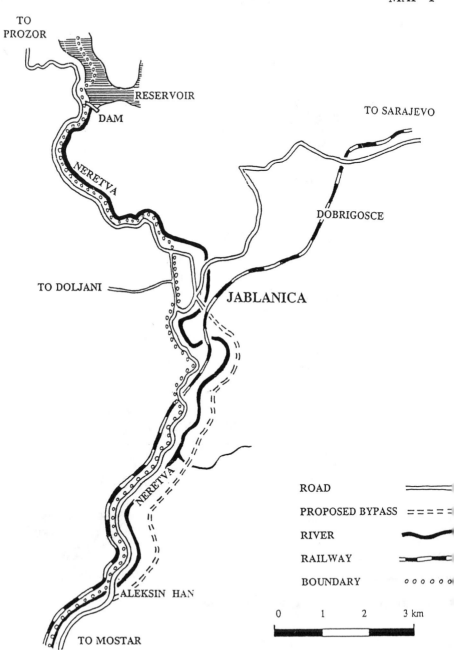

TO
PROZOR

RESERVOIR

DAM

TO SARAJEVO

NERETVA

DOBRIGOSCE

TO DOLJANI

JABLANICA

NERETVA

ROAD

PROPOSED BYPASS

RIVER

RAILWAY

BOUNDARY

ALEKSIN HAN

0   1   2   3 km

TO MOSTAR

Map of Gorazde-Rogatica-Zepa

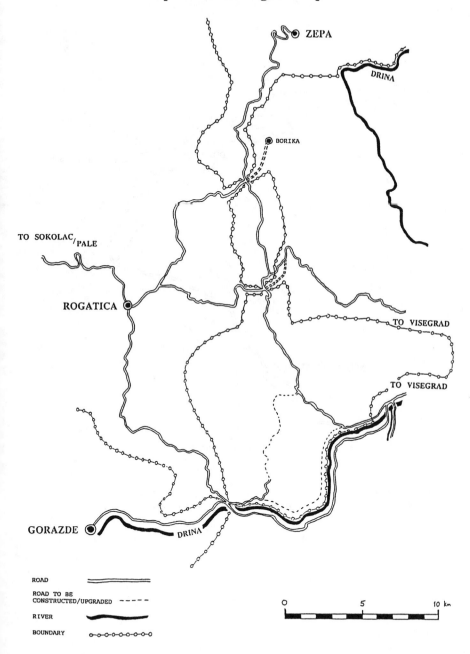

Map of Dolac-Travnik-Novi Travnik

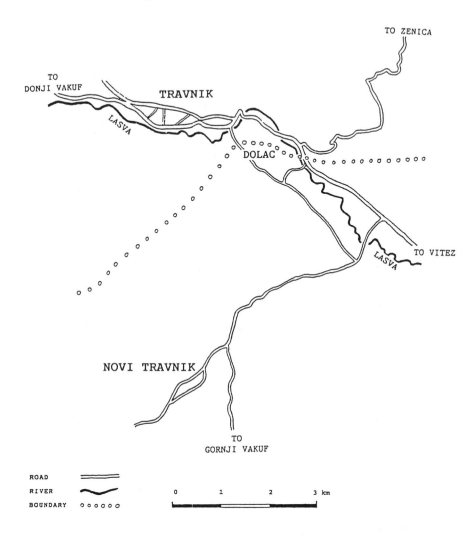

Map of Capljina-Ljubinje-Metkovic-Neum-Stolac

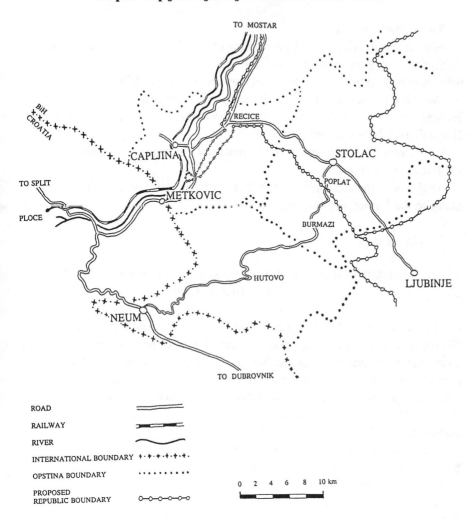

ROAD	
RAILWAY	
RIVER	
INTERNATIONAL BOUNDARY	+·+·+·+·+·+·
OPSTINA BOUNDARY	··········
PROPOSED REPUBLIC BOUNDARY	o—o—o—o—o—o

0   2   4   6   8   10 km

63. Agreement Relating to Bosnia and Herzegovina*

The Undersigned,

Guided by the principles of the Charter of the United Nations, the Universal Declaration of Human Rights and the Declaration of the Rights of Persons belonging to National or Ethnic, Religious and Linguistic Minorities,

Recalling the Statement of Principles by the International Conference on the Former Yugoslavia at its session in London and the Programme of Action on Humanitarian Issues agreed to at that session,

Considering the decisions of the United Nations Security Council relating to the former Yugoslavia,

Reaffirming their commitment to peace and security among the successor States to the former Yugoslavia,

Hereby agree as follows:

I. Constitutional Agreement of the Union of Republics of Bosnia and Herzegovina

(a) The constitutional Agreement of the Union of Republics of Bosnia and Herzegovina is set out in Appendix I hereto. The three parties agree that it shall enter into force one week of the Security Council has taken into account the present Agreement, has confirmed that the Union of Republics of Bosnia and Herzegovina will continue as a member of the United Nations as specified in Security Council Resolution 859 (1993) and has authorized United Nations support for the implementation of the present Agreement.

(b) The three parties understand that the Security Council will consider the broader question of sanctions in respect to an overall solution of the outstanding questions related to the former Yugoslavia. Nevertheless they understand that the Security Council, taking into account the present Agreement, will, in parallel with implementation of the peace plan, authorize a phased lifting of those sanctions applied to the Federal Republic of Yugoslavia (Serbia and Montenegro) specifically in respect to the situation in Bosnia and Herzegovina, provided there is clear evidence of the good faith implementation of all aspects of the present Agreement, in particular the withdrawal of forces to the agreed boundaries of the three Constituent Republics as shown in Annex A, Part I.

---

*   The undersigned are A. Izetbegovic, R. Karadzic, M. Boban, M. Bulatovic, S. Milosevic, and F. Tudjman; and, as witnesses, T. Stoltenberg and D. Owen.

(c) Agreed arrangements concerning the Constitutional Agreement are set out in Parts 1 and 2 of Appendix II hereto.

II. TERMINATION OF THE CONFLICT

The parties reaffirm the Agreement for a Complete Cessation of All Combat activities signed by their military commanders on 30 July 1993 set out in Part 1 of Appendix III hereto, and the Military Agreement for Peace in Bosnia and Herzegovina signed by their military commanders on 11 August 1992 set out in Part 2 of Appendix III, and decide that the latter shall be amended as set out in Part 3 of Appendix III and shall enter into force in the day after the Security Council has authorized United Nations support for the implementation of the present Agreement.

III. COOPERATION IN RESPECT OF HUMANITARIAN EFFORTS

(a) Maximum cooperation shall be extended to the United Nations High Commissioner for Refugees, the International Committee of the Red Cross, The United Nations Protection Force, the European Community Monitoring Mission and other humanitarian organizations working to provide assistance to refugees and displaced persons.

(b) Full cooperation shall also be extended to the United Nations High Commissioner for Refugees in drawing up and implementing programmes for the return of refugees and displaced persons to their homes.

IV. PRELIMINARY AGREEMENT WITH THE REPUBLIC OF CROATIA FOR IMPLEMENTING THE 1965 CONVENTION ON THE TRANSIT TRADE OF LAND-LOCKED COUNTRIES

As soon as the Constitutional Agreement enters into force, the Union of Republics of Bosnia and Herzegovina shall conclude with the Republic of Croatia the Preliminary Agreement for implementation the 1965 Convention on the Transmit Trade of Land-Locked Countries set out in Appendix IV hereto.

V. AGREEMENT FOR THE EXCHANGE OF TERRITORIES

(a) A separate agreement has been reached between the Muslim and the Serb parties that the road linking Gorazde to Zepa referred to in paragraph 2 of Part I of Annex A to the Constitutional Agreement shall be three kilometres wide and shall have two crossovers between points within the Serb majority Republic. There have also been agreed adjustments to the map as shown in Annex A, Part I.

(b) It has been further agreed between the Muslim and the Serb parties to form a working group for outstanding matters related to the territorial delimitation between the two Republics in the envisaged Union of Republics of Bosnia and Herzegovina, including the areas of Brcko, Bosanska Krajina, the Neretva Valley, Eastern Bosnia and the Ozren mountain, including the natural right of the two Republics to access to the sea. This is in addition to the commitment already made to find a permanent solution to the governance of the Sarajevo District within two years. After reaching a mutually acceptable resolution to the territorial delimitation of the three Constituent Republics within the Union, and during the initial two-year period of the Union's existence, there shall be a provision for a referendum to be held on a mutually agreed date within the Republics of the Union on the question of whether citizens of any particular Constituent Republic agree to remain in the Union or to leave the Union. In the case of a dissolution of the Union, all rights of the Union of the Republics of Bosnia and Herzegovina, including membership of the United Nations, shall be automatically vested in the Republic with a predominantly Muslim majority.[I]

(c) The Croat and Muslim parties have also agreed to form a working group for matters related to the territorial delimitation between the two Constituent Republics in the Union of Republics of Bosnia and Herzegovina as a matter of common developmental interest.[II]

VI. ACCESS TO THE SEA

Separate agreements have been reached:

(a) between the Muslim and Croat parties for the establishment of an exit to the sea for the Muslim majority Republic through he Croat majority Republic via the Access Authority Throughway from Poplat to Neum and for the Muslim majority Republic to hold a tract of land on the shore of the Adriatic on the isthmus of Kosa (Klek) and establish a Joint Auth-

---

[I]   This was further elaborated in a Joint Muslim-Serb Declaration signed in Geneva on 16 September 1993 and set out in Annex V hereto.

[II] This was further elaborated in a Joint Muslim-Croat Declaration signed in Geneva on 14 September 1992 and set out in Annex VI hereto.

ority between the two republics to develop the tourist industry in that area;

(b) between the Croat and Muslim parties that a port facility for the Muslim majority Republic shall be between Visici and Celjevo on the Neretva capable of taking vessels trans-shipping from Ploce and also directly from other ports in the Adriatic, and that the southern border of the Muslim majority Republic shall be moved down from Recice to just above Visici. Initially there shall be an Access Authority Throughway along the road from Recice to Tasovcici and to the turn-off to Celjevo. The land for the part shall be defined as being south of the houses along the road to Celjevo, west of the houses along the road to Vesici, to the north of the built-up area of Visici and than following the east bank of the Neretva River. If the port is developed the Muslim majority Republic will be expected to build a flyover at the Celjevo crossroad and a new road along an agreed route to Recice avoiding as far as possible existing settlements, and this road, with the land one half kilometre on either side, and the port area will be part of the Muslim majority Republic;

(c) the Republic of Croatia has agreed to a 99-year lease for a separate port facility of the Muslim majority Republic at the port of Ploce, and the details governing this port facility shall be set out in the agreement between the Republic of Croatia and the Union of Republics of Bosnia and Herzegovina set out in Appendix VII hereto;

(d) that as soon as relations between the Republic of Croatia and the Federal Republic of Yugoslavia (Serbia and Montenegro) are normalised there shall be a treaty covering an exchange of territory involving also the Union of Republics of Bosnia and Herzegovina to take account of the need for strategic assurances for Dubrovnik and of the strategic importance of Prevlaka to the Bay of Kotor, the need for the Serb majority Republic to have access to the sea in the area between Ostri Rt and Molunat, and the need for the Republic of Croatia to be compensated with territory so that there shall be no net loss of territory to the Republic of Croatia.

VII. POLITICAL AGREEMENTS

It is agreed by all three parties that the first elections in the Constituent Republics shall take place, under the supervision of the United Nations and the European Community, no later than two years after the entry into force of the Constitutional Agreement. All elections to the legislative bodies of Constituent Republics and of opstinas shall be by proportional representations. All political parties registered in any of the Constituent Republics may organize themselves and act freely throughout the territory of the Union of Republics of Bosnia and Herzegovina, provided their activities are in accordance with the Constitutional Agreement.

64. APPENDIX I
CONSTITUTIONAL AGREEMENT OF THE UNION OF REPUBLICS OF BOSNIA AND HERZEGOVINA

I. THE UNION OF REPUBLICS OF BOSNIA AND HERZEGOVINA

Article 1
The Union of Republics of Bosnia and Herzegovina is composed of three Constituent Republics and encompasses three constituent peoples: the Muslims, Serbs and Croats, as well as a group of other peoples. The Union of Republics of Bosnia and Herzegovina will be a member state of the United Nations, and as a member state it shall apply for membership of other organisations of the United Nations system.

Article 2
The flag and emblem of the Union of Republics of Bosnia and Herzegovina shall be specified by a law adopted by the Union Parliament.

Article 3
(a) Citizenship of Bosnia and Herzegovina shall be determined by a law adopted by the Union Parliament.
(b) Every person who on the entry onto force of this Constitutional Agreement was entitled to be a citizen of the Republic of Bosnia and Herzegovina shall be entitled to be a citizen of a Constituent Republic as well as of the Union of Republics of Bosnia and Herzegovina.
(c) Dual citizenship shall be allowed.
(d) Decision about citizenship shall be made by the designated organs of the Constituent Republics, subject to the competent courts.

Article 4
Neither the Union of Republics of Bosnia and Herzegovina nor any of the Constituent Republics shall maintain any military force, and any forces existing

on the date of entry into force of this Constitutional Agreement shall be progressively disarmed and disbanded under the supervision of the United Nations and the European Community.

II. THE CONSTITUENT REPUBLICS AND THEIR RESPONSIBILITIES

Article 1

(a) The boundaries of the Constituent Republics shall be as set out in Annex A, Part I. Except as provided in (b) boundaries of the Republics may only be changed by the procedure provided for amending this Constitutional Agreement.

(b) Marginal changes in the boundaries set out in Annex A may be made by the Presidency on the recommendation of a Boundary Commission, which shall receive evidence from those specifically affected by them. The Commission shall consist of five persons appointed by the Secretary-General of the United Nations, of whom three shall be persons recommended by representatives of the three constituent peoples.

(c) The areas specified in Annex A, Part II, even though within the territory and under the jurisdiction of a Constituent Republic, shall be vested as specified in Article VII.2 (b) for the purpose of ensuring continued access to buildings of the Union in Sarajevo, to the sea at Neum and to the Sava River.

(d) There shall be no border controls on boundaries between the Constituent Republics, and there shall be free movement of persons, goods and services throughout the territory of the Union of Republics of Bosnia and Herzegovina.

Article 2

(a) Each of the Constituent Republics shall adopt its own constitution, which shall provide for democratic forms of government, including democratically elected legislatures and chief executives and independent judiciaries, as well as for the highest standards of human rights and fundamental freedoms. No provision of these constitutions may be inconsistent with this Constitutional Agreement.

(b) The initial elections in each Constituent Republic shall be supervised by the United Nations and the European Community.

Article 3

All governmental functions and powers, except those assigned by this Constitutional Agreement to the Union of Republics of Bosnia and Herzegovina or to any of its institutions, shall be those of the Constituent Republics.

Article 4

All acts taken by a competent governmental authority of any of the Constituent Republics shall be accepted as valid by the other Constituent Republics.

III. THE COMMON INSTITUTIONS OF THE UNION OF REPUBLICS OF BOSNIA AND HERZEGOVINA

Article 1

(a) The Presidency of the Union of Republics of Bosnia and Herzegovina shall consist of the President, or of an appointee of the legislature, of each of the Constituent Republics.

(b) The Chairmanship of the Presidency shall rotate every four months among the members of the Presidency. The Chairman shall represent the Union of Republics of Bosnia and Herzegovina.

(c) The presidency shall take all its decisions by consensus.

Article 2

(a) The head of the Council of Ministers of the Union of Republics of Bosnia and Herzegovina shall be the Prime Minister, who shall be appointed and may be removed by the Presidency. The post shall rotate every year so as to be occupied in turn by the nominee of the President of a different Constituent Republic.

(b) The Presidency shall also appoint and may remove a Foreign Minister. The post shall rotate every year so as to be occupied in turn by the nominee of the President of a different Constituent Republic.

(c) The Prime Minister and the Foreign Minister shall be from different Constituent Republics.

(d) Other Minister may be appointed by the Presidency. They and the Prime Minister and the Foreign Minister shall constitute the Council of Minister, with responsibility for the policies of the Union of Republics of Bosnia and Herzegovina in relation to foreign affairs, international trade and the functioning of the common institutions, as well as any other function and institutions that the union Parliament may from time to time specify by law.

Article 3

(a) The Parliament of the Union of Republics of Bosnia and Herzegovina shall be composed of 120 representatives, one third each to be elected by the respective legislatures of the Constituent Republics.

(b) The Union Parliament may by a simple majority of the members from each Constituent Republic adopt laws within the competence of the Union of Republics of Bosnia and Herzegovina.

Article 4

The Union of Republics of Bosnia and Herzegovina shall have the following courts:

(i) A Supreme Court, composed of four judges appointed by the Presidency, no two of whom shall be from the same peoples, which, except as specified in para. (iii), shall be the final court of appeals from the courts of the Constituent Republics.

(ii) A Constitutional Court, composed of three judges appointed by the Presidency, no two of whom shall be from the same Constituent Republic, which shall be competent to resolve by consensus disputes among the Constituent Republics, between any of these and the Union of Republics of Bosnia and Herzegovina or any of its common institutions, and among any of these institutions. Should the Court not be constituted or be unable to resolve a dispute, it shall be referred for a binding decision by a standing arbitral tribunal composed of judges of the International Court of Justice or members of the permanent Court of Arbitration, one each of whom shall be elected be the President of each of the Constituent Republics and two of whom shall be elected by the Presidency or, if it is unable to do so, by the Secretary-General of the United Nations and by the President of the Council of Ministers of the European Community.

(iii) A Court of Human Rights to be established in accordance with Resolution 93 (6) of the Committee of Ministers of the Council of Europe, whose precise composition and competence shall be as set out in the agreed Annex B.

Article 5

Joint authorities between two or more of the Constituent Republics may be established by agreement of the Republics concerned if approved by a law adopted by the Union Parliament.

IV. International Relations

Article 1

(a) The Union of Republics of Bosnia and Herzegovina shall apply for membership of European and international institutions and organisations, as decided by the Presidency.

(b) Any Constituent Republics may apply for membership of an international organization if such membership would not be inconsistent with the interests of the Union of Republics of Bosnia and Herzegovina or of either of the other Constituent Republics.

Article 2

(a) The Union of Republics of Bosnia and Herzegovina shall remain a party to all international treaties in force for the Republic of Bosnia and Herzegovina on the date of the entry into force of this Constitutional Agreement, unless the Union Parliament decides that steps to denounce any such treaty shall be taken. However, treaties entered into after 18 November 1990 shall be considered by the Union Parliament within a period of three months from the entry into force of this Constitutional Agreement and shall only remain on force if the Union Parliament so decides.

(b) The Union of Republics of Bosnia and Herzegovina shall continue all diplomatic relations until the Presidency decides to continue or discontinue them.

(c) Union of Republics of Bosnia and Herzegovina may become a party to international treaties if such participation is approved by the Union Parliament. The Parliament may by law provide for participation in certain types of international agreements by decision of the Presidency. To the extent such participation would involve responsibilities that are to be carried out by the Constituent Republics, their advance approval must be secured, except in respect of the treaties referred to in Article V.3.

(d) Any Constituent Republic may, if eligible, become a party to an international treaty if such participation would not be inconsistent with the interests of the Union of Republics of Bosnia and Herzegovina or of either of the other Constituent Republics.

V. Human Rights and Fundamental Freedoms

Article 1

(a) Subject to Article V.2, all persons within the territory of the Union of Republics of Bosnia and Herzegovina shall be entitled to enjoy the rights and freedoms provided for in the instruments listed in Annex C.

(b) Should there be any discrepancy between the rights and freedoms specified in any of these instruments, or between any of these and the rights and freedoms specified in any other legal provision in force, the provision providing the greater protection for human rights and fundamental freedoms shall be applied.

Article 2

All courts, administrative agencies and other governmental organs of the Union of Republics of Bosnia and Herzegovina and of the Constituent Republics shall apply and conform the rights and freedoms specified in the instruments listed in Parts I and IV of Annex C. The rights specified in the instruments listed in Parts II and III of Annex C shall be considered as aspirations to be attained as rapidly as possible; all legislative, judicial, administrative and other governmental organs of the Union and Republican Governments shall take these rights appropriately into account in promulgating, executing and interpreting any legislative provisions designed to or otherwise suitable or implementing such rights and in otherwise carrying out the functions of these organs.

Article 3

The Union of Republics of Bosnia and Herzegovina shall as soon as possible become a party to each of the international treaties listed in Annex C.

Article 4

All organs of the Union and Republican Governments shall cooperated with the supervisory bodies established by any of the instruments listed in Annex C, as well as with the International Human Rights Monitoring Mission for Bosnia and Herzegovina established by the United Nations.

Article 5

(a) All citizens have the right to settle in any part of the territory of the Union of Republics of Bosnia and Herzegovina. They shall have the right to have restored to them any property of which they were deprived in the course of ethnic cleansing and to be compensated for any property which cannot be restored to them.

(b) The Union Parliament, as well as the legislature of the Constituent Republics, shall enact laws to assist in implementing these rights.

Article 6

To assist in implementing the rights and freedoms specified in this Chapter and in particular in Article V.5 (a), ombudsmen shall be appointed and carry out functions initially as specified in Annex D and thereafter as specified in a law adopted by the Union Parliament.

VI. FINANCES

Article 1

(a) The Union Parliament shall each year, on the proposal of the Prime Minister and with the subsequent approval of the Presidency, adopt a budget covering the expenditures required to carry out only those functions of the Union of Republics of Bosnia and Herzegovina relating to the maintenance of its common institutions and compliance with its international obligations, as well as such other functions as may from time to time be agreed by the Union Parliament.

(b) If no such budget is adopted in due course, the budget for the previous year shall be used on a provisional basis.

Article 2

(a) The expenditures provided for in the budget shall, except to the extent that other revenues are available or as otherwise specified in a law adopted by the Union Parliament, be covered in equal part by each of the Constituent Republics.

(b) Other sources of revenues, such as custom duties, fees for services or taxes on specified activities, may be determined by law.

VII. THE CONSTITUTIONAL AGREEMENT

Article 1

(a) This Constitutional Agreement may be amended by decision of the Union Parliament, when such amendment has been approved by each of the Constituent Republics according to its constitutional processes.

(b) No amendments may be adopted that abolish or diminish any of the rights or freedoms specified in Chapter V.

Article 2

(a) This Constitutional Agreement may not be abolished and none of the Constituent Republics may withdraw from the Union of Republics of Bosnia and Herzegovina without the prior agreement of all of the Republics. Such a decision may be appealed to the Security Council by any of the Constituent Republics, and the Council's decision shall be final.

(b) Should any of the Constituent Republics withdraw from the Union of Republics of Bosnia and Herzegovina, the areas specified in Annex A, Part II that are within the territory of such Republic shall remain a part of the Union of Republics of Bosnia and Herzegovina. Should the Union be dissolved or should both the Serb and the Croat majority Republics withdraw from the Union, then the areas specified in Annex A, Part II that are within the territories of those Constituent Republics shall become part of the Muslim majority Republic.

Article 3

This Constitutional Agreement shall enter into force when approved as part of the over-all peace settlement by representatives of the three constituent peoples, and on a date specified by them.

Annex A, Part I
The Boundaries of the Constituent Republics

1. The boundaries of the Constituent Republics shall be as indicated on the map below, subject to any changes that may be made in accordance with Article II.1 (b) of the Constitutional Agreement. The Boundary Commission shall ensure that the territory of the Muslim majority Republic shall not be less than 30% of the entire territory of the Union of Republics of Bosnia and Herzegovina.
2. The road marked on the Map that links Gorazde to Zepa shall constitute part of the Muslim majority Republic, which shall be responsible for its upkeep and policing.
3. As much as possible of the town of Gornji Vakuf shall be in the Muslim majority Republic, subject to the Croat majority Republic retaining road access to Prozor from the north of Gornji Vakuf, and to Novi Travnik along the road running north from the village of Ploca towards the road junction to the north of Bistrica. Construction of new roads may be necessary, and the Special Representative of the UN Secretary-General (SRSG), after appropriate consultations, shall arbitrate in the case of disputes.
4. Similarly, the SRSG shall be charged with arbitrating the boundary between the Muslim majority Republic and the Croat majority Republic where it follows a line drawn south of the River Lasva in Travnik, in order that as many Croatian villages as is feasible are included in the Croat majority Republic.
5. At the request of any Constituent Republic, the Presidency may decide that a religious or cultural building located in another Constituent Republic shall be under the special protection and responsibility of the requesting Republic.

Annex A, Part II
Areas Vested in the Union of Republics of Bosnia and Herzegovina

1. The area defined by the present opstina of Neum, and that part of the present opstina of Stolac that lies below the southern border of the Muslim majority Republic.
2. That part of the railway line from Tuzla that passes across Brcko to the railway bridge on the Sava.
3. Those public buildings in the Sarajevo District and in the surrounding area that are designated by the Presidency to be used by the Union Parliament, the Council of Ministers, the Supreme, Constitutional and Human Rights Courts, and the administrative institutions of the Union.

Annex B
Composition and Competence of the Human Rights Court

Article 1

The Human Rights Court of Bosnia and Herzegovina (the "Court") shall operate within the framework of the mechanism established by the Council of Europe by Resolution 93 (6) of its Council of Ministers, as that Resolution may be amended from time to time.

Article 2

(a) The Court shall initially consist of nine judges.

(b) The Presidency shall appoint four of the judges of the Court, one from each recognized group: Muslims, Serbs, Croats and Others. These judges shall enjoy tenure and shall not require reappointment.

(c) The Committee of Ministers of the Council of Europe shall appoint five of the judges of the Court in accordance with the above-cited resolution. These judges may not be citizens of the Union of Republics of Bosnia and Herzegovina nor of neighbouring States.

(d) If the Court concludes that its business requires the participation of more judges to avoid undue delays in the disposition of cases, the Government shall make arrangements with the Council of Europe for the appointment of additional judges, in accordance with the above-specified proportion of national and foreign judges.

Article 3

(a) The Court shall regulate its own procedure and its organisation.

(b) Each panel of the Court is to have the composition specified for the Court in Article 2(b)-(c) of this Annex.

(c) The equality of the parties shall be ensured in every proceeding.

(d) The Court shall allow written and oral pleadings in every proceeding pursuant to Articles 5-7 of this Annex.

Article 4

The competence of the Human Rights Court shall extent to any question concerning a constitutional or other legal provision relating to human rights or fundamental freedoms or to any of the instruments listed in Annex C to the Constitutional Agreement.

Article 5

Any party to a proceeding in which another court of the Union of Republics of Bosnia and Herzegovina or of any of its Constituent Republics has pronounced a judgment that is not subject to any other appeal (for a reason other than the lapse of time limit for which the moving party is responsible), may appeal such judgment to the Court on the basis of any question within its competence. The decision of the Court in such an appeal shall be final and binding.

Article 6

(a) An appeal may also be taken to the Court if a proceeding is pending for what it considers an unduly long time in any other court of the Union of Republics of Bosnia and Herzegovina or of any of its Constituent Republics.

(b) The Court shall decide whether to accept such an appeal after a preliminary consideration of whether the proceeding in the other court has been pending too long and whether the subject of the appeal is within its competence.

Article 7

Any appellate court of the Union of Republics of Bosnia and Herzegovina or of any of its Constituent Republics may, at the request of any party to a proceeding pending before it, or on its own motion in relation to such a proceeding, address to the Court a question arising out of the proceeding if the question related to any matter within the competence of the Court. The response of the Court is binding on the requesting court.

Article 8

The Court shall continue to function until the Union of Republics of Bosnia and Herzegovina becomes a party to the European Convention on Human Rights and Fundamental Freedoms, unless the Council of Europe mechanism referred to in Article 1 of this Annex ceases at some earlier date to be in force in respect of the Union of Republics of Bosnia and Herzegovina.

Annex C
Human Rights Instruments Incorporated into
the Constitutional Agreement

A. General Human Rights, especially Civil and Political Rights

1. 1948 Convention on the Prevention and Punishment of the Crime of Genocide;
2. 1948 Universal Declaration of Human Rights, Articles 1-21;
3. 1949 Geneva Conventions I-IV on the Laws of War, and the 1977 Geneva Protocols I-II thereto;
4. 1950 European Convention for the Protection of Human Rights and Fundamental Freedoms, and Protocols 1-10 thereto;
5. 1951 Convention relating to the Status of Refugees and the 1966 Protocol thereto;
6. 1965 International Convention on the Elimination of All Forms of Racial Discrimination;
7. 1966 International Covenant on Civil and Political Rights and its 1966 and 1989 Optional Protocols thereto;
8. 1979 International Convention on the Elimination of All Forms of Discrimination against Women;
9. 1981 [UN] Declaration on the Elimination of all Forms of Intolerance and of Discrimination Based on Religion or Belief;
10. 1984 Convention against Torture and Other Cruel, Inhuman or Degrading Treatment or Punishment;
11. 1987 European Convention on the Prevention of Torture and Inhuman or Degrading Treatment or Punishment;
12. 1989 Convention on the Rights of the Child.

B. Protection of Groups and Minorities

13. 1990 Council of Europe Parliamentary Assembly Recommendation on the Rights of minorities, paras. 10-13;
14. 1992 [UN] Declaration on the Rights of Persons Belonging to National, Ethnic, Religious and Linguistic Minorities.

C. Economic, Social and Cultural Rights

15. 1948 Universal Declaration of Human Rights, Articles 22-27;
16. 1961 European Social Charter and the Protocol 1 thereto;
17. 1966 International Covenant on Economic, Social and Cultural Rights.

D. Citizenship and Nationality

18. 1957 Convention on the Nationality of Married Women;
19. 1961 Convention on the Reduction of Statelessness.

Annex D
Initial Appointment and Functions of the Ombudsmen

I. GENERAL PROVISIONS

Article 1

(a) The Ombudsmen are to protect human dignity, rights and liberties as provided in the Constitutional Agreement and in the instruments listed in Annex C thereto, and in the constitutions and legislations of the Constituent Republics, and in particular shall act to reverse the consequences of the violation of these rights and liberties and especially of ethnic cleansing.

(b) In carrying out their function, the Ombudsmen must be guided by law and by the principles of morality and justice.

Article 2

Each Ombudsman shall exercise his functions individually, except as otherwise provided herein. Two or more Ombudsmen may cooperate in carrying out any of their functions.

Article 3

The Ombudsmen are independent in carrying out their functions and no governmental organ or any other person may interfere with such functions.

Article 4

(a) There shall be four Ombudsmen, one from each recognized group: Muslims, Serbs, Croats and Others. Until the Parliament adopts a law relating to the appointment and functioning of the ombudsmen, they shall be appointed and may be removed by the Co-Chairmen of the Steering Committee of the International Conference on the Former Yugoslavia, after consultations with the members of the Presidency.

(b) Each of the Ombudsmen shall, with the approval of the presidency, appoint one or more Deputies.

(c) The terms of service of the Ombudsmen and their Deputies shall be the same respectively as those of the President and of judges of the Supreme Court.

(d) Each Ombudsman shall also appoint additional staff within the framework of the budget approved therefore by the Parliament or initially by the Presidency.

II. THE COMPETENCE AND THE POWERS OF THE OMBUDSMEN

The Ombudsmen may follow the activities of any common institution of the Union of Republics of Bosnia and Herzegovina or of any organ of a Constituent Republic or of governmental units subordinate thereto, as well as of an other institution or person by whom human dignity, rights or liberties may be negated or ethnic cleansing may be accomplished or its effects preserved.

Article 6

In the course of carrying out his functions an Ombudsman may examine all official documents, including secret ones, as well as judicial and administrative files and require any person (including any official) to cooperate, in particular by transmitting relevant information, documents and files. Ombudsmen may also attend court and administrative hearings, as well as meetings of other organs and enter and inspect any place where persons deprived of their liberty are confined or work.

Article 7

The Ombudsmen, their Deputies and any other person who carries out inquiries pursuant to Article 6, are required to maintain the secrecy of whatever they learned in the course of such inquiry, and must treat all documents and files in accordance with the applicable rules.

III. REPORTS OF THE OMBUDSMEN

Article 8

(a) Each Ombudsman shall present an annual report to the Presidency of the Union of Republics of Bosnia and Herzegovina, to the president of each of the Constituent Republics and the Co-Chairmen of the Steering Committee of the International Conference on the Former Yugoslavia.

(b) An Ombudsman may also present at any time special reports to any competent authorities.

IV. REGULATIONS OF THE OMBUDSMEN

Article 9

Each Ombudsman shall draw up, or the Ombudsmen may collectively draw up, Regulations that specify their organization and the method of exercising their function, which shall be promulgated in the Official Journal of the Union of Republics of Bosnia and Herzegovina, as well as in the official journals of the Constituent Republics. These Regulations may be changed by a law adopted by the Parliament.

65. APPENDIX II
AGREED ARRANGEMENTS CONCERNING THE CONSTITUTIONAL AGREEMENT OF THE UNION OF REPUBLICS OF BOSNIA AND HERZEGOVINA

PART 1

1. The name of each Constituent Republic will be determined by the competent authorities of that Republic.
2. Access Authority:

   (a) Pursuant to Article III.5 of the Constitutional Agreement there shall established, immediately on the entry into force of that Agreement, an access Authority, charged with assisting in the implementation of Article II.1 (d) of the Agreement requiring free movement of persons, goods and services throughout the territory of the Union of Republics of Bosnia and

Herzegovina.

(b) The purpose of the Authority will be to guarantee full freedom of movement in certain essential areas between and within the Constituent Republics, and also to and from these Republics to the Republic of Croatia and the Republic of Serbia.

(c) The members of the Authority shall be three persons appointed by the Presidency, one from each Constituent Republics. Its headquarters shall be in or around the city of Sarajevo.

(d) Even though the Authority is to be in operation as soon as possible following the entry into force of the Constitutional Agreement, inevitably there will be an initial period when UNPROFOR will have sole responsibility for freedom of movement along designated "Blue Routes" around Sarajevo and "Throughways" ensuring freedom of movement along the key roads and railway lines throughout the country. Thereafter there will be a period of overlapping responsibility for the Authority's designated routes will be phased out, and these responsibilities assumed by the traffic police of the Authority. This transfer of responsibility requires the agreement of all members of the Authority. The traffic police will be seconded to the Authority from the police force of the Constituent Republics.

(e) The following shall be the routes to be controlled by the Access Authority:

   (i)   The road and railway line from Metkovic on the border of Croatia to the centre of the city of Sarajevo;

   (ii)   The railway from the city of Sarajevo to Doboj and Samac;

   (iii) The so-called "Una" railway from Bosanski Novi through Bihac southwards to the border of Croatia;

   (iv)   The road from Nevesinje to Mostar airport;

   (v)   The road from Srebrenica to Kladanj;

   (vi)   The road from Gorazde through Cajnice to the border of Montenegro;

   (vii) Sarajevo Airport;

   (viii) The so-called "Transit Road" through the south of the city of Sarajevo;

   (ix)   The road between Sarajevo and the crossing-point north of Trnovo which gives access to Gorazde;

   (x)   The road between Bosanski Brod (via Derventa, Doboj, Zenica) and Sarajevo;

(xi)   The road from the border of the Republic of Croatia near Velika Kladusa (via Cazin, Bihac, Kljuc, Jajce, Donji Vakuf) to Mostar;

(xii) The road between Donji Vakuf (via Travnik) and Zenica;

(xiii) The road from Poplat to Neum.

PART 2

A. Sarajevo District

1. For an interim period, specified in paragraph 2 below, there shall be established the Sarajevo District the outer boundary of which shall be as delineated in the attached map. This boundary shall be subject to adjustment by the Boundary Commission in accordance with Article II.1 (b) of the Constitutional Agreement. The Commission shall first of all consider the areas Cekrcici, Ratkovci, Catici and Drazevici for inclusion in the Sarajevo District and shall thereafter also consider the inclusion of the opstinas of Kiseljak and Kresevo.

2. The period of UN participation in the governance of the Sarajevo District is planned for two years. The parties commit themselves to finding a permanent solution during this period. The period of UN presence can therefore be shortened if so recommended by the Presidency, it being understood that the participation of the United Nations in the governance of that District shall at all times be as determined by the Security Council of the United Nations.

3. Sarajevo District shall have the governmental functions and powers specified for Constituent Republics in the Constitutional Agreement, except that it shall not be represented in the Presidency. The opstinas within the Sarajevo District shall have those governmental functions and powers that opstinas have under current legislation, subject to the authority of the UN Administrator, to be used only in exceptional circumstances. Laws adopted by the Union Parliament shall apply also within Sarajevo District.

4. Sarajevo District shall be governed by a UN Administrator appointed by the Secretary-General of the United Nations. The UN Administrator shall work under the over-all supervision of the Special Representative of the Secretary-General and in close operation with the Joint Commission for the Sarajevo District established by the Military Agreement for Peace in Bosnia and Herzegovina. The UN Administrator shall be advised by an Advisory Body, which shall be composed of 4 representatives of the Muslim people, 3 representatives of the Serb people, 2 representatives of the Croat people, and 1 representative of the District's minorities; the latter shall be nominated by the Co-Chairmen. The Advisory Body shall make its recommendations by consensus.

5. The UN Administrator shall establish courts of first instance and an appellate court in each opstina included in Sarajevo District. Appeals from these courts may be taken to the courts of the Union of Republics of Bosnia and Herzegovina in the same way as appeals from courts of the Constituent Republics.

6. Within Sarajevo District the Boundary Commission shall propose new opstina boundaries, taking into account the following factors:

(a) The boundaries existing of 1 January 1991;
(b) The tentative changes in boundaries that were implemented after 1 January 1991;
(c) The ceasefire line;
(d) Population distribution, as reflected in census figures and other data;
(e) The wishes of those specifically affected, determined by a plebiscite or otherwise;
(f) The view of the Advisory Body and the UN Administrator.

The proposals of the Boundary Commission for the opstina boundaries shall be submitted for decision to the Presidency.

B. Mostar City Opstina

1. For an interim period, specified in paragraph 2 below, there shall be established the Mostar City Opstina the outer boundary of which shall be as determined in accordance with the procedure specified in the attachment hereto. This boundary shall be subject to adjustment by the Boundary Commission in accordance with Article II.1 (b) of the Constitutional Agreement.

2. The period of European Community participation in the governance of the Mostar City opstina is planned for two years. The parties commit themselves to finding a permanent solution during this period. The period of European Community presence can therefore be shortened if so recommended by the Presidency, it being understood that the participation of the European Community in the governance of the Mostar City Opstina shall at all times be as determined by the Council of Ministers of the European Community.

3. Mostar City Opstina, which shall have within it the buildings for the capital of the Croat majority Republic, shall have the governmental function and powers specified for Constituent Republics in the Constitutional Agreement. The Mostar City Opstina shall have those governmental functions and powers that opstinas have under current legislation, subject to the authority of the EC Administrator, to be used only in exceptional circumstances. Laws adopted by the Union Parlia-

ment shall apply also within Mostar City Opstina.

4. Mostar City Opstina shall be governed by an EC Administrator appointed by the President of the European Council. The EC Administrator shall work in close consultation with the Special Representative of the Secretary-General and in close cooperation with the Regional Joint Commission established by the Military Agreement for Peace in Bosnia and Herzegovina. The EC Administrator shall be advised by an Advisory Body, which shall be composed of 3 representatives of the Croat people, 3 representatives of the Muslim people, 2 representatives of the Serb people, and 1 representative of the City's minorities; the latter shall be nominated by the Co-Chairmen. The Advisory Body shall make its recommendations by consensus.

5. The EC Administrator shall establish courts of first instance and an appellate court on the Mostar City Opstina. Appeals from these courts may be taken to the courts of the Union of Republics of Bosnia and Herzegovina in the same way as appeals from courts of the Constituent Republics.

6. Mostar City Opstina shall be demilitarized under the arrangements of a Regional Joint Commission in accordance with the Military Agreement for Peace in Bosnia and Herzegovina. UNPROFOR as all other UN agencies shall operate in the City as in the rest of the Country.

C. Police Forces

1. Each existing or new opstina in the Sarajevo District and the Mostar City Opstina shall organize and control its own uniformed police force, which shall have a proportionally balanced ethnic composition and shall be subjected to supervision by respectively the Administrator for the Sarajevo District or the Mostar City Opstina.

2. Each Constituent Republic shall organize and control its own uniformed police force, which shall have a proportionally balanced ethnic composition, any necessary coordination shall be the responsibility of the Presidency.

3. The parties understand that as part of the UNPROFOR deployment in Bosnia and Herzegovina there is to be a large civilian police element, whose principal task will be to monitor the police of the Constituent Republics and of the opstinas in the Sarajevo District and the Mostar City Opstina, so that each: has an appropriately balanced ethnic composition; does not oppress members of minority ethnic groups; contributes positively to the reversal of "ethnic cleansing" by protecting persons returning after having been forced to flee; carries out the judgements of courts, in particular the Human Rights Court; assists the Interim Human Rights Commissioner, the Deputy Commissioners and the human rights

monitors; and that the numbers and equipment of the police are in keeping with normal European standards.

D. *Protection of Human Rights and the Reversal of Ethnic Cleansing*

1. The right is established of a refugee or displaced person to freely return as part of an overall process of normalisation. All statements or commitments made under duress, particularly those relating to the relinquishment of rights to land or property, shall be treated as wholly null and void.
2. The parties understand that there is to be an International Human Rights Monitoring Mission, to be established by the Secretary-General of the United Nations, which is to be headed by a Human Rights Commissioner for Bosnia and Herzegovina based in Sarajevo. Deputy Commissioners are to based in various parts of the country. The Commissioner is to be supported by international human rights monitors, deployed throughout the territory of the Union of Republics of Bosnia and Herzegovina; in order to provide protection in urgent cases, they may intercede with the Presidency and the governments of the Constituent Republics, with the Administrators of Sarajevo District and Mostar City Opstina and with UNPROFOR; they may refer issues to the ombudsmen and to other human rights agencies as needed and are to work closely with the United Nations High Commissioner for Refugees (UNHCR), the International Committee of the Red Cross (ICRC) and other humanitarian agencies. The Commissioner is expected to submit regular reports to the Secretary-General, who is to report periodically to the Security Council and to other international bodies, including the United Nations Commission on Human Rights and its Special Rapporteur.

ATTACHMENT

A. *The Outer Boundary of the Sarajevo District*

The outer boundary of the Sarajevo District shall be as indicated on the map below, subject to any changes that may be made in accordance with paragraph A.1 of Part 2 of the present Appendix.

B. *The Outer Boundary of the Mostar City Opstina*

It has been suggested that the Mostar City Opstina be defined as including the six mjesna zajednica of Aleksa Santic, Carina, Cernica, Brankovac, Donja Mahala and Luka I. This needs however, to be determined by consultation in Mostar with all interested parties, which is to be done locally as soon as circumstances permit. If there is failure to agree in the delimitation of the Mostar City Opstina it is agreed that the Special Representative of the Secretary-General of the United Nations shall make the final determination.

66. APPENDIX III
MILITARY AGREEMENTS

Part 1
Agreement for a Complete Cessation of All Combat Activities Among the Parties in Conflict*

THE UNDERSIGNED MILITARY COMMANDERS, as representatives of their respective Parties in conflict,

Respecting the recent decisions of their commanders-in-chief in Geneva, made under the auspices of the International Conference on the Former Yugoslavia,

Mindful of their obligation under relevant Security Council resolutions, including to ensure UNPROFOR's safety and freedom of movement,

Recognizing the absolute urgency of the present situation and pledging their full efforts to see that their Agreement is honoured,

Have agreed as follows:

Article I
Cessation of all Combat Activities

1. Beginning upon signature of this Agreement, all forces of the three Parties shall cease firing and shall freeze all military activities, including military movements, deployments of forces and establishment of fortifications.

2. Written orders mandating such cessation of combat activities shall be issued, as soon as possible following signature of this Agreement, by each of the undersigned military commanders.

---

* The undersigned are Gen. Rasim Delic, Lt. Gen. Ratko Mladic, and Gen. Milivoj Petkovic; and, as UNPROFOR witnesses, Gen. Jean Cot, Force Commander, and Lt. Gen. Francis Briquemont, Commander, B & H Command.

Article II

Humanitarian Aid and Freedom of Movement

Written orders shall be issued by the undersigned military commanders, as soon as possible following signature of this Agreement, permitting:

(a) free passage for UNPROFOR;
(b) free passage for UNPROFOR convoys and convoy escorts, subject to routine control of numbers of personnel and weapons entering and leaving territory under the control of a Party; and
(c) free passage for humanitarian aid convoys, subject to reasonable control of the contents and personnel that are part of the convoy at one checkpoint.

UNPROFOR acknowledges that each Party has legitimate concerns over movements within territories under its control. UNPROFOR shall provide notification of convoy movements.

Article III

Verification of Compliance with this Agreement

1. The undersigned military commanders shall confirm to UNPROFOR the issuance of orders required by this Agreement, and their acknowledgement by subordinate commanders. Full assistance shall be extended to UNPROFOR to permit it to monitor the implementation of this Agreement. UNPROFOR officers in the field may be consulted to provide assistance in implementation of this Agreement.

2. The undersigned military commanders, or their authorized representatives, shall continue to meet daily at a specified time while their commanders-in-chief are meeting in Geneva or, when necessary, on the request of any of the Parties. In accordance with the recommendation made in Geneva by the commanders-in-chief of the Parties, the draft "Military Agreement on the Cessation of Hostilities" shall be discussed among other issues.

3. For urgent matters, the military commanders shall make available through reliable communications on a 24-hour a day basis, a representative who is authorized to take decisions or reach those with such authority.

This Agreement, done pursuant of the commanders-in-chief of the Parties in Geneva, shall enter into force upon its signature.

DONE AT Sarajevo airport, on the 30th day of July, 1993, in two versions, one in English and the other in the language of the Parties. Where there are differences of interpretation between the versions, the English version shall control.

Part 2
Military Agreement for Peace in Bosnia and Herzegovina[*]

THE UNDERSIGNED MILITARY COMMANDERS, as representatives of the Parties in conflict,

Pursuant to Section II of the Agreement relating to Bosnia and Herzegovina to be concluded in Geneva,

Desiring to work out arrangements for bringing about compliance with a cessation of hostilities, and for monitoring it so as to ensure that its is effective and lasting,

Hereby agree as follows:

Article I
Measures for Compliance

1. The Parties shall comply in good faith with all provisions in this Agreement. If a dispute arises, UNPROFOR shall be notified and may make a determination on the merits of the dispute.

2. The Parties shall adhere to the Target Time-Table from implementing this agreement, attached as Appendix I, except when UNPROFOR deems that changes are necessary.

3. The Parties shall full support monitoring an control measures to verify compliance with this Agreement, including:

   (a) establishment of the Joint Commission, which shall operate in accordance with the procedure set out in Appendix II;
   (b) establishment of Regional Joint Commissions, which shall operate in accordance with the procedures set-out in Appendix II;
   (c) establishment of "hot lines" between commanders in conflict areas, and between commanders and UNPROFOR;

---

[*] The undersigned are Gen. Rasim Delic, Lt. Gen. Ratko Mladic, Gen. Milivoj Petkovic, and Lt. Gen. Francis Briquemont.

(d) ensuring military observers full freedom of movement and access to military installations; and

(e) monitoring and movement by helicopter, in accordance with clearance arrangements to be determined by the Joint Commission.

Article II
Separation of Forces

1. Principles for Initial Separation of Forces

(a) Separation of forces shall be achieved progressively and shall include monitoring by UNPROFOR on infantry and heavy weapons on both sides of confrontation lines, that are within range of the confrontation lines.

(b) The concepts of separation of forces and withdrawal of heavy weapons shall be linked. Heavy weapons shall be defined as weapons having a calibre of 12.7 or more millimetres.

(c) Details of implementation, including items "to be agreed", shall be resolved in the Joint Commissions.

(d) Special priority shall be given to Sarajevo.

2. Ceasefire

In accordance with Article I of the Agreement for a Complete Cessation of All Combat Activities of 30 July 1993, the forces of the Parties shall:

(a) cease firing and make no offensive actions;

(b) freeze their positions on existing lines;

(c) make no forward deployments of personnel or materiel. Rotations of units shall be permitted on a one-for-one basis, under UNPROFOR monitoring; and

(d) make no establishment or enhancement of fortifications.

3. Declaration of Forces

The Parties shall provide to UNPROFOR the following information:

(a) numbers and locations of all heavy weapons that are within range of the confrontation lines;

(b) maps and other detailed documentation on all mines, that surround or are within the confrontation lines;

(c) traces depicting the position of front lines;

(d) positions and descriptions of fortifications; and

(e) positions and numbers of soldiers.

4. Withdrawal of Forces

(a) UNPROFOR, in consultation with the Joint Commission, shall mark the confrontation lines.

(b) The forces of the Parties shall withdraw, in a balanced manner but one that is consistent with their different composition. The manner and extent of withdrawal shall be worked out by UNPROFOR, in consultation with the Joint Commission.

(c) The Areas of Separation shall be increased over time but the continued withdrawal of the forces of the Parties to their respective regions, in consultation with UNPROFOR in the Joint Commission. As this progressive withdrawal takes place, a number of units shall demobilize UNPROFOR, in consultation with the Joint Commission, shall monitor the process of agreed demobilisation.

(d) The forces of the Parties shall be prohibited from entering the Areas of Separation, except while conducting joint patrols with UNPROFOR or clearing mines. Areas of Separation shall be open to civilian movement, under UNPROFOR control.

5. Withdrawal of Heavy Weapons

(a) In accordance with locations and a time schedule to be agreed within the Joint Commission, the heavy weapons of the Parties shall be withdrawn from their current positions and concentrated in new locations. Such locations shall be agreed in light of their suitability for monitoring and the range of the heavy weapons.

(b) UNPROFOR shall monitor the process of withdrawal. Heavy weapons that are withdrawn to locations that are out of range of position of the other parties shall be monitored by UNPROFOR; heavy weapons that remain within range of such positions shall be controlled by UNPROFOR.

(c) Ammunition shall be stored and monitored separately from heavy weapons. The distance between ammunition and heavy weapons shall be agreed within the Joint Commission.

6. Confinement of Infantry to Barracks

As selected infantry forces are withdrawn from the lines of confrontation, a number of such forces, to be determined by UNPROFOR in consultation with the Joint Commission, shall be confined to barracks.

7. Clearing mines

Designated units of the Parties shall, within areas of separation and elsewhere clear all mines they have laid, in accordance with mutual agreement in the Joint Commission.

Article III

Monitoring of Borders

1. The borders of the Union of Republics of Bosnia and Herzegovina shall be monitored in accordance with the agreement of the political representatives of all Parties and relevant Security Council resolutions.

Article IV

Restoration of Infrastructure

1. Principles for Restoration of Infrastructure

   (a) Inferring with the supply of water, gas, or electricity as a weapon or mean of pressure is unacceptable. Infrastructure shall not be attacked or degrading in any way, and shall not be used for any military purpose.
   (b) Restoration of infrastructure shall not be conditioned on implementation of the military provisions in this Agreement or of other provisions in the Agreement Relating to Bosnia and Herzegovina.
   (c) Infrastructure shall be restored for the benefit of all civilians, irrespective of ethnic origin, and shall be re-established across international borders, in accordance with agreements reached by the civil authorities.
   (d) UNPROFOR and other international agencies, as appropriated, may provide guidance and assistance in restoration of infrastructure.
   (e) Special priority shall be given to restoration of infrastructure for all the citizens of Sarajevo.

2. Identifying Priorities and Making Repairs

(a) The Infrastructure Management Group, composed of representatives of each party, shall identify infrastructure repair priorities according to needs, local resources and the resources of aid agencies. Repairs shall be executed in conjunction with civilian authorities and relevant local agencies of all Parties.
(b) The Parties shall provide and fulfill guarantees of security to make such repairs. Access shall be guaranteed by the Parties.
(c) Parties shall provide access to infrastructure sites consistent with security. Parties shall provide liaison repair teams, after local agreement by joint committees. A common instruction for passage down chains of command shall be developed to demonstrate equal endorsement of support for restoration of infrastructure and to allow free access for reconnaissance, workers and expert teams.

3. Infrastructure sites shall include:

(a) Power grids;
(b) Steam power stations, coal mines, and hydroelectric power stations;
(c) Bridges;
(d) Gas lines;
(e) Telecommunications;
(f) Railway lines;
(g) Routes; and
(h) Water supply.

Article V
Providing Freedom of Movement

1. Principles for Freedom of Movement

(a) UNPROFOR and international humanitarian organisations, especially aid convoys, shall have freedom of movement and priority use of roads and transportation facilities. UNPROFOR may provide escort for convoys and other vehicles as it deems necessary.
(b) The Parties shall ensure the security and freedom of movement of civilian and commercial traffic. Special attention shall be paid to ensure a traffic throughway to the Bihac area, and right of passage to enclaves in Eastern

Bosnia, and access to commercial ports on the Adriatic.

(c) In consultation with the Joint Commission, UNPROFOR may monitor, patrol and establish checkpoints to enhance freedom of movement. UNPROFOR may conduct joint patrols with each Party of the territory that it controls.

2. Special Measures to open Specified Routes

As a first step in establishing freedom of movement, special measures shall be taken to open the routes specified in paragraph 3 of this Article. Such measures shall be agreed upon in joint commissions and shall include the following:

(a) UNPROFOR may conduct recess and facilitate repairs;

(b) Military movements of the parties shall be permitted only in coordination with UNPROFOR, as well as with the commanders of the Parties;

(c) UNPROFOR shall maintain a heightened presence, including establishing checkpoints at the entrance and exit of such routes and elsewhere where it deems necessary in order to ensure safe passage;

(d) UNPROFOR may conduct inspections at UNPROFOR checkpoints and seize war-related materials carried during unauthorized movements. The Parties may be present during such inspections; and

(e) A corridor extending 500 meters to the left and right of the specified routes shall be demilitarized, in accordance with measures agreed by the Joint Commission.

3. Routes with Special Measures shall be established between or to the following destinations:

(a) The road and railway line from Metkovic on the border of the Republic of Croatia to the centre of the city of Sarajevo;

(b) The road from Sarajevo city to Zenica, via Rajlovac-Ilijas-Visiko;

(c) The road and railway from the city of Sarajevo to Samac via Doboj, and from Doboj to Tuzla;

(d) The road from Bihac to Livno;

(e) The road from Nevisinje to Mostar;

(f) The road from Zepa/Srebrenica to Kladanj;

(g) The road from Visegrad to Sarajevo via Gorazde and Pale;

(h) The road from Stolac to Trebinje via Ljubinje;

(i) The Road from Doboj to Teslic;

(j) Sarajevo Airport;
(k) Banja Luka Airport;
(l) Tuzla Airport;
(m) Mostar Airport.

This Agreement:

(a) shall enter into and remain in force in accordance with the Agreement Relating to Bosnia and Herzegovina to be concluded in Geneva; and
(b) shall supersede and replace the Agreement for Peace Bosnia and Herzegovina set out in Appendix III to the Agreement to be concluded in Geneva.

DONE AT Sarajevo Airport, on the eleventh day of August, 1993, in two versions, the English version being the authentic one.

APPENDIX I
TARGET TIME-TABLE FOR IMPLEMENTING THIS AGREEMENT

D Day = Seven days after midnight of the day the Agreement relating to Bosnia and Herzegovina is signed in Geneva.

Phase One: D - 7 to D Day
Cessation of All Combat Activities, in accordance with the Agreement of 30 July 1993, continues to be observed.

Phase Two: D Day to + 7
1. Full Ceasefire observed (Article II, paragraph 1).
2. Declaration of forces provided (Article II, paragraph 2).
3. Joint Commission, hot lines, and other monitoring and control measures established (Article I).
4. Principles for Freedom of Movement observed (Article V, paragraph 1).

Phase Three: D + 8 to D + 29
1. Lines of confrontation marked (ARTICLE II, paragraph 4 (a)).
2. Infrastructure restoration begins (Article IV).
3. Routes with Special Measures to Ensure Safe Passage are opened (Article V, paragraphs 2 and 3).

4. Withdrawal of Forces and Heavy Weapons begins (Article II, paragraphs 4 (b) and 4 (d), and Article II).
5. Confinement of Infantry to Barracks begins (Article IV, paragraph 6).
6. Monitoring of Borders begins (Article III).

Phase Four: D + 29 to D + 60
Continued withdrawal of forces to their respective regions. Demobilization of units. Area of Separation expanded (Article II, paragraph 4 (c)).

APPENDIX II
PROCEDURES FOR THE JOINT COMMISSION

1. The Joint Commission shall operate under the chairmanship of UNPROFOR. Each party shall designate the representative of its choosing, whether civil or military, to the Joint Commission. Deputies and assistants, civilian or military, may be present to assist their representatives.
2. Other than authorized members of each delegation, meetings of the Joint Commission shall be closed. Media may be present only by express agreement of each Party.
3. Each Party's representative shall be authorized to act fully on behalf of that Party and to take decisions with respect to implementation of this Agreement.
4. The Joint Commission shall meet when and where UNPROFOR decides, in consultation with the Parties.
5. Decision of the Joint Commission shall be taken by consensus. UNPROFOR may decide certain matters that it deems principally within its competence, in consultation with the concerned Parties.
6. UNPROFOR shall report on the proceedings of the Joint Commission to the United Nations, through the Special Representative of the Secretary-General for the Former Yugoslavia.
7. These procedures shall guide the operation of Regional Joint Commissions and other implementing bodies. Amendments to these procedures may be made by UNPROFOR in consultation with the Parties.

Part 3
Amendments to the 11 August 1993 Military Agreement for Peace in Bosnia and Herzegovina

The Military Agreement for Peace in Bosnia and Herzegovina, which was concluded by the military commanders of the parties in Sarajevo on 11 August

1993 and which is set out in Part 2 of the Present Appendix, is hereby amended as follows:

1. *Article I, sub-paragraph 3 (b)*, to read as follows:

   (b) establishment of a Joint Commission for the Sarajevo District and other Regional Joint Commissions, which shall operate in accordance with the procedures set out in Appendix II;

2. *Article II, sub-paragraph 4(c)*, to read as follows:

   (c) The Areas of Separation shall be increased over time by the continued withdrawal of the forces of the Parties to their respective regions, in consultation with UNPROFOR in the Joint Commission. As this progressive withdrawal takes place, a number of units shall demobilize. Sarajevo District and Pale Opstina shall be demilitarized. UNPROFOR, in consultation with the Joint Commission, shall monitor the process of agreed demobilization and demilitarization.

3. *Entry-Force Clause*: delete paragraph (b).
4. *Appendix I, first paragraph*, to read as follows:

   D Day = Seven days after midnight (New York time) of the day on which the Security Council approves the arrangements implementing the Military Agreement of 11 August, as amended.

5. *Appendix I, second paragraph, paras. 1 and 2* to read as follows:

   1. Full Ceasefire observed (Article II, paragraph 2,)
   2. Declaration of forces provided (Article II, paragraph 3.)

6. *Appendix I, third paragraph, para. 4*, to read as follows:

   4. Withdrawal of Forces and Heavy Weapons begins (Article II, paragraphs 4(b), 4 (d) and 5.)

67. APPENDIX IV
PRELIMINARY AGREEMENT BETWEEN THE REPUBLIC OF CROATIA AND THE UNION OF REPUBLICS OF BOSNIA AND HERZEGOVINA FOR IMPLEMENTING THE 1965 CONVENTION ON TRANSIT TRADE OF LAND-LOCKED STATES

The Republic of Croatia and The Union of Republics of Bosnia and Herzegovina,

Considering that, as successors of the Socialist Federal Republic of Yugoslavia which had been party to the Convention of Transit Trade of Land-Locked States concluded in New York on 8 July 1965 (hereinafter the "Convention"), the Republic of Croatia and the Union of Republics of Bosnia and Herzegovina should apply between them the provisions of the Convention,

Further considering that the Union of Republics of Bosnia and Herzegovina is to be considered a "land-locked State" within the meaning of that Convention and that with respect to Bosnia and Herzegovina the Republic of Croatia is a "transit State" within the meaning of the Convention,

Desiring to conclude an agreement, on a basis of reciprocity - in accordance with Article 3(1) (a) of the Convention on the High Seas quoted in the Preamble of the Transit Trade Convention and with Article 15 of that Convention - to establish, as foreseen in paragraph 2 of Article 2 of the Convention, the rules governing traffic in transit and the use of means of transport passing across Croatian territory between the territory of the Union of Republics of Bosnia and Herzegovina and the Adriatic Sea, and when passing across territory of the Union of Republics of Bosnia and Herzegovina in transit between places of entry and exit which are both on Croatian territory, as well as to regulate other matters foreseen in the Convention,

Hereby agree as follows:

Article 1

(a) Freedom of transit under the terms of this Preliminary Agreement shall be granted to both Parties on the basis of reciprocity.

(b) The Croatian ports of Ploce and Rijeka are designated as those to which the Union of Republics of Bosnia and Herzegovina is to have access, as foreseen in the Convention, and the routes, by road and as appropriate by rail, between Ploce and Sarajevo and between Rijeka and Bihac are the ones as to which special rules are to be adopted.

(c) The roads on the territory of the Union of Republics of Bosnia and Herzegovina:

(i) between the Croatian border near Velika Kladusa (via Cazin, Bihac, Kljuc, Jajce, Dinji Vakuf, Bugonjo, Jablanica and Mostar) and the Croatian border on the south, as well as the road between Bonji Vakuf (via Travnik) and Zenica where this road links with the road under (ii) below;

(ii) between Bosanski Brod (via Dervanta, Doboj, Zenica, Sarajevo and Mostar and the Croatian border in the south;

shall be the ones to which the freedom of transit, in accordance with the Convention, shall be granted to the Republic of Croatia.

(d) The same freedom of transit shall be granted to the Republic of Croatia on the so-called "Una railway line" on the territory of the Union of Republics of Bosnia and Herzegovina between Bosanski Novi (via Bihac) and the Croatian border on the south in the direction of Knin.

(e) The reference to specific ports of Croatia and the roads and railway line within the Union of Republics of Bosnia and Herzegovina, and specific points of entry from Croatia and the Union of Republics of Bosnia and Herzegovina and from Bosnia and Herzegovina to Croatia, are not intended to exclude the facilitation by both states of transit trade through other ports of entry.

Article 2

The Parties shall immediately start negotiating, with a view to concluding by 1 December 1993, an agreement relating to all aspects of the implementation of the Convention and this Preliminary Agreement, covering in particular the following subjects:

1. Specification of the primary routes, by road as well as by rail, from the ports to the cities specified in Article 1 (a);
2. Rules governing the means of transport over the routes and the railroad specified in Article 1 (Art. 2 (2) of the Convention);
3. Facilities existing, or to be built, within the specified ports that are to be specially dedicated to traffic of the Union of Republics of Bosnia and Herzegovina might be permitted to operate and develop with the consent of the Republic of Croatia;
4. Possible imposition of special transit dues, tariffs or charges (Arts, 3 and 4 of the Convention)
5. Special customs and other measures to facilitate transit trade (Art. 5 of the Convention);
6. Condition of storage of goods in transit (Art. 6 of the Convention);

7. Possible establishment of free zones in the designated ports (Art. 8 of the Convention);
8. Exceptions on grounds of public health, security and protection of intellectual property (Art 11 of the Convention);
9. Exceptions of the Agreement in time of war (Art. 13 of the Convention);
10. Application of the Agreement in time of war (Art. 13 of the Convention);
11. Settlement of disputes pursuant to Article 16 of the Convention.

Article 3

Pending the conclusion of the Agreement referred to in Article 2, the Republic of Croatia and the Union of Republics of Bosnia and Herzegovina shall facilitate, as far as it is possible, their mutual transit trade, as defined in this Agreement.

DONE this --- day of --- 1993, in ...., in three copies, each in the English, Croatian and Serbian languages, which shall be equally authentic.

68. APPENDIX V
JOINT DECLARATION*

Momir Bulatovic, Alija Izetbegovic, Radovan Karadzic and Slobodan Milosevic,

Accepting the principles of the London Conference and taking into account the solutions proposed by the Geneva Peace Conference on the constitutional arrangement of the future Union of Bosnia and Herzegovina,

Determined to immediately arrive at the cessation of hostilities and to create the conditions for peace in Bosnia and Herzegovina,

Convinced that the solution of this crisis has to be found through political, not military, means,

Prepared to immediately approach the normalization of relations with the Croatian people in the light of the solutions proposed by the Peace Conference in Geneva,

---

* Done at Geneva on 16 September 1993. The undersigned are Momir Bulatovic, Alija Izetbegovic, Radovan Karadzic, and Slobodan Milosevic: and, as witnesses, Thorvald Stoltenberg and David Owen.

Have hereby agreed to:

I

1. Provide for the prompt cessation of all hostilities and military conflicts between the units of the Army of Bosnia and Herzegovina and the Bosnian Serb Army in accordance with the Agreement of 30 July, 1993, immediately and by no later than September 18, 1993 at 12.00 hours, and establish direct communication (hot lines) between military commanders at all levels.
2. Provide for the bilateral and unconditional disbanding of all detainee camps and for the release of detainees in territories under the control of the Army of Bosnia and Herzegovina and the Bosnian Serb Army immediately, commencing with the release of those detained in Tarcin (207 detainees) and Kula (207 detainees), and by no later than September 21, 1993, at 12.00 hours, and bilaterally assume the responsibility for their protection and care.
3. Create bilaterally the conditions for free and unhindered passage of all relief convoys and activities of humanitarian organisation, and the free and unhindered movement of all civilians.
4. Form a working group for the supervision and safeguarding of human rights in territories under the control of the Army of Bosnia and Herzegovina and the Bosnian Serb Army in accordance with the principles and proposed solutions of the Peace Conference on Bosnia and Herzegovina.
5. Form a working group for outstanding matters related to the territorial delimitation between the two Republics in the envisaged Union of Bosnia and Herzegovina, including the areas of Brcko, Bosanski Krajina, the Neretva Valley, Eastern Bosnia and the Ozren mountain, including the natural rights of the two Republics to access to the sea. This is in addition to the commitment already made to find a permanent solution to the governance of the Sarajevo District within two years. After reaching a mutually acceptable resolution to the territorial delimitation of the three republics within the Union, and during the initial two year period of the Union's existence, there shall be a provision for a referendum to be held on a mutually agreed date within the Republics of the Union of the question of whether citizens of any particular republic agree to remain in the Union or the leave the Union.

In the case of a dissolution of the Union, all the rights of the Union of the Republics of Bosnia and Herzegovina, including membership of the United Nations, shall be automatically vested in the Republic with a predominantly Muslim majority.

II

In order to arrange stable relations and as a common contribution to regional peace the signatories have decided to form:

1. A working group to deal with humanitarian, status, material and other questions related to the position of refugees and displaced persons from Bosnia and Herzegovina;
2. A working group for the drawing up of agreements, including agreements in the use of power and port facilities, traffic arteries, communications and other economic potentials.

III

For the sake of a prompt, comprehensive and credible implementation of all the measures and activities envisaged in this Joint Declaration, the signatories have decided to appoint trustees having full authority and responsibility for the complete implementation of the accords envisaged in this Declaration.

Alija Izetbegovic has appointed as his trustee Haris Silajdzic.

Radovan Karadzic has appointed as his trustee Momcilo Krajisnik.

The signatories and the trustees will seek and secure the assistance and cooperation of international political, humanitarian and other organisations and factors for the sake of the comprehensive implementation of all measures envisaged in this Declaration, and in the interest of the establishment of permanent peace and stability in this part of the world.

To this end, it is agreed that the three Bosnian Parties will be invited by the Co-Chairmen of the International Conference on the Former Yugoslavia to meet on Tuesday 21 September at 11 am at Sarajevo Airport to consider signing the peace package as a whole, which includes The Agreement Relating to Bosnia and Herzegovina (Geneva, September 1993), with this Joint Declaration and the Joint Declaration signed on Tuesday 14 September by the Croats and the Muslims annexed to the Peace Package. The Co-Chairmen will, in the intervening days, seek further agreement by shuttling among the parties in the former Yugoslavia.

69. APPENDIX VI
JOINT DECLARATION*

The Presidents of the Republic of Croatia Dr. Franjo Tudjman and of the Presidency of the Republic of Bosnia and Herzegovina Mr. Alija Izetbegovic,

Accepting the principles of the London Conference and taking into account the solutions proposed by the Geneva Peace Conference on the constitutional arrangement of the future Union of Bosnia and Herzegovina,

Taking into account the historical interests of the Croatian and Muslim peoples,

Determined to immediately arrive at the cessation of hostilities and to create the conditions for peace in Bosnia and Herzegovina,

Convinced of the need for a continuous strengthening of confidence between the Croatian and Muslim peoples, and for efficient steps in that regard,

Prepared to immediately approach the normalisation of relations with the Croatian people in the light of the solutions proposed by the Peace Conference in Geneva,

Have hereby agreed to:

I

1. Provide for the prompt cessation of all hostilities and military conflicts between the units of the Army of Bosnia and Herzegovina and the HVO in accordance with the Agreement of 30 July, 1993, immediately and by no later than September 18, 1993 at 12.00 hours.

2. Provide for the bilateral and unconditional disbanding of all detainee camps and for the release of detainees in territories under the control of the Army of Bosnia and Herzegovina and HVO immediately, and by no later than September 21, 1993, at 12.00 hours and bilaterally assume the responsibility for their protection and care.

3. Create bilaterally the conditions for free and unhindered passage of all relief convoys and activities of humanitarian organisations.

---

* Done at Geneva on 14 September 1993. The undersigned are the President of the Republic of Croatia, Dr. Franjo Tudjman, and the President of the Presidency of Bosnia and Herzegovina, Mr. Alija Izetbegovic. The Declaration was agreed upon and adopted in the presence of, on behalf of the Republic of Croatia, Mr. Hrvoje Sarinic, Dr. Zeljiko Matic, Dr. Miomir Zuzul, and Mr. Hidajet Biscevic; and, on behalf of the Republic of Bosnia and Herzegovina, Dr. Haris Silajdzic, Dr. Ejup Ganic, Dr. Muhamed Filipovic, and Dr. Ivo Komsic.

4. Form a working group for the supervision and safeguarding of human rights in territories under the control of the Army of Bosnia and Herzegovina and the HVO in accordance with the principles and proposed solutions of the Peace Conference on Bosnia and Herzegovina.

5. Form a working group for matters related to the territorial delimitation between the two Republics in the envisaged Union of Bosnia and Herzegovina, including the access to the sea, as a matter of common developmental interest.

6. Form a working group for drawing up and monitoring the implementation of comprehensive measures for building and enhancing confidence and coexistence between the Croatian and Muslim peoples, including media and other activities and programmes aimed at overcoming distrust.

II

In order to arrange stable relations between the two states as a common contribution to regional peace, the President Dr Franjo Tudjman and Mr Alija Izetbegovic have decided to form:

1. A working group to deal with humanitarian, status, material and other questions related to the position of refugees and displaced persons from Bosnia and Herzegovina in the Republic of Croatia, and their return to Bosnia and Herzegovina;
2. A working group for the drawing up of interstate agreements, including agreements in the use of power and port facilities, traffic arteries, communications and other economic potentials.

The two Presidents have agreed that they would bring their influence to bear in providing for the appropriate support of international political and financial organisations in the reconstruction and development of the two States.

III

For the sake of a prompt, comprehensive and credible implementation of all the measures and activities envisaged in this Joint Declaration, the Presidents Dr Franjo Tudjman and Mr Alija Izetbegovic have decided to appoint their personal trustees having full authority and responsibility for the complete implementation of the accords envisaged in this Declaration.

The President Dr. Franjo Tudjman has appointed, as his trustee, Dr. Mate Granic, Vice Premier and Minister of Foreign affairs of the Republic of Croatia.

The President Mr. Alija Izetbegovic has appointed as his trustee Haris Silajdzic, Minister of Foreign Affairs of Bosnia and Herzegovina.

The Presidents and their personal trustees will seek and secure the assistance and cooperation of international political, humanitarian and other organizations and factors for the sake of the comprehensive implementation of all measures envisaged in this Declaration, and in the interest of the establishment of permanent peace and stability in this part of the world.

70. APPENDIX VII
AGREEMENT BETWEEN THE REPUBLIC OF CROATIA AND THE UNION OF REPUBLICS OF BOSNIA AND HERZEGOVINA GRANTING THE UNION ACCESS TO THE ADRIATIC THROUGH THE TERRITORY OF THE REPUBLIC OF CROATIA

The Republic of Croatia and The Union of Republics of Bosnia and Herzegovina,

Considering that it is desirable that the Union of Republics of Bosnia and Herzegovina (hereinafter the "Union") and in particular the Muslim majority Republic have assured and unrestricted access to the Adriatic Sea on the surface and in the air through and over the territory of the Republic of Croatia (hereinafter "Croatia"),

Hereby agree as follows:

Article 1
(a) Croatia shall lease to the Muslim majority Republic for the duration of this Agreement the plot of land within the Port of Ploce, including the docks and the parts of the harbour pertaining thereto described in Annex A hereto (hereinafter referred to as the "Leased Area").

(b) Croatia agrees that the Leased Area shall enjoy the status of a free zone in which no duties or taxes imposed by Croatia shall apply.

Article 2
(a) Croatia shall allow access to and from the Leased Area:

(i) By ships from the Adriatic Sea, through the territorial waters of Croatia, subject to such ships complying with any applicable international regulations;

(ii) By ships or barges up the Neretva River up to the point where that River enters the territory of the Muslim majority Republic;

(iii) By railroad on the line between Ploce to Sarajevo up to the point where that railroad line enters the territory of the Union;

(iv) By road between Ploce to Sarajevo up to the point where that road enters the territory of the Union.

(b) Ships, barges, railroad cars and trucks and other road vehicles using the routes referred to in paragraph (a) that carry the flag of the Union or are marked by an emblem of the Union or of the Muslim majority Republic shall not be entered or inspected by any public authority of Croatia.

(c) Limits in the sizes and specification of the characteristics of the ships, barges, railroad cars, and trucks and other road vehicles referred to in paragraph (b) and of the volume of traffic in the routes referred to in paragraph (a) may be set by the Joint Commission established in accordance with Article 4.

(d) Should the limits set in accordance with paragraph (c) restrict the volume of traffic that the Muslim majority Republic considers it necessary to maintain, then it may, at its cost and in accordance with plans approved by the Joint Commission, arrange for the capacity of the routes referred to in paragraph (a) to be increased.

(e) With respect to any traffic or persons or goods carried out pursuant to this Article, all responsibilities for compliance with international laws and obligations shall be assumed by the Muslim majority Republic or the Union.

Article 3

Croatia grants to the Union and in particular to the Muslim majority Republic the right to authorize any types of aircraft to overfly the territory of Croatia, including its territorial waters, along the corridor specified in Annex B hereto, subject to such aircraft complying with any applicable international air traffic regulations.

Article 4

(a) The Parties hereby establish a Joint Commission to assist in implementing the present Agreement by:

(i) establishing any rules and standards required for implementing the Agreement, and in particular Article 2 (c), including for any construction;

(ii) arrange for any monitoring required to prevent abuses of the Agreement;

(iii) settle, subject to Article 6, any disputes regarding the interpretation or the application of the Agreement.

(b) Croatia and the Muslim majority Republic shall appoint three members each to the Joint Commission and they shall by joint agreement appoint three more members, one of whom shall be the Chairman, if no agreement can be reached on one or more of the joint appointments within three months, the Secretary-General of the United Nations shall make those appointments at the request of either party.

(c) The Joint Commission shall adopt its own rules of procedure. Its decisions shall require five concurring votes.

Article 5

The present agreement is without prejudice to any rights or obligations flowing from the Preliminary Agreement between the Parties hereto for implementing the 1965 Convention on the Transit Trade of Land-Locked States or any agreement that may be concluded between the Parties to implement or to supersede that Preliminary Agreement.

Article 6

Unless otherwise agreed, any legal dispute concerning the interpretation of this Agreement may be submitted by either Party to the International Court of Justice.

Article 7

(a) This Agreement shall remain in force for a period of 99 years, except as otherwise agreed by the Parties.

(b) Should the Union be dissolved, it shall be succeeded as a Party to this Agreement by the Muslim majority Republic.

DONE this --- day of --- 1993, in ---, in three copies, each in the English, Croatian and Serbian languages, which shall be equally authentic.

C. THE EUROPEAN UNION ACTION PLAN

71. DECLARATION ON THE FORMER YUGOSLAVIA[*]

A humanitarian disaster is threatening Bosnia and Herzegovina this winter. The war and the atrocities must end. That is why the European Union has put forward and action plan to ensure the convoying of aid and the resumption of negotiations. The plan has been accepted by all parties as the basis for negotiation. There is now a real possibility of achieving peace, provided the parties concerned really wish it. In order to achieve peace, all parties must demonstrate the necessary flexibility and negotiate in good faith without wasting any more time.

The European Union is providing the major part of the humanitarian effort. Its joint action is currently being implemented. The European Union continues to insist that Tuzla airport be re-opened. Although the humanitarian convoys are subject to less obstruction, the parties concerned are still far from fulfilling the obligations entered into 29 November in Geneva. They must adhere strictly to them.

At political level, enormous obstacles have still to be overcome. The Bosnians are entitled to a viable territory including access to the sea, and an appeal is made to the Croatian side on this point. The arrangement on Sarajevo, as agreed on board HMS Invincible, will have to guarantee, under United Nations supervision, free access and free movement for all its citizens throughout the city. The claim by the Bosnian side to a third of the territory of Bosnia and Herzegovina is legitimate and must be met.

The Serbs must be aware of the responsibility which they take upon themselves should they continue adopting an inflexible attitude. They must realize that only real territorial concessions by them in Bosnia and Herzegovina and acceptance of the modus vivendi in Croatia will induce the European Union to work, as it promised to do in Geneva, for the progressive and conditional suspension of sanctions in line with implementation. In the meantime, the European Union will endeavour to promote a more rigorous application of sanctions.

The European Council required all parties to act in a constructive spirit and expects third States to dissuade the parties involved from resorting to the military option. The European Union again confirms that it is ready to play its role in implementing the peace plan. As regards the Bosnian side, the European

---

[*]   Presidency Conclusions, Brussels, 10 and 11 December 1993.

Union will endeavour to obtain credible assurances regarding the effective implementation of a peace settlement. In this context, it will endeavour to ensure that the necessary facilities are established under the authority of the United Nations Security Council using, inter alia, the resources of NATO. The Member States of the European Union will make their contribution to these arrangements and appeal to the other States concerned to provide their support as well.

The European Council confirmed its confidence in the negotiations, who are concentrating their efforts to push through the Action Plan, which constitutes the basis for negotiation, it invited the Serb Bosnian and Croat leaders to meet the Council in Brussels on 22 December.

72. EUROPEAN UNION'S REQUESTS TO THE PARTIES[*]

Requests to *all the parties*:

a) War must end. Basis is the European Union Action Plan, as put forward in Geneva at the 29 November meeting.
b) The parties must negotiate in good faith, show the necessary flexibility and reach agreement quickly.
c) The parties have to fulfil scrupulously their commitments of November 29 concerning free access of humanitarian aid and respects for humanitarian law.
d) Maintaining the Union of the Republics of Bosnia and Herzegovina remains European Union's preference.

The *Serbs* are requested to:

a) deliver the difference between the Invincible acquis and the Moslems one-third (= 3-4 % more territory), which must be a viable territory containing in particular,

- Invincible acquis including the access to the Sava at Brcko,
- more territory in Central Bosnia and round the eastern enclaves,
- a stable link between the enclaves and the main Muslim land at Sarajevo;

---

[*] Brussels, 20 December 1993.

b) agree to the modus vivendi of the UNPAs;

c) guarantee full freedom of movement in entire Sarajevo and renounce partition of the city;

d) stop the shelling of Sarajevo and the enclaves, stop the encirclement of Tuzla;

e) accept opening of Tuzla airport for humanitarian use.

The Serbian side should be told that their inflexible attitude in the negotiations is the main stumbling block. The European Union maintains its promise to work towards a gradual and conditional suspension of UN sanctions. But they must realise that they can expect suspension only if they agree to and implement a peace package as described and the modus vivendi.

If they do not show sufficient flexibility, the sanctions regime will be upheld and reinforced, Furthermore a continued shelling of protected zones will meet with the specific response provided for by relevant UN-Security Council resolutions.

The *Croats* are requested to:

a) show flexibility in order to make a viable Muslim territory possible, without the Invincible acquis being put into question;

b) agree to the modus vivendi in the UNPAs;

c) give sea access at Prevlaka or revert to Invincible sea access package including on Neum reverting to Union, or to Muslims in case Herzeg-Bosna quits Union. In both cases access to port facilities in Ploce as a greed on Invincible, including a river port at the Neretva has to be conceded;

d) refrain from linking recognition of Croatia by Serbia-Montenegro to aspects of Bosnia settlement;

e) renounce partition of Mostar.

The Croatian side should be told that negotiations on increased economic an trade relations with EU will only take place after fulfilment of these demands and implementation in good faith.

The *Muslims* are requested to:

a) stick to their quantitative territorial demands (overall one third, taking into account, as appropriated, an internationally administered Sarajevo);

b) renounce Muslim sovereignty over Neum and accept sea access at Prevlaka or revert to Invincible sea access package including clause on Neum
reverting to Union or to Muslims in case Herzeg-Bosna quits Union;

c) accept that most additional territory would be granted in Central Bosnia in
order to make the main Muslim land viable;

d) accept that a viable and stable link of the Eastern enclaves will be made to
Sarajevo (not to Tuzla);

e) stop the offensive against territories allotted to the Croats.

The Muslims should be told that EU is taking up their legitimate demands to
have a third of Bosnia as a viable territory with a stable link to the Eastern
Bosnian enclaves and with access to sea and to Sava. EU will endeavour to
ensure that the necessary facilities are established under authority of UN Security Council using, inter-alia, to resources of NATO. EU will contribute to this
and also to economic reconstruction.

But this requires also flexibility of the side of the Bosnian government and its
support for EU's efforts. Despite all humanitarian efforts - of which EU bears
the brunt - a humanitarian disaster cannot be avoided if a political solution is not
reached quickly. In this respect leaders of *all* parties have a heavy responsibility.

73. INTRODUCTORY REMARKS BY THE PRESIDENT OF THE COUNCIL*

Ladies and Gentlemen, Some weeks ago we met in Geneva. There the European Union presented to you an action plan to ensure the convoying of aid and
the resumption of negotiations. You accepted that plan as a basis for action and
negotiation. If some progress was achieved, it was unfortunately short-lived.

Humanitarian aid is far from getting through without let a hindrance. Progress in the political negotiations, in particular on the future of Bosnia and
Herzegovina, has still not materialized.

Faced with the danger of seeing the impetus of Geneva peter out, the European Council on 10 and 11 December took a three point-decision:

- in a declaration made at the highest level, the Council clearly indicated the
areas where additional efforts were indispensable;
- in the spirit of that declaration, the Council of Ministers decided to spell out
certain aspects of the action plan, in particular the territorial aspect; and

---

* Brussels, 22 December 1993.

- decided to invite the parties on that twofold basis to a further meeting with the twelve Foreign Affairs Minister of the Union.

Ladies and Gentlemen, the European Council has stressed above all else: a humanitarian disaster is threatening Bosnia and Herzegovina, the war and the atrocities must end. The Serbs must stop their encirclement of Tuzla and halt the bombing of Sarajevo and the enclaves, which cannot continue without some form of retort. An end must be put to the chain of offensives and counter-offensives. The military option is unacceptable.

Furthermore, we call for a complete end to the obstruction of convoys, as agreed in Geneva. In addition, we ask yet again the Serbian side to allow Tuzla airport to be reopened, for duly monitored humanitarian purposes only. For its part, the Union remains ready to ensure the operation of Tuzla airport just as it is preparing itself to provide the material means to ensure that the convoy routes become passable again.

We dare to hope that Christmas will be marked by a cessation of hostilities and by a humanitarian truce, which could subsequently be consolidated.

Ladies and Gentlemen, in its Action Plan, the Union spelled out the content of a modus vivendi in the Croatian areas under UNPROFOR mandate.

The Croat and Serb sides have started negotiating on that basis. We should like to believe that an agreement will be reached soon, and we are urging the parties to lose no time in concluding the negotiations.

Ladies and Gentlemen, the negotiations on the fate of Bosnia and Herzegovina are marking time. They are, however, crucial. Here we are at the very crux of the drama in former Yugoslavia. Without agreement in Bosnia and Herzegovina, the humanitarian drama will continue, and there will continue to be no real solution to the other disputes arising from the disintegration of Yugoslavia. Thus is why the European Council, here more than anywhere else, requires all the parties to act constructively. In order to overcome certain remaining obstacles, the European Union wishes to clarify here and now certain points of its plan.

Our plan of action shows that the Serbian side will be required to accept specific and substantial territorial adjustments on a par with the demands made by the Bosnian Presidency in the eve of the meeting on board HMS Invincible.

The territorial concessions in its favour must be sufficient to attribute it one-third of the entire territory of Bosnia and Herzegovina.

Zones - such as Sarajevo - which might come under an international mandate will have to be taken into account, in a proportion yet to be determined, in the calculation of that third. These territorial concessions must be sought principally in Central Bosnia, while taking into account the territorial adjustments which would be made elsewhere. In this respect, I am thinking in particular of the adjustments which would be made in Eastern Bosnia around the enclaves, which should, moreover, be linked securely to Sarajevo.

To guarantee the viability of this territory, the European Union considers that access by sea and waterway must be assured. Access to Sava will be guaranteed by a corridor towards to town and port of Breko, as planned on board HMS Invincible. In addition, access to the sea will have to be assured both by making port facilities freely available, notably at Ploce, and by territorial access to the Adriatic Sea either to the North of Prevlaka, or at Neum in accordance with the arrangements arrives at on HMS Invincible.

The European Union wishes at the same time to point out what it is prepared to contribute.

It is maintaining its offers concerning Sarajevo and Mostar where we are urging the parties to give up the idea of partitioning. It is for the parties to decide on this, but we insist that the UN participate in the administration of Sarajevo in accordance with the modalities in the Geneva agreements. The arrangements as agreed on board HMS Invincible will also have to guarantee, under UN supervision, free access and free movement throughout the city for all its citizens. The European Union also reiterates its offer to participate in the administration of Mostar City Opstina, which once again pre-supposes that the city will not be divided.

We would also remind to the Serbs that only real territorial concessions by them in Bosnia and Herzegovina and acceptance of the modus vivendi in Croatia will induce the European Union to work, as it promised to do in Geneva, for the progressive and conditional suspension of sanctions in line with implementation. In the meantime, it will endeavour to promote more rigorous application of them. If the deadlock persisted, it would have no other solution that to continue to step up the system of sanctions.

Finally, we would once again confirm that we are ready to assume our share in implementing the peace plan to be reached by the parties. As regards the Bosnian side, the European Union will endeavour to obtain credible assurances regarding the effective implementation of a peace settlement. In this context, it will act to ensure that the necessary facilities are established, under the authority of the UN security Council, using, inter alia, the resources of NATO. The member States of the European Union will contribute to these arrangements and will ensure that the other States concerned also join it.

Ladies and Gentlemen, we shall shortly be holding discussions with each of you, which will enable us to clarify certain points and hear your comments. After lunch, we will come together again to conclude this meeting.

I cannot insist strong enough that each and every one of you should gauge the importance of our meeting today. The European Union is seeking to help you out of the drama which is ruining your countries and decimating your peoples. But if we are to be able to help you, you yourselves must first want a solution and work out the concessions in order to arrive at it. Despite all the humanitarian efforts which the European Union has been the first to make, the humanitarian disaster can be avoided only by a political agreement. All the sides have responsibility in ensuring that such an agreement is worked out urgently.

If the deadlock were to persist at the end of the day, we would be forced to explain to causes for it and point the finger at those responsible.

D. THE CONTACT GROUP PLAN

74. COMMUNIQUE OF THE MEETING OF FOREIGN MINISTERS IN GENEVA, 13 MAY 1994

The Foreign Ministers of Greece, Belgium and Germany and European Commissioner Hans van den Broek, comprising the Troika of the European Union, and the Foreign Ministers of France, the Russian Federation, the United Kingdom and the United States met in Geneva on 13 May. Together with the Co-Chairmen of the Steering Committee of the International Conference on the Former Yugoslavia, they reviewed the serious situation in Bosnia and Herzegovina and their common efforts to date to end the conflict and achieve a political settlement.

The Ministers underscore their resolve and unity of purposes in working for an early and durable settlement of the Bosnian conflict. They reaffirm that the conflict in Bosnia and Herzegovina cannot be resolved by military means and must be settled through negotiations. Only a peaceful settlement will command the support of the international community and offer the peoples of Bosnia and Herzegovina the prospect of a secure future. They confirm their support of a settlement that preserves Bosnia and Herzegovina as a single Union within its internationally recognized borders, while providing for constitutional arrangements that establish the relationship between the Bosniac-Croat and the Bosnian Serb entities. The Ministers are committed to doing their utmost to promote such a settlement.

They also affirm the readiness of their countries to participate as appropriate in implementing an agreed settlement, and in supporting the reconstruction of war-ravaged Bosnia and Herzegovina.

The Ministers express their strong concern that in the wake of the recent Bosnian Serb attack in the UN-declared safe area of Gorazde, the negotiating process has been set back. They warn all the parties concerning the unacceptability and risks of pursuing military solutions. In this regard, they support the determination of the international community to take the necessary action to protect the safe areas within Bosnia and Herzegovina established in accordance with Security Council resolutions 824 and 836. They demand that the parties comply fully with the terms and conditions of the relevant Security Council resolutions, the decision taken in reliance thereon, and all agreements the parties have concluded. They express their full support for strict enforcement of these resolutions, decisions, and agreements. The Ministers demand that all parties permit the unimpeded delivery of humanitarian assistance in accordance with existing agreements. The Ministers insist on the release of those members of humanitarian organisations in detention.

The Ministers note with concern the recent military action related to Brcko and endorse efforts currently being made by UNPROFOR and underway in the United Nations Security Council to prevent offensive action in safe areas and particularly in and around Brcko and to reduce tensions in other parts of Bosnia and Herzegovina.

The Ministers agreed on immediate steps aimed at an early settlement in Bosnia and Herzegovina. They call on the parties to conclude a comprehensive cessation of hostilities and to resume in parallel without preconditions serious efforts to reach a political settlement.

The agreement on cessation of hostilities must include the separation of forces, the withdrawal of heavy weapons and the interposition of UNPROFOR troops. On the basis of previous discussions with the parties, the Ministers believe that the agreement should be for a period of four months, with provision for extension. Ministers underscored the need for the United Nations and the parties to establish necessary arrangements to insure compliance with this agreement. To complete its task in the safe areas and in support of the cessation of hostilities, UNPROFOR will need further reinforcement.

Previous negotiations have established the concept of a territorial compromise based on 51 percent for the Bosniac-Croat entity and 49 percent for the Bosnian Serb entity. Ministers urge the parties to reach an agreement on this basis.

The Ministers take note of the steps to establish the Bosniac-Croat Federation. They believe that the final arrangement for the Federation must provide it with viable, realistic, and reasonable territory consistent with the concept described above.

The existing UN Security Council resolution must be strictly enforced and complied with, and the Ministers agree that any attempt to make sanctions relief a precondition for resuming talks is unacceptable. Good faith implementation of a peace settlement that includes provision for withdrawal to agreed territorial limits will lead to phased suspension of the sanctions imposed by the United Nations.

With a view to achieving an early settlement within this framework, the Ministers invite the parties to begin substantive negotiations under the aegis of the Contact Group within the next two weeks. The Contact Group was instructed to immediately commence all the necessary substantive preparation aimed at facilitating an early settlement.

The Ministers will follow closely the course of these negotiations and the actions of the parties on the ground. They agreed to meet again as soon as necessary.

75. MINISTERIAL TEXT OF 5 JULY 1994

Ministers welcomed the map agreement agreed by the Contact Group and instructed the Group to present it to the parties. Ministers took the view that the territorial arrangements incorporated in the map represented a reasonable balance and they instructed the Contact Group to make clear to the parties that a response was needed within two weeks at the latest. Ministers urged the parties to accept the proposed map or to present mutually agreed amendments.

Ministers confirmed their support for a settlement that keeps Bosnia and Herzegovina as a Union within its internationally recognized borders and which continues the international legal personality of the Republic of Bosnia and Herzegovina. Constitutional arrangements will define the relationship between the Bosniac/Croat and the Bosnian Serb entities. The human rights specified in the principal international and European instruments are to be observed. Constitutional arrangements may be revised by mutual consent once the territorial settlement concerning Sarajevo has been concluded.

Ministers agreed that the parties should observe and prolong the ceasefire and refrain from military action. The objective is the earliest possible signature by the parties of a comprehensive cessation of hostilities as a first step in implementing an overall settlement.

Ministers agreed that the Contact Group should also set out to the parties certain incentives and disincentives as follows:

If, on this basis, both parties agree to the map:

Incentives for the Federation:
- International assurances for implementation of the territorial settlement;
- Assistance with reconstruction;
- Resettlement fund for refugees.

Incentives for the Bosnian Serbs:
- Suspension of sanctions geared to implementation of the territorial settlement. Preparation of a draft UNSC Resolution for Geneva III to be introduced immediately after Bosnian Serb acceptance of the map;
- Phasing of suspension of sanctions would include clearing application in the UN sanctions committee and opening Belgrade Airport for civilian passen-

ger service immediately on acceptance of the map. Completion of with-drawal would lead to suspension of other sanctions.

If the Federation refuses but the Bosnian Serbs agree:

Disincentives for the Federation:
- Loss of international support. Proposed reconstruction assistance for Bosnia put in jeopardy;
- Easing of sanctions on the Serbs as described above;
- Continuation of the arms embargo and its rigorous enforcement;
- Exclusion of Federation military from territory from which the Bosnian Serbs withdrew in accordance with the Contact Group map.

If the Federation agrees and the Bosnian Serbs refuse:

Disincentives for the Serbs:
- Measures to tighten existing sanctions and preparation for Geneva III of a new UNSC Resolution on extending sanctions to be introduced after rejection of the map;
- Extension and strict enforcement of exclusion zones.

If despite these measures, the Bosnian Serbs continued to reject the map, a decision in the UNSC of the lifting of the arms embargo could become unavoidable. There will be consequences for the presence of UNPROFOR.

- We commended and approved the substantive preparations done by the Contact Group following its meeting with the parties in accordance with the instructions given at the last Geneva ministerial Meeting.
- We welcomed the territorial proposal developed by the Contact Group and have directed the Group to present it to the representatives of the Bosnian Government of the Bosnian Serbs.
- This effort is strongly supported by our government as a reasonable basis of an immediate political settlement.
- We are urging the parties to consider it favourably and to give us their responses within two weeks.
- It would from part of a settlement that preserves Bosnia and Herzegovina as a single union within its internationally recognized borders, while providing for constitutional arrangements that establish the relationship between the Bosniac/Croat and Bosnian Serb entities.

- We also express once again our firm support for a settlement which provides for refugees and displaced persons to have the possibility to return freely to their homes of origin.
- Our proposal represents an important moment of opportunity, which may not come again. Those of use gathered here are united in our belief that the war can be ended now.
- We believe the consequences of failing to do so would be grave.
- With peace, however, the international community stands ready to begin implementing a settlement and rebuilding Bosnia. We urge Bosnian parties to respond quickly and positively to our offer.
- The Contact Group will be presenting Ministers' views tomorrow to the parties. Without going into details there are important incentives for the parties if they accept the proposed map:
- For the Bosnian government we are ready to assist in the implementation a territorial settlement and to help with reconstruction;
- For the Serbs, sanctions will be suspended geared to their pullback to the lines indicated on the map.

If the parties do not agree they can expect more pressure to be applied. In particular, existing UNSCRs concerning safe areas will be rigorously enforced. The necessary planning is being undertaken. As a last resort decision in the Security Council to lift the arms embargo could become unavoidable. That would have consequences for the presence of UNPROFOR.

- In the meantime, the parties should observe and prolong the ceasefire and refrain from military action.
- The parties are required to give their answer to this proposal in two weeks.
- We agreed to meet again before the end of July ....
- We also discussed the wider situation in the former Yugoslavia. We urge mutual recognition between all States within the boundaries of the former Yugoslavia. We urge the immediate resumption of talks between the Croatian government and the local Serb authorities.

E. THE PROXIMITY PEACE TALKS*

76. KEYNOTE REMARKS BY SECRETARY OF STATE WARREN CHRISTOPHER AT THE INITIALING OF THE BALKAN PROXIMITY PEACE TALKS AGREEMENT

President Izetbegovic, President Milosevic, President Tudjman, Mr. Bildt, Deputy Minister Ivanov, General Shalikashvili, Deputy Secretary White, honored colleagues and guests: We have reached a day many believed would never come. After three weeks of intensive negotiations in Dayton, the leaders of Bosnia-Herzegovina, Croatia, and Serbia have agreed to end the war in the former Yugoslavia. They have agreed that four years of destruction is enough. The time has come to build peace with justice.

Today's agreement would not have come without the vision and leadership of President Clinton. The diplomatic and military strategy that he launched this summer has borne fruit. I am gratified at the result and determined to see that it is implemented.

We have come to this hopeful moment because the parties made the fundamental choices that lasting peace will require. And we are here because our international negotiating team successfully led the parties to agreement. Assistant Secretary Holbrooke and his team took on a hard, exhausting task and succeeded in a way that will long be remembered and admired. I also want to recognize the tireless efforts of my friend and colleague National Security Advisor Tony Lake. The European Union and the members of the Contact Group - Germany, France, the United Kingdom, and Russia - were with us every critical step of the way.

No one thought these negotiations would be easy, and all of us on this stage can tell you they were not. What we wanted was a comprehensive settlement, and that is what we have achieved. The hard-won commitments we will initial today address the wrenching and fundamental issues over which the war was fought.

Today's agreement assures the continuity of a single state of Bosnia-Herzegovina, with effective federal institutions, a single currency, and full respect by its neighbors for its sovereignty. The city of Sarajevo, which has gripped the world's attention for the last four years, will no longer be divided. It will be reunified under the Federation of Bosnia and Herzegovina. Checkpoints and

---

* Wright-Patterson Air Force Base, Dayton, Ohio, November 1-21, 1995.

closed bridges will no longer divide its families. All Bosnia's people will have the right to move freely throughout the country. Refugees and displaced persons will have the right to return home or obtain just compensation. Free and democratic elections will be held next year.

The agreement contains strong human rights protections. It confirms the parties' obligation to cooperate fully in the investigation and prosecution of war crimes. It excludes indicted war criminals from military or government office.

The agreement requires the parties to withdraw their forces to agreed positions and provides for important confidence building measures among them. The parties have pledged to cooperate fully with a NATO-led peace implementation force and to ensure the safety of its personnel. And it sets the stage for a comprehensive program of economic reconstruction.

Today's agreement certainly does not erase memories of what has come before, or guarantee that the fabric of Bosnia's society will easily be restored. But still, it is a victory for us all.

The agreement is a victory for people of every heritage in the former Yugoslavia. It offers tangible hope that there will be no more days of dodging bullets, no more winters of freshly dug graves, no more years of isolation from the outside world.

The agreement is a victory for all those who believe in a multi-ethnic democracy in Bosnia-Herzegovina. Securing that goal will require an immense effort in the days ahead. But that effort can now begin as the war that has torn Bosnia apart finally comes to an end.

The agreement is a victory for all those in the world who believed that with determination, a principled peace is possible. That conviction was shared by the three brave American diplomats who gave their lives in pursuit of peace in Bosnia -- Bob Frasure, Joe Kruzel, and Nelson Drew. We honor their memories. I am so pleased that their families are with us today.

But this victory will not be secure unless we all get to work to ensure that the promise of this moment is realized. The' parties have put a solemn set of commitments on paper. In the coming days and weeks, they will have to put them into practice, extending them to every mayor, every soldier, every police officer on their territory. The United States and the international community will continue to help them succeed. It is profoundly in our self-interest to do so.

As we move forward, we must be realistic and clear-eyed. We should not assume that the people of the former Yugoslavia have resolved all their differences. But we should also remember we can now begin to leave behind the horrors of the last four years. This war was waged against civilians; it is they who are the real winners today. The American people should be proud of that achievement. The war in Bosnia has been a challenge to our interests and our values. By our leadership here, we have upheld both.

I trust that one day, people will look back on Dayton and say: This is the place where the fundamental choices were made. This is where the parties chose peace over war, dialogue over destruction, reason over revenge. And this is where each of us accepted the challenge to make those choices meaningful and to make them endure.

Thank you.

77. GENERAL FRAMEWORK AGREEMENT FOR PEACE IN BOSNIA AND HERZEGOVINA[*]

The Republic of Bosnia and Herzegovina, the Republic of Croatia and the Federal Republic of Yugoslavia (the "Parties"),

Recognizing the need for a comprehensive settlement to bring an end to the tragic conflict in the region,

Desiring to contribute toward that end and to promote an enduring peace and stability,

Affirming their commitment to the Agreed Basic Principles issued on September 8, 1995, the Further Agreed Basic Principles issued on September 26, 1995, and the cease-fire agreements of September 14 and October 5, 1995,

Noting the agreement of August 29, 1995, which authorized the delegation of the Federal Republic of Yugoslavia to sign, on behalf of the Republika Srpska, the parts of the peace plan concerning it, with the obligation to implement the agreement that is reached strictly and consequently,

Have agreed as follows:

Article I

The Parties shall conduct their relations in accordance with the principles set forth in the United Nations Charter, as well as the Helsinki Final Act and other documents of the Organization for Security and Cooperation in Europe. In particular, the Parties shall fully respect the sovereign equality of one another, shall settle disputes by peaceful means, and shall refrain from any action, by threat or

---

[*]   Initialled on 21 November 1995 by representatives of the Republic of Bosnia and Herzegovina, the Republic of Croatia, the Federal Republic of Yugoslavia; and, as witnesses, by representatives of the European Union Special Negotiator, the French Republic, the Federal Republic of Germany, the Russian Federation, the United Kingdom of Great Britain and Northern Ireland and the United States of America.

use of force or otherwise, against the territorial integrity or political independence of Bosnia and Herzegovina or any other State.

Article II

The Parties welcome and endorse the arrangements that have been made concerning the military aspects of the peace settlement and aspects of regional stabilization, as set forth in the Agreements at Annex 1-A and Annex 1-B. The Parties shall fully respect and promote fulfillment of the commitments made in Annex 1-A, and shall comply fully with their commitments as set forth in Annex 1-B.

Article III

The Parties welcome and endorse the arrangements that have been made concerning the boundary demarcation between the two Entities, the Federation of Bosnia and Herzegovina and Republika Srpska, as set forth in the Agreement at Annex 2. The Parties shall fully respect and promote fulfillment of the commitments made therein.

Article IV

The Parties welcome and endorse the elections program for Bosnia and Herzegovina as set forth in Annex 3. The Parties shall fully respect and promote fulfillment of that program.

Article V

The Parties welcome and endorse the arrangements that have been made concerning the Constitution of Bosnia and Herzegovina, as set forth in Annex 4. The Parties shall fully respect and promote fulfillment of the commitments made therein.

Article VI

The Parties welcome and endorse the arrangements that have been made concerning the establishment of an arbitration tribunal, a Commission on Human Rights, a Commission on Refugees and Displaced Persons, a Commission to Preserve National Monuments, and Bosnia and Herzegovina Public Corporations, as set forth in the Agreements at Annexes 5-9. The Parties shall fully respect and promote fulfillment of the commitments made therein.

Article VII

Recognizing that the observance of human rights and the protection of refugees and displaced persons are of vital importance in achieving a lasting peace, the Parties agree to and shall comply fully with the provisions concerning human rights set forth in Chapter One of the Agreement at Annex 6, as well as the provisions concerning refugees and displaced persons set forth in Chapter One of the Agreement at Annex 7.

Article VIII

The Parties welcome and endorse the arrangements that have been made concerning the implementation of this peace settlement, including in particular those pertaining to the civilian (non-military) implementation, as set forth in the Agreement at Annex 10, and the international police task force, as set forth in the Agreement at Annex 11. The Parties shall fully respect and promote fulfillment of the commitments made therein.

Article IX

The Parties shall cooperate fully with all entities involved in implementation of this peace settlement, as described in the Annexes to this Agreement, or which are otherwise authorized by the United Nations Security Council, pursuant to the obligation of all Parties to cooperate in the investigation and prosecution of war crimes and other violations of international humanitarian law.

Article X

The Federal Republic of Yugoslavia and the Republic of Bosnia and Herzegovina recognize each other as sovereign independent States within their international borders. Further aspects of their mutual recognition will be subject to subsequent discussions.

Article XI

This Agreement shall enter into force upon signature.

DONE AT Paris, this 21st day of November, 1995, in the Bosnian, Croatian, English and Serbian languages, each text being equally authentic.

78. ANNEX 1-A
AGREEMENT ON THE MILITARY ASPECTS OF THE PEACE SETTLEMENT*

The Republic of Bosnia and Herzegovina, the Federation of Bosnia and Herzegovina, and the Republika Srpska (hereinafter the "Parties") have agreed as follows:

Article I
General Obligations

1. The Parties undertake to recreate as quickly as possible normal conditions of life in Bosnia and Herzegovina. They understand that this requires a major contribution on their part in which they will make strenuous efforts to cooperate with each other and with the international organizations and agencies which are assisting them on the ground. They welcome the willingness of the international community to send to the region, for a period of approximately one year, a force to assist in implementation of the territorial and other militarily related provisions of the agreement as described herein.

(a) The United Nations Security Council is invited to adopt a resolution by which it will authorize Member States or regional organizations and arrangements to establish a multinational military Implementation Force (hereinafter "IFOR"). The Parties understand and agree that this Implementation Force may be composed of ground, air and maritime units from NATO and non-NATO nations, deployed to Bosnia and Herzegovina to help ensure compliance with the provisions of this Agreement (hereinafter "Annex"). The Parties understand and agree that the IFOR will begin the implementation of the military aspects of this Annex upon the transfer of authority from the UNPROFOR Commander to the IFOR Commander (hereinafter "Transfer of Authority") and that until the Transfer of Authority, UNPROFOR will continue to exercise its mandate.

(b) It is understood and agreed that NATO may establish such a force, which will operate under the authority and subject to the direction and political control of the North Atlantic Council ("NAC") through the NATO chain of command. They undertake to facilitate its operations. The Parties, therefore, hereby agree and freely undertake to fully comply with all obligations set forth in this Annex.

(c) It is understood and agreed that other States may assist in implementing the military aspects of this Annex. The Parties understand and agree that the

---

* Initialled by representatives of the Republic of Bosnia and Herzegovina, the Federation of Bosnia and Herzegovina and the Republika Srpska; and, as endorsement, by representatives of the Republic of Croatia and the Federal Republic of Yugoslavia.

modalities of those States' participation will be the subject of agreement between such participating States and NATO.

2. The purposes of these obligations are as follows:

(a) to establish a durable cessation of hostilities. Neither Entity shall threaten or use force against the other Entity, and under no circumstances shall any armed forces of either Entity enter into or stay within the territory of the other Entity without the consent of the government of the latter and of the Presidency of Bosnia and Herzegovina. All armed forces in Bosnia and Herzegovina shall operate consistently with the sovereignty and territorial integrity of Bosnia and Herzegovina;

(b) to provide for the support and authorization of the IFOR and in particular to authorize the IFOR to take such actions as required, including the use of necessary force, to ensure compliance with this Annex, and to ensure its own protection; and

(c) to establish lasting security and arms control measures as outlined in Annex 1-B to the General Framework Agreement, which aim to promote a permanent reconciliation between all Parties and to facilitate the achievement of all political arrangements agreed to in the General Framework Agreement.

3. The Parties understand and agree that within Bosnia and Herzegovina the obligations undertaken in this Annex shall be applied equally within both Entities. Both Entities shall be held equally responsible for compliance herewith, and both shall be equally subject to such enforcement action by the IFOR as may be necessary to ensure implementation of this Annex and the protection of the IFOR.

Article II
Cessation of Hostilities

1. The Parties shall comply with the cessation of hostilities begun with the agreement of October 5, 1995 and shall continue to refrain from all offensive operations of any type against each other. An offensive operation in this case is an action that includes projecting forces or fire forward of a Party's own lines. Each Party shall ensure that all personnel and organizations with military capability under its control or within territory under its control, including armed civilian groups, national guards, army reserves, military police, and the Ministry of Internal Affairs Special Police (MUP) (hereinafter "Forces") comply with this Annex. The term "Forces" does not include UNPROFOR, the International Police Task Force referred to in the General Framework Agreement, the IFOR or other elements referred to in Article I, paragraph 1 (c).

2. In carrying out the obligations set forth in paragraph 1, the Parties undertake, in particular, to cease the firing of all weapons and explosive devices except as authorized by this Annex. The Parties shall not place any additional minefields, barriers, or protective obstacles. They shall not engage in patrolling, ground or air reconnaissance forward of their own force positions, or into the Zones of Separation as provided for in Article IV below, without IFOR approval.

3. The Parties shall provide a safe and secure environment for all persons in their respective jurisdictions, by maintaining civilian law enforcement agencies operating in accordance with internationally recognized standards and with respect for internationally recognized human rights and fundamental freedoms, and by taking such other measures as appropriate. The Parties also commit themselves to disarm and disband all armed civilian groups, except for authorized police forces, within 30 days after the Transfer of Authority.

4. The Parties shall cooperate fully with any international personnel including investigators, advisors, monitors, observers, or other personnel in Bosnia and Herzegovina pursuant to the General Framework Agreement, including facilitating free and unimpeded access and movement and by providing such status as is necessary for the effective conduct of their tasks.

5. The Parties shall strictly avoid committing any reprisals, counterattacks, or any unilateral actions in response to violations of this Annex by another Party. The Parties shall respond to alleged violations of the provisions of this Annex through the procedures provided in Article VIII.

Article III
Withdrawal of Foreign Forces

1. All Forces in Bosnia and Herzegovina as of the date this Annex enters into force which are not of local origin, whether or not they are legally and militarily subordinated to the Republic of Bosnia and Herzegovina, the Federation of Bosnia and Herzegovina, or Republika Srpska, shall be withdrawn together with their equipment from the territory of Bosnia and Herzegovina within thirty (30) days. Furthermore, all Forces that remain on the territory of Bosnia and Herzegovina must act consistently with the territorial integrity, sovereignty, and political independence of Bosnia and Herzegovina. In accordance with Article II, paragraph 1, this paragraph does not apply to UNPROFOR, the International Police Task Force referred to in the General Framework Agreement, the IFOR or other elements referred to in Article I, paragraph 1(c).

2. In particular, all foreign Forces, including individual advisors, freedom fighters, trainers, volunteers, and personnel from neighboring and other States,

shall be withdrawn from the territory of Bosnia and Herzegovina in accordance with Article III, paragraph 1.

Article IV
Redeployment of Forces

1. The Republic of Bosnia and Herzegovina and the Entities shall redeploy their Forces in three phases:

2. PHASE I

(a) The Parties immediately after this Annex enters into force shall begin promptly and proceed steadily to withdraw all Forces behind a Zone of Separation which shall be established on either side of the Agreed Cease-Fire Line that represents a clear and distinct demarcation between any and all opposing Forces. This withdrawal shall be completed within thirty (30) days after the Transfer of Authority. The precise Agreed Cease-Fire Line and Agreed Cease-Fire Zone of Separation are indicated on the maps at Appendix A of this Annex.

(b) The Agreed Cease-Fire Zone of Separation shall extend for a distance of approximately two (2) kilometers on either side of the Agreed Cease-Fire Line. No weapons other than those of the IFOR are permitted in this Agreed Cease-Fire Zone of Separation except as provided herein. No individual may retain or possess any military weapons or explosives within this four kilometer Zone without specific approval of the IFOR. Violators of this provision shall be subject to military action by the IFOR, including the use of necessary force to ensure compliance.

(c) In addition to the other provisions of this Annex, the following specific provisions shall also apply to Sarajevo and Gorazde:

Sarajevo

(1) Within seven (7) days after the Transfer of Authority, the Parties shall transfer and vacate selected positions along the Agreed Cease-Fire Line according to instructions to be issued by the IFOR Commander.

(2) The Parties shall complete withdrawal from the Agreed Cease-Fire Zone of Separation in Sarajevo within thirty (30) days after the Transfer of Authority, in accordance with Article IV, paragraph 2. The width of this Zone of Separation will be approximately one (1) kilometer on either side of the Agreed Cease-Fire Line. However, this Zone of Separation may be adjusted by the IFOR Commander either to narrow the Zone of Separation to take account of the urban area of Sarajevo or to widen the Zone of Separation up to two (2) kilometers on either side of the Agreed Cease-Fire Line to take account of more open terrain.

(3) Within the Agreed Cease-Fire Zone of Separation, no individual may retain or possess any weapons or explosives, other than a member of the IFOR or the local police exercising official duties as authorized by the IFOR in accordance with Article IV, paragraph 2(b).

(4) The Parties understand and agree that violators of subparagraphs (1), (2) and (3) above shall be subject to military action by the IFOR, including the use of necessary force to ensure compliance.

Gorazde

(1) The Parties understand and agree that a two lane all-weather road will be constructed in the Gorazde Corridor. Until such road construction is complete, the two interim routes will be used by both Entities. The Grid coordinates for these alternate routes are: (Map References: Defense Mapping Agency 1:50,000 Topographic Line Maps, Series M709, Sheets 2782-1, 2782-2, 2782-3, 2782-4, 2881-4, 2882-1, 2882-2, 2882-3, and 2882-4; Military Grid Reference System grid coordinates referenced to World Geodetic System 84 (Horizontal Datum)):

Interim Route 1: From Gorazde (34TCP361365), proceed northeast following Highway 5 along the Drina River to the Ustipraca area (34TCP 456395). At that point, proceed north on Highway 19-3 through Rogatica (34TCP393515) continuing northwest past Stienice (34TCP294565) to the road intersection at Podromanija (34TCP208652). From this point, proceed west following Highway 19 to where it enters the outskirts of Sarajevo (34TBP950601).

Interim Route 2: From Gorazde (34TCP361365), proceed south following Highway 20. Follow Highway 20 through Ustinkolina (34TCP218281). Continue south following Highway 20 passing Foca along the west bank of the Drina River (34TCP203195) to a point (34TCP175178) where the route turns west following Highway 18. From this point, follow Highway 18 south of Miljevina (34TCP097204) continuing through Trnovo (34TBP 942380) north to the outskirts of Sarajevo where it enters the town at Vaskovici (34TBP868533).

There shall be complete freedom of movement along these routes for civilian traffic. The Parties shall only utilize these interim routes for military forces and equipment as authorized by and under the control and direction of the IFOR. In this regard, and in order to reduce the risk to civilian traffic, the IFOR shall have the right to manage movement of military and civilian traffic from both Entities along these routes.

(2) The Parties understand and agree that violators of subparagraph (1) shall be subject to military action by the IFOR, including the use of necessary

force to ensure compliance.

(3) The Parties pledge as a confidence building measure that they shall not locate any Forces or heavy weapons as defined in paragraph 5 of this Article within two (2) kilometers of the designated interim routes. Where those routes run in or through the designated Zones of Separation, the provisions relating to Zones of Separation in this Annex shall also apply.

(d) The Parties immediately after this Annex enters into force shall begin promptly and proceed steadily to complete the following activities within thirty (30) days after the Transfer of Authority or as determined by the IFOR Commander: (1) remove, dismantle or destroy all mines, unexploded ordnance, explosive devices, demolitions, and barbed or razor wire from the Agreed Cease-Fire Zone of Separation or other areas from which their Forces are withdrawn; (2) mark all known mine emplacements, unexploded ordnance, explosive devices and demolitions within Bosnia and Herzegovina; and (3) remove, dismantle or destroy all mines, unexploded ordnance, explosive devices and demolitions as required by the IFOR Commander.

(e) The IFOR is authorized to direct that any military personnel, active or reserve, who reside within the Agreed Cease-Fire Zone of Separation register with the appropriate IFOR Command Post referred to in Article VI which is closest to their residence.

3. PHASE II (as required in specific locations). This phase applies to those locations where the Inter-Entity Boundary Line does not follow the Agreed Cease-Fire Line.

(a) In those locations in which, pursuant to the General Framework Agreement, areas occupied by one Entity are to be transferred to another Entity, all Forces of the withdrawing Entity shall have forty-five (45) days after the Transfer of Authority to completely vacate and clear this area. This shall include the removal of all Forces as well as the removal, dismantling or destruction of equipment, mines, obstacles, unexploded ordnance, explosive devices, demolitions, and weapons. In those areas being transferred to a different Entity, in order to provide an orderly period of transition, the Entity to which an area is transferred shall not put Forces in this area for ninety (90) days after the Transfer of Authority or as determined by the IFOR Commander. The Parties understand and agree that the IFOR shall have the right to provide the military security for these transferred areas from thirty (30) days after the Transfer of Authority until ninety-one (91) days after the Transfer of Authority, or as soon as possible as determined by the IFOR Commander, when these areas may be occupied by the Forces of the Entity to which they are transferred. Upon occupation by the Entity to which the area is transferred, a new Zone of Separation along the Inter-Entity Boundary

Line as indicated on the map at Appendix A shall be established by the IFOR, and the Parties shall observe the same limitations on the presence of Forces and weapons in this Zone as apply to the Agreed Cease-Fire Zone of Separation.

(b) The IFOR is authorized to direct that any military personnel, active or reserve, who reside within the Inter-Entity Zone of Separation register with the appropriate IFOR Command Post referred to in Article VI which is closest to their residence.

4. General. The following provisions apply to Phases I and II:

(a) In order to provide visible indication, the IFOR shall supervise the selective marking of the Agreed Cease-Fire Line and its Zone of Separation, and the Inter-Entity Boundary Line and its Zone of Separation. Final authority for placement of such markers shall rest with the IFOR. All Parties understand and agree that the Agreed Cease Fire Line and its Zone of Separation and the Inter-Entity Boundary Line and its Zone of Separation are defined by the maps and documents agreed to as part of the General Framework Agreement and not the physical location of markers.

(b) All Parties understand and agree that they shall be subject to military action by the IFOR, including the use of necessary force to ensure compliance, for:

(1) failure to remove all their Forces and unauthorized weapons from the four (4) kilometer Agreed Cease-Fire Zone of Separation within thirty (30) days after the Transfer of Authority, as provided in Article IV, paragraph 2(a) and (b) above;

(2) failure to vacate and clear areas being transferred to another Entity within forty-five (45) days after the Transfer of Authority, as provided in Article IV, paragraph 3(a) above;

(3) deploying Forces within areas transferred from another Entity earlier than ninety (90) days after the Transfer of Authority or as determined by the IFOR Commander, as provided in Article IV, paragraph 3(a) above;

(4) failure to keep all Forces and unauthorized weapons outside the Inter Entity Zone of Separation after this Zone is declared in effect by the IFOR, as provided in Article IV, paragraph 3(a) above; or

(5) violation of the cessation of hostilities as agreed to by the Parties in Article II.

5. PHASE III. The Parties pledge as confidence building measures that they shall:

(a) within 120 days after the Transfer of Authority withdraw all heavy weapons and Forces to cantonment/barracks areas or other locations as designated by the IFOR Commander. "Heavy weapons" refers to all tanks and armored vehicles, all artillery 75 mm and above, all mortars 81 mm and above, and all anti-aircraft weapons 20 mm and above. This movement of these Forces to cantonment/barracks areas is intended to enhance mutual confidence by the Parties in the success of this Annex and help the overall cause of peace in Bosnia and Herzegovina.

(b) within 120 days after the Transfer of Authority demobilize Forces which cannot be accommodated in cantonment/barracks areas as provided in subparagraph (a) above. Demobilization shall consist of removing from the possession of these personnel all weapons, including individual weapons, explosive devices, communications equipment, vehicles, and all other military equipment. All personnel belonging to these Forces shall be released from service and shall not engage in any further training or other military activities.

6. Notwithstanding any other provision of this Annex, the Parties understand and agree that the IFOR has the right and is authorized to compel the removal, withdrawal, or relocation of specific Forces and weapons from, and to order the cessation of any activities in, any location in Bosnia and Herzegovina whenever the IFOR determines such Forces, weapons or activities to constitute a threat or potential threat to either the IFOR or its mission, or to another Party. Forces failing to redeploy, withdraw, relocate, or to cease threatening or potentially threatening activities following such a demand by the IFOR shall be subject to military action by the IFOR, including the use of necessary force to ensure compliance, consistent with the terms set forth in Article I, Paragraph 3.

Article V
Notifications

1. Immediately upon establishment of the Joint Military Commission provided for in Article VIII, each Party shall furnish to the Joint Military Commission information regarding the positions and descriptions of all known unexploded ordnance, explosive devices, demolitions, minefields, booby traps, wire entanglements, and all other physical or military hazards to the safe movement of any personnel within Bosnia and Herzegovina, as well as the location of lanes through the Agreed Cease-Fire Zone of Separation which are free of all such hazards. The Parties shall keep the Joint Military Commission updated on changes in this information.

2. Within thirty (30) days after the Transfer of Authority, each Party shall furnish to the Joint Military Commission the following specific information regarding the status of its Forces within Bosnia and Herzegovina and shall keep the Joint Military Commission updated on changes in this information:

(a) location, type, strengths of personnel and weaponry of all Forces within ten (10) kilometers of the Agreed Cease-Fire Line and Inter-Entity Boundary

Line;
(b) maps depicting the forward line of troops and front lines;
(c) positions and descriptions of fortifications, minefields, unexploded ordnance, explosive devices, demolitions, barriers, and other man-made obstacles, ammunition dumps, command headquarters, and communications networks within ten (10) kilometers of the Agreed Cease-Fire Line or Inter-Entity Boundary Line;
(d) positions and descriptions of all surface to air missiles/launchers, including mobile systems, anti-aircraft artillery, supporting radars and associated command and control systems;
(e) positions and descriptions of all mines, unexploded ordnance, explosive devices, demolitions, obstacles, weapons systems, vehicles, or any other military equipment which cannot be removed, dismantled or destroyed under the provisions of Article IV, paragraphs 2(d) and 3(a); and
(f) any further information of a military nature as requested by the IFOR.
3. Within 120 days after the Transfer of Authority, the Parties shall furnish to the Joint Military Commission the following specific information regarding the status of their Forces in Bosnia and Herzegovina and shall keep the Joint Military Commission updated on changes in this information:
(a) location, type, strengths of personnel and weaponry of all Forces;
(b) maps depicting the information in sub-paragraph (a) above;
(c) positions and descriptions of fortifications, minefields, unexploded ordnance, explosive devices, demolitions, barriers, and other man-made obstacles, ammunition dumps, command headquarters, and communications networks; and
(d) any further information of a military nature as requested by the IFOR.

Article VI
Deployment of the Implementation Force

1. Recognizing the need to provide for the effective implementation of the provisions of this Annex, and to ensure compliance, the United Nations Security Council is invited to authorize Member States or regional organizations and arrangements to establish the IFOR acting under Chapter VII of the United Nations Charter. The Parties understand and agree that this Implementation Force may be composed of ground, air and maritime units from NATO and non-NATO nations, deployed to Bosnia and Herzegovina to help ensure compliance with the provisions of this Annex. The Parties understand and agree that the IFOR shall have the right to deploy on either side of the Inter-Entity Boundary Line and throughout Bosnia and Herzegovina.

2. The Parties understand and agree that the IFOR shall have the right:

(a) to monitor and help ensure compliance by all Parties with this Annex (including, in particular, withdrawal and redeployment of Forces within agreed periods, and the establishment of Zones of Separation);

(b) to authorize and supervise the selective marking of the Agreed Cease Fire Line and its Zone of Separation and the Inter-Entity Boundary Line and its Zone of Separation as established by the General Framework Agreement;

(c) to establish liaison arrangements with local civilian and military authorities and other international organizations as necessary for the accomplishment of its mission; and

(d) to assist in the withdrawal of UN Peace Forces not transferred to the IFOR, including, if necessary, the emergency withdrawal of UNCRO Forces.

The Parties understand and agree that the IFOR shall have the right to fulfill its supporting tasks, within the limits of its assigned principal tasks and available resources, and on request, which include the following:

(a) to help create secure conditions for the conduct by others of other tasks associated with the peace settlement, including free and fair elections;

(b) to assist the movement of organizations in the accomplishment of humanitarian missions;

(c) to assist the UNHCR and other international organizations in their humanitarian missions;

(d) to observe and prevent interference with the movement of civilian populations, refugees, and displaced persons, and to respond appropriately to deliberate violence to life and person; and,

(e) to monitor the clearing of minefields and obstacles.

4. The Parties understand and agree that further directives from the NAC may establish additional duties and responsibilities for the IFOR in implementing this Annex.

5. The Parties understand and agree that the IFOR Commander shall have the authority, without interference or permission of any Party, to do all that the Commander judges necessary and proper, including the use of military force, to protect the IFOR and to carry out the responsibilities listed above in paragraphs 2, 3 and 4, and they shall comply in all respects with the IFOR requirements.

6. The Parties understand and agree that in carrying out its responsibilities, the IFOR shall have the unimpeded right to observe, monitor, and inspect any Forces, facility or activity in Bosnia and Herzegovina that the IFOR believes may have military capability. The refusal, interference, or denial by any Party of this right to observe, monitor, and inspect by the IFOR shall constitute a breach of this Annex and the violating Party shall be subject to military action by the

IFOR, including the use of necessary force to ensure compliance with this Annex.

7. The Army of the Republic of Bosnia and Herzegovina, the Croat Defense Council Forces, and the Army of Republika Srpska shall establish Command Posts at IFOR brigade, battalion, or other levels which shall be co-located with specific IFOR command locations, as determined by the IFOR Commander. These Command Posts shall exercise command and control over all Forces of their respective sides which are located within ten (10) kilometers of the Agreed Cease-Fire Line or Inter-Entity Boundary Line, as specified by the IFOR. The Command Posts shall provide, at the request of the IFOR, timely status reports on organizations and troop levels in their areas.

8. In addition to co-located Command Posts, the Army of the Republic of Bosnia and Herzegovina, the Croat Defense Council Forces, and the Army of Republika Srpska shall maintain liaison teams to be co-located with the IFOR Command, as determined by the IFOR Commander, for the purpose of fostering communication, and preserving the overall cessation of hostilities.

9. Air and surface movements in Bosnia and Herzegovina shall be governed by the following provisions:

(a) The IFOR shall have complete and unimpeded freedom of movement by ground, air, and water throughout Bosnia and Herzegovina. It shall have the right to bivouac, maneuver, billet, and utilize any areas or facilities to carry out its responsibilities as required for its support, training, and operations, with such advance notice as may be practicable. The IFOR and its personnel shall not be liable for any damages to civilian or government property caused by combat or combat related activities. Roadblocks, checkpoints or other impediments to IFOR freedom of movement shall constitute a breach of this Annex and the violating Party shall be subject to military action by the IFOR, including the use of necessary force to ensure compliance with this Annex.

(b) The IFOR Commander shall have sole authority to establish rules and procedures governing command and control of airspace over Bosnia and Herzegovina to enable civilian air traffic and non-combat air activities by the military or civilian authorities in Bosnia and Herzegovina, or if necessary to terminate civilian air traffic and non-combat air activities.

(1) The Parties understand and agree there shall be no military air traffic, or non-military aircraft performing military missions, including reconnaissance or logistics, without the express permission of the IFOR Commander. The only military aircraft that may be authorized to fly in Bosnia and Herzegovina are those being flown in support of the IFOR, except with the express permission of the IFOR. Any flight activities by military fixed-wing or heli-

copter aircraft within Bosnia and Herzegovina without the express permission of the IFOR Commander are subject to military action by the IFOR, including the use of necessary force to ensure compliance.

(2) All air early warning, air defense, or fire control radars shall be shut down within 72 hours after this Annex enters into force, and shall remain inactive unless authorized by the IFOR Commander. Any use of air traffic, air early warning, air defense or fire control radars not authorized by the IFOR Commander shall constitute a breach of this Annex and the violating Party shall be subject to military action by the IFOR, including the use of necessary force to ensure compliance.

(3) The Parties understand and agree that the IFOR Commander will implement the transfer to civilian control of air space over Bosnia and Herzegovina to the appropriate institutions of Bosnia and Herzegovina in a gradual fashion consistent with the objective of the IFOR to ensure smooth and safe operation of an air traffic system upon IFOR departure.

(c) The IFOR Commander is authorized to promulgate appropriate rules for the control and regulation of surface military traffic throughout Bosnia and Herzegovina, including the movement of the Forces of the Parties. The Joint Military Commission referred to in Article VIII may assist in the development and promulgation of rules related to military movement.

10. The IFOR shall have the right to utilize such means and services as required to ensure its full ability to communicate and shall have the right to the unrestricted use of all of the electromagnetic spectrum for this purpose. In implementing this right the IFOR shall make every reasonable effort to coordinate with and take into account the needs and requirements of the appropriate authorities.

11. All Parties shall accord the IFOR and its personnel the assistance, privileges, and immunities set forth at Appendix B of this Annex, including the unimpeded transit through, to, over and on the territory of all Parties.

12. All Parties shall accord any military elements as referred to in Article I, paragraph l(c) and their personnel the assistance, privileges and immunities referred to in Article VI, paragraph 11.

Article VII
Withdrawal of UNPROFOR

It is noted that as a consequence of the forthcoming introduction of the IFOR into the Republic of Bosnia and Herzegovina, the conditions for the withdrawal of the UNPROFOR established by United Nations Security Council Resolution 743 have been met. It is requested that the United Nations, in consultation with

NATO, take all necessary steps to withdraw the UNPROFOR from Bosnia and Herzegovina, except those parts incorporated into the IFOR.

Article VIII
Establishment of a Joint Military Commission

1. A Joint Military Commission (the "Commission") shall be established with the deployment of the IFOR to Bosnia and Herzegovina.

2. The Commission shall:

(a) Serve as the central body for all Parties to this Annex to bring any military complaints, questions, or problems that require resolution by the IFOR Commander, such as allegations of cease-fire violations or other noncompliance with this Annex.

(b) Receive reports and agree on specific actions to ensure compliance with the provisions of this Annex by the Parties.

(c) Assist the IFOR Commander in determining and implementing a series of local transparency measures between the Parties.

3. The Commission shall be chaired by the IFOR Commander or his or her representative and consist of the following members:

(a) the senior military commander of the forces of each Party within Bosnia and Herzegovina;

(b) other persons as the Chairman may determine;

(c) each Party to this Annex may also select two civilians who shall advise the Commission in carrying out its duties;

(d) the High Representative referred to in the General Framework Agreement or his or her nominated representative shall attend Commission meetings, and offer advice, particularly on matters of a political-military nature.

4. The Commission shall not include any persons who are now or who come under indictment by the International Tribunal for the former Yugoslavia.

5. The Commission shall function as a consultative body for the IFOR Commander. To the extent possible, problems shall be solved promptly by mutual agreement. However, all final decisions concerning its military matters shall be made by the IFOR Commander.

6. The Commission shall meet at the call of the IFOR Commander. The High Representative may when necessary request a meeting of the Commission. The Parties may also request a meeting of the Commission.

7. The IFOR Commander shall have the right to decide on military matters, in a timely fashion, when there are overriding considerations relating to the safety of the IFOR or the Parties' compliance with the provisions of this Annex.

8. The Commission shall establish subordinate military commissions for the purpose of providing assistance in carrying out the functions described above.

Such commissions shall be at the brigade and battalion level or at other echelons as the local IFOR Commander shall direct and be composed of commanders from each of the Parties and the IFOR. The representative of the High representative shall attend and offer advice particularly on matters of a political-military nature. The local IFOR Commander shall invite local civilian authorities when appropriate.

9.   Appropriate liaison arrangements will be established between the IFOR Commander and the High Representative to facilitate the discharge of their respective responsibilities.

Article IX
Prisoner Exchanges

1.   The Parties shall release and transfer without delay all combatants and civilians held in relation to the conflict (hereinafter "prisoners"), in conformity with international humanitarian law and the provisions of this Article.

(a)   The Parties shall be bound by and implement such plan for release and transfer of all prisoners as may be developed by the ICRC, after consultation with the Parties.

(b)   The Parties shall cooperate fully with the ICRC and facilitate its work in implementing and monitoring the plan for release and transfer of prisoners.

(c)   No later than thirty (30) days after the Transfer of Authority, the Parties shall release and transfer all prisoners held by them.

(d)   In order to expedite this process, no later than twenty-one (21) days after this Annex enters into force, the Parties shall draw up comprehensive lists of prisoners and shall provide such lists to the ICRC, to the other Parties, and to the Joint Military Commission and the High Representative. These lists shall identify prisoners by nationality, name, rank (if any) and any internment or military serial number, to the extent applicable.

(e)   The Parties shall ensure that the ICRC enjoys full and unimpeded access to all places where prisoners are kept and to all prisoners. The Parties shall permit the ICRC to privately interview each prisoner at least forty-eight (48) hours prior to his or her release for the purpose of implementing and monitoring the plan, including determination of the onward destination of each prisoner.

(f)   The Parties shall take no reprisals against any prisoner or his/her family in the event that a prisoner refuses to be transferred.

(g)   Notwithstanding the above provisions, each Party shall comply with any order or request of the International Tribunal for the Former Yugoslavia for the arrest, detention, surrender of or access to persons who would otherwise be released and transferred under this Article, but who are accused of violations within the jurisdiction of the Tribunal. Each Party must detain persons reasonably suspected of such violations for a period of time sufficient to permit appropriate consultation with Tribunal authorities.

2. In those cases where places of burial, whether individual or mass, are known as a matter of record, and graves are actually found to exist, each Party shall permit graves registration personnel of the other Parties to enter, within a mutually agreed period of time, for the limited purpose of proceeding to such graves, to recover and evacuate the bodies of deceased military and civilian personnel of that side, including deceased prisoners.

Article X
Cooperation

The Parties shall cooperate fully with all entities involved in implementation of this peace settlement, as described in the general Framework Agreement, or which are otherwise authorized by the United Nations Security Council, including the International Tribunal for the Former Yugoslavia.

Article XI
Notification to Military Commands

Each Party shall ensure that the terms of this Annex, and written orders requiring compliance, are immediately communicated to all of its Forces.

Article XII
Final Authority to Interpret

In accordance with Article I, the IFOR Commander is the final authority in theatre regarding interpretation of this agreement on the military aspects of the peace settlement, of which the Appendices constitute an integral part.

79. APPENDIX A TO ANNEX 1-A*

Appendix A to Annex 1-A consists of this document together with

(a) a 1:600,000 scale UNPROFOR road map consisting of one map sheet, attached hereto; and

---

* Initialled by representatives of the Republic of Bosnia and Herzegovina, the Federation of Bosnia and Herzegovina and the Republika Srpska; and, as endorsement, by representatives of the Republic of Croatia and the Federal Republic of Yugoslavia.

(b) a 1:50,000 scale Topographic Line Map, to be provided as described below.

On the basis of the attached 1:600,000 scale map, the Parties request that the United States Department of Defense provide a 1:50,000 scale Topographic Line Map, consisting of as many map sheets as necessary, in order to provide a more precise delineation of the lines and zones indicated. Such map shall be incorporated as an integral part of this Appendix, and the Parties agree to accept such map as controlling and definitive for all purposes.

80. APPENDIX B TO ANNEX 1-A
AGREEMENT BETWEEN THE REPUBLIC OF BOSNIA AND HERZEGOVINA AND THE NORTH ATLANTIC TREATY ORGANISATION (NATO) CONCERNING THE STATUS OF NATO AND ITS PERSONNEL*

The Republic of Bosnia and Herzegovina and the North Atlantic Treaty Organisation have agreed as follows:

1. For the purposes of the present agreement, the following expressions shall have the meanings hereunder assigned to them:
-   "the Operation" means the support, implementation, preparation and participation by NATO and NATO personnel in a peace plan in Bosnia and Herzegovina or a possible withdrawal of U.N. Forces from former Yugoslavia;
-   "NATO personnel" means the civilian and military personnel of the North Atlantic Treaty Organisation with the exception of personnel locally hired;
-   "NATO" means the North Atlantic Treaty Organisation, its subsidiary bodies, its military Headquarters and all its constituent national elements/units acting in support of, preparing and participating in the Operation;
-   "Facilities" mean all premises and land required for conducting the operational, training and administrative activities by NATO for the Operation as well as for accommodations of NATO personnel.
2. The provisions of the Convention on the Privileges and Immunities of the United Nations of 13 February 1946 concerning experts on mission shall apply mutatis mutandis to NATO personnel involved in the Operation, except as other-

---

*   Signed by representative of the Republic of Bosnia and Herzegovina.

wise provided for in the present agreement. Moreover NATO, its property and assets shall enjoy the privileges and immunities specified in that convention and as stated in the present agreement.

3. All personnel enjoying privileges and immunities under this Agreement shall respect the laws of the Republic of Bosnia and Herzegovina insofar as it is compatible with the entrusted tasks/mandate and shall refrain from activities not compatible with the nature of the Operation.

4. The Government of the Republic of Bosnia and Herzegovina recognizes the need for expeditious departure and entry procedures for NATO personnel. They shall be exempt from passport and visa regulations and the registration requirements applicable to aliens. NATO personnel shall carry identification which they may be requested to produce for the authorities of the Republic of Bosnia and Herzegovina but operations, training and movement shall not be allowed to be impeded or delayed by such requests.

5. NATO military personnel shall normally wear uniforms, and NATO personnel may possess and carry arms if authorized to do so by their orders. The authorities of the Republic of Bosnia and Herzegovina shall accept as valid, without tax or fee, drivers' licenses and permits issued to NATO personnel by their respective national authorities.

6. NATO shall be permitted to display the NATO flag and/or national flags of its constituent national elements/units on any NATO uniform, means of transport or facility.

7. NATO military personnel under all circumstances and at all times shall be subject to the exclusive jurisdiction of their respective national elements in respect of any criminal or disciplinary offenses which may be committed by them in the Republic of Bosnia and Herzegovina. NATO and the authorities of the Republic of Bosnia and Herzegovina shall assist each other in the exercise of their respective jurisdictions.

8. As experts on mission, NATO personnel shall be immune from personal arrest or detention. NATO personnel mistakenly arrested or detained shall immediately be turned over to NATO authorities.

9. NATO personnel shall enjoy, together with their vehicles, vessels, aircraft and equipment, free and unrestricted passage and unimpeded access throughout the Republic of Bosnia and Herzegovina including airspace and territorial waters of the Republic of Bosnia and Herzegovina. This shall include, but not be limited to, the right of bivouac, maneuver, billet, and utilization of any areas or facilities as required for support, training, and operations. NATO shall be exempt from providing inventories or other routine customs documentation on personnel, vehicles, vessels, aircraft, equipment, supplies, and provisions entering, exiting, or transiting the territory of the Republic of Bosnia and Herzegovina in support

of the Operation. The authorities of the Republic of Bosnia and Herzegovina shall facilitate with all appropriate means all movements of personnel, vehicles, vessels, aircraft, equipment or supplies, through ports, airports or roads used. Vehicles, vessels and aircraft used in support of the Operation shall not be subject to licensing or registration requirements, nor commercial insurance. NATO will use airports, roads and ports without payment of duties, dues, tolls or charges. However, NATO shall not claim exemption from reasonable charges for services requested and received, but operations/movement and access shall not be allowed to be impeded pending payment for such services.

10. NATO personnel shall be exempt from taxation by the Republic of Bosnia and Herzegovina on the salaries and emoluments received from NATO and on any income received from outside the Republic of Bosnia and Herzegovina.

11. NATO personnel and their tangible movable property imported into or acquired in the Republic of Bosnia and Herzegovina shall also be exempt from all identifiable taxes by the Republic of Bosnia and Herzegovina, except municipal rates for services enjoyed, and from all registration fees and related charges.

12. NATO shall be allowed to import and to export free of duty or other restriction equipment, provisions, and supplies, necessary for the Operation, provided such goods are for the official use of NATO or for sale via commissaries or canteens provided for NATO personnel. Goods sold shall be solely for the use of NATO personnel and not transferable to other parties.

13. It is recognized by the Government of the Republic of Bosnia and Herzegovina that the use of communications channels shall be necessary for the Operation. NATO shall be allowed to operate its own internal mail and telecommunications services, including broadcast services. This shall include the right to utilize such means and services as required to assure full ability to communicate, and the right to use all of the electromagnetic spectrum for this purpose, free of cost. In implementing this right, NATO shall make every reasonable effort to coordinate with and take into account the needs and requirements of appropriate authorities of the Republic of Bosnia and Herzegovina.

14. The Government of the Republic of Bosnia and Herzegovina shall provide, free of cost, such facilities NATO needs for the preparation for and execution of the Operation. The Government of the Republic of Bosnia and Herzegovina shall assist NATO in obtaining, at the lowest rate, the necessary utilities such as electricity, water and other resources necessary for the Operation.

15. Claims for damage or injury to Government personnel or property, or to private personnel or property of the Republic of Bosnia and Herzegovina shall be submitted through governmental authorities of the Republic of Bosnia and Herzegovina to the designated NATO Representatives.

16. NATO shall be allowed to contract direct with suppliers for services and supplies in the Republic of Bosnia and Herzegovina without payment of tax or duties. Such services and supplies shall not be subject to sales and other taxes. NATO may hire local personnel who shall remain subject to local laws and regulations. However, local personnel hired by NATO shall:

(a) be immune from legal process in respect of words spoken or written and all acts performed by them in their official capacity;

(b) be immune from national services and/or national military service obligations;

(c) be exempt from taxation on the salaries and emoluments paid to them by NATO.

17. NATO may in the conduct of the Operation, have need to make improvements or modifications to certain infrastructure of the Republic of Bosnia and Herzegovina such as roads, utility systems, bridges, tunnels, buildings, etc. Any such improvements or modifications of a non-temporary nature shall become part of and in the same ownership as that infrastructure. Temporary improvements or modifications may be removed at the discretion of the NATO Commander, and the facility returned to as near its original condition as possible.

18. Failing any prior settlement, disputes with regard to the interpretation or application of the present agreement shall be settled between the Republic of Bosnia and Herzegovina and NATO Representatives by diplomatic means.

19. The provisions of this agreement shall also apply to the civilian and military personnel, property and assets of national elements/units of NATO states, acting in connection to the Operation or the relief for the civilian population which however remain under national command and control.

20. Supplemental arrangements may be concluded to work out details for the Operation also talking into account its further development.

21. The Government of the Republic of Bosnia and Herzegovina shall accord non-NATO states and their personnel participating in the Operation the same privileges and immunities as those accorded under this agreement to NATO states and personnel.

22. The provisions of this agreement shall remain in force until completion of the Operation or as the Parties otherwise agree.

23. This Agreement shall enter into force upon signature.

DONE at Wright-Patterson Air Force Base, Ohio on November 21, 1995.

Letter of Slobodan Milosevic, on Behalf of the Federal Republic of Yugoslavia, Addressed to Sergio Silvio Balanzino, Acting Secretary General of the North Atlantic Treaty Organisation*

Excellency: I refer to the Agreement on the Military Aspects of the Peace Settlement, which the Federal Republic of Yugoslavia has endorsed, and the Agreement Between the Republic of Bosnia and Herzegovina and the North Atlantic Treaty Organisation (NATO) Concerning the Status of NATO and its Personnel.

On behalf of the Federal Republic of Yugoslavia, I wish to assure you that the Federal Republic of Yugoslavia shall take all necessary steps, consistent with the sovereignty, territorial integrity and political independence of Bosnia and Herzegovina, to ensure that the Republika Srpska fully respects and complies with commitments to NATO, including in particular access and status of forces, as set forth in the aforementioned Agreements.

Letter of Mate Granić, Deputy Prime Minister and Minister of Foreign Affairs of the Republic Croatia, Addressed to Sergio Silvio Balanzino, Acting Secretary General of the North Atlantic Treaty Organisation**

Excellency, I refer to the Agreement on the Military Aspects of the Peace Settlement, which the Republic of Croatia has endorsed, and the Agreement Between the Republic of Bosnia and Herzegovina and the North Atlantic Treaty Organisation (NATO) Concerning the Status of NATO and its Personnel.

On behalf of the Republic of Croatia, I wish to assure you that Republic of Croatia shall take all necessary steps, consistent with the sovereignty, territorial integrity and political independence of Bosnia and Herzegovina, to ensure that personnel or organisations in Bosnia and Herzegovina which are under its control or with which it has influence fully respect and comply with the commitments to NATO, including in particular access and status of forces, as set forth in the aforementioned Agreements.

---

*   Wright-Patterson Air Force Base, Ohio, 21 November 1995.
**   Wright-Patterson Air Force Base, Ohio, 21 November 1995.

Letter of Jadranko Prlic, Prime Minister and Defense Minister of the Federation of Bosnia and Herzegovina, Addressed to Sergio Silvio Balanzino, Acting Secretary General of the North Atlantic Treaty Organisation*

Excellency: I refer to the Agreement on the Military Aspects of the Peace Settlement, which the Federation of Bosnia and Herzegovina has signed as a Party, and the Agreement Between the Republic of Bosnia and Herzegovina and the North Atlantic Treaty Organisation (NATO) Concerning the Status of NATO and its Personnel.

On behalf of the Federation of Bosnia and Herzegovina, I wish to assure you that the Federation of Bosnia and Herzegovina will adhere to and fulfill its commitments regarding access and status of forces in general, including in particular, its commitments to NATO.

Letter of Momcilo Krajisnik, President of the Republika Srpska, Addressed to Sergio Silvio Balanzino, Acting Secretary General of the North Atlantic Treaty Organisation**

Excellency: I refer to the Agreement on the Military Aspects of the Peace Settlement, which the Republika Srpska has signed as a Party, and the Agreement Between the Republic of Bosnia and Herzegovina and the North Atlantic Treaty Organisation (NATO) Concerning the Status of NATO and its Personnel.

On behalf of the Republika Srpska, I wish to assure you that the Republika Srpska will adhere to and fulfill its commitments regarding access and status of forces in general, including in particular, its commitments to NATO.

81. Appendix B to Annex 1-A
Agreement Between the Republic of Croatia and the North Atlantic Treaty Organisation (NATO) Concerning the Status of NATO and its Personnel***

The Republic of Croatia and the North Atlantic Treaty Organisation have agreed as follows:

---

* Wright-Patterson Air Force Base, Ohio, 21 November 1995.
** Wright-Patterson Air Force Base, Ohio, 21 November 1995.
*** Signed by representative of the Republic of Croatia.

1.   For the purposes of the present agreement, the following expressions shall have the meanings hereunder assigned to them:

-   "the Operation" means the support, implementation, preparation and participation by NATO and NATO personnel in a peace plan in Bosnia and Herzegovina or a possible withdrawal of U.N. Forces from former Yugoslavia;
-   "NATO personnel" means the civilian and military personnel of the North Atlantic Treaty Organisation with the exception of personnel locally hired;
-   "NATO" means the North Atlantic Treaty Organisation, its subsidiary bodies, its military Headquarters and all its constituent national elements/units acting in support of, preparing and participating in the Operation;
-   "Facilities" means all premises and land required for conducting the operational, training and administrative activities by NATO for the Operation as well as for accommodations of NATO personnel.

2.   The provisions of the Convention on the Privileges and Immunities of the United Nations of 13 February 1946 concerning experts on mission shall apply mutatis mutandis to NATO personnel involved in the Operation, except as otherwise provided for in the present agreement. Moreover NATO, its property and assets shall enjoy the privileges and immunities specified in that Convention and as stated in the present agreement.

3.   All personnel enjoying privileges and immunities under this Agreement shall respect the laws of the Republic of Croatia, insofar as it is compatible with the entrusted tasks/mandate and shall refrain from activities not compatible with the nature of the Operation.

4.   The Government of Croatia recognizes the need for expeditious departure and entry procedures for NATO personnel. They shall be exempt from passport and visa regulations and the registration requirements applicable to aliens. NATO personnel shall carry identification which they may be requested to produce for Croatian authorities but operations, training and movement shall not be allowed to be impeded or delayed by such requests.

5.   NATO military personnel shall normally wear uniforms, and NATO personnel may possess and carry arms if authorized to do so by their orders. Croatian authorities shall accept as valid, without tax or fee, drivers' licenses and permits issued to NATO personnel by their respective national authorities.

6.   NATO shall be permitted to display the NATO flag and/or national flags of its constituent national elements/units on any NATO uniform, means of transport or facility.

7. NATO military personnel under all circumstances and at all times shall be subject to the exclusive jurisdiction of their respective national elements in respect of any criminal or disciplinary offenses which may be committed by them in the Republic of Croatia. NATO and Croatian authorities shall assist each other in the exercise of their respective jurisdictions.

8. As experts on mission, NATO personnel shall be immune from personal arrest or detention. NATO personnel mistakenly arrested or detained shall immediately be turned over to NATO authorities.

9. NATO personnel shall enjoy, together with their vehicles, vessels, aircraft and equipment, free and unrestricted passage and unimpeded access throughout Croatia including Croatian airspace and territorial waters. This shall include, but not be limited to, the right of bivouac, maneuver, billet, and utilization of any areas or facilities as required for support, training, and operations. NATO shall be exempt from providing inventories or other routine customs documentation on personnel, vehicles, vessels, aircraft, equipment, supplies, and provisions entering, exiting, or transiting Croatian territory in support of the Operation. The Croatian authorities shall facilitate with all appropriate means all movements of personnel, vehicles, vessels, aircraft or supplies, through ports, airports or roads used. Vehicles, vessels and aircraft used in support of the Operation shall not be subject to licensing or registration requirements, nor commercial insurance. NATO win use airports, roads and ports without payment of duties, dues, tolls or charges. However, NATO shall not claim exemption from reasonable charges for services requested and received, but operations/movement and access shall not be allowed to be impeded pending payment for such services.

10. NATO personnel shall be exempt from taxation by the Republic of Croatia on the salaries and emoluments received from NATO and on any income received from outside the Republic of Croatia.

11. NATO personnel and their tangible movable property imported into or acquired in Croatia shall also be exempt from all identifiable taxes by the Republic of Croatia, except municipal rates for services enjoyed, and from all registration fees and related charges.

12. NATO shall be allowed to import and export free of duty or other restriction equipment, provisions, and supplies, necessary for the Operation, provided such goods are for the official use of NATO or for sale via commissaries or canteens provided for NATO personnel. Goods sold shall be solely for the use of NATO personnel and not transferable to other parties.

13. NATO shall be allowed to operate its own internal mail and telecommunications services, including broadcast services. Telecommunications channels and other communications needs which may interfere with Croatian telecommunica-

tion services shall be coordinated with appropriate Croatian authorities free of cost. It is recognized by the Government of Croatia that the use of communications channels shall be necessary for the Operation.

14. The Government of Croatia shall provide, free of cost, such facilities NATO needs for the preparation for and execution of the Operation. The Government of Croatia shall assist NATO in obtaining, at the lowest rate, the necessary utilities such as electricity, water and other resources necessary for the Operation.

15. Claims for damage or injury to Croatian Government personnel or property, or to private personnel or property shall be submitted through Croatian governmental authorities to the designated NATO Representatives.

16. NATO shall be allowed to contract direct with suppliers for services and supplies in the Republic of Croatia without payment of tax or duties. Such services and supplies shall not be subject to sales or other taxes. NATO may hire local personnel who shall remain subject to local laws and regulations. However, local personnel hired by NATO shall:

(a) be immune from legal process in respect of words spoken or written and all acts performed by them in their official capacity;

(b) be immune from national services and/or national military service obligations;

(c) be exempt from taxation on the salaries and emoluments paid to them by NATO.

17. NATO may in the conduct of the Operation, have need to make improvements or modifications to certain Croatian infrastructure such as roads, utility systems, bridges, tunnels, buildings, etc. Any such improvements or modifications of a non-temporary nature shall become part of and in the same ownership as that infrastructure. Temporary improvements or modifications may be removed at the discretion of the NATO Commander, and the facility returned to as near its original condition as possible.

18. Failing any prior settlement, disputes with regard to the interpretation or application of the present agreement shall be settled between Croatia and NATO Representatives by diplomatic means.

19. The provisions of this agreement shall also apply to the civilian and military personnel, property and assets of national elements/units of NATO states, acting in connection to the Operation or the relief for the civilian population which however remain under national command and control.

20. Supplemental arrangements may be concluded to work out details for the Operation also taking into account its further development.

21. The Government of Croatia shall accord non-NATO states and their personnel participating in the Operation the same privileges and immunities as those

accorded under this agreement to NATO states and personnel.

22. The provisions of this agreement shall remain in force until completion of the Operation or as the Parties otherwise agree.

23. This Agreement shall enter into force upon signature.

DONE at Wright-Patterson Air Force Base, Ohio on November 21, 1995.

82. APPENDIX B TO ANNEX 1-A
AGREEMENT BETWEEN THE FEDERAL REPUBLIC OF YUGOSLAVIA AND THE NORTH ATLANTIC TREATY ORGANIZATION (NATO) CONCERNING TRANSIT ARRANGEMENTS FOR PEACE PLAN OPERATIONS*

Considering that the North Atlantic Treaty Organization is conducting contingency planning in coordination with the United Nations to support the implementation of a peace plan in Bosnia and Herzegovina or a possible withdrawal of U.N. Forces from former Yugoslavia, and may be requested by the United Nations to execute either such operation;

Considering the necessity to establish adequate transit arrangements for the execution/implementation of this Operation;

It is agreed that:

1. For the purposes of the present agreement, the following expressions shall have the meanings hereunder assigned to them:

- "the Operation" means the support, implementation, preparation and participation by NATO and NATO personnel in a peace plan in Bosnia and Herzegovina or a possible withdrawal of U.N. Forces from former Yugoslavia;

- "NATO personnel" means the civilian and military personnel of the North Atlantic Treaty Organization with the exception of personnel locally hired;

- "NATO" means the North Atlantic Treaty Organization, its subsidiary bodies, its military Headquarters and all its constituent national elements/units acting in support of, preparing and participating in the Operation.

2. The Government of the Federal Republic of Yugoslavia shall allow the free transit over land, rail, road, water or through air of all personnel and cargo,

---

* Signed by representative of the Federal Republic of Yugoslavia.

equipment, goods and material of whatever kind, including ammunition required by NATO for the execution of the Operation, through the territory of the Federal Republic of Yugoslavia including Federal Republic of Yugoslavia airspace and territorial waters.

3.   The Government of the Federal Republic of Yugoslavia shall provide or assist to provide, at the lowest cost, such facilities or services as determined by NATO as are necessary for the transit.

4.   NATO shall be exempt from providing inventories or other routine customs documentation on personnel, equipment, supplies, and provisions entering, exiting, or transiting the Federal Republic of Yugoslavia territory in support of the Operation. The Federal Republic of Yugoslavia authorities shall facilitate with all appropriate means all movements of personnel, vehicles and/or supplies, through ports, airports or roads used. Vehicles, vessels and aircraft in transit shall not be subject to licensing or registration requirements, nor commercial insurance. NATO shall be permitted to use airports, roads and ports without payment of duties, dues, tolls or charges. NATO shall not claim exemption for reasonable charges for services requested and received, but transit shall not be allowed to be impeded pending negotiations on payment for such services. The modes of transport will be communicated by NATO to the Government of the Federal Republic of Yugoslavia in advance. The routes to be followed will be commonly agreed upon.

5.   The provision of the Convention on the Privileges and Immunities of the United Nations of 13 February 1946 concerning experts on mission shall apply mutatis mutandis to NATO personnel involved in the transit, except as otherwise provided for in the present agreement. Moreover NATO, its property and assets shall enjoy the privileges and immunities specified in that Convention and as stated in the present agreement.

6.   All personnel enjoying privileges and immunities under this Agreement shall respect the laws of the Federal Republic of Yugoslavia, insofar as respect for said laws is compatible with the entrusted tasks/mandate and shall refrain from activities not compatible with the nature of the Operation.

7.   The Government of the Federal Republic of Yugoslavia recognizes the need for expeditious departure and entry procedures for NATO personnel. They shall be exempt from passport and visa regulations and the registration requirements applicable to aliens. NATO personnel shall carry identification which they may be requested to produce for Federal Republic of Yugoslavia authorities, but transit shall not be allowed to be impeded or delayed by such requests.

8.   NATO military personnel shall normally wear uniforms, and NATO personnel may possess and carry arms if authorized to do so by their orders. The Fed-

eral Republic of Yugoslavia authorities shall accept as valid, without tax or fee, drivers' licenses and permits issued to NATO personnel by their respective national authorities.

9. NATO shall be permitted to display the NATO flag and/or national flags of its constituent national elements/units on any NATO uniform, means of transport or facility.

10. NATO military personnel under all circumstances and at all times shall be subject to the exclusive jurisdiction of their respective national elements in respect of any criminal or disciplinary offenses which may be committed by them in the Federal Republic of Yugoslavia. NATO and the Federal Republic of Yugoslavia authorities shall assist each other in the exercise of their respective jurisdictions.

11. As experts on mission, NATO personnel shall be immune from personal arrest or detention. NATO personnel mistakenly arrested or detained shall immediately be turned over to NATO authorities.

12. NATO personnel and their tangible movable property in transit through the Federal Republic of Yugoslavia shall also be exempt from all identifiable taxes by the Government of the Federal Republic of Yugoslavia.

13. NATO shall be allowed to operate its own telecommunications services. This shall include the right to utilize such means and services as required to assure full ability to communicate, and the right to use all of the electro-magnetic spectrum for this purpose, free of cost. In implementing this right, NATO shall make every reasonable effort to coordinate with and take into account the needs and requirements of appropriate Federal Republic of Yugoslavia authorities.

14. Claims for damage or injury to Federal Republic of Yugoslavia Government personnel or property, or to private persons or property shall be submitted through the Federal Republic of Yugoslavia governmental authorities to the designated NATO Representatives.

15. Failing any prior settlement, disputes with regard to the interpretation or application of the present agreement shall be settled between the Federal Republic of Yugoslavia and NATO Representatives by diplomatic means.

16. The provisions of this agreement shall also apply to the civilian and military personnel, property and assets of national elements/units of NATO states, acting in connection to the Operation of the relief for the civilian population which however remain under national command and control.

17. Supplemental arrangements may be concluded to work out details for the transit also taking into account its further development.

18. The Government of the Federal Republic of Yugoslavia shall accord for the transit of non-NATO states and their personnel participating in the Operation the

same privileges and immunities as those accorded under this agreement to NATO states and personnel.

19. The provisions of this agreement shall remain in force until completion of the Operation or as the Parties otherwise agree.

20. This Agreement shall enter into force upon signature.

DONE at Wright-Patterson Air Force Base, Ohio on November 21, 1995.

83. ANNEX 1-B
AGREEMENT ON REGIONAL STABILIZATION*

The Republic of Bosnia and Herzegovina, the Republic of Croatia, the Federal Republic of Yugoslavia, the Federation of Bosnia and Herzegovina, and the Republika Srpska (hereinafter the "Parties") have agreed as follows:

Article I
General Obligations

The Parties agree that establishment of progressive measures for regional stability and arms control is essential to creating a stable peace in the region. To this end, they agree on the importance of devising new forms of cooperation in the field of security aimed at building transparency and confidence and achieving balanced and stable defense force levels at the lowest numbers consistent with the Parties' respective security and the need to avoid an arms race in the region. They have approved the following elements for a regional structure for stability.

Article II
Confidence- and Security-Building Measures in Bosnia and Herzegovina

Within seven days after this Agreement (hereinafter "Annex") enters into force, the Republic of Bosnia and Herzegovina, the Federation of Bosnia and Herzegovina, and the Republika Srpska shall at an appropriately high political level commence negotiations under the auspices of the Organization for Security and Cooperation in Europe (hereinafter "OSCE") to agree upon a series of measures to enhance mutual confidence and reduce the risk of conflict, drawing fully upon the 1994 Vienna Document of the Negotiations on Confidence- and Security-Building Measures of the OSCE. The objective of these negotiations is

---

* Initialled by representatives of the Republic of Bosnia and Herzegovina, the Republic of Croatia, the Federal Republic of Yugoslavia, the Federation of Bosnia and Herzegovina and the Republika Srpska.

to agree upon an initial set of measures within forty-five (45) days after this Annex enters into force including, but not necessarily limited to, the following:

(a) restrictions on military deployments and exercises in certain geographical areas;

(b) restraints on the reintroduction of foreign Forces in light of Article III of Annex 1-A to the General Framework Agreement;

(c) restrictions on locations of heavy weapons;

(d) withdrawal of Forces and heavy weapons to cantonment/barracks areas or other designated locations as provided in Article IV of Annex 1-A;

(e) notification of disbandment of special operations and armed civilian groups;

(f) notification of certain planned military activities, including international military assistance and training programs;

(g) identification of and monitoring of weapons manufacturing capabilities;

(h) immediate exchange of data on the holdings of the five Treaty on Conventional Armed Forces in Europe (hereinafter "CFE") weapons categories as defined in the CFE Treaty, with the additional understanding that artillery pieces will be defined as those of 75 mm calibre and above; and

(i) immediate establishment of military liaison missions between the Chiefs of the Armed Forces of the Federation of Bosnia and Herzegovina and the Republika Srpska;

Article III
Regional Confidence- and Security-Building Measures

To supplement the measures in Article II above on a wider basis, the Parties agree to initiate steps toward a regional agreement on confidence- and security-building measures. The Parties agree:

(a) not to import any arms for ninety (90) days after this Annex enters into force;

(b) not to import for 180 days after this Annex enters into force or until the arms control agreement referred to in Article IV below takes effect, whichever is the earlier, heavy weapons or heavy weapons ammunition, mines, military aircraft, and helicopters. Heavy weapons refers to all tanks and armored vehicles, all artillery 75 mm and above, all mortars 81 mm and above, and all anti-aircraft weapons 20 mm and above.

Article IV
Measures for Sub-Regional Arms Control

1. Recognizing the importance of achieving balanced and stable defense force levels at the lowest numbers consistent with their respective security, and understanding that the establishment of a stable military balance based on the lowest

level of armaments will be an essential element in preventing the recurrence of conflict, the Parties within thirty (30) days after this Annex enters into force shall commence negotiations under the auspices of the OSCE to reach early agreement on levels of armaments consistent with this goal. Within thirty (30) days after this Annex enters into force, the Parties shall also commence negotiations on an agreement establishing voluntary limits on military manpower.

2.   The Parties agree that the armaments agreement should be based at a minimum on the following criteria: population size, current military armament holdings, defense needs, and relative force levels in the region.

(a) The agreement shall establish numerical limits on holdings of tanks, artillery, armored combat vehicles, combat aircraft, and attack helicopters, as defined in the relevant sections of the CFE Treaty, with the additional understanding that artillery pieces will be defined as those of 75 mm calibre and above.

(b) In order to establish a baseline, the Parties agree to report within thirty (30) days after this Annex enters into force their holdings as defined in sub-paragraph (a) above, according to the format prescribed in the 1992 Vienna Document of the OSCE.

(c) This notification format shall be supplemented to take into account the special considerations of the region.

3.   The Parties agree to complete within 180 days after this Annex enters into force the negotiations above on agreed numerical limits on the categories referred to in paragraph 2(a) of this Article. If the Parties fail to agree to such limits within 180 days after this Annex enters into force, the following limits shall apply, according to a ratio of 5:2:2 based on the approximate ratio of populations of the Parties:

(a) the baseline shall be the determined holdings of the Federal Republic of Yugoslavia (hereinafter the "baseline");

(b) the limits for the Federal Republic of Yugoslavia shall be seventy-five (75) percent of the baseline;

(c) the limits for the Republic of Croatia shall be thirty (30) percent of the baseline;

(d) the limits for Bosnia and Herzegovina shall be thirty (30) percent of the baseline; and

(e) the allocations for Bosnia and Herzegovina will be divided between the Entities on the basis of a ratio of two (2) for the Federation of Bosnia and Herzegovina and one (1) for the Republika Srpska.

4. The OSCE will assist the Parties in their negotiations under Articles II and IV of this Annex and in the implementation and verification (including verification of holdings declarations) of resulting agreements.

Article V
Regional Arms Control Agreement

The OSCE will assist the Parties by designating a special representative to help organize and conduct negotiations under the auspices of the OSCE Forum on Security Cooperation ("FSC") with the goal of establishing a regional balance in and around the former Yugoslavia. The Parties undertake to cooperate fully with the OSCE to that end and to facilitate regular inspections by other parties. Further, the Parties agree to establish a commission together with representatives of the OSCE for the purpose of facilitating the resolution of any disputes that might arise.

Article VI
Entry into Force

This Annex shall enter into force upon signature.

84. ANNEX 2
AGREEMENT ON INTER-ENTITY BOUNDARY LINE AND RELATED ISSUES*

The Republic of Bosnia and Herzegovina, the Federation of Bosnia and Herzegovina and the Republika Srpska (the "Parties") have agreed as follows:

Article I
Inter-Entity Boundary Line

The boundary between the Federation of Bosnia and Herzegovina and the Republika Srpska (the "Inter-Entity Boundary Line") shall be as delineated on the map at the Appendix.

Article II
Adjustment by the Parties

The Parties may adjust the Inter-Entity Boundary Line only by mutual consent. During the period in which the multinational military Implementation

---

* Initialled by representatives of the Republic of Bosnia and Herzegovina, the Federation of Bosnia and Herzegovina and the Republika Srpska; and, as endorsement, by representatives of the Republic of Croatia and the Federal Republic of Yugoslavia.

Force ("IFOR") is deployed pursuant to Annex 1-A to the General Framework Agreement, the Parties shall consult with the IFOR Commander prior to making any agreed adjustment and shall provide notification of such adjustment to the IFOR Commander.

Article III
Rivers

1.   Where the Inter-Entity Boundary Line follows a river, the line shall follow natural changes (accretion or erosion) in the course of the river unless otherwise agreed. Artificial changes in the course of the river shall not affect the location of the Inter-Entity Boundary Line unless otherwise agreed. No artificial changes may be made except by agreement among the Parties.

2.   In the event of sudden natural changes in the course of the river (avulsion or cutting of new bed), the line shall be determined by mutual agreement of the Parties. If such event occurs during the period in which the IFOR is deployed, any such determination shall be subject to the approval of the IFOR Commander.

Article IV
Delineation and Marking

1.   The line on the 1:50,000 scale map to be provided for the Appendix delineating the Inter-Entity Boundary Line, and the lines on the 1:50,000 scale map to be provided for Appendix A to Annex 1-A delineating the Inter-Entity Zone of Separation and the Agreed Cease-Fire Line and its Zone of Separation, which are accepted by the Parties as controlling and definitive, are accurate to within approximately 50 meters. During the period in which the IFOR is deployed, the IFOR Commander shall have the right to determine, after consultation with the Parties, the exact delineation of such Lines and Zones, provided that with respect to Sarajevo the IFOR Commander shall have the right to adjust the Zone of Separation as necessary.

2.   The Lines and Zones described above may be marked by representatives of the Parties in coordination with and under the supervision of the IFOR. Final authority for placement of such markers shall rest with the IFOR. These Lines and Zones are defined by the maps and documents agreed to by the Parties and not by the physical location of markers.

3.   Following entry into force of this Agreement, the Parties shall form a joint commission, comprised of an equal number of representatives from each Party, to prepare an agreed technical document containing a precise description of the Inter-Entity Boundary Line. Any such document prepared during the period in

which the IFOR is deployed shall be subject to the approval of the IFOR Commander.

Article V
Arbitration for the Brcko Area

1. The Parties agree to binding arbitration of the disputed portion of the Inter-Entity Boundary Line in the Brcko area indicated on the map attached at the Appendix.

2. No later than six months after the entry into force of this Agreement, the Federation shall appoint one arbitrator, and the Republika Srpska shall appoint one arbitrator. A third arbitrator shall be selected by agreement of the Parties' appointees within thirty days thereafter. If they do not agree, the third arbitrator shall be appointed by the President of the International Court of Justice. The third arbitrator shall serve as presiding officer of the arbitral tribunal.

3. Unless otherwise agreed by the Parties, the proceedings shall be conducted in accordance with the UNCITRAL rules. The arbitrators shall apply relevant legal and equitable principles.

4. Unless otherwise agreed, the area indicated in paragraph 1 above shall continue to be administered as currently.

5. The arbitrators shall issue their decision no later than one year from the entry into force of this Agreement. The decision shall be final and binding, and the Parties shall implement it without delay.

Article VI
Transition

In those areas transferring from one Entity to the other in accordance with the demarcation described herein, there shall be a transitional period to provide for the orderly transfer of authority. The transition shall be completed forty-five (45) days after the Transfer of Authority from the UNPROFOR Commander to the IFOR Commander. as described in Annex 1-A.

Article VII
Status of Appendix

The Appendix shall constitute an integral part of this Agreement.

Article VIII
Entry into Force

This Agreement shall enter into force upon signature.

Appendix to Annex 2[*]

The Appendix to Annex 2 consists of this document together with (a) a 1:600,000 scale UNPROFOR road map consisting of one map sheet, attached hereto; and (b) a 1:50,000 scale Topographic Line Map, to be provided as described below.

On the basis of the attached 1:600,000 scale map, the Parties request that the United States Department of Defense provide a 1:50,000 scale Topographic Line Map, consisting of as many map sheets as necessary, in order to provide a more precise delineation of the Inter-Entity Boundary Line. Such map shall be incorporated as an integral part of this Appendix, and the Parties agree to accept such map as controlling and definitive for all purposes.

---

[*]   Initialled by representatives of the Republic of Bosnia and Herzegovina, the Federation of Bosnia and Herzegovina and the Republika Srpska; and, as endorsement, by representatives of the Republic of Croatia and the Federal Republic of Yugoslavia.

Proximity Peace Talks Representative Map

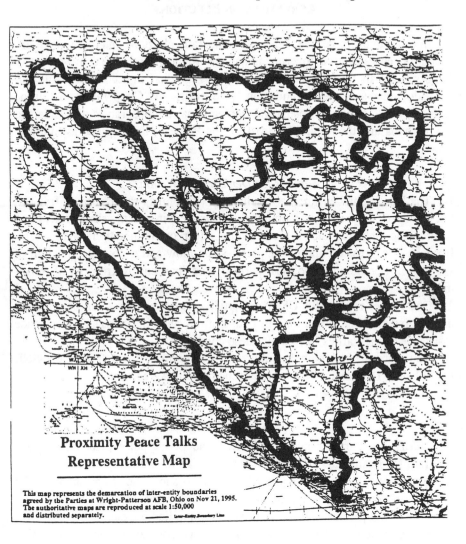

**Proximity Peace Talks
Representative Map**

This map represents the demarcation of inter-entity boundaries
agreed by the Parties at Wright-Patterson AFB, Ohio on Nov 21, 1995.
The authoritative maps are reproduced at scale 1:50,000
and distributed separately.　　　　——— Inter-Entity Boundary Line

85. ANNEX 3
AGREEMENT ON ELECTIONS[*]

In order to promote free, fair, and democratic elections and to lay the foundation for representative government and ensure the progressive achievement of democratic goals throughout Bosnia and Herzegovina, in accordance with relevant documents of the Organization for Security and Cooperation in Europe (OSCE), the Republic of Bosnia and Herzegovina, the Federation of Bosnia and Herzegovina and the Republika Srpska ("the Parties") have agreed as follows:

Article I
Conditions for Democratic Elections

1. The Parties shall ensure that conditions exist for the organization of free and fair elections, in particular a politically neutral environment; shall protect and enforce the right to vote in secret without fear or intimidation; shall ensure freedom of expression and of the press; shall allow and encourage freedom of association (including of political parties); and shall ensure freedom of movement.
2. The Parties request the OSCE to certify whether elections can be effective under current social conditions in both Entities and, if necessary, to provide assistance to the Parties in creating these conditions.
3. The Parties shall comply fully with paragraphs 7 and 8 of the OSCE Copenhagen Document, which are attached to this Agreement.

Article II
The OSCE Role

1. *OSCE.* The Parties request the OSCE to adopt and put in place an elections program for Bosnia and Herzegovina as set At forth in this Agreement.
2. *Elections.* The Parties request the OSCE to supervise, in a manner to be determined by the OSCE and in cooperation with other international organizations the OSCE deems necessary, the preparation and conduct of elections for the House of Representatives of Bosnia and Herzegovina; for the Presidency of Bosnia and Herzegovina; for the House of Representatives of the Federation of Bosnia and Herzegovina; for the National Assembly of the Republika Srpska; for the Presidency of the Republika Srpska; and, if feasible, for cantonal legislatures and municipal governing authorities.

---

[*]   Initialled by representatives of the Republic of Bosnia and Herzegovina, the Federation of Bosnia and Herzegovina and the Republika Srpska.

3. *The Commission.* To this end, the Parties request the OSCE to establish a Provisional Election Commission ("the Commission").

4. *Timing.* Elections shall take place on a date ("Election Day") six months after entry into force of this Agreement or, if the OSCE determines a delay necessary, no later than nine months after entry into force.

Article III
The Provisional Election Commission

1. *Rules and Regulations.* The Commission shall adopt electoral rules and regulations regarding: the registration of political parties and independent candidates; the eligibility of candidates and voters; the role of domestic and international election observers; the ensuring of an open and fair electoral campaign; and the establishment, publication, and certification of definitive election results. The Parties shall comply fully with the electoral rules and regulations, any internal laws and regulations notwithstanding.

2. *Mandate of the Commission.* The responsibilities of the Commission, as provided in the electoral rules and regulations, shall include:

(a) supervising all aspects of the electoral process to ensure that the structures and institutional framework for free and fair elections are in place;

(b) determining voter registration provisions;

(c) ensuring compliance with the electoral rules and regulations established pursuant to this Agreement;

(d) ensuring that action is taken to remedy any violation of any provision of this Agreement or of the electoral rules and regulations established pursuant to this Agreement, including imposing penalties against any person or body that violates such provisions; and

(e) accrediting observers, including personnel from international organizations and foreign and domestic non-governmental organizations, and ensuring that the Parties grant accredited observers unimpeded access and movement.

3. *Composition and Functioning of the Commission.* The Commission shall consist of the Head of the OSCE Mission, the High Representative or his or her designee, representatives of the Parties, and such other persons as the Head of the OSCE Mission, in consultation with the Parties, may decide. The Head of the OSCE Mission shall act as Chairman of the Commission. In the event of disputes within the Commission, the decision of the Chairman shall be final.

4. *Privileges and Immunities.* The Chairman and Commission shall enjoy the right to establish communications facilities and to engage local and administrative staff, and the status, privileges and immunities accorded to a diplomatic agent and mission under the Vienna Convention on Diplomatic Relations.

Article IV
Eligibility

1. *Voters.* Any citizen of Bosnia and Herzegovina aged 18 or older whose name appears on the 1991 census for Bosnia and Herzegovina shall be eligible, in accordance with electoral rules and regulations, to vote. A citizen who no longer lives in the municipality in which he or she resided in 1991 shall, as a general rule, be expected to vote, in person or by absentee ballot, in that municipality, provided that the person is determined to have been registered in that municipality as confirmed by the local election commission and the Provisional Election Commission. Such a citizen may, however, apply to the Commission to cast his or her ballot elsewhere. The exercise of a refugee's right to vote shall be interpreted as confirmation of his or her intention to return to Bosnia and Herzegovina. By Election Day, the return of refugees should already be underway, thus allowing many to participate in person in elections in Bosnia and Herzegovina. The Commission may provide in the electoral rules and regulations for citizens not listed in the 1991 census to vote.

Article V
Permanent-Election Commission

The Parties agree to create a permanent Election Commission with responsibilities to conduct future elections in Bosnia and Herzegovina.

Article VI
Entry into Force
This Agreement shall enter into force upon signature.

Attachment to Annex 3 on Elections
Document of the Second Meeting of the Conference on the Human Dimension of the Conference on Security and Cooperation in Europe, Copenhagen, 1990

Paragraphs 7 and 8:

(7) To ensure that the will of the people serves as the basis of the authority of government, the participating States will

(7.1) - hold free elections at reasonable intervals, as established by law;
(7.2) - permit all seats in at least one chamber of the national legislature to be freely contested in a popular vote;

(7.3) - guarantee universal and equal suffrage to adult citizens;

(7.4) - ensure that votes are cast by secret ballot or by equivalent free voting procedure, and that they are counted and reported honestly with the official results made public;

(7.5) - respect the right of citizens to seek political or public office, individually or as representatives of political parties or organizations, without discrimination;

(7.6) - respect the right of individuals and groups to establish, in full freedom, their own political parties or other political organizations and provide such political parties and organizations with the necessary legal guarantees to enable them to compete with each other on a basis of equal treatment before the law and by the authorities;

(7.7) - ensure that law and public policy work to permit political campaigning to be conducted in a fair and free atmosphere in which neither administrative action, violence nor intimidation bars the parties and the candidates from freely presenting their views and qualifications, or prevents the voters from learning and discussing them or from casting their vote free of fear of retribution;

(7.8) - provide that no legal or administrative obstacle stands in the way of unimpeded access to the media on a non-discriminatory basis for all political groupings and individuals wishing to participate in the electoral process;

(7.9) - ensure that candidates who obtain the necessary number of votes required by law are duly installed in office and are permitted to remain in office until their term expires or is otherwise brought to an end in a manner that is regulated by law in conformity with democratic parliamentary and constitutional procedures.

(8) The participating States consider that the presence of observers, both foreign and domestic, can enhance the electoral process for States in which elections are taking place. They therefore invite observers from any other CSCE participating States and any appropriate private institutions and organizations who may wish to do so to observe the course of their national election proceedings, to the extent permitted by law. they will also endeavor to facilitate similar access for election proceedings held below the national level. Such observers will undertake not to interfere in the electoral proceedings.

86. ANNEX 4
CONSTITUTION OF BOSNIA AND HERZEGOVINA

Based on respect for human dignity, liberty, and equality,

Dedicated to peace, justice, tolerance, and reconciliation,

Convinced that democratic governmental institutions and fair procedures best produce peaceful relations within a pluralist society,

Desiring to promote the general welfare and economic growth through the protection of private property and the promotion of a market economy,

Guided by the Purposes and Principles of the Charter of the United Nations,

Committed to the sovereignty, territorial integrity, and political independence of Bosnia and Herzegovina in accordance with international law,

Determined to ensure full respect for international humanitarian law,

Inspired by the Universal Declaration of Human Rights, the International Covenants on Civil and Political Rights and on Economic, Social and Cultural Rights, and the Declaration on the Rights of Persons Belonging to National or Ethnic, Religious and Linguistic Minorities, as well as other human rights instruments,

Recalling the Basic Principles agreed in Geneva on September 8, 1995, and in New York on September 26, 1995,

Bosniacs, Croats, and Serbs, as constituent peoples (along with Others), and citizens of Bosnia and Herzegovina hereby determine that the Constitution of Bosnia and Herzegovina is as follows:

Article I
Bosnia and Herzegovina

1. *Continuation.* The Republic of Bosnia and Herzegovina, the official name of which shall henceforth be "Bosnia and Herzegovina," shall continue its legal existence under international law as a state, with its internal structure modified as provided herein and with its present internationally recognized borders. It shall remain a Member State of the United Nations and may as Bosnia and Herzegovina maintain or apply for membership in organizations within the United Nations system and other international organizations.

2. *Democratic Principles.* Bosnia and Herzegovina shall be a democratic state, which shall operate under the rule of law and with free and democratic elections.

3. *Composition.* Bosnia and Herzegovina shall consist of the two Entities, the Federation of Bosnia and Herzegovina and the Republika Srpska (hereinafter "the Entities").

4. *Movement of Goods, Services, Capital, and Persons.* There shall be freedom of movement throughout Bosnia and Herzegovina. Bosnia and Herzegovina and the Entities shall not impede full freedom of movement of persons, goods, services, and capital throughout Bosnia and Herzegovina. Neither Entity shall establish controls at the boundary between the Entities.

5. *Capital.* The capital of Bosnia and Herzegovina shall be Sarajevo.

6. *Symbols.* Bosnia and Herzegovina shall have such symbols as are decided by its Parliamentary Assembly and approved by the Presidency.

7. *Citizenship.* There shall be a citizenship of Bosnia and Herzegovina, to be regulated by the Parliamentary Assembly, and a citizenship of each Entity, to be regulated by each Entity, provided that:

(a) All citizens of either Entity are thereby citizens of Bosnia and Herzegovina.

(b) No person shall be deprived of Bosnia and Herzegovina or Entity citizenship arbitrarily or so as to leave him or her stateless. No person shall be deprived of Bosnia and Herzegovina or Entity citizenship on any ground such as sex, race, color, language, religion, political or other opinion, national or social origin, association with a national minority, property, birth or other status.

(c) All persons who were citizens of the Republic of Bosnia and Herzegovina immediately prior to the entry into force of this Constitution are citizens of Bosnia and Herzegovina. The citizenship of persons who were naturalized after April 6, 1992 and before the entry into force of this Constitution will be regulated by the Parliamentary Assembly.

(d) Citizens of Bosnia and Herzegovina may hold the citizenship of another state, provided that there is a bilateral agreement, approved by the Parliamentary Assembly in accordance with Article IV(4)(d), between Bosnia and Herzegovina and that state governing this matter. Persons with dual citizenship may vote in Bosnia and Herzegovina and the Entities only if Bosnia and Herzegovina is their country of residence.

(e) A citizen of Bosnia and Herzegovina abroad shall enjoy the protection of Bosnia and Herzegovina. Each Entity may issue passports of Bosnia and Herzegovina to its citizens as regulated by the Parliamentary Assembly. Bosnia and Herzegovina may issue passports to citizens not issued a passport by an Entity. There shall be a central register of all passports issued by the Entities and by Bosnia and Herzegovina.

Article II
Human Rights and Fundamental Freedoms

1. *Human Rights.* Bosnia and Herzegovina and both Entities shall ensure the highest level of internationally recognized human rights and fundamental free-

doms. To that end, there shall be a Human Rights Commission for Bosnia and Herzegovina as provided for in Annex 6 to the General Framework Agreement.

2. *International Standards.* The rights and freedoms set forth in the European Convention for the Protection of Human Rights and Fundamental Freedoms and its Protocols shall apply directly in Bosnia and Herzegovina. These shall have priority over all other law.

3. *Enumeration of Rights.* All persons within the territory of Bosnia and Herzegovina shall enjoy the human rights and fundamental freedoms referred to in paragraph 2 above; these include:

(a) The right to life.
(b) The right not to be subjected to torture or to inhuman or degrading treatment or punishment.
(c) The right not to be held in slavery or servitude or to perform forced or compulsory labor.
(d) The rights to liberty and security of person.
(e) The right to a fair hearing in civil and criminal matters, and other rights relating to criminal proceedings.
(f) The right to private and family life, home, and correspondence.
(g) Freedom of thought, conscience, and religion.
(h) Freedom of expression.
(i) Freedom of peaceful assembly and freedom of association with others.
(j) The right to marry and to found a family.
(k) The right to property.
(l) The right to education.
(m) The right to liberty of movement and residence.

4. *Non-Discrimination.* The enjoyment of the rights and freedoms provided for in this Article or in the international agreements listed in Annex I to this Constitution shall be secured to all persons in Bosnia and Herzegovina without discrimination on any ground such as sex, race, color, language, religion, political or other opinion, national or social origin, association with a national minority, property, birth or other status.

5. *Refugees and Displaced Persons.* All refugees and displaced persons have the right freely to return to their homes of origin. They have the right, in accordance with Annex 7 to the General Framework Agreement, to have restored to them property of which they were deprived in the course of hostilities since 1991 and to be compensated for any such property that cannot be restored to them. Any commitments or statements relating to such property made under duress are null and void.

6. *Implementation.* Bosnia and Herzegovina, and all courts, agencies, governmental organs, and instrumentalities operated by or within the Entities, shall apply and conform to the human rights and fundamental freedoms referred to in paragraph 2 above.

7. *International Agreements.* Bosnia and Herzegovina shall remain or become party to the international agreements listed in Annex I to this Constitution.

8. *Cooperation.* All competent authorities in Bosnia and Herzegovina shall cooperate with and provide unrestricted access to: any international human rights monitoring mechanisms established for Bosnia and Herzegovina; the supervisory bodies established by any of the international agreements listed in Annex I to this Constitution; the International Tribunal for the Former Yugoslavia (and in particular shall comply with orders issued pursuant to Article 29 of the Statute of the Tribunal); and any other organization authorized by the United Nations Security Council with a mandate concerning human rights or humanitarian law.

Article III
Responsibilities of and Relations Between The Institutions of Bosnia and Herzegovina And the Entities

1. *Responsibilities of the Institutions of Bosnia and Herzegovina.* The following matters are the responsibility of the institutions of Bosnia and Herzegovina:

(a) Foreign policy.

(b) Foreign trade policy.

(c) Customs policy.

(d) Monetary policy as provided in Article VII.

(e) Finances of the institutions and for the international obligations of Bosnia and Herzegovina.

(f) Immigration, refugee, and asylum policy and regulation.

(g) International and inter-Entity criminal law enforcement, including relations with Interpol.

(h) Establishment and operation of common and international communications facilities.

(i) Regulation of inter-Entity transportation.

(j) Air traffic control.

2. *Responsibilities of the Entities.*

(a) The Entities shall have the right to establish special parallel relationships with neighboring states consistent with the sovereignty and territorial integrity of Bosnia and Herzegovina.

(b) Each Entity shall provide all necessary assistance to the government of Bosnia and Herzegovina in order to enable it to honor the international obligations of Bosnia and Herzegovina, provided that financial obligations incurred by one Entity without the consent of the other prior to the election of the Parliamentary Assembly and Presidency of Bosnia and Herzegovina shall be the responsibility of that Entity, except insofar as the obligation is necessary for continuing the membership of Bosnia and Herzegovina in an international organization.

(c) The Entities shall provide a safe and secure environment for all persons in their respective jurisdictions, by maintaining civilian law enforcement agencies operating in accordance with internationally recognized standards and with respect for the internationally recognized human rights and fundamental freedoms referred to in Article II above, and by taking such other measures as appropriate.

(d) Each Entity may also enter into agreements with states and international organizations with the consent of the Parliamentary Assembly. The Parliamentary Assembly may provide by law that certain types of agreements do not require such consent.

3. *Law and Responsibilities of the Entities and the Institutions.*

(a) All governmental functions and powers not expressly assigned in this Constitution to the institutions of Bosnia and Herzegovina shall be those of the Entities.

(b) The Entities and any subdivisions thereof shall comply fully with this Constitution, which supersedes inconsistent provisions of the law of Bosnia and Herzegovina and of the constitutions and law of the Entities, and with the decisions of the institutions of Bosnia and Herzegovina. The general principles of international law shall be an integral part of the law of Bosnia and Herzegovina and the Entities.

4. *Coordination.* The Presidency may decide to facilitate inter-Entity coordination on matters not within the responsibilities of Bosnia and Herzegovina as provided in this Constitution, unless an Entity objects in any particular case.

5. *Additional Responsibilities.*

(a) Bosnia and Herzegovina shall assume responsibility for such other matters as are agreed by the Entities; are provided for in Annexes 5 through 8 to the General Framework Agreement; or are necessary to preserve the sovereignty, territorial integrity, political independence, and international personality of Bosnia and Herzegovina, in accordance with the division of responsibilities between the institutions of Bosnia and Herzegovina. Additional institutions may be established as necessary to carry out such responsibilities.

(b) Within six months of the entry into force of this Constitution, the Entities shall begin negotiations with a view to including in the responsibilities of the institutions of Bosnia and Herzegovina other matters, including utilization of energy resources and cooperative economic projects.

Article IV
Parliamentary Assembly

The Parliamentary Assembly shall have two chambers: the House of Peoples and the House of Representatives.

1. *House of Peoples.* The House of Peoples shall comprise 15 Delegates, two-thirds from the Federation (including five Croats and five Bosniacs) and one-third from the Republika Srpska (five Serbs).

(a) The designated Croat and Bosniac Delegates from the Federation shall be selected, respectively, by the Croat and Bosniac Delegates to the House of Peoples of the Federation. Delegates from the Republika Srpska shall be selected by the National Assembly of the Republika Srpska.

(b) Nine members of the House of Peoples shall comprise a quorum, provided that at least three Bosniac, three Croat, and three Serb Delegates are present.

2. *House of Representatives.* The House of Representatives shall comprise 42 Members, two-thirds elected from the territory of the Federation, one-third from the territory of the Republika Srpska.

(a) Members of the House of Representatives shall be directly elected from their Entity in accordance with an election law to be adopted by the Parliamentary Assembly. The first election, however, shall take place in accordance with Annex 3 to the General Framework Agreement.

(b) A majority of all members elected to the House of Representatives shall comprise a quorum.

3. *Procedures.*

(a) Each chamber shall be convened in Sarajevo not more than 30 days after its selection or election.

(b) Each chamber shall by majority vote adopt its internal rules and select from its members one Serb, one Bosniac, and one Croat to serve as its Chair and Deputy Chairs, with the position of Chair rotating among the three persons selected.

(c) All legislation shall require the approval of both chambers.

(d) All decisions in both chambers shall be by majority of those present and voting. The Delegates and Members shall make their best efforts to see that the majority includes at least one-third of the votes of Delegates or Members from the territory of each Entity. If a majority vote does not include one-third of the votes of Delegates or Members from the territory of each Entity, the Chair and Deputy Chairs shall meet as a commission and attempt to obtain approval within three days of the vote. If those efforts fail, decisions shall be taken by a majority of those present and voting, provided that the dissenting votes do not include two thirds or more of the Delegates or Members elected from either Entity.

(e) A proposed decision of the Parliamentary Assembly may be declared to be destructive of a vital interest of the Bosniac, Croat, or Serb people by a majority of, as appropriate, the Bosniac, Croat, or Serb Delegates selected in accordance with paragraph l(a) above. Such a proposed decision shall require for approval in the House of Peoples a majority of the Bosniac, of the Croat, and of the Serb Delegates present and voting.

(f)   When a majority of the Bosniac, of the Croat, or of the Serb Delegates objects to the invocation of paragraph (e), the Chair of the House of Peoples shall immediately convene a Joint Commission comprising three Delegates, one each selected by the Bosniac, by the Croat, and by the Serb Delegates, to resolve the issue. If the Commission fails to do so within five days, the matter will be referred to the Constitutional Court, which shall in an expedited process review it for procedural regularity.

(g) The House of Peoples may be dissolved by the Presidency or by the House itself, provided that the House's decision to dissolve is approved by a majority that includes the majority of Delegates from at least two of the Bosniac, Croat, or Serb peoples. The House of Peoples elected in the first elections after the entry into force of this Constitution may not, however, be dissolved.

(h) Decisions of the Parliamentary Assembly shall not take effect before publication.

(i) Both chambers shall publish a complete record of their deliberations and shall, save in exceptional circumstances in accordance with their rules, deliberate publicly.

(j) Delegates and Members shall not be held criminally or civilly liable for any acts carried out within the scope of their duties in the Parliamentary Assembly.

4. *Powers.* The Parliamentary Assembly shall have responsibility for:

(a) Enacting legislation as necessary to implement decisions of the Presidency or to carry out the responsibilities of the Assembly under this Constitution.

(b) Deciding upon the sources and amounts of revenues for the operations of the institutions of Bosnia and Herzegovina and international obligations of Bosnia and Herzegovina.

(c) Approving a budget for the institutions of Bosnia and Herzegovina.

(d) Deciding whether to consent to the ratification of treaties.

(e) Such other matters as are necessary to carry out its duties or as are assigned to it by mutual agreement of the Entities.

Article V
Presidency

The Presidency of Bosnia and Herzegovina shall consist of three Members: one Bosniac and one Croat, each directly elected from the territory of the Federation, and one Serb directly elected from the territory of the Republika Srpska.

1. *Election and Term.*

(a) Members of the Presidency shall be directly elected in each Entity (with each voter voting to fill one seat on the Presidency) in accordance with an election law adopted by the Parliamentary Assembly. The first election, however, shall take place in accordance with Annex 3 to the General Framework Agreement. Any vacancy in the Presidency shall be filled from the relevant Entity in accordance with a law to be adopted by the Parliamentary Assembly.

(b) The term of the Members of the Presidency elected in the first election shall be two years; the term of Members subsequently elected shall be four years. Members shall be eligible to succeed themselves once and shall thereafter be ineligible for four years.

2. *Procedures.*

(a) The Presidency shall determine its own rules of procedure, which shall provide for adequate notice of meetings of the Presidency.

(b) The Members of the Presidency shall appoint from their Members a Chair. For the first term of the Presidency, the Chair shall be the Member who received the highest number of votes. Thereafter, the method of selecting the Chair, by rotation or otherwise, shall be determined by the Parliamentary Assembly, subject to Article IV(3).

(c) The Presidency shall endeavor to adopt all Presidency Decisions (i.e., those concerning matters arising under Article III(l)(a) - (e)) by consensus. Such decisions may, subject to paragraph (d) below, nevertheless be adopted by two Members when all efforts to reach consensus have failed.

(d) A dissenting Member of the Presidency may declare a Presidency Decision to be destructive of a vital interest of the Entity from the territory from which he was elected, provided that he does so within three days of its adoption. Such a Decision shall be referred immediately to the National Assembly of the Republika Srpska, if the declaration was made by the Member from that territory; to the Bosniac Delegates of the House of Peoples of the Federation, if the declaration was made by the Bosniac Member; or to the Croat Delegates of that body, if the declaration was made by the Croat Member. If the declaration is confirmed by a two thirds vote of those persons within ten days of the referral, the challenged Presidency Decision shall not take effect.

3. *Powers*. The Presidency shall have responsibility for:

(a) Conducting the foreign policy of Bosnia and Herzegovina.

(b) Appointing ambassadors and other international representatives of Bosnia and Herzegovina, no more than two-thirds of whom may be selected from the territory of the Federation.

(c) Representing Bosnia and Herzegovina in international and European organizations and institutions and seeking membership in such organizations and institutions of which Bosnia and Herzegovina is not a member.

(d) Negotiating, denouncing, and, with the consent of the Parliamentary Assembly, ratifying treaties of Bosnia and Herzegovina.

(e) Executing decisions of the Parliamentary Assembly.

(f) Proposing, upon the recommendation of the Council of Ministers, an annual budget to the Parliamentary Assembly.

(g) Reporting as requested, but not less than annually, to the Parliamentary Assembly on expenditures by the Presidency.

(h) Coordinating as necessary with international and nongovernmental organizations in Bosnia and Herzegovina.

(i) Performing such other functions as may be necessary to carry out its duties, as may be assigned to it by the Parliamentary Assembly, or as may be agreed by the Entities.

4. *Council of Ministers*. The Presidency shall nominate the Chair of the Council of Ministers, who shall take office upon the approval of the House of Representatives. The Chair shall nominate a Foreign Minister, a Minister for Foreign Trade, and other Ministers as may be appropriate, who shall take office upon the approval of the House of Representatives.

(a) Together the Chair and the Ministers shall constitute the Council of Ministers, with responsibility for carrying out the policies and decisions of Bosnia and Herzegovina in the fields referred to in Article III(1), (4), and (5) and reporting to the Parliamentary Assembly (including, at least annually, on expenditures by Bosnia and Herzegovina).

(b) No more than two-thirds of all Ministers may be appointed from the territory of the Federation. The Chair shall also nominate Deputy Ministers (who shall not be of the same constituent people as their Ministers), who shall take office upon the approval of the House of Representatives.

(c) The Council of Ministers shall resign if at any time there is a vote of no-confidence by the Parliamentary Assembly.

5. *Standing Committee.*
(a) Each member of the Presidency shall, by virtue of the office, have civilian command authority over armed forces. Neither Entity shall threaten or use force against the other Entity, and under no circumstances shall any armed forces of either Entity enter into or stay within the territory of the other Entity without the consent of the government of the latter and of the Presidency of Bosnia and Herzegovina. All armed forces in Bosnia and Herzegovina shall operate consistently with the sovereignty and territorial integrity of Bosnia and Herzegovina.
(b) The members of the Presidency shall select a Standing Committee on Military Matters to coordinate the activities of armed forces in Bosnia and Herzegovina. The Members of the Presidency shall be members of the Standing Committee.

Article VI
Constitutional Court
1. *Composition.* The Constitutional Court of Bosnia and Herzegovina shall have nine members.
(a) Four members shall be selected by the House of Representatives of the Federation, and two members by the Assembly of the Republika Srpska. The remaining three members shall be selected by the President of the European Court of Human Rights after consultation with the Presidency.
(b) Judges shall be distinguished jurists of high moral standing. Any eligible voter so qualified may serve as a judge of the Constitutional Court. The judges selected by the President of the European Court of Human Rights shall not be citizens of Bosnia and Herzegovina or of any neighboring state.
(c) The term of judges initially appointed shall be five years, unless they resign or are removed for cause by consensus of the other judges. Judges initially appointed shall not be eligible for reappointment. Judges subsequently appointed shall serve until age 70, unless they resign or are removed for cause by consensus of the other judges.
(d) For appointments made more than five years after the initial appointment of judges, the Parliamentary Assembly may provide by law for a different method of selection of the three judges selected by the President of the European Court of Human Rights.
2. *Procedures.*
(a) A majority of all members of the Court shall constitute a quorum.
(b) The Court shall adopt its own rules of court by a majority of all members. It shall hold public proceedings and shall issue reasons for its decisions, which shall be published.

3. *Jurisdiction.* The Constitutional Court shall uphold this Constitution.

(a) The Constitutional Court shall have exclusive jurisdiction to decide any dispute that arises under this Constitution between the Entities or between Bosnia and Herzegovina and an Entity or Entities, or between institutions of Bosnia and Herzegovina, including but not limited to:-

- Whether an Entity's decision to establish a special parallel relationship with a neighboring state is consistent with this Constitution, including provisions concerning the sovereignty and territorial integrity of Bosnia and Herzegovina.

- Whether any provision of an Entity's constitution or law is consistent with this Constitution.

- Disputes may be referred only by a member of the Presidency, by the Chair of the Council of Ministers, by the Chair or a Deputy Chair of either chamber of the Parliamentary Assembly, by one-fourth of the members of either chamber of the Parliamentary Assembly, or by one-fourth of either chamber of a legislature of an Entity.

(b) The Constitutional Court shall also have appellate jurisdiction over issues under this Constitution arising out of a judgment of any other court in Bosnia and Herzegovina.

(c) The Constitutional Court shall have jurisdiction over issues referred by any court in Bosnia and Herzegovina concerning whether a law, on whose validity its decision depends, is compatible with this Constitution, with the European Convention for Human Rights and Fundamental Freedoms and its Protocols, or with the laws of Bosnia and Herzegovina; or concerning the existence of or the scope of a general rule of public international law pertinent to the court's decision.

4. *Decisions.* Decisions of the Constitutional Court shall be final and binding.

Article VII
Central Bank

There shall be a Central Bank of Bosnia and Herzegovina, which shall be the sole authority for issuing currency and for monetary policy throughout Bosnia and Herzegovina.

1. The Central Bank's responsibilities will be determined by the Parliamentary Assembly. For the first six years after the entry into force of this Constitution, however, it may not extend credit by creating money, operating in this respect as a currency board; thereafter, the Parliamentary Assembly may give it that authority.

2. The first Governing Board of the Central Bank shall consist of a Governor appointed by the International Monetary Fund, after consultation with the Presi-

dency, and three members appointed by the Presidency, two from the Federation (one Bosniac, one Croat, who shall share one vote) and one from the Republika Srpska, all of whom shall serve a six-year term. The Governor, who shall not be a citizen of Bosnia and Herzegovina or any neighboring state, may cast tie-breaking votes on the Governing Board.

3. Thereafter, the Governing Board of the Central Bank of Bosnia and Herzegovina shall consist of five persons appointed by the Presidency for a term of six years. The Board shall appoint, from among its members, a Governor for a term of six years.

Article VIII
Finances

1. The Parliamentary Assembly shall each year, on the proposal of the Presidency, adopt a budget covering the expenditures required to carry out the responsibilities of institutions of Bosnia and Herzegovina and the international obligations of Bosnia and Herzegovina.

2. If no such budget is adopted in due time, the budget for the previous year shall be used on a provisional basis.

3. The Federation shall provide two-thirds, and the Republika Srpska one-third, of the revenues required by the budget, except insofar as revenues are raised as specified by the Parliamentary Assembly.

Article IX
General Provisions

1. No person who is serving a sentence imposed by the International Tribunal for the Former Yugoslavia, and no person who is under indictment by the Tribunal and who has failed to comply with an order to appear before the Tribunal, may stand as a candidate or hold any appointive, elective, or other public office in the territory of Bosnia and Herzegovina.

2. Compensation for persons holding office in the institutions of Bosnia and Herzegovina may not be diminished during an officeholder's tenure.

3. Officials appointed to positions in the institutions of Bosnia and Herzegovina shall be generally representative of the peoples of Bosnia and Herzegovina.

Article X
Amendment

1. *Amendment Procedure.* This Constitution may be amended by a decision of the Parliamentary Assembly, including a two-thirds majority of those present and voting in the House of Representatives.

2. *Human Rights and Fundamental Freedoms.* No amendment to this Constitution may eliminate or diminish any of the rights and freedoms referred to in Article II of this Constitution or alter the present paragraph.

Article XI
Transitional Arrangements

Transitional arrangements concerning public offices, law, and other matters are set forth in Annex II to this Constitution.

Article XII
Entry into Force

1. This Constitution shall enter into force upon signature of the General Framework Agreement as a constitutional act amending and superseding the Constitution of the Republic of Bosnia and Herzegovina.
2. Within three months from the entry into force of this Constitution, the Entities shall amend their respective constitutions to ensure their conformity with this Constitution in accordance with Article III(3)(b).

Annex I
Additional Human Rights Agreements to Be Applied in
Bosnia and Herzegovina

1. 1948 Convention on the Prevention and Punishment of the Crime of Genocide
2. 1949 Geneva Conventions I-IV on the Protection of the Victims of War, and the 1977 Geneva Protocols I-II thereto
3. 1951 Convention relating to the Status of Refugees and the 1966 Protocol thereto
4. 1957 Convention on the Nationality of Married Women
5. 1961 Convention on the Reduction of Statelessness
6. 1965 International Convention on the Elimination of All Forms of Racial Discrimination
7. 1966 International Covenant on Civil and Political Rights and the 1966 and 1989 Optional Protocols thereto
8. 1966 Covenant on Economic, Social and Cultural Rights
9. 1979 Convention on the Elimination of All Forms of Discrimination against Women
10. 1984 Convention against Torture and Other Cruel, Inhuman or Degrading Treatment or Punishment

11. 1987 European Convention on the Prevention of Torture and Inhuman or Degrading Treatment or Punishment
12. 1989 Convention on the Rights of the Child
13. 1990 International Convention on the Protection of the Rights of All Migrant Workers and Members of Their
14. 1992 European Charter for Regional or Minority Languages
15. 1994 Framework Convention for the Protection of National Minorities

Annex II
Transitional Arrangements

1. *Joint Interim Commission.*
(a) The Parties hereby establish a Joint Interim Commission with a mandate to discuss practical questions related to the implementation of the Constitution of Bosnia and Herzegovina and of the General Framework Agreement and its Annexes, and to make recommendations and proposals.
(b) The Joint Interim Commission shall be composed of four persons from the Federation, three persons from the Republika Srpska, and one representative of Bosnia and Herzegovina.
(c) Meetings of the Commission shall be chaired by the High Representative or his or designee.
2. *Continuation of Laws.* All laws, regulations, and judicial rules of procedure in effect within the territory of Bosnia and Herzegovina when the Constitution enters into force shall remain in effect to the extent not inconsistent with the Constitution, until otherwise determined by a competent governmental body of Bosnia and Herzegovina.
3. *Judicial and Administrative Proceedings.* All proceedings in courts or administrative agencies functioning within the territory of Bosnia and Herzegovina when the Constitution enters into force shall continue in or be transferred to other courts or agencies in Bosnia and in accordance with any legislation governing the competence of such courts or agencies.
4. *Offices.* Until superseded by applicable agreement or law, governmental offices, institutions, and other bodies of Bosnia and Herzegovina will operate in accordance with applicable law.
5. *Treaties.* Any treaty ratified by the Republic of Bosnia and Herzegovina between January 1, 1992 and the entry into force of this Constitution shall be disclosed to Members of the Presidency within 15 days of their assuming office; any such treaty not disclosed shall be denounced. Within six months after the Parliamentary Assembly is first convened, at the request of any member of the

Presidency, the Parliamentary Assembly shall consider whether to denounce any other such treaty.

Declaration on Behalf of the Republic of Bosnia and Herzegovina*

The Republic of Bosnia and Herzegovina approves the Constitution of Bosnia and Herzegovina at Annex 4 to the General Framework Agreement.

Declaration on Behalf of the Federation of Bosnia and Herzegovina**

The Federation of Bosnia and Herzegovina, on behalf of its constituent peoples and citizens, approves the Constitution of Bosnia and Herzegovina at Annex 4 to the General Framework Agreement.

Declaration on Behalf of the Republika Srpska***

The Republika Srpska approves the Constitution of Bosnia and Herzegovina at Annex 4 to the General Framework Agreement.

87. ANNEX 5
AGREEMENT ON ARBITRATION****

The Federation of Bosnia and Herzegovina and the Republika Srpska agree to honor the following obligations as set forth in the Agreed Basic Principles adopted at Geneva on September 8, 1995, by the Republic of Bosnia and Herzegovina, the Republic of Croatia, and the Federal Republic of Yugoslavia, the latter representing also the Republika Srpska:

- *Paragraph 2.4.* "The two entities will enter into reciprocal commitments ... (c) to engage in binding arbitration to resolve disputes between them."

---

*   Initialled by representative of the Republic of Bosnia and Herzegovina.
**   Initialled by representative of the Federation of Bosnia and Herzegovina.
***   Initialled by representative of the Republika Srpska.
**** Initialled by representatives of the Federation of Bosnia and Herzegovina and the Republika Srpska.

- *Paragraph 3.* "The entities have agreed in principle to the following: ... 3.5 The design and implementation of a system of arbitration for the solution of disputes between the two entities."

88. ANNEX 6
AGREEMENT ON HUMAN RIGHTS*

The Republic of Bosnia and Herzegovina, the Federation of Bosnia and Herzegovina and the Republika Srpska (the "Parties") have agreed as follows:

CHAPTER ONE: RESPECT FOR HUMAN RIGHTS

Article I
Fundamental Rights and Freedoms
The Parties shall secure to all persons within their jurisdiction the highest level of internationally recognized human rights and fundamental freedoms, including the rights and freedoms provided in the European Convention for the Protection of Human Rights and Fundamental Freedoms and its Protocols and the other international agreements listed in the Appendix to this Annex. These include:
(1) The right to life.
(2) The right not to be subjected to torture or to inhuman or degrading treatment or punishment.
(3) The right not to be held in slavery or servitude or to perform forced or compulsory labor.
(4) The rights to liberty and security of person.
(5) The right to a fair hearing in civil and criminal matters, and other rights relating to criminal proceedings.
(6) The right to private and family life, home, and correspondence.
(7) Freedom of thought, conscience and religion.
(8) Freedom of expression.
(9) Freedom of peaceful assembly and freedom of association with others.
(10) The right to marry and to found a family.
(11) The right to property.
(12) The right to education.

---

*   Initialled by representatives of the Republic of Bosnia and Herzegovina, the Federation of Bosnia and Herzegovina and the Republika Srpska.

(13) The right to liberty of movement and residence.

(14) The enjoyment of the rights and freedoms provided for in this Article or in the international agreements listed in the Annex to this Constitution secured without discrimination on any ground such as sex, race, color, language, religion, political or other opinion, national or social origin, association with a national minority, property, birth or other status.

CHAPTER TWO: THE COMMISSION ON HUMAN RIGHTS

PART A: GENERAL

Article II
Establishment of the Commission

1.   To assist in honoring their obligations under this Agreement, the Parties hereby establish a Commission on Human Rights (the "Commission"). The Commission shall consist of two parts: the Office of the Ombudsman and the Human Rights Chamber.

2.   The Office of the Ombudsman and the Human Rights Chamber shall consider, as subsequently described:

(a) alleged or apparent violations of human rights as provided in the European Convention for the Protection of Human Rights and Fundamental Freedoms and the Protocols thereto, or

(b) alleged or apparent discrimination on any ground such as sex, race, color, language, religion, political or other opinion, national or social origin, association with a national minority, property, birth or other status arising in the enjoyment of any of the rights and freedoms provided for in the international agreements listed in the Appendix to this Annex, where such violation is alleged or appears to have been committed by the Parties, including by any official or organ of the Parties, Cantons, Municipalities, or any individual acting under the authority of such official or organ.

3.   The Parties recognize the right of all persons to submit to the Commission and to other human rights bodies applications concerning alleged violations of human rights, in accordance with the procedures of this Annex and such bodies. The Parties shall not undertake any punitive action directed against persons who intend to submit, or have submitted, such allegations.

Article III
Facilities, Staff and Expenses

1.   The Commission shall have appropriate facilities and a professionally competent staff. There shall be an Executive Officer, appointed jointly by the Ombudsman and the President of the Chamber, who shall be responsible for all necessary administrative arrangements with respect to facilities and staff. The Executive Officer shall be subject to the direction of the Ombudsman and the President of the Chamber insofar as concerns their respective administrative and professional office staff.

2.   The salaries and expenses of the Commission and its staff shall be determined jointly by the Parties and shall be borne by Bosnia and Herzegovina. The salaries and expenses shall be fully adequate to implement the Commission's mandate.

3.   The Commission shall have its headquarters in Sarajevo, including both the headquarters Office of the Ombudsman and the facilities for the Chamber. The Ombudsman shall have at least one additional office in the territory of the Federation and the Republika Srpska and at other locations as it deems appropriate. The Chamber may meet in other locations where it determines that the needs of a particular case so require, and may meet at any place it deems appropriate for the inspection of property, documents or other items.

4.   The Ombudsman and all members of the Chamber shall not be held criminally or civilly liable for any acts carried out within the scope of their duties. When the Ombudsman and members of the Chamber are not citizens of Bosnia and Herzegovina, they and their families shall be accorded the same privileges and immunities as are enjoyed by diplomatic agents and their families under the Vienna Convention on Diplomatic Relations.

5.   With full regard for the need to maintain impartiality, the Commission may receive assistance as it deems appropriate from any governmental, international, or non-governmental organization.

PART B: HUMAN RIGHTS OMBUDSMAN

Article IV
Human Rights Ombudsman

1.   The Parties hereby establish the Office of the Human Rights Ombudsman ("Ombudsman").

2.   The Ombudsman shall be appointed for a non-renewable term of five years by the Chairman-in-Office of the Organization for Security and Cooperation in Europe (OSCE), after consultation with the Parties. He or she shall be indepen-

dently responsible for choosing his or her own staff. Until the transfer described in Article XIV below, the Ombudsman may not be a citizen of Bosnia and Herzegovina or of any neighboring state. The Ombudsman appointed after that transfer shall be appointed by the Presidency of Bosnia and Herzegovina.

3.   Members of the Office of the Ombudsman must be of recognized high moral standing and have competence in the field of international human rights.

4.   The Office of the Ombudsman shall be an independent agency. In carrying out its mandate, no person or organ of the Parties may interfere with its functions.

Article V
Jurisdiction of the Ombudsman

1.   Allegations of violations of human rights received by the Commission shall generally be directed to the Office of the Ombudsman, except where an applicant specifies the Chamber.

2.   The Ombudsman may investigate, either on his or her own initiative or in response to an allegation by any Party or person, non-governmental organization, or group of individuals claiming to be the victim of a violation by any Party or acting on behalf of alleged victims who are deceased or missing, alleged or apparent violations of human rights within the scope of paragraph 2 of Article II. The Parties undertake not to hinder in any way the effective exercise of this right.

3.   The Ombudsman shall determine which allegations warrant investigation and in what priority, giving particular priority allegations of especially severe or systematic violations and those founded on alleged discrimination on prohibited grounds.

4.   The Ombudsman shall issue findings and conclusions promptly after concluding an investigation. A Party identified as violating human rights shall, within a specified period, explain in writing how it will comply with the conclusions.

5.   Where an allegation is received which is within the jurisdiction of the Human Rights Chamber, the Ombudsman may refer the allegation to the Chamber at any stage.

6.   The Ombudsman may also present special reports at any time to any competent government organ or official. Those receiving such reports shall reply within a time limit specified by the Ombudsman, including specific responses to any conclusions offered by the Ombudsman.

7.   The Ombudsman shall publish a report, which, in the event that a person or entity does not comply with his or her conclusions and recommendations, will be

forwarded to the High Representative described in Annex 10 to the General Framework Agreement while such office exists, as well as referred for further action to the Presidency of the appropriate Party. The Ombudsman may also initiate proceedings before the Human Rights Chamber based on such Report. The Ombudsman may also intervene in any proceedings before the Chamber.

Article VI
Powers

1. The Ombudsman shall have access to and may examine all official documents, including classified ones, as well as judicial and administrative files, and can require any person, including a government official, to cooperate by providing relevant information, documents and files. The Ombudsman may attend administrative hearings and meetings of other organs and may enter and inspect any place where persons deprived of their liberty are confined or work.

2. The Ombudsman and staff are required to maintain the confidentiality of all confidential information obtained, except where required by order of the Chamber, and shall treat all documents and files in accordance with applicable rules.

PART C: HUMAN RIGHTS CHAMBER

Article VII
Human Rights Chamber

1. The Human Rights Chamber shall be composed of fourteen members.

2. Within 90 days after this Agreement enters into force, the Federation of Bosnia and Herzegovina shall appoint four members and the Republika Srpska shall appoint two members. The Committee of Ministers of the Council of Europe, pursuant to its resolution (93)6, after consultation with the Parties, shall appoint the remaining members, who shall not be citizens of Bosnia and Herzegovina or any neighboring state, and shall designate one such member as the President of the Chamber.

3. All members of the Chamber shall possess the qualifications required for appointment to high judicial office or be jurists of recognized competence. The members of the Chamber shall be appointed for a term of five years and may be reappointed.

4. Members appointed after the transfer described in Article XIV below shall be appointed by the Presidency of Bosnia and Herzegovina.

Article VIII
Jurisdiction of the Chamber

1.   The Chamber shall receive by referral from the Ombudsman on behalf of an applicant, or directly from any Party or person, non-governmental organization, or group of individuals claiming to be the victim of a violation by any Party or acting on behalf of alleged victims who are deceased or missing, for resolution or decision applications concerning alleged or apparent violations of human rights within the scope of paragraph 2 of Article II.

2.   The Chamber shall decide which applications to accept and in what priority to address them. In so doing, the Chamber shall take into account the following criteria:

(a) Whether effective remedies exist, and the applicant has demonstrated that they have been exhausted and that the application has been filed with the Commission within six months from such date on which the final decision was taken.

(b) The Chamber shall not address any application which is substantially the same as a matter which has already been examined by the Chamber or has already been submitted to another procedure or international investigation or settlement.

(c) The Chamber shall also dismiss any application which it considers incompatible with this Agreement, manifestly ill-founded, or an abuse of the right of petition.

(d) The Chamber may reject or defer further consideration if the application concerns a matter currently pending before any other international human rights body responsible for the adjudication of applications or the decision of cases, or any other Commission established by the Annexes to the General Framework Agreement.

(e) In principle, the Chamber shall endeavor to accept and to give particular priority to allegations of especially severe or systematic violations and those founded on alleged discrimination on prohibited grounds.

(f) Applications which entail requests for provisional measures shall be reviewed as a matter of priority in order to determine (1) whether they should be accepted and, if so (2) whether high priority for the scheduling of proceedings on the provisional measures request is warranted.

2.   The Chamber may decide at any point in its proceedings to suspend consideration of, reject or strike out, an application on the ground that (a) the applicant does not intend to pursue his application; (b) the matter has been resolved; or (c) for any other reason established by the Chamber, it is no longer justified to

continue the examination of the application; provided that such result is consistent with the objective of respect for human rights.

Article IX
Friendly Settlement

1.   At the outset of a case or at any stage during the proceedings, the Chamber may attempt to facilitate an amicable resolution of the matter on the basis of respect for the rights and freedoms referred to in this Agreement.

2.   If the Chamber succeeds in effecting such a resolution it shall publish a Report and forward it to the High Representative described in Annex 10 to the General Framework Agreement while such office exists, the OSCE and the Secretary General of the Council of Europe. Such a Report shall include a brief statement of the facts and the resolution reached. The report of a resolution in a given case may, however, be confidential in whole or in part where necessary for the protection of human rights or with the agreement of the Chamber and the parties concerned.

Article X
Proceedings before the Chamber

1.   The Chamber shall develop fair and effective procedures for the adjudication of applications. Such procedures shall provide for appropriate written pleadings and, on the decision of Chamber, a hearing for oral argument or the presentation of evidence. The Chamber shall have the power to order provisional measures, to appoint experts, and to compel the production of witnesses and evidence.

2.   The Chamber shall normally sit in panels of seven, composed of two members from the Federation, one from the Republika Srpska, and four who are not citizens of Bosnia and Herzegovina or any neighboring state. When an application is decided by a panel, the full Chamber may decide, upon motion of a party to the case or the Ombudsman, to review the decision; such review may include the taking of additional evidence where the chamber so decides. References in this Annex to the Chamber shall include, as appropriate, the Panel, except that the power to develop general rules, regulations and procedures is vested only in the Chamber as a whole.

3.   Except in exceptional circumstances in accordance with its rules, hearings of the Chamber shall be held in public.

4.   Applicants may be represented in proceedings by attorneys or other representatives of their choice, but shall also be personally present unless excused by the Chamber on account of hardship, impossibility, or other good cause.

5.   The Parties undertake to provide all relevant information to, and to cooperate fully with, the Chamber.

Article XI
Decisions

1.   Following the conclusion of the proceedings, the Chamber shall promptly issue a decision, which shall address:

(a) whether the facts found indicate a breach by the Party concerned of its obligations under this Agreement; and if so

(b) what steps shall be taken by the Party to remedy such breach, including orders to cease and desist, monetary relief (including pecuniary and non-pecuniary injuries), and provisional measures.

2.   The Chamber shall make its decision by a majority of members. In the event a decision by the full Chamber results in a tie, the President of the Chamber shall cast the deciding vote.

3.   Subject to review as provided in paragraph 2 of Article X, the decisions of the Chamber shall be final and binding.

4.   Any member shall be entitled to issue a separate opinion on any case.

5.   The Chamber shall issue reasons for its decisions. Its decisions shall be published and forwarded to the parties concerned, the High Representative described in Annex 10 to the General Framework Agreement while such office exists, the Secretary General of the Council of Europe and the OSCE.

6.   The Parties shall implement fully decisions of the Chamber.

Article XII
Rules and Regulations

The Chamber shall promulgate such rules and regulations, consistent with this Agreement, as may be necessary to carry out its functions, including provisions for preliminary hearings, expedited decisions on provisional measures, decisions by panels of the Chamber, and review of decisions made by any such panels.

CHAPTER THREE: GENERAL PROVISIONS

Article XIII
Organizations Concerned with Human Rights

1.   The Parties shall promote and encourage the activities of non-governmental and international organizations for the protection and promotion of human rights.

2. The Parties join in inviting the United Nations Commission on Human Rights, the OSCE, the United Nations High Commissioner for Human Rights, and other intergovernmental or regional human rights missions or organizations to monitor closely the human rights situation in Bosnia and Herzegovina, including through the establishment of local offices and the assignment of observers, rapporteurs, or other relevant persons on a permanent or mission-by-mission basis and to provide them with full and effective facilitation, assistance and access.

3. The Parties shall allow full and effective access to non-governmental organizations for purposes of investigating and monitoring human rights conditions in Bosnia and Herzegovina and shall refrain from hindering or impeding them in the exercise of these functions.

4. All competent authorities in Bosnia and Herzegovina shall cooperate with and provide unrestricted access to the organizations established in this Agreement; any international human rights monitoring mechanisms established for Bosnia and Herzegovina; the supervisory bodies established by any of the international agreements listed in the Appendix to this Annex; the International Tribunal for the Former Yugoslavia; and any other organization authorized by the U.N. Security Council with a mandate concerning human rights or humanitarian law.

Article XIV
Transfer

Five years after this Agreement enters into force, the responsibility for the continued operation of the Commission shall transfer from the Parties to the institutions of Bosnia and Herzegovina, unless the Parties otherwise agree. In the latter case, the Commission shall continue to operate as provided above.

Article XV
Notice

The Parties shall give effective notice of the terms of this Agreement throughout Bosnia and Herzegovina.

Article XVI
Entry into Force

This Agreement shall enter into force upon signature.

Appendix
Human Rights Agreements

1. 1948 Convention on the Prevention and Punishment of the Crime of Genocide
2. 1949 Geneva Conventions I-IV on the Protection of the Victims of War, and the 1977 Geneva Protocols I-II thereto
3. 1950 European Convention for the Protection of Human Rights and Fundamental Freedoms, and the Protocols thereto
4. 1951 Convention relating to the Status of Refugees and the 1966 Protocol thereto
5. 1957 Convention on the Nationality of Married Women
6. 1961 Convention on the Reduction of Statelessness
7. 1965 International Convention on the Elimination of All Forms of Racial Discrimination
8. 1966 International Covenant on Civil and Political Rights and the 1966 and 1989 Optional Protocols thereto
9. 1966 Covenant on Economic, Social and Cultural Rights
10. 1979 Convention on the Elimination of All Forms of Discrimination against Women
11. 1984 Convention against Torture and Other Cruel, Inhuman or Degrading Treatment or Punishment
12. 1987 European Convention on the Prevention of Torture and Inhuman or Degrading Treatment or Punishment
13. 1989 Convention on the Rights of the Child
14. 1990 Convention on the Protection of the Rights of All Migrant Workers and Members of Their Families
15. 1992 European Charter for Regional or Minority Languages
16. 1994 Framework Convention for the Protection of National Minorities

89. ANNEX 7
AGREEMENT ON REFUGEES AND DISPLACED PERSONS[*]

The Republic of Bosnia and Herzegovina, the Federation of Bosnia and Herzegovina, and the Republika Srpska (the "Parties") have agreed as follows:

---

[*]   Initialled by representatives of the Republic of Bosnia and Herzegovina, the Federation of Bosnia and Herzegovina and the Republika Srpska.

CHAPTER ONE: PROTECTION

Article I
Rights of Refugees and Displaced Persons

1. All refugees and displaced persons have the right freely to return to their homes of origin. They shall have the right to have restored to them property of which they were deprived in the course of hostilities since 1991 and to be compensated for any property that cannot be restored to them. The early return of refugees and displaced persons is an important objective of the settlement of the conflict in Bosnia and Herzegovina. The Parties confirm that they will accept the return of such persons who have left their territory, including those who have been accorded temporary protection by third countries.

2. The Parties shall ensure that refugees and displaced persons are permitted to return in safety, without risk of harassment, intimidation, persecution, or discrimination, particularly on account of their ethnic origin, religious belief, or political opinion.

3. The Parties shall take all necessary steps to prevent activities within their territories which would hinder or impede the safe and voluntary return of refugees and displaced persons. To demonstrate their commitment to securing full respect for the human rights and fundamental freedoms of all persons within their jurisdiction and creating without delay conditions suitable for return of refugees and displaced persons, the Parties shall take immediately the following confidence building measures:

(a) the repeal of domestic legislation and administrative practices with discriminatory intent or effect;

(b) the prevention and prompt suppression of any written or verbal incitement, through media or otherwise, of ethnic or religious hostility or hatred;

(c) the dissemination, through the media, of warnings against, and the prompt suppression of, acts of retribution by military, paramilitary, and police services, and by other public officials or private individuals;

(d) the protection of ethnic and/or minority populations wherever they are found and the provision of immediate access to these populations by international humanitarian organizations and monitors;

(e) the prosecution, dismissal or transfer, as appropriate, of persons in military, paramilitary, and police forces, and other public servants, responsible for serious violations of the basic rights of persons belonging to ethnic or minority groups.

4. Choice of destination shall be up to the individual or family, and the principle of the unity of the family shall be preserved. The Parties shall not interfere with the returnees' choice of destination, nor shall they compel them to remain

in or move to situations of serious danger or insecurity, or to areas lacking in the basic infrastructure necessary to resume a normal life. The Parties shall facilitate the flow of information necessary for refugees and displaced persons to make informed judgments about local conditions for return.

5.   The Parties call upon the United Nations High Commissioner for Refugees ("UNHCR") to develop in close consultation with asylum countries and the Parties a repatriation plan that will allow for an early, peaceful, orderly and phased return of refugees and displaced persons, which may include priorities for certain areas and certain categories of returnees. The Parties agree to implement such a plan and to conform their international agreements and internal laws to it. They accordingly call upon States that have accepted refugees to promote the early return of refugees consistent with international law.

Article II
Creation of Suitable Conditions for Return

1.   The Parties undertake to create in their territories the political, economic, and social conditions conducive to the voluntary return and harmonious reintegration of refugees and displaced persons, without preference for any particular group. The Parties shall provide all possible assistance to refugees and displaced persons and work to facilitate their voluntary return in a peaceful, orderly and phased manner, in accordance with the UNHCR repatriation plan.

2.   The Parties shall not discriminate against returning refugees and displaced persons with respect to conscription into military service, and shall give positive consideration to requests for exemption from military or other obligatory service based on individual circumstances, so as to enable returnees to rebuild their lives.

Article III
Cooperation with International Organizations and International Monitoring

1.   The Parties note with satisfaction the leading humanitarian role of UNHCR, which has been entrusted by the Secretary-General of the United Nations with the role of coordinating among all agencies assisting with the repatriation and relief of refugees and displaced persons.

2.   The Parties shall give full and unrestricted access by UNHCR, the International Committee of the Red Cross ("ICRC"), the United Nations Development Programme ("UNDP"), and other relevant international, domestic and non-governmental organizations to all refugees and displaced persons, with a view to facilitating the work of those organizations in tracing persons, the provision of medical assistance, food distribution, reintegration assistance, the provision of

temporary and permanent housing, and other activities vital to the discharge of their mandates and operational responsibilities without administrative impediments. These activities shall include traditional protection functions and the monitoring of basic human rights and humanitarian conditions, as well as the implementation of the provisions of this Chapter.

3. The Parties shall provide for the security of all personnel of such organizations.

Article IV
Repatriation Assistance

The Parties shall facilitate the provision of adequately monitored, short-term repatriation assistance on a nondiscriminatory basis to all returning refugees and displaced persons who are in need, in accordance with a plan developed by UNHCR and other relevant organizations, to enable the families and individuals returning to reestablish their lives and livelihoods in local communities.

Article V
Persons Unaccounted For

The Parties shall provide information through the tracing mechanisms of the ICRC on all persons unaccounted for. The Parties shall also cooperate fully with the ICRC in its efforts to determine the identities, whereabouts and fate of the unaccounted for.

Article VI
Amnesty

Any returning refugee or displaced person charged with a crime, other than a serious violation of international humanitarian law as defined in the Statute of the International Tribunal for the Former Yugoslavia since January 1, 1991 or a common crime unrelated to the conflict, shall upon return enjoy an amnesty. In no case shall charges for crimes be imposed for political or other inappropriate reasons or to circumvent the application of the amnesty.

CHAPTER TWO: COMMISSION FOR DISPLACED PERSONS AND REFUGEES

Article VII
Establishment of the Commission

The Parties hereby establish an independent Commission for Displaced Persons and Refugees (the "Commission"). The Commission shall have its headquarters in Sarajevo and may have offices at other locations as it deems appropriate.

Article VIII
Cooperation

The Parties shall cooperate with the work of the Commission, and shall respect and implement its decisions expeditiously and in good faith, in cooperation with relevant international and nongovernmental organizations having responsibility for the return and reintegration of refugees and displaced persons.

Article IX
Composition

1.   The Commission shall be composed of nine members. Within 90 days after this Agreement enters into force, the Federation of Bosnia and Herzegovina shall appoint four members, two for a term of three years and the others for a term of four years, and the Republika Srpska shall appoint two members, one for a term of three years and the other for a term of four years. The President of the European Court of Human Rights shall appoint the remaining members, each for a term of five years, and shall designate one such member as the Chairman. The members of the Commission may be reappointed.

2.   Members of the Commission must be of recognized high moral standing.

3.   The Commission may sit in panels, as provided in its rules and regulations. References in this Annex to the Commission shall include, as appropriate, such panels, except that the power to promulgate rules and regulations is vested only in the Commission as a whole.

4.   Members appointed after the transfer described in Article XVI below shall be appointed by the Presidency of Bosnia and Herzegovina.

Article X
Facilities, Staff and Expenses

1. The Commission shall have appropriate facilities and a professionally competent staff, experienced in administrative, financial, banking and legal matters, to assist it in carrying out its functions. The staff shall be headed by an Executive Officer, who shall be appointed by the Commission.

2.   The salaries and expenses of the Commission and its staff shall be determined jointly by the Parties and shall be borne equally by the Parties.

3.   Members of the Commission shall not be held criminally or civilly liable for any acts carried out within the scope of their duties. Members of the Commission, and their families, who are not citizens of Bosnia and Herzegovina shall be

accorded the same privileges and immunities as are enjoyed by diplomatic agents and their families under the Vienna Convention on Diplomatic Relations.

4. The Commission may receive assistance from international and nongovernmental organizations, in their areas of special expertise falling within the mandate of the Commission, on terms to be agreed.

5. The Commission shall cooperate with other entities established by the General Framework Agreement, agreed by the Parties, or authorized by the United Nations Security Council.

Article XI
Mandate

The Commission shall receive and decide any claims for real property in Bosnia and Herzegovina, where the property has not voluntarily been sold or otherwise transferred since April 1, 1992, and where the claimant does not now enjoy possession of that property. Claims may be for return of the property or for just compensation in lieu of return.

Article XII
Proceedings before the Commission

1. Upon receipt of a claim, the Commission shall determine the lawful owner of the property with respect to which the claim is made and the value of that property. The Commission, through its staff or a duly designated international or nongovernmental organization, shall be entitled to have access to any and all property records in Bosnia and Herzegovina, and to any and all real property located in Bosnia and Herzegovina for purposes of inspection, evaluation and assessment related to consideration of a claim.

2. Any person requesting the return of property who is found by the Commission to be the lawful owner of that property shall be awarded its return. Any person requesting compensation in lieu of return who is found by the Commission to be the lawful owner of that property shall be awarded just compensation as determined by the Commission. The Commission shall make decisions by a majority of its members.

3. In determining the lawful owner of any property, the Commission shall not recognize as valid any illegal property transaction, including any transfer that was made under duress, in exchange for exit permission or documents, or that was otherwise in connection with ethnic cleansing. Any person who is awarded return of property may accept a satisfactory lease arrangement rather than retake possession.

4.   The Commission shall establish fixed rates that may be applied to determine the value of all real property in Bosnia and Herzegovina that is the subject of a claim before the Commission. The rates shall be based on an assessment or survey of properties in the territory of Bosnia and Herzegovina undertaken prior to April 1, 1992, if available, or may be based on other reasonable criteria as determined by the Commission.

5.   The Commission shall have the power to effect any transactions necessary to transfer or assign title, mortgage, lease, or otherwise dispose of property with respect to which a claim is made, or which is determined to be abandoned. In particular, the Commission may lawfully sell, mortgage, or lease real property to any resident or citizen of Bosnia and Herzegovina, or to either Party, where the lawful owner has sought and received compensation in lieu of return, or where the property is determined to be abandoned in accordance with local law. The Commission may also lease property pending consideration and final determination of ownership.

6.   In cases in which the claimant is awarded compensation in lieu of return of the property, the Commission may award a monetary grant or a compensation bond for the future purchase of real property. The Parties welcome the willingness of the international community assisting in the construction and financing of housing in Bosnia and Herzegovina to accept compensation bonds awarded by the Commission as payment, and to award persons holding such compensation bonds priority in obtaining that housing.

7.   Commission decisions shall be final, and any title, deed, mortgage, or other legal instrument created or awarded by the Commission shall be recognized as lawful throughout Bosnia and Herzegovina.

8.   Failure of any Party or individual to cooperate with the Commission shall not prevent the Commission from making its decision.

Article XIII
Use of Vacant Property

The Parties, after notification to the Commission and in coordination with UNHCR and other international and nongovernmental organizations contributing to relief and reconstruction, may temporarily house refugees and displaced persons in vacant property, subject to final determination of ownership by the Commission and to such temporary lease provisions as it may require.

Article XIV
Refugees and Displaced Persons Property Fund

1. A Refugees and Displaced Persons Property Fund (the "Fund") shall be established in the Central Bank of Bosnia and Herzegovina to be administered by the Commission. The Fund shall be replenished through the purchase, sale, lease and mortgage of real property which is the subject of claims before the Commission. It may also be replenished by direct payments from the Parties, or from contributions by States or international or nongovernmental organizations.

2. Compensation bonds issued pursuant to Article XII(6) shall create future liabilities on the Fund under terms and conditions to be defined by the Commission.

Article XV
Rules and Regulations

The Commission shall promulgate such rules and regulations, consistent with this Agreement, as may be necessary to carry out its functions. In developing these rules and regulations, the Commission shall consider domestic laws on property rights.

Article XVI
Transfer

Five years after this Agreement takes effect, responsibility for the financing and operation of the Commission shall transfer from the Parties to the Government of Bosnia and Herzegovina, unless the Parties otherwise agree. In the latter case, the Commission shall continue to operate as provided above.

Article XVII
Notice

The Parties shall give effective notice of the terms of this Agreement throughout Bosnia and Herzegovina, and in all countries known to have persons who were citizens or residents of Bosnia and Herzegovina.

Article XVIII
Entry into Force

This Agreement shall enter into force upon signature.

90. ANNEX 8
AGREEMENT ON COMMISSION TO PRESERVE NATIONAL MONUMENTS*

The Republic of Bosnia and Herzegovina, the Federation of Bosnia and Herzegovina and the Republika Srpska (the "Parties") have agreed as follows:

Article I
Establishment of the Commission

The Parties hereby establish an independent Commission to Preserve National Monuments (the "Commission"). The Commission shall have its headquarters in Sarajevo and may have offices at other locations as it deems appropriate.

Article II
Composition

1.   The Commission shall be composed of five members. Within 90 days after this Agreement enters into force, the Federation of Bosnia and Herzegovina shall appoint two members, and the Republika Srpska one member, each serving a term of three years. The Director-General of the United Nations Educational, Scientific and Cultural Organization shall appoint the remaining members, each for a term of five years, and shall designate one such member as the Chairman. The members of the Commission may be reappointed. No person who is serving a sentence imposed by the International Tribunal for the Former Yugoslavia, and no person who is under indictment by the Tribunal and who has failed to comply with an order to appear before the Tribunal, may serve on the Commission.
2.   Members appointed after the transfer described in Article IX below shall be appointed by the Presidency of Bosnia and Herzegovina.

Article III
Facilities, Staff and Expenses

1.   The Commission shall have appropriate facilities and a professionally competent staff, generally representative of the ethnic groups comprising Bosnia and Herzegovina, to assist it in carrying out its functions. The staff shall be headed by an executive officer, who shall be appointed by the Commission.
2.   The salaries and expenses of the Commission and its staff shall be determined jointly by the Entities and shall be borne equally by them.

---

*   Initialled by representatives of the Republic of Bosnia and Herzegovina, the Federation of Bosnia and Herzegovina and the Republika Srpska.

3. Members of the Commission shall not be held criminally or civilly liable for any acts carried out within the scope of their duties. Members of the Commission, and their families, who are not citizens of Bosnia and Herzegovina shall be accorded the same privileges and immunities as are enjoyed by diplomatic agents and their families under the Vienna Convention on Diplomatic Relations.

Article IV
Mandate

The Commission shall receive and decide on petitions for the designation of property having cultural, historic, religious or ethnic importance as National Monuments.

Article V
Proceedings before the Commission

1. Any Party, or any concerned person in Bosnia and Herzegovina, may submit to the Commission a petition for the designation of property as a National Monument. Each such petition shall set forth all relevant information concerning property, including:
(a) the specific location of the property;
(b) its current owner and condition;
(c) the cost and source of funds for any necessary repairs to the property;
(d) any known proposed use; and
(e) the basis for designation as a National Monument.
2. In deciding upon the petition, the Commission shall afford an opportunity for the owners of the proposed National Monument, as well as other interested persons or entities, to present their views.
3. For a period of one year after such a petition has been submitted to the Commission, or until a decision is rendered in accordance with this Annex, whichever occurs first, all Parties shall refrain from taking any deliberate measures that might damage the property.
4. The Commission shall issue, in each case, a written decision containing any findings of fact it deems appropriate and a detailed explanation of the basis for its decision. The Commission shall make decisions by a majority of its members. Decisions of the Commission shall be final and enforceable in accordance with domestic law.
5. In any case in which the Commission issues a decision designating property as a National Monument, the Entity in whose territory the property is situated (a) shall make every effort to take appropriate legal, scientific, technical, administrative and financial measures necessary for the protection, conservation, presen-

tation and rehabilitation of the property, and (b) shall refrain from taking any deliberate measures that might damage the property.

Article VI
Eligibility

The following shall be eligible for designation as National Monuments: movable or immovable property of great importance to a group of people with common cultural, historic, religious or ethnic heritage, such as monuments of architecture, art or history; archaeological sites; groups of buildings; as well as cemeteries.

Article VII
Rules and Regulations

The Commission shall promulgate such rules and regulations, consistent with this Agreement, as may be necessary to carry out its functions.

Article VIII
Cooperation

Officials and organs of the Parties and their Cantons and Municipalities, and any individual acting under the authority of such official or organ, shall fully cooperate with the Commission, including by providing requested information and other assistance.

Article IX
Transfer

Five years after this Agreement enters into force, the responsibility for the continued operation of the Commission shall transfer from the Parties to the Government of Bosnia and Herzegovina, unless the Parties otherwise agree. In the latter case, the Commission shall continue to operate as provided above.

Article X
Notice

The Parties shall give effective notice of the terms of this Agreement throughout Bosnia and Herzegovina.

Article XI
Entry into Force

This Agreement shall enter into force upon signature.

91. ANNEX 9
AGREEMENT ON ESTABLISHMENT OF BOSNIA AND HERZEGOVINA
PUBLIC CORPORATIONS*

Bearing in mind that reconstruction of the infrastructure and the functioning of transportation and other facilities are important for the economic resurgence of Bosnia and Herzegovina, and for the smooth functioning of its institutions and the organizations involved in implementation of peace settlement, the Federation of Bosnia and Herzegovina and the Republika Srpska (the "Parties") have agreed as follows:

Article I
Commission on Public Corporations

1. The Parties hereby establish a Commission on Public Corporations (the "Commission") to examine establishing Bosnia Herzegovina Public Corporations to operate joint public facilities, such as for the operation of utility, energy, postal and communication facilities, for the benefit of both Entities.
2. The Commission shall have five Members. Within fifteen days after this Agreement enters into force, the Federation of Bosnia and Herzegovina shall appoint two Members, and the Republika Srpska one Member. Persons appointed must be familiar with the specific economic, political and legal characteristics of Bosnia and Herzegovina and be of high recognized moral standing. Recognizing that the Commission will benefit from international expertise, the Parties request the President of the European Bank for Reconstruction and Development to appoint the remaining two Members and to designate one as the Chairman.
3. The Commission shall in particular examine the appropriate internal structure for such Corporations, the conditions necessary to ensure their successful, permanent operation, and the best means of procuring long-term investment capital.

Article II
Establishment of a Transportation Corporation

1. The Parties, recognizing an immediate need to establish a Public Corporation to organize and operate transportation facilities, such as roads, railways and ports, for their mutual benefit, hereby establish a Bosnia and Herzegovina

---

* Initialled by representatives of the Federation of Bosnia and Herzegovina and the Republika Srpska.

Transportation Corporation (the "Transportation Corporation") for such purpose.

2. The Transportation Corporation shall have its headquarters in Sarajevo and may have offices at other locations as it deems appropriate. It shall have appropriate facilities and choose a professionally competent Board of Directors, Officers and Staff, generally representative of the ethnic groups comprising Bosnia and Herzegovina, to carry out its functions. The Commission shall choose the Board of Directors, which shall in turn appoint the Officers and select the Staff.

3. The Transportation Corporation is authorized to construct, acquire, hold, maintain and operate and dispose of real and personal property in accordance with specific plans that it develops. It is also authorized to fix and collect rates, fees, rentals and other charges for the use of facilities it operates; enter into all contracts and agreements necessary for the performance of its functions; and take other actions necessary to carry out these functions.

4. The Transportation Corporation shall operate transportation facilities as agreed by the Parties. The Parties shall, as part of their agreement, provide the Corporation with necessary legal authority. The Parties shall meet within fifteen days after this Agreement enters into force to consider which facilities the Corporation will operate.

5. Within thirty days after this Agreement enters into force, the Parties shall agree on sums of money to be contributed to the Transportation Corporation for its initial operating budget. The Parties may at any time transfer to the Transportation Corporation additional funds or facilities that belong to them and the rights thereto. The Parties shall decide the means by which the Transportation Corporation will be authorized to raise additional capital.

Article III
Other Public Corporations

The Parties may decide, upon recommendation of the Commission, to use establishment of the Transportation Corporation as a model for the establishment of other joint public corporations, such as for the operation of utility, energy, postal and communication facilities.

Article IV
Cooperation

The Commission, the Transportation Corporation and other Public Corporations shall cooperate fully with all organizations involved in implementation of the peace settlement, or which are otherwise authorized by the United Nations

Security Council, including the International Tribunal for the Former Yugo-slavia.

Article V
Ethics

Members of the Commission and Directors of the Transportation Corpor-ation may not have an employment or financial relationship with any enterprise that has, or is seeking, a contract or agreement with the Commission or the Corporation, respectively, or otherwise has interests that can be directly affected by its actions or inactions.

Article VI
Entry into Force

This Agreement shall enter into force upon signature.

92. ANNEX 10
AGREEMENT ON CIVILIAN IMPLEMENTATION OF THE PEACE SETTLEMENT*

The Republic of Bosnia and Herzegovina, the Republic of Croatia, the Federal Republic of Yugoslavia, the Federation of Bosnia and Herzegovina, and the Republika Srpska (the "Parties") have agreed as follows:

Article I
High Representative

1.   The Parties agree that the implementation of the civilian aspects of the peace settlement will entail a wide range of activities including continuation of the humanitarian aid effort for as long as necessary; rehabilitation of infrastructure and economic reconstruction; the establishment of political and constitutional institutions in Bosnia and Herzegovina; promotion of respect for human rights and the return of displaced persons and refugees; and the holding of free and fair elections according to the timetable in Annex 3 to the General Framework Agreement. A considerable number of international organizations and agencies will be called upon to assist.

2.   In view of the complexities facing them, the Parties request the designation of a High Representative, to be appointed consistent with relevant United Nati-

---

*   Initialled by representatives of the Republic of Bosnia and Herzegovina, the Republic of Croatia, the Federal Republic of Yugoslavia, the Federation of Bosnia and Herzegovina, and the Republika Srpska.

ons Security Council resolutions, to facilitate the Parties' own efforts and to mobilize and, as appropriate, coordinate the activities of the organizations and agencies involved in the civilian aspects of the peace settlement by carrying out, as entrusted by a U.N. Security Council resolution, the tasks set out below.

Article II
Mandate and Methods of Coordination and Liaison

The High Representative shall:

(a) Monitor the implementation of the peace settlement;

(b) Maintain close contact with the Parties to promote their full compliance with all civilian aspects of the peace settlement and a high level of cooperation between them and the organizations and agencies participating in those aspects.

(c) Coordinate the activities of the civilian organizations and agencies in Bosnia and Herzegovina to ensure the efficient implementation of the civilian aspects of the peace settlement. The High Representative shall respect their autonomy within their spheres of operation while as necessary giving general guidance to them about the impact of their activities on the implementation of the peace settlement. The civilian organizations and agencies are requested to assist the High Representative in the execution of his or her responsibilities by providing all information relevant to their operations in Bosnia-Herzegovina.

(d) Facilitate, as the High Representative judges necessary, the resolution of any difficulties arising in connection with civilian implementation.

(e) Participate in meetings of donor organizations, particularly on issues of rehabilitation and reconstruction.

(f) Report periodically on progress in implementation of the peace agreement concerning the tasks set forth in this Agreement to the United Nations, European Union, United States, Russian Federation, and other interested governments, parties, and organizations.

(g) Provide guidance to, and receive reports from, the Commissioner of the International Police Task Force established in Annex 11 to the General Framework Agreement.

2. In pursuit of his or her mandate, the High Representative shall convene and chair a commission (the "Joint Civilian Commission") in Bosnia and Herzegovina. It will comprise senior political representatives of the Parties, the IFOR Commander or his representative, and representatives of those civilian organizations and agencies the High Representative deems necessary.

3.   The High Representative shall, as necessary, establish subordinate Joint Civilian Commissions at local levels in Bosnia and Herzegovina.

4.   A Joint Consultative Committee will meet from time to time or as agreed between the High Representative and the IFOR Commander.

5.   The High Representative or his designated representative shall remain in close contact with the IFOR Commander or his designated representatives and establish appropriate liaison arrangements with the IFOR Commander to facilitate the discharge of their respective responsibilities.

6.   The High Representative shall exchange information and maintain liaison on a regular basis with IFOR, as agreed with the IFOR Commander, and through the commissions described in this Article.

7.   The High Representative shall attend or be represented at meetings of the Joint Military Commission and offer advice particularly on matters of a political-military nature. Representatives of the High Representative will also attend subordinate commissions of the Joint Military Commission as set out in Article VIII(8) of Annex 1A to the General Framework Agreement.

8.   The High Representative may also establish other civilian commissions within or outside Bosnia and Herzegovina to facilitate the execution of his or her mandate.

9.   The High Representative shall have no authority over the IFOR and shall not in any way interfere in the conduct of military operations or the IFOR chain of command.

Article III
Staffing

1.   The High Representative shall appoint staff, as he or she deems necessary, to provide assistance in carrying out the tasks herein.

2.   The Parties shall facilitate the operations of the High Representative in Bosnia and Herzegovina, including by the provision of appropriate assistance as requested with regard to transportation, subsistence, accommodations, communications, and other facilities at rates equivalent to those provided for the IFOR under applicable agreements.

3.   The High Representative shall enjoy, under the laws of Bosnia and Herzegovina, such legal capacity as may be necessary for the exercise of his or her functions, including the capacity to contract and to acquire and dispose of real and personal property.

4.   Privileges and immunities shall be accorded as follows:

(a) The Parties shall accord the office of the High Representative and its premises, archives, and other property the same privileges and immunities as are enjoyed by a diplomatic mission and its premises, archives, and other property under the Vienna Convention on Diplomatic Relations.

(b) The Parties shall accord the High Representative and professional members of his or her staff and their families the same privileges and immunities as are enjoyed by diplomatic agents and their families under the Vienna Convention on Diplomatic Relations.

(c) The Parties shall accord other members of the High Representative staff and their families the same privileges and immunities as are enjoyed by members of the administrative and technical staff and their families under the Vienna Convention on Diplomatic Relations.

Article IV
Cooperation

The Parties shall fully cooperate with the High Representative and his or her staff, as well as with the international organizations and agencies as provided for Article IX of the General Framework Agreement.

Article V
Final Authority to Interpret

The High Representative is the final authority in theater regarding interpretation of this Agreement on the civilian implementation of the peace settlement.

Article VI
Entry into Force

This Agreement shall enter into force upon signature.

93. ANNEX 11
AGREEMENT ON INTERNATIONAL POLICE TASK FORCE*

The Republic of Bosnia and Herzegovina, the Federation of Bosnia and Herzegovina, and the Republika Srpska ("Parties") have agreed as follows:

---

* Initialled by representatives of the Republic of Bosnia and Herzegovina, the Federation of Bosnia and Herzegovina, and the Republika Srpska.

Article I
Civilian Law Enforcement

1.   As provided in Article III(2)(c) of the Constitution agreed as Annex 4 to the General Framework Agreement, the Parties shall provide a safe and secure environment for all persons in their respective jurisdictions, by maintaining civilian law enforcement agencies operating in accordance with internationally recognized standards and with respect for internationally recognized human rights and fundamental freedoms, and by taking such other measures as appropriate.

2.   To assist them in meeting their obligations, the Parties request that the United Nations establish by a decision of the Security Council, as a UNCIVPOL operation, a U.N. International Police Task Force (IPTF) to carry out, throughout Bosnia and Herzegovina, the program of assistance the elements of which are described in Article III below.

Article II
Establishment of the IPTF

1.   The IPTF shall be autonomous with regard to the execution of its functions under this Agreement. Its activities will be coordinated through the High Representative described in Annex 10 to the General Framework Agreement.

2.   The IPTF will be headed by a Commissioner, who will appointed by the Secretary General of the United Nations in consultation with the Security Council. It shall consist of persons of high moral standing who have experience in law enforcement. The IPTF Commissioner may request and accept personnel, resources, and assistance from states and international and nongovernmental organizations.

3.   The IPTF Commissioner shall receive guidance from the High Representative.

4.   The IPTF Commissioner shall periodically report on matters within his or her responsibility to the High Representative, the Secretary General of the United Nations, and shall provide information to the IFOR Commander and, as he or she deems appropriate, other institutions and agencies.

5.   The IPTF shall at all times act in accordance with internationally recognized standards and with respect for internationally recognized human rights and fundamental freedoms, and shall respect, consistent with the IPTF's responsibilities, the laws and customs of the host country.

6.   The Parties shall accord the IPTF Commissioner, IPTF personnel, and their families the privileges and immunities described in Sections 18 and 19 of the 1946 Convention on the Privileges and Immunities of the United Nations. In

particular, they shall enjoy inviolability, shall not be subject to any form of arrest or detention, and shall have absolute immunity from criminal jurisdiction. IPTF personnel shall remain subject to penalties and sanctions under applicable laws and regulations of the United Nations and other states.

7.   The IPTF and its premises, archives, and other property shall be accorded the same privileges and immunities, including inviolability, as are described in Articles II and III of the 1946 Convention on the Privileges and Immunities of the United Nations.

8.   In order to promote the coordination by the High Representative of IPTF activities with those of other civilian organizations and agencies and of the (IFOR), the IPTF Commissioner or his or her representatives may attend meetings of the Joint Civilian Commission established in Annex 10 to the General Framework Agreement and of the Joint Military Commission established in Annex 1, as well as meetings of their subordinate commissions. The IPTF Commissioner may request that meetings of appropriate commissions be convened to discuss issues within his or her area of responsibility.

Article III

IPTF Assistance Program

1.   IPTF assistance includes the following elements, to be provided in a program designed and implemented by the IPTF Commissioner in accordance with the Security Council decision described in Article I(2):

(a)   monitoring, observing, and inspecting law enforcement activities and facilities, including associated judicial organizations, structures, and proceedings;

(b)   advising law enforcement personnel and forces;

(c)   training law enforcement personnel;

(d)   facilitating, within the IPTF' s mission of assistance, the Parties' law enforcement activities;

(e)   assessing threats to public order and advising on the capability of law enforcement agencies to deal with such threats.

(f)   advising governmental authorities in Bosnia and Herzegovina on the organization of effective civilian law enforcement agencies; and

(g)   assisting by accompanying the Parties' law enforcement personnel as they carry out their responsibilities, as the IPTF deems appropriate.

2.   In addition to the elements of the assistance program forth in paragraph 1, the IPTF will consider, consistent with responsibilities and resources, requests from the Parties or enforcement agencies in Bosnia and Herzegovina for assistance described in paragraph 1.

3. The Parties confirm their particular responsibility to ensure the existence of social conditions for free and fair elections, including the protection of international personnel in Bosnia and Herzegovina in connection with the elections provided for in Annex 3 to the General Framework Agreement. They request the IPTF to give priority to assisting the Parties in carrying out this responsibility.

Article IV
Specific Responsibilities of the Parties

1. The Parties shall cooperate fully with the IPTF and shall so instruct all their law enforcement agencies.

2. Within 30 days after this Agreement enters into force, the Parties shall provide the IPTF Commissioner or his or her designee with information on their law enforcement agencies, including their size, location, and force structure. Upon request of the IPTF Commissioner, they shall provide additional information, including any training, operational, or employment and service records of law enforcement agencies and personnel.

3. The Parties shall not impede the movement of IPTF personnel or in any way hinder, obstruct, or delay them in the performance of their responsibilities. They shall allow IPTF personnel immediate and complete access to any site, person, activity, proceeding, record, or other item or event in Bosnia and Herzegovina as requested by the IPTF in carrying out its responsibilities under this Agreement. This shall include the right to monitor, observe, and inspect any site or facility at which it believes that police, law enforcement, detention, or judicial activities are taking place.

4. Upon request by the IPTF, the Parties shall make available for training qualified personnel, who are expected to take up law enforcement duties immediately following such training.

5. The Parties shall facilitate the operations of the IPTF in Bosnia and Herzegovina, including by the provision of appropriate assistance as requested with regard to transportation, subsistence, accommodations, communications, and other facilities at rates equivalent to those provided for the IFOR under applicable agreements.

Article V
Failure to Cooperate

1. Any obstruction of or interference with IPTF activities, failure or refusal to comply with an IPTF request, or other failure to meet the Parties' responsibilities or other obligations in this Agreement, shall constitute a failure to cooperate with the IPTF.

2.   The IPTF Commissioner will notify the High Representative and inform the IFOR Commander of failures to cooperate with the IPTF. The IPTF Commissioner may request that the High Representative take appropriate steps upon receiving such notifications, including calling such failures to the attention of the Parties, convening the Joint Civilian Commission, and consulting with the United Nations, relevant states, and international organizations on further responses.

Article VI
Human Rights

1.   When IPTF personnel learn of credible information concerning violations of internationally recognized human rights or fundamental freedoms or of the role of law enforcement officials or forces in such violations, they shall provide such information to the Human Rights Commission established in Annex 6 to the General Framework Agreement, the International Tribunal for the Former Yugoslavia, or to other appropriate organizations.

2.   The Parties shall cooperate with investigations of law enforcement forces and officials by the organizations described in paragraph 1.

Article VII
Application

This Agreement applies throughout Bosnia and Herzegovina to law enforcement agencies and personnel of Bosnia and Herzegovina, the Entities, and any agency, subdivision, or instrumentality thereof. Law enforcement agencies are those with a mandate including law enforcement, criminal investigations, public and state security, or detention or judicial activities.

Article VIII
Entry Into Force

This Agreement shall enter into force upon signature.

94. AGREEMENT ON INITIALLING THE GENERAL FRAMEWORK AGREEMENT
FOR PEACE IN BOSNIA AND HERZEGOVINA*

The Republic of Bosnian and Herzegovina, the Republic of Croatia and the
Federal Republic of Yugoslavia ("the Parties"),

Recognizing the need now for a comprehensive settlement to bring an end to
the tragic conflict in the region,

Welcoming the progress achieved during the Peace Proximity Talks held at
Wright-Patterson Air Force Base, Ohio,

Desiring to promote peace and prosperity throughout Bosnia and Herzegovina and the region,

Have agreed as follows:

Article I

The negotiation of the General Framework Agreement for Peace in Bosnia
and Herzegovina and its Annexes has been completed. The Parties, and the Entities that they represent, commit themselves to signature of these Agreements in
Paris in their present form, in accordance with Article III, thus establishing their
entry into force and the date from which the Agreements shall have operative
effect.

Article II

The initialling of each signature block of the General Framework Agreement
for Peace in Bosnia and Herzegovina and its Annexes today hereby expresses the
consent of the Parties, and the Entities that they represent, to be bound by such
Agreements.

Article III

Prior to signature of the General Framework Agreement for Peace in Bosnia
and Herzegovina in Paris, the Annexes may be renumbered, with the necessary
conforming changes made.

Article IV

This Agreement shall enter into force upon signature.

---

* Signed by representatives of the Republic of Bosnia and Herzegovina, the Republic of
Croatia, and the Federal Republic of Yugoslavia.

DONE at Wright-Patterson Air Force Base, Ohio, this 21st day of November 1995, in the English language, in quadruplicate.

95. SIDE-LETTERS

Letter of 20 November 1995 of the Delegation of the Republika of Srpska, Addressed to Slobodan Milošević, Head of the Delegation of the Federal Republic of Yugoslavia*

Dear Mr. President, We write you regarding the Peace Agreement and the documents which are to be initialled at the conclusion of the peace negotiations in Ohio. Since it is requested, in a number of documents prepared for adoption, that the FR of Yugoslavia be the guarantor of the obligations taken by the RS in the peace process, we kindly ask you to assume, on behalf of the FRY, the role of the guarantor that the Republika Srpska shall fulfill all the obligations it took.

Letter of 21 November 1995 of Mate Granic, Minister of Foreign Affairs of the Republic of Croatia, Addressed to Klaus Kinkel, Federal Minister for Foreign Affairs of Germany

Dear Mr. Minister, I refer to the Agreement on the Military Aspects of the Peace Settlement and the Agreement on Inter-Entity Boundary Line and Related Issues, which constitute Annex 1-A and Annex 2 to the General Framework Agreement for Peace in Bosnia and Herzegovina. The Republic of Croatia has endorsed both of these Agreements.

On behalf of the Republic of Croatia, I wish to assure you that the Republic of Croatia shall take all necessary steps, consistent with the sovereignty, territorial integrity and political independence of Bosnia and Herzegovina, to ensure that personnel or organizations in Bosnia and Herzegovina which are under its control or with which it has influence fully respects and comply with the provisions of the aforementioned Annexes.

---

*   Signed by Momčilo Krajišnik, Nikola Koljević and Aleksa Buha.

**Letter of 21 November 1995 of Mate Granic, Minister of Foreign Affairs
of the Republic of Croatia, Addressed to Herve de Charette,
Minister for Foreign Affairs of France**

Dear Mr. Minister, I refer to the Agreement on the Military Aspects of the
Peace Settlement and the Agreement on Inter-Entity Boundary Line and Related
Issues, which constitute Annex 1-A and Annex 2 to the General Framework
Agreement for Peace in Bosnia and Herzegovina. The Republic of Croatia has
endorsed both of these Agreements.

On behalf of the Republic of Croatia, I wish to assure you that the Republic
of Croatia shall take all necessary steps, consistent with the sovereignty, territorial integrity and political independence of Bosnia and Herzegovina, to ensure
that personnel or organizations in Bosnia and Herzegovina which are under its
control or with which it has influence fully respects and comply with the provisions of the aforementioned Annexes.

**Letter of 21 November 1995 of Mate Granic, Minister of Foreign Affairs
of the Republic of Croatia, Addressed to Andre Kozyrev,
Minister for Foreign Affairs of Russia**

Dear Mr. Minister, I refer to the Agreement on the Military Aspects of the
Peace Settlement and the Agreement on Inter-Entity Boundary Line and Related
Issues, which constitute Annex 1-A and Annex 2 to the General Framework
Agreement for Peace in Bosnia and Herzegovina. The Republic of Croatia has
endorsed both of these Agreements.

On behalf of the Republic of Croatia, I wish to assure you that the Republic
of Croatia shall take all necessary steps, consistent with the sovereignty, territorial integrity and political independence of Bosnia and Herzegovina, to ensure
that personnel or organizations in Bosnia and Herzegovina which are under its
control or with which it has influence fully respects and comply with the provisions of the aforementioned Annexes.

**Letter of 21 November 1995 of Mate Granic, Minister of Foreign Affairs
of the Republic of Croatia, Addressed to Malcom Rifkind, QC MP
Secretary for Foreign Affairs of the United Kingdom**

Dear Mr. Secretary, I refer to the Agreement on the Military Aspects of the
Peace Settlement and the Agreement on Inter-Entity Boundary Line and Related
Issues, which constitute Annex 1-A and Annex 2 to the General Framework

Agreement for Peace in Bosnia and Herzegovina. The Republic of Croatia has endorsed both of these Agreements.

On behalf of the Republic of Croatia, I wish to assure you that the Republic of Croatia shall take all necessary steps, consistent with the sovereignty, territorial integrity and political independence of Bosnia and Herzegovina, to ensure that personnel or organizations in Bosnia and Herzegovina which are under its control or with which it has influence fully respects and comply with the provisions of the aforementioned Annexes.

Letter of 21 November 1995 of Mate Granic, Minister of Foreign Affairs of the Republic of Croatia, Addressed to Warren Christopher, Secretary of State of the United States of America

Dear Mr. Secretary, I refer to the Agreement on the Military Aspects of the Peace Settlement and the Agreement on Inter-Entity Boundary Line and Related Issues, which constitute Annex 1-A and Annex 2 to the General Framework Agreement for Peace in Bosnia and Herzegovina. The Republic of Croatia has endorsed both of these Agreements.

On behalf of the Republic of Croatia, I wish to assure you that the Republic of Croatia shall take all necessary steps, consistent with the sovereignty, territorial integrity and political independence of Bosnia and Herzegovina, to ensure that personnel or organizations in Bosnia and Herzegovina which are under its control or with which it has influence fully respects and comply with the provisions of the aforementioned Annexes.

Letter of 21 November 1995 of Milan Milutonovic, Minister of Foreign Affairs of the Federal Republic of Yugoslavia, Addressed to Klaus Kinkel, Federal Minister for Foreign Affairs of Germany

Dear Mr. Minister, I refer to the Agreement on the Military Aspects of the Peace Settlement and the Agreement on Inter-Entity Boundary Line and Related Issues, which constitute Annex 1-A and Annex 2 to the General Framework Agreement for Peace in Bosnia and Herzegovina. The Federal Republic of Yugoslavia has endorsed both of these Agreements.

On behalf of the Federal Republic of Yugoslavia, I wish to assure you that the Federal Republic of Yugoslavia shall take all necessary steps, consistent with the sovereignty, territorial integrity and political independence of Bosnia and Herzegovina, to ensure that the Republika Srpska fully respects and complies with the provisions of the aforementioned Annexes.

Letter of 21 November 1995 of Milan Milutonovic, Minister of Foreign Affairs of the Federal Republic of Yugoslavia, Addressed to Herve de Charette, Minister for Foreign Affairs of France

Dear Mr. Minister, I refer to the Agreement on the Military Aspects of the Peace Settlement and the Agreement on Inter-Entity Boundary Line and Related Issues, which constitute Annex 1-A and Annex 2 to the General Framework Agreement for Peace in Bosnia and Herzegovina. The Federal Republic of Yugoslavia has endorsed both of these Agreements.

On behalf of the Federal Republic of Yugoslavia, I wish to assure you that the Federal Republic of Yugoslavia shall take all necessary steps, consistent with the sovereignty, territorial integrity and political independence of Bosnia and Herzegovina, to ensure that the Republika Srpska fully respects and complies with the provisions of the aforementioned Annexes.

Letter of 21 November 1995 of Milan Milutonovic, Minister of Foreign Affairs of the Federal Republic of Yugoslavia, Addressed to Andre Kozyrev, Minister for Foreign Affairs of Russia

Dear Mr. Minister, I refer to the Agreement on the Military Aspects of the Peace Settlement and the Agreement on Inter-Entity Boundary Line and Related Issues, which constitute Annex 1-A and Annex 2 to the General Framework Agreement for Peace in Bosnia and Herzegovina. The Federal Republic of Yugoslavia has endorsed both of these Agreements.

On behalf of the Federal Republic of Yugoslavia, I wish to assure you that the Federal Republic of Yugoslavia shall take all necessary steps, consistent with the sovereignty, territorial integrity and political independence of Bosnia and Herzegovina, to ensure that the Republika Srpska fully respects and complies with the provisions of the aforementioned Annexes.

Letter of 21 November 1995 of Milan Milutonovic, Minister of Foreign Affairs of the Federal Republic of Yugoslavia, Addressed to Malcolm Rifkind, QC MP, Secretary for Foreign Affairs of the United Kingdom

Dear Mr. Secretary, I refer to the Agreement on the Military Aspects of the Peace Settlement and the Agreement on Inter-Entity Boundary Line and Related Issues, which constitute Annex 1-A and Annex 2 to the General Framework Agreement for Peace in Bosnia and Herzegovina. The Federal Republic of Yugoslavia has endorsed both of these Agreements.

On behalf of the Federal Republic of Yugoslavia, I wish to assure you that the Federal Republic of Yugoslavia shall take all necessary steps, consistent with the sovereignty, territorial integrity and political independence of Bosnia and Herzegovina, to ensure that the Republika Srpska fully respects and complies with the provisions of the aforementioned Annexes.

Letter of 21 November 1995 of Milan Milutonovic, Minister of Foreign Affairs of the Federal Republic of Yugoslavia, Addressed to Warren Christopher, Secretary of State of the United States of America

Dear Mr. Secretary, I refer to the Agreement on the Military Aspects of the Peace Settlement and the Agreement on Inter-Entity Boundary Line and Related Issues, which constitute Annex 1-A and Annex 2 to the General Framework Agreement for Peace in Bosnia and Herzegovina. The Federal Republic of Yugoslavia has endorsed both of these Agreements.

On behalf of the Federal Republic of Yugoslavia, I wish to assure you that the Federal Republic of Yugoslavia shall take all necessary steps, consistent with the sovereignty, territorial integrity and political independence of Bosnia and Herzegovina, to ensure that the Republika Srpska fully respects and complies with the provisions of the aforementioned Annexes.

Letter of 21 November 1995 of Mate Granic, Minister of Foreign Affairs of the Republic of Croatia, Addressed to Boutros Boutros-Ghali, Secretary General of the United Nations

Dear Mr. Secretary General, I refer to the Agreement on the Military Aspects of the Peace Settlement attached as Annex 1-A to the General Framework Agreement for Peace in Bosnia and Herzegovina. Recognizing the importance of a comprehensive peace settlement to bring an end to the tragic conflict in the region, I have the honor to provide the following undertaking to promote achievement of that objective.

On behalf of the Republic of Croatia, I wish to assure the United Nations that, in order to facilitate accomplishment of the mission of the multinational military Implementation Force ("IFOR") referred to in Annex 1-A, the Republic of Croatia shall strictly refrain from introducing into or otherwise maintaining in Bosnia and Herzegovina any armed forces or other personnel with military capability.

Letter of 21 November 1995 of Mate Granic, Minister of Foreign Affairs of the Republic of Croatia, Addressed to Sergio Silvio Balanzino, Acting Secretary General of the North Atlantic Treaty Organization

Dear Mr. Secretary General, I refer to the Agreement on the Military Aspects of the Peace Settlement attached as Annex 1-A to the General Framework Agreement for Peace in Bosnia and Herzegovina. Recognizing the importance of a comprehensive peace settlement to bring an end to the tragic conflict in the region, I have the honor to provide the following undertaking to promote achievement of that objective.

On behalf of the Republic of Croatia, I wish to assure the North Atlantic Treaty Organization that, in order to facilitate accomplishment of the mission of the multinational military Implementation Force ("IFOR") referred to in Annex 1-A, the Republic of Croatia shall strictly refrain from introducing into or otherwise maintaining in Bosnia and Herzegovina any armed forces or other personnel with military capability.

Letter of 21 November 1995 of Milan Milutonovic, Minister of Foreign Affairs of the Federal Republic of Yugoslavia, Addressed to Boutros Boutros-Ghali, Secretary General of the United Nations

Dear Mr. Secretary General, I refer to the Agreement on the Military Aspects of the Peace Settlement attached as Annex 1-A to the General Framework Agreement for Peace in Bosnia and Herzegovina. Recognizing the importance of a comprehensive peace settlement to bring an end to the tragic conflict in the region, I have the honor to provide the following undertaking to promote achievement of that objective.

On behalf of the Federal Republic of Yugoslavia, I wish to assure the United Nations that, in order to facilitate accomplishment of the mission of the multinational military Implementation Force ("IFOR") referred to in Annex 1-A, the Federal Republic of Yugoslavia shall strictly refrain from introducing into or otherwise maintaining in Bosnia and Herzegovina any armed forces or other personnel with military capability.

Letter of 21 November 1995 of Milan Milutonovic, Minister of Foreign Affairs of the Federal Republic of Yugoslavia, Addressed to Sergio Silvio Balanzino, Acting Secretary General of the North Atlantic Treaty Organization

Dear Mr. Secretary General, I refer to the Agreement on the Military Aspects of the Peace Settlement attached as Annex 1-A to the General Framework Agreement for Peace in Bosnia and Herzegovina. Recognizing the importance of a comprehensive peace settlement to bring an end to the tragic conflict in the region, I have the honor to provide the following undertaking to promote achievement of that objective.

On behalf of the Federal Republic of Yugoslavia, I wish to assure the North Atlantic Treaty Organization that, in order to facilitate accomplishment of the mission of the multinational military Implementation Force ("IFOR") referred to in Annex 1-A, the Federal Republic of Yugoslavia shall strictly refrain from introducing into or otherwise maintaining in Bosnia and Herzegovina any armed forces or other personnel with military capability.

Letter of 21 November 1995 of Alija Izetbegovic, President of the Republic of Bosnia and Herzegovina, Addressed to Warren Christopher, Secretary of State of the United States of America

Dear Mr. Secretary, Upon initialing of the General Framework Agreement for Peace in Bosnia and Herzegovina, I will undertake several confidence-building measures to develop ties between the Federal Republic of Yugoslavia and Bosnia and Herzegovina and to build support for the peace settlement. Toward these important ends, I am pleased to make the following commitments on behalf of the government and people of Bosnia and Herzegovina.

Release Of All Detained Non-Combatants

All detained non-combatants will be released immediately from work brigade, detention site or other formal or informal custody, as required by UN Security Council Resolution 1019 of November 9, 1995. Specifically, pursuant to the resolution, all detention camps throughout the territory of Bosnia and Herzegovina will be immediately closed, and representatives of the International Committee of the Red Cross shall be permitted (I) to register any persons detained against their will, and (II) to have access to any site it may deem important.

Customs Union

As a matter of priority, my government will participate in senior expert-level meetings to pursue the harmonization of customs policies toward establishment of a customs union between the two countries.

Hot Line

With technical assistance as offered by the United States, my government will establish a direct, secure telephone link between the Presidency of Bosnia and Herzegovina and the Presidency of the Federal Republic of Yugoslavia.

Direct Flights

My government will grant permission through appropriate national and international agencies for direct flights between Sarajevo and Belgrade. I understand that interested countries intend to encourage international carriers to add these routes to their schedule.

High-Level Visits

I undertake to have my government organize a program of high-level visits to Sarajevo and other important sites for officials and other distinguished persons from the Federal Republic of Yugoslavia. I understand that Ambassadors from Contact Group and other interested countries will be available to participate as appropriate to help sustain international and domestic interest in the strengthening of ties between the two countries.

Economic Development

My government will take the steps necessary to establish a bilateral Commission on Economic Integration and Infrastructure Development for bilateral cooperation on nationally- and internationally-funded projects affecting both countries. In particular, the Commission will promote co-financing, joint ventures, and appropriate multilateral arrangements to develop the transportation, energy, and communications sectors in both countries.

Chamber of Commerce

My government will actively seek the establishment of a joint Chamber of Commerce to promote trade and economic development in both countries by coordinating, where appropriate, the activities of the respective Chambers of Commerce in each country and by promoting ties with Chambers of Commerce in other countries.

Cultural and Educational Exchange

My government will actively develop student exchanges between the two countries, as well as nominate students to participate in joint exchange programs with the United States. Similarly, with support from the United States and other interested governments, my government will promote visits between the Federal Republic of Yugoslavia and Bosnia and Herzegovina for scientific, cultural, sporting, youth and similar groups. We will fully participate in the establishment and operation of a bilateral Commission on Cultural and Educational Exchange to develop programs in these areas.

Military Exchanges

In the context of regional arms control and related military confidence-building measures agreed elsewhere by Bosnia and Herzegovina and the Federal Republic of Yugoslavia, my government will promote familiarization and staff exchange visits for officers from the armed forces of the other country. These visits will explore, among other measures, the establishment of liaison offices to each other's respective defense chiefs.

Commission of Inquiry

My government will actively support the establishment and activities of an international commission of inquiry into the recent conflict in the former Yugoslavia. This will include participation by the governments of the states involved, as well as distinguished international experts to be named by agreement among the Republics of former Yugoslavia. The Commission's mandate will be to conduct fact-finding and other necessary studies into the causes, conduct, and consequences of the recent conflict on as broad and objective a basis as possible, and to issue a report thereon, to be made available to all interested countries and organizations. My government will cooperate fully with this Commission.

**Letter of 21 November 1995 of Slobodan Milosevic,
Addressed to Warren Christopher,
Secretary of State of the United States of America**

Dear Mr. Secretary, Upon initialing of the General Framework Agreement for Peace in Bosnia and Herzegovina, I will undertake several confidence-building measures to develop ties between the Federal Republic of Yugoslavia and Bosnia and Herzegovina and to build support for the peace settlement. Toward these important ends, I am pleased to make the following commitments on behalf of the government and people of the Federal Republic of Yugoslavia.

Release Of All Detained Non-Combatants

All detained non-combatants will be released immediately from work brigade, detention site or other formal or informal custody, as required by UN Security Council Resolution 1019 of November 9, 1995. Specifically, pursuant to the resolution, all detention camps throughout the territory of Bosnia and Herzegovina will be immediately closed, and representatives of the International Committee of the Red Cross shall be permitted (I) to register any persons detained against their will, and (II) to have access to any site it may deem important.

Customs Union

As a matter of priority, my government will participate in senior expert-level meetings to pursue the harmonization of customs policies toward establishment of a customs union between the two countries.

Hot Line

With technical assistance as offered by the United States, my government will establish a direct, secure telephone link between the Presidency of Bosnia and Herzegovina and the Presidency of the Federal Republic of Yugoslavia.

Direct Flights

My government will grant permission through appropriate national and international agencies for direct flights between Sarajevo and Belgrade. I understand that interested countries intend to encourage international carriers to add these routes to their schedule.

High-Level Visits

I undertake to have my government organize a program of high-level visits to Belgrade and other important sites for officials and other distinguished persons from Bosnia and Herzegovina. I understand that Ambassadors from Contact Group and other interested countries will be available to participate as appropriate to help sustain international and domestic interest in the strengthening of ties between the two countries.

Economic Development

My government will take the steps necessary to establish a bilateral Commission on Economic Integration and Infrastructure Development for bilateral cooperation on nationally- and internationally-funded projects affecting both countries. In particular, the Commission will promote co-financing, joint ventures, and appropriate multilateral arrangements to develop the transportation, energy, and communications sectors in both countries.

Chamber of Commerce

My government will actively seek the establishment of a joint Chamber of Commerce to promote trade and economic development in both countries by coordinating, where appropriate, the activities of the respective Chambers of Commerce in each country and by promoting ties with Chambers of Commerce in other countries.

Cultural and Educational Exchange

My government will actively develop student exchanges between the two countries, as well as nominate students to participate in joint exchange programs with the United States. Similarly, with support from the United States and other interested governments, my government will promote visits between the Federal Republic of Yugoslavia and Bosnia and Herzegovina for scientific, cultural, sporting, youth and similar groups. We will fully participate in the establishment and operation of a bilateral Commission on Cultural and Educational Exchange to develop programs in these areas.

Military Exchanges

In the context of regional arms control and related military confidence-building measures agreed elsewhere by Bosnia and Herzegovina and the Federal Republic of Yugoslavia, my government will promote familiarization and staff exchange visits for officers from the armed forces of the other country. These visits will explore, among other measures, the establishment of liaison offices to each other's respective defense chiefs.

Commission of Inquiry

My government will actively support the establishment and activities of an international commission of inquiry into the recent conflict in the former Yugoslavia. This will include participation by the governments of the states involved, as well as distinguished international experts to be named by agreement among the Republics of former Yugoslavia. The Commission's mandate will be to conduct fact-finding and other necessary studies into the causes, conduct, and consequences of the recent conflict on as broad and objective a basis as possible, and to issue a report thereon, to be made available to all interested countries and organizations. My government will cooperate fully with this Commission.

Letter of 21 November 1995 of Alija Izetbegovic, President of the Republic of Bosnia and Herzegovina, Addressed to Slobodan Milosevic, President of the Republic of Serbia*

Dear Mr. President,I refer to the General Framework Agreement for Peace in Bosnia and Herzegovina and in particular its Annex 9 on Public Corporations. My government intends to see established passenger and freight rail service on a regular schedule along the rail line extending through Bosanska Krupa, Bosanska Novi, Bosanska Dubica, and Bosanska Gradiska in a cooperative arrangement that accords with Article II of Annex 9. My government will support and facilitate as appropriate the functioning of this railroad.

---

* Cc to Warren Christopher, Secretary of State of the United States of America.

Letter of 21 November 1995 of Slobodan Milosevic, Addressed to Alija Izetbegovic, President of the Republic of Bosnia and Herzegovina*

Dear Mr. President,I refer to the General Framework Agreement for Peace in Bosnia and Herzegovina and in particular its Annex 9 on Public Corporations. As head of the joint delegation of the Federal Republic of Yugoslavia and of the Republika Srpska, I state our intention to see established passenger and freight rail service on a regular schedule along the rail line extending through Bosanska Krupa, Bosanska Novi, Bosanska Dubica, and Bosanska Gradiska in a cooperative arrangement that accords with Article II of Annex 9. Those governments will support and facilitate as appropriate the functioning of this railroad.

96. CONCLUDING STATEMENT BY THE PARTICIPANTS IN THE BOSNIA PROXIMITY PEACE TALKS

The Bosnia Proximity Peace Talks were held at Wright-Patterson Air Force Base, Ohio, from November 1 to November 20, 1995, under the auspices of the Contact Group.

During these talks, delegations from the Republic of Bosnia and Herzegovina, the Republic of Croatia, and the Federal Republic of Yugoslavia engaged in hours of discussions aimed at reaching a peaceful settlement to the conflict in Bosnia and Herzegovina.

As a result of these constructive and difficult negotiations, the parties reached agreement on the terms of a General Framework Agreement and the following Annexes thereto:

Annex 1A: Military Aspects of the Peace Settlement
Annex 1B: Regional Stabilization
Annex 2:   Inter-Entity Boundary
Annex 3:   Elections
Annex 4:   Constitution of Bosnia and Herzegovina
Annex 5:   Arbitration
Annex 6:   Human Rights
Annex 7:   Refugees and Displaced Persons
Annex 8:   Commission to Preserve National Monuments

---

*   Cc to Warren Christopher, Secretary of State of the United States of America.

Annex 9: Bosnia and Herzegovina Public Corporations
Annex 10: Civilian Implementation
Annex 11: International Police Task Force

On November 20, President Izetbegovic, for the Republic of Bosnia and Herzegovina, President Tudjman, for the Republic of Croatia, President Milosevic, for the Republic of Yugoslavia and for the Republic of Srpska, and President Zubak, for the Federation of Bosnia and Herzegovina, initialled the Framework Agreement and its Annexes, thus establishing the initialled documents as definitive, and signifying their consent to be bound thereby and their commitment to sign the Framework Agreement and its Annexes without delay.

The parties agree to reconvene in Paris under the auspices of the Contact Group to sign the Framework Agreement and its annexes shortly.

As evidence of their common endeavor to bring peace to the region, the participants stress the utmost importance of maintaining the cease-fire, of cooperating with all humanitarian and other organizations in Bosnia and Herzegovina, and of ensuring the safety and freedom of movement of personnel of such organizations. In particular, the delegations of the Republic of Bosnia and Herzegovina, the Republic of Croatia, the Federal Republic of Yugoslavia (also on behalf of the Republic of Srpska), and the Federation of Bosnia and Herzegovina have committed themselves to refrain from any hostile act against or interference with members of United Nations Protections Force, the international force to be deployed in accordance with the General Framework Agreement, and personnel of humanitarian organizations and agencies. They specifically commit themselves to assist in locating the French pilots missing in Bosnia and Herzegovina and ensure their immediate and safe return.

The participants express their deep appreciation to the Government and the people of the United States of America for the hospitality extended to them throughout the talks.

5. PEACEMAKING IN CROATIA

A. THE VANCE PLAN

Editor's Note: The United Nations' plan for dealing with the United Nations Protected and Related Areas in the Republic of Croatia, known as the "Vance Plan", is the basis for peacemaking and peacekeeping activities in the area. The text of the "Vance Plan" is reproduced below.

97. CONCEPT FOR A UNITED NATIONS PEACE-KEEPING OPERATION IN YUGOSLAVIA*

GENERAL PRINCIPLES

1. A United Nations peace-keeping operation in Yugoslavia would be an interim arrangement to create the conditions of peace and security required for the negotiation of an overall settlement of the Yugoslav crisis. It would not prejudge the outcome of such negotiations.
2. The operation would be established by the United Nations Security Council, acting on a recommendation by the Secretary-General. Before making such a recommendation, the Secretary-General would need to be satisfied that all concerned in the conflict were, in a serious and sustained way, abiding by the arrangements, including an unconditional ceasefire, agreed at Geneva on 23 November 1991. He would also need to receive, through his Personal Envoy, categorical assurances that all the Yugoslav parties concerned in the conflict

---

* As Discussed with Yugoslav Leaders by the Honourable Cyrus R. Vance, Personal Envoy of the Secretary-General and Marrack Goulding, Under-Secretary-General for Special Political Affairs, November/December 1991.

447

accepted the concepts which he intended to recommend to the Security Council and that they would provide all necessary assistance and cooperation to enable the peace-keeping operation to carry out its functions.

3. The military and police personnel required for the operation would be contributed, on a voluntary basis in response to a request from the Secretary-General, by the Government of member States of the United Nations. The contributing States would be approved by the Security Council, in the recommendation of the Secretary-General after consultation with the Yugoslav parties.

4. All members of the peace-keeping operation would be under the operational command of the Secretary-General and would not be permitted to receive operational orders for the national authorities. They would be required to be completely impartial between the various parties to the conflict. Those personnel who were armed would have standing instructions to use force to the minimum extent necessary and normally only in self-defence.

5. In accordance with its normal practice, the Security Council would probably establish the operation for an initial period of six months. Subject to the Council's agreement, the operation would remain in Yugoslavia until a negotiated settlement of the conflict was achieved. The Secretary-General would submit regular reports to the Security Council, normally every six months. These reports would contain his recommendations on extension of the operation's mandate.

6. The operation would be financed collectively by the member States of the United Nations. But the various Yugoslav authorities would be expected to make available to the United Nations, free of charge, as much as possible of the accommodation and other facilities and supplies, such as food and fuel, that would be required by the operation. They would also be asked to conclude with the United Nations agreements concerning the privileges, immunities and facilities which the operation and its members would need in order to carry out their functions, especially complete freedom of movement and communications.

BASIC CONCEPT

7. United Nations troops and police monitors would be deployed in certain areas in Croatia, designated as "United Nations Protected Areas". These areas would be demilitarized; all armed forces in them would be either withdrawn or disbanded. The role of the United Nations troops would be to ensure that the areas remained demilitarized and that all persons residing in them were protected from fear of armed attack. The role of the United Nations police monitors would be to ensure that the local police forces carried out their duties without discrimination

against persons of any nationality or abusing anyone's human rights. As the United Nations Force assumed its responsibilities in the United Nations Protected Areas (UNPAs), all JNA forces deployed elsewhere in Croatia would be relocated outside that republic. The United Nations Force would also, as appropriated, assist the humanitarian agencies of the United Nations in the return of all displaced persons who so desired to their homes in the UNPAs.

THE UNITED NATIONS PROTECTED AREAS

8. The UNPAs would be areas in Croatia in which the Secretary-General judged that special arrangements were required during an interim period to ensure that a lasting ceasefire was maintained. They would be areas in which Serbs constitute the majority or a substantial minority of the population and where intercommunal tensions have led to armed conflict in the recent past. As already stated, the special arrangements in these areas would be of an interim nature and would not prejudge the outcome of political negotiations for a comprehensive settlement of the Yugoslav crisis.

9. There would be three UNPAs: Eastern Slavonia, Western Slavonia and Krajina. They would comprise the following *opstina* or parts of *opstina*:

Eastern Slavonia:
Beli Manastir;
Those parts of Osijek which lie east of Osijek City;
Vukovar;
Certain villages in the extreme eastern part of Vinkovci.

Western Slavonia:
Grubisno Polje;
Daruvar;
Pakrac;
The western parts of Nova Gradiska;
The eastern part of Novska.

Krajina:
Kostajnica;
Petrinja;
Dvor;
Glina;
Vrgin Most;

Vojnic;
Slunj;
Titova Korenica;
Donji Lapac;
Gracac;
Obrovac;
Benkovac;
Knin.

Before deployment of the Force began, the exact boundaries of the UNPAs would be decided by an advance party of the United Nations Force, after consulting local leaders.

THE DEPLOYMENT AND FUNCTIONS OF THE UNITED NATIONS FORCE

10. The functions of protecting the inhabitants of the UNPAs would be shared between the United Nations Force's infantry units and its civilian police monitors. The infantry would ensure that the UNPAs remained demilitarized. The police monitors would ensure that the local police carried out their duties without discrimination against any nationality and with full respect for the human rights of all residents of the UNPAs.

11. The infantry units would be deployed throughout the UNPAs. They would be lightly armed but would use armoured personnel carriers and helicopters. They would control access to the UNPAs by establishing check-points on all roads and principal tracks leading into them and at important junctions inside them. At these check-points they would stop and, if necessary, search vehicles and individuals to ensure that no military formations or armed groups entered the UNPAs and that no weapons, ammunition, explosives or other military equipment were brought into them. They would patrol extensively inside the UNPAs on foot, and by vehicle and helicopter. They would also investigate any complaints made to them about violations of the demilitarized status of the UNPAs. Any confirmed violations would be taken up with the offending party and would, if necessary, be reported by the Secretary-General to the Security Council. If serious tension were to develop between nationalities in a UNPA, the United Nations Force would interpose itself between the two sides in order to prevent hostilities.

12. The civilian police monitors would also be deployed throughout the UNPAs. They would be unarmed. They would have no executive responsibility for the maintenance of public order but they would closely monitor the work of the local

police forces. To this end, they would be re-located with police headquarters in each region and *opstina* and would accompany the local police on their patrols and in their performance of their other duties. They would investigate any complaints of discrimination or other abuse of human rights and would report to the Chief of the United Nations Force any confirmed cases of discrimination or abuses. They would require free and immediate access to all premises and facilities of, or under the control of, the local police forces.

13. The United Nations Force would also include a group of military observers. They would be unarmed, in accordance with normal United Nations practice. They would initially be deployed in the UNPAs to verify the demilitarization of those areas. As soon as demilitarization had been effected, the military observers would be transferred to parts of Bosnia and Herzegovina adjacent to Croatia. Their functions there would be to patrol extensively, to liaise with the local authorities and to warn the Chief of the United Nations Force if inter-communal tension threatened to disturb the peace and tranquillity established by the Force in the UNPAs. Their good offices would be available to help to resolve local difficulties and to investigate allegations of inter-communal tension or aggression. The exact locations in which the military observers would operate would be decided by the advance party of the United Nations Force, after consulting local authorities. There would also be a small detachment of military observers at Dubrovnik.

14. The military and police personnel of the United Nations Force would arrive in Yugoslavia as soon as possible after the Security Council decided to establish the Force. They would be deployed simultaneously in all three UNPAs. The Force's assumption of responsibility for the protection of these areas would be synchronized with the demilitarization process. To this end, close coordination would be required with the commanders of the forces currently deployed in each of the UNPAs and agreed timetables would be established in order to link deployment of the United Nations Force with the demilitarization of each area.

DEMILITARIZATION OF THE UNPAS

15. On the basis of the agreed timetables, demilitarization of the UNPAs would be implemented as rapidly as possible, in the following way:

(a) All units and personnel of the Yugoslav National Army (JNA) and the Croatian National Guard, as well as any Territorial Defence units or personnel not based in the UNPAs, would be withdrawn from them.

(b)   All Territorial Defence units and personnel based in the UNPAs would be disbanded and demobilized. Disbandment would involve the temporary dissolutions of the units' command structures. Demobilization would mean that the personnel involved would cease to wear any uniform or carry weapons, though they could continue to be paid by the local authorities.

(c)   The weapons of the Territorial Defence units and personnel based in the UNPAs would be handed over to units of JNA or the Croatian National Guard, as the case might be, before those units withdrew from the UNPAs.

Alternatively, they could be handed over to the United Nations Force for safe custody during the interim period, if that arrangement was preferred by the units concerned.

(d)   All paramilitary, irregular or volunteer units or personnel would either be withdrawn from the UNPAs or, if resident in them, be disbanded and demobilized.

16. It would be the responsibility of each unit, before it withdrew or was disbanded, to remove any mines which it had laid while deployed in the UNPAs.

17. The implementation of the above arrangements for demilitarization of the UNPAs would be verified by the United Nations Force.

DECLARATION OF THE YUGOSLAV NATIONAL ARMY

18. In parallel with the assumption by the United Nations Force of its protective functions in the UNPAs, any JNA units deployed elsewhere in Croatia would be relocated to places outside that republic. A timetable for this relocation would be agreed between the Chief of the United Nations Force and the Federal Secretary for National Defence of the Socialist Federal Republic of Yugoslavia. All Serbian territory, paramilitary, irregular and volunteer units (other than those disbanded and demobilized in the UNPAs) would similarly withdraw from Croatia. These withdrawals would be verified by the military observers of the United Nations Force.

LOCAL POLICE FORCES

19. The maintenance of public order in the UNPAs would be the responsibility of local police forces who would carry only side-arms. Each of these forces would be formed from residents of the UNPA in question, in proportions reflect-

ing the national composition of the population which lived in it before the recent hostilities. The local police forces would be responsible to the existing *opstina* councils in the UNPAs. Any existing regional police structures would remain in place, provided that they were consistent with the principle described above concerning the national composition of the local police forces.

RETURN OF DISPLACED PERSONS TO THEIR HOMES

20. In accordance with established international principles, the United Nations policy is to facilitate the return to their homes of all persons displaced by the recent hostilities who so desire. The lead in this matter is being taken by he humanitarian agencies of the United Nations. If a United Nations Force were established in Yugoslavia, it would provide all appropriate support to this effort in the UNPAs. The United Nations police monitors would have an especially important role in this regard.

ORGANIZATION OF A UNITED NATIONS FORCE

21. If peace-keeping operation were established to carry out the above-described functions, it would be commanded by a civilian Chief of Mission who would receive his instructions from, and report to the Secretary-General of the United Nations. As already stated, the Secretary-General would himself report regularly to the Security Council whose guidance he would seek if any difficulties arose in implementation of the Force's mandate. Under the authority of the Chief of Mission, there would be a Force Commander, with the rank of Major General, who would command the military elements, and a Police Commissioner, who would command the police monitors. The headquarters of the Force would be located at Banja Luka, with sub-offices at Belgrade and Zagreb.

22. To carry out the functions described above, the Force would require approximately 10 infantry battalions, 100 military observers and 500 police monitors, together with the necessary civilians and military support personnel. This would indicate a strength of somewhat over 10,000 persons.

B. IMPROVEMENT OF RELATIONS BETWEEN THE REPUBLIC OF CROATIA AND THE FEDERAL REPUBLIC OF YUGOSLAVIA (SERBIA AND MONTENEGRO)

Editor's Note: Under the auspices of the Co-Chairmen, important statements and declarations were made by leaders of the Republic of Croatia and the Federal Republic of Yugoslavia (Serbia and Montenegro) on the improvement of relations between their countries. Some of these statements and declarations are reproduced below.

98. BELGRADE JOINT COMMUNIQUE OF 11 SEPTEMBER 1992[*]

I

We have today reaffirmed our total commitment to the decision taken in London at the International Conference on the Former Yugoslavia, in particular that all outstanding issues should be resolved by peaceful means, on the basis of existing borders, and in a process of urgent and continuing negotiations.

II

Concerning Bosnia and Herzegovina, we have agreed on the following practical steps and objectives:

a) There should be strict observation of the commitments to the collection and supervision of heavy weapons by the agreed expiration date of September 12, 1992;
b) The provision of power and water to Sarajevo, under international management, should be urgently agreed;
c) Every party on the ground must not only commit itself, but take all practical steps, to bring the earliest possible end to all hostilities in and around Sarajevo;
d) We welcome the imminent resumption of talks, without preconditions, on constitutional arrangements for Bosnia and Herzegovina with the participation of all parties. These will take place in Geneva, in a continuous and uninterrupted process, until full agreement is reached;

---

[*] Issued by FRY President Dobrica Cosic and FRY Prime Minister Milan Panic, and witnessed by Co-Chairmen Cyrus R. Vance and David L. Owen.

e) We agree on the desirability of stationing observers on the borders of States neighbouring Bosnia and Herzegovina, as requested by Prime Minister Panic;

f) An agreement in principle has been achieved regarding the placing of observers at military airfields, and a definitive agreement will be reached after consulting the United Nations and Governments concerned.

III

With respect to humanitarian issues:

a) We declare our total condemnation of all practices related to "ethnic cleansing", and commit ourselves to helping reverse that which has already happened;

b) We agree that all statements or commitments made under duress, particularly those relating to land and property, are wholly null and void;

c) We urge all concerned parties to cooperate fully, promptly and unconditionally with current efforts, in particular by the ICRC and the UNHCR, to free all detainees, to close all detention centres and to secure safe passage to former detainees to secure and safe areas;

d) We further urge all parties to facilitate the safe delivery of all humanitarian assistance;

e) We strongly support the efforts of all agencies, local and international, to relieve the plight of displaced persons in all territories of the former Yugoslavia.

IV

With respect to relations with Croatia:

a) We welcome the agreement on the imminent reopening of the road between Belgrade and Zagreb and its symbolic designation as a "Road of Peace";

b) We are committed to make all efforts to improve security around Maslenica Bridge so that repairs can be effected and the bridge reopened for traffic as soon as possible;

c) We agree that the status of the "Yugoslav Pipeline" should be the subject of urgent discussion, in the framework of the International Conference's Working Groups;

d) We welcome President Cosic's offer to the Presidents of Croatia, Macedonia and Slovenia to establish mixed committees to normalize and promote economic and practical cooperation. The International Conference's Working Groups on Economic Relations and on Succession Issues will usefully contribute to this work;

e) An agreement in principle has been achieved regarding the Prevlaka Peninsula. A definitive agreement will be reached after consulting the UN Secretary-General, the UN Security Council and the concerned Governments;

f) We note the importance of the work of the Joint Commission established by UNPROFOR to deal with issues related to the "Pink Zones" and urge intensified cooperation with those efforts;

g) We also call on all parties to adhere strictly to the United Nations peacekeeping plan, and in particular to support UNPROFOR's efforts in the Protected Areas to eliminate illegal activities of irregular and para-military formations and criminal elements, both Serbian and Croatian;

h) Given its importance in the provision of water and power to the region, we recognize the urgent need to reach agreement on problems relating to the Peruca Dam.

V

We pledge our mutual cooperation in order to steadily advance the peace process, to reduce the level of violence and curb the flow of arms. We pledge ourselves to swiftly implement the decisions of the International Conference on the Former Yugoslavia.

99. JOINT DECLARATION OF 30 SEPTEMBER 1992[*]

Meeting under the auspices of the Co-Chairmen of the International Conference of the Former Yugoslavia in Geneva, the undersigned Presidents wish to announce the following:

1. The two Presidents reaffirmed the commitments of the International Conference in London on the inviolability of existing borders, other than through

---

[*] Issued in Geneva by President Dobrica Cosic of the FRY and President Franjo Tudjman of the Republic of Croatia, and witnessed by Co-Chairmen Cyrus R. Vance and David L. Owen.

changes reached by peaceful agreement, and agreed to intensify work towards the normalisation of relations between the Federal Republic of Yugoslavia and the Republic of Croatia, on the basis of mutual recognition. All questions concerning succession to the former SFRY will be resolved within the framework of the International Conference or, as appropriate, bilaterally.

2. Authorities of the Republic of Croatia and the Federal Republic of Yugoslavia, in close collaboration with the United Nations Protection Force, will undertake urgent, joint measures to ensure the peaceful return to their homes in the United Nations Protected Areas of all persons displaced therefrom who so wish. To that end they propose the prompt establishment of a quadripartite mechanism - consisting of authorities of the Government of Croatia, local Serb representatives, representatives of UNPROFOR and the UNHCR - to assure that this process moves forward. Equally, the Serb and Croat people formerly residing on the territory of the Republic of Croatia and the Federal Republic of Yugoslavia should have the right to return in peace to their former homes. Agreement was reached with regard to more resolute action concerning the return of displaced persons to their homes, and to allowing for a voluntary and human resettlement of those persons wishing to do so between the two States.

3. The two Presidents agree that the Yugoslav Army will leave Prevlaka by October 20, 1992 in accordance with the Vance Plan. Security in the area will be resolved by demilitarization and the deployment of UN Monitors. The overall security of Boka Kotorska and Dubrovnik will be resolved through subsequent negotiations.

4. The two Presidents agree to establish a Joint Interstate Committee for the consideration of all open issues and for the normalisation of relations between the sovereign Republic of Croatia and the Federal Republic of Yugoslavia. In order that a durable peace may be established as soon as possible, particular attention will be given to normalising traffic and economic links.

5. The two Presidents confirm their conviction that all problems between their two states must be settled peacefully. They pledge their best efforts to this end. In that connection, they will exert all their influence towards a just, peaceful solution of the current crisis enveloping Bosnia and Herzegovina.

6. The two Presidents declare their total condemnation of all practices related to "ethnic cleansing", and commit themselves to helping reverse that which has already happened. They also declare that all statements or commitments made under duress, particularly those relating to land and property, are wholly null and void. They urge all concerned parties to cooperate fully, promptly and unconditionally with current efforts, in particular by the ICRC and the UNHCR, to free all detainees, close all detention centres, and assure

safe passage to former detainees to secure and safe areas. They further urge all parties to facilitate the safe delivery of all humanitarian assistance.

7. The two Presidents welcome the early stationing of international observers on airfields in their respective countries as a confidence-building measure.

8. The two Presidents agree to meet again on October 20 with the Co-Chairmen. They express their gratitude to the Co-Chairmen for convening today's meeting.

100. STATEMENT OF 30 SEPTEMBER 1992 BY THE CO-CHAIRMEN ON THE ESTABLISHMENT OF THE MIXED MILITARY WORKING GROUP IN SARAJEVO*

The Co-Chairmen have been pursuing discussion with the delegations participating in the talks on Bosnia and Herzegovina to bring about, as part of the efforts to reach an overall cessation of hostilities in the country, the demilitarization of Sarajevo and the cessation of hostilities, it being understood that the search for future constitutional arrangements for Bosnia and Herzegovina will continue within the framework of the International Conference on the former Yugoslavia.

The delegations have agreed that discussion will commence immediately involving their military commanders and local authorities, meeting under the good offices of UNPROFOR and the Geneva Conference.

---

* Issued by the Co-Chairmen.

C. CEASEFIRE AGREEMENTS

Editor's Note: On 22 January 1993, hostilities re-erupted. In the light of Security Council Resolutions calling for a cessation of hostilities, and for a return to the situation obtained before 22 January 1993, the Co-Chairmen and other officials of the Conference made pain-staking efforts to bring about a cessation of hostilities. On 15-16 July, an Agreement was concluded between the two sides but it was not followed up by the Croatian side. The text of this Agreement is reproduced below. It took until 29 March 1994 to get the parties to agree. The text of the Ceasefire Agreement of 29 March 1994 is reproduced below.

101. CEASEFIRE AGREEMENT OF 15-16 JULY 1993

1. There will be no Croatian armed forces or police in the areas specified on the attached map after 31 July 1993.
2. UNPROFOR shall move into the areas specified on the attached map.
3. In the villages of Islam Groki, Smokovic and Kasio, Serb police together with UNCIVPOL will be present, the number of Serb police shall be agreed with UNPROFOR.
4. With the withdrawal of the Croatian armed forces and police according to point one, Maslenica Bridge, Zemunik Airport and Peruca Dam shall be under the exclusive control of UNPROFOR. The building of the pontoon bridge may proceed after the signature of this agreement by both sides.
5. Both sides agree to intensify their efforts to reach a negotiated solution to all problems existing between them, starting with a ceasefire agreement to be negotiated by UNPROFOR.

102. CEASEFIRE AGREEMENT OF 29 MARCH 1994[*]

The parties signing this document agree that all armed hostilities between the parties should end immediately and that a ceasefire on all contact lines existing between the parties on 29 March 1994, hereafter referred to as the Contact Line, should be fully respected from 0900 hours 04 April 1994.

In order to achieve and assure a lasting cessation of hostilities, the parties have agreed to accept and comply with the latter and spirit of the following paragraphs:

---

[*] Signed by H. Sarinic and D. Rakic; and, as witnesses, by K. Eide, G. Ahrens, and B. De Lapresle.

1. All armed hostilities shall end immediately and a ceasefire on the Contact Line will start at 0900 hours on 04 April 1994.

2. From the date of the signature of this Agreement, the tactical situation of the forces deployed on the Contact Line and within 10 km of that line in either direction shall be frozen, and no movement of units shall take place within the area so defined except in execution of this Agreement or as authorised in advance by UNPROFOR. Transit through the area by units with more than three vehicles shall be notified to UNPROFOR during the first 14 days after the signature of this agreement.

3. Not later than 0900 hours 15 April, all indirect fire weapons shall be deployed out of range of the Lines of Separation (as defined in paragraph 4 below): mortars and AA-guns not less than 10 km, artillery and tanks not less than 20 km. As an exception some indirect fire weapons from both parties may be stored inside the 20 km line. This storage of weapons shall be as stated in Annex B, "Rules of Disengagement", paragraph 4.

4. Not later than 0900 hours on 08 April 1994, all units in the Contact Line shall be separated. The separation will be based on a mutual withdrawal not less than 1,000 meters from the Contact Line to their respective Line of Separation, hereafter called the "Lines of Separation". Those lines will be as drawn on maps, accepted by the parties and attached at Annex D.

   Units should be withdrawn as far away as needed to ensure they can not target each other with direct fire weapons. The line to which they redeploy should be easy to define on the ground. (Preferably a geographic feature, such as a road, river, ridge line etc.) The area between the lines of separation will be under exclusive control of UNPROFOR and except as provided in this agreement and Annex B there shall be no military, paramilitary, militia or police personnel from any of the parties therein. The parties shall be obliged, however, to assist UNPROFOR with prevention of crime and the maintenance of law and order between the Lines of Separation as stated in Annex B, paragraphs 9 and 10.

5. The ceasefire will be monitored by UNPROFOR and ECMM. UNPROFOR Military Observers shall be accorded full freedom of movement on both sides of the Lines of Separation in order to confirm that all weapons systems specified in this agreement are deployed beyond the minimum distances from the Lines of Separation. The freedom of movement in areas described above includes the right to visit military and paramilitary units and facilities with four hours advance notice. ECMM operating in accordance with its Memorandum of Understanding shall be accorded full freedom of movement on all the territories related to this Memorandum. UNPROFOR, operating accord-

ing to its mandate, shall be accorded full freedom of movement in all the relevant territories and the same right to visit military and paramilitary units and facilities as described above. The freedom of movement includes the unrestricted use of helicopters in the above mentioned areas.

6. Joint Commissions shall be established at all levels. Their first task will be to determine on the ground the Lines of Separation in accordance with the principles set out in paragraph 4. This is to be achieved by 13 April 1994. Their main mission is to investigate immediately any violation of the ceasefire. The aim of investigation is to determine responsibility for the violation. The Commission investigating the violation will be informed by the party determined to the responsible for the violation about all disciplinary or other action taken in respect of the incident. These Commissions shall be established before the ceasefire starts. Each Commission shall be chaired by a representative of UNPROFOR who will issue convening orders to parties present, as soon as possible after the receipt of the convening orders by the headquarters of the members. Details about membership, meeting places and documentation as agreed upon are to be found in Annex B.

7. Should any breach of the ceasefire or other provision of this agreement occur, neither party shall retaliate, but shall rely on the procedures foreseen in paragraph 6 above.

8. The participants agree to open a number of crossing points along the Contact Line. These new crossings together with existing crossings are listed in Annex A. At all these crossings UNPROFOR will man a checkpoint. Any checkpoints or other positions of the two sides must be established as far away as needed from the United Nations checkpoint to ensure that small arms and heavy machine gun-fire cannot be target the UNPROFOR checkpoint. At the UNPROFOR checkpoints facilities will be established to hold meetings of the Joint Commission. All crossings shall be opened by no later than 3 hours after the ceasefire starts.

9. Not later than 0900 hours on 19 April 1994, the parties will meet and negotiate the modalities for a reduction of forces in a 10 km zone on either side of the Contact Line. This reduction shall be completed within 5 days after an agreement has been reached.

Annexes:

A. Contact Line crossing points.
B. Rules of disengagement.
C. Agreement on the establishment of Joint Commissions.
D. Agreed maps

Annex A to the Ceasefire Agreement of 29 March 1994

Common Name	Location	Sector
Osijek	Approx 5 km from Osijek on the road to Sarvas	East
Osijek	Approx 5 km from Osijek on the road to Bilje	East
Vinkovci	Approx 2 km from Vinkovci on the road to St. Jankovci	East
Vinkovci	On the road to Brsadin	East
Lipovac	On the highway	East
Nova Gradinska	Highway South West of Nova Gradinska	West
Novska	Highway Est of Novska	West
Lipik	Min Road South of Lipik	West
Sisak	South of Sisak	North
Turanj	South East of Karlovac	North
Vojnovac	West of Slunj	North
Glinska Poljana	North West of Petrinja	North
Brest	North of Petrinja	North
Otocac	South east of Vrhovine	South
Medak	North West of Medak	South
Zemunik (d.Zemunik)	Near Zemunik Airport	South
Pakovo Selo	On the road Dmris-Sibenik	South
Peruca Dam	Along Prolici/Vrlika road	South
Jasenice	East of Jasenice	South

Annex B to the Ceasefire Agreement of 29 March 1994
Rules of Disengagement and other Matters related to the Ceasefire Agreement of 29 March 1994

1. The parties shall provide UNPROFOR with lists stating unit by unit the number of tanks, AA-guns, artillery pieces and other indirect weapons which are to be deployed beyond their maximum range and outside the 10 and 20 km lines. These lists should also state the exact locations with grid references (UTM) to which the weapons will be redeployed.

The parties shall provide UNPROFOR with marked maps and minefield records for all minefields within the Lines of Separation; they will remove mines upon the request and under supervision of UNPROFOR.

The parties shall provide UNPROFOR with the names of the policemen referred to in paragraph 10 below.

The above information shall be given to the UNPROFOR Sector Commanders not later than 72 hours after the signing of the Ceasefire Agreement.

2. UNPROFOR will establish temporary control on the 10 and 20 km lines in accordance with paragraph 3 of the Ceasefire Agreement. All redeploying units and their weapons must pass through and report at such control points.

At these points a Croat or a Serb liaison officer shall be present on their respective side.

3. Paragraph 3 in the Ceasefire Agreement stipulates that "all indirect fire weapons shall be deployed out of range of the Lines of Separation".

This means the maximum range for each weapon as defined in their respective technical manual. No indirect fire weapon will be allowed inside the minimum zone of separation (10 and 20 km) mentioned in the same paragraph.

4. As the only exception from paragraph above the Croatian Army will be allowed to store indirect fire weapons at Starigrad, Zadar and Sibenik, where they will remain under UNPROFOR supervision. The Serb forces will be allowed to store indirect fire weapons at Beli Manstir, Dalj, Vukovar, Benkovac and Granac.

5. The lines of separation shall be as drawn on maps by UNPROFOR and accepted by the parties. After separation is completed, these lines may be amended on the ground as proposed by UNPROFOR and accepted by the party concerned. Such a proposal may be based on suggestions from either of the parties.

This will be done by Joint Commissions, established in accordance with the special agreement on Joint Commissions (Annex C).

6. Where the Contact Line runs through a town or a village the Lines of Separation may be drawn closer than 2 km from each other. They may here be drawn as close as possible but in a way enables UNPROFOR to interpose between the parties with sufficient safety and which prevents the parties from observing and firing directly at each other. If the parties cannot agree on the location of lines, UNPROFOR has the right to arbitrate and establish these lines. Crossings between the lines inside towns or villages are to be checked or/and blocked by UNPROFOR.

7. Paragraph 5 of the Ceasefire Agreement states that "The freedom of movement in areas described above includes the right to visit military and paramilitary units and facilities with four hours advance notice."

The areas referred to above extend to a distance from the Lines of Separation that is the same as the maximum range of the longest range indirect fire weapon redeployed according to the lists mentioned in paragraph 1 above.

8. On 9 April 1994, the parties will begin to list all mines affecting the deployment of UNPROFOR elements within the area of separation. All such personnel will enter the area unarmed, move under UNPROFOR escort, and clear mines under UNPROFOR supervision. The final removal of mines will begin and be carried out as decided in the Joint Commissions.

9. Police armed with sidearms only shall be allowed to enter and work in the area between the Lines of Separation under UNPROFOR supervision, in a number agreed by the Joint Commissions at central level and in accordance with rules laid down by the same Joint Commission.

10. Pending implementation of paragraph 9 above, each side may retain up to 200 individual policemen in such areas between the Lines of Separation as agreed between the side and UNPROFOR. Such policemen shall display sequentially numbered photo identification which shall be issued by UNPROFOR no later than 7 April and shall be armed with sidearms only. No more than 75 policemen shall be deployed in any one sector.

11. The parties agree to ensure the access of bona fide visitors to the Jasenovac cemetery.

Annex C to the Ceasefire Agreement of 29 March 1994
Agreement on the Establishment of Joint Commissions

1. The parties signing this document and UNPROFOR agree to establish Joint Commissions to support the maintenance of the ceasefire agreed between the parties in 29 March 1994.

2. The tasks and guidelines for these commissions are laid down in the Ceasefire Agreement of 29 March 1994 and its annexes. These guideline do not prevent the Joint Commissions already in operation from continuing with their present tasks or from dealing with other matters agreed upon by the participants.

3. On the local level Joint Commissions shall be established before 0900 hours on 04 April 1994 at the crossing points UNPROFOR decides, chosen among those listed in Annex A to the Ceasefire Agreement.

4. In those local Joint Commissions the parties may be represented by three members and may each bring their own interpreter. UNPROFOR will be represented by three members and will chair the meetings. UNPROFOR may bring one interpreter. ECMM may be represented with two members.

5. At Sector level UNPROFOR may be represented by three members, including the chairman, who will be the Sector Commander or the Acting Sector Commander, and may bring one interpreter. The parties may each be represented with three members and may bring one interpreter. ECMM may be represented

with two members.

6. At Central level UNPROFOR may be represented by three members, including the chairman, and may bring one interpreter. The parties may each be represented with three members and may bring one interpreter, ECMM may be represented with two members.

7. The meeting place for Sector and Central level shall be decided by UNPROFOR and will usually be one of the crossing points used by local level Joint Commissions.

8. At all places where crossing points are established, separation of forces as described in Paragraph 8 of the main document must take place immediately.

D. NEGOTIATIONS

Editor's Note: Following the Ceasefire Agreement of 29 March 1994, negotiators of the International Conference on the Former Yugoslavia made repeated efforts to bring the parties to negotiations. On 5 August 1994, the following Press Release was issued by the Conference's negotiators. In December, agreement was reached between the parties on a number of economic issues. This Agreement is also reproduced in this section.

103. PRESS RELEASE OF 5 AUGUST 1994 OF THE INTERNATIONAL CONFERENCE ON THE FORMER YUGOSLAVIA

During a meeting on 5 August 1994 and following the Ceasefire Agreement of 29 March 1994 agreement was reached to continue the process of negotiations within the framework of a general normalisation of relations.

The meeting was attended by Mr. Hrvoje Sarinic, Mr. Ivic Pasalle, Mr. Borislav Mikelic and Mr. Milan Babic. It was held at the UNPROFOR Headquarters in Knin, under the auspices of the International Conference on the Former Yugoslavia.

Agreement was reached on the immediate establishment of expert groups what will prepare the following themes for the negotiation of the two delegations:

a) Humanitarian questions (missing persons and displaced persons);
b) The opening of the Zagreb-Belgrade highway;
c) The provision of water supplies;
d) The solution of pensions and saving rights;
e) the solution of questions relating to the restoration of the hydro-electric power systems;
f) The solution of questions relating to the Adriatic oil pipeline;
g) The solution of questions relating to transportation (by rail, road and air);
h) The solution of question relating to trade.

The next meeting will be decided in the light of the work of the expert groups.

104. AGREEMENT ON ECONOMIC ISSUES OF 2 DECEMBER 1994[*]

I. WATER

1. Subject of the Agreement:
1.1   The following water supply systems:
    (a) Obrovac - Zadar - Benkovac - Kakma - Biograd - Filip Jakov;
    (b) Cikola - Drnis;
    (c) Medak - Gospic - Korenica;
    (d) Petrinja - Sisak;
    (e) Gacka - Vrhovine;
    (f) Sumetlica - Pakrac - Lipik.
The Joint Commission will be examining other water-supply systems, using the same criteria for inclusion.

2.   The systems mentioned in paragraph 1.1 shall be restored and opened for the unimpeded and regular supply of water within the optimal capacity of the existing systems.

3.   Requirements prior to the opening of the water supply systems mentioned in paragraph 1.1:
3.1   All technical information requested by UNPROFOR in order to make the above mentioned water supply systems operational shall be made available without delay. This will in particular include:
    (a) Layout and technical specifications for installations, pipelines, power-lines and associated facilities;
    (b) Information concerning assessments of damage;
    (c) Assessments concerning repair work needed as well as requirements for such work;
    (d) Information concerning requirements for de-mining of any installations connected to these water supply systems and their surrounding areas.
3.2   De-mining will be carried out where necessary.
3.3   Full security will be guaranteed for all installations, facilities and working teams involved during the period of restoration of the water supply systems as well as after the have been put into operation. Within the Zone of Separation

---

[*]   Signed by H. Sarinic, D. Owen, P. Peeters, P. Galbraith, B. Mikelic, T. Stoltenberg, P.J. von Stülpnagel, and L. Kerestedzhiyants.

UNPROFOR will, for the duration of its mandate, provide this security in accordance with the Ceasefire Agreement.

3.4   UNPROFOR or experts appointed by UNPROFOR, with the cooperation of the signatories to this agreement, will carry out inspections of all facilities and installations in order to assess damage, requirements for repair work and spare parts as well as the time required to make the water supply systems operational.

3.5   UNPROFOR and experts appointed by UNPROFOR shall be given full access to all facilities in order to carry out such inspections.

3.6   A timetable will be established by UNPROFOR after consultations for the repair work of each water supply system.

3.7   The repair work required will be commenced as soon as the results of the inspections of each supply system are available. Wherever such inspections have already been carried out repair work will commence immediately. UNPROFOR will supervise the repair work and assist where appropriate.

4.   Requirements following the completion of repair work of the water supply systems:

4.1   The regular supply of water will commence immediately after the completion of work required at each supply system and when the Joint Commission has declared each system operational.

4.2   The methods and location for measuring the quantity and monitoring the quality of water shall be determined for each water system of the areas listed by the Joint Commission based on relevant technical considerations. The price of the water to the user will be agreed in the Joint Commission before the beginning of delivery of the water.

II. ELECTRICITY

1.   Subject of the Agreement:
1.1   The high-tension transmission lines.
1.2   The generator poles of the Obrovac power plant.

2.   The high-tension transmission lines.
2.1   The following high-tension transmission lines shall be opened for unimpeded and regular use:
    (a) The Mraclin - Brinje 220 kV transmission line;
    (b) The Gradiska - Meduric 110 kV transmission line;
    (c) The Obrovac - Zadar 110 kV transmission line;
    (d) The Meline - Obrovac - Konjsko 400 kV transmission line;

(e) The Tumbri - Ernestinovo 400 kV transmission line;

(f) The construction of a / new 400 kV transformer station / transmission facility on the 400 kV transmission line / at Ernestinovo.

3.   Requirements prior to the restoration of the objects mentioned in paragraph 2.1:

3.1   International expert teams, where appropriate under the auspices of UNPROFOR, shall inspect all segments of the transmission lines that are subject to the Agreement.

3.2   These inspections shall assess the repair work and de-mining required for the unimpeded and regular use of the transmission lines.

3.3   The de-mining and repair of the transmission lines will commence as soon as the results of the inspection of each line are available, under the supervision and with the assistance of UNPROFOR and/or international experts where appropriate.

3.4   The transmission lines shall be opened as soon as they are declared operational by the Joint Commission.

4.   Requirements following the opening of the transmission lines:

4.1   UNPROFOR and/or international experts shall have free access to the transmission lines and related facilities for the purpose of verifying and securing unimpeded and regular use.

5.   Joint Commission.

5.1   The Joint Commission will discuss and agree on the terms of payment as well as where necessary other questions relating to the work required to make the objects mentioned in paragraph 2.1 operational and to secure their unimpeded and regular use.

5.2   The Joint Commission will discuss and agree on the opening of additional transmission lines.

6.   The generator poles of the Obrovac power plant.

6.1   The generator poles for the Obrovac power plant, which have been repaired at the Koncar plant in Zagreb and are currently stored in Rijeka, shall be returned to the Obrovac power plant.

7.   Requirements prior to the return of the generator poles to the Obrovac power plant:
7.1   The generator poles mentioned above shall be tested at the Koncar plant in the presence of international experts, to verify that they are in working order.

8.   Timing of the return of the generator poles:
8.1   The generator poles shall be returned to the Obrovac power plant as soon as the Co-Chairmen of the ICFY declare that the highway is operating according to this agreement.

9.   Requirements following the return of the generator poles to the Obrovac power plant:
9.1   The generator poles, once installed in the Obrovac power plant, shall be inspected by UNPROFOR and/or international experts prior to being put into operation.

III. THE HIGHWAY

1.   Subject of the Agreement:
1.1   The Highway as it affects the UNPAs East and West.

2.   Permissible traffic under the Agreement:
2.1   Only that permitted under the Ceasefire Agreement of 29 March 1994 within the UNPAs East and West.

3.   Modalities of passages:
3.1   (a) All traffic under the Agreement will be granted free and safe passage. Vehicles may travel separately or together.
        (b) In order to ensure free and safe passage through UNPAs Sectors West and/or East UNPROFOR will, within its mandate, monitor these parts of the highway. UNPROFOR may stop and inspect any vehicles and/or individuals, whenever it considers that such vehicles and/or individuals endanger the implementation of this Agreement. Local police shall be obliged to provide assistance whenever required by UNPROFOR in order to ensure the free and safe traffic through UNPAs Sector West and/or East.
        (c) A bus service may be established between UNPAs Sectors West and East and may also be established along the other parts of the highway covered by this Agreement.

(d) UNPROFOR/ECMM will conduct unarmed patrols of the highway between UNPAs Sector West and East and between UNPAs Sector West and Zagreb in order to verify compliance with this Agreement.

(e) UNPROFOR/ECMM will in consultation with the relevant authorities establish procedures in order to provide assistance in case of accidents, break-down of vehicles, violations of traffic regulations, etc.

3.2 Until otherwise agreed, no road-toll will be charged inside the UNPAs from vehicles originated outside the UNPAs and outside the UNPAs from vehicles originating inside them.

IV. THE OIL PIPELINE

1. Subject of the Agreement:
1.1 The segment of the oil pipeline passing through UNPA Sectors North, West and East.

2. The pipeline shall be open for unrestricted and regular usage at this stage only through UNPA North.

3. Requirements prior to the opening of the pipeline:
3.1 An international expert team under the auspices of UNPROFOR or experts appointed by UNPROFOR shall be allowed to inspect the entire length of the segments subject to this Agreement.

3.2 This inspection will identify any repair work and any de-mining operations required in order to recommence the usage of the pipeline.

3.3 The requirements identified through the inspections mentioned above as well as any maintenance work required will be carried out without delay, under the supervision and with the assistance of UNPROFOR or experts or contractors appointed by UNPROFOR where appropriate. Free access will be given to all persons and equipment involved in carrying out this work.

3.4 A joint commercial company will be established as soon as possible to sell and distribute oil and oil products at market prices in the UNPAs. The pipeline through UNPA North will be opened as soon as this company is established and the Joint Commission has declared that the pipeline is operational. The other segment of the pipeline will be opened when circumstances permit.

V. Further Negotiations

1.   Negotiations shall be continued immediately in order to reach agreement on the following topics:
1.1   The return of refugees and displaced persons;
1.2   Pensions;
1.3   The opening of the Zagreb - Okucani - Belgrade railway;
       The opening of the Zagreb - Knin - Split railway;
       The opening of the Zagreb - Knin - Split road.

2.   Negotiations will be continued as soon as possible on other topics on which there is a consensus to negotiate.

VI. Provisions for Implementation
A. Joint Commission

1.   Subject of the Agreement:
1.1   A Joint Commission.

2.   The Joint Commission will be responsible for implementing all parts of this document as well as other and similar agreements which may be concluded as a follow-up to this document.

3.   Membership
3.1   Membership of the Joint Commission will be as follows: Two Co-Chairmen of the Joint Commission appointed by the Co-Chairmen of the Steering Committee of the ICFY. One representative appointed by each of the signatories to this Agreement. One representative of UNPROFOR. Each member of the Joint Commission will be accompanied by one associate and may call on other experts to attend the meetings.

4.   Decision-Making
4.1   Any disputes or breach of the provisions of this Agreement as well as any other matter that requires further clarification or deliberation shall be brought to the attention and resolution by the Joint Commission. Should any dispute or breach of the provisions of this Agreement occur no retaliation or unilateral action shall take place. In cases where agreement cannot be reached by consensus, the Co-Chairmen of the Joint Commission will try to arbitrate. In the event

that their proposal is not acceptable an appeal can be made to the Co-Chairmen of the Steering Committee of the ICFY, whose arbitration shall be final.

B. IMPLEMENTATION

The implementation of this Agreement shall start immediately upon its signing and shall be completed within one month wherever feasible, while the implementation of all other items shall start within the same period.

Letter to Mr. Sarinic of 2 December 1994[*]

Dear Mr. Sarinic, We are writing to you about how UNPROFOR will conduct itself under the Agreement.

Whenever it is foreseen in this Agreement that UNPROFOR is to carry out certain tasks, it is understood that UNPROFOR is requested by all concerned to carry out those tasks to the best of its abilities and within its available resources and mandate, and that all concerned will extend their utmost cooperation to UNPROFOR in carrying out such tasks.

In UNPA West there will be no checkpoints on the highway. Instead there will be joint patrolling of the highway by UNPROFOR vehicles accompanied by one person from your police.

If it is decided to establish a bus service between UNPAs Sector West and East or along other parts of the highway covered by this agreement UNPROFOR/ECMM will be present on these buses, if requested.

Letter to Mr. Mikelic of 2 December 1994[**]

Dear Mr. Mikelic, We are writing to you about how UNPROFOR will conduct itself under the Agreement.

Whenever it is foreseen in this Agreement that UNPROFOR is to carry out certain tasks, it is understood that UNPROFOR is requested by all concerned to carry out those tasks to the best of its abilities and within its available resources and mandate, and that all concerned will extend their utmost cooperation to

---

[*] Signed by D. Owen, T. Stoltenberg and P. Peeters; and, as witnesses, by P. Galbraith and L. Kerestedzhiyants.

[**] Signed by D. Owen, T. Stoltenberg and P. Peeters; and, witnesses, by P. Galbraith and L. Kerestedzhiyants.

UNPROFOR in carrying out such tasks.

In UNPA West there will be no checkpoints on the highway. Instead there will be joint patrolling of the highway by UNPROFOR vehicles accompanied by one person from your police.

UNPROFOR is not permitted at this stage to let goods pass through the UNPAs originating from, or destined to, the territory of the FRY (Serbia and Montenegro) or territory controlled by the Bosnian Serbs and therefore at the two checkpoints within UNPA East your police will be asked to provide assistance and to work alongside UNPROFOR. Control will however have to be exercised by UNPROFOR in order to ensure compliance with this Agreement.

If you decide to establish a bus service between UNPAs Sector West and East or along other parts of the highway covered by this agreement UNPROFOR/ ECMM will be present on these buses, if requested.

E. THE STOLTENBERG PLAN

105. THE STOLTENBERG PLAN

I. INTRODUCTION

1. In paragraph 4 of its resolution 981 (1995) of 31 March 1995, the Security Council requested me to continue my consultations with all concerned on the detailed implementation of the mandate of the United Nations Confidence Restoration Operation in Croatia, which is known as UNCRO, as set cut in paragraph 3 of that resolution, "and to report to the Council not later than 21 April for its approval". The present report is submitted pursuant to that request.

2. Prior to the adoption of Security Council resolution 981 (1995), I had requested Mr. Thorvald Stoltenberg, Co-Chairmen of the Steering Committee of the International Conference on the Former Yugoslavia, acting as my Special Envoy, to carry out consultations on the mandate. My Special Envoy had meetings with representatives of the Government of Croatia and of the local Serb authorities. Following the adoption of resolution 981 (1995), he continued his consultations and met with all concerned, including military authorities on both sides. The consultations have been carried out in close contact with my Special Representative for the Former Yugoslavia, Mr. Yasushi Akashi, and the Force Commander of the United Nations Peace Forces in Zagreb, Lieutenant-General Bernard Janvier.

II. BASIS OF DISCUSSIONS

3. The basis for the consultations has been paragraph 3 of resolution 981 (1995), and the documents referred to therein, namely:

   (a) Report of the Secretary-General (S/1995/222 and Corr. 1 and 2), particularly paragraph 72;
   (b) United Nations peace-keeping plan for the Republic of Croatia (S/23280, annex III);
   (c) Relevant resolutions of the Security Council;
   (d) Ceasefire agreement of 29 March 1994 (S/1994/867);
   (e) Economic agreement of 2 December 1994 (S/1994/1375).

4. The consultations have also been based on the assumption that the deployment of UNCRO and its operations will require the cooperation of all concerned.

III. CONSIDERATIONS

5.   Following his consultations with political and military leaders representing the Government of Croatia and the local Serb Authorities, my Special Envoy has recommended the implementation of Security Council resolution 981 (1995) along the lines set out below.

6.   My Special Envoy has, in pursuance of his mandate, concentrated his efforts on the tasks to be carried out and on the methods by which they would be implemented. In the light of the serious political differences between the Government of Croatia and the local Serb authorities, it is his view that a pragmatic approach is the only way in which the support and cooperation required for implementation of the new Operation's mandate can be obtained.

7.   The plan meets the objective of implementing a new mandate with fewer personnel. In the course of his consultations, my Special Envoy repeatedly reminded his interlocutors of the concerns of the troop-contributing countries, whose evaluation of the plan will be decisive for their readiness to contribute personnel to the Operation.

8.   My Special Envoy also emphasized that cooperation by the authorities concerned and their continuing commitment for existing agreements are prerequisites for obtaining assistance from the United Nations and for the effective implementation of the tasks assigned to the new Operation.

9.   With regard to the new Operation's tasks at the international borders, my Special Envoy has carefully considered the differing views expressed in the course of his consultations. He emphasized the importance of defining precise modalities of implementation which can obtain the cooperation of all concerned, which take into account the safety and security of the troops and which remain strictly within the framework of the tasks assigned.

10. Finally, my Special Envoy has strongly emphasized that the United Nations can only assist in solving the conflict. It is up to the Government of Croatia and the local Serb authorities to make the decisions and pursue the policies required to achieve a peaceful solution. Progress will ultimately require direct contacts and constructive cooperation between those specifically involved.

IV. PLAN FOR THE IMPLEMENTATION OF THE MANDATE OF UNCRO

11. The plan proposed to me by my Special Envoy, following his consultations, is based on the six main tasks identified for UNCRO in paragraph 3 of resolution 981 (1995). They are described in the following subsections.

A. Performing fully the functions envisaged in the ceasefire agreement of 29 March 1994 between the Government of Croatia and the local Serb authorities (S/1994/367)

Functions

12. In accordance with the functions envisaged in the ceasefire agreement of 29 March 1994 UNCRO will:

   (a) Monitor the area between the forward troop deployment lines, which are the lines of separation agreed to in the ceasefire agreement;
   (b) Verify that all weapons systems specified in the agreement are deployed in accordance with its provisions. This refers to heavy weapons deployed beyond the 10-kilometre and 20-kilometre lines and in weapon storage sites;
   (c) Occupy checkpoints at all crossing points specified in Annex A to the agreement;
   (d) Chair the Joint Commission at all levels;
   (e) Conduct the liaison activities required to ensure the implementation of the agreement.

Implementation

13. In order to perform these functions fully, UNCRO will have exclusive control of the area between the forward troop deployment lines and will establish static posts as well as carrying out patrols on foot, by vehicle and by helicopter. UNCRO will also have full freedom of movement to monitor the deployment of troops and weapons systems as specified in the ceasefire agreement.
14. Because of the reduced number of troops available to UNCRO, the commitment of all concerned to the ceasefire agreement will be decisive for UNCRO's ability to perform its functions fully while ensuring the safety of its troops.
15. The functions envisaged in the ceasefire agreement will be implemented in the following way:

   (a) Static observation posts and checkpoints will be established by UNCRO in the areas most vulnerable to conflict and at locations where they are required to support patrolling activities and ensure the safety of the monitoring force;

(b) UNCRO will man all the crossing-points specified in Annex A to the ceasefire agreement to ensure access for transit, resupply, humanitarian assistance, etc., as well as the crossing of civilians;

(c) Patrols on foot, by vehicle and by helicopter will be conducted between and around these static UNCRO positions;

(d) Static and mobile patrols as well as helicopter patrols will be carried out in order to monitor compliance on both sides with the provisions of the ceasefire agreement related to specific weapons systems;

(e) Mine clearance will be conducted within the area between the forward troop deployment lines in accordance with established principles; UNCRO personnel will supervise and assist relevant authorities in the clearing of mines;

(f) Civilian police monitors (CIVPOL) will supervise the local police which, under the ceasefire agreement, is obliged to assist UNCRO in the prevention of crime and maintenance of law and order in the area between the forward troop deployment lines;

(g) CIVPOL will patrol the area between the forward troop deployment lines in order to enhance confidence and identify policing requirements;

(h) UNCRO will chair Joint Commissions at all levels;

(i) UNCRO will conduct liaison activities with military and police authorities at all levels.

B. Facilitating implementation of the economic agreement of 2 December 1994 concluded under the auspices of the Co-Chairmen of the Steering Committee of the International Conference on the Former Yugoslavia (S/1994/1375)

Functions

16. In order to advance the process of reconciliation and the restoration of normal life, UNCRO will:

(a) Facilitate and support the opening of transportation networks, as well as of water and energy facilities, within the limits of its resources;

(b) Support the negotiation and implementation of further economic and humanitarian measures which are included in the economic agreement or which may be agreed in subsequent negotiations.

Implementation

17. UNCRO will implement these functions in the following way:

    (a) A security presence will be provided for the repair, opening and functioning of the networks and facilities mentioned above;

    (b) Administrative, technical, logistic and engineering advice and support will be provided;

    (c) UNCRO will supervise mine-clearance activities required to restore, open and operate the networks and facilities mentioned above;

    (d) UNCRO will co-chair with the International Conference on the Former Yugoslavia the Joint Commission established by the economic agreement;

    (e) UNCRO will coordinate the implementation of economic projects agreed in negotiations.

C. Facilitating implementation of all relevant Security Council resolutions, including the functions identified in paragraph 72 of the above-mentioned report (S/1995/222 and Corr. 1 and 2)

18. The Security Council resolutions referred to in subparagraph 3 (c) of resolution 981 (1995) are taken to include those relevant to the functioning of UNCRO (freedom of movement, security, self-defence, including close air support) and those directly relevant to the mandate set out in paragraph 3 of that resolution.

Functions

19. In order to maintain conditions of peace and security and to restore confidence, thereby also facilitating the negotiation of a political solution, UNCRO will:

    (a) Provide assistance to needy individuals and communities (Croat, Serb and others), in cooperation with international agencies;

    (b) Monitor the human rights situation of individuals and communities (Croat, Serb and others) to ensure that there is no discrimination and that the human rights are protected;

    (c) Facilitate the voluntary return of refugees and displaced persons (Croat, Serb and others) in accordance with established international principles and in coordination with the Office of the United Nations High Commissioner for Refugees (UNHCR);

(d) Support local confidence-building measures, including socio-economic and reconstruction activities, people-to-people contacts and information exchanges of mutual benefit.

Implementation

20. UNCRO, through military, civilian and CIVPOL personnel, as appropriate, will implement the above-mentioned functions in the following way:

Humanitarian Tasks

(a) Humanitarian aid will be distributed in conjunction with UNHCR and other international and non-governmental organizations;

(b) UNCRO will assist medical evacuations, prisoner exchanges, family and humanitarian visits and transfers and coordinate responses to emergency humanitarian situations;

(c) UNCRO will facilitate the primary role of UNHCR with regard to the travel of refugees, through territory in which UNCRO is deployed, to refugee camps and holding centres;

(d) UNCRO will supervise the clearance of mines by the parties when needed to meet humanitarian requirements;

Human Rights

(e) UNCRO will contribute to deterring human rights abuse by maintaining an overall presence; closely monitor and co-locate with local police forces; monitor judicial institutions to enhance respect for human rights; seek corrective action in case of human rights abuses; and provide an operational link to human rights bodies;

(f) UNCRO will monitor and protect the welfare and human rights of people in villages of particular sensitivity;

Return of Refugees and Displaced Persons

(g) Appropriate support will be provided to UNHCR for the voluntary return of refugees and displaced persons to their homes in conditions of safety, security and dignity and in accordance with established international principles;

Confidence-building

(h) UNHCR will promote local economic, social and reconstruction projects of mutual benefit and support the negotiation and implementation of such projects;

(i) UNHCR will promote people-to-people contacts, including humanitarian, media, local, commercial and administrative exchanges, and be available to provide security to those activities where appropriate.

D. Assisting in controlling, by monitoring and reporting, the crossing of military personnel, equipment, supplies and weapons, over the international borders between the Republic of Croatia and the Republic of Bosnia and Herzegovina, and the Republic of Croatia and the Federal Republic of Yugoslavia (Serbia and Montenegro) at the border crossings for which UNCRO is responsible, as specified in the United Nations peace-keeping plan for the Republic of Croatia (S/23280, Annex III)

Functions

21. UNCRO will carry out these monitoring and reporting functions at designated border-crossing points. Traffic crossing over the international borders will be monitored for military personnel, equipment, supplies and weapons. All information concerning the movement of military personnel, equipment, supplies and weapons will be reported to the Security Council through the Secretary-General.

Implementation

22. The above-mentioned functions will be implemented in the following way:

(a) UNCRO will carry out its tasks at designated border crossing-points by deploying with a strength sufficient to perform these tasks and maintain troop safety and security. These deployments will include a number of permanent and temporary border crossing-points;

(b) All vehicles and personnel will stop at the border crossing-points. They will be visually checked in order to verify whether they carry military personnel, equipment, supplies and weapons;

(c) In cases where military personnel, equipment, supplies and weapons are detected, UNCRO will give notice that the crossing of such personnel and items would be in violation of Security Council resolutions and will be reported to the Security Council;

(d) UNCRO will compile any information on the crossing of such personnel and items and report this information to the Security Council through the Secretary-General.

E. Facilitating the delivery of international humanitarian assistance to the Republic of Bosnia and Herzegovina through the territory of the Republic of Croatia

Functions

23. UNCRO's tasks will be concentrated on providing advice and assistance to agencies involved in international humanitarian deliveries to Bosnia and Herzegovina through the territory of Croatia.

Implementation

24. To implement these functions, UNCRO will:

(a) Facilitate convoy clearances from the Government of Croatia and from the local Serb authorities;

(b) Facilitate route clearance from the Government of Croatia and the local Serb authorities;

(c) Escort humanitarian convoys as required for their security and protection;

(d) Maintain routes when required and within the limits of its resources.

F. Monitoring the demilitarization of the Prevlaka peninsula in accordance with resolution 779 (1992)

Functions

25. In order to monitor the demilitarization of the Prevlaka peninsula, United Nations military observers will patrol and maintain a permanent presence on the most southerly portion of the peninsula. They will also monitor the area 5 kilometres on either side of the border and report on the presence of any military forces.
26. Full freedom of movement, including freedom of access into and out of the areas, will be essential.
27. This task will continue, as at present, to be performed by unarmed military observers only. It will require the cooperation of both sides and their commitment to demilitarization.

Implementation

28. The functions will be carried out as follows:

   (a) United Nations military observers will patrol and sustain a continuous presence in the vicinity of the Prevlaka/Ostra peninsula;
   (b) United Nations military observers will monitor the area 5 kilometres on each side of the border between BN 898149 and BN 966998 by patrolling;
   (c) Liaison activities will be continued with the military and civil authorities of the parties at all levels in order to resolve violations or disputes;
   (d) Theatre headquarters (UNPF-HQ) will convene the Joint Inter-State Commission to mediate and resolve any disputes that are beyond the competence of a lower level of authority.

V. RESOURCE REQUIREMENTS

29. My Special Representative and the Theatre Force Commander at the United Nations Peace Force Headquarters (UNPF-HQ) have analyzed the functions and responsibilities enumerated in sections IV.A to F above and assess that an overall total of some 8,750 troops would be required for their implementation, on the assumption that the military and civilian staff of the operation will enjoy the necessary cooperation of all concerned,. The troops will be deployed in accord-

ance with operations requirements determined by UNPF-HQ and UNCRO. The requirements for civilian staff, United Nations military observers and CIVPOL, as well as administrative and logistical support elements, will be submitted to the Advisory Committee on Administrative and Budgetary Questions in the context of an overall budget submission for UNPF-HQ, UNCRO, the United Nations Protection Force (UNPROFOR) and the United Nations Preventive Deployment Force (UNPREDEP), in accordance with the recommendation made in paragraph 84 of my report of 22 March 1995 (S/1995/222). It is expected that the strength of the United Nations forces currently in Croatia can be reduced to the proposed level of 8,750 and their deployment completed by 30 June 1995.

VI. STATUS-OF-FORCES AGREEMENT

30. In accordance with paragraph 11 of resolution 981 (1995), discussions have been pursued with the Government of Croatia concerning a status-of-forces agreement for the presence of UNPF-HQ, UNCRO and, for a transitional period, UNPROFOR, on its territory, as well as for the use of Croatian territory for the support of UNPROFOR in Bosnia and Herzegovina and UNPREDEP in the former Yugoslav Republic of Macedonia. Difficulties have arisen as a result of demands by the Croatian authorities which are incompatible with the model status-of-forces agreement (A/45/594 of 9 October 1990) and with Security Council resolutions 908 (1994) and 981 (1995).
31. On 1 April my Special Representative wrote to the President of Croatia referring to paragraph 11 of resolution 981 (1995) and requesting the early meeting of representatives to finalize the matter. Following a meeting on 10 April, UNPF-HQ forwarded a draft agreement to the Croatian authorities on 14 April. A further meeting is expected to take place in the course of the current week.

VII. OBSERVATIONS

32. In spite of serious differences of approach, my Special Envoy's assessment is that there is enough common ground between the Government of Croatia and the local Serb authorities to make it possible to implement resolution 981 (1995). The ceasefire agreement provides a level of stability on the basis of which negotiations and efforts of reconciliation can take place. The economic agreement will, when fully implemented, provide an essential contribution too the normalization of life and the restoration of confidence. These two agreements are pillars of common interest which can reinforce the future process of reconciliation and

normalisation for the people living in this area. In this regard, I lay special emphasis on measures intended to provide protection and to advance the process of reconciliation as well as the new Operation's ability to promote such measures.

33. The situation on the ground is volatile. Without the requisite sense of responsibility on the part of all concerned, it could quickly deteriorate further. However, in spite of these circumstances and the serious political differences which continue to exist, both the Government of Croatia and the local Serb authorities are aware that the alternative to this plan would be more violence and a resumption of war.

34. As was to some degree the case in February 1992 when UNPROFOR was originally established, the plan set out above does not have the formal acceptance and full support of either the Government of Croatia or the local Serb authorities. The risk therefore remains that either or both sides will fail to cooperate with the United Nations in its implementation. In these circumstances, it is not without misgiving that I present these proposals to the Council On the other hand the proposed plan provides for a pragmatic implementation of paragraph 3 of Security Council resolution 981 (1995) and the alternative to its adoption would be the withdrawal of United Nations forces and the resumption of war. If the two sides seriously wish to avoid a renewal of the conflict, it is up to them to provide the necessary conditions for the new Operation to discharge its responsibility successfully.

35. I therefore recommend that the Security Council approve the arrangements set out in the present report and authorize the deployment of UNCRO to implement them.

F. EASTERN SLAVONIA, BARANJA, AND WESTERN SIRMIUM

106. GUIDING BASIC PRINCIPLES FOR NEGOTIATIONS ON A SETTLEMENT OF EASTERN SLAVONIA, BARANJA AND WESTERN SIRMIUM

1. A transition period shall be established for the region.

2. A transitional authority shall be established by the United Nations Security Council to administer the region during the transition period. Such authority shall include a mechanism to represent the interests of the Government of Croatia, the local Serbs, returning Croatian refugees and displaced persons, and ethnic minorities.

3. International forces shall be stationed within the region during the transition to maintain the peace and enforce compliance with the final settlement. The region shall otherwise be demilitarized during the transition.

4. The transitional authority will facilitate the return of refugees and displaced persons to their homes. It will also take steps to reestablish Creation institutions in the region (such as telephone service, post offices, banks, utilities, pension offices, passport and citizenship offices, etc.).

5. The transitional authority shall establish a transitional police force in which Croats and Serbs are represented. Other ethnic groups shall also be represented in the police force in the regions where they are present.

6. Internationally recognized human rights and fundamental freedoms will receive the highest respect from all levels of government throughout the Republic of Croatia.

7. All Croatian citizens and persons eligible for Croatian citizenship, including all refugees and displaced persons, have the right to return freely to their places of residence and reside there in conditions of security.

8. All persons have the right to have restored to them any property of which they were deprived by unlawful acts or forced to abandon and to be compensated for any property which cannot be restored to them.

9. The right to return, to recover property, to receive compensation for non-recoverable property, and to receive assistance in reconstruction of damaged property shall be equally available to all Croatian citizens and persons eligible for Croatian citizenship, without regard to ethnicity.

10. The international community will provide guarantees of the terms to and of the human rights protections established in the settlement. These guarantees would include the presence of international monitors for an agreed period of time in the region both during and following the transition. This work shall not be impeded.

11. After the end of the transitional period, elections for local administration shall be held.

107. BASIC AGREEMENT ON THE REGION OF EASTERN SLAVONIA, BARANJA, AND WESTERN SIRMIUM*

The parties agree as follows:

1. There shall be a transitional period of 12 months which may be extended at most to another period of the same duration if so requested by one of the parties.

2. The U.N. Security Council is requested to establish a Transitional Administration, which shall govern the Region during the transitional period in the interest of all persons resident in or returning to the Region.

3. The U.N. Security Council is requested to authorize an international force to deploy during the transitional period to maintain peace and security in the Region and otherwise to assist in implementation of this Agreement. The Region shall be demilitarized according to the schedule and procedure determined by the international force. This demilitarization shall be completed not later than 30 days after deployment of the international force and shall include military forces, weapons, and police, except for the international force and for police operating under the supervision of, or with the consent of the Transitional Administration.

4. The Transitional Administration shall ensure the possibility for the return of refugees and displaced persons to their homes of origin. All persons who have left the Region or who have come to the Region with previous permanent residence in Croatia shall enjoy the same rights as all other residents of the Region. The Transitional Administration shall also take the steps necessary to reestablish the normal functioning of all public services in the Region without delay.

5. The Transitional Administration shall help to establish and train temporary police forces, to build professionalism among the police and confidence among all ethnic communities.

6. The highest levels of internationally-recognized human rights and fundamental freedoms shall be respected in the Region.

---

* Signed on 12 November 1995 by Milan Milanovic, Head of the Serb Negotiating Delegation, and Hrvoje Sarinic, Head of the Croatian Government Delegation, and witnessed Peter W. Galbraith, United States Ambassador, and Thorvald Stoltenberg, United Nations Mediator.

7. All persons have the right to return freely to their place of residence in the Region and to live there in conditions of security. All persons who have left the Region or who have come to the Region with previous permanent residence in Croatia have the right to live in the Region.

8. All persons shall have the right to have restored to them any property that was taken from them by unlawful acts or that they were forced to abandon and to just compensation for property that cannot be restored to them.

9. The right to recover property, to receive compensation for property that cannot be returned, and to receive assistance in reconstruction of damaged property shall be equally available to all persons without regard to ethnicity.

10. Interested countries and organizations are requested to take appropriate steps to promote the accomplishment of the commitments in this Agreement. After the expiration of the transition period and consistent with established practice, the international community shall monitor and report on respect for human rights in the Region on a long-term basis.

11. In addition, interested countries and organizations are requested to establish a commission, which will be authorized to monitor the implementation of this Agreement, particularly in human rights and civil rights provisions, to investigate all allegations of violations of this Agreement, and to make appropriate recommendations.

12. Not later than 30 days before the end of the transitional period, elections for all local government bodies, including for municipalities, districts, and counties, as well as the right of the Serbian community to appoint a joint Council of municipalities, shall be organized by the Transitional Administration. International Organizations and institutions (e.g. the Organization for Security and Cooperation in Europe, the United Nations) and interested states are requested to oversee the elections.

13. The Government of the Republic of Croatia shall cooperate fully with the Transitional Administration and the international force. During the transitional period the Croatian Government authorizes the presence of international monitors along the international border of the Region in order to facilitate free movement of persons across existing border crossings.

14. This Agreement shall enter into force upon the adoption by the U.N. Security Council of a resolution responding affirmatively to the requests made in this Agreement.

6. PEACEMAKING IN THE FORMER YUGOSLAV REPUBLIC OF MACEDONIA

Editor's Note: The efforts of the International Conference on the Former Yugoslavia have been directed at the prevention of conflict in the Former Yugoslav Republic of Macedonia. In the recommendation of the Co-Chairmen, steps were taken that led to the establishment of the first-ever preventive deployment of United Nations Peace-keeping Forces: in the Former Yugoslav Republic of Macedonia.

The Co-Chairmen also spearheaded a major negotiation effort to deal with the dispute between the Former Yugoslav Republic of Macedonia and Greece. The Co-Chairmen prepared and submitted to the two sides a comprehensive draft Convention to regulate relations between them. The text of the draft Convention is reproduced below.

108. EXERCISE OF GOOD OFFICES BY THE CO-CHAIRMEN OF THE STEERING COMMITTEE IN RESPECT OF THE DIFFERENCE WHICH HAS ARISEN IN CONNECTION WITH THE REQUEST FOR ADMISSION TO MEMBERSHIP IN THE UNITED NATIONS OF THE STATE ADMITTED AS THE FORMER YUGOSLAV REPUBLIC OF MACEDONIA

Letter of 30 April 1993 of Co-Chairmen David Owen and Cyrus Vance, Addressed to the Secretary-General of the United Nations Boutros Boutros-Ghali

Dear Mr. Secretary-General, In your letter of 13 April 1993 referring to Security Council resolution 817 (1993), you requested us to use our good offices to settle the difference which has arisen in connection with the request for admission to membership in the United Nations of the State that was admitted under the name of the Former Yugoslav Republic of Macedonia and to promote confidence-building measures among the parties.

You also requested us to keep you informed of the steps we undertake in this connection, and of the relevant developments. Accordingly, we are sending to you the attached report on our efforts up to the end of April. We shall endeavour to pursue the matter while we are in Athens and also to continue our discussion on the name of the country. We shall keep you advised of our discussions.

For the time being the attached report is for your information and is not yet at a stage where it can be published.

Progress Report of the Secretary-General Submitted Pursuant to Resolution 817 (1993)

INTRODUCTION

On 7 April 1993, the Security Council adopted resolution 817 (1993) (copy attached) on the application for admission to the United Nations of the State later admitted as the Former Yugoslav Republic of Macedonia. In that resolution the Council:

> [Noted] ... that a difference has arisen over the name of the State, which needs to be resolved in the interest of the maintenance of peaceful and good-neighbourly relations in the region,

and

> [Welcomed] ... the readiness of the Co-Chairmen of the Steering Committee of the International Conference on the Former Yugoslavia, at the request of the Secretary-General to use their good offices to settle the above-mentioned difference, and to promote confidence-building measures among the parties,

On 12 April, the Co-Chairmen wrote to the Secretary-General stating their readiness to help settle the difference and to promote confidence-building measures among the parties. They stated that they would do so expeditiously and report to the Secretary-General within two months at the latest.

I. DISCUSSIONS WITH THE PARTIES

On 12 April, the Co-Chairmen held two meetings with a Greek delegation led by Foreign Minister Papaconstantinou. On the same day, the Co-Chairmen also met with a delegation from the Former Yugoslav Republic of Macedonia, led by the Deputy Prime Minister and Acting Foreign Minister Crvenkovski. The Co-Chairmen met again with the delegations on 13 April.

The discussion took place against the background of earlier work done within

the framework of the European Community conference on the former Yugoslavia, and in particular:

- Opinion No. 6 on the recognition of the Socialist Republic of Macedonia by
  the European Community and its member States rendered by the Arbitra-
  tion Commission presided over by Mr. R. Badinter (annex II);
- Draft Treaty for the Confirmation of the Existing Frontiers, prepared by Sir
  Robin O'Neill, Envoy of the President of the European Community (annex
  III).

During the course of the discussion, the two delegations raised issues that
they wished the Co-Chairmen to consider. The two sides also provided written
submission in support of their positions.

In particular, the Greek delegation expressed concern about the contents of
the Preamble, Article 3 and Article 49 of the Constitution of the State represented by the other delegation. It also made suggestions with respect to the content of the draft Treaty for the Confirmation of the Existing Frontier (annex III).

The Delegation of the Former Yugoslav Republic of Macedonia suggested
that the two countries sign an Agreement of Friendship and Cooperation, and
provided a draft for the consideration of the Co-Chairmen. Among the specific
issues of concern the delegation raised were the need to ensure the free flow of
goods, peoples and ideas without discrimination; the need to re-establish as
quickly as possible between the parties the treaty relations that had previously
existed between Greece and the Socialist Federal Republic of Yugoslavia; and
provisions of Greek legislation which, it claimed, hindered the exercise of civil
property and legal rights of citizens on the basis of ethnic background.

Following this initial round of discussions, the Co-Chairmen arranged for
technical discussions to be held from 14 to 26 April between their legal expert
and the legal experts of the two delegations. During the course of these technical
discussions, various position papers and information materials were provided by
the two delegations.

Based on those technical discussions, a working paper was prepared and
submitted to the two delegations on 21 April for their comments.

Additionally, Lord Owen, accompanied by Mr. Vance's Special Adviser,
held talks with the parties in their capitals. On 22 and 23 April, he met with
President Gligorov in Skopje and Prime Minister Mitsotakis and Special Envoy
Papoulias in Athens.

Discussions on the working papers were held with the two delegations
between 27 and 29 April at United Nations Headquarters in New York.

II. DRAFT TREATY

On 29 April, the Co-Chairmen submitted to the two sides a draft Treaty Confirming the existing Frontier and Establishing Measures for Confidence Building, Friendship and Neighbourly Cooperation (annex IV).

Annex I
Security Council
Resolution 817 (1993)

Adopted by the Security Council at its 3196th meeting, on 7 April 1993

THE SECURITY COUNCIL,

Having examined the application for admission to the United Nations in document S/25147,

Noting that the applicant fulfils the criteria for membership in the United Nations laid down in Article 4 of the Charter,

Noting however that a difference has arisen over the name of the State, which needs to be resolved in the interest of the maintenance of peaceful and good-neighbourly relations in the region,

Welcoming the readiness of the Co-Chairmen of the Steering Committee of the International Conference on the Former Yugoslavia, at the request of the Secretary-General, to use their good offices to settle the above-mentioned difference, and to promote confidence-building measures among the parties,

Taking note of the contents of the letters contained in documents S/25541, S/25542 and S/25543 received from the parties,

1. *Urges* the parties to continue to cooperate with the Co-Chairmen of the Steering Committee of the International Conference on the Former Yugoslavia in order to arrive at a speedy settlement of their difference;

2. *Recommends* to the General Assembly that the State whose application is contained in document S/25147 be admitted to membership in the United Nations, this State being provisionally referred to for all purposes within the United Nations as "the Former Yugoslav Republic of Macedonia" pending settlement of the difference that has arisen over the name of the State;

3. *Requests* the Secretary-General to report to the Council on the outcome of the initiative taken by the Co-Chairmen of the Steering Committee of the International Conference on the Former Yugoslavia.

Annex II
Opinion No. 6 of the Conference on Yugoslavia Arbitration Commission on the Recognition of the Socialist Republic of Macedonia by the European Community and its Member States*

In a letter dated 20 December 1991 to the President of the Council of the European Communities, the Minister of Foreign Affairs of the Republic of Macedonia asked the member States of the Community to recognise the Republic.

The Arbitration Commission proceeded to consider this application in accordance with the Declaration of Yugoslavia and the Guidelines on the Recognition of New States in Eastern Europe and in the Soviet Union adopted by the Security Council on 16 December 1991 and the rules of procedure adopted by the Arbitration Commission on 22 December.

For the purposes of its deliberations the Commission took note of the following materials supplied by the Socialist Republic of Macedonia:

1. Declaration of 19 December 1991 by the Assembly of the Republic of Macedonia, appended to the above-mentioned letter from the Minister of Foreign Affairs;
2. Letter of 20 December 1992 from the Minister of Foreign Affairs of Republic of Macedonia;
3. Answers to the Commission's questionnaire sent to the Republics concerned on 24 December 1991;
4. Report on the results of the referendum held on 8 September 1991;
5. Declaration of 17 September 1991 by the Assembly of the Republic of Macedonia;
6. Constitution of the Republic of Macedonia of 17 November 1991 and amendments passed on 6 January 1992;
7. Letter of 11 January 1992 sent by telecopier by the Minister of Foreign Affairs to the Chairman of the Arbitration Commission in response to the Commission's request of 10 January 1992 for additional information.

Having regard to the information before it, and having heard the Rapporteur, the Arbitration Commission delivers the following opinion:

---

* Signed by R. Badinter in Paris on 11 January 1992.

1. In his answers to the Commission's questionnaire the Minister of Foreign Affairs made the following statements on behalf of Republic of Macedonia:

(a) In response to the question what measures Macedonia had already taken, or intended to take, to give effect to the principles of the United Nations Charter, the Helsinki Final Act and the Charter of Paris:

> "The Constitutional Act to give effect to the Constitution of the Republic of Macedonia states that the Republic of Macedonia bases its international position and its relations with other States and international organisations on the generally accepted principle of international law (Article 3).
>
> The Constitutional Act to give effect to the Constitution of the Republic of Macedonia defines that the Republic of Macedonia, as an equal legal successor of the Socialist Federal Republic of Yugoslavia together with the other republics, takes over the rights and obligations arising from the creation of SFRY (Article 4)."

(b) In response to the question what measure Macedonia had already taken, or intended to take, to guarantee the rights of the ethnic and national groups and minorities on its territory:

> "The Constitution of the Republic of Macedonia provides for the establishment of a council for Inter-Ethnic Relations, which shall consider issues of inter-ethnic relations in the Republic. The Council composed of all the nationalities on a parity basis, apart from the President of the Assembly, consists of two members from the ranks of the Macedonians, the Albanians, the Turks, the Vlachs and the Roms, as well as two members from the ranks of other nationalities in Macedonia. The Assembly is obliged to take into consideration the appraisals of proposals of the Council and to pass decisions regarding them (Article 78)."

(c) In response to the question whether Macedonia would undertake not to alter its frontiers by means of force:

> "Yes, the Republic of Macedonia respects the inviolability of the territorial borders which could be changed only in a peaceful manner and by mutual consent.
>
> The Assembly of the Republic of Macedonia, in its declaration of 17 September 1991, states that the Republic of Macedonia, strictly respecting the principles of inviolability of frontiers, as a guarantee for peace and security in the region and wider, confirms its policy of neither expressing not having territorial claims against any neighbouring country (Article 4)."

(d) In response to the question whether Macedonia was willing to abide by all the undertakings given on disarmament and the non-proliferation of nuclear weapons:

> "Yes, the Republic of Macedonia undertakes all relevant obligations referring to disarmament and nuclear non-proliferation, as well as security and territorial stability."

(e) In response to the question whether Macedonia was prepared to settle by agreement all questions relating to state succession in Yugoslavia and regional disputes, or by recourse to arbitration if necessary:

> "Yes, the Republic of Macedonia accepts this obligation and strives for the resolution of all issues relating to the succession of States and to regional disputes, and in case this cannot be reached, by arbitration."

(f) In response to the question what measures Macedonia had already taken, or intended to take, to honour this undertaking:

> "The Constitutional Act for implementation of the Constitution of the Republic of Macedonia regulates the question of succession and states that the Republic of Macedonia as an equal successor with the other Republics of the SFRY will assume the rights and obligations of the SFRY under the agreement with the other republics for the legal succession of the SFRY and mutual relations (Article 4)."

(g) In response to the question whether, and in what form, Macedonia had accepted the draft Convention of 4 November 1991 prepared by the Conference on Yugoslavia:

> "The Assembly of the Republic of Macedonia, on a proposal by the Government of the Republic of Macedonia, passed a Declaration on 19 December 1991 accepting the draft Convention prepared by the Conférence on Yugoslavia (Article 3)."

(h) In response to the question whether acceptance applied more specifically to Chapter II of the draft Convention:

> "Yes, the Republic of Macedonia accepts the provisions of Chapter II of the draft Convention concerning human rights and the rights of national or ethnic groups."

2. Following a request made by the Arbitration Commission on 10 January 1992 the Minister of Foreign Affairs of the Republic of Macedonia stated in a letter of 11 January that the Republic would refrain from any hostile propaganda against a neighbouring country which was a Member State of the European Community.

3. The Arbitration Commission also notes that on 17 November 1991 the Assembly of the Republic of Macedonia adopted a Constitution embodying the democratic structures and the guarantees for human rights which are in operation

in Europe.

For the protection of minorities in particular the Constitution contains a number of special provisions, whose main features at least should be mentioned:

(a) The main provision is to be found in Article 48 (1), which states than members of the several nationalities have the right to the free expression, cultivation and development of their national identity; the same applies to national "attributes".

(b) In Article 48 (2) the Republic guarantees that the ethnic, cultural, linguistic and religious identity of the several nationalities will be protected.

(c) Article 48 (3) gives members of the several nationalities the right to set up cultural and artistic institutions and educational and other associations that will enable them to express, cultivate and develop their national identity.

(d) Under Article 48 (4) they also have the right to be educated in their own language at both primary and secondary levels.

These provisions are to be given effect by statute. In schools where instruction is to be given in the language of one of the other nationalities, the Macedonian language must also be taught.

(e) In this connection Article 45 is important since its provides that any citizen may set up a private school at any educational level except primary. Article 19 (4) provides that religious communities are also entitled to establish schools. In both these cases, however, the precise extent of the rights in question has still to be determined by legislation.

(f) In the matter of language and script, Article 7 (2) provides that in communities where the majority of the inhabitants belong to another nationality, the language and script of the other nationality must be used for official purposes, alongside the Macedonian language and the Cyrillic alphabet. Article 7 (3) makes the same provision for communities where a substantial number of inhabitants belong to a given nationality. In both these cases, however, the rights in question have still to be determined in precise terms by legislation.

(g) Article 9 (1) of the Constitution prohibits any discrimination on grounds of race, colour, national or social origin, or political or religious convictions.

On 6 January 1992 the Assembly of the Republic of Macedonia amended the Constitution of 17 November 1991 by adopting the following Constitutional Act:

"These amendments are an integral part of the Constitution of the Republic of Macedonia and shall be implemented on the day of their adoption.

Amendment I
1. The Republic of Macedonia has no territorial claims against neighbouring States.
2. The borders of the Republic of Macedonia could not be changed only in accordance with the Constitution, and based on the principle of voluntariness and generally accepted international norms.
3. Item 1 of the Amendment is added to Article 3; and Item 2 replaces paragraph 3 of Article 3 of the Constitution of the Republic of Macedonia.

Amendment II
1. The Republic shall not interfere in the sovereign rights of other States and their internal affairs.
2. This Amendment is added to paragraph 1 of Article 49 of the Constitution of the Republic of Macedonia."

5. The Arbitration Commission consequently takes the view:

- that the Republic of Macedonia satisfies the tests in the Guidelines on the Recognition of New States in Eastern Europe and in the Soviet Union and the Declaration on Yugoslavia adopted by the Council of the European Communities on 16 December 1991;
- that the Republic of Macedonia has, moreover, renounced all territorial claims of any kind in unambiguous statement binding in territorial law that the use of the name "Macedonia" cannot therefore imply any territorial claim against another State; and
- that the Republic of Macedonia has given a formal undertaking in accordance with international law to refrain, both in general and pursuant to Article 49 of its Constitution in particular, from any hostile propaganda against any other State: this follows from a statement which the Minister of Foreign Affairs of the Republic made to the Arbitration Commission on 11 January 1992 in response to the Commission's request for clarification of Constitution Amendment II of 6 January 1992.

Annex III
Treaty for the Confirmation of the Existing Frontier

THE STATES PARTIES TO THIS TREATY,

Recalling the principles of the inviolability of frontiers and the territorial integrity of States which are incorporated in the Final Act of the Conference on Security and Cooperation in Europe signed in Helsinki,

Bearing in mind the relevant provisions of the UN Charter and, in particular those referring to the obligations of States to refrain in their international relations from the threat or use of force against the territorial integrity or independence of any state,

Inspired by a spirit of good neighbourliness and a desire to avoid conflicts between them,

Desiring to develop their mutual relations and to lay firm foundations for the climate of friendship and lasting understanding,

Considering their mutual interest for the maintenance of international peace and security,

Desiring to confirm the existing frontier between them as an enduring international frontier,

Desiring to ensure that the frontier is a bond of friendship between them,

Have agreed as follows:

Article 1

The two States/Parties to this treaty hereby confirm their common existing frontier as an enduring and inviolable international frontier.

Article 2

The Two States/Parties undertake to respect the sovereignty the territorial integrity and the political independence of each other.

Article 3

The two States/Parties shall refrain from threats or the use of force aimed at the violation of the common existing frontier, in accordance with the purposes and principles of the Charter of the United Nations, and agree that neither of them will assert or support claims to any part of the territory of the other State or claims for a change of the present frontier.

Article 4

The two States/Parties will work together and cooperate to maintain and ensure the lawful and free movement of goods and persons through the frontier, in conformity with the obligations which the Parties have assumed under the relevant International Conventions.

Annex IV

Treaty Confirming the Existing Frontier and Establishing Measures for Confidence Building, Friendship and Neighbourly Cooperation - Co-Chairmen's Draft, 29 April 1993

The Republic of Greece and [..........],

Recalling the principles of the inviolability of frontiers and the territorial integrity of States incorporated in the Final Act of the Conference on Security and Cooperation in Europe, signed in Helsinki,

Bearing in mind the provisions of the United Nations Charter and, in particular those referring to the obligations of States to refrain in their international relations from the threat or use of force against the territorial integrity or independence of any State,

Guided by the spirit and the principles of democracy and fundamental freedoms and respect for human rights and dignity, in accordance with the Charter of the United Nations, as well as the Helsinki Final Act, the Charter of Paris for a new Europe and other pertinent acts of the Conference on Security and Cooperation in Europe,

Inspired by a spirit of good neighbourliness and the desire to avoid conflicts between them,

Considering their mutual interest in the maintenance of international peace and security, especially in their region,

Desiring to confirm the existing frontier between them as an enduring international border, and to ensure that that frontier constitutes a bond of friendship between them,

Recalling their obligation not to intervene, on any pretext or in any form, in the internal affairs of the other,

Desiring to develop their mutual relations and to lay firm foundations for a climate of friendship and lasting understanding,

Realizing that economic cooperation is an important element for the development of mutual relations on a stable and firm basis, as well as desiring to develop and promote future cooperation,

Have agreed as follows:

A. FRIENDLY RELATIONS AND CONFIDENCE-BUILDING MEASURES

Article 1

1. The Parties hereby formally recognize each other and shall, upon ratification of this Agreement, promptly establish diplomatic relations at the ambassadorial level.
2. The Parties shall consult regularly on the development and promotion of their bilateral relations. For this purpose they hereby establish an Interministerial Joint Commission, which shall meet at least once a year, alternately in their respective capitals.
3. Each Party shall designate a senior official who shall at all times be immediately available to the other, for the purpose of promptly considering and bringing to the attention of the competent authorities any matter or incident involving the security, tranquillity or general order of their mutual frontier. These officials shall meet from time to time and shall develop any agreed procedures necessary to carry out their responsibilities.

Article 2

The Parties hereby confirm their common existing frontier as an enduring and inviolable international border.

Article 3

Each Party undertakes to respect to sovereignty, the territorial integrity and the political independence of the other Party.

Article 4

The Parties shall refrain, in accordance with the purpose and principles of the Charter of the United Nations, from the threat or use of force designed to violate their existing frontier, and they agree that neither of them will assert of support claims to any part of the territory of the other Party or claims for a change of their existing frontier.

Article 5

[..........] hereby agrees to use that name for all official purposes.

Article 6

1. [...........] hereby solemnly declares that nothing in its Constitution, and in particular in the Preamble thereto or in Article 3, can be interpreted as constituting or will ever constitute the basis of any claim by [...........] to any territory not within its existing frontiers.

2. [...........] hereby solemnly declares that nothing in its Constitution, and in particular Article 49, can be interpreted as constituting or will ever constitute the basis of any claim by [...........] specifically to protect the rights of any persons in other States who are not its citizens.

3. [...........] furthermore solemnly declares that the interpretations given in paragraphs 1 and 2 of Article 6 of this international Agreement will not be superseded by any other interpretation of its Constitution.

Article 7

1. Each Party shall promptly take effective measures to prohibit hostile activities or propaganda by State-controlled agencies and to discourage acts by private entities that are likely to incite violence, hatred or hostility against each other, and especially activities of an irredentist nature against the other party.

2. Each Party undertakes not to use symbols, names, flags, monuments or emblems constituting part of the historic or cultural patrimony of the other party; in this regard [...........] agrees, as a confidence-building measure, not to use the Vergina Sun in any way. Furthermore, each party shall respect the official geographic names and toponyms in the other country, as recommended by the United Nations Conference for the Standardization of Geographic Names, and shall endeavour to use only these designations in their official documents, publications and maps.

3. If either party brings to the attention of the other any alleged violation of paragraph 1 or 2, the latter shall promptly take the necessary corrective action or indicate why it does consider that it need to do so.

B. HUMAN AND CULTURAL RIGHTS

Article 8

1. In the conduct of their affairs the Parties shall be guided by the spirit and principles of democracy and fundamental freedoms and respect for human rights and dignity and the rule of law, in accordance with the Charter of the United Nations, the Universal Declaration of Human Rights, the European Convention for the Protection of Human Rights and Fundamental Freedoms, the International Convention on the Elimination of All Forms of Racial Discrimination, the

Convention on the Rights of the Child, the Helsinki Final Act, the Document of the Copenhagen Meeting of the Conference on the Human Dimension of the Conference on Security and Cooperation in Europe and the Charter of Paris for a New Europe.

2. No provision of the instruments listed in paragraph 1 shall be interpreted so as to give any right to perform an action contrary to the aims and principles of the United Nations Charter, or of the Helsinki Final Act, including the principles of territorial integrity of States.

Article 9

The Parties shall cooperate in maintaining and cherishing the European cultural heritage.

Article 10

Convinced that the development of human relations is necessary for improving understanding and good-neighbourliness of their two peoples, the Parties shall encourage contacts at all appropriate levels and shall not discourage meetings between their citizens.

C. EUROPEAN INSTITUTIONS

Article 11

1. The Republic of Greece shall endeavour to support, wherever possible, the admission of [..........] to those European institutions of which Greece is a member.

2. The Parties agree that he ongoing economic transformation of [..........] should be supported through international cooperation, as far as possible by a closer relationship of [..........] with the European Economic Area and the European Community.

D. TREATY RELATIONS

Article 12

1. The Parties shall apply in their relations the provision of the following bilateral agreement that had been concluded between the former Socialist Federal Republic of Yugoslavia and the Republic of Greece on 18 June 1959:

(a) Convention concerning mutual legal relations;
(b) Agreement concerning the reciprocal recognition and the enforcement of judicial decisions; and
(c) Agreement concerning hydro-electric questions.

At the request of either Party they shall consult concerning the renegotiation of any of these agreements, with a view to replacing them by ones concluded directly between the Parties.

2. The Parties shall consult with each other in order to examine the status and applicability of the other bilateral agreement that had formerly been in force between the Republic of Greece and the former Socialist Federal Republic of Yugoslavia, with a view either to renewing or renegotiating those agreements within six months of the entry into force of this Agreement.

3. The Parties may conclude additional bilateral agreements in areas of mutual interest.

Article 13

Having regard to the fact that [..........] is a land-locked State, the parties shall, when concluding the agreement provided for in Article 14, take into account, as far a practicable, the provisions of the 1965 Convention on Transit Trade of Land-Locked States.

Article 14

1. The two Parties shall encourage the development of friendly and good neighbourly relations between them and shall reinforce their economic cooperation in all sectors, including that of water resources management. In particular they shall promote, on a reciprocal basis, road, rail, maritime and air transport and communication links, using the best available technologies, and facilitate the transmit of their goods between them and through their territories and ports.

2. To this end they shall initiate within one month from the entry into force of this Agreement, negotiations aimed at signing, within six months or as soon as possible thereafter, of agreements of cooperation of the aforementioned areas, taking into account the obligations of the Republic of Greece deriving from its membership in the European Community and from other international instruments. Such agreements shall relate to visas, work permits, economic cooperation both in the bilateral and multilateral level, including cooperation between [..........] and the European Community and other international institutions.

E. ECONOMIC, COMMERCIAL, ENVIRONMENTAL AND LEGAL RELATIONS

Article 15

1. The Parties shall strengthen their economic relations in all fields.

2. The Parties shall in particular support development and cooperation in the fields of capital investments, as well as industrial cooperation between enterprises. Special attention shall be paid to cooperation between small and medium-size companies and enterprises.

Article 16

1. The Parties shall develop and improve scientific and technical cooperation, as well as cooperation in the field of education.

2. The Parties shall intensify their exchanges of information and of scientific and technical documentation, and shall strive to improve mutual access to scientific and research institutions, archives, libraries and similar institutions.

3. The Parties shall support initiatives by scientific institutions and by individuals aimed at improving cooperation.

Article 17

The Parties shall emphasize their mutual cooperation in the agro-industrial field, with particular reference to health-food production.

Article 18

The Parties are aware that it is desirable to improve the utilization of land, especially between neighbouring States, and shall cooperate to this end.

Article 19

1. The Parties shall take great care to avoid dangers to the environment and the preserve natural living conditions, especially in the lakes and rivers shared by the two States.

2. The Parties shall cooperate to eliminate all forms of pollution in border areas.

3. The Parties shall strive to develop and harmonize strategies and programmes for regional and international cooperation for protecting the environment.

Article 20

The parties shall cooperate to alleviate the consequences of disasters.

Article 21

1. The Parties shall improve and promote business and tourist travel.

2. The parties shall make joint efforts to improve and accelerate customs and border formalities, including simplifications on the issue of visas to each other's citizens, consistent with the obligations of the Republic of Greece arising from its membership of the European Community and from relevant instruments of the Community.

3. The Parties shall endeavour to improve and modernize existing border crossing as required by the flow of traffic, and construct new ones as necessary.

Article 22

1. The Parties shall develop, intensify and improve their consular relations and legal cooperation, and within this framework provide legal assistance to each other in criminal, civil, social and administrative affairs, respecting their respective legal orders as well as bilateral and multilateral treaties and conventions.

2. The Parties shall cooperate in their fight against organized crime, terrorism, economic crimes, narcotic crimes, illegal trade in cultural property, offenses against civil air transport and counterfeiting.

F. FINAL CLAUSES

Article 23

1. The Parties shall settle any disputes exclusively by peaceful means in accordance with the Charter of the United Nations.

2. Unless otherwise agreed by the Parties, any difference or dispute that arises between them concerning the interpretation or implementation of this Agreement may be submitted by either of them to the International Court of Justice.

Article 24

This Agreement is not directed against any other State or entity. It does not infringe on the rights and duties resulting from bilateral and multilateral agreements already in force that the Parties have concluded with other States or international organisations.

Article 25

1. This Agreement is subject to ratification. The instruments of ratification shall be exchanged as soon as possible. The Agreement shall come into force on the day of such exchange.

2. This Agreement shall remain in force indefinitely. Articles 2-7 may not be terminated, except by mutual agreement.

In Witness Whereof the Parties have, through their authorized representatives, signed four copies of this Agreement in the English language, witnessed by Mr. Cyrus Vance and Lord Owen.

109. LETTER DATED 13 SEPTEMBER 1995 FROM THE SECRETARY-GENERAL ADDRESSED TO THE PRESIDENT OF THE SECURITY COUNCIL[*]

I am writing to inform you and your colleagues in the Council about the latest developments regarding the difference between Greece and the former Yugoslav Republic of Macedonia.

My Special Envoy, Mr. Cyrus Vance, has continued his efforts pursuant to Security Council resolution 845 (1993). I am pleased to inform you that the Foreign Ministers of the two parties signed a wide-ranging interim accord today at United Nations Headquarters in New York, in the presence of myself and Mr. Vance.

Attached are copies of the interim accord, of three sets of letters concerning the interim accord and various provisions thereof as well as of a statement of the Special Envoy authorized by the two parties.

I shall of course inform the members of the Council of any further developments regarding the difference between Greece and the former Yugoslav Republic of Macedonia.

Annex I
Interim Accord[**]

Minister Karolos Papoulias, representing the Party of the First Part (the "Party of the First Part") and Minister Stevo Crvenkovsky, representing the Party of the Second Part (the "Party of the Second Part"), hereby DECLARE AND AGREE as follows:

Recalling the principles of the inviolability of frontiers and the territorial

---

[*] UN Doc. S/1995/794. Signed by Boutros Boutros-Ghali.

[**] Signed by the Representative of the Party of the First Part and the Representative of the Party of the Second Part; and, as witnesses, in accordance with Security Council resolution 845 (1993), by Cyrus Vance, Special Envoy of the Secretary-General of the United Nations.

integrity of States incorporated in the Final Act of the Conference on Security and Cooperation in Europe, signed in Helsinki,

Bearing in mind the provisions of the Charter of the United Nations and, in particular, those referring to the obligation of States to refrain in their international relations from the threat or use of force against the territorial integrity of political independence of any State,

Guided by the spirit and principles of democracy and fundamental freedoms and respect for human rights and dignity, in accordance with the Charter of the United Nations, as well as the Helsinki Final Act, the Charter of Paris for a new Europe and pertinent acts of the organization for Security and Cooperation in Europe,

Considering their mutual interest in the maintenance of international peace and security, especially in their region,

Desiring to confirm the existing frontier between them as an enduring international border,

Recalling their obligation not to intervene, on any pretext or in any form, in the internal affairs of the other,

Desiring to develop their mutual relations and to lay firm foundations for a climate of peaceful relations and understanding,

Realizing that economic cooperation is an important element for the development of mutual relations on a stable and firm basis, as well as desiring to develop and promote future cooperation,

Desiring to reach certain interim agreements that will provide a basis for negotiating a permanent Accord,

Have agreed as follows:

A. FRIENDLY RELATIONS AND CONFIDENCE-BUILDING MEASURES

Article 1

1. Upon entry into force of this Interim Accord, the Party of the First Part recognizes the Party of the Second Part as an independent and sovereign State, under the provisional designation set forth in a letter of the Party of the First Part of the date of this Interim Accord, and the Parties shall at an early date establish diplomatic relations at an agreed level with the ultimate goal of relations at ambassadorial level.

2. The Party of the First Part shall as promptly as possible establish a liaison office in Skopje, the capital of the Party of the Second Part, and the Party of the

Second Part shall as promptly as possible establish a liaison office in Athens, the capital of the Party of the First Part.

Article 2

The Parties hereby confirm their common existing frontier as an enduring and inviolable international border.

Article 3

Each Party undertakes to respect the sovereignty, the territorial integrity and the political independence of the other Party. Neither Party shall support the action of a third party directed against the sovereignty, the territorial integrity or the political independence of the other Party.

Article 4

The Parties shall refrain, in accordance with the purposes and principles of the Charter of the United Nations, from the threat or use of force, including the threat or use of force designed to violate their existing frontier, and they agree that neither of them will assert or support claims to any part of the territory of the other Party or claims for a change of their existing frontier.

Article 5

1. The Parties agree to continue negotiations under the auspices of the Secretary-General of the United Nations pursuant to Security Council resolution 845 (1993) with a view to reaching agreement on the difference described in that resolution and in Security Council resolution 817 (1993).

2. Recognizing the difference between them with respect to the name of the Party of the Second Part, each Party reserves all of its rights consistent with the specific obligations undertaken in this Interim Accord. The Parties shall cooperate with a view to facilitating their mutual relations notwithstanding their respective positions as to the name of the Party of the Second Part. In this context, the Parties shall take practical measures, including dealing with the matter of documents, to carry out normal trade and commerce between them in a manner consistent with their respective positions in regard to the name of the Party of the Second Part. The Parties shall take practical measures so that the difference about the name of the Party of the Second Part will not obstruct or interfere with normal trade and commerce between the Party of the Second Part and third parties.

Article 6

1. The Party of the Second Part hereby solemnly declares that nothing in its Constitution, and in particular in the Preamble thereto or in Article 3 of the Constitution, can or should be interpreted as constituting or will ever constitute the basis of any claim by the Party of the Second Part to any territory not within its existing borders.

2. The Party of the Second Part hereby solemnly declares that nothing in its Constitution, and in particular in Article 49 as amended, can or should be interpreted as constituting or will ever constitute the basis for the Party of the Second Part to interfere in the internal affairs of another State in order to protect the status and rights of any persons in other States who are not citizens of the Party of the Second Part.

3. The Party of the Second Part furthermore solemnly declares that the interpretations given in paragraphs 1 and 2 of this Article will not be superseded by any other interpretation of its Constitution.

Article 7

1. Each Party shall promptly take effective measures to prohibit hostile activities or propaganda by State-controlled agencies and to discourage acts by private entities likely to incite violence, hatred or hostility against each other.

2. Upon entry into force of this Interim Accord, the Party of the Second Part shall cease to use in any way the symbol in all its forms displayed on its national flag prior to such entry into force.

3. If either Party believes one or more symbols constituting part of its historic or cultural patrimony is being used by the other Party, it shall bring such alleged use to the attention of the other Party, and the other Party shall take appropriate corrective action or indicate why it does not consider it necessary to do so.

Article 8

1. The Parties shall refrain from imposing any impediment to the movement of people or goods between their territories or through the territory of either Party to the territory of the other. Both Parties shall cooperate to facilitate such movements in accordance with international law and custom.

2. The Parties agree that the European Union and the United States may be requested to use their good offices with respect to developing practical measures referred to in paragraph 2 of Article 5 so as to assist the Parties in the implementation of Article 8.

B. Human and Cultural Rights

Article 9

1. In the conduct of their affairs the Parties shall be guided by the spirit and principles of democracy, fundamental freedoms, respect for human rights and dignity, and the rule of law, in accordance with the Charter of the United Nations, the Universal Declaration of Human Rights, the European Convention for the Protection of Human Rights and Fundamental Freedoms, the International Convention on the Elimination of All Forms of Racial Discrimination, the Convention on the Rights of the Child, the Helsinki Final Act, the document of the Copenhagen Meeting of the Conference on the Human Dimension of the Conference on Security and Cooperation in Europe and the Charter of Paris for a New Europe.
2. No provision of the instruments listed in paragraph 1 above shall be interpreted to give any right to take any action contrary to the aims and principles of the Charter of the United Nations, or of the Helsinki Final Act, including the principle of the territorial integrity of States.

Article 10

Convinced that the development of human relations is necessary for improving understanding and good-neighbourliness of their two peoples, the Parties shall encourage contacts at all appropriate levels and shall not discourage meetings between their citizens in accordance with international law and custom.

C. International, Multilateral and Regional Institutions

Article 11

1. Upon entry into force of this Interim Accord, the Party of the First Part agrees not to object to the application by or the membership of the Party of the Second Part in international, multilateral and regional organizations and institutions of which the Party of the First Part is a member; however, the Party of the First Part reserves the right to object to any membership referred to above if and to the extent the Party of the Second Part is to be referred to in such organization or institution differently than in paragraph 2 of United Nations Security Council resolution 817 (1993).
2. The Parties agree that the ongoing economic development of the Party of the Second Part should be supported through international cooperation, as far as possible by a close relationship of the Party of the Second Part with the European Economic Area and the European Union.

D. TREATY RELATIONS

Article 12

1. Upon entry into force of this Interim Accord, the Parties shall in their relations be directed by the provisions of the following bilateral agreements that had been concluded between the former Socialist Federal Republic of Yugoslavia and the Party of the First Part on 18 June 1959:

(a) The convention concerning mutual legal relations,
(b) The agreement concerning the reciprocal recognition and the enforcement of judicial decisions, and
(c) The agreement concerning hydro-economic questions.

The Parties shall promptly consult with a view to entering into new agreements substantially similar to those referred to above.
2. The Parties shall consult with each other in order to identify other agreements concluded between the former Socialist Federal Republic of Yugoslavia and the Party of the First Part that will be deemed suitable for application in their mutual relations.
3. The Parties may conclude additional bilateral agreements in areas of mutual interest.

Article 13

Having regard to the fact that the Party of the Second Part is a landlocked State, the Parties shall be guided by the applicable provisions of the United Nations Convention on the Law of the Sea as far as practicable both in practice and when concluding agreements referred to in Article 12.

Article 14

1. The Parties shall encourage the development of friendly and good-neighbourly relations between them and shall reinforce their economic cooperation in all sectors, including that of water resources management. In particular they shall promote, on a reciprocal basis, road, rail, maritime and air transport and communication links, using the best available technologies and facilitate the transit of their goods between them and through their territories and ports. The Parties shall observe international rules and regulations with respect of transit, telecommunications, signs and codes.
2. To this end the Parties agree to enter forthwith into negotiations aimed at promptly implementing agreements of cooperation in the aforementioned areas,

taking into account the obligations of the Party of the First Part deriving from its membership in the European Union and from other international instruments. Such agreements shall relate to visas, work permits, "green-card" insurance, airspace transit and economic cooperation.

E. ECONOMIC, COMMERCIAL, ENVIRONMENTAL AND LEGAL RELATIONS

Article 15

1. The Parties shall strengthen their economic relations in all fields.
2. The Parties shall in particular support development and cooperation in the field of capital investments, as well as industrial cooperation between enterprises. Special attention shall be paid to cooperation between small and medium-size companies and enterprises.

Article 16

1. The Parties shall develop and improve scientific and technical cooperation, as well as cooperation in the field of education.
2. The Parties shall intensify their exchanges of information and of scientific and technical documentation, and shall strive to improve mutual access to scientific and research institutions, archives, libraries and similar institutions.
3. The Parties shall support initiatives by scientific institutions and by individuals aimed at improving cooperation in the sciences.

Article 17

1. The Parties shall take great care to avoid dangers to the environment and to preserve natural living conditions in the lakes and rivers shared by the two Parties.
2. The Parties shall cooperate in eliminating all forms of pollution in border areas.
3. The Parties shall strive to develop and harmonize strategies and programmes for regional and international cooperation for protecting the environment.

Article 18

The Parties shall cooperate in alleviating the consequences of disasters.

Article 19

1. The Parties shall cooperate in improving and promoting business and tourist travel.

2. Consistent with the obligations of the Party of the First Part arising from its membership in the European Union and from relevant instruments of the Union, the Parties shall make joint efforts to improve and accelerate customs and border formalities, including simplification in the issuance of visas to each other's citizens, taking into account Article 5, paragraph 2, of this Interim Accord.

3. The Parties shall endeavour to improve and modernize existing border crossings as required by the flow of traffic, and construct new border crossings as necessary.

Article 20

The Parties shall cooperate in the fight against organized crime, terrorism, economic crimes, narcotics crimes, illegal trade in cultural property, offences against civil air transport and counterfeiting.

F. Final Clauses

Article 21

1. The Parties shall settle any disputes exclusively by peaceful means in accordance with the Charter of the United Nations.

2. Any difference of dispute that arises between the Parties concerning the interpretation or implementation of this Interim Accord may be submitted by either of them to the International Court of Justice, except for the difference referred to in Article 5, paragraph 1.

Article 22

This Interim Accord is not directed against any other State or entity and it does not infringe on the rights and duties resulting from bilateral and multilateral agreements already in force that the Parties have concluded with other States or international organizations.

Article 23

1. This Interim Accord shall enter into force and become effective on the thirtieth day following the date on which it is signed by the representatives of the Parties as set forth below.

2. This Interim Accord shall remain in force until superseded by a definitive agreement, provided that after seven years either Party may withdraw from this Interim Accord by a written notice, which shall take effect twelve months after its delivery to the other Party.

IN WITNESS WHEREOF the Parties have, through their authorized representatives, signed three copies of this Interim Accord in the English language, which shall be registered with the Secretariat of the United Nations. Within two months of the date of signature, the United Nations is to prepare, in consultation with the Parties, translations into the language of the Party of the First Part and the language of the Party of the Second Part, which shall constitute part of the registration of this Accord.

DONE AT New York on the 13th day of September 1995

Annex II
Letter dated 13 September 1995 from Cyrus R. Vance, Special Envoy of the Secretary-General, addressed to the Minister for Foreign Affairs of the former Yugoslav Republic of Macedonia

I enclose herewith a copy of a letter addressed to me today by Minister Papoulias concerning the implementation of article 1, paragraph 1, of the interim accord of today's date.

Annex III
Letter dated 13 September 1995 from Karolos Papoulias, Minister for Foreign Affairs of Greece, addressed to the Special Envoy of the Secretary-General

In implementation of article 1, paragraph 1, of the interim accord of today's date, the Government of Greece recognizes the party of the second part within its internationally recognized borders, with the provisional name of the former Yugoslav Republic of Macedonia, pending settlement of the difference that has arisen over the name of the State.

Annex IV
Letter dated 13 September 1995 from Stevo Crvenkovski, Minister for Foreign Affairs of the former Yugoslav Republic of Macedonia, addressed to the Special Envoy of the Secretary-General

I hereby acknowledge receipt of your letter of today's date, under cover of which you transmitted to me a copy of a letter addressed to you today by Minister Papoulias concerning the implementation of article 1, paragraph 1, of the interim accord of today's date.

Annex V
Letter dated 13 September 1995 from Karolos Papoulias, Minister for Foreign Affairs of Greece, addressed to the Special Envoy of the Secretary-General

With regard to article 7, paragraph 2, of the interim accord of today's date, the Government of Greece would like to confirm that the symbol referred to in the above-mentioned article of the said accord is the Sun or Star of Vergina, in all its historical forms.

Annex VI
Letter dated 13 September 1995 from Cyrus R. Vance, Special Envoy of the Secretary-General, addressed to the Minister for Foreign Affairs of Greece

I hereby acknowledge receipt of your letter of today's date concerning article 7, paragraph 2, of the interim accord of today's date. I have made the other party aware of the content of your letter.

Annex VII
Letter dated 13 September 1995 from Stevo Crvenkovski, Minister for Foreign Affairs of the former Yugoslav Republic of Macedonia, addressed to the Special Envoy of the Secretary-General

This is to inform you that, in connection with the interim accord of today's date, my Government wishes to make clear that no instrument that has not been signed on its behalf can be considered as binding on it.

Annex VIII
Letter dated 13 September 1995 from Cyrus R. Vance, Special Envoy of the Secretary-General, addressed to the Minister for Foreign Affairs of the former Yugoslav Republic of Macedonia

I hereby acknowledge the receipt of your letter of today's date concerning the legal effect of the instruments exchanged in connection with the interim accord of today's date. I have made the other party aware of the content of your letter.

Annex IX
Statement of Cyrus R. Vance, Special Envoy of the Secretary-General of the United Nations, upon signature of the interim accord between Greece and the former Yugoslav Republic of Macedonia on 13 September 1995

I am very pleased to welcome the signing of the interim accord between the two neighbouring States. The accord establishes a new relationship between them that will be based on concepts of international law and peaceful, friendly relations.

The Hellenic Republic has authorized me to make the following statement on its behalf in so far as this statement refers to actions to be taken by it, and the former Yugoslav Republic of Macedonia has authorized me to make the following statement on its behalf in so far as this statement refers to actions to be taken by it.

The accord provides that each party will respect the sovereignty, territorial integrity and political independence of the other and confirms their common existing frontier as an enduring and inviolable international border.

The accord further provides for recognition by the Hellenic Republic of the former Yugoslav Republic of Macedonia as an independent and sovereign State, and that the two countries will establish liaison offices in each other's capital.

The accord also provides that the former Yugoslav Republic of Macedonia will cease to use in any manner the symbol that is now on its national flag. It also provides specific and binding assurances that the Constitution of the former Yugoslav Republic of Macedonia is consistent with the principles of international law and good-neighbourly relations mentioned earlier.

The accord provides for unimpeded movement of people and goods between the two countries. In this connection I can confirm that the accord, by its terms, provides for terminating the measures that had been imposed by the Hellenic Republic on 16 February 1994, and provides for replacing these measures by an open and cooperative economic relationship.

The necessary steps required to implement the accord fully will commence upon signature and will take place over the next few weeks, with the effective date of its operative provisions 30 days from today.

The accord provides that the parties will continue negotiations under the auspices of the Secretary-General of the United Nations with respect to the outstanding difference between them referred to in relevant Security Council resolutions.

Finally, the accord contains other important provisions relating to areas of cooperation between the parties, a commitment to settle disputes exclusively by peaceful means, and the timing and terms of implementation.

As the Special Envoy of the Secretary-General of the United Nations, under whose auspices this lengthy mediation effort has been conducted, I congratulate the parties on the important step they have taken to achieve a new relationship, which will promote peace and security between them and in their entire region.

PART TWO

INTRODUCTION

Between September 1992 and June 1995, the Co-Chairmen submitted numerous reports to the Security Council through the United Nations Secretary-General. A brief summary of the content of these reports is provided in Part One below. Part Three contains a list of Security Council Resolutions on the Former Yugoslavia up to September 1994.

1. SUMMARY OF CONTENTS OF REPORTS TO THE SECURITY COUNCIL

S/24634 (8 Oct. 1992)
Letter dated 92/10/08 from the Permanent Representative of the United Kingdom to the United Nations addressed to the President of the Security Council
Transmits report of the Chairman of the Working Group on Confidence and Security-building and Verification Measures to the Co-Chairmen of the Steering Committee of the International Conference on the Former Yugoslavia concerning aerial confidence measures including the ban on the military use of aircraft in Bosnia and Herzegovina. Includes Agreement on modalities for the Implementation of the Measures Agreed to Facilitate the Resumption of Humanitarian Flights into Sarajevo

S/24795 (11 Nov. 1992)
Report of the Secretary-General on the International Conference on the Former Yugoslavia
Includes joint declaration signed by the President of Croatia and the President of the Federal Republic of Yugoslavia, Geneva, 30 Sept. 1992

S/25015 (24 Dec. 1992)
Report of the Secretary-General on the International Conference on the Former Yugoslavia

S/25050 (6 Jan. 1993)
Report of the Secretary-General on the activities if the International Conference on the Former Yugoslavia
Includes draft agreement relating to Bosnia and Herzegovina, 6 Jan. 1993

S/25100 (14 Jan. 1993)
Letter dated 93/01/13 from the Secretary-General addressed to the President of the Security Council
"Annex: Report of the Secretary-General on the activities of the International Conference on the Former Yugoslavia"

S/25221 (2 Feb. 1993)
Report of the Secretary-General on the activities of the International Conference on the Former Yugoslavia
Includes draft interim arrangements for Bosnia and Herzegovina, 2 Feb. 1993

S/25248 (8 Feb. 1993)
Report of the Secretary-General on the New York Round of the Peace Talks on Bosnia and Herzegovina, 3-8 February 1993

S/25403 (12 Mar. 1993)
Report of the Secretary-General on the activities of the International Conference on the Former Yugoslavia
Includes Vance-Owen Peace Plan for the Republic of Bosnia and Herzegovina, 1993

S/25479 (26 Mar. 1993)
Report of the Secretary-General on the activities of the International Conference on the Former Yugoslavia: peace talks on Bosnia and Herzegovina
Includes Vance-Owen Peace Plan for the Republic of Bosnia and Herzegovina, 1993

S/25490 (30 Mar. 1993)
Report of the Secretary-General on the International Conference on the Former Yugoslavia: Recent activities of the working groups

S/25708 (30 Apr. 1993)
Report of the Secretary-General on the activities of the Co-Chairmen of the Steering Committee of the International Conference on the Former Yugoslavia

S/25709 (3 May 1993)
Report of the Secretary-General on the activities of the International Conference on the Former Yugoslavia: peace talks, Athens, 1-2 May 1993

S/26066 (8 July 1993)
Letter dated 93/07/08 from the Secretary-General addressed to the President of the Security Council
Transmits report by the Co-Chairmen of the Steering Committee of the International Conference on the Former Yugoslavia, on the subject of Bosnia and Herzegovina. Includes revised Constitutional Principles for Bosnia and Herzegovina, Agreement for Peace in Bosnia and Herzegovina and revised Interim Arrangement

S/26233 (3 Aug. 1993)
Letter dated 93/08/03 from the Secretary-General addressed to the President of the Security Council
Transmits report by the Co-Chairmen of the Steering Committee of the International Conference on the Former Yugoslavia. Includes Agreement for a Complete Cessation of All Combat Activities among the Parties in Conflict, Sarajevo, 30 July 1993

S/26260 (6 Aug. 1993)
Letter dated 93/08/06 from the Secretary-General addressed to the President of the Security Council
Transmits report of the Co-Chairmen of the Steering Committee on the activities of the International Conference on the Former Yugoslavia. Includes Constitutional Agreement on the Union of Republics of Bosnia and Herzegovina

S/26337 (20 Aug. 1993)
Letter dated 93/08/20 from the Secretary-General addressed to the President of the Security Council
Transmits report of the Co-Chairmen of the Steering Committee on the activities of the International Conference on the Former Yugoslavia

S/26395 (1 Sept. 1993)
Letter dated 93/09/01 from the Secretary-General addressed to the President of the Security Council
Transmits report by the Co-Chairmen of the Steering Committee on the activities of the International Conference on the Former Yugoslavia

S/26486 (23 Sept. 1993)
Letter dated 93/09/23 from the Secretary-General addressed to the President of the Security Council
Transmits report of the Co-Chairmen of the Steering Committee on the activities of the International Conference on the Former Yugoslavia. Includes draft Agreement between the Republic of Croatia and the Union of Republics of Bosnia and Herzegovina granting the Union access to the Adriatic through the territory of the Republic of Croatia

S/26922 (29 Dec. 1993)
Letter dated 93/12/28 from the Secretary-General addressed to the President of the Security Council
Transmits report of the Co-Chairmen of the Steering Committee of the International Conference on the Former Yugoslavia

S/1994/64 (21 Jan. 1994)
Letter dated 94/01/21 from the Secretary-General addressed to the President of the Security Council
Transmits report of the Co-Chairmen of the Steering Committee of the International Conference on the Former Yugoslavia

S/1994/83 (26 Jan. 1994)
Letter dated 94/01/25 from the Secretary-General addressed to the President of the Security Council
Transmits report of the Co-Chairmen of the Steering Committee of the International Conference on the Former Yugoslavia on the activities of the working groups and other organs of the Conference. Include the agreed minutes signed by representatives from the Government of the former Yugoslav Republic of Macedonia, Serbs in Macedonia, the International Conference on the Former Yugoslavia and the Conference on Security and Co-operation in Europe. Also includes opinions no 14-15 issued by the Arbitration Commission

S/1994/173 (14 Feb. 1994)
Letter dated 94/02/14 from the Secretary-General addressed to the President of the Security Council
Transmits report of the Co-Chairmen of the Steering Committee on the activities of the International Conference on the Former Yugoslavia

S/1994/811 (8 July 1994)
Letter dated 94/07/08 from the Secretary-General addressed to the President of the Security Council

S/1994/1074 (19 Sept. 1994)
Letter dated 94/09/19 from the Secretary-General addressed to the President of the Security Council

S/1994/1124 (3 Oct. 1994)
Letter dated 94/10/03 from the Secretary-General addressed to the President of the Security Council

S/1994/1246 (3 Nov. 1994)
Letter dated 94/11/02 from the Secretary-General addressed to the President of the Security Council

S/1994/1375 (2 Dec. 1994)
Letter dated 94/12/02 from the Secretary-General addressed to the President of the Security Council

S/1994/1454 (29 Dec. 1994)
Letter dated 94/12/29 from the Secretary-General addressed to the President of the Security Council

S/1995/6 (5 Jan. 1995)
Letter dated 95/01/04 from the Secretary-General addressed to the President of the Security Council

S/1995/104 (3 Feb. 1995)
Letter dated 95/02/03 from the Secretary-General addressed to the President of the Security Council

S/1995/175 (2 Mar. 1995)
Letter dated 95/03/02 from the Secretary-General addressed to the President of the Security Council

S/1995/255 (31 Mar. 1995)
Letter dated 95/03/95 from the Secretary-General addressed to the President of the Security Council

S/1995/302 (13 Apr. 1995)
Letter dated 95/01/13 from the Secretary-General addressed to the President of the Security Council

S/1995/320 (18 Apr. 1995)
Report of the Secretary-General submitted pursuant to Paragraph 4 of Security Council Resolution 981 (1995)

S/1994/406 (18 May 1995)
Letter dated 95/05/18 from the Secretary-General addressed to the President of the Security Council

S/1995/510 (25 June 1995)
Letter dated 95/06/25 from the Secretary-General addressed to the President of the Security Council

S/1995/626 (26 July 1995)
Letter dated 95/07/27 from the Secretary-General addressed to the President of the Security Council

S/1995/645 (3 Aug. 1995)
Letter dated 95/08/03 from the Secretary-General addressed to the President of the Security Council

S/1995/768 (6 Sept. 1995)
Letter dated 95/09/06 from the Secretary-General to the President of the Security Council

S/1995/835 (29 Sept. 1995)
Further report of the Secretary-General pursuant to Security Council resolution 1009 (1995)

S/1995/944 (10 Nov. 1995)
Letter dated 95/11/10 from the Secretary-General addressed to the President of the Security Council
Transmits report by the Co-Chairmen of the Steering Committee of the International Conference on the Former Yugoslavia concerning the operations of the International Conference's Mission to Yugoslavia. The report contains the certification referred to in Security Council resolution 988 (1995)

S/1995/987 (23 Nov. 1995)
Report of the Secretary-General pursuant to Security Council resolutions 981 (1995), 982 (1995) and 983 (1995)
Includes UN map no. 3684 rev. 7: U.N. Peace Forces development as of November 1995 (Nov. 1995)

S/1995/988 (27 Nov. 1995)
Report of the Secretary-General pursuant to Security Council resolution 1019 (1995) on violations of international humanitarian law in the areas of Srebrenica, Zepa, Banja Luka and Sanski Most

S/1995/1031 (13 Dec. 1995)
Report of the Secretary-General pursuant to Security Council resolution 1026 (1995)

S/1995/1034 (14 Dec. 1995)
Letter dated 95/12/14 from the Secretary-General addressed to the President of the Security Council
Reports that Bosnia and Herzegovina, Croatia, Yugoslavia and other parties formally signed the General Framework Agreement for Peace in Bosnia and Herzegovina and the annexes thereto, 14 Dec. 1995, Paris

S/1995/1050 (20 Dec. 1995)
Letter dated 95/12/20 from the Security-General addressed to the President of the Security Council
Refers to the operative paragraph 19 of the Security Council resolution 1031 (1995) and reports that the transfer of authority from the United Nations Protection Force to the Implementation Force took place in Sarajevo at 11:00 a.m. local time, 20 Dec. 1995

S/1996/65 (30 Jan. 1996)
Report of the Secretary-General pursuant to Security Council resolution 1027 (1995)

2. REPORTS TO THE SECURITY COUNCIL

110. REPORT OF THE SECRETARY-GENERAL ON THE INTERNATIONAL CONFERENCE ON THE FORMER YUGOSLAVIA[*]

I. ORGANIZATION AND STRUCTURE OF THE INTERNATIONAL CONFERENCE

1. The International Conference on the Former Yugoslavia (ICFY) is an innovative enterprise combining the efforts of the United Nations and the European Community (EC), as well as other international organisations such as the Conference on Security and Cooperation in Europe (CSCE) and the Organisation of the Islamic Conference (OIC) to deal with a situation fraught with danger for international peace and security. ICFY combines active preventive diplomacy, peacemaking, peace-keeping, and also has a potential peace enforcement component. The International Conference is organized to remain in being until a final settlement of the problems of the former Yugoslavia has been reached. It builds on the work already done by the European Community's Conference on Yugoslavia. Its permanent Co-Chairmen are the Head of State or Government of the Presidency of the European Community and the Secretary-General of the United Nations. A Steering Committee which manages the operational work of the Conference is co-chaired by the representative of the Secretary-General of the United Nations, Mr. Cyrus Vance and a representative of the Presidency of the European Community, Lord Owen. Its membership includes representatives of a troika of the European Community, a troika of the CSCE, the five permanent members of the United Nations Security Council, a representative from the Organisation of the Islamic Conference, two representatives from neighbouring States, and Lord Carrington.

---

[*] UN Doc. S/24795, 11 November 1992.

2. Mr. Vance and Lord Owen are assisted by the Chairperson of the Conference's six Working Groups. They work in continuous session at the United Nations Office in Geneva. In addition to their own activities, the Co-Chairmen direct the Working Groups and prepare the basis for a general settlement and associated measures. The Conference also has an Arbitration Commission and a small secretariat.

II. Activities of the Steering Committee

A. First Meeting

3. The first meeting of the Steering Committee was held in Geneva at 3 September 1992, under the Co-Chairmenship of Mr. Vance and Lord Owen. The Co-Chairmen paid a tribute to the earlier work by Lord Carrington and the United Nations. They stressed that the International Conference would be a completely joint effort by the United Nations and the European Community. They emphasized their intention to hold all the Yugoslav Republics to the commitments made at the London session of the International Conference and called for a rapid implementation of the Conference's recommendations in tightening sanctions.
4. Following reports from the Chairpersons of the six Working Groups, it was decided that the Working Group Chairpersons would be responsible for their own method of work; that flexible representation for relevant countries might be better than fixed patterns; and that they should use expert opinion as and when needed.
5. An initial discussion of cost-sharing took place. The Co-Chairmen indicated that the secretariat would be kept as lean as possible.

B. Second Meeting

6. The Co-Chairmen convened a second meeting of the Steering Committee on 27 October 1992. The Co-Chairmen reported on recent developments. The Chairpersons of the Working Groups briefed the Committee on their activities. The Steering Committee also dealt with the composition and terms of reference of the Arbitration Commission, and with financial issues, including the budget and a proposed scale of cost apportionment.

C. *Information to Members of the Steering Committee and other Delegations*

7. The members of the Steering Committee and members of the Security Council receive information notes twice weekly on developments in the Conference. The information notes cover the activities of the Co-Chairmen, the Working Groups, and recent developments in the former Yugoslavia. Delegations are also briefed regularly by the Co-Chairmen or their Special Advisers on the activities of the Conference. Other delegations receive information once a week and are invited to the briefings as observers.

III. THE CO-CHAIRMEN OF THE STEERING COMMITTEE

A. *Humanitarian issues*

8. Upon their arrival in Geneva on 3 September, the Co-Chairmen devoted special attention to the situation brought about by the loss of the United Nations humanitarian aircraft near Sarajevo. On 4 September they sent a message of condolence to the Italian Foreign Minister and requested the Chairman of their Working Group on Confidence and Security-Building and Verification Measures to initiate an urgent inquiry, and to inform them of its findings and recommendations. They also consulted with the United Nations High Commissioner for Refugees and addressed a meeting she had organized on humanitarian assistance, which, they stressed, was of deep concern to them.

9. On Saturday 5 September, the Co-Chairmen intensified their efforts to clarify the circumstances surrounding the loss of the aircraft and to determine measures that could be taken to facilitate the resumption of humanitarian flights. They issued a public appeal which stated that:

> "they consider it of great importance that conditions be re-established as rapidly as possible to permit the resumption of United Nations humanitarian flights."

10. The Co-Chairmen, assisted by the Chairperson of the Humanitarian Issues Working Group and the Chairman of the Working Group on Confidence and Security-Building and Verification Measures, continued to make strenuous efforts to facilitate the resumption of humanitarian flights. Details of their activities are provided in subsequent sections of the present report. As a result of these efforts humanitarian flights could be resumed on 3 October.

11. The Co-Chairmen have continued to give the highest priority to humanitarian issues. They and their staff have kept in almost daily contact with the United Nations High Commissioner for Refugees and members of her staff, with the

President of the International Committee of the Red Cross and his staff, and with other humanitarian organisations. In this regard the location of the International Conference at Geneva has been valuable. These contacts have enabled the Co-Chairmen to monitor the humanitarian situation in the former Yugoslavia closely and the international community at large about the humanitarian plight of the victims of the conflict in Bosnia and Herzegovina.

12. The Co-Chairmen have issued several public appeals for humanitarian protection and assistance to victims of the conflict. Thus, on 24 September, they issued a public statement expressing their deep concern about reports they had received from the Banja Luka region indicating a build-up of tension, bomb incidents, and intimidation with the potential threat of violence and the development of the ethnic-cleansing campaign. The Co-Chairmen, therefore, called in Ambassador Pavicevic of the Federal Republic of Yugoslavia (FRY) and Dr. Koljevic, the Bosnian Serb representative, and urged that immediate steps be taken to reduce tensions in the area. In view of the urgency of the situation, the Co-Chairmen decided to travel to Banja Luka the following day to assess the situation on the ground and to speak to representatives of the local communities and humanitarian agencies.

13. On 31 October 1992 the Co-Chairmen again issued a public statement, this time condemning the continuing assaults on innocent civilians fleeing from the fighting in and around Jajce. They called upon all parties to cease and desist from further attacks on persons displaced by the fighting. They noted that many of the civilians were seeking refuge in Travnik, were the UNHCR and other humanitarian organizations were providing help. They stated: "These blameless persons, as well as the relief workers, must not be harmed. We call upon the political and military leaders of all parties to issue instructions so that the lives of these innocent persons and of the relief workers are not further endangered. We ask that other leaders join us in this urgent appeal".

B. Diplomatic activities

14. The Co-Chairmen have engaged in extensive diplomatic activities to promote peace and the resolution of humanitarian problems in the area of the former Yugoslavia. They have naturally given priority to the current conflict in Bosnia and Herzegovina. The humanitarian, military, and political aspects of this tragic conflict have been at the top of their agenda. They have been in steady contact with the principal leaders in the former Yugoslavia, as well as leaders of the neighbouring countries. They have contacted Governments in a position to assist the peace process and have brought together in Geneva Presidents Cosic and

Tudjman on the one hand, and Presidents Cosic and Izetbegovic, on the other. They have also sought to deal with the central relationship between Croatia and the Federal Republic of Yugoslavia - in the light of last year's bitter conflict between Croats and Serbs, whose aftermath is still felt. The Co-Chairmen have also given close attention to the potentially explosive situation in the Serbian province of Kosovo and in Macedonia.

15. With regard to the brutal conflict in Bosnia and Herzegovina, the Co-Chairmen have sought throughout to ensure that efforts to resolve civil strife should not become hostage to the normalization of relations between Croatia and the Federal Republic of Yugoslavia. They have therefore pursued parallel initiatives. Their efforts have been directed simultaneously at two basic objectives - first, a cessation of hostilities, and second, the preparation of options for the constitutional future of the country.

16. As regards the crucial Serb-Croat relationship, the Co-Chairmen have worked to help improve relations between the Federal Republic of Yugoslavia and the Republic of Croatia. They organized two sets of meetings in Geneva between President Cosic and Tudjman on 30 September and 20 October. Following each of those meetings the two Presidents signed joint declarations which contained important statements of principles and arrangements for practical cooperation. Some important results have come out of this process including the demilitarization of the Prevlaka peninsula and the establishment of liaison offices in Belgrade and Zagreb.

17. Regarding the situation in Kosovo and Macedonia, the Co-Chairmen had believed from the outset that they needed careful handling. They, therefore, asked the Chairmen of the Working Group on Ethnic and National Communities and Minorities to give these situations special attention. The Co-Chairmen have visited both areas and have had discussions with leaders on the spot and in Geneva.

18. The broad range of diplomatic activities pursued by the Co-Chairmen have included the following:

9-12 September
Co-Chairmen visited Zagreb, Sarajevo and Belgrade (Mr. Vance also visited Ljubljana)

12-13 September
Lord Owen attended EC Foreign Ministers informal meeting

16 September
Co-Chairmen met with Macedonian Minister of the Interior, L. Frckovski;
Co-Chairmen met with Mr. I. Rugova, Kosovo Albanian leader

18 September
Mr. Vance met with Chairman of Arbitration Commission, Mr. R. Badinter

21 September
Mr. Vance met with Director of UNICEF, Mr. J. Grant.

22-23 September
Co-Chairmen visited Athens for talks with Prime Minister Mitsotakis

25-26 September
Co-Chairmen visited Zagreb and Banja Luka to examine humanitarian
situation

28 September
Visit by Co-Chairman to Belgrade

28 September
Co-Chairmen visited Belgrade for discussion with FRY leaders

29 September
Co-Chairmen met with President Izetbegovic of Bosnia and Herzegovina in
Geneva; Mr. Vance met with ICRC President, C. Sommaruga

30 September
FRY President Cosic and Croatian President Tudjman met in Geneva under
the auspices of the Co-Chairmen

2 October
Co-Chairmen met with Macedonian Foreign Minister, Mr. D. Maleski, in
Geneva

3 October
Mr. Vance met with UNHCR, Mrs. S. Ogata, and ICRC President, C.
Sommaruga; Lord Owen briefed Council of Europe

6 October
Mr. Vance met with Deputy Prime Minister of Croatia Mr. M. Granic in Geneva

8 October
Co-Chairmen met with UNCHR Rapporteur, Mr. T. Mazowiecki

10 October
Co-Chairmen visited Moscow for talks with Russian Federation Foreign Minister, Mr. A. Kozyrev

14 October
Mr. Vance briefed United Nations Security Council

16 October
Co-Chairmen met with Macedonian President, K. Gligorov in Geneva.

17 October
Co Chairman met with Federal Republic of Yugoslavia Prime Minster, M. Panic in Geneva

19 October
FRY Presidents Cosic and Bosnia and Herzegovina President Izetbegovic met in Geneva under the auspices of the Co-Chairmen

20 October
Second meeting of Presidents Tudjman and Cosic in Geneva under the auspices of the Co-Chairmen

21 October
Co-Chairmen met with President Izetbegovic in Geneva

24 October
Lord Owen met with Irish Prime Minister in Dublin

26 October
Mr. Vance met with ICRC President, C. Sommaruga

28 October
Constitutional paper for Bosnia and Herzegovina launched

28-30 October
Co-Chairmen visited Belgrade, Zagreb, Pristina, Tirana, Skopje and Podgorica for discussion

4-5 November
Co-Chairmen visited Ankara for discussions with Turkish leaders

9 November
Lord Owen briefed EC Foreign Affairs Council in Brussels

19. The diplomatic activities undertaken by the Co-Chairmen, or carried out under their auspices, have led to the adoption of the following document:

(a) The Belgrade joint communiqué of 11 September 1992 issued by Federal Republic of Yugoslavia President Cosic, and Federal Republic of Yugoslavia Prime Minister Panic and witnessed by the Co-Chairmen (annex I);

(b) The joint declaration issued in Geneva on 30 September 1992 by President Cosic of the Federal Republic of Yugoslavia and President Tudjman of the Republic of Croatia, and witnessed by the Co-Chairmen (annex II);

(c) The statement issued by the Co-Chairmen on 30 September 1992 on the establishment of the Mixed Military Working Group in Sarajevo (annex III);

(d) The statement issued by the Co-Chairmen on 13 October 1992 concerning the removal of Bosnian Serb combat aircraft from Banja Luka airfield and from the territory of Bosnia and Herzegovina to the Federal Republic of Yugoslavia (annex IV);

(e) The joint statement of 19 October issued by the Federal Republic of Yugoslavia President Cosic and President Izetbegovic of Bosnia and Herzegovina (annex V);

(f) The joint declaration issued on 20 October 1992 by Federal Republic of Yugoslavia President Cosic and President Tudjman of Croatia and witnessed by the Co-Chairmen (annex VI);

(g) Agreements with Croatia, FRY, Government of Bosnia and Herzegovina and Bosnian Serb representatives on deployment of observers at airfields in context of ban on military flights over Bosnia and Herzegovina. This agreement has already been dealt with in the report of the

Secretary-General pursuant to Security Council resolution 781 (1192) (S/24767 of 5 November 1992).

C. Supervision of Heavy Weapons in Bosnia and Herzegovina

20. Following their arrival in Geneva on 3 September the Co-Chairmen also gave urgent attention to seeking the implementation of the agreement signed in London on 27 August by Mr. Douglas Hurd, Secretary of State for Foreign and Commonwealth Affairs and Dr. Radovan Karadzic, President of the Serbian Democratic Party, concerning the concentration and supervision of heavy weapons around Sarajevo, Bihac, Jajce and Gorazde. They asked Under-Secretary-General Goulding to stop in Geneva on 5 and 6 September in his way back to New York to brief them on the problems entailed in implementation of the agreement.

21. Mr. Goulding reported that in contact with the Bosnian Serb leadership on Tuesday and Wednesday, 1 and 2 September, the United Nations Protection Force (UNPROFOR) had succeeded in obtaining the Bosnian Serb side's agreement that the term "heavy weapons" should be interpreted to include all artillery with a calibre of 100 mm or more, all tanks armed with cannon, all multiple rocket-launchers, and all mortars with a calibre of 82 mm or more. Mr. Goulding recommended, and the Co-Chairmen agreed, that the period of 96 hours provided for in the agreement of 27 August should be deemed to have begun when this definition was agreed, namely at noon on Wednesday 2 September.

22. On 15 September 1992, Mr. Vance issued the following statement:

> "UNPROFOR has told me that the Serb side has stated that it has concentrated its heavy weaponry - artillery, tanks, 82 mm mortar and above - at 11 sites around Sarajevo. These are now being put under UNPROFOR monitoring. In Bihac, where such weapons are to be concentrated at three sites, the local commander has declared all his heavy weaponry, but has so far declined to concentrate his 82 mm mortars, and discussions are continuing. Fighting around Jajce has thus far prevented UNPROFOR from making effective contact with the local Serb command. The Serb side has withdrawn from most of Gorazde, also removing its heavy weaponry. Although the process is not yet complete, we believe this is a start."

Further information on this issue is contained in the Secretary-General's forthcoming report on peace-keeping.

IV. WORKING GROUP ON BOSNIA AND HERZEGOVINA

23. This Working Group is chaired by Mr. Martti Ahtisaari. Its task is to promote a cessation of hostilities and a constitutional settlement in Bosnia and

Herzegovina.

24. The Working Group took up this dual task on 18 September, and since that time has had 40 formal meetings, each between the Chairman and the representatives of one or another of the parties, since, so far, some of these have been unwilling to negotiate directly with the others. In addition, there have been almost an equal number of informal consultations, between the Co-Chairmen, the Chairman of the Working Group or members of the secretariat, and the leaders or other members of the delegations. As a result of these multiple and extensive contacts, a good understanding has been acquired of the positions of the parties on many of the important issues before the Working Group.

25. As the Working Group's task is a dual one, some meetings have been devoted to both the promotion of a cessation of hostilities in Bosnia and Herzegovina and the promotion of a constitutional settlement in that country, while at others only one of these subjects was discussed. It was always understood that the two aspects of the work are closely related.

A. Cessation of Hostilities

26. The discussion relating to the cessation of hostilities led to an agreement, which the Co-Chairmen reported on 30 September that military commanders and local authorities of the three sides would meet under the auspices of UNPROFOR and the International Conference on the Former Yugoslavia to work towards the demilitarization of Sarajevo and a cessation of hostilities in the city. General Morillon made several efforts to get his Mixed Military Working Group under way, but the Presidency of Bosnia declined to participate before water and electricity were restored to Sarajevo. The Co-Chairmen made strong representations to remove this precondition.

27. The Mixed Military Working Group finally met for the first time on Friday 23 October at Sarajevo airport. It has since held three further meetings. The activities of the Mixed Military Working Group are dealt with in the Secretary-General's forthcoming report on peace-keeping.

28. On 13 October, Lord Owen secured from Dr. Radovan Karadzic an undertaking to remove all Bosnian Serb combat aircraft from Banja Luka airfield and from the territory of Bosnia and Herzegovina to the Federal Republic of Yugoslavia. The implementation of this undertaking has been dealt with in the report of the Secretary-General of 5 November 1992 pursuant to Security Council resolution 781 (1992) (S/24767).

B. Constitutional arrangements

1. Framework of the negotiations

29. It will be recalled that the European Communities (EC) Conference on Yugoslavia (EC-COY) initiated a series of talks in February 1992 on the Future Constitutional Arrangements for Bosnia and Herzegovina. Ten rounds took place under the chairmanship of Ambassador José Cutileiro of Portugal, and senior representatives of the three main Bosnian political parties participated.

30. At the fifth round of these talks a "Statement of Principles for new constitutional arrangements for Bosnia and Herzegovina" was tentatively agreed to on 18 March 1992, and these were supplemented by some additional principles on human rights developed on 31 March at the sixth round. However, these tentative agreements were repudiated soon thereafter. No further constitutional agreements were reached at later talks held under the auspices of the EC-COY.

31. The International Conference assigned the continuation of the negotiation of a constitutional settlement in Bosnia and Herzegovina to the Bosnia and Herzegovina Working Group.

32. In starting the Working Group's consideration of this subject, the Chairman distributed a number of papers to the parties:

1. Checklist of principles relating to the Constitution;
2. Revised checklist of international human rights instruments relevant to a Constitution for Bosnia and Herzegovina (BiH);
3. List of human rights that might be considered for inclusion in, or other protection under, the BiH Constitution;
4. Preliminary thoughts for discussion on implementation, enforcement, and guarantees of human rights provisions of the BiH Constitution;
5. Distribution of governmental responsibilities between central government and constituent units - request for indication of preference.

At the request of the Chairman of the Working Group, the parties have given their oral or written reactions to the papers on human rights prepared by the secretariat, as well as written responses to the questionnaire on the distribution of governmental responsibilities. All of these were communicated to the other delegations with the consent of the submitting delegation. The parties have also submitted, on a no-distribution basis, their respective positions regarding the constituent units or regions into which they consider Bosnia and Herzegovina should be arranged.

33. On the basis of the positions of the three parties derived from these meetings and conversations, and from their close consultations with the Chairman of the Bosnia and Herzegovina Working Group, the Co-Chairmen have reached the conclusions discussed below and presented to the parties a paper on a possible constitutional structure for Bosnia and Herzegovina (annex VII below).

2. Structure of the State

(a) Basic Considerations

34. It was recognized from the beginning that the views of the three parties diverged widely on the structure of the future Bosnia and Herzegovina. One of the parties initially advocated a centralized, unitary State, arranged into a number of regions possessing merely administrative functions. Another party considered that the country should be divided into three independent States, respectively for the Muslim, Serb and Croat peoples, with each of these States having its own international legal personality, which States might form a loose confederation for the purpose of coordinating certain of their activities. The third party supported a middle position.

35. The basis for the consideration of this issue was the Statement of Principles adopted by the International Conference on the Former Yugoslavia in London (LC/C2 (FINAL)), and especially its total condemnation of forced expulsions of populations and the reversal of those which had already taken place (paragraph vi), as well as respect for the inviolability of all borders and the rejection of all efforts to change borders by force (para. vii). These principles had also been reiterated in paragraphs (c) and (e) of the above-cited Statement on Bosnia.

36. The population of Bosnia and Herzegovina is inextricably intermingled. Thus, there appears to be no viable way to create three territorially distinct States based on ethnic or confessional principles. Any plan to do so would involve incorporating a very large number of members of the other ethnic/confessional groups, or consist of a number of separate enclaves of each ethnic/confessional group. Such a plan could achieve homogeneity and coherent boundaries only by a process of enforced population transfer - which has already been condemned by the International Conference on the Former Yugoslavia as well as by the General Assembly (resolution 46/242, preamble and para. 6) and the Security Council (resolutions 771 (1992) and 779 (1992)). Consequently, the Co-Chairmen deemed it necessary to reject any model based on three separate, ethnic/confessionally based States. Furthermore, a confederation formed of three such States would be inherently unstable, for at least two would surely forge

immediate and stronger connections with neighbouring States of the former Yugoslavia than they would with the other two units of Bosnia and Herzegovina.

37. The Co-Chairmen also recognized, however, that a centralized state would not be accepted by at least two of the principal ethnic/confessional groups in Bosnia and Herzegovina, since it would not protect their interests in the wake of the bloody civil strife that now sunders the country.

38. Consequently, the Co-Chairmen believe that the only viable and stable solution that does not acquiesce in already accomplished ethnic cleansing, and in further internationally unacceptable practices, appears to be the establishment of the decentralized State. This would mean a State in which many of its principal functions, especially those directly affecting persons, would be carried out by a number of autonomous provinces. The central government, in turn, would have only those minimal responsibilities that are necessary for a state to function as such, and to carry out its responsibilities as a member of the international community. The proposed decentralisation also appears to reflect the wish of all the parties, as indicated by their responses to the questionnaire on the distribution of governmental responsibilities mentioned in paragraph 32 above.

(b) Number of Provinces

39. In considering the number of units, tentatively referred to as "provinces", into which Bosnia and Herzegovina might be arranged, account must of course be taken of the views of the parties. One party still insists on three as the appropriate number, as corresponding to the number of the principal "constituent nations" in the country. However, the party that originally favoured a centralized State with the existing 95 administrative units, now suggests that in a decentralized structure the number of provinces could be between 6 and 18.

40. In deciding what number or range of numbers to propose to the parties various considerations must be taken into account. These include the desirability that each of the provinces be an administratively and economically viable unit, a goal that would be difficult to achieve if the number of units were to exceed 10. Exceeding 10 would probably mean that some would have populations of less that a quarter million. On the one hand, if the number of the provinces were too few, it would be difficult to realize ethnic homogeneity without either violating the principle of geographic coherence or accepting the results of ethnic cleansing. Consequently, to meet these criteria the number of provinces might range from 7 to 10, with the precise number to be established by negotiation among the parties, in the light of proposed boundaries of the provinces.

(c) Boundaries of the Provinces

41. The boundaries of the provinces should be drawn so as to constitute areas as geographically coherent as possible, taking into account ethnic, geographical (i.e., natural features, such as rivers), historical, communications (i.e., the existing road and railroad networks), economic viability, and other relevant factors (annex VII below, sect. I.B.1). Given the demographic composition of the country, it is likely that many of the provinces (but not necessarily all) will have a considerable majority of one of the three major groups. Thus, a high percentage of each group would be living in a province in which it constitutes a numerical majority, although most of the provinces would also have significant numerical minorities.

42. Utilizing the maps supplied by each of the parties on a confidential basis, proposals are being developed for a possible arrangement of Bosnia and Herzegovina into provinces that would reflect the above-mentioned considerations. It is intended to do this as soon as possible, with the assistance of expert advisers.

(d) Nature of the Boundaries

43. The boundaries of the provinces are to be set out in the constitution and would be subject to change only by amending that instrument with majorities (either in the legislature, or in a referendum, or both) indicating that the three principal groups all accept the change (see annex VII below, sect. I. B.2).

44. The boundaries between provinces are not to have the nature of state borders, i.e., there are to be no borders or other controls that would hinder the free movement of people and goods throughout the entire country (annex VII below, sect. I.B.4).

(e) Recognition of Ethnic and other Groups

45. It is common ground among the parties that Bosnia and Herzegovina is populated by three major "constituent peoples" or ethnic/confessional groups, namely the Muslims, the Serbs and the Croats, and also by a category of "others". Two of the parties contend that in designing a government for the country a predominant roles must be given to these "constituent peoples". The other party considers that there should be no such overt recognition, although it admits that the political processes of the country have been and are likely to continue to be characterized by religious and ethnic factors. The paper on a proposed constitutional structure therefore proposes that the Constitution recog-

nize the existence of the groups in two ways: by providing that certain posts or functions be assigned by rotation or by equitable balancing among the recognized groups (see, for example, annex VII below, sect. IV. A.2 (a)), and also by the conscious protection of group or minority rights (annex VII, sect VI.A.2 (b), and appendix, part C).

3. Distribution of governmental functions

46. The task of making recommendations as to the distribution of governmental responsibilities and functions between the central government and the provinces was eased through the completion of the above-mentioned questionnaire by the delegation of each of the parties, and by the fact that their responses corresponded to a considerable extent. In particular, all responses indicated a preference for a considerably decentralized State, with only minimal responsibilities entrusted to the central authorities.

47. The Central government (annex VII, sect. II.A) would be responsible for: foreign affairs (including membership in international organisations), international commerce, national defence and citizenship. Only a single citizenship is to exist in the country, although any person may hold dual citizenship (annex VII, sect. VI.C). The central government would have the power to tax for these limited purposes. Although it is intended to establish provinces that are all economically viable, if that cannot be fully realized or if some provisions are much poorer than others, than resource transfers among them may have to be envisaged, possibly using taxes collected by the central government.

48. It is proposed that certain tasks be carried out in a centralized fashion, not by the central government, but rather by independent authorities administered by representatives of all the provinces. These could be assigned operational and some regulatory tasks. In particular, the Central Bank, which is to be both the issuer of the national currency and the principal regulator of banks and similar financial institutions in the country, would be such an authority. Other authorities might be established, or constitute parts of international authorities, for operating certain transnational communication links (annex VII, sect. II.B).

49. A few functions might be carried out jointly, or on the basis of responsibility shared between the central and the provincial governments (Annex VII, sect. II. II.C).

50. As already indicated, most governmental functions would be carried out at the provincial, or even local, level. This relates to the police, which is in almost all respects to be completely controlled by the provinces (annex VII, sect. V. 2). In addition, almost all activities in which individuals are directly affected by the government, such as educational and cultural activities, the licensing of trades,

professions and business and the provision of health, social care, and insurances would be carried out at the local level. These are the functions that are of particular concern to those seeking to maintain the separate heritages of the peoples constituting Bosnia and Herzegovina. Of course, as indicated in paragraph 64 (b) below, the rights of the minorities likely to be scattered throughout each of the provinces would be adequately safeguarded. As far as possible, the provinces would be responsible for their own economies and infrastructure.

4. Structure of the Government

51. Both the central and the provincial governments are to be structured along classical links, i.e., they are to have legislative, executive and judicial branches.

(a) The Central Government

52. The national legislature is to consist of two Houses:

    (a) The Lower House is to be elected by proportional representation in the country considered as a whole (annex VII, sect. IV.A.1 (a)). Consequently, it is likely that its composition will initially correspond to the ethnic composition of the country. It is possible that eventually political parties may develop that are not primarily ethnically based, but rather reflect political or regional orientation or other concerns (e.g., environmental ones). The Lower House is to appoint the Prime Minister (annex VII, sect. IV.A.2 (c)) and, eventually, the ombudsmen (annex VII, sect. VI.B.2). It will also share responsibility for legislating with the Upper House, although it might be provided - as in many countries - that the Lower House, as the only directly elected national body, should predominate in any case of divergence between the two Houses, and that it should have a particular responsibility for taxation and the budget.

    (b) The Upper House is the be appointed by and from the provincial governments (annex VII, sect. IV.A.1 (b)). Since most of the provinces will probably have a population in which one ethnic group or another is in the majority, the composition of that House is also likely to reflect roughly the ethnic composition of the country as a whole.

53. Executive power is to be divided among a number of persons and bodies:

(a) The Presidency is to consist of the Governors (i.e. the chief executives) of all the provinces - which will thus reflect roughly the ethnic composition of the country (see para. 52 (b) above) (annex VII, sect. IV.A.2(a)). It is to be chaired by the President. The powers of this body are to be restricted to making a number of senior appointments: that of the President, of the highest appellate judges and of the military chiefs, and also the approval of the Ministers named by the Prime Minister. All these appointments are to take into account either rotation among the several groups (for unique positions such as the Presidency) or balance (for collective bodies such as the Cabinet). It will be possible to appeal alleged violations of these principles to the Constitutional Court which, at least initially, is to include a predominance of foreign judges (annex VII, sect, IV.A.3 (c)).

(b) The President is to be selected by the Presidency, whether from its own ranks or from the outside (e.g., a distinguished citizen, not necessarily political aligned) for a limited term, and will be subject to group rotation - i.e. two members of the same group cannot succeed each other. His/her function as Head of State is to be largely ceremonial, but the actual powers assigned to him/her are to be specified in detail in the Constitution (annex VII, sect. IV.A.2(b)).

(c) The Prime Minister is to be the head of Government, and is to be elected by the Lower House (annex VII, sect. IV.A.2 (c)), thus conforming to the pattern of most parliamentary democracies. As indicated, the division of powers between the Prime Minister and the President will have to be detailed in the Constitution.

(d) The Ministers would form the Cabinet with the Prime Minister and are to be appointed by him/her but, instead of being approved by the Lower House, would be approved by the Presidency - the body charged with maintaining group balance. It has not been stated that they need be members of either House of the legislature, although that could be provided.

(e) The national civil service, which is likely to be small because of the limited functions of the central government, would be subject to normal civil service/administrative governance. Its composition would have to take account of the obligation to maintain group balance.

54. The judiciary is to be a shared responsibility of the central and the provincial governments, In particular, it is proposed that the courts of "first instance" (i.e.,

the courts to which cases are first submitted), as well as those considering the first level of appeal from these, be constituted exclusively by the provinces. A further appeal would lie to one or more of the highest courts (e.g., civil and criminal, administrative, labour) that would be created at the national level and whose judges would be appointed by the Presidency. This appeal would encompass only questions concerning the Constitution or those arising out of national legislation or international treaties. On question of purely provincial concern, the highest appellate level would therefore be the provincial one (annex VII, sects. IV.A.3 (a) and IV.B.3).

55. In addition to these courts, there would be the two senior courts with, at least initially, a predominance of foreign judges:

   (a) One would be the Human Rights Court (annex VII, sect. VI. VI.B.3), to which an appeal can be taken on any constitutionally defended human rights issue from the final, otherwise unappealable, decision of any other court. It might also be provided that an appeal can be taken if such other court delays the proceedings unduly, and also that such other court might address questions to the Human Rights Court, with the answers binding on the court that addressed the question. The national judges on this Court would be appointed by the Presidency in such a way that each group is represented. A somewhat larger number of judges would be appointed by the President of the European Court of Human Rights and the President of the European Commission of Human Rights. This would be done by a special arrangement with the Council of Europe, for which purposes political bodies of the Council are already considering a new, general mechanism (i.e., one that would not apply just to Bosnia and Herzegovina) proposed by Lord Owen to the Parliamentary Assembly of the Council. It is hoped that the competent bodies of the Council will act quite soon to create the necessary mechanisms, and the Constitution of Bosnia and Herzegovina would then appropriately refer to it.
   (b) The other court would be the Constitutional Court (annex VII, sect. IV.A.3), whose primary function would be to decide disputes between constitutional entities (e.g., the Presidency. the President, the Prime Minister, Ministers, the Lower and Upper House of the Legislature). It would also be competent to decide appeals concerning the exercise of the Presidency's appointing power (annex VIII, sect. IV.A.2(a)) and it would also serve as the court of final appeal on constitutional questions arising in litigation in other courts. The Court would be composed of national judges appointed by the Presidency and of a majority of foreign

judges, appointed in the first instance by the International Conference on the Former Yugoslavia and later by any international body designated by the Conference (e.g., the President of the International Court of Justice or the United Nations Secretary-General). A court along these lines was already foreseen in the Principles agreed to by the parties on 18 March (see paragraph 30 above).

(b) The Provincial Governments

56. It is not anticipated that the Constitution will specify in any detail the provisions of the provincial constitutions or of the provincial governmental structures. As appropriate for a decentralized system, these matters should be left for decision by the provincial governments and voters. The provisions of the provincial constitutions, however, and of any laws adopted under them would have to be subject to the federal Constitution and laws. Any disputes concerning such matters would be decided by the Constitutional Court (annex VII, sect. III.B.).

57. Each province is expected to have a legislature, but whether it were unicameral or bicameral would be determined by the provincial constitution (annex VII sect. IB.B.1). Of course, under the human rights provision of the Constitution, it would be necessary that the method of electing the legislature be fully democratic.

58. Similarly, it is not to be specified in the Constitution how the provincial Governors (annex VII, sect. IV.B.2) are to attain those posts, for example by direct, popular election, or by appointment of one or both houses of the provincial legislature.

59. The provincial courts (annex Vii, sect. IV.B.3), i.e. those of first instance and the intermediate appellate courts, will constitute part of the judicial system of the country as a whole and be subject to the highest courts established on the national level, including the Constitutional and the Human Rights Courts (paras. 54 and 55 above). However, the details of the structuring of provincial courts would not be specified in the Constitution, although they might be subject to some national legislation.

5. Organization and Control of Executive Force

60. As the central Government is to be solely responsible for national defence, the military forces are to be entirely under its control (annex VII, sect. V.A.1.). It remains to be decided which official will exercise that control, but we believe that the senior staff, which is to be appointed by the Presidency (annex VII, sect.

IV.A.2(a)), must be balanced in respect of the recognized groups and that the post of Chief of Staff must rotate among them. In addition, all military units are to be fully integrated and function on a non-discriminatory basis. At least of an initial period (see para. 69 below), these requirements of balance, rotation, integration, and non-discrimination are to be supervised by any international authority designated by the International Conference on the Former Yugoslavia, because it is recognized that melding three armed forces which currently are engaged in bitter combat is unlikely to be successful without outside assistance and mediation (annex VII, sect. V.A.2).

61. The Constitution is to provide that the above-described forces controlled by the central Government are to have exclusive possession of military power in Bosnia and Herzegovina (annex VII, sect. V.C.). Therefore, neither the provinces, nor any other public or private entities are to be allowed to form armed units or to possess heavy weapons. What weapons the provincial police may possess might be the subject of national legislation.

62. All uniformed police are to be controlled by the provinces or by local authorities under them (annex VII, sect. V.B.1.(a)). All police forces are to be fully integrated, and this requirement, too, would initially be supervised by an international authority designated by the International Conference, for the reasons indicated in respect of the military (annex VII, sect. V.B.1(b)). At the national level there is to be no uniformed, armed police, but only a coordinating office to assist the provincial police authorities and to maintain contacts with international and foreign police authorities (annex VII, sect. V.B.2) (e.g., Interpol); this responsibility would include ensuring implementation of any treaty-based responsibilities that Bosnia and Herzegovina may have (e.g., those relating to the combat of terrorism and the illegal trade in prohibited narcotic drugs).

6. Human Rights

63. Statements made by the parties in the previous talks (paras. 29 and 30 above) and their oral and written observations in the Working Group agreed that the parties wish the Constitution to reflect, and the country to observe, the highest internationally accepted standards of human rights. They had also agreed that these rights be based on the international instruments formulated by, or under the aegis of, the United Nations, the Council of Europe, and the Conference on Security and Cooperation in Europe as already foreseen in the Statement of Principles of the International Conference (LC/C2 (FINAL), para. (iv)). Similarly, they agree that the implementation of these rights in Bosnia and Herzegovina should, at least for a time, be supervised through international

mechanisms. A list of such instruments and a description of such mechanisms were furnished to the parties (para. 32 above, items 2-4) and their reactions were uniformly positive.

64. It is therefore proposed that the Constitution set out a number of human rights, grouped essentially into three categories:

(a) General human, especially civil and political, rights as expressed in instruments such as the 1966 International Covenant on Civil and Political Rights and the Protocols thereto, and in the 1950 European Convention for the Protection of Human Rights and Fundamental Freedoms and in the protocols thereto (annex VII, sect. VI.A.2(a), and appendix, part A);

(b) Group and especially "minority" rights, as expressed in instruments such as the 1992 draft Declaration on the rights of persons belonging to national or ethnic, religious and linguistic minorities (A/47/501) and in the 1990 Recommendation 1134 (1990) of the Parliamentary Assembly of the Council of Europe, on the rights of minorities (annex VII, sect. VI.A.2(b), and appendix, part B);

(c) Economic, social and cultural rights, as expressed in the 1966 International Covenant on Economic, Social and Cultural Rights and in the 1961 European Social Charter and the Protocol thereto; it is foreseen that many of the rights under this heading will be stated only as aspirations, as their immediate implementation may be beyond the economic means and other capabilities of the new country (annex VII, sect, VI.A.2(c), and appendix, part C).

65. It is proposed that these rights be expressly included in the Constitution, in appropriated detail for such an instrument. In any event, the international treaties and some instruments in which these rights are to be expressed, and which would be listed in the Constitution or in an annex thereto, would be incorporated into the Constitution by reference (annex VII, sect.VI.A.1, and appendix). It is also foreseen that the Constitution is to require the new State to become a party to the listed treaties as quickly as possible. As the Socialist Federal Republic of Yugoslavia, the predecessor State, was a party to most of the United Nations treaties in question, it will only be necessary in respect of these to file a notice of succession with the Secretary-General. As to the treaties originating with the Council of Europe, Bosnia and Herzegovina will not be eligible to become a party thereto until it becomes a member of the Council (annex VII, appendix, para. A(b)).

66. One of the questions that particularly interested the parties was how to ensure that these extensive human rights to be embodied in the Constitution would actually be implemented. Among the devices discussed with them, and which are in part reflected in the paper annexed hereto, are to following:

(a) All persons in Bosnia and Herzegovina, whether citizens or not, would at all times have unimpeded access to the courts (annex VII, sect. VI.B.4);

(b) Both the provincial and the national courts would be required to apply the constitutionally guaranteed human rights, as set out in the Constitution or in the international instruments incorporated therein by reference as directly applicable law, regardless of whether implementing legislation had already been enacted (annex VII, sect. VI.B.4, and appendix, para. (a));

(c) There are to be four ombudsmen, one representing each of the recognized groups, who are to have wide powers to investigate, either on the basis of complaints or on their own initiative, all questions relating to the implementation of human rights, including those arising out of ethnic cleansing, to contact the authorities responsible for any abuses, and to report to the legislature and to other appropriated governmental bodies; they would also have the right to enter the courts. Initially, the ombudsmen are to be appointed by ICFY, and later by the Lower House of the national legislature, as is customary in many countries (annex VII, sect. VI.B.2);

(d) There is to be a Human Rights Court, which has already been described in paragraph 55 (a) above (annex VII, sect. VI.B.3);

(e) There is also to be an International Commission on Human Rights for Bosnia and Herzegovina, which is not to be an instrument created by the Constitution, but by ICFY. It would be guaranteed wide powers to investigate and to hear complaints in the country, and to report thereon to the appropriate international bodies (annex VII, sect. VI.B.1);

(f) Finally, as Bosnia and Herzegovina will be required to become a party to a number of international human rights treaties that establish various types of supervisory, monitoring, and dispute-settlement mechanisms (which are especially marked in the appendix to annex VII below), it will automatically become subject to the operations of these bodies, which will provide another measure of international supervision. Incidentically these measures, unlike some of the others which are meant to operate only on an interim, transitional basis (see para. 69 below), would continue to function permanently, as they do for other States parties to these treaties.

7. Transitional International Control Measures

67. Although a Constitution along the lines outlined in annex VII below would be designed to establish Bosnia and Herzegovina as a State functioning in a normal way in the international community as soon as possible, it is recognized that it will be necessary during a limited period for certain aspects of the operations of the country to be subject to some international supervision and control. This will be necessary in the light of the continuing violence and other activities taking place in the country, which are likely to make it extremely difficult for the contending parties to settle into normal cooperation as foreseen in the Constitution. It also seems to reflect the desires of the parties, who have indicated that certain international controls will be necessary for some time.

68. Consequently, a number of transitional international control measures are foreseen (annex VII, sect. I.D.1(a)-(f)):

(a) Two of these would be the proposed Constitutional Court and the Human Rights Court, described in paragraphs (a) and (b) above;

(b) Another measure would be the proposed International Human Rights Commission for Bosnia and Herzegovina, described in paragraph 66 (e) above;

(c) The ombudsmen, described in paragraph 66 (c) above, who are initially to be appointed by ICFY;

(d) The supervision of the balance and integration of the military forces and of the non-discrimination requirements relating to the provincial police are described in paragraphs 60 and 62 above.

69. Various provisions are foreseen for the duration of these transitional measures (annex VII, sect. I.D.2 (a)-(d)). For some, a particular time limit has been suggested, while others would be at the discretion of ICFY or its designated successor. Finally, all these measures (except for the purely international Human Rights Commission, which will not be a body created by the Constitution), including these for which there is no explicit termination provision, can be removed from the Constitution by amendment. Any such amendment, however, will require sufficiently high majorities to ensure that all three major groups agree that such elimination is indeed timely (annex VII, sect. III.A.3(c)).

8. Further Measures

70. Immediately after the Co-Chairmen's proposals concerning a constitutional structure for Bosnia and Herzegovina (annex VII) were presented to the parties represented in the Bosnia and Herzegovina Working Group on 28 October, the Chairman of the Working Group started holding consultations with them concerning these proposals. In due course it is hoped that negotiations will commence among them, either directly or through the Chairman of the Working Group. During such negotiations, the provisions outlined in the Co-Chairmen's proposal will be drafted in the form of constitutional texts by the parties with the assistance of the secretariat of ICFY. During this process, it will of course, be necessary to settle many of the details that have so far been left open or merely outlined.

71. An important element in the constitutional negotiations will be the need to reach agreement on the number and the precise boundaries of the several provinces (see paras. 39-41 above), so that these can be incorporated into the Constitution. At an appropriated time proposals regarding boundaries will be submitted to the parties (see para. 42 above).

72. Once the three parties represented in the Working Group agree to the Constitution, it is expected that they will be prepared to adopt it within the framework of the Conference. At that point, a date for entry into force must also be agreed upon, which will have to take into account the necessary preparatory steps to allow for implementation of the Constitution as soon as the country is governed by that instrument.

V. Working Group on Humanitarian Issues

73. The Working Group on Humanitarian Issues is chaired by the United Nations High Commissioner for Refugees, Mrs. Sadako Ogata. Its task is to promote humanitarian relief in all its aspects, including refugees.

74. It is estimated that within the region of the former Yugoslavia alone some 3 million people - displaced persons, refugees and people in besieged cities and regions - are directly affected by the crisis and are to a large extent dependent on external assistance for their survival. The main theatre of compelled displacement, as a result of fighting, ethnic cleansing and lack of means for survival, continues to be the Republic of Bosnia and Herzegovina. With the onset of winter, the plight of the civilian population, whether already displaced or not, is becoming harsher every day.

75. The Working Group has, therefore, concentrated a substantive part of its work on the situation in Bosnia and Herzegovina. There the needs are undoubtedly the greatest and the most urgent. Moreover, by trying to improve the situation in humanitarian terms, perhaps fewer people would be compelled to look for safety and assistance in the already over-burdened adjacent States, and beyond.

76. On 18 and 19 September, the Chairperson met with the Bosnian parties, in Geneva, and obtained written assurances for the safe resumption of the vital airlift to Sarajevo (which at that time had been suspended owing to the shooting down of the Italian aircraft on 3 September), for the safe passage of road convoys, for the release and safe transmit of detainees, and for the unhindered supply of basic necessities such as water and electricity to besieged cities, in particular Sarajevo.

77. On 3 October, the vital airlift to Sarajevo was resumed. Furthermore, UNHCR obtained the names of local authorities responsible for the safe passage of road convoys. Thanks to the unrelenting efforts of the ICRC, in early October, some 1,670 detainees (from Trnopolje and Bileca) regained their freedom, after obtaining safe passage to Croatia and Montenegro respectively, where they are now temporarily under UNHCR's care.

78. On 15 and 16 October, and on 5 November, the Chairperson of the Working Group convened further meetings with the Bosnian parties to review the implementation of the September commitments, and to discuss the ever-increasing needs of the civilian population and the ways to reach them in the most efficient and safest manner. The Chairperson confronted the parties with the fact that harassment at checkpoints and other obstacles continue to hamper UNHCR's safe humanitarian access through road convoys. They reconfirmed their commitment to full collaboration in ensuring the safe and unhindered passage of relief convoys.

79. The Chairperson reminded the parties of their commitment under the Programme of Action on Humanitarian Issues, adopted in London, to proceed unconditionally with the release of detainees, many of whom continue to be in detention. Reportedly not all detainees have yet been notified to ICRC. The cooperation of third States in temporarily receiving the detainees has regrettably become a crucial factor in implementing their release. The International Conference counts on the cooperation of the international community to offer temporary protection to this most vulnerable group of people. Despite the urgent appeals of UNHCR, ICRC and others, thousands of prisoners are still awaiting a solution amidst terrible conditions. The biggest group consists of 3,700 persons of the Muslim faith held in the Manjaca camp.

80. In her Working Group, Mrs. Ogata is vigorously taking part in the condemnation by the entire International Conference of the ongoing practice of ethnic cleansing. She has continued to insist on the right of people to stay, in conditions of security, and in the responsibility of everyone to ensure respect for this right. She asked the Serbian side in particular to take measures to protect the remaining non-Serbian population in Banja Luka town, where the harassment of non-Serbs has reportedly thus far been less violent than elsewhere.

81. The discussion in the Working Group lend support to the practical arrangements which necessarily have to be worked out on the ground, for instance regarding the priorities of assistance, the safe passage of road convoys and the modalities of the release of detainees. Secondly, these discussions serve to constantly remind the parties of their commitment, to respect to London Agreements, and to respect humanitarian law and human rights.

VI. WORKING GROUP ON ETHNIC AND NATIONAL COMMUNITIES AND MINORITIES

82. This Working Group is chaired by Ambassador Geert Ahrens. Its task is to recommend initiatives for resolving ethnic questions in the former Yugoslavia. A special group on the former autonomous province of Kosovo has been set up.

83. The Working Group started its work with a plenary meeting on 15 September 1992 in which government delegations from Slovenia, Croatia, Bosnia and Herzegovina, and Macedonia participated. The delegation from Belgrade, comprising Federal, Serbian and Montenegrin government representatives did not attend, owing to technical reasons. In the plenary meeting all those present reconfirmed their commitment to the Conference Principles, particularly to the Treaty Provisions for the Convention adopted in The Hague. During the same week, there were also talks in Geneva with ethnic and national communities and minorities, namely, Albanians from Kosovo, Albanians from Macedonia, Muslims from Serbia, Muslims and Albanians from Montenegro, Hungarians from Vojvodina, Croats from Vojvodina, and Serbs from Croatia. These talks showed pictures of continuous and, in some places, dangerous ethnic conflicts that were to be taken up urgently with the Governments concerned.

84. A Working Group delegation visited Belgrade from 22 to 24 September. Talks with Federal Ministers showed a general readiness to address critical issues, but also a certain hesitation to accept Conference mediation. Another plenary meeting was held in Geneva on 2 November 1992, at which the Federal delegation from Belgrade declared its commitment to the Principles of the London Conference. Participant were also brought up to date on the Group's latest

activities.

85. The Sub-Group on Macedonia held three meetings between Government representatives and Albanians in Geneva on 17 September, in Skopje on 15 October and in Geneva on 3 and 4 November. The very intensive work that had been done in the summer of 1992 was continued. Although some further progress could be achieved, the overall situation of the Republic (economic blockade, as the Government put it, non-recognition and, as a consequence, upsurge of nationalism) makes it increasingly difficult for the Government to compromise of ethnic questions. In the opinion of the Chairman of the Working Group, everything has to be done to uphold the so far positive internal development in Macedonia which is in real danger. The next round of talks is scheduled to take place in Skopje on 24 November.

86. The Sub-Group on Vojvodina had talks in Geneva, Belgrade and Subotica which was visited on 24 September and where both Hungarians and Croatians were present. The Sub-Group has not yet been able to start trilateral talks owing to some hesitation in Belgrade, However, there were positive signs from Belgrade, mainly regarding the Hungarians from Vojvodina, and a first round of trilateral talks involving Government representatives, ethnic Hungarians from Vojvodina and a Working Group delegation is scheduled for 10 to 11 November in Novi Sad. Concerning the Croats from Vojvodina, there is reason for hope that trilateral talks will be held in the near future.

87. In the overall situation of the Vojvodina Hungarians, there seems not to have been further deteriorations, whereas the ethnic Croats in Vojvodina are under severe pressure.

88. Regarding Sandjak, although trilateral talks have not yet been held, here also there is hope that these will materialize in a short time. The situation in this region, which is related to the Bosnian war, is alarming. Large numbers of Muslims have already left. Hopefully, the presence of CSCE observers there will help to defuse the tense situation on the ground, which is a serious obstacle to meaningful dialogue.

89. On the Serbs in Croatia, the Working Group had a talk with Mr. Goran Hadzic, "President of the Republic of Krajina", and several meetings with Croatian representatives. In Belgrade on 25 September, Mr. Hadzic said that he was quite prepared for talks on human rights, economic and communication issues, but not on any form of Serbian autonomy inside Croatia. He further said that the Krajina would rather resort to renewed warfare than become a part of Croatia again. It was not possible so far to convince Mr. Hadzic or any other Knin representative that a solution has to be found on the basis of the London Principles. At a forthcoming Working Group visit to Zagreb from 17 to 19 November, preliminary talks with UNPROFOR and UNHCR on how to proceed

and cooperate on the Krajina problems will continue. The continuation of contacts with both Croatian and Serbian politicians is also envisaged.

90. Intensive work was done in the Special Group on Kosovo. The basic approach agreed to by both sides is to try a pragmatic breakthrough in one important sector - the ethnic Albanians chose education - in order to improve the political atmosphere for talks on more fundamental issues where positions are at present irreconcilable. After difficult and tedious preparations, in which the release of the Chairman of the Albanian Teachers Association from prison could be achieved, the first Conference-sponsored talks between the Federal and the Serbian Governments from Belgrade on one side and ethnic Albanian representatives from Kosovo on the other took place. On 14 October all parties agreed to the following statement:

> "1. Representatives of the Government of the FRY and Serbia led by the Federal Minister of Education, Mr. Ivic, and representatives of the Albanians met in Pristina on 13 and 15 October with the participation of the Geneva Conference Special Group on Kosovo, under the Chairmanship of Ambassador Ahrens. A representative of the CSCE mission was also present.
> 2. After detailed discussion of the problem of education in the Albanian language, the participants agreed that the present situation must be changed. They further agreed on the urgent desirability of the return to normal working conditions for schools and other educational institutions.
> 3. It was agreed that, to achieve this, it would be necessary to adopt a pragmatic approach requiring urgent resolution, without prejudice to the positions of the parties on broader political issues.
> 4. The Albanian representatives agreed to provide a list of schools and other educational institutions to be covered by the measures mentioned in (2); as well a list of teaching plans and programmes.
> 5. The Group agreed to meet again in Belgrade on 22 October. At that meeting discussions will be held on all the issues mentioned with the aim of reaching the necessary decisions for immediate actions."

91. These talks were continued accordingly on 22 October in Belgrade, after meeting with both President Cosic and Mr. Rugova. The participants reaffirmed their commitment to the necessity of changing the existing situation in the field of education, and the urgent need for a return to normal conditions in schools and other educational institutions in Kosovo, as set out in their statement of 14 October. They agreed that this commitment refers to all four levels of education: pre-school, elementary school, secondary school and higher education. On Albanian insistence, there was agreement that all problems related to education in Albania at all levels are related and must be treated as a whole. The Serbian and Federal representatives made plain the material and financial constraints affecting their areas of responsibility. Within those constraints, there will be no discrimination as between the support which they will provide for instruction in

both the Albanian and the Serbian languages. However, no agreement could be reached so far on conditions under which school buildings should be opened, teachers should be reinstated and entrance examinations should be handled. The Working Group has done its best to arrange proper coordination with the CSCE efforts in former Yugoslavia. A representative of the CSCE participated in both of the Kosovo talks, in Pristina on 13 October and in Belgrade on 22 October. On 21 October there was also a conversation with the leader of the CSCE mission in Belgrade. The activities of the CSCE observers on the ground complement the negotiating endeavours of the International Conference.

92. Personal contact has been established between the Working Group's Chairman and the Special Rapporteur of the United Nations Commission on Human Rights, Mr. Mazowiecki.

VII. WORKING GROUP ON SUCCESSION ISSUES

93. The task of the Working Group is to resolve succession issues arising from the emergence of new states in the territory of the former Yugoslavia. Its work is complemented by the Working Group on Economic Issues, which is preparing an inventory of State assets and liabilities affected by the succession.

94. The Working Group was first chaired by Mr. Henry Darwin. The Co-Chairmen learned with profound regret of his death, of a heart attack, on 17 September 1992. The untimely death of this distinguished jurist deprives the Conference of one of its outstanding members. The Co-Chairmen expressed their sincere condolences to the members of Mr. Darwin's family and their gratitude for the unique contribution he had made to the search for a peaceful settlement in Yugoslavia.

95. On 8 October 1992, the Co-Chairmen announced that they had selected Jorgen Bojer, a senior Danish diplomat, to chair the Working Group.

96. In meetings in Geneva from 7 to 9 September 1992, the Working Group considered the issue of citizenship and concluded that the existence of a Republican citizenship, even under the former Yugoslav law, meant that no former Yugoslav citizen would become stateless as a consequence of the emergence of new states; however, certain aspects of citizenship, and particularly the conditions for changing citizenship between Republics in the light of the new situation, would require further study.

97. The Working Group also considered the definition of State property which is to be regarded as affected by the succession of States. Divergent views were expressed on this issue in the Working Group. The Working Group held preliminary discussion on the criteria that might be appropriate for the distribution of

sate property among the States involved.

98. Other points being discussed in the Working Group include possible criteria for distributing any balance of assets and liabilities among the new Republics, pensions, archives, overseas properties, and succession of the treaties and to international organisations.

99. The next meeting of the Working Group is scheduled to be held at Geneva from 24 November to 27 November 1992.

VIII. WORKING GROUP ON ECONOMIC ISSUES

100. This Working Group is chaired by M. Jean Durieux. Its task is to address the economic issues arising from the emergence of new States in the territory of the former Yugoslavia. The Group's work on future economic relations between the Republics of the former Yugoslavia has had to be suspended in the light of conflict in the area and the imposition of economic sanctions. In the interim, the Group has established six expert sub-groups to prepare an inventory of assets and liabilities of the former Yugoslavia, which could be completed in the first months of 1993. A seventh working group on war damages will be convened at a later stage.

101. The Working Group has prepared a report which has evaluated the economic situation in Macedonia and the Republic's short term needs for external assistance.

102. At the request of the Co-Chairmen of the Steering Committee, the Working Group is exploring the possibility of organizing, at the beginning of 1993, a conference, at the Prime Ministerial level, to discuss the economic reconstruction of the area of the former Yugoslavia, keeping in mind the relevant pronouncements of the United Nations Security Council.

IX. WORKING GROUP ON CONFIDENCE AND SECURITY-BUILDING AND VERIFICATION MEASURES

103. This Working Group is chaired by Mr. Vincente Berasategui. Its tasks are to develop confidence-building measures covering military movements, arms control and arms transfers and limitations, and measures for their monitoring and verification.

104. The Working Group began its work as requested by the Co-Chairmen immediately after the downing, on 3 September, of a Italian aircraft participating in the humanitarian airlift to Sarajevo and the suspension of all humanitarian flights that followed. It held 14 meetings from 4 September to 6 October. The prime

objective of the Working Group was to seek measures that could be taken by all the parties in the former Yugoslavia, and particularly those in Bosnia and Herzegovina, to facilitate the resumption of humanitarian flights into Sarajevo by restoring confidence to the operators of those flights. At the same time, measures were sought that would engage the parties in the region in a cooperative efforts. All parties in the former Yugoslavia were represented, including the three sides in Bosnia and Herzegovina. Furthermore, in attendance were the main contributors to the airlift, including Italy, representatives of the EC, CSCE, UNHCR and UNPROFOR.

105. A set of measures was adopted on 15 September and modalities for their implementation on 24 September. The measures included several already agreed upon at the London session of the International Conference in August and several are reproduced in the annex to Security Council document S/24634 of 8 October 1992 and are referred to in the preambular part of resolution 781 (1992).

106. In pursuance of the measures agreed upon and in accordance with their related modalities, all the parties in the former Yugoslavia transmitted to the Chairman several rounds of information which, in an important indication of transparency, were eventually exchanged among all participants in the Working Group, including the representatives of those countries operating humanitarian flights. The parties have reported, *inter alia*, on the headquarters and commanders in force in a 45-km radius of this site where the Italian aircraft went down and in a 45-km area on either side of the agreed flight route. Furthermore, two parties in Bosnia and Herzegovina have agreed to withdraw all their anti-aircraft artillery from a 45-km area on each side of the route agreed upon for humanitarian flights. One party states it would withdraw from that area anti-aircraft artillery of 40 mm and above, and light anti-aircraft artillery (below 40 mm) from a 10-km area on each side of the route agreed upon for humanitarian flights.

107. The modalities agreed upon for the implementation of those measures have not been completely complied with and some information has still not been forwarded. In order to assist in maintaining the level of the confidence already achieved by the measures agreed upon, the Working Group will keep under review the further implementation of the measures agreed upon directly relevant to the now resumed humanitarian flights. The review of the measures adopted by the Working Group to facilitate the resumption of the humanitarian flights will be co-ordinated closely with the activities in this area conducted by UNHCR and UNPROFOR.

108. On 10 October 1992, within the context of the activities of the working Group on Confidence and Security-Building and Verification Measures, representatives of Croatia and the Federal Republic of Yugoslavia confirmed paragraph 7 of the Joint Declaration signed by the Presidents on 30 September 1992 (annex II below), and agreed on certain practical measures relating to the deployment of the European Community Monitoring Mission (ECMM) and UNPROFOR military observers on airfields in this respective countries as a confidence-building measure.

109. The Working Group will continue to meet to pursue long-term confidence-building measures as envisaged by the International Conference in London (see Specific Decisions by London Conference - LC/C7, and Confidence, Security-Building and Verification - LC/C11). These documents will continue to serve as the terms of reference for the further work of the Group. Efforts will be made to seek common ground among the parties in the region on such measures in the field of confidence-building which would support the political process launched by the Co-Chairmen.

X. Cooperation with UNPROFOR

110. The Co-Chairmen have maintained close contacts with Under-Secretary-General Goulding, and with General Nambiar, General Morillon and their colleagues in UNPROFOR. UNPROFOR has deployed a Military Liaison Officer to the Office of the Co-Chairmen, at the request of the latter, on order to ensure smooth day-to-day cooperation and coordination.

XI. Cooperation with Human Rights and Humanitarian Bodies

111. The Co-Chairmen recognize that human rights and humanitarian issues are at the core of the current crisis on the former Yugoslavia and should be given the utmost priority.

112. In recognition of this, the Co-Chairmen, in making proposals for the proposed constitutional structure for Bosnia and Herzegovina, have advanced far-reaching ideas on human rights norms that should be included in the future Constitution; the role of the Constitutional Court; the role of a Special Human Rights Court; the need for an International Commission on Human Rights for Bosnia and Herzegovina; the need for ombudsmen; the need or the protection of minorities; and the importance of the rectification of international human rights treaties.

113. The Co-Chairmen have already taken the lead in alerting the international community to human rights and humanitarian issues in the former Yugoslavia. In his remarks to the United Nations Security Council in New York on 14 October, Mr. Vance stated:

> "We are facing an extremely difficult and complex situation whose humanitarian consequences are already appalling. I want to report frankly that with the approach of winter thousands of lives are at risk unless the international community is able to avert a disaster. A catastrophe of untold dimensions could be unfolding.
> I also want to express our team's deep anguish and concern at what is taking place on the ground in Bosnia and Herzegovina. It is hard to believe that basic rules of human rights and humanitarian law are flouted so consistently in the last decade of the twentieth century."

In his remarks to the Steering Committee of the International Conference in Geneva on 27 October, Mr. Vance stated:

> "We continue to be deeply worried about the humanitarian situation in the country."

He specifically invited the Steering Committee to:

> "consider what more can be done to make it perfectly clear that 'ethnic cleansing' is not and will not be accepted by the international community; and what steps can be taken to reverse that has already been done".

114. The Co-Chairmen have been cooperating with the Special Rapporteur of the Commission of Human Rights, Mr. Tadeusz Mazowiecki. The day after their arrival in Geneva, on 4 September, the Co-Chairmen had an extensive meeting, lasting two hours, with the Special Rapporteur. They discussed a broad range of issues. The Co-Chairmen met with the Special Rapporteur again on 8 October to review developments and to coordinate their efforts. The Bosnia and Herzegovina and the Special Rapporteur have designated contact persons in an effort to assure efficient coordination. The Co-Chairmen have designated, on their side, the Chairpersons on the International Conference's Working Group on Humanitarian Issues, the United Nations High Commissioner for Refugees, Mrs. Ogata, and the Chairman of the Working Group on Minorities, Ambassador Ahrens. In addition, the Chairmen of other Working Groups of the Conference, including the Working Group on Bosnia and Herzegovina, have also had meetings with Mr. Mazowiecki or his staff.

115. In order to facilitate coordination at the working level, the Co-Chairmen have established an informal contact group on human rights and humanitarian issues, which has done useful work. Participation is being extended to include nominees from the Office of the Co-Chairmen, UNHCR, ICRC, UNPROFOR, the Special Rapporteur of the Commission on Human Rights, and the Commis-

sion of Experts recently established by the United Nations Security Council to examine and analyse evidence of grave breaches of the Geneva Conventions and other violations of international and humanitarian law committed in the territory of the former Yugoslavia.

XII. FINANCIAL ASPECTS

116. The participants in the International Conference have agreed to bear the costs related to the administrative implementation of the Conference's work programme and the provision of the secretariat.

117. At the 2nd meeting of the Steering Committee on 27 October, the Co-Chairmen announced that they had agreed on a budget of US$ 3.37 million for the six-month period ending 28 February 1993. A scale of cost apportionment among the participating States is close to agreement. To date, two States have made payments towards costs. The Organisation of the Islamic Conference has also made a financial contribution. In addition, a number of Governments have also helped financially, either by covering some of the personnel and other costs, or by providing, at no cost to the budget, such services as aircraft for missions to the former Yugoslavia and other countries. The Co-Chairmen are deeply appreciative of this support.

118. It was also agreed at the 2nd meeting of the Steering Committee to establish an open-ended ad hoc working group on financial matters, open to all States participating in the International Conference. It will meet, as required, to review budgetary trends and outlook.

XIII. SECRETARIAT

119. Based on the recommendation of the London session of the International Conference, a small secretariat has been established at the United Nations Office in Geneva. It is staffed by personnel from the United Nations and from the European Community. The Secretariat is fully equipped and functioning.

XIV. OBSERVATIONS

120. Solutions to the problems of the former Yugoslavia will not be easy. Patient and persistent work is required. As can be seen from the preceding sections of this report, the process is being pursued in earnest. The Co-Chairmen of the Steering Committee and the Chairpersons of the Working Groups will need

the full cooperation of all the parties involved and the support of the international community.

Annex I
Belgrade Joint Communique of 11 September 1992 issued by Federal Republic of Yugoslavia President Cosic and Federal Republic of Yugoslavia Prime Minister Panic and witnessed by the Co-Chairmen*

1. We have today reaffirmed our total commitment to the decision taken in London at the International Conference on the Former Yugoslavia, in particular that all outstanding issues should be resolved by peaceful means, on the basis of existing borders, and in a process of urgent and continuing negotiations.
2. Concerning Bosnia and Herzegovina, we have agreed on the following practical steps and objectives: (a) there should be strict observation of the commitments to the collection and supervision of heavy weapons by the agreed expiration date of 12 September 1992; (b) the provision of power and water to Sarajevo, under international management, should be urgently agreed; (c) every party on the ground must not only commit itself, but take all practical steps, to bring the earliest possible end to all hostilities in and around Sarajevo; (d) we welcome the imminent resumption of talks, without preconditions, on constitutional arrangements for Bosnia and Herzegovina with the participation of all parties. These will take place in Geneva, in a continuo^Ps and uninterrupted process, until full agreement is reached; (e) we agree on the desirability of stationing observers on the borders of States neighbouring Bosnia and Herzegovina, as requested by Prime Minister Panic; (f) an agreement in principle has been achieved regarding the placing of observers at military airfields, and a definitive agreement will be reached after consulting the United Nations and Governments concerned.
3. With respect to humanitarian issues:

   (a) We declare our total condemnation of all practices related to "ethnic cleansing", and commit ourselves to helping reverse that which has already happened;
   (b) We agree that all statements or commitments made under duress, particularly those relating to land and property, are wholly null and void;

---

* Previously issued in document A/46/971 - S/24553.

(c) We urge all concerned parties to cooperate fully, promptly and unconditionally with current efforts, in particular by the ICRC and the UNHCR, to free all detainees, to close all detention centres and to secure safe passage of former detainees to secure and safe areas;

(d) We further urge all parties to facilitate the safe delivery of all humanitarian assistance;

(e) We strongly support the efforts of all agencies, local and international, to relieve the plight of displaced persons in all territories of the former Yugoslavia.

4. With respect to relations with Croatia:

(a) We welcome the agreement on the imminent reopening of the road between Belgrade and Zagreb and its symbolic designation as a "road of peace";

(b) We are committed to make all efforts to improve security around Maslenica Bridge so that repairs can be effected and the bridge reopened for traffic as soon as possible;

(c) We agree that the status of the "Yugoslav Pipeline" should be the subject of urgent discussion, in the framework of the working groups of the International Conference;

(d) We welcome President Cosic's offer to the Presidents of Croatia, Macedonia and Slovenia to establish mixed committees to normalize and promote economic and practical cooperation. The International Conference's working groups on economic relations and on succession issues will usefully contribute to this work;

(e) An agreement in principle has been achieved regarding the Prevlaka Peninsula. A definitive agreement will be reached after consulting the UN Secretary-General, the UN Security Council and the Governments concerned;

(f) We note the importance of the work of the joint commission established by the United Nations Protection Force (UNPROFOR) to deal with issues related to the "pink zones" and urge intensified cooperation with those efforts;

(g) We also call on all parties to adhere strictly to the United Nations peacekeeping plan, and in particular to support the efforts of UNPROFOR in the protected areas to eliminate illegal activities of irregular and paramilitary formations and criminal elements, both Serbian and Croatian;

(h) Given its importance in the provision of water and power to the region, we recognize the urgent need to reach agreement on problems relating to the Peruca Dam.

5. We pledge our mutual cooperation in order to steadily advance the peace process, to reduce the level of violence and curb the flow of arms. We pledge ourselves to swiftly implement the decisions of the International Conference on the Former Yugoslavia.

Annex II
Joint Declaration issued in Geneva on 30 September 1992 by President Cosic of the Federal Republic of Yugoslavia and President Tudjman of the Republic of Croatia, and witnessed by the Co-Chairmen*

Meeting under the auspices of the Co-Chairmen of the International Conference of the Former Yugoslavia in Geneva, the undersigned Presidents wish to announce the following:

1. The two Presidents reaffirmed the commitments of the International Conference in London on the inviolability of existing borders, other than through changes reached by peaceful agreement, and agreed to intensify work towards the normalisation of relations between the Federal Republic of Yugoslavia and the Republic of Croatia, on the basis of mutual recognition. All questions concerning succession to the former SFRY will be resolved within the framework of the International Conference or, as appropriate, bilaterally.
2. Authorities of the Republic of Croatia and the Federal Republic of Yugoslavia, in close collaboration with the United Nations Protection Force, will undertake urgent, joint measures to ensure the peaceful return to their homes in the United Nations Protected Areas of all persons displaced therefrom who so wish. To that end they propose the prompt
establishment of a quadripartite mechanism - consisting of authorities of the Government of Croatia, local Serb representatives, representatives of UNPROFOR and the UNHCR - to assure that this process moves forward. Equally, the Serb and Croat people formerly residing on the territory of the Republic of Croatia and the Federal Republic of Yugoslavia should have the right to return in peace to their former homes. Agreement was reached with

---

* Previously issued in document S/24476.

regard to more resolute action concerning the return of displaced persons to their homes, and to allowing for a voluntary and human resettlement of those persons wishing to do so between the two States.

3. The two Presidents agree that the Yugoslav Army will leave Prevlaka by 20 October 1992 in accordance with the Vance Plan. Security in the area will be resolved by demilitarization and the deployment of UN Monitors. The overall security of Boka Kotorska and Dubrovnik will be resolved through subsequent negotiations.

4. The two Presidents agree to establish a Joint Interstate Committee for the consideration of all open issues and for the normalisation of relations between the sovereign Republic of Croatia and the Federal Republic of Yugoslavia. In order that a durable peace may be established as soon as possible, particular attention will be given to normalising traffic and economic links.

5. The two Presidents confirm their conviction that all problems between their two states must be settled peacefully. They pledge their best efforts to this end. In that connection, they will exert all their influence towards a just, peaceful solution of the current crisis enveloping Bosnia and Herzegovina.

6. The two Presidents declare their total condemnation of all practices related to "ethnic cleansing", and commit themselves to helping reverse that which has already happened. They also declare that all statements or commitments made under duress, particularly those relating to land and property, are wholly null and void. They urge all concerned parties to cooperate fully, promptly and unconditionally with current efforts, in particular by the ICRC and the UNHCR, to free all detainees, close all detention centres, and assure safe passage to former detainees to secure and safe areas. They further urge all parties to facilitate the safe delivery of all humanitarian assistance.

7. The two Presidents welcome the early stationing of international observers on airfields in their respective countries as a confidence-building measure.

8. The two Presidents agree to meet again on October 20 with the Co-Chairmen. They express their gratitude to the Co-Chairmen for convening to-day's meeting.

Annex III
Statement issued by the Co-Chairmen on 30 September 1992 on the establishment of the Mixed Military Working Group in Sarajevo

The Co-Chairmen have been pursuing discussion with the delegations participating in the talks on Bosnia and Herzegovina to bring about, as part of the efforts to reach an overall cessation of hostilities in the country, the demilitarization of Sarajevo and the cessation of hostilities, it being understood that the search for future constitutional arrangements for Bosnia and Herzegovina will continue within the framework of the International Conference on the former Yugoslavia.

The delegations have agreed that discussion will commence immediately involving their military commanders and local authorities, meeting under the good offices of UNPROFOR and the Geneva Conference.

Annex IV
Statement issued by the Co-Chairmen on 13 October 1992 concerning the removal of Bosnian Serb combat aircraft from Banja Luka airfield and from the territory of Bosnia and Herzegovina to the Federal Republic of Yugoslavia

The Co-Chairmen have been urgently discussing concrete steps which can be taken to achieve a cessation of hostilities in Bosnia and Herzegovina, and this is also being vigorously pursued in the Mixed Military Working Group under the chairmanship of General Morillon, UNPROFOR Commander in Bosnia and Herzegovina.

At a meeting with Lord Owen today, 13 October, Dr. Karadzic offered to remove all Bosnian Serb combat aircraft from Banja Luka airfield and from the territory of Bosnia and Herzegovina to the Federal Republic of Yugoslavia (Serbia and Montenegro) as a sign of his delegation's desire to achieve a cessation of hostilities and to facilitate the implementation of United Nations Security Council resolution 781 (1992). Prime Minister Panic of the Federal Republic of Yugoslavia has agreed under a special bilateral agreement to accept these aircraft on Federal Republic of Yugoslavia airfields which will have UNPROFOR observers, and has confirmed his agreement to the Co-Chairmen. It has been agreed that an UNPROFOR representative will travel to Banja Luka with a high-level representative of the Federal Republic of Yugoslavia Air Force to work out the practical arrangements on the ground.

Annex V
Joint Statement of 19 October 1992 issued by Federal Republic
of Yugoslavia President Cosic and President Izetbegovic of
Bosnia and Herzegovina*

Having met at 19 October 1992 in Geneva under the auspices of the Co-Chairmen of the International Conference on the Former Yugoslavia, Dobrica Cosic, President of the Federal Republic of Yugoslavia and Alija Izetbegovic, President of the Republic of Bosnia and Herzegovina, wish to make the following statement:

1. The two Presidents welcomed the invitation of the Co-Chairmen to hold this meeting and expressed their appreciation to them. The two presidents are of the view that the International Conference on the Former Yugoslavia represents the forum for resolving outstanding problems in the area of the former Yugoslavia and pledge their support for the efforts of the Co-Chairmen. They reaffirmed all commitments entered into at the International Conference in London. Their meeting took place in an open, frank atmosphere and addressed a wide range of issues in a comprehensive fashion.

2. They reaffirm the commitments of the International Conference in London on the inviolability of existing borders other than through changes reached by peaceful agreement. They further reaffirm that comprehensive political solution in Bosnia and Herzegovina must be found by agreement between the Republic's three constituent peoples within the International Conference in Geneva. All questions concerning succession of the former Socialist Federal Republic of Yugoslavia will be resolved within the framework of the International Conference or, as appropriated, bilaterally.

3. The two Presidents agree that efforts should be intensified at all levels and by all parties involved in the conflict in Bosnia and Herzegovina to effectuate an immediate cessation of hostilities.

4. They agree on the urgent need to end the blockade of and to demilitarize Sarajevo and other cities with the assistance and under the supervision of the United Nations Protection Force. In this connection the two Presidents express the hope that the work of the Mixed Military Working Group in Bosnia and Herzegovina would be carried out intensively with participation at senior military level. The Mixed Military Working Group should meet in continuous and uninterrupted sessions.

---

*   Previously issued in document A/47/571-S/24702.

5. They welcome the statement by the Co-Chairmen of the International Conference issued in Geneva on 13 October last and will within their respective competences see that it is carried out as soon as possible. President Cosic informed President Izetbegovic that he had received a report today to the effect that Bosnian Serbs' military aircraft had been confined to hangars; upon his return to Belgrade he intended to sign an agreement with Bosnian Serb representatives transferring these aircrafts from Bosnia and Herzegovina to the Federal Republic of Yugoslavia. The two Presidents further agreed on the desirability of promptly stationing observers at military airfields as provided for in United Nations Security Council resolution 781 (1992) as well as their common State border.

6. The two Presidents agree on the need for all the parties in the conflict to bring under effective command and control all armed units on the territory of the Republic of Bosnia and Herzegovina and to eliminate all paramilitary groups and criminal and mercenary elements emanating from whatever source.

7. They declare their total condemnation of "ethnic cleansing" and commit themselves to helping reverse that which has already taken place. They will also use their best endeavours to bring about conditions for the return of refugees and displaced persons to their permanent residences. They further declare that all statements or commitments made under duress, particularly those relating to land and property, are null and void. They urge all concerned parties to cooperate fully, promptly and unconditionally with current efforts, in particular by the International Committee of the Red Cross and the Office of the United Nations High Commissioner for Refugees to free all detainees, close all detention centres and assure safe passage of former detainees to secure and safe areas. They further urge all parties to facilitate the safe delivery of all humanitarian assistance to the populace of Bosnia and Herzegovina.

8. The two Presidents note the adoption of United Nations Security Council resolution 780 (1992) establishing an impartial commission of experts to examine, gather and evaluate evidence of war crimes and crimes against humanity. They express their firm conviction that all perpetrators of criminal acts committed during the armed conflict in Bosnia and Herzegovina should be punished in accordance with all relevant legal provisions.

9. The two Presidents agree to meet again with the Co-Chairmen at a date to be determined. They thank the Co-Chairmen for today's meeting and also express their appreciation at the presence of UNPROFOR Force Commander, Lt.-Gen. Satish Nambiar.

Annex VI
Joint Declaration issued on 20 October 1992 by the Federal Republic of Yugoslavia President Cosic and President Tudjman of Croatia and witnessed by the Co-Chairmen*

The President of the Federal Republic of Yugoslavia, Mr. Dobrica Cosic, and the President of the Republic of Croatia, Dr. Franjo Tudjman, met in Geneva on 20 October 1992, under the auspices of the Co-Chairmen of the International Conference on the Former Yugoslavia, Cyrus Vance and Lord Owen. The two Presidents reviewed the implementation of their joint declaration of 30 September and, in order to provide for its further implementation, declare as follows:

1. They note with satisfaction that various specific measures have already been taken to implement several fundamental issues covered in the joint declaration, that is, the agreement on Prevlaka; the stationing of observers at airfields in the Federal Republic of Yugoslavia and in the Republic of Croatia; and the establishment of the Joint Inter-State Committee and its five commissions.

2. They note that the Joint Committee has held its first meeting. In order to promote and enhance the work of the Committee, and with a view to ensuring conditions for normalization of relations, they agree to establish liaison offices of the Inter-State Committee in each other's capitals, Belgrade and Zagreb. Under the direction of the Committee, the liaison offices will coordinate work on all open questions between the Republic of Croatia and the Federal Republic of Yugoslavia and, as a priority, will address the following:

- Reopening of road, rail and telecommunications links between the Republic of Croatia and the Federal Republic of Yugoslavia, as well as re-establishing international links across the two countries;
- Resolving matters of personal property, pension and remittances, and other problems related to the economic well-being of their people;
- Examining issues related to dual citizenship.

3. Reaffirming their commitment in paragraph 2 of their joint declaration of 30 September, the two Presidents agree that the quadripartite mechanism established therein should start its work as soon as possible. Its priority task should be to organize and facilitate the return and the resettlement, under humane condi-

---

* Previously issued in document A/47/572-S/24704.

tions, of displaced persons and groups. The two Presidents further agree that their representatives will provide for an exchange of information on missing persons.

4. The two Presidents agree to establish a Joint Inter-State Commission for the consideration of the overall security of Boka Kotorska and Dubrovnik. Joint customs controls will be established on the border.

5. The two Presidents agree to discuss, within their respective competences, all elements concerning the implementation of the Vance plan at their next meeting with the two Co-Chairmen.

6. The two Presidents reaffirm their determination to exert all their influence towards a just, peaceful solution of the conflict in Bosnia and Herzegovina. They urge all parties to the conflict to direct all necessary efforts towards a cessation of hostilities and the negotiation of constitutional arrangements for Bosnia and Herzegovina on the basis of agreement between the three constituent peoples. With respect to the delivery of humanitarian aid, President Cosic informed the meeting that his Government had made the necessary preparations for the secure delivery of such aid along the Belgrade-Sarajevo route.

7. The two Presidents express their gratitude to the Co-Chairmen for having convened today's meeting and agree to meet again on a date to be specified.

Annex VII
Proposed constitutional structure for Bosnia and Herzegovina

Bosnia and Herzegovina (BiH) to be a decentralized State with significant functions carried by 7 to 10 autonomous provinces whose boundaries taken into account ethnic and other considerations.

I. OVERALL STRUCTURE

A. Bosnia and Herzegovina to be a decentralized State within its present international borders (i.e., those it had within the former Socialist Federal Republic of Yugoslavia).

B. Bosnia and Herzegovina to be divided into 7 to 10 autonomous provinces:

1. Boundaries of provinces to be drawn so as to constitute areas as geographically coherent as possible, taking into account ethnic, geographical (i.e. natural features, such as rivers), historical, communication (i.e., the existing road and railway networks), economic viability, and other rel-

evant factors. It is likely that many of the provinces (but not necessarily all) will have a considerable majority of one of the three major ethnic groups, and most will have a significant representation of minorities;

2. The provincial boundaries to be set in the Constitution, and may not be changed without amending it with high majority requirements (III.A.3). Similarly, no province to be permitted to secede without such an agreement;

3. None of the provinces to have a name that specifically identifies it with one of the major ethnic groups;

4. There are to be no border controls at inter-provincial boundaries, and full freedom of movement is to be allowed throughout the entire country.

C. The Constitution is to recognize that there are three major "ethnic" (national/religious) groups, as well as a group of "others".

D. The Constitution is to provide that on a transitional basis certain of the constitutional bodies be manned by persons appointed by the International Conference on the Former Yugoslavia and certain functions be internationally supervised.

1. These include:

   (a) The Constitutional Court (IV.A.3(c));
   (b) The ethnic balancing and integration of the military forces (V.A.2);
   (c) The non-discriminatory composition of the police (V.B.1(b));
   (d) The International Commission of Human Rights for Bosnia and Herzegovina (VII. B. 1);
   (f) The Human Rights Court (VI.B.3).

2. The duration of these arrangements could be:

   (a) Limited to a specified period (e.g., IV.A.2(b));
   (b) Determined by ICFY or a succession (e.g., VI.A.2);
   (c) Determined by objective factors (e.g., VI.B.3);
   (d) If not otherwise provided (e.g., IV.A.3(c)), until the Constitution is amended to eliminate or change the applicable provision, for which high enough majorities should be set so that they can only be obtained by a substantial consensus of the groups (III.A.3(c)).

II. Distribution of Governmental Functions

A. The central government is to have exclusive responsibility for:

    1. Foreign affairs (including membership in international organisations);
    2. National defence (V.A);
    3. International commerce (custom duties; quotas);
    4. Citizenship (including dual) (VI.C.1-2);
    5. Taxation for central government purposes.[a]

B. "Independent" authorities, consisting of representatives of all the provinces, are to have responsibility for:

    1. Central bank;

        (a) Issues of currency;
        (b) Regulatory functions over provincial banks.

    2. Infrastructure for international and inter-provincial communications: railroads,[b] canals,[b] pipelines,[b] air control, post, telephone and telegraph;
    3. Electric power grid.

C. The central government and the province are to share responsibility for:

    1. Environmental controls, with the central government setting minimum standards, which each province can raise;
    2. Judiciary (IV.A.3 and IV.B.3).

D. The provinces are generally to have exclusive responsibility for:

    1. Education, including higher (i.e., universities);
    2. Cultural institutions and programmes;
    3. Radio and television;
    4. Licensing of professions and trades;

---

[a] If the provinces are not all economically viable, or if some are much poorer than others, then some sort of resource transfer among them may have to be envisaged, possibly utilizing the taxing power of the central government.

[b] Possibly as part of an international authority.

5. Natural resources use, e.g., agriculture; forestry; hunting and fishing; mining;
6. Health care, social services and insurance;
7. Provincial communications, e.g., local roads; airports;
8. Energy production;
9. Control of commercial and savings banks and other financial institutions;
10. Police (V.B.1);
11. Taxation for provincial purposes.

The provinces are not to be allowed to entertain formal international or inter-provincial ties, except with permission of the central government; they are to have no international legal personality.

III. Constitutions

A. Central:

1. To be negotiated and adopted within the framework of ICFY;
2. Supreme law of Bosnia and Herzegovina and of all the provinces;
3. Difficult to amend (i.e., high majority requirements in both Houses of legislature and possibly a referendum with high absolute and/or relative majority requirements), with the following provisions enjoying special protection (e.g., still higher majority requirements or even unanimity):

   (a) Human and group right provisions (VI.A.2 (a)-(b)) and the related procedural devices (VI.B);
   (b) Boundaries of provinces or permission for any to secede (I.B.2);
   (c) Certain provisions for transitional international supervision (I.D. 2(d)).

B. Provincial: Each province to adopt its own, subject only to the national Constitution in accordance with any decisions of the Constitutional Court (IV.A.3 (c)(i)).

IV. GOVERNMENTAL STRUCTURES

A. *Central Government*

1. Legislature

   (a) Lower House: Elected on basis of proportional representation in Bosnia and Herzegovina as a whole;[c]
   (b) Upper House: Appointed by and from the provincial governments.

Legislation, including approval of important international engagements and of constitutional changes (III.A.3), should generally require action by both Houses, although their respective functions may not be identical in respect of all of these and different majorities might be specified for different actions.

2. Executive

   (a) A "Presidency" to consist of the "Governors" of all the provinces, chaired by the President, with no executive functions but responsibility solely for senior appointments, in particular: President (IV.A.2(b)); Ministers (IV.A.2(d)); judges of highest appellate court(s) (IV.A.3(a)); national appointees to the Human Rights Court (VI.B.3) and the Constitutional Court (IV.A.3(c)); chiefs of military staff (V.A.2), all of which are to require either group rotation or balance,[d] as to which an appeal will lie to the Constitutional Court (IV.A.3(c) (iv)). No unanimity or consensus requirement, to avoid possibility of paralysis;
   (b) A President (a largely ceremonial Head of State)[e] chosen by the Presidency for a limited term and subject to rotation among the groups;
   (c) A Prime Minister (head of Government)[e] elected by the Lower House of the legislature;
   (d) Ministers appointed by the Prime Minister with the approval of the Presidency, with due account for group balance, the Foreign and

---

[c] This means that each group can form one or more parties - but there might also be parties on purely political, provincial or ideological bases.

[d] It will be necessary to indicate whether the word "balance" means "equal" or "proportional" representation.

[e] The Constitution will have to specify precisely the division of responsibilities between the President and the Prime Minister.

Defence Ministers in any event to be from different groups;

(e) A civil service constituted on principle of group balance.[d]

3. Judiciary

(a) The highest appellate court(s), with group balance to be required. (The courts of first instance and the intermediate appellate courts are to be provincial (IV.B.3).);[f]

(b) A Human Rights Court (VI.B.3);

(c) A Constitutional Court, primarily[g] for resolving disputes:

(i)   Between the central Government and one or more provinces;

(ii)   Between provinces;

(iii) Between principal authorities of the central government;

(iv) Concerning the group rotation or balance of appointments made by the Presidency (IV.A.2(a)).

The Constitutional Court would also serve as a court of appeals on constitutional questions from the highest appellate courts (VI.A.3(a)). The Court is to consist of one national judge from each group, appointed by the Presidency, and of five foreign judges appointed in the first instance by ICFY, with replacements to be appointed by an appropriate international authority designated by ICFY.

B. Provincial (Determined by each provincial constitution)

1. Legislature: Preferably a single chamber, possibly two but elected on different bases.

2. Executive: A single "Governor" from each province.

3. Judiciary: Courts of first instance (civil, criminal, administrative, labour, etc.) and intermediate appellate courts.

---

[f]   Normally appeals to the national appellate courts would have to be on a question of national (i.e., involving the Constitution, national legislation or international treaties), so that for most other issues the provincial appellate court would be the highest instance reached.

[g]   The Constitutional Court, whose primary function would be to settle disputes among the constitutional authorities, would be a court of first instance for such cases - i.e. such disputes would be brought to it directly and could be disposed of as quickly as the matter required - in preference to the Court's appellate jurisdiction specified in the sentence following the several subparagraphs.

V. EXECUTIVE FORCE

A. Military:

1. Entirely under control of central government executive.
2. Central staff to be group balanced with rotating occupation of key posts and all units to be integrated (i.e., not established on group lines); the initial arrangements relating to balancing and integration to be supervised by ICFY and thereafter by an appropriate authority designated by ICFY.

B. Police:

1. Provincial: All uniformed police to be at provincial or local level:

   (a) Police controlled by provincial executive;
   (b) Police to observe same rules as to non-discrimination, etc., as all branches of government (VI.A.2 (b)); the initial arrangements relating to non-discrimination to be supervised by ICFY and thereafter by an appropriate authority designated by ICFY.

2. National: only an administrative body (i.e., no uniformed, armed forces) in order to:

   (a) Coordinate provincial police;
   (b) Assist in technical functions (e.g., crime laboratories);
   (c) Coordinate with international and foreign police authorities.

C. Prohibition on other armed forces: Aside from the military and, as appropriate, the police, no other public or private armed units may be formed in the country.

VI. HUMAN AND GROUP/MINORITY RIGHTS

A. Substantive:

1. Source: The highest level of internationally recognized rights, as set out in instruments (primarily treaties and some intergovernmental organisations declarations - originating with United Nations, Council of

Europe and CSCE) to be specified in the Constitution (see the appendix hereto).

2. Types

    (a)   General human, especially civil and political rights;

    (b)   Group, especially minority[h] rights, including obligation to maintain group balance in governmental decision-making bodies as well as in the various central and provincial civil, police and other services (or, at the minimum, strict non-discrimination);

    (c)   Economic, social and cultural rights - which to a considerable extent may have to be set out as aspirations and goals, and not be subject to the rigid protection of the other above-mentioned rights.

B. Procedural: The general human, civil and political, and group rights to be protected by a number of domestic and international procedural arrangements, including:[i]

1. An International Commission on Human Rights on Bosnia and Herzegovina, with wide powers to investigate and to hear complaints, the obligation to report to competent international (United Nations, CSCE, Council of Europe) bodies, including, if appropriate, the Security Council. To be established by ICFY for a limited period (e.g., five years, subject to prolongation by ICFY or another appropriate international authority designated by it).

2. Four ombudsmen, one from each group, to be initially appointed by ICFY and later by the Lower House of the legislature. They are to have adequate staffs and be equipped with strong powers to investigate, be obliged to make reports to all competent governmental authorities at any level, and be empowered to appeal to or intervene in courts to protect rights; they are to have special responsibility to reverse ethnic cleansing.

---

[h]   This term will require special attention and definition in respect of Bosnia and Herzegovina, because on the one hand no ethnic or other group has an absolute majority in the country as a whole, so that in a sense all are minorities, but it is likely that in many regions one group will have a clear majority.

[i]   In addition to the arrangements listed below, account must also be taken of the international supervision provided on a normal basis by the special organs created by the human rights treaties to which Bosnia and Herzegovina will be obliged to become a party (to be specified in the Constitution (VI.A.1) - see para. (c) of the appendix hereto).

3. A Human Rights Court to which appeals can be taken from any court (provincial or national) on human rights issues, which would initially be established as part of a Council of Europe mechanism and consist of one national judge from each group appointed by the Presidency and at least five foreign judges, appointed by the Presidents of he European Court of Human Rights and the European Commission of Human Rights - to be maintained at least until Bosnia and Herzegovina becomes a member of Council of Europe and party to the European Convention on Human Rights, and perhaps even beyond.

4. Unimpeded access by individuals and recognized groups to courts under all circumstances, and with right to rely directly on constitutional provisions and on those of international treaties to which Bosnia and Herzegovina is a party or which are referred to in the Constitution, whether or not there is implementing legislation.

C. Citizenship (Closely connected with many of the human and group rights provisions):

1. Citizenship of Bosnia and Herzegovina: to be determined by central government, in accordance with the Constitution and national laws;
2. Dual citizenship to be allowed;
3. No "provincial citizenship";
4. No official ethnic identification of citizens (e.g., on identity cards).

Appendix
International Human Rights Treaties and Other Instruments[a]
to be Incorporated by Reference into the Constitution of
Bosnia and Herzegovina

The purpose of such incorporation would be:

(a) To make their provisions immediately applicable to Bosnia and Herzegovina and enforceable by its courts. In this connection it should be noted that normally States are bound only by treaties and only by those to which they voluntarily become parties. Although States can bind them-

---

[a] In the list herein, treaties are printed in italics and other instruments (e.g., declarations) are not.

selves to observe other instruments, such as declarations, many such
instruments are not so formulated as to allow them to be easily used as a
source of positive law. Also requiring a State to abide by such instruments puts it into a somewhat invidious position as almost no States
have voluntarily entered into, or become subject to, such obligations.
Consequently, before requiring Bosnia and Herzegovina to bind itself
constitutionally to abide by any non-treaty instruments, each such instrument should be examined carefully to determine whether it is suitable;

(b) To oblige Bosnia and Herzegovina to become a party to those of the
listed instruments that are treaties, as and when possible, i.e. immediately in respect of United Nations treaties, and upon becoming a member of he Council of Europe in respect of its treaties. As to those treaties
to which the former Yugoslavia was a party,[b] Bosnia and Herzegovina
will only have to submit a statement of succession to the United Nations
Secretary-General;

(c) To allow international monitoring or other supervision by the bodies
⸱ created by certain of these treaties.[c]

It is understood that the parties to the constitutional negotiation may agree to list
additional instruments in the Constitution.[d]

A. General human rights, especially civil and political rights

(a) United Nations system instruments:

1. *1948 Convention on the Prevention and Punishment of the Crime of
   Genocide**
2. 1948 Universal Declaration of Human Rights, Articles 1-21
3. *1966 International Covenant on Civil and Political Rights** and its *1966*
   (right of petition to the Human Rights Committee) and perhaps its *1989*
   (abolition of death penalty) *Optional Protocols* [HUMAN RIGHTS COM-

---

[b]   In this list, those treaties are marked with an asterisk (*).

[c]   Such bodies are indicated in this list by print in small capitals.

[d]   This list does not include about a dozen instruments, include a number of CSCE declarations that would fit under categories A or B, that do not appear to meet the criteria in
paragraph (a) above or as to which it otherwise appears doubtful that inclusion in the BiH
Constitution should be demanded, but which were included in a list of human rights instruments provided to the parties for their information.

MITTEE]

4. *1965 International Convention on the Elimination of All Forms of Racial Discrimination** [COMMITTEE ON THE ELIMINATION OF RACIAL DISCRIMINATION (CERD)]

5. *1979 International Convention on the Elimination of All Forms of Discrimination against Women** [COMMITTEE ON THE ELIMINATION OF DISCRIMINATION AGAINST WOMEN (CEDAW)]

6. *1989 Convention on the Rights of the Child** [COMMITTEE ON THE RIGHT OF THE CHILD]

7. *1984 Convention against Torture and Other Cruel, Inhuman or Degrading Treatment or Punishment* [COMMITTEE AGAINST TORTURE]

8. *1951 Convention relating to the Status of Refugees** and the *1966 Protocol* thereto* [UNITED NATIONS HIGH COMMISSIONER FOR REFUGEES]

(b) Council of Europe instruments:

9. *1950 European Convention for the Protection of Human Rights and Fundamental Freedoms*, and *Protocols 1-10* thereto [EUROPEAN COMMISSION ON HUMAN RIGHTS AND EUROPEAN COURT OF HUMAN RIGHTS]

10. *1987 European Convention on the Prevention of Torture and Inhuman or Degrading Treatment or Punishment* [EUROPEAN COMMITTEE FOR THE PREVENTION OF TORTURE AND INHUMAN OR DEGRADING TREATMENT OR PUNISHMENT - operates in respect to art. 3 of instrument 9 above]

(c) Conference on Security and Cooperation in Europe (CSCE) instruments:

11. 1975 Final Act of the [Helsinki] Conference on Security and Cooperation in Europe, Part 1 (a) (VII) and Basket III [HELSINKI REVIEW PROCESS, as enhanced by the human dimension review mechanism established by paras. 1-4 of the Vienna Concluding Document, paras. (41)-(42) of the Document of the Copenhagen Meeting, and Part I of the Document of the Moscow Meeting].

B. Protection of minorities[e]

(a) United Nations system instruments:

  12. 1992 draft Declaration on the Rights of Persons Belonging to National, Ethnic, Religious and Linguistic Minorities

(b) Council of Europe instruments:

  13. 1990 Council of Europe Parliamentary Assembly Recommendation on the Rights of minorities, paras. 10-13

(c) CSCE instruments:

C. Economic, social and cultural rights

(a) United Nations system instruments:

  2*. 1948 Universal Declaration of Human Rights, articles 22-27.
  14. *1966 International Covenant on Economic Social and Cultural Rights** [Economic and Social Council COMMITTEE ON ECONOMIC, SOCIAL AND CULTURAL RIGHTS]

(b) Council of Europe instruments:

  15. *1961 European Social Charter and Protocol 1 thereto* [COMMITTEE OF EXPERTS]

(c) CSCE instruments:

      ...

[e]   The instruments listed herein are those dealing specifically with the rights of minorities. In addition, a number of the instruments listed in section A also have relevant provisions on this subject.

D. Citizenship and Nationality[f]

(a) United Nations system instruments:

16. *1957 Convention on the Nationality of Married Women**
17. *1961 Convention of the Reduction of Statelessness*

(b) Council of Europe instruments:

...

(c) CSCE instruments

...

111. REPORT OF THE SECRETARY-GENERAL ON THE INTERNATIONAL CONFERENCE ON THE FORMER YUGOSLAVIA*

INTRODUCTION

1. On 11 November 1992, the Secretary-General submitted a report to the Security Council on the activities of the International Conference on the Former Yugoslavia since it began work in Geneva on 3 September 1992 (S/24795). The Security Council considered that report at its 3134th to 3137th meetings, held on 13 and 16 November 1992. On 16 November, the Security Council adopted resolution 787 (1992) in which it expresses its appreciation for the report presented to it by the Co-Chairmen of the Steering Committee of the International Conference, and requested the Secretary-General to continue to keep the Council regularly informed of developments and of the work of the Conference. The present report provides information on activities undertaken within the International Conference since the submission of the previous report.

---

[f] The instruments listed herein are those dealing specifically with question relating to citizenship and nationality, In addition, a number of the instruments listed in section A also have relevant provisions on this subject.

* UN Doc. S/25015, 24 December 1992.

I. Activities of the Steering Committee

2. The third meeting of the Steering Committee of the International Conference was held, in expanded form and at ministerial level, in Geneva on 16 December 1992. There was an in-depth discussion of the situation in the former Yugoslavia and particularly Bosnia and Herzegovina. In a message to the meeting (see annex I) the Secretary-General stated that: "the current situation demands statesmanship of the highest order. Understandable emotion must be balanced by a sober appreciation of risks and benefits. Short-term nostrums must be examined in the light of their contribution to long-range stability." He added that "the road ahead lies through continuous negotiations in good faith, in the spirit of the Charter of the United Nations and the principles of the International Conference, not in actions which would serve to continue or escalate the violence".

3. Addresses by the Co-Chairmen of the Steering Committee are contained in annexes II and III. Detailed briefings were given by Generals Nambiar and Morillon, the United Nations High Commissioner for Refugees, Mrs. Sadako Ogata, the President of the International Committee of the Red Cross (ICRC), Mr. C. Sommaruga, and Mr. Martti Ahtisaari, Chairman of the Working Group on Bosnia and Herzegovina. A number of Ministers gave their view and put questions to Generals Nambiar and Morillon, which were answered.

4. General Nambiar reported in the implementation of the various mandates of the United Nations Protection Force (UNPROFOR), including in the United Nations protected areas in Croatia and Bosnia and Herzegovina. General Morillon reported on the situation in Sarajevo and on the efforts of UNPROFOR to secure observance of the cessation of hostilities agreed on 12 November 1992 by the three parties in Bosnia and Herzegovina. He states that, while fighting continued in the Republic, the level of hostilities had been reduced since the conclusion of that agreement.

5. The United Nations High Commissioner for Refugees, Mrs. Ogata, reported on humanitarian relief activities. In Bosnia and Herzegovina it had been possible thus far to meet about 80 per cent of objectives in the food sector and about half the objectives on winterization. The President of ICRC, Mr. Sommaruga, provided information regarding the release of detainees held by the three parties to the conflict in Bosnia and Herzegovina. He expected 4,245 prisoners to be released during the same week: 2,780 by the Bosnian Serbs, 1,027 by the Bosnian Government and 538 by the Bosnian Croats.

6. Mr. Ahtisaari reported on discussions about a new institutional structure for Bosnia and Herzegovina, particularly on efforts to settle constitutional principles

and to delimit the boundaries of provinces. He expressed his conviction that a negotiated settlement of the situation in Bosnia and Herzegovina could be achieved.

7. It emerged from the meeting that the Minister wished the Co-Chairmen of the Steering Committee and the Chairpersons of the Working Groups to press ahead with strategies for peaceful solutions to problems in the former Yugoslavia. Many participants expressed the view that negotiated solutions were possible and preferable to expanding the war. In that regard the view was expressed repeatedly that pressure must be increased upon all parties to cooperate. It was specifically suggested that sanctions should be rigorously enforced, especially on the Danube. The appointment of an Executive Coordinator on Sanctions was proposed and received favourably by the Steering Committee.

8. Participants repeatedly urged all the sides involved in the conflict in Bosnia and Herzegovina to cooperate with ICRC, and to honour their agreements to release all their prisoners and detainees. They expressed their strong disapproval of breaches of the air interdiction zone over Bosnia and Herzegovina and wished measures to be taken to bring about compliance with it.

9. There was a clear sense at the meeting that there could be no compromise on basic principles of respect for human rights and non-acceptance of forcible change of borders. Participants reacted strongly to reports of grievous violations of human rights, including ethnic cleansing and allegations regarding ill-treatment of women. Broad support was expressed for the establishment of an international criminal court to try persons accused of war crimes.

10. Views were mixed about lifting the arms embargo in favour of the Government of Bosnia and Herzegovina. Most speakers opposed lifting the embargo. Safety zones or safe havens were also briefly touched upon.

11. The United States Government offered 25 observers to help to fill the gap in airfield monitors. That action was warmly received. The Co-Chairmen appealed to other Governments in a position to do so to make similar offers.

II. CO-CHAIRMEN OF THE STEERING COMMITTEE

A. Peacemaking

12. The Co-Chairmen of the Steering Committee have continued their contacts with the heads of State of Bosnia and Herzegovina, Croatia and the Federal Republic of Yugoslavia in an effort to promote peaceful solutions to problems in

the former Yugoslavia. They have also held meetings with other leaders in the former Yugoslavia and in neighbouring countries. They also visited Croatia and Bosnia and Herzegovina during this period.

13. On 6 November they had a private meeting in Geneva with President Cosic of the Federal Republic of Yugoslavia. On 7 November they met in Geneva with President Gligorov of the Former Yugoslav Republic of Macedonia. On 19 and 20 November they visited the United Nations protected areas in Croatia. On 23 November they met in Geneva with Prime Minister Mitsotakis of Greece. On 25 November they met in Geneva with Prime Minister Panic of the Federal Republic of Yugoslavia. During the weekend of 28 and 29 November they met privately in Brioni with President Tudjman of Croatia. On 2 December they held a private meeting in Jeddah with President Izetbegovic of Bosnia and Herzegovina. They visited Zagreb for discussions with President Tudjman and Izetbegovic and others on 17 December.

B. Human Rights and Humanitarian Issues

14. The Co-Chairmen have continued to use their good offices on humanitarian matters as well as on issues of human rights. On 30 November the Co-Chairmen sent a message to the Commission on Human Rights, convened in a special session to discuss the situation of human rights in the former Yugoslavia. In their message they condemned ethnic cleansing and other violations of human rights and invited the Commission to give attention to the important question of protecting the rights of minorities which, they stated, was of great importance to the future stability and security in the area of the former Yugoslavia.

15. On 4 December Mr. Vance addressed a high-level meeting of the Humanitarian Issues Working Group. He emphasized that securing respect for basic human rights and humanitarian law must remain a high priority in dealing with the situation in Bosnia and Herzegovina as well as throughout the former Yugoslavia. Noting that solidarity with human beings in distress was a central tenet of the post-1945 world order, he expressed profound respect, admiration and gratitude of the work of the Office of the United Nations High Commissioner for Refugees (UNHCR), ICRC and non-governmental organizations (NGOs) as well as to the soldiers of UNPROFOR and to aircrews flying dangerous humanitarian missions.

16. The Co-Chairmen have also made determined efforts to help bring about a forensic examination of a mass grave site at Ovcara near Vukovar. They were in contact on that matter with the Secretary-General, the Special Rapporteur of the

Commission on Human Rights and the Commission of Experts established by the Security Council to deal with allegations of violation of humanitarian law. The Commission of experts has made arrangements for a forensic examination, which has begun at the site.

C. Cooperation with Regional Organizations

17. The Co-Chairmen have maintained contacts with concerned regional organizations including the organization of the Islamic Conference (OIC) and the Conference on Security and Cooperation in Europe (CSCE). They attended a special session of Ministers for Foreign Affairs of OIC held in Jeddah on 1 and 2 December to consider the situation in Bosnia and Herzegovina.

18. Mr. Vance delivered a statement on behalf of the Secretary-General, which described the events taking place in Bosnia and Herzegovina as a direct challenge to international public order. The statement noted that, despite specific injunctions by the Security Council, violence was continuing, human rights were being flouted, relied efforts were being obstructed, United Nations peacekeepers were being attacked and ethnic cleansing was continuing. The statement of the Secretary-General referred to the measures being taken by the United Nations to bring an end to the conflict and suggested the following ways in which OIC could be supportive. First, it could support the call to the parties in Bosnia and Herzegovina to negotiate a political settlement on the basis of the constitutional outline presented by the Co-Chairmen, Second, it could back the Security Council's call for a cessation of hostilities and the work of the Mixed Military Working Group aimed at unblocking and demilitarizing Sarajevo and other towns. Third, it could help to ensure compliance with sanctions.

19. In his address to that meeting, Lord Owen dealt with the Islamic suspicion that the world was not defending the rights of the Muslims of Bosnia and Herzegovina in the same way it would if they were of another religion. "I do not believe this charge has any substance," he stated. As for comparisons with the international community's response to the invasion of Kuwait, he said that the situation in the former Yugoslavia was different, "politically, military and geographically". He added that to lift the embargo for Bosnia and Herzegovina, could well trigger a resumption of arms supplies, overtly or covertly, to Serbia and Montenegro by its traditional suppliers.

20. Lord Owen stated that the Co-Chairmen were determined to see violations of the no-fly order cease, although he noted that no combat missions by fixedwing aircraft had been recorded since 12 October.

21. Lord Owen addressed a session of CSCE held in Stockholm on 14 December 1992. Assessing the chances for a negotiated settlement, he states: "I believe this is particularly a moment for the international community to hold its nerve and to continue with the present strategy." He added that there was also an extreme need to do everything to pressure all the parties to come constructively to the negotiating table: "This is the time", he continued, "to have continued faith in the negotiating of a peaceful settlement."

III. Working Group on Bosnia and Herzegovina

22. The previous report of the Secretary-General contained information about the ideas that the Co-Chairmen had presented to the parties on a possible constitutional structure for Bosnia and Herzegovina (S/24795, annex VII). The principal points of the constitutional proposals were the following:

(a) Bosnia and Herzegovina would be a decentralized state with 7 to 10 autonomous provinces whose boundaries would take into account ethnic and other considerations. All governmental functions relating to normal contact of public authorities with citizens, for example, education and health care, would be assigned to the provinces;

(b) The Constitution would recognize the existence of three major "ethnic" or "national/religious" groups, as well as a group of "others";

(c) Both the central and the provincial governments would have democratically elected and democratically chosen heads of government and an independent judiciary. In all the central government organs, the principle of group balancing or rotation would be observed;

(d) There would be a Constitutional Court to decide disputes between the provinces and organs of the central Government. It would be composed of four judges, one chosen from each of the Bosnian groups, and of a majority of foreign judges appointed by the Conference;

(e) Any military establishment would be entirely under the central government, while the police would be entirely provincial. No other armed forces would be allowed;

(f) An important feature of the Constitution would be its insistence on the highest level of internationally proclaimed human rights. Their implementation would be ensured and monitored by a variety of national and partially or wholly international organs;

(g) Other important features of the Constitution would be various international control mechanisms, such as the predominance of non-Bosnian judges in the Constitutional and Human Rights Courts. Most of these mechanisms would remain in force until the Constitution was amended to eliminate them, which could only happen by agreement of all the three major groups.

23. Consultations have since been held separately with delegations from each of the parties. The Bosnian Government appears satisfied with the general outline of the Co-Chairmen's proposals, although from the extensive discussion held with the delegation as a whole and with some of its members it appears that it considers that they provide for excessive decentralization and that ethnic and other group considerations are overemphasized.

24. In written comments that were also confirmed at subsequent meetings, the Bosnian Croat delegation indicated that the constitutional proposals were a relatively acceptable basis for further talks, subject to three principal reservations: it considered that (a) the constitutional arrangements should more adequately reflect that Bosnia and Herzegovina was a State of three constituent nations; (b) it should not be a protectorate of either the United Nations or of the international community; and (c) the State should be demilitarized. Specific amendments were proposed to implement those principles, which among other things would foresee the formation of three so-called "constituent units", each composed of two or more provinces that would in effect be governed together, and these constituent units would in most respects play the role foreseen for the provinces in the Co-Chairmen's proposal. An important incidental effect of that change would be to make decisions of many of the organs of the central Government depend on a consensus of the three major ethnic groups, except in respect of matters that all three of them agreed did not affect their vital interests. All the international control measures foreseen by the Co-Chairmen would be eliminated except for the possibility of participation by the European Court of Human Rights in the Bosnian Human Rights Court, for a limited period.

25. The Bosnian Serb delegation, on 19 November, presented what was in effect a counter-proposal to that of the Co-Chairmen, which it insisted, on the basis of instruction of its Assembly, be considered together with the latter. The essential feature of the counter-proposal is that Bosnia and Herzegovina would be divided, on an exclusively ethnic basis, into three sovereign States, each with international legal personality and only loosely confederated in a central unit, which itself would also have limited international legal personality. Although it is

foreseen that the so-called "constituent States" would delegate certain functions on the area of economics, in particular international trade, to the central Government, each of the States would have its own currency. All the organs of the central Government would be constituted by appointees of the constituent States on an equal basis and would generally be able to take decisions only by consensus or at least with the agreement of the majority to each State's representatives. This would even be true of the Constitutional and Human Rights Courts, neither of which would have any non-Bosnian members. An important role would be assigned to a dozen commissions consisting of representatives of each of the three States that would monitor the functions of the central Government and coordinate the corresponding functions of the constituent States. Although human rights would be guaranteed at the highest international level, as prescribed by United Nations and CSCE instruments, there would be no device for international monitoring of compliance, in this or in other respects.

26. As soon as the Conference's constitutional proposals were submitted to the parties, they indicated that it would be essential for, and of great assistance in, considering the proposals to have an indication of the precise geographic context in which they would be applied. The Chairman of the Conference's Working Group on Bosnia and Herzegovina thereupon renewed the Conference's earlier request to the parties to provide, if possible in the form of maps, their conception as to the boundaries to be drawn within the country. These maps were to be the starting point for the possible development within the Conference of a set of relevant proposals.

27. In spite of these urgent requests and the evident interest of the parties in having the Co-Chairmen's constitutional proposals complemented by those concerning the maps, it was not until the second week of December that each of the parties presented some ideas concerning the geographic division of the country. The map presented by the Bosnian government delegation indicated a division of the country into 13 provinces, the populations of which would vary between 564,000 and 67,000. All of these would have an ethnically varied population, although, in each, one of the ethnic groups would predominate, sometimes distinctly, sometimes just barely. The delegation also submitted a written explanation indicating the considerations that had motivated the boundaries it suggested: historical, economic, commercial, climatic, geological, cultural and ethnic.

28. The Bosnian Serb delegation submitted a map, accompanied by a brief written explanation, that showed the proposed delimitation between the Serb republic and other constituent units. The former would include about 75 per cent

of the area of the country, with a population of some 1,6 million Serbs, i.e. almost all the Bosnian Serbs, plus about 300,000 Muslims and 100,000 Croats. The basis for the territory claimed was explained as all areas in which Serbs actually constituted the majority and owned the greatest percentage of the land; plus those areas in which they would have constituted such a majority except for the genocide committed during World War II and the policies of the subsequent Titoist regime; plus other areas under Serb control at present. There was no indication of how the Serb-claimed territory, which constitutes a continuous area, might be subdivided into provinces or how the other three areas might be so divided or how these might be divided between the Muslims and the Croats.

29. The Bosnian Croat delegation submitted a map merely indicating those territories, consisting of one large, one medium-sized and four small ones, within which Croats allegedly constituted a majority of 60 per cent or more. No indication was given as far as to how provincial boundaries might be drawn in that light, although in accompanying oral explanations it was stated that the Croats would expect to end up with two provinces and that other concentrations of Croat populations would necessarily be assigned to provinces with other majorities.

30. The government and the Croat delegations agreed to attempt to submit a joint proposal as to the delimitation of the provinces.

31. The Co-Chairmen and the Chairman of the Working Group on Bosnia and Herzegovina intend to use the maps submitted or to be submitted by the parties to narrow the differences between them.

IV. WORKING GROUP ON HUMANITARIAN ISSUES

32. A high-level meeting of the Humanitarian Issues Working Group was held on 4 December 1992 to assess the effectiveness of the humanitarian assistance operation and to recommend further measures. The meeting was attended by all States of the region of the former Yugoslavia, the donor community, other interested States and international governmental and non-governmental organizations. The Chairperson of the Working Group, the United Nations High Commissioner for Refugees, Mrs. Ogata, invited the meeting to review the implementation of the Comprehensive Humanitarian Response launched on 29 July 1992, both as to protection and material assistance.

33. A working document that the Chairperson submitted to the meeting drew attention, among other things, to the following:

(a) There were some 3 million refugees, displaced persons and other victims of the conflict who were in need of humanitarian assistance;

(b) There was a persistent threat of ethnic cleansing in many parts of Bosnia and Herzegovina, particularly in the north-western part of the country. Harassment and persecution continued unabated. There were shocking reports of sexual abuse of women;

(c) Admission to safety abroad had come under pressure;

(d) International relief efforts were increasingly complex, dangerous and frustrating. Security condition affecting humanitarian access remained fragile. Harassment and delays at checkpoints, indiscriminate fighting and political manipulations had continued to be major obstacles;

(e) Deliveries of relief assistance were not reaching all the victims and covered only a portion of their survival needs;

(f) There was a serious shortfall of 2,300 places for providing temporary refuge abroad for detainees;

(g) The inadequate level of support to the World Health Organization (WHO) and the United Nations Children's Fund (UNICEF) portions of the Consolidated Appeal continued to be a cause of concern.

34. During the meeting, delegations expressed their continued support for the Comprehensive Response and confirmed that it continued to constitute the framework for the humanitarian relief effort in the former Yugoslavia.

35. The meeting heard appeals to all parties to the conflict to abide by human rights and humanitarian principles and for an immediate cessation of all hostilities. Calls were also made for unconditional and unhindered humanitarian access to those in need, which was considered a cornerstone of the Comprehensive Response.

36. Delegation expressed their serious concern at the plight of the 3 million people who had been forced to flee from their homes and the risk of a further deterioration of their already tragic situation and a spread of the conflict.

37. The heinous practice of ethnic cleansing was vigorously condemned. There were renewed calls to the parties in the conflict to continue the release of those persons still unlawfully detained contrary to the commitments made at the London session of the International Conference.

38. Some delegations intervened on the issue of creating safety zones in Bosnia and Herzegovina, on which a study had been called for in Security Council resolution 787 (1992). The complexity of the issue was widely recognized. The Chairperson assured delegations that their observations would be taken fully into

account in her further consultation with the Secretary-General on that issue.

39. While several delegations expressed their appreciation for the amount of assistance reaching Bosnia and Herzegovina, there was general agreement that additional urgent measures, particularly relating to shelter and health, were necessary to save lives during the winter period. Further progress needed to be made in achieving unhindered access, as well as in addressing crucial infrastructural needs.

40. The meeting also recognized temporary protection needs, particularly with respect to vulnerable cases. In that regard the Chairperson stated that she was grateful for the additional offers of places for ex-detainees that had been announced at the meeting. She encouraged Governments to make further commitments.

41. The Chairperson continued that, while she had been very cautious in identifying vulnerable categories for temporary protection, she expected that, owing to the deteriorating situation on the ground, pressure in that regard would mount. She reiterated her appeal to Governments to continue to admit to safety all those in need of protection. Time was running out for the innocent victims of the conflict. She expected the urgency of the situation described at the meeting to guide Governments in their deliberations in the coming days towards decisive political actions.

V. WORKING GROUP ON ETHNIC AND NATIONAL COMMUNITIES AND MINORITIES

42. At its second plenary meeting in Geneva on 2 November 1992, delegations from Bosnia and Herzegovina, Croatia, the former Yugoslav Republic of Macedonia, Slavonia and a federal delegation from Belgrade declared their continued adherence to the London documents, particularly to chapter II of the draft Convention of 4 November 1991, negotiated in The Hague. Since then the Working Group's activities have taken place in the different sub-groups, particularly the Subgroup on Macedonia and the Special Group on the Former Autonomous Province of Kosovo set up under the chairmanship of Ambassador Ahrens, at the London session of the International Conference.

A. Former Yugoslav Republic of Macedonia

43. On 24 November, the Subgroup on the former Yugoslav Republic of Macedonia held high-level talks in Skopje with President Gligorov, Prime Minister Crvenkovski and the President of the Republican Parliament Mr. Andov, as well as with parliamentary leaders of all political parties. On 8 December, the Subgroup had a meeting with the leader of the Opposition Party, VMRO, Mr. Georgievski. There were trilateral talks with representatives of the government and of the Albanians from the former Yugoslav Republic of Macedonia in Geneva on 3 and 4 November and again on 1 and 2 December, and in Skopje on 24 November and 8 December. Trilateral talks with government representatives and representatives of the Macedonian Serbs took place in Skopje on 24 November and in Geneva at 2 December. On 8 December, the Subgroup met in Skopje with the media. The meeting was chaired by the Director-General of the Macedonian Radio and Television. Through the good offices of the Council of Europe, Mr. Werner Haug, Chairman of the European Population Committee of the Council of Europe, joined the Subgroup for a first exchange of view on a republic-wide census that is to take place at the earliest possible date. Mr. Haug held talks with all interested sides in Geneva on 1 December and in Skopje from 8 to 10 December.

44. All these contacts, which are to be continued with high intensity, showed that there is still a good chance to solve ethnic conflicts inside the republic by peaceful means. All sides are still on good speaking terms with one another and show a remarkable willingness for crisis management and reasonable compromise. All are, however, under increasing pressure from more radical elements that grow in strength the longer the unfortunate recognition issue remains unsolved. The Chairman of the Working Group considers that, in the interest of the endangered stability of the republic, the early arrival of United Nations peace-keeping troops as well as the presence of long-term CSCE observers, which include members of the European Community Monitoring Mission (ECMM), would be most helpful.

45. As figures on the percentage of Macedonian Albanians in the overall population given by the Government and the Macedonian Albanians differ widely from 21 to 48 per cent, an early census is most desirable. The Macedonian Albanians did not participate in the 1991 census, but are willing to do so now under the condition of international participation. Against the background of a worsening economic crisis, the Government will, however, need international assistance to finance the census.

46. In the trilateral talks with the Macedonian Albanians, some real progress could be achieved, for example, on the aforementioned census issue, on secondary education and on problems related to the display of Macedonian Albanian national emblems. There is also agreement that a new law on local self-administration should be worked out that would provide more decentralization, thus giving minorities a greater say in local affairs. There are, however, other Macedonian Albanian requests that have remained unfulfilled. On most of them discussions will continue. It was agreed that the editor of the Albanian-language television programme, which is only one hour a day on one of the channels, will work out proposals on how to improve this unsatisfactory situation. These proposals will be considered by the Subgroup in the first part of January 1993. Macedonian Albanians and Serbs are not satisfied with their overall constitutional position. The Government is at present not prepared to consider further constitutional changes. There might be a better basis for such discussion after the census has taken place. The earliest date for the census is November 1993.

B. Kosovo

47. The Special Group on Kosovo has weekly meetings ever since the education talks, mentioned in the previous report, started. Four of these meetings took place in Pristina, one in Belgrade, one in Novi Sad and three in Geneva. The attendance varies, because the Government of the Serbian Republic has refused to accept Geneva as a venue. The Special Group drew the attention of the Serbian Government repeatedly to the fact that that attitude violated the working paper agreed to by all the participants at the London Conference. The paper states that sessions of the working group are held in Geneva.

48. At the latest meeting in Pristina on 9 December, attended by all parties including the Serbian Government, participants held discussions that showed different standpoints on both fundamental and educational issues. Participants confirmed their statement of 14 October 1992 quoted in the previous report (S/24795, para. 90). The Kosovar Albanians, however, voiced their deep disappointment that nothing had changed on the ground.

49. The Kosovar Albanian representatives proposed the opening of school premises at all levels at once and without preconditions. Any questions concerning education in Albanian should be dealt with after the reopening of the premises. The Government said that that was not possible and that there had to be agreement on some points before the premises could be handed over. There were altogether three points: (a) teaching programmes; (b) the status of teaching

personnel; and (c) a solution to problems related to examinations and time spent in the parallel education system maintained by the Kosovar Albanians. Against this background, participants started to discuss teaching plans. There was agreement that so far there was no problem with the university level because such teaching plans were decided by the faculties and the universities themselves. On teaching plans for elementary and secondary education, the Kosovar Albanians had given Ambassador Ahrens corresponding documents that were briefly considered by participants. The Federal Minister of Education, Mr. Ivic, stated that the teaching programmes were complete but that the teaching plans were missing. The Kosovar Albanians replied that they would present those teaching plans although they saw no need to do so. They stressed that they had handed those materials to the Special Group only for consideration by all sides in the Group and they did not want any form of legalization by the Serbian Government.

50. The Group agreed to have a thorough exchange on the teaching programmes and plans at the next meeting at which the status of teachers and examinations and time spent in the parallel system would also be discussed. These discussions will take place against the background of the statement of 14 October 1992, which stressed the urgency of changes on the ground.

51. The Kosovar Albanians complain that nothing has changed on the ground. The negotiation strategy, of having a quick breakthrough in one important sector, i.e. education, chosen by Federal Prime Minister Panic, and agreed to by Mr Rugova, the Kosovar Albanian leader, was meant to create a better atmosphere, so that it would become possible to move from there to other areas and, finally, to the extraordinarily complicated fundamental issues related to the status of Kosovo. However, this has so far not borne fruit. Education can hardly remain the only subject of discussion in the Special Group. Accordingly, on 24 November, the Group held talks with a delegation of Kosovar Albanian medical experts in order to deal with that sector in which urgent improvement is also necessary. Other such sectors, for instance public media and the economy, were taken up with Kosovar Albanian representatives on 17 December. The Federal Government has indicated its readiness to participate in such wider talks and also to start discussion on the status of Kosovo once the revision of the federal and the Serbian Constitutions begin after the elections of 20 December 1992.

52. The Chairman of the Working Group considers that, realistically, no progress in Kosovo can be expected in any sector before these elections have taken place and before there are again clear political structures in Belgrade. At present, only stocktaking and crisis management seem to be possible. This is the purpose of the intense activities of the Special Group, greatly helped by the

CSCE long-term observer on the spot, who participates in the Special Group talks, and by the intense international attention devoted to Kosovo.

C. Vojvodina

53. The Subgroup on Vojvodina held talks, on 10 and 11 November, concerning the Hungarian minority in the province. After a discussion in the Hungarian Ministry of Foreign Affairs in Budapest, there was a series of meetings between the Federal Government of Yugoslavia and the Democratic Union of Vojvodina Hungarians, led by Mr. Agoston, other Hungarian organizations and representatives of all walks of life. The Subgroup was also received by the head of the provincial government. From these meetings, it became clear that the situation of the Hungarians has deteriorated in the course of the crisis. The main complaints are the resettlement of Serbian refugees in Hungarian towns and villages and an overproportional and disproportionate draft of Hungarians into the Yugoslav army. A follow-up on the Novi Sad meeting and serious negotiations on satisfying compromises will not, in the view of the Chairman of the Working Group, be possible before the elections of 20 December.

54. On 10 and 12 November, the Subgroup also met with the Chairman of the Croatian Party in Vojvodina, Mr. Tonkovic, and six Catholic priests from southern Vojvodina, where human rights violations are more frequent than in the north. It was agreed with the CSCE long-term observers in Subotica that they would take up the individual human rights cases. The Subgroup has approached the Federal Government on behalf of the Vojvodina Croats, but so far no conference-sponsored talks have been possible. The matter will be taken up after 20 December.

55. On 15 December, a delegation of the Subgroup headed by Ambassador Rey participated in a Novi Sad-type meeting with the Slovak minority in Vojvodina, which took place in Backi Petrovac as proposed by the Federal Government. It also held talks with Vojvodina Hungarian and Croatian representatives.

D. Sandjak

56. The Subgroup on the Sandjak held talks with a delegation of the Muslim National Council of Sandjak. The Co-Chairmen wrote to President Milosevic of Serbia and to President Bulatovic of Montenegro on behalf of the Sandjak Muslims, who, particularly as a consequence of the war in Bosnia and Herzegovina, are victims of serious human rights violations. A trilateral meeting in Novi

Pazar, envisaged by the Federal Government following repeated insistence by the Subgroup, has so far not taken place.

E. Croatia

57. The Working Group held several contacts with the Croatian Government representatives and Serbs from Croatia. Endeavours have to be intensified as soon as the overall political situation, particularly in the United Nations protected areas, allows. In the meantime, the Working Group will continue its contacts with Croatian government representatives and with Serbs living in Croatia. Some complaints by Serbs about violation of their rights have reached the Group.

VI. WORKING GROUP ON SUCCESSION ISSUES

58. The Working Group on Succession Issues met under its new Chairman, Ambassador Jorgen Bojer, from 24 to 27 November. Delegations from all successor States on the territory of the former Yugoslavia participated.

59. The Working Group adopted a text on the question of citizenship, which stressed that no former citizen of the Socialist Federal Republic of Yugoslavia will become stateless.

60. The Working Group also discussed the issues on pension and other acquired rights of those former Socialist Federal Republic of Yugoslavia citizens who live in a successor State of which they are not citizens. Other matters dealt with by the Working Group included the rights of refugees and displaced persons, how to define State property and the relationship of the successor States with the international financial institutions. The discussion of these topics will be continued at the next meeting of the Working Group scheduled to be held in January 1993.

VII. WORKING GROUP ON ECONOMIC ISSUES

61. The Working Group on Economic Issues convened on 11 November to consider:

(a) Amendments to the inventory of assets, liabilities and archives of the former Socialist Federal Republic of Yugoslavia proposed by the six subgroups meeting in Brussels at the end of October;

(b) A projected high-level conference on the economic future of the republics of former Yugoslavia;

(c) The need to look at proposals for practical policy initiatives in the economic field.

62. Work on the valuation of assets, liabilities and archives of the former Yugoslav federation is proceeding, although the intensive bilateral consultations held earlier had shown that large differences remained between the delegation of Serbia-Montenegro and the others in what the content of the inventory should be. The Serbian view of what should count as an asset of the former Socialist Federal Republic of Yugoslavia is quite extensive; the view of the other delegations is much more restrictive.

63. A delegation comprising two officials and four representatives of a consulting firm has been in Belgrade to examine financial assets and liabilities of the former federation. The delegation was granted access to most of the information sources and databases it wanted to cover, including the statistics of the National Bank of Yugoslavia. Another similar fact-finding mission has been dispatched to Belgrade to look at federal archives. There have been unconfirmed reports that the Government of the Federal Republic of Yugoslavia is opposed to any division of the archives of the former federation.

64. The principles of a high-level conference on the economic future of the republics of former Yugoslavia, focusing on recovery and reconstruction, was well received, although questions were raised as to the correct timing of such an event.

65. Future meetings of the Working Group will consider a number of practical policy initiatives submitted by the different delegations and by the Chairman, as well as the question of the proper timing of the proposed high-level conference.

VIII. WORKING GROUP ON CONFIDENCE- AND SECURITY-BUILDING
AND VERIFICATION MEASURES

66. The Working Group on Confidence- and Security-building and Verification Measures met regularly in November and early December (a) to review the implementation of several of the confidence- and security-building measures adopted on 15 September 1992 to facilitate the continued operation of the humanitarian flights into Sarajevo (see S/24634, annex) and (b) to seek common

ground among all the parties in former Yugoslavia on long-term measures to build confidence in the military sphere.

67. With respect to the 15 September Confidence- and Security-building Measures agreement, efforts focused on the parties' compliance with the ban on radar lock-ons of humanitarian flights and other flights authorized by UNPROFOR; the withdrawal of anti-aircraft artillery and surface-to-air missiles from an area of 45 kilometres each side of the route agreed for the humanitarian flights and the declarations of locations of all anti-aircraft artillery and surface-to-air missiles throughout Bosnia and Herzegovina. Information was received from all the parties on the ground in Bosnia and Herzegovina. The parties took a step forward by agreeing to exchange the information they had submitted. Efforts will continue to be exerted to gain full compliance with the 15 September agreement.

68. The London Conference document on confidence, security-building and verification (LC/C11) has been the basis for consideration of longer-term confidence- and security-building measures.

69. Over the last month, the Working Group has received possible measures to facilitate, within its mandate, the reduction of tension among the parties by beginning its consideration of the question of other long-term confidence-building measures. Among them, the Working Group has before it a proposal for a preliminary exchange of information on the types of weapon systems and armed forces levels in the possession of each party in the region. It is hoped thereby to begin to prepare the ground for eventual mutually acceptable confidence- and security-building measures, which might have the desired effect of building genuine confidence in the military field among the parties in the former Yugoslavia.

Annex I
Message from the Secretary-General to the Ministerial Meeting of the Steering Committee of the International Conference on the Former Yugoslavia dated 16 December 1992

As Co-Chairman of the International Conference on the Former Yugoslavia, I welcome you to the Palais des Nations and send you my best wishes for a productive meeting. This expanded meeting of our Conference's Steering Committee convenes at an opportune moment. The conflict in Bosnia and Herzegovina continues in spite of strenuous efforts to halt it, although the intensity of the hostilities has been reduced. Displaced persons, refugees and other affected persons are facing the rigours of expanded conflict.

The current situation demands statesmanship of the highest order. Understandable emotion must be balanced by a sober appreciation of risks and benefits. Short term nostrums must be examined in the light of their contribution to long range stability.

Much has been done to stem the conflict and to provide vital humanitarian assistance to its victims. Humanitarian organizations deserve our admiration and gratitude for their unceasing efforts. Your continuing support for their work is still essential.

The Co-Chairmen of the Steering Committee are laying the foundations for their peaceful settlement. Their emphasis has rightly been, and continues to be, on peacemaking, peacekeeping, preventive diplomacy and peace-building. The road ahead lies through continuous negotiations in good faith, in the spirit of the Charter of the United Nations and the principles of the International Conference, not in actions which would serve to continue or escalate the violence. I wish you success in your endeavours.

Annex II
Opening statement of Mr. Cyrus Vance to the Ministerial Meeting of the Steering Committee

Lord Owen and I extend to you our warmest good wishes and welcome you to this Ministerial Meeting of the Steering Committee of the International Conference.

Your presence here today demonstrates the deep concern of the international community over the grave situation in former Yugoslavia. Conflict persists in Bosnia and Herzegovina. More than 3 million refugees and displaced persons from the three communities continue to depend on international aid for their survival. Over the last three months more than 7,000 troops have joined the command of the United Nations Protective Force (UNPROFOR) in Bosnia and Herzegovina, helping to bring urgently needed humanitarian assistance to the civilian populace. While much has been done, the conflict endures, with the risk of spreading to other areas of the Balkans.

The conflict in Bosnia and Herzegovina is but the most recent explosion in the violent break-up of post-Tito Yugoslavia. The roots of the violence lie deep in the region's complex history of mutual grievances, political ambitions, territorial claims, religious differences, and ethnic rivalries.

But to say that the causes of the conflict are complex does not relieve us of the responsibility to seek just and equitable solutions. It is essential that we bend every effort to unify our actions to bring the fighting to an end, to prevent the conflict from spreading, to provide humanitarian assistance to all, and to find a lasting political solution to the problems of Bosnia and Herzegovina and the former Yugoslavia as a whole.

In the 104 days since the International Conference began, we and our many colleagues, civilian and military, and other institutions and organizations, have worked to push forward on a wide range of problems. All are difficult, but all are essential.

They have included:

(a) Improving relations between Croatia and the Federal Republic of Yugoslavia;

(b) Initiating serious dialogue among the leaders of Croatia, the Federal Republic of Yugoslavia, and Bosnia and Herzegovina;

(c) Working to stabilize the situation in the United Nations protected areas in Croatia, including such thorny problems as the return of refugees;

(d) Demilitarizing the Prevlaka Peninsula in the context of an agreed withdrawal of the Yugoslav army from Croatian territory on 20 October;

(e) Deploying a large United Nations peace-keeping operation in Bosnia and Herzegovina to protect humanitarian convoys;

(f) Establishing a Mixed Military Working Group in Sarajevo to bring about a cessation of hostilities and to address other important military issues;

(g) Constructing a constitutional framework for Bosnia and Herzegovina;

(h) Working to strengthen existing sanctions and measures for enforcement;

(i) Deploying preventive peace-keeping troops in Macedonia, as well as conducting preventive diplomacy in Kosovo, Sandjak, and Vojvodina;

(j) Actively cooperating with the United Nations Commission on Human Rights and its Special Rapporteur, as well as with the Commission of Experts on violations of humanitarian law, including war crimes.

Promoting a cessation of hostilities and constitutional settlement in Bosnia and Herzegovina, remain our priority objectives. It has not been easy, and I must tell you that all three sides have at different times created obstacles to the realization of these goals. Nonetheless, some progress, although not nearly enough, has been made. After lengthy and strenuous efforts by the United Nations Commanders, a tripartite Mixed Military Working Group has been established in Sarajevo. The results have not been negligible and the overall level of violence has been reduced, although not ended.

From the outset Lord Owen and I have proceeded on the basis that our essential task is to bring about a durable political solution. Practically speaking, there are no serious alternatives to a negotiated political settlement. It is important, therefore, that our actions work consistently to this end. We hope very much that this meeting will send a clear message to all parties concerned that incentives are available to those who cooperate in the peace process, and that costs will be borne by those who do not. Let me briefly share with you our thinking on a range of specific issues which concern us all.

Macedonia is undergoing an acute crisis. To help defuse it, the Security Council has just approved the Secretary-General's recommendation that a United Nations peace-keeping operation - a preventive deployment - be established in Macedonia. An infantry battalion consisting of some 700 armed troops, with logistic support, military observers, and United Nations civilian police will perform this task. The Co-Chairmen join the Security Council in attaching great urgency to some immediate deployment.

Kosovo is no less pressing a problem. It is doubtful whether at present we could receive the required consent to insert United Nations peace-keeping forces into this province of Serbia, but in any event the Conference on Security and Cooperation in Europe (CSCE) already maintains a presence in Kosovo. We welcome the CSCE decision in Stockholm to enlarge its civilian monitor mission. Given the heightened tension on all sides involved in the Kosovo issue, conflict could break out there as much by misadventure as by design. Therefore the good offices role of the CSCE mission is of critical importance. Over the long run serious improvements must be made in Kosovo. During the last three months the Conference's Special Group on Kosovo has carried out intensive discussions with all sides on a broad range of social, educational, and political issues. We believe that these efforts will help to improve stability and will bear fruit. Restoration of genuine autonomy to Kosovo remains a principal goal.

With respect to the no-fly zone over Bosnia and Herzegovina, we believe that breaches of the Security Council's resolution need to be examined. In this connection it is essential to understand the factual situation. The fact is that UNPROFOR thus far has not seen any use of fixed-wing fighter aircraft in support of combat operations in Bosnia and Herzegovina since the no-fly-zone resolution was passed more that two months ago. UNPROFOR has tracked helicopters on a number of occasions and has been informed of allegations that helicopters have been used in an offensive role. This, however, has not been confirmed by UNPROFOR. These facts should be taken into account in any consideration of a Chapter VII determination, The Security Council must also consider the probable consequences of an enforcement action, particularly the endangerment of UNPROFOR personnel, and staff of the office of the United Nations High Commissioner of Refugees (UNHCR), the European Community Monitoring Mission (ECMM) and unarmed humanitarian workers in Bosnia and Herzegovina and elsewhere in the former Yugoslavia.

Another important issue is the suggested lifting of the arms embargo. Two weeks ago in Jeddah, Lord Owen and I were able to assess the depth of feeling of the Islamic countries in favour of this actions. Yet I must tell you that, in our view, such action would be unwise. It would widen and deepen the war in Bosnia and Herzegovina. It would encourage the delivery of more sophisticated and more destructive weapons to all the warring parties, and could also lead to the spread of the conflict throughout the Balkan region.

Another subject under consideration is that of security zones or safe havens for civilians caught up in the fighting. Advocates of this policy offer several variants and it is not always clear what is being proposed. I believe we should examine such proposals carefully, but Lord Owen and I cannot support any policy that would contribute to ethnic cleansing. We continue to believe the best "safe haven" lies in an overall cessation of hostilities.

With respect to the refugee situation, Mrs. Ogata will be reporting on her activities and the requirements on the ground. Inside and outside of Bosnia and Herzegovina more than 3 million refugees and displaced persons still need assistance. Inside the country, thanks to the heroic efforts of UNHCR workers, UNPROFOR and others, food and other supplies are getting through to many places that had not been reached before. But international relief efforts remain dangerous, and still encounter obstruction and intimidation. More must be done by all of us to improve the lot of innocent civilians.

Human rights issues have been at the forefront of our concerns since our first day in Geneva. In a message we sent to the UN Commission on Human Rights on November 30 we again condemned ethnic cleansing and other violations of human rights and invited the Commission to give attention to the important question of protecting the rights of minorities.

We have cooperated with the International Committee of the Red Cross (ICRC), and we pay tribute to President Sommaruga and his colleagues for their noble and unsung work day in and day out - particularly on prisoners release and evacuation. In view of the urgency of this matter, and deep interest in it, he will report on the latest developments.

We have also taken action on allegations of war crimes and other breaches of international humanitarian law. We have sought to help the Commission of Experts bring about a forensic examination of the mass grave site of Ovcara near Vukovar and this is in train this week. Lord Owen and I believe that atrocities committed in the former Yugoslavia are unacceptable, and persons guilty of war crimes should be brought to justice. We therefore recommend the establishment of an international criminal court.

This is the path we have followed since assuming our mission, and we shall continue to press ahead the strategies I have indicated. Finally, in his remarks Lord Owen will address the steps we plan to take in the immediate future to expedite our endeavours.

Thank you.

Annex III
Speech by the Right Honourable the Lord Owen to the Ministerial Meeting of the Steering Committee

As Co-Chairmen we are both convinced that we should press for an overall settlement to be achieved as soon as humanly possible. This will have to include the restoration of full autonomy for Kosovo where the situation is particularly dangerous. Realism tells us that there are many formidable problems ahead.

We never doubted that the parties in Bosnia and Herzegovina cannot negotiate a settlement on their own and that there will have to be considerable pressure brought to bear on all three parties at various times. Many of the countries sitting around this table have a part to play in that process.

One of our concerns is that the Bosnia and Herzegovina Government is sadly increasingly becoming representative only of the Muslim population. We are travelling tomorrow to Zagreb to meet with President Tudjman and President Izetbegovic in an attempt to bring together the Bosnian Muslims and Bosnian Croats into a more representative Presidency. We will try, though we know it will be very difficult, to persuade both sides to come to some measure of agreement on a provincial map for Bosnia and Herzegovina.

So far we have failed to get the Bosnia and Herzegovina Government, at political level, to come around the same table with the Bosnian Serbs and Bosnian Croats. With so much of the territory in which they would normally be in the majority under the control of the Bosnian Serbs they are afraid of negotiating now, as they see it, from a position of weakness. We will, I expect, need the support of countries particularly in the Islamic world to encourage President Izetbegovic to participate constructively in January. But if he is to compromise we will have to be able to demonstrate that we are capable of rolling back the present Bosnian Serb frontline and obtaining their agreement to live under a rule of law that allows for ethnic cleansing to be reserved.

The Bosnian Croatian position presents for the moment the least difficulty and indeed could become a helpful factor in negotiations but there are still parts of the Croatian Army in Bosnia and Herzegovina and some unauthorised flights from Zagreb.

The overriding challenge is, however, to roll back the Bosnian Serbs and here General Mladic is becoming even more important. He is a determined officer. While he probably listens to President Cosic and General Panic he is not controlled by them. He answers to President Milosevic.

It is Belgrade, above all, that controls the main pressure points on the Bosnian Serbs. Dr. Karadzic ultimately answers to Belgrade and in effect the Bosnian Serb military efforts and economy, apart from food, is critically dependent on decisions taken in Belgrade. We are right therefore in believing that Belgrade has - if it cares to exercise it - the capacity to deliver a settlement.

That is why it is fundamentally important that all existing sanctions against Serbia and Montenegro are maintained and indeed reinforced. We cannot afford to allow sanctions to be evaded as happened a few weeks ago with the oil embargo. We need a person who can string together intelligence information from different countries and report evasion and potential sanctions busting to the Sanctions Committee. Having adopted at last stop and search in the Adriatic we must have stop and search on the Danube. It is prudent too for us all to plan for new and tougher sanctions. They may be needed against an intransigent new Serbian Government, but we as Co-Chairmen do not believe that they should be applied or even threatened until we have given whatever new government emerges in Belgrade the opportunity to contribute positively to the negotiation process. Whatever happens on 20 December, President Cosic will remain the President.

We intend to proceed on a determined and persistent path towards a negotiated settlement.

Between Christmas and New Year, Mr. Boutros Boutros-Ghali will be visiting Geneva and during that time he has agreed to meet with us and President Cosic and also separately with President Tudjman. We may or may not seek to bring the Presidents together.

If no candidate in the Serbian Presidential elections obtains more than 50 per cent of the vote there will have to be a run-off, and the most likely time for a second election is thought to be 3 January. The results would not be known before 4 or 5 January and there will be a public holiday because of the Orthodox Christmas on 7 and 8 January. We may find therefore that we have not an authoritative government to deal with in Belgrade until the week beginning 11 January. Yet neither of us believes it is acceptable in terms of the situation on the ground in Bosnia and Herzegovina or indeed in terms of world opinion for us to wait until then.

We are therefore inviting to Geneva on 2 January President Izetbegovic, Dr. Karadzic and Mr. Boban and asking them to bring their senior military commander. We want not only a sustainable cessation of hostilities and the demilitarisation of Sarajevo, but also to try to reach an agreement on a pullback from the military front line in a way which reinforces and goes with the grain of an overall political settlement. We will also be trying to ensure free access of all citizens in and out of cities and towns that have been under siege and the free movement of humanitarian aid. We will be inviting Belgrade and Zagreb to send representation at the level they think appropriate to these talks. We will plan to follow these talks up when the political situation is clearer in Belgrade with further meetings in the middle of January.

We believe that only when this process has been undertaken will we be able to analyse the potential for a genuine negotiated settlement which fulfils the principles laid down for this Conference at the end of August in London. If any party in Bosnia and Herzegovina or any government in Zagreb or Belgrade is obstructing such a settlement we will not hesitate to bring their attitude and action to the attention of this Conference. We cannot fix deadlines or milestones but when a new administration is established in the United States it may well be appropriate to adopt new measures in the Security Council and even meet again at Ministerial level.

At this stage, however, neither Cyrus Vance nor I are faint-hearted about the prospect of a negotiated settlement. A great deal of time and effort has been invested in a negotiated settlement since we met together for the first time here on 3 September. We intend to capitalise on that investment. We do believe, however, that four additional new measures should be considered.

(a) Firstly, consideration of the establishment of an international Criminal Court through a Resolution by the Security Council. It would surely be wrong if the practitioners of ethnic cleansing are not brought to justice.

(b) Secondly, consideration of a Chapter VII determination to make it possible to enforce a no-fly ban by the Security Council if and only if infringements continue. This is a two stage process for the implications of any actual enforcement for UN troops, UNHCR and others on the ground in BiH demand the deepest analysis by members of the Security Council. The Secretary-General will also need to be fully involved in any decisions in the timing and the type of any enforcement action and his decision to ask NATO for planning assistance will help this process.

(c) Thirdly, consideration to toughening existing sanctions through a mechanism for using delicate intelligence and other information so as to report evasions to the UN Sanctions Committee at the earliest moment.

(d) Fourthly, consideration to a Security Council Resolution on Kosovo making it clear that all parties should show restraint but that any further internal suppression would be considered a threat to the peace and that negotiated autonomy is an essential and urgent priority.

We both remain firmly against making any change in the Security Council arms embargo which was passed in September 1991 and covers the whole territory of the former Yugoslavia. Now is the time to test the parties inside Bosnia and Herzegovina and the countries surrounding Bosnia and Herzegovina at the negotiating table. It must never be forgotten that peace will only come to the former Yugoslavia through negotiations. To bring that about we need a judicious use of moral, political, economic and military pressures.

112. Report of the Secretary-General on the Activities of the International Conference on the Former Yugoslavia*

1. Since my last report was issued on 24 December 1992 (S/25015), a number of important developments have taken place, about which I felt it important to inform the Security Council immediately.

---

* UN Doc. S/25050, 6 January 1993.

PEACE TALKS: 2-4 JANUARY 1993

2. In view of heightening international concern over the situation in Bosnia and Herzegovina, the Co-Chairmen of the Steering Committee issued invitations to the three sides in Bosnia and Herzegovina to come to Geneva from 2 January 1993 onward for talks on the following matters: "to discuss a sustainable cessation of hostilities; demilitarization of Sarajevo; an agreement on a pull-back from the military front line in a way that reinforces and goes with the grain of an overall political settlement; ensuring free access of all citizens in and out of besieged cities and towns; and the free movements of humanitarian aid". The Governments of the Republic of Croatia and the Federal Republic of Yugoslavia were also invited to send representatives to the talks at the level they considered appropriate.

BACKGROUND

3. In preparation for these talks, the Co-Chairmen of the Steering Committee invited President Tudjman of Croatia and President Izetbegovic of Bosnia and Herzegovina to Geneva for consultations on Sunday, 27 December, and Monday, 28 December 1992. Those consultations concentrated on the provincial structure in Bosnia and Herzegovina as an intrinsic part of future constitutional arrangements.

4. Also in preparation for the talks, the Co-Chairmen invited President Cosic of the Federal Republic of Yugoslavia and President Tudjman of the Republic of Croatia for consultations in Geneva on Monday, 28 December.

5. I considered it crucial that the parties should cooperate with the Co-Chairmen of the Steering Committee. I and the Co-Chairmen of the Steering Committee, Cyrus Vance and Lord Owen, accordingly had talks, individually, on Monday, 28 December, with President Cosic, President Tudjman and President Izetbegovic. I expressed to each of them my grave concern over developments in Bosnia and Herzegovina and the risk of escalation and expansion of the conflict. I strongly appealed to each of them to help the Co-Chairmen in their search for peaceful solutions.

6. In the light of my conversations with them, I wrote to the President of the Security Council on 30 December 1992 describing my impression that there were subtle signs of progress in the peace process and expressing my grave concern at the growing momentum for stronger military measures by the interna-

tional community in Bosnia and Herzegovina. I stated my conviction - which I continue to hold - that this momentum should be slowed in order to allow the still fragile peace process an opportunity to take root.

7. My discussions with the three Presidents and the Co-Chairmen led me to the conclusion that the designation of Sarajevo as a demilitarized open city could be advantageous to the peace process in Bosnia and Herzegovina.

THE TALKS

8. Talks among the three sides to the conflict in Bosnia and Herzegovina were held in Geneva from 2 to 4 January 1993. The delegations were represented at the highest political and military levels. Also present were President Cosic of the Federal Republic of Yugoslavia with a delegation and President Tudjman of Croatia with a delegation. A list of the participants is set out in annex I to the present document.

9. This was the first time since the Co-Chairmen began their activities in Geneva on 3 September 1992, that the three sides to the conflict in Bosnia and Herzegovina had sat down together around the table for peace talks.

10. In their opening address to the talks on 2 January, the Co-Chairmen, Cyrus Vance and Lord Owen, appealed to the participants that "this is a historic meeting. It is our best chance for peace and we must ensure that it succeeds. From the beginning, we have sought to work together with you in the quest for peace. Now, for the first time, we have the leaders of all delegations assembled here, together with their political and military advisers. You can act decisively to bring an end to the plight of the people of Bosnia and Herzegovina, who have suffered so grievously". The Co-Chairmen stressed the importance of Sarajevo as an "open city". The remarks of the Bosnia and Herzegovina are annexed (see annexes II and III).

11. The Co-Chairmen placed before the delegates a draft map on the delimitation of 10 provinces in Bosnia and Herzegovina (see annex V, appendix), as well as a set of constitutional principles to underlie the future constitutional framework of Bosnia and Herzegovina (see annex V). The Co-Chairmen also circulated a paper prepared by the International Committee of the Red Cross showing the numbers and locations of prisoners held by the three sides in Bosnia and Herzegovina and urged their immediate release (see annex (IV).

12. At the opening session of the talks, the leaders of the five delegations all made statements signalling their desire for peace in Bosnia and Herzegovina and

promising to cooperate with the Co-Chairmen. Following these opening statements, the talks continued in two working groups. Working Group I, chaired by Mr. Martti Ahtisaari, considered the draft map on the provincial structure and the constitutional principles. Working Group II, chaired by the United Nations Protection Force Commander Lieutenant-General Satish Nambiar, discussed issues related to observance of a cessation of hostilities.

ACTIVITIES OF WORKING GROUP I

13. Working Group I held meetings on 2, 3 and 4 January 1993. Individual, bilateral and trilateral meetings were also conducted by Mr. Ahtisaari. The meetings all proceeded in an in-depth manner, without invective, Mr. Ahtisaari and the Co-Chairmen made extensive and determined efforts to bring the parties closer together in the delimitation of provinces and constitutional principles.

14. In the light of the discussions in the Working Group and of contacts with the delegations, Mr. Ahtisaari and the Co-Chairmen drew up and placed before the parties on 4 January a draft agreement relating to Bosnia and Herzegovina (see annex V). It dealt with the delimitation of provinces, a constitutional framework for Bosnia and Herzegovina and cooperation in respect of humanitarian efforts. Appended to it was a map suggesting a future provincial structure for Bosnia and Herzegovina.

ACTIVITIES OF WORKING GROUP II

15. Working Group II held meetings on 2, 3 and 4 January. The deliberations proceeded in a constructive atmosphere. The Group discussed the following items: principles of cessation of hostilities, restoration of infrastructure; opening of routes and freedom of movement; separation of forces; demilitarization of Sarajevo.

16. At the first meeting, on 2 January, the Co-Chairmen invited the delegations to make introductory presentations. Subsequently, at the start of the discussion on each item, General Nambiar raised issued on which he invited each delegation to comment in turn. In the light of their reactions, he prepared and submitted to the Working Group, on 4 January, elements of an agreement for peace in Bosnia and Herzegovina that would consist of an introductory part and annexes on the following points:

1. Measures for the achievement of an unconditional cessation of hostilities throughout Bosnia and Herzegovina;
2. Measures for the restoration of infrastructure on Bosnia and Herzegovina;
3. Measures for the opening of routes;
4. Arrangements on the separation of forces;
5. Measures for the demilitarization of Sarajevo;
6. Measures for the monitoring of the borders of Bosnia and Herzegovina;
7. Return of forces to designated provinces.

17. Following discussion of these elements in the Working Group, General Nambiar produced a revised version of the document, which he presented to the plenary session of the peace talks on 4 January. He stated that, in his view, the document represented a reasonable and constructive approach to dealing with the issues discussed in the Working Group. The Chairman's framework agreement for peace in Bosnia and Herzegovina is reproduced in annex VI to the present document.

PLENARY SESSION ON 4 JANUARY 1993

18. At a plenary session of the talks on 4 January, the Co-Chairmen reminded the participants that the success or failure of the talks depended primarily on them. The ultimate choice was theirs: peace over war. The Co-Chairmen explained that they had reached a stage where they believed that they should put to the parties a comprehensive package that would form the basis to sign the documents contained in annexes V and VI to the present report, which they explained, were inextricably linked. They explained further, that if, at any time, the three parties proposed agreed changes in either of the two papers or the provincial map, those changes would be incorporated.
19. The Co-Chairmen expressed the hope that all three parties would sign the two documents. However, if any party wished to think about the issues involved overnight, they would be ready to hold another plenary session on Tuesday, 5 January. Alternatively, if one or more parties wished to take the document back for consultations, a further plenary meeting would be called in Geneva on Sunday, 10 January, at 11 a.m. after the recess for the Orthodox Christmas.
20. Some of the parties asked for further discussions on parts of the two documents proposed by the Co-Chairmen, as well as on the map. Accordingly, it was decided that the Conference would recess until Sunday, 10 January, at 11 a.m.

The Co-Chairmen urged most strongly that there be maximum military restraint in the intervening days. They also urged maximum restraint in the participants' public statements.

CONCLUDING OBSERVATIONS

21. The peace talks represented a historic step forward in the pursuit of peace in Bosnia and Herzegovina. Discussions took place on the three critical components for achieving peace in Bosnia and Herzegovina; the constitutional principles; the delimitation of provinces; and arrangements for implementing and monitoring a cessation of hostilities.

22. All the delegations participating in the talks pledged their cooperation with the Co-Chairmen in the search for peaceful solutions. The peace process has thus taken on a qualitatively new dimension. Henceforth it should be easier to establish clearly who is cooperating and who is not. I believe that the Security Council should let it be known clearly to all sides in Bosnia and Herzegovina that it is their duty to cooperate with the Co-Chairmen in bringing the conflict in Bosnia and Herzegovina to an end swiftly, and that there would be penalties for obstruction.

23. In the view of the ongoing talks in Geneva, it remains my sincere belief that, if the Council decides to adopt a resolution enforcing the ban on non-authorized flights over Bosnia and Herzegovina, it would be helpful if its implementation could be delayed for a reasonable period of time.

Annex 1
Composition of Delegations

BOSNIAN CROAT
Mate Boban
Mile Akmadzic
Commander Milovoj Petkovic

BOSNIA AND HERZEGOVINA
Alija Izetbegovic
Haris Silajdzic
Commander-in-Chief Sefar Halilovic
Kasim Trnka

BOSNIAN SERB
Radovan Karadzic
General Ratko Mladic
Aleksa Buha
Vladimir Lukic
Sveto Plavsic

FEDERAL REPUBLIC OF YUGOSLAVIA
Dobrica Cosic
Svetozar Stojanovic
Ljubisa Rakic
Vladimir Pavicevic
Dragoslav Rancic
Radovan Radinovic

CROATIA
Franjo Tudjman
Gojko Susak
Jure Radic
General Anton Tus
Neven Madey

Annex II
Opening Statement of Mr. Cyrus Vance

This is an historic meeting. It is our best chance for peace and we must ensure that it succeeds. From the beginning we have sought to work together with you in the quest for peace. Now, for the first time, we have the leaders of all delegations assembled here, together with their political and military advisers. You can act decisively to bring an end to the plight of the people of Bosnia and Herzegovina, who have suffered so grievously.

The process we are starting today can make the difference between peace and war; between life and death for thousands of people. Those gathered around this table have it in their power to prevent us from sliding into escalation, or expansion, of the conflict. You, the leaders around this table, can control what comes next. Peace can come about only with your cooperation, We, in the International Conference, are here to assist you; the decision to choose peace or war rests with you.

It is your historic responsibility to see to it that peace prevails. We therefore welcome you and thank you for accepting our invitation to join us in these peace talks.

Peaceful solutions are within our grasp. The groundwork has been laid within the International Conference in the form of the principles agreed to and the commitments made by all of the parties, many of which have unfortunately not been fulfilled. The road to peace lies in implementation of these principles and commitments. Time is running short.

We expect that the outcome of the process starting today will be the achievement, and consolidation, of tangible measures for peace. Let us, in this regard, remind you of the principles and commitments that already unite you:

(a) You agreed to the principles of the International Conference adopted on 26 August. You committed yourselves that all parties should cease fighting and should engage actively in negotiations. You agreed on respect for the highest standards of human rights and on non-recognition of advantages gained by force;

(b) You agreed in London to the Statement on Bosnia adopted on 27 August. It calls, *inter alia*, for a full and permanent cessation of hostilities; recognition of Bosnia and Herzegovina by the former Yugoslav republics; respect for the integrity of present frontiers, unless changes by mutual agreement; guarantees for the rights of all communities and minorities; and the establishment of democratic and legal structures in Bosnia and Herzegovina;

(c) The three Bosnia and Herzegovina sides agreed to participate continuously and unconditionally in negotiations for the achievement of a cassation of hostilities and a constitutional settlement;

(d) The three Bosnia and Herzegovina sides also agreed to the unconditional and unilateral release, under international supervision, of all civilians detained, and the closure of detention camps without delay. To date, 137 prisoners have been released by the Bosnian Government; 5,040 prisoners have been released by the Bosnian Serbs; and 357 released by the Bosnian Croats. Unfortunately, 2,757 prisoners are still known to be held in captivity. According to the International Committee of the Red Cross (ICRC), 887 prisoners are still held by the Bosnian Government; 1,333 prisoners by the Bosnian Serbs; and 537 by the Bosnian Croats. A paper is being circulated to you which provides further information on where the detainees are being held. Your immediate release of all detainees is essential. It would not only be an indication of your peaceful intentions, but could also help to stop the drums of war, which are beating so loudly around us as we meet here today;

(e)   The three sides agreed, on 30 September 1992, to the establishment of a Mixed Military Working Group to discuss the demilitarization of Sarajevo, the cessation of hostilities in Bosnia and Herzegovina and other military issues. Talks to achieve these objectives have been going on in Sarajevo since October and 17 meetings of the Mixed Military Working Group have so far been held;

(f)   The three sides also agreed, with effect from 12 November 1992, to an unconditional ceasefire throughout Bosnia and Herzegovina. On 13 December, you reaffirmed your commitment to the unconditional ceasefire - a commitment which has not been realized fully;

(g)   The three sides have made political and moral commitments to allow humanitarian assistance to reach all civilians in need.

We are assembled here today to bring about the implementation of these agreements.

In our letter inviting you to this meeting, we stated that our objectives are:

"to discuss a sustainable cessation of hostilities; demilitarization of Sarajevo; an agreement on a pull-back from the military front line in a way that reinforces and goes with the grain of an overall political settlement; ensuring free access of all citizens in and out of besieged cities and towns; and the free movement of humanitarian aid".

In this regard, let us remind you of the following points:

(a)   The drafting of a new constitution for Bosnia and Herzegovina is vital for the future of the country. The re-establishment of peace, assured respect for human and minority rights and the future institutional structure of the country depend upon it. Within the Working Group on Bosnia and Herzegovina, chaired by Mr. Ahtisaari, you have had extensive opportunities to offer suggestions on the constitutional principles and structures that should underlie future institutional arrangements in Bosnia and Herzegovina. Out of this process, 10 principles have been distilled concerning the constitutional framework for Bosnia and Herzegovina. They will be circulated to you later. Our task in these meetings will be to confirm these principles and to convert these principles as rapidly as possible into the full text of a Constitution;

(b) You have had opportunities to offer your views, and to provide corresponding maps on the delimitation of provinces. Discussion on maps have been taking place at the highest levels in recent days. In the light of those discussions, and in response to your wishes, we will be circulating to you a map indicating a proposed delimitation of the provinces (see annex V, appendix). A crucial task of our meetings is to finalize such a map;

(c) Within the Mixed Military Working Group, which has been meeting in Sarajevo since October, various measures have been discussed with regard to the implementation of the ceasefire accord of 12 November, and related humanitarian issues. Our task at these meetings will be to reach specific agreement for the observance of the cessation of hostilities, for monitoring it, and on measures that can help to relieve the plight of civilians. The designation of Sarajevo as an open city is one of the important ideas that have been suggested and we hope that the highest priority will be given to it.

Let us now turn to the organization of our work. We shall first give the floor to the heads of the three Bosnia and Herzegovina sides, followed by the heads of the other two delegations.

After these statements, two Working Groups will commence their work. Mr. Ahtisaari will chair Working Group I. General Nambiar will chair Working Group II.

At the opening of Working Group I, the Chairman will describe the map circulated on the proposed delimitation of provinces and will explain the 10 proposed constitutional principles. The Chairman will then lead the discussion towards the finalization of the map and the constitutional principles, as well as the establishment of a mechanism for preparing a full Constitution.

At the opening of Working Group II, the Chairman will invite discussions on measures for the designation of Sarajevo as an open city - on which you will be hearing shortly from Lord Owen; measures for the implementation of the cessation of hostilities, for relieving the plight of civilians and for stabilizing the situation in Sarajevo and other parts of Bosnia and Herzegovina.

The two Working Groups will meet in parallel sessions this afternoon, on Sunday and on Monday. On Monday at 8 p.m. we shall reconvene in plenary session to consider the recommendations of the two Working Groups, which shall be presented by their Chairmen. We shall continue in plenary session on the morning of Tuesday, 5 January, when, we hope that progress will be reached on the issues mentioned earlier.

Finally, on humanitarian matters, we appeal to you to do everything possible to facilitate access of the Office of the United Nations High Commissioner for Refugees (UNHCR) and other humanitarian organizations to civilians in need. We also appeal to you to increase your efforts in order to ensure security for humanitarian convoys and relief staff. Their security, and the need to respect their humanitarian mission, is a major concern of the international community. We also invite you to give particular attention to ensuring that humanitarian relief reaches, and is used for the benefit of, those for whom it is intended.

Annex III
Opening Statement of Lord Owen

We thought it would be helpful in this plenary session if we outlined how we saw the two Working Groups proceeding. Their work is interrelated, but there is also a lot of detailed work which has to take place on which progress can be made independently. The Co-Chairmen intend to move between the two Working Groups and will in this way hope to minimize any problems of overlap.

As to the maps which you should now all have in front of you, there are no suggested provinces. We have sought to arbitrate on many conflicting claims and we have been very conscious of the need to follow the criteria that we established on 27 October, "Boundaries of provinces to be drawn so as to constitute areas as geographically coherent as possible, taking into account ethnic, geographical (i.e. natural features, such as rivers), historical, communication (i.e. the existing road and railroad networks), economic viability and other relevant factors." We have had to choose between conflicting claims and we cannot stress enough how vital it is that everyone accepts that there cannot be agreement without compromise, sometimes painful compromise.

In connection with the attached map (see annex V, appendix), it is proposed that a number of "throughways" be established, in respect of which the parties agree and will guarantee full freedom of movement and in respect of which the United Nations Protection Force (UNPROFOR) or another appropriate international force will, until the constitution enters into force and for a period thereafter:

(a) Patrol these roads in order to ensure that the free flow of traffic is not obstructed by any provincial or other authorities;

(b) Control the crossings of these roads from one province into another to ensure that military forces or specified war *matériel* do not move through such crossings.

These provisions must be understood in the context of the proposed constitutional principle that "full freedom of movement shall be allowed throughout Bosnia and Herzegovina".

We are proposing the following "throughways":

1. On the road from Banja Luka to Bijeljina as it passes through Province 3, which we understand might be called Posavina Province;

2. On the road from Bihac to Livoc as it passes through Province 2, which we understand might be called Banja Luka Province;

3. On the road from Ljubinje to the port of Neum as it passes through Province 8, which we understand might be called Mostar Province;

4. On the road from Sekovici to Han Pijesak as it passes through Province 5, which we understand might be called Tuzla Province;

5. If the road from Pale to Jahorina is extended so as to cross the road from Trvono to Foca and to proceed to Kalinovik, it is envisaged that a "throughway" would be established, or a land corridor negotiated, where it proceeds through Province 7, Sarajevo Province. A "throughway" would also be established for the Trnovo to Foca road through Province 6, which we understand might be called East Herzegovina Province.

We envisage all the provinces except Sarajevo as having separate legislatures elected by normal democratic methods. In Sarajevo, the capital city, we believe that there would be considerable merit to underline its position as an "open city" if the three major "ethnic" groups as the constituent units of the State were represented in the Government of the province in the same way that we have proposed they should be represented in the presidency of the country. The boundaries of Sarajevo Province, that we propose would be the existing boundary, less the *Opstina* of Pale but with the addition of Kresevo, part of Kiseljak and Visoko.

We believe that Sarajevo should be demilitarized at the earliest possible date, and we hope that the detailed discussions that have already taken place in the Mixed Military Working Group can now be brought to the point of agreement.

The area of separation in the western and southern districts of Sarajevo provides for the withdrawal of heavy weapons and is linked to an absolute ceasefire, cessation of hostilities, freedom of movement for all civilians and the restoration of public utilities. Three free passage routes (blue routes) have been proposed with mutually agreed measures to guarantee and ensure the safe passage and free movement of civilians and humanitarian aid to and from Sarajevo. These routes would effectively lift the blockade of the city and establish free movement between Sarajevo and Zenica, Mostar and Zvornik.

After the cessation of hostilities the concept of blue routes for crossing existing confrontation lines will have to be extended to cover the whole country until free passage on all roads is established. Also there will be an urgent need for action to restore public utilities, maintenance of the peace will in part depend on preventing the further introduction of military personnel, heavy weapons and ammunition for such weapons. Under Security Council resolution 787 (1992) the deployment of United Nations observers to border crossing-points has been authorised, and it will be necessary for them to observe, search and report on cargoes transiting the borders. The responsibility for preventing the movement of any such personnel and weaponry will lie with legal authorities in Croatia and the Federal Republic of Yugoslavia (Serbia and Montenegro). While it will not be possible to deploy the full resources required for such a task immediately, priority will be accorded to deploying available observers to major crossing-points.

Separation of the armed forces throughout Bosnia and Herzegovina will have to be negotiated in the light of the boundaries of the new provinces. It is envisaged that there will be no military forces in Sarajevo province. Bosnian-Serb forces might withdraw to province 2,4 and 6. Bosnian Croat forces could be deployed in province 3, and the remaining forces would hopefully reach agreement as to their deployment in provinces 1, 5, 8, 9 and 10. Under our constitutional principles (No. 8) Bosnia and Herzegovina is to be progressively demilitarized.

Sadly, some of the boundaries of provinces will inevitably be treated as a front line with roadblocks and other manifestations of confrontation but as confidence in the cessation of hostilities grows, it would be hoped that the barriers will soon come down. Confidence-building measures will have to be developed along with the corralling, United Nations supervision and eventual dismantling of much of the heavy weaponry.

This is a comprehensive agenda that faces us over the next few days but we hope that we will nevertheless be able to settle on heads of agreement before we recess.

The ban on military flights over Bosnia and Herzegovina would continue with only Casevac and Medevac flights allowed and all combat aircraft grounded. But it would be hoped that UNHCR and UNPROFOR flights to Sarajevo will be extended to Cazin, Banja Luka and Tuzla airports and communications flight for government officials will be authorized.

Interim measures for the government of the provinces, the government of the country and the establishment of the presidency will have to be agreed.

Once the new Constitution is agreed and a stable peace and normal civil life has been established, United Nations/European Community (EC)-supervised elections will be instituted.

Annex IV
Unconditional and Unilateral Release of All Prisoners
Paper Presented by the International Committee of the Red Cross

1. During the London session of the International Conference and pursuant to a subsequent agreement signed at the International Committee of the Red Cross (ICRC) Headquarters on 1 October 1992, the parties to the conflict agreed to release all prisoners. Today the situation is as follows:

Prisoners held by the Bosnian Government: 137 released, 887 still held;
Prisoners held by the Bosnian Croats: 357 released, 537 still held;
Prisoners held by the Bosnian Serbs: 5,040 released, 1,333 still held.

2. The release process came to a standstill after the Bosnian Serbs released all prisoners held at Manjaca, except 532 who were transferred to Batkovic (camp closed on 18 December) and the two other parties did not release all their prisoners as promised during talks with President Sommaruga on 9 December. The respective positions are as follows:

(a) The Bosnian Government says it stands ready to release all prisoners, except war criminals, after an amnesty has been proclaimed. The following places of detention are concerned:

Held by the Government of Bosnia and Herzegovina:

Bihac	7
Breza	1
Konjic	106
Tarcin	285
Tuzl	135
Tesanj	9
Travnik	3
Visoko	62
Zenica	279

(b) The Bosnian Croats claim that 532 prisoners were transferred out of Manjaca before he closure of the camp and that they are not holding any prisoners themselves. In reality the situation is as follows:

Held by the Bosnian Croat authorities:

Livno	120 (civilians assigned to residence)
Mostar Rodoc	9
Orasje	161
Rascani	247 (civilians assigned to residence)

The 532 prisoners have been visited by the ICRC in Batkovic, except 131, who were reported exchanged near Sokolac.

(c) The Bosnian Serbs claim that they have made enough unilateral gestures. They hold the following prisoners:

Held by Bosnian Serb authorities:

Banja Luka Tunjice	54
Batkovic	1163
Doboj	97
Kotor Varos	18
Manjaca	-
Vlasenica	1

In view of the promise made by each party, the closure of all the above places of detention can no longer be contingent on considerations of reciprocity. All the prisoners must be released under ICRC auspices in unilateral and unconditional operations. It is also of utmost importance that all three parties to the conflict provide ICRC with proper notification of all other prisoners they hold and give the necessary facilities so that immediate visits can be made to all prisoners held within Bosnia and Herzegovina.

Annex V
Draft Agreement Relating to Bosnia and Herzegovina*

THE UNDERSIGNED,

Guided by the principles of the Charter of the United Nations, the Universal Declaration of Human Rights[1] and the Declaration on the Rights of Persons belonging National or Ethnic, Religious and Linguistic Minorities,[2]

Recalling the Statement of Principles and the Statement on Bosnia adopted by the International Conference on the Former Yugoslavia at its session in London and the Programme of Action on Humanitarian Issues agreed to at that session,

Considering the decisions of the United Nations Security Council relating to the former Yugoslavia,

Reaffirming their commitment to peace and security among the successor States to the former Yugoslavia.

Hereby agree as follows:

I. DELIMITATION OF PROVINCES

The delimitation of Bosnia and Herzegovina into provinces shall be in accordance with the attached map.

---

* The undersigned are A. Izetbegovic, R. Karadzic, and M. Boban; and, as witnesses, C.R. Vance and D. Owen.
[1] General Assembly resolution 217 A (III).
[2] General Assembly resolution 47/135.

II. CONSTITUTIONAL FRAMEWORK FOR BOSNIA AND HERZEGOVINA

Tripartite negotiations shall proceed on a continuous basis in Geneva, under the auspices of the International Conference on the Former Yugoslavia, in order to finalise a Constitution for Bosnia and Herzegovina in accordance with the following principles:

(1) Bosnia and Herzegovina shall be a decentralized State, with most governmental functions carried out by its provinces.

(2) The provinces shall not have any international legal personality and may not enter into agreements with foreign States or with international organizations.

(3) Full freedom of movement shall be allowed throughout Bosnia and Herzegovina, to be ensured in part by the maintenance of internationally controlled throughways.

(4) The Constitution shall recognize three "constituent peoples", as well as a group of "others".

(5) All matters of vital concern to any of the constituent peoples shall be regulated in the Constitution, which as to these points may be amended only by consensus of these constituent peoples; ordinary governmental business is not to be veto-able by any group.

(6) The provinces and the central Government shall have democratically elected legislatures and democratically chosen chief executives and an independent judiciary. The Presidency shall be composed of three elected representatives each of the three constituent peoples. The initial elections are to be United Nations/European Community/Conference on Security and Cooperation in Europe supervised.

(7) A Constitutional Court, with a member from each group and a majority of non-Bosnian members initially appointed by the International Conference on the Former Yugoslavia, shall resolve disputes between the central Government and any province, and among organs of the former.

(8) Bosnia and Herzegovina is to be progressively demilitarized under United Nations/European Community supervision.

(9) The highest level of internationally recognized human rights shall be provided for in the Constitution, which shall also provide for the ensurance of implementation through both domestic and international mechanisms.

(10) A number of international monitoring or control devices shall be provided for in the Constitution, to remain in place at least until the three constituent peoples by consensus agree to dispense with them.

III. COOPERATION IN RESPECT OF HUMANITARIAN EFFORTS

1. Maximum cooperation shall be extended to the High Commissioner for Refugees, the International Committee of the Red Cross, the United Nations Protection Force, the European Community Monitoring Mission and other humanitarian organizations working to provide assistance to refugees and displaced persons.

2. Full cooperation shall also be extended to the High Commissioner for Refugees in drawing up and implementing programmes for the return of refugees and displaced persons to their homes.

Appendix

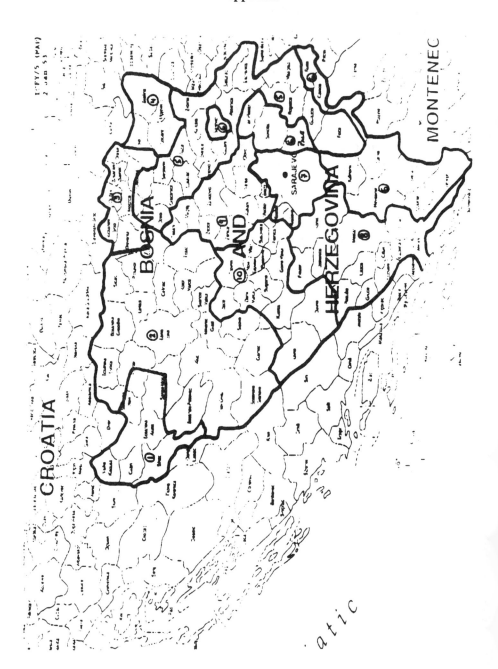

Annex IV
Agreement for Peace in Bosnia and Herzegovina*

THE UNDERSIGNED,

Welcoming the invitation of the Co-Chairmen of the Steering Committee of the International Conference on the Former Yugoslavia to participate in talks for the restoration of peace in Bosnia and Herzegovina,

Taking account of the constructive atmosphere of the peace talks held in Geneva from 2 to 5 January and the assistance of the Force Commander of the United Nations Protection Force, Lieutenant-General Satish Nambiar,

Keeping in mind the principles of the International Conference and the resolutions of the United Nations Security Council, in particular resolutions 752 (1992) and 787 (1992) pertaining to withdrawal of all outside forces from Bosnia and Herzegovina,

Wishing to bring the conflict in Bosnia and Herzegovina to an end without any further delay and to re-establish peace throughout the country,

Desiring to work out arrangements for bringing about compliance with a cessation of hostilities, and for monitoring it so as to ensure that it is effective and lasting,

Hereby agree on the following:

1. Measures for the achievement of an unconditional cessation of hostilities throughout Bosnia and Herzegovina, as set out in Annex I to the present agreement;
2. Measures for the restoration of infrastructure in Bosnia and Herzegovina, as set out in annex II to the present agreement;
3. Measures on the opening of routes, as set out in annex III to the present agreement;
4. Arrangements on the separation of forces, as set out in annex IV to the present agreement;
5. Measures for the demilitarization of Sarajevo, as set out in annex V to the present agreement;

---

* The undersigned are Sefar Halilovic, Ratko Mladic, and Milivoj Petkovic; and, as witnesses, Radovan Radinovic, Anton Tus, C.R. Vance, and D. Owen.

6. Measures for the monitoring of the borders of Bosnia and Herzegovina, as set out in annex VI to the present agreement;
7. Return of forces to the designated provinces, as set out in annex VII to the present agreement.

Annex I
Cessation of Hostilities

Broad Principles

All parties agree to support the broad principles required to support a cessation of hostilities. These broad principles will be translated into concrete action through additional discussion within the Mixed Military Working Group. Several of the principles will be dealt with on a stand-alone basis, although they remain an integral part of the overall framework of the cessation of hostilities.

The broad principles are:

- A ceasefire must be put in place and remain effective. This is to be implemented 72 hours from the time of signature of the agreement.
- Monitoring and control measures are to be put in place to ensure compliance and should include as a minimum:

    - Links between Commanders in conflict areas (hot lines);
    - Provision of United Nations Protection Force/European Community Monitoring Mission liaison and monitors;
    - Establishment of joint crisis management teams;
    - Opening of confrontation line crossing-points. For use by the United Nations Protection Force and monitoring agencies.

- The separation of forces is to be achieved.
- Routes supporting the general freedom of movement of people, commerce and humanitarian aid are to be opened.
- The restoration of infrastructure will proceed as a priority. Restoration will not be linked to any negotiations.

Essential Elements

- Signature of declaration - initiates all follow-on action (D-3). The 72 hours permit passage of information;
- Cessation of hostilities effective (D-Day);
- Declaration of forces - this is to take place in D-1 and should include:
  - Numbers and locations of all heavy weapons,
  - Detailed documentation of mine fields,
  - Locations of front lines (traces),
  - Defensive works and positions;
- Establish demarcation line (joint actively);
- Move in United Nations Protection Force to establish security (commencing D+1):
  - Monitor lines of conflict,
  - Monitor heavy weapons,
  - Reporting system (all parties);
- Withdrawal of heavy weapons:
  - Of calibre 12.7 mm and above; 5 days for Sarajevo and 15 days for remaining areas,
  - Locations to be determined based on effective ranges of weapon systems,
  - All such withdrawals will be supervised by the United Nations Protection Force and subsequently monitored at the designated locations by the United Nations Protection Force in order to prevent their use;
- Separation of forces:
  - Abandon defensive works on confrontation line,
  - Area of separation to be agreed,
  - Distance in which no forces, except police, allowed,
  - Distance within which no defensive works will be manned.

Separation of forces and withdrawal of heavy weapons are linked.

- Mixed Military Commission is established to deal with any clarifications and breaches of the cessation of hostilities.

Annex II
Restoration of Infrastructure

All parties agree that denial or use of civil utilities as a weapon of war is unacceptable, and all affirm their commitment to the full restoration of the civil infrastructure across Bosnia and Herzegovina, and in particular, Sarajevo.

The provision of humanitarian aid cannot be linked in any way with the military steps of the process of demilitarization or cessation of hostilities. Being humanitarian in nature, its priority is strictly governed by the ability of all three parties to support its implementation.

Restoration will be the first priority. Therefore, immediate efforts must be placed on the restoration of infrastructure. This is equally applicable to the city of Sarajevo as well as the rest of Bosnia and Herzegovina. It includes where applicable:

- Power grids;
- Power stations;
- Bridges;
- Gas;
- Telecommunications;
- Railway lines;
- Routes;
- Water supply.

Guarantees of security will be requested and must be provided and the restoration of power/water/heat will be fully supported by the warring parties.

A joint committee is already in place in Sarajevo; the work of this committee is to be facilitated with immediate effect to enable early restoration of utilities in Sarajevo.

Assistance will be provided through all the appropriated agencies, including United Nations and civilian expertise. However, within Bosnia and Herzegovina, a joint commission composed of representatives of all sides is to identify the priorities, define the needs and execute the work in conjunction with civil authorities. To this end, vital installations will be identified in conjunction with Bosnia and Herzegovina joint commission:

- Access will be guaranteed after local arrangements are made;
- Forces will be withdrawn from sites consistent with security;

- Warring parties will provide, when necessary, liaison for the repair teams;
- Civil agencies/workers will be assisted.

Parties will work to re-establish infrastructure, including railways/power grids/water supplies, across borders with neighbouring republics.

Respect for infrastructure facilities must be developed and they must remain free from attack or use as defensive positions.

All parties agree to develop a common instruction for passage down chains of command to demonstrate an equal endorsement of support.

Annex III
Opening of Routes

The opening of routes is directly related to the political issue which concerns the freedom of movement of all people in the context of constitutional principles. It is equally applicable to Sarajevo as well as all other areas of Bosnia and Herzegovina.

It is to be achieved through:

- Security guarantees by all parties to ensure non-interference and protection of personnel and material using the routes;
- Non-interference on the route;
- Checkpoints, patrols, and monitoring by United Nations Protection Force/European Community Monitoring Mission, as appropriate;
- Supervised inspection at entry points;
- Freedom of passage of humanitarian aid;
- Absolute freedom of movement of United Nations forces.

The concept of blue routes for Sarajevo is appended hereto. This format is applicable for the establishment of all other similar types of routes within Bosnia and Herzegovina. Additional routes can be negotiated under the aegis of the Mixed Military Working Group.

APPENDIX

SARAJEVO "BLUE ROUTE" CONCEPT

The parties have decided to establish three free passage routes with mutually agreed measures to guarantee and ensure safe passage for freedom of movement of civilians, commercial goods and humanitarian aid to and from Sarajevo.

These routes are:

- Sarajevo-Zenica-Sarajevo;
- Sarajevo-Mostar-Sarajevo;
- Sarajevo-Zvornik-Sarajevo.

Outline plan for blue routes

1.   Execution

1.1   Prerequisites

The following prerequisites are to be required:

1.1.1 Cessation of hostilities.

1.1.2 Complete freedom of movement for United Nations Protection Force on the three blue routes.

1.2   Use of the Blue Routes

1.2.1 Timings

Routes will be open during daylight hours for convoys. United Nations Protection Force will use the route 24 hours a day.

1.2.2 Access for Civilians

All civilians, regardless of sex, age, or ethnic origin, and without weapons or ammunition, will be allowed to use the routes. Private and commercial vehicles will also be permitted on each route subject to inspection outlined on paragraph 1.5.1 below.

1.2.3 Access for Humanitarian Aid

All international and local humanitarian aid agencies will be allowed to use the routes. Humanitarian aid includes, but is not limited to, food, water, medical supplies and fuel.

1.2.4 Access for Commercial Goods

Normal commerce will be progressively restored to and from Sarajevo.

1.3 Establishment of Routes

1.3.1 Sarajevo-Zenica-Sarajevo

This route incorporates Sarajevo-Rajlovac-Ilijas-Visoko-Zenica.

1.3.2 Sarajevo-Mostar-Sarajevo

This route incorporates Sarajevo-Ilidza-Hadzici-Tarcin-Jablanica-Mostar.

1.3.3 Sarajevo-Zvornik-Sarajevo

This route incorporates Sarajevo-Bentbasa-Mokro-Sololac-Vlasenica-Zvornik.

1.4 Checkpoints

Checkpoints will be established and manned by United Nations Protection Force at the entrance and exit of each route and when crossing a line of confrontation. Each United Nations Protection Force checkpoint will be located near or with the checkpoint of the force controlling the territory involved consistent with the security requirements of the factions. No side will be permitted to erect a new checkpoint.

1.5   Control Measures

1.5.1 Inspection Procedures

(a)   Inspections will be conducted by United Nations Protection Force. Each side is permitted to monitor the events in close coordination with the United Nations Protection Force.

(b)   War-related material, weapons or ammunition are forbidden. If found, the items will be confiscated and subsequently destroyed under control of the United Nations Protection Force and the parties.

(c)   Humanitarian aid convoys may be subjected to inspections. (Note: commercial traffic has been excluded)

(d)   Checkpoints will be activated only during daylight hours as a safety measure for civilians and convoys.

1.5.2 Escorts

(a)   Each convoy will be escorted with the appropriate United Nations Protection Force vehicles.

(b)   Convoys and escorts will take priority over military activities.

(c)   The army controlling the territory involved may provide civilian police as an additional means of security.

1.5.3 Patrols

(a)   United Nations Protection Force will patrol the blue routes as necessary.

(b)   Patrols will consist of at least two vehicles suitably equipped and will contain an appropriate communications net.

(c)   All United Nations Protection Force patrols will be permitted to cross all checkpoints.

1.6   Implementation

1.6.1 Suggested Timeframe

D-3   - Security Council endorses the plan
D+1   - Erecting checkpoints
       - Inspection procedures agreed

    - Routes cleared of all obstacles
    - Repairs carried out as required
    - Reconnoitre by the United Nations Protection Force
D+5 - Opening of blue routs for civilians and humanitarian aid

Annex IV
Separation of Forces

The parties agree that the separation of forces is an element of the overall cessation of hostilities. An agreement will be based on the steps and control measures and sequence of events outlined below:

Steps

The concrete steps envisaged in the process include:

- An absolute ceasefire;
- Temporary freezing of the military situation, pending agreement in return of forces to designated provinces;
- No forward deployments or offensive action;
- No move of additional forces, explosives and weapons forward will be permitted. Rotation on an individual basis is acceptable;
- Withdrawal of heavy weapons (direct and indirect fire) of all parties from areas of confrontation to areas of range, decided upon by the parties in conjunction with the United Nations Protection Force;
- Physical separation of forces in contact;
- Security and monitoring of the demilitarized zone.

Control Measures

The control measures required include:

- Declaration of forces in being, including location of minefields;
- Monitoring of front lines;
- Declaration of heavy weapons in separation areas;
- Establishing agreed lines in which forces may be located;

- Staged withdrawal of forces culminating in their relocation to designated provinces.

Sequence of Events

- Ceasefire under aegis of the overall cessation of hostilities;
- Establishment and patrol of the demarcation line by United Nations Protection Force personnel;
- Withdrawal of designated weapons systems of all parties;
- Search and clearance of the affected area by joint patrols;
- Conduct of joint and United Nations-only patrols within the area. Composition of the patrols to be negotiated at the Mixed Military Working Group.

UNPROFOR Concept for Heavy Weapons Control

- All heavy weapons 12.7 mm calibre and above are included.
- These weapons will be withdrawn out of effective range to areas decided between the United Nations Protection Force and the parties.
- The withdrawal will be monitored by the United Nations Protection Force.
- Once in location the weapons will be monitored to ensure that they are not used.
- The United Nations Protection Force will not physically take over the weapons.
- Where terrain such as towns preclude moving weapons out of range, they will be gathered in agreed location under United Nations Protection Force control to ensure that they are not used.

Annex V
Demilitarization of Sarajevo

The demilitarization of Sarajevo is based on one requirement: an effective cessation of hostilities.

The other elements are:

- Establishment of control on an designated line;
- Restoration of civil utilities;

- Land routes and freedom of movement;
- Separation of forces along lines of confrontation.

Control measures include:

- Patrol and monitoring of the demarcation line;
- Checkpoints at major crossings until confidence is restored;
- Mixed patrols in the demilitarized zone.

A military/civil joint commission as previously proposed should oversee the implementation of the accord.

Appended hereto is a draft agreement covering first stage of a potential agreement on the demilitarization of Sarajevo. This stage covers the airport area as already discussed at the Mixed Military Working Group.

APPENDIX

PROPOSED AGREEMENT ON THE FIRST STAGE OF DEMILITARIZATION
OF SARAJEVO

The authorized representatives of all three conflicting sides with the presence of the United Nations Protection Force representative agree on the implementation of an area in the western and southern districts of Sarajevo.

Cessation of Hostilities

The cessation of hostilities will be implemented as follows:

(a) The freezing of the military situation on the existing lines;
(b) No offensive action allowed;
(c) No forward redeployments;
(d) All heavy weapons will be withdrawn from positions from which they can engage;
(e) No movement or any additional forces although rotation of personnel on a one-for-one basis shall be permitted;
(f) No movement or resupply of ammunitions, explosives or incendiary devices.

Freedom of Movement for all Civilians

The agreement on blue routes will re-establish the freedom of movement of all civilians in support of this plan.

Restoration of Civil Utilities

A Joint Commission composed of representatives from each side will identify priorities, define needs and execute the implementation of civil utilities. Details can be found in annex II, Restoration of infrastructure.

Removal of Heavy Weapons

(a) *Area.* All heavy weapons will be withdrawn to designated locations from the following: Mojmilo, Dobrinja, Lukavica, Gornji, Kotorac, Vojkovici, Hrasnica, Sokolovici, Butmir, Ilidza, Otes, Stup, Nedarici.

(b) *Joint Commission.* A Joint Commission will be created.

    (1) The mission of this Joint Commission will be to execute and implement details of this plan and subsequent phases.

    (2) This Joint Commission will be composed of:

        (a) A United Nations Protection Force command and support element;

        (b) A team of each side commanded by an officer senior enough to make decisions and designated as the authorised commander for the troops in the areas affected;

        (c) A joint communications system which includes a command set and the necessary guaranteed communications link to each individual headquarters.

(c) *Time-frame.* From each district the withdrawal of heavy weapons out of the designated area will be carried out in two stages within a period of five days:

    (1) Stage 1 - Withdrawal of all direct fire weapons of 12.7 mm calibre and above (tanks, armoured personnel carriers, anti-tank, anti-aircraft and heavy machine guns).

(2) Stage 2 - Withdrawal of all heavy indirect fire weapons (mortars, field artillery).

(d) *Control measures*. The following implementation and control measures will be used:

(1) United Nations Protection Force will patrol the area of separation between the conflicting sides.
(2) United Nations Protection Force forces will be deployed on the confrontation lines and in agreed mixed checkpoints proposed by the Joint Commission.
(3) All parties are to identify weapons by type and location and will provide the United Nations Protection Force with detailed maps of areas considered to be under their respective control.
(4) Complete freedom of movement for all United Nations Protection Force personnel and vehicles within the affected areas.
(5) The Joint Commission will establish mixed patrols as appropriate.

Annex VI
Monitoring of Borders

Pursuant to United Nations Security Council resolution 787 (1992), Paragraph 5, to prevent interference from outside the Republic of Bosnia and Herzegovina, the United Nations Protection Force/European Community Monitoring Mission will monitor borders with neighbouring republics.

Principles

- United Nations Protection Force/European Monitoring Mission forces will monitor crossings to prevent weapons, munitions, military personnel or irregular forces from entering the country.
- Borders with adjoining republics will be monitored.
- United Nations Protection Force actions to observe, search and report will be facilitated by the authorities of the Republic of Croatia and the Federal Republic of Yugoslavia.

Annex VII
Return of Forces to Designated Provinces

To enable the process of return to normalcy, and as a direct follow-on from the cessation of hostilities and the separation of forces, a return of forces to designated provinces will be conducted. This can start as part of the withdrawal of heavy weapons but, given the winter weather conditions, it is hard to fix a definite date for the completion of this process. We should, however, aim to achieve the return of forces within 45 days.

This stage will be coordinated with an agreed demobilization of forces in being.

The United Nations Protection Force/European Community Monitoring Mission will monitor the withdrawal of these forces in conjunction with national and provincial authorities.

The Mixed Military Working Group would be the technical negotiating agency.

113. LETTER DATED 13 JANUARY 1993 FROM THE SECRETARY-GENERAL ADDRESSED TO THE PRESIDENT OF THE SECURITY COUNCIL[*]

I have the honour to convey the attached report in the peace talks convened by the Co-Chairmen of the Steering Committee of the International Conference on the Former Yugoslavia, which adjourned yesterday in Geneva.

As the report shows, potentially important progress has been achieved, particularly on the question of constitutional arrangements for Bosnia and Herzegovina. While the talks have been adjourned, the Co-Chairmen intend to continue discussions with the parties in the area in the coming days, while awaiting confirmations of Mr. Karadzic's agreement to the proposed constitutional principles. It is therefore my earnest hope that members of the Security Council will continue to extend their strong support to the Co-Chairmen in their efforts to consolidate and build upon the progress achieved.

[*] UN Doc. S/25100, 14 January 1993. Signed by Boutros Boutros-Ghali.

Annex
Report of the Secretary-General on the Activities of the
International Conference on the Former Yugoslavia

1. In my last report on the talks held between 2 and 4 January 1993 (S/25050), I informed the Security Council that the Co-Chairmen of the Steering Committee had recessed the talks until Sunday, 10 January, and had urged that there be maximum military and political restraint in the intervening days. I commented that the peace process had taken no a qualitatively new dimension and reiterated my sincere belief that, if the Council decided to adopt a resolution enforcing the ban on non-authorized flights over Bosnia and Herzegovina, it would be helpful if its implementation could take effect after a reasonable period of time.

2. Unfortunately, as the Security Council already knows, on 8 January 1993, the Deputy Prime Minister of Bosnia and Herzegovina, Mr. Hakija Turajlic, was killed in Sarajevo while under the protection of the United Nations Protection Force (UNPROFOR). I immediately issued a statement condemning this reprehensible act which, I emphasized, made it all the more necessary for the parties to cooperate in the peace talks and to conclude the agreements placed before them by the Co-Chairmen. I also initiated an investigation of the incident by appointing a Special Commission of Inquiry headed jointly by Shabzada Yaqub-Khan, former Foreign Minister of Pakistan and current Special Representative of the Secretary-General for Western Sahara, and Lieutenant-General Lars-Eric Walgren, Commander of the United Nations Interim Force in Lebanon (UNIFIL).

3. On 9 January, the Co-Chairmen also condemned the killing of Mr. Turajlic which, they added, underlined the need to end the war in Bosnia and Herzegovina. On the same day the Co-Chairmen wrote to Mr. Karadzic expressing their anger at the killing of Mr. Turajlic, which they deplored. They further informed Mr. Karadzic that they expected him to take immediate action to identify those responsible for that heinous crime. They stated that swift and sure action must be taken to detain and bring to trial those involved in the incident. In addition, they asked that he and General Mladic issue unambiguous orders to their forces that that type of conduct would not be condoned. They added that the suffering, death and dislocation in Bosnia and Herzegovina had gone on for too long and that the time had come to end the killing. They emphasized that the peace process must go forward.

I. Statement by the President of the Security Council

4. On 8 January, at the 3160th meeting of the Security Council, the President of the Council made a statement (S25079) declaring that the Council fully supported the efforts of the Co-Chairmen of the Steering Committee of the International Conference on the Former Yugoslavia aimed at achieving an overall political settlement of the crisis through a complete cessation of hostilities and the establishment of the constitutional framework for Bosnia and Herzegovina. In this connection, the Council reaffirmed the need to respect full the sovereignty, territorial integrity and political independence of Bosnia and Herzegovina. The Council fully endorsed the view of the Secretary-General described in his report (S/25050) that it was the duty of all the parties involved in the conflict in Bosnia and Herzegovina, despite the recent provocation, to cooperate with the Co-Chairmen in bringing the conflict to an end swiftly. The Council appealed to all the parties involved to cooperate to the fullest with the peace efforts and warned any party that would oppose an overall political settlement about the consequences of such an attitude. It stated that lack of cooperation and non-compliance with the relevant solutions would compel it to review the situation in an urgent and most serious manner and to consider further necessary measures.

II. Resumption of the Peace Talks

A. First Plenary Meeting

5. At the resumption of the talks, on 10 January 1993, the Co-Chairmen began by sharing their profound sorrow at the heinous killing of Mr. Turajlic on 8 January, and condemned that outrageous action. They equally condemned the brutal killing on 7 January of Minister Jossip Gogala, who headed the Internal Revenue Service of Bosnia and Herzegovina. They then noted that, at the adjournment of the peace talks on 4 January, they had placed before the delegations a comprehensive package which, they believed, represented a fair, just and lasting peace in Bosnia and Herzegovina. The package consisted of a draft agreement relating to Bosnia and Herzegovina which dealt with the delimitation of provinces, a constitutional framework and humanitarian issues; and a draft agreement for peace in Bosnia and Herzegovina which dealt with observance and monitoring of the cessation of hostilities (see S/25050, annexes V and VI). They reminded the delegations that, in presenting the package, they had explained that its two agreements were inextricably linked and had indicated that, if all three parties proposed mutually agreed changes, the changes would be incorporated.

They noted that Mr. Boban had accepted and signed the two agreements. President Izetbegovic had accepted the constitutional principles and the agreement dealing with observance of a cessation of hostilities. He had not accepted, however, certain of the proposed provincial boundaries. Mr. Karadzic, they further noted, had deferred expressing his views with respect to both of the documents until the resumption of the peace talks. The Co-Chairmen reiterated that a historic responsibility rested upon all those present. They emphasized that peace depended on them and expressed the hope that they would discharge that high responsibility to the people of Bosnia and Herzegovina and agree with the two peace agreements that had been placed before them.

6. Following the introductory statement by the Co-Chairmen, Mr. Boban reaffirmed his delegation's acceptance of the two agreements, which he had already signed. Mr. Silajdzic stated that his delegation formally accepted the constitutional principles proposed by the Co-Chairmen (see appendix I). Mr. Karadzic stated that the two agreements were acceptable as a basis for discussion, but that further talks were necessary to settle details with regard to the constitutional principles and the proposed limitation of provinces. With regard to the former, he tabled a document containing eight suggested principles (see appendix II).

7. Following the statement of Mr. Karadzic, the Co-Chairmen invited the other delegations to make comments. Mr. Boban appealed to the other delegations to accept and sign the package, as his delegation had done. Mr. Silajdzic sought clarification as to whether the Bosnian Serb delegation was accepting or was rejecting the Co-Chairmen's constitutional principles. The Co-Chairmen replied that Mr. Karadzic had raised issues for discussion with regard to those principles.

8. The Co-Chairmen then proceeded to examine the 10 constitutional principles *seriatim*, comparing the text of those they had proposed with those submitted by Mr. Karadzic and seeking clarifications from him about the meaning of his suggestions. During the ensuing discussion, the Co-Chairmen reaffirmed the importance of the concept of "three constituent peoples" and also made extensive references to other elements of the annex to the constitutional principles which had been circulated on 4 January ("Proposed constitutional structure for Bosnia and Herzegovina").

9. With regard to principle No. 1 the Co-Chairmen commented that they did not see any real difference between what they had proposed and what Mr. Karadzic had offered. The differences appeared to be mainly semantic. Both Co-Chairmen and Mr. Ahtisaari made it clear, however, that the concept of a "State within a State" would not be permitted under principle No. 1. In response to a comment by Mr. Silajdzic, the Co-Chairmen reaffirmed that Bosnia and Herzegovina has

to remain an independent, sovereign State within its internationally recognized boundaries.

10. With regard to principle No. 2, which was omitted from Mr. Karadzic's list, Mr. Ahtisaari explained that it was not intended to restrict the role of the provinces on matters within their competence. In this regard, he read the following statement, which, he stated, would form part of the records of the Conference explaining principle No. 2:

> "Only Bosnia and Herzegovina is to have international legal personality. Provinces cannot conclude formal international treaties. They would, however, be allowed to enter into administrative arrangements with each other or with foreign States, as long as the subject of the agreement was one within the exclusive competence of the province concerned and did not infringe in the rights of any other province or of the central Government. Thus, agreements could be concluded in relation to education, cultural institutions and programmes, radio and television, licensing of professions and trades, natural resources use, health care, provincial communications, and energy production, etc. Should any question arise between one or more of the provinces wishing to conclude arrangements with each other or with a foreign entity, and the central Government or certain other provinces, as to the legality of such an arrangement, the question could be decided by the Constitutional Court at the request of any of the provinces or of the central Government."

11. With regard to principles Nos. 3 to 9, the Co-Chairmen noted that the views expressed by Mr. Karadzic related more to issues of detail than of substance. In this regard they explained that, once the constitutional principles had been accepted, a Working Group would be established to draft the Constitution proper. In the Working Group, the three sides, meeting under the chairmanship of Mr. Ahtisaari and operating by consensus, would formulate the precise text of the Constitution. Therefore, nothing would be imposed upon any delegation, which would be given every opportunity to express its views, to make proposals and to work out arrangements acceptable to all delegations. The Co-Chairmen further explained that, in the event of difficulties being encountered in reaching agreement on the details of the new Constitution, these would be referred to them and they would then use their good offices to help to resolve such difficulties.

12. With regard to principle No. 10 proposed by the Co-Chairmen but omitted from Mr. Karadzic's list, they explained that it was introduced for the benefit of all three sides participating in the discussion. The Co-Chairmen then reviewed in detail the international monitoring and control arrangements envisaged with regard to the following matters:

(a) Interprovincial throughways;
(b) The Constitutional Court;

    (c) The progressive demilitarization of the country;

    (d) The non-discriminatory composition of the police;

    (e) The International Commission of Human Rights for Bosnia and Herzegovina;

    (f) The Ombudsmen;

    (g) The Human Rights Court.

13. The Co-Chairmen specifically explained that, with regard to the composition of bodies dealing with constitutional issues, human rights or international guarantees, details of the composition and procedures of those bodies would be worked out in the actual drafting of the Constitution.

B. Second Plenary Meeting

14. At the second plenary meeting, on 12 January, the Co-Chairmen welcomed President Milosevic (Serbia) and President Bulatovic (Montenegro) to the peace talks. They noted that, on 10 January, they had listened to comments on the agreement placed before the sides and had provided clarifications on the constitutional principles. Those clarifications had been reflected in the minutes of the plenary meeting, which had been circulated and formed part of the record of the Conference.

15. They further noted that, since the last plenary session, they had carried out extensive consultations. In the light of those consultations, they had combined the first and fourth principles into one, while retaining the identical wording. The 10 principles had accordingly become 9. The new version was before the delegations (see appendix III).

16. Mr. Karadzic stated that his delegation had held extensive consultations on the documents proposed by the Co-Chairmen. It had suggested some changes to those documents which had not been incorporated. It therefore repeated the following suggestions:

    (a) The insertion of a preambular reference in the draft agreement on Bosnia and Herzegovina reaffirming the 1966 International Covenants on Human Rights;

    (b) The agreement to be signed should indicate that the map proposed by the Co-Chairmen was a basis for discussion;

    (c) The following provision contained in working paper ICFY/4 circulated by the Co-Chairmen on 2 January 1993 should be reinstated in the constitutional principles:

> "The constitution shall recognize the three major 'ethnic' groups as the constituent units of the State, as well as a group of 'others'."

If those three points were accommodated, his delegation would accept the documents proposed by the Co-Chairmen.

17. The Co-Chairmen stated that the preambular reference to the International Covenant could be considered when the documents were prepared for signature. If there was agreement on the principles, then the discussion would proceed with regard to the map, until an accord was reached in it, so that the second change proposed by Mr. Karadzic would not be necessary.

18. Mr. Karadzic reiterated that the matter was of the greatest importance. If there was no compromise on the proposals his delegation had made, it could not accept the constitutional principles and would have to refer the matter to its Assembly and possibly to a referendum.

19. President Cosic stated that, in view of the fact that the constitutional principles guaranteed equal rights for all peoples, and taking into account that the Constitution itself would be worked on through consensus, the constitutional principles were acceptable to his delegation. He appealed for continued efforts to be made in the search for peace. President Milosevic stated that he shared the views of President Cosic and that the constitutional principles proposed by the Co-Chairmen were acceptable to him.

20. Mr. Silajdzic stated that, even as the peace talks were going on, Sarajevo had been shelled and people were dying. People were also dying from hunger and cold. He stated that the most urgent issue was to place all heavy weapons under United Nations control. The Co-Chairmen pointed out that the issue of heavy weapons had been already addressed in the documents proposed by them and that there seemed to have been a general understanding on dealing with such weapons as part of the package.

21. Mr. Boban requested that the floor be given to Prime Minister Akmadzic of Bosnia and Herzegovina. He warmly welcomed the peace efforts of the Co-Chairmen and expressed appreciation for their statements of condolences at the heinous murder of Mr. Turajlic and Mr. Gogala. After stating that there was no consensus on the composition of the delegation of Bosnia and Herzegovina, which could be decided only by the people of the country, he reiterated that the Bosnian Croat delegation accepted the document proposed by the Co-Chairmen. He appealed for efforts to continue to bring the parties closer together.

22. President Tudjman expressed his surprise at the fact that, after all, the efforts made, agreement had not been reached on the constitutional principles. He noted that that could mean not only continuation of the war, but also its expansion. He referred to an agreement he had proposed between the Republic of Croatia and

the Federal Republic of Yugoslavia, and he urged the Co-Chairmen to use their good offices to help to achieve normalisation of relations between the two countries.

23. At the invitation of the Co-Chairmen, the Chairperson of the Humanitarian Issues Working Group, Mrs. Ogata, United Nations High Commissioner for Refugees, made an appeal to the delegations present for their cooperation on humanitarian activities in the former Yugoslavia, especially in Sarajevo. She particularly stressed the importance of free and unhindered access to people in need of humanitarian assistance; safe passage for humanitarian convoys; and safety and respect for all humanitarian relief staff.

24. Following these statements, the Co-Chairmen then adjourned the meeting. They stated that they would have bilateral talks with the delegations. They requested that all delegations be available for consultations upon short notice. If the Co-Chairmen felt that there was reason to convene another plenary meeting, they would do so. They again strongly appealed for military and political restraint. They noted in that regard that the three sides in Bosnia and Herzegovina had agreed on 10 November 1992 to a cessation of hostilities throughout Bosnia and Herzegovina and had confirmed that agreement on 13 December.

25. Several hours after the conclusion of the plenary session, Mr. Karadzic issued a statement that he had decided to agree with the proposed constitutional principles provided that his "assembly" confirmed that agreement within several days.

APPENDIX I

CONSTITUTIONAL PRINCIPLES FOR BOSNIA AND HERZEGOVINA PROPOSED BY THE CO-CHAIRMEN ON 2 JANUARY 1993

(1) Bosnia and Herzegovina shall be a decentralized State, with most governmental functions carried out by its provinces.

(2) The provinces shall not have any international legal personality and may not enter into agreements with foreign States or with international organizations.

(3) Full freedom of movement shall be allowed throughout Bosnia and Herzegovina, to be ensured in part by the maintenance of internationally controlled throughways.

(4) The Constitution shall recognize three constituent "peoples", as well as a group of "others".

(5) All matters of vital concern to any of the constituent peoples shall be regulated in the Constitution, which as to these points may be amended only by consensus of these constituent peoples; ordinary governmental business is not to be

veto-able by any group.

(6) The provinces and the central Government shall have democratically elected legislature and democratically chosen chief executives and an independent judiciary. The Presidency shall be composed of three elected representatives each of the three constituent peoples. The initial elections are to be United Nations/European Community/Conference on Security and Cooperation in Europe supervised.

(7) A Constitutional Court, with a member from each group and a majority of non-Bosnian members initially appointed by the International Conference on the Former Yugoslavia, shall resolve disputes between the central Government and any province, and among organs of the former.

(8) Bosnia and Herzegovina is to be progressively demilitarized under United Nations/European Community supervision.

(9) The highest level of internationally recognized human rights shall be provided for in the Constitution, which shall also provide for the ensurance of implementation through both domestic and international mechanisms.

(10) A number of international monitoring or control devices shall be provided for in the Constitution, to remain in place at least until the three constituent peoples by consensus agree to dispense with them.

APPENDIX II

CONSTITUTIONAL PRINCIPLES FOR BOSNIA AND HERZEGOVINA PROPOSED BY THE BOSNIAN SERB DELEGATION ON 10 JANUARY 1993

(1) Bosnia and Herzegovina shall be a composite State, with most of the State functions carried out by its provinces.

(2) Full freedom of movement shall be allowed throughout Bosnia and Herzegovina, to be ensured in part by the maintenance of internationally controlled throughways.

(3) The Constitution shall recognize three constituent peoples as its three constituent units, as well as a group of others.

(4) All matters of vital concern to any of the constituent peoples shall be regulated in the constitutional agreement, which would be adopted by consensus of these constituent peoples; ordinary governmental business is not to be veto-able by any group.

(5) The provinces and the central Government shall have democratically elected legislature and democratically chosen chief executives and an independent judiciary. Central authorities shall be composed on a parity basis with a consensual or highly qualified majority in the decision-making process. The Presidency shall

be composed of three elected representatives each of the three constituent peoples. The initial elections are to be United Nations/European Community/ Conference on Security and Cooperation in Europe supervised.

(6) A Constitutional Court, with a member from each constituent people, shall resolve disputes between the central Government and any province, and among organs of the former. A number of foreign experts may be nominated to the Constitutional Court at the proposal of each constituent people on an equal basis.

(7) Bosnia and Herzegovina is to be progressively demilitarized under United Nations/European Community supervision.

(8) The highest level of internationally recognized human rights shall be provided for in the Constitution, which shall also provide for the ensurance of implementation through both domestic and international mechanisms.

APPENDIX III
CONSOLIDATED CONSTITUTIONAL PRINCIPLES FOR BOSNIA AND HERZEGOVINA PROPOSED BY THE CO-CHAIRMEN

(1) Bosnia and Herzegovina shall be a decentralized State, the Constitution shall recognize three constituent peoples, as well as a group of others, with most governmental functions carried out by its provinces.

(2) The provinces shall not have any international legal personality and may not enter into agreements with foreign States or with international organizations.

(3) Full freedom of movement shall be allowed throughout Bosnia and Herzegovina, to be ensured in part by the maintenance of internationally controlled throughways.

(4) All matters of vital concern to any of the constituent peoples shall be regulated in the Constitution, which as to these points may be amended only by consensus of these constituent peoples; ordinary governmental business is not to be veto-able by any group.

(5) The provinces and the central Government shall have democratically elected legislature and democratically chosen chief executives and an independent judiciary. The Presidency shall be composed of three elected representatives each of the three constituent peoples. The initial elections are to be United Nations/European Community/Conference on Security and Cooperation in Europe supervised.

(6) A Constitutional Court, with a member from each group and a majority of non-Bosnian members initially appointed by the International Conference on the Former Yugoslavia, shall resolve disputes between the central Government and any province, and among organs of the former.

(7) Bosnia and Herzegovina is to be progressively demilitarized under United Nations/European Community supervision.

(8) The highest level of internationally recognized human rights shall be provided for in the Constitution, which shall also provide for the ensurance of implementation through both domestic and international mechanisms.

(9) A number of international monitoring or control devices shall be provided for in the Constitution, to remain in place at least until the three constituent peoples by consensus agree to dispense with them.

114. REPORT OF THE SECRETARY-GENERAL ON THE ACTIVITIES OF THE INTERNATIONAL CONFERENCE ON THE FORMER YUGOSLAVIA*

INTRODUCTION

1. Since my last report to the Security Council (S/25100, annex), a further round of the peace talks on Bosnia and Herzegovina was held in Geneva from 23 to 30 January. The participants included the leaders from the three sides in Bosnia and Herzegovina, President Alija Izetbegovic, Mr. Radovan Karadzic and Mr. Mate Boban, the President of the Republic of Croatia, Mr. Franjo Tudjman, and the President of the Federal Republic of Yugoslavia (Serbia and Montenegro), Mr. Dobrica Cosic.

2. At the opening session of the latest round of the peace talks, and subsequently, the Co-Chairmen of the Steering Committee faced an added complication, namely the resumption of hostilities within the Republic of Croatia. This development was reflected in some of the statements and replies made at the opening session. The Co-Chairmen maintained the momentum of the peace talks, while at the same time seeking to halt the fighting in Croatia, as a well as fighting between Bosnian government and Bosnian Croat forces in central Bosnia. They did this through personal appeals and through bilateral and trilateral meetings with the leaders directly concerned.

3. The peace talks, however, were inevitable adversely affected by events outside the Conference. These events demonstrated yet again the close interconnections of all developments in the former Yugoslavia and the necessity to find a comprehensive settlement for the entire range of problems assailing the former Yugoslav lands.

---

*   UN Doc. S/25221, 2 February 1993.

I. Framework for the Peace Talks

4. Efforts to bring peace to Bosnia and Herzegovina have proceeded throughout on the basis of the principles of the Charter of the United Nations, the relevant decisions of the Security Council and the principles of the International Conference, adopted at its London session in August 1992.

5. The fundamental objectives of the talks have been, and remain, that the conflict must be stopped and prevented from spreading, while respecting human rights and fundamental freedoms. This had been a principal goal of the Co-Chairmen, who have repeatedly condemned ethnic cleansing and have pledged their determinations to bring about its reversal (see Annex I). They have strongly supported efforts to provide humanitarian relief and assistance to victims of the conflict. They have also urged the establishment of an international criminal court to try persons accused of crimes against humanity in connection with the armed conflict in the former Yugoslavia.

6. The Co-Chairmen continue to believe that the strict application of sanctions and respect for the arms embargo are crucial for the containment of the conflict and the restoration of peace. They firmly believe that a selective lifting of the arms embargo would not only prolong and deepen the war, but could lead to its spilling over to neighbouring countries. It was precisely with a view to preventing the spread of the conflict that they recommended a preventive deployment of United Nations peace-keeping forces in the former Yugoslav Republic of Macedonia.

7. The Co-Chairmen are resolute in their conviction that there is no realistic alternative to dealing with the conflict in Bosnia and Herzegovina other than through negotiation in good faith by all sides to reach a comprehensive settlement.

8. At the end of the previous round of the peace talks the position was that Mr. Boban had signed the agreement setting out the constitutional principles, the provincial map and the agreement on military and related issues. President Izetbegovic had accepted the constitutional principles and the agreement on military and related issues; he did not, however, accept the provincial map. Mr. Karadzic had not yet answered whether he would accept the constitutional principles but indicated that his response would be given later; he did not accept the provincial map and had some questions about the agreement on military and related issues.

II. Constitutional Principles

9. On 23 January 1993, the Co-Chairmen recorded the clear position that all three Bosnian sides unconditionally accepted the constitutional principles (see S/25100, appendix III). On 30 January, all three sides signed an agreement containing the constitutional principles (see annex II).

III. Provincial Boundaries

10. In my report of 11 November 1992, I informed the Council that the Co-Chairmen were working on establishing provincial boundaries, taking into account the views of the three sides (S/24795, para.42). After several weeks of painstaking discussion, during which each side continued to insist on its own position, the Co-Chairmen came to the view that the most practical way of advancing the peace process would be for the Co-Chairmen to put forward a provincial map for Bosnia and Herzegovina. They did this on 2 January 1993. The map put forward by the Co-Chairmen was set out in my report of 12 January 1993 (S/25050, annex V, appendix). The Co-Chairmen assured the three sides that, if all of them could agree on any changes to the proposed map, such changes would be incorporated.

11. On 23 January the Co-Chairmen indicated that they were at the disposal of the three sides to assist them in any further discussion they might wish to have on the Co-Chairmen's map. Mr. Boban reiterated that he accepted the map and noted that he had already signed it. President Izetbegovic sought changes in the map. Mr. Karadzic also sought changes and suggested that the populations involved be consulted. The Co-Chairmen replied that, since there had been massive displacements of populations largely as a result of deliberate ethnic cleansing in Bosnia and Herzegovina, consultations with the populations involved could not be carried out fairly in the prevailing circumstances.

12. Chairman of the Working Group on Bosnia and Herzegovina, Mr. Martti Ahtisaari, then had extensive discussions with the three Bosnian sides, during which he invited them to comment on the proposed provincial boundaries. In these discussions, Mr. Boban confirmed that he accepted the boundaries proposed by the Co-Chairmen. President Izetbegovic reversed his position on the provincial boundaries until the central and provincial government structure would be clarified. Mr. Karadzic sought to include more areas where Serbs lived into the three provinces with Serb majorities.

13. Following the foregoing discussion, the Co-Chairmen held individual, bilateral and trilateral meetings with the three sides in order to help to bridge their

positions. After a series of individual, bilateral and trilateral meetings, the Co-Chairmen informed the three sides at a plenary meeting on 30 January that, in the light of the discussions that had taken place, they had come to the conclusion that the provincial map they had submitted earlier should be maintained. They then invited the three sides to sign that map (see annex III).

14. Mr. Boban reconfirmed his acceptance of the map submitted by the Co-Chairmen and signed it. President Izetbegovic stated that he could not accept the map because, in his view, it had the effect of rewarding the ethnic cleansing that had taken place as it would leave military forces in areas from which populations had forcibly been removed and to which they could not return unless such forces were removed. Mr. Karadzic stated that large parts of the map were acceptable and that he could accept it formally if was understood that the populations in certain areas would be democratically consulted. The Co-Chairmen ruled that that condition was tantamount to not accepting the map.

IV. MILITARY AND RELATED ISSUES

15. In my report of 6 January 1993, I informed the Council about the state of discussions on the agreement on military and related issues put to the three sides by the Co-Chairmen (S/25050, annex VI). During the recently concluded session of the peace talks 23-30 January), discussions took place on a few provisions of the agreement. Clarifications were provided by the Co-Chairmen and a few minor textual modifications were made.

16. On 30 January the Co-Chairmen invited the three sides to sign this agreement (see annex IV). Mr. Boban and Mr. Karadzic signed it. Notwithstanding his earlier acceptance (S/25100, annex, para 5) President Izetbegovic stated that he would not sign the agreement because he felt that the arrangements on the control of heavy weapons were not strong enough. The Co-Chairmen invited him to consult with the United Nations Protection Force (UNPROFOR) Force Commander to obtain clarifications that the Co-Chairmen felt would meet his concern and enable him to sign the agreement.

V. INTERIM INSTITUTIONAL ARRANGEMENTS

17. During the latest round of the peace talks (23-30 January), the Co-Chairmen, in response to a suggestion, also took up the issue of interim arrangements for governing both Bosnia and Herzegovina as a whole and also each of the provinces during a transitional period.

18. An initial round of discussions on the interim institutional arrangements was held between the Bosnian Croat and the Bosnian government sides, concerning the six provinces in which the Croats or the Muslims would constitute the majority or plurality populations, namely Mostar, Bihac, Zenica, Tuzla, Posavina and Travnik. It was agreed between them that the Governors of Bihac, Zenica and Tuzla would be Muslim while the Governors of Mostar, Posavina and Travnik would be Croats. The two sides indicated they were prepared to approve an arrangement along those lines.

19. In the light of their subsequent discussion with the three sides, the Co-Chairmen submitted to them on 29 January a working paper entitled "Interim arrangements for Bosnia and Herzegovina" (see Annex V). The three sides were invited to submit any comments they might wish to make on the working paper.

VI. POSITION OF THE EUROPEAN COMMUNITY

20. On 1 February 1993, the European Community issued the following declaration:

> "The European Community and its member States express their full and unequivocal support for the comprehensive plan for a peaceful settlement in Bosnia and Herzegovina, put forward by the International Conference on the Former Yugoslavia, in accordance with the commitments reached at the London Conference.
>
> The peace plan and the draft interim arrangements for governing the Republic of Bosnia and Herzegovina until free and fair elections will take place, represent a coherent and comprehensive settlement, taking into account the legitimate interests of the three constituent communities of that republic.
>
> The European Community and its member States strongly urge all three parties of Bosnia and Herzegovina to accept the peace plan and the draft interim arrangements. The parties must also fully cooperate in implementing them.
>
> The European Community and its member States call upon the Security Council of the United Nations to give its full support to this plan and its implementation. The European Community and its member States are prepared to contribute actively to this end.
>
> The European Community and its member States reiterate their full support for the sovereignty, territorial integrity, and multi-ethnic character of the Republic of Bosnia and Herzegovina. They will continue their efforts to help the republic to recover from the present tragedy." (S/25225)

VII. OBSERVATIONS

21. I endorse the agreements put forward by the Co-Chairmen, which constitute a just and viable settlement for all sides.

22. The Co-Chairmen have stated that they intend to continue their negotiations with the parties. I will report to the Security Council on further developments.

Annex I
The Co-Chairmen of the Steering Committee and Human Rights Issues in the Former Yugoslavia

I. HUMAN RIGHTS AS A CORE ELEMENT OF THE PEACEMAKING STRATEGY

1. From the outset of the chairmanship of the Steering Committee of the International Conference on the Former Yugoslavia, the Co-Chairmen, Cyrus Vance and Lord Owen, have placed human rights and humanitarian issues at the core of the peacemaking process in the former Yugoslavia. At a press conference on 23 October 1992, the Co-Chairmen insisted that the international community would not tolerate the taking of territory by force, nor acquiesce in ethnic cleansing. Responding to reports that Bosnia and Herzegovina had in fact been carved up by Serbian and Croatian forces, the Co-Chairmen said that the status quo on the ground was not acceptable and that international recognition and lifting of the sanctions would not take place until a political solution had been found.

2. "This is not going to be settled by people who have taken up arms, and have abandoned humanitarian principles, and trampled on international law", Lord Owen told the assembled correspondents. "We do not accept this status quo as permanent", he added, "and we intend to see that it is changed". Mr. Vance agreed, saying "That is the way that we will act; that is what we expect to happen; and we will not be turned back in our determination to see that happen."

3. On 13 November 1992, Mr. Vance said to the Security Council:

"You have called for a political settlement consistent with the principles of the Charter and of international norms on human rights. You have rightly condemned forcible expulsions, illegal detentions, and all attempts to change the demographic composition of territories.

...

I mentioned these statements of principles in order to emphasize a simple but crucial point: the international community cannot accept non-compliance with these guidelines.

As Co-Chairmen of the Steering Committee, our mandate requires that we maintain lines of communication with all sides while preserving our neutrality and independence. Other United Nations bodies are looking into violations of human rights and humanitarian law. We are cooperating with them and will continue to do so. I do, however, want to underscore my firm conviction that there can be no compromise when it comes to respect for the principles of the Charter, and of the international norms of human rights and humanitarian law." (S/PV.3134)

4. Lord Owen told the Security Council on the same day:

"How can we as Co-Chairmen and you as members of the Council implement the principles and objectives agreed at the London Conference at the end of August?

European history is, sadly, no stranger to conflict nor to ethnic disputes. Memories of the Holocaust are still with us. The odious practice of 'ethnic cleansing' that we are witnessing in the former Yugoslavia is not something therefore which any European can ignore, merely passing by on the other side.

Europe knows that, were this flagrant 'ethnic cleansing' to be tolerated, were all its perpetrators to be allowed to escape without being brought to justice, and were its victims not to be helped to return to their homes and land, then we Europeans would pay a terrible price." (ibid.)

II. Prisoners and Detainees

5. The Co-Chairmen have worked closely with the International Committee of the Red Cross (ICRC) to secure the release of prisoners and detainees in the former Yugoslavia. They have used every occasion to highlight the plight of prisoners and detainees in their contacts with Governments and with the parties, in their public statements and in the reports submitted to the Security Council and the General Assembly. At the commencement of the peace talks on Bosnia and Herzegovina on 2 January 1993, the Co-Chairmen made the following appeal to the parties to the conflict:

"... Your immediate release of all detainees is essential. It would not only be an indication of your peaceful intentions, but could also help to stop the drums of war, which are beating so loudly around us as we meet here today..." (S/25050, annex I)

6. They arranged for the distribution of an appeal by ICRC for the release of prisoners and detaineed (see S/25050, annex IV).

III. War Crimes

7. On the issue of grave breaches of humanitarian law, the Co-Chairmen have been in frequent contact with the Chairman of the Committee of Experts established by the Secretary-General to examine information pertaining to these breaches. Working-level contacts have also been maintained between the Co-Chairmen's staff and the staff of the Commission of Experts.

8. The Co-Chairmen conducted meetings with the Commission of Experts, the Secretary-General and the Special Rapporteur for Yugoslavia of the Commission

on Human Rights to help bring about a forensic examination of the mass grave site at Ovcara in Croatia. The Co-Chairmen's efforts helped to bring about a decision by the Commission of Experts to arrange for a prompt forensic examination of the mass grave site. In a public statement on 17 December 1992 the Commission of Experts stated:

> "A major step taken by the Commission has been to request an NGO, 'Physicians for Human Rights', to investigate a mass grave near Vukovar taking into account calls made by ... the Co-Chairmen of the Conference on the Former Yugoslavia ..."

IV. INTERNATIONAL CRIMINAL COURT

9. The Co-Chairmen have repeatedly advocated the establishment of an international criminal court to deal with the grave breaches of humanitarian law. On 16 December 1992, Mr. Vance stated to the Ministerial Meeting of the Steering Committee of the Conference:

> "Lord Owen and I believe that atrocities committed in the former Yugoslavia are unacceptable, and persons guilty of war crimes should be brought to justice. We, therefore, recommend the establishment of an international criminal court."

V. CONSTITUTIONAL ARRANGEMENTS

10. The Co-Chairmen have also placed human rights issues at the core of their proposals for the future constitutional framework of Bosnia and Herzegovina. They have proposed that the Constitution set out a number of human rights, grouped in three categories:

(a) General human, especially civil and political, rights as expressed in instruments such as the 1966 International Covenant on Civil and Political Rights[a] and the Protocols thereto, and in the 1950 European Convention for the Protection of Human Rights and Fundamental Freedoms and in the Protocols thereto;

(b) Group and especially "minority" rights, as expressed in instruments such as the 1992 United Nations Declarations on the Rights of Persons belonging to National or Ethnic, Religious and Linguistic Minorities[b]

---

[a]   General Assembly resolution 2100 A (XXI), Annex.
[b]   General Assembly resolution 47/135.

and in the 1990 Recommendation 1134 (1990) on the rights of minorities of the Parliamentary Assembly of the Council of Europe;

(c) Economic, social and cultural rights, as expressed in the 1966 International Covenant on Economic, Social and Cultural Rights[c] and in the 1961 European Social Charter and the Protocol thereto.

11. To ensure the protection of human rights, the Co-Chairmen have proposed that:

(a) All persons in Bosnia and Herzegovina, whether citizens or not, will at all times have unimpeded access to the courts;

(b) Both the provincial and the national courts will be required to apply the constitutionally guaranteed human rights, as set out in the Constitution or in the international instruments incorporated therein by reference as directly applicable law;

(c) There will be four ombudsmen, one representing each of the recognized groups. These ombudsmen will have wide powers to investigate, either on the basis of complaints or on their own initiative, all questions relating to the implementation of human rights, including those arising out of ethnic cleansing, and to report to the legislature and to other appropriate governmental bodies. Initially, the ombudsmen are to be appointed by the International Conference on the Former Yugoslavia, and later by the Lower House of the national legislature;

(d) There will be a Constitutional Court and a Human Rights Court;

(e) There is also to be an International Commission on Human Rights for Bosnia and Herzegovina. This Commission will be authorized to investigate and to hear complaints and to report thereon to the appropriate international bodies;

(f) Bosnia and Herzegovina will be required to become a party to a number of international human right treaties that establish supervisory, monitoring and dispute-settlement mechanisms.

12. Addressing the Organisation of the Islamic Conference on 1 December 1992, Lord Owen stated:

"You have already seen in our proposals for a new constitution for Bosnia and Herzegovina that we are not prepared to accept that land can be taken by force by the Bosnian Serbs - land which far exceeds anything that they could justifiably claim in

---

[c] General Assembly resolution 2100 A (XXI), Annex.

the past to have contained a majority of Serbs.

You will also have seen in those same constitutional proposals the toughest provision for enforcing human rights and interlocking mechanisms for the reversal of the odious practice of ethnic cleansing.

I can assure you that the citizens of the European Community did not live through the trauma of the 1930s and 1940s without vowing to themselves that they would never again tolerate within Europe the vile things which we have seen practised in Bosnia and Herzegovina. We are determined, with your help, to end the practices and reverse the consequences."

VI. HUMAN RIGHTS AND HUMANITARIAN ISSUES

13. The Co-Chairmen have cooperated closely with the Special Rapporteur of the United Nations Commission on Human Rights. The day after their arrival in Geneva, on 4 September 1992, they had an extensive meeting with the Special Rapporteur. They met with the Special Rapporteur again on 8 October. Working-level contacts have been maintained throughout by the Co-Chairmen's staff and the staff of the Special Rapporteur.

14. In a message which the Co-Chairmen sent to the Commission on Human Rights on 30 November they stated:

"Regrettably the disgraceful practice of ethnic cleansing had not ceased and violations of international norms on human rights and humanitarian law are rampant. We condemn these violations in the most categorical terms.

We hope that your session will help in bringing an end to the violations of human rights and humanitarian law taking place. We also hope that you will give attention to the important question of protecting the rights of minorities. This issue is of great importance to the future stability and security in the area of the former Yugoslavia."

15. The Co-Chairmen have used their influence to highlight the importance of human rights issues, They initiated contact with the Council of Europe immediately after they started operations, so as to draw upon the expertise and assistance of the human rights machinery of the Council of Europe. Addressing the Council on 3 October 1992, Lord Owen made the following proposal:

"Let me put one practical suggestion to this body.

...

A non-member State could subscribe to the Council of Europe ad hoc mechanisms by means of a unilateral declaration which would then be in its Constitution, but which would have to be accepted by the Committee of Ministers of the Council of Europe. The mechanism could consist of a body which would be set up for a transitional period pending the accession of the subscribing State to the Council of Europe fully and to the European Convention of Human Rights. The body might be composed of judges of the European Court of Human Rights, members of the European Commission on Human Rights and persons from the subscribing State, individuals, group of individuals or non-governmental organizations alleging violations of human rights in a subscribing State. The body would be able to examine the admissibility and merits of the allegations received. It could make findings of fact and state its opinion, in the first place by reference to the Convention of Human Rights and the case-law developing under it, but also by reference to other international human rights treaties and agreement to which the subscribing State was already a contracting party - for example, United Nations covenants - and other legal instruments relating to human rights. The opinion of the body could be made binding on the subscribing State. I hope that they would not choose it to be only an advisory opinion but that they would entrench this body in their Constitution until such time as they were able to become members of the Council of Europe."

16. As a result of an initiative by the Co-Chairmen the Human Rights Committee (established by the International Covenant on Civil and Political Rights) requested reports from the Federal Republic of Yugoslavia (Serbia and Montenegro), Bosnia and Herzegovina and Croatia on human rights matters of international concern. The Human Rights Committee undertook searching examinations of the human rights situation in these countries from 3 to 6 November 1992 and made important recommendations to the three States.

17. The Co-Chairmen have on a number of occasions reacted to urgent humanitarian situations. On 24 September 1992, they issued a public statement expressing their deep concern about reports that they had received from the Banja Luka region indicating a build-up of tension, bomb incidents and intimidations with the potential threat of violence and the development of an ethnic-cleansing campaign. In view of the urgency of the situation, the Co-Chairmen travelled to Banja Luka the following day to assess the situation on the ground and to speak to representatives of the local communities and humanitarian agencies.

18. The Co-Chairmen have continually emphasized the importance and urgency of humanitarian relief and protection. Addressing the Security Council on 13 November 1992, Mr. Vance stated:

> "... On humanitarian aid, countless thousands of lives depend on our help and, despite the increasing pressure placed upon the UNHCR and the International Committee of the Red Cross (ICRC), we cannot afford to slacken our efforts. To this end, the international community must insist on unhindered access to persons who need humanitarian aid, especially food, medical supplies and shelter - particularly in view of the approaching winter. The release of prisoners and detainees, particularly from Bosnia and Herzegovina, now depends primarily on providing immediately refuge for them abroad." (S/PV.3134)

19. Addressing a special meeting of the Humanitarian Issues Working Group on 4 December Mr. Vance also stated:

> "What we are faced with in former Yugoslavia is a situation that challenges (international standards of conduct for the protection of human rights) ... internally as well as

externally. Internally, the vile practice of ethnic cleansing has led to terrible human loss and suffering. The rule of law and the reign of principle have been replaced by disgraceful forms of behaviour, externally, notwithstanding the generosity of many countries and organizations, basic principles have come under stress, including the principles of non-refoulement of refugees, and of solidarity with human beings in distress."

Annex II
Agreement Relating to Bosnia and Herzegovina[*]

THE UNDERSIGNED,

Guided by the principles of the Charter of the United Nations, the Universal Declaration of Human Rights[a] and the Declaration on the Rights of Persons belonging National or Ethnic, Religious and Linguistic Minorities,[b]

Recalling the Statement of Principles and the Statement on Bosnia adopted by the International Conference on the Former Yugoslavia at its session in London and the Programme of Action on Humanitarian Issues agreed to at that session,

Considering the decisions of the United Nations Security Council relating to the former Yugoslavia,

Reaffirming their commitment to peace and security among the successor States to the former Yugoslavia,

Hereby agree as follows:

I. CONSTITUTIONAL FRAMEWORK FOR BOSNIA AND HERZEGOVINA

Tripartite negotiations shall proceed on a continuous basis in Geneva, under the auspices of the International Conference in the Former Yugoslavia, in order to finalise a Constitution for Bosnia and Herzegovina in accordance with the following principles:

(1) Bosnia and Herzegovina shall be a decentralized State, the Constitution shall recognize three constituent peoples, as well as a group of others, with most governmental functions carried out by its provinces.

---

[*] Geneva, 30 January 1993. Signed by A. Izetbegovic, R. Karadzic and M. Boban; and, as witnesses, by C.R. Vance and D. Owen.
[a] General Assembly resolution 217 A (III).
[b] General Assembly resolution 47/135.

(2) The provinces shall not have any international legal personality and may not enter into agreements with foreign States or with international organizations.

(3) Full freedom of movement shall be allowed throughout Bosnia and Herzegovina, to be ensured in part by the maintenance of internationally controlled throughways.

(4) All matters of vital concern to any of the constituent peoples shall be regulated in the Constitution, which as to these points may be amended only by consensus of these constituent peoples; ordinary governmental business is not to be veto-able by any group.

(5) The provinces and the central Government shall have democratically elected legislature and democratically chosen chief executives and an independent judiciary. The Presidency shall be composed of three elected representatives of each of the three constituent peoples. The initial elections are to be United Nations/European Community/ Conference on Security and Cooperation in Europe supervised.

(6) A Constitutional Court, with a member from each group and a majority of non-Bosnian members initially appointed by the International Conference on the Former Yugoslavia, shall resolve disputes between the central Government and any province, and among organs of the former.

(7) Bosnia and Herzegovina is to be progressively demilitarized under United Nations/European Community supervision.

(8) The highest level of internationally recognized human rights shall be provided for in the Constitution, which shall also provide for the ensurance of implementation through both domestic and international mechanisms.

(9) A number of international monitoring or control devices shall be provided for in the Constitution, to remain in place at least until the three constituent peoples by consensus agree to dispense with them.

II. COOPERATION IN RESPECT OF HUMANITARIAN EFFORTS

1. Maximum cooperation shall be extended to the High Commission for Refugees, the International Committee of the Red Cross, the United Nations Protection Force, the European Community Monitoring Mission and other humanitarian organizations working to provide assistance to refugees and displaced persons.

2. Full cooperation shall also be extended to the High Commissioner for Refugees in drawing up and implementing programmes for the return of refugees and displaced persons to their homes.

Annex III

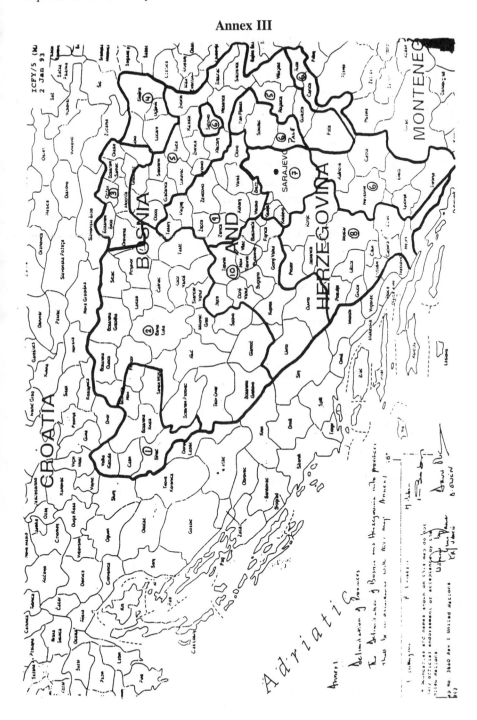

Annex IV
Agreement for Peace in Bosnia and Herzegovina[*]

THE UNDERSIGNED,

Welcoming the invitation of the Co-Chairmen of the Steering Committee of the International Conference on the Former Yugoslavia to participate in talks for the restoration of peace in Bosnia and Herzegovina,

Taking account of the constructive atmosphere of the peace talks held in Geneva from 2 to 5 January and the assistance of the Force Commander of the United Nations Protection Force, Lieutenant-General Satish Nambiar,

Keeping in mind the principles of the International Conference and the Resolutions of the United Nations Security Council, in particular Resolutions 752 (1992) and 787 (1992) pertaining to withdrawal of all outside forces from Bosnia and Herzegovina,

Wishing to bring the conflict in Bosnia and Herzegovina to an end without any further delay and to re-establish peace throughout the country,

Desiring to work out arrangements for bringing about compliance with a cessation of hostilities, and for monitoring it so as to ensure that it is effective and lasting,

Hereby agree on the following:

1. Measures for the achievement of an unconditional cessation of hostilities throughout Bosnia and Herzegovina, as set out in Annex I to the present agreement;
2. Measures for the restoration of infrastructure in Bosnia and Herzegovina, as set out in annex II to the present agreement;
3. Measures on the opening of routes, as set out in annex IV to the present agreement;
4. Arrangements on the separation of forces, as set out in annex IV to the present agreement;
5. Measures for the demilitarization of Sarajevo, as set out in annex V to the present agreement;
6. Measures for the monitoring of the borders of Bosnia and Herzegovina, as set out in annex VI to the present agreement;

---

[*] Geneva, 30 January 1993. Not signed by A. Izetbegovic, signed R. Karadzic and M. Boban; and, as witnesses, by C.R. Vance and D. Owen.

7. Return of forces to the designated provinces, as set out in annex VII to the present agreement.

ANNEX I: CESSATION OF HOSTILITIES

Broad Principles

All parties agree to support the broad principles required to support a cessation of hostilities. These broad principles will be translated into concrete action through additional discussion within the Mixed Military Working Group. Several of the principles will be dealt with on a stand-alone basis, although they remain an integral part of the overall framework of the cessation of hostilities.

The broad principles are:

- A ceasefire must be put in place and remain effective. This is to be implemented 72 hours from midnight (New York time - EST) of the day on which the Security Council endorses this plan.
- Monitoring and control measures are to be put in place to ensure compliance and should include as a minimum:
  - Links between Commanders in conflict areas (hot lines);
  - Provision of United Nations Protection Force/European Community Monitoring Mission liaison and monitors;
  - Establishment of joint crisis management teams;
  - Opening of confrontation line crossing-points. For use by the United Nations Protection Force and monitoring agencies.
- The separation of forces is to be achieved.
- Routes supporting the general freedom of movement of people, commerce and humanitarian aid are to be opened.
- The restoration of infrastructure will proceed as a priority. Restoration will not be linked to any negotiations.

Essential Elements

- Security Council endorses the plan - initiates all follow-on action (D-3). The 72 hours permit passage of information;
- Cessation of hostilities effective (D-Day);
- Declaration of forces - this is to take place in D-1 and should include:
  - Numbers and locations of all heavy weapons,
  - Detailed documentation of mine fields,

- Locations of front lines (traces),
- Defensive works and positions;
- Establish demarcation line (joint actively);
- Move in United Nations Protection Force forces to establish security (commencing D+1):
  - Monitor lines of conflict,
  - Monitor heavy weapons,
  - Reporting system (all parties);
- Withdrawal of heavy weapons:
  - Of calibre 12.7 mm and above; 5 days for Sarajevo and 15 days for remaining areas;
  - Locations to be determined based on effective ranges of weapon systems.
  - All such withdrawals will be supervised by the United Nations Protection Force and subsequently monitored at the designated locations by the United Nations Protection Force in order to prevent their use.
- Separation of forces:
  - Abandon defensive works on confrontation line,
  - Area of separation to be agreed,
  - Distance in which no forces, except police, allowed,
  - Distance within which no defensive works will be manned.
- The separation of forces and withdrawal of heavy weapons are linked.
- Mixed Military Commission is established to deal with any clarifications and breaches of the cessation of hostilities.

ANNEX II: RESTORATION OF INFRASTRUCTURE

All parties agree that denial or use of civil utilities as a weapon of war is unacceptable, and all affirm their commitment to the full restoration of the civil infrastructure across Bosnia and Herzegovina, and in particular, Sarajevo.

The provision of humanitarian aid cannot be linked in any way with the military steps of the process of demilitarization or cessation of hostilities. Being humanitarian in nature, its priority is strictly governed by the ability of all three parties to support its implementation.

Restoration will be the first priority. Therefore, immediate efforts must be placed on the restoration of infrastructure. This is equally applicable to the city of Sarajevo as well as the rest of Bosnia and Herzegovina. It includes where applicable:

- Power grids;
- Power stations;
- Bridges;
- Gas;
- Telecommunications;
- Railway lines;
- Routes;
- Water supply.

Guarantees of security will be requested and must be provided and the restoration of power/water/heat will be fully supported by the warring parties.

A joint committee is already in place in Sarajevo; the work of this committee is to be facilitated with immediate effect to enable early restoration of utilities in Sarajevo.

Assistance will be provided through all the appropriated agencies, including United Nations and civilian expertise. However, within Bosnia and Herzegovina, a joint commission composed of representatives of all sides is to identify the priorities, define the needs and execute the work in conjunction with civil authorities. To this end, vital installations will be identified in conjunction with Bosnia and Herzegovina joint commission:

- Access will be guaranteed after local arrangements are made.
- Forces will be withdrawn from sites consistent with security.
- Warring parties will provide, when necessary, liaison for the repair teams.
- Civil agencies/workers will be assisted.

Parties will work to re-establish infrastructure, including railways/power grids/water supplies, across borders with neighbouring republics.

Respect for infrastructure facilities must be developed and they must remain free from attack or use as defensive positions.

All parties agree to develop a common instruction for passage down chains of command to demonstrate an equal endorsement of support.

ANNEX III: OPENING OF ROUTES

The opening of routes is directly related to the political issue which concerns the freedom of movement of all people in the context of constitutional principles. It is equally applicable to Sarajevo as well as all other areas of Bosnia and Herzegovina.

It is to be achieved through:

- Security guarantees by all parties to ensure non-interference and protection of personnel and material using the routes;
- Non-interference on the route;
- Checkpoints, patrols, and monitoring by United Nations Protection Force/European Community Monitoring Mission, as appropriate;
- Supervised inspection at entry points;
- Freedom of passage of humanitarian aid;
- Absolute freedom of movement of United Nations forces.

The concept of blue routes for Sarajevo is appended hereto. This format is applicable for the establishment of all other similar types of routes within Bosnia and Herzegovina. Additional routes can be negotiated under the aegis of the Mixed Military Working Group.

APPENDIX: SARAJEVO "BLUE ROUTE" CONCEPT

The parties have decided to establish three free passage routes with mutually agreed measures to guarantee and ensure safe passage for freedom of movement of civilians, commercial goods and humanitarian aid to and from Sarajevo.
These routes are:

- Sarajevo-Zenica-Sarajevo;
- Sarajevo-Mostar-Sarajevo;
- Sarajevo-Zvornik-Sarajevo.

Outline Plan for Blue Routes

1. Execution
1.1 Prerequisites

The following prerequisites are to be required:

1.1.1 Cessation of hostilities.

1.1.2 Complete freedom of movement for United Nations Protection Force on the three blue routes.

1.2 Use of the blue routes

1.2.1 Timings

Routes will be open during daylight hours for convoys. United Nations Protection Force will use the route 24 hours a day.

1.2.2 Access for Civilians

All civilians, regardless of sex, age, or ethnic origin, and without weapons or ammunition, will be allowed to use the routes. Private and commercial vehicles will also be permitted on each route subject to inspection outlined on paragraph 1.5.1 below.

1.2.3 Access for Humanitarian Aid

All international and local humanitarian aid agencies will be allowed to use the routes. Humanitarian aid includes, but is not limited to, food, water, medical supplies and fuel.

1.2.4 Access for Commercial Goods

Normal commerce will be progressively restored to and from Sarajevo.

1.3 Establishment of Routes

1.3.1 Sarajevo-Zenica-Sarajevo

This route incorporates Sarajevo-Rajlovac-Ilijas-Visoko-Zenica.

1.3.2 Sarajevo-Mostar-Sarajevo

This route incorporates Sarajevo-Ilidza-Hadzici-Tarcin-Jablanica-Mostar.

1.3.3 Sarajevo-Zvornik-Sarajevo

This route incorporates Sarajevo-Bentbasa-Mokro-Sololac-Vlasenica-Zvornik.

1.4 Checkpoints

Checkpoints will be established and manned by United Nations Protection Force forces at the entrance and exit of each route and when crossing a line of confrontation. Each United Nations Protection Force checkpoint will be located near or with the checkpoint of the force controlling the territory involved consistent with the security requirements of the factions. No side will be permitted to erect a new checkpoint.

1.5 Control Measures

1.5.1 Inspection Procedures

   (a) Inspections will be conducted by United Nations Protection Force forces. Each side is permitted to monitor the events in close coordination with the United Nations Protection Force.
   (b) War-related material, weapons or ammunition are forbidden. If found, the items will be confiscated and subsequently destroyed under control of the United Nations Protection Force and the parties.
   (c) Humanitarian aid convoys may be subjected to inspections.
   (d) Checkpoints will be activated only during daylight hours as a safety measure for civilians and convoys.

1.5.2 Escorts

   (a) Each convoy will be escorted with the appropriate United Nations Protection Force vehicles.
   (b) Convoys and escorts will take priority over military activities.
   (c) The army controlling the territory involved may provide civilian police as an additional means of security.

1.5.3 Patrols

   (a) United Nations Protection Force forces will patrol the blue routes as necessary.
   (b) Patrols will consists of at least two vehicles suitably equipped and will contain an appropriate communications net.
   (c) All United Nations Protection Force patrols will be permitted to cross all checkpoints.

1.6 Implementation

1.6.1 Suggested Timeframe

D-3   - Security Council endorses the plan
D+1 - Erecting checkpoints
     - Inspection procedures agreed
     - Routes cleared of all obstacles
     - Repairs carried out as required
     - Reconnoitre by the United Nations Protection Force
D+5 - Opening of blue routes for civilians and humanitarian aid

ANNEX IV: SEPARATION OF FORCES

The parties agree that the separation of forces is an element of the overall cessation of hostilities. An agreement will be based on the steps and control measures and sequence of events outlined below:

Steps

The concrete steps envisaged in the process include:

- An absolute ceasefire.
- Temporary freezing of the military situation, pending agreement in return of forces to designated provinces.
- No forward deployments or offensive action.
- No move of additional forces, explosives and weapons forward will be permitted. Rotation on an individual basis is acceptable.
- Withdrawal of heavy weapons (direct and indirect fire) of all parties from areas of confrontation to areas of range, decided upon by the parties in conjunction with the United Nations Protection Force.
- Physical separation of forces in contact.
- Security and monitoring of the demilitarized zone.

Control Measures

The control measures required include:

- Declaration of forces in being, including location of minefields.
- Monitoring of front lines.
- Declaration of heavy weapons in separation areas.
- Establishing agreed lines in which forces may be located.
- Staged withdrawal of forces culminating in their relocation to designated provinces.

Sequence of Events

- Ceasefire under aegis of the overall cessation of hostilities.
- Establishment and patrol of the demarcation line by United Nations Protection Force personnel.
- Withdrawal of designated weapons systems of all parties.
- Search and clearance of the affected area by joint patrols.
- Conduct of joint and United Nations-only patrols within the area. Composition of the patrols to be negotiated at the Mixed Military Working Group.

UNPROFOR Concept for Heavy Weapons Control

- All heavy weapons 12.7 mm calibre and above are included.
- These weapons will be withdrawn out of effective range to areas decided between the United Nations Protection Force and the parties.
- The withdrawal will be monitored by the United Nations Protection Force.
- Once in location the weapons will be monitored to ensure that they are not used.
- The United Nations Protection Force will not physically take over the weapons.
- Where terrain such as towns preclude moving weapons out of range, they will be gathered in agreed location under United Nations Protection Force control to ensure that they are not used.

ANNEX V: DEMILITARIZATION OF SARAJEVO

The demilitarization of Sarajevo is based on one requirement: an effective cessation of hostilities.

The other elements are:

- Establishment of control on an designated line;
- Restoration of civil utilities;
- Land routes and freedom of movement;
- Separation of forces along lines of confrontation.

Control measures include:

- Patrol and monitoring of the demarcation line;
- Checkpoints at major crossings until confidence is restored;
- Mixed patrols in the demilitarized zone.

A military/civil joint commission as previously proposed should oversee the implementation of the accord.

Appended hereto is a draft agreement covering first stage of a potential agreement on the demilitarization of Sarajevo. This stage covers the airport area as already discussed at the Mixed Military Working Group.

APPENDIX: PROPOSED AGREEMENT ON THE FIRST STAGE OF DEMILITARIZATION OF SARAJEVO

The authorized representatives of all three conflicting sides with the presence of the United Nations Protection Force representative agree on the implementation of an area in the western and southern districts of Sarajevo.

Cessation of Hostilities

The cessation of hostilities will be implemented as follows:

(a) The freezing of the military situation on the existing lines.
(b) No offensive action allowed.
(c) No forward redeployments.
(d) All heavy weapons will be withdrawn from positions from which they can engage.
(e) No movement or any additional forces although rotation of personnel on a one-for-one basis shall be permitted.
(f) No movement or resupply of ammunitions, explosives or incendiary devices.

Freedom of movement for all civilians

The agreement on blue routes will re-establish the freedom of movement of all civilians in support of this plan.

Restoration of civil utilities

A Joint Commission composed of representatives from each side will identify priorities, define needs and execute the implementation of civil utilities. Details can be found in annex II, Restoration of infrastructure.

Removal of heavy weapons

(a) *Area*. All heavy weapons will be withdrawn to designated locations from the following: Mojmilo, Dobrinja, Lukavica, Gornji, Kotorac, Vojkovici, Hrasnica, Sokolovici, Butmir, Ilidza, Otes, Stup, Nedarici.

(b) *Joint Commission*. A Joint Commission will be created.

    (1) The mission of this Joint Commission will be to execute and implement details of this plan and subsequent phases.
    (2) This Joint Commission will be composed of:

        (a) A United Nations Protection Force command and support element;
        (b) A team of each side commanded by an officer senior enough to make decisions and designated as the authorised commander for the troops in the areas affected;
        (c) A joint communications system which includes a command set and the necessary guaranteed communications link to each individual headquarters.

(c) *Time-frame*. From each district the withdrawal of heavy weapons out of the designated area will be carried out in two stages within a period of five days:

    (1) Stage 1 - Withdrawal of all direct fire weapons of 12.7 mm calibre and above (tanks, armoured personnel carriers, anti-tank, anti-aircraft and heavy machine guns).
    (2) Stage 2 - Withdrawal of all heavy indirect fire weapons (mortars, field artillery).

(d) *Control measures*. The following implementation and control measures will be used:

(1) United Nations Protection Force forces will patrol the area of separation between the conflicting sides.

(2) United Nations Protection Force forces will be deployed on the confrontation lines and in agreed mixed checkpoints proposed by the Joint Commission.

(3) All parties are to identify weapons by type and location and will provide the United Nations Protection Force with detailed maps of areas considered to be under their respective control.

(4) Complete freedom of movement for all United Nations Protection Force personnel and vehicles within the affected areas.

(5) The Joint Commission will establish mixed patrols as appropriate.

ANNEX VI: MONITORING OF BORDERS

Pursuant to United Nations Security Council resolution 787 (1992), Paragraph 5, to prevent interference from outside the Republic of Bosnia and Herzegovina, the United Nations Protection Force/European Community Monitoring Mission will monitor borders with neighbouring republics.

Principles

- United Nations Protection Force/European Monitoring Mission forces will monitor crossings to prevent weapons, munitions, military personnel or irregular forces from entering the country.
- Borders with adjoining republics will be monitored.
- United Nations Protection Force actions to observe, search and report will be facilitated by the authorities of the Republic of Croatia and the Federal Republic of Yugoslavia.

ANNEX VII: RETURN OF FORCES TO DESIGNATED PROVINCES

To enable the process of return to normalcy, and as a direct follow-on from the cessation of hostilities and the separation of forces, a return of forces to designated provinces will be conducted. This can start as part of the withdrawal of heavy weapons but, given the winter weather conditions, it is hard to fix a definite date for the completion of this process. We should however aim to achieve the return of forces within 45 days.

This stage will be coordinated with an agreed demobilization of forces in being.

The United Nations Protection Force/European Community Monitoring Mission will monitor the withdrawal of these forces in conjunction with national and provincial authorities.

The Mixed Military Working Group would be the technical negotiating agency.

Annex V
Interim Arrangements for Bosnia and Herzegovina[*]

INTRODUCTION

In 1990, the Bosnian Parliament adopted amendment LXXIII to the Constitution of the Republic of Bosnia and Herzegovina. Following the outbreak of hostilities in 1992, this provision of the Constitution was invoked and the Presidency was expanded from 7 to 10 members with the inclusion of the Prime Minister, The President of the Assembly and the Commander-in-Chief of the Armed Forces. The powers of the Parliament were transferred to the Presidency.

Following the signing of the peace agreement and their endorsement by the United Nations Security Council, it is proposed that each of the three parties represented at the Conference (the "parties") nominate three representatives to serve in an interim central Government. The confirmation of these nine representatives will be subject to the approval of the Co-Chairmen of the Steering Committee of the International Conference on the Former Yugoslavia (the "Co-Chairmen"). Once the composition of the interim central Government has been confirmed, it is proposed that the Presidency, acting in accordance with its powers under amendment LXXIII, will transfer its powers and authority to this interim central Government.

Those aspects of the existing Constitution which relate to the Presidency will then be suspended. To the extent practicable, the other provisions of the existing Constitution of Bosnia and Herzegovina will continue to apply, in particular those provisions relating to the courts and legal system.

During the interim period, which is defined as the period between the transfer

---

[*]   29 January 1993.

of authority to the interim central Government and the holding of free and fair elections, a new Constitution for Bosnia and Herzegovina will be drafted by the parties with the assistance of the Co-Chairmen and will be the basis upon which the elections will take place.

In each province, there will be an interim provincial government composed of a Governor, Vice-Governor and 10 other members.

Throughout the interim period, *opstina* authorities will retain their existing powers. The *opstina* boundaries will remain as at present except where they are crossed by provincial boundaries or where the boundaries have been changed by agreement under the auspices of the International Conference on the Former Yugoslavia.

This document contains proposals for the functioning of an International Access Authority, the national power authority, the National Bank, the Post, Telegraph and Telecommunications Authority of Bosnia and Herzegovina and an independent National Civil Aviation authority.

I. INTERIM CENTRAL GOVERNMENT

A. In the interim period, there will be a nine-member interim central Government.

1. Three representatives will be nominated by each of the parties. These nominations will then be conformed by the Co-Chairmen.
2. The interim central Government will take decisions by consensus. In the event that a decision will be referred to the Co-Chairmen for their urgent consideration.
3. The interim central Government will be located in Sarajevo, within that *opstina* designated as the capital. In addition to its national responsibilities, the interim central Government will administer the capital and have responsibility for its policy.
4. The position of President of the interim central Government will rotate every four months among the representatives of the parties. The President of the interim central Government will perform the role of head of State.

B. The principal responsibilities of the interim central Government will be as follows:

1. Preparations for the holding of free and fair elections, on the basis of the new Constitution, under international supervision;

2. Relations with the Mixed Military Working Group, the United Nations Protection Force (including the United Nations Civilian Police), the European Community Monitoring Mission and the International Conference on the Former Yugoslavia;

3. Coordination with the Office of the United Nations High Commissioner for Refugees, The International Committee of the Red Cross, the World Health Organization and other relevant agencies on the return and rehabilitation of refugees and displaced persons.

4. Foreign Affairs (including membership in international organizations);

5. International commerce (customs duties, quotas);

6. Citizenship;

7. Raising of any taxes required to carry out its functions.

C. The interim central Government will be responsible or appointing ministers and determining the role of such ministries as are deemed appropriate.

D. The Co-Chairmen will be involved with the parties in the preparation of the Constitution for Bosnia and Herzegovina and will also be available to assist the interim central Government in its work.

II. Interim Provincial Governments

A. During the interim period, each province will have an interim provincial government composed of a Governor, a Vice-Governor and 10 other members. The Governor, the Vice-Governor and the 10 other members of the interim provincial government will be nominated by the parties on the basis of the composition of the population of the province[a] provided that none of the three constituent peoples will be left unrepresented in any province. The interim provincial governments will be composed as in annex A.

B. Decisions will normally be taken by a simple majority, except that the adoption of the provincial constitution and the setting of *opstina* boundaries will be taken by consensus.

---

[a] To determine these relative percentages, the 1991 census will be used.

C. The principal functions of the interim provincial governments will be:

1. The drafting of provincial constitutions in accordance with the new Constitution of Bosnia and Herzegovina;
2. The preparation of free and fair elections, which should be held as soon as possible, on the basis of proportional representation and under international supervision;
3. Relations with the Mixed Military Working Groups, the United Nations Protection Force (including the United Nations Civilian Police), the European Community Monitoring Mission and the International Conference on the Former Yugoslavia;
4. Coordination with the Office of the United Nations High Commissioner for Refugees, The International Committee of the Red Cross, the World Health Organization and other relevant agencies on the return and rehabilitation of refugees and displaced persons;
5. Supervision of Police Force;
6. Restoration of infrastructure;
7. Raising of any taxes necessary to carry out their functions.

D. There will be attached to the staff of each provincial Governor a United Nations Protection Force Military Liaison, including a United Nations Civilian Police Liaison Officer, to assist in the carrying out of the above tasks.

III. Interim Arrangements for the Protection of Human Rights

A. The three parties have accepted principle No. 8 of the Constitutional Framework for Bosnia and Herzegovina which states that the highest level of internationally recognized human rights shall be provided for in the Constitution. The international community has repeatedly condemned ethnic cleansing and has demanded that its results be reversed. In order that the provisions of principle No. 8 be implemented in the interim period, the following measures will be taken, with particular emphasis placed on reversing ethnic cleansing wherever it has occurred.

1. All statements or commitments made under duress, particularly those relating to the relinquishment of rights to land and property, are wholly null and void.
2. Four ombudsmen will be appointed immediately by the Co-Chairmen, as per paragraph VI.B.2 of the *Proposed Constitutional Structure for Bosnia*

and Herzegovina (ICFY/6, annex).

3. All citizens, through their representatives, will have the right to request international monitoring in areas where they believe that human rights were being, are being, or are about to be infringed. This may involve the monitoring of the area by the United Nations Civilian Police or other appropriate bodies such as the European Community Monitoring Mission, with or without the assistance of United Nations Protection Force military personnel. In the same way, they will also be able to make representations to the Mixed Military Working Group to request a redeployment of any armed forces in their area.

IV. Appointment of a Representative of the Co-Chairmen on Bosnia and Herzegovina

The Co-Chairmen shall appoint a representative in Bosnia and Herzegovina, who will be resident in Sarajevo and available as and when necessary to he interim central Government and the interim provincial governments.

V. Establishment of an International Access Authority

A. Principle 3 of the Constitutional Framework for Bosnia and Herzegovina states that "full freedom of movement shall be allowed throughout Bosnia and Herzegovina, to be ensured in part by the maintenance of internationally controlled throughways".

In order to implement this principle, an international access authority will be established with representatives from the interim central Government and the interim provincial governments, which:

1. Will have sole responsibility for all railway lines in Bosnia and Herzegovina and those roads which are declared as internationally controlled throughways.
2. Will regulate the operation of port facilities on the River Sava.

The Authority's essential purpose will be to guarantee full freedom of movement between and within the provinces of Bosnia and Herzegovina and also to and from these provinces to the Republic of Croatia and to the Republic of Serbia (the proposed routes are set forth in annex B).

B. It is intended that the International Access Authority will be in operation as soon as possible during the interim period. Following the endorsement of the Agreement on Peace in Bosnia and Herzegovina by the United Nations Security Council, all designated throughways will come under the overlapping responsibility of the United Nations Protection Force. A period of overlapping responsibility is envisaged for the United Nations Protection Force and that of the International Access Authority. During this period of overlapping responsibility, the United Nations Protection Force's involvement will be phased out and its responsibilities assumed by traffic police employed by the International Access Authority, This transfer of responsibility will only happen by agreement of all those involved in the International Access authority.

VI. FUNCTIONING OF THE NATIONAL POWER AUTHORITY

A. Board of Directors will be appointed by the interim central Government and the interim provincial governments to manage Electro Priveda, the existing national power authority, which will be responsible for the transmission and distribution of electricity in Bosnia and Herzegovina. The Board will be responsible for ensuring the uninterrupted supply of electricity to the whole of the country and to make appropriated links with neighbouring countries.

1. The interim central Government and each of the interim provincial governments will appoint one representative to the Board of Directors of Elektro Priveda.
2. Elektro Priveda will continue to have its headquarters in Sarajevo.

VII. FUNCTIONING OF THE NATIONAL BANK OF BOSNIA AND HERZEGOVINA

The functions of the Governor and Council of the National Bank (Naroda Banka) of Bosnia and Herzegovina will be taken over by a Board of Governors. The National Bank will continue to have responsibility, *inter alia*, for issuing currency and for exercising a regulatory function over provincial banks, as well as for relations with international financial institutions.

1. The interim central Government and each of the interim provincial governments will appoint one representative to the Board of Governors of the National Bank.
2. The National Bank will remain located in Sarajevo.

VIII. FUNCTIONING OF THE NATIONAL POST, TELEGRAPH AND
TELECOMMUNICATIONS AUTHORITY

A Board of Directors will be appointed by the interim central Government
and the interim provincial governments to manage to National Post, Telegraph
and Telecommunications services throughout Bosnia and Herzegovina, and
necessary international links. It will also have responsibility for the allocation of
radio and television transmission frequencies in Bosnia and Herzegovina.

1. The interim central Government and each of the interim provincial governments will appoint one representative to the Board of Directors of the
   National Post, Telegraph and Telecommunications Authority.
2. The National Post, Telegraph and Telecommunications Authority will be
   located in Sarajevo.

IX. ESTABLISHMENT OF AN INDEPENDENT NATIONAL
CIVIL AVIATION AUTHORITY

An independent National Civil Aviation Authority will be established as soon
as possible by the interim central Government and the interim provincial governments.

The National Civil Aviation Authority will, when appropriate, assume responsibilities for the control of all civilian traffic in the airspace of Bosnia and
Herzegovina, as well as for relations with the International Civil Aviation
Organization and other relevant international authorities. Initially, a period of
overlapping responsibilities is envisaged for the United Nations Protection Force
and the National Civil Aviation Authority.

The United Nations Protection Force will continue operating and controlling
Sarajevo airport until other arrangements are agreed with the United Nations
Protection Force.

1. The interim central Government and each of he interim provincial governments will appoint one representative to the Board of Directors of the
   National Civil Aviation Authority.
2. The National Civil Aviation Authority will have its headquarters in Sarajevo.

ANNEX A: STRUCTURE OF INTERIM PROVINCIAL GOVERNMENTS

For the purposes of this annex, the parties will be designated "Party A", "Party B" and "Party C", denoting the delegations of Mate Boban, Alija Izetbegovic and Radovan Karadzic respectively.

Province No. 1
Province capital: Bihac
Governor: Nominated by Party B
Vice-Governor: Nominated by Party C
Other members of interim provincial government:
seven members nominated by Party B, two members, nominated by Party C, one member nominated by Party A

Province No. 2
Province capital: Banja Luka
Governor: Nominated by Party C
Vice-Governor: Nominated by Party B
Other members of interim provincial government:
seven members nominated by Party C, two members nominated by Party B, one member nominated by Party A

Province No. 3
Province capital: Bosanski Brod
Governor: Nominated by Party A
Vice-Governor: Nominated by Party C
Other members of interim government:
Five members nominated by Party A, three members nominated by Party C, two members nominated by Party B

Province No. 4
Province capital: Bijeljina
Governor: Nominated by Party C
Vice-Governor: Nominated by Party B
Other members of interim provincial government:
five members nominated by Party C, four members nominated by Party B, one member nominated by Party A

Province No. 5
Province capital: Tuzla
Governor: Nominated by Party B
Vice-Governor: Nominated by Party C
Other members of interim provincial government:
five members nominated by Party B, three members nominated by Party C, two
members nominated by Party A

Province No. 6
Province capital: Nevesinje
Governor: Nominated by Party C
Vice-Governor: Nominated by Party B
Other members of interim provincial government
seven members nominated by Party C, two members nominated by Party B, one
member nominated by Party A

Province No. 7
Province of Sarajevo
    Because of its special position with the capital in its midst, it is proposed that
each of the parties will nominate three members in the interim provincial government.
    The *opstina* boundaries in Sarajevo will be referred immediately to a commit-
tee to which each party will nominate a member. The Committee will meet in
Sarajevo under the chairmanship of the Co-Chairmen's representative, and will
report to the Co-Chairmen before Sunday, 7 February 1993. The Co-Chairmen
will arbitrate in the event of any differences.
    It is envisaged that one of the *opstina*s will be called the "Capital *opstina*"
and encompass the government buildings, historic buildings, the university,
hospital, the railway station and sports facilities and will come under the administration of the interim central Government.

Province No. 8
Province capital: Mostar
Governor Nominated by Party A
Vice-Governor: Nominated by Party B
Other members of interim provincial government:
six members nominated by Party A, three members nominated by Party B, one
member nominated by Party C

Province No. 9
Province capital: Zenica
Governor: Nominated by Party B
Vice-Governor: Nominated by Party A
Other members of interim provincial government:
six members nominated by Party B, two members nominated by Party A, two members nominated by Party C

Province No. 10
Province capital: Travnik
Governor: Nominated by Party A
Vice-Governor: Nominated by Party B
Other members of interim provincial government:
five members nominated by Party B, four members nominated by Party A, one member nominated by Party C

ANNEX B: THROUGHWAYS TO BE CONTROLLED BY THE INTERNATIONAL ACCESS AUTHORITY

- That part of the road from Bihac to Livno that passes through Banja Luka Province;
- That part of the road from Bihac to Jajce that passes through Banja Luka Province;
- That part of the road from Banja Luka to Brcko that passes through Posavina Province;
- Those parts of the roads from Tuzla to Orasje and from Tuzla to Brcko that pass through Posavina and Bijeljina Provinces;
- Those parts of the roads from Han Pijesak to Sekovici and from Sekovici to Zvornik that pass through Tuzla Province;
- That part of the road from Pale to Kalinovik that passes through Sarajevo Province;
- That part of the road from Foca to Sarajevo that passes through East Herzegovina Province;
- The road from Sarajevo to Mostar and to the Croatian border towards Split;
- That part of the road from Ljubinja to Neum that passes through Mostar Province.

International road border crossings affecting the International Access Authority:

- Bihac Province: Velika Kladusa, towards Karlovac and Zagreb;
- Banja Luka Province: Bosanski Gradisja, towards Zagreb-Belgrade auto-route;
- Posavina Province: Orasje, towards Zagreb-Belgrade autoroute;
- Bijeljina Province: Sremska Race, towards Zagreb-Belgrade autoroute;
- Tuzla Province: Zvornik, towards Zagreb-Belgrade autoroute;
- Mostar Province: Osoje, towards Split.

115. REPORT OF THE SECRETARY-GENERAL ON THE NEW YORK ROUND OF THE PEACE TALKS ON BOSNIA AND HERZEGOVINA (3-8 FEBRUARY 1993)[*]

INTRODUCTION

1. In my report of 2 February (S/25221) to the Security Council, I related the efforts of the Co-Chairmen of the Steering Committee of the International Conference on the Former Yugoslavia to help bring about peace in Bosnia and Herzegovina. I endorsed the peace package put forward by the Co-Chairmen as a just and viable settlement for all sides.

2. The Co-Chairmen, Cyrus Vance and Lord Owen, decided to hold a round of the peace talks in New York in order to be closer to members of the Security Council so that the good offices of the Council could be used to advantage in helping the three sides to overcome their outstanding differences. Accordingly, since coming to New York on 1 February, the Co-Chairmen have had extensive discussions with members of the Security Council, meeting in groups, and have also negotiated intensively over Friday, Saturday and Sunday, 5 to 7 February, with the three sides.

I. DISCUSSIONS WITH MEMBERS OF THE SECURITY COUNCIL

3. The Co-Chairmen met the President of the Security Council on 2 February. The same day they met with the five permanent members of the Council. On the following day, they met with the non-aligned members of the Council and also with the remaining five members.

---

[*] UN Doc. S/25248, 8 February 1993.

4. The Co-Chairmen explained the process that had led them to propose their peace package and the factors that had influenced the contents of that package. They also reported the attitudes of the three sides participating in the peace talks.
5. The Co-Chairmen emphasized to the members of the Security Council their rejection of ethnic cleansing, their strongly held view that human rights and fundamental freedoms must be woven into the peace package, their insistence that Bosnia and Herzegovina should remain a sovereign, independent, integral and multi-ethnic State in which all parts of the population could live in peace in accordance with their respective cultures and traditions.
6. The Co-Chairmen further explained that their priorities were to stop the conflict; to develop a Constitution for Bosnia and Herzegovina in accordance with the constitutional principles that had been signed by the three sides (see S/25100, appendix III), and to devise interim arrangements for the period until elections could be held pursuant to the new Constitution - all to be consistent with the principles laid down by the Security Council and at the London sessions of the International Conference. The Co-Chairmen also explained their concerns about the danger of the conflict spreading. In this regard, the Co-Chairmen have continued to maintain the view that even a selective lifting of the arms embargo would not be in the interest of peace or of human rights but could, instead, lead to a devastating conflagration engulfing the Balkan region.
7. The Co-Chairmen conveyed their assessment to the members of the Security Council that the peace package that they had put forward was enforceable. In their estimation, a United Nations force of 15,000 to 25,000 would be required to implement the package in Bosnia and Herzegovina.
8. The Co-Chairmen repeatedly and strongly urged the members of the Security Council to establish an international criminal court to try persons accused of grave breaches of international humanitarian law in former Yugoslavia.
9. The Co-Chairmen also met with the Contact Group of the Organisations of the Islamic Conference (OIC) and developed many of the same points. During the weekend of 6 and 7 February 1992, the Co-Chairmen also spoke to Foreign Minister Djukic of the Federal Republic of Yugoslavia (Serbia and Montenegro) and briefed him on their efforts. He said that he and his Government continued to express fullest support for the Co-Chairmen and their plan.

II. MEETINGS WITH THE THREE BOSNIAN SIDES

10. The Co-Chairmen held several rounds of discussions with each of the three Bosnian sides.

A. The Bosnian Government Side

11. The Bosnian government side took the position throughout the New York round of the talks that it was not willing to discuss either the provincial boundaries or the interim governmental arrangements. It also declined to meet together with the other two sides. The delegation raised the issue of the non-implementation of agreements reached at the London session of the International Conference and also the non-implementation of prior decision of the Security Council. The delegation suggested that work should rather concentrate henceforth on the drafting of a new Constitution for Bosnia and Herzegovina. The Co-Chairmen told the delegation that the most optimistic estimate was that that would take three months.

12. With respect to interim governmental arrangements, the Bosnian government side wanted them to be built around the existing Government. It reintroduced into the discussion written comments (annex I) that it had presented earlier on a preliminary version of the working paper on interim governmental arrangements (see S/25221, annex V). The Co-Chairmen explained that most of the points contained in the written comments had already been accommodated in the working paper on interim governmental arrangements and also indicated why others had not been included.

13. The government delegation proposed that Serb heavy weaponry be placed immediately under international control and offered to do the same. The Co-Chairmen told the delegation that the only way that could be achieved quickly was through adopting their comprehensive peace settlement. As to further measures to deal with heavy weapons, the Co-Chairmen explained that an enforceable no-fly ban would be necessary in the event of a cessation of hostilities and that they were exploring with the United Nations Protection Force (UNPROFOR) the possibility that aircraft assigned to enforcing the no-fly zone might also be empowered to take action against any heavy weapons that have not been declared to UNPROFOR or which were breaching the ceasefire.

14. The Co-Chairmen discussed those elements that they hoped might be included in a future Security Council resolution supporting the peace package. In particular, the Co-Chairmen stressed that UNPROFOR and all other United Nations agencies would need to be authorized to have unobstructed access to anywhere in Bosnia and Herzegovina.

15. In these discussions, the Co-Chairmen indicated that they felt that it would enhance the authority of the proposed International Human Rights Commission for Bosnia and Herzegovina if its establishment was to be directly recommended by the Security Council and could address human rights and humanitarian issues

with particular attention to measures for the protection of refugees and displaced persons who wished to return to their homes.

16. The Co-Chairmen also stressed that the establishment of an international criminal court to deal with persons accused of grave breaches of international humanitarian law in the former Yugoslavia would reassure people that, even after a cessation of hostilities, it would be possible to bring perpetrators of war crimes and crimes against humanity to justice.

B. The Bosnian Serb Side

17. The Bosnian Serb side continued to maintain that many predominantly Serb areas had been excluded from Serb majority provinces. It continued to take the position that it would be ready to accept and to sign the map proposed by the Co-Chairmen (see S/25221, annex III) only if the populations of contested areas were consulted. The Co-Chairmen continued to reject this on the ground, as stated in my previous report (S/25221, para. 11), that there had been so much ethnic cleansing and displacement of population in Bosnia and Herzegovina that it would be wholly impractical to hold democratic consultations.

18. The Bosnian Serb side also submitted to the Co-Chairmen a map suggesting wholesale changes in the proposed provincial boundaries. The Co-Chairmen said the other parties were most unlikely to agree, but they agreed to raise again with the Bosnian government delegation the suggestion, first put on the table in Geneva, to create two new provinces on the eastern border (see annex II). Of particular importance was that the expanded province No. 4 would be likely to have a majority of Muslims and include a number of towns like Brcko and Janja were Muslims were in the majority while, in the province No. 4 suggested by the Co-Chairmen, the Serbs were likely to form the majority.

19. With regard to interim arrangements, the Bosnian Serb side stated that it could not accept any arrangements that were based on the premise that the existing Constitution of Bosnia and Herzegovina continued to be valid or that the interim Government would be a continuation of the current Presidency. They continued to prefer not to call it the interim central Government but rather the "central coordinating body".

C. The Bosnian Croat Side

20. It will be recalled that the Bosnian Croat side has already signed the constitutional principles, the map specifying the proposed provincial boundaries and the agreement dealing with military and security issues.

21. In their discussions with the Bosnian Croat side, the Co-Chairmen sought to explore whether any adjustments could be made in the proposed provincial boundaries that would make them more acceptable to the other two sides. The Bosnian Croat side indicated that it was prepared to entertain some changes. It put forward a number of suggestions, particularly in the eastern border of Travnik Province (No. 10) and the western border of Posavina province (No. 3). A revised map showing the possible changes is contained in annex III to the present document.

III. THE PEACE PACKAGE

22. The Co-Chairmen indicated to the parties their intention to establish a boundary commission, with the participation of the three sides, that would determine the precise delimitation of the provinces consequent on the proposed map, and that might, in addition assist the sides in negotiating any possible adjustments.

23. From the foregoing account of the New York round of the peace talks, it will be seen that the possibility of reaching agreed solutions among the three Bosnian sides was reduced by the refusal of the Bosnian government delegation to meet with the other sides or to discuss provincial boundaries. In the circumstances, the Co-Chairmen were left with the option of maintaining the peace package in the form it was presented to the Security Council in my last report (S/25221), annexes II-IV) or to modify it so as to address as far as possible the often-repeated concerns of the two sides that had not yet accepted the map dealing with provincial boundaries.

24. It was the considered judgement of the Co-Chairmen, taking into account the work done at the New York round of the peace talks, that some modifications were possible in the proposed provincial boundaries that might be acceptable to all the parties. Accordingly, they submitted to the Bosnian Croat side, as the party most affected, a revised map of the provincial boundaries. The map was then presented to the Bosnian Serbs and they rejected it and also reconfirmed their position on the original map put forward by the Co-Chairmen. The Bosnian Government side was given a copy of the revised map for information, but since it was not agreed by all the parties the Co-Chairmen remain committed to their original proposal.

Annex I
Comments on the "Interim Arrangements for Bosnia and Herzegovina" of the Delegation of the Republic of Bosnia and Herzegovina to the International Conference on the Former Yugoslavia, dated 28 January 1993

1. The interim period for the establishment of peace until the adoption of the new Constitution and until the democratic elections take place opens a series of legal and practical questions. We do appreciate the efforts of the Co-Chairmen to restore as soon as possible all the vital functions and the whole territory of Bosnia and Herzegovina. We would like to draw your attention to the most important implications in the case of the application of the interim arrangements.

2. During the process of the international recognition of Bosnia and Herzegovina all the relevant political factors in the world, including the Badinter Commission, established that Bosnia and Herzegovina fulfils all democratic standards. The legitimacy of its democratically elected organs has not been questioned at all. Even in the situation of the aggression the legitimacy and legality of a State that is defending itself has been maintained. On the contrary, the proposed interim arrangements envisage the suspension of the democratically elected organs and the interruption of the continuity of the constitutional order.

3. This proposal produces two negative effects - it deprives the legally and democratically constituted organs of their legitimacy and at the same time it legalizes the "para-State" structures. Thus, legitimate self-defence is negated and aggression is rewarded.

4. The document does not envisage any democratic and institutional framework for the elections of the representatives of three constituent peoples. It also ignores the group "others" and, thus, deprives a considerable part of the populations of its basic democratic right to be represented in the Government. The proposal envisages decision-making by consensus in the coordinating bodies without offering any solution to overcome blockades when consensus cannot be reached. The proposal also ignores the existence of a series of other institutions which are a part of the legal system such as the Central Bank of Bosnia and Herzegovina, the Post and Telecommunications of Bosnia and Herzegovina, the National Power Authority, etc.

5. All these proposals suggest the completion of the ethnic division and of the destruction of Bosnia and Herzegovina that was started by the delimitation of provinces on the ethnic principles and was continued by the proposed constitutional arrangements.

6. In order to avoid these and other negative consequences, we propose that the interim solutions be established according to the current constitutional arrangements.

7. According to amendment LXXIII to the Constitution of the Republic of Bosnia and Herzegovina, the Presidency of Bosnia and Herzegovina along with the President of the parliament and the Government and Commander-in-Chief of the Bosnia and Herzegovina Army have the role of the Parliament in the situation of war. This body, whose national composition can be balanced, can at the proposal of the International Conference on the Former Yugoslavia appoint an interim Government and establish its term of reference as well as those of the proposed coordinating bodies. The same body can appoint the coordinating bodies of the provinces in the same way. The Presidency enlarged for that purpose, would, on the basis of its current constitutional mandate, amend the existing Constitution by issuing a decree with the force of mandate, amend the exiting Constitution by issuing a decree with the force of law. The composition of the interim Government, i.e. of another corresponding body would be ethnically balanced, as envisaged by this proposal. No individual involved in the aggression, war crimes or crimes against humanity and international law could be appointed members of such a body.

8. Since it is impossible and unprecedented that one ministerial function is carried out by three people, the possible solutions are as follows:

   (a) Either the representatives of the three nations alternate after a shorter term in office;
   (b) The functions of the minister and his two deputies should be clearly defined.

9. These solutions are to be applied until the end of war. Upon the establishment of peace, the Parliament and other legal institutions of the system should carry out their functions.

Annex II

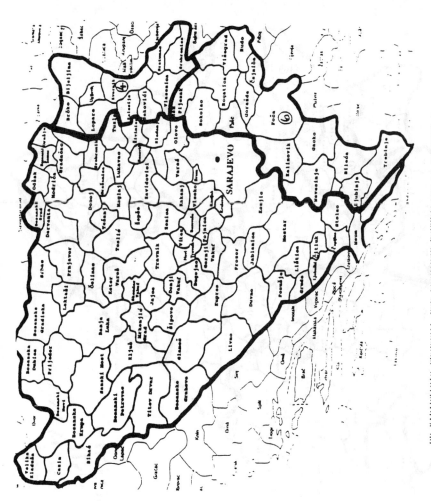

DR KARADZIC'S PROPOSAL FOR PROVINCE BOUNDARIES IN EASTERN BOSNIA

Proposed province boundaries: ⎯⎯⎯

Annex III

116. REPORT OF THE SECRETARY-GENERAL ON THE ACTIVITIES OF THE INTERNATIONAL CONFERENCE ON THE FORMER YUGOSLAVIA*

INTRODUCTION

1. In my last report, of 8 February 1993 (S/25248), I informed the Security Council about the round of the peace talks on Bosnia and Herzegovina held in New York from 3 to 8 February 1993. Since then, the Co-Chairmen of the Steering Committee of the International Conference on the Former Yugoslavia, Cyrus Vance and Lord Owen, have stayed in New York and continued to work for agreement on the comprehensive peace package (S/25221, annexes II-IV). This resumed round of the peace talks lasted from 1 to 6 March 1993.

2. The recent efforts of the Co Chairmen centred on the three elements of the peace package, and an additional component on interim arrangements: first, building on the constitutional principles for Bosnia and Herzegovina; second, settling the boundaries of provinces in the areas where agreement has not yet been forthcoming from the government delegation and the Bosnian Serb side; third, addressing questions that had prevented the Bosnian Government from signing the military agreement; and, in addition, promoting agreement among the three Bosnian sides on arrangements for the governance of the country in the interim period between the signing of a peace settlement and the holding of elections under a new Constitution.

I. CONSTITUTIONAL ISSUES

3. As members of the Council are aware, the three sides in Bosnia and Herzegovina signed, on 30 January 1993, the nine constitutional principles on the basis of which a new Constitution for Bosnia and Herzegovina is to be drafted. The agreed constitutional principles are reproduced in annex I below.

II. PROVINCIAL BOUNDARIES

4. In my report of 2 February 1993, I transmitted to the Council a provincial map that the Co-Chairmen of the Steering Committee had placed before the three sides and had invited them to sign. The Bosnian Croat side signed the map on 30 January 1993 (S/25221, annex III).

---

* UN Doc. S/25403, 12 March 1993.

5. In my report of 8 February 1993, I transmitted to the Council a revised map that the Co-Chairmen had put forward to the three sides (S/25248, annex III). The Bosnian Croat side had signed the revised map on 7 February.

6. The Bosnian Government side and the Bosnian Serb side did not sign the map during the resumed round which ended on 6 March. With respect to the comprehensive peace-package, a statement issued by the Bosnian Government upon the conclusion of this resumed round, 6 March, said: "... Progress had and continues to be made, and President Izetbegovic look(s) forward to returning to the United States toward the end of next week with the intention of moving the discussion forward to a successful conclusion ... We will continue our cause towards peace in good faith. We call upon other associated with the process to do the same." The Co-Chairmen made clear to all three sides that the provisional map would be the basis for the implementation of all interim arrangements until a final map has been agreed. The provisional provincial map recommended by the Co-Chairmen is reproduced in annex II below.

7. During the resumed round from 1 to 6 March, all aspects of the problem were extensively discussed and a number of new suggestions arose. In the light of their discussions with the three sides the Co-Chairmen suggested the establishment of a Boundary Commission, to be set up by the Secretary-General in consultation with the Co-Chairmen. The Commission would receive and, if necessary, hear evidence from those affected by the proposed provincial boundaries and advise in the demarcation of the provinces to be included in the new Constitution. The Boundary Commission would consist of five persons: one each to be recommended by the three parties and two, one of whom shall be the Chairman, to be recommended by the Co-Chairmen. The decisions of the Commission would be adopted by consensus.

III. MILITARY AND RELATED ISSUES

8. In my report of 2 February 1993, I informed the Council that on 30 January the Co-Chairmen had invited the three sides to sign an agreement for peace in Bosnia and Herzegovina that dealt with the cessation of hostilities; the restoration of infrastructure; the demilitarization of Sarajevo; the monitoring of borders; and the return of forces to designated provinces (S/25221, annex IV). The Bosnian Croats and the Bosnian Serbs signed the agreement on 30 January. The Bosnian Government stated on 30 January that it would not sign the agreement because it felt that the arrangements as to the control of heavy weapons were not strong enough. The Co-Chairmen invited President Izetbegovic to consult with the Force Commander of the United Nations Protections Force (UNPROFOR) to

obtain clarification that the Co-Chairmen believed would meet his concerns and enable him to sign the agreement.

9. The agreement for peace was formulated at a time when the Co-Chairmen were seeking additional resources so as to guarantee implementation of the agreement, allow physical control of heavy weapons, and permit sufficient deployment to ensure physical separation of opposing forces. Subsequently, there have been some important developments:

(a) A Canadian battalion has now been deployed to Sarajevo and is positioned near the airport.

(b) Some countries have indicated that in the event of the achievement of an agreed peace settlement they would be prepared to help the United Nations implement that settlement. For instance, in a statement made on 10 February 1993, United States Secretary of State Warren Christopher stated that "the President has taken steps to make clear to all concerned that the United States is prepared to do its share to help implement and enforce an agreement that is acceptable to all parties. If there is a viable agreement containing enforcement provisions, the United States would be prepared to join with the United Nations, NATO, and others in implementing and enforcing it, including possible United States military participations. This is a shared problem, and it must be a shared burden".

(c) Discussion have taken place involving the Department of Peace-keeping Operations of the United Nations Secretariat, the UNPROFOR Commander and his colleagues, and representatives of NATO headquarters and of the Supreme Headquarters of the Allied Powers in Europe (SHAPE).

10. Furthermore, General Nambiar wrote to the Co-Chairmen on 2 March saying that, once substantial numbers of additional troops arrived in Bosnia and Herzegovina, it would be possible to deal fully with the concerns of both the Bosnian Government and the Bosnian Serbs. He considered that physical control of heavy weapons could be undertaken, thus meeting the concerns of the Bosnian Government, and that there would be adequate deployment of ground troops, which would meet one of the concerns of the Bosnian Serbs.

11. In the light of these developments, the Bosnian Government agreed to, and signed, the military agreement on 3 March. The text agreed to and signed by all sides is reproduced in annex III below.

IV. INTERIM ARRANGEMENTS

12. In my report of 2 February 1993, I informed the Security Council about the discussion the Co-Chairmen had held with the three Bosnian sides with regard to interim institutional arrangements. I noted that the Co-Chairmen had submitted a working paper on this subject and had invited the sides to comment on it (S/25221, annex V).

13. The latest round of discussion have proceeded on the basis that until the entry into force of the new Constitution and the holding of elections thereunder, the present Constitution of Bosnia and Herzegovina should, except to the extent required to implement sections IV A and B below, continue in force. Also, the present powers of the *opstinas* would continue, as would their boundaries, except as required to conform to the agreed provisional provincial boundaries, or when changed by consensus.

A. Human Rights and the Reversal of "Ethnic Cleansing"

14. During the interim period, all persons in Bosnia and Herzegovina should be entitled to all rights provided for in the existing Constitution and in legislation in force, as well as to all rights provided for in specified international instruments on human rights. To the extent that there are any discrepancies, the provision providing the greater protection of human rights should be applied. All statements or commitments made under duress, particularly those related to the relinquishment of rights to land or property, should be treated as wholly null and void.

13. The implementation of the above-mentioned human rights should be ensured through:

   (a) The courts of Bosnia and Herzegovina, to which all persons would have unimpeded access;
   (b) An Interim Human Rights Court for Bosnia and Herzegovina, along the lines of that proposed by the Co-Chairmen for establishment by the new Constitution; and
   (c) The four ombudsmen proposed by the Co-Chairmen for inclusion in the new Constitution, who would need to be supported by adequate staff and facilities.

16. In addition, it has been agreed that there should be an International Human Rights Minority Mission, to be established by the Secretary-General and to be

headed by an Interim Human Rights Commissioner for Bosnia and Herzegovina, who would be based in Sarajevo. Deputy Commissioners would be based in various parts of the country. The Commissioners would be supported by international human rights monitors, deployed throughout the country and particularly in areas affected by "ethnic cleansing". They would observe the situation of human rights throughout Bosnia and Herzegovina, would intercede with the interim Presidency, with provincial authorities and with UNPROFOR to provide protection in urgent cases, would refer issues to the ombudsmen and to other human rights agencies as needed, and would work closely with the Office of the United Nations High Commissioner for Refugees (UNHCR), the International Committee of the Red Cross and other humanitarian agencies. The Commissioner would submit regular reports to the Secretary-General who would, in turn, report periodically to the Security Council and to other international bodies, including the United Nations Commission on Human Rights and its Special Rapporteur.

17. The central and other authorities should be required to give the fullest access, in respect of all relevant persons and places, to the Interim Human Rights Commissioner, the Deputy Commissioners and the human rights monitors, as well as to UNHCR, ICRC and other international humanitarian organizations.

18. It is also envisaged that as part of the UNPROFOR deployment in Bosnia and Herzegovina there should be a sufficiently large United Nations Civilian Police (UNCIVPOL) element whose tasks would be to see that: the police in all parts of the country have an appropriately balanced ethnic composition; do not oppress members of minority ethnic groups; contribute positively to the reversal of "ethnic cleansing" by protecting persons returning after having been forced to flee; carry out the judgements of courts, in particular the Human Rights Court; and assist the Interim Human Rights Commissioner, the Deputy Commissioners and the human rights monitors.

19. The question of war indemnities was raised by the Bosnian Government but no conclusion was reached.

B. Government arrangements

1. Background

20. During the period between the entry into force of the peace settlement and the holding of free and fair elections, there is a need for an interim institutional mechanism so that the country can function effectively. The drafting of a new

Constitution for the Republic of Bosnia and Herzegovina is expected to take months. Also, it is very likely to take more than a year for the many refugees and displaced persons to return to their homes. Nevertheless, free and fair elections must be held within two years; the date will be fixed by the interim Presidency in consultation with the Co-Chairmen.

21. At the time of the November 1990 general elections in Bosnia and Herzegovina, the Constitution provided for the election to the collective Presidency of two representatives from each of the three constituent peoples, together with one "other". The two Muslim members elected from the SDA Party were Fikret Abdic and Alija Izetbegovic. The two Serb members elected from the SDS Party were Nikola Koljevic and Biljana Plavsic. The two Croat members elected from the HDZ Party were Franjo Boras and Stjepan Kljuic. The seventh member of the Presidency, Ejup Ganic, was elected from the "other" or "Yugoslav" category.

22. The Constitution provided that the position of President of the Presidency should rotate among the three constituent peoples and that the member of the Presidency designated as President was to serve in that capacity for one year, renewable for a second year. In December 1990 Alija Izetbegovic was nominated by the SDA to serve as the first president. The Presidency then confirmed the nominations. In December 1991, the Presidency extended the mandate of President Izetbegovic for a second year.

23. In early 1992, the two Serb members of the Presidency, Nikola Koljevic and Biljana Plavsic, withdrew, to protest the decision to hold a referendum on the proposed secession of the Republic of Bosnia and Herzegovina from the Socialist Federal Republic of Yugoslavia. The Serb President of the Bosnian Parliament, Momcilo Krajisnik, also withdrew. The Bosnian Serbs then declined to participate in the referendum, which was held on 29 February and 1 March 1992.

24. Following the outbreak of hostilities in Bosnia and Herzegovina in April 1992, the remaining members of the Presidency invoked a provision of the Constitution which apparently provides that during times of war, the seven-member Presidency could be expanded to include the Prime Minister, the President of the Parliament, and the Commander-in-Chief of the Armed Forces. By the same decision, the collective Presidency also assumed the powers and responsibilities of the parliament (S/24248, annex I).

2. Interim Presidency

25. Constitutional principle 5, signed by the three sides on 30 January 1993, provides that "the Presidency shall be composed of three elected representatives

of each of the three constituent peoples" (see annex I below). Since this nine member structure is to operate under the new Constitution, the Co-Chairmen have sought to apply the agreed structure in the arrangements for the interim period. During a meeting in Zagreb on 17 December, 1992, President Izetbegovic and Mr. Boban specifically agreed to a nine-member structure for the interim period.

26. Keeping these factors in mind, the Co-Chairmen have discussed with the three sides the ideas that they should nominate representatives to serve in an interim Presidency. The position of the President, to be elected by the interim Presidency, would rotate. The President, would perform the role of head of State. The interim Presidency would be located in Sarajevo. The principal responsibilities of the interim Presidency would be as set out in document S/25221, annex V, section I. It would, naturally, be expected to act to ensure respect for human rights, in cooperation with the International Human Rights Monitoring Mission. It would also be expected to deal with the establishment and functioning of an International Access Authority, a National Power Authority, a National Bank, a National Post, Telegraph and Telecommunications Authority, an independent National Civil Aviation Authority, as suggested in document S/25221, annex V, sections V-IX, In addition to its national responsibilities, the interim central Government would administer any capital *opstina* that might eventually be agreed to in Sarajevo and have responsibility for its policing.

27. The Co-Chairmen also discussed with the three sides interim governmental arrangements in the provinces. They suggested that during the interim period, each province should have an interim provincial government composed of a Governor, a Vice-Governor and 10 other members. All these would be nominated by the parties on the basis of the composition of the population of the respective province, provided that none of the thee constituent peoples would be left unrepresented in any province. To determine these relative percentages, the 1991 census was used. Consequently, the interim provincial governments would be composed as set out in document S/25221, annex V, a simple majority, except that the adoption of the provincial constitution and the setting of *opstina* boundaries would be taken by consensus.

28. The principal functions of the interim provincial governments would be as indicated in document S/25221, annex V, section II. They would, naturally, be expected to act to ensure respect for human rights, in cooperation with the International Human Rights Monitoring Mission. An UNPROFOR Military Liaison Officer, as well as an UNCIVPOL Liaison Officer, would be attached to the staff of each provincial government to assist in the carrying out of its functions.

29. In the light of the ideas on interim governmental arrangements put to the three sides by the Co-Chairmen, President Izetbegovic, Foreign Minister Siladzic, Mr. Boban and Prime Minister Akmadzic signed an agreement on 3 March 1993 which contained the following relevant provisions:

(a) The responsibilities of the Presidency and of the Government of the Republic of Bosnia and Herzegovina, as well as of the provinces, will be in accordance with the letter and spirit of the constitutional principles agreed and signed by the parties.

(b) The institution of the Presidency will be preserved during the interim period. There will be nine members on the interim Presidency, with three representatives from each of the three constituent peoples. Since the Republic of Bosnia and Herzegovina is to be demilitarized as provided for in constitutional principle 7, the Commander-in-Chief of the Armed Forces will not continue to serve in the interim Presidency.

(c) The nine members of the interim Presidency will designate one member to serve as President of the Presidency. The President will perform the role of head of State. The position of President will rotate every six months among the three constituent peoples, in accordance with the existing sequence of rotation (Muslim, Croat, Serb).

(d) The interim Presidency will take its decision by consensus of nine, by a qualified majority of seven, or by a simple majority of five depending on whether the decision relates to a constitutional principle, or specially important question, or to normal business of the Presidency. If the members of the interim Presidency are unable to agree on the applicable majority, they will consult the Co-Chairmen, whose decision will be binding.

(e) The two sides have each submitted three names to the Co-Chairmen to serve in the interim Presidency. The Co-Chairmen have been requested to ask the Bosnian Serbs to propose three representatives to serve on the interim Presidency.

30. In subsequent discussions with the Co-Chairmen, the Bosnian Government, the Bosnian Serb and the Bosnian Croat sides discussed the functions of the interim Presidency and the interim central Government. The Bosnian Serb side again reiterated its wish for a central coordinated body that would be a new vehicle for government. They did not wish to revert back to the institution of the Presidency, which in their view had failed them in the past. The Co-Chairmen demonstrated why the interim Presidency was different: it was not a seven-mem-

ber Presidency but a nine-member Presidency, with the three constituent peoples fully represented. There was now a proper decision-making procedure, which would prevent stalemate, or one or two constituent peoples being able to impose on the other. The distribution of powers and competencies between the centre and the provinces were also identified in keeping with the agreed decision to create a decentralized Bosnia and Herzegovina.

31. The Co-Chairmen explained further that, in the interim period, where a consensus amongst the three constituent peoples as highly desirable in the aftermath of hostilities, the role of the interim Presidency and interim government would inevitably be more like that of a coalition government. This arrangement would not prejudge negotiation over a new Constitution, whereunder the role of the Presidency and a democratically elected Parliament and government would be bound to be different and reflect more accurately the will of the people. Even so, the Presidency would be bound to have important reserve powers to safeguard the rights of the constituent peoples.

32. The Co-Chairmen explained that the interim Presidency would be responsible for appointing ministers to the interim central Government and determining the role of such ministries as are deemed appropriate, and to establish the necessary agencies and other aspects of government. The principal responsibilities of the interim Presidency and the interim central Government would be as follows:

1. Preparations for the holding of free and fair elections, on the basis of the new Constitution, under international supervision;
2. Relations with ICFY, the Mixed Military Working Group, UNPROFOR (including UNCIVPOL), and the European Community Monitoring Mission (ECMM);
3. Coordination with the Commissioner for Human Rights, the Deputy Commissioners, and human rights monitors;
4. Coordination with UNHCR, ICRC, WHO and other relevant agencies on the return and rehabilitation of refugees and displaced persons;
5. Foreign affairs (including membership on international organizations);
6. International commerce (customs duties, quotas);
7. Citizenship;
8. Raising of any taxes required to carry out its functions;
9. Coordination of the provincial police;
10. Coordination of assistance for technical functions (e.g., crime laboratories); and
11. Coordination with international and foreign police authorities.

33. There was some discussion about the organization and structure of the police in the future, The Co-Chairmen, in their constitutional proposals of 27 October 1992, had proposed that all uniformed police should be controlled by the provinces or by local authorities under them. All police forces should be fully integrated. At the national level there would be no uniformed, armed police, but a coordinating office to assist the provincial police authorities and to maintain contact with international and foreign police authorities (e.g., INTERPOL).

34. Discussions took place about arrangements for the governance of the provinces during the interim period along the lines contained in the working paper put forward by the Co-Chairmen for discussion (S/25221, annex V, section II) and on the understanding that it would be for the interim Presidency to give effect to these guidelines.

35. As to governance of the province of Sarajevo, the Bosnian Croat side accepted the Co-Chairmen's compromise of the provinces being governed by three representatives each of the three constituent peoples. There was no agreement on the part of the Bosnian Government and the Bosnian Serb sides, each proposing different alternatives. It was apparent to the Co-Chairmen that the issue required further study. The Co-Chairmen said it would be possible for the whole issue of the future Government of Sarajevo to be referred to the Boundary Commission, but that while such reference was being made, an interim provincial government still had to be established.

V. Concluding Observations

36. Significant progress was made at this latest round of the peace talks. With the Bosnian Government's signature of the military agreement, seven out of nine signatures required for the conclusion of the peace settlement plan have been obtained. Additionally, President Izetbegovic assured the Co-Chairmen of his return to New York after a few days with the intention of successfully concluding the peace talks in New York. After six months of intensive negotiations, during which time the Co-Chairmen have persistently worked for a just and durable settlement, it is now crucial that the Bosnian Government and the Bosnian Serbs agree to and sign the provincial map as quickly as possible, so that implementation may commence. Agreement on the peace plan and its rapid and robust implementation offer the best prospect for improving the situation in Bosnia and Herzegovina.

Annex I
Agreement Relating to Bosnia and Herzegovina[*]

THE UNDERSIGNED,

Guided by the principles of the Charter of the United Nations, the Universal Declaration of Human Rights[a] and the Declaration on the Rights of Persons belonging National or Ethnic, Religious and Linguistic Minorities,[b]

Recalling the Statement of Principles and the Statement on Bosnia adopted by the International Conference on the Former Yugoslavia at its session in London and the Programme of Action on Humanitarian Issues agreed to at that session,

Considering the decisions of the United Nations Security Council relating to the former Yugoslavia,

Reaffirming their commitment to peace and security among the successor States to the former Yugoslavia,

Hereby agree as follows:

I. CONSTITUTIONAL FRAMEWORK FOR BOSNIA AND HERZEGOVINA

Tripartite negotiations shall proceed on a continuous basis in Geneva, under the auspices of the International Conference in the Former Yugoslavia, in order to finalise a Constitution for Bosnia and Herzegovina in accordance with the following principles:

(1) Bosnia and Herzegovina shall be a decentralized State, the Constitution shall recognize three constituent peoples, as well as a group of others, with most governmental functions carried out by its provinces.

(2) The provinces shall not have any international legal personality and may not enter into agreements with foreign States or with international organizations.

(3) Full freedom of movement shall be allowed throughout Bosnia and Herzegovina, to be ensured in part by the maintenance of internationally controlled throughways.

---

[*] Geneva, 30 January 1993. Signed by A. Izetbegovic, R. Karadzic and M. Boban; and, as witnesses, by C.R. Vance and D. Owen.

[a] General Assembly resolution 217 A (III).

[b] General Assembly resolution 47/135.

(4) All matters of vital concern to any of the constituent peoples shall be regulated in the Constitution, which as to these points may be amended only by consensus of these constituent peoples; ordinary governmental business is not to be veto-able by any group.

(5) The provinces and the central Government shall have democratically elected legislature and democratically chosen chief executives and an independent judiciary. The Presidency shall be composed of three elected representatives of each of the three constituent peoples. The initial elections are to be United Nations/European Community/ Conference on Security and Cooperation in Europe supervised.

(6) A Constitutional Court, with a member from each group and a majority of non-Bosnian members initially appointed by the International Conference on the Former Yugoslavia, shall resolve disputes between the central Government and any province, and among organs of the former.

(7) Bosnia and Herzegovina is to be progressively demilitarized under United Nations/European Community supervision.

(8) The highest level of internationally recognized human rights shall be provided for in the Constitution, which shall also provide for the ensurance of implementation through both domestic and international mechanisms.

(9) A number of international monitoring or control devices shall be provided for in the Constitution, to remain in place at least until the three constituent peoples by consensus agree to dispense with them.

II. COOPERATION IN RESPECT OF HUMANITARIAN EFFORTS

1. Maximum cooperation shall be extended to the High Commission for Refugees, the International Committee of the Red Cross, the United Nations Protection Force, the European Community Monitoring Mission and other humanitarian organizations working to provide assistance to refugees and displaced persons.

2. Full cooperation shall also be extended to the High Commissioner for Refugees in drawing up and implementing programmes for the return of refugees and displaced persons to their homes.

Annex II

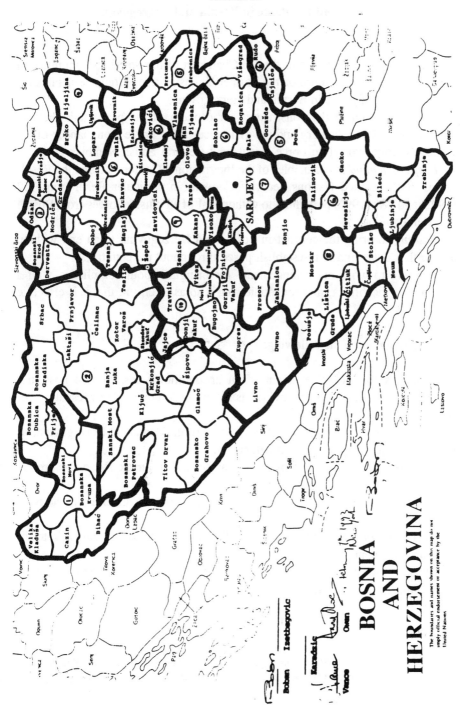

BOSNIA
AND
HERZEGOVINA

The boundaries and names shown on this map do not
imply official endorsement or acceptance by the
United Nations

Annex III
Agreement for Peace in Bosnia and Herzegovina[*]

THE UNDERSIGNED,

Welcoming the invitation of the Co-Chairmen of the Steering Committee of the International Conference on the Former Yugoslavia to participate in talks for the restoration of peace in Bosnia and Herzegovina,

Taking account of the constructive atmosphere of the peace talks held in Geneva from 2 to 5 January and the assistance of the Force Commander of the United Nations Protection Force, Lieutenant-General Satish Nambiar,

Keeping in mind the principles of the International Conference and the Resolutions of the United Nations Security Council, in particular Resolutions 752 (1992) and 787 (1992) pertaining to withdrawal of all outside forces from Bosnia and Herzegovina,

Wishing to bring the conflict in Bosnia and Herzegovina to an end without any further delay and to re-establish peace throughout the country,

Desiring to work out arrangements for bringing about compliance with a cessation of hostilities, and for monitoring it so as to ensure that it is effective and lasting,

Hereby agree on the following:

1. Measures for the achievement of an unconditional cessation of hostilities throughout Bosnia and Herzegovina, as set out in Annex I to the present agreement;
2. Measures for the restoration of infrastructure in Bosnia and Herzegovina, as set out in annex II to the present agreement;
3. Measures on the opening of routes, as set out in annex IV to the present agreement;
4. Arrangements on the separation of forces, as set out in annex IV to the present agreement;
5. Measures for the demilitarization of Sarajevo, as set out in annex V to the present agreement;
6. Measures for the monitoring of the borders of Bosnia and Herzegovina, as set out in annex VI to the present agreement;

---

[*] Geneva, 30 January 1993. Not signed by A. Izetbegovic, signed R. Karadzic and M. Boban; and, as witnesses, by C.R. Vance and D. Owen.

7. Return of forces to the designated provinces, as set out in annex VII to the present agreement.

ANNEX I: CESSATION OF HOSTILITIES

Broad Principles

All parties agree to support the broad principles required to support a cessation of hostilities. These broad principles will be translated into concrete action through additional discussion within the Mixed Military Working Group. Several of the principles will be dealt with on a stand-alone basis, although they remain an integral part of the overall framework of the cessation of hostilities.

The broad principles are:

- A ceasefire must be put in place and remain effective. This is to be implemented 72 hours from midnight (New York time - EST) of the day on which the Security Council endorses this plan.
- Monitoring and control measures are to be put in place to ensure compliance and should include as a minimum:
  - Links between Commanders in conflict areas (hot lines);
  - Provision of United Nations Protection Force/European Community Monitoring Mission liaison and monitors;
  - Establishment of joint crisis management teams;
  - Opening of confrontation line crossing-points. For use by the United Nations Protection Force and monitoring agencies.
- The separation of forces is to be achieved.
- Routes supporting the general freedom of movement of people, commerce and humanitarian aid are to be opened.
- The restoration of infrastructure will proceed as a priority. Restoration will not be linked to any negotiations.

Essential Elements

- Security Council endorses the plan - initiates all follow-on action (D-3). The 72 hours permit passage of information;
- Cessation of hostilities effective (D-Day);
- Declaration of forces - this is to take place in D-1 and should include:
  - Numbers and locations of all heavy weapons,
  - Detailed documentation of mine fields,

- Locations of front lines (traces),
- Defensive works and positions;
- Establish demarcation line (joint actively);
- Move in United Nations Protection Force forces to establish security (commencing D+1):
  - Monitor lines of conflict,
  - Monitor heavy weapons,
  - Reporting system (all parties);
- Withdrawal of heavy weapons:
  - Of calibre 12.7 mm and above; 5 days for Sarajevo and 15 days for remaining areas;
  - Locations to be determined based on effective ranges of weapon systems.
  - All such withdrawals will be supervised by the United Nations Protection Force and subsequently monitored at the designated locations by the United Nations Protection Force in order to prevent their use.
- Separation of forces:
  - Abandon defensive works on confrontation line,
  - Area of separation to be agreed,
  - Distance in which no forces, except police, allowed,
  - Distance within which no defensive works will be manned.
- The separation of forces and withdrawal of heavy weapons are linked.
- Mixed Military Commission is established to deal with any clarifications and breaches of the cessation of hostilities.

ANNEX II: RESTORATION OF INFRASTRUCTURE

All parties agree that denial or use of civil utilities as a weapon of war is unacceptable, and all affirm their commitment to the full restoration of the civil infrastructure across Bosnia and Herzegovina, and in particular, Sarajevo.

The provision of humanitarian aid cannot be linked in any way with the military steps of the process of demilitarization or cessation of hostilities. Being humanitarian in nature, its priority is strictly governed by the ability of all three parties to support its implementation.

Restoration will be the first priority. Therefore, immediate efforts must be placed on the restoration of infrastructure. This is equally applicable to the city of Sarajevo as well as the rest of Bosnia and Herzegovina. It includes where applicable:

- Power grids;
- Power stations;
- Bridges;
- Gas;
- Telecommunications;
- Railway lines;
- Routes;
- Water supply.

Guarantees of security will be requested and must be provided and the restoration of power/water/heat will be fully supported by the warring parties.

A joint committee is already in place in Sarajevo; the work of this committee is to be facilitated with immediate effect to enable early restoration of utilities in Sarajevo.

Assistance will be provided through all the appropriated agencies, including United Nations and civilian expertise. However, within Bosnia and Herzegovina, a joint commission composed of representatives of all sides is to identify the priorities, define the needs and execute the work in conjunction with civil authorities. To this end, vital installations will be identified in conjunction with Bosnia and Herzegovina joint commission:

- Access will be guaranteed after local arrangements are made.
- Forces will be withdrawn from sites consistent with security.
- Warring parties will provide, when necessary, liaison for the repair teams.
- Civil agencies/workers will be assisted.

Parties will work to re-establish infrastructure, including railways/power grids/water supplies, across borders with neighbouring republics.

Respect for infrastructure facilities must be developed and they must remain free from attack or use as defensive positions.

All parties agree to develop a common instruction for passage down chains of command to demonstrate an equal endorsement of support.

ANNEX III: OPENING OF ROUTES

The opening of routes is directly related to the political issue which concerns the freedom of movement of all people in the context of constitutional principles. It is equally applicable to Sarajevo as well as all other areas of Bosnia and Herzegovina.

It is to be achieved through:

- Security guarantees by all parties to ensure non-interference and protection of personnel and material using the routes;
- Non-interference on the route;
- Checkpoints, patrols, and monitoring by United Nations Protection Force/European Community Monitoring Mission, as appropriate;
- Supervised inspection at entry points;
- Freedom of passage of humanitarian aid;
- Absolute freedom of movement of United Nations forces.

The concept of blue routes for Sarajevo is appended hereto. This format is applicable for the establishment of all other similar types of routes within Bosnia and Herzegovina. Additional routes can be negotiated under the aegis of the Mixed Military Working Group.

APPENDIX: SARAJEVO "BLUE ROUTE" CONCEPT

The parties have decided to establish three free passage routes with mutually agreed measures to guarantee and ensure safe passage for freedom of movement of civilians, commercial goods and humanitarian aid to and from Sarajevo.
These routes are:

- Sarajevo-Zenica-Sarajevo;
- Sarajevo-Mostar-Sarajevo;
- Sarajevo-Zvornik-Sarajevo.

Outline Plan for Blue Routes

1.   Execution
1.1   Prerequisites

The following prerequisites are to be required:

1.1.1 Cessation of hostilities.

1.1.2 Complete freedom of movement for United Nations Protection Force on the three blue routes.

1.2   Use of the blue routes

1.2.1 Timings

Routes will be open during daylight hours for convoys. United Nations Protection Force will use the route 24 hours a day.

1.2.2 Access for Civilians

All civilians, regardless of sex, age, or ethnic origin, and without weapons or ammunition, will be allowed to use the routes. Private and commercial vehicles will also be permitted on each route subject to inspection outlined on paragraph 1.5.1 below.

1.2.3 Access for Humanitarian Aid

All international and local humanitarian aid agencies will be allowed to use the routes. Humanitarian aid includes, but is not limited to, food, water, medical supplies and fuel.

1.2.4 Access for Commercial Goods

Normal commerce will be progressively restored to and from Sarajevo.

1.3   Establishment of Routes

1.3.1 Sarajevo-Zenica-Sarajevo

This route incorporates Sarajevo-Rajlovac-Ilijas-Visoko-Zenica.

1.3.2 Sarajevo-Mostar-Sarajevo

This route incorporates Sarajevo-Ilidza-Hadzici-Tarcin-Jablanica-Mostar.

1.3.3 Sarajevo-Zvornik-Sarajevo

This route incorporates Sarajevo-Bentbasa-Mokro-Sololac-Vlasenica-Zvornik.

1.4   Checkpoints

Checkpoints will be established and manned by United Nations Protection Force forces at the entrance and exit of each route and when crossing a line of confrontation. Each United Nations Protection Force checkpoint will be located near or with the checkpoint of the force controlling the territory involved consistent with the security requirements of the factions. No side will be permitted to erect a new checkpoint.

1.5   Control Measures

1.5.1 Inspection Procedures

    (a)   Inspections will be conducted by United Nations Protection Force forces. Each side is permitted to monitor the events in close coordination with the United Nations Protection Force.

    (b)   War-related material, weapons or ammunition are forbidden. If found, the items will be confiscated and subsequently destroyed under control of the United Nations Protection Force and the parties.

    (c)   Humanitarian aid convoys may be subjected to inspections.

    (d)   Checkpoints will be activated only during daylight hours as a safety measure for civilians and convoys.

1.5.2 Escorts

    (a)   Each convoy will be escorted with the appropriate United Nations Protection Force vehicles.

    (b)   Convoys and escorts will take priority over military activities.

    (c)   The army controlling the territory involved may provide civilian police as an additional means of security.

1.5.3 Patrols

    (a)   United Nations Protection Force forces will patrol the blue routes as necessary.

    (b)   Patrols will consists of at least two vehicles suitably equipped and will contain an appropriate communications net.

    (c)   All United Nations Protection Force patrols will be permitted to cross all checkpoints.

1.6 Implementation

1.6.1 Suggested Timeframe

D-3   - Security Council endorses the plan
D+1 - Erecting checkpoints
       - Inspection procedures agreed
       - Routes cleared of all obstacles
       - Repairs carried out as required
       - Reconnoitre by the United Nations Protection Force
D+5 - Opening of blue routes for civilians and humanitarian aid

ANNEX IV: SEPARATION OF FORCES

The parties agree that the separation of forces is an element of the overall cessation of hostilities. An agreement will be based on the steps and control measures and sequence of events outlined below:

Steps

The concrete steps envisaged in the process include:

- An absolute ceasefire.
- Temporary freezing of the military situation, pending agreement in return of forces to designated provinces.
- No forward deployments or offensive action.
- No move of additional forces, explosives and weapons forward will be permitted. Rotation on an individual basis is acceptable.
- Withdrawal of heavy weapons (direct and indirect fire) of all parties from areas of confrontation to areas of range, decided upon by the parties in conjunction with the United Nations Protection Force.
- Physical separation of forces in contact.
- Security and monitoring of the demilitarized zone.

Control Measures

The control measures required include:

- Declaration of forces in being, including location of minefields.
- Monitoring of front lines.
- Declaration of heavy weapons in separation areas.
- Establishing agreed lines in which forces may be located.
- Staged withdrawal of forces culminating in their relocation to designated provinces.

Sequence of Events

- Ceasefire under aegis of the overall cessation of hostilities.
- Establishment and patrol of the demarcation line by United Nations Protection Force personnel.
- Withdrawal of designated weapons systems of all parties.
- Search and clearance of the affected area by joint patrols.
- Conduct of joint and United Nations-only patrols within the area. Composition of the patrols to be negotiated at the Mixed Military Working Group.

UNPROFOR Concept for Heavy Weapons Control

- All heavy weapons 12.7 mm calibre and above are included.
- These weapons will be withdrawn out of effective range to areas decided between the United Nations Protection Force and the parties.
- The withdrawal will be monitored by the United Nations Protection Force.
- Once in location the weapons will be monitored to ensure that they are not used.
- The United Nations Protection Force will not physically take over the weapons.
- Where terrain such as towns preclude moving weapons out of range, they will be gathered in agreed location under United Nations Protection Force control to ensure that they are not used.

ANNEX V: DEMILITARIZATION OF SARAJEVO

The demilitarization of Sarajevo is based on one requirement: an effective cessation of hostilities.

The other elements are:

- Establishment of control on an designated line;
- Restoration of civil utilities;
- Land routes and freedom of movement;
- Separation of forces along lines of confrontation.

Control measures include:

- Patrol and monitoring of the demarcation line;
- Checkpoints at major crossings until confidence is restored;
- Mixed patrols in the demilitarized zone.

A military/civil joint commission as previously proposed should oversee the implementation of the accord.

Appended hereto is a draft agreement covering first stage of a potential agreement on the demilitarization of Sarajevo. This stage covers the airport area as already discussed at the Mixed Military Working Group.

APPENDIX: PROPOSED AGREEMENT ON THE FIRST STAGE OF DEMILITARIZATION OF SARAJEVO

The authorized representatives of all three conflicting sides with the presence of the United Nations Protection Force representative agree on the implementation of an area in the western and southern districts of Sarajevo.

Cessation of Hostilities

The cessation of hostilities will be implemented as follows:

(a) The freezing of the military situation on the existing lines.
(b) No offensive action allowed.
(c) No forward redeployments.
(d) All heavy weapons will be withdrawn from positions from which they can engage.
(e) No movement or any additional forces although rotation of personnel on a one-for-one basis shall be permitted.
(f) No movement or resupply of ammunitions, explosives or incendiary devices.

Freedom of movement for all civilians

The agreement on blue routes will re-establish the freedom of movement of all civilians in support of this plan.

Restoration of civil utilities

A Joint Commission composed of representatives from each side will identify priorities, define needs and execute the implementation of civil utilities. Details can be found in annex II, Restoration of infrastructure.

Removal of heavy weapons

(a) *Area*. All heavy weapons will be withdrawn to designated locations from the following: Mojmilo, Dobrinja, Lukavica, Gornji, Kotorac, Vojkovici, Hrasnica, Sokolovici, Butmir, Ilidza, Otes, Stup, Nedarici.

(b) *Joint Commission*. A Joint Commission will be created.

  (1) The mission of this Joint Commission will be to execute and implement details of this plan and subsequent phases.
  (2) This Joint Commission will be composed of:
      (a) A United Nations Protection Force command and support element;
      (b) A team of each side commanded by an officer senior enough to make decisions and designated as the authorised commander for the troops in the areas affected;
      (c) A joint communications system which includes a command set and the necessary guaranteed communications link to each individual headquarters.

(c) *Time-frame*. From each district the withdrawal of heavy weapons out of the designated area will be carried out in two stages within a period of five days:

  (1) Stage 1 - Withdrawal of all direct fire weapons of 12.7 mm calibre and above (tanks, armoured personnel carriers, anti-tank, anti-aircraft and heavy machine guns).
  (2) Stage 2 - Withdrawal of all heavy indirect fire weapons (mortars, field artillery).

(d) *Control measures*. The following implementation and control measures will be used:

(1) United Nations Protection Force forces will patrol the area of separation between the conflicting sides.

(2) United Nations Protection Force forces will be deployed on the confrontation lines and in agreed mixed checkpoints proposed by the Joint Commission.

(3) All parties are to identify weapons by type and location and will provide the United Nations Protection Force with detailed maps of areas considered to be under their respective control.

(4) Complete freedom of movement for all United Nations Protection Force personnel and vehicles within the affected areas.

(5) The Joint Commission will establish mixed patrols as appropriate.

ANNEX VI: MONITORING OF BORDERS

Pursuant to United Nations Security Council resolution 787 (1992), Paragraph 5, to prevent interference from outside the Republic of Bosnia and Herzegovina, the United Nations Protection Force/European Community Monitoring Mission will monitor borders with neighbouring republics.

Principles

United Nations Protection Force/European Monitoring Mission forces will monitor crossings to prevent weapons, munitions, military personnel or irregular forces from entering the country.

Borders with adjoining republics will be monitored.

United Nations Protection Force actions to observe, search and report will be facilitated by the authorities of the Republic of Croatia and the Federal Republic of Yugoslavia.

ANNEX VII: RETURN OF FORCES TO DESIGNATED PROVINCES

To enable the process of return to normalcy, and as a direct follow-on from the cessation of hostilities and the separation of forces, a return of forces to designated provinces will be conducted. This can start as part of the withdrawal of heavy weapons but, given the winter weather conditions, it is hard to fix a definite date for the completion of this process. We should however aim to achieve the return of forces within 45 days.

This stage will be coordinated with an agreed demobilization of forces in being.

The United Nations Protection Force/European Community Monitoring Mission will monitor the withdrawal of these forces in conjunction with national and provincial authorities.

The Mixed Military Working Group would be the technical negotiating agency.

117. REPORT OF THE SECRETARY-GENERAL ON THE ACTIVITIES OF THE INTERNATIONAL CONFERENCE ON THE FORMER YUGOSLAVIA: PEACE TALKS ON BOSNIA AND HERZEGOVINA*

1. The present report refers only to the efforts of the Co-Chairmen of the Steering Committee on the International Conference on the Former Yugoslavia regarding Bosnia and Herzegovina, without entering into other questions under the purview of the Conference.

2. The Co-Chairmen of the Steering Committee of the International Conference on the Former Yugoslavia, Cyrus Vance and Lord Owen, have deployed their best endeavours for seven months to bring peace, with justice and respect for human rights, to Bosnia and Herzegovina. They and their colleagues have laboured night and day to help the parties to the conflict to reach an honourable and durable settlement. In my earlier reports to the Security Council, I have provided extensive information on the detailed efforts of the Co-Chairmen.

3. In my last report of 12 March (S/25403), I noted that the recent efforts of the Co-Chairmen centred on the following elements of the peace package: first, building on the constitutional principles for Bosnia and Herzegovina; second, settling the boundaries of provinces in the areas where agreement has not yet been forthcoming from the Government and the Bosnian Serb sides; third, advancing toward implementation of the military agreement; and, fourth, promoting agreement along the three Bosnian sides on arrangements for the governance of the country in the interim period between the signing of a peace settlement and the holding of elections under a new Constitution. The Co-Chairmen have consistently sought to advance agreement on the package as a whole because they consider that partial solutions are likely to be exploited for partisan advan-

---

*   UN Doc. S/25479, 26 March 1993.

tages. Only a comprehensive approach can lead to lasting peace.

4. Since the issuance of my last report, the Co-Chairmen have held another round of peace talks with the three sides to the conflict. The latest round lasted from 16 to 25 March 1993. The efforts of the Co-Chairmen, and the positions of the three sides, are set out below.

I. INTERIM ARRANGEMENTS

5. In all the meetings that the Co-Chairmen have had with the Bosnian Government side, as well as in meetings with the Bosnian Serbs, over the last few months, a fundamental difference constantly emerged over issues of legitimacy of the State of Bosnia and Herzegovina. The Government side insists that since Bosnia and Herzegovina is an independent, sovereign State recognized as such by the United Nations, the existing constitutional order, government and governmental institutions should all be preserved and endorsed in any peace settlement by all the parties. The Bosnian side's view is that a civil war is raging because of the circumstances surrounding the creation of Bosnia and Herzegovina. They were adamant that they cannot rejoin the existing system which, they considered, brought on the war and was the reason for their withdrawing from the Assembly, the Government, the Presidency and for persuading Bosnian Serbs to boycott the referendum. In view of the Co-Chairmen the only way a settlement could be reached would be for all sides to concentrate on specific arrangements for the interim period.

6. In an effort to deal with these fundamental points, the Co-Chairmen arranged meetings during the preceding round of the talks between the Bosnian Government side and the Bosnian Croat side in order to promote agreement. Those meetings led to the signature, on 3 March 1993, of an agreement on interim governmental agreements between the Bosnian Government and the Bosnian Croat sides. The relevant points of that agreement, and the related discussion on interim governmental arrangements, were summarized in my previous report to the Security Council (S/25403, paras. 29-35).

7. During the latest round of the peace talks, the Co-Chairmen arranged meetings between the Bosnian Serb side and the Bosnian Croat side in an attempt to agree on provisions for the interim governmental arrangements. Meetings for this purpose were also arranged again between the Bosnian Government side and the Bosnian Croat side.

8. In the light of the view expressed, the Co-Chairmen arranged a further meeting between the Bosnian Government side and the Bosnia Croat side on 24 March 1993 to discuss a working paper on interim governmental arrangement.

After five hours of meeting, the two sides reached agreement, which they signed on 25 March 1993 (annex I). As part of that agreement, they also signed on the same occasion, a revised map of provincial boundaries (annex III).

9. On 25 March 1993, when President Izetbegovic signed the agreement on interim arrangements and the provincial map, he made a declaration which is reproduced in full in annex V.

II. Sarajevo

10. As regards arrangements for the governance of Sarajevo, it emerged in discussion that a way forward might be to increase the size if the proposed Sarajevo province making it less dominated by the city and therefore more like that of the other nine provinces. Both the Bosnian Government and the Bosnian Croats felt that in addition to the inclusion of most of the *opstina* of Kiseljak and that of Kresevo, as in the original map, the inclusion of the whole *opstinas* of Visolo, Breza and Vares and a small border area of Kakanj would make for a better balanced province. They believed also that within Sarajevo province there was a case for defining a capital city district which would continue to allow for an open and undivided city as previously proposed by the Co-Chairmen, but which was somewhat larger than the capital *opstina* that was referred to in my previous report to the Security Council (S/25403, para.26). Both sides believed that in such a case Sarajevo province should be governed during the interim under the same proportional formula which had been suggested should apply to the other nine provinces. Sarajevo city itself would be governed by an Interim Executive Mayor and Interim Executive Board, under the nominal supervision of the Presidency. These ideas for Sarajevo were discussed with the Bosnian Serbs and then in detail with the Bosnian Croats together with the Bosnian Government, who both accepted them and expressed their readiness, on that basis, to sign a revised map (annex III).

11. The positions of the three sides on other issues are outlined below.

III. The Bosnian Government

12. The Bosnian Government side, led by President Alija Izetbegovic, met the Co-Chairmen in New York on 18 March 1993. The main subject of discussion was the need for the Assembly that had been suspended since the war and whose powers had been assumed by the Presidency to be reactivated during the interim period. The Co-Chairmen pointed out that neither the Bosnian Croats nor the Bosnian Serbs had been prepared to accept that the Assembly should have any

role in the interim period.

13. On 19 March 1993, the Co-Chairmen had a further discussion about the interim Presidency and its relation to the Government. The Co-Chairmen explained that in a decentralized state a number of the existing Ministries and Ministerial functions would no longer be necessary, and a smaller list of Ministries was discussed. That list was then subsequently discussed separately, and together, with the Bosnian Croats and Bosnian Serbs. The outcome of these discussions was the agreement on interim arrangements mentioned earlier (annex I).

IV. THE BOSNIAN SERBS

14. The Bosnian Serb side, which remained involved in the talks regarding the interim governmental agreement and the revised map of provincial boundaries, was invited to sign them at a plenary session of the talks held on 25 March, but declined to do so. It stated, however, that it would refer these documents to its assembly for its consideration and decision. The Co-Chairmen encouraged it to do so and to act promptly.

15. The Bosnian Serb side asserts that it wishes for peace and claims that it is being forced to fight because of specific attacks by Bosnian Government forces, whether in Sarajevo or Eastern Bosnia. At the current round of the peace talks it proposed to the Co-Chairmen that all three sides should agree on an end to the war and that, for its part, it would state publicly that the status quo would not prejudice the final territorial settlement. The Co-Chairmen felt, in the light of the situation on the ground, that there was no point in pursuing hollow declarations and that there was no escaping the need for withdrawal of the Bosnian Serb armed forces from those parts of the territory of Bosnia and Herzegovina which they at present claimed for themselves and which lay outside the three provinces in the map in which the Serbs could expect to be the majority in the provincial government. For similar reasons the Co-Chairmen rejected the Bosnian Serb suggestion that United Nations forces should be invited into the territory which they at present occupy outside these provinces but from which they would withdraw their forces. The Co-Chairmen noted that the territories involved would, under the proposals, remain under the adminstration and control of the Bosnian Serbs, with Serb police remaining.

16. With regard to the governance of Sarajevo, the Bosnian Serb side's initial position was that it should be governed by Muslims and Serbs on a 50-50 basis but that they would accept a capital *opstina* governed on a 3:3:3 basis. They expressed some interest in the idea put forward by the Co-Chairmen that the

Boundary Commission should be asked to consider future arrangements in Sarajevo. They also expressed interest in the idea of a capital city concept for an inner part of Sarajevo to be governed by an Executive Major and an Executive Board.

17. The Bosnian Serb side openly admitted to the Co-Chairmen that as far as they are concerned the independent State of Bosnia and Herzegovina has never existed and does not exist. It did not disguise the fact that it considers that it is being forced by the international community to live within Bosnia and Herzegovina against its wishes. That being the case, it wished to retain as much of its present "Republika Srpska" as possible and to restrict the functions of the central governmental institutions of Bosnia and Herzegovina to a minimum. Notwithstanding the fact that it signed the nine Constitutional Principles on 30 January 1993, it continued to argue for Bosnia and Herzegovina to be divided into what would effectively be three separate states. It takes the view that the Constitutional Principles are relevant only to the drafting of a new constitution and are not applicable for the interim period. Its position, for all practical purposes, amounts to a strategy of continuing its "Republika Srpska" by merging the three provinces in which it would have a majority and which it continues to argue should be contiguous on the map and linked in all aspects of government.

18. In discussing with the Co-Chairmen the laws to be applied in the interim in the three provinces where there is a Serb majority, the Bosnian Serb side insisted on the continuation of what it said were the over 700 acts of legislation adopted by its "Republika Srpska". The Co-Chairmen arranged for their legal advisers to meet to examine this legislation in more detail. Since it is envisaged that there would be freedom for different provincial legislation, provided it was not incompatible with the constitution of Bosnia and Herzegovina, some different legislation in these three provinces might be acceptable in the interim provided it did not conflict with the legislation necessary for Bosnia and Herzegovina as a whole in the interim.

19. As to the structure of central government for the interim, the Bosnian Serb said they were not prepared to accept the case of an Interim President to the Head of State or the need for a Presidency, or even for any form of interim central government. They argued, instead, for a central coordinating body which would have as few functions as possible, involving coordination among the three peoples' interim constituent structures. They were not even prepared to envisage as interim Ministry or Minister for Foreign Affairs. The Co-Chairmen said that such a position was totally incompatible with the Constitutional Principles which they had signed and would have the effect of convincing any fair-minded person that they had no intention of living within the single state of Bosnia and Herzeg-

ovina, not just for the interim, but would obstruct negotiations for a final Constitution compatible with the agreed principles.

20. The Bosnian Serb side did, however, express support for the ideas of the Co-Chairmen - which has been endorsed by the other two sides - that an international human rights monitoring mission should be established in Bosnia and Herzegovina with open access to all provinces. The Bosnian Serbs were not convinced of the case for establishing ombudsmen at the national level and considered that each of the three sides should appoint four ombudsmen for each of the sides' constituent structures. Also, they believed that any Human Rights Court should operate similarly in the three peoples' constituent structures. The Co-Chairmen made it clear that the provinces were separate constitutional entities with their own separate provincial constitutions and parliaments, which could not be emerged into one Parliament.

21. It was clear to the Co-Chairmen that the position of the Bosnian Serbs had hardened appreciably since the Geneva round of negotiations in January on many of the political aspects of an overall settlement.

V. THE BOSNIAN CROATS

22. The Bosnian Croat side has signed all the elements of the peace package put forward by the Co-Chairmen: the Constitutional Principles, the map of provincial boundaries, the military agreement, and the interim arrangements.

23. As it has done in earlier rounds of the peace talks, the Bosnian Croat side, led by Mr. Mate Boban and including Bosnia and Herzegovina Prime Minister Mile Admadzic, continued to support the peace package and to urge the other two sides to sign the comprehensive peace package - so that implementation could begin as soon as possible and the war be brought to an end.

24. With regard to the suggestion by the Bosnian Government delegation that the existing Parliament should be reconvened, the Bosnian Croat delegation refused because it maintained that the Parliament has been an extremely divisive institution which had, in its view been one of the principal causes for the outbreak of the conflict. They also maintained that the three constituent peoples represented in the interim Presidency had to be in overall control, though the main executive functions could be carried out by the Interim Government, albeit with many of its functions removed in view of the increased powers to be exercised by the provinces during the interim.

VI. Assessment

25. The Co-Chairmen considered that the Interim arrangements paper (annex I) should now form part of the package alongside the Constitutional Principles (annex II), the map (annex III) and the military agreement (annex IV) and put this package for final signature to the three sides at a plenary meeting held on 25 March 1993 as representing a fair compromise among complex and conflicting demands.

26. At the final plenary meeting of this round of the peace talks, on 25 March 1993, the Co-Chairmen urged all three sides to build upon the work that had been done and upon the progress made so as to put an end to the conflict, to bring relief to its innocent victims, and to set the country on a new course. The Co-Chairmen particularly urged all three sides to exercise maximum restraint and to do everything possible to ensure respect for the norms of international humanitarian law.

27. In these circumstances, the Co-Chairmen have concluded that the responsible course of action is for them to recommend that any enforcement action of the no-fly zone, or toughening of sanctions, or the placing of United Nations military observers (UNMOs) around the border of Bosnia and Herzegovina, in Croatia and the Federal Republic of Yugoslavia (Serbia and Montenegro), should now be accompanied by the Security Council's unqualified endorsement of the peace package (annexes I-IV).

28. I recommend the early establishment of an International Human Rights Monitoring Mission as described in my previous Report (S/25403), which all three sides have expressly accepted. Pursuant to the recommendation of the Co-Chairmen, discussions are continuing to develop an implementation peace-keeping plan that could, when all three sides have signed the whole package, be endorsed by the Security Council. Furthermore, the Co-Chairmen recommend the establishment of the Boundary Commission mentioned in the previous report of the Secretary-General.

VII. Concluding Observations

29. The moment has arrived for the international community to come to grips with the process that has been conducted by the Co-Chairmen and with the results obtained. After seven months of the most intensive negotiation, 10 out of the 12 signatures required have been obtained. Only one side - the Bosnian Serbs - now lags behind in signature of the provincial map and the agreement on interim arrangements.

30. The Co-Chairmen's peace packages the only mechanism available for the re-establishment of peace, with justice and respect for human rights, in Bosnia and Herzegovina. Final agreement on the peace plan, and its rapid and robust implementation, offer the best prospect for improving the situation in Bosnia and Herzegovina. I strongly urge the Security Council to approve the whole peace package and to call upon the Bosnian Serbs to sign the remaining two parts so that attention may be concentrated henceforth on the implementation of the plan.

Annex I
Agreement on Interim Arrangements[*]

A. INTERIM PRESIDENCY AND INTERIM CENTRAL GOVERNMENT

1. During the interim period between the conclusion of the peace package and the holding of elections under a new Constitution, the Republic of Bosnia and Herzegovina, as well as its Provinces, shall be governed under the prevailing legal system and in accordance with the letter and spirit of the Constitutional Principles agreed and signed by the parties. During this period, in the direct aftermath of hostilities, when a consensus amongst the three constituent peoples is the only acceptable basis for reaching any fundamental decisions, the Interim Presidency and Interim Government shall function on a coalition basis. This arrangement shall not prejudge the provisions to be negotiated for the new Constitution, under which the role of the Presidency and the Government chosen from a democratically elected Parliament is expected to be different and will reflect more accurately the will of the people.[a] Even so, under the Constitutional Principles the Presidency will be bound to have an important role to safeguard the rights of the constituent peoples.

2. During the interim period there shall be a nine-member Interim Presidency, with three representatives from each of the three constituent peoples. The Interim Presidency is to be the highest authority of the State but will not be involved in the day to day detail of government.

3. The nine members of the Interim Presidency shall designate one member to serve as President of the Presidency. The President shall perform the role of head of state. The position of President shall rotate every six months among the

[*] New York, 25 March 1993. Not signed by R. Karadzic, signed by A. Izetbegovic and M. Boban; and, as witnesses, by C.R. Vance and D. Owen.

[a] See S/24795, paras. 52-55 and annex VII, part IV.A.

three constituent peoples in accordance with the sequence of rotation: Muslim, Croat, Serb.

4. The Interim Presidency shall take decisions by consensus of nine, or by a qualified majority of seven, or by a simple majority of five depending on whether the decision relates to a constitutional principle, to a specially important question, or to normal business of the Presidency. If the members of the interim Presidency are unable to agree on the applicable majority, they will consult the Co-Chairmen of the Steering Committee of the International Conference on the Former Yugoslavia, whose decision shall be binding.

5. The Interim Presidency shall appoint a Prime Minister and the following eight Ministers:

    (a) Minister of Foreign Affairs;
    (b) Minister of Finance, with responsibility also for Customs and Excise Duties;
    (c) Minister of Justice and Citizenship;
    (d) Minister of International Commerce;
    (e) Minister of Communications and Transport;
    (f) Minister for Refugee Affairs;
    (g) Minister for Reconstruction;
    (h) Minister for Environmental Protection.

6. Of these nine Ministers, for the interim period each shall be members of each of the three constituent peoples. This arrangement does not set a precedent for the final Constitution to be negotiated, whereunder the Government will be formed following elections and will reflect the view of the electorate. The Prime Minister may not be a member of the same constituent people as the President of the Presidency; the term of office of the Prime Minister shall coincide with that of the President. The Presidency shall also appoint Deputy Ministers, Under-Secretaries and other senior officials in the proportion 4:3:2. No member of the Presidency shall simultaneously serve also as Minister in the Government. Decision on appointments or dismissals shall require a majority of seven members of the Interim Presidency.

7. The Interim Presidency shall also be responsible for determining the role of such ministries as are deemed appropriate, and for establishing the functions and governance of any necessary independent agencies - such as the International Access Authority (see part I below), a National Power Authority, the National Bank, a National Civil Aviation Authority, and a National Post, Telegraph and Telephone Authority - and other aspects of government. The Presidency shall be

responsible for setting policy guidelines and overseeing the work of the Interim Central Government and any other agencies which it might establish, all of which shall be answerable to it.

8. The principal responsibilities of the Interim Presidency and the Interim Central Government shall be:

(a) Preparations for the holding of free and fair elections, on the basis of the new Constitution, under international supervision;

(b) Ensuring respect for human rights, in cooperation with the International Human Rights monitoring Mission (para. H.3 below);

(c) Relations with the International Conference on the Former Yugoslavia (ICFY), the Mixed Military Working Group, the United Nations Protection Force (UNPROFOR) (including the United Nations Civilian Police (UNCIVPOL)), and the European Community Monitoring Mission (ECMM);

(d) Coordination with the Office of the United Nations High Commissioner for Refugees (UNHCR), the International Committee of the Red Cross (ICRC), the World Health Organization (WHO) and other relevant agencies on the return and rehabilitation of refugees and displaced persons;

(e) Foreign affairs (including membership in international organizations);

(f) International commerce;

(g) Citizenship;

(h) In respect of the provincial police:

    (i) provide coordination;

    (ii) assist in technical functions (e/g. crime laboratories); and

    (iii) coordination with international and foreign police authorities;

(i) Raising of any taxes required to carry out its functions.

B. BOUNDARY COMMISSION

A Boundary Commission shall be set up by the Secretary-General in consultation with the Co-Chairmen. The Commission shall receive and, if necessary, hear evidence from those affected by the proposed provisional provincial boundaries and advise on the demarcation of the Provinces to be specified in the new Constitution. The Commission shall consist of five persons: one each to be recommended by the three parties and two, one of whom shall be the Chairman, to be recommended by the Co-Chairmen. The Commission shall use as its basic document the provisional provincial map (appendix A). It shall be empowered to consider the mainly marginal changes to the provisional boundaries. The decisions of the Commission shall be adopted by consensus.

C. SARAJEVO

1. The Capital City of Sarajevo will remain within the enlarged Sarajevo Province and its citizens will be represented in the governing of the Province. The concept of an undivided, open capital city being run by its citizens but with an overall responsibility to the whole country is one that is well understood. The Capital City will consist of the build-up areas of parts of the opstinas Novi Grad, Centar Sarajevo, Novo Sarajevo and Stari Grad. The provincial boundaries are as specified in appendix B but they will be referred to the Boundary Commission for review and any agreed changes will be introduced prior to implementing the new Constitution.
2. There shall be an independent Interim executive Mayor and an Interim Executive Board to be nominated by the parties on the basis of the composition of the population of the Capital City in the 1991 census, provided that none of the three constituent peoples and others are left unrepresented. The Capital City shall be governed under the overall responsibility of the Presidency, but the Presidency shall not interfere with day-to-day management of the Capital City. The Presidency shall be responsible for the quality and character of the Capital City. There can be no changes in the Constitution in the Capital City or its boundaries without the agreement on the Presidency. Within the Capital City important religious buildings shall be considered as inviolable to the same extent as Embassies.
3. Under the new Constitution, the citizens of the Capital City will be represented in the Lower House and Upper House on the same basis as other citizens of Bosnia and Herzegovina in the Province of Sarajevo.

D. INTERIM PROVINCIAL GOVERNMENTS

1. During the interim period, each Province shall have an Interim Provincial Government composed of a Governor, a Vice-Governor, and ten other members, all of whom are to be nominated by the parties, with any representation of others to be decided by the Interim Presidency, on the basis of the composition of the population of the Province (based on the results of the 1991 census), provided that none of the three constituent peoples may be left unrepresented in any Province and that the Governor shall be a member of the most numerous constituent people and the Vice-Governor of the second most numerous. The Interim Presi-

dency shall oversee the establishment of the Interim Provincial Governments.

2. Decisions of the Interim Provincial Governments shall normally be taken by a simple majority, except that the adoption of the Provincial Constitution and the setting of opstina boundaries shall require a consensus.

3. The principal responsibilities of the Interim Provincial Governments shall be:

(a) The drafting of the Provincial Constitutions, which must be in accord with the new Constitution of Bosnia and Herzegovina;

(b) Ensuring respect for human rights, in cooperation with the International Human Rights Monitoring Mission;

(c) Preparation for the holding of free and fair elections, to be held as soon as possible, under the new Constitution of Bosnia and Herzegovina and the applicable Provincial Constitution, on the basis of proportional representation and under international supervision;

(d) Relations with the Mixed Military Working Group, UNPROFOR (including UNCIVPOL), ECMM and ICFY;

(e) Coordination with UNHCR, ICRC, WHO and other relevant agencies on the return and rehabilitation of refugees and displaced persons;

(f) Supervision of the provincial police forces;

(g) Restoration of infrastructure;

(h) Raising of any taxes necessary to carry out their functions.

4. Attached to the staff of each provincial Governor there will be UNPROFOR Military Liaison Officers, as well as an UNCIVPOL Liaison Officer, to assist in the carrying out of the above tasks.

5. The legal system of each Province during the Interim period shall be that now prevailing in its territory, provided that no legal provision at the provincial level may be in conflict with the Interim Arrangements specified herein.

6. Similarly, the present powers of the opstinas shall continue, as shall their boundaries, except as required to conform to the provisional provincial boundaries set out in annex A or when changed by a consensus decision of the Interim Provincial Government.

E. WITHDRAWAL OF FORCES

Sarajevo Province shall be immediately demilitarized. All Serb forces shall withdraw into province 2, 4 and 6; HVO forces into Province 3; Bosnian Army forces into Province 1. Both Bosnian Army and HVO forces shall be deployed in Provinces 5, 8, 9 and 10 under arrangements agreed between them. The process of demilitarization shall apply to all forces in all these nine Provinces, and shall be carried out under the supervision of UNPROFOR and in accordance with the detailed arrangements and timetables in the agreement for Peace in Bosnia and Herzegovina, or as negotiated in the Mixed Military Working Group.

F. INTERNATIONAL BORDERS

International border crossing points initially are to be controlled by UNPROFOR. The question of policing the borders shall be further discussed on the content of the new Constitution. The Interim Presidency and the Interim Central Government, through the Ministry of Finance, shall be responsible for customs and excise arrangements, and shall have the normal powers to stop, search, detain and bring prosecutions to enforce these arrangements.

G. POLICE FORCES

During the interim period, all police forces shall conform to the proposals made by the Co-Chairmen in respect of the constitutional structure.[b] Therefore, all uniformed police shall be controlled by the Interim Provincial Government or by local authorities under them, and shall reflect the proportions of the constituent peoples in the respective Provinces. At the national level there shall be no uniformed, armed police, but only a coordinating office in the Ministry of Justice to assist the provincial police authorities and to maintain contacts with international and foreign police authorities (e.g., Interpol).

H. PROTECTION OF HUMAN RIGHTS AND THE REVERSAL OF ETHNIC CLEANSING

1. During the interim period, all persons in Bosnia and Herzegovina shall be entitled to all rights provided for in the existing Constitution and in applicable legislation in force, as well as to all rights provided for in specified international instruments on human rights (set out in appendix C). To the extent that there are any discrepancies, the provision providing the greater protection of human rights shall be applied. All statements or commitments made under duress, particularly those related to the relinquishment of rights to land or property, should be

---

[b]   See S/24795, annex VII, part V.B.

treated as wholly null and void.

2. The implementation of the above-mentioned human rights shall be ensured through:

(a) The national and provincial courts of Bosnia and Herzegovina, to which all persons shall have unimpeded access;

(b) An Interim Human Rights Court for Bosnia and Herzegovina, to be established immediately along the lines of that proposed by the Co-Chairmen for inclusion in the new Constitution;[c] and

(c) The immediate appointment of four Ombudsmen, supported by adequate staff and facilities.[d]

3. In addition, there shall be an International Human Rights Minority Mission, to be established by the Secretary-General and to be headed by an Interim Human Rights Commissioner for Bosnia and Herzegovina, to be based in Sarajevo. Deputy Commissioners are to be based in various parts of the country. The Commissioner is to be supported by international human rights monitors, deployed throughout the country and particularly in areas affected by "ethnic cleansing". They shall be permitted to observe the situation of human rights throughout Bosnia and Herzegovina; in order to provide protection in urgent cases they shall be allowed to intercede with the interim Presidency, the Interim central Government and the Interim Provincial Governments and with UNPROFOR; they may refer issues to the Ombudsmen and to other human rights agencies as needed, and are to work closely with UNHCR, ICRC and other humanitarian agencies. The Commissioner is expected to submit regular reports to the Secretary-General who is to report periodically to the Security Council and to other international bodies, including the United Nations Commission on Human Rights and its Special Rapporteur.

4. The interim Presidency, the Interim Central Government and the Interim Provincial Governments shall be required to give the fullest access, in respect of all relevant persons and places, to he Interim Human Rights Commissioner, the Deputy Commissioners and the human rights monitors, as well as to UNHCR, ICRC and other international humanitarian organizations.

5. It is understood that as part of the UNPROFOR deployment in Bosnia and Herzegovina there will be a large UNCIVPOL element whose principal task would be to monitor the police of the Provinces so that each: has an appropriate-

---

[c]   Ibid., part VI.B.3.

[d]   Ibid., part VI.B.2.

ly balanced ethnic composition; does not oppress members of minority ethnic groups; contributes positively to the reversal of "ethnic cleansing" by protecting persons returning after having been forced to flee; carries out the judgements of courts, in particular the Human Rights Court; and assist the Interim Human Rights Commissioner, the Deputy Commissioners and the human rights monitors (para. H.3 above).

I. INTERNATIONAL ACCESS AUTHORITY

1. Principle 3 of the agreed Constitutional Principles states that "full freedom of movement shall be allowed throughout Bosnia and Herzegovina, to be ensured in part by the maintenance of internationally controlled throughways". In order to implement this principle, the Interim Presidency shall establish an International Access Authority to:

    (a)   Have the sole responsibility for all railway lines in Bosnia and Herzegovina;

    (b)   Have responsibility, in cooperation with UNPROFOR, for these roads which are declared to be internationally controlled throughways, as specified in appendix D;

    (c)   Regulate the operation of port facilities on the River Sava.

2. The essential purpose of the International Access Authority will be to guarantee full freedom of movement between and within the provinces and also to and from the Provinces to the Republic of Croatia and the Republic of Serbia. It is intended that the authority be in operation as soon as possible during the interim period. Following the conclusions of the peace package, all designated throughways shall come under the responsibility of UNPROFOR; thereafter there will be a period of overlapping responsibility of UNPROFOR and the Authority, during which UNPROFOR's involvement will be phased out and its responsibilities assumed by traffic police employed by the Authority. This transfer of responsibility requires the agreement of all members of the Authority.

3. The Interim Presidency and each of the Interim Provincial Governments shall appoint one representative to the Interim Access Authority.

4. The Authority shall enter into force on signature by all three parties and the adoption by the Security Council of a resolution providing for implementation of the peace package.

APPENDIX A

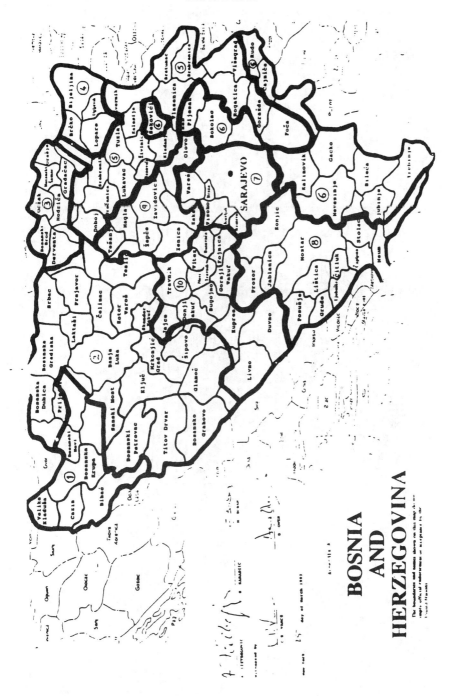

BOSNIA
AND
HERZEGOVINA

APPENDIX B

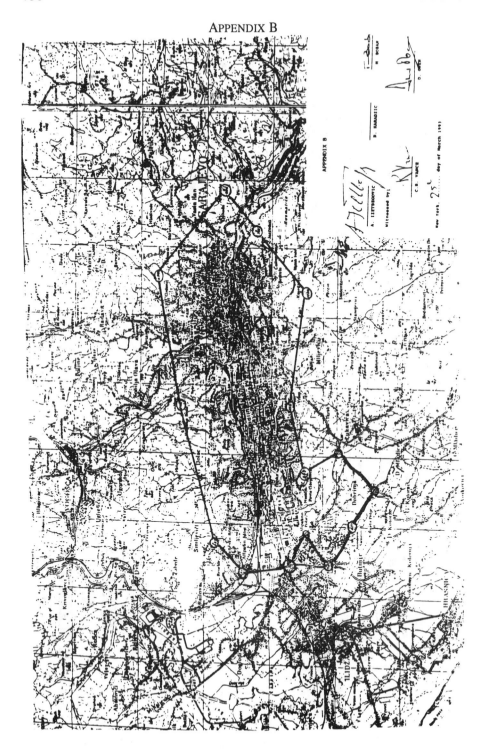

APPENDIX C

INTERNATIONAL HUMAN RIGHTS TREATIES AND OTHER INSTRUMENTS TO BE
APPLIED IN BOSNIA AND HERZEGOVINA DURING THE INTERIM PERIOD

A. General Human Rights, especially Civil and Political Rights

1. 1948 Convention on the Prevention and Punishment of the Crime of Genocide;
2. 1948 Universal Declaration of Human Rights, Articles 1-21;
3. 1966 International Covenant on Civil and Political Rights and its 1966 and 1989 Optional Protocols;
4. 1965 International Convention on the Elimination of All Forms of Racial Discrimination;
5. 1979 International Convention on the Elimination of All Forms of Discrimination against Women;
6. 1989 Convention on the Rights of the Child;
7. 1984 Convention against Torture and Other Cruel, Inhuman or Degrading Treatment or Punishment;
8. 1951 Convention relating the status of Refugees and the 1966 Protocol thereto;
9. 1950 European Convention for the Protection of Human Rights and Fundamental Freedoms, and Protocols 1-10 thereto;
10. 1987 European Convention on the Prevention of Torture and Inhuman or Degrading Treatment or Punishment.

B. Protection of Minorities

11. 1992 draft Declaration on the rights of persons belonging to national, ethnic, religious and linguistic minorities;
12. 1990 C/E Parliamentary Assembly Recommendation 1134 (1990) on the rights of minorities.

C. Economic, Social and Cultural Rights

13. 1948 Universal Declaration of Human Rights, Articles 22-27;
14. 1966 International Covenant on Economic, Social and Cultural Rights;
15. 1961 European Social Charter and the Protocol 1 thereto.

D. Citizenship and Nationality

16. 1957 Convention on the Nationality of Married Women;
17. 1961 Convention on the Reduction of Statelessness.

APPENDIX D

THROUGHWAYS TO BE CONTROLLED BY THE
INTERNATIONAL ACCESS AUTHORITY

- that part of the road from Bihac to Livno that passes through Banja Luka Province;
- that part of the road from Bihac to Jajce that passes through Banja Luka Province;
- that part of the road from Banja Luka to Brcko that passes through Posavina Province;
- those parts of the roads from Tuzla to Orasje and from Tuzla to Brcko that pass through Posavina and Bijeljina Provinces;
- those parts of the roads from Han Pijesak to Sekovici and from Sekovici to Zvornik that pass through Tuzla Province;
- that part of the road from Pale to Kalinovik that passes through Sarajevo Province;
- that part of the road from Foca to Sarajevo that passes through East Herzegovina Province;
- the road from Sarajevo to Mostar and to the Croatian border towards Split;
- that part of the road from Ljubinja to Neum that passes through Mostar Province;
- the road from Sarajevo through Orlovo to Tuzla;
- the road from Gorazde, through Cajnice, to the border.

International road border crossings affecting the International Access Authority:

- Bihac Province - Velika Kladusa, towards Karlovac and Zagreb;
- Banja Luka Province - Bosanski Gradisja, towards Zagreb-Belgrade autoroute;
- Posavina Province - Orasje, towards Zagreb-Belgrade autoroute;
- Bijeljina Province - Sremska Race, towards Zagreb-Belgrade autoroute;
- Tuzla Province - Zvornik, towards Zagreb-Belgrade autoroute;
- Mostar Province - Osoje, towards Split.

Annex II
Agreement Relating to Bosnia and Herzegovina[*]

THE UNDERSIGNED,

Guided by the principles of the Charter of the United Nations, the Universal Declaration of Human Rights[a] and the Declaration on the Rights of Persons belonging National or Ethnic, Religious and Linguistic Minorities,[b]

Recalling the Statement of Principles and the Statement on Bosnia adopted by the International Conference on the Former Yugoslavia at its session in London and the Programme of Action on Humanitarian Issues agreed to at that session,

Considering the decisions of the United Nations Security Council relating to the former Yugoslavia,

Reaffirming their commitment to peace and security among the successor States to the former Yugoslavia,

Hereby agree as follows:

I. CONSTITUTIONAL FRAMEWORK FOR BOSNIA AND HERZEGOVINA

Tripartite negotiations shall proceed on a continuous basis in Geneva, under the auspices of the International Conference in the Former Yugoslavia, in order to finalise a Constitution for Bosnia and Herzegovina in accordance with the following principles:

(1) Bosnia and Herzegovina shall be a decentralized State, the Constitution shall recognize three constituent peoples, as well as a group of others, with most governmental functions carried out by its provinces.

(2) The provinces shall not have any international legal personality and may not enter into agreements with foreign States or with international organizations.

(3) Full freedom of movement shall be allowed throughout Bosnia and Herzegovina, to be ensured in part by the maintenance of internationally controlled throughways.

---

[*] Previously reproduced in S/25403, annex I. Geneva, 30 January 1993. Signed by A. Izetbegovic, R. Karadzic, and M. Boban; and, as witnesses, by C.R. Vance and D. Owen.

[a] General Assembly resolution 217 A (III).

[b] General Assembly resolution 47/135.

(4) All matters of vital concern to any of the constituent peoples shall be regulated in the Constitution, which as to these points may be amended only by consensus of these constituent peoples; ordinary governmental business is not to be veto-able by any group.

(5) The provinces and the central Government shall have democratically elected legislature and democratically chosen chief executives and an independent judiciary. The Presidency shall be composed of three elected representatives of each of the three constituent peoples. The initial elections are to be United Nations/European Community/Conference on Security and Cooperation in Europe supervised.

(6) A Constitutional Court, with a member from each group and a majority of non-Bosnian members initially appointed by the International Conference on the Former Yugoslavia, shall resolve disputes between the central Government and any province, and among organs of the former.

(7) Bosnia and Herzegovina is to be progressively demilitarized under United Nations/European Community supervision.

(8) The highest level of internationally recognized human rights shall be provided for in the Constitution, which shall also provide for the ensurance of implementation through both domestic and international mechanisms.

(9) A number of international monitoring or control devices shall be provided for in the Constitution, to remain in place at least until the three constituent peoples by consensus agree to dispense with them.

II. COOPERATION IN RESPECT OF HUMANITARIAN EFFORTS

1. Maximum cooperation shall be extended to the High Commission for Refugees, the International Committee of the Red Cross, the United Nations Protection Force, the European Community Monitoring Mission and other humanitarian organizations working to provide assistance to refugees and displaced persons.

2. Full cooperation shall also be extended to the High Commissioner for Refugees in drawing up and implementing programmes for the return of refugees and displaced persons to their homes.

Annex III

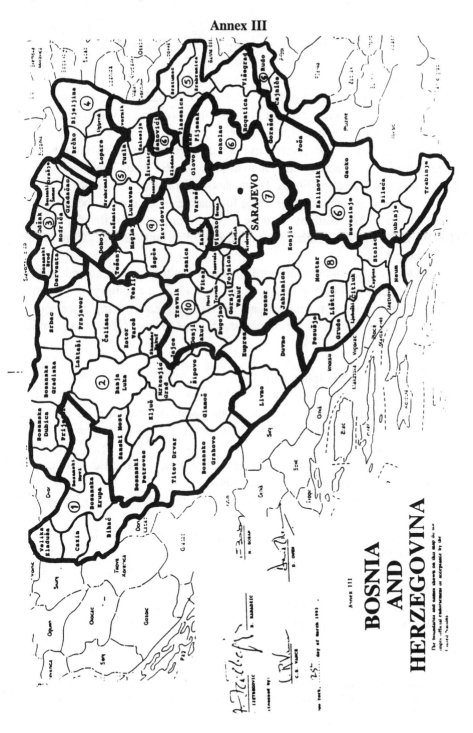

BOSNIA
AND
HERZEGOVINA

The boundaries and names shown on this map do not
imply official endorsement or acceptance by the
United Nations.

Annex IV
Agreement for Peace in Bosnia and Herzegovina[*]

THE UNDERSIGNED,

Welcoming the invitation of the Co-Chairmen of the Steering Committee of the International Conference on the Former Yugoslavia to participate in talks for the restoration of peace in Bosnia and Herzegovina,

Taking account of the constructive atmosphere of the peace talks held in Geneva from 2 to 5 January and the assistance of the Force Commander of the United Nations Protection Force, Lieutenant-General Satish Nambiar,

Keeping in mind the principles of the International Conference and the Resolutions of the United Nations Security Council, in particular Resolutions 752 (1992) and 787 (1992) pertaining to withdrawal of all outside forces from Bosnia and Herzegovina,

Wishing to bring the conflict in Bosnia and Herzegovina to an end without any further delay and to re-establish peace throughout the country,

Desiring to work out arrangements for bringing about compliance with a cessation of hostilities, and for monitoring it so as to ensure that it is effective and lasting,

Hereby agree on the following:

1. Measures for the achievement of an unconditional cessation of hostilities throughout Bosnia and Herzegovina, as set out in Annex I to the present agreement;
2. Measures for the restoration of infrastructure in Bosnia and Herzegovina, as set out in annex II to the present agreement;
3. Measures on the opening of routes, as set out in annex IV to the present agreement;
4. Arrangements on the separation of forces, as set out in annex IV to the present agreement;
5. Measures for the demilitarization of Sarajevo, as set out in annex V to the present agreement;
6. Measures for the monitoring of the borders of Bosnia and Herzegovina, as set out in annex VI to the present agreement;

---

[*] Previously reproduced in S/25403, annex III. Geneva, 30 January 1993. Not signed by A. Izetbegovic, signed R. Karadzic and M. Boban; and, as witnesses, by C.R. Vance and D. Owen.

7. Return of forces to the designated provinces, as set out in annex VII to the present agreement.

ANNEX I: CESSATION OF HOSTILITIES

Broad Principles

All parties agree to support the broad principles required to support a cessation of hostilities. These broad principles will be translated into concrete action through additional discussion within the Mixed Military Working Group. Several of the principles will be dealt with on a stand-alone basis, although they remain an integral part of the overall framework of the cessation of hostilities.

The broad principles are:

- A ceasefire must be put in place and remain effective. This is to be implemented 72 hours from midnight (New York time - EST) of the day on which the Security Council endorses this plan.
- Monitoring and control measures are to be put in place to ensure compliance and should include as a minimum:
  - Links between Commanders in conflict areas (hot lines);
  - Provision of United Nations Protection Force/European Community Monitoring Mission liaison and monitors;
  - Establishment of joint crisis management teams;
  - Opening of confrontation line crossing-points. For use by the United Nations Protection Force and monitoring agencies.
- The separation of forces is to be achieved.
- Routes supporting the general freedom of movement of people, commerce and humanitarian aid are to be opened.
- The restoration of infrastructure will proceed as a priority. Restoration will not be linked to any negotiations.

Essential Elements

- Security Council endorses the plan - initiates all follow-on action (D-3). The 72 hours permit passage of information;
- Cessation of hostilities effective (D-Day);
- Declaration of forces - this is to take place in D-1 and should include:
  - Numbers and locations of all heavy weapons,
  - Detailed documentation of mine fields,

  - Locations of front lines (traces),
  - Defensive works and positions;
- Establish demarcation line (joint actively);
- Move in United Nations Protection Force forces to establish security (commencing D+1):
  - Monitor lines of conflict,
  - Monitor heavy weapons,
  - Reporting system (all parties);
- Withdrawal of heavy weapons:
  - Of calibre 12.7 mm and above; 5 days for Sarajevo and 15 days for remaining areas,
  - Locations to be determined based on effective ranges of weapon systems,
  - All such withdrawals will be supervised by the United Nations Protection Force and subsequently monitored at the designated locations by the United Nations Protection Force in order to prevent their use.
- Separation of forces:
  - Abandon defensive works on confrontation line,
  - Area of separation to be agreed,
  - Distance in which no forces, except police, allowed,
  - Distance within which no defensive works will be manned.
- The separation of forces and withdrawal of heavy weapons are linked.
- Mixed Military Commission is established to deal with any clarifications and breaches of the cessation of hostilities.

ANNEX II: RESTORATION OF INFRASTRUCTURE

All parties agree that denial or use of civil utilities as a weapon of war is unacceptable, and all affirm their commitment to the full restoration of the civil infrastructure across Bosnia and Herzegovina, and in particular, Sarajevo.

The provision of humanitarian aid cannot be linked in any way with the military steps of the process of demilitarization or cessation of hostilities. Being humanitarian in nature, its priority is strictly governed by the ability of all three parties to support its implementation.

Restoration will be the first priority. Therefore, immediate efforts must be placed on the restoration of infrastructure. This is equally applicable to the city of Sarajevo as well as the rest of Bosnia and Herzegovina. It includes where applicable:

- Power grids;
- Power stations;
- Bridges;
- Gas;
- Telecommunications;
- Railway lines;
- Routes;
- Water supply.

Guarantees of security will be requested and must be provided and the restoration of power/water/heat will be fully supported by the warring parties.

A joint committee is already in place in Sarajevo; the work of this committee is to be facilitated with immediate effect to enable early restoration of utilities in Sarajevo.

Assistance will be provided through all the appropriated agencies, including United Nations and civilian expertise. However, within Bosnia and Herzegovina, a joint commission composed of representatives of all sides is to identify the priorities, define the needs and execute the work in conjunction with civil authorities. To this end, vital installations will be identified in conjunction with Bosnia and Herzegovina joint commission:

- Access will be guaranteed after local arrangements are made.
- Forces will be withdrawn from sites consistent with security.
- Warring parties will provide, when necessary, liaison for the repair teams.
- Civil agencies/workers will be assisted.

Parties will work to re-establish infrastructure, including railways/power grids/water supplies, across borders with neighbouring republics.

Respect for infrastructure facilities must be developed and they must remain free from attack or use as defensive positions.

All parties agree to develop a common instruction for passage down chains of command to demonstrate an equal endorsement of support.

ANNEX III: OPENING OF ROUTES

The opening of routes is directly related to the political issue which concerns the freedom of movement of all people in the context of constitutional principles. It is equally applicable to Sarajevo as well as all other areas of Bosnia and Herzegovina.

It is to be achieved through:

- Security guarantees by all parties to ensure non-interference and protection of personnel and material using the routes;
- Non-interference on the route;
- Checkpoints, patrols, and monitoring by United Nations Protection Force/European Community Monitoring Mission, as appropriate;
- Supervised inspection at entry points;
- Freedom of passage of humanitarian aid;
- Absolute freedom of movement of United Nations forces.

The concept of blue routes for Sarajevo is appended hereto. This format is applicable for the establishment of all other similar types of routes within Bosnia and Herzegovina. Additional routes can be negotiated under the aegis of the Mixed Military Working Group.

APPENDIX: SARAJEVO "BLUE ROUTE" CONCEPT

The parties have decided to establish three free passage routes with mutually agreed measures to guarantee and ensure safe passage for freedom of movement of civilians, commercial goods and humanitarian aid to and from Sarajevo.
These routes are:

- Sarajevo-Zenica-Sarajevo;
- Sarajevo-Mostar-Sarajevo;
- Sarajevo-Zvornik-Sarajevo.

Outline Plan for Blue Routes

1. Execution
1.1 Prerequisites

The following prerequisites are to be required:

1.1.1 Cessation of hostilities.

1.1.2 Complete freedom of movement for United Nations Protection Force on the three blue routes.

1.2 Use of the blue routes

1.2.1 Timings

Routes will be open during daylight hours for convoys. United Nations Protection Force will use the route 24 hours a day.

1.2.2 Access for Civilians

All civilians, regardless of sex, age, or ethnic origin, and without weapons or ammunition, will be allowed to use the routes. Private and commercial vehicles will also be permitted on each route subject to inspection outlined on paragraph 1.5.1 below.

1.2.3 Access for Humanitarian Aid

All international and local humanitarian aid agencies will be allowed to use the routes. Humanitarian aid includes, but is not limited to, food, water, medical supplies and fuel.

1.2.4 Access for Commercial Goods

Normal commerce will be progressively restored to and from Sarajevo.

1.3 Establishment of Routes

1.3.1 Sarajevo-Zenica-Sarajevo

This route incorporates Sarajevo-Rajlovac-Ilijas-Visoko-Zenica.

1.3.2 Sarajevo-Mostar-Sarajevo

This route incorporates Sarajevo-Ilidza-Hadzici-Tarcin-Jablanica-Mostar.

1.3.3 Sarajevo-Zvornik-Sarajevo

This route incorporates Sarajevo-Bentbasa-Mokro-Sololac-Vlasenica-Zvornik.

1.4 Checkpoints

Checkpoints will be established and manned by United Nations Protection Force forces at the entrance and exit of each route and when crossing a line of confrontation. Each United Nations Protection Force checkpoint will be located near or with the checkpoint of the force controlling the territory involved consistent with the security requirements of the factions. No side will be permitted to erect a new checkpoint.

1.5 Control Measures

1.5.1 Inspection Procedures

  (a) Inspections will be conducted by United Nations Protection Force forces. Each side is permitted to monitor the events in close coordination with the United Nations Protection Force.
  (b) War-related material, weapons or ammunition are forbidden. If found, the items will be confiscated and subsequently destroyed under control of the United Nations Protection Force and the parties.
  (c) Humanitarian aid convoys may be subjected to inspections.
  (d) Checkpoints will be activated only during daylight hours as a safety measure for civilians and convoys.

1.5.2 Escorts

  (a) Each convoy will be escorted with the appropriate United Nations Protection Force vehicles.
  (b) Convoys and escorts will take priority over military activities.
  (c) The army controlling the territory involved may provide civilian police as an additional means of security.

1.5.3 Patrols

  (a) United Nations Protection Force forces will patrol the blue routes as necessary.
  (b) Patrols will consists of at least two vehicles suitably equipped and will contain an appropriate communications net.
  (c) All United Nations Protection Force patrols will be permitted to cross all checkpoints.

1.6 Implementation

1.6.1 Suggested Timeframe

D-3   - Security Council endorses the plan
D+1 - Erecting checkpoints
      - Inspection procedures agreed
      - Routes cleared of all obstacles
      - Repairs carried out as required
      - Reconnoitre by the United Nations Protection Force
D+5 - Opening of blue routes for civilians and humanitarian aid

ANNEX IV: SEPARATION OF FORCES

The parties agree that the separation of forces is an element of the overall cessation of hostilities. An agreement will be based on the steps and control measures and sequence of events outlined below:

Steps

The concrete steps envisaged in the process include:

- An absolute ceasefire.
- Temporary freezing of the military situation, pending agreement in return of forces to designated provinces.
- No forward deployments or offensive action.
- No move of additional forces, explosives and weapons forward will be permitted. Rotation on an individual basis is acceptable.
- Withdrawal of heavy weapons (direct and indirect fire) of all parties from areas of confrontation to areas of range, decided upon by the parties in conjunction with the United Nations Protection Force.
- Physical separation of forces in contact.
- Security and monitoring of the demilitarized zone.

Control Measures

The control measures required include:

- Declaration of forces in being, including location of minefields.
- Monitoring of front lines.
- Declaration of heavy weapons in separation areas.
- Establishing agreed lines in which forces may be located.
- Staged withdrawal of forces culminating in their relocation to designated provinces.

Sequence of Events

- Ceasefire under aegis of the overall cessation of hostilities.
- Establishment and patrol of the demarcation line by United Nations Protection Force personnel.
- Withdrawal of designated weapons systems of all parties.
- Search and clearance of the affected area by joint patrols.
- Conduct of joint and United Nations-only patrols within the area. Composition of the patrols to be negotiated at the Mixed Military Working Group.

UNPROFOR Concept for Heavy Weapons Control

- All heavy weapons 12.7 mm calibre and above are included.
- These weapons will be withdrawn out of effective range to areas decided between the United Nations Protection Force and the parties.
- The withdrawal will be monitored by the United Nations Protection Force.
- Once in location the weapons will be monitored to ensure that they are not used.
- The United Nations Protection Force will not physically take over the weapons.
- Where terrain such as towns preclude moving weapons out of range, they will be gathered in agreed location under United Nations Protection Force control to ensure that they are not used.

ANNEX V: DEMILITARIZATION OF SARAJEVO

The demilitarization of Sarajevo is based on one requirement: an effective cessation of hostilities.

The other elements are:

- Establishment of control on an designated line;
- Restoration of civil utilities;
- Land routes and freedom of movement;
- Separation of forces along lines of confrontation.

Control measures include:

- Patrol and monitoring of the demarcation line;
- Checkpoints at major crossings until confidence is restored;
- Mixed patrols in the demilitarized zone.

A military/civil joint commission as previously proposed should oversee the implementation of the accord.

Appended hereto is a draft agreement covering first stage of a potential agreement on the demilitarization of Sarajevo. This stage covers the airport area as already discussed at the Mixed Military Working Group.

APPENDIX: PROPOSED AGREEMENT ON THE FIRST STAGE OF DEMILITARIZATION OF SARAJEVO

The authorized representatives of all three conflicting sides with the presence of the United Nations Protection Force representative agree on the implementation of an area in the western and southern districts of Sarajevo.

Cessation of Hostilities

The cessation of hostilities will be implemented as follows:

(a) The freezing of the military situation on the existing lines.
(b) No offensive action allowed.
(c) No forward redeployments.
(d) All heavy weapons will be withdrawn from positions from which they can engage.
(e) No movement or any additional forces although rotation of personnel on a one-for-one basis shall be permitted.
(f) No movement or resupply of ammunitions, explosives or incendiary devices.

Freedom of movement for all civilians

The agreement on blue routes will re-establish the freedom of movement of all civilians in support of this plan.

Restoration of civil utilities

A Joint Commission composed of representatives from each side will identify priorities, define needs and execute the implementation of civil utilities. Details can be found in annex II, Restoration of infrastructure.

Removal of heavy weapons

(a) *Area*. All heavy weapons will be withdrawn to designated locations from the following: Mojmilo, Dobrinja, Lukavica, Gornji, Kotorac, Vojkovici, Hrasnica, Sokolovici, Butmir, Ilidza, Otes, Stup, Nedarici.
(b) *Joint Commission*. A Joint Commission will be created.

  (1) The mission of this Joint Commission will be to execute and implement details of this plan and subsequent phases.
  (2) This Joint Commission will be composed of:

    (a) A United Nations Protection Force command and support element;
    (b) A team of each side commanded by an officer senior enough to make decisions and designated as the authorised commander for the troops in the areas affected;
    (c) A joint communications system which includes a command set and the necessary guaranteed communications link to each individual headquarters.

(c) *Time-frame*. From each district the withdrawal of heavy weapons out of the designated area will be carried out in two stages within a period of five days:

  (1) Stage 1 - Withdrawal of all direct fire weapons of 12.7 mm calibre and above (tanks, armoured personnel carriers, anti-tank, anti-aircraft and heavy machine guns).
  (2) Stage 2 - Withdrawal of all heavy indirect fire weapons (mortars, field artillery).

(d) *Control measures*. The following implementation and control measures will be used:

(1) United Nations Protection Force forces will patrol the area of separation between the conflicting sides.

(2) United Nations Protection Force forces will be deployed on the confrontation lines and in agreed mixed checkpoints proposed by the Joint Commission.

(3) All parties are to identify weapons by type and location and will provide the United Nations Protection Force with detailed maps of areas considered to be under their respective control.

(4) Complete freedom of movement for all United Nations Protection Force personnel and vehicles within the affected areas.

(5) The Joint Commission will establish mixed patrols as appropriate.

ANNEX VI: MONITORING OF BORDERS

Pursuant to United Nations Security Council resolution 787 (1992), Paragraph 5, to prevent interference from outside the Republic of Bosnia and Herzegovina, the United Nations Protection Force/European Community Monitoring Mission will monitor borders with neighbouring republics.

Principles

- United Nations Protection Force/European Monitoring Mission forces will monitor crossings to prevent weapons, munitions, military personnel or irregular forces from entering the country.
- Borders with adjoining republics will be monitored.
- United Nations Protection Force actions to observe, search and report will be facilitated by the authorities of the Republic of Croatia and the Federal Republic of Yugoslavia.

ANNEX VII: RETURN OF FORCES TO DESIGNATED PROVINCES

To enable the process of return to normalcy, and as a direct follow-on from the cessation of hostilities and the separation of forces, a return of forces to designated provinces will be conducted. This can start as part of the withdrawal of heavy weapons but, given the winter weather conditions, it is hard to fix a definite date for the completion of this process. We should however aim to achieve the return of forces within 45 days.

This stage will be coordinated with an agreed demobilization of forces in being.

The United Nations Protection Force/European Community Monitoring Mission will monitor the withdrawal of these forces in conjunction with national and provincial authorities.

The Mixed Military Working Group would be the technical negotiating agency.

Annex V
Statement of the Republic of Bosnia and Herzegovina[*]

By signing the Vance-Owen Plan for the Republic of Bosnia and Herzegovina (the nine principles, the military agreement, the maps of the proposed provinces and the document in the interim period) the State delegation of the Republic of Bosnia and Herzegovina states the following:

1. Regardless of the fact whether or not all parties will sign the documents today, the Delegation of Bosnia and Herzegovina considers that the International Community was and will remain obligated to protect the independence and the territorial integrity of Bosnia and Herzegovina as an attacked country, in accordance with the Charter of the United Nations, International Law, decisions of the London Conference, and especially according to all relevant resolutions of the United Nations Security Council concerning the aggression against Bosnia and Herzegovina.

2. Our signatures on the proposed documents will become invalid and will be considered null and void if the following conditions are not met:

   a) All interested parties, especially the aggressor side does not sign the documents without any alterations or reservations within a reasonable time frame.
   b) The International Community does not undertake, within a timely fashion the effective measures of implementation of the signed agreement, to the degree and in the manner which the situation will impose.
   c) If the aggression continues.

[*] See UN Doc. A/47/913-S/25474. New York, 25 March 1993. For the delegation for the Government of the Republic of Bosnia and Herzegovina, signed by Alija Izetbegovic, President of the Republic of Bosnia and Herzegovina.

3. Any provisions of the signed documents cannot be interpreted and not be understood as the diminishing integrity and sovereignty of the Republic of Bosnia and Herzegovina as an independent and undivided whole State. On the contrary, the signed agreement must be understood and can only be interpreted as the means and way to protect and strengthen that integrity.

4. It is understood that individuals declared as war criminals, or for whom there is a grounded suspicion that they were instigators or organizers or executors of war crimes on the territory of Bosnia and Herzegovina, will not and cannot be nominated for the highest positions of authority of the State, both in the Interim Presidency and Interim Government.

5. The Delegation of the Government of the Republic of Bosnia and Herzegovina asks the international community and the UN Security Council to continue with the intention of successfully completing the establishment of the Court for War Crimes committed on the territory of Bosnia and Herzegovina and the former Yugoslavia.

6. Upon the signing of today's documents, the Delegation of Bosnia and Herzegovina expresses that the aggression and its consequences be stopped and reversed with peaceful means, but at the same time the Delegation will not surrender its legitimate right to self defence in accordance with Article 51 of the UN Charter.

In this regard, if the peace efforts remain without results, the Presidency and the Government will undertake all necessary measures to defend its people, and in that case, expect the Security Council without further delay to lift the arms embargo on Bosnia and Herzegovina.

7. The Delegation of Bosnia and Herzegovina expresses its appreciation to the United States of America and to its special envoy to these talks Ambassador Reginald Bartholomew, for the constructive contributions in overcoming the difficulties which arose during the course of these talks.

8. We are issuing this statement concurrent with the signing of today's documents and are handing it over to the International Conference on the Former Yugoslavia with the request that it be included and attached with the official documents of the Conference.

118. Report of the Secretary-General on the International Conference on the Former Yugoslavia: Recent Activities of the Working Groups[*]

Introduction

1. In recent reports submitted to the Security Council, I informed the Council about developments in the peace talks on Bosnia and Herzegovina being conducted by the Co-Chairmen of the Steering Committee of the International Conference on the Former Yugoslavia (S/25050, S/25221, S/25403).

2. In two earlier reports, I had informed the Council about other activities undertaken within the framework of the International Conference (S/24795 of 11 November 1992 and S/25015 of 24 December 1992). The present report provides information on the activities of the Working Group of the Conference since the beginning of 1993.

I. Working Group on Bosnia and Herzegovina

3. The activities with regard to the situation in Bosnia and Herzegovina have been dealt with in my recent reports to the Council (S/25050, S/25221, S/25248 and S/25403).

II. Working Group on Humanitarian Issues

4. The Working Group on Humanitarian issues, chaired by Mrs. S. Ogata, the United Nations High Commissioner for Refugees, has continued to address the plight of refugees, displaced persons and other victims of conflict. As humanitarian lead agency in the former Yugoslavia, UNHCR maintains intensive contacts with all relevant counterparts in the region. Contacts at the governmental level take place through Mrs. Ogata's Special Representative, who travels to the various capitals on a regular basis, and through her Chiefs of Mission in those capitals. These contacts are complemented and supported by official sessions of the Working Group at Geneva and in the field, as required. The Working Group has proven to be a useful forum for negotiations with the Bosnian parties.

5. On 11 January 1993, Mrs. Ogata addressed a plenary session of the peace talks on Bosnia and Herzegovina, attended by the Bosnian parties and by the

---

[*] UN Doc. S/25490, 30 March 1993.

Presidents of Croatia, the Federal Republic of Yugoslavia (Serbia and Montenegro), Serbia and Montenegro. From 24 to 27 January, she visited Zagreb, Belgrade and Sarajevo to meet with President Cosic, Milosevic and Tudjman, with the Bosnian leadership, and with Generals Nambiar and Morillon of the United Nations Protection Force (UNPROFOR). Upon returning to Geneva, she held separate working group sessions with President Izetbegovic, the Bosnian Croats (Mr. Boban) and the Bosnian Serbs (Dr. Karadzic).

6. Regarding Bosnia and Herzegovina, many of these contacts have concentrated on the need for unimpeded humanitarian access to all victims of conflict. During the period under review, the relief effort has been severely jeopardized. Harassment and endless delays at check-points have become daily occurrences. Fighting between Bosnian Croat and government forces was a serious set-back for the relief operation in central Bosnia, which accommodates the majority of displaced persons. UNHCR had to temporarily withdraw its staff from the Serbian-held Banja Luke regions because of security threats. Access to the government-held Bihac region was temporarily blocked by local Serb authorities in the Krajina region in Croatia, after fighting broke out in the pink zone adjacent to UNPA South. On 2 February, operations on the crucial Mostar road had to be suspended, after the killing of a UNHCR driver. On several occasions the airlift to Sarajevo had to be suspended due to security incidents, e.g., in 6 February, after a German plane was hit by anti-aircraft artillery. Most serious has been the denial of access to government-held enclaves in eastern Bosnia, inducing the Bosnian Government on 12 February to refuse further acceptance of humanitarian assistance in Sarajevo and Tuzla. After a new partial suspension, UNHCR and UNPROFOR managed to gain access to some of the enclaves, while American air drops, carried out in coordination with UNHCR, started relieving the dire conditions in other enclaves.

7. Despite these serious problems, the international relief effort, conducted by United Nations agencies, UNPROFOR, International Committee of the Red Cross and various non-governmental organizations has thus far prevented mass starvation. However, fighting and persecution continue to cause new victims and displacement, especially in eastern Bosnia. In close cooperation, the humanitarian organizations are preparing for the arrival of thousands of victims in Tuzla, central Bosnia. Of great concern are the sharply declining economic conditions in this region, as tensions between Bosnian Croat force and the government side are negatively affecting the circulation of commercial goods.

8. Newly arriving refugees are adding to the already enormous burden of adjacent countries, where socio-economic conditions have continued to decline. For this reason, Mrs. Ogata convened on 25 March 1993 a meeting of the Humanitarian Issues Working Group, uniting all countries of the region, the interna-

tional donor community and other interested states, the Department of Humanitarian Affairs and international governmental and non-governmental organizations at this meeting the overall humanitarian situation was assessed, and a new consolidated appeal for the period 1 April - 31 December 1993 was launched.

III. Working Group on Ethnic and National Communities and Minorities

9. Since the Working Group on ethnic and national Communities and Minorities met in December with representatives of Muslims from Sandjak and of the Hungarians, Croats and Slovaks from Vojvodina, no new meeting could be arranged, due to elections and changes of the Governments in Serbia, Montenegro and in the Federal Republic of Yugoslavia.

10. On 10 March, the Chairman of the Group, Ambassador Ahrens, and members of the Working Group, had a first meeting in Belgrade with Mrs. Savonic, the new Minister for Human Rights and minorities in the Federal Government. In this first exchange of views, Mrs. Slavonic showed a positive attitude towards the activities of the Group. The Chair stressed the importance of resuming, as soon as possible, the work of the Group on all items that had been on its agenda, so far.

11. The Group had planned to meet the same day in Belgrade with representatives of the Hungarian minority in Vojvodina, but the meeting had to be cancelled because the Hungarians were apparently unable to attend. A meeting in Belgrade with Serbs from the Gorski Kotar area in Croatia, scheduled for 10 March 1993, was also called off.

12. Since the beginning of the year, two trilateral meetings were held on minority issues in the former Yugoslav Republic of Macedonia. The first took place from 20 to 22 January, in Skopje, the second on 10 and 11 February, in Geneva. Before the meeting in Skopje, the Group stopped for talks in Tirana, where they were received by President Berisha. Voicing his concern about the development in the south-east part of the former Yugoslavia, President Berisha expressed strong support for the endeavours of the group, adding that everything should be done to stabilize the situation of the former Yugoslav Republic of Macedonia and in Kosovo.

13. The talks on the former Yugoslav Republic of Macedonia continue to follow the pattern of slow but steady progress, Improvements could be achieved, for instance, on the use of minority languages and the reopening of a number of secondary school classes in Albanian. Progress is under way concerning the situation in the media sector, a census with participation of the Albanians and on

self-administration.

14. The European Community Commission is considering financial support for the census. On 8 March, Ambassador Rey attended a meeting in Brussels with representatives of the European Community Commission and the Council of Europe on organizational and financial aspects of the census. Everything will be done to have the census organized before the end of the year.

15. A further trilateral meeting on the former Yugoslav Republic of Macedonia was planned to take place in Skopje on 10 and 11 March. It was the intention of the Group to clarify at that meeting remaining issues concerning the media sector as well as to take up all other pending issues such as the law on local self-government, the law on foreigners, the three laws on elementary, secondary and university education, as well as certain problems related to the implementation of the law on citizens and legislation related to the organization of administration and of the organization of the courts. Invoking technical problems, the Government asked for postponement of the meeting. It is the Group's hope that work in the outstanding issues can be pursued as soon as possible in the spirit of cooperation which has so far characterized the talks.

16. When in Belgrade, Ambassador Ahrens met, on 10 March, with Patriarch Pavle on matters related to religious services for the Serbian ethnic group in the former Yugoslav Republic of Macedonia.

Special Group on Kosovo

17. The special Group on Kosovo met in Geneva from 26 to 28 January and in Belgrade on 17 and 18 February. As in past meetings, the talks were limited to the subject of education, on which the Group still endeavours to reach pragmatic solutions in the hope of improving the overall climate between the parties, which continued to be far from positive.

18. The Kosovar Albanians presented their teaching plans. These were rejected by the Government on the ground that they contained an underlying assumption of independence for Kosovo. The Government made new proposals on the reinstatement of teachers and on the recognition of years spent in the parallel school system run by the Albanians. They were rejected by the Kosovar Albanian side, which insists on the "unconditional" reopening of school premises before they would be ready to address other issues.

19. In the talks on Kosovo, fundamental issues are constantly hindering the pragmatic approach for solutions in the field of education. The Group will pursue its efforts, but at the same time it is necessary to address fundamental issues in the light of the principles agreed upon at the London Conference.

20. When in Belgrade on 10 March, the Chair emphasized to Mr. Jovanovic, the Federal Minister for Foreign Affairs, the necessity of this double track approach. While agreeing in principle, the Foreign Minister stressed the desirability for success on the educational issues as a first step before other issues were approached. On 17 March, Ambassador Ahrens had a discussion with Mr. Bukoshi, who spoke on behalf of Albanians from Kosovo. There was agreement that everything should be tried to achieve progress in the ongoing talks. Mr Bukoshi informed Ambassador Ahrens that authorities in Kosovo had taken away the passport of Professor Statovci, a member of the Kosovar Albanian negotiating team since the beginning, on whose participation the Kosovar Albanians had to insist.

IV. Working Group in Succession Issues

21. The Working Group on Succession Issues, which is chaired by Ambassador J. Bojer, has met twice in 1993 a joint meeting of the Economic Issues and State Succession Working Groups was held in Geneva.

22. In the January meeting, delegations from all successor States of the former Yugoslavia participated. The delegations of Bosnia and Herzegovina and the former Yugoslav Republic of Macedonia were both delayed. On he basis of a working paper by the late Chairmen of the State Succession Working Group, Mr. Henry Darwin, the participants continued drafting texts on succession with respect to citizenship, acquired rights and pensions. State archives and diplomatic and consular property were also discussed.

23. In the meeting in March, delegations from Croatia, from the former Yugoslav Republic of Macedonia and from Slovenia took part. A representative of Bosnia and Herzegovina was present during part of the meeting as an observer. The delegation of Bosnia and Herzegovina stated that its non-participation was due to the impossibility for its delegates, who had remained in Zagreb since the previous meeting in January, to go to Sarajevo to receive instructions prior to the meeting owing to UNPROFOR's practice concerning transport of government representatives in and out of Sarajevo. The delegation of the Federal Republic of Yugoslavia (Serbia and Montenegro) had, on 4 March, asked for a postponement of the meeting until after 22 March because of the change of government in Belgrade. The Chairman decided not to postpone the meeting at such short notice, as other delegations had already undertaken extensive preparations for the meeting. There were no representatives of the Federal Republic of Yugoslavia present at the meeting.

24. On substantive issues, the three delegations formally participating drafted

texts on succession with respect to state archives and rules concerning distribution of immovable and movable properties administered by the former Federal Secretariat for Foreign Affairs of the Socialist Federal Republic of Yugoslavia. Pension obligations was the third major issue discussed at the meeting.

25. At the joint meeting of the Economic Issues and State Succession Working Groups on 12 March, the participants discussed the implications of the conclusions in Mr. Durieux's "Chairman's Report on the Valuation of the Assets and Liabilities of the Former SFRY", of 26 February 1993, on the coordination of the future work of the two working groups.

26. The plan for the next meeting of the Working Group of Succession Issues, scheduled to take place from 5 to 7 April 1993 at Geneva, is to carry on the drafting of texts on succession with respect to financial assets and liabilities of the former Socialist Federal Republic of Yugoslavia, rules for the distribution of immovable and movable properties (abroad), State archives, pensions, and legal problems related to the draft single inventory of the assets and liabilities of the Socialist Federal Republic of Yugoslavia.

V. WORKING GROUP ON ECONOMIC ISSUES

27. The Working Group on Economic Issues is chaired my Mr. J. Durieux.

Meeting: Brussels, 20 and 21 January 1993

28. The six subgroups charged with the valuation of the assets and liabilities of the former Federation met to review the latest draft of a report on this valuation. The meeting revealed uneven progress across the six subgroups with some basic information still missing and some estimated values being contested. The gap between the undisputed part of the inventory and those parts which some of the delegations felt ought not to be considered in the framework of State succession remained wide.

29. Subsequent to this meeting some further information and comments were received which were included in the report. The final draft of the report was submitted to the Co-Chairmen on 4 March.

Meeting: Geneva, 17 February 1993

30. The main item on the agenda was the proposed high-level conference on the economic future of the countries of the former Yugoslavia. All delegations except Slovenia (the delegation of Bosnia and Herzegovina did not attend)

thought the Conference to be a useful idea, but felt that a number of conditions would need to be satisfied before it could be held, notably an effective ceasefire, the emergence of a global political settlement, progress on the lifting of sanctions and activation of he PHARE programme. Further work on the draft paper on the economic situation of the countries of the former Federation as well as submissions from the Republics will follow, but progress is now dependent upon political factors.

VI. WORKING GROUP ON CONFIDENCE- AND SECURITY-BUILDING AND VERIFICATION MEASURES

31. Working Group on Confidence- and Security-Building and Verification Measures, chaired by Mr. V. Beresategui, recommended its activity this year on 18 January 1993. At that meeting, the Working Group heard a report from UNHCR on incidents which had jeopardized its humanitarian airlift and which were in violation of the 15 September 1992 agreement on confidence-building measures (see S/24634). UNHCR strongly appealed to all sides to respect the humanitarian nature of the airlift.

32. In December 1992, the Working Group had begun consideration of a proposal for a preliminary exchange of information among parties in the former Yugoslavia on weapons systems and levels of armed forces, in order to facilitate confidence-building measures. At the meeting on 18 January, the Chairman of the Working Group announced that, after consultation with the Co-Chairmen of the Steering Committee, he was deferring further work, in the light of the crucial stage of the negotiations on a peace plan for Bosnia and Herzegovina.

119. REPORT OF THE SECRETARY-GENERAL ON THE ACTIVITIES OF THE CO-CHAIRMEN OF THE STEERING COMMITTEE OF THE INTERNATIONAL CONFERENCE ON THE FORMER YUGOSLAVIA[*]

INTRODUCTION

1. The present report deals with the activities of the Co-Chairmen of the Steering Committee of the International Conference on the Former Yugoslavia since the issuance of the report of the Secretary-General of 26 March 1993 (S/25479).

---

[*]   UN Doc. S/25708, 30 April 1993.

I. THE SITUATION IN BOSNIA AND HERZEGOVINA

2. The Bosnia and Herzegovina have continued their efforts to help alleviate the humanitarian situation in Bosnia and Herzegovina; to persuade the Bosnian Serb side to sign the two remaining documents of the peace plan; and to prepare for the implementation of the peace plan upon completion of signature.

3. Between 21 and 25 April, Lord Owen accompanied by Mr. Vance's Special Adviser, led a delegation on behalf of the Co-Chairmen to the area of the former Yugoslavia. On Wednesday, 21 April, Lord Owen had a one-hour meeting at Zagreb Airport with the Croatian Defence Minister, Gojko Susak. Talks focused on the fighting in central Bosnia and Herzegovina between Bosnian Croats and Bosnian government troops.

4. Lord Owen went on to Belgrade that day for a two-hour meeting with the President of the Federal Republic of Yugoslavia, Dobrica Cosic. Detailed discussion were held on the "throughway concept". Lord Owen then met with President Slobodan Milosevic, particularly concentrating on the issue of the map and the northern corridor. With his military adviser, and the UNPROFOR military adviser to the Conference, he met for three hours with General Ratko Mladic.

5. Later that evening Lord Owen had a further meeting with President Cosic and President Milosevic, who were joined by Dr. Radovan Karadzic, leader of the Bosnian Serbs.

6. On Thursday, 22 April, Lord Owen's programme focused on the situation between the Republic of Greece and the former Yugoslav Republic of Macedonia, meeting with President Gligorov in Skopje and Prime Minister Mitsotakis in Greece. On Friday, 23 April, he flew to Skopje to see President Gligorov again, and then flew to Montenegro for a meeting with President Bulatovic. Later, he met President Milosevic in Belgrade.

7. On Saturday, 24 April, Lord Owen had a meeting with the Bosnian Serbs on a session lasting over three hours, which was attended on the Bosnian Serb side by Dr. Karadzic, the Bosnian Serb "Assembly" President Momcilo Krajisnik and General Mladic. Subsequently, he met again with Presidents Cosic and Milosevic.

8. Lord Owen left Belgrade on Saturday afternoon, arriving in Zagreb at about 3 p.m. He then held a series of meetings, the first with Croatian Defence Minister Susak and the Bosnian Croat leader, Mr. Mate Boban. The problem of central Bosnia was discussed, along with the possibility of instituting a military arrangement to reduce the tension between the two allied forces.

9. Lord Owen met a 5 p.m. that day with the President of Bosnia and Herzegovina, Alija Izetbegovic. Lord Owen then proceeded to the residence of the President of the Republic of Croatia, Franjo Tudjman, where he had a round of talks with Mr. Tudjman, Mr. Boban, the Croatian Defence Minister and other ministers. A second round of talks was held at 9 p.m., with the addition of President Izetbegovic. That session produced, at about 1 a.m., a ceasefire agreement, including an agreement between the two military leaders on the coordination of efforts to eliminate conflict between their forces in central Bosnia (annex I).

10. On Sunday morning, 25 April, Lord Owen met with the UNPROFOR Force Commander, Lieutenant-General Lars-Eric Wahlgren, in a two-hour meeting to discuss the implementation of the Vance-Owen plan.

11. At midday Sunday, Lord Owen returned to Belgrade at the request of President Cosic and President Milosevic, President Bulatovic also joined the group, for a meeting that lasted more than six hours. Halfway through the meeting, the group was joined by Dr. Karadzic and Mr. Krajisnik, whose Bosnian Serb "Assembly" was due to consider and vote on the peace plan. Lord Owen stayed overnight in Belgrade and that night Presidents Cosic, Milosevic and Bulatovic wrote a letter to the Bosnians urging them to accept the peace plan. At 6 a.m. Monday, 26 April, the "Assembly" did not accept the peace plan, but decided to put the issue to a referendum. Lord Owen visited Bonn, Copenhagen, London and Paris before returning to New York on Wednesday, 28 April.

12. The Co-Chairmen then continued their efforts to persuade the Bosnian Serb side to sign the outstanding two documents of the peace plan. On Thursday, 29 April, there were informed that the Bosnian Serb decision to hold a referendum had been superseded by a decision to hold a fresh meeting on Wednesday, 5 May. They were also informed of the decision of the Serbian and Montenegrin Parliaments to support the three presidents, In the light of these developments, the Co-Chairmen, Cyrus Vance and Lord Owen, together with Co-Chairmen-designate, Mr. Thorvald Stoltenberg, decided to convene a meeting, starting on Saturday 1 May, in Athens, with the generous hospitality of Prime Minister Mitsotakis. The following agreed to attend:

- President A. Izetbegovic (Bosnia and Herzegovina);
- President F. Tudjman (Croatia);
- President D. Cosic (Federal Republic of Yugoslavia (Serbia and Montenegro));
- President S. Milosevic (Serbia);
- President M. Bulatovic (Montenegro);

- Mr. M. Boban;
- Dr. R. Karadzic.

The meeting will begin on Saturday evening, 1 May, and the Co-Chairmen will report separately on it.

II. THE SITUATION IN THE UNITED NATIONS PROTECTED AREAS IN CROATIA

13. In its resolution 802 (1993), adopted on 25 January 1993 in the wake of the 22 January military incursion by Croatia into part of a pink zone and a UNPA round the Maslenica bridge, the Security Council demanded the immediate cessation of hostile activities by Croatian armed forces and the withdrawal of the Croatian armed forces from these areas. The Security Council also demanded that the heavy weapons seized by the Serbs from the UNPROFOR controlled storage areas in the wake of the Croatian incursion be returned immediately to UNPROFOR.

14. By its resolution 807 (1993), of 19 February, the Security Council reiterated these demands and urged the parties and others concerned fully to cooperate with the Co-Chairmen in discussions to ensure full implementation of the United Nations peace-keeping mandate in Croatia.

15. At the conclusion of negotiations conducted under the auspices of the Co-Chairmen from mid-February, successively in New York, Geneva, Zagreb, Belgrade, New York and Geneva, on 6 April, an agreement in implementation of Security Council resolution 802 (1993) was signed by a representative of the Croatian Government and a representative of the Serb local authorities, the agreement provided for a cessation of hostilities four days after its entry into force. Within five days of the cessation of hostilities, the Croatian armed forces should start returning to the lines of confrontation existing before the outbreak of hostilities on 22 January and complete this return within a further five days. In parallel to the withdrawal of the Croatian government armed forces, all Serb heavy weapons (i.e., not only those seized from UNPROFOR control after 22 January) are to be placed under the supervision of UNPROFOR in accordance with the Vane plan. The Maslenica bridge, Zemunik airport and the Peruca dam are to be placed under complete UNPROFOR control for the purpose of restoring them to general civilian use.

16. Under the agreement, the parties undertake to commence talks under the auspices of the Co-Chairmen, no later than 15 days after its entry into force (i.e., just after the completion of implementation of the military provisions), and to implement the remaining provisions of the Vance plan and of all relevant

Security Council resolutions, including 762 (1992).

17. The agreement provided that it would enter into force when both parties have assured the Co-Chairmen that neither of them will station any police within any area from which Croatian government armed forces withdraw; in those areas, UNPROFOR shall for the time being exclusively fulfil all police functions. The Croatians orally gave that assurance at the time of signature; the Serb assurance requires the approval of their Assembly. That approval has so far not been forthcoming and further talks took place in Geneva with Serb representatives on Friday, 30 April. Additional meetings are planned to take place next week. Some of the related issues between Serbia and Croatia may be discussed in the margins of the Athens meeting.

III. The Difference Between the Republic of Greece and the Former Yugoslav Republic of Macedonia

18. On 12 and 13 April, the Co-Chairmen held discussions in New York with delegations from he Former Yugoslav Republic of Macedonia and from Greece. Between 14 and 25 April, technical work was carried out among legal experts from the secretariat of the International Conference on the Former Yugoslavia and the two delegations with a view to preparing a draft agreement for consideration. Additionally, Lord Owen accompanied by Mr. Vance's Special Adviser, held talks with the parties in their capitals. The Co-Chairmen had further discussions with delegations from the Former Yugoslav Republic of Macedonia and from Greece from 26 to 29 April. Information on these discussions will be contained in a separate report from the Co-Chairmen to the Secretary-General as soon as they are ready to make a final report.

IV. Succession Issues

19. At the request of the Chairman of the Conference's Working Group on Succession Issues, and with a view to settling relations among the successor Republics in the former Yugoslavia, the Co-Chairmen, on 20 April 1993, submitted a request to the Conference's Arbitration Commission for an advisory opinion on the following six questions:

1. In the light of the inventory on the report by the Chairman of the Working Group on Economic Issues, what assets and liabilities should be divided between the successor States to the former Socialist Federal Republic of Yugoslavia during the succession process?

2. In what date(s) did succession of States occur for the various States that have emerged from the Socialist Federal Republic of Yugoslavia?

3. (a) What legal principles apply to the division of State property, archives and debts of the Socialist Federal Republic of Yugoslavia in connection with the succession of States when one or more of the parties concerned refuse(s) to cooperate?

   (b) In particular, what should happen to property
   - not located on the territory of the States concerned, or
   - situated on the territory of the States taking part in the negotiations?

4. Under the legal principles that apply, might any amounts owed by one or more parties in the form of war damages affect the distribution of State property, archives and debts in connection with the succession process?

5. (a) In view of the dissolution of the Socialist Federal Republic of Yugoslavia, is the National Bank of Yugoslavia entitled to take decisions affecting property, rights and interests that should be divided between the successor States to the Socialist Federal Republic of Yugoslavia in connection with the succession of States?

   (b) Have the central banks of the States emerging from the dissolution of the Socialist Federal Republic of Yugoslavia succeeded to the rights and obligations of the National Bank of Yugoslavia deriving from international agreements concluded by the latter, i n particular the 1988 Financial Agreement with (the) (foreign) commercial banks?

6. (a) On what condition can States, within whose jurisdiction property formerly belonging to the Socialist Federal Republic of Yugoslavia is situated, oppose the free disposal of that property or take other protective measures?

   (b) On what condition and under what circumstances would such States be required to take such steps?

120. REPORT OF THE SECRETARY-GENERAL ON THE ACTIVITIES OF THE INTERNATIONAL CONFERENCE ON THE FORMER YUGOSLAVIA: PEACE TALKS, ATHENS, 1-2 MAY 1993[*]

INTRODUCTION

1. In my previous report (S/25708), I informed the Security Council that the Co-Chairmen of the Steering Committee, Cyrus Vance and Lord Owen, together with the Co-Chairman-designate, Thorvald Stoltenberg, had decided, on 29 April 1993, to convene a round of peace talks in Athens on 1 and 2 May with the generous hospitality of Prime Minister Mitsotakis and the Greek Government. In addition to Mr. Vance, Lord Owen, and Mr. Stoltenberg, the following leaders headed delegations at the talks:

- President A. Izetbegovic (Bosnia and Herzegovina);
- President F. Tudjman (Republic of Croatia);
- President D. Cosic (Federal Republic of Yugoslavia (Serbia and Montenegro));
- President S. Milosevic (Serbia);
- President M. Bulatovic (Montenegro);
- Mr. M. Boban;
- Dr. R. Karadzic.

The following attended as observers:

- Observer from the host Government: E. Karagiannis;
- Observer from the European Community: B. Weber;
- Special Envoy: R. Bartholomew (United States of America);
- Special Envoy: V. Churkin (Russian Federation).

I. ADDRESS BY PRIME MINISTER CONSTANTINOS MITSOTAKIS

2. On Saturday evening, 1 May, the Prime Minister of Greece, Mr. Mitsotakis, addressed the participants with a strong appeal to them to bring peace to Bosnia and Herzegovina. He urged boldness and courage on the part of the political leaders.

---

[*] UN Doc. S/25709, 3 May 1993.

II. OPENING REMARKS BY CYRUS VANCE

3. Following the address of Prime Minister Mitsotakis, Mr. Vance welcomed the participants and expressed the gratitude of the Co-Chairmen to Prime Minister Mitsotakis and his Government for their hospitality. He underlined the critical importance of a positive outcome of the talks and stated: "The time is overdue to act decisively to bring peace to Bosnia and Herzegovina and to begin the reconstruction of the former Yugoslavia ... What is urgently needed now is to bring the plan into force. To do this, Dr. Karadzic needs to sign the remaining two documents of the plan, namely, the provisional provincial map and the agreement on interim arrangements." He noted that the Co-Chairmen had provided clarification to a number of questions that had been raised and stated: "In the light of the answers given, we are convinced that there is no reasonable ground for further delay in completing the signing of the peace plan."

III. FACTORS RELEVANT TO THE IMPLEMENTATION OF THE PEACE PLAN

4. Lord Owen then made a statement in which he noted that during recent discussions with all the parties, the Co-Chairmen had provided explanations and amplifications on various aspects of the peace plan. The text of this statement is reproduced in annex I. The text of Lord Owen's remarks was distributed to the participants. Also distributed with it was a paper on the concept for the Northern Corridor, which is reproduced in annex II.
5. At the second session of the peace talks, held on Sunday, 2 May, Mr. Vance, speaking on behalf of the Co-Chairmen, provided additional amplifications on the concept of the Northern Corridor, which are reproduced in annex III.
6. On 2 May the Co-Chairmen wrote a letter to President Izetbegovic, Mr. Boban, and Dr. Karadzic on the status of the above-mentioned explanation and amplifications, the text of which is reproduced in annex IV.

IV. SIGNING OF THE PEACE PLAN

7. On 2 May Dr. Karadzic signed the Agreement on Interim Arrangements and the provisional provincial map. At the time of signing, he made and signed a statement, the text of which is reproduced in annex V.
8. Following Dr. Karadzic's signing of the above-mentioned documents, the Co-Chairmen called upon the participants to do their utmost for its faithful implementation. They called for maximum military restraint and urged the Bosnian sides to observe a cessation of hostilities throughout Bosnia and Herzegovina.

9. The participants paid a warm tribute to Cyrus Vance for his enormous contribution to the pursuit of peace in the former Yugoslavia.

CONCLUDING OBSERVATIONS

10. The completion of signature of the peace plan marks a decisive moment in efforts to stop the conflict in Bosnia and Herzegovina. Everything possible must now be done to bring the peace plan into force and to implement it in accordance with its letter and spirit.

Annex I
Statement by Lord Owen on behalf of the Co-Chairmen

During my recent discussions with all the parties in Belgrade and Zagreb, we focused on many aspects of the peace plan. I believe it would help all the parties if I were now to repeat some of the points of clarification that arose during this trip.

INTERIM ARRANGEMENTS

The agreement on interim arrangements, annex I of the Secretary-General's report of 26 March 1993, document S/25479, is in the view of the Co-Chairmen fully consistent with constitutional principle 4, which has been signed by all the parties and states:

> "All matters of vital concern to any of the constituent peoples shall be regulated in the Constitution, which as to these points may be amended only by consensus of these constituent peoples; ordinary governmental business is not to be veto-able by any group."

This is made very clear in annex I, A. Interim Presidency and Interim Central Government, in paragraph 1 of which it states:

> "in the direct aftermath of hostilities, when a consensus amongst the three constituent peoples is the only acceptable basis for reaching any fundamental decisions, the Interim Presidency and Interim Government shall function on a coalition basis.
> In signing this agreement we are asking as section I, paragraph 5, of the Secretary-General's report of 26 March (S/25479) makes clear, that all sides should 'concentrate on agreeing on specific arrangements for the interim period'."

PROCEDURES INSIDE THE INTERIM PRESIDENCY

Annex I of S/25479, Agreement on interim arrangements, states in paragraph 4:

> "The Interim Presidency shall take decisions by consensus of nine, or by a qualified majority of seven, or by a simple majority of five depending on whether the decision relates to a constitutional principle, to a specially important question, or to normal business of the Presidency. If the members of the interim Presidency are unable to agree on the applicable majority, they will consult the Co-Chairmen of the Steering Committee of the International Conference on the Former Yugoslavia (the 'Co-Chairmen'), whose decision shall be binding."

I was asked if I could indicate in advance whether the rules of procedure for operating the Interim Presidency would be a decision taken by consensus of the nine members an d my instant response was that it would be, but I checked with Mr. Vance and he agreed without demur that this would be our decision.

INTERIM PRESIDENT

In discussions over the rotating Interim President, where each of the constituent peoples will hold the Interim Presidency for six months, a fear was expressed that if elections were held after a year, one of the constituent peoples would not be able to hold the position of Interim President. I think it might help to put this issue in perspective if I remind you what was said on 12 March 1993 in the Secretary-General's report, document S/25403, paragraph 20:

> "During the period between the entry into force of the peace settlement and the holding of free and fair elections, there is a need for an interim institutional mechanism so that the country can function effectively. The drafting of a new Constitution for the Republic of Bosnia and Herzegovina is expected to take months. Also, it is very likely to take more than a year for the many refugees and displaced persons to return to their homes. Nevertheless, free and fair elections must be held within two years; the date will be fixed by the interim Presidency in consultation with the Co-Chairmen."

It is the view of the Co-Chairmen that elections will not be held for at least 18 months and that therefore all three constituent peoples will have the opportunity to hold the Interim Presidency.

WITHDRAWAL OF FORCES

After consulting the Force Commander, General Wahlgren, it has been explained to all the parties at both the political and the military level that, when forces withdraw under the plan to named provinces and towns where they have been protecting villages and towns where their own constituent peoples are in the majority, they will be replaced by UNPROFOR and not by opposing forces. Nevertheless, the administration and in particular the police forces in the areas from which they have withdrawn shall, as stated in section G of annex I to S/25479, "be controlled by the Interim Provincial Governments or local authorities under them, and shall reflect the proportions of the constituent peoples in the respective provinces." UNCIVPOL's principal task, as is made clear in section H, paragraph 5, "would be to monitor the police of the Provinces so that each: has an appropriately balanced ethnic composition; [and] does not oppress members of minority ethnic groups". It is important also to remember that minorities in any province will have access to the service of their own ombudsmen appointed to cover the whole of Bosnia and Herzegovina who shall be supported by adequate staff and facilities at provincial level, particularly in a province where another constituent people is in the majority.

THE PROVISIONAL PROVINCIAL MAP

It needs to be stressed that the reason for referring to the boundaries of the provinces as "provisional" is that the final boundaries will be adopted by consensus by the parties for the new Constitution in the framework of the International Conference on the Former Yugoslavia. It will be perfectly possible for the parties in the improved atmosphere associated with the cessation of hostilities and in the spirit of cooperation hopefully built up during the period of interim coalition government to negotiate amongst themselves changes of the provincial boundaries.

In addition, the Conference will have before it recommendation from the Boundary Commission (section B). The Commission shall receive and, if necessary, hear evidence form those people who feel they are adversely affected by the proposed provincial boundaries. The Commission is empowered to consider only marginal changes and its decisions will be adopted by consensus. But it does introduce an important area of flexibility and it will be possible for villages or towns that feel they have been wrongly placed on one side or another of the provisional boundary to have their positions reviewed.

The capital city of Sarajevo will exceptionally have its provisional boundaries specifically referred to the Boundary Commission for review (section C) and there is no marginal qualification made to the text. In this case "any agreed changes will be introduced prior to implementing the new Constitution."

It is the view of the Co-Chairmen that these arrangements provide for considerable flexibility in the defining of the provincial boundaries; also the Constitution will no doubt provide for a mechanism whereby boundaries could be changed at some future date after adoption of the Constitution by consensus.

NORTHERN CORRIDOR

One of the most controversial issues between the parties has been the concern about free access from Banja Luka Province to Bijeljina Province. The main road through Posavina and Tuzla Province will be a United Nations-throughway controlled not by the provincial police but by UNPROFOR and with an area of 5 kilometres on either side of the road demilitarized under the responsibility of UNPROFOR. A paper describing the detailed arrangements approved by the UNPROFOR Force Commander whereby UNPROFOR propose to control the road has already been circulated to the parties to demonstrate how they will guarantee free passage along the road and is attached to this explanation in annex II. In this regard, it should be noted that ever since 19 February 1993, under Security Council resolution 807 (1993), UNPROFOR has been acting under Chapter VII of the Charter of the United Nations and the Force Commander has given assurances that there will be consultations amongst the parties prior to deploying United Nations forces to control the Northern Corridor. All of these matters will be specifically covered and put for the endorsement of the Council in the resolution on implementation arrangements.

Also, as in relation to the demilitarization of Sarajevo, (annex V, page 28 of S/25403 of the Agreement for Peace in Bosnia and Herzegovina), a Joint Commission Chaired by UNPROFOR will oversee the implementation of the arrangements for the Northern Corridor. This will mean that all three of the parties will be represented on the Commission and can bring before it any alleged violations.

INTERNATIONAL ACCESS AUTHORITY

The Agreement on Interim Arrangements provides in section I for the interim Presidency to establish an International Access Authority in order to implement principle 3 of the Agreed Constitutional Principles and to allow full freedom of movement between and within the Provinces and also to and from the provinces to the Republic of Croatia and to the Republic of Serbia. It is intended that the Authority be in operation as soon as possible during the interim period. Following the conclusion of the package, all designate throughways shall come under the responsibility of UNPROFOR, thereafter there will be a period of overlapping responsibility of UNPROFOR and the Authority, during which

UNPROFOR's involvement will be phased out and its responsibilities assumed by traffic police employed by the Authority.

I would draw attention to the fact that other throughways have also provided assurance, particularly that between Gorazde and Cajnice. The Blue Routes are also important, particularly that between Pale and Zvornik.

In Zagreb and Belgrade I had preliminary discussions as to whether or not it would be possible to extend the International Access Authority to related roads and railways in Croatia, Serbia and Montenegro. Such a development depends on discussions between their government and is outside the context of the interim agreement and therefore of this peace plan.

Nevertheless, the Co-Chairmen hope that in the margins of this Conference it might be possible to hold some further discussions about this wider concept with the Governments concerned to see if there is a possible basis for agreement.

I hope that with the clarifications it will now be possible for the Bosnian Serb delegation to agree to sign the two outstanding documents, the interim agreement and the provincial map, and thereby ensure with these two additional signatures that we have the 12 signatures necessary for full endorsement of the peace plan.

Once the peace plan has been agreed in full by all the parties, we as Co-Chairmen shall report to the Secretary-General, who has then been requested by the Security Council to report at the earliest possible date on proposals for the implementation of the peace plan. On the passing of a Security Council resolution on implementation, the peace plan will start to operate.

In the meantime, we hope all three parties on signature will agree to join the Coordination Body which was established recently in Zagreb to work together in the spirit of the peace plan as far as circumstances will allow before the stage of formal implementation and the start of the Interim Presidency.

Annex II
Concept for the Northern Corridor

The Northern Corridor will consist of the internationally controlled throughway linking Banja Luka Province and Bijeljina Province and a demilitarized zone extending 5 kilometres either side of the throughway in the territory of Bosnia and Herzegovina.

The demilitarized zone concept includes:

- Adherence to the broad principles for the cessation of hostilities agreed by all parties and included in S/25221 (annex I);

- Implementation of the measures to separate forces and withdraw heavy weapons agreed by all parties and included in S/25221 (annex IV);
- The implementation of a zone extending in Bosnia and Herzegovina territory for 5 kilometres either side of the throughway in which no military force's personnel, equipment or installations, other than those of the United Nations forces, will be authorized.

Demilitarized zone measures will include:

- Patrolling by the United Nations implementation force to ensure compliance by all parties;
- Other than United Nations forces, the only personnel allowed to carry arms in the demilitarized zone will be provincial civil police officers on duty. The only arms these officers will be authorized to carry will be personal sidearms (handguns). Provincial police officers will have no powers on the northern throughway.

The throughway concept is:

- A security guarantee initially by UNPROFOR and later the International Access Authority to all parties traversing Posavina and Tuzla Province via Brcko to ensure non-interference with and protection of personnel and material using the throughway;
- No interference on the throughway. No provincial police will be able to stop any vehicle and if they have any complaint about speeding or other matters, they would have to notify an UNPROFOR patrol or later and International Access Authority Police;
- Checkpoints, patrol and monitoring, along the length of the throughway, initially by the United Nations implementation force and then a period of joint working with the International Access Authority Police;
- The supervised inspection at the entry points at each end of the throughway by United Nations force;
- Freedom of passage of humanitarian aid;
- Freedom of movement for United Nations forces.

Throughway measures will include:

- Timings: the throughway will be open at all times. United Nations forces and International Access Authority Police will use the throughway at any time and have total authority over maintenance, sign posting and other

technical matters;
- Access for civilians: all civilians, regardless of sex, age or ethnic origin but provided they are carrying no weapons or ammunition will be allowed to use the throughway. Private and commercial vehicles will also be permitted to use the throughway. All will be subject to the inspection measures outlined below;
- Access for humanitarian aid: all international and local humanitarian aid agencies will be allowed to use the throughway;
- Checkpoints: the only authorized checkpoints will be those established and manned by the United Nations force. Provincial authorities will not be permitted to impose their own checkpoints on the throughway. Checkpoints will initially, as a security measure for users, be open only during daylight hours for non-United Nations traffic;
- Inspection procedures: inspections will be conducted by the United Nations force at checkpoints;
- Inspections may be carried out on all users of the throughway, including humanitarian convoys.
- War-related material: the carriage or transport of all weapons, ammunition or other war-related material will not be permitted without a licence issued by the United Nations Force Commander or International Access Authority Officer responsible for the throughway. Licences will only be issued for the arms and ammunition appropriate for and destined to civil police forces. All non-licensed war-related material will be turned back a the entrance or escorted back to the point of entry;
- Escorts: traffic may initially, as a security measure for users, move through a checkpoint and along the throughway by United Nations-escorted convoy only;
- Patrols: the throughway will be patrolled by the United Nations force or International Access authority official police vehicles which have appropriate communications.

Implementation time-frame: The United Nations will, in line with "Agreement on Peace" signed by all three parties, aim to erect checkpoints and reconnoitre the throughway by $D+1$, then open the throughway for civilian through traffic by no later than $D+15$.

International Access Authority: An International Access Authority will be established as part of the process for implementing interim arrangements for Bosnia and Herzegovina. Details were included in the United Nations Secretary-General's report to the Security Council on 2 February 1993 (S/25221). One of the Authority's tasks will be to take on sole responsibility for all roads declared as internationally controlled throughways. A period of overlapping responsibility is envisaged for the United Nations force and that of the Access Authority. This transfer of authority will only be completed by agreement of all those involved in the Access Authority.

The United Nations Implementation Force. The Northern Corridor will be one of the highest priorities for the United Nations Force tasked to implement the Vance-Owen Plan for Bosnia and Herzegovina. The Northern Corridor will be the highest standing priority for the United Nations formation tasked to be responsible of the Posavina and Tuzla Province. This United Nations formation will be specifically selected for its capability to undertake this task.

The broader context. With the agreement of the Republic of Croatia and FRY (Serbia and Montenegro), the International Access Authority's role would broaden. Its existing responsibility for all rail routes in Bosnia and Herzegovina, including in the Northern Corridor the important routes from Banja Luka to the border at Bosanski Samac and from Tuzla to the border at Brcko, would extend to include the links between these routes and the Zagreb-to-Belgrade rail route and to the railway through Knin to the coast in Croatia. Similarly, its responsibility for roads would extend from the international crossing points at Bosankska Gradiska and Orasje to the links between these roads and to Belgrade along the autoroute.

Annex III
Statement by Cyrus Vance[*]

Last night it was suggested that it would be helpful for the parties to have further clarification of the penultimate paragraph of the "Concept for the Northern Corridor", annexed to Lord Owen's statement of yesterday (1 May 1993) to this Conference on behalf of the Co-Chairmen. The Co-Chairmen fully recognize the need to provide clear assurance of the security of the population in the areas concerned. Some of the fiercest fighting in the war has taken place around Brcko and, sadly, is still continuing. We urge all the parties to start to show the same restraint in this area as has been recently shown in some other strongly contested areas.

With a ceasefire established and increased freedom of movement, the tasks of securing the throughway through Posavina and Tuzla Province will be accorded

---

[*] Athens, 2 May 1993.

highest priority along with the demilitarization of Sarajevo Province. This means that as soon as the cessation of hostilities takes place elements of existing UNPROFOR forces already deployed in Bosnia and Herzegovina will be tasked to quickly redeploy to the Northern Corridor, in order to ensure free movement of traffic as put forward in the framework in this Conference and detailed in the Concept Paper. Additional forces, provided under a new mandate to be approved by the Security Council, would also be deployed to the Northern Corridor without delay. It is envisaged that these forces would be armoured infantry, capable of mobile operations and possessing sufficient combat power to ensure that they can carry out their task. The final concept of operations will be developed by the responsible military commander. But these forces, continuing to act under the provisions of Chapter VII of the United Nations Charter, will be tasked to maintain a strong presence along the throughway and throughout the demilitarized zone, in the form of checkpoints, patrols and escorts. An effective mobile reserve would also be provided to ensure that the forces will be able to react to unforeseen or hostile developments.

The force will be composed of high calibre troops capable of conducting sustained mobile and forceful action if required. It is our view that the force should include highly professional contingents from North America, Western Europe and the Russian Federation.

It is the Co-Chairmen's considered view that this substantial and specific commitment of international military resources will effectively assure the freedom of movement, and thus the overall security, of the inhabitants of the areas concerned.

Annex IV
Letter of 2 May 1993 from the Co-Chairmen to the Leaders of the Three Bosnian Delegations*

Dear ...,

A great responsibility lies upon the leaders and representatives of the three constituent peoples to prevent further bloodshed, and to begin the reconstruction of Bosnia and Herzegovina. Peace will not only put an end to further killings, but will also allow the return of refugees and displaced person to their homes.

At our meetings in Athens on 1 and 2 May, the Co-Chairmen provided clari-

---

* The undersigned are Cyrus Vance, Thorvald Stoltenberg and David Owen.

fications and answers to questions that had been raised with them about the content and implementation of the United Nations/European Community peace plan. The statements made by the Co-Chairmen are attached.

The purpose of this letter is to confirm that the above-mentioned statements of the Co-Chairmen form part of the official records and involve the full authority of the International Conference on the Former Yugoslavia. As has always been the case, the Secretary-General of the United Nations would reflect the discussions and the documents on his report to the Security Council on the deliberations of the Athens round of the peace talks. These documents will also form the basis for the future work of the International Conference, will guide the drafting of the future constitution for Bosnia and Herzegovina, and will also provide guidance to the commanders and personnel of UNPROFOR.

Yours sincerely,

Annex V
Statement by Dr. Karadzic*

By signing the Vance-Owen Peace Plan (the nine principles, the military agreement, the maps of the proposed provinces and the document on the interim period), the delegation of the Republic of Srpska states the following:

1. Our signature on the proposed documents will become invalid and will be considered null and void unless the following condition is met:

   The Assembly of the Republic of Srpska meeting on Wednesday, 5 May supports the decision of their delegation taken here in Athens on 2 May 1993.
2. After the meeting of the Assembly of the Republic of Srpska and if they support the peace plan, we will be ready to nominate three people to sit in the Coordination Body to work together in the spirit of the peace plan. There are a number of issues which we will wish to raise including those related to the provisional provincial map and the work of the Boundary Commission.

---

* Athens, 2 May 1993. The undersigned are, for the delegation for the Government of the Republic of Srpska, Radovan Karadzic, President of the Republic of Srpska; and, as witnesses, Cyrus Vance, David Owen, and Thorvald Stoltenberg.

3. We are issuing this statement concurrent with our signing of today's documents and are handing it over to the International Conference on the Former Yugoslavia with the request that it be included and attached with the official documents of the Conference.

121. LETTER DATED 8 JULY 1993 FROM THE SECRETARY-GENERAL ADDRESSED TO THE PRESIDENT OF THE SECURITY COUNCIL[*]

I have the honour to convey the attached report addressed to me on 6 July 1993 by the Co-Chairmen of the Steering Committee of the International Conference on the Former Yugoslavia.

The report refers only to Bosnia and Herzegovina, without entering into other questions within the purview of the Conference.

I should be grateful if you would bring this information to the attention of the members of the Security Council.

Annex
Report of the Steering Committee of the International Conference on the Former Yugoslavia

INTRODUCTION

1. The activities of the Co-Chairmen of the Steering Committee of the International Conference on the Former Yugoslavia were last reported to the Security Council in document S/25709. The present report covers events concerning Bosnia and Herzegovina since early May 1993.

I. DEVELOPMENTS AFFECTING THE VANCE-OWEN PEACE PLAN

2. It will be recalled that, up to the first week of May 1993, the efforts of the Co-Chairmen of the Steering Committee, with the support of the Security Council, had been directed towards completing signature by the three Bosnian sides of the Vance-Owen Peace Plan, consisting of constitutional principles, a military agreement, a provisional provincial map and an agreement on interim arrangements. Signature of the peace plan was completed on 2 May when Mr. Karadzic

---

[*]   UN Doc. S/26066, 8 July 1993. Signed by Boutros Boutros-Ghali.

signed the provisional provincial map and the agreement on interim arrangements. However, Mr. Karadzic's signature was annulled almost immediately by the Bosnian-Serb assembly meeting at Pale (5 May) and to subsequent "referendum" (15 and 16 May), despite President Milosevic and Prime Minister Mitsotakis intervening in favour of it. Immediately after the assembly meeting, the Federal Republic of Yugoslavia (Serbia and Montenegro) announced that it was cutting off all but humanitarian supplies to the Bosnian Serbs.

3. One of the prerequisites for going ahead with the implementation of the Vance-Owen Peace Plan in the absence of agreement by the Bosnian Serbs was the continuation of cooperation between the Muslims and Croats. Unfortunately, by the second week of May, major fighting broke out again between the Croats and Muslims in central Bosnia. The Co-Chairmen immediately left New York on 14 May in order to travel to central Bosnia for meetings with President Izetbegovic, Mr. Boban, President Tudjman and their military advisers. This meeting took place on 18 May in Medugorje, near Mostar. At the meeting, the Co-Chairmen sought to achieve to following objectives:

 (a) A cessation of hostilities between the Muslims and the Croats;
 (b) Cooperation between the Muslims and the Croats in the implementation of the Peace Plan in the six predominantly Muslim or Croat provinces;
 (c) Further meetings of the Coordination Body to pursue the implementation of the Peace Plan;
 (d) The organization of regular meetings of the Presidency of Bosnia and Herzegovina;
 (e) The formation of a Government with agreed allocations of ministries and diplomatic posts.

4. President Izetbegovic and Mr. Boban reached understandings on all of these points and it was agreed to hold a follow-up meeting in Sarajevo to pursue the implementation of these decisions. On 20 May the United States and Russian Foreign Ministers met to discuss the situation in Bosnia and were joined by their United Kingdom, French and Spanish colleagues on 21 May, with a joint statement being published on 22 May. Unfortunately, the perception was conveyed during these meetings in some press reports that the roll-back of the Bosnian Serbs was no longer a priority issue on the international agenda.

5. The Co-Chairmen travelled to the follow-up meeting of the Coordination Body scheduled to be held in Sarajevo on 3 June. While there, they met Mr. Karadzic, who had welcomed the Washington statement, and his colleagues in Pale in order to see if it would be helpful to invite him to join the Coordination Body. However, they found that Mr. Karadzic had interpreted the Washington

statement as meaning the Bosnian Serbs no longer had to negotiate about the Vance-Owen Peace Plan. He was insistent on the need for the "Republika Srpska" to be recognized, and the Co-Chairmen did not feel it appropriate to pursue the question of inviting him to designate representatives on the Coordination Body. Unfortunately, the meeting planned between President Izetbegovic and Mr. Boban in Sarajevo on 4 June could not be held. The helicopter in which Mr. Boban was flying to Sarajevo was shot at and received two direct hits, one near the fuel tank. He returned to Split. The Co-Chairmen met with President Izetbegovic and then immediately travelled to Split for discussions with Mr. Boban. The objectives of the Co-Chairmen remained the same, namely the progressive implementation of the Peace Plan to the extent possible in the circumstances.

6. Meanwhile fighting in central Bosnia increased between the Muslims and the Croats as each tried to contest as much territory as possible. It became increasingly evident that the cooperation between the Muslims and Croats, which had lasted with varying degrees since the referendum in March 1992, no longer existed. In Belgrade, President Milosevic informed them that Mr. Karadzic was ready to negotiate on the basis of the Vance-Owen peace process. In Zagreb, Mr. Boban indicated that he was willing to meet President Izetbegovic only if Mr. Karadzic also participated in the discussion. This, combined with the fighting on he ground, made it abundantly clear that a new stage had been reached in the conflict in Bosnia and Herzegovina.

7. At the invitation of the Co-Chairmen, the Presidency of Bosnia and Herzegovina met in Geneva on 13 and 14 June. This was the first time that the full Presidency had met for nearly 14 months. The presidency has since held several meetings in Geneva, Zagreb and Sarajevo.

8. The Co-Chairmen brought together for discussions in Geneva on 15 and 15 June Presidents Bulatovic, Milosevic, Tudjman and Izetbegovic. Mr. Karadzic and Mr. Boban were not present at the discussions with President Izetbegovic, but were available for consultations. President Izetbegovic listened carefully over several hours to a proposal that Bosnia and Herzegovina should be a confederated State, and asked that he should be provided with further elements which he could put before his people. He did not negotiate. At the conclusion of the talks on 16 June, it was decided that all the participants should meet again on 23 June, after Mr. Karadzic and Mr. Boban had met to work out their ideas.

9. During their meetings with the Presidency of Bosnia and Herzegovina, the Co-Chairmen emphasized to them the need for all parties involved on the conflict in Bosnia and Herzegovina to engage in a constructive negotiation process, especially because of the deterioration in the situation on the ground politically

and military and in humanitarian terms. Some members of the Presidency them-selves emphasized that the situation could not be allowed to continue because of the suffering of the people on the ground.

II. CONFEDERATION PROPOSALS

10. Presidents Milosevic and Tudjman informed the Co-Chairmen at their meeting on 23 June that consultations had taken place between Mr. Boban and Mr. Karadzic and hat a draft providing for the organization of Bosnia and Herzegovina into a confederation of three constituent republics had been prepared. The constitutional principles already agreed upon as part of the Vance-Owen Peace Plan had been the basis for this document. The Co-Chairmen discussed the draft put forward and suggested additional elements designed to foster the cohesiveness and integrity of Bosnia and Herzegovina as a State Member of the United Nations. These included:

(a) The establishment of a Confederated Council of Ministers whose Chairman would be Prime Minister, rotating at agreed intervals among the three Republics with a similar rotation for the Foreign Minister;

(b) The referral of disputes that cannot be settled in the Constitutional Court by consensus for binding arbitration by a Chamber of five drawn from judges of the International Court of Justice;

(c) The international monitoring of throughways so as to ensure freedom of movement.

11. The Co-Chairmen felt that the draft principles were of sufficient importance to give them to the members of the Presidency of Bosnia and Herzegovina for their information (see appendix I), the Co-Chairmen themselves took no position on this document, seeing their role as one of clarifying the issues. The Co-Chairmen then arranged for the Presidency of Bosnia and Herzegovina to meet with Presidents Milosevic and Tudjman so that the two presidents could explain their thinking. The meetings, throughout, had the character of an exchange of views.
12. Following the conclusion of the meeting between the Presidency of Bosnia and Herzegovina and Presidents Milosevic and Tudjman, the Co-Chairmen had a further meeting with the Presidency. The presidency met again in Zagreb on Friday 25 June. It went to Brussels on Saturday, 26 June for meetings with the European Community troika and returned to Geneva for further discussion with the Co-Chairmen on Monday morning, 28 June. By then both President Izetbegovic and seven members of the presidency had met with Presidents Milosevic

and Tudjman and the European Community troika.

13. In the afternoon of 28 June the Co-Chairmen also had discussions with Mr. Boban and Mr. Karadzic. During those discussions, the two leaders largely reconfirmed their acceptance of the Vance-Owen Plan's military agreement subject to reference to the Mixed military Working Group for updating and consequential amendment. They also agreed on texts that maintained key parts of the Vance-Owen agreement on interim arrangements (see appendices II and III), the texts were distributed to all members of the Presidency of Bosnia and Herzegovina, including President Izetbegovic. The Co-Chairmen again did not take any position on these texts.

14. In the light of their discussion with the Co-Chairmen, all members of the Presidency of Bosnia and Herzegovina met in Sarajevo on 29 June. They decided to appoint a group of three of their members to make policy suggestions for the Presidency in reacting to the proposals of the Serbs and the Croats mentioned above. The Presidency announced its intention to pursue this matter and indicated that it would wish to meet again with the Co-Chairmen.

III. MEETING OF THE STEERING COMMITTEE OF THE INTERNATIONAL CONFERENCE

15. The Co-Chairmen convened a meeting of the Steering Committee of the International Conference on the Former Yugoslavia on 1 July:

The Co-Chairmen stressed the following points:

(a) The deteriorating security situation facing the United Nations Protection Force (UNPROFOR), the Office of the United Nations High Commissioner for Refugees (UNHCR) and humanitarian workers;
(b) The lack of resources for humanitarian operations;
(c) the lack of troops in UNPROFOR to fulfil the various mandates entrusted to it by the Security Council;
(d) The importance of continuing the search for negotiated solutions;
(e) The dangers of escalation of the conflict if the parties turn their backs on the search for negotiated solutions.

16. The Co-Chairmen circulated to the Steering Committee the revised constitutional principles, military agreements and interim arrangements put forward by the Serbs and Croats (see appendices I-III). During the meeting, they gave a detailed presentation of how, as a result of their clarification meetings, they thought a confederation of three Republics on Bosnia and Herzegovina might

look in terms of territorial boundaries. They stressed that no specific map had been put forward but that the Serbs and Croats were offering to negotiate directly along the lines that had already explained to President Izetbegovic and the collective Presidency. The Co-Chairmen indicated what elements they had stressed on behalf of the Muslim people during their discussion on the Serb-Croat proposals:

(a) The importance of any republic with a predominantly Muslim population being given an equitable and economically viable share of territory, with guaranteed access to the Sava river and Adriatic Sea;
(b) The need to ensure road and rail access routes for Sarajevo;
(c) The need for contiguous territorial links for Srebrenica, Zepa and Gorazde, the three "safe areas" in eastern Bosnia;
(d) The need to ensure that the Bihac area was of sufficient size to be viable and to have guaranteed road access to central Bosnia, and also out to Croatia;
(e) The importance of extending a republic with a predominantly Muslim population as far south as possible so as to make credible any guarantee of access to the Croatian port of Ploce.

IV. THE CHALLENGES AHEAD

17. In Bosnia and Herzegovina not only is there currently widespread fighting but the humanitarian operations of international organizations are obstructed or sabotaged for military purposes, while the personnel of UNPROFOR, UNHCR and other organizations are increasingly targeted deliberately by members of the armed forces. While all of this is going on, the support of the international community for humanitarian operations is dwindling, with a wide gap between the needs of humanitarian operations and the sums actually received. There is therefore a serious challenge of role and of means affecting the United Nations and other organizations in Bosnia and Herzegovina.

18. The following facts vividly bring out the situation on the ground.

A. *The Humanitarian Situation*

19. UNHCR has funds for humanitarian operations for only a few more weeks. The winter of 1992-1993 was mild in Bosnia and Herzegovina. The chances are very high that the coming winter will be more severe, taking into account the usual kind of winter in the country. The problem facing UNHCR and other

humanitarian organizations now is that they can hardly meet the needs of this summer, much less the needs of the coming winter. Since there is no sign of abatement of the conflict, it must be assumed that there will be a continued need for humanitarian relief in the winter. How to meet this need is difficult to foresee.

20. There is clear evidence of the deliberate targeting of humanitarian personnel. Aid convoys are deliberately blocked as part of the military strategies of all three sides. Humanitarian relief is diverted for military purposes. UNHCR and other humanitarian organizations are unable to operate in some parts of the country.

B. The Peace-keeping Situation

21. The focus of the military conflict has shifted from a relative localized Serbian-Muslim confrontation in the east to a wide-ranging Croat-Muslim confrontation in the centre. This phase of the conflict has disrupted UNHCR and commercial traffic to the point were food has become scarce in the area. Refugee populations are swelling. Humanitarian agencies advise that many civilians, having exhausted their savings and food stocks over the last winter are destitute.

22. In Bosnia and Herzegovina UNPROFOR has been given the tasks o^N protecting humanitarian convoys and deterring attacks against the safe areas. With the deployment of United Nations military observers to Gorazde, UNPROFOR has a presence in each of the safe areas that enables it to monitor the situation. However the stark realities are that there is little prospect for implementing the safe areas policy before new resources arrive and that the civilian population will face devastating hardship next winter unless UNPROFOR focuses on efforts to restore utilities and humanitarian relief deliveries.

23. At the same time, there is concrete evidence that members of UNPROFOR are becoming the targets of deliberate attacks with a resulting rise in the casualty rates. UNPROFOR has now incurred 548 casualties, including 51 fatalities, in the former Yugoslavia. The casualty rate has significantly increased recently.

24. UNPROFOR's resources and equipment are badly strained. UNPROFOR has an urgent need for more troops and for armoured vehicles, medical evacuation capabilities, night vision and other surveillance equipment, signals equipment and communications equipment.

CONCLUSION

25. Member of the Security Council will wish to consider the deteriorating situation on the ground against the prospects for a negotiated settlement. While it is obviously of paramount importance to sustain the humanitarian efforts for as long as possible, there is a real risk that, if the present downward spiral continues, it will be impossible for the United Nations to remain in Bosnia and Herzegovina.

APPENDIX I

CONSTITUTIONAL PRINCIPLES FOR BOSNIA AND HERZEGOVINA

(1) Bosnia and Herzegovina shall be a Confederation, the Constitution shall recognize three constituent peoples, as well as a group of others, with most governmental functions carried out by its provinces.

(2) The Republics shall not enter into agreements with foreign States or with international organizations if it can damage the interests of other Republics.

(3) Full freedom of movement shall be allowed throughout Bosnia and Herzegovina, to be ensured in part by the maintenance of internationally monitored throughways.

(4) All matters of vital concern to any of the constituent peoples and their Republics shall be regulated in the Constitutions of the Republics and the tripartite constitutional agreement of confederation which, as to these points may be amended only by consensus.

(5) The Republics shall have democratically elected legislature and democratically chosen chief executives and an independent judiciary. The Presidency of the Confederation shall be composed of three presidents of the Republic. There shall be a Confederal Council of Ministers composed of nine members, three from each of the Republics. The Chairman of the Confederal Council shall be Prime Minister. The Confederal Council shall include a Foreign Minister. The posts of Prime Minister and Foreign Minister shall rotate at agreed intervals among the three Republics. The Confederal Parliament shall be indirectly elected by the legislatures of the three Republics. The initial elections are to be United Nations/European Community/Conference on Security and Cooperation in Europe supervised.

(6) A Constitutional Court, with a member from each Republic, shall resolve disputes between the Republics and the Confederation, and among organs of the latter. In the event that the Constitutional Court cannot settle disputes by consensus, they shall be referred for binding arbitration by a Chamber of five drawn

from judges of the International Court of Justice.

(7) Bosnia and Herzegovina is to be progressively demilitarized under United Nations/European Community supervision.

(8) The highest level of internationally recognized human rights shall be provided for in the Constitution, which shall also provide for the ensurance of implementation through both domestic and international mechanisms.

(9) A number of international monitoring or control devices shall be provided for in the Constitution, to remain in place at least until the three Republics by consensus agree to dispense with them.

APPENDIX II

AGREEMENT FOR PEACE IN BOSNIA AND HERZEGOVINA

Provided that there is agreement on the constitutional principles and on a new map of the boundaries of the Republics within Bosnia and Herzegovina, the Serb and Croat sides accept the document "Agreement for peace in Bosnia and Herzegovina", subject to reference to the Mixed Military Working Group for updating and any consequential amendments, for example in relations to the agreed map.

APPENDIX III

INTERIM ARRANGEMENTS

A. COORDINATION BODY

A Coordination Body for the implementation of peace in Bosnia and Herzegovina (hereafter the Coordination Body) will be established in Bosnia and Herzegovina to an end and to work for reconstruction and full respect for human rights within the framework of the Vance-Owen peace process and the continuing work of the International Conference on the Former Yugoslavia.

The Coordination Body shall be composed of nine members, three each to be appointed from time to time by the parties representing respectively the Muslim, the Serb and the Croat peoples of Bosnia and Herzegovina.

The Coordination Body shall take its decision by a consensus of nine, or by a qualified majority of seven, or by simple majority of five, depending on whether the decision relates to a constitutional principle, to a specially important question or to normal business of the Coordination Body. The precise mechanism is to be laid down in the rules of procedure, which will be adopted by consensus.

The Coordination Body shall be chaired by the Co-Chairmen until the start of the interim period. The Coordination Body shall at the start of the interim period elect from its number three Presidents, who shall hold the chairmanship of the Coordination Body on a monthly basis, during which time they shall exercise the functions of Head of the Confederation of Bosnia and Herzegovina.

The Coordination Body shall elect a person to be Foreign Minister and this post will rotate every four months. The Foreign minister shall be answerable to the Coordination Body.

B. BOUNDARY COMMISSION

A Boundary Commission shall be set up by the Secretary-General in consultation with the Co-Chairmen. The Commission shall receive and, if necessary, hear evidence from those affected by the proposed provisional boundaries of the Republics and advise on the demarcation of the Republics to be specified in the new Constitution. The Commission shall consist of five persons: one each to be recommended by the three parties and two, one of whom shall be the Chairman, to be recommended by the Co-Chairmen. The Commission shall use as its basic document the provisional map of the Republics. It shall be empowered to consider the mainly marginal changes to the provisional boundaries. The decisions of the Commission shall be adopted by consensus. Any disagreement shall be referred to the Coordination Body.

C. INTERNATIONAL BORDERS

International border crossing-points are to be the responsibility of the Republics; initially, until the new Constitution comes into effect, in accordance with Secretary-General Security Council resolution 838 (1993), international observers shall be deployed to monitor effectively the implementation of the relevant Security Council resolutions. Monitors shall be drawn from the United Nations and, if appropriate, from Member States acting nationally or through regional organizations. Customs and excise arrangements shall be the responsibility of the Republic. The Coordination Body will establish the quota for funding the confederal budget.

D. POLICE FORCES

All uniformed police shall be controlled by the Republics and shall reflect the proportions on the constituent peoples of the respective Republics. Any necessary coordination shall be the responsibility of the Coordination Body.

E. PROTECTION OF HUMAN RIGHTS AND THE REVERSAL OF ETHNIC CLEANSING

1. During the interim period, all persons in Bosnia and Herzegovina shall be entitled to all rights provided for in the existing Constitution and in applicable legislation in force, as well as to all rights provided for in specified international instruments on human rights (set out in document S/24795, annex VII, appendix). To the extent that there are any discrepancies, the provision providing the greater protection of human rights shall be applied. All statements or commitments made under duress, particularly those related to the relinquishment of rights to land or property, should be treated as wholly null and void.

2. The implementation of the above-mentioned human rights shall be ensured through:

   (a) The courts of the Republics of Bosnia and Herzegovina, to which all persons shall have unimpeded access;

   (b) An Interim Human Rights Court for Bosnia and Herzegovina, to be established immediately along the lines of that proposed by the Co-Chairmen for inclusion in the new Constitution;[a] and

   (c) The immediate appointment of four Ombudsmen, supported by adequate staff and facilities.[b]

3. In addition, there shall be an International Human Rights Minority Mission, to be established by the Secretary-General and to be headed by an Interim Human Rights Commissioner for Bosnia and Herzegovina, to be based in Sarajevo. Deputy Commissioners are to be based in various parts of the country. The Commissioner is to be supported by international human rights monitors, deployed throughout Bosnia and Herzegovina; in order to provide protection in urgent cases they shall be allowed to intercede with the Coordination Body and

---

[a]   See S/24795, annex VII, sect.VI.B.3.

[b]   Ibid., sect.VI.B.2.

the governments of the Republics, and with UNPROFOR; they may refer issues to the ombudsmen and to other human rights agencies as needed, and are to work closely with UNHCR, International Committee of the Red Cross (ICRC) and other humanitarian agencies. The Commissioner is expected to submit regular reports to the Secretary-General who is to report periodically to the Security Council and to other international bodies, including the United Nations Commission on Human Rights and its Special Rapporteur.

4. The Coordination Body and the governments of the Republics shall be required to make certain that all authorities give the fullest access, in respect of all relevant persons and places, to the Interim Human Rights Commissioner, the Deputy Commissioners and the human rights monitors, as well as to UNHCR, ICRC and other international humanitarian organizations.

5. It is understood that as part of the UNPROFOR deployment in Bosnia and Herzegovina there will be a large civilian police element whose principal task would be to monitor the police of the Republics so that each: has an appropriately balanced ethnic composition (see sect. D above); does not oppress members of minority ethnic groups; contributes positively to the reversal of "ethnic cleansing" by protecting persons returning after having been forced to flee; carries out the judgements of courts, in particular the Human Rights Court (see sect. E.2 (b) above); and assist the Interim Human Rights Commissioner, the Deputy Commissioners and the human rights monitors (see sect. E.3 above). All of these monitors would be responsible to the United Nations Secretary-General's Special Representative.

F. INTERNATIONAL ACCESS AUTHORITY

1. Principle 3 of the agreed constitutional principles states that "full freedom of movement shall be allowed throughout Bosnia and Herzegovina, to be ensured in part by the maintenance of internationally controlled throughways". In order to implement this principles, the Coordination Body shall establish an International Access Authority:

   (a) To have sole responsibility for all railway lines in Bosnia and Herzegovina that traverse more than one Republic;
   (b) To have responsibility, in cooperation with UNPROFOR, for these roads which are declared to be internationally controlled throughways;
   (c) To regulate, where necessary, the operation of port facilities on the River Sava.

2. The essential purpose of the International Access Authority will be to guarantee full freedom of movement between and within the Republics and also to and from the Republics to the Republic of Croatia and the Republic of Serbia. It is intended that the Authority be in operation as soon as possible during the interim period. Following the conclusion of the peace package, all designated throughways shall come under the responsibility of UNPROFOR; thereafter there will be a period of overlapping responsibility of UNPROFOR and the Authority, during which UNPROFOR's involvement will be phased out and its responsibilities assumed by traffic police employed by the Authority. This transfer of responsibility requires the agreement of all members of the Authority.

3. The Coordination Body shall appoint the Interim Access Authority.

4. The Authority shall have its headquarters in Sarajevo.

122. LETTER DATED 3 AUGUST 1993 FROM THE SECRETARY-GENERAL ADDRESSED TO THE PRESIDENT OF THE SECURITY COUNCIL[*]

I have the honour to convey the attached report addressed to me on 2 August 1993 by the Co-Chairmen of the Steering Committee of the International Conference on the Former Yugoslavia.

Annex
Report of the Co-Chairmen of the Steering Committee of the International Conference on the Former Yugoslavia

INTRODUCTION

1. The Secretary-General reported to the Security Council on 8 July on the activities of the Co-Chairmen of the Steering Committee of the International Conference on the Former Yugoslavia (S/26066). The present report contains information on the latest efforts of the Co-Chairmen to stop the conflict in Bosnia and Herzegovina, as well as on other activities of the Conference.

---

[*]   UN Doc. S/26233, 3 August 1993. Signed by Boutros Boutros-Ghali.

I. BOSNIA AND HERZEGOVINA

2. The Co-Chairmen have continued their search for a negotiated settlement to the conflict in Bosnia and Herzegovina. They have maintained contacts with the different sides to the conflict, seeking to serve as a channel of communication and to clarify ideas and proposals advanced by the parties during the discussions.

3. During their contacts with Presidents Izetbegovic, Mr. Boban and Mr. Karadzic, as well as in related contacts with Presidents Milosevic, Bulatovic and Tudjman, the Co-Chairmen impressed upon them the urgency of reconvening peace talks to strive for a negotiated and durable solution. As a part of this process, the Co-Chairmen arranged for a meeting, held in Geneva on Saturday, 17 July, between President Milosevic and President Tudjman.

4. Having regard to developments on the ground, especially the deteriorating humanitarian situation and the persistence of conflict, the Co-Chairmen invited the Bosnian sides, together with Presidents Milosevic, Bulatovic and Tudjman, to come to Geneva for talks on Friday, 23 July 1993. The Co-Chairmen also appealed to Bosnian leaders to order their forces to refrain from further hostilities and to help to alleviate the humanitarian situation, especially by assisting in the restoration of utilities in Sarajevo and in allowing access for humanitarian convoys.

5. Owing to the hostilities then taking place around Sarajevo, President Izetbegovic requested, and the Co-Chairmen agreed to, a postponement of the talks from Friday, 23 July to Sunday, 25 July 1993. For similar reasons, a further deferral was made to Tuesday, 27 July, when all sides came to Geneva for peace talks. Seven other members of the Presidency of Bosnia and Herzegovina also attended, as did President Milosevic, Bulatovic and Tudjman. Furthermore, President Izetbegovic brought with him five leaders of political parties, with whom the Co-Chairmen met and held discussions.

6. The peace talks began on 27 July and were continuing as at 2 August 1993. The discussions concentrated on steps to secure a ceasefire and on ways and means of dealing with humanitarian issues; future constitutional arrangements; and the allocation of territory to the constituent units.

A. Cessation of Hostilities and Humanitarian Issues

7. Following discussion on 27, 28 and 29 July, President Izetbegovic, Mr. Karadzic and Mr. Boban agreed to issue immediate directives to their military commanders to implement a full cessation of hostilities. They further agreed that, in order to reinforce that directive, the commanders of the three military

forces should meet immediately at Sarajevo Airport under the chairmanship of the United Nations. Furthermore, the commanders should meet each day while the talks continued so as to discuss the causes of any conflict and to correct the situation. The commanders were also requested to discuss whether any modifications were needed to the military agreements contained in the Vance-Owen Peace Plan (see S/25479, annex IV) that all three sides have reaffirmed.

8. The military commanders of the three sides met at Sarajevo Airport on 30 July 1993 under the auspices of the Force Commander of the United Nations Protection Force (UNPROFOR). At the end of their meeting that day, they signed an agreement providing that all forces of the three parties cease firing and freeze all military activities, including military movements, deployment of forces and establishment of fortifications. The agreement also provides for permitting free passage for UNPROFOR convoys and convoy escorts and free passage for humanitarian aid convoys. The text of the agreement signed is reproduced in appendix I to the present report.

B. *Constitutional Agreement*

9. During the discussion on constitutional issues, all sides submitted working papers, which were distributed and discussed. Taking these submissions into account and having regard to the issues raised on the discussions, a consolidated working paper was discussed and examined article by article, with all sides participating in an open and constructive manner.

10. After intensive discussion on a number of drafts submitted by the parties, with amendments submitted by all three parties, they agreed on 30 July to a Constitutional Agreement for a Union of Republics of Bosnia and Herzegovina to form part of an overall peace settlement. The text of the Constitutional Agreement is reproduced in appendix II to the present report.

C. *Access Authority*

11. The Co-Chairmen stressed the vital importance of ensuring freedom of movement throughout the country. They proposed establishing an Access Authority, as foreseen under the Vance-Owen Peace Plan, with throughways to ensure access in sensitive areas of the country after UNPROFOR withdraws. They also stressed that the "blue routes" concept in the Agreement for Peace in the Vance-Owen Peace Plan would also be maintained and that would ensure, within a few days, access through Sarajevo city and the surrounding areas out to key cities.

12. The railway and road from Ploce to Doboj which, after it crosses the Croatian border, follows the route Mostar-Jablanica-Sarajevo-Zenica-Doboj, criss-crosses all three of the constituent republics. For this reason, the Co-Chairmen strongly felt that it should be run by the Access Authority. There would be guaranteed road access along the designated "blue routes" (Sarajevo-Ilidza-Hadzici-Tarcin-Jablanica-Mostar, Sarajevo-Rajlovac-Ilijas-Visoko-Zenica, Sarajevo-Bentbasa-Mokro-Sokolac-Vlasenica-Zvornik) as soon as UNPROFOR started to implement the military plan. This time interval while UNPROFOR was present in the country would allow a number of bypass roads to be constructed to give guaranteed access within the territory of each constituent republic.

D. The Map

13. The Co-Chairmen's detailed discussions on the map started on 21 July 1993. They are determined to ensure that the suggestion made during their earlier clarification talks that any Muslim-majority republic should have at least 30 per cent of the territory of Bosnia and Herzegovina and have guaranteed access to the Sava river and to the sea at Ploce should be fulfilled.
14. The discussions on the map are continuing.

II. CROATIA

15. Following the military actions of the Croatian armed forces in January 1993, the Security Council, by its resolution 802 (1993), ordered, among other things, that Croatian government forces be withdrawn from the areas within or adjacent to the United Nations protected areas. Since then, successive rounds of discussions have been organized within the framework of the International Conference, as well as under the auspices of UNPROFOR, to bring about compliance with Security Council resolution 802 (1993).
16. On 15-16 July 1993, an agreement relevant to the implementation of that resolution was signed by Serb local authorities and by representatives of the Croatian Government. The Agreement followed contacts that the Co-Chairmen had had earlier with president Milosevic and President Tudjman, followed by discussions held in Zagreb and Erdut. The Agreement of 15-16 July provided that there would be no Croatian armed forces or police in the areas specifies in the Agreement after 31 July 1993. UNPROFOR would move in those areas. In the villages of Islam Grcki, Smokovic and Kasic, Serb police together with United Nations Civilian Police (UNCIVPOL) would be present. With the with-

drawal of the Croatian armed forces and police, according to the first paragraph of the Agreement, Maslenica Bridge, Zemunik Airport and Peruca Dam would be under the exclusive control of UNPROFOR. The building of a pontoon bridge could proceed after the signature of the agreement by both sides. Both sides agreed to intensify their efforts to reach a negotiated solution to all problems existing between them, starting with a ceasefire agreement to be negotiated by UNPROFOR. The text oft he Agreement is set out in appendix III to the present report.

17. Following the signature of the Agreement, efforts continued to get the two sides to sign a ceasefire agreement. On 20 July 1992, Croatian and Serb delegations met in Vienna in a plenary session and reviewed a draft ceasefire agreement that had been produced by UNPROFOR. Initially the talks went well, with few significant differences between the parties. A military working group was established to examine in detail the areas involved and the exact lines of withdrawal. However, after both sides consulted their authorities, it emerged that the Croatian Government considered that the ceasefire agreement was not linked to the agreement of 15-16 July, while the Serbs insisted that the Croatian forces should withdraw in accordance with that agreement before they would sign any global ceasefire. Despite the best efforts of the negotiations, it proved impossible to find a formula to reconcile these positions, and on 22 July the talks were adjourned until further notice.

18. Subsequently, on 23 July 1993 the Croatian authorities signed a unilateral undertaking to the agreement of 15-16 July in order for UNPROFOR units to start deploying in the Zemunik/Maslenica area not later than 0900 hours on 26 July. UNPROFOR forces would assume control of the whole area by not later than 31 July. The other areas would be taken over by UNPROFOR after the signing of a former ceasefire agreement. The undertaking further provided that, in the villages mentioned in the Agreement of 15-16 July UNCIVPOL would be present together with five Serb policemen in each village, armed with sidearms only. Those policemen would be allowed to cross the present confrontation line and enter the villages on 1 August. The task of the undertaking is set out in appendix IV to the present report. The Serb local authorities rejected the undertaking, as not falling within the scope of the agreement of 15-16 July.

19. The crux of the problem has been that the Croatian Government has not yet withdrawn from the areas from which they promised to withdraw in the Agreement on 15-16 July, while the Serbs repeatedly warned that, unless the Agreement is complied with by 31 July, they would feel free to shell the Maslenica Bridge and surrounding areas.

20. Numerous contacts have been made with the Croatian authorities in Zagreb and the Co-Chairmen of the International Conference have had discussions on the matter with President Tudjman.

21. On 25 July the Deputy Force Commander of UNPROFOR obtained an undertaking from the Serb leadership to refrain from all armed hostilities until 31 July 1993, in order to allow the Croatian armed forces and police to withdraw from the areas specified in the Agreement of 15-16 July. The text of the undertaking is set out in appendix IV to the present report.

22. Repeated efforts to let the Croatian authorities to comply with the 15-16 July Agreement were unsuccessful and the Serbs continued to indicate that they would feel free to resume armed hostilities after 31 July.

23. On 30 July 1993, Croatian Defence Minister Susak informed the Deputy Force Commander of UNPROFOR as follows:

(a) United Nations military observers can go into all areas specified in the Agreement of 15-16 July;

(b) Armed troops can deploy into the area of the "blue zones", i.e. Maslenica Bridge, Zemunik Airport and Serbian villages;

(c) Discussions can continue after 31 July.

24. The Serb leadership considers that none of the proposals complied with the Agreement of 15-16 July.

25. The Security Council considered its situation on 30 July 1993. Having heard with deep concern a report from the Special Representative of the Secretary-General for the Former Yugoslavia, the Security Council demanded that the Croatian forces withdraw forthwith in conformity with the agreement of 15-16 July and that they permit the immediate deployment of UNPROFOR. The Council also demanded that the Krajina Serb forces refrain from entering the area. The Council called for maximum restraint from all the parties, including the observance of a ceasefire. The Council warned of the serious consequences of any failure to implement the Agreement of 15-16 July.

26. Following the issuance of the statement, the Co-Chairmen have been in contact with the parties and with others in a position to influence the situation so as to promote compliance with the decisions of the Security Council.

III. HUMANITARIAN ISSUES

27. Since the last report of the Secretary-General, Mrs. Sakado Ogata, United Nations High Commissioner for Refugees and Chairperson of the Humanitarian

Issues Working Group, has maintained close contact with Governments of the region and with the Bosnian parties, through her Special Envoy and Chiefs of Missions. On 14 July 1993 she visited Sarajevo to express support to its besieged population and to re-emphasize to President Izetbegovic her commitment to continue humanitarian operations in Bosnia and Herzegovina, where possible.

28. On 16 July 1993, Mrs. Ogata chaired a meeting of the Humanitarian Issues Working Group in Geneva, attended by senior representatives of all Governments of the region, of a large number of interested States, and of several inter-governmental and non-governmental organizations. The meeting was addressed by Mrs. Ogata, Mr. Stoltenberg, Lord Owen, Mr. Nakajima of the World Health Organization (WHO), President Sommaruga of the International Committee of the Red Cross (ICRC) and by senior representatives of the World Food Programme (WFP) and the United Nations Children's Fund (UNICEF). Mrs. Ogata informed the meeting of the serious obstacles affecting the international relief effort, including the ongoing denial and obstruction of humanitarian access in many areas of Bosnia and Herzegovina, and attacks on and harassment of relief staff. She highlighted the intensification of war and persecution and the dire conditions of the population of Sarajevo and Mostar and in central Bosnia. Warning that, under these conditions a humanitarian catastrophe would be unavoidable during the coming winter months, she called on all Bosnian parties to respect the humanitarian and impartial nature of the international relief effort and to ensure unimpeded and safe access.

29. A further serious obstacle Mrs. Ogata mentioned was the shortfall in funding for all United Nations agencies participating in the relief effort. The shortfall had already resulted in cutbacks in various support programmes including in Croatia and Yugoslavia (Serbia and Montenegro), which were facing substantial and rising social and economic difficulties. Mrs. Ogata emphasized the need for continuous and increased burden-sharing with all regional countries of asylum, while calling in these and other States to continue to provide admission and proper treatment, under safe conditions, to persons in need of protection irrespective of their ethnic or religious origin.

30. Expressing concern about the difficulties faced by UNPROFOR and by the Office of the United Nations High Commissioner for Refugees (UNHCR) and other humanitarian organizations, the meeting reaffirmed its commitment to the international relief effort in the entire region. Many delegates expressed their willingness to participate in, or otherwise support, a UNHCR-proposed consortium to provide shelter to the increasing number of displaced persons, particularly in central Bosnia, and to undertake essential infrastructural repairs, where feasible. The continuing need to provide temporary protection was recognized,

as well as the need to ease the burden of the refugee-receiving States in the region. Financial pledges were made, totalling US $ 126 million, of which $ 63 million were for UNHCR's programme for the former Yugoslavia. While these pledges are encouraging, they will unfortunately not permit UNHCR and other humanitarian organizations to sustain the international relief effort for former Yugoslavia beyond October 1993. Moreover, while the number of people dependent on external assistance is rising daily, parties to the conflict in Bosnia and Herzegovina are rendering it increasingly difficult to reach the victims and to ease their plight.

IV. ARBITRATION COMMISSION

31. As the Secretary-General reported earlier to the Security Council (see S/25708, para. 19), the Working Group on Succession Issues had submitted to the Arbitration Commission six legal questions for its opinion. On 16 July 1993, the arbitration Commission issued three advisory opinions, giving its views on four of the questions. These opinions are reproduced in appendix VI to the present report. The Commission also indicated that it would give responses relating to the other two questions shortly.

V. CONCLUDING OBSERVATIONS

32. During the latest round of peace talks on Bosnia and Herzegovina unprecedented positive steps have been registered.

(a) The leadership of the three sides negotiated for the first time intensively, cordially and in a constructive manner for seven days continuously, and continues to do so;

(b) All three sides agreed to a constitutional framework for Bosnia and Herzegovina on 30 July;

(c) The political leadership of the three sides directed their military commanders to observe a ceasefire and an agreement to that effect was signed by the military commanders on 30 July;

(d) The political leadership of the three sides directed their military commanders to observe a ceasefire and an agreement to that effect was signed by the military commanders on 30 July;

(e) Fighting in Bosnia and Herzegovina has been decreasing greatly while the talks are on;

(f) Electricity and water are again available in Sarajevo although there are still technical problems. The gas pipeline has now been turned on by the Hungarian authorities;

(g) Humanitarian convoys are getting through. The current success rate is 80 per cent;

(h) The delimitation of constituent parts of the State of Bosnia and Herzegovina has been taking shape and every effort is being made to see to it that the areas allocated to the Muslim-majority Republic, which contain most of the wealth and the industrial base of the country, should not be less than 30 per cent of the overall territory.

APPENDIX I
AGREEMENT FOR A COMPLETE CESSATION OF ALL COMBAT ACTIVITIES AMONG THE PARTIES IN CONFLICT OF 30 JULY 1993[*]

THE UNDERSIGNED MILITARY COMMANDERS, as representatives of their respective Parties in conflict,

Respecting the recent decisions of their commanders-in-chief in Geneva, made under the auspices of the International Conference on the Former Yugoslavia,

Mindful of their obligations under relevant Security Council resolutions, including to ensure UNPROFOR's safety and freedom of movement,

Recognizing the absolute urgency of the present situation and pledging their full efforts to see that this Agreement is honoured,

Have agreed as follows:

Article I
Cessation of all Combat Activities

1. Beginning upon signature of this Agreement, all forces of the three Parties shall cease firing and shall freeze all military activities, including military movements, deployments of forces and establishment of fortifications.

2. Written orders mandating such cessation of combat activities shall be issued, as soon as possible following signature of this Agreement, by each of the undersigned military commanders.

---

[*] Signed by General Rasim Delic, Lieutenant-General Ratko Mladic, and General Milivoj Petkovic, and as UNPROFOR witnesses by General Jean Cot, Force Commander, and Lieutenant General Francis Briquemont, Commander Bosnia and Herzegovina.

Article II
Humanitarian Aid and Freedom of Movement

Written orders shall be issued by the undersigned military commanders, as soon as possible following signature of this Agreement, permitting:

(a) Free passage for UNPROFOR;

(b) Free passage for UNPROFOR convoys and convoy escorts, subject to routine control of numbers of personnel and weapons entering and leaving territory under the control of a Party; and

(c) Free passage for humanitarian aid convoys, subject to reasonable control of the contents and personnel that are part of the convoy at one checkpoint.

UNPROFOR acknowledges that each Party has legitimate concerns over movements within territories under its control. UNPROFOR shall provide notification of convoy movements.

Article III
Verification of Compliance with this Agreement

1. The undersigned military commanders shall confirm to UNPROFOR the issuance of orders required by this Agreement, and their acknowledgement by subordinate commanders. Full assistance shall be extended to UNPROFOR to permit it to monitor the implementation of this Agreement. UNPROFOR officers in the field may be consulted to provide assistance in implementation of this Agreement.

2. The undersigned military commanders, or their authorized representatives, shall continue to meet daily at a specified time while their commanders-in-chief are meeting in Geneva or, when necessary, on the request of any of the Parties. In accordance with the recommendation made in Geneva by the commanders-in-chief of the Parties, the draft "Military Agreement on the Cessation of Hostilities" shall be discussed among other issues.

3. For urgent matters, the military commanders shall make available through reliable communications on a 24-hour a day basis, a representative who is authorized to take decisions or reach those with such authority.

THIS AGREEMENT, done pursuant of the commanders-in-chief of the Parties in Geneva, shall enter into force upon its signature.

DONE at Sarajevo Airport, on the 30th day of July, 1993, in two versions, one in English and the other in the language of the Parties. Where there are differences of interpretation between the versions, the English version shall control.

APPENDIX II

CONSTITUTIONAL AGREEMENT OF THE UNION OF REPUBLICS OF
BOSNIA AND HERZEGOVINA

I. THE UNION OF REPUBLICS OF BOSNIA AND HERZEGOVINA

Article 1

The Union of Republics of Bosnia and Herzegovina is composed of three Constituent Republics and encompasses three constituent peoples: the Muslims, Serbs and Croats, as well as a group of other peoples. The Union of Republics of Bosnia and Herzegovina will be a member state of the United Nations, and as a member state it shall apply for membership of other organizations of the United Nations system.

Article 2

The flag and emblem of the Union of Republics of Bosnia and Herzegovina shall be specified by a law adopted by the Union Parliament.

Article 3

(a) Citizenship of Bosnia and Herzegovina shall be determined by a law adopted by the Union Parliament.

(b) Every person who on the entry into force of this Constitutional Agreement was entitled to be a citizen of the Republic of Bosnia and Herzegovina shall be entitled to be a citizen of a Constituent Republic as well as of the Union of Republics of Bosnia and Herzegovina.

(c) Dual citizenship shall be allowed.

(d) Decision about citizenship shall be made by the designated organs of the Constituent Republics, subject to the competent courts.

Article 4

Neither the Union of Republics of Bosnia and Herzegovina nor any of the Constituent Republics shall maintain any military force, and any forces existing on the date of entry into force of this Constitutional Agreement shall be progressively disarmed and disbanded under the supervision of the United Nations and the European Community.

II. THE CONSTITUENT REPUBLICS AND THEIR RESPONSIBILITIES

Article 1

(a) The boundaries of the Constituent Republics shall be as set out in Annex A, Part I. Except as provided in (b) boundaries of the Republics may only be changed by the procedure provided for amending this Constitutional Agreement.

(b) Marginal changes in the boundaries set out in Annex A may be made by the Presidency on the recommendation of a Boundary Commission, which shall receive evidence from those specifically affected by them. The Commission shall consist of five persons appointed by the Secretary-General of the United Nations, of whom three shall be persons recommended by representatives of the three constituent peoples.

(c) The areas specified in Annex A, Part II, even though within the territory and under the jurisdiction of a Constituent Republic, shall be vested as specified in Article VII.2 (b) for the purpose of ensuring continued access to buildings of the Union in Sarajevo, to the sea at Neum and to the Sava River.

(d) There shall be no border controls on boundaries between the Constituent Republics, and there shall be free movement of persons, goods and services throughout the territory of the Union of Republics of Bosnia and Herzegovina.

Article 2

(a) Each of the Constituent Republics shall adopt its own constitution, which shall provide for democratic forms of government, including democratically elected legislatures and chief executives and independent judiciaries, as well as for the highest standards of human rights and fundamental freedoms. No provision of these constitutions may be inconsistent with this Constitutional Agreement.

(b) The initial elections in each Constituent Republic shall be supervised by the United Nations and the European Community.

Article 3

All governmental functions and powers, except those assigned by this Constitutional Agreement to the Union of Republics of Bosnia and Herzegovina or to any of its institutions, shall be those of the Constituent Republics.

Article 4

All acts taken by a competent governmental authority of any of the Constituent Republics shall be accepted as valid by the other Constituent Republics.

III. THE COMMON INSTITUTIONS OF THE UNION OF REPUBLICS OF
BOSNIA AND HERZEGOVINA

Article 1

(a) The Presidency of the Union of Republics of Bosnia and Herzegovina shall consist of the President, or of an appointee of the legislature, of each of the Constituent Republics.

(b) The Chairmanship of the Presidency shall rotate every four months among the members of the Presidency. The Chairman shall represent the Union of Republics of Bosnia and Herzegovina.

(c) The Presidency shall take all its decisions by consensus.

Article 2

(a) The head of the Council of Ministers of the Union of Republics of Bosnia and Herzegovina shall be the Prime Minister, who shall be appointed and may be removed by the Presidency. The post shall rotate every year so as to be occupied in turn by the nominee of the President of a different Constituent Republic.

(b) The Presidency shall also appoint and may remove a Foreign Minister. The post shall rotate every year so as to be occupied in turn by the nominee of the President of a different Constituent Republic.

(c) The Prime Minister and the Foreign Minister shall be from different Constituent Republics.

(d) Other Ministers may be appointed by the Presidency. They and the Prime Minister and the Foreign Minister shall constitute the Council of Minister, with responsibility for the policies of the Union of Republics of Bosnia and Herzegovina in relation to foreign affairs, international trade and the functioning of the common institutions, as well as any other function and institutions that the union Parliament may from time to time specify by law.

Article 3

(a) The Parliament of the Union of Republics of Bosnia and Herzegovina shall be composed of 120 representatives, one third each to be elected by the respective legislatures of the Constituent Republics.

(b) The Union Parliament may by a simple majority of the members from each Constituent Republic adopt laws within the competence of the Union of Republics of Bosnia and Herzegovina.

Article 4

The Union of Republics of Bosnia and Herzegovina shall have the following courts:

(i)   A Supreme Court, composed of four judges appointed by the Presidency, no two of whom shall be from the same peoples, which, except as specified in para. (iii), shall be the final court of appeals from the courts of the Constituent Republics.

(ii)   A Constitutional Court, composed of three judges appointed by the Presidency, no two of whom shall be from the same Constituent Republic, which shall be competent to resolve by consensus disputes among the Constituent Republics, between any of these and the Union of Republics of Bosnia and Herzegovina or any of its common institutions, and among any of these institutions. Should the Court not be constituted or be unable to resolve a dispute, it shall be referred for a binding decision by a standing arbitral tribunal composed of judges of the International Court of Justice or members of the permanent Court of Arbitration, one each of whom shall be elected be the President of each of the Constituent Republics and two of whom shall be elected by the Presidency or, if it is unable to do so, by the Secretary-General of the United Nations and by the President of the Council of Ministers of the European Community.

(iii)   A Court of Human Rights to be established in accordance with Resolution 93 (6) of the Committee of Ministers of the Council of Europe, whose precise composition and competence shall be as set out in the agreed annex B.

Article 5

Joint authorities between two or more of the Constituent Republics may be established by agreement of the Republics concerned if approved by a law adopted by the Union Parliament.

IV. INTERNATIONAL RELATIONS

Article 1

(a) The Union of Republics of Bosnia and Herzegovina shall apply for membership of European and international institutions and organizations, as decided by the Presidency.

(b) Any Constituent Republics may apply for membership of an international organization if such membership would not be inconsistent with the interests of the Union of Republics of Bosnia and Herzegovina or of either of the other Constituent Republics.

Article 2

(a) The Union of Republics of Bosnia and Herzegovina shall remain a party to all international treaties in force for the Republic of Bosnia and Herzegovina on the date of the entry into force of this Constitutional Agreement, unless the Union Parliament decides that steps to denounce any such treaty shall be taken. However, treaties entered into after 18 November 1990 shall be considered by the Union Parliament within a period of three months from the entry into force of this Constitutional Agreement and shall only remain in force if the Union Parliament so decides.

(b) The Union of Republics of Bosnia and Herzegovina shall continue all diplomatic relations until the Presidency decides to continue or discontinue them.

(c) The Union of Republics of Bosnia and Herzegovina may become a party to international treaties if such participation is approved by the Union Parliament. The Parliament may by law provide for participation in certain types of international agreements by decision of the Presidency. To the extent such participation would involve responsibilities that are to be carried out by the Constituent Republics, their advance approval must be secured, except in respect of the treaties referred to in Article V.3.

(d) Any Constituent Republic may, if eligible, become a party to an international treaty if such participation would not be inconsistent with the interests of the Union of Republics of Bosnia and Herzegovina or of either of the other Constituent Republics.

V. HUMAN RIGHTS AND FUNDAMENTAL FREEDOMS

Article 1

(a) Subject to Article V.2, all persons within the territory of the Union of Republics of Bosnia and Herzegovina shall be entitled to enjoy the rights and freedoms provided for in the instruments listed in Annex C.

(b) Should there be any discrepancy between the rights and freedoms specified in any of these instruments, or between any of these and the rights and freedoms specified in any other legal provision in force, the provision providing the greater protection for human rights and fundamental freedoms shall be applied.

Article 2

All courts, administrative agencies and other governmental organs of the Union of Republics of Bosnia and Herzegovina and of the Constituent Republics shall apply and conform the rights and freedoms specified in the instruments listed in Parts I and IV of Annex C. The rights specified in the instruments listed in Parts II and III of Annex C shall be considered as aspirations to be attained as rapidly as possible; all legislative, judicial, administrative and other governmental organs of the Union and Republican governments shall take these rights appropriately into account in promulgating, executing and interpreting any legislative provisions designed to or otherwise suitable or implementing such rights and in otherwise carrying out the functions of these organs.

Article 3

The Union of Republics of Bosnia and Herzegovina shall as soon as possible become a party to each of the international treaties listed in Annex C.

Article 4

All organs of the Union and Republican Governments shall cooperate with the supervisory bodies established by any of the instruments listed in Annex C, as well as with the International Human Rights Monitoring Mission for Bosnia and Herzegovina established by the United Nations.

Article 5

(a) All citizens have the right to settle in any part of the territory of the Union of Republics of Bosnia and Herzegovina. They shall have the right to have restored to them any property of which they were deprived in the course of ethnic cleansing and to be compensated for any property which cannot be restored to them.
(b) The Union Parliament, as well as the legislature of the Constituent Republics, shall enact laws to assist in implementing these rights.

Article 6

To assist in implementing the rights and freedoms specified in this Chapter and in particular in Article V.5 (a), Ombudsmen shall be appointed and carry out functions initially as specified in Annex D and thereafter as specified in a law adopted by the Union Parliament.

VI. FINANCES

Article 1

(a) The Union Parliament shall each year, on the proposal of the Prime Minister and with the subsequent approval of the Presidency, adopt a budget covering the expenditures required to carry out only those functions of the Union of Republics of Bosnia and Herzegovina relating to the maintenance of its common institutions and compliance with its international obligations, as well as such other functions as may from time to time be agreed by he Union Parliament.

(b) If no such budget is adopted in due course, the budget for the previous year shall be used on a provisional basis.

Article 2

(a) The expenditures provided for in the budget shall, except to the extent that other revenues are available or as otherwise specified in a law adopted by the Union Parliament, be covered in equal part by each of the Constituent Republics.

(b) Other sources of revenues, such as custom duties, fees for services or taxes on specified activities, may be determined by law.

VII. THE CONSTITUTIONAL AGREEMENT

Article 1

(a) This Constitutional Agreement may be amended by decision of the Union Parliament, when such amendment has been approved by each of the Constituent Republics according to its constitutional processes.

(b) No amendments may be adopted that abolish or diminish any of the rights or freedoms specified in Chapter V.

Article 2

(a) This Constitutional Agreement may not be abolished and none of the Constituent Republics may withdraw from the Union of Republics of Bosnia and Herzegovina without the prior agreement of all of the Republics. Such a decision may be appealed to the Security Council by any of the Constituent Republics, and the Council's decision shall be final.

(b) Should any of the Constituent Republics withdraw from the Union of Republics of Bosnia and Herzegovina, the areas specified in Annex A, Part II that are within the territory of such Republic shall remain a part of the Union of Republics of Bosnia and Herzegovina. Should the Union be dissolved or should both the Serb and the Croat majority Republics withdraw from the Union, then the areas specified in Annex A, Part II that are within the territories of those Constituent Republics shall become part of the Muslim majority Republic.

Article 3

This Constitutional Agreement shall enter into force when approved as part of the overall peace settlement by representatives of the three constituent peoples, and on a date specified by them.

LIST OF ANNEXES

A. (See art. II.I (a) and (c)) Part I: Boundaries of the constituent Republics;
   Part II: Areas vested in the Union of Republics of Bosnia and Herzegovina
B. (See art. III.4 (iii)) Composition and competence of the Human Rights Court
C. (See art. V.1 (a)) List of human rights instruments
D. (See art. V.6) Initial appointment and functions of the Ombudsmen

APPENDIX III
AGREEMENT*

1. There will be no Croatian armed forces or police in the areas specified on the attached map after 31 July 1993.
2. UNPROFOR shall move into the areas specified on the attached map.
3. In the villages of Isalm Gorcki, Smokovic and Kasic, Serb police together with UNPROFOR will be present; the number of Serb police shall be agreed with UNPROFOR.
4. With the withdrawal of the Croatian armed forces and police according to paragraph 1 above, Maslenica Bridge, Zemunik Airport and Peruca Dam shall be under the exclusive control of UNPROFOR. The building of the pontoon bridge may be proceed after the signature of this agreement by both sides.
5. Both sides agree to intensify their efforts to reach a negotiated solution to all problems existing between them, starting with a ceasefire agreement to be negotiated by UNPROFOR.

---

* Signed for the Krajina authorities by S. Jarcevic on 15 July 1993 and for the Government of Croatia by Ivica Murdrinic on 16 July 1993; and as witnesses, on behalf of the International Conference on the Former Yugoslavia, for the Krajina authorities by K. Vollebaek and G. Ahrens, and for the Government of Croatia by K. Vollebaek and General Eide.

APPENDIX IV

COMPLEMENTARY AGREEMENT, DATED 23 JULY 1993, TO THE AGREEMENT
OF 15-16 JULY 1993*

The areas mentioned in the agreement of 15-16 July 1993 will be under the control of UNPROFOR. UNPROFOR units will start to deploy in the Zemunik-Maslenica area not later than 0900 hours on 26 July 1993. UNPROFOR forces will assume control of the whole area by not later than 31 July 1993. The other areas will be taken over by UNPROFOR after the signing of a formal ceasefire agreement.

In the villages mentioned in the agreement of 15-16 July 1993, UNCIVPOL will be present together with five Serb policemen in each village, armed with side-arms only. Those police men will be allowed to cross the present confrontation line and enter the village on 1 August 1993.

APPENDIX V

SERBIAN REPUBLIC OF KRAJINA**

1. In order to implement paragraph 1 of the Erdut agreement, i.e. to enable the unobstructed withdrawal of Croatian forces from the area indicated in the map annexed to the Erdut agreement, the Serbian Army of Krajina has ceased all armed hostilities since 18 July 1993. We strongly commit ourselves to refrain from all armed hostilities until 31 July 1993.

2. For the purpose of controlling the cessation of armed hostilities in this period, we are inviting the UNPROFOR Command to deploy urgently its forces and observers along the whole of the confrontation line, as has been agreed between the Serbian Army of Krajina and UNPROFOR.

3. We comply with UNPROFOR's request that, in compliance with the spirit of the Erdut agreement, their forces be deployed in the areas from which the Croatian forces will withdraw, on condition that we are previously given assurance by the UNPROFOR Command that they will withdraw form these areas until 2400 hours on 31 July 1993 if until then the Croatian side does not fully implement the agreement of 15 and 16 July 1993; in other works, if the Croatian side does not withdraw from all the areas indicated on the map annexed to the

---

* Signed for the Government of Croatia by Slavko Degoricija and General Stipetic; and as witnesses, on behalf of UNPROFOR, by General Eide and General Cot.
** Signed on original Serbian version by Dorde Bjegovic, Prime Minister. Reproduction of this appendix does not imply any official endorsement by the United Nations.

Erdut agreement.

4. We accept UNPROFOR's obligation to inform us on time on the plan of deployment of UNPROFOR forces in the specified areas.

5. We express our readiness to agree with the other side in the lasting ceasefire and restoration of peace after the Erdut agreement has been implemented.

Appendix VI
Letter Dated 26 July 1993 from the Chairman of the Arbitration Commission of the International Conference on the Former Yugoslavia Addressed to the Co-Chairmen of the Steering Committee of the International Conference on the Former Yugoslavia*

In response to the letter dated 20 April 1993, the Arbitration Commission of the International Conference on the Former Yugoslavia on 16 July 1993 issued three opinions relating to questions Nos. 2, 3, 4 and 6.

Attached hereto are the texts of opinion Nos. 11, 12 and 13 in their original language, French, as well as in an unofficial English translation.

In accordance with the possibility provided to it under article 7.5 of the rules of procedure of 26 April 1993, the Arbitration Commission has deferred consideration to questions Nos. 1 and 5 for one month.

ENCLOSURE

A. Opinion No. 11**

On 20 April 1993 the Co-Chairmen of the Steering Committee of the International Conference on the Former Yugoslavia referred six questions of the Chairman of the Arbitration Commission, seeking the Commission's opinion.

Question No. 2 was:

"On what date(s) did State succession occur for the various States that have emerged from the Socialist Federal Republic of Yugoslavia?"

On 12 May, the Co-Chairmen of the Steering Committee of the International Conference transmitted to the Chairman of the Commission a declaration by the Government of the Federal Republic of Yugoslavia raising a number of objec-

---

*   Signed by Robert Badinter.
** Paris, 16 July 1993.

tions to the reference to the Commission. The members of the Commission unanimously adopted a document reacting to the assertions made by the Federal Republic of Yugoslavia; this was addressed to the Co-Chairmen of the Steering Committee of the International Conference on 26 May 1993. None of the States parties to the proceedings has contested the Commission's right to answer questions referred to it.

The Commission has taken cognizance of the memorandum, observations and other materials communicated by the Republic of Bosnia and Herzegovina, the Republic of Croatia, the former Yugoslav Republic of Macedonia and the Republic of Slovenia, which have been passed on to all the successor States of the Socialist Federal Republic of Yugoslavia. The Federal Republic of Yugoslavia has submitted no memorandum or observations on the questions referred.

1. In accordance with the generally accepted definition contained in article 2 of the 1978 and 1983 Vienna Conventions on the Succession of States, "'date of the succession of States' mean the date upon which the successor State replaces the predecessor State in the responsibility for the international relations of the territory to which the succession of States relates".

2. In the case in point there is a particular problem arising for the circumstances in which State succession occurred:

First, the predecessor^QState, the Socialist Federal Republic of Yugoslavia, has ceased to exist and, as the Commission found on its opinion No, 9, none of the successor States can claim to be the sole continuing State.

Second, the demise of the Socialist Federal Republic of Yugoslavia, unlike that of other recently dissolved States (USSR, Czechoslovakia), resulted not from an agreement between the parties but from a process of disintegration that lasted some time, starting, in the Commission's view, on 29 November 1991, when the Commission issued opinion No. 1, and ending on 4 July 1992, when it issued opinion No. 8.

3. However, while these circumstances need to be taken into account in determining the legal arrangements applying to State succession (see arts. 18, 31 and 41 of the Vienna Convention of 8 April 1983 on Succession of States in respect of State Property, Archives and Debts), they are immaterial in determining the date of State succession, which, as the Commission indicated in paragraph 1 above, is the date upon which each successor State replaced the predecessor State. Since, in the case on point, the successor States of the Socialist Federal Republic of Yugoslavia are new States, and since they became independent on different dates, the relevant date is, for each of them, that on which they became States.

As the Commission indicated in opinion No. 1, this is a question of fact that is to be assessed in each case in the light of the circumstances in which each of the States concerned was created.

4. The issue is the same as regards to the Republics of Croatia and Slovenia, both of which declared their independence on 25 June 1991 and suspended their declarations of independence for three months on 7 July 1991, as provided by the Brioni Declaration. In accordance with the declaration, the suspension ceased to have effect on 8 October 1991. Only then did these two Republics definitively break all links with the organs of the Socialist Federal Republic of Yugoslavia and become sovereign State in international law. For them, then, 8 October 1991 is the date of State succession.

5. Macedonia asserted its rights to independence on 25 January 1991, but it did not declare its independence until after the referendum held on 8 September 1991, the consequences of which were drawn in the Constitution adopted on 17 November 1991, effective on the same day. That is the date on which the Republic of Macedonia became a sovereign State, having no institutional link with the Socialist Federal Republic of Yugoslavia. So 17 November 1991 is the date of State succession as regards to Macedonia.

6. In opinion No. 4, issued on 11 January 1991, the Arbitration Commission came to the view that "the will of the peoples of Bosnia and Herzegovina to constitute the Socialist Republic of Bosnia and Herzegovina as a sovereign and independent State [could] not be held to have been fully established". Since then, in a referendum held on 29 February and 1 March 1992, the majority of the people of the Republic have expressed themselves in favour of a sovereign and independent Bosnia. The result of the referendum was officially promulgated on 6 March, and since that date, notwithstanding the dramatic events that have occurred in Bosnia and Herzegovina, the constitutional authorities of the Republic have acted like those of a sovereign State in order to maintain its territorial integrity and their full and exclusive powers. So 6 March 1992 must be considered the date on which Bosnia and Herzegovina succeeded the Socialist Federal Republic of Yugoslavia.

7. There are particular problems in determining the date of State succession in respect of the Federal Republic of Yugoslavia because that State considers itself to be the continuation of the Socialist Federal Republic of Yugoslavia rather than a successor State.

As has been affirmed by all international agencies which have had to state their views on this issue, and as the Commission itself has indicated more than once, this is not a position than can be upheld.

The Commission opines that 27 April 1992 must be considered the date of State succession in respect of the Federal Republic of Yugoslavia because that was the date on which Montenegro and Serbia adopted the Constitution of the new entry and because the relevant international agencies then began to refer to "the former Socialist Federal Republic of Yugoslavia", affirming that the process of dissolution of the Socialist Federal Republic of Yugoslavia had been completed.

8. The Arbitration Commission is aware of the practical problems that might ensue from determining more than one date of State succession because of the long-drawn-out process whereby the Socialist Federal Republic of Yugoslavia was dissolved. One implication is that different dates would apply for the transfer of State property, archives and debts, and of other rights and interests, to the several successor States of the Socialist Federal Republic of Yugoslavia.

9. The Commission would point out, however, that the principles and rules of international law in general relating to State succession are supplemental, and that States are at liberty to resolve difficulties that might ensue from applying them by entering into agreements that would permit an equitable outcome.

10. The Arbitration Commission consequently takes the view:

- That the dates upon which the States emerged stemming from the Socialist Federal Republic of Yugoslavia succeeded the Socialist Federal Republic of Yugoslavia are:
- 8 October 1991, in the case of the Republic of Croatia and the Republic of Slovenia;
- 17 November 1991 in the case of the former Yugoslav Republic of Macedonia;
- 6 March 1992 in the case of he Republic of Bosnia and Herzegovina;
- 27 April 1992 in the case of the Federal Republic of Yugoslavia (Serbia-Montenegro);
- That, unless the States concerned agree otherwise, these are the dates upon which State property, assets and miscellaneous rights, archives, debts and various obligations of the former Socialist Federal Republic of Yugoslavia pass to the successor States.

B. OPINION NO. 12[*]

On 20 april 1993, the Co-Chairmen of the Steering Committee of the International Conference of the Former Yugoslavia referred six question to the Chair-

---

[*]   Paris, 16 July 1993.

man of the Arbitration Commission, seeking the Commission's opinion. Question No. 3 was:

"(a) What legal principles apply to the division of State property, archives and debts of the Socialist Federal Republic of Yugoslavia in connection with the succession of States when one or more of the parties concerned refuse(s) to cooperate?

(b) In particular, what should happen to property

- not located on the territory on any of the States concerned; or
- situated on the territory of the States taking part in the negotiations?"

Question No. 6 was:

"(a) On what conditions can States, within whose jurisdiction property formerly belonging to the Socialist Federal Republic of Yugoslavia is situated, block the free disposal of that property or take other protective measures?

(b) On what conditions and under what circumstances would such States be required to take such steps?"

The Commission considers that these two questions form an entity and should be answered in one and the same opinion.

On 12 May 1993, the Co-Chairmen of the Steering Committee of the International Conference transmitted to the Chairman of the Commission a declaration by the Government of the Federal Republic of Yugoslavia raising a number of objections to the reference to the Commission. The members of the Commission unanimously adopted a document reacting to the assertions made by the Federal Republic of Yugoslavia; this was addressed to the Co-Chairmen of the Steering Committee of the International Conference on 26 May 1993. None of the States party to the proceedings has contested the Commission's right to answer questions referred to it.

The Commission has taken cognizance of the memorandum, observations and other materials communicated by the Republic of Bosnia and Herzegovina, the Republic of Croatia, the former Yugoslav Republic of Macedonia and the Republic of Slovenia, which have been passed on to all the successor States of the Socialist Federal Republic of Yugoslavia. The Federal Republic of Yugoslavia has submitted no memorandum or observations on the questions referred.

1. In its opinion No. 9, the Arbitration Commission recalled the few well-established principles of international law applicable to State succession.

The fundamental rule is that States must achieve an equitable result by negotiation and agreement. The principles is applicable to the distribution of the State property, archives and debts of the Socialist Federal Republic of Yugoslavia.

2. If one or more of the parties concerned refused to cooperate, it would be in breach of that fundamental obligation and would be able internationally, with all the legal consequences this entails, notably the possibility for States sustaining loss to take non-forcible countermeasures, in accordance with international law.

3. It follows from the principles formulated above that the other States concerned must consult with each other and achieve, by agreement between them, a comprehensive equitable result reserving the rights of the State or States refusing to cooperate.

Such an agreement is *res inter alios acta* in relation to third States, be they States refusing to cooperate or other States. In accordance with the established principles of international law enshrined in article 34 of the Vienna Convention on the Law of Treaties, whereby "a treaty does not create either obligations or rights for a third State without its consent", third States on whose territory property covered by State succession is situated are not required to take action in pursuance of such agreements.

However, such third States may, in the exercise of their sovereignty, give effect to them if they satisfy the conditions set out in paragraph 2 above.

4. Even in the absence of such agreements, third States may take such interim measures of protection as are needed to safeguard the interest of the successor States by virtue of the principles applicable to State succession.

5. Third States would be required to do so if an international agency with powers in the matter took decisions that were binding on States within whose jurisdiction property having belonged to the former Socialist Federal Republic of Yugoslavia was situated.

6. The Arbitration Commission consequently takes the view that:

- Refusal by one or more successor States to cooperate in no way alters the principles applicable to State succession as set out in opinion No. 9;
- Other States concerned may conclude one or more agreements conforming to those principles in order to secure to equitable distribution of the States property, archives and debts of the Socialist Federal Republic of Yugoslavia;
- Such agreement would not be binding on States which were not party to them, nor on other States in whose territory property having belonged to the Socialist Federal Republic of Yugoslavia was situated;
- However, this answer is without prejudice to the rights of successor States sustaining loss by virtue of the refusal of one or more of the parties concerned to cooperate, to take countermeasures in accordance with international law, to the right of third States to take the necessary safeguard

measures to protect the successor States and to such obligations as might be incumbent on third States to give effect to decisions taken by international agency having powers in the matter.

C. Opinion No. 13[*]

On 20 April 1993, the Co-Chairmen of the Steering Committee of the International Conference on the Former Yugoslavia referred six questions to the Chairman of the Arbitration Commission, seeking the Commission's opinion. Question No. 4 was:

"Under the legal principles that apply, might any amounts owed by one or more parties in the form of war damages affect the distribution of State property, archives and debts in connection with the succession process?"

On 12 May 1993, the Co-Chairmen of the Steering Committee of the International Conference transmitted to the Chairman of the Commission a declaration by the Government of the Federal Republic of Yugoslavia raising a number of objections to the reference to the Commission. The members of the Commission unanimously adopted a document reacting to the assertions made by the Federal Republic of Yugoslavia; this was addressed to the Co-Chairmen of the Steering Committee of the International Conference on 26 May 1993. None of the States parties to the proceedings has contested the Commission's right to answer questions referred to it.

The Commission has taken cognizance of the memorandum, observations and other materials communicated by the Republic of Bosnia and Herzegovina, the Republic of Croatia, the former Yugoslav Republic of Macedonia and the Republic of Slovenia, which have been passed on to all the successor States of the Socialist Federal Republic of Yugoslavia. The Federal Republic of Yugoslavia has submitted no memorandum or observations on the questions referred.

1. In opinion No. 9 the Arbitration Commission appreciates that there are few well-established principles of international law that apply to State succession. Application of these principles is largely to be determined case by case, depending on the circumstances proper to each form of succession, although the 1978 and 1983 Vienna Conventions do offer some guidance.
2. The Commission would point out in particular that articles 18, 31 and 41 of the Convention of 8 April 1983 are relevant where State succession occurs as a

[*]   Paris, 16 July 1993.

result of the dissolution of a pre-existing State. While equity has some part to play in the division of State property, archives, and debts between successor States, these articles do not require that each category of assets or liabilities be divided in equitable proportions by only that the overall outcome be an equitable division.

3. However, this equitable outcome is to be obtained by reference to the law of State succession. The rules applicable to State succession, on the one hand, and the rules of State responsibility, on which the question of war damages depends, on the other, fall within two district areas of international law.

4. The equitable division of the assets and liabilities of the former Socialist Federal Republic of Yugoslavia between the successor States must therefore be effected without the question of war damages being allowed to interfere in the matter of State succession, in the absence of an agreement to the contrary between some or all of the States concerned or of a decision imposed upon them by an international body.

5. The Arbitration Commission would, however underline the fact that its reply to the question referred to it is in no way prejudicial to the respective responsibilities of the parties concerned in international law. The possibility cannot be excluded in particular of setting off assets and liabilities to be transferred under the rules of State succession on the one hand against war damages on the other.

6. Subject to the observations made above, the Arbitration Commission consequently takes the view that amounts that might be owing by one or more parties in respect of war damages can have no direct impact on the division of State property, archives or debts for purposes of State succession.

123. LETTER DATED 6 AUGUST 1993 FROM THE SECRETARY-GENERAL ADDRESSED TO THE PRESIDENT OF THE SECURITY COUNCIL[*]

I have the honour to convey the attached report addressed to me on 5 August 1993 by the Co-Chairmen of the Steering Committee of the International Conference on the Former Yugoslavia.

---

[*] UN Doc. S/26260, 6 August 1993. Signed by Boutros Boutros-Ghali.

Annex
Report of the Co-Chairmen of the Steering Committee on the activities of the International Conference on the Former Yugoslavia

INTRODUCTION

1. It is almost a year since efforts began within the International Conference on the Former Yugoslavia to stop the conflict in Bosnia and Herzegovina. During that time intensive, patient, and painstaking negotiations have been held with the sides involved in the conflict to help to reconcile their positions, but the historical background to the conflict, which stretches over centuries, and an intricately interwoven ethnic make-up in Bosnia and Herzegovina, have made this an exceptionally difficult and delicate task.

2. The past year's efforts have shown that the parties to the conflict are unable to make peace by themselves and even impartial intermediaries cannot always shift one or other of the sides from adopting intransigent and unreasonable positions, when they feel their vital interests are concerned. Nor can intermediaries keep them to their word. Ceasefires are entered into in the full knowledge that they are not going to be fulfilled, and other pledges broken within hours of being made.

3. On 2 May 1993, it appeared that a settlement was in sight: in Athens Mr. Karadzic added his signature to those of President Izetbegovic and Mr. Boban on the Vance-Owen Peace Plan (see S/25479, annex IV), but by 6 May, the Bosnian Serb "Assembly" in Pale had rejected the Plan. By 21 May, it had become clear that the international will was lacking to continue pushing for the 10-Province Solution proposed under the Vance-Owen Peace Plan and the substantial Bosnian-Serb military roll-back that was implied. As a direct consequence of appearing to move to merely containing Bosnian-Serb military gains, the Bosnian Croats, whose relations with the Bosnian Muslims were already under strain both in the Government of Bosnia and Herzegovina and as supposed military allies, started to act to consolidate their "Herzeg Bosna". Relations between the Bosnian Croats and the Bosnian Muslims deteriorated day by day. This flare-up in the fighting led to a further wave of displaced persons crossing the new front lines and more roadblocks, and put increasingly strain on the ability of international agencies to deal with the dramatically deteriorating humanitarian situation. With winter not far off, the prospects for the civilian population of Bosnia and Herzegovina began to look ever more dire.

4. The revival of the concept of a Confederation for Bosnia and Herzegovina by Presidents Milosevic and Tudjman occurred when the Co-Chairmen visited Belgrade and Zagreb from 9 to 11 June 1993. The concept of a confederal solution

for Bosnia and Herzegovina had first been proposed in March 1992 by Ambassador Cutileiro in Lisbon, when Lord Carrington was the European Community Peace Envoy. This proposal came even before the outbreak of war and was initially accepted by all three sides. However, president Izetbegovic withdrew his support for the proposal, and it was from then on vigorously opposed by the Bosnian Government side in the context of the International Conference on the Former Yugoslavia peace talks in Geneva.

5. In Belgrade the Serbs' initial outline map was put forward to the Co-Chairmen, consisting of a core area in central Bosnia for a Muslim-majority republic. There was clearly defined access to the Sava in the north. In the south, the boundary ran just south of Jablanica. Access to Sarajevo was through a narrow bottleneck. The Muslim-majority republic was to have a slender finger of territory in eastern Bosnia and in the Bihac area the boundary was to be on the current line of confrontation.

6. The Co-Chairmen, after consultation with the Security Council and the European Community, attempted to clarify the Serb-Croat proposal and urge the Serbs and Croats to put forward proposals that took more account of the principles of the August 1992 London Conference, both in regard to any new Constitution, and to the size and shape of a republic in which the Muslims would be in a majority. They also emphasised the great importance of keeping as much of the Vance-Owen plan as possible in any new proposal, particularly those aspects relating to the protection of human rights and the reversal of ethnic cleansing.

7. The Co-Chairmen told the Serbs that the initial outline map would be totally unacceptable to the international community. If there was to be a new tripartite structure for the State of Bosnia and Herzegovina, the Serb and Croat sides had to be far more aware of the legitimate needs of the Muslim-majority republic. While they could not commit the international community to support this approach, the Co-Chairmen indicated to the Serb and Croat sides that, if they expected their proposals to be given serious consideration by President Izetbegovic, they would have to be reworked, and this work should be completed before they could arrange a meeting between President Izetbegovic and Presidents Milosevic, Bulatovic and Tudjman.

8. When the proposals were presented again to the Co-Chairmen on 15 and 16 June, it was an avowedly confederal solution. The Co-Chairmen advised strongly against both labelling and thinking in this way, for it would be seen as the first step towards secession. In addition, there had to be guarantees against the unilateral secession of any of the Constituent Republics. The map did, however, show some progress in extending the boundaries of a proposed Muslim-majority area towards the sea and their overall percentage of territory had been increased, but

in eastern Bosnia their territory had decreased. The Co-Chairmen insisted that the three United Nations safe areas in eastern Bosnia - Srebrenica, Zepa and Gorazde - had to be retained, and that the overall percentage should not fall below 30 per cent. Progress was made, in cooperation with the Croatian Government, on guarantees for access to the port of Ploce. The Co-Chairmen also emphasized that allocation of a port area as well as access to the Sava River remained a major concern.

9. The Serb-Croat concept was explained to President Izetbegovic by Presidents Milosevic, Tudjman and Bulatovic. He listened carefully and asked for a detailed proposal that he could put before the Presidency.

10. On 23 June in Geneva the Serb and Croat sides came forward with nine constitutional principles (see S/26066, appendix I) after detailed discussion with the Co-Chairmen. These were presented to seven members of the Presidency, who had travelled to Geneva, and who also saw the "troika" of the European Community. The Presidency came up with constitutional proposals of its own, based on a federal concept, which were presented to the Co-Chairmen on 11 July in Zagreb.

11. In the intervening period the Co-Chairmen remained in close contact with President Izetbegovic. They also had further contacts with Presidents Tudjman and Milosevic, and both Presidents agreed that any Muslim-majority republic should have at least 30 per cent of the territory of Bosnia and Herzegovina. However, a revised map presented in Belgrade on 8 July, although it had improved in some aspects, no longer included the three "safe areas" in Eastern Bosnia established under Security Council resolution 824 (1993). The Co-Chairmen warned that, if the Serb and Croat parties wanted the international community to accept their proposals, these areas had to be left in the Muslim-majority republic. They re-emphasized this point when they met Presidents Tudjman and Milosevic in Geneva on 17 July. On that occasion the two Presidents issued a statement saying that they were against the partition of Bosnia and Herzegovina, and that the only way to achieve permanent peace lay in the recognition of all the three constituent peoples.

I. THE CURRENT ROUND OF PEACE TALKS

12. It was against this background that the Co-Chairmen invited the three sides to participate in the latest round of negotiations.

13. The peace talks began on 27 July 1993 and are expected to continue on Monday 9 August. The discussions concentrated on steps to secure a ceasefire and on ways and means of dealing with humanitarian issues; future constitutional

arrangements; and the allocation of territory to the constituent entities.

14. Despite the undertakings of all three political leaders to end hostilities, the negotiations, as has been all too common, proceeded against the backdrop of continued fighting, although at a generally much reduced level. The major offensive activity throughout all but the last few days of the current negotiating period was the Bosnian Government's attack against the Bosnian Croats in central Bosnia, leading to the capture of Fojnica and of most of Gornji Vakuf. The Bosnian Serb attacks against the government forces around Sarajevo dominated the picture, started first on Zuc Hill, then on Mounts Bjelasnica and Igman. The Bosnian-Serb operations in northern Bosnia to widen their east-west corridor from the Croatian Army, continued to build up in the general Prozor area prior to possible counter-attacks against the Bosnian government forces. Western and eastern Bosnia were generally quiet.

Cessation of hostilities and humanitarian issues

15. Following discussions on 27, 28 and 29 July 1993, President Izetbegovic, Mr. Karadzic and Mr. Boban agreed to issue immediately directives to their military commanders to implement a full cessation of hostilities. They further agreed that in order to reinforce this directive, the commanders of the three military forces should meet immediately at Sarajevo Airport under the chairmanship of the United Nations. Furthermore, the commanders should meet each day while the talks continued so as to discuss the causes of any conflict and to correct the situation. The commanders were also requested to discuss whether any modifications were needed to the military agreement contained in the Vance-Owen Peace Plan, which all three sides had reaffirmed.

16. The military commanders of the three sides met at Sarajevo Airport on 30 July under the auspices of the Force commander of the United Nations Protection Force (UNPROFOR). At the end of their meeting that day, they signed an agreement providing that all forces of the three parties cease combat activities and freeze all military activities, including military movements, deployment of forces and establishment of fortifications. The agreement also provided for permitting free passage for UNPROFOR convoys and convoy escorts, and free passage for humanitarian aid convoys (see S/26233, appendix I).

17. On 4 August, the Serb side agreed in principle to the Co-Chairmen's reiteration of the proposal for the opening up of Sarajevo. The general concept is the relief of the immediate humanitarian situation and the reversal of the strangulation of the people of Sarajevo by the opening up of selected routes to all movements of humanitarian foods, material and people. Checkpoints would need to be

established to exclude any warlike goods. The Co-Chairmen put the proposal to members of the Presidency of 5 August; they agreed in principle without prejudice to their negotiating position. Both sides agreed to instruct their military commanders to enter into immediate negotiations, within the framework of the Mixed Military Working Group, with a view to reaching an early agreement on this proposal, which would have to be staged and subject to the strict upholding of the ceasefire. After a meeting in Pale on 5 August, Lieutenant General Briquemont and Mr. Karadzic issued a joint statement agreeing to the first stages in this process, to be followed up by a meeting on 6 August to consider the detail.

Constitutional Agreement

18. During the discussions on constitutional issues, all sides submitted working papers, which were distributed and discussed, taking these submissions into account, and having regard to the issues raised in the discussions, a consolidated working paper was discussed and examined in detail, with all sides participated in an open and constructive manner.

19. After intensive discussion on a number of drafts submitted by the parties, with amendments submitted by all three parties, they agreed on 30 July to a constitutional agreement for a Union of Republics of Bosnia and Herzegovina (see appendix I) and to its forming part of an overall peace settlement.

20. In reply to a letter which President Izetbegovic sent to them on 31 July asking for clarification of Chapter I, Article 1, of the Constitutional Agreement and in particular the question of the membership in the United Nations of the Union of Republics of Bosnia and Herzegovina, the Co-Chairmen wrote as follows:

"(a) Bosnia and Herzegovina is already a recognized State Member of the United Nations;

(b) The principles adopted of the London Conference, as well as the principles laid down by the Security Council, guarantee to sovereignty, independence and territorial integrity of Bosnia and Herzegovina as a State Member of the United Nations;

(c) Article I of the Constitutional Agreement, which all three parties have agreed to, states that 'the Union of Republics of Bosnia and Herzegovina will be a State Member of the United Nations'. We interpret this article in the spirit of the Charter of the United Nations, the Principles of the London Conference and the principles laid down by the Security Council and therefore confirm to you our understanding that the meaning of article 1 is that the Union of Republics of Bosnia and Herzegovina will continue as a State member of the United Nations."

21. The Co-Chairmen subsequently suggested to the Presidency that, if it was still concerned about the issue, it should ask the Security Council to put the matter beyond doubt.

22. It should be noted that the provisions of the Constitutional Agreement make it legally impossible to dissolve the Union without the free consent of all three Constituent Republics.

Annexes to the Constitutional Agreement

23. In subsequent discussions with the parties the following annexes to the Constitutional Agreement were prepared and were accepted by all three sides.

Annex B: Composition and Competence of the Human Rights Court;
Annex C: List of Human Rights Instruments incorporated in the Constitutional
           Agreement;
Annex D: Initial Appointment and Functions of the Ombudsmen.

Agreed Arrangements concerning the Constitutional Agreement of the Union of Republics of Bosnia and Herzegovina

24. All three sides agreed that "the name of each Constituent Republic will be determined by the competent authorities of that Republic". Also all three sides agreed that "the map of the three Constituent Republics set out in part I of annex A to the Constitutional Agreement will be referred to the Boundary Commission established in accordance with chapter II, article 1 (b), of that Agreement, and the Commission shall ensure that the territory of the Republic marked as No. 1 on the map shall not be less than 30 per cent of the entire territory of the Union of Republics of Bosnia and Herzegovina" (see appendix II).

Access Authority

25. During the discussions, the Co-Chairmen stressed the vital importance of ensuring freedom of movement throughout the country. They proposed establishing an Access Authority (see appendix II), as had been foreseen under the Vance-Owen Peace Plan, with Access Authority throughways to ensure access in sensitive areas of the country after UNPROFOR withdraws. The roads designated as throughways are set out in appendix II. They also stressed that the "blue route" concept in the Agreement for Peace in the Vance-Owen Peace Plan would also be maintained and this would ensure, within a few days, access though

Sarajevo city and the surrounding areas out to key cities. Immediately UNPROFOR started to implement the military plan, there would be guaranteed road access along the designated "blue routes": Sarajevo-Ilidza-Hadzici-Tarcin-Jablanica-Mostar, Sarajevo-Rajlovac-Ilijas-Visoko-Zenica, Sarajevo-Bentbasa-Mokro-Sokolac-Vlasenica-Zvornik.

26. The railway and road from Ploce to Doboj which, after it crosses the Croatian border, follows the route Mostar-Jablanica-Sarajevo-Zenica-Doboj, would criss-cross all three of the proposed Constituent Republics. For this reason, the Co-Chairmen argued strongly that it should be run by the Access Authority and this too was agreed by all sides.

27. It was suggested by the Bosnian Serbs that, during the time that UNPROFOR was present in the country, a number of bypass roads could be built to give guaranteed access within the territory of each Constituent Republic, if they believed that this was necessary.

Access of Bosnia and Herzegovina to the Sea

28. The Co-Chairmen considered this question of key importance and the participation of President Tudjman in the peace talks facilitated the negotiation between the Republic of Croatia and the three Bosnian parties of a preliminary agreement for implementing the 1965 Convention on Transit Trade of Land-Locked States in order to secure preferential access for the Union of Republics of Bosnia and Herzegovina to two Croatian ports on the Adriatic: Ploce and Rijeka. The draft agreement (see appendix IV) would in return provide Croatia with designated road and rail routes from the northern to the southern part of its territory through that of Bosnia and Herzegovina. The Co-Chairmen believe that this agreement will greatly benefit the economies of both States, and the draft has been supported by all three sides.

Military Aspects of implementing a Peaceful settlement

29. During the discussions, the three sides reaffirmed their acceptance of the Agreement for peace in Bosnia and Herzegovina, which deals with the military aspects of implementing a peaceful settlement for Bosnia and Herzegovina and further agreed that all necessary updating of the document would be undertaken by the Mixed Military Working Group under the chairmanship of UNPROFOR. This process is now under way in Sarajevo (see appendix III).

Territorial arrangements (see annex A to the Constitutional Agreement)

30. Once the Bosnian Presidency had agreed in principle to examine a possible three-republic structure for Bosnia and Herzegovina, the Co-Chairmen pursued the approach they had consistently taken through the weeks of clarification talks. Emphasizing that, while the maps were the responsibility of the parties, any solution based on three republics was inevitably going to be more ethnically based than that in the Vance-Owen Peace Plan. Yet other crucial factors had to be taken into account, including communication links, geography and economic viability. They repeatedly stressed, however, that the Muslim-majority republic should have at least 30 per cent of the territory. This commitment was agreed by all three sides.

31. A series of intense and detailed bilateral and trilateral talks were held, during which the parties set out their positions. The Serb and Croat side repeatedly referred to the fact that the Muslim-majority republic would contain most of the major population centres of Bosnia and Herzegovina, and also the majority of the industrial centres and natural resources, and that this justified the Serb-majority Republic having a higher percentage of the territory than envisaged in the Vance-Owen Peace Plan. Nevertheless, the Serbs claimed that with 30 per cent guaranteed for the Muslim-majority republic, they would be accepting a major roll-back of about 18 per cent.

32. A great deal of progress was made during the bilateral and trilateral talks when all parties engaged fully in the negotiations. After President Izetbegovic's temporary withdrawal from the negotiations because of the continued fighting, especially around Sarajevo, the Co-Chairmen did their best to make further progress and in particular to persuade the Serb and Croat sides to cede more territory, and clarify points of contention, in bilateral talks.

33. *Brcko*. A detailed Serb proposal emerged in discussions for dealing with the question of access to Brcko. A fly-over complex should be constructed on the western outskirts of Brcko, where the Tuzla-Brcko road crosses the Tuzla-Brcko railway line, involving the Tuzla-Brcko road, the Tuzla-Brcko railway line and a new road that will run from west to east. From the west side of the fly-over complex the boundary of the Muslim-majority republic would run west along a line north of the Tuzla-Brcko railway; and run south-east to the Brcka river and from there south of the Tuzla road, skirting Broad and running west of Brcka. To the north-east of this fly-over complex, the boundary of the Muslim-majority republic would run to the north-west of the town, to a point east of the junction of the Gorice-Brcko and Donji Rahic-Brcko roads and from there to the Sava river, east of the settlement of Grbavica. It would run north-west along the Brcka

river, which would form the eastern boundary. The existing railway line running from the fly-over complex to the Sava in the territory of the Serb-majority republic would come under the Access Authority. The Access Authority would also be responsible for rebuilding the destroyed railway bridge across the Sava. The Presidency is considering its attitude to this proposal as part of the overall peace settlement.

34. *Eastern Bosnia*. President Izetbegovic pressed hard for a large area of territory in this area, going much wider than the three safe areas of Gorazde, Zepa and Srebrenica. The Co-Chairmen had intense negotiations with the Serb side, which initially was reluctant to cede any territory at all. The Co-Chairmen managed to move them some way from their initial offer of giving the three special autonomous status within the Serb-majority republic. Eventually the Serb side conceded that Gorazde should be linked territorially to the central area of the Muslim-majority republic. An Access Authority throughway would link it from Sarajevo to just above Trnovo, then through Cajnice to the Montenegrin border and the Sandjak, as had been proposed in the Vance-Owen peace plan. Zepa and Srebrenica would be linked to each other and the territory around them enlarged by 100 per cent. They would be linked to the Muslim-majority republic by an Access Authority throughway to Kakanj. The Presidency is considering its attitude to this proposal of an overall peace settlement.

35. *Bihac Pocket*. The Co-Chairmen urged the Serb side to extend the boundary of the Bihac area eastward from the existing front line. They recalled that this was an area which stirred up strong emotions in the international community because of the widely documented ethnic cleansing that had been taken place in such cities as Prijedor, Sanski and Bosanski Novi. President Milosevic backed the Co-Chairmen's request for the boundaries of this area to go east of the Una river, and some concessions were made, but the basic Serb position was that this territory had been traditionally Serb prior to massacres during the Second World War. Guaranteed access from Bihac to Rijeka was agreed, as was an Access Authority throughway to Travnik and eastern Herzegovina. The Presidency is considering its attitude to this proposal as part of an overall peace plan.

36. *Posavina and Eastern Herzegovina*. The Serb and Croat sides are still continuing to negotiate on the exact boundaries between their republics in the north at Posavina along the Sava, and in the south above Dubrovnik.

37. *Central Bosnia*. The boundary between the Croat and Muslim-majority republics in this region, where fighting was intense while negotiations were continuing, was an area of great contention. The atmosphere for negotiations was not improved by the offensive the Bosnian Government army launched in this region. A Serb-Croat proposal emerged for the boundary to run along the

Lasva River from Travnik to the east. The Presidency is considering its attitude to central Bosnia and is hoping to have bilateral talks with the Croat side before the talks resume in Geneva.

38. *Sarajevo*. This was the most contentious issue during discussion on the future map, with positions deeply entrenched. The passions aroused are intense. The local loyalties, mainly Muslim and Serb, though also Croat, of those living in the city itself and in the surrounding settlements are fierce, and have been heightened by more than a year of fighting. For any side, reaching a compromise by taking a decision to give up territory that has been held by their people through these months is an intensely difficult and emotive issue.

39. The Serbs proposed that all of the inner city of Sarajevo would be in the Muslim-majority republic and to make this possible, they are prepared to leave the area of Grbavica, which they currently hold. They believe, however, that they need to compensate for this by having the housing estate at Nedarici, which they hold, and the whole of the Dobrinja housing estate, the centre of which the Bosnian Government holds, in the Serb-majority republic.

40. Both the Muslim-majority republic and the Serb-majority republic would have access to the airport, with the boundary between the two republics running down the centre of the runway. The Muslim-majority republic's access to the airport would be through Stup, to the north of the airport. The Serb side would have access to Ilidza, Ilijas and Hadzici, all areas which they wish to retain, from the south of the airport. Road access from Pale to the airport would initially be via a throughway running along the transit route through the south of the city. The Serbs intend to build a bypass as soon as possible.

41. The Serbs propose that, in order to provide guaranteed access to the city from the north, Vogosca, which is current held by the Serbs, and the area around it, would become part of the Muslim-majority republic. Of the settlements surrounding Sarajevo, the Serb-held areas of Ilijas, Rajlovac and Ilidza would form part of the Serb-majority republic. In order to link the Serb-held areas of Ilidza and Lukavica, which have a majority Serb population, the settlements of Butmir, currently held by the Bosnian Government, and Hrasnica, parts of which are held by the Government, would come within the Serb-majority republic.

42. The railways running into the city from the north and south would cross over the proposed boundaries a number of times, and since it is in the interests of all parties to allow the free flow of traffic on them, they would be under the Access Authority.

43. The Serb side would undertake to construct a bypass on the territory of the Muslim-majority republic linking the main Mostar road to the Zenica road and would be responsible for building another bypass linking the Zenica road to the

main Tuzla-Sarajevo road east of Ilijas.

44. It has been agreed by all sides that the main road running south from Sarajevo to just above Trnovo would be an Access Authority throughway and also that Sarajevo Airport would come under the Access Authority.

45. For President Izetbegovic, and many among the Presidency and the opposition leaders who attended the talks in Geneva, the very idea of dividing the area surrounding Sarajevo from the city itself in any way is inconceivable. They believe that having fought for the idea of a united country, they cannot live with a solution which, regardless of what happens in the rest of the country, divides their capital city. They sense that they have world opinion on their side on this issue. On the other hand, the Serb side is equally adamant that Sarajevo is surrounded by areas that have been traditionally Serb for centuries, and which throughout the war have remained in Serb hands, and that these areas should be in the Serb-majority republic. They intend that the capital of the Serb-majority republic would be built around the Serb settlement of Ilidza.

46. This dilemma over Sarajevo is not new to the Co-Chairmen. During these last 10 days, many of the concepts that had previously come up during the negotiations of the Vance-Owen peace plan were gone over yet again in considerable detail. These included all of the parties sharing the administration of the whole of Sarajevo (the 3-3 concept developed during the Vance-Owen negotiations), a small capital building area coming under joint administration and other similar schemes on which agreement is unlikely to be reached.

47. The Serb proposal that eventually emerged after long and difficult discussions with the Co-Chairmen, who warned them that it would present great difficulties to the other parties, was not acceptable to President Izetbegovic and a majority of the Presidency. It raised a number of problems, above and beyond the fundamental criticism of splitting the valley in which Sarajevo city itself nestles between the mountains. They had doubts over access from the city to the rest of the Muslim-majority republic, which was vital, although the Serb side had reluctantly agreed to give up the Vogasca area. They were also concerned about the Rajlovac area, which overlooks the road and rail access routes running to an from the centre.

Comment

48. Under these circumstances, the Co-Chairmen are driven to the belief that it may not be possible to negotiate a permanent solution in Sarajevo for some time. Time may be needed for the wounds of the war to heal; time to restore the damage done to communications and buildings in the Serb, Muslim and Croat areas;

time during which the three republics will learn to live and cooperate together and for the citizens of Bosnia and Herzegovina to rediscover mutual respect and tolerance.

49. Sarajevo is already designated a United Nations safe area. The Co-Chairmen believe that the Security Council and the international community will have to consider whether a temporary solution might have to be found, which may have to last one or more years. During this time it could be easier for both sides to move towards a permanent settlement, compatible with the Constitutional Agreement that has been a major product of the present period of negotiations.

II. IMPLEMENTATION

50. The Co-Chairmen have proceeded on the basis that, if agreement was reached on the concepts outlined above, from the start of implementation of the Agreement for peace in Bosnia and Herzegovina, the force established or charged by the United Nations with assisting in implementing agreement (the Implementation Force) would, after the relevant Security Council resolutions, begin implementing all key aspects of the Agreement for peace in Bosnia and Herzegovina. It has been envisaged that the Implementation Force would have its responsibilities phased out and withdraw once free and fair elections were held, which would have to take place not later than two years after the signature of the Agreement relating to Bosnia and Herzegovina. In respect of these areas designated as 'safe areas' under Security Council resolution 824 (1993), apart from Sarajevo, which is dealt with above, and Tuzla and Bihac which would not be as vulnerable as the others, the United Nations had said that it would give special protection as a temporary measure. It is possible that the United Nations Security Council might wish to continue to protect Srebrenica, Zepa and Gorazde for a period longer than after the elections, but that is a judgement which it is unlikely to make at this moment.

51. The Implementation Force would have responsibility for opening up and guaranteeing key communication links, as outlined above. It would only be following the withdrawal of the Implementation Force that sole responsibility for ensuring access and freedom of movements along roads and railways would fall to the Access Authority.

52. The Implementations Force would begin overseeing the separation of forces and the withdrawal of heavy weapons, which would facilitate the reopening of routes and the free movement of people. It would then move on to progressive demilitarization of the entire country.

53. During the implementation period, the civil elements of the Implementation Force would supervise the various civil engineering projects needed to effect the longer-term access arrangements, in particular in Brcko and Sarajevo. In the early months following a settlement, many temporary solutions would have to be adopted by local agreement. The Implementation Force would assist in devising and implementing such solutions prior to the realization of permanent solutions.

54. The Co-Chairmen cannot stress enough to the Security Council and the European Community the vital need for an effective Implementation Force. The early dispatch of a credible force will itself ensure the greatest chance of achieving the objectives of the peace settlement including the reversal of ethnic cleansing and the monitoring of human rights. The world has watched in dismay and despair as the horror has unfolded in Bosnia and Herzegovina. Nevertheless, the humanitarian effort over the last winter was immense and broadly successful. Peace now is imperative, but to ensure that it is not peace at any price, the world must pay the price of a serious and successful implementation period.

APPENDIX I

CONSTITUTIONAL AGREEMENT OF THE UNION OF REPUBLICS OF BOSNIA AND HERZEGOVINA*

I. THE UNION OF REPUBLICS OF BOSNIA AND HERZEGOVINA

Article 1

The Union of Republics of Bosnia and Herzegovina is composed of three Constituent Republics and encompasses three constituent peoples: the Muslims, Serbs and Croats, as well as a group of other peoples. The Union of Republics of Bosnia and Herzegovina will be a member state of the United Nations, and as a member state it shall apply for membership of other organizations of the United Nations system.

Article 2

The flag and emblem of the Union of Republics of Bosnia and Herzegovina shall be specified by a law adopted by the Union Parliament.

---

* Previously reproduced in document S/26233, appendix II.

Article 3

(a) Citizenship of Bosnia and Herzegovina shall be determined by a law adopted by the Union Parliament.

(b) Every person who on the entry into force of this Constitutional Agreement was entitled to be a citizen of the Republic of Bosnia and Herzegovina shall be entitled to be a citizen of a Constituent Republic as well as of the Union of Republics of Bosnia and Herzegovina.

(c) Dual citizenship shall be allowed.

(d) Decision about citizenship shall be made by the designated organs of the Constituent Republics, subject to the competent courts.

Article 4

Neither the Union of Republics of Bosnia and Herzegovina nor any of the Constituent Republics shall maintain any military force, and any forces existing on the date of entry into force of this Constitutional Agreement shall be progressively disarmed and disbanded under the supervision of the United Nations and the European Community.

II. THE CONSTITUENT REPUBLICS AND THEIR RESPONSIBILITIES

Article 1

(a) The boundaries of the Constituent Republics shall be as set out in Annex A, Part I. Except as provided in (b) boundaries of the Republics may only be changed by the procedure provided for amending this Constitutional Agreement.

(b) Marginal changes in the boundaries set out in Annex A may be made by the Presidency on the recommendation of a Boundary Commission, which shall receive evidence from those specifically affected by them. The Commission shall consist of five persons appointed by the Secretary-General of the United Nations, of whom three shall be persons recommended by representatives of the three constituent peoples.

(c) The areas specified in Annex A, Part II, even though within the territory and under the jurisdiction of a Constituent Republic, shall be vested as specified in Article VII.2 (b) for the purpose of ensuring continued access to buildings of the Union in Sarajevo, to the sea at Neum and to the Sava River.

(d) There shall be no border controls on boundaries between the Constituent Republics, and there shall be free movement of persons, goods and services throughout the territory of the Union of Republics of Bosnia and Herzegovina.

Article 2

(a) Each of the Constituent Republics shall adopt its own constitution, which shall provide for democratic forms of government, including democratically elected legislatures and chief executives and independent judiciaries, as well as for the highest standards of human rights and fundamental freedoms. No provision of these constitutions may be inconsistent with this Constitutional Agreement.

(b) The initial elections in each Constituent Republic shall be supervised by the United Nations and the European Community.

Article 3

All governmental functions and powers, except those assigned by this Constitutional Agreement to the Union of Republics of Bosnia and Herzegovina or to any of its institutions, shall be those of the Constituent Republics.

Article 4

All acts taken by a competent governmental authority of any of the Constituent Republics shall be accepted as valid by the other Constituent Republics.

III. THE COMMON INSTITUTIONS OF THE UNION OF REPUBLICS OF BOSNIA AND HERZEGOVINA

Article 1

(a) The Presidency of the Union of Republics of Bosnia and Herzegovina shall consist of the President, or of an appointee of the legislature, of each of the Constituent Republics.

(b) The Chairmanship of the Presidency shall rotate every four months among the members of the Presidency. The Chairman shall represent the Union of Republics of Bosnia and Herzegovina.

(c) The Presidency shall take all its decisions by consensus.

Article 2

(a) The head of the Council of Ministers of the Union of Republics of Bosnia and Herzegovina shall be the Prime Minister, who shall be appointed and may be removed by the Presidency. The post shall rotate every year so as to be occupied in turn by the nominee of the President of a different Constituent Republic.

(b) The Presidency shall also appoint and may remove a Foreign Minister. The post shall rotate every year so as to be occupied in turn by the nominee of the President of a different Constituent Republic.

(c) The Prime Minister and the Foreign Minister shall be from different Constituent Republics.

(d) Other Ministers may be appointed by the Presidency. They and the Prime Minister and the Foreign Minister shall constitute the Council of Minister, with responsibility for the policies of the Union of Republics of Bosnia and Herzegovina in relation to foreign affairs, international trade and the functioning of the common institutions, as well as any other function and institutions that the union Parliament may from time to time specify by law.

Article 3

(a) The Parliament of the Union of Republics of Bosnia and Herzegovina shall be composed of 120 representatives, one third each to be elected by the respective legislatures of the Constituent Republics.

(b) The Union Parliament may by a simple majority of the members from each Constituent Republic adopt laws within the competence of the Union of Republics of Bosnia and Herzegovina.

Article 4

The Union of Republics of Bosnia and Herzegovina shall have the following courts:

(i) A Supreme Court, composed of four judges appointed by the Presidency, no two of whom shall be from the same peoples, which, except as specified in para. (iii), shall be the final court of appeals from the courts of the Constituent Republics.

(ii) A Constitutional Court, composed of three judges appointed by the Presidency, no two of whom shall be from the same Constituent Republic, which shall be competent to resolve by consensus disputes among the Constituent Republics, between any of these and the Union of Republics of Bosnia and Herzegovina or any of its common institutions, and among any of these institutions. Should the Court not be constituted or be unable to resolve a dispute, it shall be referred for a binding decision by a standing arbitral tribunal composed of judges of the International Court of Justice or members of the permanent Court of Arbitration, one each of whom shall be elected be the President of each of the Constituent Republics and two of whom shall be elected by the Presidency or, if it is unable to do so, by the Secretary-General of the United Nations and by the President of the Council of Ministers of the European Community.

(iii) A Court of Human Rights to be established in accordance with Resolution 93 (6) of the Committee of Ministers of the Council of Europe, whose precise composition and competence shall be as set out in the agreed annex B.

Article 5

Joint authorities between two or more of the Constituent Republics may be established by agreement of the Republics concerned if approved by a law adopted by the Union Parliament.

IV. INTERNATIONAL RELATIONS

Article 1

(a) The Union of Republics of Bosnia and Herzegovina shall apply for membership of European and international institutions and organizations, as decided by the Presidency.

(b) Any Constituent Republics may apply for membership of an international organization if such membership would not be inconsistent with the interests of the Union of Republics of Bosnia and Herzegovina or of either of the other Constituent Republics.

Article 2

(a) The Union of Republics of Bosnia and Herzegovina shall remain a party to all international treaties in force for the Republic of Bosnia and Herzegovina on the date of the entry into force of this Constitutional Agreement, unless the Union Parliament decides that steps to denounce any such treaty shall be taken. However, treaties entered into after 18 November 1990 shall be considered by the Union Parliament within a period of three months from the entry into force of this Constitutional Agreement and shall only remain in force if the Union Parliament so decides.

(b) The Union of Republics of Bosnia and Herzegovina shall continue all diplomatic relations until the Presidency decides to continue or discontinue them.

(c) The Union of Republics of Bosnia and Herzegovina may become a party to international treaties if such participation is approved by the Union Parliament. The Parliament may by law provide for participation in certain types of international agreements by decision of the Presidency. To the extent such participation would involve responsibilities that are to be carried out by the Constituent Republics, their advance approval must be secured, except in respect of the treaties referred to in Article V.3.

(d) Any Constituent Republic may, if eligible, become a party to an international treaty if such participation would not be inconsistent with the interests of the Union of Republics of Bosnia and Herzegovina or of either of the other Constituent Republics.

V. HUMAN RIGHTS AND FUNDAMENTAL FREEDOMS

Article 1

(a) Subject to Article V.2, all persons within the territory of the Union of Republics of Bosnia and Herzegovina shall be entitled to enjoy the rights and freedoms provided for in the instruments listed in Annex C.

(b) Should there be any discrepancy between the rights and freedoms specified in any of these instruments, or between any of these and the rights and freedoms specified in any other legal provision in force, the provision providing the greater protection for human rights and fundamental freedoms shall be applied.

Article 2

All courts, administrative agencies and other governmental organs of the Union of Republics of Bosnia and Herzegovina and of the Constituent Republics shall apply and conform the rights and freedoms specified in the instruments listed in Parts I and IV of Annex C. The rights specified in the instruments listed in Parts II and III of Annex C shall be considered as aspirations to be attained as rapidly as possible; all legislative, judicial, administrative and other governmental organs of the Union and Republican governments shall take these rights appropriately into account in promulgating, executing and interpreting any legislative provisions designed to or otherwise suitable or implementing such rights and in otherwise carrying out the functions of these organs.

Article 3

The Union of Republics of Bosnia and Herzegovina shall as soon as possible become a party to each of the international treaties listed in Annex C.

Article 4

All organs of the Union and Republican Governments shall cooperate with the supervisory bodies established by any of the instruments listed in Annex C, as well as with the International Human Rights Monitoring Mission for Bosnia and Herzegovina established by the United Nations.

Article 5

(a) All citizens have the right to settle in any part of the territory of the Union of Republics of Bosnia and Herzegovina. They shall have the right to have restored to them any property of which they were deprived in the course of ethnic cleansing and to be compensated for any property which cannot be restored to them.

(b) The Union Parliament, as well as the legislature of the Constituent Republics, shall enact laws to assist in implementing these rights.

Article 6

To assist in implementing the rights and freedoms specified in this Chapter and in particular in Article V.5 (a), Ombudsmen shall be appointed and carry out functions initially as specified in Annex D and thereafter as specified in a law adopted by the Union Parliament.

VI. FINANCES

Article 1

(a) The Union Parliament shall each year, on the proposal of the Prime Minister and with the subsequent approval of the Presidency, adopt a budget covering the expenditures required to carry out only those functions of the Union of Republics of Bosnia and Herzegovina relating to the maintenance of its common institutions and compliance with its international obligations, as well as such other functions as may from time to time be agreed by he Union Parliament.

(b) If no such budget is adopted in due course, the budget for the previous year shall be used on a provisional basis.

Article 2

(a) The expenditures provided for in the budget shall, except to the extent that other revenues are available or as otherwise specified in a law adopted by the Union Parliament, be covered in equal part by each of the Constituent Republics.

(b) Other sources of revenues, such as custom duties, fees for services or taxes on specified activities, may be determined by law.

VII. THE CONSTITUTIONAL AGREEMENT

Article 1

(a) This Constitutional Agreement may be amended by decision of the Union Parliament, when such amendment has been approved by each of the Constituent Republics according to its constitutional processes.

(b) No amendments may be adopted that abolish or diminish any of the rights or freedoms specified in Chapter V.

Article 2

(a) This Constitutional Agreement may not be abolished and none of the Constituent Republics may withdraw from the Union of Republics of Bosnia and Herzegovina without the prior agreement of all of the Republics. Such a decision may be appealed to the Security Council by any of the Constituent Republics, and the Council's decision shall be final.

(b) Should any of the Constituent Republics withdraw from the Union of Republics of Bosnia and Herzegovina, the areas specified in Annex A, Part II that are within the territory of such Republic shall remain a part of the Union of Republics of Bosnia and Herzegovina. Should the Union be dissolved or should both the Serb and the Croat majority Republics withdraw from the Union, then the areas specified in Annex A, Part II that are within the territories of those Constituent Republics shall become part of the Muslim majority Republic.

Article 3

This Constitutional Agreement shall enter into force when approved as part of the overall peace settlement by representatives of the three constituent peoples, and on a date specified by them.

ANNEX A

I. THE BOUNDARIES OF THE CONSTITUENT REPUBLICS

1. The boundaries of the Constituent Republics shall be as indicated on the map below, subject to any changes that may be made in accordance with Chapter II, Article 1 (b) of the Constitutional Agreement.

II. AREAS VESTED IN THE UNION OF REPUBLICS OF BOSNIA AND HERZEGOVINA

1. The area defined by the present *opstina* of Neum, and that part of the present *opstina* of Stolac that lies below the southern border of the Constituent Republic that extend up through Sarajevo to Brcko on the Sava.
2. That part of the railway line from Tuzla that passes across Brcko to the railway bridge on the Sava.
3. Those public buildings in the city of Sarajevo and in the surrounding area that are designated by the Presidency to be used by the Union Parliament, the Council of Ministers, the Supreme, Constitutional and Human Rights Courts, and the administrative institutions of the Union.

ANNEX B
COMPOSITION AND COMPETENCE OF THE HUMAN RIGHTS COURT

Article 1
The Human Rights Court of Bosnia and Herzegovina (the "Court") shall operate within the framework of the mechanism established by the Council of Europe by Resolution 93 (6) of its Council of Ministers, as that Resolution may be amended from time to time.

Article 2
(a) The Court shall initially consist of nine judges.
(b) The Presidency shall appoint four of the judges of the Court, one from each recognized group: Muslims, Serbs, Croats and Others. These judges shall enjoy tenure and shall not require reappointment.
(c) The Committee of Minister of the Council of Europe shall appoint five of the judges of the Court in accordance with the above-cited resolution. These judges may not be citizens of the Union of Republics of Bosnia and Herzegovina nor of neighbouring States.
(d) If the Court concludes that its business requires the participation of more judges to avoid undue delays in the disposition of cases, the Government shall make arrangements with the Council of Europe for the appointment of additional judges, in accordance with the above-specified proportion of national and foreign judges.

Article 3
(a) The Court shall regulate its own procedure and its organization.
(b) Each panel of the Court is to have the composition specified for the Court in

article 2, paragraphs (b) and (c) of the present annex.

(c) The equality of the parties shall be ensured in every proceeding.

(d) The Court shall allow written and oral pleadings in every proceeding pursuant to articles 5 to 7 of this annex.

Article 4

The competence of the Human Rights Court shall extent to any question concerning a constitutional or other legal provision relating to human rights or fundamental freedoms or to any of the instruments listed in annex C to the Constitutional Agreement.

Article 5

Any party to a proceeding in which another court of the Union of Republics of Bosnia and Herzegovina or of any of its Constituent Republics has pronounced a judgment that is not subject to any other appeal (for a reason other than the lapse of time limit for which the moving party is responsible), may appeal such judgment to the Court on the basis of any question within its competence. The decision of the Court in such an appeal shall be final and binding.

Article 6

(a) An appeal may also be taken to the Court if a proceeding is pending for what it considers an unduly long time in any other court of the Union of Republics of Bosnia and Herzegovina or of any of its Constituent Republics.

(b) The Court shall decide whether to accept such an appeal after a preliminary consideration of whether the proceeding in the other court has been pending too long and whether the subject of the appeal is within its competence.

Article 7

Any appellate court of the Union of Republics of Bosnia and Herzegovina or of any of its Constituent Republics may, at the request of any party to a proceeding pending before it, or on its own motion in relation to such a proceeding, address to the Court a question arising out of the proceeding if the question related to any matter within the competence of the Court. The response of the Court is binding on the requesting court.

Article 8

The Court shall continue to function until the Union of Republics of Bosnia and Herzegovina becomes a party to the European Convention on Human Rights and Fundamental Freedoms, unless the Council of Europe mechanism referred to in article 1 of this annex ceases at some earlier date to be in force in respect of the Union of Republics of Bosnia and Herzegovina.

ANNEX C

HUMAN RIGHTS INSTRUMENTS INCORPORATED IN
THE CONSTITUTIONAL AGREEMENT

A. *General Human Rights, especially Civil and Political Rights*

1. 1948 Convention on the Prevention and Punishment of the Crime of Genocide
2. 1948 Universal Declaration of Human Rights, arts. 1-21
3. The four 1949 Geneva Conventions on the laws of war, and the two Geneva Protocols thereto of 1977
4. The 1950 European Convention for the Protection of Human Rights and Fundamental Freedoms, and Protocols 1 to 10 thereto
5. The 1951 Convention relating to the Status of Refugees and the 1966 Protocol thereto
6. The 1965 International Convention on the Elimination of All Forms of Racial Discrimination
7. The 1966 International Covenant on Civil and Political Rights and the Optional Protocols thereto of 1966 and 1989
8. The 1979 International Convention on the Elimination of All Forms of Discrimination against Women
9. The 1981 [United Nations] Declaration on the Elimination of all Forms of Intolerance and of Discrimination Based on Religion or Belief
10. The 1984 Convention against Torture and Other Cruel, Inhuman or Degrading Treatment or Punishment
11. The 1987 European Convention on the Prevention of Torture and Inhuman or Degrading Treatment or Punishment
12. The 1989 Convention on the Rights of the Child

B. *Protection of Groups and Minorities*

13. The 1990 Council of Europe Parliamentary Assembly Recommendation on the Rights of Minorities, paras. 10-13
14. The 1992 United Nations Declaration on the Rights of Persons Belonging to National, Ethnic, Religious and Linguistic Minorities

C. Economic, Social and Cultural Rights

15. The 1948 Universal Declaration of Human Rights, arts. 22-27
16. The 1961 European Social Charter and the Protocol 1 thereto
17. The 1966 International Covenant on Economic, Social and Cultural Rights

D. Citizenship and Nationality

18. The 1957 Convention on the Nationality of Married Women
19. The 1961 Convention on the Reduction of Statelessness

ANNEX D

INITIAL APPOINTMENT AND FUNCTIONS OF THE OMBUDSMEN

I. GENERAL PROVISIONS

Article 1

(a) The Ombudsmen are to protect human dignity, rights and liberties as provided in the Constitutional Agreement and in the instruments listed in Annex C thereto, and in the constitutions and legislations of the Constituent Republics, and in particular shall act to reverse the consequences of the violation of these rights and liberties and especially of ethnic cleansing.

(b) In carrying out their functions, the Ombudsmen must be guided by law and by the principles of morality and justice.

Article 2

Each Ombudsman shall exercise his functions individually, except as otherwise provided herein. Two or more Ombudsmen may cooperate in carrying out any of their functions.

Article 3

The Ombudsmen are independent in carrying out their functions and no governmental organ or any other person may interfere with such functions.

Article 4

(a) There shall be four Ombudsmen, one from each recognized group: Muslims, Serbs, Croats and Others. Until the Parliament adopts a law relating to the appointment and functioning of the ombudsmen, these shall be appointed and may be removed by the Co-Chairmen of the Steering Committee of the International Conference on the Former Yugoslavia, after consultations with the members of the Presidency.

(b) Each of the Ombudsmen shall, with the approval of the presidency, appoint one or more Deputies.

(c) The terms of service of the Ombudsmen and their Deputies shall be the same respectively as those of the President and of judges of the Supreme Court.

(d) Each Ombudsman shall also appoint additional staff within the framework of the budget approved therefore by the Parliament or initially by the Presidency.

II. THE COMPETENCE AND THE POWERS OF THE OMBUDSMEN

Article 5

The Ombudsmen may follow the activities of any common institution of the Union of Republics of Bosnia and Herzegovina or of any organ of a Constituent Republic or of governmental units subordinate thereto, as well as of an other institution or person by whom human dignity, rights or liberties may be negated or ethnic cleansing may be accomplished or its effects preserved.

Article 6

In the course of carrying out his functions an Ombudsman may examine all official documents, including secret ones, as well as judicial and administrative files and require any person (including any official) to cooperate, in particular by transmitting relevant information, documents and files. Ombudsmen may also attend court and administrative hearings, as well as meetings of other organs and enter and inspect any place where persons deprived of their liberty are confined or work.

Article 7

The Ombudsmen, their Deputies and any other person who carries out inquiries pursuant to Article 6, are required to maintain the secrecy of whatever they learned in the course of such inquiry, and must treat all documents and files in accordance with the applicable rules.

III. REPORTS OF THE OMBUDSMEN

Article 8

(a) Each Ombudsman shall present an annual report to the Presidency of the Union of Republics of Bosnia and Herzegovina, to the president of each of the Constituent Republics and the Co-Chairmen of the Steering Committee of the International Conference on the Former Yugoslavia.

(b) An Ombudsman may also present at any time special reports to any competent authorities.

IV. REGULATIONS OF THE OMBUDSMEN

Article 9

Each Ombudsman shall draw up, or the Ombudsmen may collectively draw up, Regulations that specify their organization and the method of exercising their function, which shall be promulgated in the *Official Journal of the Union of Republics of Bosnia and Herzegovina*, as well as in the *Official Journals* of the Constituent Republics. These Regulations may be changed by a law adopted by the Parliament.

Appendix II

Agreed Arrangements concerning the Constitutional Agreement of the Union of Republics of Bosnia and Herzegovina

1. The name of each Constituent Republic will be determined by the competent authorities of that Republic.

2. The map of the three Constituent Republics set out in part I of annex A to the Constitutional Agreement will be referred to the Boundary Commission established in accordance with Chapter II, Article 1 (b), of that Agreement, and the Commission shall ensure that the territory of the Republic marked as No. 1 on the map shall not be less than 30 per cent of the entire territory of the Union of Republics of Bosnia and Herzegovina.

3. Access Authority:

    (a) Pursuant to Chapter III, Article 5 of the Constitutional Agreement there shall established, immediately on the entry into force of that Agreement, an Access Authority, charged with assisting in the implementation of section II, Article 1 (d) of the Agreement requiring free movement of

persons, goods and services throughout the territory of the Union of
Republics of Bosnia and Herzegovina;

(b) The purpose of the Authority will be to guarantee full freedom of movement in certain essential areas between and within the Constituent Republics, and also to and from these Republics to the Republic of Croatia
and the Republic of Serbia;

(c) The members of the Authority shall be three persons appointed by the
Presidency, one from each Constituent Republics. Its headquarters shall
be in or around the city of Sarajevo;

(d) Even though the Authority is to be in operation as soon as possible
following the entry into force of the Constitutional Agreement, inevitably there will be an initial period when UNPROFOR will have sole responsibility for freedom of movement along designated "blue routes"
around Sarajevo and "throughways" ensuring freedom of movement
along the key roads and railway lines throughout the country. Thereafter
there will be a period of overlapping responsibility for the Authority's
designated routes will be phased out, and these responsibilities assumed
by the traffic police of the Authority. This transfer of responsibility
requires the agreement of all members of the Authority. The traffic
police will be seconded to the Authority from the police force of the
Constituent Republics;

(e) The following shall be the routes to be controlled by the Access Authority:

(i)   The road and railway line from Metkovic on the border of
        Croatia to the centre of the city of Sarajevo;

(ii)   The railway from the city of Sarajevo to Visoko and Doboj;

(iii)   The railway through Brcko to the bridge across the Sava;

(iv)   The road from Bihac to Jajce and Travnik;

(v)   The road from Nevesinje to Mostar Airport;

(vi)   The road from Srebrenica to Kladanj;

(vii)   The road from Gorazde through Cajnice to the border;

(viii) Sarajevo Airport;

(ix)   The so-called "Transit Road" through the south of the city of
        Sarajevo;

(x)   The road between Sarajevo and the crossing point north of
        Trnovo which gives access to Gorazde;

(xi)   The road between Bosanski Brod (via Derventa, Doboj, Zenica)
        and Sarajevo;

(xii)   The road from the border of the Republic of Croatia near Velika
Kladusa (via Cazin, Bihac, Kljuc, Donji Vakuf) to Mostar;
(xiii) The road between Donji Vakuf (via Travnik) and Zenica.

APPENDIX III

AGREEMENT ON THE TERMINATION OF THE CONFLICT

The Parties reaffirm their acceptance of the Agreement for peace in Bosnia
and Herzegovina (see S/25479, annex IV). The Mixed Military Working Group
that had been established by the International Conference on the Former Yugoslavia shall, under the chairmanship of the United Nations Protection Force,
update that agreement and make any necessary amendments, in particular on
relation to the Constitutional Agreement. Any new Agreement that is signed by
representatives of the Parties shall, to the extent that it so provides, replace and
supersede the preceding document.

APPENDIX IV

PRELIMINARY AGREEMENT BETWEEN THE REPUBLIC OF CROATIA AND
THE UNION OF REPUBLICS OF BOSNIA AND HERZEGOVINA FOR
IMPLEMENTING THE 1965 CONVENTION ON TRANSIT TRADE
OF LAND-LOCKED STATES[*]

*The Republic of Croatia and the Union of Republics of Bosnia and Herzeg-
ovina,*

Considering that, as successors of the Socialist Federal Republic of Yugoslavia which had been party to the Convention of Transit Trade of Land-Locked
States concluded in New York on 8 July 1965 (hereinafter the "Convention"),
the Republic of Croatia and the Union of Republics of Bosnia and Herzegovina
should apply between them the provisions of the Convention,

Further considering that the Union of Republics of Bosnia and Herzegovina
is to be considered a "land-locked State" within the meaning of that Convention
and that with respect to Bosnia and Herzegovina the Republic of Croatia is a
"transit State" within the meaning of the Convention,

[*]   The undersigned are representatives of the Republic of Croatia and the parties to the
Constitutional Agreement establishing the Union of Republics of Bosnia and Herzegovina;
and, as witnesses, Thorvald Stoltenberg and Lord David Owen.

Desiring to conclude an agreement, on a basis of reciprocity - in accordance with Article 3 (1) (a) of the Convention on the High Seas quoted in the Preamble of the Transit Trade Convention and with article 15 of that Convention - to establish, as foreseen in paragraph 2 of Article 2 of the Convention, the rules governing traffic in transit and the use of means of transport passing across Croatian territory between the territory of the Union of Republics of Bosnia and Herzegovina and the Adriatic Sea, and when passing across territory of the Union of Republics of Bosnia and Herzegovina in transit between places of entry and exit which are both on Croatian territory, as well as to regulate other matters foreseen in the Convention,

Hereby agree as follows:

Article 1

(a) Freedom of transit under the terms of this Preliminary Agreement shall be granted to both Parties on the basis of reciprocity.

(b) The Croatian ports of Ploce and Rijeka are designated as those to which the Union of Republics of Bosnia and Herzegovina is to have access, as foreseen in the Convention, and the routes, by road and as appropriate by rail, between Ploce and Sarajevo and between Rijeka and Bihac are the ones as to which special rules are to be adopted.

(c) The roads on the territory of the Union of Republics of Bosnia and Herzegovina:

(i) Between the Croatian border near Velika Kladusa (via Cazin, Bihac, Kljuc, Jajce, Dinji Vakuf, Bugonjo, Jablanica and Mostar) and the Croatian border on the south, as well as the road between Bonji Vakuf (via Travnik) and Zenica where this road links with the road under (ii) below;

(ii) Between Bosanski Brod (via Dervanta, Doboj, Zenica, Sarajevo and Mostar and the Croatian border in the south;

shall be the ones to which the freedom of transit, in accordance with the Convention, shall be granted to the Republic of Croatia.

(d) The same freedom of transit shall be granted to the Republic of Croatia on the so-called "Una railway line" on the territory of the Union of Republics of Bosnia and Herzegovina between Bosanski Novi (via Bihac) and the Croatian border on the south in the direction of Knin.

(e) The reference to specific ports of Croatia and the roads and railway line within the Union of Republics of Bosnia and Herzegovina, and specific points of entry from Croatia and the Union of Republics of Bosnia and Herzegovina and from Bosnia and Herzegovina to Croatia, are not intended to exclude the facilitation by both states of transit trade through other ports of entry.

Article 2

The parties shall immediately start negotiating, with a view to concluding by _____ 1993, an agreement relating to all aspects of the implementation of the Convention and this Preliminary Agreement, covering in particular the following subjects:

1. Specification of the primary routes, by road as well as by rail, from the ports to the cities specified in article 1;
2. Rules governing he means of transport over the routes and the railroad specified in article 1 (Art. 2 (2) of the Convention);
3. Facilities existing, or to be built, within the specified ports that are to be specially dedicated to traffic of the Union of Republics of Bosnia and Herzegovina might be permitted to operate and develop with the consent of the Republic of Croatia;
4. Possible imposition of special transit dues, tariffs or charges (arts, 3 and 4 of the Convention);
5. Special customs and other measures to facilitate transit trade (art. 5 of the Convention);
6. Conditions of storage of goods in transit (art. 6 of the Convention);
7. Possible establishment of free zones in the designated ports (art. 8 of the Convention);
8. Exceptions on grounds of public health, security and protection of intellectual property (art. 11 of the Convention);
9. Exceptions in case of emergency (art. 12 of the Convention);
10. Application of the Agreement in time of war (art. 13 of the Convention);
11. Settlement of disputes pursuant to article 16 of the Convention.

Article 4

Pending the conclusion of the agreement referred to in article 2 above, the Republic of Croatia and the Union of Republics of Bosnia and Herzegovina shall facilitate, as far as it is possible, their mutual transit trade, as defined in this Agreement.

DONE this --- day of August 1993, in ----, in three copies, each in the English, Croatian and Serbian languages, which shall be equally authentic.

124. LETTER DATED 20 AUGUST 1993 FROM THE SECRETARY-GENERAL ADDRESSED TO THE PRESIDENT OF THE SECURITY COUNCIL*

I have the honour to convey the attached report addressed to me on 20 August 1993 by the Co-Chairmen of the Steering Committee of the International Conference on the Former Yugoslavia.

Annex
Report of the Co-Chairmen of the Steering Committee on the Activities of the International Conference on the Former Yugoslavia

INTRODUCTION

1. It will be recalled that the latest round of peace talks to resolve the conflict in Bosnia and Herzegovina started on 27 July 1993. Since then the Co-Chairmen have submitted two reports to the Security Council. The present report provides information on developments in the peace talks since the submission of the last report (S/26260).

I. CONSTITUTIONAL AGREEMENT, ANNEXES AND RELATED INSTRUMENTS

2. Since the submission of the last report, the parties have continued their deliberations to settle the annexes and other instruments related to the Constitutional Agreement. All of these annexes to the Constitutional Agreement have been finalized, as well as a preliminary bilateral treaty between the Union of Republics of Bosnia and Herzegovina and the Republic of Croatia on the access of the former to two Adriatic ports.
3. The parties carefully reviewed and confirmed provisions to which they had earlier given their agreement with regard to the organization of the police and human rights, especially the right of refugees and displaced persons to return.

---

* UN Doc. S/26337, 20 August 1993. Signed by Boutros Boutros-Ghali.

4. All these instruments, which are to be appended to an agreement relating to Bosnia and Herzegovina, will be reproduced in an addendum to the present report.

II. DELIMITATION OF THE CONSTITUENT REPUBLICS

5. In their previous report to the Security Council, the Co-Chairmen note that the parties were in essential agreement on the core areas to be allocated to each of the three Constituent Republics. They provided detailed information on the main areas that were still to be resolved by the parties in their efforts to draw the boundaries of the three Constituent Republics (see S/26260, paras. 30-37). Since then the parties have continued their efforts to reach agreement in bilateral and trilateral meetings, assisted by the good offices of the Co-Chairmen. The results of these negotiation are reflected in the attached map (appendix I).

6. As at 20 August 1993, the parties had worked out arrangement to place Sarajevo (see attached map, appendix II) under the administration of the United Nations for a period of up to two years and to place Mostar under the administration of the European Community for a similar (subject to agreement of the European Community). Detailed arrangements were worked out in respect of demarcations in the town of Brcko (see attached map, appendix III), and there were lengthy discussions regarding the towns of Gornji Vakuf, Donji Vakuf, Bugojno an Travnik. The Serb side agreed to a special road linking Gorazde and Zepa which will be part of the territory of, and administered and policed by, the Muslim majority republic.

7. In the light of these developments, on 20 August 1993 the parties agreed to issue the following statement:

> "The Co-Chairmen today met President Izetbegovic. They then met Dr. Karadzic and Mr. Boban in the presence of Presidents Milosevic, Bulatovic and Tudjman. The Co-Chairmen later met all heads of delegations.
>
> Based on the constitutional and related documents already worked out, and the discussions over the last two days, the Co-Chairmen have given the three sides a package containing the constitutional papers and a map (attached) reflecting the discussions that have taken place among the parties. They will return home to explain the map and will come back to Geneva for a final meeting on Monday, 30 August 1993."

Appendix I

UNION OF REPUBLICS OF BOSNIA AND HERZEGOVINA

ZEPA-GORAZDE LINK RAOD WHICH IS PART OF
THE MUSLIM MAJORITY REPUBLIC

APPENDIX II

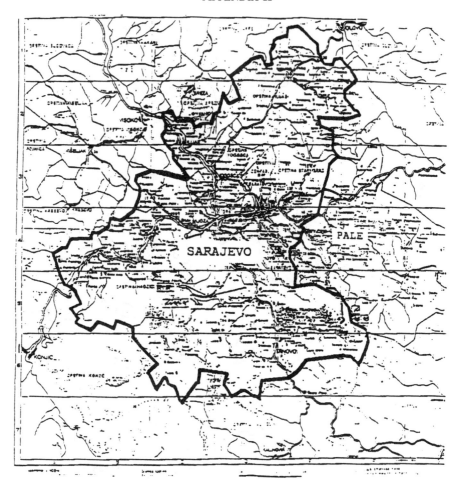

APPENDIX III

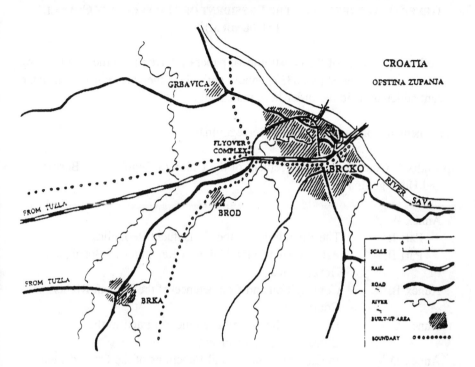

125. LETTER DATED 20 AUGUST 1993 FROM THE SECRETARY-GENERAL ADDRESSED TO THE PRESIDENT OF THE SECURITY COUNCIL (ADDENDUM)*

Following is a list of the constitutional papers referred to in the statement by the parties on 20 August (S/26337, annex, para. 7), which are reproduced in the present addendum, in the order here indicated:

Agreement relating to Bosnia and Herzegovina;

Appendix I: Constitutional Agreement of the Union of Republics of Bosnia and Herzegovina

Annex A:
Part I:	The Boundaries of the Constituent Republics
Part II:	Areas vested in the Union of Republics of Bosnia and Herzegovina
Annex B:[1]	Composition and Competence of the Human Rights Court
Annex C:[1]	Human rights instruments incorporated in the Constitutional Agreement
Annex D:[1]	Initial Appointment and Functions of the Ombudsmen

Appendix II: Agreed Arrangement concerning the Constitutional Agreement of the Union of Republics of Bosnia and Herzegovina

Part 1:	Names of Republics; Access Authority
Part 2:	A. Sarajevo District; B. Mostar; C. Police Forces; D. Protection of Human Rights and the Reversal of Ethnic Cleansing
Attachment:	
A.	The outer boundary of Sarajevo District[2]
B.	The outer boundary of the Mostar City Opstina

---

*   UN Doc. S/26337/Add.1, 23 August 1993.
[1]   Previously reproduced in document S/26260, appendix I.
[2]   Previously reproduced in document S/26337, appendix II.

Appendix III: Military Agreements

Part 1:[3]	30 July 1993 Agreement for a complete cessation of all combat activities among the parties in conflict
Part 2:	11 August 1993 military agreement for peace in Bosnia and Herzegovina
Appendix I:	Target time-table for implementation of this Agreement
Appendix II:	Procedures for the Joint Commission
Part 3:	Amendments to the 11 August 1993 military agreement for peace in Bosnia and Herzegovina

Appendix IV:[4] Preliminary Agreement between the Republic of Croatia and the Union of Republics of Bosnia and Herzegovina for implementing the 1965 Convention on the Transmit Trade of Land-Locked States

Agreement relating to Bosnia and Herzegovina[*]

THE UNDERSIGNED,

Guided by the principles of the Charter of the United Nations, the Universal Declaration of Human Rights and the Declaration of the Rights of Persons belonging to National or Ethnic, Religious and Linguistic Minorities,

Recalling the Statement of principles by the International Conference on the Former Yugoslavia at its session in London and the Programme of Action on Humanitarian Issues agreed to at that session,

Considering the decisions of the United Nations Security Council relating to the former Yugoslavia,

Reaffirming their commitment to peace and security among the successor States to the former Yugoslavia,

Hereby agree as follows:

---

[3] Previously reproduced in document S/26233, appendix I.

[4] Text previously reproduced in document S/26260, appendix IV.

[*] The undersigned are A. Izetbegovic, R. Karadzic, and M. Boban; and, as witnesses, T. Stoltenberg and D. Owen.

I. CONSTITUTIONAL AGREEMENT OF THE UNION OF REPUBLICS OF
BOSNIA AND HERZEGOVINA

(a) The Constitutional Agreement of the Union of Republics of Bosnia and
Herzegovina is set out in Appendix I hereto. it shall enter into force one week
after the Security Council has taken into account the present Agreement, has
confirmed that the Union of Republics of Bosnia and Herzegovina will continue
as a member of the United Nations and has authorized United Nations support
for the implementation of the present Agreement.
(b) Agreed arrangements concerning the Constitutional Agreement are set out in
Parts 1 and 2 of Appendix II hereto.

II. TERMINATION OF THE CONFLICT

The parties reaffirm the Agreement for a Complete Cessation of All Combat
Activities signed by their military commanders on 30 July 1993 set out in Part 1
of Appendix III hereto, and the Military Agreement for Peace in Bosnia and
Herzegovina signed by their military commanders on 11 August 1992 set out in
Part 2 of Appendix III, and decide that the latter shall be amended as set out in
Part 3 of Appendix III and shall enter into force on the day after the Security
Council has authorized United Nations support for the implementation of the
present Agreement.

III. COOPERATION IN RESPECT OF HUMANITARIAN EFFORTS

(a) Maximum cooperation shall be extended to the United Nations High Commissioner for Refugees, the International Committee of the Red Cross, The
United Nations Protection Force, the European Community Monitoring Mission
and other humanitarian organizations working to provide assistance to refugees
and displaced persons.
(b) Full cooperation shall also be extended to the United Nations High Commissioner for Refugees in drawing up and implementing programmes for the
return of refugees and displaced persons to their homes.

IV. Preliminary Agreement with the Republic of Croatia for
Implementing the 1965 Convention on the Transit Trade of
Land-Locked Countries

As soon as the Constitutional Agreement enters into force, the Union of
Republics of Bosnia and Herzegovina shall conclude with the Republic of Cro-
atia the Preliminary Agreement for implementation the 1965 Convention on the
Transmit Trade of Land-Locked Countries set out in Appendix IV hereto.

Done in Geneva, this ---- day of August 1993

Appendix I
Constitutional Agreement of the Union of Republics of
Bosnia and Herzegovina

I. The Union of Republics of Bosnia and Herzegovina

Article 1
The Union of Republics of Bosnia and Herzegovina is composed of three
Constituent Republics and encompasses three constituent peoples: the Muslims,
Serbs and Croats, as well as a group of other peoples. The Union of Republics of
Bosnia and Herzegovina will be a member State of the United Nations, and as a
member State it shall apply for membership of other organizations of the United
Nations system.

Article 2
The flag and emblem of the Union of Republics of Bosnia and Herzegovina
shall be specified by a law adopted by the Union Parliament.

Article 3
(a) Citizenship of Bosnia and Herzegovina shall be determined by a law adopted
by the Union Parliament.
(b) Every person who on the entry into force of this Constitutional Agreement
was entitled to be a citizen of the Republic of Bosnia and Herzegovina shall be
entitled to be a citizen of a Constituent Republic as well as of the Union of Republics of Bosnia and Herzegovina.
(c) Dual citizenship shall be allowed.

(d) Decision about citizenship shall be made by the designated organs of the Constituent Republics, subject to the competent courts.

Article 4

Neither the Union of Republics of Bosnia and Herzegovina nor any of the Constituent Republics shall maintain any military force, and any forces existing on the date of entry into force of this Constitutional Agreement shall be progressively disarmed and disbanded under the supervision of the United Nations and the European Community.

II. THE CONSTITUENT REPUBLICS AND THEIR RESPONSIBILITIES

Article 1

(a) The boundaries of the Constituent Republics shall be as set out in Annex A, Part I. Except as provided in (b) boundaries of the Republics may only be changed by the procedure provided for amending this Constitutional Agreement.

(b) Marginal changes in the boundaries set out in Annex A may be made by the Presidency on the recommendation of a Boundary Commission, which shall receive evidence from those specifically affected by them. The Commission shall consist of five persons appointed by the Secretary-General of the United Nations, of whom three shall be persons recommended by representatives of the three constituent peoples.

(c) The areas specified in Annex A, Part II, even though within the territory and under the jurisdiction of a Constituent Republic, shall be vested in the Union of Republics of Bosnia and Herzegovina, for the purposes of ensuring access by all citizens to buildings of the Union in Sarajevo, to the sea at Neum and to the Sava River.

(d) There shall be no border controls on boundaries between the Constituent Republics, and there shall be free movement of persons, goods and services throughout the territory of the Union of Republics of Bosnia and Herzegovina.

Article 2

(a) Each of the Constituent Republics shall adopt its own constitution, which shall provide for democratic forms of government, including democratically elected legislatures and chief executives and independent judiciaries, as well as for the highest standards of human rights and fundamental freedoms. No provision of these constitutions may be inconsistent with this Constitutional Agreement.

(b) The initial elections in each Constituent Republic shall be supervised by the United Nations and the European Community.

Article 3

All governmental functions and powers, except those assigned by this Constitutional Agreement to the Union of Republics of Bosnia and Herzegovina or to any of its institutions, shall be those of the Constituent Republics.

Article 4

All acts taken by a competent governmental authority of any of the Constituent Republics shall be accepted as valid by the other Constituent Republics.

III. THE COMMON INSTITUTIONS OF THE UNION OF REPUBLICS OF BOSNIA AND HERZEGOVINA

Article 1

(a) The Presidency of the Union of Republics of Bosnia and Herzegovina shall consist of the President, or of an appointee of the legislature, of each of the Constituent Republics.

(b) The Chairmanship of the Presidency shall rotate every four months among the members of the Presidency. The Chairman shall represent the Union of Republics of Bosnia and Herzegovina.

(c) The presidency shall take all its decisions by consensus.

Article 2

(a) The head of the Council of Ministers of the Union of Republics of Bosnia and Herzegovina shall be the Prime Minister, who shall be appointed and may be removed by the Presidency. The post shall rotate every year so as to be occupied in turn by the nominee of the President of a different Constituent Republic.

(b) The Presidency shall also appoint and may remove a Foreign Minister. The post shall rotate every year so as to be occupied in turn by the nominee of the President of a different Constituent Republic.

(c) The Prime Minister and the Foreign Minister shall be from different Constituent Republics.

(d) Other Ministers may be appointed by the Presidency. They and the Prime Minister and the Foreign Minister shall constitute the Council of Minister, with responsibility for the policies of the Union of Republics of Bosnia and Herzegovina in relation to foreign affairs, international trade and the functioning of the common institutions, as well as any other function and institutions that the Union Parliament may from time to time specify by law.

Article 3

(a) The Parliament of the Union of Republics of Bosnia and Herzegovina shall be composed of 120 representatives, one third each to be elected by the respective legislatures of the Constituent Republics.

(b) The Union Parliament may by a simple majority of the members from each Constituent Republic adopt laws within the competence of the Union of Republics of Bosnia and Herzegovina.

Article 4

The Union of Republics of Bosnia and Herzegovina shall have the following courts:

(i)   A Supreme Court, composed of four judges appointed by the Presidency, no two of whom shall be from the same peoples, which, except as specified in para. (iii), shall be the final court of appeals from the courts of the Constituent Republics.

(ii) A Constitutional Court, composed of three judges appointed by the Presidency, no two of whom shall be from the same Constituent Republic, which shall be competent to resolve by consensus disputes among the Constituent Republics, between any of these and the Union of Republics of Bosnia and Herzegovina or any of its common institutions, and among any of these institutions. Should the Court not be constituted or be unable to resolve a dispute, it shall be referred for a binding decision by a standing arbitral tribunal composed of judges of the International Court of Justice or members of the Permanent Court of Arbitration, one each of whom shall be elected by the President of each of the Constituent Republics and two of whom shall be elected by the Presidency or, if it is unable to do so, by the Secretary-General of the United Nations and by the President of the Council of Ministers of the European Community.

(iii) A Court of Human Rights to be established in accordance with Resolution 93 (6) of the Committee of Ministers of the Council of Europe, whose precise composition and competence shall be as set out in the agreed Annex B.

Article 5

Joint authorities between two or more of the Constituent Republics may be established by agreement of the Republics concerned if approved by a law adopted by the Union Parliament.

IV. INTERNATIONAL RELATIONS

Article 1

(a) The Union of Republics of Bosnia and Herzegovina shall apply for membership of European and international institutions and organizations, as decided by the Presidency.

(b) Any Constituent Republics may apply for membership of an international organization if such membership would not be inconsistent with the interests of the Union of Republics of Bosnia and Herzegovina or of either of the other Constituent Republics.

Article 2

(a) The Union of Republics of Bosnia and Herzegovina shall remain a party to all international treaties in force for the Republic of Bosnia and Herzegovina on the date of the entry into force of this Constitutional Agreement, unless the Union Parliament decides that steps to denounce any such treaty shall be taken. However, treaties entered into after 18 November 1990 shall be considered by the Union Parliament within a period of three months from the entry into force of this Constitutional Agreement and shall only remain on force if the Union Parliament so decides.

(b) The Union of Republics of Bosnia and Herzegovina shall continue all diplomatic relations until the Presidency decides to continue or discontinue them.

(c) The Union of Republics of Bosnia and Herzegovina may become a party to international treaties if such participation is approved by the Union Parliament. The Parliament may by law provide for participation in certain types of international agreements by decision of the Presidency. To the extent such participation would involve responsibilities that are to be carried out by the Constituent Republics, their advance approval must be secured, except in respect of the treaties referred to in Article V.3.

(d) Any Constituent Republic may, if eligible, become a party to an international treaty if such participation would not be inconsistent with the interests of the Union of Republics of Bosnia and Herzegovina or of either of the other Constituent Republics.

V. Human Rights and Fundamental Freedoms

Article 1
(a) Subject to Article V.2, all persons within the territory of the Union of Republics of Bosnia and Herzegovina shall be entitled to enjoy the rights and freedoms provided for in the instruments listed in Annex C.
(b) Should there be any discrepancy between the rights and freedoms specified in any of these instruments, or between any of these and the rights and freedoms specified in any other legal provision in force, the provision providing the greater protection for human rights and fundamental freedoms shall be applied.

Article 2
All courts, administrative agencies and other governmental organs of the Union of Republics of Bosnia and Herzegovina and of the Constituent Republics shall apply and conform the rights and freedoms specified in the instruments listed in Parts I and IV of Annex C. The rights specified in the instruments listed in Parts II and III of Annex C shall be considered as aspirations to be attained as rapidly as possible; all legislative, judicial, administrative and other governmental organs of the Union and Republican governments shall take these rights appropriately into account in promulgating, executing and interpreting any legislative provisions designed to or otherwise suitable or implementing such rights and in otherwise carrying out the functions of these organs.

Article 3
The Union of Republics of Bosnia and Herzegovina shall as soon as possible become a party to each of the international treaties listed in Annex C.

Article 4
All organs of the Union and Republican Governments shall cooperate with the supervisory bodies established by any of the instruments listed in Annex C, as well as with the International Human Rights Monitoring Mission for Bosnia and Herzegovina established by the United Nations.

Article 5
(a) All citizens have the right to settle in any part of the territory of the Union of Republics of Bosnia and Herzegovina. They shall have the right to have restored to them any property of which they were deprived in the course of ethnic cleansing and to be compensated for any property which cannot be restored to them.

(b) The Union Parliament, as well as the legislature of the Constituent Republics, shall enact laws to assist in implementing these rights.

Article 6

To assist in implementing the rights and freedoms specified in this Chapter and in particular in Article V.5 (a), ombudsmen shall be appointed and carry out functions initially as specified in Annex D and thereafter as specified in a law adopted by the Union Parliament.

VI. FINANCES

Article 1

(a) The Union Parliament shall each year, on the proposal of the Prime Minister and with the subsequent approval of the Presidency, adopt a budget covering the expenditures required to carry out only those functions of the Union of Republics of Bosnia and Herzegovina relating to the maintenance of its common institutions and compliance with its international obligations, as well as such other functions as may from time to time be agreed by he Union Parliament.

(b) If no such budget is adopted in due course, the budget for the previous year shall be used on a provisional basis.

Article 2

(a) The expenditures provided for in the budget shall, except to the extent that other revenues are available or as otherwise specified in a law adopted by the Union Parliament, be covered in equal part by each of the Constituent Republics.

(b) Other sources of revenues, such as custom duties, fees for services or taxes on specified activities, may be determined by law.

VII. THE CONSTITUTIONAL AGREEMENT

Article 1

(a) This Constitutional Agreement may be amended by decision of the Union Parliament, when such amendment has been approved by each of the Constituent Republics according to its constitutional processes.

(b) No amendments may be adopted that abolish or diminish any of the rights or freedoms specified in Chapter V.

Article 2

(a) This Constitutional Agreement may not be abolished and none of the Constituent Republics may withdraw from the Union of Republics of Bosnia and Herzegovina without the prior agreement of all of the Republics. Such a decision may be appealed to the Security Council by any of the Constituent Republics, and the Council's decision shall be final.

(b) Should any of the Constituent Republics withdraw from the Union of Republics of Bosnia and Herzegovina, the areas specified in Annex A, Part II that are within the territory of such Republic shall remain a part of the Union of Republics of Bosnia and Herzegovina.

Article 3

This Constitutional Agreement shall enter into force when approved as part of the overall peace settlement by representatives of the three constituent peoples, and on a date specified by them.

ANNEX A, PART I
THE BOUNDARIES OF THE CONSTITUENT REPUBLICS

1. The boundaries of the Constituent Republics shall be as indicated on the map below,* subject to any changes that may be made in accordance with Article II.1 (b) of the Constitutional Agreement. The Boundary Commission shall ensure that the territory of the Muslim majority Republic shall not be less than 30% of the entire territory of the Union of Republics of Bosnia and Herzegovina.

2. The road marked on he Map that links Gorazde to Zepa shall constitute part of the Muslim majority Republic, which shall be responsible for its upkeep and policing.

3. As much as possible of the town of Gornji Vakuf shall be in the Muslim majority Republic, subject to the Croat majority Republic retaining road access to Prozor from the north of Gornji Vakuf, and to Novi Travnik along the road running north from the village of Ploca towards the road junction to the north of Bistrica. Construction of new roads may be necessary, and the Special Representative of the UN secretary-General (SRSG), after appropriate consultations, shall arbitrate in the case of disputes.

4. Similarly, the SRSG shall be charged with arbitrating the boundary between the Muslim majority Republic and the Croat majority Republic where it follows

---

*   To be issued as document S/26337/Add.2.

a line drawn south of the River Lasva in Travnik, in order that as many Croatian villages as is feasible are included in the Croat majority Republic.

5. At the request of any Constituent Republic, the Presidency may decide that a religious or cultural building located in another Constituent Republic shall be under the special protection and responsibility of the requesting Republic.

ANNEX A, PART II
AREAS VESTED IN THE UNION OF REPUBLICS OF BOSNIA AND HERZEGOVINA

1. The area defined by the present opstina of Neum, and that part of the present opstina of Stolac that lies below the southern border of the Constituent Republic that extend up through Sarajevo to Brcko on the Sava.

2. That part of the railway line from Tuzla that passes across Brcko to the railway bridge on the Sava.

3. Those public buildings in the city of Sarajevo and in the surrounding areas that are designated by the Presidency to be used by the Union Parliament, the Council of Ministers, the Supreme, Constitutional and Human Rights Courts, and the administrative institutions of the Union.

ANNEX B
COMPOSITION AND COMPETENCE OF THE HUMAN RIGHTS COURT

Article 1
The Human Rights Court of Bosnia and Herzegovina (the "Court") shall operate within the framework of the mechanism established by he Council of Europe by Resolution 93 (6) of its Council of Ministers, as that Resolution may be amended from time to time.

Article 2
(a) The Court shall initially consist of nine judges.

(b) The Presidency shall appoint four of the judges of the Court, one from each recognized group: Muslims, Serbs, Croats and Others. These judges shall enjoy tenure and shall not require reappointment.

(c) The Committee of Minister of the Council of Europe shall appoint five of the judges of the Court in accordance with the above-cited resolution. These judges may not be citizens of the Union of Republics of Bosnia and Herzegovina nor of neighbouring States.

(d) If the Court concludes that its business requires the participation of more judges to avoid undue delays in the disposition of cases, the Government shall make arrangements with the Council of Europe for the appointment of additional judges, in accordance with the above-specified proportion of national and foreign judges.

Article 3

(a) The Court shall regulate its own procedure and its organization.
(b) Each panel of the Court is to have the composition specified for the Court in Article 2(b)-(c) of this Annex.
(c) The equality of the parties shall be ensured in every proceeding.
(d) The Court shall allow written and oral pleadings in every proceeding pursuant to Articles 5-7 of this Annex.

Article 4

The competence of the Human Rights Court shall extend to any question concerning a constitutional or other legal provision relating to human rights or fundamental freedoms or to any of the instruments listed in Annex C to the Constitutional Agreement.

Article 5

Any party to a proceeding in which another court of the Union of Republics of Bosnia and Herzegovina or of any of its Constituent Republics has pronounced a judgment that is not subject to any other appeal (for a reason other than the lapse of time limit for which the moving party is responsible), may appeal such judgment to the Court on the basis of any question within its competence. The decision of the Court in such an appeal shall be final and binding.

Article 6

(a) An appeal may also be taken to the Court if a proceeding is pending for what it considers an unduly long time in any other court of the Union of Republics of Bosnia and Herzegovina or of any of its Constituent Republics.
(b) The Court shall decide whether to accept such an appeal after a preliminary consideration of whether the proceeding in the other court has been pending too long and whether the subject of the appeal is within its competence.

Article 7

Any appellate court of the Union of Republics of Bosnia and Herzegovina or of any of its Constituent Republics may, at the request of any party to a proceeding pending before it, or on its own motion in relation to such a proceeding, address to the Court a question arising out of the proceeding if the question related to any matter within the competence of the Court. The response of the Court is binding on the requesting court.

Article 8

The Court shall continue to function until the Union of Republics of Bosnia and Herzegovina becomes a party to the European Convention on Human Rights and Fundamental Freedoms, unless the Council of Europe mechanism referred to in Article 1 of this Annex ceases at some earlier date to be in force in respect of the Union of Republics of Bosnia and Herzegovina.

ANNEX C
HUMAN RIGHTS INSTRUMENTS INCORPORATED IN
THE CONSTITUTIONAL AGREEMENT

A. General Human Rights, especially Civil and Political Rights

1. 1948 Convention on the Prevention and Punishment of the Crime of Genocide
2. 1948 Universal Declaration of Human Rights, arts. 1-21
3. The four 1949 Geneva Conventions on the laws of war, and the two Geneva Protocols thereto of 1977
4. The 1950 European Convention for the Protection of Human Rights and Fundamental Freedoms, and Protocols 1 to 10 thereto
5. The 1951 Convention relating to the Status of Refugees and the 1966 Protocol thereto
6. The 1965 International Convention on the Elimination of All Forms of Racial Discrimination
7. The 1966 International Covenant on Civil and Political Rights and the Optional Protocols thereto of 1966 and 1989
8. The 1979 International Convention on the Elimination of All Forms of Discrimination against Women
9. The 1981 [United Nations] Declaration on the Elimination of all Forms of Intolerance and of Discrimination Based on Religion or Belief
10. The 1984 Convention against Torture and Other Cruel, Inhuman or Degrading Treatment or Punishment
11. The 1987 European Convention on the Prevention of Torture and Inhuman or Degrading Treatment or Punishment

ANNEX D
INITIAL APPOINTMENT AND FUNCTIONS OF THE OMBUDSMEN

I. GENERAL PROVISIONS

Article 1

(a) The Ombudsmen are to protect human dignity, rights and liberties as provided in the Constitutional Agreement and in the instruments listed in Annex C thereto, and in the constitutions and legislations of the Constituent Republics, and in particular shall act to reverse the consequences of the violation of these rights and liberties and especially of ethnic cleansing.

(b) In carrying out their functions, the Ombudsmen must be guided by law and by the principles of morality and justice.

Article 2

Each Ombudsman shall exercise his functions individually, except as otherwise provided herein. Two or more Ombudsmen may cooperate in carrying out any of their functions.

Article 3

The Ombudsmen are independent in carrying out their functions and no governmental organ or any other person may interfere with such functions.

Article 4

(a) There shall be four Ombudsmen, one from each recognized group: Muslims, Serbs, Croats and Others. Until the Parliament adopts a law relating to the appointment and functioning of the ombudsmen, these shall be appointed and may be removed by the Co-Chairmen of the Steering Committee of the International Conference on the Former Yugoslavia, after consultations with the members of the Presidency.

(b) Each of the Ombudsmen shall, with the approval of the presidency, appoint one or more Deputies.

(c) The terms of service of the Ombudsmen and their Deputies shall be the same respectively as those of the President and of judges of the Supreme Court.

(d) Each Ombudsman shall also appoint additional staff within the framework of the budget approved therefore by the Parliament or initially by the Presidency.

II. THE COMPETENCE AND THE POWERS OF THE OMBUDSMEN

Article 5

The Ombudsmen may follow the activities of any common institution of the Union of Republics of Bosnia and Herzegovina or of any organ of a Constituent Republic or of governmental units subordinate thereto, as well as of an other institution or person by whom human dignity, rights or liberties may be negated or ethnic cleansing may be accomplished or its effects preserved.

Article 6

In the course of carrying out his functions an Ombudsman may examine all official documents, including secret ones, as well as judicial and administrative files and require any person (including any official) to cooperate, in particular by transmitting relevant information, documents and files. Ombudsmen may also attend court and administrative hearings, as well as meetings of other organs and enter and inspect any place where persons deprived of their liberty are confined or work.

Article 7

The Ombudsmen, their Deputies and any other person who carries out inquiries pursuant to Article 6, are required to maintain the secrecy of whatever they learned in the course of such inquiry, and must treat all documents and files in accordance with the applicable rules.

III. REPORTS OF THE OMBUDSMEN

Article 8

(a) Each Ombudsman shall present an annual report to the Presidency of the Union of Republics of Bosnia and Herzegovina, to the president of each of the Constituent Republics and the Co-Chairmen of the Steering Committee of the International Conference on the Former Yugoslavia.

(b) An Ombudsman may also present at any time special reports to any competent authorities.

IV. REGULATIONS OF THE OMBUDSMEN

Article 9

Each Ombudsman shall draw up, or the Ombudsmen may collectively draw up, Regulations that specify their organization and the method of exercising their function, which shall be promulgated in the *Official Journal of the Union of Republics of Bosnia and Herzegovina*, as well as in the *Official Journals* of the Constituent Republics. These Regulations may be changed by a law adopted by the Parliament.

Appendix II

Agreed Arrangements concerning the Constitutional Agreement of the Union of Republics of Bosnia and Herzegovina

PART 1

1. The name of each Constituent Republic will be determined by the competent authorities of that Republic.

2. Access Authority:

    (a) Pursuant to Article III.5 of the Constitutional Agreement there shall be established, immediately on the entry into force of that Agreement, an access Authority, charged with assisting in the implementation of Article II.1 (d) of the Agreement requiring free movement of persons, goods and services throughout the territory of the Union of Republics of

Bosnia and Herzegovina.

(b) The purpose of the Authority will be to guarantee full freedom of movement in certain essential areas between and within the Constituent Republics, and also to and from these Republics to the Republic of Croatia and the Republic of Serbia.

(c) The members of the Authority shall be three persons appointed by the Presidency, one from each Constituent Republics. Its headquarters shall be in or around the city of Sarajevo.

(d) Even though the Authority is to be in operation as soon as possible following the entry into force of the Constitutional Agreement, inevitably there will be an initial period when UNPROFOR will have sole responsibility for freedom of movement along designated "Blue Routes" around Sarajevo and "Throughways" ensuring freedom of movement along the key roads and railway lines throughout the country. Thereafter there will be a period of overlapping responsibility for the Authority's designated routes will be phased out, and these responsibilities assumed by the traffic police of the Authority. This transfer of responsibility requires the agreement of all members of the Authority. The traffic police will be seconded to the Authority from the police force of the Constituent Republics.

(e) The following shall be the routes to be controlled by the Access Authority:

(i) The road and railway line from Metkovic on the border of Croatia to the centre of the city of Sarajevo;

(ii) The railway from the city of Sarajevo to Doboj and Samac;

(iii) The so-called "Una" railway from Bosanski Novi through Bihac southwards to the border of Croatia;

(iv) The road from Nevesinje to Mostar Airport;

(v) The road from Srebrenica to Kladanj;

(vi) The road from Gorazde through Cajnice to the border of Montenegro;

(vii) Sarajevo Airport;

(viii) The so-called "Transit Road" through the south of the city of Sarajevo;

(ix) The road between Sarajevo and the crossing point north of Trnovo which gives access to Gorazde;

(x) The road between Bosanski Brod (via Derventa, Doboj, Zenica) and Sarajevo;

(xi)   The road from the border of the Republic of Croatia near Velika
        Kladusa (via Cazin, Bihac, Kljuc, Donji Vakuf) to Mostar;
(xii)   The road between Donji Vakuf (via Travnik) and Zenica;
(xiii) The road from Poplat to Neum.

PART 2

A. Sarajevo District

1. For an interim period, specified in paragraph 2 below, there shall be established the Sarajevo District the outer boundary of which shall be as delineated in
the attached map. This boundary shall be subject to adjustment by the Boundary
Commission in accordance with Article II.1 (b) of the Constitutional Agreement.
The Commission shall first of all consider the areas Cekrcici, Ratkovci, Catici
and Drazevici for inclusion in the Sarajevo District and shall thereafter also
consider the inclusion of the opstinas of Kiseljak and Kresevo.
2. The period of UN participation in the governance of the Sarajevo District is
planned for two years. The parties commit themselves to finding a permanent
solution during this period. The period of UN presence can therefore be
shortened if so recommended by the Presidency, it being understood that the
participation of the United Nations in the governance of that District shall at all
times be as determined by the Security Council of the United Nations.
3. Sarajevo District shall have the governmental functions and powers specified
for Constituent Republics in the Constitutional Agreement, except that it shall
not be represented in the Presidency. The opstinas within the Sarajevo District
shall have those governmental functions and powers that opstinas have under
current legislation, subject to the authority of the UN Administrator, to be used
only in exceptional circumstances. Laws adopted by the Union Parliament shall
apply also within Sarajevo District.
4. Sarajevo District shall be governed by a UN Administrator appointed by the
Secretary-General of the United Nations. The UN Administrator shall work
under the over-all supervision of the Special Representative of the Secretary-
General and in close cooperation with the Joint Commission for the Sarajevo
District established by the Military Agreement for Peace in Bosnia and Herzegovina. The UN Administrator shall be advised by an Advisory Body, which shall
be composed of 4 representatives of the Muslim people, 3 representatives of the
Serb people, 2 representatives of the Croat people, and 1 representative of the
District's minorities; the latter shall be nominated by the Co-Chairmen. The
Advisory Body shall make its recommendations by consensus.

5. The UN Administrator shall establish courts of first instance and an appellate court in each opstina included in Sarajevo District. Appeals from these courts may be taken to the courts of the Union of Republics of Bosnia and Herzegovina in the same way as appeals from courts of the Constituent Republics.

6. Within Sarajevo District the Boundary Commission shall propose new opstina boundaries, taking into account the following factors:

(a) The boundaries existing of 1 January 1991;

(b) The tentative changes in boundaries that were implemented after 1 January 1991;

(c) The ceasefire line;

(d) Population distribution, as reflected in census figures and other data;

(e) The wishes of those specifically affected, determined by a plebiscite or otherwise;

(f) The view of the Advisory Body and the UN Administrator.

The proposals of the Boundary Commission for the opstina boundaries shall be submitted for decision to the Presidency.

B. Mostar City Opstina

1. For an interim period, specified in paragraph 2 below, there shall be established the Mostar City Opstina, the outer boundary of which shall be as determined in accordance with the procedure specified in the attachment hereto. This boundary shall be subject to adjustment by the Boundary Commission in accordance with Article II.1 (b) of the Constitutional Agreement.

2. The period of European Community participation in the governance of the Mostar City opstina is planned for two years. The parties commit themselves to finding a permanent solution during this period. The period of European Community presence can therefore be shortened if so recommended by the Presidency, it being understood that the participation of the European Community in the governance of the Mostar City Opstina shall at all times be as determined by the Council of Ministers of the European Community.

3. Mostar City Opstina, which shall have within it the buildings for the capital of the Croat majority Republic, shall have the governmental function and powers specified for Constituent Republics in the Constitutional Agreement. The Mostar City Opstina shall have those governmental functions and powers that opstinas have under current legislation, subject to the authority of the EC Administrator, to be used only in exceptional circumstances. Laws adopted by the Union Parlia-

ment shall apply also within Mostar City Opstina.

4. Mostar City Opstina shall be governed by an EC Administrator appointed by the President of the European Council. The EC Administrator shall work in close consultation with the Special Representative of the Secretary-General and in close cooperation with the Regional Joint Commission established by the Military Agreement for Peace in Bosnia and Herzegovina. The EC Administrator shall be advised by an Advisory Body, which shall be composed of 3 representatives of the Croat people, 3 representatives of the Muslim people, 2 representatives of the Serb people, and 1 representative of the City's minorities; the latter shall be nominated by the Co-Chairmen. The Advisory Body shall make its recommendations by consensus.

5. The EC Administrator shall establish courts of first instance and an appellate court on the Mostar City Opstina. Appeals from these courts may be taken to the courts of the Union of Republics of Bosnia and Herzegovina in the same way as appeals from courts of the Constituent Republics.

6. Mostar City Opstina shall be demilitarized under the arrangements of a Regional Joint Commission in accordance with the Military Agreement for Peace in Bosnia and Herzegovina. UNPROFOR and all other UN agencies shall operate in the City as in the rest of the Country.

C. Police Forces

1. Each existing or new opstina in the Sarajevo District shall organize and control its own uniformed police force, which shall have a proportionally balanced ethnic composition and shall be subjected to supervision by the UN Administrator.

2. Each Constituent Republic shall organize and control its own uniformed police force, which shall have a proportionally balanced ethnic composition. Any necessary coordination shall be the responsibility of the Presidency.

3. The parties understand that as part of the UNPROFOR deployment in Bosnia and Herzegovina there is to be a large civilian police element, whose principal task will be to monitor the police of the Constituent Republics and of the opstinas in the Sarajevo District, so that each: has an appropriately balanced ethnic composition; does not oppress members of minority ethnic groups; contributes positively to the reversal of "ethnic cleansing" by protecting persons returning after having been forced to flee; carries out the judgements of courts, in particular the Human Rights Court; assists the Interim Human Rights Commissioner, the Deputy Commissioners and the human rights monitors; and that the numbers and equipment of the police are in keeping with normal European standards.

D. *Protection of Human Rights and the Reversal of Ethnic Cleansing*

1. The right is established of a refugee or displaced person to freely return as part of an overall process of normalisation. All statements or commitments made under duress, particularly those relating to the relinquishment of rights to land or property, shall be treated as wholly null and void.

2. The parties understand that there is to be an International Human Rights Monitoring Mission, to be established by the Secretary-General of the United Nations, which is to be headed by a Human Rights Commissioner for Bosnia and Herzegovina based in Sarajevo. Deputy Commissioners are to based in various parts of the country. The Commissioner is to be supported by international human rights monitors, deployed throughout the territory of the Union of Republics of Bosnia and Herzegovina; in order to provide protection in urgent cases, they may intercede with the Presidency and the governments of the Constituent Republics, with the Administrators of Sarajevo District and with UNPROFOR; they may refer issues to the ombudsmen and to other human rights agencies as needed and are to work closely with the United Nations High Commissioner for Refugees (UNHCR), the International Committee of the Red Cross (ICRC) and other humanitarian agencies. The Commissioner is expected to submit regular reports to the Secretary-General, who is to report periodically to the Security Council and to other international bodies, including the United Nations Commission on Human Rights and its Special Rapporteur.

ATTACHMENT

A. *The Outer Boundary of the Sarajevo District*

The outer boundary of the Sarajevo District shall be as indicated on the map below, subject to any changes that may be made in accordance with paragraph A.1 of Part 2 of the present Appendix.

B. *The Outer Boundary of the Mostar City Opstina*

The outer boundary of the Mostar City Opstina shall be as indicated on the map below, subject to any changes that may be made in accordance with paragraph 1 of Part 2 of the present Appendix.

Appendix III
Military Agreements

PART 1
AGREEMENT FOR A COMPLETE CESSATION OF ALL COMBAT
ACTIVITIES AMONG THE PARTIES IN CONFLICT OF 30 JULY 1993*

THE UNDERSIGNED MILITARY COMMANDERS, as representatives of their respective Parties in conflict,

Respecting the recent decisions of their commanders-in-chief in Geneva, made under the auspices of the International Conference on the Former Yugoslavia,

Mindful of their obligations under relevant Security Council resolutions, including to ensure UNPROFOR's safety and freedom of movement,

Recognizing the absolute urgency of the present situation and pledging their full efforts to see that this Agreement is honoured,

Have agreed as follows:

Article I
Cessation of all Combat Activities
1. Beginning upon signature of this Agreement, all forces of the three Parties shall cease firing and shall freeze all military activities, including military movements, deployments of forces and establishment of fortifications.
2. Written orders mandating such cessation of combat activities shall be issued, as soon as possible following signature of this Agreement, by each of the undersigned military commanders.

Article II
Humanitarian Aid and Freedom of Movement
Written orders shall be issued by the undersigned military commanders, as soon as possible following signature of this Agreement, permitting:

(a) Free passage for UNPROFOR;

---

* The undersigned are General Rasim Delic, Lieutenant-General Ratko Mladic, and General Milivoj Petkovic; and, as UNPROFOR witnesses, General Jean Cot, Force Commander, and Lieutenant General Francis Briquemont, Commander Bosnia and Herzegovina.

(b) Free passage for UNPROFOR convoys and convoy escorts, subject to routine control of numbers of personnel and weapons entering and leaving territory under the control of a Party; and

(c) Free passage for humanitarian aid convoys, subject to reasonable control of the contents and personnel that are part of the convoy at one checkpoint.

UNPROFOR acknowledges that each Party has legitimate concerns over movements within territories under its control. UNPROFOR shall provide notification of convoy movements.

Article III
Verification of Compliance with this Agreement

1. The undersigned military commanders shall confirm to UNPROFOR the issuance of orders required by this Agreement, and their acknowledgement by subordinate commanders. Full assistance shall be extended to UNPROFOR to permit it to monitor the implementation of this Agreement. UNPROFOR officers in the field may be consulted to provide assistance in implementation of this Agreement.

2. The undersigned military commanders, or their authorized representatives, shall continue to meet daily at a specified time while their commanders-in-chief are meeting in Geneva or, when necessary, on the request of any of the Parties. In accordance with the recommendation made in Geneva by the commanders-in-chief of the Parties, the draft "Military Agreement on the Cessation of Hostilities" shall be discussed among other issues.

3. For urgent matters, the military commanders shall make available through reliable communications on a 24-hour a day basis, a representative who is authorized to take decisions or reach those with such authority.

THIS AGREEMENT, done pursuant of the commanders-in-chief of the Parties in Geneva, shall enter into force upon its signature.

DONE at Sarajevo Airport, on the 30th day of July, 1993, in two versions, one in English and the other in the language of the Parties. Where there are differences of interpretation between the versions, the English version shall control.

PART 2
MILITARY AGREEMENT FOR PEACE IN BOSNIA AND HERZEGOVINA[*]

THE UNDERSIGNED MILITARY COMMANDERS, as representatives of the Parties in Conflict,

Pursuant to Section II of the Agreement relating to Bosnia and Herzegovina concluded in Geneva,

Desiring to work out arrangements for bringing about compliance with a cessation of hostilities, and for monitoring it so as to ensure that its is effective and lasting.

Hereby agree as follows:

Article 1

Measures for Compliance

1. The Parties shall comply in good faith with all provisions in this Agreement. If a dispute arises, UNPROFOR shall be notified and may make a determination on the merits of the dispute.

2. The Parties shall adhere to the Target Time-Table from implementing this agreement, attached as Appendix I, except when UNPROFOR deems that changes are necessary.

3. The Parties shall full support monitoring and control measures to verify compliance with this Agreement, including:

  (a) establishment of the Joint Commission, which shall operate in accordance with the procedure set out in Appendix II;

  (b) establishment of Regional Joint Commissions, which shall operate in accordance with the procedures set-out in Appendix II;

  (c) establishment of "hot lines" between commanders in conflict areas, and between commanders and UNPROFOR;

  (d) ensuring military observers full freedom of movement and access to military installations; and

  (e) monitoring and movement by helicopter, in accordance with clearance arrangements to be determined by the Joint Commission.

---

[*]   The undersigned are Gen. Rasim Delic, Lt. Gen. Ratko Mladic, Gen. Milivoj Petkovic, and Lt. Gen. Francis Briquemont.

Article 2
Separation of Forces
1. Principles for Initial Separation of Forces

   (a) Separation of forces shall be achieved progressively and shall include monitoring by UNPROFOR on infantry and heavy weapons on both sides of confrontation lines, that are within range of the confrontation lines.
   (b) The concepts of separation of forces and withdrawal of heavy weapons shall be linked. Heavy weapons shall be defined as weapons having a calibre of 12.7 or more millimetres.
   (c) Details of implementation, including items "to be agreed", shall be resolved in the Joint Commissions.
   (d) Special priority shall be given to Sarajevo.

2. Ceasefire

In accordance with Article I of the Agreement for a Complete Cessation of All Combat Activities of 30 July 1993, the forces of the Parties shall:

   (a) cease firing and make no offensive actions;
   (b) freeze their positions on existing lines;
   (c) make no forward deployments of personnel or materiel. Rotations of units shall be permitted on a one-for-one basis, under UNPROFOR monitoring; and
   (d) make no establishment or enhancement of fortifications.

3. Declaration of Forces

The Parties shall provide to UNPROFOR the following information:

   (a) numbers and locations of all heavy weapons that are within range of the confrontation lines;
   (b) maps and other detailed documentation on all mines, that surround or are within the confrontation lines;
   (c) traces depicting the position of front lines;
   (d) positions and descriptions of fortifications; and
   (e) positions and numbers of soldiers.

4. Withdrawal of Forces

    (a) UNPROFOR, in consultation with the Joint Commission, shall mark the confrontation lines.

    (b) The forces of the Parties shall withdraw, in a balanced manner but one that is consistent with their different composition. The manner and extent of withdrawal shall be worked out by UNPROFOR, in consultation with the Joint Commission.

    (c) The Areas of Separation shall be increased over time but the continued withdrawal of the forces of the Parties to their respective regions, in consultation with UNPROFOR in the Joint Commission. As this progressive withdrawal takes place, a number of units shall demobilize UNPROFOR, in consultation with the Joint Commission, shall monitor the process of agreed demobilisation.

    (d) The forces of the Parties shall be prohibited from entering the Areas of Separation, except while conducting joint patrols with UNPROFOR or clearing mines. Areas of Separation shall be open to civilian movement, under UNPROFOR control.

5. Withdrawal of Heavy Weapons

    (a) In accordance with locations and a time schedule to be agreed within the Joint Commission, the heavy weapons of the Parties shall be withdrawn from their current positions and concentrated in new locations. Such locations shall be agreed in light of their suitability for monitoring and the range of the heavy weapons.

    (b) UNPROFOR shall monitor the process of withdrawal. Heavy weapons that are withdrawn to locations that are out of range of position of the other parties shall be monitored by UNPROFOR; heavy weapons that remain within range of such positions shall be controlled by UNPROFOR.

    (c) Ammunition shall be stored and monitored separately from heavy weapons. The distance between ammunition and heavy weapons shall be agreed within the Joint Commission.

6. Confinement of Infantry to Barracks

As selected infantry forces are withdrawn from the lines of confrontation, a number of such forces, to be determined by UNPROFOR in consultation with the Joint Commission, shall be confined to barracks.

7. Clearing mines

Designated units of the Parties shall, within areas of separation and elsewhere clear all mines they have laid, in accordance with mutual agreement in the Joint Commission.

Article 3
Monitoring of Borders

1. The borders of the Union of Republics of Bosnia and Herzegovina shall be monitored in accordance with the agreement of the political representatives of all Parties and relevant Security Council resolutions.

Article 4
Restoration of Infrastructure

1. Principles for Restoration of Infrastructure

   (a) Inferring with the supply of water, gas, or electricity as a weapon or mean of pressure is unacceptable. Infrastructure shall not be attacked or degrading in any way, and shall not be used for any military purpose.
   (b) Restoration of infrastructure shall not be conditioned on implementation of the military provisions in this Agreement or of other provisions in the Agreement Relating to Bosnia and Herzegovina.
   (c) Infrastructure shall be restored for the benefit of all civilians, irrespective of ethnic origin, and shall be reestablished across international borders, in accordance with agreements reached by the civil authorities.
   (d) UNPROFOR and other international agencies, as appropriated, may provide guidance and assistance in restoration of infrastructure.
   (e) Special priority shall be given to restoration of infrastructure for all the citizens of Sarajevo.

2. Identifying Priorities and Making Repairs

   (a) The Infrastructure Management Group, composed of representatives of each party, shall identify infrastructure repair priorities according to needs, local resources and the resources of aid agencies. Repairs shall be executed in conjunction with civilian authorities and relevant local agencies of all Parties.

   (b) The Parties shall provide and fulfil guarantees of security to make such repairs. Access shall be guaranteed by the Parties.

   (c) Parties shall provide access to infrastructure sites consistent with security. Parties shall provide liaison repair teams, after local agreement by joint committees. A common instruction for passage down chains of command shall be developed to demonstrate equal endorsement of support for restoration of infrastructure and to allow free access for reconnaissance, workers and expert teams.

3. Infrastructure sites shall include:

   (a) Power grids;
   (b) Steam power stations, coal mines, and hydroelectric power stations;
   (c) Bridges;
   (d) Gas lines;
   (e) Telecommunications;
   (f) Railway lines;
   (g) Routes; and
   (h) Water supply.

Article 5
Providing Freedom of Movement

1. Principles for Freedom of Movement

   (a) UNPROFOR and international humanitarian organizations, especially aid convoys, shall have freedom of movement and priority use of roads and transportation facilities. UNPROFOR may provide escort for convoys and other vehicles as it deems necessary.

   (b) The Parties shall ensure the security and freedom of movement of civilian and commercial traffic. Special attention shall be paid to ensure a traffic throughway to the Bihac area, and right of passage to enclaves in

Eastern Bosnia, and access to commercial ports on the Adriatic.

(c) In consultation with the Joint Commission, UNPROFOR may monitor, patrol and establish checkpoints to enhance freedom of movement. UNPROFOR may conduct joint patrols with each Party of the territory that it controls.

2. Special Measures to open Specified Routes

As a first step in establishing freedom of movement, special measures shall be taken to open the routes specified in paragraph 3 of this Article. Such measures shall be agreed upon in joint commissions and shall include the following:

(a) UNPROFOR may conduct reccss and facilitate repairs;

(b) military movements of the parties shall be permitted only in coordination with UNPROFOR, as well a with the commanders of the Parties;

(c) UNPROFOR shall maintain a heightened presence, including establishing checkpoints at the entrance and exit of such routes and elsewhere where it deems necessary in order to ensure safe passage;

(d) UNPROFOR may conduct inspections at UNPROFOR checkpoints and seize war-related materials carried during unauthorized movements. The Parties may be present during such inspections; and

(e) A corridor extending 500 meters to the left and right of the specified routes shall be demilitarized, in accordance with measures agreed by the Joint Commission.

3. Routes with Special Measures shall be established between or to the following destinations:

(a) The road and railway line from Metkovic on the border of the Republic of Croatia to the centre of the city of Sarajevo;

(b) The road from Sarajevo city to Zenica, via Rajlovac-Ilijas-Visiko;

(c) The road and railway from the city of Sarajevo to Samac via Doboj, and from Doboj to Tuzla;

(d) The road from Bihac to Livno;

(e) The road from Nevisinje to Mostar;

(f) The road from Zepa/Srebrenica to Kladanj;

(g) The road from Visegrad to Sarajevo via Gorazde and Pale;

(h) The road from Stolac to Trebinje via Ljubinje;

(i) The Road from Doboj to Teslic;

(j) Sarajevo Airport;
(k) Banja Luka Airport;
(l) Tuzla Airport;
(m) Mostar Airport.

THIS AGREEMENT:

(a) shall enter into and remain in force in accordance with the Agreement Relating to Bosnia and Herzegovina to be concluded in Geneva; and
(b) shall supersede and replace the Agreement for Peace Bosnia and Herzegovina set out in Appendix III to the Agreement to be concluded in Geneva.

DONE at Sarajevo Airport, on the eleventh day of August, 1993, in two versions, the English version being the authentic one.

APPENDIX I: TARGET TIME-TABLE FOR IMPLEMENTING THIS AGREEMENT

D-Day = Seven days after midnight of the day the Agreement relating to Bosnia and Herzegovina is signed in Geneva.

Phase One: D - 7 to D-Day

Cessation of All Combat Activities, in accordance with the Agreement of 30 July 1993, continues to be observed.

Phase Two: D-Day to + 7

1. Full ceasefire observed (Article II, paragraph 1);
2. Declaration of forces provided (Article II, paragraph 2);
3. Joint Commission, hot lines, and other monitoring and control measures established (Article I);
4. Principles for Freedom of Movement observed (Article V, paragraph 1).

Phase Three: D + 8 to D + 29

1. Lines of confrontation marked (Article II, paragraph 4 (a));
2. Infrastructure restoration begins (Article IV);

3. Routes with Special Measures to Ensure Safe Passage are opened (Article V, paragraphs 2 and 3);
4. Withdrawal of Forces and Heavy Weapons begins (Article II, paragraphs 4 (b) and 4 (d), and Article II);
5. Confinement of Infantry to Barracks begins (Article IV, paragraph 6);
6. Monitoring of Borders begins (Article III).

Phase Four: D + 29 to D + 60

Continued withdrawal of forces to their respective regions. Demobilization of units. Area of Separation expanded (Article II, paragraph 4 (c)).

APPENDIX II: PROCEDURES FOR THE JOINT COMMISSION

1. The Joint Commission shall operate under the chairmanship of UNPROFOR. Each party shall designate the representative of its choosing, whether civil or military, to the Joint Commission. Deputies and assistants, civilian or military, may be present to assist their representatives.
2. Other than authorized members of each delegation, meetings of the Joint Commission shall be closed. Media may be present only by express agreement of each Party.
3. Each Party's representative shall be authorized to act fully on behalf of that Party and to take decision with respect to implementation of this Agreement.
4. The Joint Commission shall meet when and where UNPROFOR decides, in consultation with the Parties.
5. Decision of the Joint Commission shall be taken by consensus. UNPROFOR may decide certain matters that it deems principally within its competence, in consultation with the concerned Parties.
6. UNPROFOR shall report on the proceedings of the Joint Commission to the United Nations, through the Special Representative of the Secretary-General for the Former Yugoslavia.
7. These procedures shall guide the operation of Regional Joint Commissions and other implementing bodies. Amendments to these procedures may be made by UNPROFOR in consultation with the Parties.

PART 3

AMENDMENTS TO THE 11 AUGUST 1993 MILITARY AGREEMENT FOR PEACE
IN BOSNIA AND HERZEGOVINA

The Military Agreement for Peace in Bosnia and Herzegovina, which was concluded by the military commanders of the parties in Sarajevo on 11 August 1993 and which is set out in Part 2 of the Present Appendix, is hereby amended as follows:

1. *Article I, sub-paragraph 3 (b)*, to read as follows:

(b) establishment of a Joint Commission for the Sarajevo District and other Regional Joint Commissions, which shall operate in accordance with the procedures set out in Appendix II;

2. *Article II, sub-paragraph 4(c)*, to read as follows:

(c) The Areas of Separation shall be increased over time by the continued withdrawal of the forces of the Parties to their respective regions, in consultation with UNPROFOR in the Joint Commission. As this progressive withdrawal takes place, a number of units shall demobilize. Sarajevo District and Pale Opstina shall be demilitarized. UNPROFOR, in consultation with the Joint Commission, shall monitor the process of agreed demobilization and demilitarization.

3. *Entry-Force Clause*: delete paragraph (b).

4. *Appendix I, first paragraph*, to read as follows:

D-Day = Seven days after midnight (New York time) of the day on which the Security Council approves the arrangements implementing the Military Agreement of 11 August, as amended.

Appendix IV
Preliminary Agreement between the Republic of Croatia and the Union of Republics of Bosnia and Herzegovina for implementing the 1965 Convention on Transit Trade of Land-Locked States

The Republic of Croatia and the Union of Republics of Bosnia and Herzegovina,

Considering that, as successors of the Socialist Federal Republic of Yugoslavia which had been party to the Convention of Transit Trade of Land-Locked States concluded in New York on 8 July 1965 (hereinafter the "Convention"), the Republic of Croatia and the Union of Republics of Bosnia and Herzegovina should apply between them the provisions of the Convention,

Further considering that the Union of Republics of Bosnia and Herzegovina is to be considered a "land-locked State" within the meaning of that Convention and that with respect to Bosnia and Herzegovina the Republic of Croatia is a "transit State" within the meaning of the Convention,

Desiring to conclude an agreement, on a basis of reciprocity - in accordance with Article 3 (1) (a) of the Convention on the High Seas quoted in the Preamble of the Transit Trade Convention and with article 15 of that Convention - to establish, as foreseen in paragraph 2 of Article 2 of the Convention, the rules governing traffic in transit and the use of means of transport passing across Croatian territory between the territory of the Union of Republics of Bosnia and Herzegovina and the Adriatic Sea, and when passing across territory of the Union of Republics of Bosnia and Herzegovina in transit between places of entry and exit which are both on Croatian territory, as well as to regulate other matters foreseen in the Convention,

Hereby agree as follows:

Article 1
(a) Freedom of transit under the terms of this Preliminary Agreement shall be granted to both Parties on the basis of reciprocity.
(b) The Croatian ports of Ploce and Rijeka are designated as those to which the Union of Republics of Bosnia and Herzegovina is to have access, as foreseen in the Convention, and the routes, by road and as appropriate by rail, between Ploce and Sarajevo and between Rijeka and Bihac are the ones as to which special rules are to be adopted.
(c) The roads on the territory of the Union of Republics of Bosnia and Herzegovina:

(i) Between the Croatian border near Velika Kladusa (via Cazin, Bihac, Kljuc, Jajce, Dinji Vakuf, Bugonjo, Jablanica and Mostar) and the Croatian border on the south, as well as the road between Bonji Vakuf (via Travnik) and Zenica where this road links with the road under (ii) below;

(ii) Between Bosanski Brod (via Dervanta, Doboj, Zenica, Sarajevo and Mostar and the Croatian border in the south;

shall be the ones to which the freedom of transit, in accordance with the Convention, shall be granted to the Republic of Croatia.

(d) The same freedom of transit shall be granted to the Republic of Croatia on the so-called "Una railway line" on the territory of the Union of Republics of Bosnia and Herzegovina between Bosanski Novi (via Bihac) and the Croatian border on the south in the direction of Knin.

(e) The reference to specific ports of Croatia and the roads and railway line within the Union of Republics of Bosnia and Herzegovina, and specific points of entry from Croatia and the Union of Republics of Bosnia and Herzegovina and from Bosnia and Herzegovina to Croatia, are not intended to exclude the facilitation by both states of transit trade through other ports of entry.

Article 2

The parties shall immediately start negotiating, with a view to concluding by _____ 1993, an agreement relating to all aspects of the implementation of the Convention and this Preliminary Agreement, covering in particular the following subjects:

1. Specification of the primary routes, by road as well as by rail, from the ports to the cities specified in article 1;
2. Rules governing he means of transport over the routes and the railroad specified in article 1 (Art. 2 (2) of the Convention);
3. Facilities existing, or to be built, within the specified ports that are to be specially dedicated to traffic of the Union of Republics of Bosnia and Herzegovina might be permitted to operate and develop with the consent of the Republic of Croatia;
4. Possible imposition of special transit dues, tariffs or charges (arts, 3 and 4 of the Convention);
5. Special customs and other measures to facilitate transit trade (art. 5 of the Convention);
6. Conditions of storage of goods in transit (art. 6 of the Convention);

7. Possible establishment of free zones in the designated ports (art. 8 of the Convention);
8. Exceptions on grounds of public health, security and protection of intellectual property (art. 11 of the Convention);
9. Exceptions in case of emergency (art. 12 of the Convention);
10. Application of the Agreement in time of war (art. 13 of the Convention);
11. Settlement of disputes pursuant to article 16 of the Convention.

Article 4

Pending the conclusion of the agreement referred to in Article 2, the Republic of Croatia and the Union of Republics of Bosnia and Herzegovina shall facilitate, as far as it is possible, their mutual transit trade, as defined in this Agreement.

DONE this --- day of August 1993, in ----, in three copies, each in the English, Croatian and Serbian languages, which shall be equally authentic.

126. LETTER DATED 20 AUGUST 1993 FROM THE SECRETARY-GENERAL ADDRESSED TO THE PRESIDENT OF THE SECURITY COUNCIL (ADDENDUM)*

BOUNDARIES OF THE CONSTITUENT REPUBLICS

The map below will ultimately be incorporated in appendix I, annex A, Part I, to the Agreement relating to Bosnia and Herzegovina (see S/26337/Add.1). The map has been reduced to 90 per cent of the original size.

---

* UN Doc. S/26337/Add.2, 23 August 1993.

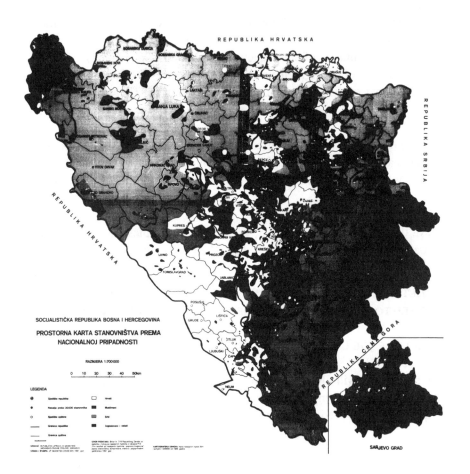

SOCIJALISTIČKA REPUBLIKA BOSNA I HERCEGOVINA

PROSTORNA KARTA STANOVNIŠTVA PREMA
NACIONALNOJ PRIPADNOSTI

RAZMJERA 1:700 000

0   10   20   30   40   50km

LEGENDA

127. LETTER DATED 1 SEPTEMBER 1993 FROM THE SECRETARY-GENERAL ADDRESSED TO THE PRESIDENT OF THE SECURITY COUNCIL*

I have the honour to convey the attached report addressed to me on 1 September 1993 by the Co-Chairmen of the Steering Committee of the International Conference on the Former Yugoslavia.

Annex
Report of the Steering Committee on the Activities of the International Conference on the Former Yugoslavia

The previous report of the Co-Chairmen of the Steering Committee of the International Conference on the Former Yugoslavia, which the Secretary-General transmitted to the Security Council on 20 August 1993 (S/26337), contained the text of a peace plan for Bosnia and Herzegovina as it had been developed by the parties up to 20 August 1993. On that date, the parties had decided to return home to explain the map and to come back to Geneva for a final meeting on 30 August 1993 (S/26337, para. 7).

I. RESUMED PEACE TALKS (31 AUGUST TO 1 SEPTEMBER)

The parties returned to Geneva and resumed their discussion with the Co-Chairmen on Tuesday, 31 August. The Co-Chairmen first saw President Izetbegovic and Mr. Silajdzic. President Izetbegovic informed the Co-Chairmen that he was authorized to sign the peace package but asked that the Muslim majority province be given territory extending to the Adriatic sea and that Muslim majority areas in the area of the River Drina, in the area east of Bihac and in Jajce, should be allocated to the Muslim majority republic, which should have a larger percentage of the national territory. Later, President Izetbegovic gave a map to the Co-Chairmen claiming 2.3 per cent of the territory of Bosnia and Herzegovina in eastern Bosnia and 1.7 per cent east of Bihac making 4 per cent in all.

The Co-Chairmen then met Dr. Karadzic and Mr. Boban in the presence of Presidents Milosevic, Tudjman and Bulatovic. Dr. Karadzic stated that he was authorized to sign the peace package as it existed. He explained that the authorization of his parliament assembly had required a two-third majority vote and that

---

* UN Doc. S/26395, 1 September 1993. Signed by Boutros Boutros-Ghali.

he could not sign the package with any change.

Mr. Boban reported that his parliamentary assembly had also authorized him to sign the package without any change provided the other two parties signed. He added that it had been felt that the Croats had accepted the package in the interest of peace.

The Co-Chairmen explained to Dr. Karadzic and Mr. Boban, in the presence of Presidents Milosevic, Tudjman and Bulatovic, that President Izetbegovic was unlikely to sign the package unless, at a minimum, there were changes granting the Muslim majority republic additional access to the Adriatic Sea and some Muslim majority areas along the river Drina.

After some discussion, the following method of proceeding was agreed:

1. The package should be retained and eventually signed as it is.
2. Bilateral negotiations could take place between the Muslims and the Serbs and also between the Muslims and the Croats.
3. Any bilateral agreements worked out should be signed at the same time as the peace package.

President Izetbegovic held bilateral talks with the Serbs in the afternoon of 31 August and with the Croats in the same evening.

On Wednesday morning, 1 September, the Co-Chairmen first met with President Izetbegovic and Mr. Silajdzic. They then saw the Muslim, Serb and Croat delegation in turn. In the afternoon, they saw the three delegations again individually, and then together in a final session.

In the course of the discussions, the parties explored the following options:

A. Exchange of Territories

1.   A collateral agreement between the Muslim and the Serb parties that the road linking Gorazde to Zepa referred to in paragraph 2 of Part I of Annex A to the Constitutional Agreement shall be three kilometres wide and shall have two crossovers between points within the Serb majority republic.

2.   After the withdrawal of all forces to the agreed boundaries of the Constituent Republics, good faith negotiations would be undertaken for the exchange of territories within the Serb majority republic, such as the Czren Mountains, where a majority of Serb people live. Similar negotiation would also take place between the Croat and Muslim parties.

B. Access to the Sea

1.   A separate agreement would be concluded between the Muslim and Croat parties for the establishment of an exit to the sea for the Muslim majority republic through the Croat majority republic via the Access Authority throughway from Poplat to Neum, and for the Muslim majority republic to acquire a tract of land on the shore of the Adriatic, either around Neum or on the Isthmus of Klek (Kosa) and, if feasible, on technical and environmental grounds, develop it as a commercial port.
2.   The Serb majority republic might make an agreement with the Republic of Croatia regarding an exchange of territories in east Herzegovina with a view to establishing an exit to the Adriatic.

C. Political Agreements

All three parties would agree that the first elections in the Constituent Republics should take place, under the supervision of the United Nations and the European Community, no later than two years after the entry into force of the Constitutional Agreement. All elections to the legislative bodies of Constituent Republics and of opstinas should be by proportional representation. All political parties registered in any of the Constituent Republics might organize themselves and act freely throughout the territory of the Union of Republics of Bosnia and Herzegovina, provided their activities are in accordance with the Constitutional Agreement.

II. OUTCOME

The original package (S/26337 and addenda) and the options mentioned above, which were distilled from the three parties' own ideas, were put by the Co-Chairmen to the three delegation individually on the afternoon of Wednesday, 1 September.

The Croat delegation stated that it accepted the original package and the collateral agreements and was ready to sign them. It suggested that a clause be added stating an understanding of the three parties on the issue of sanctions.

When the Co-Chairmen saw president Izetbegovic and asked him for his position on the original peace package and the proposed collateral agreements, he informed the Co-Chairmen that while he appreciated the efforts made, the results achieved on territorial issues had, in his view, been meagre. He stated that he could not understand why the Muslim majority areas along the River

Drina and in east of Bihac were not allocated to the Muslim majority republic; nor did he understand why the Muslims' request for territory extending to the Adriatic sea was not accepted. In the circumstances, he was not prepared to sign the peace package or the collateral agreements.

The Co-Chairmen suggested that President Izetbegovic explain his position to the other delegations directly and they were then called in, whereupon President Izetbegovic repeated that he could not sign the peace package and the collateral agreement.

Dr. Karadzic commented that on 20 August the Serbs and Croats had made five final concessions on the understanding that if there were no agreement, those concessions would be withdrawn. He noted that a good compromise package had been worked out on 20 August which the Serbs and the Croats had accepted and which should not be unravelled. He emphasized that the Serbs were withdrawing from 24 per cent of the territories they currently hold. He added that the Muslims now hold only 10 per cent but were being given over 30 per cent. He reiterated that he accepted the package and the collateral agreements, accepted implementation, and was ready to sign on the understanding that bilateral negotiations would continue. He stressed, however, that he was not ready to re-open the package and to start negotiations all over again.

Mr. Boban stated that on 20 August the parties had taken a peace package to explain it to their constituencies and had agreed to come back to Geneva for a final session on 30 August, although the Croats had felt that their rights as a constituent people had been whittled down in the package to the barest minimum, yet they were ready to sign it and the collateral agreements in the interest of peace if the others did so. He urged that the Co-Chairmen proceed with signature of the package and cautioned against any side imposing conditions. He regretted that president Izetbegovic was setting up condition after condition. He cautioned that if the package were not accepted the result would be chaos and further war.

President Izetbegovic replied that as far as he was concerned war should not continue. He was for continuing negotiations and would respect the cessation of hostilities and free passage of humanitarian convoys. He was also in favour of exchanging prisoners of war.

Following these statements, the Co-Chairmen informed the parties that they would remain at their disposal to assist them in the search for peace. However, they expressed their grave fears for the fate of the people of Bosnia and Herzegovina as well as for the personnel of UNPROFOR, UNHCR and other humanitarian organizations. They urged the parties to keep their word to observe the cessation of hostilities and noted that they would be reporting on the talks to the

Security Council and to the European Community. They felt that it was a great tragedy that the parties had come so near to agreement but that in the end it had eluded them.

III. ASSESSMENT

The assessment of the Co-Chairmen is that:

1. The choice at the end of the day was between a negotiated peace and the continuation of war. The consequence of this choice for the population of Bosnia and Herzegovina could be severe. If the conflict persists over the next winter, it might be difficult, if not impossible, to assure continued humanitarian relief and assistance in Bosnia and Herzegovina and the consequence for the civilian population could be devastating.
2. Notwithstanding the protestations of the parties, the danger is high that further conflict could break out and could even intensify and expand.
3. The personnel of UNPROFOR, UNHCR and other humanitarian workers are already encountering unacceptable security risks. There is, therefore, a distinct possibility that these organizations may not be able to continue their activities in a deteriorating situation.
4. The original package and the associated collateral agreements, in the absence of any alternative, should be kept on the table.

128. LETTER DATED 23 SEPTEMBER 1993 FROM THE SECRETARY-GENERAL ADDRESSED TO THE PRESIDENT OF THE SECURITY COUNCIL*

I have the honour to convey the attached report addressed to me on 21 September 1993 by the Co-Chairmen of the Steering Committee of the International Conference on the Former Yugoslavia on the latest developments in the search for peace in Bosnia and Herzegovina.

---

* UN Doc. S/26486, 23 September 1993. Signed by Boutros Boutros-Ghali.

Annex
Report of the Steering Committee on the activities of the
International Conference on the Former Yugoslavia

INTRODUCTION

1. The previous report of the Co-Chairmen, which the Secretary-General transmitted to the Security Council on 1 September 1993 (S/26395), dealt with the peace talks held in Geneva on 31 August and 1 September. In that report the Co-Chairmen indicated that on 1 September they had put to the parties a peace package distilled from the parties' own ideas. The Croat delegation was ready to sign the package. The Serb delegation was also ready to sign. President Izetbegovic, however, still wanted further consideration of the question of access to the Adriatic sea and of some territorial issues.

2. Noting that the choice was between a negotiated peace and the continuation of war, the Co-Chairmen warned of the danger that further conflict could take place and that it could even intensify and expand. Fighting has indeed persisted, especially in central Bosnia and around Mostar, where a number of new offensives appear to have been launched.

3. Since the submission of the preceding report, the Co-Chairmen have maintained contacts with the three sides, as well as with Presidents Bulatovic, Milosevic and Tudjman. The Co-Chairmen shuttled among them, holding meetings in Geneva, Zagreb, Podgorica, Skopje and Belgrade. The Co-Chairmen concentrated their efforts on improving relations among the parties, on the question of the access of the Muslim-majority Republic to the Adriatic Sea and on outstanding territorial questions. In the light of contacts with the parties, the Co-Chairmen invited them to a meeting aboard *HMS Invincible* in the Adriatic Sea, on 20 September 1993. All three parties attended, led by President Izetbegovic, Mr. Karadzic and Mr. Boban. Presidents Bulatovic, Milosevic and Tudjman were also present. Deputy Foreign Minister Vitaly Churkin of the Russian Federation and Ambassador Charles Redman of the United States of America were present as observers.

I. IMPROVING RELATIONS AMONG THE PARTIES

4. Since the last report of the Co-Chairmen was issued, there have been some promising political developments, even if the conflict in Bosnia and Herzegovina has not abated. On 14 September, President Izetbegovic and President Tudjman met in Geneva and issued a joint declaration agreeing to the formation of a work-

ing group for matters related to territorial delimitation between the Muslim-majority Republic and the Croat-majority Republic in the Union of Bosnia and Herzegovina, including access to the sea, as a matter of common developmental interest. They also agreed on a cessation of all hostilities and military conflicts between the units of the Army of Bosnia and Herzegovina and the Croatian Defence Council (HVO) immediately, and by no later than 18 September 1993, at 1200 hours but unfortunately, as has so often been the case in the past, this was not respected.

5.   On 16 September, President Izetbegovic met in Geneva with Mr. Karadzic's representative, Momcilo Krajisnik. They also agreed to a joint declaration and agreed to form a working group for outstanding matters related to the territorial delimitation between the Muslim-majority Republic and the Serb-majority Republic in the Union of Bosnia and Herzegovina, including the areas of Brcko, Bosanska Krajina, the Neretva Valley, eastern Bosnia at the Ozren Mountain, including the natural rights of the two Republics to access to the sea. This was in addition to the commitment already made to find a permanent solution to the governance of Sarajevo District within two years. They also agreed on the prompt cessation of all hostilities and military conflicts between the units of the Army of Bosnia and Herzegovina and the Bosnian Serb Army immediately, and by no later than 18 September 1993, at 1200 hours. They also agreed to establish direct communication (hot lines) between military commanders at all levels. Fighting between Serbs and Muslims remains at a relatively low level.

6.   The Serb and Croat sides have indicated that they plan to meet and to issue a similar declaration.

II. ACCESS TO THE SEA

7.   In view of the importance attached to providing the Muslim-majority Republic with access to the Adriatic Sea, arrangements were made for a team of experts from France and Germany to study the possibilities of building a commercial port in the coastal area between Ploce and Neum. In a report dated 20 September, which reached the Co-Chairmen the same day, the experts stated that they could not recommend the building of a port in Neum or on the peninsula of Kosa, in which the Muslim side had expressed interest. They recommended the use of a port in Ploce as a base on the Adriatic Sea with connection to Bosnia and Herzegovina through the Neretva River. That would allow traffic to come from overseas to Ploce and then to an inland port, for example Visici/Celjevo as a port of Bosnia and Herzegovina, with river/seagoing vessels directly to the Mediterranean Sea, e.g. for general cargo.

8.   The experts saw no possibility for constructing a new port in Neum, since there was no available area and the city and its narrow surrounding areas were built on a rocky slope. The road access to the hinterland was not sufficient. There was no railway line to the area of Neum and it was impossible to build a railway line to the city to serve a port. Moreover, the entrance to the bay of Neum was very small and covered with rocky islands, so that ships would have difficulties manoeuvring. Tug-boat services and pilotage would be necessary.

9.   Furthermore, the city of Neum, as well as the northern part of the bay and parts of the Mali Ston canal, was a tourist area. The main business was tourism. It was a sensitive area, owing to the fact that the current in the canal was not strong and the exchange of water with the Adriatic Sea was low. As a result of this, the ecological situation in the bay was sensitive and would react quickly to any negative environmental impact. The Mali Ston canal and the bay of Neum was, in the eyes of may environmentalists, a natural reserve and many international environmental associations were interested in protecting the area.

10. Against the background of this information, as well as of related contacts, the Co-Chairmen discussed with President Tudjman, on 18 September 1993, the possibility of the Republic of Croatia granting a 99-year lease to enable a port to be built in Ploce for the use of the Muslim-majority Republic, After consideration of various options, President Tudjman accepted that a draft lease-agreement be prepared.

11. At the meeting on *HMS Invincible* on 20 September 1993, the following agreements were reached:

   (a) The Muslim and Croat parties agreed on the establishment of an exit to the sea for the Muslim-majority Republic through the Croat-majority Republic via the Access Authority Throughway from Poplat to Neum and for the Muslim-majority Republic to hold a tract of land on the shore of the Adriatic in the isthmus of Kosa (Klek) and establish a joint authority between the two Republics to develop the tourist industry in that area;

   (b) The Croat and Muslim parties agreed that a port facility for the Muslim-majority Republic should be between Visici and Celjevo on the Neretva, capable of taking vessels transshipping from Ploce and also directly from other ports in the Adriatic, and that the southern border of the Muslim-majority Republic should be moved down from Recice to just above Visici. Initially there would be an Access Authority Throughway along the road from Recice to Tasovcici and to the turn-off to Celjevo. The land for the part would be defined as being south of the houses along the road to Celjevo, west of the houses along the road to Vesici, to the north of the built-up area of Visici and then following the east bank of the Neretva River. If the port is developed the Muslim-majority Republic would be expected to build a flyover at the Celjevo cross-road and a new road along an agreed route to Recice avoiding as far as possible existing settlements, and this road, with the land one half kilometre on either side, and the port area will be part of the Muslim-majority Republic.

(c) The Republic of Croatia agreed to a 99-year lease for a separate port facility of the Muslim-majority Republic at the port of Ploce. The details governing this port facility are set out in the agreement to be concluded between the Republic of Croatia and the Union of Republics of Bosnia and Herzegovina as set out in the appendix to the present report.

(d) It was further agreed among the parties that, as soon as relations between the Republic of Croatia and the Federal Republic of Yugoslavia (Serbia and Montenegro) were normalized there should be a treaty covering an exchange of territory involving also the Union of Republics of Bosnia and Herzegovina to take account of the need for strategic assurances for Dubrovnik and of the strategic importance of Prevlaka to the Bay of Kotor, the need for the Serb-majority Republic to have access to the sea in the area between Ostri Rt and Molunat, and the need for the Republic of Croatia to be compensated with territory so that there shall be no net loss of territory to the Republic of Croatia.

III. TERRITORIAL ISSUES

12. As the Co-Chairmen stated in their report of 1 September 1993, the Serb and the Croat sides have maintained the view that they have already made many concessions on territorial issues to the Muslim side on the understanding that the peace package of 1 September was final. They have stated categorically that, if the peace package is not signed soon by the Muslim side, they would withdraw their concessions.

13. Notwithstanding this, the Co-Chairmen continued to explore with the parties avenues for arriving at an agreed settlement. During the meeting held on *HMS Invincible* on 20 September 1993 the following further agreements were reached on territorial issues:

(a) As part of the arrangements to provide a port facility for the Muslim-majority Republic, the southern border of the Muslim-majority Republic

will be moved down from Recici to just above Visici;
(b) The Serb side agreed that the Muslim-majority Republic should have an additional area of land along the banks of the Drina river between Gorazde and Visegrad.

IV. OBSERVATIONS

14. In the light of the agreements reached on access for the Muslim-majority Republic to the Adriatic Sea and of the addition of territory for the Muslim-majority Republic, President Izetbegovic stated at the meeting on 20 September 1993 that he would put the peace package to an extended meeting of the Parliament of Bosnia and Herzegovina to be held on Monday, 27 September 1992.

APPENDIX
AGREEMENT BETWEEN THE REPUBLIC OF CROATIA AND THE UNION OF REPUBLICS OF BOSNIA AND HERZEGOVINA GRANTING THE UNION ACCESS TO THE ADRIATIC THROUGH THE TERRITORY OF THE REPUBLIC OF CROATIA

The Republic of Croatia and The Union of Republics of Bosnia and Herzegovina,

Considering that it is desirable that Union of Republics of Bosnia and Herzegovina (hereinafter the "Union") and in particular the Muslim majority Republic have assured and unrestricted access to the Adriatic Sea on the surface and in the air through and over the territory of the Republic of Croatia (hereinafter "Croatia"),

Hereby agree as follows:

Article 1
(a) Croatia shall lease to the Muslim-majority Republic for the duration of this Agreement the plot of land within the Port of Ploce, including the docks and the parts of the harbour pertaining thereto described in Annex A hereto (hereinafter referred to as the "Leased Area").
(b) Croatia agrees that the Leased Area shall enjoy the status of a free zone in which no duties or taxes imposed by Croatia shall apply.

Article 2

(a) Croatia shall allow access to and from the Leased Area:

  (i)   By ships from the Adriatic Sea, through the territorial waters of Croatia, subject to such ships complying with any applicable international regulations;

  (ii) By ships or barges up the Neretva River up to the point where that River enters the territory of the Muslim majority Republic;

  (iii) By railroad on the line between Ploce to Sarajevo up to the point where that railroad line enters the territory of the Union;

  (iv) By road between Ploce to Sarajevo up to the point where that road enters the territory of the Union.

(b) Ships, barges, railroad cars and trucks and other road vehicles using the routes referred to in paragraph (a) that carry the flag of the Union or are marked by an emblem of the Union or of the Muslim-majority Republic shall not be entered or inspected by any public authority of Croatia.

(c) Limits in the sizes and specification of the characteristics of the ships, barges, railroad cars, and trucks and other road vehicles referred to in paragraph (b) and of the volume of traffic in the routes referred to in paragraph (a) may be set by the Joint Commission established in accordance with Article 4.

(d) Should the limits set in accordance with paragraph (c) restrict the volume of traffic that the Muslim-majority Republic considers it necessary to maintain, then it may, at its cost and in accordance with plans approved by the Joint Commission, arrange for the capacity of the routes referred to in paragraph (a) to be increased.

(e) With respect to any traffic or persons or goods carried out pursuant to this Article, all responsibilities for compliance with international laws and obligations shall be assumed by the Muslim-majority Republic or the Union.

Article 3

Croatia grants to the Union and in particular to the Muslim-majority Republic the right to authorize any types of aircraft to overfly the territory of Croatia, including its territorial waters, along the corridor specified in Annex B hereto, subject to such aircraft complying with any applicable international air traffic regulations.

Article 4

(a) The Parties hereby establish a Joint Commission to assist in implementing the present Agreement by:

    (i)   Establishing any rules and standards required for implementing the Agreement, and in particular Article 2 (c), including for any construction;

    (ii) Arrange for any monitoring required to prevent abuses of the Agreement;

    (iii) Settle, subject to Article 6, any disputes regarding the interpretation or the application of the Agreement.

(b) Croatia and the Muslim-majority Republic shall appoint three members each to the Joint Commission and they shall by joint agreement appoint three more members, one of whom shall be the Chairman, if no agreement can be reached on one or more of the joint appointments within three months, the Secretary-General of the United Nations shall make those appointments at the request of either party.

(c) The Joint Commission shall adopt its own rules of procedure. Its decisions shall require five concurring votes.

Article 5

The present agreement is without prejudice to any rights or obligations flowing from the Preliminary Agreement between the Parties hereto for implementing the 1965 Convention on the Transit Trade of Land-Locked States or any agreement that may be concluded between the Parties to implement or to supersede that Preliminary Agreement.

Article 6

Unless otherwise agreed, any legal dispute concerning the interpretation of this Agreement may be submitted by either Party to the International Court of Justice.

Article 7

(a) This Agreement shall remain in force for a period of 99 years, except as otherwise agreed by the Parties.

(b) Should the Union by dissolved, it shall be succeeded as a Party to this Agreement by the Muslim majority Republic.

DONE this --- day of --- 1993, in ---, in three copies, each in the English, Croatian and Serbian languages, which shall be equally authentic.

129. LETTER DATED 28 DECEMBER 1993 FROM THE SECRETARY-GENERAL ADDRESSED TO THE PRESIDENT OF THE SECURITY COUNCIL*

I have the honour to convey the attached report addressed to me on 23 December 1993 by the Co-Chairmen of the Steering Committee of the International Conference on the Former Yugoslavia on the latest developments in the search for peace in Bosnia and Herzegovina.

Annex
Report of the Co-Chairmen of the Steering Committee on the activities of the International Conference on the Former Yugoslavia

INTRODUCTION

1. The previous report of the Co-Chairmen, which the Secretary-General transmitted to the Security Council on 23 September 1993 (S/26468) provided an account of the deliberations on the HMS *Invincible* in the Adriatic Sea, on 20 September 1993. On that occasion, President Izetbegovic, Mr. Boban and Mr. Karadzic met in the presence of the Co-Chairmen, Presidents Bulatovic, Milosevic and Tudjman, Deputy Foreign Minister Churkin and Ambassador Redman. A constitutional agreement was reached providing for a Union of Republics of Bosnia and Herzegovina. Elaborate provisions for the promotion and protection of human rights were reconfirmed, as were arrangements for implementing and monitoring a cessation of hostilities. Agreements were also worked out providing the Muslim-majority Republic with access to the Adriatic Sea via the Neretva River, giving the Muslim-majority Republic a 99-year lease in an area for the construction of a port at Ploce. (in addition to the use of the port of Rijeka) and assuring freedom of transit between the Union of Republics of Bosnia and Herzegovina and the Republic of Croatia.

2. The three sides in Bosnia and Herzegovina informed the Co-Chairmen that they would submit the "*Invincible* Package" to their respective assemblies for ratification. The Bosnian Croat and the Bosnian Serb sides subsequently informed the Co-Chairmen that their assemblies had ratified the *Invincible* Pack-

---

* UN Doc. S/26922, 29 December 1993. Signed by Boutros Boutros-Ghali.

age. The Bosnian Presidency reported that their expanded assembly did not.

3. Both the Bosnian Croat and the Bosnian Serb sides then informed the Co-Chairmen that they had made concessions on the *HMS Invincible* conditional on the acceptance of the Package by all sides. They therefore intended to withdraw their concessions because the Bosnian Presidency side had not ratified the Package. The Co-Chairmen appealed to the Bosnian Croat and the Bosnian Serb sides not to withdraw their concessions but to continue the search for peace.

I. THE CONTINUING SEARCH FOR PEACE

4. In the situation that presented itself following one side's non-ratification of the *Invincible* Package, the Co-Chairmen decided to pursue a two-track approach: to build upon the *Invincible* Package; and to explore whether, by tackling certain problems in the former Yugoslavia together, it might be possible to create more options for helping to find a settlement in Bosnia and Herzegovina. One idea that was specifically considered was the possibility of a territorial exchange between Bosnia and Herzegovina and the Republic of Croatia that would enable agreement to be reached on an outlet to the sea for the Bosnian Republic in a deep-water area, which would allow it to build its own port on its own sovereign territory.

5. The Co-Chairmen have carried out extensive discussions with the three sides, as well as with leaders of neighbouring countries, at Geneva, Belgrade, Sarajevo and Zagreb. Together with the Foreign Ministers of the European Union they met with the parties at Geneva on 29 November. The Co-Chairmen continued their meetings with the parties and the Presidents of neighbouring countries in their respective capitals. On 17 December, the Co-Chairmen attended a meeting with the Prime Minister of Bosnia and Herzegovina at Vienna, arranged by the Belgian Foreign Minister and the Commissioner of External Affairs of the European Union. The Co-Chairmen, immediately thereafter, shuttled among the parties prior to meeting them at Geneva on 21 December. The next day, 22 December, the Co-Chairmen joined the Foreign Ministers of the European Union in a meeting with the parties at Brussels. The Co-Chairmen held further discussions with the parties in the evening of 22 December and on 23 December in a determined push for a peace agreement.

II. DELIBERATIONS

6. The discussions that took place had the following aims:

(a) To build upon the *"Invincible* Package";
(b) To provide the Muslim-majority Republic with a minimum of 33.3 per cent of territory;
(c) To ensure the Muslim-majority Republic access to the sea.

7. On the first point, namely building upon the *Invincible* Package, the Co-Chairmen have taken the view that changes would only be made if they are agreed to by all three Bosnian sides.

8. On providing the Muslim-majority Republic with a minimum of 33.3 per cent of territory, the Bosnian Croats and the Bosnian Serbs, on 21 December 1993, made a joint proposal of a map that they said provided 33.3 per cent of territory for the Bosnian Republic and 17.5 per cent for the Croat-majority Republic. In the event of any shortfall in reaching these figures on the proposed map, the Bosnian Serbs undertook to make up the difference. The Co-Chairmen transmitted this map to the Bosnian Presidency on 21 December.

9. On the issue of access to the sea, the Bosnian Croat side took the position that this had been settled in the *Invincible* Package. The Bosnian Presidency, however, submitted that Neum should be allocated to the Muslim-majority Republic on a sovereign basis. The Bosnian Croats were not prepared to accept this, pointing out that Neum was an exclusively Croat area. The Republic of Croatia then came up with a proposal according to which it would accord the Muslim-majority Republic and the Bosnian Serbs each an area of land on the Adriatic Sea in the vicinity of the Prevlaka peninsula. This would be an allocation of sovereign territory and, in the case of the Muslim-majority Republic, it would be accompanied by a sovereign road corridor. The area indicated for the Muslim-majority Republic and for the Bosnian Serbs would both be deep-water areas, at which deep-water ports could be built. In return, the Republic of Croatia would incorporate Neum and the Bosnian Serbs would give it some land that would widen its territory in the Dubrovnik area, thereby enhancing its security.

10. The Bosnian Presidency first indicated interest in the offer of a port in the Prevlaka area but after examining it further informed the Co-Chairmen that it was too far away and would be too expensive. Faced with this situation, the Co-Chairmen stated that the arrangements made on the *Invincible* in respect of Neum would be maintained. The Bosnian Presidency then came up with a proposal that Neum and a part of Stolac should be held by the Muslim-majority Re-

public and the Bosnian Croat Republic in condominium, that is to say, joint sovereignty. The Bosnian Croat side said it would study the proposal but only in relation to the Isthmus of Klek, not the opstina of Neum.

11. On the issue of international guarantees for any peace agreement, the Co-Chairmen have taken the position that this would be a matter to be considered by the Security Council. Nevertheless, the Co-Chairmen contacted interested Governments and international organizations to explain to them the importance attached to the question of international guarantees for the implementation of an agreement.

III. Outcome

12. The situation following the discussion held in Geneva on 21 December and in Brussels on 22 and 23 December may be summarized as follows:

   (a) There is agreement among all three sides that Bosnia and Herzegovina should be organized as a Union of three republics;

   (b) There is agreement that the Muslim-majority Republic should have 33.3 per cent of territory and the Croats should have 17.5 per cent;

   (c) At Brussels on 23 December, the Co-Chairmen appealed to all three sides to observe a holiday truce to cover the period 23 December to 15 January. All three leaders accepted this appeal and undertook to give instruction to their military commanders down to the local level to observe the ceasefire faithfully;

   (d) The three sides have agreed to return to Geneva on 15 January 1994, to continue the search for peace;

   (e) Working Groups have been established to look into the following issues and to help reach agreement on them by 15 January:

   (i) The definition of the Mostar city area that would be placed under the temporary administration of the European Union;

   (ii) Technical arrangements for providing the Muslim-majority Republic with road and rail access to Brcko and the Sava river, without prejudice to the Muslim-majority Republic's continued support for the arrangements agreed on the *HMS Invincible*;

   (iii) Access of the Muslim-majority republic to the sea;

   (iv) Continued discussions between Mr. Silajdzic and Mr. Krajisnik on territorial delimitation;

(f) The Co-Chairmen have asked all three sides to consult their respective "Assemblies" beforehand so that any agreement concluded at Geneva would come into force immediately upon signature.

130. Letter Dated 21 January 1994 from the Secretary-General Addressed to the President of the Security Council*

I have to honour to convey the attached report addressed to me on 20 January 1994 by the Co-Chairmen of the Steering Committee of the International Conference of the Former Yugoslavia and the latest developments in the search for peace in Bosnia and Herzegovina.

Annex
Report of the Co-Chairmen of the Steering Committee on the Activities of the International Conference on the Former Yugoslavia

Introduction

1. On 29 December 1993, the Security Council received a report of the Co-Chairmen giving an account of developments in the search for peace in Bosnia and Herzegovina following meetings held in Geneva on 21 December and in Brussels on 22 and 23 December (S/26922).

I. Continuing Contacts

2. Since the submission of that report, the Co-Chairmen maintained contacts with the parties to the conflict and with the Governments of neighbouring countries. The Co-Chairmen travelled to Vienna on 4 and 5 January for consultations with Prime Minister H. Silajdzic of Bosnia and Herzegovina and Foreign Minister M. Granic of the Republic of Croatia. While in Vienna, the Co-Chairmen had talks with Austrian Foreign Minister A. Mock. On 5 January, the Co-Chairmen went to Belgrade for discussions with President S. Milosevic and with Bosnian Serb leaders. On 6 January, the Co-Chairmen visited Budapest for discussions with Hungarian Foreign minister G. Jeszensky. The same day, the Co-Chairmen went to Bonn for consultations with German Foreign Minister K.

---

* UN Doc. S/1994/64, 21 January 1994. Signed by Boutros Boutros-Ghali.

Kinkel. On 7 January, the Co-Chairmen had consultations in Paris with French Foreign Minister A. Juppé. On 9 and 10 January, the Co-Chairmen had discussions in Bonn with Presidents A. Izetbegovic and F. Tudjman. On 16 January, the Co-Chairmen had meetings in Athens with Mr. K. Papoulias, the incoming President of the European Union Council of Ministers.

II. PEACE TALKS, 18 AND 19 JANUARY 1994

3. On 18 and 19 January 1994, resumed peace talks were held in Geneva with the attendance of Presidents Bulatovic, Izetbegovic, Milosevic and Tudjman, as well as Mr. Karadzic and Mr. Akmadzic.

4. It will be recalled that it had been hoped to conclude an overall settlement based on the *HMS Invincible* package, with each of the three peoples having their own majority republic within an overall union but with the additional features suggested in the European Union action plan whereby, in particular, the Muslim-majority Republic would have a minimum of 33,3 per cent of the territory of Bosnia and Herzegovina; as had emerged in discussion, the Croat-majority Republic would have 17.5 per cent; the Muslim-majority Republic would have, as has been suggested by President Tudjman, a tract of land on the peninsula of Peljesac instead of on the Isthmus of Klek and this would have a port and tourist facilities; and all sides would continue to commit themselves to upholding international norms of human rights, including the right of refugees and displaced persons to return to their homes.

5. During the round of talks on 18 and 19 January, a map proposed by the Bosnian Serbs was on the table offering the Muslim-majority Republic 33.56 per cent (see appendix I). The Republic of Croatia stated its willingness to sign linked agreements providing the Muslim-majority Republic with 99-year leases for use of a port at Ploce, a port in the Neretva River at Celevo, from which seagoing cargo boats or tourist passenger boats could link up with their facilities in Ploce or the existing small port on the Peljesac peninsula.

6. Detailed provisions committing all parties to international human rights conventions and making available specialized human rights machinery of the Council of Europe were maintained.

7. The Bosnian Serbs and the Bosnian Croats declared their willingness to pursue discussions to settle, as between them, the delimitation of territory so as to assure the Bosnian Croats 17.5 per cent of territory. President Izetbegovic, however, while not rejecting the figure of 17.5 per cent, entered a reservation that this must not be to the detriment of the Muslim-majority Republic.

8. President Izetbegovic acknowledged that the Muslim-majority Republic was

being offered 33.56 per cent. He submitted, however, that the map should be altered so as to include in the territory allocated to the Muslim-majority Republic certain areas in eastern and western Bosnia where the Muslims had been in the majority before the outbreak of the conflict, as well as certain areas in central Bosnia, while keeping within the target of 33.3 per cent.

9. The Co-Chairmen had painstaking discussions with the three sides in order to help them to overcome the remaining hurdles to a peace agreement. However, President Izetbegovic maintained his decision on territory. The Bosnian Serbs said they had made concession after concession in order to achieve peace, most recently reverting to their former position of accepting international administration for Sarajevo, and they could go no further. The Bosnian Croats insisted that the areas sought by President Izetbegovic in central Bosnia were vital for the Croat-majority Republic.

10. The Co-Chairmen felt that it was imperative that all concerned found a way to overcome this remaining hurdle over the allocation of territory. Accordingly, they consulted the parties concerning an arbitration procedure for breaking the impasse. After those consultations, the Co-Chairmen submitted to the parties a procedure (see appendix II) whereby the disputed territory could be referred to an arbitration commission and its recommendations come to the Security Council after a peace agreement has been implemented and forces withdrawn to the provisional boundaries on the map in appendix I.

11. The Bosnian Serbs and the Bosnian Croats were willing to accept these procedures. The Bosnian Muslims rejected them because, President Izetbegovic stated, too many areas of importance to the Muslim-majority Republic would be left unresolved and they were unwilling to have Serb or Croat forces remaining in the disputed territories that they consider should be in their Republic. The Bosnian Serbs said that, in the light of the Bosnian Muslim's rejection of the proposed arbitration commission, they would, in any future negotiations, be unwilling to remain within a Union of three republics, but that they would hope to be able to continue to accept United Nations administration for Sarajevo district. They felt that the Serb-majority Republic would henceforth have to be considered as independent for the Muslim-majority Republic.

12. Face with the danger of renewed and intensified conflict and aware of the deep concern in the United Nations High Commissioner for Refugees, Mrs. S. Ogata, the Co-Chairmen felt that they had to find a way to keep the parties engaged in the peace process and meet again in the near future. Accordingly, they proposed that the parties establish hot lines, that they exchange representatives in one another's headquarters in Sarajevo, Mostar and Pale and that the Bosnian parties should meet again in Geneva on 10 February 1994 to consider the effectiveness of these arrangements on other practical confidence-building

measures to reduce the level of fighting. All agreed to meet, but President Izet-begovic said he would need to consult his military on the idea of exchanging representatives. All three sides did, however, agree to return to Geneva on 10 February to examine the results of the efforts of the working group.

13. The Co-Chairmen view this further failure to finalize and agree on a peace settlement with considerable concern. There can be no escaping the reality that the three warring parties are now at risk of increased fighting and that more territorial issues could be settled on the battlefield than at the negotiation table. This is taking place at a time when their people are suffering immense hardship in the middle of winter, despite the best efforts of the Office of the United Nations High Commissioner for Refugees, the United Nations Protection Force and other agencies. While the fighting continues, very probable at an increased intensity, many people will lack the basic essentials for life: food, warmth and shelter.

Appendix I

Proposal for Bosnian Muslim Majority Republic
comprising over one third of territory of
Bosnia and Herzegovina

Area 1   4.2%

Area 2   65.4%

Area 3   24.6%

Area 4   1.4%

Area 5   1.3%

Sarajevo   3.1%
District

Total for Muslim Majority Republic,
including Sarajevo District on a
2-1 basis, = 33.56%

(Figures verified at the request of ICFY by
 Topomat SA computer services Geneva 8-1-94)

Appendix II

Article 1

(a) The provisional boundaries of the constituent republics shall be as set out in annex A, part 1. The Muslim-majority Republic shall be provided with a minimum of 33.33 per cent of the territory and the Bosnian Serb Party has undertaken to ensure that the Croat-majority Republic has 17.5 per cent. The Bosnian Muslim Party, while not rejecting the figure of 17.5 per cent, has a reservation that it must not be to the detriment of the Muslim-majority Republic. Except as provided in (b) and (c), the boundaries of the Republics may be changed only by the procedure provided for amending this Constitutional Agreement.

(b) Marginal changes in the boundaries set out in annex A may be made by agreement between the parties on the recommendation of a Boundary Commission, which shall receive evidence from those specifically affected by them. The Commission shall consist of five persons appointed by the Secretary-General of the United Nations, of whom three shall be persons recommended the representatives of the three constituent peoples.

(c) Substantial changes in the boundaries involving the following disputed territories - Bosanska Krupa, Bosanski Novi, Brcko, Bugojno, Busavaca, Donji Vakuf, Gornji Vakuf, Kiseljak, Kresevi, Novi Travnik, Sanski Most, Ustikolina, Visegrad, Vitez, Zvornik - and an exchange of territory of high population density with a predominantly Serb population in the District of Sarajevo for areas of lower population density in eastern Bosnia, in particular Zepa and Srebrenica, which might alter the 33.33 per cent allocation to the Muslim-majority Republic, can be agreed under the procedures specified in paragraph 1 (b), but, in the event no agreement is reached, any difference can be referred to a arbitration Commission appointed by the President of the International Court of justice after consultation with the parties. The recommendations of the Commission shall be addressed, in the first instance, to the parties, and only if there is disagreement be referred to the Security Council.

(d) There shall be no border controls on boundaries between the constituent republics, and there shall be free movement of persons, goods and services throughout the territory of the Union of Republics of Bosnia and Herzegovina.

131. LETTER DATED 25 JANUARY 1994 FROM THE SECRETARY-GENERAL ADDRESSED TO THE PRESIDENT OF THE SECURITY COUNCIL*

Further to my recent report on the latest developments in the search for peace in Bosnia and Herzegovina (S/1994/64), I have the honour to convey the attached report addressed to me on 24 January by the Co-Chairmen of the Steering Committee of the International Conference on the Former Yugoslavia on the activities of the working groups and other organs of the Conference.

Annex
Report of the Co-Chairmen of the Steering Committee on the activities of the working groups and other organs of the Conference

INTRODUCTION

1. The present report provides information on the activities of the working groups and the other organs of the Conference.

I. WORKING GROUP ON BOSNIA AND HERZEGOVINA

2. The activities undertaken on the situation in Bosnia and Herzegovina were dealt with in Security Council reports S/26922 and S/1994/64.

II. PEACEMAKING ACTIVITIES WITH REGARD TO THE SITUATION IN THE UNITED NATIONS PROTECTED AREAS AND RELATED AREAS IN CROATIA

3. The peacemaking efforts undertaken under the auspices of the International Conference in respect of the situation in the United Nations protected areas and related areas in Croatia have been dealt with in separate reports submitted to the Council, the last of which was issued on 1 December 1993 (S/26828).

III. WORKING GROUP ON HUMANITARIAN ISSUES

4. Through the Working Group on Humanitarian Issues, chaired by Mrs. S. Ogata, United Nations High Commissioner for Refugees, the humanitarian

---

* UN Doc. S/1994/83, 26 January 1994. Signed by Boutros Boutros-Ghali.

situation in the former Yugoslavia has been kept under constant review. In general, the situation has continued to deteriorate.

5. Recurring hostilities in and around the United Nations protected areas in Croatia and human rights abuses against the few remaining members of minority groups there caused new displacement in the second half of 1993. Additional large numbers of civilians have also been uprooted in Bosnia and Herzegovina as a result of military offensives, especially in central Bosnia, or as a result of persecution or a mixture of both, while hundreds of thousands of others continue to be trapped in besieged areas or cities, often under desperate conditions. As the political crisis in the former Yugoslavia continues, the refugee burden weighs heavily on all countries in the region, but particularly on Croatia and the Federal Republic of Yugoslavia (Serbia and Montenegro). In the latter, which is under sanctions imposed by the Security Council, there are grave humanitarian concerns about the dire plight of the vulnerable groups, whose numbers are rising.

6. The international relief effort has continued to try to address foremost the emergency needs of refugees, internationally displaced persons and other victims of conflict, in cooperation with the authorities of the countries concerned. The Working Group on Humanitarian Issues reviewed the implementation of the international humanitarian assistance programme during a meeting held in Geneva on 16 July 1993, which, as was the case with previous meetings, was attended by all countries of the region, the international donor community and other interested States, the Department of Humanitarian Affairs of the United Nations Secretariat and international governmental and non-governmental organizations participating in the relief effort. At a similar meeting held on 8 October 1993, a new consolidated appeal was launched, revising needs for the period October to December 1993 and putting forward the requirements for the first half of 1994, totalling $ 697 million. Several States announced new contributions, which was essential as the international relief effort was threatened by insufficient funding.

7. In Bosnia and Herzegovina operations of international organizations have been seriously obstructed, as reported on previous occasions to the Security Council. Humanitarian access to populations in need of assistance has been repeatedly denied or sabotaged for political or military purposes, especially by the Bosnian Serb and Bosnian Croat sides, while all sides have frequently and seriously threatened the security of the personnel of the United Nations Protection Force (UNPROFOR), the Office of the United Nations High Commissioner for Refugees (UNHCR) and other organizations. The international airlift to Sarajevo had to be interrupted several times for security reasons. Convoy operations were suspended in central Bosnia on 23 October 1993 after the killing of

an UNHCR driver and the wounding of nine UNPROFOR soldiers.

8. In view of the deteriorating situation on the ground, and the prospect of still greater humanitarian disaster during the winter, Mrs. Ogata met with the political and military leadership of the Bosnian parties, on 18 November 1993 in Geneva. Mr. Sommaruga, of the International Conference of the Red Cross (ICRC) participated in the Humanitarian Issues Working Group meeting in an observer capacity. Mrs. Ogata insisted with the leaders of the parties that the primary responsibility for averting further agony, especially in the view of the winter period, was theirs. The Bosnian Serb side refused to cooperate in the opening of Tuzla airport for humanitarian flights. However, in a joint declaration the parties did agree to suspend fighting along the major supply routes for the passing of humanitarian convoys, in order to ensure complete and secure freedom of movement for the United Nations and international humanitarian organizations, to prevent diversion of humanitarian assistance to the military and to release all civilian detainees in accordance with the principles of and arrangements by ICRC. Especially important was the commitment of the parties, reached after much debate, to allow UNHCR and ICRC to determine the content of humanitarian assistance, including priority winterization needs and all materials, supplies, gas and other fuel necessary for the survival of the civilian population. Following this meeting, convoy operations were resumed in central Bosnia.

9. On 19 November 1993, the outcome of the previous day's meeting and the state of preparations for the relief effort during the winter period were reviewed during a Working Group session held in Geneva with the donor community and other interested States, UNHCR, the World Food Programme (WFP), the United Nations Children's Fund (UNICEF), the World Health Organization (WHO), the Intergovernmental Organization for Migration (IOM) and ICRC. On 29 November, Mrs. Ogata addressed a meeting convened by the European Union in Geneva, and attended by the Bosnian parties, at the end of which a declaration was signed by the military leaders of those parties, reiterating the commitments of 18 November 1993.

10. After the November meetings there was some improvement in obtaining clearance for the passage of both fuel and shelter materials to some areas. However, serious problems of access have persisted. In December 1993, the UNHCR convoy operation achieved 45 per cent (20,000 tons) of its overall target for food and non-food items. Bureaucratic obstruction and security incidents have increased further. Of the gravest concern is what seems to have become a pattern of deliberate targeting of humanitarian personnel by all parties. While the international relief effort is undoubtedly helping large numbers of victims to survive through the winter, intensified fighting and offensive action,

especially in central Bosnia, are expected to increase further security risks and the obstruction of access to the victims.

IV. Working Group on Ethnic and National Communities and Minorities

Former Yugoslav Republic of Macedonia

11. On 27 August, Ambassador G. Ahrens, mediated "Agreed Minutes" (see appendix I) between the Government of the former Yugoslav Republic of Macedonia and representatives of the local Serbs, which addressed various issues brought up by Serbs in the former Yugoslav Republic of Macedonia. The Co-Chairmen raised these and other issues when they met President Gligorov in Skopje on 17 September, when they also visited the UNPROFOR contingent stationed there.

12. Regarding Albanians in the former Yugoslav Republic of Macedonia, a stocktaking exercise was undertaken by the International Conference on Former Yugoslavia in order to have a clear account of all the issues in which progress has been made and those which were still pending. Meetings in Skopje (24-27 August, 29 September-1 October, 11 November, 14-17 December, 6-7 January) concentrated mainly on improvements to the Law of Local Self-Government; the conditions for the use of the Albanian language in local and central state institutions; the training of Albanian teachers at university level; and the national census to be held i April 1994. Some of these issues are interlinked and of considerable scope, as for instance the Law of Local Self-Government, which requires a two-third majority for approval in Parliament. Although discussions were held in a constructive manner, the broad consensus necessary for a breakthrough in these areas has not yet materialized.

Kosovo

13. The Co-Chairmen raised the situation of Albanians in Kosovo several times during meetings with President Milosevic, and in particular urge the Yugoslav authorities to reconsider their decision not to prolong the mandate of the Conference on Security and Cooperation in Europe mission in Kosovo.

14. On 26 August, Ambassador Masset, Lord Owen's Deputy, travelled to Pristina to meet with the local Serb authorities and with representatives of the Albanians. There were also contacts on Kosovo with the Serbian authorities in Belgrade.

15. The International Conference on Former Yugoslavia made a further attempt to reconvene talks on educational problems in Kosovo and invited both parties to Geneva on 8 September. The Belgrade Government did not attend, claiming that minority issues were internal matters. Since then, it had not been possible to find a mutually agreeable venue for the parties to meet.

Sandjak

16. On 20 January, the Co-Chairmen met representatives of the Muslim community in the Sandjak led by Mr. Ugljanin, President of the Muslim National Council of the Sandjak, to discuss the problems of the Muslim Community. This followed up on the visit of Ambassador Masset to the Sandjak in October 1993.

Vojvodina

17. Ambassador Masset visited the Vojvodina in July 1993, where he met with leaders of the Croat and Hungarian communities, as well as the Serbian authorities, to discuss the problems of minorities in the area. Ambassador Masset also raised these problems with the federal and republican authorities in Belgrade.

V. WORKING GROUP ON SUCCESSION ISSUES

18. Two sessions of the Working Group on Succession Issues took place in Geneva, on 10 to 12 may and on 27 to 29 September 1993. A number of advisory opinions have also been given by the Arbitration Commission relating to several State succession issues. At the September meeting, Ambassador Jorgen Bajor was succeeded by Ambassador Alf Johnson as Chairman of the Working Group. Depending on the outcome of bilateral consultations the Chairman is carrying out with the parties, the next Working Group meeting is expected to take place in late February 1994.

19. The meetings were well attended, with 25 to 30 experts participating. Both the May and September meetings focused on succession in respect of archives and legal questions concerning the definition of the objects of succession.

20. As regards archives, the Working Group discussed in depth, at both meetings, the principles regulating the definition of archives and choice of legal rules applicable. Although the parties reserve their positions as regards these questions, a parallel process relating to the preservation and utilization of archives has started. A technical meeting jointly sponsored by the Commission of the European Community and the Austrian State Archives took place in Vienna from

13 to 17 November 1993, on security microfilming and preservation of archives concerning the succession of the former Yugoslavia. The meeting met with some success, with delegations from all five former Yugoslav States attending.

21. A common archives action plan, covering microfilming, protection and preservation of endangered archives in the former Yugoslavia, especially in Bosnia and Herzegovina, was agreed upon. The right of free access to all federal and republican archives was again explicitly recognized. In the course of the meeting each of the five delegations:

(a) Set out its priorities as to which archives should be microfilmed and protected;

(b) Expressed its readiness to exchange microfilms, particularly in the interest of State succession;

(c) Indicated its requirements regarding basis equipment (cameras, etc.), materials (microfilms, chemicals, etc.), technical assistance (management and control) and staff training.

There was general agreement on the need to set up five security microfilming units, working to European and international standards, one i each of the five States, as an indispensable first step to ensure the action plan's implementation. The initial outlay to establish the five units will probably be in the order of 3 to 5 million European currency units, with which the international community will be asked to assist. Operating expenses would then be assumed by the different republics.

22. As regards the definition of State property, an inventory of assets to be divided was drafted by four of the five delegations, with one delegation, "the Federal Republic of Yugoslavia" not being present at that particular meeting. There were divergent views as to whether it was necessary to have a jointly accepted definition of State property first on whether an inventory could be started immediately. The September meeting of the Working Group did not achieve a consensus on this issue.

23. The Chairman decided that, before a new full meeting of the Working Group could be called, bilateral consultations would be necessary. The members of the delegation arguing the necessity of a jointly agreed definition agreed in bilateral consultations wit the Chairman to the following:

(a) They would retain their position on the necessity for a definition;

(b) Nevertheless, they would, using their proposed definition as a working hypothesis, draw up an itemized list additional to the inventory already being worked out by the other parties.

24. Wit a view to allowing all the parties to see the maximum content of an inventory in order to prepare the ground for further negotiations, it was agreed that no new initiatives should be launched in the Working Group until the new list additional to the inventory had emerged. This should happen some time in early or mid-February, after which a full round of negotiations may be foreseen for the end of February 1994.

25. It has also been agreed by the parties in the Working Group that one should, to the extent possible, avoid the difficult questions relating to succession terminology, such as succession/secession/continuation, by using neutral language, i.e., the names of the States involved.

VI. WORKING GROUP ON ECONOMIC ISSUES

26. The Working Group on Economic Issues is chaired by Mr. J. Durieux. The Group last met on 17 February and on 23 March 1993 to consider a proposal for a high-level conference on the economic futures of the countries of the former Yugoslavia. Successive drafts of a document concerning the purpose and objectives of such a conference, exploring the different angles of a comprehensive reconstruction process, had previously been submitted to the Group and discussed by it. It was agreed, however, that the project could go forward only after there had been some advance in the peacemaking process.

27. At the 23 March session, the Chairman's report on an inventory for State succession, which had been submitted to the Co-Chairmen the previous month, was again discussed.

28. When the Working Group next reconvenes, foremost on its agenda will be the reconstruction and development issue. Planning for reconstruction is already under way in various forums. The Group will be considering some organizations aspects of a reconstruction process.

VII. WORKING GROUP ON CONFIDENCE- AND SECURITY-BUILDING AND VERIFICATION MEASURES

29. In January 1993, Ambassador Berasategui, the then Chairman of this Working Group, after consultation with the Co-Chairmen, deferred further work pending the outcome on negotiations on Bosnia and Herzegovina. Following the agreement of the Bosnian parties on 19 january 1994 to implement confidence-

building measures, Brigadier-General Pellnäs will travel to Split on 24 January for initial discussions with the Parties and, in the light of his report, the Co-Chairmen will decide on the future activities of the Group.

VIII. Arbitration Commission

30. Advisory opinions Nos. 11 to 13, issued by the Arbitration Commission os succession issues, were reproduced in document S/26233, appendix VI. Opinions Nos. 14 and 15, issued on 13 August 1993, also on succession issues, are reproduced in appendices II and II below.

Appendix I
Agreed Minutes*

The Macedonian Minister of the interior, Mr. Ljubomir Frckovski, met in Skopje on 27 August 1993 with a representative of serbs in Macedonia, Mr. Boro Ristic. The meeting was chaired by Ambassador G. Ahrens of the International Conference on the Former Yugoslavia, who was accompanied by Mr. A. Ritz and Mr. S. Coutinho. A representative of the CSCE Mission in Skopje, Mr. J. Gerasimov, was also present. The meeting recorded the following undertakings and understandings.

1. The government representative declared that the Serbian nationality will be treated completely equally with other nationalities living in Macedonia. The Government and the representative of the Serbs in Macedonia agreed to support consistent implementation in Macedonia of all rights formulated and made effective by the Charter of he United Nations and by the Conventions formulated under its auspices, as well as CSCE's, the Hague Declaration, the Charter of Paris and other instruments, especially the document of the Copenhagen Meeting on the Human Dimension.
2. The Serb representative declared that the Serbs in Macedonia would fulfil their aspiration only within the framework of the existing republic of Macedonia.

---

* Signed, for the Government, by Ljubomir Frckovski, and for the Serbs, by Boro Ristic; and, as witnesses, by Geert Ahrens (International Conference on the Former Yugoslavia) and Jakov Gerasimov (Conference on Security and cooperation in Europe).

3. The government representative declared that the Government is, in principle, prepared to satisfy the request of the serbs to be mentioned in the preamble and in article 78 of the Macedonian Constitution and that in the meantime the Government would interpret the Macedonian Constitution as if the Serbs had been mentioned in the preamble and in article 78. Consequently, their constitutional status will be equal in every respect to that of the other nationalities listed in the Constitution. The Serb representative insisted the Government, within 18 months, start and finish the process in Parliament which will make the constitutional position of the Serbs equal to that of all nationalities already quoted in the Constitution and that, in case the Parliament or the Government do no t accept the request of the Serbs, the Serbs in Macedonia will consider all dispositions of the present document as void.

4. The government representative declared that, according to the Law on Pre-School and Elementary Education, Serbian language instruction will be provided in each elementary school in which parents of at least 15 children make a request to that effect. For secondary schools, which according to the law are not obligatory, the Government declared that Serbian language instruction will be provided if at least 25 pupils make a request to that effect. The CSCE representative declared that the readiness of his organization to monitor the expression of choice by the parents, if so requested by either the Government or the parents, so that undue pressures be avoided. The Serb representative requested that the announcements for the admission of pupils to secondary schools (gymnasiums) specifically mention that instruction would be in the Serbian language in the following classes:

(a) Two classes in Skopje;
(b) Two classes in Kumanovo;
(c) One class or some other secondary school in Negotino or Kavadarci.

The Government is obliged to provide textbooks and other auxiliary teaching tools to the classes conducted in Serbian.

5. The government representative declared that the Government will guarantee to the Serbs in Macedonia constitutional religious freedom, including the freedom of choice of church.

6. The government representative declared that Serbian language media will be supported in the same way as the media of other nationalities.

7. The government representative announced that in April 1994, a national census would be conducted in Macedonia, monitored by a panel of international experts headed by the Chairman of the European Population Committee of the Council of europe. The Serb representative took note of this with satisfaction

and promised full cooperation.

8. The government representative declared that the Government will take measures to protect historical monuments as well as the cultural inheritance of the Serbs in Macedonia and will help and support cultural organizations and institutions of the Serbs in Macedonia on an equal basis wit the other nationalities.

9. The government representative announced that, to facilitate the implementation of the undertaking in paragraph 1 of these Minutes, the Government will promptly submit a request to the Council of europe for assistance in the earliest possible implementation of the human rights protection mechanism for non-member States provided for in resolution 93 (6) of the Committee of Ministers of the Council. This mechanism is to bridge the period until Macedonia becomes a full member of the council of Europe.

The International Conference on the Former Yugoslavia stated that it considered these undertakings and understandings as reflecting the requests and complaints put before the International Conference on the Former Yugoslavia by the Serbs from Macedonia. The International Conference on the Former Yugoslavia was prepared to discuss any problems arising in the course of implementing these undertakings and understandings, should either party so request.

APPENDIX II
ARBITRATION COMMISSION - OPINION NO 14*

On 20 April 1993, the Co-Chairmen of the Steering Committee of the Conference on Yugoslavia referred six questions to the Chairman of the Arbitration Commission, seeking the Commission's opinion.

Question 1 was:

"In the light of the inventory in the report by the Chairman of the Working Group on Economic Issues, what assets and liabilities should be divided between the successor States to the former Socialist Federal Republic of Yugoslavia in connection with the succession process?"

On 12 May 1993, the Co-Chairmen of the Steering Committee of the Conference transmitted to the Chairman of the Commission a declaration by the Government of the Federal Republic of Yugoslavia raising a number of objections to the reference to the Commission. The members of the Commission unanimously adopted a document reacting to the assertions made by the FRY; this was

---

* Paris, 13 August 1993.

addressed to the Co-Chairmen of the Steering Committee of the Conference on 26 May 1993. None of the States parties to the proceedings has contested the Commission's right to answer questions referred to it.

The Commission has taken cognizance of the memorandum, observations and other materials communicated by the Republic of Bosnia and Herzegovina, the Republic of Croatia, the former Yugoslav Republic of Macedonia and the Republic of Slovenia, which have been passed on to all the successor States of the SFRY. The FRY has submitted no memorandum or observations on the questions referred.

1. The Arbitration Commission notes that the Draft Single Inventory of the assets and liabilities of the SFRY as at 31 December 1991 drawn up by the Working Group of the International Conference of the Former Yugoslavia on 26 February 1993 divides the assets and liabilities into two categories - agreed items and non-agreed items.

As the Commission recalled in Opinion no 9, the first principle applicable to state succession is that the successor States should consult with each other and agree a settlement of all questions relating to the succession.

Assets and liabilities listed in the Inventory of 26 February 1993 upon which the successor States have reached agreement should accordingly be divided between them.

2. As regards non-agreed items, the Arbitration Commission considers that it does not have sufficient information on which to base a decision as to each asset and liability listed in the Inventory. Moreover, it considers that these are not legal issues which it could profitably seek to resolve as part of its consultative remit and that it should confine itself to determining the general principles to be applied.

3. The Commission would nevertheless draw attention to the well-established rule of state succession law that immovable property situated on the territory of a successor State passes exclusively to that State. Subject to possible compensation if such property is divided very unequally between the successor States to the SFRY, the principle of the *locus in quo* implies that there is no need to determine the previous owner of the property: public property passes to the successor States on whose territory it is situated. The origin or initial financing of the property and any loans or contributions made in respect of it have no bearing on the matter.

4. As regards other state property, debts and archives, a commonly agreed principle to be found in several provisions of the Vienna Convention of 8 April 1983 on the Succession of States in respect of State Property, Archives and Debts

requires that they be divided between the successor States to the SFRY if, at the date of succession, they belonged to the SFRY, and the question of the origin and initial financing of the property, debts and archives, or of any loans or contributions made in respect of them, is irrelevant.

5. To determine whether the property, debt and archives belonged to the SFRY, reference should be had to the domestic law of the SFRY at operation at the date of succession - notably to the 1974 Constitution.

There are, however, two particular problems arising from the federal structure of the Yugoslav State and from the concept of "social ownership" - a concept which, while it does exist in other countries, was particularly highly developed in the SFRY.

6. On the first point, there is no doubt that the 1974 Constitution transferred to the constituent republics ownership of many items of property which in consequence cannot be held to have belonged to the SFRY, whatever their origin or initial financing.

7. As for "social ownership", it was held for the most part by "associated labour organizations" - bodies with their own legal personality, operating in a single republic and coming within its exclusive jurisdiction. Their property, debts and archives are not to be divided for purposes of state succession: each successor State exercises its sovereign powers in respect of them.

If and to the extent that other organizations operated "social ownership" either at federal level or in two or more republics, their property, debts and archives should be divided between the successor States in question if they exercised public prerogatives in behalf of the SFRY or of individual republics. On the other hand, organizations operating at the federal level or in two or more republics but not exercising such prerogatives should be considered private-sector enterprises to which state succession does not apply.

8. The answer to the question referred is without prejudice to whatever compensation might be necessary to achieve an equitable overall outcome.

9. Should the application of these principles or the determination of the ownership of an item of property at the date of state succession give rise to problems, it would be for the states concerned to resort to arbitration or some other mode of peaceful settlement of their disputes, but it does not behove the Arbitration Commission in the exercise of its consultative function to detail whet rules would apply to a particular contentious issue between States emerging from the dissolution of the SFRY.

10. The Arbitration Commission consequently takes the view that the assets and liabilities to be divided between the successor States to the SFRY for purposes of state succession are (i) those which the successor States are agreed in regarding

as being such and (ii) the state property, debts and archives which at the date of state succession belonged to the SFRY in accordance with the law in operation there, excluding property belonging to individual republics or the "associated labour organizations" depending on them.

APPENDIX III

ARBITRATION COMMISSION - OPINION NO 15[*]

On 20 April 1993, the Co-Chairmen of the Steering Committee of the Conference on Yugoslavia referred six questions to the Chairman of the Arbitration Commission, seeking the Commission's opinion.

Question 5 was:

"(a) In view of the dissolution of the Socialist Federal Republic of Yugoslavia, is the National Bank of Yugoslavia entitled to take decisions affecting property, rights and interests that should be divided between the successor States to the Socialist Federal Republic of Yugoslavia in connection with state succession?

(b) Have the central banks of the States emerging from the dissolution of the Socialist Federal Republic of Yugoslavia succeeded to the rights and obligations of the National Bank of Yugoslavia deriving from international agreement concluded by the latter, in particular the 1988 financial agreement with foreign commercial banks?"

On 12 May 1993, the Co-Chairmen of the Steering Committee of the Conference transmitted to the Chairman of the Commission a declaration by the Government of the Federal Republic of Yugoslavia raising a number of objections to the reference to the Commission. The members of the Commission unanimously adopted a document reacting to the assertions made by the FRY; this was addressed to the Co-Chairmen of the Steering Committee of the Conference on 26 May 1993. None of the States parties to the proceedings has contested the Commission's right to answer questions referred to it.

The Commission has taken cognizance of the memorandum, observations and other materials communicated by the Republic of Bosnia and Herzegovina, the Republic of Croatia, the former Yugoslav Republic of Macedonia and the Republic of Slovenia, which have been passed on to all the successor States of the SFRY. The Federal Republic of Yugoslavia has submitted no memorandum or observations on the questions referred.

While they are linked, questions 5 (a) and 5 (b) are distinct enough to be answered separately.

---

[*] Paris, 13 August 1993.

I. QUESTION 5 (A)

1. Although municipal laws are merely facts in international law (*Certain German interests in Polish Upper Silesia*, 1926 PCIJ, Ser. A. No 7, 12), account must nevertheless be taken of the structure and responsibilities of the NBY as set out in the SFRY Constitution of 21 February 1974 and in the NBY Statute of November 1989.

As the bank of issue of the SFRY, the NBY participated in the exercise of the prerogatives of sovereignty. Moreover, as a composite of banking institutions - central, republican and provincial - its was responsible for carrying out common currency issue, credit and foreign exchange policy, and it had close institutional relations with Parliament.

The NBY, then, partook of the state power of the SFRY, whose dissolution led simultaneously to the disintegration of the collective structure of the NBY.
2. None of the organs of the NBY, therefore, can take legitimate decisions in respect of property, rights and interests that should be divided between the successor States of the SFRY.

No decision in such matters taken by the Governor of the NBY on his own authority would have any legal validity once the former collective organization has ceased to exist.
3. Only if, outside the pre-existing institutional framework, collaboration between the central banks of the states emerging from the dissolution of the SFRY had continued could the NBY be considered to be a coordinating agency acting in their behalf for purposes of *jurisdictio inter volentes* to effect - rather than obstruct - the division of the property rights and interests of the former SFRY.
4. As this is not the case, the Arbitration Commission takes the view that the NBY is not entitled to take decisions affecting property, rights and interests to be divided between the successor States in accordance with the principles of state succession.

II. QUESTION 5 (B)

5. Given the answers to question 5 (a), decisions taken by the NBY as an organ of the SFRY committed that State. The rights and obligations deriving from those decisions consequently pass to the successor States and must be divided between them in accordance with the principles of international law rehearsed by the Commission in Opinion No 9. This does not apply to ordinary commitment entered into by the NBY acting as a bank with its own legal personality.

6. This distinction is applicable to rights and obligations of the NBY deriving from international agreement it has entered into. The answer to the first part of the question 5 (b) therefore depends in each case upon the nature of the agreement and upon the NBY's commitments.

7. However, the Arbitration Commission would underline the fact that the rights and obligations of the NBY, as an organ of the SFRY, which are therefore subject to state succession (*supra* para. 5), do not pass automatically to the central banks of the states emerging from the dissolution of the SFRY: it is for each of the successor States to determine, by virtue of its sovereign constitutional powers, how these rights are to be exercised and these obligations discharged - rights and obligations which they may assume either direct or through their central banks.

8. As regards the financial agreement of 20 September 1988 between the NBY and Manufacturers Hanover Limited, acting for the international creditors, the Commission would point out that the NBY acted together with other Yugoslav banking institutions presenting themselves expressly as legal persons accepting on their own behalf the obligations deriving from the agreement (notably sections 1.01 and 10.01) and that the parties to the agreement made the discharge of their obligations subject to the law of a third State (sections 14.12) and, in the event of a dispute, to the jurisdiction of various ordinary Yugoslav or foreign courts (section 14.08).

In the event of any dispute over the interpretation or application of the agreement, it is therefore for the parties to refer it to one of the courts that have jurisdiction under the agreement itself.

9. The Commission notes, however, that the successor States to the SFRY have succeeded it in so far as it had assumed the obligations of guarantor under the agreement of 20 September 1988.

Should the application of this principle give rise to problems, it would be for the States concerned to resort to arbitration or some other mode of peaceful settlement of their disputes.

10. The Arbitration Commission consequently takes the view:

    (i) that problems arising from the rights and obligations of the NBY deriving from international agreements concluded by it are to be resolved by reference to the terms of the agreements and, in the case of dispute, are to be referred to the appropriate courts; and

    (ii) that this holds good in particular for rights and obligations deriving from the financial agreement of 1988 entered into by the NBY and other Yugoslav banking institutions with foreign national banks.

132. Letter Dated 14 February 1994 from the Secretary-General Addressed to the President of the Security Council*

I have the honour to convey the attached report addressed to me on 12 February 1994 by the Co-Chairmen of the Steering Committee of the International Conference on the Former Yugoslavia.

Annex
Report of the Co-Chairmen of the Steering Committee on the Activities of the International Conference on the Former Yugoslavia

INTRODUCTION

1. In their previous report (S/1994/64), the Co-Chairmen dealt with the round of peace talks held in Geneva from 18 to 19 January. On that occasion, a map proposed by the Bosnian Serbs had been on the table offering the Muslim majority republic 33.56 %, and the Republic of Croatia had stated its willingness to sign linked agreements providing the Muslim majority republic with 99-year leases for use of a port at Ploce, a port on the Neretva River at Celevo from which seagoing cargo boats or tourist passenger boats could link up with their facilities in Ploce or the existing small port on the Peljesac peninsula.

2. President Izetbegovic had acknowledged that the Muslim majority republic was being offered 33.56 %. He had submitted, however, that he map should be altered so as to include in the territory allocated to the Muslim majority republic certain areas in eastern and western Bosnia where the Muslims had been in the majority before the outbreak of the conflict, as well as certain areas in central Bosnia, while keeping within the target of 33.3 %.

3. Since the parties has agreed on all other aspects of a peace package other than some areas of territory in respect of which there were conflicting claims, the Co-Chairmen had submitted to the parties the idea that the areas in question should be referred to an arbitration commission appointed by the President of the International Court of Justice after consultations with the parties. The recommendations of the Commission would be addressed, in the first instance, to the parties and, only if there was disagreement, the matter would be referred to the Security Council.

---

* UN Doc. S/1994/173, 14 February 1994. Signed by Boutros Boutros-Ghali.

4. The Bosnian Croats and the Bosnian Serbs had expressed their willingness to accept these procedures. The Bosnian Presidency had taken the position that military forces should be withdrawn from the areas in question before an arbitration procedure could be accepted.

5. In those circumstances, and faced with the danger of renewed and intensified conflict, the Co-Chairmen had proposed that the parties establish hot-lines, that they exchange representatives in one another's headquarters in Sarajevo, Mostar and Pale, and that the parties should meet again in Geneva on 10 February 1994 to consider the effectiveness of those arrangements and other practical confidence-building measures. to reduce the level of fighting.

CONFIDENCE-BUILDING MEASURES

6. In accordance with the decision taken by the parties on 19 January, a working group coordinated by Brigadier-General Bo Pellnäs held two meetings in Sarajevo on 25 January and on 5 february. All three Bosnian parties took part. The Bosnian Presidency delegation was led by Prime Minister H. Silajdzic, the Bosnian Croat delegation by Mr. M. Akmadzic, and the Bosnian Serb delegation by Professor N. Koljevic. Observers of UNPROFOR, UNHCR and ICRC also took part.

7. On 25 January, an agreement was signed among the three parties providing for the restoration of the electricity system. The parties agreed to the principle of immediate repair of the electricity system. The solemnly promised that their respective forces would not, after the signing of the agreement, destroy any aspect or facility of the electricity system, nor would they prevent any work conducted by repair and maintenance teams. Additionally, the forces of the parties would not in any way interfere with or withhold the provision for electricity to any of the other parties. The agreement called for the immediate restoration of electricity lines or systems in six areas.

8. Other items on the agenda of the Working Group included the establishment of hot-lines; the establishment of standing liaison teams; regular meetings between Commanders; and Joint Military Commissions. On the issue of hot-lines, it was reported that lines of communications already existed between the BiH Army and HVO as well as HVO and the BSA. The Bosnian Serbs accepted to establish communications with the BiH Army, and UNPROFOR was asked to follow up on this subject and to facilitate the necessary arrangements.

SARAJEVO

9. During a meeting with Dr. Karadzic in Pale on 5 February, General Pellnäs received an assurance from the Bosnian Serbs that they were ready to agree to United Nations administration of Sarajevo District as defined in the peace plan under discussion in Geneva in advance of a final settlement in Bosnia and Herzegovina. This important development was about to be discussed that same day in the confidence-building meeting at Sarajevo Airport when a shell landed in the market place in Sarajevo and the meeting had to be suspended. In view of this political development concerning Sarajevo, which the Co-Chairmen had first put to the Bosnian Serbs in Geneva on 19 January, and in the light of that day's tragedy, the Co-Chairmen took action to follow up urgently the implementation of a separate political and military peace agreement for Bosnia and Herzegovina.
10. On 6 February, the Co-Chairmen travelled to Zvornik, in Bosnia and Herzegovina, to follow up this development with the Bosnian Serbs. After five hours of discussions with Bosnian Serb leaders, including Dr. Karadzic, the following agreement was reached with them:

> "In order to bring peace to sarajevo now, the Bosnian Serbs are ready, in the circumstances where it is not yet possible to reach an overall peace settlement, to negotiate for United Nations administration and the demilitarization of Sarajevo District prior to a final settlement for Bosnia and Herzegovina. The details can be discussed as part of the meeting in Geneva on 210 February on confidence-building measures with a view to establishing a mixed military-political Joint Commission to meet at Sarajevo Airport."

TALKS IN GENEVA, 10-12 FEBRUARY

11. Representatives of the Bosnian Presidency, the Bosnian Croats and the Bosnian Serbs, together with Observers from the Governments of the Republic of Croatia and the Federal Republic of Yugoslavia (Serbia and Montenegro), met in Geneva from 10-12 February to review the above developments and to continue the search for peace in Bosnia and Herzegovina. The Bosnian Presidency delegation was led by Prime Minister H. Silajdzic, the Bosnian Croat delegation by Mr. M Akmadzic and the Bosnian Serb delegation by Dr. R. Karadzic. Deputy Foreign Minister V. Churkin and Ambassador C. Redman attended as Observers.
12. Plenary as well as bilateral meetings were held. At the first plenary meeting, the Co-Chairmen invited the parties to review further confidence-building measures, bearing in mind the agreement that has been reached in Sarajevo on 9 February between the representatives of the Army of Bosnia and Herzegovina

and the Bosnian Serb Army, meeting under the auspices of General Rose, the UNPROFOR (BH) Commander. The agreement provided

> "... that there should be an immediate ceasefire in and around the city (as from 1200A 10 February 1994), that there should be a positioning of UNPROFOR troops in sensitive areas and key locations, and that there should be the monitoring and placing of all heavy weapons under UNPROFOR control."

The Co-Chairmen emphasized upon all concerned the importance of their respecting their commitments, and urged them, in the strongest possible terms, to help defuse the situation in Bosnia and Herzegovina and to set a course for the re-establishment of peace.

13. Noting that the two meetings on confidence-building had been held at a high level and conducted in a positive and constructive manner, the Co-Chairmen encouraged the Bosnian parties to regularize those meetings and to meet at fixed intervals. The parties undertook to do so.

14. The Co-Chairmen then invited the Bosnian parties to review the outstanding areas holding up the signature of a peace agreement. Bilateral meetings were held between the delegations of the Bosnian Presidency and the Bosnian Croats, the delegations of the Bosnian Presidency and the Bosnian Serbs and the delegation of the Bosnian Croats and the Bosnian Serbs. After these bilateral meetings, a plenary meeting was held to review the results of the bilateral meetings.

15. At the final plenary meeting on 12 January, the Co-Chairmen summarized the results of the discussions. They noted that on future constitutional arrangements, all three sides had expressly reiterated their acceptance of a Union of Republics, consisting of a Croat majority republic, a Muslim majority republic and a Serb majority republic.

16. The Bosnian Presidency and the Bosnian Croats reiterated their agreement that Mostar would be placed under the administration of the European Union. The Bosnian Presidency and the Bosnian Serbs reiterated their acceptance that Sarajevo would be placed under the administration of the United Nations. It was further agreed that during the period of European Union administration of Mostar and United Nations administration of Sarajevo final territorial delimitations would be worked out.

17. With regard to the definition of the Mostar City area to be placed under the administration of the European Union, the Bosnian Presidency and the Bosnian Croats agreed that the Working Group which had been established in Brussels on 23 December to look into this issue should meet on 16 February in Medjugorje, at the Headquarters of the Spanish Battalion.

18. In respect of Sarajevo, the Co-Chairmen invited the Bosnian Presidency and the Bosnian Serbs to consider the possibility of concluding a separate agreement

on Sarajevo in advance of an overall peace agreement. The Bosnian Serbs indicated their readiness to negotiate such a separate agreement. The Bosnian Presidency, however, said that while it was willing to pursue discussions on Sarajevo, there would be no such decisions until Serb withdrawal of heavy weapons was complete, and that any agreement worked out should be part of the overall peace settlement.

19. The Co-Chairmen tried a number of avenues to get the parties to move towards agreement on the territories still under dispute. They first invited the parties t indicate whether the number of disputed areas could be reduced. This did not prove possible and indeed the parties began to suggest additions to the list of disputed areas. The Co-Chairmen then invited the parties to consider whether it might be possible to move to a peace agreement by arranging for some of the area to be treated as protected areas, while a few of them could be placed under international administration. These possibilities were kept open, but discussion of them was affected by the Bosnian Serb's contention that the Bosnian Presidency, having agreed to 33.3 %, was trying to pocket the 33.56 already offered and still to maintain a list of disputed areas. A similar contention was put forward by the Bosnian Croats who also asked for recognition that they should have 17.5 % of territory. The Bosnian Presidency, however, maintained its claims. It added that it could only accept the Croats having 17.5 % on the condition that it was not prejudicial to the Presidency's claims.

20. The Co-Chairmen again consulted the parties on the proposed arbitration procedure. All three sides said that they accepted the concept of arbitration, but the Bosnian Presidency maintained its position that before an arbitration procedure could be used there should be withdrawal of military forces from the areas in question. The Bosnian Croats and the Bosnian Serbs accepted that there needed to be a withdrawal of forces, accompanied by the insertion of United Nations civilian police, in order to encourage people who lived there before the war to return, but that the areas had to be within the provisional boundaries of the republics. The Bosnian Presidency maintained that the disputed areas could not be considered as falling within the provisional republican boundaries.

21. The Co-Chairmen consulted the parties on other possible avenues for overcoming the hurdle over the disputed territories. Among the possibilities mentioned was the establishment of an International Joint Control Commission whose tasks would be to ensure that nothing was done in any of the disputed areas to alter their character or status, or which could be prejudicial to their eventual allocation while the arbitration procedure functioned. Another possibility mentioned was referral of the disputed areas to the Security Council or to a group of members of the Council. The parties were asked to suggest other poss-

ible procedures for reaching agreement on the outstanding territorial issues. No such suggestion was forthcoming.

22. In the circumstances, it was agreed that the parties should consult bilaterally, and should also have discussions with the special envoys of the Russian Federation and the United States of America. In the light of those further consultations, the Co-Chairmen would assess the situation with a view to inviting the parties back to Geneva for further talks towards the end of February or the beginning of March.

133. LETTER DATED 8 JULY 1994 FROM THE SECRETARY-GENERAL ADDRESSED TO THE PRESIDENT OF THE SECURITY COUNCIL*

I have the honour to convey the attached report addressed to me on 6 July 1994 by the Co-Chairmen of the Steering Committee of the International Conference on the Former Yugoslavia.

The report refers only to Bosnia and Herzegovina, without entering into other questions within the purview of the Conference.

I should be grateful if you would bring this information to the attention of the members of the Security Council.

Annex
Report of the Co-Chairmen of the Steering Committee on the Activities of the International Conference on the Former Yugoslavia

I. INTRODUCTION

1. The International Conference on the Former Yugoslavia (ICFY) was established in August 1992 to remain in being until a final settlement of the problems of the former Yugoslavia has been achieved. Its seat is at the United Nations Office in Geneva. The Co-Chairmen of the Conference are the Secretary-General of the United Nations and the Head of State/Government of the Presidency of the European Union. The activities of the Conference are supervised by a Committee co-chaired by representatives of the Secretary-General of the United Nations and the Presidency of the European Union. The current Chairmen of the Steering Committee are Lord Owen and Mr. Thorvald Stoltenberg. The day-to-day activities of the Conference are carried out by the Co-Chairmen of the Steer-

---

* UN Doc. S/1994/811, 8 July 1994. Signed by Boutros Boutros-Ghali.

ing Committee and in working groups and task forces. Highlights of the activities of the Conference from January to June 1994 are provided below.

II. STEERING COMMITTEE OF THE INTERNATIONAL CONFERENCE ON THE FORMER YUGOSLAVIA

2. Meetings of the Steering Committee of the Conference were held on 2 February, 30 March and 16 May 1994. Issues discussed included: reports by the Co-Chairmen and the Chairpersons of Working Groups; review of developments; humanitarian issues; and budgetary matters.

3. On 16 May, the budget of the Conference for the six-month period from 1 June 1994 to 30 November 1994 was laid down before the Steering Committee, as was a consolidated financial statement (see appendix I).

III. CONFIDENCE-BUILDING AND SECURITY ISSUES

A. Ad hoc Working Group

4. An ad hoc working group on confidence-building measures in respect of Bosnia and Herzegovina held two meetings at Sarajevo, on 25 and 26 January and on 5 February 1994. Both meetings were held at the airport and were chaired by Brigadier-General Bo Pellnäs of the International Conference of the Former Yugoslavia. The delegations of the parties were led by Prime Minister H. Silajdzic, Professor N. Koljevic and Mr. A. Akmadzic. The following results were achieved.

(a) *Restoration of Power Lines.* On 26 January an agreement was signed whereby the parties accepted that six major power lines/systems should be restored immediately. The parties also agreed not to destroy any existing system or to prevent any efforts to repair power lines.

(b) *Hot Lines.* The working group reviewed existing communication lines between the Army of Bosnia and Herzegovina and the Croatian Defence Council (HVO), as well as between HVO and he Bosnian Serb Army (BSA). During the second meeting BSA and the Army of Bosnia and Herzegovina agreed to establish communication links.

(c) *Regular Meetings between Commanders.* The parties agreed that such meetings should take place at the army level and that the first meeting should take place on 25 February, to be chaired by General Rose of UNPROFOR.

B. Consultations with Foreign Ministers of Neighbouring Countries

5. With a view to promoting confidence-building and security measures in the region, the Co-Chairmen of the Steering Committee arranged a consultation with the Foreign Ministers of neighbouring countries, which was held at the United Nations Office in Geneva on 9 February 1994. The meeting, which was of an informal character, reviewed the economic situation in the area, with particular regard to the consequences of sanctions on the economies of neighbouring countries. It also discussed the possibility of future cooperation on confidence-building and security issues. It was decided that further meetings would be held between the Co-Chairmen and the Foreign Ministers of neighbouring countries to discuss these issues and that the Co-Chairmen would commission a study on confidence-building and security measures.

C. Study on Confidence-building and Security Measures

6. Accordingly, a study was commissioned from the Institute for Security Studies of the western European Union and submitted to the Co-Chairmen on 22 April 1994. The study examines how far measures for regional stability involving both former Yugoslav successor States and their neighbours - and drawing on the experience of confidence- and security-building measures and arms control developed in the Conference on Security and Cooperation in Europe (CSCE) and the Treaty on Conventional Forces in Europe - could be applied' in post-conflict former Yugoslavia to consolidate and reinforce a political settlement. In addition, it examines what regional arms transfer control regimes could be developed to assist stability in the post-conflict situation. It includes an examination of the role of various international organizations to see what contribution they could make to the negotiation and implementation of such measures.
7. The study recalls that at the CSCE Council meeting in Rome on 30 November and 1 December 1993, CSCE Foreign Ministers decided to examine the possible contribution of CSCE to security in south-eastern Europe through arms control, disarmament and confidence-building. This idea was linked to the functions of the CSCE Forum for Security Cooperation (FSC), which was given the possibility by the CSCE Helsinki Document 1992 (A/47/361-S/24370, annex, chap. V, para. 46, sect. 6) of setting up negotiations on regional measures, including, where appropriated, reductions or limitations of armaments.
8. The study sets out five elements to be included in any process aimed at progressively achieving regional stability: three groups on confidence- and security-building measures and a two-stage arms control process. The first group of

confidence- and security building measures are those which can be used for stabilizing ceasefire agreements. The second group are those introduced to reinforce a political settlement. The third group of confidence- and security- building measures are those which could in the longer term and on a larger scale, enhance stability in the Balkans. The two rounds of arms control proposed include a first set of measures to limit the growth of armed forces in former Yugoslavia and the second round to impose ceilings, and possibly reduction, in order to prevent an arms race and the emergence of new threats.

1. Confidence- and Security-Building Measures
(a) Measures for the Stabilization of a Ceasefire

9. In this category, the study lists the following elements:

   (a) Agreement on the technical terms of a ceasefire (timing, area, forces affected and weapon categories);
   (b) Measures of constraint, including:
       (i) The disengagements of forces;
       (ii) The establishment of a demilitarized zone 2 kilometres wide (1 kilometre on each side of the confrontation line);
       (iii) The freezing of troop movements (and ultimately troop reductions) within a zone extending to 10 kilometres on either side of the confrontation line;
       (iv) The withdrawal of heavy weapons from wider zones (10 kilometres from the confrontation line for mortar and air defence systems, 20 kilometres for tanks and artillery);
   (c) Supervision of the ceasefire by United Nations Protection Force (UNPROFOR) and European Union (EU) monitors, including the right of inspections by UNPROFOR of all relevant military and paramilitary units and exclusive control of the demilitarized zone by UNPROFOR;
   (d) Establishment of joint commissions, chaired by an UNPROFOR representative, to investigate any ceasefire violations.

(b) Measures to Reinforce a Political Settlement

10. The following elements are listed in this category:

   (a) The disarming and disbanding of irregular forces and constraints on paramilitary forces;

   (b) The furthering of transparency by an exchange of military information (concerning the number and strength of military units, their location, weapons systems and equipment, and command structures);

   (c) Wider constraints on military activities (movements, deployment and exercises);

   (d) The establishment of direct communications links (hot lines) between relevant headquarters;

   (e) The establishment of joint mediating teams (or the strengthening of existing joint commissions).

11. The study suggests that the above measures be supplemented by wider measures to be introduced at the time of a political settlement:

   (a) The limitation of military flights and provision for international control of air traffic;

   (b) An aerial observation system consisting of overflights by a third party (which in the longer term could be turned into an Open Skies regime for the former Yugoslavia;

   (c) The reinforcement of confidence through the exchange of observers of military activities;

   (d) The verification of stabilization through both regular and challenge inspections (notably with regard to heavy weapons sites and storage facilities). Starting from the experience already gained by UNPROFOR in the monitoring of heavy weapons, these should be grouped in areas where redeployment would be difficult and take time.

(c) Wider Confidence- and Security-Building Measures Involving Neighbouring States

12. According to the study, this third group of confidence- and security-building measures include those which, in the longer term, should cover the whole Balkan region. They should be considered after a period of some months of peace following the political settlement. Their primary aim would be to bring the five successor States of the former Yugoslavia to accept the confidence- and security-building measures already agreed to in CSCE, as set out in the Vienna document 1992, but they would need to go beyond this in order to satisfy the security needs of all the Yugoslav successor States and their neighbours, and would therefore have to cover a wider area than former Yugoslavia. It is suggested that they could be negotiated at a regional table within FSC.

2. Arms Control

13. The study advocates that the first round of negotiations on control and verification measures be held within the framework of he International Conference on the Former Yugoslavia and involve only the successor States. The second round of negotiations on arms control measures - the introduction of ceilings which could involve reductions - should take place at a regional table within FSC and include the successor States and all immediate neighbours of the former Yugoslavia.

3. Territorial and Minority Rights Issues

14. The study cautions that arms control by itself will not be effective in producing peace and stability if unsettled disputes concerning territories and borders remain and if substantial progress in minority rights is not made.

IV. SUCCESSION ISSUES

15. Twenty-two experts from all the parties participated in a session of the Working Group on Succession Issues chaired by Ambassador A. Jonsson and held in Geneva from 16 to 18 March 1994. The delegation of the Federal Republic of Yugoslavia (Serbia and Montenegro) presented its preliminary inventory as well as an outline of the methodology applied in preparing it. The preliminary inventory consisted of some 2,600 items comprising some 75 per cent of the total value of the assets.

16. The overall division process was discussed, including the question of valuation and the key of division. The questions of archives, outstanding non-allocated debts of the Socialist Federal Republic of Yugoslavia and war damages were also discussed.

17. On 6 May 1994 the Federal Republic of Yugoslavia (Serbia and Montenegro) provided an expanded version of its inventory comprising some 8,000 items.

18. Following the intensive consultations, the Chairman of the Working Groups concluded that a new initiative was called for. This conclusion was based, among other things, on the following considerations: (a) negotiations on State succession issues have been going on since the second quarter of 1992; (b) extensive work has been done in clarifying the position of the parties and their interpretation of their rights and obligations under international law; and (c) much information the underlying economic factors has been gathered.

19. Mindful of these considerations and the principles of the London Conference, and in the light of calls from several quarters, it was decided to develop a proposal that could help solve the succession problems. The Chairman of the Working Group intends to present the proposal in the form of a comprehensive draft succession treaty, regulating matters such as archives, citizenship, treaties, assets and liabilities on 1 August 1994. Accordingly, the parties were urged to provide before 1 July any information on legal or economic matters they deemed useful.

20. The Chairman of the Working Group intends to leave time for reflection after the 1 August presentation of the initiative. The parties will be asked to provide their comments and suggestions by 1 October 1994, shortly after which a meeting will be held at Geneva, to which the parties will be invited to present their view orally.

V. Ethnic and National Communities and Minorities

21. The Working Group on Ethnic and National Communities and Minorities, under the Chairmanship of Ambassador G. Ahrens, has continued its activities, *inter alia*, in the former Yugoslav Republic of Macedonia. Cooperation with UNPROFOR and the CSCE mission continues to be excellent.

22. The Working Group's efforts in the former Yugoslav Republic of Macedonia have been more difficult in recent months owing to: political polarization that made it difficult to get measures adopted by Parliament; growing economic problems in the Republic; and a pre-election climate - elections are to be held later this year.

23. Against this background, the Working Group had separate contacts with the Government and with Albanian representatives, concentrating on matters where progress seemed possible before the elections. The recent visits of the Group to Skopje (7-8 January, 2-3 February, 20-23 April and 20-24 May) were relatively successful, and seven issues were identified where solutions were considered possible. The Government agreed on the selection of these issues:

    (a) *Census*. For over one year, an International Census Expert Group formed by the International Conference on the Former Yugoslavia and the Council of Europe has been actively engaged in assisting in preparation for a census in the Republic. The census is necessary because widely different figures about the ethnic composition of the country's population create tensions. On 21 April 1994 the Conference received assurances for the Government that it would incorporate into the draft census law all the proposals made by the International Census Expert Group. On 18 May, the law was passed in Parliament and the Expert Group is now engaged in technical preparations. The Working Group on Ethnic and National Communities and Minorities visited the former Yugoslav Republic of Macedonia in the second week of June in order to explain the census to the populations of different nationalities with a view to securing participation. The census began on 21 June. Representatives of the Conference will be present in Skopje throughout the census (21 June - 5 July 1994);

(b) *Print Media.* The Government had assured the International Conference on the Former Yugoslavia that it would very soon find the financial means to make the daily appearance of the Albanian language newspaper, *Flaka E Vellazerimit*, possible. It subsequently commenced daily publication at the beginning of June;

(c) *Television.* The Conference is expecting a proposal for initial financing of a separate televisions channel for emissions in language other than Macedonian. This plan will involve several phases so that the most important parts of the Republic might be covered first. The Government is in favour of such a project, provided that initial financing comes from abroad. As soon as the Conference receives the proposals by Macedonian Tevision, it will approach possible donor countries and organizations;

(d) *Radio.* A parallel project, as for television, is being pursued for radio, which will be less costly than the television channel. The Government is prepared to support this project on the same basis as the television project;

(e) *Pedagogical Academy.* The Government has told representatives of the International Conference of the Former Yugoslavia that, as of the academic year 1994/5 there would be offered, at the existing Pedagogical Academy, training courses for Albanian language teaching on the arts, music, geography and history in classes from the fifth grades onwards. The University Council had yet to be involved. The International Conference on the Former Yugoslavia will meet with the Chairmen of the Council on Skopje soon;

(f) *School materials and Documentation.* The Government informed the Conference that a new draft law had been sent to the Parliament, according to which, in Albanian language classes, only the more important documentation and not the less important materials would have to be translated into Macedonian. As it is a general principle of law not to pursue offences once it is clear that the offence in question will no longer be punished according to the legislation under preparation, the International Conference on the Former Yugoslavia has appealed to the competent authorities to stop the fining of Albanian teachers for not translating materials;

(g) *National flags and Symbols.* There is agreement that Albanians may, under certain circumstances, show Albanian national flags, together with the flag of the Republic.

24. After the census, the International Conference on the Former Yugoslavia will continue discussion on a number of other issues which have been on the table for a while and include some difficult political questions relating to aspects of the Constitution and the Law on Local Self-Government.

VI. Economic Issues

25. The Working Group on Economic Issues convened on 28 and 29 March 1994. The meeting was called to discuss the role to be played by the International Conference on the Former Yugoslavia and the Working Group in the process of rehabilitation, reconstruction and development. At the outset the delegation of Slovenia made clear its intention not to participate fully in discussions concerning reconstruction but rather only to observe. The remaining delegations all shared the view that a role existed for some form of multilateral oversight of the process, while each expressed reservation relating to their own priorities and views of the precondition for reconstruction. The Chairman of the Working Group, Mr. Jean Durieux, presented his idea of an ad hoc structure, created specifically for the needs of reconstruction with the double role of coordination and monitoring. This ad hoc structure would be multilateral and placed under the aegis of the International Conference on the Former Yugoslavia.

26. On the second day, the meeting was attended by representatives of UNPROFOR, the Office of the United Nations High Commissioner for Refugees (UNHCR) and the International Management Group, who contributed to a discussion on the rehabilitation of Sarajevo and the high-level cooperation committee convened by UNPROFOR each week, as well as other issues relating to the respective roles of the different interested parties.

27. The Working Group met again on 5 and 6 May with reconstruction on the agenda, and in particular the question of the organization to be established to ensure that the process is carried out in a coherent manner, making the most

effective use of external public assistance and maximizing the contribution of private investment. The Working Group was also to consider what parts of its previous work remained relevant and could be used in the context of rapid implementation of a reconstruction programme.

28. After extensive discussion of the various positions, the delegations agreed on the general lines of a text prepared by the Chairman on the position of the Group regarding the questions posed by reconstruction. The delegations were to submit any proposed amendments in written form.

29. The next meeting of the Working Group was held on 6 and 7 June, when the agenda consisted of the following: a statement by each delegation on the state of advancement of economic reform on their country; presentations by representatives of the World Bank and the European Bank for Reconstruction and Development on their view of the problems posed by reconstruction; and the relations of the Group with the UNPROFOR Department of Civil Affairs, UNHCR and the International Management Group.

VII. Humanitarian Issues

30. The Working Group on Humanitarian Issues, chaired by the United Nations High Commissioner for Refugees. Mrs. S. Ogata, has continued to function as a framework reviewing the humanitarian situation in the former Yugoslavia with the different parties in the region, and with the governmental and intergovernmental actors supporting the international relief effort led by UNHCR.

31. In all countries of the region, this effort has helped large numbers of refugees, displaced person and other victims in need of humanitarian assistance though the third winter of conflict in former Yugoslavia in spite of often enormous obstacles. In Bosnia and Herzegovina, the humanitarian situation has improved markedly since February, as a result of the Sarajevo ceasefire agreement and the cessation of hostilities between the Bosnian Government and Bosnian Croat forces. Freedom of civilian movement across some confrontation lines is gradually improving, thanks to agreements brokered by the Department of Civil Affairs of UNPROFOR and with the assistance of UNHCR. Though normal commercial traffic has not yet resumed, commercial goods have arrived in central Bosnia on convoys organized by local humanitarian organizations. UNHCR and other international humanitarian organizations have been able to operate convoys more smoothly than in the past, although security risks and obstruction of access remain.

32. Hostilities around the Maglaj pocket and the attacks on Gorazde in April were serious setbacks encountered during the spring, which resulted in numer-

ous casualties and new displacements. In both cases, humanitarian access to bring in relief supplies and to evacuate the wounded, could only be obtained after heightening international pressure. The International Committee of the Red Cross has continued to work towards the release of all civilian detainees. A matter of grave concern has been the reported ongoing risk of intimidation and violent harassment of Muslim and ethnic Croat civilians, in north-western Bosnia and Herzegovina.

33. On 2 February, Mrs. Ogata briefed the Steering Committee of the International Conference of the Former Yugoslavia in Geneva on developments in the humanitarian field. From 14 to 17 March 1994 she travelled to the region and discussed humanitarian concerns with President Gligorov at Skopje, President Milosevic at Belgrade, Present Bulatovic at Podgorica, President Izetbegovic at Sarajevo, members of the Croatian Government at Zagreb and local Croatian and Serb authorities on both sides of the front line in Sector West. Topics of discussion included the difficult situation in the former Yugoslav Republic of Macedonia; the effects of international sanctions on the most vulnerable; refugee protection issues in Serbia and Montenegro; convoy access to the Maglaj pocket and elsewhere in Bosnia and Herzegovina; the opening of Tuzla airport for humanitarian flights; continuing violations of human rights and, in that connection, the ongoing and vital need to grant refugees admission to safety; and the situation of displaced persons in Croatia, including their desire to return to their homes. At Sarajevo, Mrs. Ogata met with General Rose, and at Zagreb with Mr. Akashi, to review the important assistance provided by UNPROFOR to the international relief effort in Bosnia and Herzegovina.

34. Upon Mrs. Ogata's return on 18 March, the status of the international assistance effort was discussed at a meeting of the Working Group on Humanitarian Issues, held in Geneva with representatives of States from the region and of many countries and the United Nations and other organizations supporting or involved with the relief effort. Besides ongoing concerns, the positive developments in Sarajevo and central Bosnian were noted, which could create conditions that open the way for rehabilitation and recovery assistance. It was also noted that rehabilitation and reconstruction would play an important role in creating conditions conducive to the return of refugees and displaced persons.

35. The latter complex issue was discussed in an informal meeting on temporary protection, held at Geneva on 23 March, where UNHCR advised Governments to improve further the standards of treatment of beneficiaries of temporary protection in the areas, for example, of family reunion and work, in view of the prolonged period of exile and pending further developments which could lead to return in safety and dignity.

36. On 11 May, following an assessment mission to the region, the Department of Humanitarian Affairs of the United Nations Secretariat and UNHCR launched a revised consolidated inter-agency appeal, for $ 532 million, representing the unmet requirements until the end of 1994 of the main United Nations agencies participating in the relief effort. It covers the cost in international humanitarian assistance in sectors such as food and nutrition, health, shelter, domestic needs, community services and education, to 4.1 million beneficiaries in the five States of former Yugoslavia. As to Bosnia and Herzegovina, the appeal foresees continued relief assistance to displaced persons and other war-affected populations, but positive developments in parts of the country may allow a shift from dependency to self-sufficiency. Pending the consolidation and expansion of these developments, full donor support remains crucial. Constant reassessment of the needs is carried out to take the evolving situation fully into account.

VIII. Peacemaking in the United Nations Protected Areas and Related Areas

37. At the beginning of January, negotiators of the International Conference on the Former Yugoslavia developed a strategy to the continuation of negotiations, based on a three-phased approach of ceasefire, followed by economic confidence-building measures, leading finally to negotiation of the political questions. This strategy had been agreed to by the parties in Norway in November 1993. The strategy and the associated negotiating arrangements were coordinated with UNPROFOR.

38. Following the signature in Geneva, on 19 January 1994 of an agreement in cooperation between Zagreb and Belgrade, the Conference negotiators became involved in intensive bilateral negotiations at Zagreb, Belgrade and Knin, on a number of economic issues and predominantly on the question of the opening of the Zagreb-to-Belgrade highway, which runs through United Nations Protected Area (UNPA) Sectors West and East. They identified the main problems to be resolved if the highway were to be opened and made significant progress towards a workable model, should the opening take place. Subjects such as the restoration of telephone links between Zagreb and Belgrade were also discussed. There were numerous contacts with the Sanctions Assistance Mission in Croatia to understand the implications of sanctions on the opening of communications routes and to ensure that these provisions were not inadvertently broken during the negotiation process.

39. At the local Serb elections on 23 January 1994, the Conference negotiators continued to concentrate on certain economic questions, seeking to define com-

mon ground between the parties. On the Croatian side, the main interest was in the opening of communications routes and major infrastructure, while on the Serb side, the interest was in the lifting of paragraph 12 of Security Council resolution 820 (1993) of 17 April 1993, thus allowing the Serbs to trade independently of the Government of Croatia. In addition to the negotiations on the opening of the Zagreb to Belgrade highway and other routes, the Conference negotiators attempted to start the process with a package dealing, *inter alia* with preparation for the agricultural season, provision of seed, fertilizer and fuel to the Serbs and issues related to energy and water supplies, such as attempts to start with the return of generator poles to the Serbs in Obrovac and the restoration of the water supply by the Serbs to Zadar. The Serb side also demanded that pensions be paid be the Government of Croatia to those persons who had earned them before the outbreak of hostilities, and the Government showed interest in this.

40. During the latter half of February there were a number of incidents that raised tensions between the parties. In early March, negotiating activity centered on attempts to set up a two day meeting with only military representation to agree on a ceasefire, and on efforts to arrange the removal of a Croatian patrol that had infiltrated Serb-held territory near Gospic and was then pinned down. On the economic side, the International Conference on the Former Yugoslavia arranged for the inspection by international experts of he Obrovac generator poles and the Zadar water supply system. The latter point was intended as a confidence-building measure and was the only one on which any progress was made, with a team of Norwegian experts conducting the inspections between 21 and 25 March.

41. On 22 March, the parties met at the Russian Embassy in Zagreb and started negotiations on a ceasefire. The negotiations were co-chaired by Ambassadors Eide and Ahrens of the International Conference on the Former Yugoslavia, assisted by military negotiators for the International Conference on the Former Yugoslavia and UNPROFOR. Russian Deputy Foreign Minister Churkin and United States Ambassador Galbraith also participated throughout the negotiations and made a significant contribution to the process. Progress was made, but the parties were unable to reach an agreement and there was an adjournment of one week.

42. On 29 March, the parties returned to the Russian Embassy in Zagreb and signed a ceasefire agreement after a long and very difficult session (S/1994/367, annex). At that time, they agreed to return to the Embassy two weeks later to commence negotiations on economic measures of common interest. However, a few days later the Serb side indicated that the Embassy was no longer acceptable

as a venue. Therefore, the meeting scheduled for 12 April to commence economic negotiations had to be cancelled. Since then, the parties have been unable to agree on a venue for the negotiations.

43. In early April, the Conference negotiators, in cooperation with the Ambassadors of the Russian Federation and the United States of America in Zagreb, drafted a programme of economic measures to form the basis for the forthcoming negotiations. This working document was presented to the parties by the Conference negotiators, accompanied by the Ambassador of the Russian Federation, and was largely accepted by the Government of Croatia, However, on 10 April, the local Serb authorities said that it did not reflect their position and that they would provide their own input. This has yet to be received. However, the Conference negotiators have repeatedly stated their readiness to include further Serb proposals in order to make the document as comprehensive and balanced as possible.

44. On 21 April, a new "Government" was formed at Knin. The Conference negotiators had their first contacts with the new local Serb interlocutors, meeting Mr. Mikelic, the new "Prime Minister", at Petrinje on 30 April and Mr. Babic, the new "Foreign Minister", at Belgrade on 4 May. Since then, they have continued to have a number of meetings with both sides in an attempt to find common ground on the question of a venue for economic negotiations. Eventually, agreement was reached on a meeting to be held at Plitvice. Efforts are under way to resolve disagreements on peripheral issues that have thus far kept the meeting from taking place.

IX. PEACEMAKING IN BOSNIA AND HERZEGOVINA

45. In paragraph 12 of the report submitted the Security Council on 29 December 1993 by the Co-Chairmen of the Steering Committee (S/26922), the state which peacemaking efforts in respect of the situation in Bosnia and Herzegovina had reached was summarized as follows:

"(a) There is agreement among all three sides that Bosnia and Herzegovina should be organized as a Union of three republics;
  (b) There is agreement that the Muslim-majority Republic should have 33.3 per cent of territory and the Croats should have 17.5 per cent;
  (c) In Brussels on 23 December, the Co-Chairmen appealed to all three sides to observe a holiday truce to cover the period 23 December to 15 January. All three leaders accepted this appeal and undertook to give instruction to their military commanders down to the local level to observe the ceasefire faithfully;
  (d) The three sides have agreed to return to Geneva on 15 January 1994, to continue the search for peace;

(e) Working Groups have been established to look into the following issues and to help reach agreement on them by 15 January;

  (i) The definition of the Mostar city area that would be placed under the temporary administration of the European Union;

  (ii) Technical arrangements for providing the Muslim-majority Republic with road and rail access to Brcko and the Sava river, without prejudice to the Muslim-majority Republic's continued support for the arrangements agreed on the *HMS Invincible*;

  (iii) Access of the Muslim-majority republic to the sea;

  (iv) Continued discussions between Mr. Silajdzic and Mr. Krajisnik on territorial delimitation."

46. During a resumed round of talks on 18 and 19 January, a map proposed by the Bosnian Serbs was on the table offering the Muslim-majority Republic 33.56 per cent while the Bosnian Serbs and the Bosnian Croats declared their willingness to pursue discussion to settle between them the delimitation of territory so as to assure the Bosnian Croats 17.5 per cent.

47. In paragraph 8 of their report to the Security Council dated 21 January 1994 (S/1994.64), the Co-Chairmen reported the following:

"President Izetbegovic acknowledged that the Muslim-majority Republic was being offered 33.56 per cent. He submitted, however, that the map should be altered so as to include in the territory allocated to the Muslim-majority Republic certain areas in eastern and western Bosnia where the Muslims had been in the majority before the outbreak of the conflict, as well as certain areas in central Bosnia, while keeping within the target of 33.3 per cent."

48. The Co-Chairmen consulted the parties concerning an arbitration procedure for breaking the impasse. After those consultations, the Co-Chairmen submitted to the parties as procedure, whereby the disputed territory could be referred to an arbitration commission whose recommendations would then go to the Security Council. The Bosnian Serbs and the Bosnian Croats were willing to accept these procedures. President Izetbegovic rejected them because too many areas of importance to the Muslim-majority Republic would be left unresolved and they were unwilling to have Serb or Croat forces remaining in the disputed territories, which they consider should be a part of their Republic.

49. At another round of talks on 12 February the Co-Chairmen tried a number of avenues to get the parties to move towards agreement on the territories still under dispute. They first invited the parties to indicate whether the number of disputed areas could be reduced. This did not prove possible. The Co-Chairmen then invited the parties to consider whether it might be possible to move to a peace agreement by arranging for some of the areas to be treated as protected areas, while a few of them could be placed under international administration. These possibilities were kept open, but discussion of them was affected by the

Bosnian Serbs' contention that the Bosnian Presidency, having agreed to 33.3 per cent, was trying to pocket the 33.56 per cent already offered and still to maintain a list of disputed areas. A similar contention was put forward by the Bosnian Croats who asked for recognition also from the Bosnian Muslims that they should have 17.5 per cent of the territory. The Bosnian Presidency, however, maintained its claims. It added that it could only accept the Croats having 17.5 per cent on the condition that it was not prejudicial to the Presidency's claims.

50. The Co-Chairmen again consulted the parties on the proposed arbitration procedure. All three sides said that they accepted the concept of arbitration, but the Bosnian Presidency maintained its position that before an arbitration procedure could be used there should be withdrawal of military forces from the areas in question. The Bosnian Croats and the Bosnian Serbs accepted that there needed to be a withdrawal, of forces, accompanied by the insertion of United Nations civilian police, in order to encourage people who lived there before the war to return, but that the areas had to be within the provisional boundaries of the Republics. The Bosnian Presidency maintained that the disputed areas could not be considered as falling within the provisional boundaries of the Republics.

51. The Co-Chairmen consulted the parties on other possible avenues for overcoming the hurdle over the disputed territories. Among the possibilities mentioned was the establishment of an International Joint Control Commission whose task would be to ensure that nothing was done in any of the disputed areas to alter their character or status, or which could be prejudicial to their eventual allocation while the arbitration procedure functioned. Another possibility mentioned was referral of the disputed areas to the Security Council or to a group of members of the Council. The parties were asked to suggest other possible procedures for reaching agreement on the outstanding territorial issues. No such suggestion was forthcoming.

52. In the circumstances, it was agreed that the parties should consult bilaterally and should also have discussions with the special envoys of the Russian Federation and the United States of America. In the light of those further consultation, the Co-Chairmen would assess the situation with a view to inviting the parties back to Geneva for further talks.

53. Subsequently, the Bosnian Muslims and the Bosnian Croats held discussions in Vienna and Washington, D.C., and on 1 March, the following agreements were signed by Dr. Silajdzic, Prime Minister of the Republic of Bosnia and Herzegovina, Dr. Granic, Deputy Prime Minister and Minister for Foreign Affairs of the Republic of Croatia, and Mr. Zubak, Head of the Bosnian Croat delegation (S/1994/255):

(a) Framework Agreement establishing a Federation in the area of the Republic of Bosnia and Herzegovina with a Majority Bosniac and Croat Population;

(b) Outline of a Preliminary Agreement for a Confederation between the Republic and the Federation.

54. After further negotiations between the same delegations in Vienna and Washington, the "Constitution of the Federation of Bosnia and Herzegovina" was signed in Washington on 18 March. The Constitution provides that:

> "Bosniacs and Croats, as constituent peoples (along with others) and citizens of the Republic of Bosnia and Herzegovina, in the exercise of their sovereign rights, transform the international structure of the territories with a majority of Bosniac and Croat population in the Republic of Bosnia and Herzegovina into a Federation, which is composed of federal units with equal rights and responsibilities."

It further provides that:

> "The decisions on the constitutional status of the territories of the Republic of Bosnia and Herzegovina with a majority of Serb populations shall be made in the course of negotiations towards a peaceful settlement and at the International Conference on the Former Yugoslavia."

The Constitution of the Federation was subsequently approved by the Assembly of the Republic of Bosnia and Herzegovina, acting as the Constituent Assembly of the Federation; consequently, the Constitution entered into force. Follow-up agreements were signed at Vienna on 11 May.

55. With a view to facilitating further negotiations among the parties to the conflict in Bosnia and Herzegovina, consultations were undertaken on the establishment of a Contact Group that would work together with the parties to help bring about a comprehensive settlement. The Contact Group, as eventually established, consists of representatives of the Russian Federation and the United Sates of America and designees of the International Conference on the Former Yugoslavia, representing both the United Nations and the European Union. The Conference designees are representatives from France, Germany and the United Kingdom of Great Britain and Northern Ireland, as well as legal advisers from the secretariat of the International Conference on the Former Yugoslavia. The Contact Group held its first round of discussion with representatives of the parties on 25 and 26 may. Since then, it has met on its own and has also had further contacts with the parties.

56. The members of the Contact Group have been guided by the past work done within the International Conference on the Former Yugoslavia, by the European Union Action Plan and by the communiqué issued by the Foreign Ministers of

Belgium, France, Germany, Greece, the Russian Federation, the United Kingdom and the United States, who met at Geneva 3 May (see S/1994/579, annex). The Co-Chairmen of the Steering Committee had an exchange of views with the Foreign Ministers on that occasion.

57. The Contact Group has thus far concentrated on the preparation of a map for the allocation of territory on the basis of 51 per cent for the Bosniac-Croat Federation and 49 per cent for the Bosnian Serbs; discussion of future constitutional arrangements; and the development of incentives and disincentives to encourage acceptance of a peace package and to discourage rejection thereof.

58. The Foreign Ministers of France, Germany, Greece, the Russian Federation, the United Kingdom and the United States met in Geneva on 5 July and considered recommendations of the Contact Group. The Ministers welcomed the territorial proposal developed by the Contact Group and directed it to present the proposal to the representatives of the Bosnian Government and the Bosnian Serbs. The Ministers strongly supported the territorial proposal "as a reasonable basis for a immediate political settlement". The Ministers considered that the proposal "represents and important moment of opportunity, which may not come again". They said there were united in the belief that the war could be ended now and that the consequences of failing to do so would be grave.

59. The territorial proposals of the Contact Group together with indications of incentives and disincentives, were communicated to delegations of the Bosnian Government and the Bosnian Serbs on 6 July at Geneva. They have been asked to give their response within two weeks.

60. The Ministers indicated that there were important incentives for the parties to accept the proposed map. They said that for the Bosnian Government they were ready to assist in the implementation of a territorial settlement and to help with reconstruction, and that for the Serbs, sanctions would be suspended geared to their pullback to the lines indicated on the map.

61. The Ministers further indicated that if the parties did not agree they could expect more pressure to be applied. In particular, existing Security Council resolutions concerning safe areas would be rigorously enforced. They said that the necessary planning was being undertaken. The Ministers added that as a last resort, a decision in the Security Council to lift the arms embargo could become unavoidable and that would have consequences for the presence of UNPROFOR.

62. The Ministers called upon the parties to observe and prolong the ceasefire and to refrain from military action.

63. The Ministers agreed to meet again before the end of July.

APPENDIX

FINANCIAL STATUS OF THE INTERNATIONAL CONFERENCE ON
THE FORMER YUGOSLAVIA AS AT 30 APRIL 1994

(rounded to the nearest $ 100)

I. Contributions received	*US $*
First financial period - six months	3,096,700
(total budget $ 3,374,000)	
Second financial period - six months	2,329,200
(total budget $ 2,710,000)	
Third financial period - six months	1,196,100
(total budget $ 2,028,000)	
Fourth financial period	-
(has not been budgeted or assessed)	
Fifth financial period - six month	-
(total budget $ 1,600,000)	
Total contributions	6,622,000

*II. Estimate of Expenditures and Commitments Not Including Programme
Support Costs*

First financial period	2,531,800
Second financial period	1,513,800
Third financial period	1,594,500
Fourth financial period	357,200
Fifth financial period	-
Total expenditures	5,997,300

134. Letter Dated 19 September 1994 from the Secretary-General Addressed to the President of the Security Council*

I have the honour to convey to you the attached report addressed to me on 19 September 1994 by the Co-Chairmen of the Steering Committee of the International Conference on the Former Yugoslavia, dealing with the establishment of an International Conference on the Former Yugoslavia Mission to the Federal Republic of Yugoslavia (Serbia and Montenegro).

I should be grateful if you would bring this information to the attention of the members of the Security Council.

Annex
Report of the Co-Chairmen of the Steering Committee of the International Conference on the Former Yugoslavia on the Establishment and Commencement of Operations on an International Conference on the Former Yugoslavia Mission to the Federal Republic of Yugoslavia (Serbia and Montenegro)

I. Introduction

1. The conflict in Bosnia and Herzegovina is in its third year. Successive blueprints for peace have been drawn up with the parties and then subsequently repudiated by one side or the other: the Carrington-Cutileiro plan; the Vance-Owen Plan; "the Invincible Package"; the European Action Plan. In January-February 1994, the parties agreed, in talks held under the auspices of the Co-Chairmen of the Steering Committee of the International Conference on the Former Yugoslavia, on a constitutional framework and modalities for the implementation and monitoring of a cessation of hostilities and on the greater part of a map for the allocation of the territory. However, disagreement persisted on, at most, 2 per cent of the territory. Various methods were suggested by the Co-Chairmen, to no avail, to overcome the impasse on this small percentage of the territory. They included arbitration under the auspices of the Security Council.

---

* UN Doc. S/1994/1074, 19 September 1994. Signed by Boutros Boutros-Ghali.

II. Contact Group Proposal

2. In the light of this experience with successive peace plans, consultations took place involving the Co-Chairmen of the Steering Committee and Governments with influence on the parties. This led to the signing of the Washington accords for the establishment of the Bosniac-Croat Federation (see S/1994/255, annex I) and the establishment of a contact group consisting of five countries, namely France, Germany, the Russian Federation, the United Kingdom of Great Britain and Northern Ireland, and the United States of America, working with the International Conference. The Contact Group was guided in its work by the resolutions of the Security Council, by declarations adopted by Foreign Ministers of the Contact Group countries meeting in Geneva on 13 May an on 5 and 30 July, by the provisions of the European Union Action Plan and by the previous efforts of the International Conference.

3. The Contact Group drew up a map for the allocation of territory between the Bosniac-Croat Federation and the Bosnian Serb entity and submitted it to the two sides on 6 July. The map allocated 51 per cent to the Bosniac-Croat Federation and 49 per cent to the Bosnian Serb entity. The Contact Group, reinforced by the support of the Security Council and the Council of Ministers of the European Union, as well as by the Governments and organizations worldwide, informed the parties that the proposed map would have to be accepted as presented, unless the parties could agree between themselves on changes. At the end of July, the Bosniac-Croat Federation accepted the proposed map. The Republic of Croatia and the Federal Republic of Yugoslavia (Serbia and Montenegro) also accepted the map. Leaders of the Federal Republic of Yugoslavia (Serbia and Montenegro) urged the Bosnian Serb leadership to accept the Contact Group map. To date the Bosnian Serb leadership has not done so.

4. The Contact Group countries had made it quite clear from the outset that there would be incentives for acceptance of its proposal and discentives for rejection.

III. Closure by the Federal Republic of Yugoslavia (Serbia and Montenegro) of its Border with the Bosnian Serbs

5. On 4 August 1994, the following measures were ordered by the Government of the Federal Republic of Yugoslavia (Serbia and Montenegro), to come into effect the same day:

"(a) To break off political and economic relations with the Republika Srpska;
(b) To prohibit the stay of the members of the leadership of the Republic Srpska (Parlia-

ment, Presidency and Government) in the territory of the Federal Republic of Yugo-slavia;

(c) As of today the border of the Federal Republic of Yugoslavia is closed for all trans-port towards the Republika Srpska, except food, clothing and medicine."

IV. FOLLOW-UP BY THE CO-CHAIRMEN

6. At the request of the Secretary-General, the United Nations Co-Chairman of the Steering Committee, Mr Stoltenberg, visited Belgrade and Pale from 12 to 14 August. He discussed with President Milosevic the implementation of the measures announced for the closure of the border and their verification. Lord Owen and Mr. Stoltenberg followed up by visiting Belgrade, Podgorica and Zagreb from 4 to 6 September.

7. The Co-Chairmen discussed the border closure at length with President Milosevic and Foreign Minister Janovic in Belgrade on 4 September, and with President Bulatovic in Podgorica on 5 September. On 5 September, the day after the Co-Chairmen's conversation in Belgrade, Mr. Janovic sent the Co-Chairmen a letter recalling a proposal that had been made by the Government of the Feder-al Republic of Yugoslavia (Serbia and Montenegro) to the effect that representa-tives of international humanitarian organizations, in conjunction with representa-tives of the local Red Cross, could "establish joint controls" at places where humanitarian assistance "is organized and dispatched from". The Foreign Minis-ter requested the Co-Chairmen to propose "relevant humanitarian organ-izations", to work in conjunction with the local Red Cross to establish joint con-trols of the type mentioned.

8. At the Co-Chairmen's request, a member of their staff, Mr. Pellnäs, had detailed technical discussions in Belgrade on 4 September with Mr. Kertas, the head of Customs of the Federal Republic of Yugoslavia (Serbia and Montenegro) and on 5 September in Podgorica with Mr. Bosko Bojeric, the Deputy Interior Minister of Montenegro. In the light of the report they received, the Co-Chair-men decided to explore the possibility of sending to the Federal Republic of Yugoslavia (Serbia and Montenegro) an International Conference on the Former Yugoslavia Mission composed of personnel provided through national humani-tarian organizations who would control the effective delivery of humanitarian assistance at designated crossing-points and who would have freedom of access elsewhere in the Federal Republic of Yugoslavia (Serbia and Montenegro). It would report to the Co-Chairmen and, through them, to the Secretary-General and the Presidency of the European Union, on the implementation of the border closure.

9. From the preparatory work done by Mr. Pellnäs, it was concluded that an International Conference on the Former Yugoslavia Mission could aim initially for 135 international members. The Federal Republic of Yugoslavia (Serbia and Montenegro) offered to provide free of charge 65 drivers and also offered 7 cars to start with. The Federal Republic of Yugoslavia (Serbia and Montenegro) also said it would arrange for 65 interpreters to be paid by the Mission. The Mission Coordinator would be Mr. Bo Pellnäs (Sweden), acting in a civilian capacity. Its financing would come from voluntary contributions and countries would be expected to pay for the persons they sent.

10. The Co-Chairmen kept the Contact Group, which was then meeting in Berlin, fully briefed on these developments. The Contact Group welcomed and supported their efforts.

11. The Co-Chairmen immediately sounded out the Nordic Countries and obtained commitment that they would supply 60 persons to be in Belgrade within one week. They also obtained definite promises of $ 200,000 start-up money from two of the Nordic countries.

12. In view of these developments, the Co-Chairmen, on 8 September, informed the Foreign Minister of the Federal Republic of Yugoslavia (Serbia and Montenegro) that they were ready to set up an International Conference on the Former Yugoslavia Mission along the lines discussed with him and President Milosevic, and President Bulatovic on 4 and 5 September. The Co-Chairmen noted that Mr. Pellnäs had worked out a number of details about the proposed Mission in meetings with the head of Customs of the Federal Republic of Yugoslavia (Serbia and Montenegro) and with the Deputy Interior Minister of Montenegro. The Co-Chairmen added that Mr. Pellnäs would consult with other relevant humanitarian organizations and other countries. They further informed the Foreign Minister that the Nordic countries were ready to put some people in quickly. The Co-Chairmen said that they hoped to be able to provide more details early in the following week, by which time Mr. Pellnäs would hopefully be in a position go to Belgrade and to discuss the matter in more detail.

13. At the request of the Co-Chairmen, Mr. Pellnäs arrived in Belgrade on Wednesday, 14 September accompanied by seven persons from France, Germany, Norway, the Russian Federation, Sweden and the United States. Mr. Pellnäs immediately met with representatives of the Yugoslav authorities. Meetings continued the following day. The Yugoslav authorities agreed that all traffic would be stopped between 1900 hours and 0600 hours on all crossings except the two used for humanitarian traffic. All ferry traffic would also be stopped. Moreover, the number of international staff assigned to the Mission could be raised to 200.

14. Mr. Pellnäs was assured by the Yugoslav authorities of full access to all parts of the Federal Republic of Yugoslavia (Serbia and Montenegro). They gave Mr. Pellnäs a formal commitment to provide the Mission with sufficient helicopter resources. They accepted the establishment of a radio communication net as requested by Mr. Pellnäs. They also agreed to his request that the drivers provided by the Federal Republic of Yugoslavia (Serbia and Montenegro) should be police officers.

V. Terms of Reference of the Mission

15. On Friday, 16 September Mr. Pellnäs saw the Foreign Minister of the Federal Republic of Yugoslavia (Serbia and Montenegro) and submitted to him, on behalf of the Co-Chairmen, the following arrangements for the establishment of the International Conference on the Former Yugoslavia Mission:

"1. The Coordinator of the Mission is to be a member of the International Conference on the Former Yugoslavia staff, Mr. Bo Pellnäs, answerable to us as Co-Chairman of the Steering Committee of the International Conference on the Former Yugoslavia. The Mission will consist of such international civilian staff made available to the International Conference on the Former Yugoslavia whom we select after discussion with your Government, and those of Serbia and Montenegro.

2. The Mission will be organized out of Belgrade, initially from the Norwegian Embassy, and will have three sections in the field: one in Montenegro and two in Serbia. Each section will initially be organized into teams of four persons: two international staff, one local interpreter to be paid by the Mission and one local driver to be supplied and paid by your Government. It may be necessary to move teams quickly from one section to another as the Mission requires and for this purpose the helicopters which your Government has agreed to provide will be helpful.

3. International staff of the Mission, who will carry International Conference on the Former Yugoslavia certificates, will have the status of members of a diplomatic mission. Property and premises, including temporary ones, established by the Mission for its members shall not be seized or interfered with.

4. Teams and members of the Mission will be granted full freedom of movement. Their movements and their right to remain in any place shall not be subject to any requirement of prior notice or authorization.

5. Taking into account that the responsibility of controlling the crossings remains with your Government, members of the Mission will be enabled to work with representatives of the Yugoslav Red Cross at places from which any humanitarian assistance is organized or dispatched; to work alongside customs officers; to look into any vehicles crossing; and to have examined any item conveyed by individuals or vehicles across the border which they suspect might not be classified as purely humanitarian. For this purpose the members of the Mission are to have the possibility of examining customs, commercial, transport and related documentation, access to facilities where goods are loaded or, if inspection during loading is not feasible, the right to require unloading of vehicles and the assistance in specific cases of your authorities in carrying out examinations.

6. The Government is to ensure the security and safety of members of the Mission, without thereby interfering with their movement and work.

7. The Mission will be authorized to maintain communications between their teams, their sections, their Belgrade offices and Geneva by communication satellites as well as by radio transmitters.

If the above-mentioned conditions forming the basis for our proposals in this letter no longer exist, we reserve our right as Co-Chairmen to withdraw the Mission at any time we determine."

16. On Saturday, 17 September, Foreign Minister Jovanovic formally transmitted to the Co-Chairmen, through Mr. Pellnäs, his Government's "full acceptance" of the above-mentioned arrangements proposed by the Co-Chairmen. The International Conference on the Former Yugoslavia Mission in the Federal Republic of Yugoslavia (Serbia and Montenegro) was thus formally established as of 17 September 1994.

VI. MISSION CONCEPT

17. The Mission is being organized with personnel provided through national humanitarian organizations. It will have three sections working in the field, which will be given resources corresponding to the number of crossings within their area of responsibility, it being understood that it would be possible to carry out a quick change of resources between the sections, in order to achieve a concentrated presence in areas where needed.

18. The sections will be organized into groups of four teams, each team consisting of two international members, an interpreter, a driver and a car. The interpreter and the driver will be provided by the authorities of the Federal Republic of Yugoslavia (Serbia and Montenegro).

19. The Mission will exercise its right to go wherever it wishes, without any form of prior notification, to follow the work of customs officers of the Federal Republic of Yugoslavia (Serbia and Montenegro) and to actually look into vehicles crossing the border.

VII. COMMENCEMENT OF OPERATIONS

20. Following the initial party of 8 that assembled in Belgrade on 14 September, a second contingent of 19 persons arrived in Belgrade on Friday, 16 September, from Norway and the United Kingdom. A third contingent of 10, from France, Denmark, Spain and the United Kingdom, will arrive on Monday, 19 September. A further contingent of 15 persons from Finland will arrive on Tuesday, 20

September. As of Tuesday, 20 September, 52 international members of the Mission will thus have arrived in Belgrade. The Mission has already assembled some local drivers, local interpreters and vehicles provided by the Government of the Federal Republic of Yugoslavia (Serbia and Montenegro). In addition the Government is making helicopters available for use of the Mission.

21. Mr. Pellnäs has had extensive discussions in Belgrade with the authorities of the Federal Republic of Yugoslavia (Serbia and Montenegro) as well as with Serbian and Montenegrin authorities. A number of meetings have been held with the head of Customs of the Federal Republic of Yugoslavia (Serbia and Montenegro).

22. On 17 September, Mr. Pellnäs flew to Podgorica for a meeting with the Montenegrin authorities. As agreed in the talks with Mr. Kertas, a helicopter was provided by the authorities of the Federal Republic of Yugoslavia (Serbia and Montenegro). Mr. Pellnäs had a meeting in Podgorica with the Deputy Interior Minister. Mr. Pellnäs briefed him on what had been agreed during his talks in Belgrade and asked for his support of the Mission in Montenegro. Mr. Bojevic made a very firm commitment to Mr. Pellnäs, promising his Government's full cooperation and support. He also promised to take every possible step to ensure the safety and security of the members of the Mission. He informed Mr. Pellnäs about actions that had been taken against two private businessmen who had been caught smuggling fuel into Bosnia and Herzegovina. Both had been sent to prison. The seized vehicles and fuel had been sold and the proceeds given to the Montenegrin Red Cross.

23. On 16 September, the Mission sent out its first reconnaissance team of two members, who visited the border crossing between Zvornik and Kotroman and also made a visit to Pripolje, which is to be the base for one of the three field sections within the Mission. The teams had complete freedom of movement and thus arrived unannounced at the crossings. It saw very little traffic south of Zvornik and reported that the crossings appeared to be seriously controlled. They saw all crossing cars being checked. They observed no trucks at any of the crossing points. The team also reported that the border now had all the signs of a national border, with flags, barriers and, at places, even some defensive military positions.

24. On 17 September, the Mission sent out a team to Pripolje to start preparations in an area judged to have the highest priority. On 18 September, the Mission established a presence in Niksic with one team, while another team started working at the packing centre for humanitarian aid in Belgrade. As soon as the necessary logistical arrangements are in place, the remaining teams will be deployed to reinforce the Pripolje and Niksic centres and also to commence

operations from Banja Koviljaca, between Loznica and Zvornik.

25. Out of the 10 members arriving on Monday, 19 September, the core of a headquarters will be organized and the commanders of the three field section centres will be chosen and sent out. The 15 Finnish members due to arrive on Tuesday, 20 September will be put at the disposal of the three section commanders.

26. Further meetings between the Federal Customs authorities and the experts supporting the Mission will be held on Monday, 19 September, in order to develop working procedures further.

VIII. OBSERVATIONS

27. Mr. Pellnäs has reported to the Co-Chairmen that the federal Government and the federal authorities have fully cooperated with the Mission and have sought in every way to facilitate its work. The teams sent out by the Mission have had complete freedom of movements.

28. The Mission's first impressions from the border areas visited coincide with reports it has received from visitors from other international organizations and seem to verify that the federal Government is taking every action to seal off the border between the Federal Republic of Yugoslavia (Serbia and Montenegro) and Bosnia and Herzegovina effectively.

135. LETTER DATED 3 OCTOBER 1994 FROM THE SECRETARY-GENERAL ADDRESSED TO THE PRESIDENT OF THE SECURITY COUNCIL*

I have the honour to transmit the attached report which was addressed to me on 3 October 1993 by the Co-Chairmen of the Steering Committee of the International Conference on the Former Yugoslavia, concerning the operation of the International Conference's Mission to the Federal Republic of Yugoslavia (Serbia and Montenegro). This report by the Co-Chairmen contains the certification referred to in Security Council resolution 943 (1994).

I should be grateful if you would bring this information to the attention of the members of the Security Council.

---

* UN Doc. S/1994/1124, 3 October 1994. Signed by Boutros Boutros-Ghali.

Annex
Operations of the International Conference on the Former Yugoslavia Mission to the Federal Republic of Yugoslavia (Serbia and Montenegro) - Report of the Co-Chairmen of the Steering Committee -

I. INTRODUCTION

1. This report is submitted in follow-up to the earlier report transmitted to the Security Council on 19 September 1994 (S/1994/1074). Paragraph 5 of that report referred to the measures ordered by the Federal Republic of Yugoslavia (Serbia and Montenegro) on 4 August 1994, and its commitment to close its border "for all transport towards the Republika Srpska, except food, clothing and medicine".

II. ORGANIZATION AND DEPLOYMENT OF THE MISSION

2. The terms of reference of the Mission are spelled out in detail in the above-mentioned report (S/1994/1074), paragraph 15, and in particular point 5. As at 3 October 1994, 93 international members of the Mission have been deployed within the Federal Republic of Yugoslavia (Serbia and Montenegro). They come from the following countries: Belgium, Denmark, Finland, France, Germany, Ireland, Norway, Portugal, Russian Federation, Spain, Sweden, United Kingdom of Great Britain and Northern Ireland and United States of America. The Mission and the Co-Chairmen are actively in contact with several countries and it is expected that by the middle of this week 105 international personnel will have been deployed. There are confirmed promises of another 56 persons, who are expected to arrive within the next 10 days. There are also further promises of an additional 10. As at 3 October, the Mission had 36 teams operating from Banja Koviljaca, Zlatibor, Niksic and Belgrade.

3. The Mission has persons at the packing depots in Belgrade for humanitarian aid and at the borders, where procedures have been agreed with the Federal Customs Authorities. As for as transit traffic to the Republic of Croatia is concerned, agreements have been made covering customs documentation and the sealing of load-carrying vehicles to reduce the obvious risk of a diversion of supplies to the Bosnian Serbs. The Mission has made visits to all parts of the border between the Federal Republic of Yugoslavia (Serbia and Montenegro) and Bosnia and Herzegovina, including, in the last few days, those areas reserved for the military, and has covered all significant roads crossing the border by day and night.

III. CERTIFICATION

4. Based on the Mission's on-site observation, on the advice of the Mission Coordinator, Mr. Bo Pellnäs, and in the absence of any contrary information from the air whether airborne reconnaissance system of the North Atlantic Treaty Organisation (NATO), or from national technical means, the Co-Chairmen conclude that the Government of the Federal Republic of Yugoslavia (Serbia and Montenegro) is meeting its commitment to close the border between the Federal Republic of Yugoslavia (Serbia and Montenegro) and the areas of the Republic of Bosnia and Herzegovina under the control of the Bosnian Serb forces.

136. LETTER DATED 2 NOVEMBER 1994 FROM THE SECRETARY-GENERAL ADDRESSED TO THE PRESIDENT OF THE SECURITY COUNCIL*

I have the honour to transmit the attached report which was addressed to me on 2 November 1994 by the Co-Chairmen of the Steering Committee of the International Conference on the Former Yugoslavia, concerning the operations of the International Conference's Mission to the Federal Republic of Yugoslavia (Serbia and Montenegro). This report by the Co-Chairmen contains the certification referred to in paragraph 3 of Security Council resolution 943 (1994) (see para. 27).

I should be grateful if you would bring this information to the attention of the members of the Security Council.

Annex
Operations of the International Conference on the Former Yugoslavia
Mission to the Federal Republic of Yugoslavia (Serbia and Montenegro)
- Report of the Co-Chairmen of the Steering Committee -

I. INTRODUCTION

1. The present report is submitted pursuant to paragraph 3 of Security Council resolution 943 (1994), adopted on 23 September. In that resolution the Security Council requested that the Secretary-General submit every 30 days for its review a report from the Co-Chairmen of the Steering Committee of the International

---

* UN Doc. S/1994/1246, 3 November 1994. Signed by Boutros Boutros-Ghali.

Conference on the Former Yugoslavia on the border closure measures taken by the authorities of the Federal Republic of Yugoslavia (Serbia and Montenegro).
2. It will be recalled that, on 4 August 1994, the following measures were ordered by the Government of the Federal Republic of Yugoslavia (Serbia and Montenegro) to come into effect the same day:

> "(a) To break off political and economic relations with the Republica Srpska;
> (b) To prohibit the stay of the members of the leadership of the Republica Srpska (Parliament, Presidency and Government) in the territory of the Federal Republic of Yugoslavia;
> (c) As of today the border of the Federal Republic of Yugoslavia is closed for all transport towards the Republica Srpska, except food, clothing and medicine."

3. On 19 September 1994 and on 3 October 1994, the Secretary-General transmitted to the Security Council reports from the Co-Chairmen of the Steering Committee of the International Conference on the Former Yugoslavia on the state of implementation of the above-mentioned measures (S/1994/1074 and S/1994/1124). The report dated 3 October 1994 contained the following certification from the Co-Chairmen:

> "Based on the Mission's on-site observation, on the advice of the Mission Coordinator, Mr. Bo Pellnäs, and in the absence of any contrary information from the air whether airborne reconnaissance system of the North Atlantic Treaty Organisation (NATO), or from national technical means, the Co-Chairmen conclude that the Government of the Federal Republic of Yugoslavia (Serbia and Montenegro) is meeting its commitment to close the border between the Federal Republic of Yugoslavia (Serbia and Montenegro) and the areas of the Republic of Bosnia and Herzegovina under the control of the Bosnian Serb forces".

Developments in the past 30 days are dealt with below.

II. LEGISLATION/REGULATION ON THE BORDER CLOSURE

4. The legislation of the authorities of the Federal Republic of Yugoslavia (Serbia and Montenegro) closing the border with the Bosnian Serbs continues in force. No new legislation or decrees have been issued. However, following a considerable amount of liaison work between the authorities and the Mission to improve the routines and procedures of the customs authorities of the Federal Republic of Yugoslavia (Serbia and Montenegro), some customs officers have been changed and the cooperation and efficiency of customs improved.

III. Organization, Financing and Work of the Mission

5. As of 2 November, 118 international personnel were on duty with the Mission. The Mission personnel to date have come from Belgium, Denmark, Finland, France, Germany, Ireland, Norway, Portugal, Russian Federation, Spain, Sweden, United Kingdom of Great Britain and Northern Ireland and United States of America.

6. Since the start of the Mission, 16 members have completed their contracts and left the Mission area. They have not been replaced by the countries from which they came. Another 12 members will arrive from Canada between 4 and 11 November. Twenty additional members from the United States, as well as 20 from the Sanctions Assistance Missions Communication Centre (SAMCOMM), Brussels has confirmed but their late date of arrival is not yet known. The delay in the arrival of the Mission personnel promised has forced the Mission to change its operational procedures slightly. Caravans have been provided to all border crossings and members of the Mission are currently required to stay on duty on these points for 12 hours at a time. With time for transport, this means that the Mission member still have at least 14 working hours per day. With this, however, it has been possible to cover the main border crossings 24 hours a day despite the shortage of personnel.

7. The Mission is still operating under tight financial constraints. At a meeting of the Expanded Steering Committee of the International Conference on the Former Yugoslavia, held on 5 October 1994, the following decisions were taken regarding the financing of the Mission:

    (a) Costs for personnel should be covered by the sending State;
    (b) Voluntary contributions to the common costs were welcome;
    (c) Residual common costs should be financed through assessed contributions.

8. The following pledges of voluntary contributions have been made:

	(US dollars)
Canada	100,000
Denmark	100,000
Norway	100,000
Sweden	100,000
Switzerland	150,000 (in the form of airlifts Geneva-Belgrade)

United States   400,000
United States   500,000 (in the form of communications equipment)

The following funds have actually been received:

Canada   100,000
Denmark   100,000
Norway   100,000
Switzerland   (15 airlifts Geneva-Belgrade)
United States   400,000

9. On 1 November a note was sent to members of the Expanded Steering Committee asking that countries wishing to make further voluntary contributions inform the secretariat of the Conference by 17 November 1994. Voluntary contributions pledged by 11 November 1994 will be set off against the projected budget for the Mission.

IV. Freedom of Movement of the Mission

10. The Mission continues to enjoy freedom of movement within the Federal Republic of Yugoslavia (Serbia and Montenegro). A matter of concern has been the difficulty the Mission encountered to enter a factory compound with a connecting bridge at Raca 5 kilometres north-west of Briboj. The bridge, however, was under observation and from 20 October it was watched 24-hours a day. On 21 October, Mission members were allowed to enter and to see the complete complex. The Mission Coordinator personally visited the factory on 27 October.
11. On a few occasions, members of the Mission have been threatened by people crossing the border check-points. In the assessment of the Mission Coordinator, this may indicate that the efforts made by the Mission are having an impact and are making life difficult for smugglers. Negative reactions have also been experienced on two occasions at the packing centres in Belgrade and Niksic.

V. Cooperation of the Authorities of the Federal Republic of Yugoslavia (Serbia and Montenegro) with the Mission

12. In the assessment of the Mission Coordinator, the cooperation of the authorities of the Federal Republic of Yugoslavia (Serbia and Montenegro) continues to be satisfactory. While minor problems may still exist at the local and lower

levels - and will probably continue to do so - this, in the assessment of the Mission Coordinator, does not influence or change the overall broadly satisfactory picture.

VI. INFORMATION RECEIVED FROM NATIONAL AND OTHER SOURCES

13. The Mission Coordinator has made a standing request to Governments possessing the technical capacity to provide it with information relevant to its mandate. The Coordinator has received some such information and measures have been taken to follow-up and to check the information received. The operating principle of the Mission is to base itself on its own observations and on information that it has verified.

VII. PROBLEMS ENCOUNTERED AND REPRESENTATIONS MADE TO THE AUTHORITIES

14. As the cooperation between the Mission and the authorities of the Federal Republic of Yugoslavia (Serbia and Montenegro) results in improved control along the border, the number of detected smuggling attempts consequently rises.
15. In the northern part of the border between Serbia and the territory held by the Bosnian Serbs, the main problem being encountered is the sometimes rather intensive traffic across the border, with small-scale attempts at smuggling in cars and buses. At some of the border crossings, the quality of the work carried out by the customs officers has occasionally not been satisfactory.
16. A small passenger train, which on some occasions in the past was used between Sremska Raca and Bijeljina, has, at the request of the Mission, been stopped.
17. Freight trains between Belgrade and Bar, in Montenegro, which pass through the territory held by the Bosnian Serbs for about 12 kilometres have now started to be controlled and sealed by the Mission at stations on each side of the border. This control, however, demands quite a lot of personnel and consequently constitutes a strain on the Mission resources.
18. In Montenegro, efforts to smuggle goods across the border appear to be better organized than in Serbia. What seems to be attempts by individuals in the northern part of the Mission area is here carried out by companies bringing truckloads to the border. On four occasions trucks have been found trying to bypass border controls. On 13 October, 10 trucks managed to bypass the checkpoint at Ilijino Brdno and on 21 October another 3 trucks have been intercepted by the police, the goods confiscated and drivers arrested. The Mission has raised

these concerns with both the Federal Republic of Yugoslavia (Serbia and Montenegro) and Montenegrin officials. The Mission Coordinator discussed the matter during a meeting he had with President Bulatovic of Montenegro. As a result, efforts to block bypassing more effectively are continuing and will eventually prevent further attempts by smugglers to avoid the border checkpoint. At present those efforts are contested by local individuals, destroying steel bars that were erected. Measures will therefore continue to be taken that hopefully will discourage any attempt to reopen these tracks.

19. A number of "duty free shops" along the border in Montenegro dealing mainly in cigarettes have, at the request of the Mission, been closed by the authorities of the Federal Republic of Yugoslavia (Serbia and Montenegro).

20. On 14 October International Conference on the Former Yugoslavia members reported a helicopter flying at low altitude into the territory held by the Bosnian Serbs at Krstac in Montenegro. Information concerning possible helicopter flights across the border into Bosnia and Herzegovina was submitted to the Security Council on 25 and 27 October (See S/1994/5/Add.75, annex I, serial Nos. 3015-1018, annex II, serial No. 3007, and S/1994/5/ Add. 76, annex I, serial Nos. 3027 and 2038; annex II, serial No. 3026).

21. The Co-Chairmen have taken a very serious view of this and discussed the matter in detail with President Milosevic during a meeting with him in Belgrade on Wednesday 26 October 1994. President Milosevic replied that the allegations were being investigated and that the results would be communicated to the Mission. He insisted that no such flights took place with the consent, knowledge or acquiescence of the Government of the Federal Republic of Yugoslavia (Serbia and Montenegro). He emphasized that the authorities of the Federal Republic of Yugoslavia (Serbia and Montenegro) were resolute in their determination to enforce the border closure. He added that it was not in the interest of the Federal Republic of Yugoslavia (Serbia and Montenegro) if unauthorized helicopter flights were confirmed. He informed the Co-Chairmen when they saw him again on Friday, 28 October, that a double control system had since been instituted for any military or police helicopter flight. Furthermore, special elements of the police had been placed in the area of the Tara mountains, where some of the helicopter flights were reported to have taken place, in order to guard against any possibility of unauthorized conduct going against the express instructions of the Government to close the border. President Milosevic reaffirmed that the policy of the Government was to seal the border against the Bosnia Serbs, except for food, clothing an medicine.

22. On 31 October, the Mission Coordinator was called in by President Milosevic to discuss the issue of the helicopter flights. President Milosevic once again

confirmed his resolve to control the border and reiterated the measures he had undertaken to achieve that goal. He informed the Mission Coordinator that the investigations were still going on, that some changes of personnel had been made and that the means of control and of technical surveillance of the border had been strongly reinforced. He assured the Mission Coordinator that the control of Serbian and Montenegrin airspace now would make it impossible to fly any unannounced flights. Any aircraft making such an attempt would be detected and forced to land. The Mission Coordinator's assessment as of 2 November is that:

"Notwithstanding the fact that reported helicopter flights as well as trucks passing the border constitute violations of the border closure, I conclude that the Federal Republic of Yugoslavia (Serbia and Montenegro) continues to meet its commitment to close the border towards the Bosnian Serbs. The measures that the authorities have said they are taking, would take, should be satisfactory. During the following 30-day period the International Conference on the Former Yugoslavia Mission will try to verify if these measures, especially those with regard to control of the airspace, are effective and suited to preventing further violations of this kind."

VIII. REPRESENTATIONS ON BEHALF OF HUMANITARIAN ORGANIZATIONS

23. The Mission Coordinator has sought to assist the Office of the United Nations High Commissioner for Refugees (UNHCR) and the International Committee of the Red Cross (ICRC) in their efforts to get the authorities of the Federal Republic of Yugoslavia (Serbia and Montenegro) to implement the border closure in such a manner as would not adversely affect their ongoing programmes in eastern Bosnia. On 6 October 1994, the Co-Chairmen received from the UNHCR Special Envoy for the Former Yugoslavia a copy of a letter sent that day to the Foreign Minister of the Federal Republic of Yugoslavia (Serbia and Montenegro) on difficulties being encountered by UNHCR. The Special Envoy's letter stated that, as a result of measures adopted by the Government of the Federal Republic of Yugoslavia (Serbia and Montenegro), the Federal Customs Authorities had begun denying passage to humanitarian assistance other than food, medicine and clothing. The Special Envoy continued:

"Other types of humanitarian assistance have been a part of UNHCR since its inception, as they are of the programmes of ICRC and other humanitarian organizations. All such assistance has the approval of the Committee established by Co-Chairmen resolution 724 (1991), I should be most grateful if you would take action to ensure that the decision restricting passage across your border with Bosnia and Herzegovina welcomed by the Security Council in resolution 943 (1994) does not have the incidental, and I am sure unintentional, effect of also restricting the delivery of legitimate humanitarian assistance approved by the Security Council".

24. On 6 October 1994, Co-Chairmen wrote to the Foreign Minister of the Federal Republic of Yugoslavia (Serbia and Montenegro) referring to the above-mentioned letter of the Special Envoy of UNHCR, asking him to use his good offices to help UNHCR and ICRC to continue their humanitarian activities. The Co-Chairmen asserted:

> "The general principle that UNHCR and ICRC, as international humanitarian organizations operating within the framework of Security Council resolutions, should not in any way be impeded in their humanitarian activities by the measures announced by the Government of the Federal Republic of Yugoslavia on 4 August 1994".

25. Based on representations from UNHCR and a letter dated 19 October 1994 received from the Chairmen of the Security Council Committee established pursuant to resolution 724 (1991) concerning Yugoslavia, the Co-Chairmen discussed the matter with President Milosevic during meetings in Belgrade. On 20 October 1994 the Co-Chairmen handed over to President Milosevic a letter on the subject written to him, with the Co-Chairmen's full support, by the High Commissioner for Refugees, Mrs. Ogata. President Milosevic said he would look into the issue. The Mission Coordinator discussed the issue with President Milosevic on 31 October. President Milosevic indicated his willingness to find a solution to the problem. The Mission Coordinator will meet the Director of Customs of the Federal Republic of Yugoslavia (Serbia and Montenegro) and representatives of UNHCR and ICRC on 3 November to discuss the issue.

IX. TRANSIT TRAFFIC

26. The procedures for traffic transiting the territory held by the Bosnian Serbs into the territory held by Serbs in Croatia have now been firmly established. Transports are divided into two categories, one consisting of humanitarian aid (described as "food, clothes and medicine") and the second being fuel. The first is handled by the International Conference on the Former Yugoslavia Mission as all other humanitarian aid, which means that it is checked and loaded under International Conference on the Former Yugoslavia observation and then sealed by the Mission. Because of the nature of the goods transported on these trucks, it has not been deemed necessary to take special measures to control the delivery in Croatia. The second category, fuel, is transported on 52 specially designated trucks escorted by police, transit into Croatia. The tachometers are sealed by the Mission when trucks leave Belgrade two or three times a week, and are removed by the Mission when the trucks return to the starting point. The first sets of

recovered print-outs from the tachometers were sent to the United Kingdom on 1 November for analysis.

X. CERTIFICATION

27. In the light of the foregoing developments during the past 30 days, based on the Mission's on-site observation, on the advice of the Mission Coordinator, Mr. Bo Pellnäs, and in the absence of any contrary information from the air, whether the airborne reconnaissance system of the North Atlantic Treaty Organisation (NATO) or national technical means, the Co-Chairmen conclude that the Government of the Federal Republic of Yugoslavia (Serbia and Montenegro) is continuing to meet its commitment to close the border between the Federal Republic of Yugoslavia (Serbia and Montenegro) and the areas of the Republic of Bosnia and Herzegovina under the control of the Bosnian Serb forces.

137. LETTER DATED 2 DECEMBER 1994 FROM THE SECRETARY-GENERAL ADDRESSED TO THE PRESIDENT OF THE SECURITY COUNCIL*

I have the honour to transmit the report addressed to me on 2 December 1994 by the Co-Chairmen of the Steering Committee of the International Conference on the Former Yugoslavia, on the conclusion of an Economic Agreement between the Croatian Government and the Serb local authorities (see annex).

I should be grateful if you would bring this information to the attention of the members of the Security Council.

Annex
Report of the Co-Chairmen of the Steering Committee of the International Conference on the Former Yugoslavia on the Conclusion of an Economic Agreement between the Croatian Government and the Serb Local Authorities

INTRODUCTION

1. One of the priorities of the International Conference on the Former Yugoslavia since its establishment has been the promotion of better relations between

---

* UN Doc. S/1994/1375, 2 December 1994. Signed by Boutros Boutros-Ghali.

the Government of the Republic of Croatia and the Croatian Serbs. As part of this process, the Co-Chairmen of the Steering Committee and negotiators of the International Conference on the Former Yugoslavia have maintained constant contacts with the leadership in Zagreb and in Knin. Efforts for the normalization of relations between the Governments of the Federal Republic of Yugoslavia (Serbia and Montenegro) and the Republic of Croatia were also part of this process. It will be recalled, in this connection, that the Belgrade Joint Communiqué of 11 September 1992 by Presidents Cosic and Tudjman, which were negotiated under the auspices of the Co-Chairmen, helped defuse trouble spots at places such as the Prevlaka peninsula and the Peruca dam and provided a framework for future cooperation. The Co-Chairmen have also been instrumental in arranging meetings between Presidents Milosevic and Tudjman, and between the Foreign Ministers of the Federal Republic of Yugoslavia (Serbia and Montenegro) and the Republic of Croatia.

2. The Ceasefire Agreement of 29 March 1994, negotiated under the auspices of the International Conference on the Former Yugoslavia, with the participation of the Ambassadors of the United States of America and of the Russian Federation in Zagreb, brought active hostilities between Croatian Government forces and Croatian Serb forces to an end. The ceasefire, which is still largely respected, has stopped the deaths and destruction that were commonplace before. Since the conclusion of the Ceasefire Agreement of 29 March 1994, the Co-Chairmen and negotiators of the International Conference on the Former Yugoslavia, in close consultations with the leadership in Zagreb, Knin and Belgrade, have sought to develop confidence by encouraging and steering negotiations on practical issues of economic cooperation, while simultaneously keeping in mind the need for negotiated political solutions.

3. Negotiators of the International Conference on the Former Yugoslavia have had innumerable meetings in Zagreb, in Knin and elsewhere to advance agreements on water, power, the reopening of pipelines, highways and railways, the return of refugees and displaced persons and the payment of pensions. Based on the work done by negotiators of the International Conference on the Former Yugoslavia between March and October 1994, the Co-Chairmen assembled delegations from the Croatian Government and the Serb local authorities at Camp Pleso of the United Nations Protection Force (UNPROFOR) in Zagreb on 27 October to discuss drafts on these topics.

4. The Croatian Government delegation was headed by Mr. H. Sarinic. The delegation of the Serb local authorities was headed by Mr. B. Mikelic. The discussions were characterized by a businesslike and constructive attitude on the part of both delegations.

5. The outcome of the meeting was a consolidated draft Agreement on water, electricity, the oil pipeline, the Zagreb-Belgrade Highway and railways. There were some technical points that needed to be checked and each side agreed to meet in the following days with the International Conference on the Former Yugoslavia, and UNPROFOR representatives.

6. The Ambassadors of the Russian Federation and the United States of America in Zagreb were present at the talks and were briefed in bilateral meetings the Co-Chairmen had with each delegation just before their departure.

7. The Co-Chairmen held resumed discussions with the two delegations in Knin on Thursday, 3 November. The whole draft agreement was discussed and a substantial measure of agreement achieved on some parts. In preparation for a resumed session, a expert group on electricity-related issues met under the chairmanship of the International Conference on the Former Yugoslavia in Split on 7 November, and an expert group on oil-related issues met in Topusko on 11 November.

8. The Co-Chairmen met with the two delegations again on 15 November at UNPROFOR's Camp Pleso in Zagreb. The Co-Chairmen also had consultations with the Ambassadors of the Russian Federation and the United States in Zagreb, as well as with the Special Representative of the Secretary-General Mr. Yasushi Akashi. On 16 November, the Co-Chairmen, together with the Ambassadors of the Russian Federation and the United States and Ambassadors Ahrens and Eide of the International Conference on the Former Yugoslavia, saw President Tudjman and Mr. Sarinic. Ambassador Ahrens and Ambassador Eide travelled to Belgrade the same day for a meeting with Mr. Mikelic.

9. In the light of those discussions, a proposed Agreement on water, electricity, the oil pipelines, the Highway and railways was finalized and transmitted to the two sides with accompanying letters making it clear that the Co-Chairmen, together with the Ambassador of the Russian Federation, Mr. Kerestedzhiyants, and the Ambassador of the United States of America, Mr. Galbraith, were conducting themselves within the framework of the Vance plan and all relevant Security Council resolutions. The Croatian side accepted the document. The Croatian Serbs submitted it to their "Assembly", which met on Saturday, 19 November, but they asked for some further amendments which the Co-Chairmen judged as ruling out further negotiations at that juncture.

10. Following the Co-Chairmen's decision, President Milosevic met with the Croatian Serb leaders and this was followed by a number of contacts with the Co-Chairmen which were sufficiently encouraging for the Co-Chairmen to arrange to meet with President Tudjman in Zagreb in the morning of Friday, 25 November. The outcome of this meeting was a recasting of the proposed Agreement which the Co-Chairmen took immediately to Belgrade for discussion with

President Milosevic and Mr. Mikelic. The Co-Chairmen flew back to Zagreb and saw President Tudjman that evening. The Co-Chairmen then flew next morning to see Mr. Mikelic in Belgrade.

11. On the basis of those discussions, the Co-Chairmen submitted to the two delegations the text of a recast Agreement, together with accompanying letters to Mr. Sarinic and Mr. Mikelic.

12. The Agreement, as signed by the two delegations together with the Co-Chairmen, General Peeters of UNPROFOR and Ambassador Paul Joachim von Stülpnagel, Head of the European Monitoring Mission, and witnessed by Ambassador Galbraith and Ambassador Kersetedzhiyants, is contained in appendix I. The letters to Mr. Sarinic and Mr. Mikelic also appear in appendixes II and III.

APPENDIX I
AGREEMENT*

I. WATER

1. Subject of the Agreement:

1.1 The following water supply systems:

(a) Obrovac - Zadar - Benkovac - Kakma - Biograd - Filip Jakov;
(b) Cikola - Drnis;
(c) Medak - Gospic - Korenica;
(d) Petrinja - Sisak;
(e) Gacka - Vrhovine;
(f) Sumetlica - Pakrac - Lipik.

The Joint Commission will be examining other water-supply systems, using the same criteria for inclusion.

2. The systems mentioned in paragraph 1.1 shall be restored and opened for the unimpeded and regular supply of water within the optimal capacity of the existing systems.

---

* Signed on 2 December 1994 by H. Sarinic, D. Owen, P. Peeters, P. Galbraith, B. Mikelic, T. Stoltenberg, P.J. von Stülpnagel, and L. Kerestedzhiyants.

3. Requirements prior to the opening of the water supply systems mentioned in paragraph 1.1:

3.1 All technical information requested by UNPROFOR in order to make the above mentioned water supply systems operational shall be made available without delay. This will in particular include:

(a) Layout and technical specifications for installations, pipelines, power-lines and associated facilities;
(b) Information concerning assessments of damage;
(c) Assessments concerning repair work needed as well as requirements for such work;
(d) Information concerning requirements for de-mining of any installations connected to these water supply systems and their surrounding areas.

3.2 De-mining will be carried out where necessary.

3.3 Full security will be guaranteed for all installations, facilities and working teams involved during the period of restoration of the water supply systems as well as after the have been put into operation. Within the Zone of Separation UNPROFOR will, for the duration of its mandate, provide this security in accordance with the Ceasefire Agreement.

3.4 UNPROFOR or experts appointed by UNPROFOR, with the cooperation of the signatories to this agreement, will carry out inspections of all facilities and installations in order to assess damage, requirements for repair work and spare parts as well as the time required to make the water supply systems operational.

3.5 UNPROFOR and experts appointed by UNPROFOR shall be given full access to all facilities in order to carry out such inspections.

3.6 A timetable will be established by UNPROFOR after consultations for the repair work of each water supply system.

3.7 The repair work required will be commenced as soon as the results of the inspections of each supply system are available. Wherever such inspections have already been carried out repair work will commence immediately. UNPROFOR will supervise the repair work and assist where appropriate.

4. Requirements following the completion of repair work of the water supply systems:

4.1 The regular supply of water will commence immediately after the completion of work required at each supply system and when the Joint Commission has declared each system operational.

4.2 The methods and location for measuring the quantity and monitoring the quality of water shall be determined for each water system of the areas listed by the Joint Commission based on relevant technical considerations. The price of the water to the user will be agreed in the Joint Commission before the beginning of delivery of the water.

II. ELECTRICITY

1. Subject of the Agreement:

1.1 The high-tension transmission lines.
1.2 The generator poles of the Obrovac power plant.

2. The high-tension transmission lines.

2.1 The following high-tension transmission lines shall be opened for unimpeded and regular use:

  (a) The Mraclin - Brinje 220 kV transmission line;
  (b) The Gradiska - Meduric 110 kV transmission line;
  (c) The Obrovac - Zadar 110 kV transmission line;
  (d) The Meline - Obrovac - Konjsko 400 kV transmission line;
  (e) The Tumbri - Ernestinovo 400 kV transmission line;
  (f) The construction of a / new 400 kV transformer station / transmission facility on the 400 kV transmission line / at Ernestinovo.

3. Requirements prior to the restoration of the objects mentioned in paragraph 2.1:

3.1 International expert teams, where appropriate under the auspices of UNPROFOR, shall inspect all segments of the transmission lines that are subject to the Agreement.

3.2 These inspections shall assess the repair work and de-mining required for the unimpeded and regular use of the transmission lines.

3.3 The de-mining and repair of the transmission lines will commence as soon as the results of the inspection of each line are available, under the supervision and with the assistance of UNPROFOR and/or international experts where appropriate.

3.4 The transmission lines shall be opened as soon as they are declared operational by the Joint Commission.

4. *Requirements following the opening of the transmission lines:*

4.1 UNPROFOR and/or international experts shall have free access to the transmission lines and related facilities for the purpose of verifying and securing unimpeded and regular use.

5. *Joint Commission.*

5.1 The Joint Commission will discuss and agree on the terms of payment as well as where necessary other questions relating to the work required to make the objects mentioned in paragraph 2.1 operational and to secure their unimpeded and regular use.
5.2 The Joint Commission will discuss and agree on the opening of additional transmission lines.

6. *The generator poles of the Obrovac power plant.*

6.1 The generator poles for the Obrovac power plant, which have been repaired at the Koncar plant in Zagreb and are currently stored in Rijeka, shall be returned to the Obrovac power plant.

7. *Requirements prior to the return of the generator poles to the Obrovac power plant:*

7.1 The generator poles mentioned above shall be tested at the Koncar plant in the presence of international experts, to verify that they are in working order.

8. *Timing of the return of the generator poles:*

8.1 The generator poles shall be returned to the Obrovac power plant as soon as the Co-Chairmen of the ICFY declare that the highway is operating according to this agreement.

9. *Requirements following the return of the generator poles to the Obrovac power plant:*

9.1 The generator poles, once installed in the Obrovac power plant, shall be inspected by UNPROFOR and/or international experts prior to being put into operation.

III. THE HIGHWAY

1. Subject of the Agreement:

1.1 The Highway as it affects the UNPAs East and West.

2. Permissible traffic under the Agreement:

2.1 Only that permitted under the Ceasefire Agreement of 29 March 1994 within the UNPAs East and West.

3. Modalities of passages:

3.1 (a) All traffic under the Agreement will be granted free and safe passage. Vehicles may travel separately or together.

(b) In order to ensure free and safe passage through UNPAs Sectors West and/or East UNPROFOR will, within its mandate, monitor these parts of the highway. UNPROFOR may stop and inspect any vehicles and/or individuals, whenever it considers that such vehicles and/or individuals endanger the implementation of this Agreement. Local police shall be obliged to provide assistance whenever required by UNPROFOR in order to ensure the free and safe traffic through UNPAs Sector West and/or East.

(c) A bus service may be established between UNPAs Sectors West and East and may also be established along the other parts of the highway covered by this Agreement.

(d) UNPROFOR/ECMM will conduct unarmed patrols of the highway between UNPAs Sector West and East and between UNPAs Sector West and Zagreb in order to verify compliance with this Agreement.

(e) UNPROFOR/ECMM will in consultation with the relevant authorities establish procedures in order to provide assistance in case of accidents, break-down of vehicles, violations of traffic regulations, etc.

3.2 Until otherwise agreed, no road-toll will be charged inside the UNPAs from vehicles originated outside the UNPAs and outside the UNPAs from vehicles originating inside them.

IV. THE OIL PIPELINE

1. Subject of the Agreement:

1.1 The segment of the oil pipeline passing through UNPA Sectors North, West and East.

2. The pipeline shall be open for unrestricted and regular usage at this stage only through UNPA North.

3. Requirements prior to the opening of the pipeline:

3.1 An international expert team under the auspices of UNPROFOR or experts appointed by UNPROFOR shall be allowed to inspect the entire length of the segments subject to this Agreement.

3.2 This inspection will identify any repair work and any de-mining operations required in order to recommence the usage of the pipeline.

3.3 The requirements identified through the inspections mentioned above as well as any maintenance work required will be carried out without delay, under the supervision and with the assistance of UNPROFOR or experts or contractors appointed by UNPROFOR where appropriate. Free access will be given to all persons and equipment involved in carrying out this work.

3.4 A joint commercial company will be established as soon as possible to sell and distribute oil and oil products at market prices in the UNPAs. The pipeline through UNPA North will be opened as soon as this company is established and the Joint Commission has declared that the pipeline is operational. The other segment of the pipeline will be opened when circumstances permit.

V. FURTHER NEGOTIATIONS

1. Negotiations shall be continued immediately in order to reach agreement on the following topics:

1.1 The return of refugees and displaced persons;
1.2 Pensions;

1.3 The opening of the Zagreb - Okucani - Belgrade railway;
    The opening of the Zagreb - Knin - Split railway;
    The opening of the Zagreb - Knin - Split road.

2.   Negotiations will be continued as soon as possible on other topics on which there is a consensus to negotiate.

VI. PROVISIONS FOR IMPLEMENTATION

A. JOINT COMMISSION

1.   Subject of the Agreement:

1.1 A Joint Commission.

2.   The Joint Commission will be responsible for implementing all parts of this document as well as other and similar agreements which may be concluded as a follow-up to this document.

3.   Membership

3.1 Membership of the Joint Commission will be as follows: Two Co-Chairmen of the Joint Commission appointed by the Co-Chairmen of the Steering Committee of the ICFY. One representative appointed by each of the signatories to this Agreement. One representative of UNPROFOR. Each member of the Joint Commission will be accompanied by one associate and may call on other experts to attend the meetings.

4.   Decision-making

4.1 Any disputes or breach of the provisions of this Agreement as well as any other matter that requires further clarification or deliberation shall be brought to the attention and resolution by the Joint Commission. Should any dispute or breach of the provisions of this Agreement occur no retaliation or unilateral action shall take place. In cases where agreement cannot be reached by consensus, the Co-Chairmen of the Joint Commission will try to arbitrate. In the event that their proposal is not acceptable an appeal can be made to the Co-Chairmen of the Steering Committee of the ICFY, whose arbitration shall be final.

B. IMPLEMENTATION

The implementation of this Agreement shall start immediately upon its signing and shall be completed within one month wherever feasible, while the implementation of all other items shall start within the same period.

*Accompanying Letter Addressed to Mr Sarinic**

2 December 1994

Dear Mr Sarinic, We are writing to you about how UNPROFOR will conduct itself under the Agreement.

Whenever it is foreseen in this Agreement that UNPROFOR is to carry out certain tasks, it is understood that UNPROFOR is requested by all concerned to carry out those tasks to the best of its abilities and within its available resources and mandate, and that all concerned will extend their utmost cooperation to UNPROFOR in carrying out such tasks.

In UNPA West there will be no checkpoints on the highway. Instead there will be joint patrolling of the highway by UNPROFOR vehicles accompanied by one person from your police.

If it is decided to establish a bus service between UNPAs Sector West and East or along other parts of the highway covered by this agreement UNPROFOR/ECMM will be present on these buses, if requested.

*Accompanying Letter Addressed to Mr Mikelic**

2 December 1994

Dear Mr Mikelic, We are writing to you about how UNPROFOR will conduct itself under the Agreement.

Whenever it is foreseen in this Agreement that UNPROFOR is to carry out certain tasks, it is understood that UNPROFOR is requested by all concerned to carry out those tasks to the best of its abilities and within its available resources

---

* Signed by D. Owen, T. Stoltenberg, and P. Peeters; and as witnesses by P. Galbraith and L. Kerestedzhiyants.
* Signed by D. Owen, T. Stoltenberg, and P. Peeters; and as witnesses by P. Galbraith and L. Kerestedzhiyants.

and mandate, and that all concerned will extend their utmost cooperation to UNPROFOR in carrying out such tasks.

In UNPA West there will be no checkpoints on the highway. Instead there will be joint patrolling of the highway by UNPROFOR vehicles accompanied by one person from your police.

UNPROFOR is not permitted at this stage to let goods pass through the UNPAs originating from, or destined to, the territory of the FRY (Serbia and Montenegro) or territory controlled by the Bosnian Serbs and therefore at the two checkpoints within UNPA East your police will be asked to provide assistance and to work alongside UNPROFOR. Control will however have to be exercised by UNPROFOR in order to ensure compliance with this Agreement.

If you decide to establish a bus service between UNPAs Sector West and East or along other parts of the highway covered by this agreement UNPROFOR/ECMM will be present on these buses, if requested.

138. LETTER DATED 29 DECEMBER 1994 FROM THE SECRETARY-GENERAL ADDRESSED TO THE PRESIDENT OF THE SECURITY COUNCIL[*]

I have the honour to convey the attached biannual report addressed to me on 22 December 1994 by the Co-Chairmen of the Steering Committee of the International Conference on the Former Yugoslavia (see annex).

I should be grateful if you would bring this information to the attention of the members of the Security Council.

Annex
Biannual Report of the Co-Chairmen of the Steering Committee on the Activities of the International Conference on the Former Yugoslavia

INTRODUCTION

1. The International Conference on the Former Yugoslavia (ICFY) was established in August 1992 to remain in being until a final settlement of the problems of the former Yugoslavia has been achieved. Its seat is at the United Nations Office in Geneva. The Co-Chairmen of the Conference are the Secretary-General of the United Nations and the Head of State/Government of the Presidency of the European Union. The activities of the Conference are supervised by a

---

[*] UN Doc. S/1994/1454, 29 December 1994. Signed by Boutros Boutros-Ghali.

Committee co-chaired by representatives of the Secretary-General of the United Nations and the Presidency of the European Union. The current Chairmen of the Steering Committee are Lord Owen and Mr. Thorvald Stoltenberg. The day-to-day activities of the Conference are carried out by the Co-Chairmen of the Steering Committee and in working groups and task forces.

2. Since its establishment, the ICFY has provided a forum for discussion and negotiation, usually directly between the parties in conflict or in disagreement, throughout the former Yugoslavia. The ICFY helped to negotiate a new Cease-fire Agreement in Croatia on 29 March 1994 and successive blueprints for peace in Bosnia and Herzegovina; recommended the preventive deployment of the United Nations Protection Force (UNPROFOR) in the former Yugoslav Republic of Macedonia; negotiated joint understandings between the Governments of the Republic of Croatia and the Federal Republic of Yugoslavia (Serbia and Montenegro); provided a framework for addressing humanitarian issues; negotiated confidence-building measures, negotiated a draft treaty on succession issues; defused tensions involving ethnic and national communities and minorities; and sponsored efforts looking towards reconstruction and economic development in the area. In the six-month period covered by the present report, the ICFY has:

(a) Negotiated an Economic Agreement between the Government of the Republic of Croatia and the Serb local authorities, which was signed on 2 December 1994. Pursuant to that Agreement, the Zagreb-Belgrade international highway was reopened on 21 December 1994;

(b) Worked, with representatives of the Russian Federation and the United States of America, on a draft agreement, looking towards political solutions in the Republic of Croatia;

(c) Worked closely with the Contact Group of five nations for Bosnia and Herzegovina and helped to develop the map and constitutional arrangements;

(d) Established and operated the ICFY Mission to the Federal Republic of Yugoslavia (Serbia and Montenegro), regarding the provision of only humanitarian goods to territory controlled by Bosnian Serbs;

(e) Provided a framework for dealing with humanitarian problems in the Working Group chaired by the United Nations High Commissioner for Refugees, Mrs Sakado Ogata;

(f) Initiated and worked to ensure a population census in the former Yugoslav Republic of Macedonia, which was needed as a basis for discussions among the various population groups. The ICFY has also contributed to defusing tensions in the country in the run-up to and during elections held in October;

(g) Negotiated a draft treaty on succession issues;

(h) Exercised its good offices to promote mutual recognition among successor States in the former Yugoslavia;

(i) Brought together the Foreign Ministers of the Republic of Croatia and the Federal Republic of Yugoslavia (Serbia and Montenegro) for what is hoped will be regular meetings in their respective capitals.

Information on these and other activities on the Conference from July to December 1994 is provided below.

II. STEERING COMMITTEE

3. Meetings of the Steering Committee of the Conference were held on 6 July, 1 August and 5 October. Issues discussed included: reports by the Co-Chairmen and the Chairpersons of Working Groups; review of developments; humanitarian issues and budgetary matters. Pursuant to a decision adopted by the Steering Committee on 5 October, a budget for the six-month period 1 December 1994 to 31 May 1995 was worked out and assessments sent to members of the Steering Committee. The next meeting of the Steering Committee will be held in January 1995.

III. CROATIA

4. One of the priorities of the International Conference on the Former Yugoslavia since its establishment has been the promotion of better relations between the Government of the Republic of Croatia and the Croatian Serbs. As part of this process, the Co-Chairmen of the Steering Committee and negotiators of the International Conference on the Former Yugoslavia have maintained constant contacts with the leadership in Zagreb and in Knin. The Ceasefire Agreement of 29 March 1994, negotiated under the auspices of the International Conference on the Former Yugoslavia, brought intermittent hostilities between Croatian Government forces and Croatian Serb forces to an end. The ceasefire, which is still largely respected, has reduced the number of violations, deaths and destructions. Since the conclusion of the Ceasefire Agreement of 29 March 1994, the Co-Chairmen and ICFY negotiators, in close consultations with the leadership in Zagreb, Knin and Belgrade, have sought to develop confidence by encouraging and steering negotiations on practical issues of economic cooperation, while simultaneously keeping in mind the need for negotiated political solutions.

5. During a meeting organized by ICFY negotiators on 5 August, agreement was reached to continue the process of negotiations within the framework of a general normalization of relations and on the establishment of expert groups to prepare the following themes for negotiations:

(a) Humanitarian question (missing persons and displaced persons);
(b) The re-opening of the Zagreb-Belgrade highway;
(c) The provision of water supplies;
(d) The solution of pension and savings rights;
(e) The solution of questions relating to the restoration of hydro-electric power systems;
(f) The solution of questions relating to the Adriatic oil pipeline;
(g) The solution of question relating to transportation (by rail, road and air);
(h) The solution of question relating to trade.

6. On 2 December 1994, an Agreement was concluded between the Government of Croatia and the Serb local authorities dealing with water, electricity, the highway and the oil pipeline, and providing for further negotiations on the return of refugees and displaced persons, pensions the opening of other railways and roads. The text of the Agreement appears in appendix I to the report submitted to the Security Council on 2 December 1993 (S/1994/1375, annex).

7. The Co-Chairmen and ICFY negotiators have deployed intensive and sustained efforts for the implementation of the Agreement. A complication during this process was the danger of a resumption of hostilities in Croatia. This danger had been acute since mid-summer 1994 when fighting broke out in the Bihac pocket. It intensified in November and December in and around the area of Bihac as not only were Croatian Serb forces supporting Bosnian Serb forces, but a significant number of regular Croatian Army forces were engaged in active hostilities in Bosnia and Herzegovina. The Co-Chairmen's efforts to keep the implementation of the Economic Agreement on track played a crucial role in preventing the resurgence of conflict and in keeping the parties on the path of peaceful cooperation. Pursuant to the Agreement, on 21 December, at 1400 hours. UNPROFOR opened the highway for unhindered safe passages, removed its barriers and commenced regular patrol. A United Nations Civilian Police (UNCIVPOL) Highway Patrol Command has been established, comprising 150 UNCIVPOL monitors who will patrol and monitor the highway, initially during daylight hours, then 24 hours a day, seven days a week.

8. The Co-Chairmen and two ICFY negotiators, with the Ambassadors of the Russian Federation and the United States of America to Croatia (commonly called the Z-4), have continued to promote discussion of ideas for a political

settlement to the conflict in Croatia, A draft document is in an advanced stage of preparation.

9. The Co-Chairmen have also been active on other aspects of the situation in the former Yugoslavia that have a bearing on the situation in the United Nations Protected and related Areas. The Co-Chairmen have used their good offices to promote mutual recognition among succession States in the former Yugoslavia. The Co-Chairmen have also used their good offices to arrange meetings between the Foreign Ministers of the Federal Republic of Yugoslavia (Serbia and Montenegro) and of Croatia. The first public meeting took place in Zagreb on 4 November. The next meeting is due to be held in Belgrade, with meetings thereafter alternating between their capitals.

IV. BOSNIA AND HERZEGOVINA

10. The conflict in Bosnia and Herzegovina is regrettably now in its third year. Successive blueprints for peace have been drawn up with the parties and then subsequently repudiated by one side or the other: the Carrington-Cutileiro Plan of March 1992; in the framework of the ICFY, the Vance-Owen Plan of May 1993; the "HMS INVINCIBLE" package of September 1993; the European Union Action Plan of October 1993. On 18 and 19 January 1994, the parties to the conflict met together in the same room in Geneva for talks held under the auspices of the Co-Chairmen of the Steering Committee of the ICFY. The Bosnian Serbs put forward a map, as part of the union of three republics, for a predominantly Bosniac republic covering 33.5 per cent of the country, and they also agreed that a predominantly Croat Republic should cover 17.5 per cent. However, disagreement persisted on 1 to 2 per cent of the territory, and the Bosnian Serbs were reluctant to accept in advantage of a final agreement the demilitarization of Sarajevo and its surroundings, which represented some 3.2 per cent on the map and which the parties had agreed should be administered by the United Nations. It may be mentioned, in this connection, that one aspect of the package then under discussion, namely, European Union administration of Mostar, was realized with the signing of an Agreement on 10 June 1994, and with the installation of the European Union Administrator, Mr. Hans Koschnik.

11. On 6 February, the Bosnian Serbs informed the Co-Chairmen that they would now accept negotiations on the demilitarization of Sarajevo and its administration by the United Nations. Tragically, a mortar bomb had exploded on the previous day in the marketplace in Sarajevo. This was followed by the introduction of a heavy-weapons exclusion zone in Sarajevo. With the involvement of the North Atlantic Treaty Organisation (NATO) and the redeployment of a Russian

UNPROFOR contingent from Sector East to Sarajevo, it became necessary for the Governments of France, Germany, the Russian Federation, the United Kingdom of Great Britain and Northern Ireland and the United States of America to become more deeply involved in the peace process. The United States took the lead in establishing the Bosnia-Croat Federation (see S/1994/255, attachment I) and of a Confederation between Croatia and the Federation. The signing of the Washington Agreement took place on 1 March 1994. Meanwhile, a Contact Group had been established involving, at ministerial level, the Foreign Ministers of the Russian Federation, the United States, the United Kingdom, France, Germany and Greece, as a member of the European Union troika, the European Union Commissioner for Foreign Affairs and the two Co-Chairmen. The Contact Group has been guided in its work by the resolutions of the Security Council, by declaration adopted by Foreign Ministers of the Contact Group countries and by the provisions of the European Union Action Plan, and has built on the previous negotiations of the ICFY. The Conference is represented on the Contact Group at ambassadorial level by its legal adviser and an assistant to the Co-Chairmen.

12. The Contact Group drew up a map for the allocation of territory between the Bosnia-Croat Federation and the Bosnian Serb entity and submitted it to the two sides on 6 July. The map allocated 51 per cent to the Bosnia-Croat Federation and 49 per cent to the Bosnian Serb entity. The Contact Group at ministerial level reinforced by the support of the Security Council and the Council of Ministers of the European Union, as well as by Governments and organizations worldwide, informed the parties could agree between themselves on any changes. The Bosnia-Croat Federation accepted the proposed map as did Croatia. The Bosnian Serb leadership rejected the map, but, as with the Vance-Owen Plan in May 1993, the leaders of the Federal Republic of Yugoslavia (Serbia and Montenegro) urged the Bosnian Serb leadership to accept the Contact Group map.

13. The Co-Chairmen of the Steering Committee of the Conference have done their utmost to support the efforts of the Contact Group to bring about acceptance. At the request of the Secretary-General, the United Nations Co-Chairmen of the Steering Committee, Mr. Stoltenberg, visited Belgrade and Pale from 12 to 14 August, He discussed with President Slobodan Milosevic the implementation of the measures announced by the Federal Republic of Yugoslavia (Serbia and Montenegro) on 4 August 1994 for the closure of the border towards the Bosnian Serbs and their verification.

14. Lord Owen and Mr. Stoltenberg followed up by visiting Belgrade, Podgorica and Zagreb from 4 to 6 September 1994. They were determined not to miss the opportunity, as had been done in May 1994, to help the Government of

the Federal Republic of Yugoslavia (Serbia and Montenegro) to take action to persuade the Bosnian Serb leadership to accept the Contact Group plan so that the peace process could go forward. The Co-Chairmen managed to negotiate the establishment of an ICFY Mission to the Federal Republic of Yugoslavia (Serbia and Montenegro) to assist in the implementation of the decision taken on 4 August 1994 by the Government of the Federal Republic of Yugoslavia (Serbia and Montenegro), namely:

"As of today the border of the Federal Republic of Yugoslavia is closed for all transport towards the Republika Srpska, except food, clothing and medicine."

Reference is made in this regard to the reports on the establishment and operations of the Mission submitted to the Security Council (see S/1994/1074, S/1994/1124, S/1994/1246 and S/1994/1372).

15. The Co-Chairmen continue to work closely with the Contact Group and with other Governments and leaders whose influence could help the Bosnian Parties to terminate their conflict and to achieve a negotiated political settlement. In that regard, the Co-Chairmen have attended meetings of the Security Council and the European Foreign Affairs Council. They also keep close touch with UNPROFOR and with the Special Representative of the Secretary-General, Mr. Yasushi Akashi.

V. HUMANITARIAN ISSUES

16. The Humanitarian Issues Working Group, chaired by Mrs. Ogata, has continued to serve as a framework for the review and response of humanitarian needs in the former Yugoslavia. The Working Group has proved to be a useful forum where the different parties to the conflict and other Governments and international organizations meet, on a periodic basis, to highlight the humanitarian dimension of the problem and better channel international relief efforts. Since the previous biannual report, the Group has met in Geneva five times.

17. On 7 July 1994, the United Nations High Commissioner for Refugees convened a meeting of the Working Group. Since prospects for the return of Bosnian refugees and displaced persons had gained prominence in those months, that meeting was devoted primarily to discussing voluntary repatriation as well as the difficult funding situation. On that occasion, the Office of the United Nations High Commissioner for Refugees (UNHCR) submitted a note on assistance in voluntary repatriation to Bosnia and Herzegovina. It was generally felt that the time had come to begin planning for return. It was decided that an expert meeting on return would be convened by the end of August to study the issue

further.

18. The expert meeting on repatriation was held in Geneva on 18 August. A paper on the establishment on an information system for potential returnees was presented. It suggested that the information system should include up-to-date data on issues such as the security situation, the legal situation, immovable property and accommodation, services, economic opportunities and entitlements for return. UNHCR also submitted for comment a survey of information relating to voluntary repatriation to Bosnia and Herzegovina. There was consensus on the need for a cautious approach concerning voluntary repatriation. It was concluded that a second meeting would be convened at a later stage depending on the political and military developments on the ground.

19. As the situation in Bosnia and Herzegovina has significantly deteriorated over the last few months, the difficulties involved in carrying out the relief work have increased. The freedom of movement of both UNPROFOR and of UNHCR convoys has been severely restricted by the Serb authorities in Bosnia. The airlift operation has also been jeopardized by numerous suspensions when the necessary security guarantees could not be obtained. This suspensions, together with different forms of bureaucratic harassment delaying land convoys to Sarajevo, has impeded the provision of adequate assistance to the city.

20. UNHCR has re-emphasized the imperative need to have an open access route at all times to Sarajevo. Since the last biannual report only an unacceptable low number of convoys have been able to reach the Bihac enclave because of access restrictions by Croatian Serb authorities. UNHCR has recently been obliged to take the decision that it can no longer continue to assist the territories controlled by the Croatian Serbs as long as convoys are not allowed to proceed regularly to the Bihac enclave. Since then, only a few UNHCR convoys have been able to enter the enclave after significant difficulties and protracted negotiations.

21. With regard to the situation in the eastern enclaves, lack of access and developments in the security circumstances have resulted in a situation in which normal deliveries, which should be about 1,700 metric tons of load, were 30 per cent shorter in October and almost 50 per cent shorter in November. However, in the last few weeks access problems have eased somewhat.

22. On a more positive note, the situation in the Federal areas is less acute as a result of the increasing resumption of commercial traffic and a good harvest following successful distribution of the UNHCR seed programme earlier in the year. This has led to very significant price reductions for a number of important basic goods.

23. However, human rights abuses against minority groups in Bosnian Serb-held areas remain pervasive. More than 3,300 people, the great majority Muslim,

have been forced to leave to Banja Luka since July, Some 6,000 have also been expelled from Bijeljina and Janja and forced across the frontline into Tuzla. Draft-age males continue to be separated from their families and sent to perform work obligations, often on the front line. Human rights atrocities and violations of humanitarian law continue to be perpetrated.

24. As these gloomy developments took place, the United Nations Revised Consolidated Inter-Agency Appeal for $ 721 million was launched to cover humanitarian operation needs for 2.2 million people from January to June 1995. Then, on 25 November, the Chairperson of the Humanitarian Working Group, Mrs. Ogata, gave an update on the present situation, focusing on issues such as new displacements of civilians, the need for the continuation of temporary protection, the overall deterioration of the security situation and the need to continue funding United Nations humanitarian assistance in the republics of the former Yugoslavia. On that occasion, in a reference to her 18 March 1994 statement that "there is light at the end of the tunnel", Mrs. Ogata said, less optimistically, that "if there was light at the end of the tunnel, it is now extremely faint". She concluded:

> "While the victims wait for a lasting peace that cannot come to soon, we must all continue to alleviate their human suffering. The humanitarian space is shrinking. With your active support we can and will keep it open."

VI. ETHNIC AND NATIONAL COMMUNITIES AND MINORITIES

A. The Former Yugoslav Republic of Macedonia

25. The Co-Chairmen remain concerned about the general economic and political situation in the former Yugoslav Republic of Macedonia. The Preventive deployment recommended to the Secretary-General of the United Nations by the Co-Chairmen of the Conference in 1992 has played an important part. Mr. Cyrus Vance continues with his mediation efforts in relation to the Governments of Greece and the former Yugoslav Republic of Macedonia. The Co-Chairmen believe, however, that there is a need for more economic preventive action.

Census

26. Following the independence of the former Yugoslav Republic of Macedonia, the lack of a generally accepted source of information on the ethnic composition of its population, and its size, soon indicated the need for a new census of population and housing. This was recognized at an early stage by the ICFY and its

Working Group on Ethnic and National Communities and Minorities, which, in September 1992, took the issue as one of its major priorities and undertakings in the country. The national authorities, and the representatives of Albanian and other nationalities, were in favour of a new census being conducted, provided adequate financial assistance and international observation would be made available.

27. Originally initiated by the ICFY, this project was backed by the Council of Europe, which set up and international group of experts to assist the former Yugoslav Republic of Macedonia's statistical office in the preparation of a draft census act as well as the census and the field work itself. The European Union, through Eurostat, and the United Nations, through the Economic Commission for Europe, were associated in the work of the group from the outset. The European Union, through its Programme of Assistance for Economic Restructuring in the Countries of Central and Eastern Europe (PHARE), and the Council of Europe, through contributions to a special account opened for the purpose, helped to cover the costs of the operation (local, observation and continued assistance by the experts). Nineteen countries participated in the observation network. The Conference was present in all the meetings of the expert group and led, on the eve of the census, a delegation that visited all the difficult municipalities (15 altogether). In sometimes very difficult meetings, doubts about the fairness of the census, particularly by ethnic Albanians, were dispelled through arrangements with the Government reached at the highest level.

28. Begun on 21 June, the census was declared completed on 11 July. As provided under the terms of the Memorandum of Understanding signed by the financing organization and the President of the State Census Commission, a network of 40 observers from 19 European countries followed the preparation of the census and the field work, including the aggregation of the first results and post-enumeration check. The observers operated in all 34 municipalities and were present in 669 enumeration districts (almost 10 per cent of all districts) and 2,282 households. Of the latter, 1,264 (55,4 per cent) were Macedonian, 608 (26,6 per cent) Albanian and 410 (18 per cent) others. The observation was thus broadly based and largely representative of the country as a whole.

29. The general impression of the observers was that the overall results of the census were of acceptable reliability despite difficulties in some areas, particularly those with a large Albanian population, poor quality maps and some confusion on the citizenship question.

30. The pressure on the observation teams appear to have had a positive influence on the operation in general and to have helped to increase confidence on the part of the population at large.

Elections

31. In early October 1994, the leadership of the biggest Albanian party in the former Yugoslav Republic of Macedonia. the Party for Democratic Prosperity (PDP), threatened to boycott the elections scheduled for 16 and 30 October on the grounds that, in their view, 145,000 Albanians would not be allowed to participate in the elections as they did not appear on the electorial lists. During the weeks prior to the elections, the Working Group had several contacts with the Government and with Albanian representatives to try to overcome those difficulties. The electorial lists were improved by the Government and all the nationalities participated in the elections, which were judged by the observers of the Conference on Security and Cooperation in Europe (CSCE) to have been free and fair. However, it was acknowledged that some administrative irregularities had taken place.

32. The second round of parliamentary elections was boycotted by the ethnic Macedonian opposition parties, however. As a consequence, the ruling three-party Alliance for Macedonia, which in the past had formed a coalition Government with the ethnic Albanian PDP, secured an overwhelming majority of seats in the new parliament. Technically, therefore, it did not need a coalition partner to form a new Government. However, as the absence of minority representation in the Government could endanger the constructive approach in inter-ethnic relations in the former Yugoslav Republic of Macedonia, the Working Group held talks in Skopje from 16 to 19 November with the President of the Republic and with representatives of the Alliance, as well as with the leaders of the Albanian Groups represented in the new Parliament. The Co-Chairmen and ICFY negotiators strongly encouraged all their interlocutors to have Macedonian Albanian representation in the Government. On 16 December, the announcement of the new Government included four Macedonian Albanians. Three were appointed to the Ministries of Development, Labour and Social Policy, and Culture; one was appointed Minister Without Portfolio.

Pedagogical Academy

33. In April 1994, the Government committed itself to providing, at the University of Skopje, a programme to train teachers to teach subjects in the Albanian language at secondary level starting with the school year 1994/95. Over recent months ICFY representatives intervened repeatedly, including at the highest levels of the Government and of the University, and obtained assurances that the training programme would begin soon. The Co-Chairmen visited Skopje for

discussions with President Kiro Gligorov and Foreign Minister Stevo Crvenkovski on 18 December. President Gligorov informed them that the Government had already taken the decision to establish a Pedagogical Academy for Albanian courses within the University of Skopje. It would offer four-year courses. An announcement would be made the following week on the hiring of professors for the Academy. The President said that the Government would welcome international assistance for the development of the Academy. The Co-Chairmen undertook to raise the matter with the European Union and the United Nations Educational, Scientific and Cultural Organization (UNESCO) and to do whatever they could to generate international assistance.

Television

34. In September 1994, the Director General of Radio and Television informed ICFY negotiators that by the end of the year television broadcasts in the languages of the nationalities would be increased substantially from one to three hours per day in Albanian, from one to two hours per day in Turkish, from half an hour to one hour in Serbian, Roma and Vlach. There is, however, a need to expand the corresponding producing facilities for which external financial support is required. During their discussions with President Gligorov on 18 December, he informed the Co-Chairmen that the Government was endeavouring to provide more time on radio and television for programmes in the Albanian language. A new head of television of the former Yugoslav Republic of Macedonia had recently been appointed and he had already been in contact with representatives of the Albanian community. The Government needed resources to update its technical equipment as well as to develop additional programmes in the Albanian language. The Co-Chairmen said they would do whatever they could. With the assistance of an independent expert, a project to equip further studio space has been worked out and the Conference is now engaged in trying to find the necessary sponsoring from abroad to finance it.

B. Kosovo

35. The Co-Chairmen have kept the situation in Kosovo in the Federal Republic of Yugoslavia (Serbia and Montenegro) constantly in focus. They have discussed it frequently during their meetings with the leadership in Belgrade and have also met with the leadership of the Kosovar Albanians. During the period covered in the present report, meetings with Mr. Ibrahim Rugova took place in Oslo and Geneva.

36. The Co-Chairmen have sought to promote negotiated solutions within the framework of the Federal Republic of Yugoslavia (Serbia and Montenegro) and the principles of the International Conference. In that regard, they have endeavoured to bring about contacts between the Serbian leadership and the Kosovar Albanian leadership. The Co-Chairmen have advanced some ideas with them for such contacts and are awaiting a response from the Kosovar Albanian leadership in order to take the next steps. The Co-Chairmen will persist in their endeavours to promote peaceful and negotiated solutions.

VII. SUCCESSION ISSUES

37. The Succession Issues Working Group of the Conference has continued its efforts. Meticulous and persistent work has brought the parties within reach of agreement on draft treaty provisions dealing with citizenship, pension, acquired rights, treaty succession and archives. On the division of assets and liabilities, however, divergences of view exist among the parties and it will most likely be necessary for the Co-Chairmen to put forward proposals on their disposition.

38. After a review of developments to date, the Co-Chairmen, together with the Chairman of the Working Group, Ambassador Alf Jonsson (Denmark), have decided to proceed as follows:

(a) The draft succession treaty has been case into two portions, which could constitute independent treaties or be parts of a single treaty, depending on future negotiations among the successor States;

(b) The first portion deals with citizenship, pensions, acquired rights, archives, treaty succession and arbitration mechanisms. It contains provisions that have been discussed in detail with the parties and on which there is a large measure of agreement. It was sent to the parties with a request for written comments in what is hoped will be a process of finalization of the draft treaty on this issues;

(c) The second portion deals with the disposition of assets and liabilities. Consultations are continuing on how they could be distributed among the successor republics. The Co-Chairmen will decide how to proceed with the second portion in the light of those consultations.

VIII. ECONOMIC ISSUES

39. During the period covered by the present biannual report, the Economic Working Group met once, on 12 and 13 July 1994.

40. The first item on the agenda for the meeting was a discussion on the economic impact of measures undertaken for refugees and displaced persons and measures to include them in the process of reconstruction. Each delegation (with the exception of Slovenia, which participated as an observer) outlined the measures currently being taken to provide for refugees and displaced persons. There was a discussion of the similarities, from an economic perspective, of the situation of a refugee and that of the long-term unemployed, as well as some recognition of the need for the integration of reconstruction plans with those for the reinsertion of refugees and displaced persons. A UNHCR official gave a presentation on the programmes supported by the High Commissioner to help returnees to help themselves.

41. The second point on the agenda covered reconstruction in Sarajevo and Mostar and focused on the presentation by a representative of the office of the United Nations Special Coordinator for Sarajevo, which emphasized the importance of good coordination for the success of reconstruction, not only among donors, but also on the ground between the relevant authorities. He outlined the organization of the agency for reconstruction being established by the Bosnian Government, as well as of Ambassador Eagleton's staff. There were a number of points of common interest between the reconstruction of Sarajevo and that of Mostar, notably in the field of infrastructure. The delegations argued for the need to involve local enterprises in providing material and expertise for reconstruction.

42. The Economic Working Group has not met since its meeting in July. The Chairman of the Working Group believes that an improvement in the political situation is necessary before further efforts are made.

IX. SANCTIONS

43. The Co-Chairmen and ICFY personnel have cooperated with international institutions monitoring the implementation of sanctions. In that regard, the Director of the ICFY secretariat has participated in meetings of the Sanctions Liaison Group held in Vienna. On these occasions he briefed the Group on the activities of the Conference in support of sanctions and provided detailed briefings on the efforts of the ICFY Mission to the Federal Republic of Yugoslavia (Serbia and Montenegro) regarding the provision on only humanitarian goods to territory controlled by Bosnian Serbs.

139. LETTER DATED 4 JANUARY 1995 FROM THE SECRETARY-GENERAL ADDRESSED TO THE PRESIDENT OF THE SECURITY COUNCIL*

I have the honour to transmit the attached report, which was addressed to me on 4 January 1995 by the Co-Chairmen of the Steering Committee of the International Conference on the Former Yugoslavia, concerning the operations of the International Conference's Mission to the Federal Republic of Yugoslavia (Serbia and Montenegro). This report by the Co-Chairmen contains the certification referred to in paragraph 3 of Security Council resolution 943 (1994).

I should be grateful if you would bring this information to the attention of the members of the Security Council.

Annex
Operations of the International Conference on the Former Yugoslavia Mission to the Federal Republic of Yugoslavia (Serbia and Montenegro) - Report of the Co-Chairmen of the Steering Committee -

I. INTRODUCTION

1. The present report is submitted pursuant to paragraph 3 of Security Council resolution 943 (1994) of 23 September 1994. In that resolution, the Security Council requested that the Secretary-General submit every 30 days for its review a report from the Co-Chairmen of the Steering Committee of the International Conference on the Former Yugoslavia on the border closure measures taken by the authorities of the Federal Republic of Yugoslavia (Serbia and Montenegro).

2. It will be recalled that, on 4 August 1994, the following measures were ordered by the Government of the Federal Republic of Yugoslavia (Serbia and Montenegro) to come into effect the same day:

"(a) To break off political and economic relations with the Republika Srpska;
(b) To prohibit the stay of the members of the leadership of the Republika Srpska (Parliament, Presidency and Government) in the territory of the Federal Republic of Yugoslavia;
(c) As of today the border of the Federal Republic of Yugoslavia is closed for all transport towards the Republika Srpska, except food, clothing and medicine."

3. On 19 September 1994, 3 October, 2 November and 5 December 1994, the Secretary-General transmitted to the Security Council reports from the Co-

---

* UN Doc. S/1995/6, 5 January 1995. Signed by Boutros Boutros-Ghali.

Chairmen of the Steering Committee of the International Conference on the Former Yugoslavia on the state of implementation of the above-mentioned measures (S/1994/1074 and S/1994/1124; S/1994/1246; S/1994/ 1372). The report dated 5 December 1994 contained the following certification from the Co-Chairmen:

> "In the light of the foregoing developments during the past 30 days, based on the Mission's on-site observation, on the advice of the Mission Coordinator, Mr. Bo Pellnäs, and in the absence of any contrary information from the air, whether the airborne reconnaissance system of the North Atlantic Treaty Organization (NATO), or national technical means, the Co-Chairmen conclude that the Government of the Federal Republic of Yugoslavia (Serbia and Montenegro) is continuing to meet its commitment to close the border between the Federal Republic of Yugoslavia (Serbia and Montenegro) and the areas of the Republic of Bosnia and Herzegovina under the control of the Bosnian Serb forces".

Developments in the past 30 days are dealt with below.

II. LEGISLATION/REGULATION ON THE BORDER CLOSURE

4. The legislation of the authorities of the Federal Republic of Yugoslavia (Serbia and Montenegro) closing the border with the Bosnian Serbs continues in force. It should be noted that the legislation adopted by the Federal Republic of Yugoslavia (Serbia and Montenegro) only closed the border "for all transport towards the Republika Srpska, except food, clothing and medicine". This point has been made in each of the four preceding reports submitted by the Co-Chairmen to the Security Council (S/1994/1074, para. 5; S/1994/1124, para.1; S/1994/1246, para. 2; S/1994/1372, para.2). The terms of reference of the Mission were reproduced in the report of 19 September 1994 (S/1994/1074, para. 15), where it is expressly stated that "the responsibility of controlling the crossings remains with your Government, members of the Mission will be enabled to work with representatives of the Yugoslav Red Cross at places from which any humanitarian assistance is organized or dispatched; to work alongside customs officers; to look into any vehicles crossing; and to have examined any item conveyed by individuals or vehicles across the border which they suspect might not be classified as purely humanitarian".

5. Keeping in mind the government legislation and the above-mentioned terms of reference, the Mission has concentrated on transport toward the "Republika Srpska", while paying attention to transit traffic. As was stated in the report of 3 October 1994 (S/1994/1124, para. 3), "as far as transit traffic to the Republic of Croatia is concerned, agreements have been made covering customs documentation and the sealing of load-carrying vehicles to reduce the obvious risk of a diversion of supplies to the Bosnian Serbs". This is further elaborated upon in

the report of 2 November (S/1994/1246, para. 26), the relevant parts of which were as follows:

> "The procedures for traffic transiting the territory held by the Bosnian Serbs into the territory held by Serbs in Croatia have now been firmly established. Transports are divided into two categories, one consisting of humanitarian aid... and the second being fuel ... The second category, fuel, is transported on 52 specially designated trucks escorted by police, transit into Croatia. The tachometers are sealed by the Mission when trucks leave Belgrade two or three times a week, and are removed by the Mission when the trucks return to the starting point. The first sets of recovered print-outs from the tachometers were sent to the United Kingdom on 1 November for analysis".

Analysis has shown that all the vehicles concerned kept to their authorized route. Nevertheless, the only check against them offloading oil at rest points was the accompanying police.

6. Some comments have been made about the relevance of Security Council resolution 820 (1993), and especially paragraph 12 thereof, to the activities of the Mission. On this point, the Co-Chairmen have based themselves on the following interpretation provided by their legal adviser:

> "Paragraph 12 of resolution 820 (1993) empowers the Government of the Republic of Croatia to control authorizations for imports to, exports from and transshipments through the United Nations Protected Areas (UNPAs) in the Republic of Croatia only for the purpose of ensuring that no goods prohibited in respect of the Federal Republic of Yugoslavia (Serbia and Montenegro) by that resolution or by resolutions 757 (1992) and 787 (1992) are imported to, exported from, or transshipped through those areas of the Republic of Co-Chairmen under the control of the Bosnian Serbs forces without proper authorization from the Government of Bosnia and Herzegovina".

7. Apart from the legal aspects of this matter, there is also a political aspect of vital importance. The closure by the Federal Republic of Yugoslavia (Serbia and Montenegro) of the border towards the Republika Srpska had the objective of persuading the Bosnian Serb leadership to accept the Contact Group plan for Bosnia and Herzegovina. That objective would surely have been defeated had the Government of the Federal Republic of Yugoslavia (Serbia and Montenegro) simultaneously pursued policies that could have thrown the Croatian Serbs into the arms of the Bosnian Serbs. It was precisely for those reasons that the Co-Chairmen intensified efforts for the conclusion of an economic agreement between the Croatian Government and the local Serb authorities which could enable the UNPAs to be supplied with oil from within the Republic of Croatia. In section IV of the agreement signed on 2 December 1994 by the Croatian Government and the local Serb authorities (see S/1994/1375, appendix I) it is provided that:

"A joint commercial company will be established as soon as possible to sell and distribute oil and oil products at market prices in the UNPAs. The pipeline through UNPA North will be opened as soon as this company is established and the Joint Commission has declared that the pipeline is operational. The other segment of the pipeline will be opened when circumstances permit."

8. With the establishment of a joint commercial oil company, the issue of oil transiting into the UNPAs will no longer arise. The Co-Chairmen shuttled between Zagreb and Belgrade between 15 and 18 December in an attempt to reach agreement on the oil company and the opening of the Zagreb-Belgrade highway. On Sunday, 18 December, in Belgrade, it appeared to the Co-Chairmen that the opening of the highway was again to be delayed. They therefore instructed the Coordinator of the Mission to stop all oil-transiting into the UNPAs. On Wednesday, 21 December, the highway was opened and the Co-Chairmen instructed that electricity supply materials necessary for the implementation of that part of the agreement relating to electricity and water should transit to Knin. On 23 December there were further negotiations in Belgrade over a joint commercial oil company. On 29 December, when the highway through the western UNPA was certified by the United Nations Protection Force (UNPROFOR) to be fully opened, the Co-Chairmen instructed that, following the previously agreed procedures (see para. 5 above), oil should be supplied only to the western UNPA. Since this supply was clearly linked to implementation of the 2 December agreement, UNPROFOR agreed to check the oil-carrying vehicles on entering and leaving the western UNPA. The Co-Chairmen also informed the Croatian Government on 2 January 1995 that the generating poles in Zagreb should be sent to the Obrovac power station. The Co-Chairmen continued negotiating on the joint commercial oil company in Knin, Zagreb and Belgrade between 2 and 4 January and will keep the Security Council informed on progress (see appendix).

III. ORGANIZATION, FINANCING AND WORK OF THE MISSION

9. As at 3 January 1995, 178 international Mission personnel were on duty with the Mission. The Mission personnel to date have come from Belgium, Canada, the Czech Republic, Denmark, Finland, France, Germany, Greece, Ireland, the Netherlands, Norway, Portugal, Russian Federation, Spain, Sweden, United Kingdom of Great Britain and Northern Ireland and United States of America.

IV. FREEDOM OF MOVEMENT OF THE MISSION

10. The Mission continues to enjoy freedom of movement within the Federal Republic of Yugoslavia (Serbia and Montenegro). The security situation for the Mission members did not cause concern as December ended. The Sector Commander, Sector Belgrade, did, however, receive a threatening call in December. The Mission Coordinator gave all information to the authorities and they took swift and forceful action.

V. COOPERATION OF THE AUTHORITIES OF THE FEDERAL REPUBLIC OF YUGOSLAVIA (SERBIA AND MONTENEGRO) WITH THE MISSION

11. In the assessment of the Mission Coordinator, the cooperation of the authorities of the Federal Republic of Yugoslavia (Serbia and Montenegro) continues to be very satisfactory.

VI. INFORMATION RECEIVED FROM NATIONAL AND OTHER SOURCES

12. The operating principle of the Mission is to base itself on its own observations and on information that it has verified. The Mission Coordinator has maintained a standing request to Governments possessing the technical capacity to provide it with information relevant to its mandate. The Coordinator has received some such information on which follow-up measures have been taken.
13. The information received has basically been of two kinds: that which describes events in terms so general that make it totally impossible to find out where and when the event allegedly took place, and detailed information stating both place and time. Almost all detailed information up until now has proved to be inaccurate since the Mission has had teams on a 24-hour basis on the crossings where incidents are said to have occurred. In some cases, violations allegedly took place before the Mission had members on a 24-hour basis at the actual spots. When it has thus been possible to check information received, it has turned out that it is mostly unfounded and this raises serious questions about the accuracy of the general kind of information.

VII. PROBLEMS ENCOUNTERED AND REPRESENTATIONS MADE TO THE AUTHORITIES

14. The Mission now covers 20 major crossings 24 hours a day. Some minor crossings are being sealed during night time, in a way that makes it virtually impossible to use them. The Mission now encounters very few substantial problems along the border. Its members, in many cases, are very tired because of the long period of hard work under often harsh conditions, but continue to carry out their tasks with keenness and high morals. The coverage of the border is now such that there is a good picture of what is going on. The Mission Coordinator finds the situation most satisfactory and reported that his latest proposals to the Federal Republic of Yugoslavia (Serbia and Montenegro) authorities have been fully accepted and forceful action was being taken by them, including by the military. The Mission Coordinator personally inspected border crossings over the three-day period, from 18 to 20 December 1994.

15. In the last report it was stated that sufficient measures to meet the Mission's demands had not yet been taken by the military authorities. At a meeting on 8 December with the Deputy Chief of the General Staff, General Kovacevic, the Mission Coordinator, was informed about actions taken by the Yugoslav Army. General Kovacevic claimed that the border battalions had been reinforced; the rules for division of responsibilities between the police, customs and the military had been clarified; and the cooperation between them reinforced. The Mission teams along the border confirmed a noticeable increase in military presence along the order as well as improved cooperation with the Mission.

16. On Friday, 16 December, the Mission Coordinator had a meeting with General Babic, Commander of the Second Yugoslav Army, and Admiral Zec, Commander Herceg Novi Military District. During this meeting, General Babic presented a map that indicated that 20 minor border crossings inside military border areas were to be permanently blocked. General Babic stated that the work was already being carried out. It was agreed that the Mission could seal a barrier that was to be erected across the road in the so-called Nudo Valley. Observations on the ground and talks between the Mission's Special Envoy in Podgorica and the Chef de Cabinet of president Bulatovic revealed that the barricades were not constructed as promised by General Babic. They could still be removed fairly quickly and were, as a matter of fact, not completely blocking the roads. At a further meeting with General Babic in Podgorica on 20 December, the Mission Coordinator raised this issue, and he once again assured the Mission Coordinator that all 20 crossings were to be thoroughly and permanently blocked. At 1900 hours on 21 December the Mission Coordinator received reports that confirmed

that all crossings in Sector Charlie had been effectively blocked. In fact the number of such physical barriers erected from where the border leaves the Drina river down to Herceg Novi is 32. The physical blocking of bypass roads and minor dirt-track roads has had a good effect. With only one exception, every reported effort by smugglers to bypass police or military checkpoints has failed. In the view of the Mission Coordinator, this was a major achievement since it literally made it impossible to take any cars or trucks across the Montenegrin border to Bosnia and Herzegovina except at seven checkpoint where Mission, customs and police personnel are present on a 24-hour basis. Any substantial support from the Yugoslav Army to the Bosnian Serbs across the Montenegrin border was thus made impossible.

17. The reports from the Mission members, as well as the observations of the Mission Coordinator, verify an intensified presence of the Yugoslav Army also along the Drina. The Mission Coordinator has been informed that 30 percent of the border troops along the borders with Hungary and Romania have been transferred to the Bosnian border, together with their equipment, such as cars and radios. The Mission Coordinator also understands that 1,500 additional security personnel have been hired in order to shut down smuggling operations aggressively in towns and cities and prevent goods from reaching the border. During the week from 17 to 24 December, according to government sources, not less than 30 tons of fuel were confiscated. In the view of the Mission Coordinator, the control of the Drina is effective and as a result the amount of confiscated fuel is reported to be substantial.

18. On 18 December, Mission members detected a smuggling operation across the bridge at Mali Zvornik, with cars passing the border repeatedly, after being filled up at a garage some 100 metres away from that crossing. Neither the police nor the customs took action in spite of demands from the Mission members. The Mission Coordinator brought this to the attention of the authorities in Belgrade and demanded action. In response, the authorities have closed down this operation, made arrests and banned the several vehicles involved from making any further crossings into Bosnia and Herzegovina while the border sanctions are in effect. The Mission Coordinator's demand was given a positive response and sufficient action now seems to be taken.

19. On some occasions, however, military patrols from the Yugoslav Army had been neglecting to take action against smugglers that have come across. The Mission Coordinator has asked the authorities to correct this shortcoming immediately.

20. At a meeting with the Federal Republic of Yugoslavia (Serbia and Montenegro) Director of Customs, Mr. Kertes, on 13 December, informed the Mission

Coordinator that a special command with special teams under his direct authority had been organized. These teams were tasked to patrol the entire border, controlling not only the border itself, but also all police customs and military personnel working along the border. Their first efforts were concentrated on Montenegro.

21. The Mission Coordinator reported that it was obvious that the customs authorities were trying hard to improve customs procedures. While there may still have been some shortcomings among individuals, the overall picture was satisfactory. The customs work had been especially good at Sremska Raca, Badovinci and in Belgrade. Nevertheless, during the week of 12 to 18 December, at a point some 8 kilometres south-east of Bratunac, a Mission foot patrol found four large pontoon boats in an area where the teams earlier had been advised not to go for "security reasons". There were no signs that the boats had been used. Two Bosnian Serb soldiers, however, were observed on the other side of the Drina. The Mission Coordinator demanded that the boats be taken away.

22. In the opinion of the Mission Coordinator customs procedures otherwise have improved lately by stricter control of buses passing the border. Although buses have been a concern to the Mission, so far the controls carried out have revealed only one attempt to smuggle fuel in extra tanks. The situation in Montenegro continues to be satisfactory with Mission personnel present 24 hours a day at all major crossings and with good cooperation from the authorities. The Mission members working with the trains passing through Bosnia and Herzegovina are satisfied with the cooperation given to them by the railway authorities. The sealing of trains un Uscica and in Priboj continues without any problems.

23. In the night of 31 December 1994 to 1 January 1995, 16 fuel tankers and 7 other trucks were seized by the military in the Nudo Valley, south of the Vilusi border crossing. This large-scale attempted smuggling operation seems to have been a calculated attempt to take advantage of an anticipated festive atmosphere at border crossings on New Year's Eve. It started by a bulldozer coming up to the 3-metre-high barrier from the Bosnian side. It was turned back by the military and did so without protests. After this the trucks started to come into the valley. The warrant officer in charge of the area called for reinforcements and positions were taken up by the military to prevent any efforts to free drivers and trucks. As at 3 January, the trucks had not yet been extricated from the valley, which would require drivers to reverse for 2 kilometres uphill on a very narrow mountain road, running on a shelf between the mountain side and a steep slope.

24. At the border crossing at Metaljka, trucks with coal, said to be humanitarian aid, started to cross the border on 16 December, despite protests from Mission personnel on the ground and also from the Sector Headquarters. The Mission Coordinator made representations to the authorities and has reason to believe

that this traffic has now been effectively stopped.

25. On the night of 26/27 December, 14 buses passed from Bosnia and Herzegovina into Serbia at Sremska Raca, carrying soldiers. In the darkness, it was not possible for the Mission personnel to see what sort of army badges - if any - were worn. Information received by the Mission Coordinator from reliable sources indicates that the soldiers were Croatian Serbs from UNPA Sector East returning after their tour of duty in UNPA Sector South. While transit into the Federal Republic of Yugoslavia (Serbia and Montenegro) does not come within the mandate of the Mission, the Mission Coordinator has written to the authorities in Belgrade informing them that any attempt to take soldiers back across the border would be a violation.

26. Lack of resources has been a major cause of concern. Insufficient four-wheel-drive cars, low standards of accommodation, long-lasting power cuts, difficult road communications between headquarters and teams on the ground and an inability to purchase generators for caravans has made life very hard for many members of the Mission. If the Security Council decides to continue with the Mission, then the Co-Chairmen will have to make expenditures for improving facilities. They wish to put on record their thanks for the dedication and unstinting efforts put in by all members of the Mission and in particular its Coordinator, Bo Pellnäs, who has asked to retire and will be replaced by Mr. Auno Juhani Nieminen of Finland on 15 January 1995.

27. With the new barriers in place on Montenegro and the increased surveillance and enforcement along the Drina, the Mission Coordinator believes that the authorities of the Federal Republic of Yugoslavia (Serbia and Montenegro) are meeting their commitment to close the border effectively. While some small-scale smuggling may be possible, the above measures have made it highly unlikely that any cars or trucks could cross the border, except at those places where the Mission maintains a 24-hour presence. It may still be possible for the local population to take small boats across the Drina at night, although the risk of being detected has increased substantially. The possibilities of bringing fuel or other goods down to the river most probably have anyhow ceased to exist. The authorities have made major efforts to meet our demands and the Mission Coordinator has emphasized that no information or reports about fuel passing the border in Montenegro have been received during the last five weeks.

28. The roads in part of the Mission area are now becoming increasingly dangerous. At places it will from time to time not be possible to pass through. Hard surface ice on the asphalt on steep slopes where the road turns sharply without fences has, unfortunately, caused accidents involving Mission personnel already, but with minor injuries only. The Mission Coordinator has authorized Sector

leaders to stop teams going to some border crossings when they judge weather conditions to be too dangerous. The Mission Coordinator reported on 31 December:

> "I am very satisfied with the efforts undertaken by the Federal Republic of Yugoslavia (Serbia and Montenegro) authorities during the last month. The most significant of those being the physical barriers on bypasses and small dirt track roads between the Drina and the Adriatic at 32 places, Those barriers, together with the already fallen snow, will make it very difficult to pass the border with any kind of vehicle, except on the official border crossings where the International Conference on the former Yugoslavia has a 24-hour presence.
>
> The reinforced surveillance of the Drina by the military border battalions is also efficient. The constant patrolling of the border by special combined teams (Federal Republic of Yugoslavia (Serbia and Montenegro) customs, police, military) has also improved the work of the 'normal' border teams at the official crossings. It is therefore my conclusion that the Federal Republic of Yugoslavia (Serbia and Montenegro) authorities are meeting their commitment to close the border effectively."

VIII. CERTIFICATION

29. In the light of the foregoing developments during the past 30 days, based on the Mission's on-site observation, on the advice of the Mission Coordinator, Mr. Bo Pellnäs, and in the absence of any contrary information from the air, whether the airborne reconnaissance system of NATO or national technical means, the Co-Chairmen conclude that the Government of the Federal Republic of Yugoslavia (Serbia and Montenegro) is continuing to meet its commitment to close the border between the Federal Republic of Yugoslavia (Serbia and Montenegro) and the areas of the Republic of Bosnia and Herzegovina under the control of the Bosnian Serb forces.

APPENDIX
TIMETABLE FOR THE IMPLEMENTATION OF THE ECONOMIC AGREEMENT OF 2 DECEMBER 1994

The Co-Chairmen of the Steering Committee of the International Conference on the Former Yugoslavia have agreed with Mr. Sarinic and Mr. Mikelic on the following implementation timetable for the agreement signed on 2 December 1994.

1. The Zagreb-Lipovac highway, which opened for daytime travel on 21 December 1994 will, as from Friday, 6 January 1995, 6 a.m., be permanently opened on a 24-hour basis.

2. From Thursday, 5 January 1995, the generator poles shall be tested at the Koncar factory in Zagreb in the presence of international experts to verify that they are in working order, and will be transported by road to the Obrovac Power plant on Monday 9 January.

3. Repair work on all damaged electricity and water facilities will process as quickly as possible according to a timetable to be agreed and monitored by the Joint Commission, the first phase of which should be operational by 24 February 1995.

4. Legal and commercial experts will conduct further negotiations on the statutes for a joint commercial oil company with a view to reaching early agreement.

5. UNPROFOR experts accompanied by two experts from Croatian Railways and two experts from the local authorities will immediately inspect the Zagreb-Okucani-Brod-Mirkovci railway line and report by Tuesday, 10 January 1995, on the schedule for the urgent repair of the line. The repair work will be conducted under UNPROFOR supervision and will draw on equipment and expertise that will be made available at no charge from Croatian Railways and the local authorities.

6. The same technical procedure as above will be followed with a view to drawing up a schedule for the opening of Zagreb-Knin-Split railway and the report will be made available as soon as possible.

7. The oil pipeline through UNPA Sector North will be inspected by UNPROFOR experts as soon as weather conditions permit, the problem being that demining is hazardous when snow is on the ground.

8. On 5 January 1995, the Joint Commission will meet in Split, chaired by Ambassador Eide and the United Nations Head of Civil Affairs, Mr. Moussali, on behalf of the Co-Chairmen of the Steering Committee. This meeting will deal with all aspects of implementation of the agreement signed on 2 December 1994.

9. On Wednesday, 11 January 1995, Co-Chairmen of the Steering Committee of the International Conference on the Former Yugoslavia will meet at the United Nations headquarters at Pleso Camp with Mr. Sarinic and Mr. Mikelic to continue negotiations.

140. LETTER DATED 3 FEBRUARY 1995 FROM THE SECRETARY-GENERAL ADDRESSED TO THE PRESIDENT OF THE SECURITY COUNCIL*

I have the honour to transmit the attached report, which was addressed to me on 2 February 1995 by the Co-Chairmen of the Steering Committee of the International Conference on the Former Yugoslavia, concerning the operations of the International Conference's Mission to the Federal Republic of Yugoslavia (Serbia and Montenegro). This report by the Co-Chairmen contains the certification referred to in paragraph 5 of Security Council resolution 970 of 12 January 1995.

I should be grateful if you would bring this information to the attention of the members of the Security Council.

Annex
Operations of the International Conference on the Former Yugoslavia Mission to the Federal Republic of Yugoslavia (Serbia and Montenegro) - Report of the Co-Chairmen of the Steering Committee -

I. INTRODUCTION

1. The present report is submitted pursuant to paragraph 5 of Security Council resolution 970 (1995) of 12 January 1995. In that resolution, the Council requested that the Secretary-General submit every 30 days for its review a report from the Co-Chairmen of the Steering Committee of the International Conference on the Former Yugoslavia on the border closure measures taken by the authorities of the Federal Republic of Yugoslavia (Serbia and Montenegro).

2. It will be recalled that, on 4 August 1994, the following measures were ordered by the Government of the Federal Republic of Yugoslavia (Serbia and Montenegro) to come into effect the same day:

"(a) To break off political and economic relations with the Republika Srpska;
(b) To prohibit the stay of the members of the leadership of the Republika Srpska (Parliament, Presidency and Government) in the territory of the Federal Republic of Yugoslavia;
(c) As of today the border of the Federal Republic of Yugoslavia is closed for all transport towards the Republika Srpska, except food, clothing and medicine."

---

* UN Doc. S/1995/104, 3 February 1995. Signed by Boutros Boutros-Ghali.

3. On 19 September 1994, 3 October, 2 November, 5 December 1994, and 5 January 1995, the Secretary-General transmitted to the Security Council reports from the Co-Chairmen of the Steering Committee of the International Conference on the Former Yugoslavia on the state of implementation of the above-mentioned measures (S/1994/1074 and S/1994/1124; S/1994/1246; S/1994/1372; S/1995/6). The report dated 5 January 1995 contained the following certification from the Co-Chairmen:

> "In the light of the foregoing developments during the past 30 days, based on the Mission's on-site observation, on the advice of the Mission Coordinator, Mr. Bo Pellnäs, and in the absence of any contrary information from the air, whether the airborne reconnaissance system of the North Atlantic Treaty Organization (NATO), or national technical means, the Co-Chairmen conclude that the Government of the Federal Republic of Yugoslavia (Serbia and Montenegro) is continuing to meet its commitment to close the border between the Federal Republic of Yugoslavia (Serbia and Montenegro) and the areas of the Republic of Bosnia and Herzegovina under the control of the Bosnian Serb forces".

Developments in the past 30 days are dealt with below.

II. Legislation/Regulation on the Border Closure

4. The legislation of the authorities of the Federal Republic of Yugoslavia (Serbia and Montenegro) closing the border with the Bosnian Serbs continues in force.

5. Sector Belgrade of the Mission has spent a great deal of time trying to perfect ways of preventing trade, disguised as aid, from crossing the border with Bosnia and Herzegovina. One way of doing this is the imposition of weight limits on products that were thought most likely to be traded, i.e., fruit from Bulgaria and Turkey, cooking oil and sweets. These impositions have been done with the full approval of the Yugoslav Red Cross and the Federal Customs Authorities. Further product lines are likely to have weight limits imposed in the coming weeks, all in an effort to reduce the profit element in the "donations". Also in an endeavour to prevent the possibility of smuggling, the Sector has requested that the Customs apply more vigorous searching and confiscation procedures at the checking areas. For the most part this has been implemented.

III. Organization, Financing and Work of the Mission

6. As of 1 February 1995, 188 international Mission personnel were on duty with the Mission. The Mission personnel to date have come from the following

countries: Belgium, Canada, Czech Republic, Denmark, Finland, France, Germany, Greece, Ireland, Italy, Netherlands, Norway, Portugal, Russian Federation, Spain, Sweden, United Kingdom of Great Britain and Northern Ireland and United States of America.

7. On 13 January 1995, Mr. Tauno Nieminen of Finland assumed the position of Coordinator. For operational and administrative reasons, effective 11 January 1995, a new Sector named Sector Bajina Basta was established by dividing sector Bravo into two operational areas. This new sector is responsible for the area from the boundary with Sector Alpha in the north to 1 kilometre north of the village of Raca, including 24-hour coverage of the Skelani and Kotroman border crossing-points and the railway stations in Uzice and Priboj. Sector Bravo retains operational responsibility for the remainder of the Sector Bravo areas of operations.

8. In many areas of Sectors Bravo and Charlie, roads are covered by snow, causing difficulties and hazardous driving conditions. With temperatures in some areas as low as 20 degrees Celsius below zero and sporadic power cuts, sometimes lasting up to 13 hours, living conditions inside the caravans at some of the border crossing-points have become extremely difficult. One team was forced to spend 72 hours at the Sastavci border crossing-point because of snow blocking the access road.

IV. Freedom of Movement of the Mission

10. The Mission continues to enjoy freedom of movement within the Federal Republic of Yugoslavia (Serbia and Montenegro). As opportunities have diminished for smugglers and those profiting from trading in humanitarian goods with the improved checking for contraband at the border, there is an attendant security problem to be dealt with. An increase in the verbal abuse and threats has been reported by teams in Sector Belgrade and brought to the attention of the authorities. The customs authorities are aware of the problem and of the possibility of the threats being translated into actions. They are seeking approval for some of their officers to carry arms. The Mission teams are often working in an emotionally charged atmosphere and have on occasions to deal with people who have been drinking.

V. Cooperation of the Authorities of the Federal Republic of Yugoslavia (Serbia and Montenegro) with the Mission

10. In the assessment of the Mission Coordinator, the cooperation of the authorities of the Federal Republic of Yugoslavia (Serbia and Montenegro) continues to be satisfactory. Customs work, although sometimes uneven, continue to improve at most of the border crossing-points.

VI. Information Received from National and Other Sources

11. The operating principle of the Mission is to base itself on its own observations and on information that it has verified. The Mission Coordinator has maintained a standing request to Governments possessing the technical capacity to provide it with information relevant to its mandate. The Coordinator has not received any such information since the last report.

VII. Problems Encountered and Representations Made to the Authorities

12. The Mission now covers 19 major crossings 24 hours a day. Mission patrols have noticed that the Yugoslav Army has continued active patrolling and all the routes to the Drina River have been covered. In sector Charlie, especially, snow drifts along the main roads have made driving conditions treacherous and most minor roads remain impassable.

13. The Mission has received an update on the smuggling attempts at the end of December in the Nudo Vally, where 16 tankers and 7 trucks were seized by the military. The incident is treated as a customs offence. All fuel has been transferred to Jugopetrol in Kotor. The confiscated cigarettes are held at the customs warehouse in Niksic. It is believed that the organizers are from the Trebinje and Bilenica area in the "Republika Srpska" and hence they could be difficult to find and prosecute. Drivers will be prosecuted for attempting to cross the border at a crossing-point not authorized for lorries.

14. At Mali Zvornik, there have been numerous incidents in which persons have attempted to cross into Bosnia on foot carrying fuel. This appears to have been an organized attempt to violate the embargo and has been prevented by the militia.

15. At Mali Zvornik, the Mission team noticed on 13 January that no further than 200 metres from the border control point preparations were going on for a large-scale smuggling operation. Some vehicles were refilling hidden tanks, with

approximately 80 to 100 litres of fuel per vehicle. When the local federal police were called, they, together with the authorities at the border control point, confiscated 500 litres of fuel and 1,250 litres of alcohol.

16. As the border crossing point at Badovinci, in particular, numerous carts and buses have been denied entry into the "Republika Srpska", mainly for carrying large quantities of beer or extra fuel. Customs at Scepan Polje, together with the special customs team, checked a Volkswagen pick-up vehicle. They found 4,600 packages of Partner filter cigarettes. The owners of the goods were charged and the cigarettes were taken away.

17. On 18 January, the Mission Coordinator, together with his Senior Political Adviser, met the Head of Customs, Mr. Kertes. The Mission Coordinator drew his attention to the requirements under Security Council 970 (1995), particularly emphasizing the content of paragraphs 3 and 5. Since 19 January, the import of goods from the "Republika Srpska Krajine" through the "Republika Srpska" has been totally stopped. Until then, trucks mainly loaded with timber and coals were crossing the border from Bosnia to Serbia.

18. The Mission Coordinator requested Mr. Kertes to take action in order to close down the ferry in Jamena. For some weeks, this ferry has been used by only a very few vehicles and persons crossing the river each day. Mr. Kertes agreed that the ferry should be closed down by dismantling the engine. For the last few days the ferry has not operated, but the motor-boat that has been used to push the ferry is still operational.

19. A Mission mobile patrol noticed on 17 January that on the Nudo Valley road a new barricade had been erected by the authorities near Grahovo, 6 kilometres further back from the old barricade. On 19 January, the Mission patrol discovered that the new barricade had been partially removed, letting traffic through on one lane. At the site of the previous rock and gravel barricade, near the border, moveable metal barriers had been erected, guarded by two police and six military personnel. Local cars and buses have been allowed to pass through this border crossing-point.

20. On 20 January, the Mission's acting Special Envoy in Montenegro met with Mr. Zoran Celebic, Chief of Cabinet. Mr. Celebic informed him that the villagers in the Nudo Valley had made several complaints to the Montenegrin Government about the blockade at the border with Bosnia. The Government of Montenegro had therefore decided to remove the barricade and to replace it with concertina wire and metal traffic obstacles. The police, along with the military, were manning the point on a 24-hour basis. Mr. Celebic also stated that only in emergency cases would people be allowed to pass through this point.

21. The Mission Coordinator met with General Kovacevic, Deputy Chief of the General Staff, on 21 January. In their meeting, the Mission Coordinator stated

that the Montenegrin decision to dismantle the stone barrier in the Nudo Valley was a very disturbing development, violating the explicit commitment made by General Babic to Mr. Pellnäs. He furthermore referred to the Security Council resolution 970 (1995), which specifically mentioned the closing of crossing-points, insisting that there must be a permanent, effective barricade put up and that this must be done promptly. General Kovacevic promised to investigate the matter.

22. On 25 January, the Mission Coordinator met with Second Army Commander Babic to discuss the Nudo Valley situation. He expressed great concern that the permanent barrier had been replaced with a moveable barrier without any consultation with the Mission, despite the specific commitments that had been made to Mr. Pellnäs. General Babic acknowledged that he had made a commitment to block permanently the Nudo Valley road. However, he noted that the people in the Nudo Valley had traditionally looked to Trebinje in Bosnia for their schooling, medical and other services, and that the closure of the border had thus been especially disruptive. He submitted that a well-guarded checkpoint with a Mission presence would maintain the effective closure of the border. It would also make it more sustainable because the people would feel their needs had been taken into account. In this regard, Mission personnel reported that local attitudes towards the Mission had noticeably improved since the permanent barrier had been removed.

23. In the assessment of the Mission Coordinator, the practical difficulties caused by the border closure were real. Apart from adding an extra hour of travel time, the alternative route via Vilusi was often unusable because of ice and snow. In the circumstances, the Mission Coordinator is working out an arrangement whereby the Nudo crossing would have a moveable barrier with a 24-hour Mission, police and customs presence, as well as with a permanent military unit on guard. The permanent barrier would be reinstated should there be any attempt to abuse the checkpoint.

24. The Mission has been emphasizing the checking of buses, because they, at this point, seem to have the largest potential for violations. In this regard, improvements are already beginning to be seen in the degree and thoroughness of inspections. In Badovinci the quality of checking has normally been high. However, on 18 January, a 5-seater bus carrying 11 passengers fully loaded with wine, spirits, soap powder, cooking oil, etc. was allowed to proceed to Bosnia at the Badovinci crossing-point. The customs official on duty claimed that duty had been paid at the Hungarian/Yugoslav border and that he would let it go through in spite of the protests by the Mission team. Later, the regional customs officer was disciplined and the Mission received assurances that similar incidents would

not take place again.

25. The Mission teams are still reporting that the quality of customs work at some border crossing-points is uneven. At Sremska Raca customs presence has been increased to allow for more thorough checks of buses. The overall customs checks of vehicles appear to have been tightened up.

VIII. CERTIFICATION

26. In the light of the foregoing developments during the past 30 days, based on the Mission's on-site observation, on the advice of the Mission Coordinator, Mr. T.J. Nieminen, and in the absence of any contrary information from the air, whether the airborne reconnaissance system of NATO or national technical means, the Co-Chairmen conclude that the Government of the Federal Republic of Yugoslavia (Serbia and Montenegro) is continuing to meet its commitment to close the border between the Federal Republic of Yugoslavia (Serbia and Montenegro) and the areas of the Republic of Bosnia and Herzegovina under the control of the Bosnian Serb forces.

141. LETTER DATED 2 MARCH 1995 FROM THE SECRETARY-GENERAL ADDRESSED TO THE PRESIDENT OF THE SECURITY COUNCIL*

I have the honour to transmit the attached report which was addressed to me on 1 March 1995 by the Co-Chairmen of the Steering Committee of the International Conference on the Former Yugoslavia concerning the operations of the International Conference's Mission to the Federal Republic of Yugoslavia (Serbia and Montenegro). This report by the Co-Chairmen contains the certification referred to in paragraph 5 of Security Council resolution 970 (1995) of 12 January 1995.

I should be grateful if you would bring this information to the attention of the members of the Security Council.

* UN Doc. S/1995/175, 2 March 1995. Signed by Boutros Boutros-Ghali.

Annex
Operations of the International Conference on the Former Yugoslavia Mission to the Federal Republic of Yugoslavia (Serbia and Montenegro) - Report of the Co-Chairmen of the Steering Committee -

I. INTRODUCTION

1. The present report is submitted pursuant to paragraph 3 of Security Council resolution 943 (1994) of 23 September 1994 and paragraph 5 of Council resolution 970 (1995 of 12 January 1995. In those resolutions, the Council requested that the Secretary-General submit every 30 days for its review a report from the Co-Chairmen of the Steering Committee of the International Conference on the Former Yugoslavia on the border closure measures taken by the authorities of the Federal Republic of Yugoslavia (Serbia and Montenegro).

2. It will be recalled that, on 4 August 1994, the following measures were ordered by the Government of the Federal Republic of Yugoslavia (Serbia and Montenegro) to come into effect the same day:

> "(a) To break off political and economic relations with the Republika Srpska;
> (b) To prohibit the stay of the members of the leadership of the Republica Srpska (Parliament, Presidency and Government) in the territory of the Federal Republic of Yugoslavia;
> (c) As of today the border of the Federal Republic of Yugoslavia is closed for all transport towards the Republika Srpska, except food, clothing and medicine."

3. On 19 September 1994, 3 October, 2 November, 5 December 1994, and 5 January and 2 February 1995, the Secretary-General transmitted to the Security Council reports from the Co-Chairmen of the Steering Committee of the International Conference on the Former Yugoslavia on the state of implementation of the above-mentioned measures (S/1994/1074 and S/1994/1124; S/1994/1246; S/1994/1372; S/1995/6; S/1995/104). The report dated 2 February 1995 contained the following certification from the Co-Chairmen:

> "In the light of the foregoing developments during the past 30 days, based on the Mission's on-site observation, on the advice of the Mission Coordinator, Mr. T.J. Nieminen, and in the absence of any contrary information from the air, whether the airborne reconnaissance system of the North Atlantic Treaty Organization (NATO), or national technical means, the Co-Chairmen conclude that the Government of the Federal Republic of Yugoslavia (Serbia and Montenegro) is continuing to meet its commitment to close the border between the Federal Republic of Yugoslavia (Serbia and Montenegro) and the areas of the Republic of Bosnia and Herzegovina under the control of the Bosnian Serb forces".

In a supplementary note provided to the Security Council on 7 February 1995, the Co-Chairmen stated as follows:

"The 30-day report from the Co-Chairmen covered a period of only 19 days under resolution 970 (1995) and this is why they did not change the certification wording on this occasion. They are however, ready to certify that during the last 30-day period from 2 to 31 January based on the Mission's on-site observation, on the advice of the Mission Coordinator, Mr. T.J. Nieminen, and in the absence of any contrary information from the air, whether the airborne reconnaissance system of the North Atlantic Treaty Organization or national technical means, there were no transshipments across the border between the Federal Republic of Yugoslavia (Serbia and Montenegro) and the Republic of Bosnia and Herzegovina."

Developments in the past 30 days are dealt with below.

II. LEGISLATION/REGULATION ON THE BORDER CLOSURE

4. The legislation of the authorities of the Federal Republic of Yugoslavia (Serbia and Montenegro) closing the border with the Bosnian Serbs continues to be in force.

5. On 13 February 1995, the Mission Coordinator signed a Memorandum of Understanding with the Director of Customs of the Federal Republic of Yugoslavia (Serbia and Montenegro), Mr. M. Kertes, about the control of buses. It was agreed that all buses must be partially checked at a minimum level of 20 per cent. It was also agreed that buses based in the "Republika Srpska" with additional fuel tanks will not be allowed to enter the Federal Republic of Yugoslavia (Serbia and Montenegro). Similarly, buses based in the Federal Republic of Yugoslavia (Serbia and Montenegro) will not be allowed to enter the "Republika Srpska" with fuel in additional tanks. The Mission Coordinator considers this to be a very tight level of control. The 20 per cent goal of examinations is still to be attained at some border crossing-points.

6. The Mission has received from the authorities of the Federal Republic of Yugoslavia (Serbia and Montenegro) the following analysis of confiscation by them along the border with the Republic of Bosnia and Herzegovina for the period from 4 August 1994 to 31 January 1995.

Goods	At the border crossing-points	Elsewhere	Total
Petrol	21.9 tons	23.5 tons	45.5 tons
Diesel	16.4 tons	283.1 tons	399.5 tons
Cigarettes	0.805 tons	43.3 tons	44.1 tons
Construction material	-	161.2 tons	161.2 tons
Wood construction material	-	11.1 cu m	11.1 cu m
Alcohol	326 litres	3.824 litres	4.150 litres
Foodstuff	10 kg	9.5 tons	9.5 tons
Textiles/clothing/footwear	120 kg	9.5 tons	10 tons
Livestock	-	37	37
Other goods	15 tons	36.6 tons	51.6 tons

7. In 138 cases during the above-mentioned period (4 August 1994-31 January 1995), violation resulted in administrative fines or prosecutions. A system has now been established to provide the categories or confiscations and offences on a monthly basis which can be used for comparison purposes. This analysis also includes the Nudo Valley incident at the end of December 1994. The Mission Coordinator hopes to obtain these figures separately. Warrants for the arrest of the Nudo Valley organizers have been issued.

III. ORGANIZATION, FINANCING AND WORK OF THE MISSION

8. As at 1 March 1995, 189 international Mission personnel were on duty with the Mission. The Mission personnel to date have come from the following countries: Belgium, Canada, Czech Republic, Denmark, Finland, France, Germany, Greece, Ireland, Italy, Netherlands, Norway, Portugal, Russian Federation, Spain, Sweden, United Kingdom of Great Britain and Northern Ireland and United States of America.

9. A provisional border crossing point at Nudo Valley was activated on a 24 hour-basis effective from 7 February. Better weather conditions over the Podgora mountains allowed the remanning of the Sula border crossing point in sector Bravo on 9 February. The Mission is now covering 21 border crossings 24 hours a day. Of those, 2 are train stations.

10. The Mission headquarters has been reorganized. The senior staff includes to senior advisers, one for political issues who is also deputy to the head of mission and one for customs policy matters who is also special envoy to the Montenegrin Government. The rest of the headquarters personnel is divided between the

operations department and the administrative department. Standard operating procedures have been written to provide the Mission monitors with guidelines, ensuring that tasks and duties are dealt with in an uniform, standard and professional manner.

11. The UHF radio network installation has been completed in the area of operations of sectors Belgrade and Alpha. Work is under way in the remaining sectors.

A. *Auditing of the Mission's Accounts*

12. Appendix I to the present report contains a summary of the finances made available to the Mission up to 26 February 1995. The accounts of the Mission are currently being audited by an independent accounting firm. The initial audit will cover the period from 17 September 1994 until 9 January 1995 and the results will be made known.

B. *Additional Observers needed by the Mission*

13. The approved budget of the Mission for the period from 1 December 1994 to 31 May 1995 is US $ 3.1 million, based on 170 observers, 85 interpreters and 85 vehicles. Contributions received to date are only US $ 1.1 million. Based on previous patterns, there are uncertainties about payment from some countries, estimated at $ 0.7 million, leaving the Mission with an estimated expected amount of $ 1.3 million until the end of May. With the target of 225 observers the subsequent requirement for additional funding for the period is estimated at $ 2,445,000, leaving the Mission with and under-funding of Security Council 945,000 for the next three months, assuming that expected payments are actually made, and on time.

14. Unless the assessed funds arrive shortly, particularly from the main contributors, the Mission may well have to cease operation and terminate within the month. Without the approval and receipt of the needed additional funding of $ 945,000, it will not be able to sustain the operation until the end of May.

15. The Mission strength as of the date of this report is 189 international observers, It is expected that this number will increase to approximately 225, including the impending arrival of some 20 observers from the United States, 5 from the Russian Federation and 2 from the United Kingdom. Provided that these members join the Mission, it will be able to cope with its current tasks and duties, However, even with these additions unusually heavy demands will still be made on Mission personnel, who are currently working an average of 12 hours

daily, 6 to 7 days a week.

16. Having also evaluated staffing levels required to meet its obligations, the Mission would require an additional 25 observers, bringing the total number of monitors to 250 with a corresponding increase in the number of interpreters and vehicles. The incremental cost of adding these additional members is estimated at $ 200,000 for a three-month period.

17. The following is a table of funding requirements until 31 May 1995:

US dollars

- Operating funds from March to May ($500,000 x 3 months)	1,500,000
- Termination costs	70,000
- Improvement of border control points working conditions from caravans to portacabins	200,000
- Payment of outstanding obligations	250,000
- Cost of pledge staffing: 190 to 225 monitors	225,000
Total funds required, March-May	2,245,000

Current funding of the Mission: (not including voluntary start-up contributions)

Assessed contributions	3,130,000
Less:	
Contingencies for non/late payment of assessed contributors[a]	(700,000)
Assessed contributions received	(1,300,000)
Expected payment of assessments until the end of May	1,300,000
Supplementary funds required	945,000
Plus:	
Funds required to increase staffing from 225 to 250	200,000
Total supplementary funds required from participating States	1,145,000

[a] Certain contributing States have developed a pattern of non-payment or late payment of assessed contributions.

A summary showing the current status of contributions is presented in appendix II to the present report.

C. Question of an Aerial Component for the Mission

18. As will be related in section VII below, alleged helicopter incidents between 1 and 4 February have attracted a great deal of publicity. This raises the issue of whether the Mission should be provided with an aerial component.
19. Radar coverage of the border between the Federal Republic of Yugoslavia (Serbia and Montenegro) and the "Republika Srpska" from Surcin extends as far as the Montenegrin border under optimum conditions. The ability to detect helicopters is dependent upon several factors: height and size of target, weather returns, terrain and the tuning and power of the radar equipment.
20. In addition to the acceptance by the authorities of the Federal Republic of Yugoslavia (Serbia and Montenegro) to permit unimpeded access for the United Nations military observers (UNMOs) to existing facilities (which would be in the interest of the desire of the Government of the Federal Republic of Yugoslavia (Serbia and Montenegro) to confirm their total closure of the "Republika Srpska" border), further means could be employed to achieve increased certainty of coverage:

- By employment of a NATO airborne sensor, either fixed wing or helicopter;
- Through the use of mobile radar facilities placed to optimum positions along the borders.

21. The Mission's understanding is that AWACS are primarily tasked to watch for fixed-wing violations, the lower detection threshold of their radar being set above that of a slow-moving helicopter. This is to avoid the clutter of additional targets that fast-moving road vehicles would produce.
22. Should an airborne watch be preferred, then there are a number of aircraft besides AWACS that could be considered. Specialist advice would need to be sought to determine how this can be achieved.
23. Alternatively, mobile low-altitude radar systems could be employed. This is sophisticated, complex equipment, which the Mission does not have the technical means to operate and support. A number of radars would be required to cover the length of the border. As the latter is in a predominantly mountainous region, radars would have to be accurately sited to ensure total coverage of the numerous valleys and ridges that exist, each unit would likely consist of a radar head, power plant, control room, communications, accommodation and a staffing by up to 50 technicians, supported by an extensive logistical and administrative structure.

24. In the opinion of the Mission, the cost of a mobile radar operation, in terms of both manpower and equipment would be high and the Mission Coordinator therefore recommended to the Co-Chairmen that the UNMO system already in place - with the specific assurances from the authorities of the Federal Republic of Yugoslavia (Serbia and Montenegro) of unhindered access to the radar screens - should continue verification of Security Council resolution 781 (1992).

25. In the absence of any evidence of helicopters flying from the Federal Republic of Yugoslavia (Serbia and Montenegro) to Bosnia and Herzegovina, the Co-Chairmen do not recommend that scarce resources for the Mission be expended for radar equipment to monitor helicopter flights but instead that Governments should meet their financial obligations and provide the resources needed to allow the number of Mission observers to rise to 250 with increased mobile patrolling, and that the UNMO system already in place should continue its monitoring of the airspace.

IV. FREEDOM OF MOVEMENT OF THE MISSION

26. The Mission continues to enjoy freedom of movement within the Federal Republic of Yugoslavia (Serbia and Montenegro).

27. On 3 February, threats were heard by the Chief of Police at Sremska Raca against Mission observers. The threats were coming from the "Republika Srpska" side. In the evening the police were seen to be carrying rifles and wearing flack jackets and helmets. Also, Sector Alpha reported that the situation at Badovinci was tense during the first week of February and the locals were becoming angry with the customs, police and Mission observers. Tensions subsided later, but Mission staff are alert for any recurrence.

28. A shooting incident occurred on 14 February in the North of Section Charlie in Montenegro. Upon return from a foot patrol near the Bosnian border, the personnel went into their vehicle and proceeded to return to Pluzine along the same unimproved dirt road it had used to reach its dismount point. After driving 500 metres, the vehicle approached a number of large rocks which ineffectively blocked the road. The observers got out of their vehicle and as they began to move the rocks a weapon report rang out. The next report was preceded by the sound of an impact within metres of the patrol's general location and was considered a good indication that the rifle fire was purposely aimed in the direction of the patrol. During the four minutes required to hastily move the rocks, five rifle reports were heard. An unknown individual pointing a hunting rifle at the patrol was spotted. All Mission personnel and equipment evacuated the area without damage or injury and proceeded to the Pluzine police station to inform

the local authorities. It is the patrol's general impression that the incident was not designed to inflict physical harm on Mission members even though the circumstances were characteristic of an ambush.

29. On 15 February, the Mission Coordinator's Special Envoy (a member of the patrol involved in the shooting incident) and two other members of the patrol were invited to meet the interior Minister of Montenegro. The Deputy Interior Minister and the Chief of the Niksic Police, together with his deputy were also present. The shooting incident was discussed in some detail: a 17-year-old youth had been arrested. He had admitted firing in the area at the time and the place of the incident, but stated that he was not aware of the patrol's presence and that Mission involvement was purely an accident. He will be charged with possessing a firearm under age and without a licence, and for firing in an area likely to endanger life. His elder brother, who legally owns the gun, may also face prosecution. The Mission Coordinator has passed his commendation to the Montenegrin authorities for their prompt and effective action in this matter.

V. COOPERATION OF THE AUTHORITIES OF THE FEDERAL REPUBLIC OF YUGOSLAVIA (SERBIA AND MONTENEGRO) WITH THE MISSION

30. In the assessment of the Mission Coordinator, the cooperation of the authorities of the Federal Republic of Yugoslavia (Serbia and Montenegro) continues to be satisfactory.

31. On 6 February 1995, the Mission Coordinator together with his Senior Political Advisor, Special Envoy and Press Officer, met with the President of Montenegro, Mr. Bulatovic; the Commander of the Second Army, General Babic; and the Commander of the Herzeg Novi Military District, Admiral Zec. They all reaffirmed their commitment to continue the high level of cooperation with the Mission and the effective closure of the border between Montenegro and Bosnia and Herzegovina. On 22 February 1995, the Mission Coordinator paid a courtesy call on President Milosevic.

32. In the assessment of the Mission Coordinator, as most border crossing points, the level of customs inspection of vehicles is good. Customs officials are confiscating goods which have not been declared prior to the vehicles being examined and are turning away vehicles trying to cross the border several times per day. The amount of fuel confiscated seems to be increasing. Customs at Sremska Raca has informed the Mission that, on average, contraband valued at DM 60,000 is seized at the border crossing point each week. This excludes the value of any fuel confiscated.

VI. Information Received from National and Other Sources

33. The operating principle of the Mission is to base itself on its own observations and on information that it has verified. The Mission Coordinator has maintained a standing request to Governments possessing the technical capacity to provide it with information relevant to its mandate.

34. The Mission Coordinator has received information from different sources that there might be an underwater oil pipeline across the Drina River. No exact location of this possible pipeline has been given. Mission mobile patrols have been searching for any signs of a pipeline on the banks of the Drina, but no signs of it have been discovered.

VII. Problems Encountered and Representations Made to the Authorities

35. The Mission now covers 21 major crossings 24 hours a day. Appendix III to the present report contains a comprehensive and updated list of border crossings between the Federal Republic of Yugoslavia (Serbia and Montenegro) and the Republic of Bosnia and Herzegovina.

A. *No-fly Zone over Bosnia and Herzegovina*

36. The alleged helicopter incidents between 1 and 4 February, in particular the reported sightings of 15 to 20 helicopters near Srebrenica on 3 February, have been thoroughly investigated. There has been no confirmation of any helicopters crossing the border either from NATO or national Governments during this period, nor from UNMOs in a position to monitor the airspace through their presence in the radar control room at Surcin Airport, Belgrade. Between 2 and 15 February, the UNMOs were denied the facility to watch over a local radar operator but were not banned from the radar room itself. When the Co-Chairmen, Lord Owen and Thorvald Stoltenberg, met President Milosevic in Belgrade on 15 February to discuss wider questions, they asked him to make more information available for the days of the alleged helicopter sightings and on the capabilities of the radar at Surcin. That same afternoon they were informed that the Chief UNMO in Belgrade had been called in to review the tapes.

37. The Mission Coordinator subsequently reported to the Co-Chairmen that after reviewing the radar tapes for the days in question, the UNMOs had found nothing except one approved MEDEVAC flight which was observed by a Mission team at Ljubovica. Nine reports from the Srebrenica area from the

period from 1 to 4 February were evaluated. The radar tapes were evaluated 10 minutes before and 10 minutes after each actual report. The review was carried out by UNMO air traffic controllers in good cooperation with, and support from, the local representatives of the Surcin airport authorities and the Yugoslav air Force liaison officer. Of the nine reports only the third report showed a short track which covered an approved MEDEVAC helicopter flight from Batajnica to Pale. The observers of the International Conference on the Former Yugoslavia at Ljubovica observed a helicopter at the expected travel time, and the timings also fit in with the ground operations done at Srebrenica. The conclusion was therefore that the radar track did not indicate a border-crossing violation and the flight was not a ground-observed violation.

38. In meetings with the Mission Coordinator, on 8 and 13 February, Mr. Kertes, the Head of the Customs Authorities of the Federal Republic of Yugoslavia (Serbia and Montenegro), categorically denied involvement of the Federal Republic of Yugoslavia (Serbia and Montenegro) in any of the alleged helicopter flights near Srebrenica. He also vigorously rejected suggestions that "Republika Srpska" helicopters could have crossed into the Federal Republic of Yugoslavia (Serbia and Montenegro), stating that instructions had been given to shoot down any "Republika Srpska" helicopter that might try to cross the border, The Mission also held meetings on Tuesday, 14 February, with the United Nations Protection Force (UNPROFOR) at Belgrade, and on 15 February a mission operations officer was in attendance at a meeting between the representatives of UNPROFOR and air traffic control personnel at Surcin. The Coordinator of the Mission has checked repeatedly with Mission monitors along the border in the most likely areas of possible crossings and none has either seen or heard any helicopters crossing the border during that period. The Coordinator of the Mission has double-checked with heads of Mission sectors Alpha and Bajina Basta, both of whom reaffirmed that none of their observers saw or heard any helicopters near to or crossing the border between Serbia and the "Republika Srpska" during the dates or times in question. On 17 February, the Mission Coordinator met with the Deputy Minister of Defence Mr. Bjelica, the Deputy Chief of the General Staff, General Kovacevic and the Commander of the First Army, General Ojdanic. They all categorically denied any involvement of the Federal Republic of Yugoslavia (Serbia and Montenegro) in any of the flights near Srebrenica. On 22 February, President Milosevic also assured the Mission Coordinator that no helicopters from the Federal Republic of Yugoslavia (Serbia and Montenegro) were involved.

39. At the meeting with he Mission Coordinator, the authorities of the Federal Republic of Yugoslavia (Serbia and Montenegro) requested that the results of the investigations into the alleged helicopter incidents should be made known at the

highest level where the accusations against them were originally made. They also requested assistance from UNPROFOR and the International Conference on the Former Yugoslavia to unlock blocked overseas accounts in order to enable procurement of radar equipment spare parts.

40. It will be recalled that, following negotiations between the then Co-Chairmen, Cyrus Vance and Lord Owen, and the then Government of the Federal Republic of Yugoslavia (Serbia and Montenegro), and in particular President Cosic and Prime Minister Panic, an agreement was signed on 2 November 1992, between General Zivota Panic, CGS JA, and Lt. General Satish Nambiar, Force Commander UNPROFOR, concerning access to the airfields at Surcin and Batajnica (Belgrade), Podgorica (Montenegro), Pristina (Kosovo) and Kraljevo (now closed). It also included access to Nis, Poikve (10 kilometres south-east of Bajina Basta) and Berane (formerly Ivangrad, in Montenegro). Currently UNMO controllers are based at Surcin (Belgrade) whilst airfield monitors are deployed at the Batajnica, Podgorica, Ponikve and Pristina airfields.

41. When NATO began to police the no-fly zone around March 1993, they tried to stop helicopter flights as well as the flying of fixed-wing aircraft. Whereas under the voluntary agreement fixed-wing flying stopped, helicopter flying began to build up and NATO aircraft, despite taking action to force down some helicopters, soon found that helicopters violations continued regardless of their actions. There have been in total 3,935 violations since April 1992. The violations are broken down as follows: 14 per cent for the Croats, 33 per cent for the Bosnians, 46 per cent for the Serbs and 7 per cent unknown.

42. At the meeting on 15 February between the air traffic control authorities of the Federal Republic of Yugoslavia (Serbia and Montenegro), representatives from UNPROFOR and the Mission, full access for the UNMOs was restored with an improvement in availability of facilities being assured. The Mission Coordinator has reported that at that meeting it was confirmed by the civil aviation authorities of the Federal Republic of Yugoslavia (Serbia and Montenegro) that UNMOs would be assured full and unimpeded admission to the ATC radar room at Surcin airport and the sole use of a free radar scope. The voice and radar tapes would also be made available for analysis by the UNMOs. In fact the representative of the Federal Republic of Yugoslavia (Serbia and Montenegro) requested that UNMOs should review the tapes for the whole period to avoid any further accusations or suspicions.

43. From the Missions's point of view, with the lack of any confirmation, or of visual or other evidence, it has concluded that there is no evidence that the helicopters sighted near Srebrenica came from the Federal Republic of Yugoslavia (Serbia and Montenegro). In its resolution 781 (1992), the Security Council

gives the mandate for UNPROFOR to monitor compliance of the ban of military flights in the airspace of Bosnia and Herzegovina. Within the Federal Republic of Yugoslavia (Serbia and Montenegro), this is done by UNMOs consisting of 5 controllers and 16 airfield monitors tasked to report on violations of the no-fly zone.

B. Other Issues

44. On 1 February, the ferry at Jamena was loaded on trucks parked on the "Republika Srpska" side of the river. The motor boat has also been removed. The Colonel in charge of the military in the vicinity of Jamena and Sremska Raca said that the Yugoslav Army is increasing the number and size of its patrols in the area. The military accompanied the Mission's mobile observer team in the area on 4 February in full-body armour and with rifles - which had not been done hitherto.

45. Near Jamena a Yugoslav Army patrol in mid-February caught two smugglers, with 43 boxes of cigarettes and DM 8,000. One smuggler managed to escape. All the goods were confiscated. In order to suppers smuggling, the authorities of the Federal Republic of Yugoslavia (Serbia and Montenegro) occasionally saturate areas along the Drina with Yugoslav Army ambushes, irregular guard posts and special police operations.

46. At Sremska Raca, on 9 February, a truck had 100,000 cigarettes in a concealed container. The cigarettes and the truck were confiscated and taken to Novi Sad for inspection. On 10 February, two trucks approached the crossing point at considerable speed, and as the barrier was up, they passed straight through. The assessment of the Mission observers was that the trucks were waiting for the right moment as there were only a few vehicles at the crossing point. Customs officials gave conflicting reasons for the incident. On 11 February a military truck was allowed to cross without being checked. On 27 February, two buses, each containing about 50 young men, crossed the border going on holiday following their basic training. No obvious military equipment or clothing was seen on the buses. Both buses had Vukovar plates.

47. At Badovinci, on 11 February, a Bosnian Serb police officer in uniform, and with a side-arm was allowed to cross the border. On the same day, another violation occurred when a van full of stationery was allowed to cross into the "Republika Srpska".

48. At Trbusnica, on 26 February, a car full of goods was allowed to cross the border. The customs officials' justification for this was that the goods were for the Army. This incident has been reported to the Head of Customs of the Federal

Republic of Yugoslavia (Serbia and Montenegro) for an explanation.

49. On 11 February, an incident occurred at the Sastavci crossing, when two cars crossed the border into "Republika Srpska" using the bypass road. The cars appeared at the Sastavci border crossing point by were rejected for arriving to late at the crossing point which had already closed. The Mission team noticed the cars when they returned to the bypass road and crossed into the "Republika Srpska". The local police and the Mission teams jointly investigated the matter. Tracks were discovered on the bypass road indicating that it had been used by several cars. As a result two official requests were made: (a) that the bypass be effectively closed; and (b) that the owners of the vehicles be prosecuted.

50. At Metaljka, on 16 February, some excessive foodstuffs were stopped from crossing the border. Observers witnessed some of these goods re-entering Bosnia via a small bypass track which is usable only for pedestrians. The goods were loaded into vehicles on the other side of the border.

51. A helicopter (Mi-B) with Red Cross insigne flew across the border from Montenegro to Bosnia along the Drina Valley at Scepan Polje on 21 February at 1030 hours. The flight had not been authorized by the United Nations. The Yugoslav Army has been unable to confirm the mission status (authorized or unauthorized) of the helicopter sighting. During the Mission Coordinator's meeting on 28 February with Mr. Kertes, he informed the Mission Coordinator that the Montenegrin police had confirmed the flight of a helicopter, but insisted that it had only taken place along the border and had not crossed into Bosnia.

52. At Vracenovici, a van passed through the border crossing-point after its closing, on 20 February, at 2055 hours. It was not checked and the Mission observers estimate that it was carrying 10 large tyres.

53. The Mission Coordinator has been informed by UNPROFOR Belgrade of a number of air crossings of the border that have taken place between 21 and 27 February 1995. Since being allowed full and unimpeded access to the radar room at Surcin, UNMO controllers have detected several slow-moving contacts which appear to have crossed the border between Bosnia and the Federal Republic of Yugoslavia (Serbia and Montenegro). These contacts have been tracked travelling only from west to east. Precise details of these reports have been submitted by UNPROFOR through their chain of command. The UNMO controller had access to the raw radar of the military scope at all times. At the time the weather was good and the ground speed of the contacts was between 45 and 95 knots. Crossings were made at various points between Bijeljina and Priboj during the day and at night. None of these crossings had been visually witnessed by Mission members, The Mission is following up these reports.

54. At the Vilusi border crossing point, on 8 February, the police confiscated three hand grenades, over 200 rounds of small-arms ammunition, a knife and miscellaneous military equipment from a car. On 9 February, at the Viluso bypass, the Mission mobile patrol encountered a car leaving the barrier in the direction of the Federal Republic of Yugoslavia (Serbia and Montenegro). On the "Republika Srpska" side of the barrier, the patrol observed two men loading a car with about 200 litres of fuel and about 500 cartons of cigarettes. The patrol radioed for police assistance, but the smugglers had left before the police arrived. The Mission mobile patrol gave the identification of the vehicles to the police.

55. There are signs that the so-called Vilusi bypass is frequently used by smugglers. Contraband is carried around the barrier on the road. On 16 February, a Mission mobile patrol noticed a smuggler in the vicinity of the bypass. The observer suggested that the smuggler turn himself in to the police at the border crossing point, which he did. His goods were confiscated and, according to the police, he was arrested. A second barrier closer to the main road has been built to prevent continued smuggling activities. Customs teams and police have been patrolling in the area.

56. In the Nudo valley, the police have received instructions to man the Nudo crossing, and a customs officer arrived at Nudo on 3 February. The Mission Coordinator sent a letter to the Second Army Commander, General Babic, on 30 January, proposing that a "provisional" checkpoint be established on the Nudo valley road. In addition, the Mission Coordinator proposed that a movable barrier be installed on the track leading south from the Nudo valley and that some additional barricades be constructed on the tracks in the border area to the north of Vilusi, as soon as the weather conditions permitted.

57. On 7 February, a provisional crossing point was established in the Nudo valley with the customs, the police and the Mission observers maintaining a 24-hours presence. The checkpoint can be used only by people living in the Nudo valley. The main border crossing point for traffic towards Trebinje in Bosnia and Herzegovina remains at Vilusi. Under this arrangement, the Mission Coordinator made it clear that abuse of the checkpoint for smuggling purposes would automatically require re-establishment of a permanent barricade, should the Mission conclude that this is the only effective way to ensure compliance with the Government's border closure policy.

58. To enhance the closure of the Montenegrin border, the military has built six additional barricades on tracks north of Vracenovici and blocked one more track south of Kratac.

59. On 3 February, the Mission Coordinator, together with his Senior Political Advisor, met the head of Customs of the Federal Republic of Yugoslavia (Serbia

and Montenegro), Mr. M. Kertes. They discussed requirements contained within the Security Council resolution 970 (1995), paragraph 3, and especially the contents of the phrase "international humanitarian agencies". At the same time the Memorandum on Definitions of Humanitarian Aid, signed by Mr. Kertes and Mr. Pellnäs on 4 November 1994 (S/1994/1372, appendix), was discussed. No changes in the prevailing practices were made.

60. During the 30 days, from 14 January to 14 February 1995, sector Belgrade sealed a total of 925 trucks with a total weight of 19,109 metric tons. The average number of trucks sealed, each 30 days, in the first 100 days was 1,185, with a weight of 15,995 tons. During the period from 14 January to 14 February, there were fewer loads but with increased tonnage. Around 70 per cent of the trucks sealed belong to the Yugoslav Red Cross, whose trucks account for around 80 per cent of the total tonnage.

61. At several border crossing-points during the last week of February, many vehicles with 4 to 6 sacks of fertilizer were crossing the border to Bosnia. According to information from the local customs authorities, fertilizer suppliers in Badovinci are paying anyone who is willing to deliver any number of sacks of fertilizers to their shops in Bosnia and Herzegovina. A great number of vehicles have been denied crossing for the second time a day. Excess amounts of fertilizer, beer and fuel continue to be the main violations reported.

VIII. CERTIFICATION

62. In the light of the foregoing developments during the past 30 days, based on the Mission's on-site observation, on the advice of the Mission Coordinator, Mr. T.J. Nieminen, and in the absence of any contrary information from the air, whether the airborne reconnaissance system of NATO or national technical means, the Co-Chairmen conclude that the Government of the Federal Republic of Yugoslavia (Serbia and Montenegro) is continuing to meet its commitment to close the border between the Federal Republic of Yugoslavia (Serbia and Montenegro) and the areas of the Republic of Bosnia and Herzegovina under the control of the Bosnian Serb forces. The Co-Chairmen also conclude that during the past 30 days no transshipments were detected by the Mission across the border between the Federal Republic of Yugoslavia (Serbia and Montenegro) and the Republic of Bosnia and Herzegovina.

IX. FUNDING

63. The Co-Chairmen wish to draw particular attention to the fact that the resources available for the Mission have been exhausted and that unless contributions outstanding are received urgently the Co-Chairmen will have no alternative but to wind down the Mission.

APPENDIX I
FINANCIAL STATUS AS AT 28 FEBRUARY 1995

Contributions	*US dollars*
1.1 Voluntary contributions	735,988.08[a]
1.2 Assessed contributions	1,153,975.83
Total	1,889,963.91

Statement of Account with Swiss Bank Corporations

2.1 Funds transferred to the International Conference on the Former Yugoslavia Belgrade	1,872,186.55
2.2 Expenses paid by bank on behalf of the Mission	1,758.27
2.3 Banking charges	31.04
2.4 Balance of funds with Bank	15,988.05
Total	1,889,963.91

[a] Voluntary contributions totalled $ 800,000. At the start of the Mission, an amount of $64,011.92 was taken directly to Belgrade without passing through the bank account of the International Conference on the Former Yugoslavia.

APPENDIX II
STATUS OF ASSESSMENTS AS AT 28 FEBRUARY 1995
(United States dollars)

Contributing States	Percentage Share	Proportional Share of Costs	Contributions Received	Outstanding Balance
Albania	0.01	313.00	0.00	313.00
Austria	0.75	23,487.00	23,458.86	28.14
Belgium	1.53	47,914.00	47,913.00	1.00
Bosnia and Herzegovina	0.04	1,253.00	0.00	1,253.00
Bulgaria	0.13	4,071.00	0.00	4,071.00
Canada	3.11	197,394.00	0.00	97,394.00
China	0.77	24,114.00	24,113.00	1.00
Croatia	0.13	4,017.00	0.00	4,071.00
Denmark	0.94	29,437.00	0.00	29,437.00
Federal Republic of Yugoslavia (Serbia and Montenegro)	0.14	4,384.00	0.00	4,384.00
France	8.68	271,825.00	271,285.00	0.00
Germany	12.92	404,606.00	404,606.00	0.00
Greece	0.51	15,971.00	15,971.00	0.00
Hungary	0.18	5,637.00	0.00	5,637.00
Ireland	0.26	8,142.00	8,143.00	(1.00)
Italy	6.21	194,474.00	0.00	194,474.00
Japan	12.43	389,887.00	0.00	389,887.00
Luxembourg	0.09	2,818.00	0.00	2,818.00
Netherlands	2.17	67,956.00	67,957.00	(1.00)
Norway	0.55	17,224.00	17,224.00	0.00
Portugal	0.29	9,082.00	9,082.00	0.00
Romania	0.17	5,324.00	0.00	5,324
Russian Federation	6.71	210,132.00	0.00	210,132.00
Saudi Arabia	0.96	30,064.00	0.00	30,064.00
Senegal	0.01	313.00	0.00	313.00
Slovakia	0.13	4,071.00	0.00	4,071.00
Slovenia	0.09	2,818.00	0.00	2,818.00
Spain	2.57	89,878.00	0.00	89,878.00
Sweden	1.11	34,761.00	0.00	34,761.00
Switzerland	1.16	36,327.00	36,327.00	0.00
Turkey	0.27	8,455.00	0.00	8,455.00
United Kingdom of Great Britain and Northern Ireland	7.26	227,356.00	227,355.97	0.03
United States of America	25.00	782,906.00	0.00	782,906.00
Organization of the Islamic Conference	2.40	75,159.00	0.00	75,159.00
TOTALS	100.00	3,131,624.00	1,153,975.83	1,977,648.00

Note: The table reflects the current status of contributions for the period from 1 December 1994 to 31 May 1995. It does not include voluntary start-up contributions.

APPENDIX III
BORDER POINTS IN THE MISSION, UPDATED AS AT 1 MARCH 1995

BCP   = Border crossing-point, manned and controlled by ICFY and the
         FRY authorities
         (19 + 2 Train stations)

CCP   = Controlled crossing-point, manned and controlled by the FRY
         authorities
         (13)

Ucp   = Uncontrolled (unmanned/used or potential) crossing-point
         (71)

(JA   = The Yugoslav Army's military compounds from where they
         patrol the CCPs)

How to read:

BCP BE 01 = border crossing point Belgrade 01;
CCP A 08   = controlled crossing point Alpha 08;
UPP BB 01 = Uncontrolled crossing point Bajina Basta 01;

and so on.

BCPs, CCPs and UCPs in Sector Belgrade

BCP BE 01   Jamina (CQ 487 711)
             military ferry (not used)
             24 hours
             1 caravan
BCP BE 02   Sremska Raca (CQ 636743)
             bridge, open 24 hours
             24 hours
             2 caravans
             (Railway closed), UNHCR/ICRC/YRC
             capsat
             telephone
             customs

BCPs, CCPs and UCPs in Sector Alpha

BCP A 04	Badovinci (CQ 687 599)
	bridge, no lorries, open 0600-1900
	24 hours
	2 caravans
	telephone/customs+police
UCP A 04A	small boat crossing (CQ 715 784)
UCP A 04B	small boat crossing (CQ 715 781)
UCP A 04C	Balatin (CQ 716 ...)
	closed ... ferry
UCP A 04D	(CQ 696 640)
	smuggling incident
	for ex ...
UCP A 05	.... (CQ 6.. ...)
	closed .... ferry
UCP A 05A	small boat crossing (CQ 617 556)
UCP A 05B	small boat crossing (CQ 6.. 5..)
UCP A 05C	small boat crossing (CQ 678 5..)
	with the access to secondary check from the river
BCP A 06	Trbusnica (CQ 556 338)
	bridge, no lorries, open 0600-1900
	24 hours
	2 caravans
	telephone/customs
UCP A 06A	small boat crossing (CQ 616 445)
UCP A 06B	small boat crossing (CQ 5.. ...)
UCP A 06C	.... ferry (CQ 567 381)
	with cable access the river Drina
UCP A 06D	small boat crossing (CQ 5.. 3.2)
UCP A 07	Banja .... (CQ ... 306)
	closed .... ferry
UCP A 07A	.... (CQ ... ...)
	small boat crossing
CCP A 08	Donia .... (CQ 526 210)
	closed railway, sealed, controlled by military 24 hours

BCP A 09	Mali Zvornik (CQ 507 187)
	bridge, open 0600-1900, only UNHCR
	24 hours
	2 caravans
	telephone/customs
CCP A 10	Stari Most Zvornik (CQ 493 145)
	bridge for pedestrians and emergency vehicles,
	open 0600-1900
	controlled by police 24 hours
CCP A 11	Da.. Zvornik (CQ 491 145)
	bridge for pedestrians controlled by military 24 hrs
UCP A 11A	(CQ 546 654)
UCP A 11B	(CQ ... ...)
BCP A 12	Ljudovija (CQ 688 960)
	bridge, no lorries, open 0600-1900
	24 hours
	2 caravans
	capsat
	telephone/customs
UCP A 12A	.... (CQ 778 ...)
	with observed boats

BCP's CCP's and UCPs in Sector Bajina Basta

UCP BB 00A	Vitinovac (CP ... ...)
	25 km N of R.... track
UCP BB 00B	Gornja Tre..ca (CP 781 871)
	22 km N of R.... , track
UCP BB 01	Fakovici (CP ... 421)
	15 km N of R..., wire across the river Drina
	4 pontoons restored on the river bank fry side
UCP BB 01A	...nice (CP ... ...)
	12 km N of R...., wire across the river Drina
UCP BB 02	Kod Kameria (CP ... ...)
	9,5 km N of R...., wire across the river Drina
UCP BB 03	Ok.... (CP ... ...)
	9 km N of R... wire across the river Drina
UCP BB 03A	Gadom (CP ... ...)
	7,7 km N of R...., track

UCP BB 04   O..... (CP ... ...)
            7,5 km N of R...., wire across the river Drina
UCP BB 4A   Vranjkovina (CP ... ...)
            4 km N of R.... , track
UCP BB 04B Ban... (CP ... ...)
            3,3 km N of R...., track
UCP BB 05   Ovcinja (CP ... ...)
            1 km N of R..., wire across the river Drina
UCP BB 05A Ovcinja (CP ... ...)
            N of ..., wire across the river Drina
UCP O5B   Rogacica (CP ... ...)
            Rogacica, track
UCP BB 06   Don... (CP ... ...)
            2 km S of R..., wire across the River Drina
            used almost daily
UCP BB 07   Petrica (CP ... ...)
            3 km S of R.... , wire across the river Drina
UCP BB 08   Crivka Danja (cp ... ...)
            5 km S of R..., wire across the river Drina
UCP BB 09   Crivka Co... (CP ... ...)
            7 km S of R..., wire across the river Drina
BCP BB 10   Skelani (831 703)
            bridge, no buses and lorries
            open 0600-1900
            24 hours
            1 caravan
            1 wooden cabin
            telephone
UCP BB 10A ...... (CP ... ...)
            7 km from Skelani, wire across the river Drina
CCP BB 10B Peruca Dam (CP 723 692)
            12 Km W of Skelani, dam, pedestrian bridge,
            open 0600-1900
            controlled by police (24 hrs) and customs
UCP BB 10C Watermill ruin (CP 612 654)
            5,5 km SW of Rasiste
UCP BB 10CA Veliri Stolac (CP 623 644)
            Huge tree across the dirt road

UCP BB 10D   Captains Water (CP 636 632)
6,4 km SW of Rasiste, track

UCP BB 10E   T... (CP ... ...)
7,3 km SW of Rasiste, track

UCP BB 10F   Feci... (CP 666 888)
3 km SW of Jezdici, track

UCP BB 10G   Raj... (CP 669 584)
3 km of Jezdici, track

UCP BB 10H   Boliste (CP674 576)
4 km SW of Jezdici, track

UCP BB 10I   Boliste Stn (CP 674 570)
1 km S of Boliste, track

UCP BB 10J   Bare (CP(6.. 558)
Bare, track

UCP BB 10K   Bijevice (CP 692 55.)
Bijevice, track

UCP BB 10L   Tetribica (CP ..5 525)
Tetribica, track

UCP BB 10LA   Zagvoznica (CP 736 ...)
track

UCP BB 10LB   Ijpa (CP ... ...)
track

UCP BB 10..   Radoni (CP 768 575)
1 km NW of Kotroman, track

BCB BB 11   Kotroman (CP 769 468)
Main road, only UNHCR, open 0600-1900
24 hours
2 caravans
telephone/police

UCP BB 12   Pan... (CP 778 44.)
3 km SE of Kotroman., track

UCP BB 13   Ociles tunnel (CP ... ...)
2 km W of Jablanica, railway

TRAIN STN   Uzice (Rail team - sealing of trains)
24 hours
2 caravans
capsat
telephone

TRAINS STN   Priboj (rail team - sealing of trains)
                24 hours
                1 container
                capsat
                telephone

BCPs, CCPs and UCPs in sector Bravo

CCP B 14A   River Ford (CP 788 330)
                pedestrian wire bridge, controlled by military 24 hrs
BCP B 15   Raca (FAP bridge) (CP 783 321)
                big concrete bridge, pedestrians, 24 hrs
UCP B 15A   Foot bridge (CP 7862..)
                1 km south of Fab bridge (pedestrians)
CCP B 15B   Stone bridge (CP 785 294)
                pedestrian bridge, controlled by military 24 hrs
BCP B 16   UVAC (CP 783 288)
                bridge/surface road
                no lorries, open 0600-1900
                24 hours
                2 caravans
                telephone/customs
UCP B 16A   railway bridge (CP 7.. ...)
                100 m south of B 16)
CCP B 16B   Hospital checkpoint (CP 800 270)
                surface road, open 0600-1900
                controlled by police 24 hrs
BCP B 17   Sastavci (CP 728 250)
                surface road, no lorries
                open 09-1900
                24 hours
                1 container
                capsat
UCP B 17A   Okpalje (CP 614 3..)
                track

BCP B 18	Metaijka (CP 497 213)
	surface road, no lorries
	open 0600-1900
	24 hours
	2 caravans
	1 container
	capsat
UCP B 18A	...evica (CP ... ...)
	track
BCP B 19	Sula (CP 414 069)
	surface road, no lorries, open 0600-1900
	manned by police 24 hrs
	24 hours
	2 caravans
	capsat
UCP B 20	Slatina/Slatina road (CP 451 531 / 418 534)
	track

BCPs, CCPs and UCPs in Sector Charlie

UCP C 00	Likica Do (CP 313 ...)
	blown bridge
	no crossing possible
(JA 01	Police Crkvicko (CN 281993) JA military compound
	stone wall, military patrol, controlling the movements)
BCP C 01	Scepan Polje (CP 254 018)
	police and customs, no lorries
	open 0600-1900, locked - sealed 1900-0600
	chain barrier
	24 hrs
	2 caravans
	capsat
(JA 02	Mratinje (CN 218 928) JA military compound
	stone wall, active control of all traffic)
CCP C 01A	Mratinje (CN 216 938) JA military checkpoint
	no obstacles
	manned 24 hrs

UCP C 01B	Stubica I (CN 147 .27)
	stone wall, military patrol controlling the movements
	(unobserved since ... to snow)
CCP C 01C	Stubica II (CN ... 873) JA military checkpoint
	wooden gate
	manned 24 hrs
(JA 03	Stabna (CN 173 810) JA military compound
	stone wall, active control of all traffic)
BCP	Krstac (4 km NE of Krstac) (CN 097 667)
	police and customs, no lorries
	open 0600-1900
	Montenegrin villages beyond
	metal saw horses
	24 hours
	2 caravans
(JA 04	Krstac (CN 122 639) JA military compound
	steel pole of the road)
	manned 24 hrs
CCP C 03	G. Crkvice (BN 973 ..5) JA military checkpoint
	stone wall, controlling the movements
	manned 24 hrs
(JA 05	Crkvice (BN 996 ...) JA military compound
	active traffic control
UCP C 04A	Kovacs (BN 9.. 5..)
	Stone wall, military patrol controlling the movements
	patrolled daily
UCP C 04 B	Brcka Pec I (BN 962 555)
	stone wall, military patrol controlling the movements
	patrolled daily
UCP C 04C	Brcka Pec II (BN 961 563)
	stone wall, military patrol controlling the movements
	patrolled daily
UCP C 04D	....ca (BN 0.. ...)
	stone wall, military patrol controlling the movements
	patrolled daily
UCP C 04 E	Vici Do I (BN ... 523)
	stone wall, military patrol controlling the movements
	patrolled daily

UCP C 04F	Vici Do II (BN 957 514)
	stone wall, military patrol controlling the movements
	patrolled daily
(JA 06	Pilatovci (BN 967 408) JA military compound
	observing and patrolling)
UCP C 06	K....ca (BN ... ...)
	stone wall, military patrol controlling the movements
	patrolled daily
UCP C 07	.... (BN 9.. 417)
	stone wall, military patrol controlling the movements
	patrolled daily
BCP C 08	Vracknovici (BN 944 468)
	police and customs, no lorries
	open 0600-1900
	metal saw horses
	24 hours
	2 caravans
(JA 07	Kliakovica (BN 942 419) JA military compound
	observing and patrolling
CCP C 09	Kliakovica I (BN 942 410) JA military checkpoint
	stone wall, controlling the movements heading west
	manned 24 hrs
CCP C 09A	Kliakovica II (BN 942 410) JA military checkpoint
	steel pole gate, controlling the movements heading north
	manned 24 hours
UCP C 09B	Prikovici (BN ... ...)
	stone wall
	patrolled daily
CCP C 09C	River road (old railway road) (BN 938 365)
	stone wall military patrol controlling the movements
	manned 24 hrs
UCP C 10	Ra... DO (BN 966 ...)
	stone wall, military patrol controlling the movements
	patrolled daily
BCP C 11	Vilusi (or Ilijino Brdo) (CN 006 318)
	police and customs, open 24 hours
	metal saw horses, UNHCR/ICRC/YRC
	24 hours
	1 caravan

UCP C 11A   First Vilusi By-pass (CN 011 329)
              two stone walls. paloce patrol, cooperative patrols
UCP C 11B   Second Viluso By-pass (CN 010 326)
              steel pole gate (locked and sealed)
              police and ICFY observe and patrol
BCP C 12   Nudo (BN 989 298) (Provisional BCP)
              police and customs, only for the locals,
              no lorries, open 0530-1930
              metal saw horses
              24 hours
              2 caravans
(JA 08   Nudo (CN 007 278) JA military compound
              observing an patrolling)
UCP C 12 A   Jarcista (CN ... ...)
              stone wall, military patrol controlling the movements
              seasonal patrols due to snow
BCP C 13   Vrbanj (BN 952 150)
              no buses and lorries, open 0600-1900
              police/military/customs
              Montenegrin villages beyond BCP
              metal saw horses
              24 hours
              2 caravans
              capsat
              satphone
(JA 09   Kamkno (BN 972 057) JA military compound
              observing and patrolling

142. Letter Dated 31 March 1995 from the Secretary-General Addressed to the President of the Security Council*

I have the honour to transmit the attached report, which was addressed to me on 30 March 1995 by the Co-Chairmen of the Steering Committee of the International Conference on the Former Yugoslavia, concerning the operations of the International Conference's Mission to the Federal Republic of Yugoslavia (Serbia and Montenegro). This report by the Co-Chairmen contains the certifi-

---

* UN Doc. S/1995/255, 31 March 1995. Signed by Boutros Boutros-Ghali.

cation referred to in paragraph 5 of Security Council resolution 970 (1995) of 12 January 1995.

I should be grateful if you would bring this information to the attention of the members of the Security Council.

Annex
Operations of the International Conference on the Former Yugoslavia Mission to the Federal Republic of Yugoslavia (Serbia and Montenegro)

I. INTRODUCTION

1. The present report is submitted pursuant to paragraph 5 of Security Council resolution 970 (1995), adopted on 12 January 1995. In that resolution, the Security Council requested that the Secretary-General submit every 30 days for its review a report from the Co-Chairmen of the Steering Committee of the International Conference on the Former Yugoslavia on the border closure measures taken by the authorities of the Federal Republic of Yugoslavia (Serbia and Montenegro).

2. It will be recalled that on 4 August 1994 the following measures were ordered by the Government of the Federal Republic of Yugoslavia (Serbia and Montenegro) to come into effect the same day:

> "(a) To break off political and economic relations with the 'Republika Srpska';
> (b) To prohibit the stay of the members of the leadership of the 'Republika Srpska' (Parliament, Presidency and Government) in the territory of the Federal Republic of Yugoslavia;
> (c) As of today the border of the Federal Republic of Yugoslavia is closed for all transport towards the 'Republika Srpska', except food, clothing and medicine."

3. On 19 September, 3 October, 2 November and 5 december and 5 January, 3 February and 2 March 1995, the Secretary-General transmitted to the Security Council reports from the Co-Chairmen of the Steering Committee of the International Conference on the Former Yugoslavia on the state of implementation of the above-mentioned measures (S/1994/1074; S/1994/1124; S/1994/1246; S/1994/1372; S/1995/6; S/1995/104 and S/1995/175). The report dated 2 March 1995 contained the following certification from the Co-Chairmen:

> "In the light of the foregoing developments during the past 30 days, based on the Mission's on-site observation, on the advice of the Mission Coordinator, Mr. T.J. Nieminen, and in the absence of any contrary information from the air, whether the airborne reconnaissance system of the North Atlantic Treaty Organization (NATO) or national technical means, the Co-Chairmen conclude that the Government of the Federal Republic of Yugoslavia (Serbia and Montenegro) is continuing to meet its commit-

ment to close the border between the Federal Republic of Yugoslavia (Serbia and Montenegro) and the areas of the Republic of Bosnia and Herzegovina under the control of the Bosnian Serb forces. The Co-Chairmen also conclude that during the past 30 days no transshipments were detected by the Mission across the border between the Federal Republic of Yugoslavia (Serbia and Montenegro) and the Republic of Bosnia and Herzegovina."

4. Developments in the past 30 days are dealt with below. Developments in the remainder of the 100-day period will be covered in a follow-up report.

II. Legislation/Regulation on the Border Closure

5. The legislation of the authorities of the Federal Republic of Yugoslavia (Serbia and Montenegro) closing the border with the Bosnian Serbs continues to be in force.

6. On 27 March 1995 the Mission Coordinator signed a memorandum of understanding with the Director of Customs of the Federal Republic of Yugoslavia (Serbia and Montenegro), Mr. M. Kertes, to improve control and provide firmer assurances on supplies of humanitarian aid through the Yugoslav Red Cross. In the opinion of the Mission Coordinator, the improvements in control are significant and substantial. With the Yugoslav Red Cross exclusively determining the destination of the goods to limited agencies in the "Republika Srpska", any commercial link that might have existed in the past between supplier and recipient will be much more difficult to sustain. More importantly, the stricter inspection at loading should ensure that no contraband, including war *matériel*, is concealed in the consignments. These inspection arrangements are now more or less on a par with those applying to the Office of the United Nations High Commissioner for Refugees (UNHCR) and the International Committee of the Red Cross.

7. The Mission has received from the authorities of the Federal Republic of Yugoslavia (Serbia and Montenegro) the following analysis of confiscations along the border with the Republic of Bosnia and Herzegovina for February 1995:

Petrol (gasoline)	12.4 tons
Diesel	13.2 tons
Cigarettes	1.3 tons
Construction material	648 kilograms
Alcohol	2,208 litres
Food items	389 kilograms
Textiles, clothing, footwear	576 kilograms
Fertilizer	19.0 tons

Coffee	110 kilograms
Other goods	1.2 tons
Vehicles	2

For the first time, confiscations of fertilizer have been included in the information provided by the authorities for the month of February.

8. During the month of February, there were 215 customs offence procedures initiated and 41 were finalized. Fines and penalties amounted to 127,300 dinars. During the previous six months, from 4 August 1994 to 31 january 1995, 138 offence penalties were initiated, of which 71 were finalized. Fines and penalties during this six-month period amounted to 341,450 dinars. These figures give some indication of the sharply increased number of interceptions of smuggling attempts and confiscations. In the opinion of the Mission Coordinator this reflects a tightened degree of control on the border to Bosnia and Herzegovina by the customs authorities of the Federal Republic of Yugoslavia (Serbia and Montenegro) during the last month.

III. Organization, Financing and Work of the Mission

9. As of 1 April 1995, 163 international Mission personnel will be on duty with the Mission. The Mission personnel to date have come from the following countries: Belgium, Canada, Czech Republic, Denmark, Finland, France, Germany, Greece, Ireland, Italy, Netherlands, Norway, Portugal, Russian Federation, Spain, Sweden, United Kingdom of Great Britain and Northern Ireland and United States of America. Because of financial difficulties, no new observers are being taken on to replace those who leave. The number of observers will continue to fall until the minimal threshold of 150 is reached or until such time as the current financial constraints are eased. By the Mission's own calculations, an observer complement below 150 may not be able to provide sufficiently credible information to certify whether the Government of the Federal Republic of Yugoslavia (Serbia and Montenegro) is in compliance with its decision to close its border with Bosnian Serb-held areas of Bosnia and Herzegovina to all but shipments of humanitarian aid.

10. A new six-month budget for the Mission commencing 1 April was drafted after the 10 March meeting of the Steering Committee. This US\$ 3.66 million budget would, if fulfilled, bring the complement of international observers to 250. An appeal was made to countries members of the Steering Committee to pay their contributions before the end of March to forestall the possible closure of the Mission. The Mission Coordinator personally made this point to

embassies in Belgrade during an information briefing on 15 March.

11. The Mission has reacted swiftly to the new fiscal reality presented by the funding crisis by reducing operating costs by 136,000 Deutsch Mark per month over January costs. Vehicle and office space rental charges have been reduced and telecommunication expenditures have been cut significantly. As an example of measures undertaken, over the course of the last month the Mission has been able to terminate most of its reliance on hired cars and it is now operating and servicing its own smaller fleet of vehicles. While expenses continue to be reviewed in detail by the Mission, the magnitude of savings that will be generated by future cutbacks is not significant in relation to the overall, persistent problem of inadequate funding.

12. The ferry at Jamena has not been operating since mid-January and was taken out of the water on the "Republika Srpska" side of the river on 1 February. The high-water level of the Seva river has hindered the effective blockade of the ferry ramp on the Serbian side. On 2 March a second barrier was completed on the ramp and sealed by Mission personnel. This enabled the Mission to close the border crossing-point on 4 March and change its status to a controlled crossing-point. The area will be patrolled by Mission mobile patrols, while it will be controlled by the police of the Federal Republic of Yugoslavia (Serbia and Montenegro).

13. In order to reduce personnel requirements, the border crossing-point at Raca (Sector Bravo) was closed on 23 March. The crossing-point is a bridge behind the FAP Factory near Priboj. The bridge is sealed by a barrier and will be patrolled by Mission mobile patrols while it will be controlled by the police of the Federal Republic of Yugoslavia (Serbia and Montenegro).

14. The Mission is now covering 19 border crossings 24 hours a day. Of those, two are train stations. There are no other major changes to the list of border crossings between the Federal Republic of Yugoslavia (Serbia and Montenegro) provided as appendix III to the previous report (S/1995/175). In order to staff all remaining border crossings fully, the Mission has been forced to curtail much of its mobile patrolling on the border.

IV. FREEDOM OF MOVEMENT OF THE MISSION

15. The Mission continues to enjoy fully freedom of movement within the Federal Republic of Yugoslavia (Serbia and Montenegro).

16. On 14 March, a shooting incident occurred at Krstac (Sector Charlie) where individuals crossing the border from the "Republika Srpska" and the police of the Federal Republic of Yugoslavia (Serbia and Montenegro) were engaged in an

extended shoot-out close to the border crossing-point. Mission personnel, protected by the police, had to withdraw and continue their observation from a safe place. On 15 March, the situation was considered to have calmed down and the team returned to the border crossing-point. The Chief of the Montenegrin Cabinet called the Mission Coordinator on 17 March to apologize for the fact that the safety of the Mission personnel had been jeopardized by the incident.

17. Between 16 and 18 March, the situation at the Metaljka and Sastavci border crossing-points (Sector Bravo) became tense when some local civilians, while being thoroughly checked by Customs, threatened Mission personnel. Police chiefs and liaison officers of the army of the Federal Republic of Yugoslavia (Serbia and Montenegro) on the scene expressed their concern and asked Mission personnel not to leave the border crossing-points without police escorts. Excellent cooperation with the police and the army should be noted in this case. Tension eased on 20 March.

18. On 22 March, a Mission team in Belgrade port was threatened by a local citizen who forced the team's car door open and threatened to use a gun. The team decided to withdraw instantly, until the security of Mission personnel could be ensured. Immediate contacts were made by the Mission Coordinator with Mr. Kertes, who promised to restore security at once. On 23 March, the team returned to Belgrade port, where the police and local security were present and the situation returned to normal.

20. Since 25 march, as hostilities resumed in Bosnia and Herzegovina, Mission personnel at Trbusnica and Mali Zvornik (Sector Alpha) and Metaljka and Sula (Sector Bravo) have reported periodically hearing shelling from the Bosnian side of the border. They also heard and observed increased air activity - both helicopter and fixed-wing - on the Bosnian side of the border. The situation is being closely monitored by Mission headquarters.

21. In the early morning of 26 March, two off-duty Mission personnel were physically assaulted in Banja Koviljaca (Sector Alpha) by four drunk local citizens. One of them sustained minor injuries and has now returned to duty. The report was forwarded to the police. One of the perpetrators has been already apprehended.

V. COOPERATION OF THE AUTHORITIES OF THE FEDERAL REPUBLIC OF YUGOSLAVIA (SERBIA AND MONTENEGRO) WITH THE MISSION

22. The cooperation with the authorities of the Federal Republic of Yugoslavia (Serbia and Montenegro) continues to be good.

VI. Information Received from National and Other Sources

23. The operating principle of the Mission is to base itself on its own observations and on information that it has verified. The Mission Coordinator has maintained a standing request to Governments possessing the technical capacity to provide it with information relevant to its mandate.

24. With reference to the last monthly report concerning an alleged underwater oil pipeline across the Drina river, the search was continued. The only remotely relevant report on the issue was submitted from Sector Alpha on 26 March, where a mobile patrol team discovered remnants of an old pipeline on the beach, near Citluk (CQ 545055). It extended from the water with an open end, corroded and rusted, with no trace of recent use.

25. Another information report was received on 16 March alleging that:

   (a) A temporary bridge was set up near Jaguatica on the Drina on 17 February 1995 and has been used since then to transport material to the Bosnian Serb Army. Mission mobile and foot patrols proceeded to the area and found that the course of the river was about 20 metres below a steep cliff, and no bridge was found. The Mission assessment is that, taking into consideration the nature of the terrain and the location of the area (just opposite the Muslim "Zepa pocket" on the other side of the river), it appears very unlikely that there could be continuous shipping of goods across this part of the Drina;

   (b) Military *matériel* has been passing through four border crossing-points after they close for the day. The Mission assessment is that all four border crossing-points are under observation by Mission personnel 24 hours a day, every day. Therefore it is extremely unlikely that something might pass through the boundary without the Mission's knowledge.

VII. Problems Encountered and Representations Made to
the Authorities

26. On 28 February, a Mission mobile patrol conducted a day survey from Badovinci north to the Sava river. In the process they discovered a smuggling operation in progress 4 kilometres north of Badovinci. The liaison officers of the army of the Federal Republic of Yugoslavia (Serbia and Montenegro) and the Serbian Special Police were present and confiscated one metal boat, a BMW car and seven 225-litre drums of fuel.

27. The impact of delays caused by thorough Customs searches is reflected in an incident that happened at Badovinci (Sector Alpha) on 7 March. Local farmers established a blockade with their tractors on the cross-border road in protest at farm vehicles not being given priority to cross. Additional militia and the army of the Federal Republic of Yugoslavia (Serbia and Montenegro) were summoned, though it appeared that everyone in the protest remained on amicable terms. The next day a meeting was held between the Head of Sector and local authorities and the problem was solved by giving the farmers with tractors priority in crossing the border during the early hours of the morning.

28. During some period in March, the performance of the customs officers at the four border crossing-points in Sector Alpha declined noticeably. On the surface, it appeared that the checking level of buses was maintained and that there were numerous denials of vehicles. Under the surface, however, it appeared that confiscations had dropped substantially, that the thorough searches of vehicles were not up to the previous standards and the a more relaxed attitude was taken generally about allowing significant excess quantities across the border. The Mission Coordinator met the Director Customs of the Federal Republic of Yugoslavia (Serbia and Montenegro) on 27 March to discuss the situation. The Director of Customs had already given very strict instructions to the customs personnel on the ground. He also indicated several personnel changes, i.e. dismissals of customs officers who were "too relaxed in their performance". In all other sectors, the Mission Coordinator confirms good cooperation, good standards of performance and very good work generally by customs.

29. On 13 March, it was reported from Badovinci that two buses with unarmed but uniformed soldiers were allowed to cross into Bosnia and Herzegovina. The Mission Coordinator lodged a formal, high-level protest concerning this matter the following day. Senior authorities of the Federal Republic of Yugoslavia (Serbia and Montenegro) promised to take immediate action, and similar incidents have not been reported since.

30. There have been some attempts in Sector Charlie, particularly in the Vracenovici - Crkvice area, to dismantle the barriers that are blocking the tracks in the border areas with Bosnia and Herzegovina. The police, together with military personnel, have been rebuilding and reinforcing barriers in the area. The Special Envoy of the Mission Coordinator has had discussion with the Second Army Headquarters of the Federal Republic of Yugoslavia (Serbia and Montenegro) to ensure that a correct up-to-date barrier plan is in place. It has been agreed that a greater degree of delegation of responsibility for minor adjustments to the barrier plan needs to be made and that contacts at working level should be between the Head of Sector Charlie and the Liaison Officer of the army of the Federal Republic of Yugoslavia (Serbia and Montenegro). On 20 March, two barriers in

this area were partially dismantled and traces of trucks were visible. On 22 March, a Mission mobile patrol found fresh traces trucks around the restored barriers. On 24 March, a mobile patrol spotted a smuggling attempt from the Bosnia and Herzegovina side (two trucks with timber). The would-be smugglers had to withdraw to Bosnia and Herzegovina. On 26 March, mobile patrols once again discovered traces of smuggling activity - spills of fuel and truck traces around bypasses. A liaison officer of the army of the Federal Republic of Yugoslavia (Serbia and Montenegro) claimed that the army did not have enough manpower to cover all bypasses.

31. Bold smuggling attempts are still taking place on the Vilusi and Vracenovici bypasses (Sector Charlie), where the barriers were partially dismantled on 13 March. This problem was solved at the local level by agreement between the army, the police and the Mission. On 15 march the barriers were restored and reinforced. The areas are now also being patrolled frequently by the army and the police. The result so far is that two attempts to smuggle fuel across the border have been uncovered.

32. Another possible breach has been detected by the local customs in Belgrade, when they screened (X-ray) 50 per cent of a postal shipment on 11 March and refused a large proportion of the packages, which they considered to be trade.

33. During the period from 13 to 19 March, traffic volume at all border crossing-points between the Federal Republic of Yugoslavia (Serbia and Montenegro) and the "Republika Srpska" were recorded. Below are the Mission's main findings and observations:

    (a) A daily average of 28,850 persons crossed the border at the border crossing-points in both directions during the week, either on foot or in vehicles. The busiest border crossing-points, accounting for more than half of the total traffic volume were Sremska Raca (A02) in Sector Belgrade and Badovinci (A04) and Trbusnica (A06), both in Sector Alpha;

    (b) At Sremska Raca, the average daily traffic across the border in both directions was 6,832 persons travelling in 1,113 cars, 167 buses, 167 trucks and 16 tractors or walking. In Badovinci the number of persons crossing averaged 4,697 persons either on foot, or in one of the 1,822 cars, 32 buses and 488 tractors crossing. At Trbusnica, the average number of persons crossing in both directions was 4,345 persons in 1,745 cars, 23 buses and 131 tractors or on foot;

    (c) At the remaining 16 border crossing-points average daily traffic flow ranged from a low of 38 persons, 13 cars, 1 bus and 2 tractors at border crossing point Sula (B10) in Sector Bravo to 3,655 persons in 1,345 cars, 37 buses, 8 trucks and 75 tractors in Mali Zvornik (A09) in Sector Alpha. The Mali Zvornik foot bridge (A10) was used by an average of 3,360 pedestrians crossing the border in both directions on a daily basis;

(d) At the train stations in Proboj and Uzice a daily average of 183 railway cars was sealed and 9 trains crossed the border in both directions;

(e) During the period from 1 to 26 March, Sector Belgrade sealed 1,643 trucks and trailers with a total volume of 22,622 tons of humanitarian aid. During the same period, Sector Charlie also sealed 221 trucks carrying 198 tons of humanitarian aid. Trucks are permitted to cross the border into "Republika Srpska" only at Sremska Raca in Sector Belgrade and Vilusi in Sector Charlie, with occasional UNHCR convoys allowed at Mali Zvornik in Sector Alpha and Kotroman in Sector Bajina Basta. Trucks are subject to normal customs checks at the border crossing-point when leaving the Federal Republic of Yugoslavia (Serbia and Montenegro) and are not allowed to carry fuel in belly tanks. During the period from 1 to 26 March, 108 trucks were denied crossing to "Republika Srpska" for extra fuel or minor customs violations;

(f) Also during the same period, customs reached an overall thorough checking level of 21 per cent on unscheduled long-distance buses entering "Republika Srpska" with 368 of 1,768 buses being fully checked and the remaining being controlled with very good partial checks. In total, 101 buses were denied crossing, mainly for carrying excess amount of commercial goods, including fuel, and 1,858 cars and 299 tractors were denied for similar reasons.

34. In March, United Nations airfield monitors working at civilian radar screens at Surcin Airport near Belgrade observed 26 tracks of likely helicopter flights moving from Bosnia and Herzegovina into the Federal Republic of Yugoslavia (Serbia and Montenegro). While none was observed by Mission personnel from the ground, these clearly constituted border violations. Officers of the Federal Republic of Yugoslavia (Serbia and Montenegro) continued to deny their existence or origin even in the face of comprehensive, credible technical information. There are no reports of those helicopters travelling from the Federal Republic of Yugoslavia (Serbia and Montenegro) back into Bosnia and Herzegovina. Therefore, for the airspace above the border, the Federal Republic of Yugoslavia (Serbia and Montenegro) is not closing its border with Bosnia. This is particularly perplexing inasmuch as the efforts of the Federal Republic of Yugoslavia (Serbia and Montenegro) to enhance its closure of the land border during March and in keeping with its commitment have been broadly effective. The Mission

will be looking once again at whether anything can be done to enhance the information available on border crossings by air.

VIII. CERTIFICATION

35. In light of the foregoing developments during the past 30 days, based on the Mission's on-site observation, and based on the advice of the Mission Coordinator, Mr. T.J. Nieminen, and in the absence of any contrary information from the air, whether the airborne reconnaissance system of the North Atlantic Treaty Organization (NATO) or national technical means, and aside from the reported tracking of helicopters crossing the border, the Co-Chairmen conclude that the Government of the Federal Republic of Yugoslavia (Serbia and Montenegro) is continuing to meet its commitment to close the land border between the Federal Republic of Yugoslavia (Serbia and Montenegro) and the areas of the Republic of Bosnia and Herzegovina under the control of the Bosnian Serb forces. The Co-Chairmen also conclude that during the past 30 days there were no commercial transshipments across the border between the Federal Republic of Yugoslavia (Serbia and Montenegro) and the Republic of Bosnia and Herzegovina.

36. The Co-Chairmen will provide an additional report before the expiration of the 100-day period.

143. LETTER DATED 13 APRIL 1995 FROM THE SECRETARY-GENERAL ADDRESSED TO THE PRESIDENT OF THE SECURITY COUNCIL[*]

I have the honour to transmit the attached report, which was addressed to me on 11 April 1995 by the Co-Chairmen of the Steering Committee of the International Conference on the Former Yugoslavia, concerning the operations of the International Conference's Mission to the Federal Republic of Yugoslavia (Serbia and Montenegro). This report by the Co-Chairmen contains the certification referred to in paragraph 5 of Security Council resolution 970 (1995) of 12 January 1995.

I should be grateful if you would bring this information to the attention of the members of the Security Council.

---

[*]   UN Doc. S/1995/302, 13 April 1995. Signed by Boutros Boutros-Ghali.

Annex
Operations of the International Conference on the Former Yugoslavia Mission to the Federal Republic of Yugoslavia (Serbia and Montenegro)

I. INTRODUCTION

1. The present report is submitted as indicated in paragraph 36 of the annex to the letter dated 31 March 1995 from the Secretary-General addressed to the President of the Security Council (S/1995/255).

2. It will be recalled that on 4 August 1994 the following measures were ordered by the Government of the Federal Republic of Yugoslavia (Serbia and Montenegro) to come into effect the same day:

> "(a) To break off political and economic relations with the 'Republika Srpska';
> (b) To prohibit the stay of the members of the leadership of the 'Republika Srpska' (Parliament, Presidency and Government) in the territory of the Federal Republic of Yugoslavia;
> (c) As of today the border of the Federal Republic of Yugoslavia is closed for all transport towards the 'Republika Srpska', except food, clothing and medicine."

3. In its resolution 970 (1995), adopted on 12 January 1995, the Security Council requested that the Secretary-General submit every 30 days for its review a report from the Co-Chairmen of the Steering Committee of the International Conference on the Former Yugoslavia on the border closure measures taken by the authorities of the Federal Republic of Yugoslavia (Serbia and Montenegro). Pursuant to paragraph 5 of that resolution, the Secretary-General transmitted to the Council reports from the Co-Chairmen in the state of implementation of the above-mentioned measures on 3 February (S/1995/ 104), 2 March (S/1995/175) and 31 March (S/1995/255). The report dated 31 March 1995 contained the following certification from the Co-Chairmen:

> "In light of the foregoing developments during the past 30 days, based on the Mission's on-site observation, and based on the advice of the Mission Coordinator, Mr. T.J. Nieminen, and in the absence of any contrary information from the air, whether the airborne reconnaissance system of the North Atlantic Treaty Organization (NATO) or national technical means, and aside from the reported tracking of helicopters crossing the border, the Co-Chairmen conclude that the Government of the Federal Republic of Yugoslavia (Serbia and Montenegro) is continuing to meet its commitment to close the land border between the Federal Republic of Yugoslavia (Serbia and Montenegro) and the areas of the Republic of Bosnia and Herzegovina under the control of the Bosnian Serb forces. The Co-Chairmen also conclude that during the past 30 days there were no commercial transshipments across the border between the Federal Republic of Yugoslavia (Serbia and Montenegro) and the Republic of Bosnia and Herzegovina."

4. Security Council resolution 970 (1995) provides that the restrictions and their measures referred to in paragraph 1 of resolution 943 (1994) of XX September 1994 shall be suspended for a further period of 100 days from the adoption of resolution 970 (1995). The present report supplements the three previous 30-day reports and discusses developments during the first 10 days of April.

II. LEGISLATION/REGULATIONS ON THE BORDER CLOSURE

5. The legislation of the authorities of the Federal Republic of Yugoslavia (Serbia and Montenegro) closing the border between the Federal Republic of Yugoslavia (Serbia and Montenegro) and the areas of the Republic of Bosnia and Herzegovina under the control of the Bosnian Serbs continues to be in force.

6. The Mission has received from the Authorities of the Federal Republic of Yugoslavia (Serbia and Montenegro) the following analysis of confiscations along the border with Bosnia and Herzegovina for March 1995:

Petrol	10.4 tons
Diesel	110.7 tons
Motor oil	194 litres
Cigarettes	2.4 tons
Construction materials	3.8 tons
Wood	10 cubic metres
Alcohol	nil
Food	9.9 tons
Textiles/clothing/footwear	490 kg
Motor vehicles	5
Coffee	82 kg
Other goods	22.2 tons

There were 84 customs offence procedures initiated during the month and 72 were finalized. Fines and penalties amounted to 251,400 dinars. The confiscations of diesel oil included one large consignment of 100 tons in Sector Charlie on XX March. Apart from alcohol most of the other categories of confiscations show an increase over the previous month. While the number of new offence cases initiated is down from the previous month they are above the average of the previous seven months, and there is a monthly in crease in the number of cases finalized as well as in the value of penalties.

III. ORGANIZATION, FINANCING AND WORK OF THE MISSION

7. As at April 10 1995, 152 international Mission personnel were on duty with the Mission. The Mission personnel to date have come from the following countries: Belgium, Canada, Czech Republic, Denmark, Finland, France, Germany, Greece, Ireland, Italy, Netherlands, Norway, Portugal, Russian Federation, Spain, Sweden, United Kingdom of Great Britain and Northern Ireland and United States of America. Because of financial difficulties, no new observers have been taken on to replace those who leave. The participating countries have been asked to replace any observers who depart the Mission after 15 April on a one-for-one basis. By the Mission's own calculations, an observer complement below 150 may not be able to provide sufficiently credible information to certify whether the Government of the Federal Republic of Yugoslavia (Scrbia and Montenegro) is in compliance with its decision to close the border with Bosnian Serb-held areas of Bosnia and Herzegovina to all but shipments of humanitarian aid. Depending on the receipt of funding the Mission will determine at the earliest possible date if and when it will request observers above the 150 minimum.

8. Around the end of March an unusually heavy snowfall was experienced in the mountainous regions of the area of operations. The snow caused roadblocks and multiple avalanches, thus impeding most mobile patrols and preventing the relief of teams at several border crossing-points. The team from the Sula border crossing-point was withdrawn on 30 March at 1430 because of the blizzard. Sula was remanned again on 31 March at 1530. The observers at the Sastanvci border crossing-point were stranded for 102 hours before they were relieved on 2 April. From 31 March to late on 1 April it was not possible to relieve teams at Scapan Polje and Kratac.

IV. FREEDOM OF MOVEMENT OF THE MISSION

9. The Mission continues to enjoy full freedom of movement within the Federal Republic of Yugoslavia (Serbia and Montenegro).

10. On 6 April, four kilometres north of Uvac near a pedestrian bridge over the river ford (Sector Bravo), a mobile patrol, led by the Head of Sector, received incoming rifle fire (about 10 rounds went into the water some 20 metres below the vehicle and 5 or 6 rounds impacted 5-6 metres above the car). The gunfire came from a Bosnian civilian, who is living on the other side of the bridge. On the Federal Republic of Yugoslavia (Serbia and Montenegro) side there were three policemen, one customs official and two Yugoslav Army soldiers on the

spot, but they did not react in any way. The patrol had to withdraw from the scene and the next day the Head of Sector submitted a strong protest to the local authorities (Yugoslav Army, militia). They regretted the incident very much and apologized for their personnel's reaction. They assured the Head of Sector that a Yugoslav Army liaison officer will always be present with Mission patrols in this area to look after their security. On the same day the Mission Coordinator called the Director of Customs of the Federal Republic of Yugoslavia (Serbia and Montenegro) who expressed his deep concern and promised to take necessary measures immediately to defuse the situation. Nevertheless, the Mission Coordinator instructed Sector Bravo not to approach the place until security was fully restored.

11. On 8 April, the Mission teams working in Belgrade port (Sector Belgrade) were subjected to threats from angry drivers. Security was inadequate and that had to withdraw to the hotel with a police escort.

V. COOPERATION OF THE AUTHORITIES OF THE FEDERAL REPUBLIC OF YUGOSLAVIA (SERBIA AND MONTENEGRO) WITH THE MISSION

12. The cooperation with the authorities of the Federal Republic of Yugoslavia (Serbia and Montenegro) continues to be good.

13. With reference to the Mission's previous monthly reports it should be noted that:

(a) Violations cited in those reports are in most cases isolated exceptions, and need to be read in the context of overall satisfactory compliance by the authorities of the Federal Republic of Yugoslavia (Serbia and Montenegro). Swift disciplinary measures taken by the authorities against deficient police or customs officials suggest that the violations are errors (wilful or accidental) on the part of individual officers acting against government policy;

(b) Smuggling attempts can be expected along any frontier which has restricted passage. The authorities have reacted quickly and have taken action against individuals involved in smuggling attempts. The Mission has no evidence to suggest that unauthorized goods cross the border between the Federal Republic of Yugoslavia (Serbia and Montenegro) and Bosnia and Herzegovina in any appreciable quantity;

(c) It can be expected that locals in isolated areas may tamper with border barricades which cause them inconvenience. They may do it for freedom of movement or for purposes of smuggling but the authorities react quickly to rebuild, restore or repair the barricades. In most cases these uncontrolled border crossings are in very remote locations where the difficult terrain would make truck crossings very difficult or virtually impossible.

14. Since agreeing to a new Memorandum of Understanding on Yugoslav Red Cross consignments, inspection facilities for their loads are now more or less in line with the other international aid agencies, making it even more difficult to conceal any significant quantity of contraband. It is worth noting as well that the Customs Authorities of the Federal Republic of Yugoslavia (Serbia and Montenegro) regularly receive inquiries and requests mainly about definitions of humanitarian aid goods allowed to cross the border. Normally the authorities will deal with these matters themselves, but in case of doubt will consult the Mission. During the period from 1 to 31 March the Customs received 63 requests and rejected all of them. They consulted the Mission on another 15 cases of which 10 were approved and 5 were disallowed. The Mission coordinator has stressed that the Mission exercises the right to refuse to seal any vehicle when its monitors are not notified with the cargo or the searching procedure.

VI. INFORMATION RECEIVED FROM NATIONAL AND OTHER SOURCES

15. The operating principle of the Mission is to base itself on its own observations and on information that it has verified. The Mission Coordinator has maintained a standing request to Governments possessing the technical capacity to provide it with information relevant to its mandate.

16. On 2 April, the Mission received information from an unknown source that the Bosnian Serb Army had acquired a substantial resupply of ammunition or other war *matériel* across the border, carried in civilian trucks which normally carry humanitarian aid. It was alleged that about 30 humanitarian aid trucks crossed the border at border crossing-point Sremska Raca (Sector Belgrade) on 30 March and 46 trucks on 31 March, all without proper checks. It was further alleged that this information was corroborated from independent sources. The Mission has checked this matter thoroughly and can confirm that, because of the inspection and loading procedures in place with the Office of the United Nations High Commissioner for Refugees and the International Committee of the Red Cross, as well as from standard customs inspections of trucks which arrive at Belgrade port already loaded, it is virtually impossible to conceal any significant quantity of ammunition or other war *matériel* in their consignments. The Mission has also carefully reviewed procedures regarding Yugoslav Red Cross

consignments on the two days in question and has questioned the monitors who were working at Belgrade port and Novi Sad (two principal points for loading, inspecting and sealing). It was confirmed that they had been present during all customs inspections and that the Customs had diligently searches and inspected all the trucks either by using a probe (feeler) or by moving some of the cargo at random.

17. In this regard, it may be noted that in the whole history of the Mission there have been no discoveries of weapons, ammunition or anything similar, apart from one instance at the end of February (Sector Charlie) when one man was apprehended by the Federal Republic of Yugoslavia (Serbia and Montenegro) Customs while attempting to cross the border with a gun, one hand grenade and some ammunition.

VI. Problems Encountered and Representations Made to the Authorities

18. On 2 April, a mobile patrol observed a number of boats on the Bosnian side of the Drina River near Culine, 10 km south of Mali Zvornik (Sector Alpha). A special militia patrol was notified. Close monitoring of this site was continued, and on 5 April another mobile patrol, taking a high ground observation post, was able to observe on the Bosnian side across Culine what appeared to be a Bosnian Serb fuel supply depot, including 1 military fuel tanker, 4 military trucks, 3 rubber boats (approximate capacity 12 pax), 2 barges, 2 big metal reservoirs and a number of metal containers on the island in the middle of the river. On 6 April, another mobile patrol confirmed the finding and notified the local authorities. Since then, a special militia team of police and army has established a 24-hour surveillance of the place. The Mission mobile patrols continue to monitor this site closely.

19. On 2 April, a Sula border crossing-point team (Sector Bravo) reported that a truck with one uniformed policeman of the Federal Republic of Yugoslavia (Serbia and Montenegro), previously rejected, was allowed to cross to the Bosnian side of the border. The local police commander, presented with a protest, confirmed that it was a mistake by his personnel.

20. On 2 april, at Strpci Station (Sector Bajina Basta) a Mission team encountered an individual with a submachine gun who presented himself as a driver for a military commanding officer from the Bosnian side and warned team members not to use binoculars or cameras trained at the Bosnian side, saying: "We do not want to shoot at you". The authorities were notified about this individual, along with the fact that the team had not used any cameras.

21. On 3 April, at Drzavna Ada, 3 km south of Badovinci (Sector Alpha) a large boat was spotted on the Bosnian side of the river Drina by a mobile patrol, as well as a Yugoslav Army ambush in the Federal Republic of Yugoslavia (Serbia and Montenegro) side waiting in case it came across.

22. On 5 April, the Head of Sector Bravo together with a local police chief and a Yugoslav Army liaison officer visited the FAP truck factory near Priboj and witnessed truck frames in production. They found no evidence of military production.

23. On 5 April, a mobile patrol discovered a new possible point for potential smuggling at a disused railroad line across the boundary in the vicinity of Vracanovici (Sector Charlie). Two empty trucks were observed there on rendezvous with another car, entering the Bosnian side and heading to Bileca. The police of the Federal Republic of Yugoslavia (Serbia and Montenegro) were notified, as was the Yugoslav Army liaison officer. Discussions about the modalities of coverage of this point are still in progress.

24. On 7 April, a mobile patrol near Jamena (Sector Belgrade) observed three new pontoons tied together plus one tug boat on the Bosnian side. Three military personnel were seen as well, busily servicing the tug boat. Nevertheless, there were no traces of activity on the Federal Republic of Yugoslavia (Serbia and Montenegro) side: the seals on the barriers were intact. The police and Yugoslav Army seemed unaware of what the Bosnian Serb side was doing.

25. On 7 April, at Badovinci (Sector Alpha) it was reported that under the bridge the police of the Federal Republic of Yugoslavia (Serbia and Montenegro) captured nine men and three women on bicycles who were trying to smuggle to Bosnia and Herzegovina approximately 1.2 tons of fuel, which was confiscated on the spot.

26. On 8 April, near Citluc (Sector Alpha) the Commanding Officer of a special militia team notified a mobile patrol that there was a potential smuggling site on the Bosnian side where a large barge capable of carrying a loaded truck had been spotted. The place is being closely monitored by mobile patrols.

27. On 8 April, from Vilusi (Sector Charlie) the observers reported that they had observed one truck with approximately 5 to 60 crates of empty beer bottles crossing into Federal Republic of Yugoslavia (Serbia and Montenegro) at night without being checked. In two hours the same truck, already with full bottles, crossed back into Bosnia and Herzegovina without being checked again. On 9 April, the matter was reported to the local authorities for appropriate action.

28. During the period from 2 to 7 April, United Nations airfield monitors working at radar screens at Surcin Airport near Belgrade observed an additional 25 unexplained slow-moving radar contacts from Bosnia and Herzegovina to the Federal Republic of Yugoslavia (Serbia and Montenegro). As in March, none

was observed by Mission personnel from the ground even though additional mobile patrols were mounted to search the skies during likely hours of crossing in the most travelled reaches of the Drina (between Mali Svornik and Ljubovija). As in the past, there were no reports of likely helicopter flights travelling from the Federal Republic of Yugoslavia (Serbia and Montenegro) back into Bosnia and Herzegovina. When presented with this information on 10 April, the Customs Director of the Federal Republic of Yugoslavia (Serbia and Montenegro), Mihalj Kertes, confirmed only the crossing, and return, of a helicopter from Bosnia and Herzegovina into the Federal Republic of Yugoslavia (Serbia and Montenegro) on 5 April and one on 6 April, but denied the existence of the other 23 possible helicopter flights.

29. At a later meeting, on 10 april, the Mission Coordinator, together with his Senior Political Adviser and Press Officer, met with the Director of Customs, the Deputy Director of Customs, the Assistant to the Chief of the Yugoslav Army General Staff for Air Force, the Assistant to the Chief of the Yugoslav Army General Staff for Radars and Electronic Monitoring Systems, the Yugoslav Army Head of Regional Flight Control and the Deputy Director of Civilian Air-traffic Control of the Federal Republic of Yugoslavia (Serbia and Montenegro). At the meeting the authorities categorically denied any involvement of the Federal Republic of Yugoslavia (Serbia and Montenegro) in the alleged air crossings. In view of the countervailing claims by senior officials of the Federal Republic of Yugoslavia (Serbia and Montenegro) as to the veracity of UNPROFOR technical data, it was agreed that experts should be asked to review the radar tapes for the period of 2 to 7 april.

30. Some 80 radar contacts have been reported by UNPROFOR to the Mission since 19 October 1994. Each track has been plotted to show its point of detection, the point of border crossing and the place where the radar track faded. Analysis of the positions and timing of these events shows no apparent pattern. Despite the recent extraordinary efforts by Mission personnel to confirm visually these possible violations of the air border, not one helicopter has been sighted from the ground. None the less, the characteristics of these radar contacts are, according to United Nations military observers, indicative of helicopters.

VIII. Certification

31. In the light of the foregoing developments based on the Mission's on-site observation, and in the absence of any contrary information from the air, whether the airborne reconnaissance system of NATO or national technical means, and aside from the reported tracking of possible helicopters crossing the

border, the Co-Chairmen conclude that the Government of the Federal Republic of Yugoslavia (Serbia and Montenegro) is continuing to meet its commitment to close the land border between the Federal Republic of Yugoslavia (Serbia and Montenegro) and the areas of the Republic of Bosnia and Herzegovina under the control of Bosnian Serb forces. The Co-Chairmen also conclude that during the period covered by this report there have been no commercial transshipments across the border between the Federal Republic of Yugoslavia (Serbia and Montenegro) and the Republic of Bosnia and Herzegovina.

144. REPORT OF THE SECRETARY-GENERAL SUBMITTED PURSUANT TO PARAGRAPH 4 OF SECURITY COUNCIL RESOLUTION 981 (1995)*

I. INTRODUCTION

1. In paragraph 4 of its resolution 981 (1995) of 31 March 1995, the Security Council requested me to continue my consultations with all concerned on the detailed implementation of the mandate of the United Nations Confidence Restoration Operation in Croatia, which is known as UNCRO, as set cut in paragraph 3 of that resolution, "and to report to the Council not later than 21 April for its approval". The present report is submitted pursuant to that request.

2. Prior to the adoption of Security Council resolution 981 (1995), I had requested Mr. Thorvald Stoltenberg, Co-Chairmen of the Steering Committee of the International Conference on the Former Yugoslavia, acting as my Special Envoy, to carry out consultations on the mandate. My Special Envoy had meetings with representatives of the Government of Croatia and of the local Serb authorities. Following the adoption of resolution 981 (1995), he continued his consultations and met with all concerned, including military authorities on both sides. The consultations have been carried out in close contact with my Special Representative for the Former Yugoslavia, Mr. Yasushi Akashi, and the Force Commander of the United Nations Peace Forces in Zagreb, Lieutenant-General Bernard Janvier.

---

* UN Doc. S/1995/320, 18 April 1995.

II. Basis of Discussions

3. The basis for the consultations has been paragraph 3 of resolution 981 (1995), and the documents referred to therein, namely:

    (a) Report of the Secretary-General (S/1995/222 and Corr. 1 and 2), particularly paragraph 72;

    (b) United Nations peace-keeping plan for the Republic of Croatia (S/23280, annex III);

    (c) Relevant resolutions of the Security Council;

    (d) Ceasefire agreement of 29 March 1994 (S/1994/867);

    (e) Economic agreement of 2 December 1994 (S/1994/1375).

4. The consultations have also been based on the assumption that the deployment of UNCRO and its operations will require the cooperation of all concerned.

II. Considerations

5. Following his consultations with political and military leaders representing the Government of Croatia and the local Serb Authorities, my Special Envoy has recommended the implementation of Security Council resolution 981 (1995) along the lines set out below.

6. My Special Envoy has, in pursuance of his mandate, concentrated his efforts on the tasks to be carried out and on the methods by which they would be implemented. In the light of the serious political differences between the Government of Croatia and the local Serb authorities, it is his view that a pragmatic approach is the only way in which the support and cooperation required for implementation of the new Operation's mandate can be obtained.

7. The plan meets the objective of implementing a new mandate with fewer personnel. In the course of his consultations, my Special Envoy repeatedly reminded his interlocutors of the concerns of the troop-contributing countries, whose evaluation of the plan will be decisive for their readiness to contribute personnel to the Operation.

8. My Special Envoy also emphasized that cooperation by the authorities concerned and their continuing commitment for existing agreements are prerequisites for obtaining assistance from the United Nations and for the effective implementation of the tasks assigned to the new Operation.

9. With regard to the new Operation's tasks at the international borders, my Special Envoy has carefully considered the differing views expressed in the

course of his consultations. He emphasized the importance of defining precise modalities of implementation which can obtain the cooperation of all concerned, which take into account the safety and security of the troops and which remain strictly within the framework of the tasks assigned.

10. Finally, my Special Envoy has strongly emphasized that the United Nations can only assist in solving the conflict. It is up to the Government of Croatia and the local Serb authorities to make the decisions and pursue the policies required to achieve a peaceful solution. Progress will ultimately require direct contacts and constructive cooperation between those specifically involved.

IV. PLAN FOR THE IMPLEMENTATION OF THE MANDATE OF UNCRO

11. The plan proposed to me by my Special Envoy, following his consultations, is based on the six main tasks identified for UNCRO in paragraph 3 of resolution 981 (1995). They are described in the following subsections.

A. *Performing fully the functions envisaged in the ceasefire agreement of 29 March 1994 between the Government of Croatia and the local Serb authorities (S/1994/367)*

Functions

12. In accordance with the functions envisaged in the ceasefire agreement of 29 March 1994 UNCRO will:

(a) Monitor the area between the forward troop deployment lines, which are the lines of separation agreed to in the ceasefire agreement;
(b) Verify that all weapons systems specified in the agreement are deployed in accordance with its provisions. This refers to heavy weapons deployed beyond the 10-kilometre and 20-kilometre lines and in weapon storage sites;
(c) Occupy checkpoints at all crossing points specified in Annex A to the agreement;
(d) Chair the Joint Commission at all levels;
(e) Conduct the liaison activities required to ensure the implementation of the agreement.

Implementation

13. In order to perform these functions fully, UNCRO will have exclusive control of the area between the forward troop deployment lines and will establish static posts as well as carrying out patrols on foot, by vehicle and by helicopter. UNCRO will also have full freedom of movement to monitor the deployment of troops and weapons systems as specified in the ceasefire agreement.

14. Because of the reduced number of troops available to UNCRO, the commitment of all concerned to the ceasefire agreement will be decisive for UNCRO's ability to perform its functions fully while ensuring the safety of its troops.

15. The functions envisaged in the ceasefire agreement will be implemented in the following way:

  (a) Static observation posts and checkpoints will be established by UNCRO in the areas most vulnerable to conflict and at locations where they are required to support patrolling activities and ensure the safety of the monitoring force;

  (b) UNCRO will man all the crossing-points specified in Annex A to the ceasefire agreement to ensure access for transit, resupply, humanitarian assistance, etc., as well as the crossing of civilians;

  (c) Patrols on foot, by vehicle and by helicopter will be conducted between and around these static UNCRO positions;

  (d) Static and mobile patrols as well as helicopter patrols will be carried out in order to monitor compliance on both sides with the provisions of the ceasefire agreement related to specific weapons systems;

  (e) Mine clearance will be conducted within the area between the forward troop deployment lines in accordance with established principles; UNCRO personnel will supervise and assist relevant authorities in the clearing of mines;

  (f) Civilian police monitors (CIVPOL) will supervise the local police which, under the ceasefire agreement, is obliged to assist UNCRO in the prevention of crime and maintenance of law and order in the area between the forward troop deployment lines;

  (g) CIVPOL will patrol the area between the forward troop deployment lines in order to enhance confidence and identify policing requirements;

  (h) UNCRO will chair Joint Commissions at all levels;

  (i) UNCRO will conduct liaison activities with military and police authorities at all levels.

B. *Facilitating implementation of the economic agreement of 2 December 1994 concluded under the auspices of the Co-Chairmen of the Steering Committee of the International Conference on the Former Yugoslavia (S/1994/1375)*

Functions

16. In order to advance the process of reconciliation and the restoration of normal life, UNCRO will:

(a) Facilitate and support the opening of transportation networks, as well as of water and energy facilities, within the limits of its resources;
(b) Support the negotiation and implementation of further economic and humanitarian measures which are included in the economic agreement or which may be agreed in subsequent negotiations.

Implementation

17. UNCRO will implement these functions in the following way:

(a) A security presence will be provided for the repair, opening and functioning of the networks and facilities mentioned above;
(b) Administrative, technical, logistic and engineering advice and support will be provided;
(c) UNCRO will supervise mine-clearance activities required to restore, open and operate the networks and facilities mentioned above;
(d) UNCRO will co-chair with the International Conference on the Former Yugoslavia the Joint Commission established by the economic agreement;
(e) UNCRO will coordinate the implementation of economic projects agreed in negotiations.

C. *Facilitating implementation of all relevant Security Council resolutions, including the functions identified in paragraph 72 of the above-mentioned report (S/1995/222 and Corr. 1 and 2)*

18. The Security Council resolutions referred to in subparagraph 3 (c) of resolution 981 (1995) are taken to include those relevant to the functioning of UNCRO (freedom of movement, security, self-defence, including close air

support) and those directly relevant to the mandate set out in paragraph 3 of that resolution.

Functions

19. In order to maintain conditions of peace and security and to restore confidence, thereby also facilitating the negotiation of a political solution, UNCRO will:

   (a) Provide assistance to needy individuals and communities (Croat, Serb and others), in cooperation with international agencies;
   (b) Monitor the human rights situation of individuals and communities (Croat, Serb and others) to ensure that there is no discrimination and that the human rights are protected;
   (c) Facilitate the voluntary return of refugees and displaced persons (Croat, Serb and others) in accordance with established international principles and in coordination with the Office of the United Nations High Commissioner for Refugees (UNHCR);
   (d) Support local confidence-building measures, including socio-economic and reconstruction activities, people-to-people contacts and information exchanges of mutual benefit.

Implementation

20. UNCRO, through military, civilian and CIVPOL personnel, as appropriate, will implement the above-mentioned functions in the following way:

Humanitarian Tasks

   (a) Humanitarian aid will be distributed in conjunction with UNHCR and other international and non-governmental organizations;
   (b) UNCRO will assist medical evacuations, prisoner exchanges, family and humanitarian visits and transfers and coordinate responses to emergency humanitarian situations;
   (c) UNCRO will facilitate the primary role of UNHCR with regard to the travel of refugees, through territory in which UNCRO is deployed, to refugee camps and holding centres;
   (d) UNCRO will supervise the clearance of mines by the parties when needed to meet humanitarian requirements;

Human Rights

(e) UNCRO will contribute to deterring human rights abuse by maintaining an overall presence; closely monitor and co-locate with local police forces; monitor judicial institutions to enhance respect for human rights; seek corrective action in case of human rights abuses; and provide an operational link to human rights bodies;

(f) UNCRO will monitor and protect the welfare and human rights of people in villages of particular sensitivity;

Return of Refugees and Displaced Persons

(g) Appropriate support will be provided to UNHCR for the voluntary return of refugees and displaced persons to their homes in conditions of safety, security and dignity and in accordance with established international principles;

Confidence-building

(h) UNHCR will promote local economic, social and reconstruction projects of mutual benefit and support the negotiation and implementation of such projects;

(i) UNHCR will promote people-to-people contacts, including humanitarian, media, local, commercial and administrative exchanges, and be available to provide security to those activities where appropriate.

D. *Assisting in controlling, by monitoring and reporting, the crossing of military personnel, equipment, supplies and weapons, over the international borders between the Republic of Croatia and the Republic of Bosnia and Herzegovina, and the Republic of Croatia and the Federal Republic of Yugoslavia (Serbia and Montenegro) at the border crossings for which UNCRO is responsible, as specified in the United Nations peace-keeping plan for the Republic of Croatia (S/23280, Annex III)*

Functions

21. UNCRO will carry out these monitoring and reporting functions at designated border-crossing points. Traffic crossing over the international borders will be monitored for military personnel, equipment, supplies and weapons. All

information concerning the movement of military personnel, equipment, supplies and weapons will be reported to the Security Council through the Secretary-General.

Implementation

22. The above-mentioned functions will be implemented in the following way:

   (a) UNCRO will carry out its tasks at designated border crossing-points by deploying with a strength sufficient to perform these tasks and maintain troop safety and security. These deployments will include a number of permanent and temporary border crossing-points;
   (b) All vehicles and personnel will stop at the border crossing-points. They will be visually checked in order to verify whether they carry military personnel, equipment, supplies and weapons;
   (c) In cases where military personnel, equipment, supplies and weapons are detected, UNCRO will give notice that the crossing of such personnel and items would be in violation of Security Council resolutions and will be reported to the Security Council;
   (d) UNCRO will compile any information on the crossing of such personnel and items and report this information to the Security Council through the Secretary-General.

E. *Facilitating the delivery of international humanitarian assistance to the Republic of Bosnia and Herzegovina through the territory of the Republic of Croatia*

Functions

23. UNCRO's tasks will be concentrated on providing advice and assistance to agencies involved in international humanitarian deliveries to Bosnia and Herzegovina through the territory of Croatia.

Implementation

24. To implement these functions, UNCRO will:

   (a) Facilitate convoy clearances from the Government of Croatia and from the local Serb authorities;

(b) Facilitate route clearance from the Government of Croatia and the local Serb authorities;

(c) Escort humanitarian convoys as required for their security and protection;

(d) Maintain routes when required and within the limits of its resources.

F. *Monitoring the demilitarization of the Prevlaka peninsula in accordance with resolution 779 (1992)*

Functions

25. In order to monitor the demilitarization of the Prevlaka peninsula, United Nations military observers will patrol and maintain a permanent presence on the most southerly portion of the peninsula. They will also monitor the area 5 kilometres on either side of the border and report on the presence of any military forces.

26. Full freedom of movement, including freedom of access into and out of the areas, will be essential.

27. This task will continue, as at present, to be performed by unarmed military observers only. It will require the cooperation of both sides and their commitment to demilitarization.

Implementation

28. The functions will be carried out as follows:

(a) United Nations military observers will patrol and sustain a continuous presence in the vicinity of the Prevlaka/Ostra peninsula;

(b) United Nations military observers will monitor the area 5 kilometres on each side of the border between BN 898149 and BN 966998 by patrolling;

(c) Liaison activities will be continued with the military and civil authorities of the parties at all levels in order to resolve violations or disputes;

(d) Theatre headquarters (UNPF-HQ) will convene the Joint Inter-State Commission to mediate and resolve any disputes that are beyond the competence of a lower level of authority.

V. Resource Requirements

29. My Special Representative and the Theatre Force Commander at the United Nations Peace Force Headquarters (UNPF-HQ) have analyzed the functions and responsibilities enumerated in sections IV.A to F above and assess that an overall total of some 8,750 troops would be required for their implementation, on the assumption that the military and civilian staff of the operation will enjoy the necessary cooperation of all concerned. The troops will be deployed in accordance with operations requirements determined by UNPF-HQ and UNCRO. The requirements for civilian staff, United Nations military observers and CIVPOL, as well as administrative and logistical support elements, will be submitted to the Advisory Committee on Administrative and Budgetary Questions in the context of an overall budget submission for UNPF-HQ, UNCRO, the United Nations Protection Force (UNPROFOR) and the United Nations Preventive Deployment Force (UNPREDEP), in accordance with the recommendation made in paragraph 84 of my report of 22 March 1995 (S/1995/222). It is expected that the strength of the United Nations forces currently in Croatia can be reduced to the proposed level of 8,750 and their deployment completed by 30 June 1995.

VI. Status-of-Forces Agreement

30. In accordance with paragraph 11 of resolution 981 (1995), discussions have been pursued with the Government of Croatia concerning a status-of-forces agreement for the presence of UNPF-HQ, UNCRO and, for a transitional period, UNPROFOR, on its territory, as well as for the use of Croatian territory for the support of UNPROFOR in Bosnia and Herzegovina and UNPREDEP in the former Yugoslav Republic of Macedonia. Difficulties have arisen as a result of demands by the Croatian authorities which are incompatible with the model status-of-forces agreement (A/45/594 of 9 October 1990) and with Security Council resolutions 908 (1994) and 981 (1995).

31. On 1 April my Special Representative wrote to the President of Croatia referring to paragraph 11 of resolution 981 (1995) and requesting the early meeting of representatives to finalize the matter. Following a meeting on 10 April, UNPF-HQ forwarded a draft agreement to the Croatian authorities on 14 April. A further meeting is expected to take place in the course of the current week.

VII. OBSERVATIONS

32. In spite of serious differences of approach, my Special Envoy's assessment is that there is enough common ground between the Government of Croatia and the local Serb authorities to make it possible to implement resolution 981 (1995). The ceasefire agreement provides a level of stability on the basis of which negotiations and efforts of reconciliation can take place. The economic agreement will, when fully implemented, provide an essential contribution too the normalization of life and the restoration of confidence. These two agreements are pillars of common interest which can reinforce the future process of reconciliation and normalisation for the people living in this area. In this regard, I lay special emphasis on measures intended to provide protection and to advance the process of reconciliation as well as the new Operation's ability to promote such measures.

33. The situation on the ground is volatile. Without the requisite sense of responsibility on the part of all concerned, it could quickly deteriorate further. However, in spite of these circumstances and the serious political differences which continue to exist, both the Government of Croatia and the local Serb authorities are aware that the alternative to this plan would be more violence and a resumption of war.

34. As was to some degree the case in February 1992 when UNPROFOR was originally established, the plan set out above does not have the formal acceptance and full support of either the Government of Croatia or the local Serb authorities. The risk therefore remains that either or both sides will fail to cooperate with the United Nations in its implementation. In these circumstances, it is not without misgiving that I present these proposals to the Council. On the other hand the proposed plan provides for a pragmatic implementation of paragraph 3 of Security Council resolution 981 (1995) and the alternative to its adoption would be the withdrawal of United Nations forces and the resumption of war. If the two sides seriously wish to avoid a renewal of the conflict, it is up to them to provide the necessary conditions for the new Operation to discharge its responsibility successfully.

35. I therefore recommend that the Security Council approve the arrangements set out in the present report and authorize the deployment of UNCRO to implement them.

**145. LETTER DATED 18 MAY 1995 FROM THE SECRETARY-GENERAL
ADDRESSED TO THE PRESIDENT OF THE SECURITY COUNCIL***

I have the honour to transmit the attached report which was addressed to me
on 17 May 1995 by the Co-Chairmen of the Steering Committee of the International Conference on the Former Yugoslavia, concerning the operations of the
International Conference's Mission to the Federal Republic of Yugoslavia
(Serbia and Montenegro). This report by the Co-Chairmen contains the certification referred to in Security Council resolution 988 (1995).

I should be grateful if you would bring this information to the attention of the
members of the Security Council.

Annex

**Operations of the International Conference on the Former Yugoslavia
(ICFY) Mission to the Federal Republic of Yugoslavia
(Serbia and Montenegro)**

I. INTRODUCTION

1. The present report is submitted pursuant to Security Council Resolution 988
(1995) adopted on 21 April 1995. In paragraph 5 of the resolution, the Security
Council underlined the importance it attached to the work of the ICFY Mission,
expressed its concern that a shortage of resources hampered the effectiveness of
that work and requested the Secretary-General to report to it within 30 days of
the adoption of the resolution on measures to increase the effectiveness of the
work of the ICFY Mission, including on the question of helicopter flights. The
Security Council also requested Member States to make available the necessary
resources to strengthen the Mission's capacity to carry out its task. The report of
a special inquiry into helicopters flights was submitted to the Security Council on
.... (S/). The question of measures to increase the effectiveness of the
Mission is dealt with in Section IV below. In paragraph 13 of its resolution, the
Council requested that the Secretary-General submit every 30 days for its review
a report from the Co-Chairmen of the Steering Committee of the International
Conference on the Former Yugoslavia on the border closure measures taken by
the authorities of the Federal Republic of Yugoslavia (Serbia and Montenegro).
Developments during the past 30 days are dealt with in this report.

---

* UN Doc. S/1995/406, 18 May 1995. Signed by Boutros Boutros-Ghali.

2. In paragraph 16 of its resolution, the Security Council, furthermore, encouraged the Co-Chairmen of the ICFY Steering Committee to ensure that the ICFY Mission keep the Government of the Republic of Bosnia and Herzegovina, the Government of the Republic of Croatia and the authorities of the Federal Republic of Yugoslavia (Serbia and Montenegro) fully informed about the findings of the ICFY Mission. Pursuant to this provision, the Co-Chairmen have instructed the Head of the ICFY Mission to bring to their attention any findings of special concern to any of the three countries so that the Co-Chairmen can transmit it to them. In this regard, they have written to the Foreign Minister of the Republic of Croatia to report in more details about the Sremska Raca border crossing point earlier in May.

3. It will be recalled that on 4 August 1994 the following measures were ordered by the Government of the Federal Republic of Yugoslavia (Serbia and Montenegro) to come into effect the same day:

"a. To break off political and economic relations with the 'Republica Srpska';
 b. To prohibit the stay of the members of the leadership of the 'Republica Srpska' (Parliament, Presidency and Government) in the territory of the Federal Republic of Yugoslavia;
 c. As of today the border of the Federal Republic of Yugoslavia is closed for all transport towards the 'Republica Srpska', except food, clothing and medicine."

4. On 19 September 1994, on 3 October 1994, on 2 November 1994, on 5 December 1994, on 5 January 1995, on 3 February 1995, on 2 March 1995, on 31 March 1995 and on 13 April 1995, the Secretary-General transmitted to the Security Council reports from the Co-Chairmen of the Steering Committee of the International Conference on the Former Yugoslavia on the state of implementation of the above-mentioned measures (S/1994/1074; S/1994/1124; S/1994/1246; S/1994/1372; S/1995/6; S/1995/104; S/1995/175; S/1995/255 and S/1995/302). The report dated 13 April 1995 contained the following certification from the Co-Chairmen:

"In the light of the foregoing developments based on the Mission's on-site observation, and in the absence of any contrary information from the air, whether the airborne reconnaissance system of the North Atlantic Treaty Organization (NATO), or national technical means, and aside from the reported tracking of possible helicopters crossing the border, the Co-Chairmen conclude that the Government of the Federal Republic of Yugoslavia (Serbia and Montenegro) is continuing to meet its commitment to close the land border between the Federal Republic of Yugoslavia (Serbia and Montenegro) and the areas of the Republic of Bosnia and Herzegovina under the control of the Bosnian Serb forces. The Co-Chairmen also conclude that during the period covered by this report there have been no commercial transshipments across the border between the Federal Republic of Yugoslavia (Serbia and Montenegro) and the Republic of Bosnia and Herzegovina."

5. Developments in the past 30 days are provided below.

II. LEGISLATION/REGULATIONS ON THE BORDER CLOSURE

6. The legislation of the authorities of the Federal Republic of Yugoslavia (Serbia and Montenegro) closing the border with the Bosnian Serbs continues to be in effect.

7. In accordance with Federal Government law, the border crossings will be open for passenger traffic during May, June and July from 4 a.m. to 8 p.m. The border crossings at Sremska Raca and Vilusi will be open for passenger and freight traffic 24 hours a day.

8. The authorities of the Federal Republic of Yugoslavia (Serbia and Montenegro) have provided the Mission with the following list of confiscations conducted along its border with Bosnia and Herzegovina for April 1995:

Petrol	11.5 tons
Diesel	11.1 tons
Cigarettes	1 ton
Construction Material	472 kgs.
Wood	61 cubic metres
Alcohol	2,838 litres
Food	32 tons
Textiles, Clothing, Footwear	460 kgs.
Motor Vehicles	6
Electrical gadgets	13
Coffee	21 kgs.
Other goods	4.1 tons

9. There were 102 customs offences procedures initiated during the month and 84 were finalized. Fines and penalties amounted to 438,500 dinars. Confiscations during the month have gained momentum. The number of new offence cases was well above the average of the previous 8 months and there was a substantial increase in the amount of penalties of the adjudicated cases, which almost doubled those of March.

10. After fighting started in "Sector West" on 1 May a difficult situation developed at Sremska Raca border crossing. FRY customs authorities informed the Mission on 5 May that 100 trucks said to be carrying livestock, perishable and other goods and timber, were waiting on the road leading to Sremska Raca. The circumstances surrounding the incident were forwarded for consideration of the

UN Sanctions Committee. On 10 May the UN Sanctions Committee gave permission for only livestock and perishable goods to transit FRY into UNPA East in a convoy. The Mission sought to implement the decision of the Sanctions Committee scrupulously and, in the end result only 2 trucks carrying perishable goods were allowed to cross the border at Sremska Raca by 12 May. They were escorted by the Mission personnel and the FRY authorities into UNPA East. Having regard to the provisions of paragraph 16 of Resolution 988, the Co-Chairmen are writing to the Ministers of Foreign Affairs of the Republic of Bosnia and Herzegovina, the Republic of Croatia and the Federal Republic of Yugoslavia giving them a more detailed report on this matter.

11. In accordance with the Memorandum of Understanding (MOU) on the control of Yugoslav Red Cross consignments, substantial quantities of concealed goods were found and refused because they could be considered as trade. Under the MOU rules on buses, the scrutiny of long distance unscheduled buses was intensified. Buses transporting commercial quantities of goods and hidden fuel were regularly denied entry. In Sector Alpha the performance of Customs Officers at the four crossing-points improved considerably.

III. Organization, Financing and Work of the Mission

12. As of 15 May 1995, 154 international Mission personnel are on duty with the Mission. The Mission personnel to date have come from the following countries: Belgium, Canada, Czech Republic, Denmark, Finland, France, Germany, Greece, Ireland, Italy, the Netherlands, Norway, Portugal, the Russian Federation, Spain, Sweden, the United Kingdom of Great Britain and Northern Ireland and the United States of America.

13. The number of international Mission personnel is still too low to man all existing border crossings points (BCPs) and fell below the absolute minimum level of 150 monitors at the end of April and in the beginning of May. Due to the persistent shortage of personnel and the necessity of having two international monitors at each BCP, the Mission Coordinator ordered a temporary withdrawal of personnel from three BCPs. From 1-21 May, Mission monitors were no longer positioned at the following BCPs:

Sector Bajina Basta: BCP Skelani (manned only intermittently);
Sector Bravo: BCP Sula;
Sector Charlie: BCP Krstac.

14. Withdrawal from these BCPs was considered by the Mission Coordinator to be low-risk because of their remote location and the paucity of traffic crossing the border. They were manned by the local authorities, visited regularly by Mission mobile patrols, and were re-manned by the Mission as soon as resources permitted. An updated list of the border crossing points in the Mission is attached in Appendix A of this report.

15. Following the submission of the "Report of the Expert Inquiry into Alleged Helicopter Flights" (S/1995/), the Mission Coordinator has appointed a member of the Mission to be Air Operations Officer. He is a qualified Fighter (Aircraft) Controller and is suited to this important position. Working within the Mission's Operations Sector, he will endeavour to develop the means of monitoring the airspace above the border of the Federal Republic of Yugoslavia (Serbia and Montenegro) and Bosnia and Herzegovina. Initially, he will establish approved links between the Mission, United Nations, MCCC (NATO) and the FRY authorities. This will assist in the timely investigation of alleged infringements should they occur. Also using existing resources, both manpower and equipment, he will seek ways of improving visual detection from the ground. This can be achieved by improving real-time communications and alerting procedures among the Mission's monitors. Finally, he will propose means to enhance future surveillance.

IV. MEASURES TO INCREASE THE EFFECTIVENESS OF THE WORK OF THE MISSION

16. In paragraph five of Resolution 988 the Security Council underlined the importance it attached to the work of the ICFY Mission, expressed its concern that a shortage of resources hampered the effectiveness of that work and requested the Secretary-General to report to the Security Council within 30 days on measures to increase the effectiveness of the work of the ICFY Mission.

17. Unfortunately, the Mission has been undergoing a stringent financial situation, even though the position has, in the last few days, improved and as of 16 May 1995, the Mission had a cash balance of US$ 900,000 and liabilities totalling US$ 150,000. A voluntary contribution of US$ 256,000 has been promised but has not yet arrived, and the Mission is currently owed approximately US$ 3 million. It should be mentioned in this regard that some Governments have taken the position that they are not obliged to pay assessed contributions and make only voluntary contributions.

18. The precarious financial situation of the Mission has existed since the beginning of March 1995. Due to non-payment of contributions all new arrivals to the

Mission were stopped as of 6 March 1995. At that time the Mission had 194 international members covering 19 border crossing points. A special meeting of the Steering Committee of the ICFY was convened on 10 March to discuss the financial crisis. Following that meeting a new six-month budget was drawn-up for the Mission with effect from 1 April 1995. That budget provided for contributions in the sum of US$ 3.66 million and, if fulfilled, would have enabled the complement of international personnel to be increased to 250.

19. Unfortunately payments of contributions to this six-month budget have been considerably delayed with the result that by 16 May 1995 the Mission had decreased to 152 international members. The Mission has also been obliged to take a number of measures to reduce operating costs. Telephone charges were cut substantially and the number of rented vehicles at Mission Headquarters was cut by two-thirds. This cut has subsequently been off set by voluntary contributions of 60 vehicles. Other voluntary contributions have included a radio equipment network, office equipment and visual aids. Despite these savings, the Mission has still run into difficulties and had temporarily to stop staffing the three border control points referred to in Section III above.

20. The Mission continues to be in acute need of additional contributions if it is to be able to expand to 250 and to enhance the effectiveness of its work. Every team of two international observers requires the Mission to pay for a translator and a vehicle. Each team needs a weather-proof presence on the border in the form of one portacabin for each border crossing-point. The holiday caravans, used at present, cannot withstand the constant wear and do not provide shelter, or the security, necessary for the team, translators and drivers.

21. With the recent payments that have been made, and promised, it has been decided to start increasing the number of international members initially to 165, with the hope that if member states pay their contributions, the number can be increased to 250. The view has been expressed in some quarters that the Mission should be further expanded to 400 international members. In order to make this possible a much more secure financial basis would be needed.

22. On the question of an aerial capacity for the Mission, it will be recalled that in the report transmitted to the Security Council on 2 March 1995, reference was made to equipment that would be needed should it be decided that the Mission should have such a capacity to detect possible cross-border helicopter flights. The need for mobile radars and the tasking of dedicated observers to watch over the airspace at the border were referred to. Unfortunately, the finances of the Mission at this stage would not allow for such possibilities.

23. The Mission Coordinator has submitted to the Co-Chairmen various suggestions that he considers could contribute to increasing the effectiveness of the Mission, including the following:

- that the UN Peace Force loan the Mission the portacabins it needs;
- that more customs officers be recruited to bolster the Mission's expertise at truck-loading and border-crossing points;
- that each border control point be provided with either CAPSAT or satellite telephone equipment for contact with Mission Headquarters and other border control points;
- that efforts be made to provide basic amenities at border control points such as toilet facilities, clean drinking water, heat for winter and shade or cooling for the living quarters, refrigeration, cooking and basic washing facilities;
- that dedicated helicopter support (up to three helicopters) be provided to the Mission to allow it to respond more promptly to border violation reports. Contributing country(ies) could provide helicopter assets (equipment and crews), and the Mission could arrange the necessary base support and flight authorizations within the FRY.

24. If the Mission is to be able to expand to the extent desired and to increase the effectiveness of its work on land and in the air, considerably increased resources would be required, going well beyond the present capacity of the International Conference on the Former Yugoslavia. The Co-Chairmen have informed the Secretary-General of the United Nations, the European Union and the Contact Group of nations that they believe one should be moving towards transferring the work of the ICFY Mission to the OSCE. The Co-Chairmen took this responsibility on last September on behalf of ICFY because this was the only international body that could carry this essential task out, but they always saw it as a temporary arrangement. Now, as the months have passed and the difficulties of arranging proper financial support for the Mission have grown, they believe it would be preferable for these responsibilities to be conducted by a regional organization which has the confidence of all parties and could ensure that the Mission is properly funded with the necessary levels of staff, who can then work and plan without having to live from week to week without assurance that there will be sufficient funds to carry on their operations.

V. Freedom of Movement of the Mission

25. The Mission continues to enjoy full freedom of movement within the Federal Republic of Yugoslavia (Serbia and Montenegro).
26. On 13 April, Sector Alpha reported that a demonstration by the Serbian radical Party of V. Seselj took place near BCP Trbusnica. As a precautionary

measure Mission caravans were withdrawn from the BCP at 1040 hours and were placed in a secure area at the Loznica Red Cross. At 1600 hours, 300 fully equipped policemen with riot gear were positioned near the BCP; at 1625 hours the Head of Sector withdrew Mission monitors from the BCP; at 1700 hours a crowd of 400 arrived at the bridge followed by additional police reinforcements; at 1730 hours the crowd moved to the Bosnian side across the bridge; and at 1800 hours the demonstrators returned to the FRY side and proceeded to the town of Loznica while the situation at the bridge returned to normal. No violent actions or damage were reported. Mission personnel returned to the BCP at 1830 hours.

27. On 21 April, BCP Vracenovici (Sector Charlie) reported that ten rounds of small arms fire were heard in the vicinity of the BCP during the night. One round impacted very close to the BCP. On 25 April local police completed the investigation into the shooting incident. The Head of Sector was informed that it was a local celebration with habitual shooting in the air. The locals were warned afterwards to cease such celebrations in the vicinity of the BCP. This incident was assessed as not a direct targeting of Mission personnel.

28. On 2 May, the association "Orthodox Unity" sent a letter to the Mission demanding that "all the controllers who control crossings of the Serb people and transport communications should leave within the next five days from all check-points on the Drina and one on the Zagreb highway". This association is known to the FRY authorities who do not consider it a threat to the Mission.

29. On 6 May, Mission members were once again targeted. Another shooting incident occurred at a river ford four kilometres north of Uvac (Sector Bravo), in spite of the assurances of the local Chief of Police that it had warned the perpetrator of a previous shooting on 6 April and that it was now safe to visit the area again. The Mission Coordinator has subsequently instructed that no further patrolling be done in this area until confirmation is received that the individual concerned has been removed. On 7 May, the Mission Coordinator met with senior FRY authorities who offered an apology for the incident and promised to take all necessary measures to apprehend the perpetrator.

30. On 10 May, Sector Alpha reported that an incoming artillery shell from the Bosnian side impacted in the vicinity of CCP Stari Most Zvornik. No casualties were sustained by the Mission personnel since they were not present there at that time.

VI. COOPERATION OF THE AUTHORITIES OF THE FEDERAL REPUBLIC OF
YUGOSLAVIA (SERBIA AND MONTENEGRO) WITH THE MISSION

31. Cooperation with the authorities of the Federal Republic of Yugoslavia
(Serbia and Montenegro) continues to be good.
32. In the opinion of the Mission Coordinator, the FRY authorities are effectively implementing their border closure measures. The so-called "ant trade" (small
quantities carried by individuals) is not significant. The Mission's daily reports
show a consistent and regular pattern of refusals and confiscations of excess
goods (including fuel) from cars, buses, trucks and tractors. There are very high
vehicle search rates at the border crossings. The level of cooperation has especially improved between the Regional Heads of the FRY customs and the Mission
Sector Commanders.

VII. INFORMATION RECEIVED FROM NATIONAL AND OTHER SOURCES

33. The operating principle of the Mission is to base its reporting and evaluations on its own observations and on information that it has verified. The
Mission Coordinator has maintained a standing request to Governments possessing the technical capacity to provide it with information relevant to its mandate.
34. On 14 April, the Mission received information from unevaluated sources
alleging that large quantities of weapons and military supplies were being transported nightly by trucks which crossed the River Drina near Raca, usually over
pontoon bridges or ferries. It was further alleged that around 15 March an estimated 50 to 60 trucks with rocket launchers and other heavy weapons crossed
into Bosnia near this location from the Federal Republic of Yugoslavia (Serbia
and Montenegro). The Mission has received no reports from Sremska Raca
(described as Raca in the information) about any such incident. This BCP is
monitored by Mission observers 24 hours a day, every day. Furthermore, Sector
Belgrade has been deploying foot and mobile patrols along the Sava River from
Sremska Raca to the closed ferry crossing in Jamena. Nothing of the kind was
reported nor were there any traces of suspicious activity around the closed ferry
crossing on the FRY side.
35. In the course of the last two weeks of April, the Mission received information from unspecified sources with the following allegations:

- A pontoon bridge, which crosses the Drina river south of Janja (Bosnia)
  and west of Batar (Serbia), near the town of Loznica, located in a one
  kilometre prohibited zone, has been used since December 1994 to circum-

vent the "inter-Serbian embargo", and that trucks carrying fuel, weapons, ammunition and troops go across this bridge which is open to traffic every day;
- Several helicopters enter Bosnia daily, usually alone, but sometimes in formations of four to six, at the point where the River Lim enters the Drina river near the town of Priboj (Serbia), and they fly mostly at night from Niksic (Montenegro);
- A submerged pontoon bridge exists 10 kms downstream of the Drina river at Palovica, near Ljubovica and Dubravica;
- A secret crossing is operated by boats at night-time in Fakovici, between Bratunac and Skelani on the Drina river;
- A submerged oil pipeline exists and was operative in December 1994-January 1995 across the Drina river between Zvornik and the road bridge at BCP Ljubovija.

All allegations have been thoroughly investigated by the Sector's special mobile patrols, comprised of senior staff members and monitors from the nearby BCPs. Random checks and sky monitoring were conducted at alleged locations day and night. The level of the Drina river was still high and the stream was assessed as too fast for pontoon bridges. Mission monitors found no evidence to substantiate the abovementioned allegations.

VIII. PROBLEMS ENCOUNTERED AND REPRESENTATIONS MADE TO THE AUTHORITIES

36. Throughout the month all Sectors randomly monitored the sky and found no evidence of helicopter activity - even though air surveillance strictly goes beyond the responsibility of the Mission. These observations will continue under the guidance of the designated Air Operations Officer in the Mission's Headquarters. After the Mission Coordinator's meeting with President Milosevic on 11 April, and to this date, UNPROFOR Air Traffic Controllers have registered only one unexplained radar contact.

37. The Mission has a lingering problem with the police at the BCP Metaljka (Sector Bravo). This relates to the discovery of the pedestrian by-pass by the Mission monitors just behind the BCP which is not visible due to the curve in the road. Since then Mission monitors witnessed trucks stopping at this by-pass and being unloaded by persons who carried the goods (for example, beer) by hand through the by-pass. The matter was reported to the local police several times, but despite assurances that action will be taken, the situation remains unaccept-

able. At Metaljka (B18) a yellow VW Buggy crossed into "RS" at 151645 hours. It was allowed to pass by the police before the Customs Officer could check it. The Police Officer in question refused to give his name to our observers. The observers did not manage to write the registration number down as another car was blocking their view.

38. On 17 April and 12 May the Mission Coordinator raised the issue of uniformed personnel crossing the border with the Director-General of the FRY Customs, Mr. Kertes. In the reporting period the total figure of uniformed, but unarmed personnel, crossing the border in both directions reached 771. Eighteen of them were prevented from crossing because of possession of firearms. Their movement peaked somewhere around Easter and the beginning of May celebrations and dwindled recently to negligible numbers. The explanations given by the FRY authorities were that the personnel crossing the border regularly visit their relatives on both sides of the border for celebrations but nobody is allowed to cross wearing sidearms. Another explanation is that not every person in the military outfit is necessarily a soldier or policeman on active service. Many males on both sides of the boundary wear military garments or are unable to afford civilian clothes. Those explanations were accepted as satisfactory by the Mission because they coincided with what was reported from the Sectors and assessed by the Mission monitors. Nevertheless, it was underscored again that uniformed and armed personnel crossing the border would constitute a violation and would be registered as such.

39. On 10-16 April signs of activity on the Bosnian side of the Jamena ferry crossing were reported by mobile patrols. Boats, pontoons and a tug plus two or three military personnel have been regularly observed. Nevertheless, no traces of landing on the FRY side were evident and the barriers' seals have remained intact.

40. In the same period the volume of confiscations increased considerably in the Port of Belgrade due to implementation of the recent Memorandum of Understanding. Now all vehicles transporting packaged goods are required to unload and be reloaded in the presence of the Mission's monitors. Good customs performance is noted.

41. On 29 April it was reported from the Port of Belgrade that the monitors had discovered a "trade invoice", within the papers of the consignor, endorsed by the Yugoslav Red Cross. This truckload was rejected, and the matter is under investigation.

42. On 4 May, at Sremska Raca, Mission observers found, when checking the canopy wires of a Yugoslav Red Cross truck and trailer before removing the seals, that the wire had been cut and rejoined. The Customs Officers inspected

the load, with Mission observers, and found it was cement instead of flour, as shown on the documentation. The driver admitted that, after leaving Novi Sad, where the truck and trailer had been sealed by Customs and Mission monitors, he went to another warehouse where the wire was cut, and 25 tons of cement were loaded in place of the flour. The vehicle and contents have been impounded and moved to Novi Sad for further investigation.

43. On 14 April, a mobile patrol reported that the Special Police, based on information from the Mission, established a 24-hour surveillance of a Bosnian fuel depot near Cutline, as mentioned in a previous report. All approaches to the Serbian side of the river opposite the Bosnian fuel depot are being covered by the police.

44. On 17 April, a mobile patrol reported from Cutline that a boat with two fuel barrels was observed crossing the River Drina from FRY to BiH. Local police and the Yugoslav Army (JA) Liaison Officer were notified immediately. On 19 April, a mobile patrol reported from the same place that a rubber boat was observed unloading barrels on the FRY side and crossing back empty to BiH. Again the local police and the JA Liaison Officer were alerted immediately.

45. On 22 April, it was reported from BCP Ljubovija that a FRY police vehicle with two uniformed and armed (sidearm) policemen crossed into BiH. It was considered a violation and local authorities were notified accordingly.

46. In the early morning of 3 May, near the BCP Badovinci, a customs/police mobile patrol seized 1500 litres of fuel from a boat on the River Drina. On 4 May the police confiscated 2000 litres of fuel from smugglers at a small boat crossing on the River Drina, 3 kilometres north of Badovinci.

47. On 10 May, it was reported from BCP Badovinci that a JA patrol captured a boat with 10 empty barrels (200 litres each) trying to cross the River Drina. The matter is being investigated by the police. On 11 May, it was reported from the same BCP that a JA patrol brought two persons with a tractor and trailer full of empty fuel containers (around 2000 litres capacity) to the police at the BCP. The matter is being investigated as well.

48. On 4 May, at Trbusnica a car previously denied entry by a customs officer for carrying commercial goods was permitted to cross by the order of the Chief Customs Officer.

49. On 10 April, a mobile patrol reported from Backa Pec, near Krstac, that a stone barrier was partly dismantled and some truck traces were evident beyond the barrier. The JA Liaison Officer was notified immediately and on 13 April the restoration of this barrier was completed. It is now two metres high. Since then the JA has established a 24-hour presence on the majority of the by-passes in the Sector. On 11 May there were traces that the barricade had been by-passed again. The matter was raised immediately with the JA Liaison Officer.

50. On 11 April, it was reported from Vracenovici that customs seized three trucks with large belly tanks attempting to cross into the FRY. Customs officers believed that the drivers were trying to fill up in Niksic to go back to Bosnia.

51. On 18 April, near Vracenovici the barrier on the by-pass was again found partly dismantled and vehicle tracks were visible around it. The JA Liaison Officer and police were informed and the barricade was restored, although insufficiently. On 22 April the barricade was by-passed again by a vehicle. Police managed to identify and arrest some perpetrators of those smuggling attempts, according to the report of the police chief.

52. On 22 April, in Vracenovici the police allowed a truck with approximately 40 crates of beer to cross into BiH. The matter was reported to the Chief of Police and this police shift was severely reprimanded.

53. On 20 April, at BCP Scepan Polje, it was reported that customs confiscated one gun from a driver of a vehicle entering BiH.

54. On 20 April, a mobile patrol reported from Nudo and Vilusi by-passes that the barricades were partially dismantled and traces of use were visible. Local police were notified and the Police Chief promised to establish a permanent police presence on all by-passes.

55. On 21 April, the JA Liaison Officer informed Sector Charlie HQ that the JA had arrested four trucks for illegally crossing into the FRY near Crkvice. The matter is undergoing a police investigation and the drivers are being detained for a customs offence.

56. On 26 April, police arrested in Vilusi a person attempting to smuggle 120 litres of petrol into BiH. On the same day a mobile patrol reported from Vilusi by-pass that between 0330 and 0700 hours the ICFY seal was removed from the gate. It was resealed again. On 28 April a mobile patrol discovered that the gates on the above-mentioned by-pass were broken and unsealable. A JA unit was working to erect a barricade instead of the gates. New barriers are also under construction at Nudo and Vilusi by-passes.

57. On 26 April, the mobile patrol was informed, by the JA Liaison Officer, that a JA patrol had apprehended three trucks loaded with timber. They were attempting to illegally cross the border from BiH to FRY via Crkvice by-pass. The matter is being investigated by the police.

58. On 28 April, a mobile patrol discovered that the barricades at two by-passes near Crkvice were passable and there were traces of vehicles crossing them. No JA patrols or police were present there at the time. The matter will be discussed again at a meeting between the Head of Sector and local authorities in the near future.

IX. Certification

59. In light of the foregoing developments during the past 30 days, based on the Mission's on-site observation, on the advice of the Mission Coordinator, Mr. T. J. Nieminen, and in the absence of any contrary information from the air, either from the airborne reconnaissance system of the North Atlantic Treaty Organization (NATO) or national technical means, the Co-Chairmen conclude that the Government of the Federal Republic of Yugoslavia (Serbia and Montenegro) is continuing to meet its commitment to close the border between the Federal Republic of Yugoslavia (Serbia and Montenegro) and the areas of the Republic of Bosnia and Herzegovina under the control of the Bosnian Serb forces. The Co-Chairmen also conclude that during the period covered by this report there have been no commercial transshipments across the border between the Federal Republic of Yugoslavia (Serbia and Montenegro) and the Republic of Bosnia and Herzegovina.

146. Letter Dated 25 June 1995 from the Secretary-General Addressed to the President of the Security Council*

I have the honour to transmit the attached report which was addressed to me on 25 June 1995 by the Co-Chairmen of the Steering Committee of the International Conference on the Former Yugoslavia, concerning the operations of the International Conference's Mission to the Federal Republic of Yugoslavia (Serbia and Montenegro). This report by the Co-Chairmen contains the certification referred to in Security Council resolution 988 (1995).

I should be grateful if you would bring this information to the attention of the members of the Security Council.

---

* UN Doc. S/1995/510, 25 June 1995. Signed by Boutros Boutros-Ghali.

Annex
Operations of the International Conference on the Former Yugoslavia (ICFY) Mission to the Federal Republic of Yugoslavia (Serbia and Montenegro)

I. INTRODUCTION

1. The present report is submitted pursuant to paragraph 13 of Security Council resolution 988 (1995) adopted on 21 April 1995. In that resolution, the Security Council requested that the Secretary-General submit every 30 days for its review and no fewer than ten days before 5 July 1995, a report from the Co-Chairmen of the Steering Committee of the International Conference on the Former Yugoslavia on the border closure measures taken by the authorities of the Federal Republic of Yugoslavia (Serbia and Montenegro).

2. It will be recalled that on 4 August 1994 the following measures were ordered by the Government of the Federal Republic of Yugoslavia (Serbia and Montenegro) to come into effect the same day:

> "(a) To break off political and economic relations with the 'Republika Srpska';
> (b) To prohibit the stay of the members of the leadership of the 'Republika Srpska' (Parliament, Presidency and Government) in the territory of the Federal Republic of Yugoslavia;
> (c) As of today the border of the Federal Republic of Yugoslavia is closed for all transport towards the 'Republika Srpska' except food, clothing and medicine."

3. On 19 September, 3 October, 2 November and 5 December 1994, 5 January, 3 February, 2 March, 31 March, 13 April and 18 May 1995 the Secretary-General transmitted to the Security Council reports from the Co-Chairmen of the Steering Committee of the International Conference on the Former Yugoslavia on the state of implementation of the above mentioned measures (S/1994/1074; S/1994/1124; S/1994/1246; S/1994/1372; S/1995/6; S/1995/104; S/1995/175; S/1995/255; S/1995/302; and S/1995/406). The report dated 18 May 1995 contained the following certification from the Co-Chairmen:

> "In the light of the foregoing developments during the past 30 days, based on the Mission's on-site observation, on the advice of the Mission Coordinator, Mr. T.J. Nieminen, and in the absence of any contrary information from the air, either from the airborne reconnaissance system of NATO or national technical means, the Co-Chairmen conclude that the Government of the Federal Republic of Yugoslavia (Serbia and Montenegro) is continuing to meet its commitment to close the border between the Federal Republic of Yugoslavia (Serbia and Montenegro) and the areas of the Republic of Bosnia and Herzegovina under the control of Bosnian Serb forces. The Co-Chairmen also conclude that during the period covered by the present report there have been

no commercial transshipments across the border between the Federal Republic of Yugoslavia (Serbia and Montenegro) and the Republic of Bosnia and Herzegovina."

Developments since the last report are provided below.

II. LEGISLATION/REGULATIONS ON THE BORDER CLOSURE

4. The legislation of the authorities of the Federal Republic of Yugoslavia (Serbia and Montenegro) closing the border with the Bosnian Serbs continues to be in effect.

5. The authorities of the Federal Republic of Yugoslavia (Serbia and Montenegro) have provided the Mission with the following list of confiscations conducted along its border with Bosnia and Herzegovina for May 1995:

Petrol	9.9 tons
Diesel	34.9 tons
Motor oil	1 ton
Cigarettes	26.4 tons
Construction materials	155.6 tons
Wood	443 cu meters
Alcohol	3,005 litres
Food	21.8 tons
Textile, clothing, footwear	286 kg
Vehicles	6
Electrical gadgets	813
Coffee	11 kg
Fertiliser	12.6 tons
Military Boots	120 pairs
Other goods	7.8 tons

6. There were 116 new customs offence procedures initiated during the reporting period and 92 were finalized. Fines and penalties amounted to 534,350 dinars. There were substantial increases (in most categories) in confiscations this month over the previous month and well above the average of the previous 9 months. Similarly, the value of penalties emanating from cases finalized and the number of new offence cases continues to increase.

III. Organization, Financing and Work of the Mission

7. As of 22 June 1995, 185 international Mission personnel are on duty with the Mission. The Mission personnel to date have come from the following countries: Belgium, Canada, the Czech Republic, Denmark, Finland, France, Germany, Greece, Ireland, Italy, the Netherlands, Norway, Portugal, the Russian Federation, Spain, Sweden, the United Kingdom of Great Britain and Northern Ireland and the United States of America.

8. On May 29, the Mission received information of a physical kidnap threat to American observers in the border areas. All American observers were withdrawn from the border crossing points and patrol areas, and employed in safe areas only. On 2 June it was decided, as a precautionary measure, to put all French observers on the sidelines until security conditions allowed for the resumption of duties in the field. After consultation with the American and French Embassies in Belgrade, a decision was reached on 7 June which authorized selective deployment along the border of all American and French observers. The authorities of the Federal Republic of Yugoslavia (Serbia and Montenegro) have responded to Mission concerns as to its responsibility for the security of the Mission personnel with an increased security presence at border crossing points and at various headquarters.

9. The Mission is now covering 19 border crossings 24 hours a day. Of those, two are train stations. The financial situation of the Mission has now improved and the Co-Chairmen have authorized an increase in Mission personnel to 200.

IV. Freedom of Movement of the Mission

10. The Mission continues to enjoy full freedom of movement within the Federal Republic of Yugoslavia (Serbia and Montenegro).

11. Nevertheless, there have been some minor incidents, mostly in conjunction with the developments in Bosnia. In Banja Koviljaca, on 27 May, between 0200 and 0230 hours, one Mission vehicle was stolen and four others had their tyres slashed in front of the hotel where Sector Alpha HQ is situated. The police were notified immediately and a thorough investigation of the issue ensued.

12. On 26 May, observers at BCP Scepan Polje (Sector Charlie) reported hearing 20-25 rounds of small arms fire at night on the Bosnian side. The following night a hand grenade detonated 10 m from the BCP. Next day, a Mission monitor approached the river on the border to get some water and three "warning shots" from the Bosnian Serb police were fired. They spoke with the monitor across the river and the conversation ended with a promise to cease threatening

Mission observers. The chief of police was informed of those incidents and initiated an investigation which is presently going on.

13. On 26 May, in Becka Pec (10 kms north of Vracenovici, in Sector Charlie) a villager, angered by the military's constant efforts to close the road at the Mission's request, threatened to shoot the Mission patrol if it returned to the area again.

14. On 6 June, at 2228 hours, small arms fire was heard in the immediate vicinity of BCP Vracenovici (Sector Charlie). The police shift commander advised Mission members to leave the BCP with an escort. The BCP was remanned about one hour after the incident.

15. An attack on an Irish observer occurred at Nudo Border Crossing Point, Montenegro, on 11 June. Whilst checking adjacent footpaths which by-pass the crossing, the observer was assaulted with a blunt instrument and sustained head wounds and minor abrasions. He put up a spirited resistance however, and his attacker ran off in the direction of Nudo village. The wounds necessitated immediate treatment and he was taken by car to Niksic hospital where he was X-rayed and received stitches to the head wounds. He was then flown to the VMA hospital in Belgrade where he once again received immediate and expert attention and was released later in the evening. The authorities, both in Montenegro and Serbia, reacted promptly both in the matter of the Medevac and the investigation of the incident.

V. COOPERATION OF THE AUTHORITIES OF THE FEDERAL REPUBLIC OF YUGOSLAVIA (SERBIA AND MONTENEGRO) WITH THE MISSION

16. Cooperation with the authorities of the Federal Republic of Yugoslavia (Serbia and Montenegro) continues to be good.

17. On 13 February 1995, the Mission concluded a Memorandum of Understanding with the Yugoslav Federal Customs concerning search procedures on buses. According to the Memorandum all buses must be partially checked and additionally, 20 percent of long distance or highway coaches are fully checked. This means that baggage and people are off-loaded from the coach. After four months of steady improvement, the Mission Coordinator has reported that the Yugoslav authorities' compliance is now fully satisfactory. The local border officials increasingly deny buses carrying commercial quantities of goods and regularly confiscate fuel and other commodities. The Mission's good cooperative working relationship with the Yugoslav authorities on the border has also contributed to this higher level of enforcement. The Mission Coordinator signed a second Memorandum of Understanding on 3 April to improve the Yugoslav

Red Cross's internal safeguards and to give the Mission enhanced verification procedures where vehicles are loaded. This Memorandum has proven to be a very useful and necessary tool. As a result, there has been a significant increase in the amount of contraband found and fuel seized by the Yugoslav Customs from hidden compartments in vehicles during May and the first half of June.

VI. INFORMATION RECEIVED FROM NATIONAL AND OTHER SOURCES

18. The operating principle of the Mission is to base its reporting and evaluations on its own observations and on information that it has verified. The Mission Coordinator has maintained a standing request to Governments possessing the technical capacity to provide it with information relevant to its mandate. The Mission Coordinator has not received any such information since the last report.

VII. PROBLEMS ENCOUNTERED AND REPRESENTATIONS MADE
TO THE AUTHORITIES

19. In the previous report to the Security Council on 18 May 1995 (S/1995/406) two problematic areas with violations of the border closure were mentioned:

   i)   smuggling of fuel across the River Drina in the Citluk-Culine area (12 kilometres south of Mali Zvornik, Sector Alpha); and
   ii) use of the pedestrian by-pass at the border crossing point Metaljka (Sector Bravo).

The violations have continued in these areas since the last report as described in the following paragraphs. It seems that the local authorities are having some difficulty in controlling the situation in these areas.

20. On 16 May a mobile patrol in the area of Citluk witnessed a smuggling operation across the Drina river: two boats tied up and equipped with an engine, manned by three persons carrying 12-15 barrels (x 200 litres), crossed the river and were unloaded on the Bosnian side. On 18 May a mobile patrol reported from the same place that it observed one vessel crossing the Drina with 7-8 barrels which were unloaded on the Bosnian side. On both occasions the police and Yugoslav Army (JA) liaison officer were notified immediately. On 19 May the Head of Sector Alpha met the local authorities and raised this matter. They offered to coordinate the actions of the police, the JA and Special Customs Squads. The JA liaison officer requested that the Head of the Sector notify him

of the movements of the Mission's mobile patrols in this region in order that he could provide adequate security cover. He pointed out that this type of smuggler constitutes a possible danger for Mission monitors. On the same day the Mission Coordinator received a letter from the Deputy Chief of the General Staff of the Yugoslav Army, Lt-Gen B. Kovacevic. He affirmed that the perpetrators in the first incident had been apprehended by JA patrols and handed over to the police authorities. They confirmed that the suspects were known smugglers who had been punished for similar offenses. Charges had been brought against them.

21. On 26 May, a mobile patrol reported from Citluk area that it had observed from higher ground near the main road a boat with 4 (x 200 litres) barrels crossing the River Drina from Bosnia into FRY. On their way down from the observation post the patrol was stopped by a civilian carrying a mobile telephone. He ordered the patrol to stop and wait for the police to arrive; no explanations were given. The patrol proceeded and spotted another boat on the Bosnian side, 4 (x 200 litres) barrels and a man standing nearby. Sector's HQ was notified about both occurrences. On the way back the patrol observed a lorry with a boat trailer in the same area on the FRY side. When the patrol approached the cars, a vehicle manned by two policemen which had been parked nearby moved towards the patrol car. One of the policemen requested the Mission's patrol to leave the area immediately and did not allow the monitors to ask any questions. The patrol left the area and reported the incident to the Headquarters. On 27 May, the Head of Sector brought the matter to the attention of the local police commander who excused the behaviour of his men, saying that they were the new recruits and still not fully aware of the procedures. The Head of Sector found this explanation unacceptable and requested the authorities to undertake measures to clamp down on such illegal crossings.

22. Again on 8 June a Mission mobile patrol saw a boat in the area of Citluk-Culine crossing the River Drina from FRY to Bosnia. The boat seemed to be heavily loaded with ten barrels of 200 litres each. Three persons were on board. The Sector Headquarters informed the special police in Loznica.

23. On 22 May and 13 June, the Mission's Senior Customs Advisor met with the Deputy Director of the Customs of the Federal Republic of Yugoslavia (Serbia and Montenegro), Mr. B. Knezic, to discuss the smuggling activities in the Citluk-Culine area. The Mission explained that it was expecting more confiscations to take place and made demands for effective action to block these smuggling routes. Meanwhile, a barrier had been erected on the access road to the Drina in Culine. In the second meeting the FRY authorities also presented a survey of goods confiscated in the Citluk-Culine area. In twenty different instances during March-May, smugglers have been apprehended in the area and 5,220 litres of diesel fuel confiscated. Among other items confiscated are 18,000

litres of Coca Cola, various foodstuffs, accumulators, fertilizers, fodder and one 7.62 calibre pistol. Although the smuggling has not been totally prevented, the authorities are taking action when consignments are discovered.

24. In Metaljka the police apprehended, on 16 May, a smuggler with 20 litres of gasoline and 35 litres of diesel as he tried to use a well-known pedestrian by-pass behind the BCP. On 19 May, at the same BCP, a bold smuggling action took place: one car stopped near the by-pass, the driver unloaded 3 cartons, took them through the by-pass to the Bosnian side and handed them over to a BSA soldier, waiting for him on the top of the hill. Then the driver returned, got into his car and passed through the BCP unhindered, while smiling at the monitors. During a meeting with the Montenegrin authorities on 18 May, the Mission Coordinator raised the issue of the frequency of by-passing the Metaljka border crossing.

25. However, the problem of the BCP Metaljka has remained unsolved, in spite of the lengthy negotiations with the local authorities. On 24 May a driver of a car tried to enter Bosnia at Metaljka with a 20-litre jerrycan of fuel. When rejected, he went to the by-pass and took the jerrycan on the Bosnian side up to the hill, then returned and crossed into Bosnia without problems. A similar incident happened on the next day, 25 May. On both occasions the customs and police warned the Mission monitors about the danger of conducting observation at the by-pass. Again on 7 June, three jerrycans of fuel were carried across the border by using the by-pass. The FRY authorities have issued orders to the police in Montenegro to relocate the Border Crossing Point so as to prevent usage of the by-pass road.

26. Unarmed uniformed personnel continue to cross the border between the Federal Republic of Yugoslavia (Serbia and Montenegro) and Bosnia and Herzegovina. During the reporting period 688 such incidents were recorded, 610 of them at Sremska Raca. In seven separate occasions uniformed policemen were allowed to cross carrying a sidearm: on 17 May in Sremska Raca, on 31 May in Metaljka, on 31 May, 1 June and 17 June in Vracenovici, on 31 May in Vilusi and on 7 June in Badovinci. All these were registered as violations. In contrast, in Trbusnica during 22-24 May, uniformed personnel and two military vehicles were not allowed to cross to Bosnia.

27. In Sremska Raca (Sector Belgrade), the customs officials chose not to confiscate a load of tools (drill, perforator etc.) and chemicals of unknown origin, which they discovered hidden inside a declared load of pesticides, on 18 May. On 31 May, at the same BCP, it was reported that one truck had its canopy wire cut and rejoined. Upon inspection, 3,000 empty plastic bottles were found, 30 kg of bronze ballbearings, 700 kg of iron bars and various spare parts for

vehicles were hidden inside the declared load. The truck was impounded and the driver charged with a customs offence. On 16 June the FRY Customs seized 15 tons of coffee and 5 tons of detergent in Sremska Raca, demonstrating the close and diligent working relationship between the Mission and Customs Teams at the border crossing. Also on 16 June in Sremska Raca one passenger carrying a pistol was arrested.

28. Also at Sremska Raca on 28 May customs officials and the monitors discovered on the night shift a false bulkhead in a truck with a trailer. Behind the bulkhead a huge container with 12.5 tons of diesel fuel was found. The vehicle was seized, the driver arrested and the fuel confiscated. On 30 May, the customs officials discovered a false floor fuel tank with 1.2 tons of fuel in a truck which attempted to cross into Bosnia. The vehicle was impounded and the fuel confiscated. On 3 June, a false bulkhead fuel tank with 4 tons of fuel in it was discovered in a truck. The vehicle was impounded and the driver charged. On 4 and 7 June, similar incidents occurred with the same results. It seems that there are increasing numbers of attempts to smuggle significant quantities of fuel in hidden fuel tanks on trucks. The Mission Coordinator is satisfied that the controls which have been introduced and the cooperation built up between the observers in Sector Belgrade and the local Customs ensure that most of these attempts are unsuccessful and that appropriate offence action is taken.

29. On 24 May, Port of Belgrade observers reported that the customs officials discovered hidden "double floor" fuel tanks in two lorries, and in another truck a canopy wire was cut and undeclared items (beer, fertiliser) hidden inside the load. These trucks were rejected, contraband seized, and registration numbers put on the "Offense Action List" to avert further occurrences with the same vehicles. On 26 May, monitors at Novi Sad loading area reported that the customs officials discovered a load of 36 electrical motors hidden inside a declared load of flour. The vehicle was detained, contraband confiscated, and the consignor and the vehicle were "Offense Action Listed". On 29 May, about 30 boxes of chocolate and "Nivea" cream were found at Belgrade Port in a truck which declared its load as medicine. These goods were confiscated. On 2 June, at the same location, 2 tons of coffee were confiscated from two trucks and customs offence filed against the drivers.

30. On 20 May, a mobile patrol in Gradac (8 kilometres south of Ljubovija, Sector Alpha) observed a boat crossing the River Drina to Bosnia and unloading there (2 jerrycans and several bags). This was reported at once to the police. On 27 May, near Badovinci, the police arrested three smugglers attempting to cross into Bosnia with two 200 litre barrels of fuel. On 7 June a special police/customs patrol confiscated 1,500 litres of diesel fuel near the junction of the rivers Drina and Sava. Five smugglers were arrested. On 12 June in Mali Zvornik (Sector

Alpha) more than 30 bags of grain were allowed to be carried across the border to Bosnia.

31. Another troublesome by-pass was discovered by the Mission observers on 20 May near the village of Sula (Sector Bravo). At the time the by-pass was patrolled by the police, who claimed to be present there 24 hours per day. On 28 May, the Mission observers noticed that an empty truck with a trailer which was denied entry into FRY through the BCP Sula, was later spotted in the village of Sula, on FRY side, apparently having crossed the border via the by-pass. On 8 June the Head of Sector Bravo, together with the Mission Special Envoy to Montenegro, patrolled the by-pass road and met a truck loaded with goods crossing the border to Bosnia without being checked. The tracks on the road indicated that several vehicles had used the road lately. The Mission will try to solve this problem by moving the BCP Sula closer to the border so that the entrance of the by-pass can be controlled from the new location.

32. On 15 May the police captured two smugglers in Vilusi (Sector Charlie) with two vehicles, carrying a load of 60 litres of gasoline and 2,400 litres of diesel. On 19 May it was reported from the same BCP that two vehicles, with approximately 300 kg of groceries, were allowed to cross into Bosnia. Also a trailer with window frames and construction materials was allowed to cross into the FRY.

33. In Vracenovici (Sector Charlie) on 18 May a van with "supermarket" goods (juice, toilet paper etc.) was allowed to cross into Bosnia, a repeat of a similar incident on 8-10 May. The police claimed that there was a small shop beyond the BCP on the FRY side. However, the monitors were able to visually follow this van and confirmed its actual crossing into Bosnia. On 21 May a car was allowed to cross into Bosnia with about 150 kg of food, another with 15 cases of beer, and a third with at least nine boxes of fruit. On 23 May at the same BCP, a van loaded with boxes crossed unchecked into Bosnia. On the next day the same van was allowed to cross into Bosnia with approximately 400 kg of food, and a minibus with many empty beer bottle crates was allowed to enter FRY. The matter was raised again with FRY authorities, and on 26 May the Chief of Niksic police reprimanded his personnel involved. Even then the lax behaviour of the customs officers in Vracenovici (Sector Charlie) has continued. On 12 June a car full of groceries and a car with 20 crates of beer was allowed to cross to Bosnia. On 14 June a van with windows covered, crossed twice each way without being checked. Another van was allowed to cross the same day with 800 kg of cattle food.

34. On 15 May a mobile patrol reported that the barricades on the Uncontrolled Border Crossings (UCPs) Becka Pec and Vrbica (between Vracenovici and

Krstac, Sector Charlie) had been tampered with again. There were traces of spilled oil. This was reported to the JA Liaison Officer who ordered the reconstruction of the barricade. On 16 May, at the Becka Pec UCP, ten soldiers were located there and a stationary JA patrol was positioned at UCP Vrbica. On 18 May it was discovered that the barricade at Becka Pec had been dismantled once again and no JA presence was evident. On 20 May a Mission patrol noticed that the barricades on all the by-passes had been restored, with the police and Special Customs Squads present and active. The latter managed to apprehend two trucks attempting to smuggle decorative stones into Bosnia. The trucks and the load were confiscated. However, on 21 May, one of the barriers had again been removed and there were recent tracks around it. The Mission Coordinator met with Major General Obradovic in Podgorica on 18 May and told him that the area north of Vracenovici continued to be of concern, due to the ineffectiveness of the barrier plan. He promised to take steps to correct the problems at the border.

35. The Mission mobile patrol reported on 22 May that at the UCP Becka Pec 12 soldiers erected a barricade. On 23 May, the barricade there was removed and the road used. On 24 May, two JA patrols were seen near the barricade. On 26 May a strong JA presence was observed at UCPs (Becka Pec and Vrbica), as well as a couple of nearby villagers. They claimed they owned land on both sides of the border and had to use the roads through UCPs to till it. On 28 May, all barricades were checked and found intact, and the JA and police were present. On 30 May, the JA Liaison Officer informed the Sector Commander about the decision to establish permanent JA posts on the troubled UCPs Becka Pec and Vrbica. On 3 June, a mobile patrol observed that all principal by-passes between BCPs Vracenovici and Vilusi were controlled by JA permanent posts, as well as the main crossroad near Crkvice, which leads to these by-passes.

36. Since the last report no unexplained radar contacts have been reported by UNPROFOR Air Traffic Monitors. The Mission's Air Operations officer is conducting a ground survey in the Sectors to locate positions for air monitoring of the border. He will establish contacts with UNPROFOR and the local authorities in order to respond in a timely way to potential air border violations and their investigation.

37. Although the above list of violations and incidents is lengthy, the qualities and characteristics of the problems are not significant as such. There is a regular and consistent pattern of confiscations and refusals which show that the authorities are effectively implementing their border closure measures. Generally, the Customs Officials, especially the Special Customs Squads, and Police perform their duties in a highly professional manner.

VIII. CERTIFICATION

38. In the light of the foregoing developments during the reporting period, based on the Mission's on-site observation, on the advice of the Mission Coordinator, Mr. T.J. Nieminen, and in the absence of any contrary information from the air, either from the airborne reconnaissance system of NATO or national technical means, the Co-Chairmen conclude that the Government of Yugoslavia (Serbia and Montenegro) is continuing to meet its commitment to close the border between the Federal Republic of Yugoslavia (Serbia and Montenegro) and the areas of the Republic of Bosnia and Herzegovina under the control of Bosnian Serb forces. The Co-Chairmen also conclude that during the period covered by the present report there have been no commercial transshipments across the border between the Federal Republic of Yugoslavia (Serbia and Montenegro) and the Republic of Bosnia and Herzegovina.

147. LETTER DATED 27 JULY 1995 FROM THE SECRETARY-GENERAL ADDRESSED TO THE PRESIDENT OF THE SECURITY COUNCIL[*]

I have the honour to convey to you the attached biannual report addressed to me on 17 July 1995 by the Co-Chairmen of the Steering Committee of the International Conference on the Former Yugoslavia.

I should be grateful if you would bring this information to the attention of the members of the Security Council.

Annex
Biannual Report of the Co-Chairmen of the Steering Committee on the Activities of the International Conference on the Former Yugoslavia

I. INTRODUCTION

1. The International Conference on the Former Yugoslavia was established in August 1992, to remain in being until a settlement of the problems of the former Yugoslavia had been achieved. Its seat is at the United Nations Office in Geneva. The Co-Chairmen of the Conference are the Secretary-General of the United Nations and the Head of State or Government of the Presidency of the European Union. The activities of the Conference are supervised by a Steering

---

[*] UN Doc. S/1995/626, 26 July 1995. Signed by Boutros Boutros-Ghali.

Committee co-chaired by representatives of the Secretary-General of the United Nations and the Presidency of the European Union. The current Co-Chairmen of the Steering Committee are Mr. Carl Bildt (European Union) and Mr. Thorvald Stoltenberg (United Nations). Mr. Bildt replaced Lord Owen on 13 June 1995. The day-to-day activities of the Conference are carried out by the Co-Chairmen of the Steering Committee and in working groups and task forces.

2. Information on the activities of the Conference from January to June 1995 is provided below.

II. STEERING COMMITTEE

3. Meetings of the Steering Committee of the Conference were held on 31 January, 10 March and 13 June. Issues discussed included reports by the Co-Chairmen and International Conference negotiators; review of developments; humanitarian issues and budgetary matters.

III. BOSNIA AND HERZEGOVINA

4. As regards the situation in Bosnia and Herzegovina, during the past six months, the activities of the International Conference had three major objectives in view: to generate international humanitarian assistance; to promote acceptance by the Bosnian Serb leadership of the Contact Group Plan; and to support the activities of the International Conference Mission monitoring the closure of the border between Federal Republic of Yugoslavia (Serbia and Montenegro) and the Bosnian Serbs.

5. The provision of international humanitarian assistance is dealt with in section V below. As regards promotion o acceptance by the Bosnian Serb leadership of the Contact Group Plan, the Co-Chairmen and International Conference personnel have participated in, and supported, the activities of the Contact Group, both at the technical level and at the political level.

6. On 23 March, Mr. Stoltenberg and Lord Owen met the Bosnian Serb leadership, including Mr. Karadzic, Mr. Krajisnik, Mr. Koljevic and Mr. Buha, in Zvornik. The Bosnian Serb leadership said it was not prepared to accept any formulation that contained the words "acceptance of the peace plan". After discussion, Bosnian Serb leader Radovan Karadzic that he would respond to an exchange of letters in the following terms:

A

"Dear Dr. Karadzic,

We are writing to you to summarize our discussions today on the way ahead over the next few months. Negotiations with the aim of achieving a comprehensive settlement in Bosnia and Herzegovina on the basis of equitable and balanced arrangements will resume in early April.

These negotiations, which will be conducted by the Contact Group, will be on the basis of the peace plan of the Contact Group as a starting point leading to a comprehensive peace settlement, and will last for two months. It will be necessary for discussions to be held involving the parties to ensure an extension of the cessation of hostilities agreement to cover these negotiations

..."

B

"Excellencies,

Thank you for your letter, of which we have taken note. We accept the basis for negotiations proposed by the Contact Group as explained in your letter of 23 March 1995.

We are ready to discuss an extension of the cessation of hostilities agreement to cover these negotiations.

..."

Lord Owen and Mr. Stoltenberg undertook to pass the above-mentioned texts to the Contact Group and subsequently did so.

7. The Co-Chairmen participated in a ministerial meeting of the Contact Group held in The Hague on 29 May 1995. At that meeting, Ministers of the Contact Group issued a statement in which they once again strongly urged the Bosnian Serb authorities to accept the Contact Group Plan as a starting point for negotiations. They agreed to give a new impetus to the diplomatic process in order to reach a political settlement of the conflict, which they considered as the only possible solution. In that respect, they agreed to make a new effort with a view to the earliest possible recognition by the Federal Republic of Yugoslavia (Serbia and Montenegro) of Bosnia and Herzegovina and the strengthening of the border closure.

8. On the activities of the International Conference Mission monitoring the closure of the border of the Federal Republic of Yugoslavia (Serbia and Montenegro) to the Bosnian Serbs, reference is made to reports that the Co-Chairmen have submitted, through the Secretary-General, to the Security Council, during the first six months of 1995 (see S/1995/6; S/1995/104; S/1995/175; S/1995/255; S/1995/302; S/1995/406 and S/1995/510).

IV. CROATIA

9. Upon the conclusion of the economic agreement of 2 December 1994 (see S/1994/1375), negotiated under the auspices of the Conference, and the subsequent opening of the Zagreb-Lipovac highway on 21 December, the immediate priority of the Co-Chairmen of the Steering Committee and International Conference negotiators was to expedite the implementation of the remaining provisions of the agreement in cooperation with the United Nations Protection Force (UNPROFOR). On 9 January 1995, the electricity poles were returned to the Obrovac power plant and the oil pipeline running through Sector North was opened on 27 january. However, the intensive and sustained efforts by the Co-Chairmen and International Conference negotiators over the following weeks to achieve momentum in the implementation were inhibited by a progressive deterioration of the political climate between the Government of Croatia and the Croatian Serb leadership.

10. On 12 January 1995, President Tudjman presented his statement withdrawing consent to UNPROFOR's presence with effect from 31 March 1995. In the situation that followed, the so-called Zagreb Four group (Z-4), which included the Ambassadors in Zagreb of the Russian Federation and the United States of America, along with International Conference participants, presented the "Z-4 plan", on 30 January. It was received by the Government of Croatia, but the Croatian Serbs declined to receive it. On 8 February 1995, the Croatian Serb Assembly in Knin declined to freeze all further implementation of the economic agreement as a result of the Croatian Government's withdrawal of consent to the presence of UNPROFOR.

11. After 8 February, it proved increasingly difficult to effect any further implementation of the economic agreement. However, through a constant process of consultation by the Co-Chairmen and International Conference negotiators, in Zagreb, Knin and Belgrade, the text for a joint commercial oil company was finalized and agreed, the signature of which was postponed until the political climate improved. Limited progress was also made towards the opening of the Zagreb-Okucani-Mirkovici railway. Additionally, the first steps towards implementation of a number of water projects were achieved. Most significantly the highway remained in full 24-hour operation and, by mid April, it was estimated that over 250,000 vehicles had used it.

12. However, on 24 April 1995, the Croatian Serb leadership closed the highway for 24 hours because of claims that the highway was not of equal benefit to the Croatian Serbs. Shortly following its reopening, a series of incidents took place on the highway, after which the situation around the highway deteriorated rapidly. On 1 May 1995, Croatian forces conducted a military offensive in the

areas of Sector West under Croatian Serb control.

13. In the wake of this offensive, the Co-Chairmen of the Steering Committee invited representatives of the Government of the Republic of Croatia and the Croatian Serb leadership to Geneva for talks, in an effort to prevent any further deterioration of the situation and to recommence the negotiating process. Both parties have accepted the invitation in principle. However, the level of military tension and preconditions have precluded such a meeting to date.

14. The Co-Chairmen and International Conference negotiators have approached the two sides once more in an attempt to re-establish a dialogue between the Croatian Government and the Croatian Serb leadership.

V. HUMANITARIAN ISSUES

15. The cessation-of-hostilities agreement signed on 1 January 1995 between the Bosnian Government and the Bosnian Serbs was important for the Office of the United Nations High Commissioner for Refugees, by its mention of the monitoring of human rights as well as commitment to the reopening of civilian traffic across the Sarajevo Airport. After initial difficulties encountered in the implementation of the agreement, on 23 January the Bosnian Government and the Bosnian Serbs signed an agreement to reopen the routes across Sarajevo airport at the latest by 1 February. In addition to UNHCR, the United Nations Educational, Scientific and Cultural Organization (UNESCO), the World Health Organization (WHO), the United Nations Children's Fund (UNICEF), the World Food Programme (WFP), the Food and Agriculture Organization of the United Nations (FAO), the International Committee of the Red Cross (ICRC) and the Office of the Special Coordinator for Sarajevo, the local humanitarian organizations Merhamet, Dobrotvor, La Benevolencia, CARITAS and Adra would also be able to use the routes. The agreement also made provision for increased freedom of movement for the people of Sarajevo; further exchanges of prisoners of war in line with the ICRC plan; and medical evacuations from Gorazde; and freedom of residence. For the latter, the Bosnian Government agreed to include Bosnian serb social cases in the evacuation plans.

16. Overall deliveries of aid supplies in Bosnia and Herzegovina were successful at the beginning of the year, with UNHCR land convoys regularly reaching Sarajevo, Tuzla, Zenica and the eastern enclaves, and with the smooth running of the Sarajevo airlift. UNHCR was consistently able to exceed its monthly target in Sarajevo and elsewhere in central Bosnia in order to create a contingency stock in anticipation of a possible recurrence of obstructions later in the year. Furthermore, it was possible to bring winterization items and fuel to Sarajevo

and the eastern enclaves. As an encouraging sign, UNHCR was able for the first time to assist the Bosnian Government to bring the much-needed firewood into Sarajevo over the recently opened "blue routes" across the airport. Arrangements were made with FAO for the distribution of as many seed fertilizers and pesticides as feasible across Bosnia and Herzegovina before the onset of the planting season in March.

17. The subsequent worsening of the overall security situation in Bosnia and Herzegovina made movements increasingly difficult. UNHCR staff was denied access to Travnik, Bugonjo and Tesanj. The increased sniping incidents in Sarajevo and the closure, again,m of the "blue routes" across Sarajevo airport on 11 March further hampered the humanitarian efforts. The route on Mount Igman became, once more, too dangerous for use by UNHCR vehicles.

18. The airstrikes by the North Atlantic Treaty Organization (Nato) on 25 and 26 May and the ensuing escalation of the conflict and the hostage crisis deeply affected UNHCR's ability to continue to provide assistance in Bosnia and Herzegovina, to the point that operations became almost completely blocked in Serb-held territories as well as in the enclaves. The Bosnian Serb authorities stressed that UNHCR activities were considered separate from their disputes with UNPROFOR. However, travel restrictions continued to apply and, in view of the extremely insecure situation, UNHCR cancelled all convoys going over Bosnian Serb-held territory. As a consequence of the reduction of the activities and of the increased security risks, the majority of UNHCR international staff were temporarily removed from Sarajevo, Bihac and Banja Luka.

19. On 15 June, the United Nations High Commissioner for Refugees, Mrs. Sakado Ogata, and the Special Representative of the Secretary-General, Mr. Yasushi Akashi, cosigned a letter to Bosnian Serb leader Radovan Karadzic, conveying their profound concern about the developing disasters in Sarajevo, Bihac, Gorazde, Srebrenica and Zepa, calling on the Bosnian Serb leader to honour the commitments made by him over the past three years. "We can no longer tolerate the violation of exhaustively negotiated arrangement or the denial of well developed procedures. We refuse to accept lame excuses, false allegations, and suspicions or references to uncontrolled elements to justify interference with free movement of humanitarian goods and staff."

20. During the reporting period, 51 patients were evacuated for medical treatment in third countries, through the joint UNHCR/International Organization for Migration (IOM) medical evacuation programme covering Bosnia and Herzegovina. Thirty patients returned voluntarily upon completion of treatment.

21. In Sarajevo, the detention of a Bosnian Serb UNHCR staff member on 10 February by the Bosnian authorities, and its possible linkage to the release of prisoners held by the Bosnian Serbs, caused a short disruption of the supply

movement from the airport to the town. Supplies to the city could be resumed only thanks to the UNPROFOR french battalion that temporarily replaced UNHCR's local drivers pending deployment of an international team from Metkovic. The detained staff member was finally released on 20 March, under a two-for-two exchange between the Bosnian Government and the Bosnian Serbs. Following this incident, UNHCR replaced local drivers working at Sarajevo airport with an international team from Metkovic, in view of the limited and dangerous movement of local staff across the checkpoints between the airport and town.

22. Requesting a substantial increase in their current share of humanitarian aid, which is based on assessed need rather than on percentages, the Bosnian Serb authorities introduced a blanket rejection of the weekly Metkovic-Sarajevo convoy plan at the beginning of March. With the introduction of a new Bosnian Serb Coordinating Committee for Humanitarian Affairs, clearance was again obtained for the convoys to proceed as of 18 March.

23. On 8 June, the UNHCR Special Envoy, accompanied by Mr. Akashi, General Janvier and the UNPROFOR Civil Affairs Coordinator for Sarajevo, held discussions with the Bosnian Serb leaders in Pale in order to unblock the renewed standstill in the deliveries of humanitarian supplies by land to Sarajevo. An agreement was finally reached between the Bosnian Serb authorities and UNHCR to resume UNHCR convoys from Metkovic via Kiseljak to both Government- and Bosnian Serb-held parts of Sarajevo, with only one inspection foreseen at checkpoint Sierra 1. Escort would also be provided across Bosnian Serb-held territory to Sarajevo city and Raljovac. This also applied to UNHCR convoys to the Bosnian Serb -held areas of Trebinje in south-eastern Bosnia. After initial problems with lengthy administrative procedures, the Bosnian Serb authorities demanded 50 per cent of the deliveries instead of the usual 23 per cent. When clearances were finally obtained under the initial conditions, the convoys were blocked because of the Bosnian Army offensive around Sarajevo. Finally, three food convoys were able to reach the city on 21 June, under the terms of the agreement of 8 June. However, clearance from the Bosnian Serb authorities were again blocked, after two convoys to the Serb-held part of Sarajevo came under shelling when offloading. The humanitarian situation in Sarajevo was critical and an attempt was to be made to bring a convoy into Sarajevo via the Mount Igman road on 30 June, with the assistance of UNPROFOR drivers.

24. A sequence of serious incidents at Sarajevo airport, including aircraft of ICRC, UNPROFOR and UNHCR, led to the suspension of the humanitarian airlift on 11 March. Flights resumed on 24 March. On 29 March the Sarajevo

airlift saw its thousandth day, only to stop a few days later, on 8 April, because os security problems. The airlift remained suspended, and UNHCR had to rely on overland convoys, which were stopped up to cover about 60 per cent of the city needs. However, full access to the capital stopped in the aftermath of the vents of 24-25 May, following the serious deterioration of the overall situation n Sarajevo.

25. After a relatively stable humanitarian situation in the eastern enclaves, the situation became increasingly difficult, with repeated obstructions and confiscations. With the introduction of the new Bosnian Serb Coordinating Committee for Humanitarian Affairs, the bulk of the convoy plan to the eastern enclaves was again approved for the week starting 20 March, after disruptions in convoy access of some 80 per cent. Médecins sans Frontières (MSF) was also able to bring medicines to Gorazde and Srebrenica for the first time since November 1994, after the continuing refusal of the Bosnian Serbs to allow the delivery of medical supplies to the enclaves. The medical situation in Gorazde and Srebrenica had become critical - the hospital in Srebrenica was in a position to perform only extremely urgent surgeries and could no longer ensure basic medical care.

26. With the escalation of the conflict in May, the humanitarian situation in the eastern enclaves deteriorated rapidly. The last convoy to reach Gorazde was on 20 May. Because of the difficult food situation, the local authorities collected grain from outlying villages for distribution to vulnerable cases. In Srebrenica, where the situation had become critical, conditions improved somewhat with the arrival of a few convoys. A convoy reached Zepa on 21 June, the first since 24 May.

27. Obstructions from the Croatian Serbs and the Abdic forces continued for the passage of UNHCR convoys to the Bihac Pocket, with virtually all supplies blocked since May 1994. The humanitarian situation was critical. On 8 March, the UNHCR Special Envoy wrote to the Croatian Serb leader Martic, recalling their meeting in Knin on 21 February and pointing out that, since that meeting, no convoys had been approved for Bihac, with the exception of only four convoys. UNHCR had, therefore, no other choice at the moment but to suspend humanitarian assistance to areas under Croatian serb control until regular access to Bihac, particularly through the crossing point at Licko Petrovo Zelo, was granted.

28. With the events in Western Slavonia at the beginning of May, the Bihac pocket became even more isolated and chances to get convoys in became even more remote. The last assistance to arrive on 25 May (100 tons of food), in the southern part of the pocket, was distributed to the most vulnerable cases, through hospitals, social centres, public kitchens and the local Red Cross. UNHCR was finally able to deliver a convoy to the southern part of the pocket

on 29 June, passing through the checkpoint at Licko Petrovo Zelo. A second convoy obtained clearance for the following day.

29. The increased cooperation between the UNHCR, UNPROFOR Civil Affairs and UNHCR on the issue of monitoring of human rights was a positive development and a constant reminder of the necessity of monitoring the continuing forced departure of Muslims and Croats from Banja Luka. UNHCR was concerned about the adverse effects on the security situation and the conduct of its protection activities of the continued acts of violence against minorities in the Banja Luka area. Continuous pressure placed on minority communities to leave the area took the form of evictions, house bombings, and midnight shooting raids, arrest and interrogation, telephone calls, veiled threats, harassment on the streets, physical and verbal assaults of women and students. The rounding up of minority men between the ages of 17 and 70 to perform civilian work obligations, often on the first and second front lines, was also of great concern. As a result of the harassment, members of minorities did not venture out of their homes,; children did not attend school; and men and boys were in hiding. UNHCR protection officers closely monitored the situation, through field trips and visits to the minorities. UNHCR held numerous meetings with the local authorities, the Catholic Bishop and CARITAS, in its continued efforts to put an end to the situation.

30. In May, the influx of refugees from western Slavonia into Bosnian Serb-controlled territory, especially in the Banja Luka region, resulted in the worsening of treatment and forced expulsions of Croat and Muslim minorities residing there. UNHCR reported on numerous attacks, especially on the Catholic clergy, and repeatedly intervened, with mixed results, before the authorities to mediate between the two groups. Some 6,00 to 7,000 refugees from Western Slavonia were registered in the Banja Luka area; some 2,100 left Western Slavonia via the UNHCR "Operation Safe Passage"; some 750 were accommodated in collective centres, and the rest in private accommodation.

31. Some 100 Serb and Croat refugees expressed a desire to return to Western Slavonia. Fifty UNHCR cases received permission from the Croatian Office for Displaced Persons and Refugees to return and verbal permission by the Bosnian Serbs. A small group of Croatian Serbs who fled western Slavonia to Serbia also expressed their desire to return. The Croatian Government declared that these Croatian Serbs who fled Western Slavonia will be permitted to return, if it was ascertained that they were legally resident in Croatia prior to the 1991 conflict. UNHCR's involvement in the population movements from Western Slavonia after the restoration Croatian rule was limited to the counselling of the Croatian Serb population about their right to stay or the possibility to leave with the assist-

ance of international organizations. In the latter case, UNHCR ascertained the voluntary nature of such departures. UNHCR also interviewed refugees arriving from Sector West to Sector Bravo.

32. UNHCR dismantled the transit refugee camps in the Nepalese and Jordanian battalion camps in former Sector West that had accommodated refugees from northern Bosnia in the past. During the first days of May, the Croatian Army moved the 359 refugees at Pustara (Nepalese battalion) to Daruvar. Subsequently 245 proceeded to the island of Obonjan for collective accommodation, while the balance departed for private accommodation. The remaining 146 refugees at the Jordanian transit camp at Novska were evacuated to Ivanicgrad with the assistance of UNHCR.

33. UNHCR was concerned about the possible difficulties that Muslims fleeing Banja Luka may experience in entering Croatia, since there was no longer the buffer zone of Sector West, were they would have transited pending UNHCR intervention with the Croatian authorities to obtain entry, subject to resettlement. The Croatian regional Office for Displaced Persons and Refugees in Zagreb confirmed that refugees originally from Serb-held territory in Bosnia and Herzegovina could be registered if they arrived directly from their village of origin.

34. Some 4,500 Croatian Serbs from western Slavonia arrived in Sector East, where they were accommodated in 4 locations, in a combination of private houses and collective accommodations. UNHCR carried out a need assessment for the new arrivals. Principal needs, especially among the elderly, who were accommodated in sparse collective centres, were basic food and non-food-items.

35. The Regional Refugee Commissioner in Sector North informed UNHCR that the local police militia insisted that the total number of refugees from Bosnia and Herzegovina in the Sector would be kept to a minimum of 50 at any given time, and that refugees should not remain in the Sector for more than four weeks. UNHCR facilitated a more expeditious entry of refugees in Croatian-controlled territory.

36. In the Federal Republic of Yugoslavia (Serbia and Montenegro), the Federal Republic's Commissioner for Refugees prepare plans fort the permanent settlement of approximately 200,000 refugees The plan called for permanent shelters to be built, access to jobs or job training and some type of credit with the national bank for money to support families while they locally integrate. The initial budget foreseen is US$ 800 million. The Government was still unable to provide UNHCR with accurate numbers of refugees living in the Federal Republic of Yugoslavia (Serbia and Montenegro) or their places of origin. Plans for the permanent settlements did not mention citizenship rights of refugees.

37. UNHCR plans to finance US$ 400,000 worth of minor repairs to existing buildings accommodating refugees in 1995. The office of the Federal Republic

of Yugoslavia (Serbia and Montenegro) Commissioner for Refugees presented UNHCR with requests totalling over US$ 1.5 million worth of repairs and renovations for existing centres.

38. The capacity of collective centres in the Federal Republic of Yugoslavia (Serbia and Montenegro) is approximately 40,000 beds. until May 1995, refugees used some 60 per cent of these beds. Since June 1995, many of the commercially owned centres refused to accommodate refugees in the hope that rooms could be rented out to paying customers. Refugees were moved into collective centres built or renovated by UNHCR. It is expected that the remaining collective centres will be 80 per cent full by the end of August.

39. UNHCR learned with concern of cases of refugees carrying old Socialist Federal Republic of Yugoslavia passports from Bosnia and Herzegovina being prevented from leaving the Federal Republic of Yugoslavia (Serbia and Montenegro) without an exit visa, including refugees accepted for temporary protection in third countries. UNHCR repeated its request to the Federal Republic of Yugoslavia (Serbia and Montenegro) Government for an update on passport rules and regulations.

40. The number of refugees arriving through the reception centres in the Federal Republic of Yugoslavia (Serbia and Montenegro) continued to increase. During the first two quarters of 1995, 1,000 and 2,500 persons respectively per month were reported on average.

41. Some 2,500 refugees from Western Slavonia arrived in the Federal Republic of Yugoslavia (Serbia and Montenegro). It was estimated that nearly 7,000 refugees from Western Slavonia transited through the Federal Republic of Yugoslavia (Serbia and Montenegro) from Bosnian Serb-held territory to Sector East.

42. UNHCR was concerned about the mobilization in the Federal Republic of Yugoslavia (Serbia and Montenegro) of refugees from Croatia for the Croatian Serb army. Recently, this operation also started to target refugees from Bosnia and Herzegovina to be drafted in the Bosnian Serb army. UNHCR received hundreds of phone calls from refugees seeking advice. UNHCR voiced its strong protest with the Office of the Serbian Refugee Commissioner, with the Federal Ministry of Foreign Affairs and with the spokesperson of the Croatian Serbs for this blatant violation of the 1951 Convention relating to the Status of Refugees.

43. In Slovenia, a draft law on temporary refuge passed the first reading in the Parliament. The law proposed positive amendments to improve guarantees for the applicants during the procedure. Pending the adoption of the law, the Office for Immigration and Refugees continued its policy of "wait and see" and delivered mainly negative decisions on entry permissions and registration. applications, with the exception of family permissions and permission for medical

reasons. Bosnian citizens who received negative replies from the Slovenian Office for Immigration and Refugees were asked to register at the local police in an database including persons present in Slovenia as tourists. They were not issued any documents by the local police stations. UNHCR raised its concern for this category of the population, proposing measures for improvement.

44. On 2 June, the Bosnian Government organized the return of some 726 persons from the former Yugoslav Republic of Macedonia. UNHCR was not involved in the movements, except for monitoring and reporting purposes, and ensuring that all departures were voluntary. UNHCR also provided assistance on their arrival at collective centres in Lablanica.

45. On 10 March, the Steering Committee if the International Management Group adopted the statute of the Group at a meeting in Geneva. It also adopted the budget, in principle, depending on forthcoming additional cash contributions.

46. The United Nations revised consolidated inter-agency appeal for the former Yugoslavia covering January-December 1995 was issued on 2 June by nine United Nations agencies, for a total of US$ 470 million for humanitarian operations. The UNHCR component is US$ 172 million, to cover the cost of humanitarian aid for a total estimated number of 2,109,500 beneficiaries in Bosnia and Herzegovina, Croatia, the former Yugoslav Republic of Macedonia, Slovenia and Federal Republic of Yugoslavia (Serbia and Montenegro). Contributions as of 30 June include an estimated carryover of US$ 95.6 million; 1995 contributions amount to US$ 39.5 million.

VI. ETHNIC AND NATIONAL COMMUNITIES AND MINORITIES

A. The former Yugoslav Republic of Macedonia

47. The Working Group on Ethnic and National Communities and Minorities has intensified its activities in the former Yugoslav Republic of Macedonia. Its endeavours have concentrated mainly on problems of the ethnic Albanians in the Republic. After some talks with representatives of different ethnic Albanian parties in the country, it was possible to assemble members of the three political parties that are represented in Parliament around the same table. Thus, it became possible to continue the Conference-chaired trilateral talks with the Government, which was represented by the Ministers of the Interior, Education and Justice. Since the beginning of the year, there have been altogether five rounds of talks of two days' duration each in Skopje. A sixth round took place in Geneva from 5 to 7 July.

48. In these trilateral talks, a step-by step approach was followed. One of the issues discussed during the latest round of talks was higher education. There, a tense situation had arisen after an attempt to establish a private university in Tetovo with Albanian as the teaching language. Other issues on the agenda of the trilateral talks were certain aspects of elementary and secondary education, parts of the forthcoming law on local self-government, the showing of national symbols and flags and citizenship questions.

49. Some progress on ethnic Albanian requests was achieved. Ethnic Albanians were nominated to the judiciary, to the officer corps and to diplomatic and other important State functions, although the number of those nominated is still below the approximately 23 per cent of the population of the country that is of Albanian ethnicity. The main Albanian language newspaper now appears daily, thanks to government subsidies. An agreement between the Macedonian Radio and Television and the Swiss and Danish Governments, which was brokered by the Working Group, provides for as tripling of emissions in the Albanian Language and for considerable increases in other ethnicities' languages. A similar project is under consideration for the radio. In education, there was a government promise to open, later in 1995, a pedagogical faculty were future ethnic Albanian teachers will, to a certain extent, be trained in their own language.

50. There were also contacts of the Working Group with ethnic Serbs in the former Yugoslav Republic of Macedonia, talks with the Turkish ethnic group, in which there was an agreement of principle on trilateral talks along the model of the talks along the model of the talks with the ethnic Albanians, and a meeting with Macedonian-speaking Muslims in the Republic. The requests of these groups referred mainly to language education and religious issues. The Working Group also held five meetings with leaders of three opposition parties. It was received by President Berisha of the Republic of Albania on 30 May in Tirana, where Mr. Berisha declared his full support for the Work of the Group.

51. The Working Group, in preparation for the meetings in Skopje, had discussions with the Council of Europe in Strasbourg. The Council provided the Working Group with valuable advice on different subjects such as education and local self-government. The cooperation with the Council of Europe was in continuation of similar cooperation in connection with the census that took place a year ago and on which experts of the Council of Europe continue to work.

52. There has also been very close coordination with the Organization of Security and Cooperation in Europe (OSCE) High Commissioner for National Minorities, particularly on university-level education, and with the Special Representative of the Secretary-General for the Former Yugoslavia in Zagreb. When in Skopje, the Working Group had useful discussions with the Force Commander

and the Head of Civil Affairs of the United Nations Preventive Deployment Force (UNPREDEP).

B. Croatia

53. The Working Group has paid attention to the position of Serbs living in the areas of Croatia that are controlled by the Government. It held several exchanges of views with the Chief of Staff of the Office of the President of the Republic in Zagreb. There were also meetings with representatives of these Serbs. On one occasion, discussions took place between a delegation of the Working Group and approximately 70 Serbs, among whom various political groups and parties were represented. The aim of these efforts was to offer the good Offices of the Conference on problems voiced by the Serbs.

54. On the subject of future relations among ethnic and national communities and minorities in the former Yugoslavia, ta working Group also had contacts with Cabinet Ministers of the Federal Republic of Yugoslavia (Serbia and Montenegro) and was received by Patriarch Pavle of the Serbian Orthodox Church.

C. Kosovo, Sandjak and Vojvodina

55. Renewed efforts were made with a view to re-establishing a dialogue between representatives of non-Serb ethnicities living in these areas and the authorities. In this context, International Conference representatives met on several occasions with representatives of the Kosovo Albanians and of the Sandjak Muslims, as well as with the municipal authorities both in Pristina and in Novi Pazar.

56. The Conference is now studying the possible modalities for dialogue, will continue to be in touch with the parties and will watch future developments closely.

VII. SUCCESSION ISSUES

57. The Succession Issues Working Group has conducted negotiations on all aspects of succession related to the former Yugoslavia. Meticulous and persistent work has brought the parties within reach of agreement on draft treaty provisions dealing with citizenship, pensions acquired rights treaty succession and archives. The draft succession treaty has been cast into two portions, which could constitute independent treaties or be parts of a single treaty, depending on how events develop.

58. The first portion deals with citizenship, pensions, acquired rights, archives, treaty succession and arbitration mechanisms. It contains provisions that have been discussed in detail with the parties and on which there is a large measure of agreement. The draft has been given to the parties.

59. The second portion deals with the disposition of assets and liabilities. Consultations are continuing on how these could be distributed among the successor Republics. The Co-Chairmen will decide how to proceed with the second portion in the light of those consultations.

60. During the past six months, consultations with the parties, with major Governments and with creditors have continued on the second portion of the draft treaty. The Chairman of the Working Group hopes for a presentation to the parties as soon as circumstances permit.

VIII. ECONOMIC ISSUES

61. The Economic Issues Working Group was not convened in the first half of the year. The Chairman of the Working Group, together with the heads of delegations, considered that, given the present political circumstances, such a meeting would serve no purpose. The issue of economic reconstruction has been on the agenda on other forums, outside the Group. It is, for instance, the subject-matter of a European Union research project.

IX. ARBITRATION COMMISSION

62. The Arbitration Commission of the International Conference is composed of:

(a) Three members designated by the Council of Ministers of the European Community from among incumbent Presidents of Constitutional Courts existing in States members of the European Community or from among members of the highest courts in these States, it being understood that for the present these members are those from France, Germany and Italy;

(b) One member designated by the President of the International Court of Justice from among former members of the Court or persons possessing the qualifications required by Article 2 of the Statute of the Court;

(c) One member of the European Court of Human Rights, designated by the President of the Court.

63. No two members may have the same nationality. Each member serves as long as he or she holds the office on the basis of which the designation was made.

64. Whenever the Arbitration Commission is engaged in a contentious proceeding, each of the contending parties may appoint an ad hoc member to the Commission, who must either be incumbent members of Constitutional Courts or highest courts existing in States members of OSCE or have the qualification specifies in subparagraph 62 (b) or (c) above.

65. The current membership of the Arbitration Commission is as follows:

- President: Roland Dumas, President of the Constitutional Council of France (elected on 10 June 1995);
- Antonio Baldesarre, President of the Constitutional Court of Italy;
- Jutta Limbach, President of the Federal Constitutional Court of Germany;
- Kéba Mbaye, former Judge at the International Court of Justice;
- Elizabeth Palm, Judge of the European Court of Human Rights.

The Arbitration Commission is competent to:

(a) Decide, with binding force for the parties concerned, any dispute submitted to it by the parties thereto upon authorization by the Co-Chairmen of the Steering Committee of the International Conference;

(b) Give its advice as to any legal question submitted to it by the Co-Chairmen of the Steering Committee of the International Conference.

148. LETTER DATED 3 AUGUST 1995 FROM THE SECRETARY-GENERAL ADDRESSED TO THE PRESIDENT OF THE SECURITY COUNCIL*

I have the honour to transmit the attached report, which was addressed to me on 2 August 1995 by the Co-Chairmen of the Steering Committee of the International Conference on the Former Yugoslavia, concerning the operations of the International Conference's Mission to the Federal Republic of Yugoslavia (Serbia and Montenegro). This report by the Co-Chairmen contains the certification referred to in Security Council resolution 1003 (1995).

I should be grateful if you would bring this information to the attention of the members of the Security Council.

---

* UN Doc. S/1995/645, 3 August 1995. Signed by Boutros Boutros-Ghali.

Annex
Operations of the International Conference on the Former Yugoslavia
(ICFY) Mission to the Federal Republic of Yugoslavia
(Serbia and Montenegro)

I. INTRODUCTION

1. The present report is submitted pursuant to paragraph 13 of Security Council resolution 988 (1995) of 21 April 1995 and 1003 (1995) of 5 July 1995. In resolution 988 (1995), the Security Council requested that the Secretary-General submitted every 30 days, for its review, a report from the Co-Chairmen of the Steering Committee of the International Conference on the Former Yugoslavia on the border closure measures taken by the authorities of the Federal Republic of Yugoslavia (Serbia and Montenegro).

2. It will be recalled that, on 4 August 1994, the following measures were ordered by the Government of the Federal Republic of Yugoslavia (Serbia and Montenegro), to come into effect the same day:

"(a) To break off political and economic relations with the 'Republika Srpska';
  (b) To prohibit the stay of the members of the leadership of the 'Republika Srpska' (parliament, Presidency and Government) in the territory of the Federal Republic of Yugoslavia;
  (c) As of today the border of the Federal Republic of Yugoslavia is closed for all transport towards the 'Republika Srpska', except food, clothing and medicine."

3. On 19 September, 3 October, 2 November and 5 December 1994, 5 January, 3 February, 2 March, 31 March, 13 April, 18 May and 25 June 1995, the Secretary-General transmitted to the Security Council reports from the Co-Chairmen of the Steering Committee on the state of implementation of the above-mentioned measures (S/1994/1074; S/1994/1124; S/1994/1246; S/1994/1372; S/1995/6; S/1995/104; S/1995/175; S/1995/255; S/1995/302; S/1995/406 and S/1995/510). The report dated 25 June 1995 contained the following certification from the Co-Chairmen:

"In the light of the foregoing developments during the reporting period, based on the Mission's on-site observation, on the advice of the Mission's coordinator, Mr. T.J. Nieminen, and in the absence of any contrary information from the air, either from the airborne reconnaissance system of the North Atlantic Treaty Organization (NATO), or national technical means, the Co-Chairmen conclude that the Government of the Federal Republic of Yugoslavia (Serbia and Montenegro) is continuing to meet its commitment to close the border between the Federal Republic of Yugoslavia (Serbia and Montenegro) and the areas of the Republic of Bosnia and Herzegovina under the control of the Bosnian Serb forces. The Co-Chairmen also conclude that, during the period covered by the present report, there have been no commercial transshipments across the border between the Federal Republic of Yugoslavia (Serbia and Montenegro) and the Republic of Bosnia and Herzegovina."

Developments since the last report are outlined below.

II. LEGISLATION/REGULATIONS ON THE BORDER CLOSURE

4. The decision of the Federal Government to break off all economic and political relations with the "Republika Srpska" that was reached in August 1994 was amended on 13 July 1995. According to the amendment to the said decision, besides food, clothing and medicine, the following articles may be sent to the territory of the "Republika Srpska" as humanitarian aid:

Articles for hygiene and disinfectants;
Books, textbooks and other school materials;
Funeral equipment;
Articles for religious services (candles, icon lamps, incense and the like).

5. The authorities of the Federal Republic of Yugoslavia (Serbia and Montenegro) have provided the Mission wit the following list of confiscations conducted along its border with Bosnia and Herzegovina for June 1995:

Petrol	10.5 tons
Diesel	20.3 tons
Motor oil	784 litres
Cigarettes	1.3 tons
Construction materials	23.9 tons
Wood	27 cubic metres
Alcohol	703 litres
Food	6.7 tons
Textiles, clothing, footwear	236 kilograms
Animals	22
Coffee	1.6 tons
Electrical gadgets	550 kilograms
Motor vehicles	4
Other goods	11.4 tons

6. There were 67 new offence procedures initiated during the month and 120 were finalized. Fines and penalties amounted to 285,000 dinars. The volume of confiscations was down to more normal levels following the substantial increase

in May. The number of new offence cases was about the average for the previous 10 months, whilst the number of cases finalized and penalties levied were well above the average for the previous monthly periods.

III. ORGANIZATION, FINANCING AND WORK OF THE MISSION

7. As of 30 July 1995, 185 international Mission personnel were on duty with the Mission. The Mission personnel to date have come from the following countries: Belgium, Canada, Czech Republic, Denmark, Finland, France, Germany, Greece, Ireland, Italy, Netherlands, Norway, Portugal, Russian Federation, Spain, Sweden, United Kingdom of Great Britain and Northern Ireland and United States of America.

8. The present number of monitors assures 24-hour manning of the 19 border crossing points, as well as patrolling the Mission area of responsibility. The conditions of the observers at the crossing points were upgraded considerably by the end of July, when 13 portacabins loaned to the Mission by the United Nations were installed at the crossing points.

IV. FREEDOM OF MOVEMENT OF THE MISSION

9. The Mission continues to enjoy full freedom of movement within the Federal Republic of Yugoslavia (Serbia and Montenegro).

10. Nevertheless, there have been some minor incidents, when on eight different occasions Mission observers have been verbally threatened by local people. One of the incidents happened in the vicinity of Citluk (Sector Alpha) and the rest of them in Sector Charlie: one in Scepan Polje, two in Vracenovici, two in Nikaic and two while patrolling in Montenegro. The Mission considers those incidents as personal outbursts, reflecting the present uncertain situation in the former Yugoslavia. The security of personnel is closely monitored by the Mission headquarters and remains a matter of priority concern.

11. Also, on 22 July, a Mission mobile patrol was by the Drina river, 1.5 kilometres south of Badovinci, when from the western side of the river a burst of automatic fire was let off as a possible warning. The patrol withdrew but the incident was assessed as an isolated one (not necessarily directly targeting Mission members) and this area will continue to be monitored.

V. COOPERATION OF THE AUTHORITIES OF THE FEDERAL REPUBLIC OF YUGOSLAVIA (SERBIA AND MONTENEGRO) WITH THE MISSION

12. Cooperation with the authorities of the Federal Republic of Yugoslavia (Serbia and Montenegro) continues to be good.

IV. INFORMATION RECEIVED FROM NATIONAL AND OTHER SOURCES

13. The operating principle of the Mission is to base its reporting and evaluations on its own observations and on information that it has verified. The Mission Coordinator has maintained a standing request to Governments possessing the technical capacity to provide it with information relevant to its mandate. He has not received any such information since the last report.

VII. PROBLEMS ENCOUNTERED AND REPRESENTATIONS MADE TO THE AUTHORITIES

14. Unarmed uniformed personnel continue to cross the border between the Federal Republic of Yugoslavia (Serbia and Montenegro) and Bosnia and Herzegovina. During the reporting period, 492 such incidents were reported, 460 at Sremska Raca. Usually the crossings happen in small groups or individually, except on 21 July in Vracenovici, when 30 unarmed soldiers crossed the border in a bus from Bosnia and Herzegovina into the Federal Republic of Yugoslavia (Serbia and Montenegro). On two occasions, at Scepan Polje, uniformed persons were allowed to cross the border carrying a sidearm.

15. On 24 July, at Sremska Raca three civilians carrying sidearms were allowed to cross the border into the Federal Republic of Yugoslavia (Serbia and Montenegro). The vehicle registration number indicated it was from the "Republic of Serb Krajina" ("RSK").

16. The customs officials in Sector Belgrade have been active throughout the reporting period, confiscating many items intended for smuggling, especially at Belgrade port, where substantial quantities of confiscations have been reported by Mission observers. For example, 1 load with 4 tons of hidden fertilizer and another with 530 bottles of wine and 120 kilograms of chocolate were confiscated. In Novi Sad a load of cement was found hidden under flour in two trucks. In Sremska Raca, 2 trucks were impounded, 1 with a hidden bulkhead tank containing 11.3 tons of fuel and the other with a hidden tank of approximately 14.5 tons of fuel. On two occasions, the customs officials found 10 tons of cement when investigating the cut wire on loaded trucks.

17. On 26 July, at Sremska Raca, one car carrying packages of corn plus other packages crossed the border into Bosnia and Herzegovina unchecked after a conversation with a customs officer, who stated that he did not know what was in the packages.

18. On 26 July, a Mission mobile patrol by the Drina river 4 kilometres north of Trbusnica saw a metal boat full of 200 litres fuel drums moored to the far bank. The number of drums was at least 16. There were five cars, one van and numerous people in the area at the time. On the site is a cable ferry crossing. The pulley cable attached to the main cable had been moved from its old, useless position in midstream from the far bank. This made the ferry operational for the first time in about two months. Three hundred metres upstream and south of the ferry, a tractor and a trailer were reversed into the river. On the trailer were at least nine 200-litre fuel drums. There was a Yugoslav Army Liaison officer with the patrol, who returned to his barracks to task an army patrol to cover the area. The Mission mobile patrol returned to the area the next day, on 27 July. A three-man Yugoslav Army patrol was posted there and the patrol leader stated that they had not observed any activity in the area. The fuel drums had also disappeared.

19. At Badovinci and Trbusnica border crossing points (Sector Alpha) the problem of "ant trade" appeared in late June and increased in July. Cement, fertilizer and powder paint were allowed across the border to the Republic of Bosnia and Herzegovina, mostly on BiCycles. All indications suggested that this was trade-related. The customs authorities of the Federal Republic of Yugoslavia (Serbia and Montenegro) complied with the Mission's request to put an end to this kind of trade. The bicycle traffic continues to be a slight problem, with beer being now the principal cargo.

20. On 20 July, observers at the Skelani (Bajina Basta) border crossing point reported that a helicopter crossed the border into Bosnia and Herzegovina. On three separate occasions, on 23, 26 and 28 July, the Mission team at the Badovinci (Sector Alpha) crossing point reported a helicopter crossing the border, twice from Bosnia and Herzegovina to the Federal Republic of Yugoslavia (Serbia and Montenegro) and once in the other direction. On 28 July, separate helicopter crossings were sighted at the Mali Zvornik (Sector Alpha) and Vilusi (Sector Charlie) crossing points. The Mission headquarters has requested an explanation of the flights from the authorities of the Federal Republic of Yugoslavia (Serbia and Montenegro), who have confirmed them as medical evacuation flights. The Mission can neither confirm nor deny that these were medical evacuation flights. The United Nations military observers team in Belgrade has advised the Mission that, because of problems monitoring helicopters on the

Bosnia and Herzegovina side, no helicopter flights destined to cross the border either way have been given United Nations approval since 11 July 1995.

21. United Nations airfield monitors working at civilian radar screens at Surcin Airport near Belgrade notified the Mission of two unidentified radar tracks on 29 June, and of one further trace on 8 July. On 13 July the Mission Operations (Air) Officer reviewed the tapes covering all three cases. The tapes had no traces of the tracks reported by the military observers. After the review, the Mission Operations Officer was subjected to harassment at the Federal Air Traffic Control Authority over the wording of a written factual statement of his findings. Also the Federal Air Traffic Control Authority has been unnecessary obstructive over the Mission reviewing tapes. The Mission is making representations to the authorities of the Federal Republic of Yugoslavia (Serbia and Montenegro) about these matters.

22. Two barriers in the Tara mountains 10 kilometres west of the village of Mitrovac were frequently tampered with. The incidents were reported to the Yugoslav Army Liaison Officer, who ordered the reconstruction of the barricades.

23. In the previous report to the Security Council on 25 June (S/1995/510), the border crossing points at Metaljka and Sula (Sector Bravo) were mentioned as problematic areas because of the possibility of bypassing them. One way of dealing with the problem was to relocate those crossing points so as to prevent usage of the bypass roads. On 6 July, the Mission Coordinator, together with his senior Customs Advisor, met the Director General of the Federal Customs Administration and expressed his serious concern about the delay in relocating the two crossing points. Both of them, Metaljka and Sula, were moved to new locations that same afternoon.

24. On 26 June, at Vracenovici (Sector Charlie), a car with 14 bags of wool was allowed to cross into Bosnian Serb territory without a proper check.

25. On 17 July, an Nudo (Sector Charlie), the customs authorities of the Federal Republic of Yugoslavia (Serbia and Montenegro) allowed a van to cross into Bosnian Serb-held territory without it being checked. The observers noted that the van was fully loaded with crates of fruit, vegetables and meat.

VIII. CERTIFICATION

26. In the light of the foregoing developments during the reporting period, based on the Mission's on-site observation, on the advice of the Mission's coordinator, Mr. T.J. Nieminen, and in the absence of any contrary information from the air, either from the airborne reconnaissance system of the North Atlantic Treaty

Organization (NATO), or national technical means, the Co-Chairmen conclude that the Government of the Federal Republic of Yugoslavia (Serbia and Montenegro) is continuing to meet its commitment to close the border between the Federal Republic of Yugoslavia (Serbia and Montenegro) and the areas of the Republic of Bosnia and Herzegovina under the control of the Bosnian Serb forces. The Co-Chairmen also conclude that, during the period covered by the present report, there have been no commercial transshipments across the border between the Federal Republic of Yugoslavia (Serbia and Montenegro) and the Republic of Bosnia and Herzegovina.

27. Pursuant to Security Council resolutions 988 (1995) and 1003 (1995), the next report will be provided by 8 September 1995, before the expiration of the 75-day period.

149. LETTER DATED 6 SEPTEMBER 1995 FROM THE SECRETARY-GENERAL ADDRESSED TO THE PRESIDENT OF THE SECURITY COUNCIL*

I have the honour to transmit the attached report, which was addressed to me on 6 September 1995 by the Co-Chairmen of the Steering Committee of the International Conference on the Former Yugoslavia, concerning the operations of the International Conference's Mission to the Federal Republic of Yugoslavia (Serbia and Montenegro). This report by the Co-Chairmen contains the certification referred to in Security Council resolution 1003 (1995) of 5 July 1995.

I should be grateful if you would bring this information to the attention of the members of the Security Council.

Annex
Operations of the International Conference on the Former Yugoslavia (ICFY) Mission to the Federal Republic of Yugoslavia (Serbia and Montenegro)

I. INTRODUCTION

1. The present report is submitted pursuant to paragraph 13 of Security Council resolution 988 (1995) of 21 April 1995) and paragraph 2 of Council resolution 1003 (1995) of 5 July 1995. In those resolutions, the Council requested that the Secretary-General submitted every 30 days for its review, and no fewer than 10

---

* UN Doc. S/1995/768, 6 September 1995. Signed by Boutros Boutros-Ghali.

days before 18 September 1995, a report from the Co-Chairmen of the Steering Committee of the International Conference on the Former Yugoslavia on the border closure measures taken by the authorities of the Federal Republic of Yugoslavia (Serbia and Montenegro).

2. It will be recalled that, on 4 August 1994, the following measures were ordered by the Government of the Federal Republic of Yugoslavia (Serbia and Montenegro), to come into effect the same day:

> "(a) To break off political and economic relations with the 'Republika Srpska';
> (b) To prohibit the stay of the members of the leadership of the 'Republika Srpska' (parliament, Presidency and Government) in the territory of the Federal Republic of Yugoslavia;
> (c) As of today the border of the Federal Republic of Yugoslavia is closed for all transport towards the 'Republika Srpska', except food, clothing and medicine."

3. On 19 September, 3 October, 2 November and 5 December 1994, 5 January, 3 February, 2 March, 31 March, 13 April, 18 May, 25 June and 3 August 1995, the Secretary-General transmitted to the Security Council reports from the Co-Chairmen of the Steering Committee on the state of implementation of the above-mentioned measures (S/1994/1074; S/1994/1124; S/1994/1246; S/1994/1372; S/1995/6; S/1995/104; S/1995/175; S/1995/255; S/1995/302; S/1995/406; S/1995/510 and S/1995/645). The report dated 25 June 1995 contained the following certification from the Co-Chairmen:

> "In the light of the foregoing developments during the reporting period, based on the Mission's on-site observation, on the advice of the Mission's coordinator, Mr. T.J. Nieminen, and in the absence of any contrary information from the air, either from the airborne reconnaissance system of the North Atlantic Treaty Organization (NATO), or national technical means, the Co-Chairmen conclude that the Government of the Federal Republic of Yugoslavia (Serbia and Montenegro) is continuing to meet its commitment to close the border between the Federal Republic of Yugoslavia (Serbia and Montenegro) and the areas of the Republic of Bosnia and Herzegovina under the control of the Bosnian Serb forces. The Co-Chairmen also conclude that, during the period covered by the present report, there have been no commercial transshipment across the border between the Federal Republic of Yugoslavia (Serbia and Montenegro) and the Republic of Bosnia and Herzegovina."

Developments since the last report are outlined below.

II. LEGISLATION/REGULATIONS ON THE BORDER CLOSURE

4. The legislation of the authorities of the Federal Republic of Yugoslavia (Serbia and Montenegro) closing the border with the Bosnian Serbs continues to be in effect.

5. The authorities of the Federal Republic of Yugoslavia (Serbia and Montenegro) have provided the Mission with the following list of confiscations conducted along its border with Bosnia and Herzegovina for the month of July 1995:

Petrol	11.9 tons
Diesel	22.1 tons
Motor oil	155 litres
Cigarettes	611 kilograms
Construction materials	4.9 tons
Wood	532 cubic metres
Alcohol	282 litres
Food	10.1 tons
Textiles, clothing, footwear	1.5 tons
Animals	14
Coffee	531 kilograms
Electrical gadgets	121 kilograms
Motor vehicles	10
Other goods	10.6 tons

6. There were 152 new offence procedures initiated during the month of July and 137 were finalized. Fines and penalties amounted to 312,450 dinars. There was a small increase over the previous month in the mount of fuel confiscated, and other categories of goods more or less remained at last month's level. The number of new offence cases, cases finalized and penalties were well above the average of the previous monthly period.

7. Because of the regular smuggling activity across the Drina River in Sector Alpha, the Mission requested that confiscations in this sector, included in the monthly analysis, be identified separately. This revealed that 76 per cent of the fuel and 83 per cent of other goods confiscated in July along the border outside the border crossing-points occurred in Sector Alpha. These figures indicate that the authorities have taken action to stem smuggling in this high-risk area.

III. ORGANIZATION, FINANCING AND WORK OF THE MISSION

8. As of 3 September 1995, there are 196 international observers on duty in the Mission. The Mission personnel to date have come from the following countries: Belgium, Canada, Czech Republic, Denmark, Finland, France, Germany, Greece, Ireland, Italy, Netherlands, Norway, Portugal, Russian Federation, Spain, Sweden, United Kingdom of Great Britain and Northern Ireland and

United States of America. At this time, Canada, Portugal and Spain are not represented in the Mission.

9. In addition to 17 border crossing-points, the Mission mans train stations at Uzice at Priboj on a 24-hour basis to monitor all freight trains that cross into Bosnia between Uzice and Priboj. Operational command of the Priboj train element was transferred from Sector Bajina Basta to Sector Bravo on 1 September.

10. With the increase of Mission-owned vehicles and communication equipment, the Mission has established a workshop that is manned by three car mechanics and a radio technician.

11. A budget proposal for the next six-month period starting 1 October 1995 and ending 31 March 1996 has been submitted. The overall budget figure of US$ 4,179,700 is based on increasing the size of the Mission to 250 international personnel

12. During the time period between 6-17 August, approximately 150,000 refugees from the Krajina region were estimated to have entered from Bosnia into the Federal Republic of Yugoslavia (Serbia and Montenegro). About two thirds of them crossed at Sremska Raca (Sector Belgrade) and the rest at Badovinci, Trbusnica and Mali Zvornik (Sector Alpha). Several thousand men in "RSK" uniform, some of them armed, crossed in to the Federal Republic of Yugoslavia (Serbia and Montenegro). Their weapons and ammunition were confiscated by the authorities. Many of the Federal Republic of Yugoslavia (Serbia and Montenegro) authorities manning the border crossing-points worked extremely long hours and their frustration was sometimes, understandably, evident. The border crossing-points Badovinci and Trbusnica were not manned some days because of security reasons as refugees were gathering at the border crossing-points in an angry and sometimes vociferous mood. While unmanned, the border crossing-points were periodically patrolled by Mission teams. After 17 August the refugee influx practically subsided and the situation at the northern part of the border returned to normal.

IV. FREEDOM OF MOVEMENT AND SECURITY OF THE PERSONNEL

13. The Mission continues to enjoy freedom of movement within the Federal Republic of Yugoslavia (Serbia and Montenegro). However, on 10 August a Sector Alpha mobile patrol was prevented by a Yugoslav Army (VJ) patrol from proceeding south near Ljubovija. The Mission vehicle was searched by a VJ officer. A protest was lodged on 11 August with the VJ General Staff, which later apologized to the Mission for the incident. Security concerns limited sur-

veillance in the Tara Mountain and Jamena areas and there was a lack of VJ personnel for Mission patrols in Sector Bajina Basta.

14. On 15 August, the Mission team at Uzice train station (Sector Bajina Basta) reported on the arrival of two trains with more than 2,300 refugees. An irritated crowd around the container of Mission monitors at the station posed a danger of a potential conflict. Sealing of the trains was suspended and control of the train movement was conducted by counting cars and checking transit times. The next day the train team returned to its normal *modus operandi*. On 18 August, two monitors were threatened by local civilians from a disco in Bajina Basta. After being notified, the police conducted an investigation.

15. After midnight on 10 August, a Mission observer was involved in a fistfight with a local man in Priboj. On 16 August, a driver from Sector Bravo was hit on the head by a man who also threatened the driver if the latter continued to drive Mission cars. The matter was reported to the police, who identified and arrested the suspect the same day. The next day a Mission interpreter was threatened with rape by some local men if she kept working for the Mission. The incident was also reported to the police.

16. On 15 August, a Mission driver in Vilusi village (Sector Charlie) was cornered by a drunken Yugoslav Army (VJ) soldier who put a knife to the driver's throat, accusing him of being a spy. Another soldier took his intoxicate colleague away. The Yugoslav Army Liaison Officer was informed and promised to take action.

17. On 30 August, just before midnight, there were two explosions in the vicinity of the caravans at border crossing-point Nudo (Sector Charlie). The explosions were probably caused by either dynamite or concussion grenades. They did not cause any damage or casualties. There are no indications that this was anything more than an attempt to scare the observers.

V. COOPERATION OF THE AUTHORITIES OF THE FEDERAL REPUBLIC OF YUGOSLAVIA (SERBIA AND MONTENEGRO) WITH THE MISSION

18. Cooperation with the authorities of the Federal Republic of Yugoslavia (Serbia and Montenegro) has generally been good. During the influx of refugees some police and customs officers on the local level tended to distance themselves from observers. During August, the customs officers at Novi Sad on some occasions refused to use a metal probe and were reluctant to examine thoroughly bulk consignments of humanitarian aid, despite requests from Sector Belgrade observers. Following discussions between the Mission Senior Customs Adviser and the Federal Republic of Yugoslavia (Serbia and Montenegro) Deputy Direc-

tor of Customs, an agreement was reached and the normal procedures of examining humanitarian aid were resumed in accordance with the standing arrangements.

VI. INFORMATION RECEIVED FROM NATIONAL AND OTHER SOURCES

19. The operating principle of the Mission is to base its reporting and evaluations on its own observations and on information that it has verified. The Coordinator of the Mission maintains a standing request to Governments possessing the technical capacity to provide it with information relevant to its mandate.

20. On 30 August and 1 September, the Mission received information from unspecified sources that ammunition is being loaded on trucks in different locations in Serbia and that these trucks are crossing into Bosnia at Sremska Raca. The Mission has intensified patrolling around the village of Sremska Raca and has vigilantly monitored the situation at the border crossing-point but no evidence to substantiate the above-mentioned information has been found.

VII. PROBLEMS ENCOUNTERED AND REPRESENTATIONS MADE TO THE AUTHORITIES

21. Unarmed uniformed personnel continue to cross the border between the Federal Republic of Yugoslavia (Serbia and Montenegro) and Bosnia and Herzegovina. During the reporting period, 321 such incidents were reported, 269 of them at Sremska Raca, not counting the "RSK" soldiers that crossed the border in uniform.

22. At Belgrade Port and Novi Sad, Mission observers in Sector Belgrade regularly refuse to seal humanitarian aid trucks when they have strong grounds for suspecting that the consignments are commercial. In effect, this prevents the loads crossing the border into Bosnia and Herzegovina. However, it is conceivable that, despite the efforts of the observers and the customs officials, some commercial consignments might get through disguised as Yugoslav Red Cross (YRC) humanitarian aid.

23. On 2 August at Sremska Raca (Sector Belgrade) two ambulances and two cars with "RS" military plates were allowed to cross into Bosnia and Herzegovina unchecked. Customs officers at the border crossing-point stated that they had been instructed by the police not to inspect them. Also, on 4 August, an ambulance crossing into Bosnia and Herzegovina was ,stopped but not searched. On 7 August, a Belgrade-registered taxi was initially denied entry into Bosnia

and Herzegovina by Federal Republic of Yugoslavia customs officers for carrying 100 litres of fuel in two containers. After a short wait away from the border crossing-point, the taxi was allowed to cross, although the fuel had not been unloaded. On 18 August, also at the border crossing-point at Sremska Raca, an inspection of a loaded truck revealed an estimated 6,000 litres of fuel in drums in the load compartment. The vehicle was impounded and customs offence action was taken against the driver.

24. At Sremska Raca on 10 August, a train (diesel engine and four carriages) was seen heading south on the line behind the border crossing-point. Traffic was stopped at the road/rail bridge and the train crossed the border heading towards the town of Bijeljina in Bosnia and Herzegovina. Later that day the returned north across the border into the Federal Republic of Yugoslavia (Serbia and Montenegro). This railway line had not been used since the formation of the Mission. The Federal Republic of Yugoslavia (Serbia and Montenegro) authorities explained that the train was sent from Sid to Bijeljina to collect refugees who had no transport. The train crossed into Bosnia and Herzegovina again at 1940 hours on 10 August and returned the next day at 1245 hours with eight passengers and some flat-bed freight wagons. These crossings are reported as violations of the border closure as the Mission observers were unable to check the carriages. On 12 August at 0020 hours a train crossed into Bosnia and Herzegovina and returned to the Federal Republic of Yugoslavia (Serbia and Montenegro) at 0300 hours. On both occasions the Mission team checked the carriages. Another train movement took place at 1115 hours outbound and 1345 inbound. On these occasions the team was not able to check the train.

25. Smuggling of fuel continues across the Drina River north of Trbusnica (Sector Alpha), especially in the vicinity of Lesnica. The Mission's mobile patrols have on several occasions detected barrel tracks and evidence of spilt fuel on the ground at the river's edge. Numerous empty barrels and 2050 litre fuel containers have also been detected. On 22 August, the Sector patrol in the area north of the border crossing-point at Trbusnica reported evidence of fuel being smuggled in drums on boats across the Drina River. Federal Republic of Yugoslavia (Serbia and Montenegro) customs authorities were notified of the violation. On 23 August, a Sector Alpha mobile patrol 4 kilometres north of Trbusnica observed a boat with an outboard motor and loaded with large container-like objects camouflaged wit leaves and branches. A few hours later the patrol observed a smaller boat on which was loaded a large number (approximately 40) of cardboard boxes and some canisters. The boat crossed to the "RS:" side of the river. On 23 August, in the Citluk area, two boats crossed the River Drina and unloaded their cargo to a truck waiting on the "RS" side. The Mission Senior

Customs Adviser met on 25 August with the Deputy Director of the Federal Republic of Yugoslavia (Serbia and Montenegro) customs and discussed the fuel smuggling along the Drina, pointing out the apparent lack of effort by the military and the special police to control it. On 28 August, a letter was sent to the Federal Republic of Yugoslavia (Serbia and Montenegro) customs providing some details of the findings of Sector Alpha mobile patrols. On 1 September, the Mission Coordinator and his Senior Customs Adviser met with the Director General of the federal Customs Administration to express his serious concerns about the smuggling along the Drina. The Federal Republic of Yugoslavia customs authorities were fully aware of the situation and promised that joint customs, police and military teams will do their utmost to close that part of the border more effectively.

26. After having been curbed for a while, the problem of "ant trade" resurfaced in August, especially at the border crossing-point Badovinci (Sector Alpha), where bicycles are crossing carrying cement and beer. During the Mission Coordinator's meeting with the Director General of Federal Republic of Yugoslavia (Serbia and Montenegro) Customs on 1 September, it was indicated that the bicycle traffic will be reduced significantly.

27. On 21 August, observers at the border crossing-point Badovinci reported that 20 Federal Republic of Yugoslavia (Serbia and Montenegro) policemen armed with assault rifles crossed the border into Bosnia and Herzegovina. They returned two hours later and Federal Republic of Yugoslavia authorities explained that there had been a problem with some "RSK" soldiers that they had to handle.

28. During August tension increased in the Tara mountains in Sector Bajina Basta, where refugee soldiers of the Army of Bosnia and Herzegovina were alleged to have crossed the border from eastern Bosnia. Mission-patrolling was restricted in the area for security reasons.

29. At Kotroman on 3 August during the night, three vehicles, one of them an ambulance, were allowed to cross into Bosnia and Herzegovina unchecked.

30. In Sector Bravo two new river fords were detected two kilometres north of Uvac. The level of the River Lim is low and it is clear that a few small vehicles crossed the river because of the evidence of tracks on both sides of the river. Mission and VJ patrols will observe the new crossings.

31. At Sula on 1 August, two vehicles filled with goods were allowed to cross into Bosnia and Herzegovina without checking. On 31 August at the same border crossing-point, a bus was allowed to cross into Bosnia and Herzegovina without being checked.

32. At Scepan Polje (Sector Charlie) on 31 July, a vehicle as turned back for carrying excess fuel. The car returned to the village about 300 metres from the

border crossing-point. The customs and police officers the looked the other way when the driver and passenger carried four jerrycans to the border down by the river. Afterwards the officers allowed the vehicle to pass to Bosnia to retrieve the illicit cargo on the other side of the checkpoint.

33. At Vracenovici on 2 August, one car containing excess commercial goods was allowed to cross into Bosnia and Herzegovina. On 26 August at Vilusi, a truck loaded with foodstuffs - claimed to be humanitarian aid - was allowed to cross into Bosnia and Herzegovina although it had not been checked and sealed by customs/Mission teams in advance and had no proper documentation.

34. On five separate occasions uniformed policemen and soldiers were allowed to cross the border in Sector Charlie carrying their sidearms: these incidents occurred on 1 and 19 August at Vilusi, on 2 August at Vracenovici, on 19 August at Vilusi and on 19 and 22 August at Scepan Polje.

35. On 21 August, a helicopter was seen crossing the border in the vicinity of Nudo. The investigation revealed that the helicopter was privately owned locally. Probably the same helicopter crossed the border from Bosnia and Herzegovina on 1 September.

VIII. CERTIFICATION

36. In the light of the foregoing developments, based on the Mission's on-site observation, on the advice of the Mission's coordinator, Mr. T.J. Nieminen, and in the absence of any contrary information from the air, either from the airborne reconnaissance system of the North Atlantic Treaty Organization (NATO), or national technical means, the Co-Chairmen conclude that the Government of the Federal Republic of Yugoslavia (Serbia and Montenegro) is continuing to meet its commitment to close the border between the Federal Republic of Yugoslavia (Serbia and Montenegro) and the areas of the Republic of Bosnia and Herzegovina under the control of the Bosnian Serb forces. The Co-Chairmen also conclude that there have been no commercial transshipment across the border between the Federal Republic of Yugoslavia (Serbia and Montenegro) and the Republic of Bosnia and Herzegovina.

150. LETTER DATED 11 OCTOBER 1995 FROM THE SECRETARY-GENERAL ADDRESSED TO THE PRESIDENT OF THE SECURITY COUNCIL*

I have the honour to transmit the attached report, which was addressed to me on 9 October 1995 by the Co-Chairman of the Steering Committee of the International Conference on the Former Yugoslavia, concerning the operations of the International Conference's Mission to the Federal Republic of Yugoslavia (Serbia and Montenegro). This report by the Co-Chairmen contains certification referred to in Security Council resolution 1003 (1995) of 5 July 1995.

I should be grateful if you would bring this information to the attention of the members of the Security Council.

Annex
Operations of Mission of the International Conference on the Former Yugoslavia to the Federal Republic of Yugoslavia (Serbia and Montenegro)

I. INTRODUCTION

1. The present report is submitted pursuant to paragraph 13 of Security Council resolution 988 (1995) of 21 April 1995 and paragraph 2 of Council resolution 1015 (1995) of 15 September 1995. In those resolutions, the Council requested that the Secretary-General submit every 30 days for its review a report from the Co-Chairmen of the Steering Committee of the International Conference on the Former Yugoslavia on the border closure measures taken by the authorities of the Federal Republic of Yugoslavia (Serbia and Montenegro).

2. It will be recalled that, on 4 August 1994, the following measures were ordered by the Government of the Federal Republic of Yugoslavia (Serbia and Montenegro) to come into effect the same day:

(a) "To break off political and economic relations with the 'Republika Srpska';"
(b) "To prohibit the stay of the members of the leadership of the 'Republika Srpska' (Parliament, Presidency and Government) in the territory of the Federal Republic of Yugoslavia;"
(c) "As of today the border of the Federal Republic of Yugoslavia is closed for all transport towards the 'Republika Srpska' except food, clothing and medicine."

---

* UN Doc. S/1995/685, 11 October 1995. Signed by Boutros Boutros-Ghali.

3. On 19 September, 3 October, 2 November and 5 December 1994, and 5 January, 3 February, 2 March, 31 March, 13 April, 18 May, 25 June, 3 August and 6 September 1995, the Secretary-General transmitted to the Security Council reports from the Co-Chairmen of the Steering Committee of the International Conference on the Former Yugoslavia on the state of implementation of the above-mentioned measures (S/1994/1074; S/1994/1124; S/1994/1246; S/1994/1372; S/1995/6; S/1995/104; S/1995/175; S/1995/255; S/1995/302; S/1995/406; S/1995/510; S/1995/645 and S/1995/768). The report dated 6 September 1995 contained the following certification from the Co-Chairmen:

"In the light of the foregoing developments, based on the Mission's on-site observation, on the advice of the Mission Coordinator, Mr. T.J. Nieminen, and in the absence of any contrary information from the air, either from the airborne reconnaissance system of the North Atlantic Treaty Organization (NATO) or national technical means, the Co-Chairmen conclude that the Government of the Federal Republic of Yugoslavia (Serbia and Montenegro) is continuing to meet its commitment to close the border between the Federal Republic of Yugoslavia (Serbia and Montenegro) and the areas of the Republic of Bosnia and Herzegovina under the control of the Bosnian Serb forces. The Co-Chairmen also conclude that, during the period covered by the present report, there have been no commercial transshipments across the border between the Federal República of Yugoslavia (Serbia and Montenegro) and the Republic of Bosnia and Herzegovina."

Developments since the last report are outlined below.

II. LEGISLATION/REGULATIONS ON THE BORDER CLOSURE

4. The legislation of the authorities of the Federal Republic of Yugoslavia (Serbia and Montenegro) closing the border with Bosnian Serbs continues to be in effect.

5. The authorities of the Federal Republic of Yugoslavia (Serbia and Montenegro) have provided the Mission with the following list of confiscations conducted along its border with Bosnia and Herzegovina for the month of August 1995:

Petrol	13.1 tons
Diesel	16.8 tons
Motor oil	256 litres
Cigarettes	322 kg
Construction materials	38.8 tons
Wood	132 cubic metres
Alcohol	2.9 tons
Food	322 kg

Textiles, clothing, footwear	1.1 tons
Animals	43
Coffee	140 kg
Electrical gadgets	57 kg
Other goods	10.1 tons

6. There were 157 new offence procedures initiated during the month of August and 98 were finalized. Fines and penalties amounted to 211,092 dinars. In overall volume terms, the confiscations were well in excess of the previous month and the number of new offence cases and value of penalties continue to be well above the average for the previous 12 reporting periods.

III. ORGANIZATION, FINANCING AND WORK OF THE MISSION

7. As of 6 October 1995, there were 206 international observers on duty in the Mission. The Mission personnel to date have come from the following countries: Belgium, Canada, Czech Republic, Denmark, Finland, France, Germany, Greece, Ireland, Italy, Netherlands, Norway, Portugal, Russian Federation, Spain, Sweden, United Kingdom of Great Britain and Northern Ireland and United States of America. At this time, Canada, Portugal and Spain are not represented in the Mission.

8. At the beginning of September, the number of international observers was at its peak of 215. This healthy figure enabled the Sectors to increase their mobile patrols to a meaningful level. During the last week of September, 104 mobile patrols were mounted, day and night. In Sector Alpha, frequent visits to the gravel extraction beds to the north of Trbusnica, backed by the attention of the Special Police, would seem to have curtailed smuggling in that area. To the south of Zvornik, the previous regular violations around Citluk and elsewhere on the River Drina are no longer evident. In the Tara mountain region of Sector Bajina Basta, the Mission has been able to increase patrolling to the Zaovine reservoir and the surrounding region of Mitrovac. However, there remains scope for further effort and monitoring in Sectors Bravo and Charlie, where the area to be covered is vast. Absolute coverage is very much dependent upon the provision of more suitable vehicles to support the recent increase in international personnel at the Mission.

9. During the month of October, it is envisaged that all border crossing-points will be open for traffic from 0500 to 1900 hours. Sremska Raca (Sector Belgrade) and Vilusi (Sector Charlie) will be open for truck and passenger traffic 24 hours a day. Badovinci and Trbusnica border crossing-points (Sector Alpha) will

be open 24 hours a day if necessary for the crossing of refugees.

10. During the reporting period, the operational situation within the Missions's area of responsibility has been quiet, though some of the incidents involving Mission personnel during September may have occurred because of developments in Bosnia and Herzegovina.

IV. FREEDOM OF MOVEMENT AND SECURITY OF PERSONNEL

11. The Mission continues to enjoy freedom of movement within the Federal Republic of Yugoslavia (Serbia and Montenegro). However, on 7 September, at 1758 hours, a mobile patrol team in Sector Bajina Basta was stopped by the Yugoslav Army (VJ) and told they were not allowed to conduct patrols without a military escort. The Mission patrol leader showed the Mission of the International Conference on the Former Yugoslavia the diplomatic status letter to the military personnel. The military personnel in question refused to honour the letter. The patrol team was then escorted to a nearby barracks and questioned about their patrol by the military officer in charge, who identified himself as M. Radivojivic. At that time the observers were not allowed to use the radio sets to contact their Sector Headquarters, and the Missions's vehicle was searched. The problem was resolved at 1935 hours. On 11 September, the Deputy Head of Mission raised the above-mentioned restriction of movement with the Director-General of the Federal Republic of Yugoslavia Customs Administration, who stated that he would take action to prevent incidents of that nature recurring.

12. On 4 September, the Mission mobile patrol going from Sector Bajina Basta to Mitrovac/Zaovine was stopped by a policeman who acted in an aggressive and unprofessional manner. On the same day, another of the Sector's mobile patrol teams stopped at a public parking place to observe the Perucac dam. The Federal Republic of Yugoslavia police on the spot insisted that observers were not allowed to approach the dam, and ordered the team to leave. Both incidents were reported to the Police Department in Bajina Basta. The Chief of Police apologized for the behaviour of his subordinates and promised to take action. On 6 September, the Head of Sector was informed that the above-mentioned police teams had subsequently been replaced, and received assurances that problems of that nature would not recur.

13. On 4 September, at approximately 2000 hours, the observer team assigned to the Trbusnica border crossing-point (a bridge across the Drina River) was told by the Chief of the police team on duty that the bridge would be the target of a NATO airstrike. The Mission team leader attached little credence to the information and took no action. At 0200 hours, the Federal Republic of Yugoslavia

Customs team at the border crossing-point departed. At the same time, observers witnessed the Federal Republic of Yugoslavia police dispersing all civilians in the immediate vicinity of the bridge. The mission team leader then concluded that the fears of the local Federal Republic of Yugoslavia authorities might be soundly based. The team withdrew temporarily to the Sector Headquarters and returned to the border crossing-point at 0530 hours when the situation returned to normal.

14. On 10 September, the Sector Alpha Headquarters was informed by a security guard at the Podrinje Hotel, Banja Kovilijaca, that a local man carrying a pistol had entered the hotel restaurant shouting: "I'm going to kill everybody. They are bombing Majevica again. This is the end." The same individual damaged three of the Mission's vehicles parked in the nearby parking lot. Upon receiving this information, the Sector's Headquarters advised all Sector personnel not on duty to remain in their accommodation. The local police was notified at once but reacted reluctantly. They refused to provide additional security to the Sector's Headquarters and to personnel accommodated in the Podrinje Hotel. On 11 September, the Director-General of the Federal Customs Administration was informed of the incident. He said that the individual was well known as a member of the Serbian Radical Party and that the perpetrator would be apprehended and prosecuted. On 12 September the Chief of Police in Banja Kovilijaca stated that the individual had been arrested and the weapon confiscated.

15. On 18 September, a Sector Alpha mobile patrol stopped on the main road between Ljubovija and Mali Zvornik to monitor possible smuggling activity in the vicinity of Citluk. The observers were approached by two irate local men, who said that the patrol should not stop without a VJ escort. An attempt was made by one of the men to snatch the binoculars from the hands of the team leader. The two men and a woman tried to block the road but the patrol succeeded in departing the scene amid a flurry of blows at the vehicle, without injury being caused.

V. Cooperation of the Authorities of the Federal Republic of Yugoslavia (Serbia and Montenegro) with the Mission

16. Cooperation with the authorities of the Federal Republic of Yugoslavia (Serbia and Montenegro) continues to be good.

VI. Information Received from National and Other Sources

17. The operating principle of the Mission is to base its reporting and evaluations on its own observations and on information that it has verified. The Coordinator of the Mission maintained a standing request to Governments possessing the technical capacity to provide it with information relevant to its mandate. The Mission has not received any such information since the last report.

VII. Problems Encountered and Representations Made
to the Authorities

18. Unarmed uniformed personnel continue to cross the border between the Federal Republic of Yugoslavia (Serbia and Montenegro) and Bosnia and Herzegovina, although the number of such incidents has been declining constantly since the summer. During the reporting period, 188 uniformed personnel crossed the border at Sremska Raca (Sector Belgrade), four at Badovinci (Sector Alpha) and two at Scepan Polje (Sector Charlie). No one was observed crossing the border carrying a sidearm. At Vracenovici (Sector Charlie), on 24 September, one Bosnian Army soldier in uniform was removed from a bus that was crossing into the Federal Republic of Yugoslavia (Serbia and Montenegro); his weapon was confiscated and only then was he allowed to cross into the Federal Republic of Yugoslavia (Serbia and Montenegro).
19. Smuggling of fuel across the Drina River in Sector Alpha, which has been a problem, now seems to be contained by the Federal authorities. However, since the last report, the following incidents have been observed by the Mission. On 14 September, the Sector's patrol reported that they had observed a 7 metre-long boat crossing the Drina River form the Federal Republic of Yugoslavia (Serbia and Montenegro) to Bosnia and Herzegovina, 4 kilometres north of Trbusnica. The boat contained a number of fuel tanks and drums which were camouflaged by tree branches. Authorities of the Federal Republic of Yugoslavia (Serbia and Montenegro) were informed about the violation. On 15 September, the Sector's patrol monitored a 5 metre-long boat crossing the Drina River from the Federal Republic of Yugoslavia (Serbia and Montenegro) to the Bosnia and Herzegovina side in the area of Citluk. The boat was stacked with approximately 30 sacks, probably containing either cement or fertilizer. The incident was reported to the authorities of the Federal Republic of Yugoslavia (Serbia and Montenegro). On 22 September, Sector Alpha mobile patrol observed a 6-metre wooden boat crossing the Drina River 7 kilometres south of Mali Zvornik. The boat moored on the Bosnian side to off-load 30 crates of beer. On 5 October, a Mission patrol

saw two males crossing to Bosnia and Herzegovina shores at Divic in a small wooden boat which was loaded with at least 20 beer crates. The VJ Liaison Officer approached the nearest Army patrol, who said that they had seen the boat being loaded but were unable to reach it before it left the bank.

20. On 30 September, a car was observed crossing the border from Bosnia and Herzegovina into the Federal Republic of Yugoslavia (Serbia and Montenegro) using a river ford 4 kilometres north of Uvac (Sector Bravo). Three VJ soldiers controlling the crossing-point let the car pass unchecked.

21. On 21 September, a helicopter was observed crossing the border from the Federal Republic of Yugoslavia (Serbia and Montenegro) into Bosnia and Herzegovina at Scepan Polje (Sector Charlie). Probably it was the same helicopter that returned to the Federal Republic of Yugoslavia (Serbia and Montenegro) three and a half hours later crossing at Scepan Polje. On 24 September, in the same location, a low-flying helicopter was seen to cross into Bosnia and Herzegovina. The Mission Headquarters has requested an explanation of the flights from the authorities of the Federal Republic of Yugoslavia (Serbia and Montenegro), who have confirmed them as MEDEVAC flights. The Mission has no means of confirming the veracity of this information.

VIII. CERTIFICATION

22. In the light of the foregoing developments, based on the Mission's on-site observation, on the advice of the Coordinator of the Mission, Mr. T.J. Nieminen, and in the absence of any contrary information from the air, either from the airborne reconnaissance system of NATO or national technical means, the Co-Chairmen conclude that the Government of the Federal Republic of Yugoslavia (Serbia and Montenegro) is continuing to meet its commitment to close the border between the Federal Republic of Yugoslavia (Serbia and Montenegro) and the areas of the Republic of Bosnia and Herzegovina under the control of the Bosnian Serb forces. The Co-Chairmen also conclude that there have been no commercial transshipments across the border between the Federal Republic of Yugoslavia (Serbia and Montenegro) and the Republic of Bosnia and Herzegovina.

151. LETTER DATED 10 NOVEMBER 1995 FROM THE SECRETARY-GENERAL ADDRESSED TO THE PRESIDENT OF THE SECURITY COUNCIL*

I have the honour to transmit the attached report, which was addressed to me on 8 November 1995 by the Co-Chairmen of the Steering Committee of the International Conference on the Former Yugoslavia, concerning the operations of the International Conference's Mission to the Federal Republic of Yugoslavia (Serbia and Montenegro). This report by the Co-Chairman contains the certification referred to in Security Council resolution 988 (1995) of 21 April 1995.

I should be grateful if you would bring this information to the attention of the members of the Security Council.

Annex
Operations of the Mission of the International Conference on the Former Yugoslavia to the Federal Republic of Yugoslavia (Serbia and Montenegro)

I. INTRODUCTION

1. The present report is submitted pursuant to paragraph 13 of Security Council resolution 988 (1995) of 21 April 1995 and paragraph 2 of Council resolution 1015 (1995) of 15 September 1995. In those resolutions, the Council requested that the Secretary-General submit every 30 days for its review a report from the Co-Chairmen of the Steering Committee of the International Conference on the Former Yugoslavia on the border closer measures taken by the authorities of the Federal Republic of Yugoslavia (Serbia and Montenegro).
2. It will be recalled that, on 4 August 1994, the following measures were ordered by the Government of the Federal Republic of Yugoslavia (Serbia and Montenegro) to come into effect the same day:

   (a) "To break off political and economic relations with the 'Republika Srpska'";
   (b) "To prohibit the stay of the members of the leadership of the 'Republika Srpska' (Parliament, Presidency and Government) in the territory of the Federal Republic of Yugoslavia";
   (c) "As of today the border of the Federal Republic of Yugoslavia is closed for all transport towards the 'Republika Srpska' except food, clothing and medicine".

---

* UN Doc. S/1995/944, 10 November 1995. Signed by Boutros Boutros-Ghali.

3. On 19 September, 3 October, 2 November and 5 December 1994 and 5 January, 3 February, 2 March, 31 March, 13 April, 18 May, 25 June, 3 August, 6 September and 11 October 1995, the Secretary-General transmitted to the Security Council reports from the Co-Chairmen of the Steering Committee of the International Conference on the Former Yugoslavia on the state of implementation of the above-mentioned measures (S/1994/1074; S/1994/1124; S/1994/1246; S/1994/1372; S/1995/6; S/1995/104; S/1995/175; S/1995/255; S/1995/302; S/1995/406; S/1995/510; S/1995/645; S/1995/768 and S/1995/865). The report dated 11 October 1995 contained the following certification from the Co-Chairmen:

> "In the light of the foregoing developments, based on the Mission's on-site observation, on the advice of the Mission Coordinator, Mr. T.J. Nieminen, and in the absence of any contrary information from the air, either from the airborne reconnaissance system of the North Atlantic Treaty Organization (NATO) or national technical means, the Co-Chairmen conclude that the Government of the Federal Republic of Yugoslavia (Serbia and Montenegro) is continuing to meet its commitment to close the border between the Federal Republic of Yugoslavia (Serbia and Montenegro) and the areas of the Republic of Bosnia and Herzegovina under the control of the Bosnian Serb forces. The Co-Chairmen also conclude that, during the period covered by the present report, there have been no commercial transshipments across the border between the Federal Republic of Yugoslavia (Serbia and Montenegro) and the Republic of Bosnia and Herzegovina."

Developments since the last report are outlined below.

II. LEGISLATION/REGULATIONS ON THE BORDER CLOSURE

4. The decision of the Federal Republic of Yugoslavia (Serbia and Montenegro) to break off all economic and political relations with the "Republika Srpska" that was reached at the one hundred eighty-seventh session on 4 August 1994 and amended during the two hundred seventy-fifth session on 13 July 1995, was further amended at the three hundred third session on 17 October 1995. The latest amendment to the said decision stipulated that, in addition to food, clothing and medicine; articles for hygiene and disinfectants; books, textbooks and other school materials; funeral equipment; and articles for religious services, the following goods may be sent to the "Republika Srpska" as humanitarian aid:

Building materials
Plastic sheeting
Coal and wood burning stoves
Fifty tons of fuel oil (one off).

5. The authorities of the Federal Republic of Yugoslavia (Serbia and Montenegro) have provided the Mission with the following list of confiscations conducted along its border with Bosnia and Herzegovina for the month of September 1995:

Petrol	9.5 tons
Diesel	9.7 tons
Motor oil	1.1 tons
Cigarettes	380 kg
Construction materials	8.1 tons
Wood	96 cubic metres
Alcohol	1.6 tons
Food	2.8 tons
Textiles, clothing, footwear	0.9 tons
Motor vehicles	8
Animals	56
Electrical gadgets	42 kg
Other goods	8.7 tons

6. There were 147 new offence procedures initiated during the month of September and 92 were finalized. Fines and penalties amounted to 185,600 dinars. In volume terms, the confiscations were down from the previous month but the number of new offence cases and value of penalties continue to be well above the average for the previous 13 reporting periods. Confiscations in the Sector Alpha area along the Drina River continue to account for 80 per cent of the total confiscations along the border.

III. ORGANIZATION, FINANCING AND WORK OF THE MISSION

7. As of 6 November 1995, there were 217 international observers on duty in the Mission. The Mission personnel to date have come from the following countries: Belgium, Canada, Czech Republic, Denmark, Finland, France, Germany, Greece, Ireland, Italy, Netherlands, Norway, Portugal, Russian Federation, Spain, Sweden, United Kingdom of Great Britain and Northern Ireland and United States of America. At this time, Canada, Greece, Portugal and Spain are not represented in the Mission.

8. During the reporting period, approximately 4,500 refugees from Bosnia and Herzegovina crossed the border into the Federal Republic of Yugoslavia (Serbia and Montenegro) mainly through the border crossing point at Sremska Raca. The operational situation within the Mission's area of responsibility has

remained calm.

9. During the period 12 to 18 October, the Mission conducted a traffic survey at all 17 border crossing points. A similar exercise was conducted last March to determine the actual numbers of vehicles and persons crossing the border daily in both directions. This most recent survey indicates an overall 30 per cent reduction of traffic over the past seven months. Actual average daily figures are as follows:

Persons	20,444 (-29 per cent)
Buses	252 (-28 per cent)
Lorries/Trucks	143 (-28.5 per cent)
Cars	5,275 (-28 per cent)
Tractors	443 (-41 per cent)

The three busiest crossing points, accounting for more than half the traffic volume, were again Sremska Raca (Sector Belgrade), Badovinci (Sector Alpha) and Trbusnica (Sector Alpha). The downward trend was reflected at all border crossing points apart from Ljubovija (Sector Alpha), where there was a noticeable increase of all vehicular traffic. A possible explanation for this increase is that after the July fall of the Srebrenica enclave, located some 10 kilometres to the south-west of Ljubovija, Bosnian Serbs who relocated to the Srebrenica area started to use the Ljubovija border crossing point. Though not related to this traffic survey, the frequency of freight trains passing briefly through the areas of Bosnia and Herzegovina under the control of Bosnian Serb forces diminished by 33 per cent.

IV. FREEDOM OF MOVEMENT AND SECURITY OF PERSONNEL

10. With a few exceptions, the Mission continues to enjoy freedom of movement within the Federal Republic of Yugoslavia (Serbia and Montenegro). On 19 and 27 October, the movements of two Mission mobile patrols were restricted in the vicinity of Uvac (Sector Bravo) when they were denied entry through a Yugoslav Army (VJ) checkpoint. On 20 October, the Mission Coordinator and his Chief of Staff were obliged to wait 20 minutes at the same checkpoint before getting permission to pass through it. On 28 October, the Chief of Staff of the Mission called on the Deputy Head of the Yugoslav Army (VJ) Department for Relations with Foreign Attachés and International Organizations and drew his attention to the above-mentioned incidents.

11. On 20 October, an intoxicated local police officer threatened a Mission observer with a pistol at the Krstac border crossing point in Sector Charlie. A police patrol was immediately dispatched from police headquarters in Niksic to the border crossing point, where the intoxicated police officer was arrested. The Chief of the Niksic police station personally expressed his apology to the Mission Head of Sector and stated that it was an exceptional case which should not erode the existing friendly relationship between Mission personnel and the local police in the area.

12. On 21 October, one Mission mobile patrol from Sector Charlie was detained for three hours by members of VJ military at the checkpoint in Kovaci before the observers were released. The local authorities apologized, saying it was a "misunderstanding".

V. COOPERATION OF THE AUTHORITIES OF THE FEDERAL REPUBLIC OF YUGOSLAVIA (SERBIA AND MONTENEGRO) WITH THE MISSION

13. Notwithstanding the above-mentioned incidents, cooperation with the authorities of the Federal Republic of Yugoslavia (Serbia and Montenegro) continues to be generally good. However, despite repeated requests, the Mission has experienced serious delays in receiving the Government's approval for licences to extend the Mission's radio communication network.

VI. INFORMATION RECEIVED FROM NATIONAL AND OTHER SOURCES

14. The operating principle of the Mission is to base its reporting and evaluations on its own observations and on information that it has verified. The Mission Coordinator maintained a standing request to Governments possessing the technical capacity to provide the Mission with information relevant to its mandate.

15. At the end of September and in early October, the Mission Coordinator, on several occasions, received information from unidentified sources of possible attempts to violate the border closure. Immediately, the Mission took various steps to detect and prevent transgressions of United Nations resolutions pertaining to the border closure. These putative operations and the preparation of the Mission's monthly report were occurring simultaneously and therefore were not mentioned in the previous report (S/1995/865). Furthermore, because of the precision of the information received, no details can be provided in the present report for fear of compromising the sources. It is noteworthy that the precision and timeliness of some information have enabled the Mission teams to increase

their vigilance and apparently avert possible violations in eight different instances.

16. At the end of October, the Mission received information of a possible attempt to smuggle goods from the Federal Republic of Yugoslavia (Serbia and Montenegro) into Bosnia and Herzegovina in two tractor-trailers. These vehicles did not appear at the border.

VII. PROBLEMS ENCOUNTERED AND REPRESENTATIONS MADE TO THE AUTHORITIES

17. Unarmed uniformed personnel continue to cross the border between the Federal Republic of Yugoslavia (Serbia and Montenegro) and Bosnia and Herzegovina. During the reporting period, 348 unarmed uniformed personnel crossed the border at Sremska Raca (Sector Belgrade), four at Badovinci (Sector Alpha) and 10 at Trbusnica (Sector Alpha). On 30 October, a Bosnian Serb policeman in uniform carrying a sidearm was allowed to cross the border into the Federal Republic of Yugoslavia (Serbia and Montenegro) at Brbanj (Sector Charlie). He visited the local coffee-shop and returned into Bosnia and Herzegovina a few minutes later.

18. In response to a request by the Director-General of the Yugoslav Federal Customs Administration, Mihalj Kertes, the Mission Coordinator, on 13 October, approved as humanitarian aid the crossing of four tankers transporting 50 tons of heating oil, 30 tons of diesel and 30 tons of petrol. Mr. Kertes had stated that the consignment was destined for the bakery and hospital at Banja Luka to cope with the deteriorating refugee situation caused by the influx of refugees in the area. On 19 October, Federal Customs Officers at Sremska Raca (Sector Belgrade) allowed a similar consignment of four tankers to cross the border into Bosnia and Herzegovina. This time, Mission headquarters was not consulted and the act was considered a clear violation of the border closure and called for an explanation from the responsible authorities.

19. On 20 and 21 October, the Mission Coordinator raised the matter with Director-General Kertes and his Deputy, Mr. Bran Knezic. They claimed that letting the consignment cross on 19 October was based on a "misunderstanding" between the Mission and the Customs authorities. On 24 October, the Mission Coordinator called on Director-General Kertes. In the course of the discussions, Mr. Kertes explained that an agreement was reached within the Government of the Republic of Serbia to send, on a monthly basis, large quantities of oil products as humanitarian aid to the "Republika Srpska". In the context of the ongoing peace negotiations, the matter required the immediate attention of the

Co-Chairmen. On 27 October, Mr. Stoltenberg brought the matter to the attention of President Milosevic.

20. On 2 November, the Mission Coordinator and his Senior Customs Adviser called on the Deputy Prime Minister of the Federal Republic of Yugoslavia (Serbia and Montenegro), Mr. Nikola Sainovic, at the latter's request and upon instructions of President Milosevic. Mr. Sainovic explained that there was no intention to breach United Nations regulations nor to circumvent the Mission's mandate. He stressed that the Government of the Federal Republic of Yugoslavia (Serbia and Montenegro) would maintain full and strict adherence to the border closure agreement. Oil products would not be allowed to cross the border as humanitarian aid to the "Republika Srpska".

21. During October, an increased number of "humanitarian aid" consignments was denied. For example, in the first two weeks of October there was an average of six refusals per day. The most common cases were Bulgarian sugar, Romanian salt, Italian washing powder and bulk corn, which were found to be trade consignments and not humanitarian aid. Therefore, the Mission teams refused to place seals on the trucks. A list of suspected traders has been established to prevent commercial companies engaged in trading with the "Republika Srpska" from supplying consignments in the future.

22. The increased number of mobile patrols, especially along the River Drina, has enabled the observers to detect the following incidents:

    (a) On 10 October, a patrol observed smugglers loading fuel cans on a boat near Mali Zvornik. A VJ military patrol moved into the area and the smugglers managed to escape with eight 100-litre barrels in a 4-metre wooden boat, but left behind three full 100-litre barrels and one 50-litre can. On 12 October, in the area 5 kilometres south-east of Citluk, the same Mission patrol saw smugglers transporting approximately 10 crates of beer across the Drina River into Bosnia and Herzegovina;

    (b) On 16 October, another patrol sighted a large boat crossing the Drina River carrying six men and more than 50 heavily loaded cardboard boxes. A large truck awaited the boat on the Bosnian side. On 18 October, a Sector Alpha mobile patrol observed five smugglers unloading boxes from a large boat onto a large truck on the Bosnian side of the Drina River;

    (c) On 23 October, observers sighted a large boat fitted with an outboard motor on the Bosnian side of the Drina River. When the patrol approached to observe the activity, the perpetrators disappeared into the bushes leaving their boat and a large number of beer crates and cardboard boxes.

23. On 3 November, an observer saw a man with an ox-drawn wagon cross into Bosnia and Herzegovina 2 kilometres south of Kotroman (Sector Bajina Basta). The wagon carried four 200-litre drums, contents unknown.

24. On 13 October, a helicopter was observed crossing the border from the Federal Republic of Yugoslavia (Serbia and Montenegro) into Bosnia and Herzegovina in the Nudo area (Sector Charlie). The authorities of the Federal Republic of Yugoslavia (Serbia and Montenegro) described it as a CASEVAC flight, stating that the United Nations was not informed because it was an emergency. The Mission has no means of verifying this information provided by the Federal authorities. During his meeting with the Director General of Federal Customs on 24 October, the Mission Coordinator underlined the seriousness the United Nations Security Council attaches to any unauthorized helicopter flights crossing the border. On 28 October, one Mi-8 helicopter, originating from the Bosnian side and heading south-east, crossed the border south of the border crossing point at Scepan Polje (Sector Charlie). The Federal authorities have yet to explain the nature of this flight.

VIII. CERTIFICATION

25. In the light of the foregoing developments, based on the Mission's on-site observation, on the advice of the Mission Coordinator, Mr. T.J. Nieminen, and in the absence of any contrary information from the air, either from the airborne reconnaissance system of NATO or national technical means, the Co-Chairmen conclude that the Government of the Federal Republic of Yugoslavia (Serbia and Montenegro) is continuing to meet its commitment to close the border between the Federal Republic of Yugoslavia (Serbia and Montenegro) and the areas of the Republic of Bosnia and Herzegovina under the control of the Bosnian Serb forces. The Co-Chairmen also conclude that, during the period covered by the present report, there have been no commercial transshipments across the border between the Federal Republic of Yugoslavia (Serbia and Montenegro) and the Republic of Bosnia and Herzegovina.

152. Letter Dated 8 December 1995 from the Secretary-General Addressed to the President of the Security Council[*]

I have the honour to transmit the attached report, which was addressed to me on 7 December 1995 by the Co-Chairmen of the Steering Committee of the International Conference on the Former Yugoslavia, concerning the operations of the International Conference's Mission to the Federal Republic of Yugoslavia (Serbia and Montenegro). This report by the Co-Chairmen contains the certification referred to in Security Council resolutions 988 (1995) and 1015 (1995).

I should be grateful if you would bring this information to the attention of the members of the Security Council.

Annex
Operations of the Mission of the International Conference on the Former Yugoslavia to the Federal Republic of Yugoslavia (Serbia and Montenegro)

I. INTRODUCTION

1. The present report is submitted pursuant to paragraph 13 of Security Council resolution 988 (1995) of 21 April 1995 and paragraph 2 of Security Council resolution 1015 (1995) of 15 September 1995. In those resolutions, the Council requested that the Secretary-General submit every 30 days for its review a report from the Co-Chairmen of the Steering Committee of the International Conference on the Former Yugoslavia on the border closure measures taken by the authorities of the Federal Republic of Yugoslavia (Serbia and Montenegro).
2. It will be recalled that, on 4 August 1994, the following measures were ordered by the Government of the Federal Republic of Yugoslavia (Serbia and Montenegro) to come into effect the same day:

(a) "To break off political and economic relations with the 'Republika Srpska';"
(b) "To prohibit the stay of the members of the leadership of the 'Republika Srpska' (parliament, presidency and Government) in the territory of the Federal Republic of Yugoslavia;"
(c) "As of today the border of the Federal Republic of Yugoslavia is closed for all transport towards the 'Republika Srpska' except food, clothing and medicine."

---

[*] UN Doc. S/1995/1027, 11 December 1995. Signed by Boutros Boutros-Ghali.

3. On 22 November 1995, the Security Council adopted resolution 1022 (1995) and, in paragraph 2 thereof, decided that the suspension of sanctions referred to in paragraph 1 of that resolution "shall not apply to the measures imposed on the Bosnian Serb party until the day after the Commander of the international force to be deployed in accordance with the peace agreement, on the basis of a report transmitted through the appropriate political authorities, informs the Council via the Secretary-General that all Bosnian Serb forces have withdrawn behind the zones of separation established in the peace agreement".

4. On 19 September, 3 October, 2 November and 1 December 1994 and 4 January, 2 February, 2 and 31 March, 13 April, 18 May, 25 June, 3 August, 6 September, 11 October and 10 November 1995, the Secretary-General transmitted to the Security Council reports from the Co-Chairmen of the Steering Committee of the International Conference on the Former Yugoslavia on the state of implementation of the above-mentioned measures (S/1994/1074; S/1994/1124; S/1994/1246; S/1994/1372; S/1995/6; S/1995/104; S/1995/175; S/1995/255; S/1995/302; S/1995/406; S/1995/510; S/1995/645; S/1995/768; S/1995/865; and S/1995/944). The report dated 10 November 1995 contained the following certification by the Co-Chairmen:

> "In the light of the foregoing developments, based on the Mission's on-site observation, on the advice of the Mission Coordinator, Mr. T.J. Nieminen, and in the absence of any contrary information from the air, either from the airborne reconnaissance system of NATO or national technical means, the Co-Chairmen conclude that the Government of the Federal Republic of Yugoslavia (Serbia and Montenegro) is continuing to meet its commitment to close the border between the Federal Republic of Yugoslavia (Serbia and Montenegro) and the areas of the Republic of Bosnia and Herzegovina under the control of Bosnian Serb forces. The Co-Chairmen also conclude that, during the period covered by the present report, there have been no commercial transshipments across the border between the Federal Republic of Yugoslavia (Serbia and Montenegro) and the Republic of Bosnia and Herzegovina."

Developments since the last report are outlined below.

II. Legislation/Regulations on the Border Closure

5. The legislation of the authorities of the Federal Republic of Yugoslavia (Serbia and Montenegro) closing the border with the Bosnian Serbs continues to be in effect.

6. The authorities of the Federal Republic of Yugoslavia (Serbia and Montenegro) have provided the Mission with the following list of confiscations conducted along its border with Bosnia and Herzegovina for the month of October 1995:

Petrol	4.8 tons
Diesel	6 tons
Motor oil	366 litres
Cigarettes	2.7 tons
Construction materials	8.1 tons
Wood	105 cubic metres
Alcohol	975 litres
Food	890 kilograms
Coffee	431 kilograms
Textiles, clothing, footwear	344 kilograms
Motor vehicles	34
Animals	34
Technical equipment	530 kilograms
Other goods	237 kilograms

7. There were 97 new offence procedures initiated during the month of October, and 52 were finalized. Fines and penalties amounted to 97,718 dinars. The volume of confiscations was below average in virtually all categories and the number of new offence cases and sum of penalties were about the average for the previous 14 months. The Mission's Senior Customs Adviser discussed the downturn in confiscations with the Deputy Director of the Federal Customs. The latter explained that the widened definition of humanitarian aid allowed into the "Republika Srpska" probably reduced the incidence of smuggling attempts. Also the intense level of fighting in Bosnia and Herzegovina will have lessened the opportunity for trading.

III. Organization, Financing and Work of the Mission

8. As of 6 December 1995, there were 217 international observers on duty in the Mission. The Mission personnel to date have come from Belgium, Canada, the Czech Republic, Denmark, Finland, France, Germany, Greece, Ireland, Italy, the Netherlands, Norway, Portugal, the Russian Federation, Spain, Sweden, the United Kingdom of Great Britain and Northern Ireland and the United States of America. At the present time, Canada, Portugal and Spain are not represented in the Mission.

9. In the reporting period, the number of refugees from Bosnia and Herzegovina crossing the border into the Federal Republic of Yugoslavia (Serbia and Montenegro) decreased from approximately 157 during the first week of the month to 20 in the last week. The total number of refugees who crossed into the Federal

Republic of Yugoslavia (Serbia and Montenegro) during the last month was 325. The operational situation within the Mission's area of responsibility remained calm during the reporting period.

IV. FREEDOM OF MOVEMENT AND SECURITY OF THE PERSONNEL

10. The Mission continues to enjoy freedom of movement within the Federal Republic of Yugoslavia (Serbia and Montenegro). However, on 12 November, in Sector Charlie, the Yugoslav Army denied entry to a Mission mobile patrol vehicle through the military checkpoint en route to Kovaci. The observers were permitted to walk to the vicinity of the village. Previously, Mission vehicles were allowed to go through the checkpoint but on this occasion they were refused on the grounds of unspecified "military rules". The Yugoslav Army liaison officer in Niksic was immediately informed of the incident.

11. On 20 November in Sector Alpha, Yugoslav Army personnel prevented Mission observers from conducting foot patrols along the Drina river without the Yugoslav Army liaison officer. The Yugoslav Army soldiers insisted that they had received new instructions that the liaison officer should be present when the Mission patrolled this route.

12. On 22 November in Sector Belgrade, the Yugoslav Army denied a Sector Belgrade mobile patrol access for "security reasons" to the Morovic alternative road to controlled crossing-point Jamena after the usual route was deemed impassable. On 23 November, the Mission Coordinator and his Senior Customs Adviser met with the Deputy Chief of the General Staff, Lieutenant General Blagoje Kovacevic, and discussed assignments to the Mission of liaison officers by the Yugoslav Army, access to controlled crossing-point Jamena by road through the village of Morovic (access was limited because of the tense situation in Eastern Slavonia) and the above-mentioned cases where the movement of the Mission patrols has been impeded by the Yugoslav Army. General Kovacevic reaffirmed the Yugoslav Army's commitment to maintain the high level of cooperation that has existed with the Mission. He gave assurances that the problems encountered by the Mission would be resolved immediately.

13. On 24 November, at border crossing point Sremska Raca, a Mission team's local female interpreter was harassed in the ladies room by an intoxicated individual wearing a military uniform. The following day the Deputy to the Director-General of the Federal Customs Administration was informed of the incident. He replied that he would take action to avert incidents of that nature.

14. On 3 December, a mobile patrol in Sector Charlie, north of Crkvice, was blocked by a truck on the road. The truck driver threatened the Mission person-

nel. The team was under duress and the Yugoslav Army liaison officer who was escorting the team requested a military patrol from the nearest Yugoslav Army checkpoint on the border to escort the Mission patrol out of the area.

V. COOPERATION OF THE AUTHORITIES OF THE FEDERAL REPUBLIC OF YUGOSLAVIA (SERBIA AND MONTENEGRO) WITH THE MISSION

15. Cooperation with the authorities of the Federal Republic of Yugoslavia (Serbia and Montenegro) continues to be good. In response to specific difficulties, the Mission Coordinator and his staff have registered their concern to the appropriate authorities of the Federal Republic of Yugoslavia (Serbia and Montenegro).

16. In a letter of 28 November to Colonel D. Vuksic, Head of the Department for Relations with Foreign Military Attachés, the Mission Chief of Staff stressed the importance of maintaining a Yugoslav Army liaison officer in Sector Bajina Basta to replace the departing liaison officer. General Kovacevic, Deputy Chief of the General Staff, had reassured the Mission Coordinator, in an earlier meeting with him on 23 November, of his commitment to maintain full cooperation. Following up on this meeting and maintaining constant contact with the local officials in Montenegro, the Mission's Special Envoy to that republic, in a meeting on 27 November, emphasized to Colonel Cecovic, the Commander of Podgorica Army Corps, the necessity of improving cooperation throughout Sector Charlie. The Special Envoy noted the urgency of frequent consultations between the Yugoslav Army and the Mission. Replying to the Sector's specific concerns, Colonel Cecovic promised that the liaison officer would be accessible to the Mission by pager at all times. He promised to step up Yugoslav Army surveillance of the controlled border area between Crkvice and Vracenovici, which appears open to smuggling, and a friendlier disposition of the Yugoslav Army to the Mission. The Special Envoy and Colonel Cecovic agreed to meet every 14 days and within a couple of hours in the event of an emergency. On the night of 4 December, 17 truck drivers were arrested trying to transport goods in this area from Bosnia into the Federal Republic of Yugoslavia (Serbia and Montenegro). Subsequently, the Yugoslav Army liaison officer told the Sector that the border in Crkvice-Vracenovici would be closed and the International Conference on the Former Yugoslavia would have timely access to Yugoslav Army information in the area.

17. On 23 November, the Mission Coordinator discussed Security Council resolution 1022 (1995) with Deputy Defence Minister Bjelica Bogoljub, and both concluded from the meeting that the measures imposed by the Federal Republic

of Yugoslavia (Serbia and Montenegro) Government on the Bosnian Serbs would continue. Similarly, on 23 and 24 November, during talks between the Mission Coordinator and his Customs Adviser, the Federal Customs authorities agreed that the suspension of sanctions would not apply to the measures imposed on the Bosnian Serbs. Instructions to this effect have been issued by the authorities of the Federal Republic of Yugoslavia (Serbia and Montenegro) to their officials on the border with the "Republika Srpska".

VI. INFORMATION RECEIVED FROM NATIONAL AND OTHER SOURCES

18. The operating principle of the Mission is to base its reporting and evaluations on its own observations and on information that it has verified. The Mission Coordinator maintained a standing request to Governments possessing the technical capacity to provide it with information relevant to its mandate. He has not received any such information since the last report.

VII. PROBLEMS ENCOUNTERED AND REPRESENTATIONS MADE TO THE AUTHORITIES

19. Unarmed uniformed personnel continue to cross the border between the Federal Republic of Yugoslavia (Serbia and Montenegro) and Bosnia and Herzegovina. During the reporting period, 245 uniformed personnel crossed the border at Sremska Raca (Sector Belgrade), 7 at Badovinci (Sector Alpha), 36 at Trbusnica (Sector Alpha), 9 at Mali Zvornik (Sector Alpha), 6 at Ljubovija (Sector Alpha) and 1 at Scepan Polje (Sector Charlie).
20. On 7 November, a Sector Charlie mobile patrol discovered that a barrier had been dismantled at a bypass leading to the border near Vilusi.
21. Similarly, on 11 November, a Sector Bajina Basta mobile patrol noticed that a barrier 8 kilometres south-east of Kotroman had been removed on a bypass leading to the border. The local authorities were informed of both incidents and they promised to restore the barriers immediately.
22. On 13 November, a Sector Alpha mobile patrol observed a large boat on the Drina River, 7 kilometres south-east of Sremska Raca near the confluence of the Drina and the Sava. The craft, which was 9 metres in length and powered by an outboard engine, was heavily loaded with boxed items. The approximate size of a box was 30 x 40 x 15 centimetres. When the boat reached the Bosnia and Herzegovina bank it was unloaded by three persons. The boxes, which numbered around 800, appeared heavy. The patrol requested the assistance of the Yugoslav Army liaison officer and police to monitor the boat's route to the point

where it re-entered the Federal Republic of Yugoslavia (Serbia and Montenegro). However, after the smugglers completed unloading, the boat was pulled well up the Bosnia and Herzegovina bank. The local authorities witnessed this activity. The Mission Senior Customs Adviser raised the incident with the Deputy Director-General of the Federal Customs Administration during a call on him on 17 November. The Deputy Director-General confirmed that the Sava river was patrolled by military/police vessels, which should prevent direct access to Bosnia and Herzegovina. He requested a copy of the Mission report about the smuggling incident, which he assured would be brought to the attention of the authorities responsible for controlling the Sava.

23. On 14 November, a Sector Bajina Basta mobile patrol discovered that the barricade had been removed at Panjak, a southerly bypass to Kotroman border crossing point. The commander of the local military unit was apprised of the matter and he stated that a more permanent structure would be installed. On the same day, the Chief of Staff of the Mission met with the Deputy Head of the Department for Relations with Foreign Military Attachés and International Organizations of the Yugoslav Army. He drew attention to the requirement that barriers that had been removed were to be replaced as quickly as possible. Again, on 15 November, a Sector Bajina Basta mobile patrol witnessed a medium-size truck with a canvas cover over its cargo crossing into Bosnia and Herzegovina at Panjak. The Yugoslav Army liaison officer subsequently instructed the local Yugoslav Army commander to construct a more substantial barricade at Panjak. Finally, on 17 November a new barricade was erected and a trench dug beyond the obstruction.

24. On 24 November, in the Panjak unauthorized crossing point area, a Sector Bajina Basta mobile patrol observed a medium-size truck stuck in snow and mud approximately 50 metres inside the "Republika Srpska" territory. The truck had illegally crossed the Federal Republic of Yugoslavia (Serbia and Montenegro) - "Republika Srpska" border. The Yugoslav Army unit commander for Kotroman area was called in to witness the violation.

25. On 29 November, in the Panjak unauthorized crossing point area, a Sector Bajina Basta mobile patrol observed evidence of illegal crossing of the Federal Republic of Yugoslavia (Serbia and Montenegro) - "Republika Srpska" border and informed the Yugoslav Army liaison officer of this violation. Also, daily mobile patrols from the Sector Bajina Basta have seen evidence of smuggling activities in Panjak area. However patrols in the area have found no hard evidence to sustain the allegation of 10-ton trucks crossing at the two suspected border crossing points, but this possibility continues to be pursued with the Yugoslav Army. As of 6 December, the local Yugoslav Army commanders have

not provided the Mission with an explanation or course of action regarding these suspected crossings. The Mission Coordinator followed up on this matter during his meeting on 6 December with the Deputy Chief of the Yugoslav Army General Staff, expressing his concern and the urgency of resolving this situation in Panjak. The General Staff representatives promised to look into this question.

26. On 19 November, a Sector Alpha patrol sighted a boat crossing the Drina river 1 kilometre south of Mali Zvornik, with three men and about ten 100-litre barrels. The barrels were unloaded on the Bosnian side.

27. On 22 November, two Gazelle helicopters were observed by Sector Alpha mobile patrols flying 5 kilometres south of Mali Zvornik. The helicopters were heading from the "Republika Srpska" to the Federal Republic of Yugoslavia (Serbia and Montenegro). The local authorities were requested to investigate this border crossing. As of 6 December, the Mission Coordinator had received no reply.

28. In paragraph 24 of the Mission report to the Security Council of 10 November 1995 (S/1995/944), it was reported that "on 28 October one Mi-8 helicopter, originating from the Bosnian side and heading south-east, crossed the border south of the border crossing point at Scepan Polje (Sector Charlie)". The authorities of the Federal Republic of Yugoslavia (Serbia and Montenegro) informed the Mission that the helicopter was on HT 40 belonging to the "Republika Srpska". The authorities cited unfavourable weather conditions as reason for the helicopters crossing the border, entering 5 kilometres deep into the Federal Republic of Yugoslavia (Serbia and Montenegro) airspace and leaving without landing in the area of Pluzine.

29. On 29 November, at the vicinity of border crossing point Uvac (Sector Bravo), a 10-wheel transport truck was stuck in the middle of the river while attempting to cross the border illegally from the "Republika Srpska" to the Federal Republic of Yugoslavia (Serbia and Montenegro). The driver and passenger were arrested by a Yugoslav Army patrol.

VIII. CERTIFICATION

30. In the light of the foregoing developments, based on the Mission's on-site observation, on the advice of the Mission Coordinator, Mr. T.J. Nieminen, and in the absence of any contrary information from the air, either from the airborne reconnaissance system of the North Atlantic Treaty Organization (NATO) or national technical means, the Co-Chairmen conclude that the Government of the Federal Republic of Yugoslavia (Serbia and Montenegro) is continuing to meet its commitment to close the border between the Federal Republic of Yugoslavia

(Serbia and Montenegro) and the areas of the Republic of Bosnia and Herzegovina under the control of the Bosnian Serb forces. The Co-Chairmen also conclude that, during the period covered by the present report, there have been no commercial transshipments across the border between the Federal Republic of Yugoslavia (Serbia and Montenegro) and the Republic of Bosnia and Herzegovina.

153. LETTER DATED 2 JANUARY 1996 FROM THE SECRETARY-GENERAL ADDRESSED TO THE PRESIDENT OF THE SECURITY COUNCIL*

I have to the honour to convey the attached final biannual report addressed to me on 30 December 1995 by the Co-Chairmen of the Steering Committee of the International Conference on the Former Yugoslavia.

I should be grateful if you would bring this information to the attention of the members of the Security Council.

Annex
Biannual Report of the Co-Chairmen of the Steering Committee on the Activities of the International Conference on the Former Yugoslavia

I. INTRODUCTION

1. The International Conference on the Former Yugoslavia was established in August 1992, to remain in being until a settlement of the problems of the former Yugoslavia had been achieved. Its seat is at the United Nations Office at Geneva. The Co-Chairmen of the Conference are the Secretary-General of the United Nations and the Head of State or Government of the Presidency of the European Union. The activities of the Conference are supervised by a Steering Committee co-chaired by representatives of the Secretary-General of the United Nations and the Presidency of the European Union. The current Co-Chairmen of the Steering Committee are Mr. Carl Bildt (European Union) and Mr. Thorvald Stoltenberg (United Nations). The day-to-day activities of the Conference are carried out by the Co-Chairmen of the Steering Committee and in working groups and task forces.

---

* UN Doc. S/1996/4, 2 January 1996. Signed by Boutros Boutros-Ghali.

2. Pursuant to the decisions adopted at the Peace Implementation Conference (8 and 9 December) (S/1995/1029) and as indicated in the Secretary-General's report to the Security Council (S/1995/1031), the International Conference on the Former Yugoslavia will cease to exist as of 31 January 1996.

3. Information on the activities of the Conference from July to December 1995 is provided below.

4. Since the submission, on 26 July 1995, of the previous biannual report (S/1995/626), the International Conference has continued to provide a valuable framework for peacemaking, peace-building and humanitarian and human rights activities in the former Yugoslavia. These have included:

(a) The operation of the International Conference Mission which, since September 1994, has watched over the closure by the Federal Republic of Yugoslavia (Serbia and Montenegro) of its border towards areas of the Republic of Bosnia and Herzegovina controlled by Bosnian Serbs;

(b) Cooperation with the Contact Group countries in the development of a settlement for Bosnia and Herzegovina and the provision of inputs into peace negotiations among the parties to the conflict;

(c) Cooperation with the Contact Group countries in the development of a settlement for the eastern area of Croatia (Eastern Slavonia) and the provision of inputs into talks between the Croatian Government and the Serb local authorities;

(d) Use of the International Conference framework, notably its Humanitarian Issues Working Group, for alerting the international community to pressing humanitarian issues and for humanitarian appeals;

(e) The promotion of dialogue on human rights issues involving ethnic communities, nationalities and minorities in the former Yugoslavia;

(f) The consideration of economic and reconstruction issues.

II. HUMANITARIAN ISSUES

5. The Conference's Working Group on Humanitarian Issues, chaired by Mrs. Sadako Ogata, United Nations High Commissioner for Refugees, has continued its efforts to generate financing for humanitarian activities, to provide protection and assistance for refugees and displaced persons, and to help to uphold international norms on human rights and humanitarian law. Under the auspices of the Working Group, the Office of the United Nations High Commissioner for Refugees (UNHCR) and other international humanitarian agencies have helped millions of civilians caught up in the conflict, as well as refugees and displaced

persons, to survive the winters of 1992, 1993, 1994 and 1995.

6. The period covered by the present report saw a continued and unprecedented influx of refugees and displaced persons, affecting the humanitarian situation and activities. The fall of the eastern enclaves of Srebrenica on 11 July and Zepa on 25 July to the Bosnian Serb forces resulted in the exodus of 36,000 displaced persons to the Tuzla and Zenica regions. UNHCR identified 11,000 persons placed in collective centres around Tuzla. At the Tuzla airbase, UNHCR, in cooperation with the United Nations Protection Force (UNPROFOR) and a number of non-governmental organizations (NGOs), assisted the new arrivals from Srebrenica. At the end of July, a host family agreement was signed between the Bosnian Government and UNHCR for limited assistance to 4,500 host families in the Tuzla region. On 17 July, the High Commissioner for Refugees travelled to Tuzla to meet the victims from Srebrenica and review the efforts of UNHCR and other humanitarian organizations to assist them.

7. As the fall of Zepa became imminent, the local authorities and UNHCR made preparations to receive a possible influx of new arrivals in the Zenica region. An emergency response committee was formed to coordinate the relief action. UNHCR and UNPROFOR erected a transit camp in Zenica, where the registration of the new arrivals took place and assistance was distributed. Some 4,300 displaced persons were placed in collective centres, which were supplied with basic emergency items, as well as in host families.

8. The capture by Croatian HV/HVO forces of Glamoc and Grahovo in late July, led to the flight of 14,000 Serbs to northern Bosnia. Many of them subsequently made their way to Banja Luka. UNHCR dispatched relief items including food, plastic sheeting and sanitary materials to assist the newly displaced persons.

9. The stocks of aid supplied UNHCR had prepositioned in Banja Luka were quickly exhausted with the mass influx of refugees from the Krajina, and additional quantities of food and non-food emergency supplied were brought in by land from Belgrade. UNHCR made fuel available to assist the refugees with their transportation needs as most gradually moved on towards Serbia. In cooperation with the local authorities, way stations were established along the road to Serbia where aid was distributed. UNHCR established an airlift to Belgrade to replenish stocks there. In addition, the United Kingdom Government made two helicopters available to UNHCR, to be used to transport relief supplies from Zagreb to Banja Luka. On 12 August, the Deputy High Commissioner for Refugees visited Banja Luka to meet with the local authorities, review the emergency aid operation and visit some of the sites where the new refugees were accommodated. In order to cope with the needs of the many thousands of Serb displaced

persons in the Banja Luka area, a number of UNHCR field staff from other offices were temporarily deployed to the Banja Luka office. The work of UNHCR and other aid organizations was hampered by the very poor security situation in the area, with repeated hijackings at gunpoint, harassment and banditry. A letter was addressed to Bosnian Serb leader Radovan Karadzic protesting in "the most strenuous terms" at the "intolerable acts which have been perpetuated recently". The local Serb authorities pledged their support in preventing such incidents from recurring.

10. A major concern was the situation of the remaining Serb population in the Krajina, most of whom were elderly and frail and lived in remote, isolated villages. Human rights violations, including burning and looting of abandoned property, harassment and brutal violence, were brought to the attention of the Croatian Government at the highest levels on a number of occasions, together with the serious criticisms from the international community. UNHCR, UNCRO, the International Committee of the Red Cross (ICRC), the International Federation of Red Cross and Red Crescent Societies and the European Community Monitoring Mission (ECMM) identified the most vulnerable among them. The Croatian Red Cross took an active role and deployed six mobile teams to cater for and assist the needy population, with monitoring, funding and other support provided by a number of international organizations, including UNHCR. However, government resources and support for assistance to vulnerable minority cases remained minimal. The local Red Cross branches remained understaffed and with little logistical support to reach the many remote villages. UNHCR vehicle support to the Croatian Red Cross was only part of the solution; some government social welfare offices - independent of the Red Cross system but crucial to the relief work - had no access to transportation and received little or no support from their central offices in Zagreb.

11. UNHCR supported the authorities in the Federal Republic of Yugoslavia (Serbia and Montenegro) to cope with the massive influx of Krajina refugees. A UNHCR emergency relief team was deployed in Serbia to assess the needs of the refugees and coordinate the distribution of supplies. UNHCR distributed food and non-food items and fuel, together with emergency assistance. The massive influx of refugees had a substantial impact on UNHCR's assistance programme in the Federal Republic of Yugoslavia (Serbia and Montenegro) where the caseload more than doubled. In the supplement to the United Nations revised consolidated inter-agency appeal for the former Yugoslavia issued on 15 September 1995, UNHCR requested an additional US$ 24 million to meet the new requirements in the sectors of transport and logistics, domestic needs and household support, health and nutrition, shelter and community services.

12. The arrival of tens of thousands of Krajina refugees in the Banja Luka region resulted in a dramatic deterioration of the situation for the Croat and Muslim minorities, who felt that the only option left was to leave the region. UNHCR's involvement in the movement - some 22,000 left via the Srbac-Davor crossing - was limited to predeparture interviews and presence at the crossing points. UNHCR also urged the local authorities to ensure that minority men on work or military obligation were allowed to return to their homes so that families wishing to depart were not separated. UNHCR urged the authorities to meet their responsibility of accommodating all refugees, not only the ones of Croat ethnicity, the Government having linked the admission of Muslim refugees from Banja Luka to UNHCR providing accommodation for them. UNHCR took up the issue of "resettlement" of Bosnian Muslim refugees back to Bosnia and Herzegovina (Bihac) with the Croatian Government on a number of occasions, emphasizing that, as a signatory to the 1951 Geneva Convention on the Status of Refugees, Croatia had a duty to keep its doors of asylum open to refugees and that it must not forcibly repatriate those coming in from Bosnia and Herzegovina. UNHCR extended its full support to the Government in providing assistance to the refugees during their stay in Croatia, for example by providing shelter to Bosnian Muslim refugees in the UNCRO bases in Pustara and Novska in Western Slavonia.

13. After the recapture of the Bihac pocket by the Fifth Corps of the Bosnian Army on 7 August, UNHCR established a permanent presence in the Kuplensko camp, where some 20,000 former inhabitants of Velika Kladusa and Cazin loyal to Fidret Abdic arrived and lived in appalling conditions along the roadside. UNHCR, together with other humanitarian agencies, provided food and non-food assistance, shelter, water, sanitation and medical assistance and started a winterization operation to enable the refugees to survive during the cold months. The efforts were hampered by the extremely strict control imposed by the Croatian Special Police at the camp, which initially prevented some vital materials such as gravel and fuel from entering the camp. UNHCR also strongly protested incidents of *refoulement* in the camp, where male refugees were deported by the Croatian special police in Vojnic and handed over to the Bosnian police in Velika Kladusa.

14. On 30 October, UNHCR started a bus service from the camp to Velika Kladusa to enable those wishing to return home to do so. On arrival in Velika Kladusa, the local authorities have been registering the refugees. The refugees have in most cases returned to their houses, where UNHCR and other international organizations are monitoring their situation. By 15 December, over 4,200 refugees had returned to Velika Kladusa from the Kuplensko camp, using the

UNHCR-organized buses or their own means of transport. The UNHCR buses arriving in Velika Kladusa also provided onward travel to Cazin and Vrnograc.

15. Access to Sarajevo was very irregular during the summer months, with only 15 per cent of the target met in June, 30 per cent in July and 45 per cent in August. With the opening of the "blue routes" and the airlift, conditions improved. The humanitarian airlift resumed on 16 September after over five months of suspension. The airlift operation was temporarily suspended from 6 to 30 November to allow for a build-up of stock at Ancona in order to sustain a full schedule. UNHCR and the High-level Working Group agreed that the airbridge will carry whatever stock has been built up at Ancona by 10 December (up to 5,000 tons), before the operation is discontinued early next year.

16. A number of protection issues in Croatia were of great concern to UNHCR. In spite of repeated requests from the international community, including UNHCR, the Croatian Government did not establish a mechanism to enable those Krajina Serbs wishing to return to Croatia to do so. The law on abandoned property in the Krajina, which represented a serious impediment to possible large-scale return, was not re-examined by the Croatian Parliament. The Office for Displaced Persons and Refugees started to depopulate some refugee centres, particularly in the Istria region, with the purpose of closing them down. Some of the Bosnian Croat refugees from these centres were resettled in former Sectors North and South and others had the possibility of going elsewhere in Croatia. However, Bosnian Muslim refugees who opted to remain in Croatia often faced increased hardship conditions.

17. UNHCR, in coordination with ICRC, followed closely the situation of the estimated 800 Muslims from Zepa and Srebrenica who sere detained at Mitrovo Polje and Slivovica in the Federal Republic of Yugoslavia (Serbia and Montenegro). In order to prevent any possible attempt to refoule them to Bosnia and Herzegovina, UNHCR requested the authorities to consider them as refugees and therefore under UNHCR protection. UNHCR expressed its complete availability to assist them in submitting their applications for resettlement to third countries and sent 10 resettlement case workers to conduct interviews with the group. At the time of finalizing the present report, the first group had departed, without major problems and in cooperation with relevant authorities.

18. With the recent peace agreement and new territorial configuration in Bosnia and Herzegovina, several resettlement cases were put on hold, who, according to the new territorial agreement would be able to return to their places of origin. At this time consideration is given to refugees from Banja Luka and some refugees in marriages of mixed ethnicity.

19. UNHCR issued a strong statement concerning the involuntary relocation by the Bosnian authorities of displaced persons of newly acquired areas. UNHCR

worked on assessment of conditions, particularly the issue of voluntariness, in respect to the planned return of 1,000 persons to Sanski Most and Kljuc. Repeated visits were paid to Jajce, Travnik and Bugojno to monitor the progress in the return of Bosniac and Croat families, which met with difficulties with some Croat families returning to Bugojno and Travnik, but no Muslims being allowed to go back to Jajce and Stolac.

20. Faced with the dramatic escalation of the humanitarian needs in the former Yugoslavia, a supplement to the revised inter-agency appeal for the former Yugoslavia of 31 May 1995 was issued on 15 September to respond to the considerable rise in internally displaced persons and refugees following events since May 1995. The revised inter-agency target was increased from US$ 470 million by US$ 44.8 million to a total of US$ 514.8 million. The UNHCR component of US$ 206.4 million was increased to US$ 222.7 million in December.

21. A new United Nations consolidated inter-agency appeal for the former Yugoslavia was launched on 20 November, for US$ 179.6 million to fund humanitarian assistance to 3.3 million beneficiaries in the former Yugoslavia from January to April 1996. The UNHCR component is US$ 70.9 million.

22. The Humanitarian Issues Working Group of the International Conference on the Former Yugoslavia met in Geneva on 19 July and on 10 October, under the chairmanship of the High Commissioner for Refugees. At the London Implementation Conference, the High Commissioner for Refugees announced that the Working Group would meet on 16 January 1996, in view of the urgency of the tasks involved in repatriation planning.

23. The High Commissioner for Refugees undertook a mission to Sarajevo, Zagreb and Belgrade, from 4 to 6 December 1995 and held meetings with the respective Presidents and government officials to discuss the implementation of the Dayton peace agreement.

III. PEACEMAKING

24. In June 1995, following the appointment of Mr. Carl Bildt as the new European Union Co-Chairman of the Steering Committee, the Co-Chairmen undertook a review of forthcoming activities and decided that, in order to give enhanced focus on their efforts, one would spearhead peacemaking efforts concerning Bosnia and Herzegovina while the other would spearhead peacemaking efforts concerning Croatia, it being understood that they would be jointly responsible for all activities of the Conference. Pursuant to this arrangement, Carl Bildt, the European Union Co-Chairman, focused on peacemaking in Bosnia and

Herzegovina, while Thorvald Stoltenberg, the United Nations Co-Chairman, focused on peacemaking in the Republic of Croatia.

A. *Peacemaking in Bosnia and Herzegovina*

25. Between June and October 1995, Mr. Bildt worked intensively with representatives of the Contact Group countries to promote a negotiated solution to the conflict in Bosnia and Herzegovina. On 8 September 1995, in Geneva, he jointly chaired talks among Bosnian leaders at which a set of principles for a settlement of the conflict in Bosnia and Herzegovina was agreed upon. On 26 September 1995, in New York, he jointly chaired another meeting of Bosnian leaders at which a set of further principles was agreed upon.
26. From 1 to 21 November 1995, Mr. Bildt jointly chaired the proximity peace talks held in Dayton, Ohio. On 21 November 1995, a General Framework Agreement for Peace in Bosnia and Herzegovina together with 11 annexes and related documents were initialled. These documents were subsequently signed in Paris on 14 December 1995 (see S/1995/999, attachment).

B. *Peacemaking in Croatia*

27. Between July and September 1995, the United Nations Co-Chairman of the Steering Committee, Mr. Stoltenberg, was engaged in prolonged, discreet contacts to promote a peaceful, negotiated solution regarding Eastern Slavonia. On 3 October, in pursuance of his efforts, Mr. Stoltenberg, along with the Ambassador of the United States of America to the Republic of Croatia, Mr. Peter Galbraith, jointly chaired a meeting of representatives of the Government of Croatia and of the Serb local authorities in Sector East. At that meeting, agreement was reached on a set of guiding principles for future negotiations. The efforts of the Co-Chairmen continued during October and November and culminated with the signing, on 12 November, of a Basic Agreement on the Region of Eastern Slavonia, Baranja, and Western Sirmium (S/1995/951).

IV. THE INTERNATIONAL CONFERENCE ON THE FORMER YUGOSLAVIA MISSION TO THE FEDERAL REPUBLIC OF YUGOSLAVIA (SERBIA AND MONTENEGRO)

28. The International Conference Mission to the Federal Republic of Yugoslavia (Serbia and Montenegro) was established on 17 September 1994, at the invita-

tion of that Government, after the latter had made the following decisions on 4 August 1994:

    (a) "To break off political and economic relations with the Republika Srpska;"

    (b) "To prohibit the stay of the members of the leadership of the Republika Srpska (parliament, presidency and Government) in the territory of the Federal Republic of Yugoslavia;"

    (c) "As of today the border of the Federal Republic of Yugoslavia is closed for all transport towards the Republika Srpska except food, clothing and medicine."

29. The original members of the International Conference Mission to Yugoslavia arrived in Belgrade on 14 September 1994. The Mission is a civilian mission and is organized and operated correspondingly. Mr. Tauno Nieminen of Finland became the second Head of Mission on 13 January 1995. On 14 December 1995, he was succeeded in that capacity by Mr. Tarmo Kauppila, also of Finland.

30. The mandate of the Mission is to observe the closure of the border between the Federal Republic of Yugoslavia (Serbia and Montenegro) and areas of Bosnia and Herzegovina under control of the Bosnian Serbs in order to verify that only humanitarian aid is allowed to pass. The Federal Republic of Yugoslavia (Serbia and Montenegro) retains full control of its borders through its customs, police and military. These officials operate the border crossings. Mission members are present to observe, record and report accordingly.

31. On the basis of an agreement reached with the Federal Republic of Yugoslavia (Serbia and Montenegro) authorities, members of the Mission are entitled:

    (a) To work with representatives of the Yugoslav Red Cross at places from which humanitarian assistance is organized or dispatched;

    (b) To work alongside customs officers;

    (c) To look into any vehicle crossing the border;

    (d) To have examined any item conveyed by individuals or vehicles crossing the border which they suspect might not be classified as humanitarian aid;

    (e) To examine all customs, commercial, transport or related documentation;

    (f) To have complete freedom of movement with their safety and security guaranteed by the Government of the Federal Republic of Yugoslavia (Serbia and Montenegro);

    (g) To have their own communications system.

32. The Mission works with representatives of international and local humanitarian agencies in carrying out this mandate. Mission teams send daily reports to its headquarters. These reports are compiled weekly and sent to the Co-Chairmen of the Steering Committee. In addition, the Mission produces monthly reports that are also submitted to the Co-Chairmen. On the basis of the information provided by the Mission, the Co-Chairmen report each month to the Security Council through the Secretary-General.

33. The Mission's headquarters are located in Belgrade. The Mission covers the whole border area from the north of Serbia to the south of Montenegro (330 miles, approximately 527 kilometres). Nineteen border control posts are covered on a 24-hour basis. On top of static presence at border control posts, the Mission undertakes mobile day and night patrols along the border, usually in close cooperation with the army or police. The Mission is organized into five field sectors, between two and nine hours' drive from Belgrade and located as follows:

(a) *Sector Belgrade*. The Sector headquarters is located in Belgrade. This Sector is responsible for observing the loading and customs inspection of goods destined for points beyond the Federal Republic of Yugoslavia (Serbia and Montenegro) border with the Republika Srpska at predesignated loading sites in and around Belgrade, to ensure that only humanitarian aid is forwarded. The Sector's area of responsibility extends west from where the border of the Federal Republic of Yugoslavia (Serbia and Montenegro) with Bosnia and Herzegovina meets the Croatian border, to the confluence of the Drina and Sava rivers;

(b) *Sector Alpha*. The Sector headquarters is located in Banja Koviljaca. This Sector is responsible for the border area from the junction of the Drina and Sava in the north to Drlace in the south;

(c) *Sector Bajina Basta*. The Sector headquarters is located in Bajina Basta. This Sector is responsible for the border area from Drlace in the north to 3 kms north of Priboj. Sector Bajina Basta is also responsible for the checking and controlling of freight trains on the line passing into and out of "Republika Srpska" territory;

(d) *Sector Bravo*. The Sector headquarters is located in Priboj. This Sector is responsible for the border area 3 kms north of Priboj to the Tara river in Montenegro;

(e) *Sector Charlie*. The Sector headquarters is located in Niksic, Montenegro. This Sector is responsible for the border area from the Tara river in the north to the point at which the border of the Federal Republic of Yugoslavia (Serbia and Montenegro) with Bosnia and Herzegovina abuts the border of the Federal Republic of Yugoslavia (Serbia and Montenegro) with Croatia, near the Adriatic coast.

34. The Mission's current budget of $4.179 million covers the period from 1 October 1995 to 31 March 1996. This money is spent on operational costs. Some Governments provide vehicles, communications and transmissions equipment as well as other assets. In addition, States contributing monitors generally pay the salaries of their personnel. As of 14 December 1995, there were 217 international members of the Mission from 15 countries.

V. ECONOMIC AND RECONSTRUCTION ISSUES

35. The Economic Issues Working Group of the Conference convened on 10 October, with an open agenda. All five delegations attended. They were asked to consider various economic aspects of the peace implementation process, at a time when there were new hopes of a peace agreement being reached. They proceeded to look into the ways that progress made in past meetings of the group, on issues such as the lifting of restrictions on trade and financial transactions, or the conditionality that should be attached to economic reconstruction programmes, or the economic aspects of State succession, could be brought to bear on the peace implementation process.

36. Strong emphasis was laid by the Chairman on the integrated nature of most of the infrastructure inherited from the former Yugoslavia, and on the need to promote trade and economic relations among the successor States in order to consolidate peace, when it came, and to ensure the success of the future reconstruction process. The newly independent States of the former Yugoslavia were actively developing economic relations with new partners, but they could not afford to discard economic cooperation between themselves. The Chairman indicated that, in order to ensure the success of reconstruction and to ensure economic recovery, provision would have to be made for cooperation in the fields of trade and infrastructure. A multilateral forum, the Chairman considered, could prove more efficient than a series of bilateral relationships at negotiating appropriate trade and economic agreements in these fields.

VI. ETHNIC AND NATIONAL COMMUNITIES AND MINORITIES

37. During the period covered by the present report, activities have continued under the auspices of the Conference to address issues affecting ethnic and national communities and minorities.

A. The former Yugoslav Republic of Macedonia

38. In the former Yugoslav Republic of Macedonia, the Conference's Working Group on Ethnic and National Communities and Minorities has promoted a series of legislative and practical improvements in favour of the Albanians and other nationalities. This followed intensive, patient and detailed talks sponsored by the Working Group. After the Tetovo incident of 17 February 1995, when one ethnic Albanian was shot, the Working Group succeeded in assembling representatives of all Albanian parties in the Republic, together with the Ministers of the Interior, Justice and Education, around the same table. Since March, 10 rounds of talks have been organized. They were accompanied by numerous individual meetings with representatives of Parliament, other Government agencies, other ethnic groups such as the Turks, opposition figures outside Parliament, and the media.

39. The talks concentrated on new legislation under consideration for all three levels of education and on local self-government. There was also a wide discussion of language issues and of questions pertaining to citizenship and the display of national symbols. Some of this legislation has been adopted in the meantime, taking into consideration various suggestions developed in the Group.

40. In the media sector, the Working Group sponsored an agreement between the Danish and Swiss Governments on the one hand, and "Macedonian Radio and Television" on the other, which provides for the delivery of television equipment for the tripling of emission time in Albanian, and for a considerable increase in languages of other nationalities. A similar radio project has been prepared, within the framework of the Working Group, by specialists from the European Broadcasting Union.

41. In its activities, the Working Group has enjoyed valuable cooperation with the United Nations Preventive Deployment Force (UNPREDEP), the Organization for Security and Cooperation in Europe (OSCE) Mission in Skopje and the Council of Europe.

B. Croatia

42. The Working Group had for some time been trying to set up bilateral talks in Croatia along the model of the talks between the Government of the former Yugoslav Republic of Macedonia and the Albanians in that Republic. Three rounds of talks between the Croatian Government and representatives of Serb organizations in Croatia chaired by the Working Group have taken place. The first two, more general, meetings (12 July 1995 and 31 August 1995) led to an

understanding by participants that discussions should focus on concrete issues starting with education. At the third meeting (24 October 1995), which was devoted to educational questions, the Serb representatives identified areas on which they felt some improvements could be made, and it was agreed that they would work out concrete proposals for the next meeting.

C. *Federal Republic of Yugoslavia (Serbia and Montenegro)*

43. During the reporting period, International Conference personnel have maintained contacts with the authorities of the Federal Republic of Yugoslavia (Serbia and Montenegro), local authorities and the leaders of the communities involved regarding the situations in Kosovo, Sandjak and Vojvodina.

3. LIST OF SECURITY COUNCIL RESOLUTIONS ON THE FORMER YUGOSLAVIA

Editors' Note: Security Council Resolutions concerning Yugoslavia, Bosnia and Herzegovina and Croatia as from June 1991 to the 12th of January 1995

S/RES/713 (1991)
Resolution 713 (1191) / adopted by the Security Council at its 3009th meeting on 25 September 1991
Concerns the situation in Yugoslavia

S/RES/721 (1991)
Resolution 721 (1991) / adopted by the Security Council at its 3018th meeting, on 27 November 1991
Concerns deployment of a United Nations peace-keeping operation in Yugoslavia

S/RES/724 (1991)
Resolution 721 (1991) / adopted by the Security Council at its 3023rd meeting, on 15 December 1991
Concerns the situation in Yugoslavia

S/RES/727 (1992)
Resolution 727 (1992) / adopted by the Security Council at its 3028th meeting, on 8 January 1992
Concerns the situation in Yugoslavia

S/RES/740 (1992)
Resolution 740 (1992) / adopted by the Security Council at its 3049th meeting, on 7 February 1992
Concerns political settlement of the situation in Yugoslavia

S/RES/743 (1992)
Resolution 743 (1992) / adopted by the Security Council at its 3055th meeting on 21 February 1992
Concerns establishment of the United Nations Protection Force

S/RES/749 (1992)
Resolution 749 (1992) / adopted by the Security Council at its 3066th meeting, on 7 April 1992
Concerns deployment of the UN Protection Force in Yugoslavia

S/RES/752 (1992)
Resolution 752 (1992) / adopted by the Security Council at its 3075th meeting, on 15 May 1992
Concerns the situation in Bosnia and Herzegovina

S/RES/753 (1992)
Resolution 753 (1992) / adopted by the Security Council at its 3076th meeting, on 18 May 1992
Concerns admission of Croatia to membership in the United Nations

S/RES/755 (1992)
Resolution 755 (1992) / adopted by the Security Council at its 3079th meeting, on 20 May 1992
Concerns admission of Bosnia and Herzegovina to membership in the United Nations

S/RES/757 (1992)
Resolution 757 (1992)/ adopted by the Security Council at its 3082nd meeting, on 30 May 1992
Concerns sanctions against Yugoslavia

S/RES/758 (1992)
Resolution 758 (1992) / adopted by the Security Council at its 3083rd meeting on 8 June 1992
Concerns enlargement of the mandate and the size of the UN Protection Force and humanitarian assistance to Bosnia and Herzegovina

S/RES/760 (1992)
Resolution 760 (1992) / adopted by the Security Council at its 3086th meeting,
on 18 June 1992
Concerns humanitarian assistance to the victims of conflict in Yugoslavia

S/RES/761 (1992)
Resolution 761 (1992) / adopted by the Security Council at its 3087th meeting on
29 June 1992
Concerns deployment of additional elements of the UN Protection Force in
Bosnia and Herzegovina

S/RES/762 (1992)
Resolution 762 (1992) / adopted by the Security Council at its 3088th meeting,
on 30 June 1992
Concerns implementation of the UN peace-keeping plan in Yugoslavia

S/RES/764 (1992)
Resolution 764 (1992) / adopted by the Security Council at its 3093rd meeting,
on 13 July 1992
Concerns deployment of additional elements of the UN Protection Force in
Bosnia and Herzegovina

S/RES/769 (1992)
Resolution 769 (1992) / adopted by the Security Council at its 3104th meeting,
on 7 August 1992
Concerns enlargement of the mandate end strength of the UN Protection Force

S/RES/770 (1992)
Resolution 770 (1992) / adopted by the Security Council at its 3106th meeting,
on 13 August 1992
Concerns the situation in Bosnia and Herzegovina

S/RES/771 (1992)
Resolution 771 (1992) / adopted by the Security Council at its 3106th meeting,
on 13 August 1992
Concerns violations of humanitarian law in the territory of the former Yugoslavia and in Bosnia and Herzegovina

S/RES/776 (1992)
Resolution 776 (1992) / adopted by the Security Council at its 3114th meeting, on 14 September 1992
Concerns enlargement of the mandate of the UN Protection Force

S/RES/777 (1992)
Resolution 777 (1992) / adopted by the Security Council at its 3116th meeting, on 19 September 1992
Concerns the question of membership of the Federal Republic of Yugoslavia (Serbia and Montenegro) in the United Nations

S/RES/779 (1992)
Resolution 779 (1992) / adopted by the Security Council at its 3118th meeting, on 6 October 1992
Concerns implementation of the UN peace-keeping plan in Croatia

S/RES/780 (1992)
Resolution 780 (1992) / adopted by the Security Council at its 3118th meeting, on 6 October 1992
Concerns establishment of the Commission of experts to Examine and Analyse the Information submitted pursuant to Security Council Resolution 771 (1992)

S/RES/781 (1992)
Resolution 781 (1992) / adopted by the Security Council at its 3122nd meeting, on 9 October 1992
Concerns establishment of a ban on military flights in the airspace of Bosnia and Herzegovina except the flights of UN operations, including humanitarian assistance

S/RES/786 (1992)
Resolution 786 (1992) / adopted by the Security Council at its 3133rd meeting, on 10 November 1992
Concerns a ban on military flights in the airspace of Bosnia and Herzegovina

S/RES/787 (1992)
Resolution 787 (1992) / adopted by the Security Council at its 3137th meeting, on 16 November 1992
Concerns the situation in Bosnia and Herzegovina

S/RES/795 (1992)
Resolution 795 (1992) / adopted by the Security Council at its 3147th meeting,
on 11 December 1992
Concerns establishment of presence of the UN Protection Force in the former
Yugoslav Republic of Macedonia

S/RES/798 (1992)
Resolution 798 (1992) / adopted by the Security Council at its 3150th meeting,
on 18 December 1992
Supports initiative of the European Council to dispatch a fact-finding mission to
Bosnia and Herzegovina

S/RES/802 (1993)
Resolution 802 (1993) / adopted by the Security Council at its 3163rd meeting,
on 25 January 1993
Concerns the situation on the UN protected area in Croatia

S/RES/807 (1993)
Resolution 807 (1993) / adopted by the Security Council at its 3174th meeting,
on 19 February 1993
Concerns implementation of the UN peace-keeping plan in Croatia

S/RES/808 (1993)
Resolution 808 (1993) / adopted by the Security Council at its 3175th meeting,
on 22 February 1993
Concerns establishment of an International Tribunal for the Prosecution of Persons Responsible for Violations of International Humanitarian Law Committed
in the Territory of the Former Yugoslavia

S/RES/815 (1993)
Resolution 815 (1993) / adopted by the Security Council at its 3189th meeting,
on 30 March 1993
Concerns extension of the mandate of the UN Protection Force

S/RES/816 (1993)
Resolution 816 (1993) / adopted by the Security Council at its 3191st meeting,
on 31 March 1993
Concerns extension of the ban on military flights in the airspace of Bosnia and
Herzegovina

S/RES/819 (1993)
Resolution 819 (1993) / adopted by the Security Council at its 3199th meeting, on 16 April 1993
Concerns the situation in Srebrenica and the surrounding areas, Bosnia and Herzegovina

S/RES/820 (1993)
Resolution 820 (1993) / adopted by the Security Council at its 3200th meeting, on 17 April 1993
Concerns the peace plan for Bosnia and Herzegovina and the strengthening of the measures imposed by the earlier resolutions on the situation in the former Yugoslavia

S/RES/821 (1993)
Resolution 821 (1993) / adopted by the Security Council at its 3204th meeting, on 28 April 1993
Concerns non-participation of Yugoslavia (Serbia and Montenegro) in the work of the Economic and Social Council

S/RES/824 (1993)
Resolution 824 (1993) / adopted by the Security Council at its 3208th meeting, on 6 May 1993
Concerns treatment of certain towns and surroundings in Bosnia and Herzegovina as safe areas

S/RES/827 (1993)
Resolution 827 (1993) / adopted by the Security Council at its 3217th meeting, on 25 May 1993
Concerns establishment of the International Tribunal for the Prosecution of Persons Responsible for Serious Violations of International Humanitarian Law Committed in the Territory of the Former Yugoslavia since 1991

S/RES/836 (1003)
Resolution 836 (1993) / adopted by the Security Council at its 3228th meeting, on 4 June 1993
Concerns implementation of the peace plan for Bosnia and Herzegovina

S/RES/838 (1993)
Resolution 838 (1993) / adopted by the Security Council at its 3234th meeting, on 10 June 1993
Concerns options for deployment of international observers on the borders of Bosnia and Herzegovina

S/RES/843 (1993)
Resolution 843 (1993) / adopted by the Security Council at its 3240th meeting, on 18 June 1993
Concerns establishment by the Security Council Committee established pursuant to resolution 724 (1991) concerning Yugoslavia of its working group to examine requests for assistance

S/RES/844 (1993)
Resolution 844 (1993) / adopted by the Security Council at its 3241st meeting, on 18 June 1993
Concerns authorization of the reinforcement of the UN Protection Force

S/RES/847 (1993)
Resolution 847 (1993)/ adopted by the Security Council at its 3248th meeting, on 30 June 1993
Concerns extension of the mandate of the UN Protection Force and the situation in Croatia

S/RES/855 (1993)
Resolution 855(1993) / adopted by the Security Council at its 3262nd meeting, on 9 August 1993
Concerns refusal of the authorities in the Federal Republic of Yugoslavia to allow the CSCE special missions in Kosovo, Sandjak and Vojvodina

S/RES/859 (1993)
Resolution 859 (1993) / adopted by the Security Council at its 3269th meeting, on 24 August 1993
Concerns comprehensive political settlement of the situation in Bosnia and Herzegovina

S/RES/869 (1993)
Resolution 869 (1993) / adopted by the Security Council at its 3284th meeting on 30 September 1993
Concerns extension of the mandate of the UN Protection Force

S/RES/870 (1993)
Resolution 870 (1993) / adopted by the Security Council at its 3285th meeting, on 1 October 1993
Concerns extension of the mandate of he UN Protection Force

S/RES/871 (1993)
Resolution 871 (1993) / adopted by the Security Council at its 3286th meeting, on 4 October 1993
Concerns extension of the mandate of the UN Protection Force and implementation of the UN peace-keeping plan for Croatia

S/RES/900 (1994)
Resolution 900 (1994) / adopted by the Security Council at its 3344th meeting, on 4 March 1994
Concerns restoration of essential public services and normal life in and around Sarajevo, Bosnia and Herzegovina

S/RES/908 (1994)
Resolution 908 (1994) / adopted by the Security Council at its 3356th meeting, on 31 March 1994
Concerns extension of the mandate and increase of the personnel of the UN Protection Force

S/RES/913 (1994)
Resolution 913 (1994) / adopted by the Security Council at its 3367th meeting, on 22 April 1994
Concerns situation in Bosnia and Herzegovina, particularly in the safe area of Gorazde and political settlement of the situation in the former Yugoslavia

S/RES/914 (1994)
Resolution 914 (1994) / adopted by the Security Council at its 3369th meeting, on 27 April 1994
Concerns increase of the personnel of the UN Protection Force, in addition to the reinforcement approved in resolution 908 (1994)

S/RES/936 (1994)
Resolution 936 (1994) / adopted by the Security Council at its 3401st meeting, on 8 July 1994
Concerns the appointment of the Prosecutor of the International Tribunal for the Prosecution of Persons Responsible for Serious Violations of International Humanitarian Law Committed in the Territory of the Former Yugoslavia since 1991.

S/RES/941 (1994)
Resolution 941 (1994) / adopted by the Security Council at its 3428th meeting, on 23 September 1994
Concerns violations of international humanitarian law in Banja Luka, Bijeljina and other areas of Bosnia and Herzegovina under the control of Bosnian Serb forces

S/RES/942 (1994)
Resolution 942 (1994) / adopted by the Security Council at its 3428th meeting on 23 September 1994
Concerns reinforcement and extension of measures imposed by the Security Council resolutions with regard to those areas of Bosnia and Herzegovina under the control of Bosnian Serb forces, to assist the parties to give effect to the proposed territorial settlement in Bosnia and Herzegovina

S/RES/943 (1994)
Resolution 943 (1994) / adopted by the Security Council at its 3428th meeting, on 23 September 1994
Concerns closure of the border between the Federal Republic of Yugoslavia and Bosnia and Herzegovina with respect to all goods except foodstuffs, medical supplies and clothing for essential humanitarian needs

S/RES/947 (1994)
Resolution 947 (1994) / adopted by the Security Council at its 3434th meeting, on 30 September 1994
Concerns extension of the mandate of the UN Protection Force and decision to reconsider the mandate after requested by 20 Jan. 1995 of the Secretary-General's report on progress towards implementation of the UN Peace-keeping Plan for Croatia and all relevant Security Council resolutions

S/RES/958 (1994)
Resolution 958 (1994) / adopted by the Security Council at its 3461st meeting, on 19 November 1994
Concerns decisions that the authorization given in paragraph 10 of S/RES/836 (1993) to assist UNPROFOR in carrying out its mandate in Bosnia and Herzegovina shall apply also to such measures taken in Croatia

S/RES/959 (1994)
Resolution 959 (1994) / adopted by the Security Council at its 3462nd meeting, on 19 November 1994
Concerns efforts of the UN Protection Force to ensure implementation of Security Council Resolutions on safe areas in Bosnia and Herzegovina

S/RES/967 (1994)
Resolution 967 (1994) / adopted by the Security Council at its 3480th meeting, on 14 December 1994
Concerns exemption from the provisions of resolution 757 (1992), permitting the export of diphtheria anti-serum from Yugoslavia (Serbia and Montenegro) for a period of 30 days from the date of the adoption of this resolution

S/RES/970 (1995)
Resolution 970 (1995) / adopted by the Security Council at its 3487th meeting, on 12 January 1995
Concerns the closure of the international border between Yugoslavia and Bosnia and Herzegovina with respect to all goods except for essential humanitarian needs

S/RES/981 (1995)
Resolution 981 (1995) / adopted by the Security Council at its 3512th meeting, on 31 March 1995
Concerns the establishment of the UN Confidence Restoration Operation in Croatia (UNCRO)

S/RES/982 (1995)
Resolution 982 (1995) / adopted by the Security Council at its 3512th meeting, on 31 March 1995
Concerns extension of the mandate of the UN Protection Force in the Republic of Bosnia and Herzegovina and its operations in Croatia

S/RES/987 (1995)
Resolution 987 (1995) / adopted by the Security Council at its 3521th meeting,
on 19 April 1995
Concerns security and safety of the UN Protection Force

S/RES/988 (1995)
Resolution 988 (1995) / adopted by the Security Council at its 3522th meeting,
on 21 April 1995
Concerns further extension of the partial suspension of certain sanctions against
Yugoslavia

S/RES/990 (1995)
Resolution 990 (1995) / adopted by the Security Council at its 3527th meeting,
on 28 April 1995
Concerns authorization of the deployment of the UN Confidence Restoration
Operation in Croatia

S/RES/992 (1995)
Resolution 992 (1995) / adopted by the Security Council at its 3533th meeting,
on 11 May 1995
Concerns freedom of navigation on the Danube River

S/RES/994 (1995)
Resolution 994 (1995) / adopted by the Security Council at its 3537th meeting,
on 17 May 1995
Concerns withdrawal of the Croatian Government's troops from the zone of
separation in Croatia and full deployment of the UN Confidence Restoration
Operation in Croatia

S/RES/998 (1995)
Resolution 998 (1995) / adopted by the Security Council at its 3543th meeting,
on 16 June 1995
Concerns establishment of a rapid-reaction force within the UN Protection Force

S/RES/1003 (1995)
Resolution 1003 (1995) / adopted by the Security Council at its 3551st meeting,
on 5 July 1995
Concerns further extension of partial suspension of sanctions against Yugoslavia

S/RES/1004 (1995)
Resolution 1004 (1995) / adopted by the Security Council at its 3553rd meeting, on 12 July 1995
Demands withdrawal of the Bosnian Serb forces from the safe area of Srebrenica, Bosnia and Herzegovina

S/RES/1009 (1995)
Resolution 1009 (1995) / adopted by the Security Council at its 3563rd meeting, on 10 August 1995
Concerns compliance by Croatia with the agrement signed on 6 Aug. between Croatia and the UN Peace Forces/UN Protection Force, including the right of the local Serb population to receive humanitarian assistance

S/RES/1010 (1995)
Resolution 1010 (1995) / adopted by the Security Council at its 3564th meeting, on 10 August 1995
Concerns release of detained persons in Bosnia and Herzegovina

S/RES/1015 (1995)
Resolution 1015 (1995) / adopted by the Security Council at its 3578th meeting, on 15 September 1995
Concerns partial suspension of sanctions against Yugoslavia

S/RES/1016 (1995)
Resolution 1016 (1995) / adopted by the Security Council at its 3581st meeting, on 21 September 1995
Concerns military and humanitarian situation in Bosnia and Herzegovina

S/RES/1015 (1995)
Resolution 1015 (1995) / adopted by the Security Council at its 3578th meeting, on 15 September 1995
Concerns partial suspension of sanctions against Yugoslavia

S/RES/1016 (1995)
Resolution 1016 (1995) / adopted by the Security Council at its 3581st meeting, on 21 September 1995
Concerns military and humanitarian situation in Bosnia and Herzegovina

S/RES/1019 (1995)
Resolution 1019 (1995) / adopted by the Security Council at its 3591st meeting, on 9 November 1995
Concerns violations of international humanitarian law in the former Yugoslavia

S/RES/1021 (1995)
Resolution 1021 (1995) / adopted by the Security Council at its 3595th meeting, on 22 November 1995
Concerns termination of the embargo on deliveries of weapons and military equipment imposed by resolution 713 (1991)

S/RES/1022 (1995)
Resolution 1022 (1995) / adopted by the Security Council at its 3595th meeting, on 22 November 1995
Concerns suspension of measures imposed by or reaffirmed in Security Council resolutions related to the situation in the former Yugoslavia

S/RES/1027 (1995)
Resolution 1027 (1995) / adopted by the Security Council at its 3602nd meeting, on 30 November 1995
Concerns extension of the mandate of the UN Preventive Deployment Force

S/RES/1031 (1995)
Resolution 1031 (1995) / adopted by the Security Council at its 3607th meeting, on 15 December 1995
Concerns implementation of the Peace Agreement for Bosnia and Herzegovina and transfer of authority from the UN Protection Force to the multinational Implementation Force (IFOR)

S/RES/1034 (1995)
Resolution 1034 (1995) / adopted by the Security Council at its 3612th meeting, on 21 December 1995
Concerns violations of international humanitarian law and of human rights in the territory of the former Yugoslavia

S/RES/1037 (1996)
Resolution 1037 (1996) / adopted by the Security Council at its 3619th meeting, on 15 January 1995
Concerns establishment of the UN Transitional Administration for Eastern Slavonia, Baranja and Western Sirmium

S/RES/1038 (1996)
Resolution 1038 (1996) / adopted by the Security Council at its 3619th meeting, on 15 January 1995
Concerns authorization for the UN military observers to monitor the demilitarization of the Prevlaka peninsula, the former Yugoslavia

S/RES/1046 (1996)
Resolution 1046 (1996) / adopted by the Security Council at its 3630th meeting, on 13 February 1995
Concerns authorization of an increase in the strength of the UN Preventive Deployment Force